Feasting on the Word

Editorial Board

Feasting on the Word

Preaching the
Revised Common Lectionary

Year C, Volume 2

DAVID L. BARTLETT and BARBARA BROWN TAYLOR

General Editors

WESTMINSTER
JOHN KNOX PRESS
LOUISVILLE · KENTUCKY

Book design by Drew Stevens
Cover design by Lisa Buckley

First edition
Published by Westminster John Knox Press
Louisville, Kentucky

This book is printed on acid-free paper that meets the American National Standards Institute Z39.48 standard. ♾

PRINTED IN THE UNITED STATES OF AMERICA

10 11 12 13 14 15 16 17 18 — 10 9 8 7 6 5 4 3 2

Library of Congress Cataloging-in-Publication Data

Feasting on the Word : preaching the revised common lectionary / David L. Bartlett and Barbara Brown Taylor, general editors.
    p. cm.
  Includes index.
  ISBN 978-0-664-23101-9 (v. 6 alk. paper)
  ISBN 978-0-664-23100-2 (v. 5 alk. paper)
  ISBN 978-0-664-23099-9 (v. 4 alk. paper)
  ISBN 978-0-664-23098-2 (v. 3 alk. paper)
  ISBN 978-0-664-23097-5 (v. 2 alk. paper)
  ISBN 978-0-664-23096-8 (v. 1 alk. paper)
  1. Lectionary preaching.   2. Common lectionary (1992)   I. Bartlett, David Lyon, 1941-
II. Taylor, Barbara Brown.
  BV4235.L43F43 2008
  251'.6—dc22

                                                     2007047534

Contents

Publisher's Note

Feasting on the Word: Preaching the Revised Common Lectionary is an ambitious project that is offered to the Christian church as a resource for preaching and teaching.

The uniqueness of this approach in providing four perspectives on each preaching occasion from the Revised Common Lectionary sets this work apart from other lectionary materials. The theological, pastoral, exegetical, and homiletical dimensions of each biblical passage are explored with the hope that preachers will find much to inform and stimulate their preparations for preaching from this rich "feast" of materials.

This work could not have been undertaken without the deep commitments of those who have devoted countless hours to working on these tasks. Westminster John Knox Press would like to acknowledge the magnificent work of our general editors, David L. Bartlett and Barbara Brown Taylor. They are both gifted preachers with passionate concerns for the quality of preaching. They are also wonderful colleagues who embraced this huge task with vigor, excellence, and unfailing good humor. Our debt of gratitude to Barbara and David is great.

The fine support staff, project manager Joan Murchison and compiler Mary Lynn Darden, enabled all the thousands of "pieces" of the project to come together and form this impressive series. Without their strong competence and abiding persistence, these volumes could not have emerged.

The volume editors for this series are to be thanked as well. They used their superb skills as pastors and professors and ministers to work with writers and help craft their valuable insights into the highly useful entries that comprise this work.

The hundreds of writers who shared their expertise and insights to make this series possible are ones who deserve deep thanks indeed. They come from wide varieties of ministries. They have given their labors to provide a gift to benefit the whole church and to enrich preaching in our time.

Westminster John Knox would also like to express our appreciation to Columbia Theological Seminary for strong cooperation in enabling this work to begin and proceed. Dean of Faculty and Executive Vice President D. Cameron Murchison welcomed the project from the start and drew together everything we needed. His continuing efforts have been very valuable. Former President Laura S. Mendenhall provided splendid help as well. She made seminary resources and personnel available and encouraged us in this partnership with enthusiasm and all good grace. We thank her and look forward to working with Columbia's new president Stephen Hayner.

It is a joy for Westminster John Knox Press to present *Feasting on the Word: Preaching the Revised Common Lectionary* to the church, its preachers, and its teachers. We believe rich resources can assist the church's ministries as the Word is proclaimed. We believe the varieties of insights found in these pages will nourish preachers who will "feast on the Word" and who will share its blessings with those who hear.

Westminster John Knox Press

Series Introduction

A preacher's work is never done. Teaching, offering pastoral care, leading worship, and administering congregational life are only a few of the responsibilities that can turn preaching into just one more task of pastoral ministry. Yet the Sunday sermon is how the preacher ministers to most of the people most of the time. The majority of those who listen are not in crisis. They live such busy lives that few take part in the church's educational programs. They wish they had more time to reflect on their faith, but they do not. Whether the sermon is five minutes long or forty-five, it is the congregation's one opportunity to hear directly from their pastor about what life in Christ means and why it matters.

Feasting on the Word offers pastors focused resources for sermon preparation, written by companions on the way. With four different essays on each of the four biblical texts assigned by the Revised Common Lectionary, this series offers preachers sixteen different ways into the proclamation of God's Word on any given occasion. For each reading, preachers will find brief essays on the exegetical, theological, homiletical, and pastoral challenges of the text. The page layout is unusual. By setting the biblical passage at the top of the page and placing the essays beneath it, we mean to suggest the interdependence of the four approaches without granting priority to any one of them. Some readers may decide to focus on the Gospel passage, for instance, by reading all four essays provided for that text. Others may decide to look for connections between the Hebrew Bible, Psalm, Gospel, and Epistle texts by reading the theological essays on each one.

Wherever they begin, preachers will find what they need in a single volume produced by writers from a wide variety of disciplines and religious traditions. These authors teach in colleges and seminaries. They lead congregations. They write scholarly books as well as columns for the local newspaper. They oversee denominations. In all of these capacities and more, they serve God's Word, joining the preacher in the ongoing challenge of bringing that Word to life.

We offer this print resource for the mainline church in full recognition that we do so in the digital age of the emerging church. Like our page layout, this decision honors the authority of the biblical text, which thrives on the page as well as in the ear. While the twelve volumes of this series follow the pattern of the Revised Common Lectionary, each volume contains an index of biblical passages so that all preachers may make full use of its contents.

We also recognize that this new series appears in a post-9/11, post-Katrina world. For this reason, we provide no shortcuts for those committed to the proclamation of God's Word. Among preachers, there are books known as "Monday books" because they need to be read thoughtfully at least a week ahead of time. There are also "Saturday books," so called because they supply sermon ideas on short notice. The books in this series are not Saturday books. Our aim is to help preachers go deeper, not faster, in a world that is in need of saving words.

A series of this scope calls forth the gifts of a great many people. We are grateful first of all to the staff of Westminster John Knox Press: Don McKim, Jon Berquist, and Jack Keller, who conceived this project; David Dobson, who worked diligently to bring the project to completion, with publisher Marc Lewis's strong support; and Julie Tonini, who has painstakingly guided each volume through the production process. We thank Laura Mendenhall, former President of Columbia Theological Seminary, and Columbia's Dean, Cameron Murchison, who made our participation in this work possible. Our editorial board is a hardworking board, without whose patient labor and good humor this series would not exist. From the start, Joan Murchison has been the brains of the operation, managing details of epic proportions with great human kindness. Mary Lynn Darden, Dilu Nicholas, Megan Hackler, and John Shillingburg have supported both her and us with their administrative skills.

We have been honored to work with a multitude of gifted thinkers, writers, and editors. We present these essays as their offering—and ours—to the blessed ministry of preaching.

David L. Bartlett
Barbara Brown Taylor

A Note about the Lectionary

Feasting on the Word follows the Revised Common Lectionary (RCL) as developed by the Consultation on Common Texts, an ecumenical consultation of liturgical scholars and denominational representatives from the United States and Canada. The RCL provides a collection of readings from Scripture to be used during worship in a schedule that follows the seasons of the church year. In addition, it provides for a uniform set of readings to be used across denominations or other church bodies.

The RCL provides a reading from the Old Testament, a Psalm response to that reading, a Gospel, and an Epistle for each preaching occasion of the year. It is presented in a three-year cycle, with each year centered around one of the Synoptic Gospels. Year A is the year of Matthew, Year B is the year of Mark, and Year C is the year of Luke. John is read each year, especially during Advent, Lent, and Easter.

The RCL offers two tracks of Old Testament texts for the Season after Pentecost or Ordinary Time: a semicontinuous track, which moves through stories and characters in the Old Testament, and a complementary track, which ties the Old Testament texts to the theme of the Gospel texts for that day. Some denominational traditions favor one over the other. For instance, Presbyterians and Methodists generally follow the semicontinuous track, while Lutherans and Episcopalians generally follow the complementary track.

The print volumes of *Feasting on the Word* follow the complementary track for Year A, are split between the complementary and semicontinuous track for Year B, and cover the semicontinuous stream for Year C. Essays on the Old Testament lections for the Season after Pentecost that are not covered in the print volumes will be available on the *Feasting on the Word* Web site, www.feastingontheword.net.

For more information about the Revised Common Lectionary, visit the official RCL Web site at http://lectionary.library.vanderbilt.edu/ or see *The Revised Common Lectionary: The Consultation on Common Texts* (Nashville: Abingdon Press, 1992).

Feasting on the Word

Isaiah 58:1-12

¹Shout out, do not hold back!
  Lift up your voice like a trumpet!
  Announce to my people their rebellion,
    to the house of Jacob their sins.
²Yet day after day they seek me
    and delight to know my ways,
  as if they were a nation that practiced righteousness
    and did not forsake the ordinance of their God;
  they ask of me righteous judgments,
    they delight to draw near to God.
³"Why do we fast, but you do not see?
    Why humble ourselves, but you do not notice?"
  Look, you serve your own interest on your fast day,
    and oppress all your workers.
⁴Look, you fast only to quarrel and to fight
    and to strike with a wicked fist.
  Such fasting as you do today
    will not make your voice heard on high.
⁵Is such the fast that I choose,
    a day to humble oneself?
  Is it to bow down the head like a bulrush,
    and to lie in sackcloth and ashes?
  Will you call this a fast,
    a day acceptable to the LORD?

⁶Is not this the fast that I choose:
    to loose the bonds of injustice,
    to undo the thongs of the yoke,

Theological Perspective

The temptation one faces in preparing to preach this text, especially attractive on Ash Wednesday, is to read and proclaim it as if it were simply a prophetic critique of religious practices that ignore the needs of the poor. Clearly, the prophet's denunciation of a piety so rich in itself that it has become blind to the needs of others (as well at to its own poverty) burns here with a relentless intensity. Indeed, on Ash Wednesday we do well to remember that the ritual disposition of ashes, the confession of sin, our self-chosen Lenten fasts—as sincere and ardent as these practices may be—do not of themselves draw us one step nearer to God, and can in fact become ingenious contrivances for avoiding God altogether.

So how is one to read this text, which pointedly condemns any quest for righteousness before God that overlooks the plight of the poor, and contrasts such an unfaithful "fast" to God's concern for loosening "the bonds of injustice" and letting "the oppressed go free"? "Is this not the fast I choose?" asks the Lord. Indeed, it

Pastoral Perspective

In today's text, a crisis moment has arrived. Quiet diplomacy will not do. "Lift up your voice like a trumpet!" the prophet urges. "Announce to my people their rebellion, to the house of Jacob their sins."

Who wants to hear this? Nobody likes loud-mouth folk! When the prophet brings forth moral charges, none of the accused want to hear or deal with them. If everyone appears to be doing more or less the same thing, and things appear to be going their way, then why stir up trouble by making people feel uncomfortable? Let sleeping dogs lie! Why "declare" the people's transgressions?

If the prophet is encouraged to raise his voice like a trumpet, it is because quiet diplomacy has not worked. Yet will his trumpeting not call out contempt and violence against him? History is replete with stories of those who cried out and declared to the people their wrongdoing. Such efforts were called "disturbing the peace." Protesters were called

to let the oppressed go free,
    and to break every yoke?
[7]Is it not to share your bread with the hungry,
    and bring the homeless poor into your house;
when you see the naked, to cover them,
    and not to hide yourself from your own kin?
[8]Then your light shall break forth like the dawn,
    and your healing shall spring up quickly;
your vindicator shall go before you,
    the glory of the LORD shall be your rear guard.
[9]Then you shall call, and the LORD will answer;
    you shall cry for help, and he will say, Here I am.

If you remove the yoke from among you,
    the pointing of the finger, the speaking of evil,
[10]if you offer your food to the hungry
    and satisfy the needs of the afflicted,
then your light shall rise in the darkness
    and your gloom be like the noonday.
[11]The LORD will guide you continually,
    and satisfy your needs in parched places,
    and make your bones strong;
and you shall be like a watered garden,
    like a spring of water,
    whose waters never fail.
[12]Your ancient ruins shall be rebuilt;
    you shall raise up the foundations of many generations;
you shall be called the repairer of the breach,
    the restorer of streets to live in.

Exegetical Perspective

The particular verses from Isaiah appointed for Ash Wednesday are part of a longer section of Isaiah that begins with 56:1 and concludes with 59:20. The overarching theme is that the prerequisite for divine deliverance is that the people maintain righteous and just lives (cf. 56:1 and 59:16–20). Isaiah 58:1–12 stands in the middle of this longer section stressing the need for proper, inward repentance that leads to acceptable outward action (cf. 58:1 and 59:20; 58:2 and 56:1).

Within the longer unit, 58:1–12 should be extended to include verses 13–14 for several reasons. First, one of the key terms in 58:2, "delight," is repeated in 58:13–14 where the whole idea of what is pleasing to God is brought to closure. Second, "Jacob" as referent appears in 58:1 and again in 58:14. Third, the issue of pursuing one's personal agenda is addressed in 58:3 and again in 58:13. Finally, the last line of 59:14, "for the mouth of the LORD has spoken," marks the end of the prophet's declaration that begins at 58:3c with the words "Look, you serve your own

Homiletical Perspective

Ash Wednesday marks the beginning of the forty days of Lent. It is traditionally a time for Christians to enter a period of self-reflection, prayer, and preparation in anticipation of the celebrations of Easter. The symbolism of forty days has many roots, including the flood and forty years of wilderness wanderings, but inspiration for this time is probably taken from Jesus' forty days in the wilderness where he, like Moses and Elijah before him, sojourned in preparation for his ministry.

Fasting was one of the notable features of Jesus' forty days in the wilderness. A common practice throughout the Bible, fasting was believed to be a humbling act of commitment or repentance that was intensified when combined with prayer. Fasting has become a favored spiritual discipline for a wide variety of people who believe this effort can help eliminate earthly distractions as they seek to draw nearer to God. John Wesley, Mohandas Gandhi, Dorothy Day, Cesar Chavez, and Thomas Merton all

Isaiah 58:1-12

Theological Perspective

is, but what makes God's "fast" remarkable is not its social or political or even economic sensibilities but its reckless self-forgetfulness. "Why do we fast, but you do not see?" is the question of an anxious idolatry eager to make God "useful," worshiping God *for the sake of something else*, in this case, one's own salvation. Lusting for such a possibility was the great threat that continually confronted Israel and continues to tempt us today in both liberal and conservative garb. All desire the power to save themselves. All.

The form of fasting that God chooses is strangely free of this affliction. It is distinguished from idolatry in its lack of anxiety. It is free to engage another, to *see* the other, and to see the other not as something to be used or merely as an object of pity or duty, but as a gift.

That is why Karl Barth begins his treatment of human freedom not by talking of rights or duties but by speaking first of being set free for God, a freedom manifest in the way we keep the Sabbath day. How we understand what that day is for is the central clue to our understanding of what human beings are for. Isaiah 58 does not offer moralistic wisdom at this point. Rather, "the fast God chooses" describes a new vision of humanity. In the presence of this One, we are saved from the loneliness of our self-justifying ways, even as we are forbidden to give ultimate loyalty to our own agendas, however pious or political. Instead, we are invited to receive ourselves and others as gifts, discovering in God's engagement with us a life that can only be a life together. The end of such Sabbath freedom leads not "to the individual in isolation, but in relationship to his fellows."[1]

The danger of worship concerned only with one's own salvation is not its immorality or lack of authenticity, but its blindness. When we suffer from such idolatry, only "the fast God chooses" is able to render the neighbor visible to us. Simone Weil, hardly a Reformed theologian but a wise guide to much in Scripture, writes that it is God's freedom to forget self that is at the heart of the passion to which Ash Wednesday directs us, a freedom that is manifest in its extraordinary vision. She has in mind the freedom that enabled a despised Samaritan to stop and render aid when the priest and Levite had business elsewhere. Of this story (which has a definite resonance with this text in Isaiah 58) she writes: "One of the two is only a little piece of flesh, naked, inert, and bleeding beside a ditch; he is

1. Karl Barth, *Church Dogmatics*, III/4 (Edinburgh: T. & T. Clark, 1961), 69.

Pastoral Perspective

"outside agitators." They were often beaten, tortured, lynched, or otherwise silenced.

On Sunday, September 23, 2007, Burmese Buddhist monks participated in a peaceful demonstration to protest the harsh treatment of the people by the government. They were shot and killed by the military because they demonstrated. A 39-year-old Burmese protester in Rangoon, an ordinary citizen, cried loudly in the press. After crying out he came to the pessimistic view that nothing was going to change. Still, he continued to protest. Why? Because loud outcry is better than silently hiding behind closed doors in fear. Perhaps if the community will cry out loud enough and long enough, someone, somewhere will hear and respond. That is where the hope lies.

The prophet tells us that God is not seduced or impressed by the noise that comes from our solemn assemblies. This is what God wants from us: "to loose the bonds of injustice, to undo the thongs of the yoke, to let the oppressed go free." These are things the community can achieve through ongoing struggle. Pastoral and social-justice issues are inseparable. The prophet's pastoral perspective joins moral and spiritual vision with transforming political, economic, and justice systems.

One of the most challenging parts in the list of what God wants is close to where we live. "Bring the homeless poor into your house" (v. 7b). Whoa! Is the prophet giving us bad advice here? What about issues of personal boundaries? Perhaps the most challenging part of all is "not to hide yourself from your own kin" (v. 7d). Have you ever wanted to hide from your relatives? Relatives can show up unannounced, at any time, with a sense of entitlement. No doubt, stories abound.

The prophet's list of what God wants from us is far from what we conveniently offer to God. God cares about healing the whole creation. When we participate in the whole work of redemption and healing, God's light breaks through the gloom of despair, the darkness of ignorance, and the deception of arrogance, fear, and violence. "Then your light shall rise in the darkness, and your gloom be like the noonday" (v. 10b).

Still, there will be work to do, even in the new and idealized situation. History will continue to unfold, and new challenges will arise. However, there will be a significant difference: our desire will be satisfied in scorched places. Our bodies will be strengthened and our lives will be refreshed "like a watered garden" (v. 11d). This is how God's redemptive and healing power is revealed and experienced in the community.

interest on your fast day." Some commentators arrange the poem in five stanzas (58:1–3b; 3c–5; 6–9b; 9c–12; 13–14), others three (58:1–5; 6–12; 13–14), but most agree that 58:13–14 provide the proper conclusion of the poem and are not a later addition.

The historical setting of this passage cannot be precisely determined. The mention of "ancient ruins" (58:14) suggests some time after the destruction of Jerusalem in 586 BCE but before the restoration of the temple in 520–515 BCE. As attested by the book of Lamentations, worship did continue in Jerusalem by those not taken to Babylon. Since the character of "fasting" that is to be accepted as the worship of God is addressed, some form of organized ritual can be assumed. At least four fast days had been regularized by the time Zechariah arrived around 520 BCE (Zech. 8:18–19). Those may have remembered particular historical moments such as (1) the beginning of the siege of Jerusalem—the tenth day of the tenth month; (2) the capture of Jerusalem—the ninth day of the fourth month; (3) the burning of the temple and city —the tenth day of the fifth month; and (4) the murder of Gedaliah—the third day of the seventh month.[1] Since Isaiah 58 has been incorporated into the work of the great exilic Babylonian Isaiah (Second Isaiah), it seems likely that it reflects a time somewhere after the return of some of the exiles in 538 BCE but before the time of Haggai and Zechariah. Jerusalem was in a state of economic and social disarray, a continuing situation reflected still later in Ezra and Nehemiah.

The section opens with God's charge to the prophet and the statement of the problem: the people are very "religious," but all their fasting is mere outward "show" (vv. 1–3). They are in "rebellion" (NRSV has the better translation of *pesha'*) and do not practice "righteousness," *tsedaqah* (vv. 1–2). In this passage the disregard for doing righteousness is equated with selfishness, serving one's own interests (vv. 3, 13). "Oppressing" one's "workers," quarreling, and "pointing of the finger and the speaking of evil" (a judgmental act accompanied by slander) were all related to the selfish pursuit of personal rather than communal interests (vv. 3–4, 9). As the questions of the people indicate, they did not understand why God was not responding (v. 3a). Rather than the repentance that might prompt God to listen, the people were caught up in outward signs of mourning, such as fasting and putting on mourning garments, actions that in themselves were not acceptable to the Lord (vv.

regularly fasted; Roman Catholics are required to fast on Ash Wednesday; among Jews, Hindus, Muslims, and Buddhists, many fast. In contemporary Protestant religious practice, during Lent many persons practice some kind of fasting or a more popular (and, alas, regularly abused) idea of "giving up" something for the duration. Reasons for fasting abound—nearness to God, weight loss, detoxification—but they are often misunderstood (many forget that nothing *we* can do will draw us any nearer to God—God is already with us). The Lenten reading from Isaiah 58 helps us with this precise point.

Second Isaiah preaches to Israel at the end of their exile when they are overwhelmed with a sense of defeat and abandonment by YHWH. We know from Zechariah 7 that Israel's religious habits have become rote and empty. Walter Brueggemann calls it a kind of "pseudo-holiness."[1] Thus, when people complain that God is not hearing their prayers or responding to their fasting, Isaiah confronts them with the hypocrisy of their humility. He is direct: fasting should never be understood as an end in itself or a substitute for righteous living. Indeed, it is arterially related to righteous living. Our private devotions are inextricably linked to our public lives. True devotion to God demands both. If we are not living righteously, then our spiritual disciplines lose their meaning.

For the preacher confronted with growing numbers who say they are "spiritual but not religious" and who are infatuated with ever-increasing numbers of popular "spiritual" practices, Isaiah 58 and its emphasis on *righteousness* (Heb. *tsedaqah*) and *justice* (Heb. *mishpat*) is a text worth exploring. According to Abraham Heschel, there are few things as deeply ingrained in the heart of the faithful "as the thought of God's justice and righteousness. It is not an inference, but self-evident; [it is] not an added attribute to [YHWH's] essence."[2] This theme was absolutely central to Jesus' preaching. One need only reread the litany of accusations in Matthew 23 to experience Jesus' indignation over the same hypocrisies of the Pharisees.

Isaiah's audience is reoriented to YHWH's definition of fasting that seeks to "loose the chains of injustice," clothe the naked, and feed the hungry (cf. Matthew 25). The soaring words of this chapter reach their pinnacle in verses 9–11, when the prophet shows that when those who live righteously call upon YHWH, the Sovereign will satisfy their

1. James Muilenburg, "Isaiah," *The Interpreter's Bible* (Nashville: Abingdon Press, 1978), 5:678.

1. Walter Brueggemann, *Theology of the Old Testament* (Minneapolis: Augsburg Fortress Press, 1997), 462.
2. Abraham J. Heschel, *The Prophets* (New York: HarperCollins, 2001), 255.

Isaiah 58:1-12

Theological Perspective

nameless; no one knows anything about him. Those who pass by this thing scarcely notice it, and a few minutes afterward do not even know that they saw it. Only one stops and turns his attention toward it." In desiring the existence of this other, the Samaritan shares "in the state of inert matter which is his,"[2] a sharing that is in fact cruciform in shape and therefore able to *see* what healthy and even virtuous eyes otherwise had somehow missed. That is what it means to be free, not just generously compassionate or virtuously self-denying, but free to *see* the other and to recognize in him or her a child of God.

That is the strange place where this passage leaves us, promising of all things that those who keep the fast God chooses will indeed be set free, that is, will be able to call upon God, to cry for help and hear God say, "Here I am."

All true joy in life derives from this free decision of God to seek fellowship with that which is not God, just as all human fellowship is rooted in the triune love of Father, Son, and Holy Spirit. That is where Ash Wednesday's journey is taking us, the place where God's fast pours itself out for the sake of the whole world. There God's fast becomes our food, and we are set free to sit at table with others whom we have not chosen and would never choose, to eat and even delight in this fearful mercy.

Strangely, the prophet is very clear about this mercy and this irrepressible joy: "Then your light shall break forth like the dawn, and your healing shall spring up quickly. . . . Then you shall call, and the LORD will answer; you shall cry for help, and he will say, Here I am." In commenting on this passage Calvin writes, simply, "The chief part of our happiness" is that "God listens to us."[3] What the prophet knows, but the self-absorbed pietist and the ideologue forget, is that the God whose fast is to loosen the bonds of injustice delights in the life together that is the gift that belongs to all his children.

THOMAS W. CURRIE

Pastoral Perspective

We will be called "repairer of the breach" when we help heal broken relationships and make the streets safe for human dwelling.

The personal and social are inseparable. Ash Wednesday and Lent are times to think about the interrelatedness of the personal, the social, and the political. "Loose the bonds of injustice," the prophet cried, "let the oppressed go free" (v. 6). With pastoral care, Ash Wednesday celebrations will distinguish false piety from the true worship of God. False piety is characterized by our convenient offerings to God, which fall short of the moral challenges posed by violence and poverty. We are called to observe the requirements of both love and justice.

We know that violence in the streets and the world has its starting place at home among the "relatives." The U.S. Department of Justice's 1996 National Crime Victimization Survey informs us that women of all races are equally vulnerable to abuse by husbands, boyfriends, or other male members of the family. In some cultures, honor killing is sanctioned. The church covers domestic violence, for example, through silence. It fails church and community when it does not cry out loud about the violence done to women, children, and some men.

The church's ministry can address domestic violence through protest, the education of children, preaching, home visitation, pastoral conversations, committee meetings, pastoral counseling, and other venues where pastor and parishioners gather to talk about the life of faith. Violence in the home and streets is relevant talk for all seasons. Ash Wednesday and Lent are especially ripe times to raise a loud voice against family, domestic, and other forms of violence.

The focus of the whole season and of today's liturgy in particular is on taking stock of our lives, acknowledging betrayal, lamenting, confessing, and repenting. To remain silent about violence in the home and in the community is to give sanction to it. Victims will continue to be victims. Perpetrators will not be called to account, while the church continues in delusional thinking, shallow devotion, and empty ritual.

When it is true to its purpose, Lent will move us closer to being the suffering and resurrected body of Christ in the world. We will find hope in being faithful and strength in being honest. We will be made wiser by our discernment and confession, poised to struggle for wider justice, and enabled to dig deeper wells for the expression of compassion. "Then," the prophet says, "your light shall break forth like the dawn, and your healing shall spring up quickly."

ARCHIE SMITH JR.

---

2. Simone Weil, *Waiting for God*, trans. Emma Craufurd (New York: Perennial Classics, 2001), 90.
3. John Calvin, *Commentary on Isaiah*, trans. William Pringle, vol. 4 (Grand Rapids: Eerdmans, 1948), 236.

3, 5; cf. Jer. 14:11–12). They did not recognize their need for a basic change of attitude.

The prophet does not condemn all ritual forms of fasting. Fasting had a legitimate place in the religious/political life of ancient Israel. Joel called for public fasting in the face of a community crisis (Joel 1:8–2:17; cf. also Ezra 8:21–23; Neh. 1:4–11). Private fasts are noted (2 Sam. 12:15–23; Ps. 69:1–15). Rather, the prophet stresses what God desires as the proper outward expression of repentance. To do righteousness in the eyes of the prophet was to redress all forms of oppression and injustice. As signs of inward remorse, the people, especially the business leaders, were to correct the communal breakdown reflected in the reality of widespread hunger, homelessness, and insufficient clothing (vv. 6–7, 10; cf. Zech. 7:5–11; Matt. 25:35–40). Such action would represent the "fast that I [God] choose" (v. 5). Such action demonstrated a commitment to maintaining justice, the prerequisite of divine deliverance (56:1; cf. 59:9–20).

An integral part of doing righteousness was honoring the Sabbath (56:2–8). The pursuit of a personal agenda, serving one's "own interests," was totally unacceptable (v. 13). Just as breaking the bonds of injustice and freeing the oppressed were critical (v. 6), so was properly observing the Sabbath (v. 13). Each was an aspect of the fast that God expected. In Deuteronomy the rationale for the Sabbath is based on the experience of the slavery endured by Israel in Egypt (Deut. 5:12–15). The importance of Sabbath-keeping was a long-standing tradition. Jeremiah declared the desecration of the Sabbath in his day as one of the primary transgressions of the people of Judah that brought the Babylonian destruction (Jer. 17:19–27).

Those who have experienced oppression should not allow or participate in the structures of society that inflict others with the same. This passage contrasts self-serving "religiosity" (vv. 3–4) with a genuine attitude of repentance that seeks to set right wrongdoing and offer relief to those suffering within the community (vv. 6–7). God's promise to those who do fast in such a manner is that their cries for divine presence and vindication will be heard (vv. 8–12; cf. v. 3). Ash Wednesday is an appropriate time to reflect again on what should be an inseparable relationship of inward repentance and outward actions with regard for the undoing and overcoming of the destructiveness worked by human sin within the human communities in which we live.

W. EUGENE MARCH

needs and tend them like "a watered garden." Verse 12 fulfills the longed-for promise of restoration and anoints the people with the title "repairer of the breach," "restorer of streets to live in."

This idea of repairing the breach has deep meaning for the Jewish community and is best known in the phrase *Tikkun Olam* (literally "repairing the world"). The phrase *tikkun* appears in Ecclesiastes (1:5; 7:13) and the concept is rooted in rabbinic literature, especially the "Aleinu prayer" (one of the most essential prayers of Jewish worship that refers to their responsibilities as a chosen people). Tikkun Olam is a call to a kind of social action that seeks to repair the world through the establishment of the reign of God. In this it undergirds Martin Luther King Jr.'s concept of building the Beloved Community and most recently can be seen in the writings of several young Jewish activists in the book *Righteous Indignation: A Jewish Call for Justice*.[3]

One cannot read the paper or watch the news these days and not be alarmed by the polarization of nearly every segment of society. Nowhere is this more painful than in the church's implosion over cultural issues and the sad tensions among Christians, Muslims, and Jews on a national and international level. We who believe that we have much to offer the world must find a way to reject the battle to occupy the ground on the right or the left and instead seek to occupy the higher ground. In light of our current battles, fears, and accusations, it is poignant and disturbing to read Isaiah's message: "*Your fasting ends in quarreling and strife and in striking each other with wicked fists*" (v. 4). An Ash Wednesday call to a new kind of fasting oriented to "repairing the breach" of our differences could carry a powerful challenge that would make Isaiah's 2,500-year-old prophetic voice keenly relevant.

Whatever one chooses as a Lenten discipline, the message of Isaiah 58 can help bring a new orientation to that discipline. How might one turn the casual cultural concept of "giving up something for Lent" into a meaningful act of devotion? How might one redefine fasting, or perhaps "detoxification," to have more relevance to the things that pollute our relationship to God, rather than just the things that pollute our bodies? These are questions worthy of Ash Wednesday and a journey through the season of Lent.

NICK CARTER

3. O. Rose et al., eds., *Righteous Indignation: A Jewish Call for Justice* (Woodstock, VT: Jewish Lights, 2008).

Psalm 51:1-17

[1]Have mercy on me, O God,
  according to your steadfast love;
according to your abundant mercy
  blot out my transgressions.
[2]Wash me thoroughly from my iniquity,
  and cleanse me from my sin.

[3]For I know my transgressions,
  and my sin is ever before me.
[4]Against you, you alone, have I sinned,
  and done what is evil in your sight,
so that you are justified in your sentence
  and blameless when you pass judgment.
[5]Indeed, I was born guilty,
  a sinner when my mother conceived me.

[6]You desire truth in the inward being;
  therefore teach me wisdom in my secret heart.
[7]Purge me with hyssop, and I shall be clean;
  wash me, and I shall be whiter than snow.
[8]Let me hear joy and gladness;
  let the bones that you have crushed rejoice.

Theological Perspective

Psalm 51 provides a distinctive opportunity for confession and reflection upon Christian notions of sin in our current social context, as well as in the liturgical setting of Ash Wednesday. In liturgies and songs used in contemporary worship, Psalm 51 is primarily viewed as a commentary on one's individual sin and serves as encouragement for worshipers to turn inward to repent and seek reconciliation with God. The history of theological interpretation underscores the context of the passage as a reflection upon David's sin against Bathsheba. Using the story of David and Bathsheba as a lens for interpreting this text, readers are invited to consider the meaning of familiar phrases in this psalm such as "create in me a clean heart" and "restore to me the joy of your salvation" in the context of personal devotion and as these words relate to a larger community.

John Calvin read literally the superscription to Psalm 51 that attributed the psalm to David after "he had gone in to Bathsheba." Calvin viewed the psalm as David's expression of guilt for lusting after Bathsheba and believed that David would have seen the psalm as proof of his own repentance. David's sinful actions caused him a great deal of angst and contributed to the sincerity of his prayer. Although Calvin's commentary on the psalm set it in the

Pastoral Perspective

Psalm 51 has been described as a "lament" and is considered the most famous of the seven Penitential Psalms. Words from this psalm are well known to those who attend Christian churches or synagogues. "Create in me a clean heart, O God, and put a new and right spirit within me," the psalmist prays. "Do not cast me away from your presence, and do not take your holy spirit from me." These are words of a personal or communal petition to God that through divine love and mercy a new heart may be created in us that is clean and pure; that God will put a right spirit in us that will bring about a close, intimate relationship with the God who loves us and whom we love. We may even express this petition as "a desire to live directly out of God's vibrant presence."[1]

As we prayerfully consider Psalm 51, we learn that much more is offered to us in this psalm than just a way to "lament" our sins and petition for forgiveness. Psalm 51 offers us insight into a way to deepen and enhance our relationship with God. We may use this psalm as a portal for us to practice honest and courageous introspection and conversation with God. We can be guided to meaningful self-reflection, forgiveness, cleansing,

1. Tilden Edwards, *Living in the Presence: Spiritual Exercises to Open Our Lives to Awareness of God* (San Francisco: HarperSanFrancisco, 1987, 1995), 45.

⁹Hide your face from my sins,
and blot out all my iniquities.

¹⁰Create in me a clean heart, O God,
and put a new and right spirit within me.
¹¹Do not cast me away from your presence,
and do not take your holy spirit from me.
¹²Restore to me the joy of your salvation,
and sustain in me a willing spirit.

¹³Then I will teach transgressors your ways,
and sinners will return to you.
¹⁴Deliver me from bloodshed, O God,
O God of my salvation,
and my tongue will sing aloud of your deliverance.

¹⁵O Lord, open my lips,
and my mouth will declare your praise.
¹⁶For you have no delight in sacrifice;
if I were to give a burnt offering, you would not be pleased.
¹⁷The sacrifice acceptable to God is a broken spirit;
a broken and contrite heart, O God, you will not despise.

Exegetical Perspective

This psalm, justly treasured as a profound expression of the need for God's forgiveness, is an apt text to initiate a season of repentance. It is often associated with the Christian tradition's other Penitential Psalms (Pss. 6, 32, 38, 102, 130, and 143). Scholars differ over the precise category to assign it to, but many see it as a variation on an individual lament. The psalm title tries to locate the composition as David's response to Nathan's courageous confrontation with him over the injustice he committed against Uriah in order to take Bathsheba as his wife (2 Sam. 12). Perhaps this association came about to underscore the idea that all mortals, even a powerful and beloved king, stand in need of profound repentance.

In composition, the psalm falls into three distinct sections, verses 1–9, 10–14, and 15–19. The first section opens with a classic chiastic form asking for forgiveness based on God's qualities of steadfast love and abundant mercy, qualities that Israel attributes as core aspects of the divine character (see Exod. 34:6–7). With verse 3, the psalmist initiates an unequivocal confession. He acknowledges that the sin remains an issue until it is cleared away and that he has acted against God's standards (v. 4a). The psalmist acknowledges the justice of God's judgment against him and holds God "blameless" in the matter

Homiletical Perspective

It would be hard to imagine a psalm better suited for Ash Wednesday. Psalm 51 has poetry, honesty, and of course searing confession, confession of the type that must hit God right between the eyes. The psalmist's words admit fault, desire new direction, and seek relationship, all at the same time. It is a preaching treasure, especially if the preacher is willing to be brutally honest with his or her own spiritual condition when preparing and delivering the sermon.

There is a struggling Kansas City church that sits at an inner-city intersection facing three small businesses. On one corner is a car wash, on another a dry cleaning outfit, and on the third a drug addiction treatment center. The pastor used to say, "This is the one intersection in town where people come to get really clean. You can get your car cleaned, your clothes cleaned, and your body cleaned. Here at St. Mark, we offer a cleaning of the soul."

Psalm 51 was spoken, sung, and later penned by someone who understood the cleaning industry. Look at the verbs: wash, cleanse, wipe, purge, blot. They all speak to something that is very dirty or really deep, or both. *Sin* would be that dirty and deep grime that needs to be treated. What better day than the liturgical observance of Ash Wednesday to gain fresh insight on this age-old condition called sin?

Psalm 51:1-17

Theological Perspective

context of David's sin against Bathsheba, Calvin made no specific mention of the impact of David's actions upon Bathsheba herself. Instead, Calvin emphasized the wrong that David inflicted upon Uriah and especially God. Calvin thought that David's prayer served as a model for confession and for seeking reconciliation with God.

Verse 5, "Indeed, I was born guilty . . ." also showed the way that a particular sin invited David to reflect on his nature as a human being. According to Calvin, David realized that "he brought nothing but sin with him into the world, and . . . his nature was entirely depraved."[1] In his interpretation of this verse, Calvin aimed to set himself apart from Christians (particularly Pelagians) who believed that they themselves could right wrongful behavior because sin "descended from Adam only through force of imitation."[2] Calvin believed that only God could offer the mercy, loving-kindness, and compassion necessary to overcome the gap created between God and others by human sinfulness.

The idea that God's grace is most clearly understood in contrast to human sin is a theme that continues to define much of Reformed understandings of sin. Reinhold Niebuhr argued, along similar lines, that God's grace not only represented God's mercy and forgiveness but also encompassed the sinful elements that human beings could not overcome.[3]

Today biblical scholars think that Psalm 51 is more likely to have been added to the psalter by editors wanting to invite readers to hear it against the background of the story of David and Bathsheba, the murder of Bathsheba's husband Uriah, and the confrontation between Nathan and David. When reading 2 Samuel 11, one cannot miss the issues of power and authority present within the story of David and Bathsheba. The text says that David "lay with her" (2 Sam. 11:4), but those words do not convey the significance of a king's authority and the violence perpetrated against Bathsheba. Bathsheba clearly had no choice but to do as she was told. If we are to take seriously the biblical context in which we read and hear the words of Psalm 51, then additional questions about sin and God's grace must also be raised regarding this passage. Who is the audience for this psalm? Is it all those who sin? Or is this the

Pastoral Perspective

and comfort in God's presence, and to increased trust in the leading of the Holy Spirit. This psalm thus provides us with a fulfilling way to experience Ash Wednesday and Lent.

We begin the Ash Wednesday experience by being willing to be honest with ourselves about who we are, about our relationship with ourselves, and about our relationship with God. We may not be able to come to this honest self-knowledge instantly, however. We seek God's assistance in taking this careful approach to self-examination.

In the Hebrew Bible, King David offers us an example of someone who was not yet ready or able to be honest about his own behavior and relationship with God. God's love and compassion gradually brought David to a more accurate self-knowledge. God worked with David for a period of time to soften David's heart and open his eyes to the impact of his selfish and sinful behavior. God sent Nathan the prophet to tell David a parable (2 Sam. 12:1–14). David was astounded by the selfishness and sin of the rich man in the parable and was appalled when Nathan helped him understand that the rich man was none other than David himself. In this way, David gained a new awareness of himself and his deeds, realizing that his behavior had not only harmed others but had displeased God and damaged his relationship with God. Only then was David able to ask forgiveness and establish a right relationship with God.

God's interaction with us (like God's dealing with David) is based on God's love, compassion, and mercy toward us. A loving relationship between God and us is initiated and sustained by God. We can be active in the process of deepening our relationship with God by responding to God's loving care and call. When we experience the great joy of a "right" relationship with God, we have the energy and motivation to contribute to the maturing and deepening of that relationship.

Ash Wednesday and Lent take us beyond a lament for wrongdoing and a petition for God's forgiveness. We know that God can and has forgiven us for past failures, but part of God's promise to us is that God will "blot out" our transgressions. God is willing to focus, not on our past mistakes, but on our desire for a new heart, our desire to live out of God's vibrant presence. With new hearts we will not only experience God's forgiveness, but we will be able to forgive ourselves as well.

During Ash Wednesday and Lent we renew our covenant with God. This includes our honest self-

1. John Calvin, *Commentary on the Book of Psalms* (Grand Rapids: Eerdmans, 1949), 2:290.
2. Ibid.
3. Reinhold Niebuhr, *The Nature and Destiny of Man*, vol. 2, *Human Destiny* (New York: Charles Scribner's Sons, 1943; reprint 1963), 98.

Exegetical Perspective

(v. 4b). He concludes by reflecting on his entanglement in transgression. The Hebrew here is far clearer than rendered by the NRSV: "Indeed, *in guilt* I was born, *in sin* my mother conceived me" (v. 5). The point is not the sinfulness of being born or conceived, but that, from the very moment of his coming into existence, the psalmist found himself ensnarled in transgression. He cannot extricate himself from his failing before God.

Verse 6 shifts the focus of the writer from self-examination to acknowledgment of God's interest in his deepest nature. While the precise wording is difficult to translate, the general sense is clear: "Indeed, you take pleasure in truth that is deep; and by hidden wisdom you inform me." God's wisdom takes into consideration hidden, deep things (see Job 28 and the discourse on wisdom hidden in the depths) and so knows the remorse of the sinner and the desire for transformation. The psalmist continues with a series of statements rooted in the idea of God acting to remove the stain of sin. The "hyssop" of verse 7 is more likely marjoram, since the common hyssop is not native to Palestine. Branches of this plant were used in several rites where the worshiper would be sprinkled with a liquid (Num. 19:18) to signify cleansing. The writer implores God for restoration by asking to hear "joy and gladness" again (v. 8a). "Bones you have crushed" is a poetic expression for the sense of feeling the impact of judgment in one's physical self. The author appeals that God turn away from seeing his transgressions (v. 9a) and remove their impact (v. 9b). The focus is on God's gracious actions in undoing what the penitent cannot undo on his own.

The second section (vv. 10–14) begins with a series of desperate requests, acknowledging that only God can bring about the transformation of the penitent. The call for a "clean heart" (v. 10a) is a call for the center of perception to be remade over, and connecting it with new spirit echoes the renewal of the nation foreseen following the exile (see Ezek. 36:25–26). In this section, the psalmist seems to be taking the promises of restoration for the postexilic community as a whole and applying these promises to his personal situation. He continues by asking that God not reject him (v. 11a) but continue to allow his presence to afford comfort and sustenance (v. 11b); thus he may be restored to joy in divine service and obedience (v. 12). Once such a transformation is complete, the author indicates his sharing of his experience will bring others who have strayed back into obedience to God (v. 13). To underscore his

Homiletical Perspective

A quick overview of contemporary culture reveals two mistakes that affect a helpful understanding of sin. Our interpretative missteps are so commonly spoken and so completely at odds with Scripture that we might speak of them as crises. First, delighting in the deliciousness of other peoples' sins occupies much of our attention. Such a focus conveniently removes the heat that would come naturally from facing up to our own sin. We all know how easy it is to talk down at those who live some "low life," ignoring our close kinship with them as like types who are also "by nature sinful and unclean."

Second, we usually look at sin as primarily external in character. It is the eating of chocolate during Lent, the cursing of another motorist who cannot merge, or the bad habit of having one drink too many. According to Scripture, sin is much more internal than external in nature. God calls sin adultery of the heart. Jesus wants us to think more about what comes out of our mouths than what goes into them. One day he spoke in this way to suggest that what we utter arises from what we think and what we want. Sin is thus an internal problem. If we think in terms of cause and effect, we might say that *sin* is the cause and *sins* are the effect. Paul speaks of sin as a condition that underlies much of our inexplicable behavior ("I do not do what I want," he wrote one time, "but I do the very thing I hate" [Rom. 7:15]).

Those who preach Psalm 51 have the responsibility of addressing this twofold crisis. Neither the tendency to zero in on the sins of others, nor the practice of thinking about sin as mostly external, is beyond correction. People have the capacity to understand their own lives as encompassing more than mistakes, missteps, and confusion. They need to discover the language of sin. What better place to learn this language than in the church? Here they may find that sin cannot be trivialized in quite the same manner that mistakes or errors can. As for the hope of encouraging the faithful to look inward at sin instead of outward, this too can make for fruitful ministry. Think of it in this way: Most people have a basic understanding of the computer world. If they have a rudimentary comprehension of software, and the invisible way it works magic through the hardware, or of viruses, and the insidious way they instantly destroy a hard drive, these same people have a good chance of understanding how sin originates as an internal condition of our lives.

The psalmist illuminates such matters by speaking confessionally. First-person pronouns

Psalm 51:1-17

Theological Perspective

prayer of the powerful and privileged—those who abuse? What would this psalm sound like if it were rewritten from Bathsheba's perspective? Would God's grace and mercy be understood differently from the perspective of other characters in the story, such as Bathsheba and Uriah, who were most affected by David's violent actions?

One difficulty in the passage is that the psalm itself also seems to be silent with regard to Bathsheba's perspective. Both approaches to the text—considering the psalm as David's own reflections and taking the more contemporary view that the psalm was added by editors to express the way the community of faith wrestled with David's action—invite readers to think about sin and forgiveness in a larger communal setting. Verse 12, "Restore to me the joy of your salvation," speaks clearly about the importance of restoration. In the Hebrew Bible and also in later Christian tradition, restoration refers not only to the way that God acts but also to the human response to God's grace and mercy.

Ash Wednesday marks the beginning of Lent. The Lenten season invites us into reflection about our own individual and communal wrongdoings and leads us toward transformation. Psalm 51 is a rich resource for reflection that will deepen our own understanding of the ways we live in collusion with social systems that marginalize and oppress ourselves and others. We are living in a world that encourages us to consider individual desires first, even when satisfying those individual desires and needs comes at the expense of others. Evidence of this is seen in the way that decisions about human well-being are made on the basis of economic motives. In movies and other media, relationships are too often portrayed as the means to secure one's own well-being, with little thought of others' worth. Our bodies are turned into commodities and used by advertisers to lure us to buy consumer goods. Sexuality continues to be seen as the means to dominate others and for individual fulfillment, rather than as a significant part of relationships.

Traditionally, Christians observe Ash Wednesday with a service where ashes are used to mark a sign of the cross on each worshiper's forehead. When we pray this psalm on Ash Wednesday, we are marking the beginning of our commitment to find ways to participate in the restoration of relationships.

ELIZABETH L. HINSON-HASTY

Pastoral Perspective

assessment and disclosure to God; the experience of God's love, compassion, and forgiveness; the practice of forgiving ourselves (and others); a renewed effort to live in the awareness of God's presence; the restoration of a right spirit within us; the assurance of the sustaining power of the Holy Spirit; and the joy of salvation.

Psalm 51 describes a process of spiritual formation and deepening through actions like these:
—Seeing ourselves as we are, as God sees us
—Focusing on our relationship with God by being aware of God's loving and living presence
—Admitting to God (and others, if necessary) where we have fallen short in our behavior and response to God's love and care
—Being aware of God's steadfast love and abundant mercy available at all times
—Believing that God can cleanse us, create a new heart within us, and deepen the loving relationship between God and ourselves
—Knowing that God desires a relationship of truth and love and works with us continually to develop a relationship with those qualities
—Experiencing the Holy Spirit of God within us that is continually working to develop a "right" spirit
—Valuing and cherishing this deepening relationship with God
—Trusting that God is willing not only to forgive us but also to "blot out" our iniquities
—Realizing how essential this loving relationship with God is to our joy and fulfillment in life
—Being willing and available to partner with God to assist, guide, and mentor others in their relationships with God
—Relying on God to open our lips appropriately to sing God's praise

On Ash Wednesday we should be aware of and sorry for our failings, our missing God's hopes and prayers for our lives. We should also be confident in God's love, compassion, and mercy for us and in God's continued remarkable action in this world. Beginning today, we move toward a unique forty-day journey with Jesus and have the opportunity to fall more deeply in love with Love.

KATHERINE E. AMOS

Ash Wednesday

Exegetical Perspective

desire to share his experience, the psalmist implores God to deliver him from "bloodguilt" or "bloodshed" (v. 14), a term often associated with a very significant transgression of God's moral order (see Ezek. 9:9). This may be functioning as a rhetorical overstatement to dramatize the serious consequences that the author sees resulting from his transgression. The motive for God's acting to absolve the psalmist is that then the writer could respond by reporting to all who care to hear the gracious actions of God, an idea repeated in verse 15, once God has opened the penitent's lips.

In the third section (vv. 15–19) the writer summarizes his confidence in God's desire to forgive. He notes that the externals of offering a sacrifice for forgiveness are not what God truly desires (v. 16). Rather, what God is concerned with is the interior state of the penitent (v. 17). The expression at the beginning of verse 17 may well be a superlative and rendered as "Exceptional sacrifices are a broken spirit," the term "God" sometimes employed to express the superlative (see Jonah 1:3). The second clause uses two adjectives to describe the interior state of the penitent: "a broken and crushed heart, O God, you will not despise." The same verb for "broken" is employed in both 17a and 17b, and is used in circumstances of abject humility (Ps. 38:8). The psalmist is emphasizing that God's truest concern is with the inadequacy the penitent feels in light of God's overwhelming grace, and that God would never reject an approach out of such an overwhelming sense of brokenness and need.

The lectionary leaves off the conclusion of the canonical form of the psalm in verses 18–19. This portion seems to express a view contrary to the overall thrust of the psalm, namely, that God will be pleased by proper sacrifices, so many take verses 18–19 as an addition to this psalm intended to reaffirm the central role of the temple in the Second Temple period.

KENNETH G. HOGLUND

Homiletical Perspective

surround his language of washing and cleansing. Read Psalm 51 aloud, and you will not be fooled into believing that sin is merely some ugliness lodged in other people. No, this psalmist is committed to dealing impartially with himself. He does not avoid guilt. He treats sin as something more than surface grime—"Indeed, I was born guilty, a sinner when my mother conceived me" (v. 5). There is a deep consciousness of personal responsibility for the havoc his own sin wreaks, making his pleas for divine mercy all the more poignant.

There are two other homiletical possibilities. A preacher might devote some energy to the psalmist's line, "Blot out all my iniquities." People understand the concepts of equilibrium and disequilibrium. Anyone who has suffered a raging ear infection knows the imbalance that comes when an ear is out of sorts. A body in disequilibrium is a body that cannot stand up straight under its own power. A spiritual life in similar imbalance struggles in its own way. *Iniquity*, like *inequity*, has to do with unevenness or imbalance, a perfect theme for Ash Wednesday preaching.

The other line worth attending to is the poetic verse: "Create in me a clean heart, O God, and put a new and right spirit within me." Someone once said that sin lacks creativity and has a monotonous quality to it. According to this understanding, sins are mostly reruns of one another—"the same old, same old." If this is true, then it stands to reason that the only way out of this hamster wheel of reruns is to receive a gift from the outside—some gift that the Lord alone can fashion. Call it grace that is new every morning, if you want. Just be aware that it is a creation of God, and exactly what we need. In fact, it is perfect for cleaning up something as dirty as sin.

PETER W. MARTY

2 Corinthians 5:20b–6:10

[20]We entreat you on behalf of Christ, be reconciled to God. [21]For our sake he made him to be sin who knew no sin, so that in him we might become the righteousness of God.

[6:1]As we work together with him, we urge you also not to accept the grace of God in vain. [2]For he says,

"At an acceptable time I have listened to you,
and on a day of salvation I have helped you."

See, now is the acceptable time; see, now is the day of salvation! [3]We are putting no obstacle in anyone's way, so that no fault may be found with our ministry, [4]but as servants of God we have commended ourselves in every way: through great endurance, in afflictions, hardships, calamities, [5]beatings, imprisonments, riots, labors, sleepless nights, hunger; [6]by purity, knowledge, patience, kindness, holiness of spirit, genuine love, [7]truthful speech, and the power of God; with the weapons of righteousness for the right hand and for the left; [8]in honor and dishonor, in ill repute and good repute. We are treated as impostors, and yet are true; [9]as unknown, and yet are well known; as dying, and see—we are alive; as punished, and yet not killed; [10]as sorrowful, yet always rejoicing; as poor, yet making many rich; as having nothing, and yet possessing everything.

Theological Perspective

Ash Wednesday marks the beginning of a season of spiritual introspection. At least four groups for whom a pastor has concern can be addressed by this text: (1) congregations, like the one at Corinth, and possibly the pastor's own; (2) individuals, like Paul, reflecting on personal relationships; (3) pastors, like Paul, thinking about ministry; and (4) global Christianity, puzzling over religiously fueled violence and divisive divisions.

In our text each group is asked to examine itself. The congregation is charged to explore its unity as the body of Christ. Individual parishioners are to ask if the reconciling grace of God that has encountered them is having a positive effect. Or have they received grace in vain? Pastors listing Paul as an apostolic model of ministry are to assess their attitudes and attune themselves to the work of reconciliation. Finally, the congregation must receive the imperative to be reconcilers in the divided world beyond the church. The theological motifs of the passage are crucial for Christian anthropology, ecclesiology, and eschatology.

The Corinthian church is a microcosm of much of the modern church—urban, educated, diverse, and beset by numerous ethical and theological issues. Moreover, this church vacillates between the conflicting authorities of competing voices. In particular, they have found themselves divided over

Pastoral Perspective

Ashes on your forehead is one of the most powerful markings you may ever wear. College students tell me that Ash Wednesday is the one day of the year when they talk to strangers about their faith. People approach them after class, point to the ash crosses on their foreheads, and ask, "What's up with that?"

You remember the nursery rhyme: "Ring around the rosie, Pocketful of posies, Ashes, ashes, We all fall down." Strange things happen when we publicly acknowledge our mortality. It can open up conversations that might not otherwise take place. Naming mortality in a community is a way of falling down together so we can be pulled up together by the grace of God.

Paul is wearing his ashes in 2 Corinthians 6. As he summons the Corinthians to live faithfully, he shows his mortality and his vulnerability as a disciple. He has endured beatings, imprisonment, sleepless nights, hunger, and other hardships. His ashes are showing. At first glance, these ashes are not a great sales pitch for Christianity. Yet Paul is writing to his beloved Corinthians, whose neighbors are calling them impostors and who need a dose of encouragement in their new faith.

Paul's example of faithful living can be daunting. As a model Christian, he leaves the rest of us lurking in his shadow, struggling to live up to his standards.

Exegetical Perspective

Selected for the ringing summons to reconciliation with God (6:1–2) and the formulaic celebration of righteousness bestowed in Christ's death for sinners (5:21), this passage sets an important theological tone for Lent. The penitential season is not a lapse into "holiness boot camp," as though human beings make themselves righteous before God. Lent asks us to open our hearts to the grace of God.

A closer look at the reading in its context uncovers a more personal dimension to Paul's rhetorical highlights. Paul describes himself as God's ambassador, appealing to the audience for reconciliation (5:20a). The verses that follow this text (6:11–12) indicate the personal nature of this appeal. Paul hopes for a restoration of his badly frayed relationships with Christians in Corinth. Consequently, the main section of this reading (6:3–10) describes Paul's ministry in response to criticism by others (vv. 3, 8). This catalog is limited to immediate personal affronts, however. Paul sees the paradoxes of his apostolic ministry as appropriate to the message he preaches. He returns to this theme of the hardships that authenticate him as a minister of Christ when dealing with apostolic interlopers in 11:23–30.

Paul's opening appeal (5:20b) reminds readers that the stakes are not personal. As ambassador, Paul speaks for Christ. The formula in 5:21, "made him to

Homiletical Perspective

Ash Wednesday is a day for honest reckoning with human frailty, sinfulness, and the hope of reconciliation embodied in the life, death, and resurrection of Jesus Christ. This day begins the forty-day preparation for the paschal mystery of Christian redemption. Ash Wednesday confronts the gathered community with the uncertainty and difficulties of human life. For those who are marked with the ancient sign of ashes, the phrase "Remember that you are dust, and to dust you shall return" is the somber refrain that scores the entire service. The worship leader who is faithful to the solemnity of this day in the Christian year will keep the liturgy of Ash Wednesday in a minor key. The major chord of resurrection will come, but to hear the song of eternity, one must first have ears tuned to the reality of human brokenness and finitude.

Whether or not the worshiping congregation is marked with real ashes, ashes constitute the guiding image for the liturgy and proclamation on this day. This being said, one way to approach this reading from 2 Corinthians—and all the readings on Ash Wednesday—would be to surround the Scripture with *extended silence*. There is power added to what any preacher can proclaim on this day in the exercise of quietly and prayerfully hearing the biblical words with an invitation to self-examination. Words are

2 Corinthians 5:20b–6:10

Theological Perspective

which voices they will hear (1 Cor. 1–4). As 2 Corinthians demonstrates, they have not respected Paul's preaching and presence, thereby wounding him and depreciating his pastoral authority.

In response, the wounded apostle seeks to be a healer for this troubled congregation.[1] Paul appeals to the Corinthians to remember that they have received God's grace (5:18–19), that they have been forgiven of their sins (5:19), that they are now reconciled to God and one another (5:19), and therefore, with Paul, they are to act as God's representatives and witnesses (5:20). He fears that the factions that divide them and their ongoing rift with Paul make their graced state fruitless, in that they may have received that grace "in vain" (6:1). The congregation's task, therefore, is to rekindle a reconciling attitude with regard to one another, and to embrace Paul's ministry among them.

Good faith bears good relationships and good works. Thus, after thoroughly chastising the Corinthians in earlier chapters, Paul appeals to them to allow God to heal their brokenness and mend their tattered unity so that they can become the body of Christ. Forgiveness is a key theological concept in this passage. Paul reminds the Corinthians that their sins are forgiven; they are restored as a "new humanity" (5:17). They now must end their fruitless bickering by forgiving one another and seeking reconciliation with grace and not with haughtiness—including reconciliation with Paul. Being "at one with God" among themselves and with their pastor must begin "Now!" (6:2b), so that their salvation might be embodied and not useless and empty.

God has sought to reconcile not only congregations, but individual believers. God offers forgiveness to each person. Each is to become one with God and God's mission and serve as an ambassador who speaks of reconciliation and who is a reconciler. Indeed, as leaven in the loaf, the graced behavior of one can have an exponential effect on the whole. A widow's offering, an unsolicited helping hand in a crisis, a parent's forgiveness of an incorrigible child, are all images of reconciliation and peace. Small acts can result in big consequences. When Telemachus leaped into the arena in Rome as a living protest against the gladiatorial carnage, he was promptly run through with a sword and died. His one act was credited with the beginning of the end of these savage games. So, also, a humbled and repentant person can be a transforming representative of God's grace.

1. A direct allusion to Henri Nouwen's notion of the wounded healer.

Pastoral Perspective

Paul's list of trials may not resonate with everyone in the pews. The most pressing problems in our lives may seem insignificant compared to the trials on Paul's list. Yet we bump into reminders of our mortality every day, and they rub off on us. We are marked by mortality, though we may prefer not to look. Even if a particular church does not practice the imposition of ashes on Ash Wednesday, it is possible for a congregation to consider the ways that Christians metaphorically wear ashes—signs of our mortality—as we begin this holy season of Lent.

Consider those struggling with alcoholism, whose families are hoping someone will see the ashes on their foreheads and answer their cries for help. A few in our congregations may be literally imprisoned as Paul was, but many of us are imprisoned by consumerism or greed. To acknowledge this imprisonment is to name our mortality: we cannot take all those possessions with us, no matter how tightly we hold them. Some in the pews are wearing the ashes of frustration or exhaustion as they labor for justice but cannot see the fruits of these labors on the horizon. To accept mortality is to accept humanity. "Ashes, ashes, We all fall down."

Unfortunately, some in our congregations and communities do literally suffer beatings, imprisonment, or hunger. How can we lift up Paul's encouragement without validating domestic violence or famine in any way? How can we name our mortality without glorifying suffering? Christ modeled this balance for us. Christ was aware that he would suffer and die, yet he spent his days on earth fasting, praying, healing, giving—and encouraging others humbly to do the same. He did not glorify suffering, but worked to alleviate the world's suffering, while also laying down his own life for others.

Paul has been marked by his brushes with mortality too. Yet he knows the ashes are not the end of the story. A few verses earlier, he declares to the Corinthians that because they are in Christ, they are new creations (2 Cor. 5:17). How can a new creation already be smeared with ashes? Paul's litany in 6:8b–10 names paradox as central to a life of faith. We are poor yet lavishly rich. We are struggling yet rejoicing. We wear our mortality on our foreheads yet trust the promise of eternal life.

Just when we think all of the glory has to wait until we reach heaven, heaven breaks in: "Now is the acceptable time; see, now is the day of salvation!" (6:2). Paul's pep talk to the Corinthians includes a rearrangement of our assumptions about time. As Nathan Mitchell argues about the concept of time in

Ash Wednesday

be sin . . . that . . . we might become the righteousness of God," employs patterns found elsewhere in Paul (Gal. 3:13–14; Rom. 8:3–4). By taking the place of sinful humanity (on the cross), Christ made it possible for sinners to stand as righteous before God. Traditionally, the phrase "made sin" has been interpreted in two ways. Some, following Latin patristic writers, treat it as shorthand for "sin offering," a cultic action (so Rom. 3:25; 1 Cor. 5:7). The alternative is closer to Paul's view in Romans 8:3–4. It implies that Christ suffers as though he were sinner. As obedient Son of God, he would not be subject to death as punishment for sin (Rom. 5:12; 6:23), had he not chosen to die in place of the sinner.

What is the relationship between the "righteousness of God" bestowed through this exchange and the reconciliation with God in verse 20? Some see the former as a variation of Paul's customary righteousness language to accommodate the specific needs of the moment, the reconciliation between the Corinthians and the apostle. Most interpreters opt for some distinction between the two. Reconciliation picks up on the sinner's estrangement from God. Righteousness reflects the goal of the process of salvation, standing before God as new creation (5:17). As believers, Paul's audience have received that grace of being righteous before God. Yet he warns that such faith could be "in vain" (6:1). Paul then quotes Isaiah 49:8 (LXX), reminding his audience that God has already extended salvation to them (6:2). The unstated rhetorical conclusion is that they should respond in kind.

Verse 3 marks a sharp turn back to the real problems faced by Paul and his associates. He insists that their conduct has been irreproachable (vv. 3–4a). When Paul follows that claim with self-commendation (v. 4a), he is venturing into rhetorically dangerous territory. Boasting could be construed as arrogance, a charge that he will later (in 2 Cor. 10:12–18) make against "false apostles" and their claims to be superior to Paul's apostolic presence. Paul has set up the self-commendation of verse 4 in 5:12. Everyone should answer to God for what is in the heart, as Paul does. Since there are some who criticize the apostle, and those who trust in the gospel he preaches on the basis of externals, this self-recommendation is to provide his audience with a way to answer back.

Having brought the audience over to his side so that they might even count themselves coworkers with Paul and God (6:1), Paul then describes the apostolic life in a catalog of hardships endured (vv. 4c–5);

not always an improvement on silence, and on this day of all days in the liturgical year, a fast from excessive explanation and rhetorical flourish is the feast that is most appropriate.

If a brief sermon is to be offered on this day based on 2 Corinthians 5:20b–6:10, then two themes are immediately apparent: the *urgency* of the call to accept the reconciliation offered in Jesus Christ and the *inherent cost* in worldly terms of following the call of Christ.

Echoing Joel's call for the people of Israel to return to the Lord and quoting from the prophet Isaiah (Isa. 49:8), Paul cries out, "See, now is the acceptable time; see, now is the day of salvation!" Part of Paul's proclamation is that our time on earth is limited; our lives are finite. We do not have forever to live into the grace that comes our way through Jesus Christ. Paul wants the church at Corinth to see the sand falling through the hourglass. Paul wants us all to hear the pressing importance symbolized in the imposition of ashes. *Remember that you are dust, and to dust you shall return.* Now, not later, is the day to accept and respond to the reconciliation that comes through Jesus Christ! This day, not tomorrow, is the time to embrace the grace that fills the finitude of our earthly lives with eternity! Now, right now, the trumpet blows calling us to return to the Lord!

The preacher does not have to share Paul's sense of the imminence of Christ's return to preach about the importance of turning to God's reconciliation in Christ soon and very soon. Death is an obvious reality for each of us. *Remember that you are dust, and to dust you shall return.* Everyone, young and old, needs to be reminded that time can be wasted and grace accepted in vain. There is a depth of purpose and a source of joy available in Christ that makes the living of our days rich and alive, but the allure of worldly wealth, security, power, and prestige can turn our eyes from the "treasures in heaven, where neither moth nor rust consumes and where thieves do not break in and steal" (Matt. 6:20).

Paul also wants the Corinthians to take note that things are not always as they seem. Paul wants to make it clear that to look at his ministry and see hardship and earthly failure does not mean that the message of reconciliation in Christ is untrue or unrealized. A ministry beset with "afflictions, hardships, calamities, beatings, imprisonments, riots, labors, sleepless nights, hunger" (vv. 4b–5) does not necessarily mean that the ministry is failing or the message is false. In fact, such difficulties may give evidence of the commitment of the messengers to be

2 Corinthians 5:20b–6:10

Theological Perspective

Not only does Paul address congregations and individual believers; he models reconciling love with humble boldness that can be both breathtaking and dangerous. In homiletics many of us were taught that confessional preaching in which we use ourselves as illustrations or models smacks of self-serving egoism. *Preacher, you are not the subject of the message. You are merely a bearer of the Word. You are a vehicle of the message.* In this passage and many others, however, Paul exudes an incarnational theology that is rooted in his life experiences.[2] Here he rehearses the suffering that he has endured from Jerusalem to Caesarea to Crete; then, at Galatia; in the synagogues where he introduced Jesus as the Christ; and more recently at the hands of the Corinthian church.

As the theologian does so often when narrative reaches its limits, Paul becomes an emotive theologian in a cascade of antitheses, and even paradoxes (6:3–10). Like Hosea, he will not renounce his love of the Corinthians to whom he is God's representative. Not because of them, but in spite of them, and because of his own experience of being reconciled to God, he bids them join him in the work of reconciliation. What a bold and graceful challenge, especially to pastors who have so often been unjustly maligned and suffered silently, not only in the vicissitudes that life brings, but, sadly, at the hands of Christian brothers and sisters. In many respects our ministry can be measured by how we act in times of human brokenness that is attended by destructive behaviors. Surely we are, as God's representatives, "healers." Paul's fighting words resonate to the cowed pastor: "with the weapons of righteousness [I am armed]" (6:7) to endure, though buffeted about by "afflictions, hardships, calamities, etc." (6:4).

Finally, beyond the congregation, the individual, and the pastor, Paul's wisdom leads us to consider Ash Wednesday for global Christianity. The scandal of schisms among Christians across the world deserves an ashen attention. Moreover, violent action in the name of God begets cycles of endless violence. During Lent we need to include the "big picture" of global brokenness. As those who have been turned from enemies to friends by God's grace, we must embrace the peoples of the earth in our vision of reconciliation. This is implied in Paul's call for us to be ambassadors, and it is the eschatological hope of all that Jesus taught about the kingdom of God.

DONALD W. MUSSER

Pastoral Perspective

liturgy, "Time is defined by meaning instead of its duration."[1] For Paul, the time for reconciliation to God is today and every day we wake up to stumble through life. Through this reconciliation, God has promised salvation.

In this reality of rearranged time, how are we to live? Paul connects reconciliation to God with living an honorable life. You are forgiven, but what difference does it make in how you live? You are persevering by the grace of God, but how will others know? Paul suggests that our journeys will be marked by struggle, but also by our striving for purity, knowledge, patience, and kindness (6:4–6). Every time we fall short, we are met with an Ash Wednesday moment, when we say yes, both to the ashes and to the promise of God's grace and forgiveness.

Confessing our sins is a central part of Ash Wednesday worship. On this day we practice wearing our ashes by naming our sins before God and one another. Paul's list of honorable qualities in 6:6–7 can remind us how it looks to live as people reconciled to God. It can also remind us of how far we still have to go. His refrain of hope in 6:8b–10 is our assurance that running this race is not in vain.

How will you wear your ashes today? How will you lead your congregation in confessing their sins and naming their mortality? If today is the day of salvation (6:2), then what better time to wear our ashes, showing the world that we are mortal, yet reconciled with God?

CALLISTA S. ISABELLE

---

2. James William McClendon, among others, has argued that all theology is autobiography.

1. Nathan D. Mitchell, "From Liturgical Text to Tablature: Telling It Slant," paper presented at the Yale Institute of Sacred Music Kavanagh Lecture, New Haven, CT, October 9, 2007.

Exegetical Perspective

virtues exhibited (vv. 6–7); indifference to what others say (v. 8a); and paradoxes of apparent weaknesses that result in the greatest good (vv. 8b–10). The initial list of hardships endured corresponds to situations that Paul faced in spreading the gospel. Some were caused by the hostile reaction of others or by natural disasters. Others, such as working at a trade and possibly suffering both hunger and lack of sleep, were Paul's strategy. He could offer the gospel "for free," not commanding the wages of popular orators or philosophers in his day (1 Cor. 9:3–18).

The opening set of virtues in verse 6 appears to contain more general attributes of the Christian life that are signs of living according to the Spirit (cf. Gal. 5:22). The turn toward "power of God" and the military image "weapons of righteousness" (v. 7) return to the sense of apostolic ministry as struggle. Paul later speaks as though he were a general besieging a city (10:4–5). Both the weapons and the victory in promoting the gospel belong entirely to God.

Paul had been accused of inconsistency after a disastrous visit and cancellation of another visit to Corinth (1:15–2:4). Here he insists that he does not change his behavior to suit what people are saying (v. 8a). The catalog of paradoxes (vv. 8b–10) supports his claim. Each negative represents an outsider's view of the apostle. Most connect with hardships such as imprisonment, beatings, laboring, going hungry and without sleep. The apostle has nothing that would confer honor in the sense of social standing or importance. Yet for each negative, there is a positive outcome. It is, as he argued earlier, the near-death character of the apostle's life that enables life-giving faith (4:7–12).

Paul invites listeners to stand with him in recognizing the true foundation of his apostleship in the power of God. Does he succeed? If 2 Corinthians 10–13 came later, Paul would go over much of this ground again when outside "superapostles" used his weaknesses as marks of dishonor.

PHEME PERKINS

Homiletical Perspective

ambassadors for Christ in season and out of season, in good times and bad times, in ill repute and good repute. To turn back from proclaiming God's reconciliation because of obstacles on the journey would be to doubt the work of God in Jesus Christ. Paul reminds the church at Corinth that he and others continue in the hard times with "purity, knowledge, patience, kindness, holiness of spirit, genuine love, truthful speech, and the power of God" (vv. 6–7a).

Ash Wednesday calls us to face the harsh realities inherent in living in the finite world while committed to eternal things. The truthfulness of reconciliation in Christ is deeper and far more important than any worldly signs of power, prestige, or place.

A sermon on this passage might remind a Christian community that the call of Christ is to faithfulness, not to earthly success. To borrow other language from Paul, Ash Wednesday is a time to take stock in our foolishness for Christ. Are we willing to go where the Spirit of Christ leads us, even when that leading might be down the difficult road of reconciliation? Are we willing to give up the trappings of high station in order to be messengers of grace and eternal treasures? Can we come to a place of understanding that in Christ we possess everything, even as we have nothing of material value? In this world we are dust, and to dust we shall return; so can we place our trust in the One who brought to our dusty world the salvation of God?

ROBERT W. PRIM

Matthew 6:1-6, 16-21

"Beware of practicing your piety before others in order to be seen by them; for then you have no reward from your Father in heaven. 2"So whenever you give alms, do not sound a trumpet before you, as the hypocrites do in the synagogues and in the streets, so that they may be praised by others. Truly I tell you, they have received their reward. 3But when you give alms, do not let your left hand know what your right hand is doing, 4so that your alms may be done in secret; and your Father who sees in secret will reward you.

5"And whenever you pray, do not be like the hypocrites; for they love to stand and pray in the synagogues and at the street corners, so that they may be seen by others. Truly I tell you, they have received their reward. 6But whenever you

Theological Perspective

In the Canadian movie *Jesus of Montreal* (1989), actor Lothaire Bluteau plays an actor named Daniel who, in turn, portrays Jesus in a revamped version of the passion play. The enlivened telling of the life of Jesus raises the concern of the local Catholic authorities, including the cathedral priest who commissioned the work. They are all worried about the potential questions raised by the not-entirely orthodox text of the script when, in fact, the lives of the actors participating in the production are being transformed, taking on the concerns and traits of their respective characters. Likewise, members of the audience are being transformed by their encounter with the particular and authentic performance of Jesus' life and ministry, death, and resurrection. How poignant, then, is Daniel's proclamation as Jesus during a performance of the play when the disgruntled and self-righteous Catholic dignitaries are in attendance: "Beware of priests who desire to walk in long robes and love greetings in the markets, the highest seats in temples, the best rooms at feasts, who devour widows' houses, pretending prayer. They shall receive a greater damnation."[1]

Pastoral Perspective

"Beware of practicing your piety before others in order to be seen by them; for then you have no reward from your Father in heaven." This principle of doing acts of piety without concern for being seen flies in the face of many subtle and not too subtle temptations shaped by social pressures. Our postmodern culture is characterized by image and style while being distinguished by the drive of marketing, television, and other media into our lives.[1] In a culture that values size and "success," there are ample examples of megaministries that are adept at marketing their ministries and are the apparent "winners" in the "religious marketplace."

Ministers may be tempted to imitate well-known ministerial entrepreneurs who transform their spiritual gifts into salable commodities for mass consumption.[2] In this context of competition for souls, I was once struck by the remark of a pastor who said to a group of ministers, "Presentation often matters more than substance." All of us living in a culture where "perception is reality" need to beware of the temptation toward preoccupation with bolstering our image simply to make a good

1. *Jesus of Montreal* script: http://www.script-o-rama.com/movie_scripts/j/jesus-of-montreal-script-transcript.html (retrieved August 31, 2008).

1. Shayne Lee, *T. D. Jakes, America's New Preacher* (New York: New York University Press, 2005), 4–5.
2. Ibid., vii.

pray, go into your room and shut the door and pray to your Father who is in secret; and your Father who sees in secret will reward you. . . .

¹⁶"And whenever you fast, do not look dismal, like the hypocrites, for they disfigure their faces so as to show others that they are fasting. Truly I tell you, they have received their reward. ¹⁷But when you fast, put oil on your head and wash your face, ¹⁸so that your fasting may be seen not by others but by your Father who is in secret; and your Father who sees in secret will reward you.

¹⁹"Do not store up for yourselves treasures on earth, where moth and rust consume and where thieves break in and steal; ²⁰but store up for yourselves treasures in heaven, where neither moth nor rust consumes and where thieves do not break in and steal. ²¹For where your treasure is, there your heart will be also."

Exegetical Perspective

Today's Gospel reading comes from the middle of the Sermon on the Mount. It addresses the focus of Ash Wednesday and the season of Lent that it inaugurates, by naming the disciplines and practices that help to prepare one for the events of Holy Week and Easter. The passage begins with a warning in verse 1 ("Beware . . . !"), elaborates with three examples (vv. 2–18), and concludes with a summary warning (vv. 19–21). Except for the Lord's Prayer (in vv. 7–15, which is not assigned to be read in this lection) and the conclusion in verses 19–21, both of which are found also in Luke (11:2–4 and 12:33–34, respectively), this material is unique to Matthew's Gospel. The specific examples— charitable giving, prayer, and fasting—are standard examples of actions that would have been deemed worthy of praise in both Jewish and Gentile society. They are commended also for the followers of Jesus and the church of Matthew's day.

The difference for followers of Jesus was not the acts themselves, but rather the motives and manner in which they were to be carried out. Instead of being done with fanfare that would attract attention and admiration from other people, these deeds were to be done modestly and in secret. In that way they became a challenge to the "honor" and competition that characterized Roman society and that Matthew accuses the local synagogue of adopting.

Homiletical Perspective

On the Christian calendar, Ash Wednesday marks the beginning of a season of awareness of sin and death and of the possibilities of new life in Jesus Christ. For some, Lent is also a time of increased devotion—extra prayer services, added prayer disciplines, and fasting. Within this attention to devotion and discipline, this text from Matthew's Gospel offers a stern warning: the dangers of sin are as close as the expression of piety to which we are called. "Beware," says Jesus, "of practicing your piety before others" (v. 1). To preach on this warning is to bring it into the life of the gathered community, and doing so could make for a strong hortatory or prophetic sermon. To preach in this way, however, is not without its dangers.

The text itself has a hortatory character and, as redacted by the lectionary, has a particular shape. Jesus speaks to his disciples, cautioning them against practicing their righteousness before others. Three specific warnings follow, concerning almsgiving, praying, and fasting. In each case, the disciples are not to allow anyone to see what they are doing; their practice is to be done "in secret; and your Father who sees in secret will reward you" (v. 4). The selection concludes with an exhortation to build up treasures in heaven, which are invulnerable to the decay of moth and rust. At issue is the *focus* of the disciples'

Matthew 6:1-6, 16-21

Theological Perspective

The critique alludes to the ongoing tensions both between Jesus and the Pharisees (as well as other Jewish authorities) and between Daniel (in the fictitious world of this movie) and the church authorities of his time. More importantly for the Ash Wednesday text from Matthew 6, it highlights the dangers and consequences of inauthentic piety. Public or pretend displays of pious acts merit nothing. Matthew iterates the point explicitly: "Beware of practicing your piety before others in order to be seen by them; for then you will have no reward from your Father in heaven" (v. 1). In each of the directives in today's reading, the theme is the same: when you give to the needy, donate privately (vv. 2–4); when you pray, pray privately (vv. 5–6); when you fast, abstain privately (vv. 16–18); and when you store up treasures, store up treasures of the heart (vv. 19–21).

How can a text that implores private acts of righteousness be read on the day one receives (in many denominations) the imposition of ashes, a very visible and public act of piety? The thematic emphasis on private piety can be overstated. Better is the more implicit (and underlying) theme present in the calls to charity, prayer, and fasting: namely, authenticity. Understanding the Matthean mandates to private acts and the reception of ashes through the hermeneutical lens of authenticity bridges the (otherwise) apparent divide. Authenticity blurs the rigid lines of public and private, so that neither need be read legalistically. Private acts are not authentic, and public ones inauthentic, by default. Rather, the authenticity of an act of faith, or an act of piety, is determined by the desire and motivation of the one engaged in that act. Those desires and motivations cannot be judged externally.

Nonetheless, here is one helpful illustration of an authentic act (perhaps of piety, certainly of friendship) that is authentic, in large part because the act is done privately, even secretly. It comes from an unlikely source, a children's book called *The Frog and Toad Treasury*, by Arnold Lobel. Frog and Toad are good friends. In chapter after chapter, Lobel describes ways they pass time together, explore the world together, and support one another. One chapter is titled "The Surprise." The action in it takes place in October. The leaves are falling. Frog decides to go to Toad's house, secretly, and rake his leaves for him.

"I will rake all the leaves that have fallen on his lawn. Toad will be surprised."[2] Toad has the same

2. Arnold Lobel, *The Frog and Toad Treasury* (New York: Harper Collins, 1970), 42.

Pastoral Perspective

impression on others. When this is our goal, managing our public reputation trumps the quiet walk of personal integrity. We are tempted to "play the role" in the world that is "our stage."

As a pastor and seminary professor, I struggle with the problem of "appearances." Though I acknowledge that my gifts and talents are from God, "presentation" of myself "counts" in the public arena. For speaking engagements in churches, I am asked for a biographical sketch that summarizes my accomplishments and journey in ministry. Will sharing this promote the event or me? As an African American male with an academic doctorate, I see this accomplishment within a broader communal context of a marginalized people's strides toward freedom. So soon after doors of opportunity have been opened, more African American males are languishing in the criminal justice system than are achieving in the educational system. Is it personal ego to insist that my students recognize my title, or is this being a faithful witness in the struggle?

One of the rules of John Wesley, founder of the Methodist movement, was "to do good." Wesley wrote, "It is expected of all . . . that they should continue to evidence their desire of salvation. . . . By doing good; by being in every kind merciful after their power; doing good of every possible sort, and, as far as possible, to all."[3] What a marvelously simple rule to understand and to practice! However are not our motives for doing good sometimes mixed? Rules that are simple to understand are not easy to practice. Yes, we do good to help others, but do we not also "do good," hoping that we will receive some social benefit in return—receiving a tax deduction, accomplishing service learning goals, obtaining community service credit, increasing our network of contacts from our service on not-for-profit boards, or building our resume? In the complexity of our living, even simple rules can become perilously difficult.

In the face of such temptations, the Ash Wednesday Gospel text calls us to a season of examination of our motives. Even "doing good"—to give to the needy, to pray, or to fast—can become an occasion of religious posturing. There is no contradiction between the warning to examine our motives and the admonition of Matthew 5:14–16,

3. *The Doctrines and Disciplines of the African Methodist Episcopal Zion Church, with an Appendix Revised by the General Conference Greensboro, North Carolina, July 28–August 3, 2004* (Charlotte, NC: A.M.E. Zion Church, 2005), 23. John Wesley's General Rules are common to Wesleyan churches, including the African Methodist Episcopal Church, African Methodist Episcopal Zion Church, Christian Methodist Episcopal Church, and United Methodist Church.

Exegetical Perspective

The initial warning presents the only translation problem in the passage. The acts that are meant are summarized as *dikaiosynē*, which the NRSV translates as "piety," following its predecessor, the RSV. The KJV and the NKJV translate it as "charitable deeds," equating the term with the first of the three actions, instead of seeing it as encompassing all of them. The NIV and the New American Standard Version stay closer to the Greek by translating the term as "righteousness" or "deeds of righteousness." Most Spanish translations edge a step further by translating the term as *justicia*, justice. Instead of devoutness as an attitude toward God, which the English word "piety" suggests, the Greek word and such translations as "justice" or "righteousness" ground the three specific behaviors in the practice of covenant righteousness that is mandated by Torah and that denotes the presence of God's reign. The warning in verse 1 poses a stark alternative: if one does these things for honor or rewards on earth, one forfeits one's reward from God.

The three examples of the "justice" one is to practice follow the same pattern. Each begins with the assumption that one will do the act, be it almsgiving, prayer, or fasting. Then there is an instruction on how *not* to do it, followed by a positive alternative or model. The first, almsgiving (vv. 2–4), unfolds in hyperboles that reflect the tension that existed between Matthew's community and other Jews in the synagogue out of which they came. First, the text uses a term from the theater, "hypocrites," actors who play their parts with full fanfare, in order to be glorified by the audience for their impressive performances. While there is no record of people actually sounding a trumpet to herald their actions, the exaggeration encompasses all such deeds done as part of a public role to enhance one's own honor. Public acclaim is not to be the end pursued by Matthew's community. Instead, they are to continue to redistribute resources to those in need, but to do so in secret. Hyperbole again marks the teaching, for of course it is impossible for one hand not to know what the other is doing. The point, though, is to meet the needs of the poor, and not to put on a performance. God will know and reward such deeds. All three of the examples end with the same assurance—that God "who sees in secret will reward you." Nowhere does Matthew elaborate on the nature of the reward beyond the affirmation that one is in accord with God's own purposes.

Prayer is the second act of justice that is mentioned (vv. 5–6). The form and the substance of

Homiletical Perspective

piety. For those who follow Jesus, acts of devotion are not done for praise, visibility, or the building up of wealth and reputation. Instead, the focus is to be God alone. Hypocrisy consists of undertaking pious action in hope of earthly rewards, rewards that come from human beings instead of God.

To communicate this insight of the text, the preacher should ask herself several questions. First, in what forms of piety does her congregation engage? Jesus assumed that his disciples would fast, pray, and give alms; these were the marks of a good Jew. These examples, however, may or may not connect with the lives of individual parishioners or the congregational setting. There may be other forms of piety, such as a specific liturgical practice or various social ministry programs. The preacher may ask, What other works of devotion are *assumed* in this congregation as part of our faith life? Serving on a committee? Assisting with worship? Teaching Sunday school? Volunteering at the food bank? With these questions answered, the preacher might explore *why* these things are done. As most pastors will tell you, the motives for the things that churches and their people do are usually mixed. A genuine love of God can sit side by side with a desire for self-aggrandizement, a passion for justice with a selfish need for control. Under the condition of sin, it cannot be otherwise. It is, however, the preacher's task to name those impure motives and continue to call forth actions done in faith and hope. Or, in the language of the Lutheran theological tradition, it is the preacher's task to put "old beings" to death and to raise up "new beings" of life and faith.

There are, however, a few difficulties with extending the insight of the text into the sermon in this way. First, a sermon critiquing the life of the congregation requires a good deal of self-examination on the part of the preacher. Why has she chosen *these* examples to preach about? Does she harbor unresolved personal anger or disappointment in something the people are doing that might color the text and tone of the sermon? It is tempting indeed to use the pulpit to air grievances against the habits of the congregation or individual parishioners. The preacher is not Jesus and is thus subject to sin in the same way as the rest of the congregation. She, like they, must heed Jesus' warning: is the purpose of her sermon to advance her own agenda, or is it truly a word from the Lord?

In addition to examining her own motives, the honest preacher will also have to wrestle with how to handle Jesus' condemnation of the "hypocrites" in

Matthew 6:1-6, 16-2

Theological Perspective

idea. Both manage to arrive at the home of the other unseen, ascertain that no one is home, rake the leaves, and return to their own houses unnoticed. On their respective ways home, however, a wind comes.

The wind blows and blows. The piles of leaves do too, so that the leaves are scattered everywhere. At the end of the day, neither Frog nor Toad realizes what the other has done, because both return home to leaves strewn across their yards. Both pledge to rake their own leaves the next day.

"When Frog got home, he said, 'I will clean up the leaves that are all over my own lawn. How surprised Toad must be!'" Toad echoed Frog. "That night Frog and Toad were both happy when they each turned out the light and went to bed."[3]

The sense of purpose each derived from his acts of love and service (like praying or charitable giving) was not dependent on a public response or acknowledgment; it was not, in the end, even dependent on the accomplishment (given the wind). The acts were, in a word, authentic.

In contrast to Frog and Toad's private, unacknowledged, and authentic acts of service (or Matthew's call for private fasting and prayer) stands the Ash Wednesday practice of the imposition of ashes—replete with a very long and complicated history—as a public display of faith and an act of piety. However, Ash Wednesday is so much more. It marks the beginning of Lent and calls us to reflection and repentance; it invites us to begin our preparation for Good Friday and for Easter. It does all these things by the very use of ashes, which remind us of our humanity and our sinfulness: that we are of dust and to dust we shall return. In this way, the imposition of ashes does not stand in contrast to the reading from Matthew but embodies the spirit of those readings in its own painstaking authenticity.

LORI BRANDT HALE

Pastoral Perspective

where the disciples are told to let their light shine before persons so that others would glorify God. Righteous conduct must be visible and sometimes explained so that God is glorified. The opening verse of our lesson, Matthew 6:1, sets the frame for our practice of three ancient acts of Jewish piety—almsgiving, prayer, and fasting. Jesus assumes that his followers will do all three. He says, "Whenever you give alms" (v. 2), "whenever you pray" (v. 5), and "whenever you fast" (v. 16). Each of these is a spiritual discipline that, when practiced during the Lenten season, strengthens our capacity to please God in such acts of piety all through the year.

We are also instructed how to carry out these spiritual disciplines in such a way that our lives lift up the Savior rather than ourselves. We are warned not to do acts of piety to be praised by others. We are guaranteed that those who ignore this warning may get what they want but will not receive God's blessing. We are instructed how to perform these acts secretly. Finally, we are assured that the Father who sees in secret will reward openly.

The ritual of imposition of the ashes is a sobering reminder of our mortality. Receiving the ashes with the words "You are dust and to the dust you shall return" is a gentle whisper that says, "It is not about you." It is the Creator who is always to be glorified and not we who are created. Hearing the words "Repent and believe the gospel" is a strong rebuke to our tendency toward guarding our own image rather than growing in the image of God.

Might the season of Lent be a time of penitence and transformation from our selfish consumerism to unselfish contribution? What if we learned to serve together with persons of other races, classes, churches, and religions without being concerned with who gets the credit? Repenting, believing, and doing the gospel would become more important than our reputations. Despite our mixed motives, imperfections, and many mistakes, God uses those whose hearts are right. The inside-out work within us that marks profound transformation begins by giving ourselves sincerely to God through spiritual disciplines such as prayer, fasting, acts of piety, and acts of justice.

JEFFERY L. TRIBBLE SR.

3. Ibid., 51–53.

Ash Wednesday

Exegetical Perspective

this teaching echo the first. Again, the point is that prayer is not a public show to impress one's neighbors, but rather something between oneself and God. The teaching on prayer is expanded by a further negative and positive example (vv. 7–15, not included in this lection). There the contrast is between the long and flowery prayers attributed to Gentiles and the spare language of the prayer Jesus taught, which echoes prayers known in the synagogues of Matthew's day.

The final act of justice, fasting (vv. 16–18), receives a similar warning and advice. Instead of making a show of one's fasting by looking utterly miserable, one should groom and conduct oneself normally, since the reason for fasting is not to show off to others for the sake of one's own honor, but to focus on and commit oneself to God's purposes.

The concluding summary (vv. 19–21) elaborates in metaphorical form on the "reward" mentioned in each of the examples. The transience and insecurity of earthly "treasures" encompass not only literal treasures that can be stolen or destroyed, but also the praise and honor accorded by one's culture, which can prove utterly fickle. Those treasures define the goals of the people whose actions provide the negative examples of each act of *dikaiosynē* that was discussed. "Treasures in heaven," on the other hand, do not refer to rewards reserved for after death. Instead, as a good Jew, Matthew uses God's name and even explicit words for God very sparingly. Just as he writes of the "kingdom of heaven" where Mark and Luke refer to the "kingdom of God," so also here (where God is not named) the valuable treasures are those that one finds in company with God, and in accord with God's sovereign will. The quest for that accord, rather than any outward show of discipline or religious behavior, gives shape to our Lenten devotion as we prepare to follow Jesus in a life committed to God's reign.

SHARON H. RINGE

Homiletical Perspective

verses 2, 5, and 16. The text is explicitly tendentious: Jesus has an argument with how some of his fellow Jews practice their faith. When Matthew's readers, likely Jewish believers, first heard this text, they would have received this not as wholesale condemnation of Jewish life and practice, but as a word from a Jewish messiah about how Jewish believers were to act. Not so our congregations, who likely have few if any Jewish believers. The preacher should be aware of how this text can reinforce ugly stereotypes. Even if the congregation is not likely to hear the text with anti-Semitic ears, it is always easier to rush to the condemnation of others than to condemnation of the self. Protestants might point to Catholics as hypocrites, or evangelicals to mainliners, or vice versa on all counts. The preacher should resist any such temptation. Jesus' warning is meant for us "in here," not others "out there." If we concern ourselves with ourselves, we will have more than enough to worry about. The dangers of hypocrisy lie close to the surface.

The final danger, always present on Ash Wednesday, is that the preacher might focus only on sin and its consequences, or only what we are to do, while neglecting the promising character of life in Christ. If we concentrate only on the possibility for self-centeredness, it might leave the congregation wondering, "So why should I be here?" These words come from the One whose cross and resurrection defeat sin and its power. Self-centered though our piety may become, forgiveness is available through the grace of Christ. This forgiveness transforms self-centered people into God-centered people! When this happens, the disciplines of Lent—almsgiving, prayer, and fasting, among others—can be received more deeply as gifts of God that point us to God's presence in our lives and in our world. In the end, that is what faithful observance of Lent is—a grace-filled return to the Lord our God.

KIMBERLY M. VAN DRIEL

Deuteronomy 26:1-11

¹When you have come into the land that the LORD your God is giving you as an inheritance to possess, and you possess it, and settle in it, ²you shall take some of the first of all the fruit of the ground, which you harvest from the land that the LORD your God is giving you, and you shall put it in a basket and go to the place that the LORD your God will choose as a dwelling for his name. ³You shall go to the priest who is in office at that time, and say to him, "Today I declare to the LORD your God that I have come into the land that the LORD swore to our ancestors to give us." ⁴When the priest takes the basket from your hand and sets it down before the altar of the LORD your God, ⁵you shall make this response before the LORD your God: "A wandering Aramean was my ancestor; he went down into Egypt and lived there as an alien, few in number, and there he

Theological Perspective

Why does the church have to do theology? That may seem a strange question to raise for folk who have come to worship on the First Sunday in Lent, or on any occasion, but it is a question this text forces upon those who will hear it. For many worshipers, doing theology does not seem the most urgent task required of them on a Sunday morning. Is this what Lent is getting us into—theology?

The text in Deuteronomy 26 describes a liturgical act that is confessional and doxological, full of individual affirmation and corporate memory. It is an act of gratitude for God's particular grace that ends in a celebration whose embrace extends beyond Israel's own life ("the aliens who reside among you," v. 11). It describes a moment that is rooted in memory ("A wandering Aramean was my ancestor," v. 5), shaped by a journey ("The LORD brought us out of Egypt with a mighty hand," v. 8), and defined by joy ("shall celebrate with all the bounty that the LORD your God has given to you," v. 11). In rehearsing this story and affirming that *today* a declaration is made—"I have come into the land that the LORD swore to our ancestors to give us" (v. 3)—worshipers are committing theology. They are confessing that the faithfulness of God to Israel is the basis of their own life, the provision by which they may now voice their own gratitude and even claim

Pastoral Perspective

These days it is hard to know how we ever got along without computers and cell phones. A generation has now emerged that never knew a world without these appliances. We live in a world where the wisdom of the past is easily trumped by the latest bid for our loyalty. Are we the happy slaves of the new technologies? To whom do we belong?

The Deuteronomy passage provides an important perspective on pastoral care. There is the giving of the first fruit of the harvest and then a recitation of the story of deliverance. These are inseparable in the passage, suggesting that the meaning of the one (thanksgiving) frames the meaning of the other (recitation of God's acts of liberation).

What happens to a people's sense of self and history when their priorities are organized around material possessions and shifting market values? They may no longer know why they give thanks or to whom they give it. Their identity as God's people delivered from bondage may be lost so that certain acts of thanksgiving become meaningless. Hence this passage of Scripture is relevant to an understanding of ourselves as human beings who are the subjects of God's continual care and creative love. The text may help counter the illusion that we can deliver or save ourselves through our own technologies. Deuteronomy knows that when a people forget their past, they

became a great nation, mighty and populous. ⁶When the Egyptians treated us harshly and afflicted us, by imposing hard labor on us, ⁷we cried to the Lord, the God of our ancestors; the Lord heard our voice and saw our affliction, our toil, and our oppression. ⁸The Lord brought us out of Egypt with a mighty hand and an outstretched arm, with a terrifying display of power, and with signs and wonders; ⁹and he brought us into this place and gave us this land, a land flowing with milk and honey. ¹⁰So now I bring the first of the fruit of the ground that you, O Lord, have given me." You shall set it down before the Lord your God and bow down before the Lord your God. ¹¹Then you, together with the Levites and the aliens who reside among you, shall celebrate with all the bounty that the Lord your God has given to you and to your house.

Exegetical Perspective

These verses in Deuteronomy are among the best known in the book. At the center of the unit is something like a creedal affirmation (vv. 5b–10a) that rehearses the redemption and guidance of Israel from the descent into Egypt until the entry into Palestine. This recital has been placed within liturgical instructions for presenting the offering of firstfruits (vv. 1–5a, 10b–11). There is some debate whether two traditions are reflected in these verses in that verses 4 and 10 seem to indicate two different points at which the priest in charge is given the offering, and verses 3 and 5 seem to suggest two different affirmations to be made. Nonetheless, verses 1–11 should be read as one unit that is differentiated from the preceding verses (a curse against Amalek, 25:17–19) and those that follow (instructions concerning the paying of the tithe each three years, 26:12–15; cf. 14:22–29).

Chapter 26 as a whole marks the conclusion of the main body of Deuteronomy that begins with chapter 12. The section begins with instructions concerning where (at "the place that the Lord your God will choose": 12:5, 11, 14, 18, 21) and when (a variety of times when offerings are brought) Israel is to worship. The section closes, after the statement of numerous ordinances, with a return to the presentation of offerings at the place chosen by God

Homiletical Perspective

Each Lenten season we thoughtfully revisit the legacy of the cross and the defining miracle it wrought for each of us as Christians. Once again we seek to ready ourselves for the inbreaking of God's radical grace and abundance. Today's reading is a valuable summary of the story of God's promise of fulfillment for Israel after forty years of desert wandering. The themes of faithfulness, covenant, and abundance are all easily available for preachers, but the idea of inheritance may be the richest to pursue.

This passage has a rich heritage in the Jewish community. It begins with a liturgical recitation that was to become one of the essential identity stories in the "remembering" of Jewish society. This ancient narrative has a defining role for Israel and the understanding of its covenant with YHWH. It is the Israelites' inheritance; they are heirs to God's enduring promise that is now spread before them.

This is the climax of the exodus story. Imagine this: after thirty-nine years, eleven months, and one week in the wilderness, the Israelites are gathered on the plains of Moab, poised to enter the promised land. After nearly forty years of feeling lost and unsure, having had to learn a mountain of laws and rules, after being chastised for bad behavior (often well deservedly!), and after having spent a good deal of their sojourn being confused, underfed, and

Deuteronomy 26:1-11

Theological Perspective

this story as their own. As George Herbert noted in his poem about Israel's struggles in entering the promised land, "their story pens and sets us down,"[1] that is, their story reads those who remember and retell it, marking us by the same journey and shaping us by the same faithfulness.

The Greeks believed that the goddess of memory (*Mnēmosynē*) was the mother of imagination. For Israel, memory was more often the mother of faith, the way God's promises were rehearsed and named and claimed anew. To remember like that was not simply to rummage through archival or antiquarian documents, much less to preserve the past in some academic tome. The genealogies and stories ("A wandering Aramean was my ancestor . . .") identified Israel as belonging to the God who, in Calvin's words, "never forsakes his people in the middle of the journey"[2] and whose grace makes of such memories the stuff on which faith feeds. There are more than faint echoes of this passage in the words that celebrate another meal by which God's people are fed: "This do, in remembrance of me." Could theology be about a journey to that Table?

In any case, this journey marks us as people of a particular way. The church dares to undertake theology, to confess its faith, because on this journey the church believes that God has drawn near to us, spoken to us, even made provision for us out of the abundance of God's own life. Like a love letter, theology does not hunt up an excuse for professing its love or expressing its gratitude. Rather, it risks speaking the foolishness of love because it is convinced it has heard the language of love in God's passion and compassion for God's people. Remaining silent—or worse, conjuring up reasons to chatter among ourselves—is a sign of deafness, a sign that in seeking to avoid this word we have become captive to some deep and terrible power. The church confesses its faith by confessing that it has been loved, and thus has been liberated from the hell of self-absorption into the freedom of life as God's gift—the freedom to welcome "the aliens who reside" in our midst as gifts, the freedom to *know* God on the basis of God's extravagant, unwarranted, ever-surprising self-giving.

So what is one to say about all of this—that the journey of these Lenten weeks means that we really have to think long and hard about our story; that we have to practice some daily or weekly disciplines to

1. George Herbert, "The Bunch of Grapes," in *The Temple*, ed. Henry L. Carrigan Jr. (Brewster, MA: Paraclete Press, 2001), 128.
2. John Calvin, *Commentary on the Prophet Isaiah*, trans. William Pringle (Grand Rapids: Eerdmans, 1948), 4:238.

Pastoral Perspective

lose their present and future. This means that creeds and stories are part of the church's collective memory. Celebration and recitation are ways we fashion our identity as people of God. Ash Wednesday is an invitation to fashion anew our identity by reenacting the saving events that mark the Christian story.

There are three important pastoral themes to be discerned here.

Experiencing and expressing gratitude. Have you ever known people who seldom say, "Thank you," or express a sense of gratitude for the things done for or given to them? Some live as if they are entitled to the goodwill of others. Ash Wednesday is an opportunity to reverse this way of being in the world. Lent is a time to take stock of our life and that of the community, to remember the unmerited good that has come our way and to repent of the wrongs we have done. In this way we express gratitude by opening our lives to examination, purification, and correction. We express gratitude by seeking to live in right relationship with God, world, and self. Developing and expressing the attitude of gratitude, then, can become a spiritual discipline.

Remembering the ancestors. In this text, the ancestors are the particular individuals who stood out as exemplary figures for the people. Verse 5 reads, "A wandering Aramean was my ancestor . . ." Ash Wednesday and Lent offer us opportunities to recall those who have gone before us. These may be treasured friends, beloved relatives, or others who left their imprints on our lives and the life of the community. Our gratitude extends to them because through their faith they still speak and encourage us to work for a better world. We are challenged to remember global oppressions and the ancestors who resisted them. The work of our ancestors is furthered through our faithful efforts.

Remembering the past. The past represents the events that shaped us directly and indirectly, in recognized and unrecognized ways. We must struggle to remember the past so that we can learn the lessons of history and move toward a future with a greater sense of wisdom and appreciation of past struggles. When we ignore the past or fail to learn the lessons of history, then we are likely to repeat past tragedies on a different scale. When we do not learn from the past, the future becomes the past revisited.

This truth may be seen in experiences of violence and oppression. The question has been asked, "How

First Sunday in Lent

(26:2), accompanied with liturgical instructions and creedal affirmation (vv. 3–10), and a celebration of the covenant (vv. 16–18).

There is one very noticeable omission in the historical recital that accompanies the ritual act of presenting the firstfruits, namely any reference to Horeb/Sinai, the mountain of God. This has been explained in a number of ways. Some believe that 26:5b–10a represents a form of the confession by one group of Israelites who had not participated in the events at Horeb. Others, however, believe the omission results from the fact that the early chapters of Deuteronomy assume the Horeb tradition as the setting for the giving of the statutes and ordinances that constitute the bulk of chapters 12–25. Thus, there was no reason to make reference to Horeb in the recital. The problem has not been resolved among scholars. As the text now stands, it does represent a strange deviation from what could be expected from a creedal statement that in other respects so closely reflects the historical memories preserved in Genesis–Numbers.

The historical setting of Deuteronomy has at least two distinct phases, one before the fall of Jerusalem in 587 BCE and one after that pivotal event. Sometime in the seventh century, probably after the destruction of the northern kingdom Israel by the Assyrians, the core of the book of Deuteronomy was brought to the southern kingdom Judah. The commandments and statutes preserved in it reflect a settled community engaging in a variety of agricultural endeavors. The sanctuary initially was identified only as the place God chose for the divine name to dwell (26:2; cf. 12:5–7; 14:23–24; 16:2, 6, 11; et al.). Later the "place" came to be identified as Jerusalem. There was a "prophetic" edge to the core that emphasized care for the orphan, widow, and resident alien (Deut. 14:29; 16:11; 24:17, 19; 26:12–13; cf. Isa. 1:17, 23; Jer. 7:6; 22:3; Zech. 7:10).

The second historical setting is in the midst of the Babylonian exile (the middle-late sixth century BCE), when the core of Deuteronomy provided the foundation for the theological critique of Israel/Judah's history of failed loyalty to the Lord preserved as Joshua through 2 Kings. Deuteronomy 26 was remembered at various points along this line of tradition and even after the return of the exiles from Babylon. No doubt it meant different things to the many different people along the way, but to each group it was at least a vivid reminder of the expectation that proper worship of the Lord entailed the regular offering of gifts and self to God.

poorly housed—wondering why in the world they left Egypt in the first place—here they sit on the highlands overlooking the Jordan River Valley, the promised land lying in the distance! Everything they have endured, worked, and sacrificed for is at long last within their reach. The sense of God's grace and blessing in return for their faithfulness must be overwhelming.

Verses 1–4 speak of the firstfruits that are to be gathered in the new land. The tradition that emerged in Israel was that as the barley crop ripened (around Passover) the official harvest began and continued for another two months as other fruits matured. The first ripe fruit on any tree was picked and offered (with a ribbon tied around the branch) at the temple. While there is much to be said about the connection of this offering to the concept of tithing (which follows in vv. 12ff.), there is another important theme for preachers here that should not be overlooked: offering a harvest crop in worship presumes that the community not only has access to fertile ground, but that it is *settled*.

Up until this moment the people of Israel were wanderers without a land of their own; they were a people who lived in tents. It is not insignificant then that the liturgical passage that begins in verse 5 describes Israel's ancestor Jacob (and through him, Abraham) as a *wandering* Aramean (northern Syria). From this long legacy, painfully underscored by forty years in the wilderness, the people have come to this moment when they are about to be settled in their own land. Possessing land is the necessary prerequisite for any offering of firstfruits. It is the emotional and spiritual taproot of what the offerings mean and these actions cannot be understood apart from it.

There is opportunity here to explore two additional themes: our contemporary spiritual wanderings, and the irony of living in a country that seems to know no limits to the abundance it enjoys. Despite the fact that our nation is the wealthiest and most powerful on earth, there has never been a time in our history when more people have been consumed with a search for meaning. Anxiety and fear abound—our souls are unsettled—and while spiritual fixes proliferate, the signs of our rudderlessness grow. This wandering begs for a vision of a spiritual promised land that only faith—and faithfulness—can provide. There is a corollary we should not overlook: ours is a society that takes its amazing physical and financial abundance for granted. We have a promised land, and too often we take this as a sign of a special blessing from God,

Deuteronomy 26:1-11

Theological Perspective

keep that story ever fresh; that we have to work harder to be more sincere Christians; that we have to give more, practice more effective self-restraint? Is that the journey this text describes and to which Lent beckons us? Or is this text really about the celebration of God's abundance—to wandering Arameans and other confused types; to folk who live in a strange land and find themselves oppressed by hard taskmasters; to folk who feel trapped in impossible situations yet find themselves, surprisingly, delivered; to folk who are struggling clumsily to say thank you with their lives? The provisions of our God who never abandons us on the journey are, according to this text, bountiful (v. 11). That is why it is so important for the church, especially at the beginning of Lent, to undertake, above all, its theological task, which is to sing. This story in Deuteronomy ends in celebration and praise, which through its long and circuitous way, Lent prepares us also to offer. Theology is, in its purest sense, doxology—a way of singing, a way of offering praise to the One who will not let even death silence God's love for this world.

Of course, we do not *have* to sing. The church often thinks there are more important things to do. However what if we are set free to sing, what if we are set free to offer doxology, what if "this bounteous God" really is near us, offering joyful hearts and blessed peace to cheer us, keeping us in God's grace and guiding us when perplexed, freeing us from all ills in this world and the next?[3] Not to sing in the company of this God would be to fail miserably in understanding where Lent seeks to take us. It would be to starve ourselves on our own sufficiencies, rather than taste the banquet that has been prepared. Why not, rather, offer to God our thanks? Why not sit and eat? Why not do theology?

THOMAS W. CURRIE

Pastoral Perspective

can anyone who has experienced cruelty or harsh treatment oppress others?" Yet this is exactly what can happen when awareness of the past is denied or suppressed, dimmed or lost. The effects of the past can linger and influence the future in ways that escape our awareness. When we become historically aware of our situation and take responsibility for it, we have a better chance to address and correct cruel practices and the damaging effects of past experiences.

Ash Wednesday and the season of Lent provide opportunities for pastoral care at the individual, communal, and societal levels. Lent provides opportunities for individuals to gather in faith communities to remember and take responsibility for our collective history and our role in it. To do so can unleash redemptive possibilities for social transformation. We remember that Archbishop Desmond Tutu's Truth and Reconciliation Commission met to address the tragedies of individuals and families by calling perpetrators to account. In so doing, the community could address issues of long-standing suffering. Certain practices of social institutions around the world were challenged by this process and social transformation became possible, both in South Africa and elsewhere.

Pastoral care is not only for individual sufferers; it must extend to the communities and societies in which individuals and families live, move, and have their being. It includes care for the natural environment. We are relational beings, so that our care of persons and our care of nature are inseparable.

Celebration and recitation can be powerful symbols of and witness to what God has done in our midst. We may gather to give thanks and confess past wrongs of commission and omission, to acknowledge personal and collective participation in the wider dramas of life, and to seek to amend our ways. This is our appropriate response to the generous God who is ever ready to deliver us from various forms of bondage and give us resources beyond measure.

ARCHIE SMITH JR.

---

3. Obviously a paraphrase of the second verse of Martin Rinkart's hymn "Now Thank We All Our God."

Exegetical Perspective

The recital (26:5b–10a) stresses at least three things. First, God made the first move in claiming Israel for a people. Their forebear Jacob was a "wandering Aramean" with nothing to commend him (v. 5b). The term translated "wandering" in this context probably suggests the idea of becoming lost (Deut. 22:3) or going astray like roaming livestock (1 Sam. 9:3, 20). This echoes the insistence in the opening chapters of Deuteronomy on the total graciousness of God's election of Israel, a people without any merit whatsoever (Deut. 7:7; 9:4–7).

Second, the confession makes clear that Israel was victim of great oppression in Egypt, treated "harshly" and afflicted by "hard labor" (v. 6). As emphasized in the early chapters of Deuteronomy, God rescued them and brought them out of Egypt with great power ("a mighty hand and an outstretched arm") and with "signs and wonders" (v. 8; cf. 4:34; 6:22; 7:19; 11:2–3; and Exod. 6–12). God did so in order to give Israel a land (vv. 3, 9), an "inheritance" or possession (v. 1; cf. 4:21; 15:4; 19:10; 20:16; 24:4; 25:19). There was indeed a promise to the forebears, but Israel received the land as a gracious gift of God (v. 9; cf. 6:23; 8:7–10; 11:31).

Third, the intent of the recital was to make clear that the land Israel "possessed" still belonged to God. They were to "possess" and "settle" it (v. 1), but only because God gave it to them. This is an important point in Deuteronomy. The verb "possess" occurs more than thirty times in the first eleven chapters of the book (Deut. 1:8, 21, 39; 2:24, 31; 3:12, 18, 20; et al.). Israel was given land to "possess," but this did not mean that Israel owned the land. In acknowledgment, at each harvest time (probably the festival of Ingathering, held late in the summer or early fall) the worshiper was to return to God the "first of all the fruit of the ground" given by God (vv. 2–3, 10a). This was a sacrifice indicating that the God of Israel was the true owner of the land, and it was to be celebrated with the priestly functionaries, one's family, and all the resident aliens present (v. 11).

W. EUGENE MARCH

Homiletical Perspective

rather than a sign of special responsibility. Ours is a rich inheritance, but daily we rob future generations of their inheritance. In this Lenten season what does it mean to be heirs of God's promise?

Finally we come to verse 9, which remembers the language of YHWH's first promise to Moses from the burning bush (Exod. 3.8: "I have come down to deliver them . . . and to bring them up out of that land to a good and broad land, a land flowing with milk and honey, . . ."). These are the poetic symbols of fullness and fertility. Honey is made by bees and bees thrive only where flowers and fruit are abundant. Milk, drawn from cows and goats, implies the presence of good pasture land for grazing. Through the centuries, milk has signified a special privilege and blessing: it is the abundant knowledge of heavenly things, which is given in the promised land. Honey is the gift of happiness and delight that accompanies such knowledge. Interestingly, bees were among the first symbols adopted by Christians: the fervent activity of the beehive suggesting the church, the hibernation suggesting the resurrection, and the honey offering a symbol of the abundant new life in Christ.[1] Milk, honey, and firstfruits are all metaphors for God's grace. Americans have a tendency to literalize these images (as we do so often with the Bible), thereby robbing them of the deeper message they carry.

At the beginning of the Lenten season, this passage from Deuteronomy provides an important perspective. Despite our spiritual wanderings God has remained faithful and, through Christ's sacrifice, has brought us in grace to a land of spiritual milk and honey. Yet our failure to remember this truth puts us at risk of squandering our remarkable inheritance. How might we be more worthy of God's abundant grace and love that the good news of Easter lays before us? What remembering might we do?

NICK CARTER

---

1. Suzetta Tucker, "ChristStory Bee and Honey Page," *ChristStory Christian Bestiary,* http://ww2.netnitco.net/users/legend01/bee.htm.

Psalm 91:1-2, 9-16

¹You who live in the shelter of the Most High,
 who abide in the shadow of the Almighty,
²will say to the Lᴏʀᴅ, "My refuge and my fortress;
 my God, in whom I trust."
. . . .
⁹Because you have made the Lᴏʀᴅ your refuge,
 the Most High your dwelling place,
¹⁰no evil shall befall you,
 no scourge come near your tent.

¹¹For he will command his angels concerning you
 to guard you in all your ways.

Theological Perspective

Psalm 91 describes God as a "refuge," "fortress," and protector. Seen in the context of the Lenten journey, this psalm offers the comfort that God journeys with individuals and the larger community of faith. Lenten practices are intended to raise religious believers' awareness of the role of sin in our own lives and in our society and culture, and to prepare us to celebrate Easter. Lent is a time to contemplate what is at the center of all reality and to balance our awareness of sin with an understanding of God's care, loving-kindness, and compassion as our ultimate hope. The words of the psalmist will encourage people to perceive God's creative and creating presence at the center of all reality and to reorder their own priorities.

Throughout history, many religious believers thought of Psalm 91 as a magical formula that protected them from danger. The psalmist believed that no harm could come to those who called upon God's name. Both Jews and Christians copied passages of the psalm, particularly verses 11–13, enclosing them in amulets to be worn as protection.[1] The story of Jesus' temptation shows how the psalm was viewed in the ancient world as protection from danger. Luke's author tells about the devil tempting Jesus to jump

1. J. Clinton McCann Jr., "The Book of the Psalms," in *The New Interpreter's Bible* (Nashville: Abingdon Press, 1996), 3:1048.

Pastoral Perspective

Psalm 91 suggests that it is possible to choose to live in safety, security, trust, and refuge with God—that is, to "abide in the shadow of the Almighty" (v. 1). The psalm offers the opportunity to make "the Most High your dwelling place" (v. 9), but can we take this invitation seriously in the twenty-first century? We live in a world that is insecure, frightening, and unsafe. In the United States, some experienced years of relative prosperity and safety until 9/11. Others have lived in fear, experiencing unjust treatment for most of this country's history. How can we "buy into" the idea that we can dwell in the shelter and shadow of the Almighty, despite international terrorism, questionable financial security, wars and rumors of wars, religious and racial hatred, and the rampant fear and anxiety that have led to a myriad of addictions and dysfunctional behaviors?

Today is the first Sunday in the part of the church year designated as Lent. How does Psalm 91 speak to the Lenten experience? Is not Lent a time of deprivation; a time of concentration on Jesus' suffering and death; a time to face our own unworthiness and our sinful nature; a time to fast and pray? Introspection and self-examination are certainly important Lenten rituals, but as Psalm 91 suggests, there may be a more productive way to

¹²On their hands they will bear you up,
so that you will not dash your foot against a stone.
¹³You will tread on the lion and the adder,
the young lion and the serpent you will trample under foot.

¹⁴Those who love me, I will deliver;
I will protect those who know my name.
¹⁵When they call to me, I will answer them;
I will be with them in trouble,
I will rescue them and honor them.
¹⁶With long life I will satisfy them,
and show them my salvation.

Exegetical Perspective

This complex psalm may have its inspiration in some form of temple liturgy, though its present form does not seem to be a direct liturgical composition. Scholars offer widely variant interpretations of the life setting for the work, largely since we know very little about the way written prayers were employed in regular temple service in ancient Israel. Some have argued this work functioned as a prayer uttered by pilgrims upon entry to the temple precinct itself, and others that it functioned as some sort of blessing to ensure safety on a journey. It may be best to think of this psalm as a form of instruction, offering a confession of trust in God's continual care, a trust witnessed by a third party who also describes its consequences, and finally God's affirmation to the confession of trust. It is hard to fit this format with any other known form of liturgy, hence the suspicion by many that the psalm represents a creative literary adaptation of some liturgical form.

The use of pronouns allows a ready division into three main sections, though many modern English translations offer homogenous pronominal references in the interest of avoiding confusion for contemporary readers. Verses 1–2 open with a series of active participle forms that shift to first-person references. The participles are best rendered by a general reference: "One who dwells in the protection

Homiletical Perspective

Psalm 91 is at once beautiful and troubling. It offers some of the most comforting language in all of Scripture, but it also suggests a linkage between invoking the name of God and avoiding harm, a connection that rightly causes discomfort for many Christians. To look at the homiletical possibilities and requirements of Psalm 91, we will look at both facets.

Any family psychologist worth his or her salt will tell you, in one way or another, that security, freedom, and love are indispensable for raising children who will function happily in life. If these elements of caregiving are present in a child's life, that child will not have to struggle through the challenges of life in quite the same way as one who was reared in a less protective or less supportive environment.

Newborn infants like to be tightly wrapped when clothed for the day. Mothers in the know snuggle their babies up close to give them a sense of the womb. Children at play love forts, where a simple blanket over cardboard boxes can resemble a mother bird safeguarding her young. Jesus speaks of gathering the people of Jerusalem under his care, much as a mother hen gathers her chicks under her wings. Why all of these images of protective care? It is because we human beings, whether children or adults, crave a sense of security. We love to be

Psalm 91:1-2, 9-16

Theological Perspective

from the pinnacle of the temple by citing Psalm 91:11–13. "If you are the Son of God, throw yourself down from here, for it is written, 'He will command his angels concerning you, to protect you'" (Luke 4:9–10). Jesus responds with these words: "It is said, 'Do not put the Lord your God to the test'" (Luke 4:12).

In his *Commentary on the Book of Psalms*, John Calvin referred to the story of Jesus' temptation and its relevance for interpreting Psalm 91. Calvin argued that when the "whole human family were banished from Divine favour. . . . It was Christ, and he only, who, by removing the ground of separation, reconciled the angels to us."[2] Calvin thought that the overall meaning of the psalm was best understood in terms of God's providence. He observed that people sought refuge in a variety of hiding places according to the tragedies that threatened them, but the psalmist spoke of God as the only safe and impregnable fortress. For Calvin, the protection and security of God contrasted with all other confidences.

The doctrine of providence has been used to support the idea that God is working out God's purposes in the world, even if God's purposes are advanced through evil and suffering. Theologians such as Calvin and C. S. Lewis have suggested that we may never fully understand evil and suffering because of the limitations of our own human insight and the mysteriousness of God's work in the world. Significant and enduring questions have been raised with regard to God's providence, especially when human beings face tragic situations caused by natural disaster or as we inflict suffering upon one another. How could God, who cares so much for the world, let such bad things happen to good people? If we believe in God's infinite goodness, it is difficult to make the case that God's purposes can be furthered through social and economic structures that discriminate against people on the basis of race, gender, or class, or through the genocide that the world witnessed in the Holocaust. In these and many other examples, people are unable to find God's protection. So much suffering exists today that it is sometimes hard to believe that there is anything greater than us that can protect us or the world we live in. Sometimes it seems that God fails us. How can we continue to pray with the psalmist that God is our refuge, fortress, and protector, in light of these horrific events?

To claim that God cares for the world and continues to be involved in creation does not

Pastoral Perspective

experience Lent than to view this season as just a period of deprivation and self-criticism.

Psalm 91 proclaims God's bold invitation to us to live in the divine presence with protection, safety, and love. In her book *Psalms for Praying: An Invitation to Wholeness*, Nan C. Merrill reframes Psalm 91, presenting it as a conversation between God and us. Beginning the conversation with words of praise and trust, she describes our relationship with God as being "sheltered in infinite light" and "abiding in the wings of infinite Love."[1] The psalm continues to praise God for providing strength for living and a protective environment of safety and salvation.

God responds to this verse of praise and trust by acknowledging the love of those who call upon God's name. God assures the psalmist of deliverance, protection, rescue, and a reverence for our lives. During good times and in times of trouble, God promises to dwell in each heart, "as Loving Companion Presence, forever."[2]

As we read Merrill's interpretation of Psalm 91, we experience God as one who provides a shelter for each of us. This protective environment is a "safe house," in which God's abiding presence with us is eternal. This shelter not only protects us from danger but also is a place of love, nurture, and care. During Lent, this becomes even more meaningful as we grow in our awareness that God dwells in our hearts. In times of trouble, joy, sickness, health, vibrancy, sadness, loneliness, and death, we have a divine friend who walks with us, cries with us, loves us with a continuing, deep, and abiding love.

Lent is a time to acknowledge and respond to God's offer to dwell in our hearts. It is a time to pour energy into increasing our awareness of God's presence with us, no matter what the circumstances of our lives. Our prayer during Lent could be to ask God to let divine love open our hearts and increase our awareness of the presence of the Holy Spirit.

We might furthermore ask God to increase our courage as we respond to God's love by loving and protecting others. We need to learn to listen for God's voice as our relationships with God unfold. We need to seek and expect God's presence, guidance, and protection, while being continually grateful for the work of God in our lives. We need to be vulnerable to God and God's action in our lives.

Our response to God's continual invitation to relationship is really our lifetime spiritual journey.

---

2. John Calvin, *Commentary on the Book of Psalms* (Grand Rapids: Eerdmans, 1949), 3:486.

1. Nan C. Merrill, *Psalms for Praying: An Invitation to Wholeness* (New York: Continuum, 1996), 190.
2. Ibid., 191.

Exegetical Perspective

of the Most High, in the shadow of Almighty, stays for the night." This chiastic opening verse then shifts quickly to the first person: "I say to YHWH, 'My refuge and my fortress! My God! I trust in him!'" The petitioner is giving expression to his ultimate devotion to the God of Israel.

In verses 3–13, an anonymous narrator confirms the veracity of the opening speaker's trust in God. This narrator may reflect a priestly response to the confession of the petitioner. The lectionary skips over verses 3–8, which are cast in the voice of this outside confirmation of the petitioner's expression of trust in God. "So he will deliver you from the snare of the fowler," verse 3 declares, apparently reflecting the consequences of the affirmation made in verses 1–2. Having mentioned a fowler, the metaphors used in verse 4 touch on images of a mother bird protecting her young and closely parallel the description of God's actions toward Israel in Deuteronomy 32:11–12 (see also Pss. 36:7; 57:1; and 61:4). In verse 6 the narrator makes special point of the provision of divine protection from various illnesses. Verses 7–8 seem to suggest if the one with trust in God should see disaster happen, all they are seeing is God's punishment of the wicked, not something that would threaten the one who has placed trust in God.

The lectionary rejoins the psalm at verse 9, which, in a complex formulation, reverts briefly to the first-person statements that opened the psalm: "So for you—'YHWH is my refuge'—you have made the Most High your dwelling place." The first-person expression refers to the confession of verses 1–2 and then goes on to draw on the imagery of these verses in a slightly different formulation. So while there is a connection to the petitioner's expression of trust, the third-party confirmation introduced in verse 3 continues to give voice to the veracity of the petitioner's confidence in verses 9–13. It continues to offer these observations in the form of a direct address to the petitioner: "no scourge will come near your tent" (v. 10), recalling the protection of Israelite dwellings during the final plague that brought their liberation from Egypt (Exod. 12:13). In a striking image, the narrator goes on to state God will order angels to bear the believer up "so that you will not dash your foot against a stone" (v. 12). This is the promise Satan quotes during the temptation of Jesus (see Matt. 4:6; Luke 4:11), possibly reflecting how cherished this promise was to the faithful in the first century CE. The narrator concludes with assurances that the one trusting God will overcome cosmic forces of evil, expressed in metaphorical form and

Homiletical Perspective

sheltered, warmed, and embraced. When the psalmist talks about abiding "in the shadow of the Almighty," and says, "Under his wings you will find refuge," we relax into a smile. This is the promise of security.

To the imagery of a large protective mother bird with wings, the psalmist adds powerful language about the Lord's retinue of angels picking us up when we stumble: The Lord "will command his angels concerning you, to guard you in all your ways" (v. 11). These same angels "will bear you up so that you will not dash your foot against a stone" (v. 12). Picture the confidence that would come upon the elderly in our day if they knew an angel would scoop them up every time they came close to losing their balance. Such is the comfort of Psalm 91.

We must also reckon with another side to this same psalm: the language of condition in verses 9–10. "Because you have made the LORD your refuge, the Most High your dwelling place, no evil shall befall you, no scourge come near your tent." This is essentially "if-then" language. If you do or believe this, then you can be assured that a certain divine protection will be yours.

What is wrong with this setup? Why do some of us wince when we read these two verses? Because these verses appear to propose a relationship with God that has some basis in magic. They feel manipulative. These words give the impression that God hands out protective favors to those who have the Lord's name on their lips. "Those who love me, I will deliver; I will protect those who know my name" (v. 14). No wonder some rabbis refer to Psalm 91 as an "amulet psalm." Recite it over and over again, and it may help you attain or feel the presence of God. This is the feeling that is conveyed. Wear it around your neck like a protective charm, and you can ward off evil, harm, and illness all in one.

If you are balking at this theology, consider your instinct a good thing. There is plenty of scriptural evidence elsewhere that suggests God is much more than a lucky coin in one's pocket. The world is tired of hearing God's name invoked as the author of victory on this football field or that battlefield. Yet we persist in speaking this way, largely because it feels comforting to have God on our side.

When the devil tempted Jesus to jump off the pinnacle of the temple one day, these words of Psalm 91 are the very ones the devil quoted. Jesus refused to jump, saying in reply, "Do not put the Lord your God to the test" (Deut. 6:16). It was Jesus' way of saying, "You do not play lightly with God. You do

Psalm 91:1-2, 9-16

Theological Perspective

necessarily mean that God uses human and environmental suffering as a teaching tool. As we interpret this psalm, we must acknowledge that our worldview has changed since this psalm was written. The psalmist had a much simpler view of the universe and causality. Scientific study has opened up for us new ways of thinking about the creation of the world and God's involvement in it.

As God lives in relationship with the world, God is also limited in what God can determine as the end of particular events. Process theologian Burton Cooper describes God as "boundless, yet limited." Cooper encourages us to use the metaphor of the universe for the extensiveness of God's power: "As the universe is not in space but creates space, and is therefore boundless, so God's power is not simply in the universe but creates the universe and extends through it. As the universe is dynamic and yet, at any given time, has outer limits, so God's power is dynamic and yet limited."[3] It is not simply that God can act upon the world and protect us like a magical formula that saves us from danger. We also have to recognize our own responsibility and potential to help God realize God's hopes and dreams for the whole creation.

The words of the psalmist teach us that we should not be tempted to vest our interests in our own limited abilities to bring about transformation, in isolation from God's larger vision for the common good. Neither should we retreat and seek to find false refuge in theologies that have been used in the past to disregard human responsibility for the suffering of others or our planet. So much suffering that exists today *is* caused by human hands. As we reflect on Psalm 91 during Lent, we can reevaluate our way of thinking and refocus our practices, so that we can move closer to a celebration of the day that reminds us that our comfort and protection are found in fully participating in God's redemptive work in the world.

ELIZABETH L. HINSON-HASTY

Pastoral Perspective

We can focus on new ways to trust God's promises to us. We can experience God as a living, active, loving presence in our daily lives. We can center our lives on what it means to be in love with God. Here are some practical ways to use the Lenten season to deepen our relationship with God:

—Read the Scriptures in Lent as if you were one of the disciples present with Jesus as he ministered to others and fulfilled his mission on earth. Use the words of Scripture to paint pictures for you. Visualize yourself with Jesus—in the desert, with crowds of people, in the garden praying, or as the thief on the cross. Write in a journal about these experiences.

—Write a letter to God expressing your love for God and your desire to deepen your relationship with God. Tell God about your daily life experiences. Express how much you need God's guidance in your life. Tell God what it is like to live through Lent and Holy Week with Jesus.

—Write a poem, a hymn, a psalm, or a short story about your relationship with God.

—Draw or paint a picture that expresses your love for God or your feelings about the Lenten season. Draw or paint a picture that expresses God's love for you.

—Spend some time "hanging out" with God. Feel God's presence as you go through the daily routine of your day. Experience God as your Loving Companion daily. Be honest with God about your joys, sorrows, and frustrations in life.

—Contemplate what it means to make your home with God and to have God dwell in your heart. Think about how you can change and grow as a result of God dwelling in your heart. Work and pray to bring about that change in your life. Imagine yourself as that changed person. How would you act and feel?

Opening our hearts to God can increase our trust in God's invitations and promises. We can spend each day in the quiet shelter of God's love and protection and listen to the prayer of the Holy Spirit for our lives.

KATHERINE E. AMOS

---

3. Burton Cooper, *Why God?* (Atlanta: John Knox Press, 1988), 85.

precise parallelism: "you will tread on the lion and the adder, the young lion and the serpent you will trample under foot" (v. 13).

Verses 14–16 return to the first-person form of the opening verses: "because he has bound himself to me, I will rescue him" (v. 14a), but the role is reversed: rather than the first person expressing the petitioner's perspective, it now expresses the divine response to the petitioner's trust. The confirmation of God's beneficence as a response is not marked by specifics. Rather, it offers fairly stock refrains of God's actions in response to the faith expressed by a believer. God declares the intent to execute a series of actions on behalf of the petitioner: "I will deliver him because he has known my name" (v. 14b).

The use of the expression "known my name" is a common reference to those who offer worship to Israel's God (Ps. 9:10). God promises an answer when called upon and to be present in the midst of distress. God will deliver them and honor them (v. 15). God concludes this pledged response with the promise of a long life for the petitioner, and that God will show salvation to the one trusting in God (v. 16). Some commentators take this last phrase as a summation of all the actions, and count seven specific actions by God, a metaphor for the completeness of God's response to the petitioner's trust. Just as the psalm opened with two verses expressing trust, it closes with two verses completing God's response to that trust.

In the context of the Lenten season, this psalm offers the believer reassurance that trust in God brings about the assurance of a positive response from God. To call upon God, with the knowledge that God remains with us even in distress, is great comfort in this season of contrition.

KENNETH G. HOGLUND

not treat God willy-nilly, just because God pledges a sheltering providence for your life."

An inexact analogy might go something like this: Parents of a 17-year-old pledge to care for their child throughout life, affirming and supporting her through every major stage of the journey. The child clearly benefits from their generous love in a continuous way. As a teenager the child receives a used car through the kindness of the parents. They pay the insurance. They oversee its care. Now, when the daughter goes out for a spin one night, there is a difference between her testing the limits of the car at high speed around a curve and losing control, *and* this same girl driving quite considerately around the same curve, doing the best she can to maintain the car's course, and still losing control. The reckless choice is nothing less than playing lightly with all that the parents have entrusted to her.

So it is with the psalmist's reference to "no evil befalling" those who love the Lord. This pledge of God is not a promise with which we are permitted to play lightly.

In the end, a preacher will probably want to view Psalm 91 as only one expression of faith. There are other expressions that need to fill out the picture, other passages of Scripture we need to draw upon when truly bad things happen to us in life. It seems appropriate to allow the psalmist to show some exuberance for the sheltering providence he feels on this day. To know that no *final* evil will befall any one of us, even if there is no cure for that tumor in the brain of the person we love most in the world, is its own amazing comfort.

PETER W. MARTY

Romans 10:8b–13

8b"The word is near you,
  on your lips and in your heart"
(that is, the word of faith that we proclaim); 9because if you confess with your lips that Jesus is Lord and believe in your heart that God raised him from the dead, you will be saved. 10For one believes with the heart and so is justified, and one confesses with the mouth and so is saved. 11The scripture says, "No one who believes in him will be put to shame." 12For there is no distinction between Jew and Greek; the same Lord is Lord of all and is generous to all who call on him. 13For, "Everyone who calls on the name of the Lord shall be saved."

Theological Perspective

Lent laments the pervasive presence of sin among human beings. For forty days we take account of the times we have "missed the mark" (a word study of *hamartia* would be a fruitful project), done what we should not have done (Rom. 7:14–20), and not only committed sins, but have lived "in sin" (Rom. 6:1–12). Bowed like weeping willows, we admit freely that we have borne carnal fruit (Gal. 5:16–21). An ashen stigma announces our state of being, our sincere sorrow, and our intention to amend our ways.

In our text for today, although we are knee-deep in the ashes of our burned-out lives, an impossible possibility illumines the dark sky that is clouded by our smoldering sins. Paul, who self-confessedly kneels with us in our plight at the altar of sorrow, announces that near us, even in us (Rom. 10:8b), is a transforming word of salvation (v. 8c). He declares that if we call upon the Lord, we will be saved from the plight of our sin (vv. 12b–13). If, with our entire beings, we confess and believe (v. 9), we will no longer be shamed by the sooty residue of our sin (v. 11), but rather will be enlivened, forgiven, renewed, and enriched (v. 12). Furthermore, the whole world is invited to join in being raised from the ashes of sin into the luminous presence of God (vv. 12a, 13).

The theological underpinnings of this passage contain core themes of Paul's gospel. An initial

Pastoral Perspective

Want to divide a room fast? Just start talking about who is saved and who is not. Set up the criteria, then point out who is in and who is out. Soteriology is a hotbed of religious controversy. It is tempting to shy away from questions of salvation in an effort to avoid arguments. Yet these questions are on the minds and hearts of people all along the spectrum of religious belief, particularly during the season of Lent, with its focus on sin and sacrifice. Questions of soteriology are worth engaging from the pulpit. Obviously, we are not the first to ask such questions, and the voices of others can help us preach in this delicate terrain.

Did you know that righteousness has a voice? Paul gives it a voice in Romans 10:6: "But the righteousness that comes from faith says, 'Do not say in your heart . . .'" The fact that Paul has chosen to personify "Righteousness by Faith" and has this character speak in Romans 10 signifies more than meets the eye. In these verses, the character Righteousness by Faith is sharing its autobiography, including what it means to be and have and live out righteousness by faith.

Righteousness by Faith is a hard worker, a relentless companion. It stirs up faith through the Word of God (v. 8). This is no small feat when you consider the thickheaded disciples, most people in

Exegetical Perspective

Lent asks us to consider what it means for us to live out the faith that we hold in our hearts. For Paul, that faith is not a generic sentiment (spirituality, as it is called today). It is not limited to a humanistic ethical code ("help others," "work for a better world for everyone"). It is not even exhausted by the confession that there is only one God who created all things. Of course these three—spirituality, helping others, and recognizing God as the source of our being—are all important to the life of faith, but the Christian message focuses on Jesus. As Paul puts it briefly (v. 9): Jesus is more than an admirable human being. He embodies God's reality as Lord (Phil. 2:9–11). God demonstrates that by raising him from death (1 Cor. 15:45). The riches of salvation are extended through Jesus as Lord to all humanity (v. 12).

Romans 10:8–13 expresses these basic Christian truths but does not argue for them. Paul assumes that the Christians in Rome share those beliefs with him, even though he has never visited that church. At this point in the letter, Paul is engaged in an argument that seems quite foreign to most Christians today, explaining why the gospel is being embraced by non-Jews but rejected by most Jews (9:1–5; 10:1–4). Accustomed to thinking of Christianity and Judaism as separate religions, we have a hard time seeing why that matters so much to Paul.

Homiletical Perspective

The fact that this reading from Romans is paired with the temptation story in Luke makes it underused on the First Sunday in Lent. The story of Jesus in the wilderness for forty days being tempted by the devil is so definitive for the Lenten season that most preachers will find it very difficult not to gravitate in Luke's direction for the sermon on this particular Sunday in the Christian year. The reading from Paul's letter to the church in Rome, however, also has much to say to a congregation at the beginning of the season of preparation for the Christian Passover.

One way to focus a sermon on Romans 10:8b–13 would be to highlight the fact that there is more than meets the eyes when reading any one verse or passage from the Bible. These few verses, only four and a half to be exact, wonderfully illustrate the depth and breadth of Paul's teaching. It is hardly an exaggeration to say that Paul's backdrop for this small passage is the entire story of God's covenant with the Jews. This passage, coming as it does in the middle of Paul's wrestling with the fact that many of his fellow Jews have not accepted Jesus as the Messiah (Rom. 9–11), reflects the fact that Paul's mind and faith are profoundly shaped by his deep understanding and familiarity with the Old Testament and the grand narrative of the people of

Romans 10:8b–13

Theological Perspective

theme is the universal inclusiveness of the message. "All" are included; "no one" is excluded (vv. 11–13). Earlier, in chapters 1 to 8, Paul has already made his case for all persons to recognize their need ("all have sinned," Rom. 3:23). No one, he claims, is righteous according to the law. At the same time, he declares that no one is hopeless. If one confesses/believes/trusts, one can be transformed by a spiritual renewal (Rom. 10:9). Harping on sin in the pulpit, however, may sound a sour note. Seeking to create a sense of guilt and shame is hardly where the theologically astute preacher wants to focus this text. The best the preacher can do with the self-righteous, the self-indulgent, and the narcissistic is to nudge them toward the recognition of their faults, in the hope that they will see through their self-rectitude and self-centeredness, into the darkness of their own lives and the emptiness of living "for me."

While attending to the faux-righteous who are blind to their need, this text also challenges the preacher to make clear that Paul's "all" includes those in the congregation who are totally convinced of their sin, unworthiness, and alienation from God and grace. These shrouded souls often feel rejected and unloved. Paul addresses both groups, including both in the category of "sinner." That is the bad news: sin happens. All fall short.

A second theological theme in our passage is this good news: salvation is near, and it is near for all (v. 8b). Like the reign of God in Mark 1:15, salvation is "at hand." For some, this involves not resting in our false perception of our righteousness; for others, not being mired in unworthiness. Paul bids those in both groups to open ourselves to receiving the riches (v. 12) endowed by salvation. He is talking about an event, a happening, an experience of transforming grace. In the preaching event we proclaim the nearness of God, in the hope that hearers experience it in their heart (v. 8b) and confess it with their lips (v. 9).

Karl Barth, for one, urges the preacher not to attempt to stage, manipulate, or induce the manifestation of the saving God who is at hand. Rather, in his commentary on Romans,[1] he cautions against seeking to employ artificial human means (argument, persuasion, etc.) to convince sinners of their sin. The preacher needs to announce God's saving presence and proclaim that God is indeed among us. Barth says this means that no human pretense may be privileged. All the "means" of

Pastoral Perspective

the pews on Sundays, and all the rest of us as well. However the work of righteousness goes on, evoking a confession from the lips of believers. Only then, Paul explains through this character, is righteousness by faith complete (vv. 9–10).

Now for the chicken-and-egg question: Which comes first, belief or confession? One could rightly argue that you should confess, "Jesus is Lord," only if you truly believe it. Otherwise these are merely shallow words, spoken along with the masses but lacking a foundation of substantial belief.

Imagine someone who is deep in the valley of doubt and despair. With hands thrown up in desperation, she shouts, "Jesus, are you even there?" Can this be considered an attempt at a confession of faith? Are these the words that Righteousness by Faith has placed on her lips? Is not addressing such a plea for help to God a statement of loyalty and trust, even when the plea is uttered with a shaking voice? Stated another way, if we name our places of doubt, are they not somewhere on the path of confessing that Jesus is Lord? The one who calms the storm and shows his wounded hands can also hold our doubts. If the person facing doubt and despair is surrounded by a confessing community—one that names what it believes—perhaps the community can confess on behalf of the doubting one, even as he or she navigates the path toward trusting God.

"Everyone who calls on the name of the Lord shall be saved" (v. 13). The sticking point for many Christians is that we think we know exactly what that call sounds like, what pitch it is, how the sentences are formed, and what words are used. In your community, how does it sound when people call on the name of God? As you watch the news, what does it look like when people cling to the name of Jesus? Many images that come to mind are of those with broken spirits, whose wind has left their sails and who are trying to stay afloat. Sometimes we call on Jesus with strong, confident voices—and often we call on Jesus with sighs too deep for words.

"The word is near you," Paul writes, "on your lips and in your heart" (v. 8b). God is doing the heavy lifting here—bringing the Word near, planting the seeds of faith in our hearts, placing words tenderly on our lips. We do the telling—setting free those words already in our hearts and on our lips, sharing the questions central to our faith, in order to build up one another.

Confessing our faith takes practice. It is an ongoing act that changes as faith evolves throughout life. How might we help people articulate faith in a

---

1. Karl Barth, *The Epistle to the Romans*, trans. Edwyn C. Hoskins, 6th ed. (New York: Oxford University Press, 1933), 377–82.

First Sunday in Lent

He makes the task harder by employing forms of argument that are well known in ancient Jewish texts but unfamiliar to outsiders. Paul's audience in Rome comprised Christians of Jewish background, who still observed Jewish holidays and food laws, as well as a growing majority of non-Jewish believers. Paul later asks the two groups to live in harmony, accepting their differences and acknowledging their common faith in Christ (14:1–15:13). He also warns non-Jewish Christians against adopting an arrogant attitude toward Jews who do not accept Christ. Their refusal has served God's plan by spreading faith to the nations. At the end of the process, God will see to making God's people one in Christ (11:11–36).

Romans 10:8–13 continues a section that began with verse 5. There Paul had argued that fellow Jews rejected the gospel because they thought God required scrupulous observance of Jewish law and custom. They did not understand that the goal of the Law was a righteousness based on faith in Christ (vv. 1–4). Therefore Paul turns to the Law itself to prove his point. He does not deny that there are passages in the Law that demand such obedience. Moses pointed to that sort of righteousness in Leviticus 18:5 (v. 5). Then Paul shifts to a familiar rhetorical device, a "speech in character." Only this time the character speaking is "the righteousness which comes through faith" (vv. 6–7). Where does she speak? She speaks in Torah, in Moses' final speech to the children of Israel (Deut. 30:12–14).

Having set up the apparent contradiction in the words of Moses, Paul follows an established Jewish practice: find an interpretation of Torah that resolves the tension. Such arguments often hang on just a few words or phrases in a text. So Paul picks out phrases from Deuteronomy that he interprets as references to the gospel he preaches and the faith it calls for. The "word" said to be near in heart and mouth is the gospel "word of faith," being preached. The "mouth" becomes the response of believers who acclaim Christ as Lord in baptismal and worship contexts (Phil. 2:9–11; 1 Cor. 12:3). The "heart" is their conviction that God has raised Jesus from the dead (vv. 8–9). With a delicate rhetorical flourish Paul rounds out the pair in verse 10. Belief in the heart produces righteousness; confession with the mouth produces salvation. The biblical practice of synonymous parallelism (by which the same sentiment is repeated using different phrases) keeps us from concluding that there is a sequence of lesser to greater in the "righteousness—salvation" pair. Both designate the fullness of salvation.

Israel. These few verses in Romans 10 can take a reader on an illuminating journey through many different books in the Old Testament.

Any good reference Bible will allow a reader to discover that in these verses Paul is reworking a passage from Deuteronomy 30, where Moses speaks to the Israelites about the accessibility of the Law. Moses tells the people that the Law is not out of reach in heaven and or beyond hearing across the sea (Deut. 30:12–13). Paul takes this story of Moses and the Law and uses it to speak of the fact that faith is accessible through the proclamation of Christ—"'The word is near you, on your lips and in your heart' (that is, the word of faith that we proclaim)." Paul goes on to quote from Isaiah 28:16: "No one who believes in him will be put to shame" (v. 11). Paul takes the point of accessibility to salvation through Jesus a gigantic step forward by proclaiming that in Jesus there is no distinction between Jew and Greek, because "the same Lord is Lord of all and is generous to all who call on him" (v. 12). To reinforce this declaration of generosity, Paul quotes from the prophet Joel, who had already written, "Everyone who calls on the name of the LORD shall be saved" (Joel 2:32). Deuteronomy, Isaiah, and Joel are all referenced in these four and a half verses!

Paul came to his understanding of Jesus by way of the Old Testament. On the First Sunday in Lent, then, this passage can be a fine illustration of the Christian discipline of reading and meditating on the entire Word of God in Scripture. To understand the real depth of these verses is to follow the references into the whole story of God's redemptive work through the Jewish people, finding fulfillment in the life, death, and resurrection of the Jew Jesus Christ. In a phrase, a sermon on this passage might be titled "A Lenten Journey into the Scripture: Take, Read, and Follow the References."

It is interesting and important to note that Jesus too was shaped and strengthened in ministry by his deep reading of the Old Testament. Jesus matches the temptations of Satan by quoting from Deuteronomy (a reference Bible will take the reader to Deut. 8:3; 6:13; and 6:16). Reading and meditating on Scripture is a practice that equips followers of Jesus to face the allure of lesser gods and dead-end pathways in life. Disciplined and prayerful reading of the sacred stories of the Hebrew people; the life, death, and resurrection of Jesus; and the birth and early life of the church leads to wholeness and strength for the living of these days.

At least one warning should attend this call to read and meditate on the fullness of the scriptural

Romans 10:8b–13

Theological Perspective

marketing the gospel must be denied. Every expectation that we can manipulate the fulfillment of God's promise must be renounced. The Word of our salvation is announced in the silence of searching and longing hearts—as, perhaps, the impossible possibility becomes present among us. "Because it is the Word of Christ, it is beyond our hearing and our speaking, for, to hear it and to proclaim it—we must wait."[2] As, during Lent, we await Easter morn.

A third theological theme in this text is that our repentance and salvation begin and end with God. Sin is our problem; salvation is God's answer for our situation. To experience God's saving presence, we must believe in our hearts (v. 9) and confess with our lips (v. 10). A bounty of spiritual gifts accompanies God's presence (v. 12; see also Gal. 5:23–25). All this is of God, the author and agent of our salvation, as an act of grace.

The French painter John-Claude Gaugy came to America in 1966 and developed an art medium of works carved into wood. His most famous work, "The Awakening," consists of more than 400 brightly painted wood panels, depicting the personal awakening that may visit us when we ponder the prospect of the love of God and new life in Christ. Until recently, it was on display in Santa Fe, New Mexico, where visitors silently watched and listened to the unspoken word of this work of art.[3]

By grace, sometimes—by words heard and sights seen—the Word is heard and new life arises. During Lent, sober darkness clouds our lives for forty days, only to be replaced by the impossible possibility—the luminescent brightness—of the resurrection of new life in Christ.

DONALD W. MUSSER

Pastoral Perspective

culture that discourages the sharing of faith? How might we help to draw out the words that God has planted in hearts and set gently on lips?

This passage is a call to individual confession of faith in response to Christ. This passage is also a call to communal confession of belief. Creeds are sticky for many Christians. Some denominations use the Apostles' Creed or another creedal text each week. Some congregations have written their own statements of faith. Other churches recognize such diversity among members' theologies that they have chosen not to use a formulated creed. It may be helpful, as Romans 10 is read this week, to consider the many ways we call on the name of God during worship. What names do we use for God? Which images for God have been given priority in our liturgy? Have we left room in our worship for people to express their faith in creative ways?

If we view worship planning through this lens, then each particular word or act in worship may become our corporate confession of faith. Romans 10 reminds us of the care with which we are called to plan worship on behalf of a community. We also have the opportunity to remind the congregation of the many ways in which they confess their faith together, from the call to worship to the hymns.

All who call on the name of God will be saved, whether this call is perfectly in tune or just a jumbled joyful noise. Practicing this call is our task this Lenten season. To learn to make this joyful noise, we can listen to the voices of those who have gone before us: ancestors in the faith, hymn writers, and confessors. We can also listen to the voice of Righteousness by Faith, personified by Paul, which assures us of our salvation, no matter how small the mustard seed of faith may be.

CALLISTA S. ISABELLE

---

2. Ibid., 380.
3. See www.theawakeningmuseum.org.

Exegetical Perspective

In the second half of our passage (vv. 11–13) Paul makes another move characteristic of Jewish interpretation. He begins to argue from the prophets, who in Jewish tradition are treated as commentary on the Torah. Paul opens with Isaiah 28:16, a passage already quoted in Romans 9:33, and he closes with Joel 2:23. Even these two citations match the "heart—mouth" pairing of Paul's rhetoric. The first affirms that belief in "him" will not be disappointed. The "him" is deliberately vague, as it can refer both to God and to Christ as Lord. The Joel citation shifts to the mouth, that is, "calling upon the name of the Lord." This phrase too could be used in its common Old Testament sense of prayers or appeals addressed to God, or in the new Christian sense where the "Lord" in question is Christ.

Paul sandwiches a hot-button issue between these two prophetic quotations: the equivalence of Jew and non-Jew in God's plan for salvation. Belief in Christ is the sole requirement, he says. As far as God is concerned, it makes no difference whether a person remains devoted to Jewish traditions or is a non-Jew, turning to the God of Israel from the polytheistic cults of the day. In his Letter to the Galatians, Paul lashed out angrily at the suggestion that non-Jewish believers should adopt Jewish practices. His tone in Romans is milder. There is no threat of Judaizing here. Paul provides a framework for Jewish and non-Jewish believers to form a harmonious community in their one Lord.

At the same time, Paul's theological insights should lessen conflicts between Christians and Jews. Israel has not lost her covenant with God. Even though Paul holds that "righteousness through faith" is the teaching of the Law, he points out that the conversion of Israel remains part of God's plan. For Christians who take their cue from Paul, the Reformation slogan "righteousness through faith" could be a path toward reconciliation in divided communities, calling us to heal what is divided by fierce devotion to rules and ethnic claims to be the people of God.

PHEME PERKINS

Homiletical Perspective

narrative: We do *not* read the Bible simply in order to know facts and to be able to draw charts of connecting stories and people; rather, *we read the Bible to let the ongoing relationship of God to us and to the world settle into our hearts and minds.* We practice a deep, open, and disciplined reading of Scripture so that we can come to a place of trust in God's love for us expressed in Christ Jesus—and to a place of understanding of God's call upon our lives through this same Lord. To memorize verses and passages without allowing the love of God to be written on our hearts is work even the devil can do (see Luke 4:10–11 with references).

Another way to preach this passage from Romans is to proclaim with Paul the faithfulness of God to God's promises. For Paul, Jesus is the fulfillment of Torah. Jesus embodies God's abiding commitment to the salvation of God's creation. For Paul, the Law came to its proper conclusion in Jesus and thereby opened up for all people the possibility of being in right relationship with God and neighbor. The focus here is on God's faithfulness throughout the generations and toward the whole world. God's promises to God's people will never be revoked or go unfulfilled, and God's generosity is expansive beyond our imaginations. Our calling as followers of the One who embodied God's generosity is to live generous lives in response. The Lenten season invites us to self-examination regarding the extent to which God's generosity is written upon our hearts.

ROBERT W. PRIM

Luke 4:1-13

¹Jesus, full of the Holy Spirit, returned from the Jordan and was led by the Spirit in the wilderness, ²where for forty days he was tempted by the devil. He ate nothing at all during those days, and when they were over, he was famished. ³The devil said to him, "If you are the Son of God, command this stone to become a loaf of bread." ⁴Jesus answered him, "It is written, 'One does not live by bread alone.'"

⁵Then the devil led him up and showed him in an instant all the kingdoms of the world. ⁶And the devil said to him, "To you I will give their glory and all this authority; for it has been given over to me, and I give it to anyone I please. ⁷If you, then, will worship me, it will all be yours." ⁸Jesus answered him, "It is written,
'Worship the Lord your God,
    and serve only him.'"

Theological Perspective

The nature of evil, the nature of Christ, the power of temptation: each of these ideas has been named, over time, as a possible theme for the opening verses of the fourth chapter of Luke's Gospel—and for good reason. The first two verses alone suggest the possibilities. "Jesus, full of the Holy Spirit, returned from the Jordan and was led by the Spirit in the desert, where for forty days he was tempted by the devil." Here Jesus is described in relationship to the Spirit, evil is personified as the devil, and temptation lasts for forty days. It is all there.

No wonder, then, that when my gregarious middle son—just shy of four years old—encountered this text during a Lenten children's liturgy, he learned something about all of these themes, especially the one about temptation. I did not accompany him to this children's worship, but stayed in the main worship service. The congregational leader who led the children that day is a very dynamic speaker and storyteller, so I was not surprised when my son pulled me aside later that day to ask me some questions. "Hey, mom," he started, "what do you know about the devil?" My mind immediately jumped to a spectrum of theological views and theodicies. Should I start with Augustine? Should I couch my answer in general terms of conservative and progressive or liberal interpretations of the text?

Pastoral Perspective

There is a spiritual depth and power for life and ministry that is made possible as we respond in faith to trials, trouble, temptation, and testing. If given a choice, most of us will not intentionally choose a path filled with difficulty. Our prior choices may cause us to stumble onto this path. Similarly, the choices of others around us may create harsh and hostile circumstances that force us onto this path, but most of us are slow deliberately to choose the path of discipline.

Yet in the season of Lent we are invited to embrace an intentional way of life. For the forty days of Lent (not including Sundays), we follow the example of Jesus who was "led by the Spirit in the wilderness, where for forty days he was tempted by the devil" (vv. 1–2). The Spirit does not just "drop him off" in the wilderness to fend for himself; the Spirit continues to abide with him, enabling him to grow stronger through this season. In Luke 3:21–4:13, we see that the Spirit's anointing of Jesus in baptism and his faithfulness to God amid testing constitute Jesus' preparation for his mission. Being chosen and anointed is not sufficient preparation either for our ministry gathered or for our ministry scattered. We must be tested, often by being led to places of hunger and despair. Only then do we learn dependence on God, who graciously provides for all of our needs in all of life's seasons.

⁹Then the devil took him to Jerusalem, and placed him on the pinnacle of the temple, saying to him, "If you are the Son of God, throw yourself down from here, ¹⁰for it is written,

'He will command his angels concerning you,
    to protect you,'
¹¹and
'On their hands they will bear you up,
    so that you will not dash your foot against a stone.'"
¹²Jesus answered him, "It is said, 'Do not put the Lord your God to the test.'" ¹³When the devil had finished every test, he departed from him until an opportune time.

Exegetical Perspective

What did I just hear? The Gospel text assigned for the First Sunday in Lent, the season of preparation to accompany Jesus through the events of Holy Week, is the final episode in Luke's introduction to Jesus' public ministry. Jesus has already been baptized and heard the voice from heaven say, "You are my Son, the Beloved; with you I am well pleased" (Luke 3:22). We now witness Jesus sorting out what those words might mean for him. "Witness" is a problematic word, though, since Jesus is said to be alone in the wilderness, with only the Holy Spirit for company as he and the devil spar with each other with biblical texts. How do we "know" about it? The narrative is not presented as something Jesus taught, but rather as something that the "omniscient narrator" tells about Jesus. In other words, it is part of Luke's theological portrait of Jesus. Luke presents this as a real deliberation in which the devil pushes Jesus to look at three powerful possibilities his religious tradition offers to interpret God's words to him. These would certainly have been possibilities that his followers and members of the early church would have wondered about as they struggled to find categories by which to understand Jesus.

Luke assures us that Jesus is not separated from God's love, for the Holy Spirit fills him at the end of this episode (4:14) as well as at the beginning (4:1),

Homiletical Perspective

Luke's account of Jesus' resisting temptation in the wilderness invites reflection on the way the text presents the Son of God and the world in which his ministry is accomplished. For congregations observing Lent, the forty days of fasting, penitence, and prayer that mark the season will echo the forty days of Jesus' wilderness wandering. One does not, however, need to observe Lent in order for this text to work its power on the hearers. By trying to draw the congregation into the narrative, the preacher will encounter a number of opportunities for a lively preached word.

One such opportunity involves forging a connection between the wilderness experience of Jesus and that of the church. Jesus' sojourn in the wilderness recalls Israel's forty years of wandering—a point underscored by his repeated quotation of Deuteronomy. In the harsh environment of the wilderness, habits formed by slavery in Egypt are discarded and new ways of complete trust in God are formed. The preacher might ask, we are not the people of Israel, but in what ways have we experienced the wilderness? A number of different answers might surface in a congregational Bible study: time in recovery, a prison sentence, unemployment, or even the suffering of a whole community. The preacher, however, must push

Luke 4:1-13

Theological Perspective

Is he ready for process theology? (Am I ready for process theology?) Then I looked at him again and remembered that he was three.

"What do *you* know about the devil?" I asked in classic mom/professor mode. His response was instructive.

"Well," he began, "the devil talked to Jesus." Good, I thought. He was paying attention. "The devil was mean," he continued. *Mean.* I began to wonder about the relationship of "mean" to "evil." What is the difference between "mean" and "evil"? Was the devil really mean? Perhaps it is possible to be mean without being evil, but is the opposite true? Is it possible to be evil without being mean? Or did the beloved children's leader decide that her young audience could understand "mean" in ways they could not understand evil, so that my semantic questions had little importance relative to her rhetorical choice?

My musings were cut short as my son continued his hand-me-down exposition of the text. Leaning closer to me and dropping his voice to a loud whisper, he said, "if we were at a store, and you and Dad were in one aisle, and I was in another aisle, and"—his hushed tones became downright conspiratorial at this point—"there was candy . . ." He paused for effect. "The devil would say, 'You should take some!'"

I am not sure what was most startling to me in this retelling of the story of Luke 4:1–13 by my three-year-old: that he could, in fact, retell it—especially in such dramatic fashion—or that the version he had learned placed such heavy emphasis on the temptation and the personified tempter. In line with theologian Dietrich Bonhoeffer, I take my hermeneutical cues for reading this story from verse 8, in which Jesus quotes a passage from Deuteronomy: "Worship the Lord your God, and serve only him." It is a demanding passage, but Jesus quotes it and abides by it, knowing that the very meaning and shape of his role as Messiah are at stake.

With Bonhoeffer in mind, I started to respond to my son's statement with a message about Jesus' obedience to God. I thought about telling him that the story is more about the responses Jesus gives to the temptations than to the temptations themselves. Jesus' responses underscore his faithfulness to God, setting the stage for the whole of his ministry and, ultimately, his sacrifice. His responses come with the full knowledge that obedience to God will bring persecution, misunderstanding, and the cross. Many followers of Jesus wanted him to free Israel, to

Pastoral Perspective

This passage is helpfully read in relationship with Deuteronomy 6–8. There we see the Lord putting Israel in humbling circumstances and testing what is in their hearts. The first danger that Israel faces amidst its new freedom is the complacency of believing that God is no longer necessary to protect them from hunger and hostile threats. Even today, prosperity, provision, and a secular worldview that interprets all of life apart from a covenant relationship with God are often far greater temptations to spiritual forgetfulness than hardship. Comparing the testing of Jesus with the testing of Israel in the wilderness, sketched in Deuteronomy 6–8, we see a close parallel, except that Jesus' response is faithfulness. He renders to God the obedience that Israel does not give.

Looking toward the end of the Gospel narrative, the "last temptation" of Jesus is seen in Luke 22:39–46. Here Jesus' faithfulness to God's will is fully embraced in the context of his perseverance in prayer. By contrast, the disciples, like Israel, fail in the time of great trial and testing. Jesus had warned them, "Pray that you may not enter into temptation" (22:40 RSV). Much more was at stake than practicing spiritual discipline on the Mount of Olives in the face of their sorrow, however. Faithfulness to the divine mission involved persecution, suffering, and death. Hence this was a difficult path not easily embraced. Only by "joining Jesus"—being in total solidarity with him and his mission—could the disciples grow to "walk the talk."

A popular notion of the season of Lent is that we must "give up something." We are often asked, "What are you giving up for Lent?" Various responses are expected: red meat, sweets, or perhaps excess television or Internet browsing. Perhaps we need to give up that simplistic notion of Lent. Reflecting on some implications of Lent, liturgical scholars Hickman, Saliers, Stookey, and White write: "Lent is thus not giving up something but rather taking upon ourselves the intention and the receptivity to God's grace so that we may worthily participate in the mystery of God-with-us."[1] "Intentionality" and "receptivity to God's grace" are two things to take upon ourselves during Lent.

Intentionality in repentance, fellowship, prayer, fasting, Scripture meditation, acts of piety, acts of justice, and concentrating on our baptismal covenant are examples of things to "take upon

---

1. Hoyt L. Hickman, Don E. Saliers, Laurence Hull Stookey, and James F. White, *The New Handbook of the Christian Year* (Nashville: Abingdon Press, 1992), 106.

even in this moment of encounter with the devil. Unlike other cultures where a person on the verge of adulthood goes off alone on a vision quest to find a name and an identity, Jesus has already had the visionary experience. This is rather a time of sorting: what did that experience mean for his future? The account is set in the wilderness, a place where prophets like Moses and Elijah also began their ministries. It is the place where Israel itself was birthed as a people on their trek to the land that had been promised to them. Jesus' time there was a time of fasting and presumably of prayer.

That much of the story is shared by Mark and Matthew. Jesus' time in the wilderness is a time of "testing" (*peirasmos*). These are not "temptations" to do things that are desirable but not good for him (like our "temptation" to eat an extra piece of cake). Rather, these are tests to see whether even good things can lure Jesus from a focus on God's will—or can lure believers into following a more comfortable messiah. Matthew and Luke share the account of the three specific tests, albeit with the second and third in different order. In two of the three the devil's hook to catch Jesus is the challenge "if you are the Son of God . . ." Does Jesus really believe what he has heard? Will God make good on the implied commitment? Let's find out before you go charging off into dangerous places.

To feed the hungry. The devil's challenges to Jesus are not to do bad things. The first, to turn a stone into a loaf of bread, would assuage his hunger after the long fast. By implication, if he can do that, he can also turn the abundant stones that cover Israel's landscape into ample food to feed the many hungry people in a land often wracked by famine. The challenge is to be a new Moses for the people. Jesus' reply draws on Moses himself, by citing Deuteronomy 8:3. Bread is good, but not sufficient to define Jesus' mission.

To rule the world with justice. The second test in Luke's account portrays the devil in the role of "ruler of this world" (John 12:31; 14:30; 16:11) who can manage the governance of the world's kingdoms. For the price of "worshiping" or honoring that authority, the devil will hand it all to Jesus. Remember that most of the known world in Luke's day was under the heavy-handed control of Rome and its economic, administrative, and military empire. Surely a "regime change" can only be for the world's good! Yet again Jesus' answer is no. The price is too

beyond sheer identification to press the question of faithful engagement of the wilderness experience. Where have we experienced God's faithfulness in the wilderness? How has our relationship with God been transformed? How strong are the temptations of returning to old ways—to ways of relying on ourselves?

Into this mix of questions comes the person of Jesus, in whom the line between the old and the new is made unquestionably clear. The devil comes with tempting offers: to turn a stone to bread and thus sate his hunger, to worship the devil and gain influence over the world, and to test God's promises in a free-fall faith experiment. These Jesus rejects, preferring instead to trust God's word alone. Can we truly say that his experience and ours are analogous, or do we often find ourselves tested beyond our strength? The good news, however, is that the one who was tempted in the wilderness is also the crucified and resurrected one, in whom God's new life is made available to those who cannot, by their own resources, withstand temptation. The one who was tempted in the wilderness thus strengthens us in our weakness.

In addition to preaching on the wilderness, the preacher also has an opportunity to explore the dynamics of testing and temptation. The text tells a story about how evil works on the basis of distortions and lies. The devil presents wants as needs, falsehoods as truths, distrust as faith. The devil's second pitch—that all the kingdoms of the world have been given to him—*sounds* as if it could be true. That it is false, however, is revealed by the demand for false worship. At stake is who will be trusted and worshiped. Preachers might ask, where else do we hear lies that sound truthful? In advertising? From politicians or the media, or the pulpit? In the commonsense "advice" we teach our children? How might clinging to God's word unveil such lies as lies? The preacher could ask similar questions of the first and third temptations: Where else do we see wants presented as needs? Where are we tempted to think of faith as something God must earn?

Sermons exploring the dynamics of temptation could be built in a number of different ways. Their primary goal, of course, would be to teach the congregation to see the world in a new way. After all, that the devil comes with temptations is not something the world readily admits; we see it only through God's word. A preacher might focus on all three temptations, building a sermon in three parts, each exploring a different facet of temptation. Alternatively, the preacher may choose to focus on

Luke 4:1-13

Theological Perspective

restore an earthly kingdom marked by honor and glory. To say yes to the world would have required Jesus to say no to God, to the way of God, and to an idea of God's kingdom that those followers simply did not understand. It would have required him to say no to the freedom and love for humanity that are the marks of his death and resurrection.

Then it occurred to me. Maybe my little boy—who had already taken in so much—understood these very points about the story. So I asked him. "Honey, if we were at a store, and Dad and I were in one aisle, and you were in another aisle, and there was candy, and the devil said, 'You should take some!' What would you say back to the devil?"

A genuinely sweet grin lit up his entire face and without hesitation he replied, "Oh! I would say thank you!"

It is not surprising that a three-year-old missed the point, but lots of us miss the same point all the time. It is far easier than not for us to say, "Thank you," when temptation comes calling; however, the story is only partly about temptation. Today's text is also about Jesus' choice—and ours—to be obedient to God. Certainly, it is the more difficult choice for him to make, but it marks the beginning and frames the whole of his public ministry, particularly as it is described in Luke—from his initial rejection at Nazareth at the end of chapter 4 to his arrest and crucifixion in chapters 22 and 23.

Maybe one day my son will be able to understand the difficult idea that the way of God is simultaneously the way of obedience and the way of freedom. Personally, I am still working on it.

LORI BRANDT HALE

Pastoral Perspective

ourselves." Similarly, in the season of Lent, it may be helpful to recall or enact the historic practices of preparing new converts for initiation into the Christian faith at Easter. This is intentional evangelism aimed at new converts. We should always be reminded that conversion is best understood as a process and not as an event. Evangelism as initiation into discipleship in response to the reign of God[2] is primarily concerned with faith formation and not with membership recruitment or institutional survival. In partnership with the Holy Spirit, evangelism engages the whole people of God in habitual practices.[3]

By taking on "intentionality" and "receptivity to God's grace" during Lent, new converts and members gain the spiritual depth to be faithful to "the mystery of God-with-us" even in our unexpected trials and temptations. Jesus did not ask for trials and temptations; he accepted that they could not be avoided if he would do God's will. Jesus' season of testing was not for a day or two; his season of forty days of temptation suggests to us that we may have faithfully to endure seasons of long and protracted difficulty. Jesus did not have just one encounter of diabolical testing; he overcame multiple temptations. His temptations were real and riveting.

Would Jesus exploit his status and power before God as the Son of God to satisfy his own needs and desires? Would Jesus compromise his relationship with God by failing to acknowledge the ultimate sovereignty of God over all things? Would Jesus accept the bait of Satan, who interpreted the Scriptures outside of intimate knowledge of the ways of God? Jesus' intentionality and receptivity to God's grace show us the way to turn toward God, rather than away from God, during our trials and temptations. If we choose the Lenten struggle to be intentional and receptive to the grace of God, we will encounter a faithful God who leads us not only into the wilderness but also through the wilderness.

JEFFERY L. TRIBBLE SR.

2. Scott J. Jones, *The Evangelistic Love of God and Neighbor* (Nashville: Abingdon Press, 2003), 114.
3. Paul W. Chilcote and Laceye C. Warner, eds., *The Study of Evangelism: Exploring a Missional Practice of the Church* (Grand Rapids: Eerdmans, 2008), xxvi.

high, even to acknowledge the self-evident power of the devil in the political arena. Jesus' reply is from Deuteronomy 6:13, the *She'ma Israel*, which Matthew places as the last and pinnacle of Jesus' replies. *All* authority belongs only to God. Implicitly, even playing the world's game for a good purpose would be to risk serving something less than God.

To serve God faithfully. Luke's sequence of tests concludes in Jerusalem, the place where Jesus' ministry will culminate in his passion and resurrection appearances, and where the church will begin (Acts 1). The devil's challenge is compounded by a quotation from Psalm 91:11–12, which promises God's protection to those who are righteous. The temple is the place where the presumably most righteous—the priests—carry out their work. "Go there," the devil challenges, "and test it!" Many of those professionally righteous folks in Jesus' day, however, were living out their role among Israel's elites by working hand in glove with the Roman occupiers, to the detriment of Israel's poor and suffering. Surely reform is in order! Again Jesus' reply comes from Deuteronomy: "Do not put the Lord your God to the test" (Deut. 6:16).

No, but Yes. Jesus' successful completion of the tests sends the devil packing until the "opportune time" when he enters Judas to launch the events of the passion (Luke 22:3). In Luke's account of the passion and of Jesus' earthly ministry, the meaning of Jesus' baptismal commission unfolds, recalling the three tests he has undergone. Though he refused to turn stones into bread, he does feed the hungry (Luke 9:10–17). Though he refused political power, the proclamation of God's empire of justice and peace is the focus of his preaching and teaching. Though he refused to jump off the temple to see if God would send angels to catch him, he goes to the cross in confidence that God's will for life will trump the world's decision to execute him. Game, set, and match to Jesus!

SHARON H. RINGE

one temptation, probing it in depth. Since the passage is itself a narrative, using stories—from movies, books, or experience—would be particularly appropriate. The congregation may need help to see with transformed vision this world in which evil's tantalizing lies abound.

Finally, preaching this passage becomes an opportunity to explore the identity of Jesus. Much exegetical ink has been spilled about whether or not this incident ever really "happened." In the text, no one witnessed it. In the reading of the story in the liturgy, however, we *become* witnesses to who Jesus is. That Luke places the temptation narrative where he does makes questions of Jesus' identity apparent. As in the Gospel of Mathew, this story follows the baptismal narrative, in which Jesus is declared Son of God. Unlike Matthew, Luke inserts a genealogy of Jesus in between the stories, tracing Jesus' lineage to Adam, who is also in Luke's telling "a son of God" (3:38). In the story itself, the devil's come-on line begins with "*ei huios ei tou theou.*" This could be translated, "if you are the Son of God," but most likely means "since you are the Son of God." The appearance of the Holy Spirit at Jesus' baptism has answered the question of *whether* he is the Son; the question now is what kind of Son he will be. Luke's theological point here is unmistakable: this one is unlike Adam (and unlike us); the powers of evil will have no sway over this one, in whom God's saving purpose is made plain.

These exegetical details will not preach very well, but the theological point is worth developing. One common pastoral-theological question concerns the reality of evil: why it exists and why God seems to do nothing about it. In this story, that could be easy to dismiss, Luke assures us that evil will have no charge over the Son. Moreover, because God's saving purpose in Jesus was meant for the whole world, evil does not have ultimate charge over us. One common Lenten refrain is, "Return to the Lord your God" (Joel 2:13). In this story, we see that we have a God worth returning to, for in God alone is the tempter defeated.

KIMBERLY M. VAN DRIEL

Genesis 15:1-12, 17-18

¹After these things the word of the Lord came to Abram in a vision, "Do not be afraid, Abram, I am your shield; your reward shall be very great." ²But Abram said, "O Lord God, what will you give me, for I continue childless, and the heir of my house is Eliezer of Damascus?" ³And Abram said, "You have given me no offspring, and so a slave born in my house is to be my heir." ⁴But the word of the Lord came to him, "This man shall not be your heir; no one but your very own issue shall be your heir." ⁵He brought him outside and said, "Look toward heaven and count the stars, if you are able to count them." Then he said to him, "So shall your descendants be." ⁶And he believed the Lord; and the Lord reckoned it to him as righteousness.

⁷Then he said to him, "I am the Lord who brought you from Ur of the Chaldeans, to give you this land to possess." ⁸But he said, "O Lord God, how am I

Theological Perspective

This passage of Scripture is frequently interpreted metaphorically as an illustration of ancient Hebrew theology. While this is a legitimate approach, the riches of the passage might best be mined by imagining the text as a real divine conversation. Imagine Abram talking directly to God. God, the creator of the universe, comes to Abram and promises him the most important rewards a would-be patriarch could desire: a positive promise of an heir—and what an heir! Abram is to have an heir with descendants more numerous than the stars.

Perhaps it is this incredible generosity that is so difficult for many of us to accept. We like to think of ourselves as being people who inherently trust God. Yet H. Richard Niebuhr, Sterling Professor of Christian Ethics at Yale Divinity School, repeatedly maintained that the first response of humanity toward God is that of distrust. Although God is good to us, we do not trust God. Like most of us, Abram knows that he is not all that good or all that deserving. Accordingly, it is difficult for him to believe and accept that he might be blessed beyond measure. Yet miraculously God gives Abram blessings. Rather than being grateful, however, Abram is uncooperative.

Too often we find divine generosity so overwhelming that we dispute it. It is no surprise,

Pastoral Perspective

The biblical picture of God and Abram's relationship is fairly straightforward. God speaks; Abram listens. God promises; Abram believes. God commands; Abram obeys. There comes a point, however, when Abram finally says, "Wait a minute. I have a question."

We might breathe a sigh of relief at this revelation. Abram, the great model of faithfulness, is also a person who wants to know how God is going to fulfill God's promises. Abram looks at his life and says, "It is unclear to me, God, how you are going to work things out. There are some pretty big obstacles in the way. I'd like to have just a little more information."

Abram left his country and his father's house in response to God's command, "Go," and God's promise of blessing and prosperity. Abram went without asking any questions. Pushed out of the Negeb by famine, Abram went down to Egypt. He prospered there and left Egypt rich in cattle, silver, and gold. Abram journeyed back to Bethel and gave Lot first choice of land to settle. Again God commanded and promised, telling Abram, "Walk through the land and I will give it to you." Abram responded obediently. Later, Abram rescued Lot, who had become a prisoner of war, and returning from victory, Abram gave Melchizedek, king of

to know that I shall possess it?" [9]He said to him, "Bring me a heifer three years old, a female goat three years old, a ram three years old, a turtledove, and a young pigeon." [10]He brought him all these and cut them in two, laying each half over against the other; but he did not cut the birds in two. [11]And when birds of prey came down on the carcasses, Abram drove them away.

[12]As the sun was going down, a deep sleep fell upon Abram, and a deep and terrifying darkness descended upon him. . . .

[17]When the sun had gone down and it was dark, a smoking fire pot and a flaming torch passed between these pieces. [18]On that day the LORD made a covenant with Abram, saying, "To your descendants I give this land, from the river of Egypt to the great river, the river Euphrates."

Exegetical Perspective

The narrative here is composed of two parts: (1) verses 1–6, the dialogue between YHWH and Abram resulting in the promise first of a son and then of countless descendants, and (2) verses 7–21, a second dialogue, concluding in the promise of land. This passage, together with Genesis 17, is at the center of the Abraham cycle of stories, and the two passages constitute the core of the promises to Abraham. Both portions of chapter 15 bear signs of later composition, although perhaps not both in the same historical period. While portions of the passage may be older, the overall composition of verses 1–21 is almost certainly the product of an exilic context, an observation that is reinforced by the language in verses 13–16, which are omitted in the lectionary reading.

The core of verses 1–6 consists of a dialogue between YHWH and Abram, the first such dialogue recorded in the Abraham stories. The phrase "the word of the LORD came to Abram" imparts a prophetic quality to the encounter in verse 1 and is repeated in verse 4. The phrase is common in the prophetic books but appears only here in the Pentateuch. The prophetic slant of the verses is reinforced in verse 1 by the term "vision," common in the prophetic books but occurring in the Pentateuch only here and in Numbers 24.

Homiletical Perspective

A prayer written by the fifteenth-century Dutch priest Thomas à Kempis comes to mind when I consider Abram's lament and surprise upon hearing God's unambiguous, yet lofty promise in this text. Like Abram, Thomas inquires, "Lord, what is my confidence which I have in this life? Or, what is the greatest comfort that all things under heaven do yield me? Is it not thou, O Lord God, whose mercies are without number?" On this Second Sunday in Lent Abram's doubt is replaced by his hard-fought acceptance. Thomas comes to a conclusion similar to Abram in his devotional response: "Thou art my trust, and my confidence, thou art my Comforter, and in all this most faithful unto me."[1]

There is much to notice in the passage. It points us to what ultimately materializes in the stuff of the book of Hebrews. The movement from suspicion to belief describes the internal logic of Genesis 15. At the outset, the preacher-interpreter should carefully consider why Abram stages bold protest that calls into question the reliability of God's promise. What was the nature of his conversations with God prior to this? God asks Abram to gather his goods and leave his homeland without any real assurances. This

1. Thomas à Kempis, *Imitation of Christ*, ed. Paul M. Bechtel (Chicago: Moody Press, 1980), 270.

Genesis 15:1-12, 17-18

Theological Perspective

therefore, that Abram quarrels with God; yet God does not punish him. Feminist theologian Flora Keshgegian characterizes the patriarchal understanding of God as limiting. "The right relationship we have with God is a formal one," she writes of patriarchy, "of a subordinate to a superior, of a child to a formidable parent. God provides and we accept, gratefully and humbly. There is no room for reciprocity or mutuality or even closeness in such a relationship."[1] As valid as her point is, Abram finds divine understanding here. When God engages Abram, Abram does not merely accept God's promises humbly. God insists that Abram's reward is great, but it is a future promise. No child is present; old age and barrenness still prevail. Abram believes God. He is willing to wait on God's future promise of an heir, but he demands an immediate sign of the promise.

At Abram's age, time is precious. He lives daily with doubt and anxiety. For Abram to keep the faith, God must powerfully and directly reconfirm the divine covenant. Amazingly, God continues to be patient with him. The same God who called Abram out of Ur is willing to reaffirm Abram's blessing through a theophany. While God is patient, Abram is not and—in the long run—this impatience costs Abram his peace of mind.

The additional communication between God and Abram changes Abram's experience of the promise enormously. In today's passage, God tells Abram exactly what will happen, but now primarily in the deep and rich but mysterious medium of dreams. What did Abram actually see in his dream? We may never know, but we do know what Genesis records. Genesis tells us that Abram is finally convinced that the divine promises will be fulfilled, but he finds out more than he bargained for. Genesis depicts Abram fully understanding the promise, but also the struggle to come. He learns of the suffering of his descendants, along with their final vindication, the fulfillment of their blessings. With this further revelation, Abram is convinced that God will act, but his new knowledge includes the sad revelation of the suffering that is part of God's plan.

Abram and his descendants will be blessed. Terence E. Fretheim calls these constitutive blessings, by which he means that they are "community-creating, that is, that they enable Abram and Sarah to continue to be faithful but also inform, empower and continue to bless their progeny, the community

1. Flora A. Keshgegian, *God Reflected: Metaphors for Life* (Minneapolis: Fortress Press, 2008), 67.

Pastoral Perspective

Salem and priest of God Most High, a tithe of all the men and goods he had captured. Melchizedek declared, "Blessed be Abram by God Most High, maker of heaven and earth" (Gen. 14:19). Abram seems bold, courageous, obedient, humble, and faithful in all he does.

Abram has questions too. After these things, God reiterates the wonderful promise: "Do not be afraid, Abram, I am your shield; your reward shall be very great" (Gen. 15:1).

This time Abram does not respond with silent obedience. This time Abram says, "I have a question. How can this be, since I do not have a child?" In spite of everything up to this point—plenty of possessions and wealth, new land to settle in, and victory over his family's enemies—Abram says, "I am not absolutely sure. I still have questions." As Abram's questions start to surface, they also start to sound like complaints. "Are you going to give me what I really want, God? Is a slave going to be my heir? I want a legitimate son." Can a person who questions and complains also be a model of faith?

What is the character of faithfulness? So often when people face perplexing questions—when they feel the anxiety of doubt and uncertainty, when they struggle with frustration and disappointment—they think of it as a crisis of faith. We are tempted to think of faith only as unquestioning acceptance or silent submission, but as we follow Abram on his journey of faith, he clearly comes to the point where he challenges and questions God's claims. This kind of struggling with God can also be a part of faith.

In response to Abram's questions and complaints, God takes him outside for an astronomy lesson. God says, "Look at all those stars. When you get done counting them, you will know how many descendants I will give you."

Then the text says, Abram "believed the LORD; and the LORD reckoned it to him as righteousness" (v. 6). Abram seems prepared, in spite of lingering questions and contrary evidence, to take the next step forward, in confidence that God's promise will actually determine the course of his life. God declares Abram's willingness to live based on God's promise as "righteous."

What does Abram believe? That he will have a child? That God can be trusted? That there are a lot of stars in the sky?

Does Abram completely understand how God will fulfill what God has promised? Does Abram have all the answers to his questions? That seems unlikely. However Abram does believe that God will

Exegetical Perspective

The dialogue itself opens with YHWH's admonition, "Do not be afraid," a phrase that echoes the exilic oracles of salvation in Second Isaiah (41:10, 13, 14; 43:1, 5). In verse 2 Abram responds with a question that focuses YHWH's general promise of "reward" from verse 1 and emphasizes that nothing is valuable without an heir to inherit from him. The Hebrew phrase translated as "Eliezer of Damascus" is unclear, but the meaning of the Hebrew is not essential in the dialogue, since Abram's focus is on the lack of a bodily heir.

YHWH replies emphatically in verse 4 that Abram's heir will be a child of his body. As a sign of this promise, he takes Abram outside and tells him, "Look toward heaven and count the stars, if you are able to count them" (v. 5). Abram's descendants will be as many as the stars. In the process of the narrative move, the promise has shifted from a son to the promise of a multitude of descendants.

Verse 6 is clearly the culmination of the section. The verse moves from direct dialogue to third-person theological reflection. The Hebrew term translated "believed" may also be translated "trusted," a some-what more relational term. "Righteousness" is most often defined as acting appropriately or justly within a relationship, but here Abram has taken no action overtly; it is his trust in YHWH's promises that constitutes his righteousness. The term translated "reckoned" is a cultic term associated with a priest declaring that a sacrifice has been correctly and acceptably offered.[1] Thus it is not Abram's actions that have made him righteous in this case; it is his trust that puts him in a right relationship with YHWH.

Verse 7 begins the second part of the passage with YHWH again addressing Abram directly. The structure of the verse is in three parts and closely echoes the later call of Israel in Leviticus 25:38. It begins with the self-identification "I am YHWH," followed by a reminder of their previous relationship ("who brought you from Ur of the Chaldeans"), and concludes with a promise ("to give you this land to possess"). The verbal and structural similarities to the Leviticus passage again point to a later, exilic, date of composition for these verses.

As in verses 1–6, the address by YHWH is followed by a question from Abram. This time, instead of answering Abram's question directly, YHWH directs him to bring a heifer, a goat, a ram, a turtledove, and a pigeon. Abram responds and, going

---

1. Gerhard von Rad, "Die Anrechnung des Glaubens zur Gerechtigkeit," *Theologische Literaturzeitung* 76 (1951): 129–33.

Homiletical Perspective

is not the picture of a patient Abram, but rather of one whose endurance has run its course. Opposite genuine concern about his time remaining on earth and his wife Sarai's biological clock, the question the text poses is this: What likelihood could there be for Abram to become Abraham the "father of a multitude"? One has to listen to this text to sense its profound address to the human condition. Barrenness is one subject of scrutiny here. Life is difficult for Abram and Sarai, which means that the human quandary raised by this text poses some challenges for preaching.

The preacher must ask at least two questions with sensitivity and attentiveness. First, what was the nature and scope of barrenness in the ancient world? Second, are there analogues here that can help contemporary listeners who have struggled with the problem of infertility? This particular text encourages the preacher to do theology in a way that first honors the spirit and message of the ancients in their distinct historical contexts.

When read as focusing on the problem of infertility, this narrative needs to be reread using some ideological suspicion about ancient power construc-tions and social arrangements. How is fertility understood from a biblical worldview? It has been largely assumed that when couples struggle to conceive, the problem lies with the woman. However, we now know through medical breakthroughs that oftentimes the impediment lies with the man. Responsible Christian preaching has a justice obliga-tion to include men in the conversations and con-demn prejudices that scapegoat women around this subject. This passage does not say that childbearing is a right, nor does it imply that there are no other life circumstances that require believing faith.

Faithful interpretation must insist that Christian preaching not only delve into the past but also make inquiries into scientific advancement, posing criticism to science when it chooses to write off God's involvement in complex human matters. Inductive preaching could engage hypersensitive issues such as infertility by creating tension that helps the listener journey with the preacher. One's movement toward this text profoundly shapes how one hears this text. Rather than alienating hearers at the beginning of the sermon by spelling out its controlling idea, the judicious preacher will develop trust that honors the biblical narrative and its social environment. The preacher will gather relevant data to help the community understand what is at stake in relation to Scripture, situation, and issue.

Genesis 15:1-12, 17-18

Theological Perspective

of the future."[2] But here is the rub. Abram was blessed in Ur; it was his destiny to be blessed, whether or not he had his dream. So was his dream necessary? The text suggests that it was not. In our text, God's promise precedes Abram's demand of proof. When Abram asks for a sign of reassurance, God has already acted faithfully. Abram is thus like the father of the demon-possessed boy of Mark 9:24 who cries to Jesus, "I believe; help my unbelief."

Such a request is different from the distrustful demands that demonstrate disobedience (centuries after Abram, in John 4:48, Jesus the Son of God complains of an unfaithful generation that demands signs and wonders). In Mark's story, the father's belief is enough to allow change in the boy, who is of course healed. The father is also changed. He is put in right relationship with God.

Perhaps if Abram had not questioned God, but merely kept covenant with God, he could have been spared the sure knowledge of the painful process that God would employ to fulfill the covenant. As it was, Abram learned that God's promises require patient faith and steadfastness.

God comes to us ready to bless; our impatience does not change God. God comes to us hoping we will be trusting. Our positive response, though limiting, echoes God's hopefulness. Trusting God and receiving divine blessings is our reward. If we can learn from Abram simply to trust God, then we do not need signs.

We do not need to understand God's blessings fully in order to enjoy them. All we need are hopeful and patient hearts. The wise will accept those blessings gratefully. Walter Brueggemann describes such believing acceptance as "an act of faith."[3] God will tell us all there is to know if we persist, but sometimes it is best simply to accept divine assurances and their blessed time frame along with them.

DARRYL M. TRIMIEW

Pastoral Perspective

be faithful and true. Abram believes that the life God promises to give Abram is the course he should try to follow.

Abram believes but still asks questions. Immediately after God's judgment of Abram's faith as righteous, God declares, "I am the LORD who brought you from Ur of the Chaldeans, to give you this land to possess" (v. 7). What does Abram say? "How can I be sure?" "How can I know that I am to possess it?" Abram's faithfulness is a questioning faithfulness, a pleading with God for more: more information, more clarity, more courage, more commitment as we stumble along, trying to follow the steps God calls us to on our own journey of faith.

Abram asks how God is going to accomplish what God promises. Abram does not ask God questions that really only cover up his own sense of accomplishment. Abram does not whine and ask, "When am I going to get what I want to be happy? When am I going to be satisfied? What do I have to do to feel content?"

Abram questions God's activity. His questioning faith takes seriously God's presence and power in his life and challenges us to be open to God's work in our lives. Abram questions God because he deeply believes God can do something about it. Such questions about God can also help us take the next steps of our journey of faith.

Lent offers us an opportunity to think about our discipleship in light of how others have lived in response to God's call and command. What are the costs and demands they faced as they walked the way of discipleship? Like Abram, we also have questions that will not be silenced as we try to walk in faithfulness to God. Like Abram we can question God as part of our faithfulness and trust. We also live expectantly that God's promises of life, hope, and future are extended to us in Jesus Christ, who defines faithfulness by the character of his own life and death, and who calls us to take the next step and follow him.

DANIEL M. DEBEVOISE

2. Terence E. Fretheim, *God and World in the Old Testament: A Relational Theology of Creation* (Nashville: Abingdon Press, 2005), 107.
3. Walter Brueggemann, *Genesis*, interpretation series (Atlanta: John Knox 1982), 144.

Exegetical Perspective

beyond the direction of the text, splits the heifer, the goat, and the ram in two. Commentators disagree over the meaning of verse 11, some interpreting the vultures as an evil omen that Abram drives away by his diligence.[2]

The composition of verses 12–18 is unclear and disputed, with verses 13–16 omitted from the lectionary. Verse 12 is probably best seen as an introduction to verses 13–16. This would explain the tension with verse 17, which includes the temporal introduction ("When the sun had gone down and it was dark") to the ritual of verses 17–18. If verses 13–16 are to be omitted for purposes of sermon preparation, then verse 12 should also be bypassed and the passage read directly from verse 11 to verse 17, a smoother and more logical transition.

Commentators almost universally agree that the rite described in verses 17–18 is a rite of self-obligation committing the one passing between the halves of the animals (cf. Jer. 34:18ff.) to a solemn promise and invoking a fate similar to that of the halved animals if the promise is not fulfilled. The remarkable aspect of the ritual in this passage is that YHWH, represented by the smoking fire pot and flaming torch, is the one undertaking the obligation of the ritual. The promise is of land, specified by the list of current inhabitants in verses 19–20.

This is often read as a covenant text, but the statement of verse 18, that "On that day YHWH made a covenant with Abram," is belied by a close look at the text itself. In the true covenant form, there are obligations on both sides of the agreement. In this case it is only YHWH who is undertaking a promise—Abram is not obligating himself to do anything (cf. chap. 17). The ceremony is rather a solemn promise by YHWH, reinforced by a ritual ceremony.

This passage in the midst of the Abraham cycle contains the summary promises of descendants and of land. The dialogues of verses 1–6 and 7–21, including the cultic rehearsal of consequences if the promises are broken, point to the seriousness of God in making the promises and in keeping them. Abram can trust in those promises, and his trust puts him into the right relationship with the One who promises.

RICHARD A. PUCKETT

Homiletical Perspective

The topical sermon is another homiletical approach that might effectively address such a delicate topic. By developing the sermon topically and framing infertility as a public issue, the preacher-interpreter may start with the issue and then turn to the biblical text, instead of placing the text out front. In this way, thoroughgoing investigation into the public issue might generate truly evocative responses from the Bible.

Still, of utmost significance is that the preacher finds useful and creative ways to interpret and appropriate Genesis 15 to help listeners understand the overarching message of God's self-disclosure through promise revealed. Abram embraces God's revelation. God's revelation, Daniel Migliore explains, "is not the transmission of a body of knowledge . . . the knowledge given in revelation is not simply knowledge *that* or knowledge *about*, but knowledge *of*."[2] Abram trusted God without a tangible sign. Moreover, righteousness is seen as the theological upshot rewarding one human's faithfulness; the pain of barrenness is overturned; hope displaces lament; and divine generosity is expressed and claimed. Hope and humanity are held in tension throughout this passage. On the one hand, we are permitted to identify with Abram's human struggle and desire for confirmation of the promise made to him; on the other, we are called to mimic his response in verse 6: Abram believed! This confession earns him right standing with God.

Finally, the preacher might interpret this text for the life of the community through proclamation that announces the good news that God's provisions are first and foremost for our souls. Nourished souls trust God despite life's extremities. Any sermon on Abram and Sarai's struggle to obtain God's promise must help listeners encounter God as one who invites everyone to trust, have hope, and have faith. Abram's God is intimately personal, responsive to believing faith. Correspondingly, Abram's God is close kin to postmoderns who dare to exchange the barren language of "Christianese" for simple, honest talk. This is where knowledge of God begins.

KENYATTA R. GILBERT

2. Claus Westermann, *Genesis* (Minneapolis: Augsburg Publishing House, 1985), 226.

2. Daniel L. Migliore, *Faith Seeking Understanding* (Grand Rapids: Eerdmans, 1991), 20.

Psalm 27

[1]The Lord is my light and my salvation;
   whom shall I fear?
The Lord is the stronghold of my life;
   of whom shall I be afraid?

[2]When evildoers assail me
   to devour my flesh—
my adversaries and foes—
   they shall stumble and fall.

[3]Though an army encamp against me,
   my heart shall not fear;
though war rise up against me,
   yet I will be confident.

[4]One thing I asked of the Lord,
   that will I seek after:
to live in the house of the Lord
   all the days of my life,
to behold the beauty of the Lord,
   and to inquire in his temple.

[5]For he will hide me in his shelter
   in the day of trouble;
he will conceal me under the cover of his tent;
   he will set me high on a rock.

[6]Now my head is lifted up
   above my enemies all around me,

Theological Perspective

The Lenten journey can be a foray into the soul, offering us a good time to look deeply within ourselves in order to understand the dark realities that beset us. Among such realities are our fears, including our fear of the many uncertainties over which we have no control. As limited and finite creatures, we possess no absolute certainty with respect to the future contingencies of life or our ability successfully to meet unforeseen events. All consideration of theological matters must perforce go to our nature as limited creatures and our presumption about the nature of God whose providence cannot be limited. As creatures of a gracious God, we have a modicum of awareness of our limitations but also consciousness of a realm that transcends the corporeal. Accordingly, we are creatures who can hope, even as we experience the limitations of human existence. It is precisely in the face of human fears that human hopes seem most necessary. That an undeniable link between hope

Pastoral Perspective

In a world teeming with broken relationships, personal disappointments, public scandals, political games, cultural disrespect, and increased terrorist threats, trust is difficult to extend—even to God. Even the faithful know bitter disappointment and crushing pain. We are familiar with people maneuvering against us (vv. 2, 3, 6, 12). Even God's own know the feeling of abandonment or being "turned away" by God (v. 9). How can we or anyone call God "light" and "salvation"? What makes the psalmist believe in seeing "the goodness of the Lord in the land of the living" (v. 13)? Does God really deliver people from evil or hide people "in his shelter in the day of trouble" (v. 5)?

As Christians sit together in diverse seasons of life, Psalm 27 uniquely speaks to the person who has faced difficulty and yet knows the easing of initial pain. While perhaps callous for one in the throes of grief, and insufficiently challenging for someone comfortable to the point of needing reminder that

and I will offer in his tent
   sacrifices with shouts of joy;
   I will sing and make melody to the LORD.

[7]Hear, O LORD, when I cry aloud,
   be gracious to me and answer me!
[8]"Come," my heart says, "seek his face!"
   Your face, LORD, do I seek.
[9] Do not hide your face from me.

   Do not turn your servant away in anger,
      you who have been my help.
   Do not cast me off, do not forsake me,
      O God of my salvation!
[10]If my father and mother forsake me,
   the LORD will take me up.

[11]Teach me your way, O LORD,
   and lead me on a level path
   because of my enemies.
[12]Do not give me up to the will of my adversaries,
   for false witnesses have risen against me,
   and they are breathing out violence.

[13]I believe that I shall see the goodness of the LORD
   in the land of the living.
[14]Wait for the LORD;
   be strong, and let your heart take courage;
   wait for the LORD!

Exegetical Perspective

Psalm 27 begins and ends with the psalmist giving himself advice. It is as if he places a chair opposite himself and asks that empty chair, "Because the LORD is my light and salvation, whom should I fear?" (v. 1). The empty chair responds reasonably with silence. So the psalmist talks about his life (vv. 2–3). At present, evil men besiege him, intent on killing him so ruthlessly that the psalmist describes it as "devouring my flesh."

Psalm 27 combines an affirmation of faith (vv. 1–6) and an individual lament (vv. 7–14), expressing vibrant trust in God in a rough-and-tumble world bereft of safety nets. It shows a courageous life lived amid the onslaught of bullies described as oppressors, enemies, and false witnesses. The psalmist, identified in the superscription as David, receives an assurance of triumph over two very present problems: the presence of enemies and the trauma of false accusations (vv. 2–3, 6, 11–12).

Homiletical Perspective

There is some division of opinion among scholars on whether this psalm is a combination of two psalms or one unified psalm with multiple parts. Clearly there are two or even three sections to the psalm, verses 1–6, 7–12, and perhaps 13–14, although commentators generally seem to collapse verses 13–14 into the previous section.[1] In any case, the tone or affect is different in each section. Additionally, homiletically it seems that the first and second sections might ideally be reversed. It is a more compelling order for preaching: begin with a wavering, almost desperate faith, more longing than hope; conclude with a strong statement of conviction and exhortation, moving from doubt to certainty, dark to light. It is how sermons *ought* to work, how faith *ought* to work, how life *ought* to work, but they rarely cooperate in so tidy a fashion.

1. See, for example, Artur Weiser, *The Psalms: A Commentary* (Philadelphia: Westminster Press, 1962), and James L. Mays, *Psalms* (Louisville, KY: John Knox Press, 1994).

Psalm 27

Theological Perspective

and fear should exist has been given poetic rendering in William Cowper's adage "He has no hope who never had a fear."[1]

Psalm 27 offers a rich evocation of the tension between the reality of human fears and the assurance of divine help. The psalm affirms that, for the faithful, human fears may be assuaged through the presence of an everlasting God, the ultimate reality that undergirds all human aspirations and hopes. Yet the theological texture of the psalm reveals two opposing dynamics by which this tension is made manifest. On one hand, human freedom from fear is affirmed in the wake of the *clarity* of divine presence. On the other hand, human freedom from fear is affirmed even in the *opaqueness* of divine presence, when God seems hidden or obscured. When God seems obvious, hope is vindicated; when God seems hidden, hope requires faith for sustenance, faith being "the assurance of things hoped for, the conviction of things not seen" (Heb. 11:1).

In the first dynamic, the psalmist is confident of God's clear and unqualified presence. Given the presumed theological primacy of divine surfeit over human inadequacy, the psalm issues forth in the very first verse with the affirmation of who and what God is: "The LORD is my light and my salvation," after which the psalmist can ask with confident assurance, "Whom shall I fear?" By conflating these two affirmations—the affirmation of God's presence and the affirmation of human freedom from fear—into one sentence, the psalmist avers that the mere confession of human limitation and the certain prospect of human fear is only one part of any theological agenda. If indeed human creatures look within themselves and confess limitations—limitations that occasion fears—then ultimate affirmations about the Creator must in fact play a critical role in the overall assessment of faithful human existence. No description of human existence will be complete apart from a confession that the "LORD is the stronghold of my life," after which, again the psalmist can ask with unfailing confidence, "Of whom shall I be afraid?"

The subsequent request of the psalmist in light of God's assured presence is noteworthy for a vision of faithful living consistent with the theological underpinnings of the text. The "one thing I asked of the LORD" (v. 4) is redolent of Jesus' words about "only one thing . . . , the better part, which will not

---

1. *The Works of William Cowper*, ed. T. S. Grimshawe (London: Saunders & Otley, 1835), 6:63.

Pastoral Perspective

hope is in God and not self, Psalm 27 offers camaraderie and subtle guidance to someone scared or uncertain about the future. Whether this person is surviving cancer, navigating a twelve-step recovery program while tempted by old adversaries, or returning from military to civilian life still dueling PTSD demons, Psalm 27 maintains gritty honesty as it dances back and forth between fear and trust.

On the one hand, the psalmist addresses God as "light," "salvation," and "stronghold." God "hides" or protects the psalmist in times of trouble. God "teaches" and "leads" in the ways of right living. Even in times of trouble, the psalmist affirms, God is worth the wait. Psalm 27 is a breathtaking affirmation of faith and trust in God, even in the face of dangerous enemies. It inspires bold liturgical affirmations of faith as well as the singing of triumphant hymns such as "I Sing the Mighty Power of God," "God of Grace and God of Glory," "Immortal, Invisible, God Only Wise," and "A Mighty Fortress Is Our God."

On the other hand, the questions "Whom shall I fear?" and "Of whom shall I be afraid?" may not be rhetorical. Verse 2 names "evildoers," "adversaries," and "foes," while verse 3 identifies entire armies or groups of people arrayed against the psalmist, ready to fight. By verse 7, the bravado of these initial verses is gone, and the psalmist pleads with God: "Hear me . . . when I cry aloud" (v. 7). The psalmist implores God: "answer me!" (v. 7), "Do not hide your face from me. Do not turn your servant away in anger. . . . Do not cast me off, do not forsake me" (v. 9), and "Do not give me up" (v. 12). The tension between verses 1 and 12 feels palpable. Real fear lives alongside honest faith. Bona fide doubt holds hands with genuine trust. In this psalm, as in life, both are unavoidable.

Perhaps unexpectedly, both are also essential. Vigorous faith and animated doubt both insist that we take God seriously, ask God real questions, and depend upon God in tangible ways. Examined doubts refine our understanding and illuminate our experience of God as we filter our beliefs, sifting wishful thinking about the God we want from the challenging wisdom of the God who is.

Thus, though uncomfortable with this part of Lenten discipline, we follow Psalm 27's lead, holding fear and faith, doubt and trust together. We form communities where people are allowed and taught to talk honestly. In response to culture's deep and pronounced needs for connectivity and authenticity, we offer safe space, even to people whose lives, views of the world, or clothing style may not match our own.

Exegetical Perspective

The psalmist compliments the Lord by enumerating the Lord's characteristics and sometimes personalizing them: the Lord is *my* light, *my* salvation, the stronghold of *my* life, *my* helper (vv. 1, 9); beautiful (v. 4); is able to keep *me* safe in the day of trouble and hide *me* in his tabernacle (v. 5); and is full of goodness that *I* will live to see (v. 13) (italics added).

The psalmist remembers sweet worship in the Lord's house. He desires deliverance from his enemies in order to worship yet again. He longs to dwell in the Lord's house and to gaze upon the Lord's beauty. These longings need "all the days of my life" to satisfy (v. 4).

He describes God's protection in a delightfully imaginative way by saying that in the day of trouble God will set him high upon a rock, protect him with hospitality, and keep him safe in the place of worship (v. 5).

The psalmist offers a profound antidote to fear: confidence in God and confidence in himself. The psalmist makes a profound choice: he chooses not to fear. Faced with human finiteness, he channels his energy toward trust. Significantly, the psalmist's confidence grows throughout the psalm. The psalmist exercises trust by praising God, calling upon God, requesting something from God, and counseling himself not to fear.

His confidence extends to a prophetic word: the psalmist prophesies victory over his surrounding enemies. Shouting noisily and triumphantly raising his head, he proclaims that he will live and not die (vv. 6, 13)! He will worship again in the Lord's sanctuary, offering the sacrifice of joy (v. 6).

The psalmist's confidence in God burgeons into self-confidence. The psalmist expects a cheery outcome in his favor. This he knows: he will not only live but will also see the goodness of the Lord. The tuneful psalmist decides to express his thanksgiving and love with exuberance. He plans to include joyful shouting, singing, and making music to the Lord (v. 6).

After these praises, the psalm switches to lament. Turning from victorious pronouncements and thanksgiving, the psalm concentrates abruptly on problems and petitions. At the core of a lament psalm is the desire to obtain something from God. When the psalmist says, "Hear my voice" (v. 7), he desires to move the heart of God. In a humble way appropriate for Lent, he seeks God's favor with nine petitions:

v. 7   Hear my voice. Be merciful. Answer me.
v. 9   Do not hide your face from me. Do not reject or forsake me.
v. 11   Teach me. Lead me.
v. 12   Do not turn me over to my foes.

Homiletical Perspective

Two steps forward, one step back. That is, one step, if we are lucky. Certainly many psalms follow along this very trajectory, moving from doubt or anger or mistrust toward thanks and praise. It moves better, making for more powerful preaching. End on a high note. Alas, that is not how the psalm is put together.

After a little honest reflection, however, there is some real wisdom in the way in which we have received this psalm, regardless of its literary history. The psalm starts with good, solid, hopeful, well-articulated intentions as we often do ourselves, all with apparently firm foundations. Just think of all those New Year's resolutions that have come to life in great hope but quickly withered under the pressure of a lack of discipline, strength, or resolve. How many diets have been destroyed under the weight of a luscious slice of chocolate chip cheesecake? Our grand intentions are inevitably tested in the crucible of need and crisis, that is, in reality. What happens to those intentions when put under pressure? In the case of this psalm, there is a momentary wavering, but it closes with a strong reaffirmation of faith and trust in God. What matters is where we end up—faith or doubt. The psalmist ends up in faith, in trust, waiting for the Lord.

Be clear, however, this is not a psalm about how God answers our prayers. It is a prayer, even a plea, for patience, for trust, for the ability and the endurance to wait for the Lord, even when there is no sign that prayers may be answered, when the Lord's arrival is a long, undetermined way off. This radical sort of trust is hard enough to generate but so much harder to sustain in difficult times. In the aftermath of both 9/11 and the devastating hurricane Katrina, television reports and newspaper articles featured folks who had lost trust, who had lost faith in God because of these events. If there even *is* a God, they opined, those catastrophic events proved either that God is not all powerful or that God just does not care. In either case, God is not to be trusted. It is the age-old problem of theodicy. Martin Luther wrote a hymn that attempts to counter this dilemma. The lyrics request, "Grant peace, we pray in mercy, Lord." They later resume, "For there is none on earth but you, none other to defend us. You only, Lord, can fight for us."[2]

There is none other to defend us. There is no one else, only God. There is nothing I can do myself. This is not some mere antiwar protest song; it is a radical

2. *Lutheran Book of Worship* (Minneapolis: Augsburg Publishing House, 1978), hymn #471.

Psalm 27

Theological Perspective

be taken away" (Luke 10:42). That "one thing," that one irreducible abstract of faithful living, is the hope of leading a life in which one enjoys protection "in the day of trouble." Moreover, the psalmist is a part of a believing community whose corporate life is graced by the ability to behold "the beauty of the LORD" (v. 4), or to enjoy an awareness of a realm of sublime order that is constitutive of faithful existence. An asylum from mayhem or the nefarious work of evildoers is afforded those who enjoy the obvious presence of the Lord.

There is another dynamic in this psalm that proceeds from the presumption that God's presence may not always be as obvious as was the case before. The psalmist is undergoing spiritual anxiety that was not present in the first dynamic. This is evidenced by the words, "Your face, LORD, do I seek." In the first dynamic, no such effort was needed, but now the psalmist pleads, "Do not hide your face from me." The notion of *deus absconditus*, or the hidden God, affirms a theological posture that privileges revelation, rather than human initiatives such as the use of reason, as a means of discerning who God is. Ultimately, the "I am that I am" eschews the familiar settings in which human eyes have longed to see God or the philosophical categories that have been the putative places in which God might be sequestered for easier human comprehension. Many Christians will resonate with Pascal's instinct: "What can be seen on earth points to neither the total absence nor the obvious presence of divinity, but to the presence of a hidden God. Everything bears this mark."[2] Yet, such marks as might be available to us are under the provenance of a God who even in elusiveness evidences presence to faithful human creatures.

The response to the hidden God can be nothing other than a response of faith, couched in the assurance of hope. Even the hidden God will be evident to the believing community, provided they see such a God through the eyes of faith. Moreover, an active faith born of hope can inspire the psalmist to make a final declaration that manages to merge the dynamics that have been identified, that is to say, when the *hidden* becomes palpably *clear:* "I believe that *I shall see* the goodness of the LORD in the land of the living" (v. 13).

SAMUEL K. ROBERTS

Pastoral Perspective

In many churches, we spend tremendous time debating interesting questions, "believing" or "not believing" that God engages personal or political matters—for example, "believing" or "not believing" that God rescues and hides people from enemies. Yet faith is not simply about believing or not believing. It is not assent to a specific supposition; at its best, faith is not about doctrine at all. It is about the truth of what we have known. The life of faith is grounded in experience; it is about the real mystery, awe, pain, and grace that we know. As such, the faithful live at the intersection of religious ideas and real life, humbly bringing soaring trust, persistent doubts, and everything in between into conversation with Scripture, church tradition, the chorus of witnesses, and the Holy Spirit who works in and through all. In this busy age of anxiety, as in the contemplative days of Lent, we teach and provide opportunity for people to do what the psalmist is doing in Psalm 27: sharing the experience of God (vv. 1–6, 13–14) and praying raw prayer that may not seem respectful or theologically correct but is honest (vv. 7–12).

Learning to hold doubt and faith together takes patience, which is why the last verse of the psalm— "Wait for the LORD"—holds all fourteen verses together. Patient seeking, patient searching, patient development of spiritual practices that make both faith and doubt meaningful—these give us the time and skills we need to navigate pain, learn lessons, gain perspective, and perhaps even experience the world differently.

After all, those with the courage and the skills to gaze deeply at doubt, faith, and all of life generally have "eyes to see and ears to hear" what we easily miss. They see differently, turning a corner and seeing abundance before scarcity. They reach a milestone and recognize grace before loss. Rejecting the self-fulfilling belief that we live in a world based on fear, scarcity, and competition, they notice what is easily overlooked and recognize what is given each day. They do not gloss over real poverty (material, spiritual, or emotional), nor do they minimize pain or injustice. They know the power of trust and the benefits of doubt in bringing out the best in others and in themselves. Furthermore, based on who they keep discovering God to be, they too proclaim the word we all need to hear: "The LORD is my light and my salvation. . . . The LORD is the stronghold of my life."

LINDSAY P. ARMSTRONG

---

2. Blaise Pascal, *Pensées*, trans. Martin Turnell (New York: Harper & Bros., 1962), 234.

Exegetical Perspective

The psalmist expresses confidence that he will be heard. As a member of the covenant community, he carries legal standing. He calls himself the Lord's servant (v. 9). This familiarity shows his ongoing, covenantal relationship with the Lord. The psalmist has an immediate need—deliverance from a host of enemies and false accusers—along with the legal standing to have that need addressed.

Weary from his enemies' advance, the desperate psalmist needs someone immediately to protect and comfort him. No longer "making nice," he commands God: "Hear my voice when I call. Be merciful to me and answer me" (v. 7).

He receives an immediate and possibly unexpected answer. He hears his heart say, "Seek his face." Although perhaps surprised that God's strong right arm does not immediately strike his foes, this well-trained believer nonetheless responds with instant obedience: "Your face, Lord, do I seek" (v. 8).

He acknowledges God as more reliable than his closest kin (v. 10). The psalm presents the possibility that his father and mother either already forsook him or are at least capable of abandoning him. In contrast, God, as the psalmist's stronghold, greets him with ready help.

The psalm explores the delightful prospect of hiding with the Lord; together from a high rock they will watch the psalmist's enemies go by. The Lord's sheltering presence is a hiding place. Perhaps fearing abandonment, the psalmist complains that he does not like it when the Lord plays hide-and-seek with him (v. 9).

Yet with a confident attitude this psalmist awaits the Lord's timing. Staying a steady course, the quieted psalmist contentedly waits to see how God chooses to exhibit light and salvation. He refrains from mandating that divine help come in a certain way. The psalmist beautifully, poetically calls God's decisive actions on his behalf (whatever they may be) "God's goodness in the land of the living" (v. 13).

Although an individual lament psalm, Psalm 27 also serves well in public worship. Because of its broad generalities, most worshipers easily identify with it. Many of them also face false accusations and enemies intent on the kill; they too want a safe hideaway with the Lord.

The psalmist ends with more advice to that empty chair. It is as if the psalmist—now confidently standing tall, shoulders back, head lifted high—shakes his finger in admonition at the opposite chair and shouts, "Wait, I say, on the Lord; be strong and take heart and wait for the Lord!" (v. 14).

ROBIN GALLAHER BRANCH

Homiletical Perspective

posture for living. It is to be applied in every circumstance, at every level. So much energy is spent in self-defense against enemies, real and imagined; against attacks, real and imagined. You *only*, Lord, can fight for us, none other to defend us. This is the human dilemma—to believe this and not try to hedge somehow by having a backup plan. The old joke closes, "Is there anyone else up there?" No, there is not.

In the first section, the psalmist claims only the desire to be in God's presence, "to live in the house of the Lord all the days of my life, to behold the beauty of the Lord, and to inquire in his temple." Nice. Noble. Neat. Malarkey. Some years ago, I went to a regional pastors' meeting where the guest speaker did an in-service on professional burnout. Every person there was a prime candidate for burnout. The ones with especially high ideals were the most likely to suffer, but everyone there was afflicted. Some while later, I observed in an Advent sermon with a clergy group that I had enjoyed Christmas less each year since I had been ordained. I thought it was a risky statement, one that would arouse suspicions. I saw a lot of nodding heads as I looked out at this congregation of clergy. They were not dozing but agreeing with the observation. So this psalm captures the dilemma many of us face, calling in our preaching for a resolve, a faith, a trust that we can barely muster ourselves. Yet it is the only hope we have.

Judging by a similar exhortation in the second reading, "Stand firm in the Lord" (Phil. 4:1), and judging by the "deep and terrifying darkness" that descended on Abram (Gen. 15:12), this is a continuing condition among religious people. Recent memoirs of Mother Teresa confirm that faithful people have even extended times of dark and dread and doubt, but they persist in their faith.

So our psalm begins with an untested, even naive bravado, weakens for unnamed reasons, but ends on an upbeat note. So it is in much of our living. We wait for the Lord.

RICHARD C. STERN

Philippians 3:17‑4:1

[17]Brothers and sisters, join in imitating me, and observe those who live according to the example you have in us. [18]For many live as enemies of the cross of Christ; I have often told you of them, and now I tell you even with tears. [19]Their end is destruction; their god is the belly; and their glory is in their shame; their minds are set on earthly things. [20]But our citizenship is in heaven, and it is from there that we are expecting a Savior, the Lord Jesus Christ. [21]He will transform the body of our humiliation that it may be conformed to the body of his glory, by the power that also enables him to make all things subject to himself. [4:1]Therefore, my brothers and sisters, whom I love and long for, my joy and crown, stand firm in the Lord in this way, my beloved.

Theological Perspective

Protestants shaped by Luther and Calvin are often made nervous by all notions of "imitation," as if Jesus were a moral exemplar who, like any other heroic figure, is to be imitated in order that we might earn our own salvation. Luther famously called such efforts by the derisive name of "works righteousness." The worry over making the gospel into a form of moralism is quite legitimate; it seems to fling salvation by grace alone through faith alone right out the window. If Jesus is primarily a figure in whose image we are meant to copy and model ourselves, then the question naturally arises: Why him? Why not the Buddha or Confucius, why not Muhammad or Gandhi, why not Emma Lazarus or Anne Frank?

Yet the imitation theme in Scripture is undeniable. Paul urges the Philippians to imitate him, even as he himself imitates Christ Jesus. As inheritors of ancient notions about learning and thus about discipleship, both Jesus and the apostle know that true moral and spiritual formation depends on tutelage under a master—learning to follow the habits and practices of one who has become proficient in a particular trade or skill. Indeed, this is the precise meaning of the word "disciple": a learner or pupil. Like all other Christians, therefore, Paul is the pupil of Christ and

Pastoral Perspective

In the Protestant tradition in which I serve (Presbyterian), the liturgical seasons are inscrutable. They are not yet fully part of our identity; they have not yet mutated our spiritual DNA. If pressed, my congregants might report that Advent or Lent means the purple comes out, Pentecost means we all wear red (and maybe host a picnic afterward), and high holy days call for white. Unfortunately, this is akin to suggesting that Republicans are elephants and Democrats are donkeys—the understanding lacks a certain depth or subtlety. Congregants are often surprised to find out Easter is a season rather than a day, and Advent celebrates a second coming along with the first. In tacit approval of the retail season over the liturgical one, the Christmas tree usually comes down on December 26.

Lent is especially confusing to most people.

"Why do we commemorate Jesus in the wilderness if we are on the road to the cross? Did that not happen at the beginning of his ministry?"

"Why do we say forty days? It is not forty days. I counted."

"Can I still eat meat? Why do people do that?"

Then there are the two questions that seem to be the crux of everyone's understanding: "Why do we give something up for Lent?" and its counter, "I thought we were supposed to take something on for Lent—not give something up, right?"

Exegetical Perspective

Who weeps anymore over those who live as enemies of the cross of Christ? Hardly anyone I know. When you stop and think about it, the very idea seems absurd. Expressing grief because of lifestyle? Perhaps even over our own manner of living? When everything is permissible? Paul's impassioned plea strikes us as breathtakingly unreasonable. Still, if Lent is the season in which the church is invited to the task of personal reflection about the cross, then this text is for us. Here we are asked to examine our own cross-denying ways. Fortunately there is a template for us to follow. Its shape, however, is cruciform. Conforming our lives to this template will be difficult work at best. It was for the apostle Paul: "For [Christ's] sake I have suffered the loss of all things, and I regard them as rubbish, in order that I might gain Christ. . . . sharing . . . his sufferings . . . becoming like him in his death" (Phil. 3:8–10). This is the invitation of Lent.

Paul notes that an appropriate response to the daily challenges confronting Christian existence is found in imitating a certain pattern, but conforming ourselves to this pattern is a special kind of imitation. Mimesis (imitation) is never some kind of slavish reduplication of a pattern. It is rather an incarnation of a living example that the Philippians can observe in Paul, Timothy, and Epaphroditus. In turn, these three have themselves followed the

Homiletical Perspective

Lent has just begun. The journey of forty days toward the three-day Easter feast engages the individual and the community in deeper reflection of what it means to live as children of God in this world. Lent, rather than being simply a time of stricter discipline, is like a concentrated reflection on the life we are called to live throughout the year. The forty days are rooted in baptism. The readings encourage us to root ourselves in our baptismal vocation. Many churches may actually be preparing candidates for baptism at the Easter Vigil service.

In this text from Philippians, Paul focuses on some of the characteristics of life in the church, the community of the children of God. Several inter-related themes stand out: living as a community, living as an individual, and the citizenship of the children of God.

Living as community. The opening verse is striking: "join in imitating me." We would expect Paul to write "join in imitating Christ," much as he did in the preceding chapter: "Let the same mind be in you that was in Christ Jesus" (2:5). Even in chapter 2, Paul is already encouraging a communal "mind-set" over individual imitation ("be of the same mind, having the same love," 2:2). Here in verse 17, Paul holds up his life and the life of others who observe "the

Philippians 3:17-4:1

Theological Perspective

thus an imitator of him. He calls the Christians at Philippi to do and to be the same.

That Jesus is not another hero such as Socrates or Aristotle, such as Seneca or Cicero, immediately becomes evident when Paul declares that those who do not follow Jesus are "enemies of the cross of Christ." It is this ugly instrument of suffering and shame that sets Christ qualitatively apart. Whereas all other great teachers and moral exemplars are devoted to noble human ends that are to be achieved by noble human means, the cross is the uniquely divine means for accomplishing the uniquely divine end known as the kingdom of God. All human visions of peace and justice finally fail if they do not resort to force and coercion, whereupon they destroy peace and corrupt justice. The company of the cross is the one community that makes an instrument of worldly powerlessness and defeat its central emblem and banner.

In writing his pre-Christian epic titled *The Lord of the Rings*, J. R. R. Tolkien echoes this profoundly Christian understanding of what it means to be a friend rather than an enemy of the cross. The Fellowship of the Ring is a company of Nine Walkers who, with the exception of the wizard Gandalf, are fairly ordinary creatures. They are set against the Nine Riders, the wrathful wraiths and merciless slaves of the dark lord Sauron. Sauron had fashioned a Ruling Ring of absolute power in order to conquer the known world with it. Through means providential no less than fortuitous, the One Ring has come into the possession of Frodo, a seemingly insignificant hobbit and member of the Fellowship. Nearly everyone assumes that the only means of resisting Sauron's murderous determination to reclaim the ring is to use it against him—to fight fire with fire, terror with terror, coercive might with coercive might. Indeed, anyone who suggests any countercourse is regarded as foolish in the extreme. All other ways are but paths of despair.

Yet Gandalf counsels the more excellent way, the way of surrender rather than use of coercive power. In virtual echoes of Paul's summons to the folly of the cross, Gandalf urges the fellowship to

> let folly be our cloak, a veil before the eyes of the Enemy. For he [Sauron] is very wise, and weighs all things to a nicety in the scales of his malice. But the only measure that he knows is desire, desire for power; and so he judges all hearts. Into his heart the thought will not enter that any will refuse [such power], that having the Ring we may seek to destroy it. If we seek this we shall put him out of all reckoning.[1]

Pastoral Perspective

Scriptures like Philippians 3:17–4:1 cloud the problem. How are we to understand the "enemies of the cross," for instance? Do those who idolatrize their bellies do so by strict observance of the dietary laws? Or do they make idols through gluttony? Is their sin one of restriction or consumption? Have they given up too much for Lent or taken on too much?

Perhaps we should reframe this passage as a question: how should the Philippians observe Lent? They are, after all, looking forward with eager longing to the resurrection, to a savior who "will transform our lowly bodies so that they will be like his glorious body" (3:21 NIV). Where can they turn for guidance in how to live in this time of waiting?

Paul suggests, perhaps even humbly, that they turn to him, their spiritual leader. In imitating Paul, they are imitating their teacher. Pastors are uncomfortable with talk like this. If two thousand years have taught us anything, it is that spiritual leaders are deeply flawed and need guidance too. It should be remembered, however, that by this injunction to imitate Paul, we are following an ancient pedagogy—we are learning through imitation of one who is more mature than we are. In doing so, we should remember further—and more importantly in this case—that we are imitating our teacher's teacher. Though Paul never met Jesus, he regularly claims the resurrected Christ as his master (Rom. 1:1 and Gal. 1:10). In essence, Paul encourages us to imitate Christ by imitating him, a man who has encountered the resurrected Christ, a man who encourages us earlier, "Let the same mind be in you that was in Christ Jesus" (Phil. 2:5). By imitating Paul, we are thus imitating Christ. So goes the theory, at least.

We live in a time when Christians are losing their denominational identities. Packaged with this loss is a loss of clarity. Perhaps Presbyterians never imitated their pastor, but they knew what they believed by virtue of the fact that Presbyterians believed certain things. Lutherans, Methodists, and Baptists may have had similar beliefs, but the differences were crucial, and they could tell you why. Now people are as confused by denominational doctrine as they are by some people's unwillingness to have the magi show up in their nativities until Epiphany ("What is that all about!?!" someone asked me recently). This loss of clarity leads to a loss of religious identity. While some may lament this turn of events, it strikes me as a wonderful opportunity to reorient ourselves—not by doctrine, but by imitation.

pattern of Christ, who emptied himself (2:5–11). This hymn to the nature and work of Christ is foundational in Paul's letters to his emphasis upon the Christian's imitation of the Lord. In fact, the very nature of emptying ourselves as Christ did is indispensable for our journey of authentic discipleship.

Philippians 2:5–11 opens Paul's appeal to those who would disrupt the fellowship and unity of the congregation. If Christian existence is based upon the life of Christ, then we are to have a mind-set of humility just as he did. Our pattern to emulate is this: Jesus did not regard his equality with God something to be hoarded and clung to; he poured himself into the form of a servant. As such, he experienced death on the cross. Thus Jesus serves as the model to imitate. Sacrificial love for others becomes the gold standard of Christian conduct. Such a life may have many shapes over the generations. It can even have many shapes within the same generation. There is no outward form to which one can point and say, "That is it." Pouring oneself voluntarily into the shape of a servant in order to serve others out of love will be multiform. This is exactly the kind of imitation that Lent invites us again to consider.

As Christ has emptied himself, so Paul has been emptied of everything he counted as among his greatest treasures—his heritage, his own innate goodness, his religious fervor. All these pale in comparison to knowing Christ and following his example of sacrificial love. The cross is always central in the concept of imitating Christ. Such discipleship is marked by suffering and death, never boasting and arrogance. Paul's letters begin with doctrine and proceed to application. This passage in Philippians serves as a bridge between the reality of the cross and the application of cruciform living in daily life. Perhaps we need to weep more for ourselves than for anyone else.

Cruciform living is necessarily countercultural. It is the antithesis to a materialistic approach of living as seen in those whose "god is their belly" and whose "minds are set on earthly things" (3:19). If the Philippian Christians were to follow *this* kind of pattern, the end result would be destruction and eternal loss. Sadly, for many North Americans the paradigm is to worship at the altar of having stuffed lives, filled to the brim. Gluttony is not too strong a word to describe such a life. Having a voracious appetite for self-fulfillment apart from the cross is a denial of the One who emptied himself of this kind of life in order to

example you have in us." Paul is directing the gaze of the community not toward some type of individual perfection, not even toward the supreme perfection of Christ (*imitatio Christi*) but to the realization of Christ's love within the community itself. It is as if he says, "Look to those in your midst who live according to the gospel. Let their example, visible in the midst of your community, be a guide for your own life."

This is not what many of us expect or even want to hear. We prefer to hold up models of faithful living that are more remote, not those who live in the same community with us. The lives of these distant spiritual heroes do not affect us in the same way. We can keep them at a distance—it was a different time, they encountered different problems—or we can let ourselves be influenced individually by them without having to make a commitment of our own lives in community. They can be our personal "saints," who give us strength and courage but who do not take us into the harder demands of living as children of God. Of course, looking to such heroes eventually leads to discouragement, for in the end we can never be like them. So our spiritual lives slowly dry up.

Paul, on the other hand, does not point to any heroes. He points to himself (that is, someone they all know) and to others who live like him. He points us to the community as it struggles to live according to the mind that was in Jesus Christ. The community is never a perfect community. It struggles to understand how faith is lived in the world and in the particular local context. Paul holds up that struggle as the way of right living. Engage the faith in the messiness of life, he says—not just individually, but as a community. Look toward those in your own community—your neighbor, your friend, maybe even someone you do not particularly like—and learn from the way in which they struggle to live faith in community.

Living as individuals. The opposite of this discipline of the community is a self-centered interest. The enemies of the cross of Christ are those who make their own lives the focus of their attention. This is an especially hard word from Paul for our society, which values the individual self above almost anything else, catering to every single individual need as if our "needs" automatically translated into our "rights." The words need to be repeated so that those who have ears can hear: Paul calls those who live in this way "enemies of the cross."

Their end, he writes, is destruction. In the end, their self-centeredness leads them into lifelessness. They are "curved-within-themselves" (as Luther put

Philippians 3:17–4:1

Theological Perspective

Frodo and his companions finally succeed in defeating the nearly omnipotent figure of evil precisely because they choose the crosslike way. So it is with Paul's summons to imitate him in following the way of the cross, the instrument of defeat that is the only hope of real and lasting victory, because it is not a human victory but a divine victory.

The cross also identifies the enemies of Christ. It is important not to literalize Paul's declarations about making "a god of the belly," about glorying "in shame," and thus about minds "set on earthly things." If we do so, we are likely to think well of ourselves because we are not gourmands, because we have a pristine reputation, or because we do not care overmuch for our possessions. Such self-congratulatory claims can be made by many people who do not follow the way of the cross. Lent is meant precisely for the repentance of such self-praise. We are *all* given to what Paul repeatedly calls earthly-mindedness. We do not find our identity in Christ's present and future reign through his body called the church, but rather in earthly sources of our identity—our ethnicity or nationality, our gender or social status, our political commitments, or our families and careers.

For Paul to declare that "our commonwealth is in heaven" is not to make a sentimental otherworldly promise. Christians do not live for "payday some day." If we do, then Marx and Nietzsche and Freud were right to call ours a religion of illusion and deceit. On the contrary, our bodies (and therefore our earthly lives) are so essential to our souls (and thus our spiritual lives) that the two cannot be divided. We are ensouled bodies and embodied souls. We can obey Paul's call to "stand firm in the Lord" (4:1) only by following the way of the cross, only if we are seeking here and now to begin that union of our bodies and souls that shall be finished there and then.

RALPH C. WOOD

Pastoral Perspective

Clearly, as long as we have broken spiritual leaders, imitation will always be tricky, but we have an extraordinary resource at our disposal that the apostle Paul never had: the Gospels—written accounts of the teacher's teacher. We do not need Paul for imitation; we have the life of the one we call Savior for imitation, the one for whom we wait.

Using that framework, we reframe the question once again: how would Christ live through Lent? As alluded to earlier, we can use as our model either his time in the wilderness or his journey to the cross. Did he make a god of the belly? He certainly loved food, culminating his ministry with a final meal the church still reenacts. He was even accused of drunkenness and gluttony (Luke 7:34), but did his belly rule him? Certainly not. His time in the wilderness shows us that he did not "live by bread alone, but by every word that comes from the mouth of God" (Matt. 4:4). In short, he would neither distort himself for a meal nor follow a path of asceticism around food. In imitation today, then, perhaps Christ's followers should give up a habit that threatens to distort us, while picking up a habit that gives us new life.

Christ's definitive instruction about how to live in Lent comes from that resource the Philippians could not have seen for another generation, the Gospel according to Mark. Here Jesus says, "If any want to become my followers, let them deny themselves and take up their cross and follow me" (Mark 8:34), which is not simply a call to self-denial but a call to imitation—day in and day out.

Interestingly, this call is also why we celebrate the liturgical seasons. It provides the structure by which we imitate the life of Christ. In Advent, we rehearse the story of his birth and await his second coming. In Lent, we travel the wilderness with him and pick up the cross on which he will be crucified. In Easter, we celebrate that death is not the final word but that Christ has the power to "make all things subject to himself" (Phil. 3:21), that he is, in fact, a savior for when our imitation fails.

CASEY THOMPSON

---

1. J. R. R. Tolkien, *The Fellowship of the Ring*, 2nd ed. (Boston: Houghton Mifflin, 1967), 282–83.

embrace the cross. There are patterns to follow that lead to death, and another pattern that leads to life. Paradoxically, we never completely and fully attain this pattern in this life. We must always "press on" (3:12). Lent reminds us of this. The pattern is given, yet it cannot be fully duplicated in our lives. We can only strive toward it with determination, thankful for all the living examples of the pattern living around us in a community of faith.

The life of the cross leads to a heavenly commonwealth. While the Philippians were proud of their status as citizens of Rome, Paul reminded them that there is a better citizenship to be had. There is a greater Lord than Caesar. This Lord is the crossbearer who is now glorified and eternal. Our hope for an eternal future with him is grounded in the call to be like him now in servanthood to others. Cruciform living is the opposite of escapism. It is our active engagement in the suffering of the world as we empty ourselves and discover the scandal of a life never before imagined. This life points to something beyond all hope, that God is in control and will transform this life into something of a different kind altogether. There will be a new heaven and a new earth. Imitating Christ is never joyless drudgery. It is the confident hope that we shall be like him.

Lent demands a response to this hope while it invites deep reflection. Are our lives cruciform or not? Paul calls those who move toward the cross his "joy and crown" (4:1). We are asked to stand firm in the Lord. This is more than being in a secure place; it is being in a secure person. The pattern we imitate is nothing less than grace and peace. Thank God for Lent.

MARK E. HOPPER

it), shutting them off from the possibilities of community and subsequently of life. Of course some may argue that there are many things they "enjoy" without letting those things become their "gods," as Paul puts it in this passage. Such reasoning is a subtle deception. In his *Large Catechism*, Luther writes, "It is the trust and faith of the heart alone that makes both God and an idol. . . . Anything on which your heart relies and depends, I say, that is really your God."[1] If we want to know who our God is, we need only ask ourselves: on what do I depend? The answer may be disturbing.

When the glory of the individual is not the struggle of living life together in a community, not the struggle of living out one's baptismal calling in the world or carrying the cross, but simply the pursuit of one's own self-interest, then Paul calls this glory a shame. "Their glory is in their shame" (3:19), he writes.

Citizenship. The citizenship of such individuals is in their self-enclosed lives, both material and spiritual. The citizenship of the children of God is elsewhere. This is an important qualifier to the above-mentioned theme. Our life is called to be in community but even this community is not perfect—at least not yet. Life in community is lived in a deep expectation. It is lived as a struggle but a struggle of faith, that is, a struggle that is both "joy and crown" (4:1).

DIRK G. LANGE

1. Robert Kolb and Timothy J. Wengert, eds., *The Book of Concord: The Confessions of the Evangelical Lutheran Church* (Minneapolis: Augsburg Fortress Press, 2000), 386.

Luke 13:31-35

³¹At that very hour some Pharisees came and said to him, "Get away from here, for Herod wants to kill you." ³²He said to them, "Go and tell that fox for me, 'Listen, I am casting out demons and performing cures today and tomorrow, and on the third day I finish my work. ³³Yet today, tomorrow, and the next day I must be on my way, because it is impossible for a prophet to be killed outside of Jerusalem.' ³⁴Jerusalem, Jerusalem, the city that kills the prophets and stones those who are sent to it! How often have I desired to gather your children together as a hen gathers her brood under her wings, and you were not willing! ³⁵See, your house is left to you. And I tell you, you will not see me until the time comes when you say, 'Blessed is the one who comes in the name of the Lord.'"

Theological Perspective

The metaphor of the inward and outward journey has always been appropriate for the season of Lent, emphasizing deliberate reflection on the obstacles that beset us in our spiritual life and the hope for new direction as we look ahead to the promise of Easter. In the final weeks of his life, Jesus is moving ever closer to Jerusalem—the city of David—where the great prophets of the past have more often than not been ignored, reviled, or killed. Jeremiah attests to the reception that Uriah received from King Jehoiakim when the prophet dared to speak out against the kingdom of Judah: "[he] struck him down with the sword and threw his dead body into the burial place of the common people" (Jer. 26:23). Jeremiah himself almost succumbed to the same fate, left to die in a muddy cistern after speaking words of discouragement to the people (38:4–6).

Jesus was journeying toward this same end, and he knew it well. Not even the threats coming from the "fox," Herod Antipas, executioner of John the Baptist, could distract him from his final destination. His was a sacred journey ordained by God that could not be thwarted by the jealous anger of a petty Galilean tetrarch. Jesus' calling had not been confounded by Herod's father at his birth (Matt. 2:13–18), nor by the crowd in Nazareth intent on hurling him off a cliff (Luke 4:29). On the contrary, these were only

Pastoral Perspective

We live in a world obsessed with status and power, and consequently rife with political machinations. Most obvious in this regard may be the candidates for and holders of governmental office, who often try to make themselves look better than they actually are—and their opponents look worse than they are. We also encounter such machinations on a more mundane basis. At work, a colleague slyly tries to take credit for someone else's bold and profitable idea. We call this "office politics." In the community of faith, people jockey to influence the outcome of decisions about who will be the next pastor, how mission moneys will be apportioned, or what color of carpet will be installed in the fellowship hall. We call these activities "church politics."

Some people think Jesus was innocent—or ignorant—of the realities of politics. Those who think so have not read the Gospels very closely.

Jesus of Nazareth was no stranger to political machinations. He was prone to saying things like, "Indeed [when the kingdom of God arrives in its fullness], some are last who will be first, and some are first who will be last" (Luke 13:30). Nothing will more quickly alarm those on top, in comfortable positions, than the suggestion that they may not end up on top, but that some of those now relegated to the bottom, to last place, will ultimately be first.

Exegetical Perspective

The Herod of this story is Herod Antipas, the son of Herod the Great. According to Herod's will, Antipas received the Galilee and Perea upon his father's death. The Romans did not allow him to use the title king, but styled him as tetrarch (ruler of a quarter part; Luke 3:1). This, no doubt, was intended to show his subordinate status. Antipas ruled not by right but at the pleasure of the emperor. Some Jews thought that the Herodians were little more than collaborators. Their support for the dynasty was almost nonexistent. The paranoia of Herod the Great may have been pathological; nevertheless, his dynasty survived only because it was propped up by the Romans.

Jesus had no use for Antipas. During his Galilean ministry, he never entered two cities particularly associated with Antipas: Sepphoris, which was his first capital, and Tiberias, which Antipas built to replace Sepphoris. These cities represented the antithesis of the kingdom that Jesus proclaimed. They were monuments to attempts to Romanize the people of Galilee. Jesus came to call the people to repentance and faith. He called them to renew their commitment to their ancestral religious traditions. Antipas and his supporters also wished to lead the people of the Galilee to a new world—a world whose center was Rome and whose values were opposed to the values of the gospel.

Homiletical Perspective

African slaves of antebellum America, by virtue of their servitude, were compelled to cast their ken beyond mere sight—to extend their vision beyond things as they were, to a deeper, broader, higher vision, and dream of things as they could be. Hence many of their sacred songs, the Negro spirituals, stretch the contours of reality as it is given in the social order, pointing to the form of a new heaven and a new earth—a new social order, a new set of institutional arrangements—a kingdom not born of or controlled by the powers of this world. One of their spirituals describes the kingdom of God thus: "There's plenty good room, plenty good room, plenty good room in my Father's kingdom."

That, for Luke, is a central message and a recurring theme. In the Gospel for the Second Sunday in Lent Jesus speaks in tones of abject disappointment and utter heartbreak at the refusal of his own people to hear and heed the summons of God to draw near, to gather, and to come home: "O Jerusalem, Jerusalem, killing the prophets and stoning those who are sent to you! How often would I have gathered your children together as a hen gathers her brood under her wings, and you would not! Behold, your house is forsaken. And I tell you, you will not see me until you say, 'Blessed be he who comes in the name of the Lord'" (Luke 13:34–35 RSV).

Luke 13:31-35

Theological Perspective

momentary obstacles along this final trip to Jerusalem. Jesus' harsh words for Herod reflect his utmost confidence in the providence and will of God in the task that he, the Son of God, has been called to complete. For his opponents to suggest that he would somehow be killed anywhere or at any time outside the Holy City was to venture into the realm of the absurd.

While Jesus no doubt identified with the likes of Jeremiah, Uriah, Zechariah, and so many others whose voices piqued the ire of the Jerusalem elite, it is likely that the nuances of this final pilgrimage to the Holy City were informed by a prophetic insider who preceded him by seven centuries. During the reigns of kings Ahaz and Hezekiah, Isaiah sought to challenge the predominant Jerusalem theology that interpreted the Davidic monarchy and the presence of God in the temple as the final fulfillment of God's promise to Abraham. Under the sway of this theology of grace, a kind of aristocratic complacency set in, what Walter Brueggemann has called the "royal consciousness."[1] No longer was Moses' alternative community living freely under the laws of the covenant; rather, God's will came to be reified in the political apparatus of the state.

Prophets arose in the apostasy that ensued, trying to remind the kings and their bureaucrats of their covenantal duty, but to no avail. Yet a hopeful vision of a just and righteous kingdom was never far from the consciousness of some among Jerusalem's faithful. "In days to come," Isaiah wrote, "the mountain of the LORD's house shall be established as the highest of the mountains . . . ; all the nations shall stream to it" (2:2). In this time of peace, swords would be beaten into plowshares and spears into pruning hooks—images that hearken back to the original call of Adam as steward of creation (Isa. 2:4; cf. Gen. 2:15). This prophecy would never come to pass as long as the faith of Israel remained tied exclusively to the primacy of the temple, as Jeremiah knew so well. No, God would have to do "a new thing" (Isa. 43:19).

This new vision must have been on Jesus' mind as he looked toward the city that would ultimately reject him. He lamented how often he desired to gather its children "as a hen gathers her brood under her wings" (Luke 13:34). Scholars have made much of the comparison between this simile and other avian allusions in the Hebrew Scriptures, but they

Pastoral Perspective

Accordingly, the Gospel of Luke tells us, "at the very hour" Jesus utters these disturbing words, some Pharisees arrive and tell him to flee immediately—because Herod wants to kill him (v. 31).

What is peculiar about this ostensibly protective warning is that the Pharisees have, to this point in the Gospel story, not been Jesus' friends. They have been among those most threatened by the topsy-turvy kingdom Jesus heralds, among those "first" who may end up "last." Why, suddenly, are these particular Pharisees so concerned for his safety? More than likely they have ulterior motives. Possibly they are in league with Herod and hope to drive Jesus out of Herod's jurisdiction, into the arms of Pilate and Pilate's responsibility.[1] Then, like a state governor in our day passing on responsibility to federal authorities, at least Herod cannot be blamed for the results of this troublemaker's actions. Maybe Pilate can figure out a way to get rid of Jesus altogether.

It is admittedly speculative to guess at the motives of those who come to Jesus with Herod's threat. What is clear is that Jesus, in any event, responds to the outwardly friendly warning as if it were an instance of political machination. "Go and tell that fox for me . . . ," he says, revealing that he knows these Pharisees are in cahoots with the conniving, calculating Herod (v. 32). To use parlance of our day, Jesus "steps up" to Herod's oblique, veiled challenge. He lets the Pharisees and Herod know he is not politically naive. He is fully aware that the kingdom he proclaims—and enacts, by "casting out demons and performing cures today and tomorrow," especially among the poor and the typically neglected—is an affront to the powers that be.

More than that, he informs them that his challenge will go all the way to the top. He will not stop in the provinces but will proceed, on his own time, to the capital city of Jerusalem. So Pilate will be confronted soon enough. It is as though Jesus makes it clear that the discomforting politics of his kingdom will not stop at entering the doors of statehouses in Alabama, Maine, or Idaho, but will also be taken up the line to the ultimate stops, to the steps of the Congress and White House in Washington, DC. He does not imagine that Jerusalem (or Washington) will placidly welcome him. Jerusalem is "the city that kills the prophets" and murders those sent to it for its own welfare (vv. 33–34). Likewise, Washington (alongside other

---

1. See Walter Brueggemann, *The Prophetic Imagination*, 2nd ed. (Minneapolis: Fortress Press, 2001), esp. chap. 2.

1. See John Nolland, *Word Biblical Commentary: Luke 9:21–18:34*, vol. 35B (Dallas: Word, 1993), 743.

Exegetical Perspective

Like many of his contemporaries, Jesus probably regarded the Herodians as usurpers, who had no right to the kingdom promised by God to David. As a former disciple of John the Baptist, who had become very popular in his own right, Jesus was likely perceived by Antipas and the Herodians as a threat. His proclamation of the coming "kingdom of God" likely made Antipas and his supporters uncomfortable. That they planned to rid themselves of Jesus is likely, though Luke is the only evangelist to report this incident. He alone gives Antipas a role to play in the trial of Jesus (23:6–12). The ridicule that Antipas and his courtiers heaped on Jesus shows that Antipas regarded him as a rival who could no longer be allowed to be a serious threat to his rule.

What Jesus implied by calling Herod a "fox" is not clear. In Hellenistic thought, the fox is regarded as clever but sly and unprincipled. The Old Testament associates the fox with destruction (Song 2:15; Ezek. 13:4). Jewish dietary laws classified the jackal as an unclean animal. In any case, Jesus' words reflect the disdain he held for Antipas. Jesus dismissed Antipas as powerless to prevent him from carrying on the mission to establish God's rule on earth. Echoing a theme found often in the Fourth Gospel (see John 7:30; 8:20; 8:59; 10:39; 11:54), Luke has Jesus imply that his enemies have no power over him until the time set by God for Jesus' passion and death. Jesus asserts that he will continue his ministry and his journey to Jerusalem, where his divinely determined fate awaits him. Antipas can do nothing to stop him.

The reference to Jerusalem in verse 33 and Antipas's plans to have Jesus killed (v. 31) lead Luke to attach Jesus' apostrophe to the city at this point. Matthew (23:37–39) has Jesus lament Jerusalem's fate after he enters the city—a more logical placement. Luke has Jesus say these words while he is still on the way to Jerusalem. The accusation that the city kills prophets reflects popular Jewish tradition rather than the Bible, which is silent on the fate of the prophets. For example, *The Martyrdom of Isaiah,* a first-century CE pseudepigraphical work, asserts that Manasseh had Isaiah sawed in half—a legend found in the Talmud and other early Jewish works. While the Old Testament does not speak of Isaiah's death, Hebrews 11:37 may be an allusion to this legend. Of course, the Old Testament often portrays Jerusalem's behavior as symptomatic of Israel's failure to heed God's word (e.g., Isa. 3:8; Jer. 13:27; Ezek. 16:2).

Luke places the lament over Jerusalem at the end of a collection of parables (13:1–30), all of which are calls for repentance. This is very likely a key to how

Homiletical Perspective

For Jesus, God's passionate dream, compassionate desire, and bold determination is to gather God's human children closer and closer in God's embrace and love. That mission and commitment is at the center of Jesus' work. Like a mother hen, God seeks to draw, embrace, include, and welcome God's children into the family of humanity that God has intended from the dawn of Eden itself.

Luke's Gospel signals this core message early in the telling of the life of Jesus. It is to shepherds that the good news of the Messiah is first told. That is not insignificant. Shepherds in the biblical world were not nice, gentle, and respectable figures. In his magisterial book *The Birth of the Messiah*, the late Raymond Brown writes, "Far from being regarded as either gentle or noble, in Jesus' time shepherds were often considered dishonest, outside the Law." He goes on to say, "Herdsmen were added by the early rabbis to the list of those ineligible to be judges or witnesses since they frequently grazed their flocks on other people's lands."[1]

Shepherds represented those on the fringe, the margins of society. However, the gospel transcends marginality and creates the context for the emergence of a new humanity, a new human community, born not of social custom but of the Spirit of God. "I am bringing you good news of great joy for all the people: to you is born this day in the city of David a Savior, who is the Messiah, the Lord" (2:10–11 NRSV).

Luke saw a persistent intent on the part of Jesus to bring in those cast out, to raise up those beaten down, to bring those on the extremities of the social order close to the heart of God. Luke sees this at the heart of Jesus' messianic message. That is why in Luke's Gospel a peasant girl sings a song of revolution in the Savior's coming: "My soul magnifies the Lord, and my spirit rejoices in God my Savior, for he has regarded the low estate of his handmaiden" (1:46–47 RSV). In Luke, Jesus tells of a prodigal son welcomed home by a father whose compassion is extravagant and whose love seems reckless. In Luke, Jesus tells of a good Samaritan to folk who often thought that the only good Samaritan was a dead Samaritan. Luke remembers a "good thief," who finds the kingdom of God while dying on a cross next to Jesus.

When Jesus begins his ministry, he identifies his work with the prophecy of Isaiah from the days of

---

1. Raymond E. Brown, *The Birth of the Messiah* (New York: Doubleday, 1993), 420.

Luke 13:31-35

Theological Perspective

have almost always missed the mark in terms of contextual relevance. The most common reference is to Deuteronomy 32:11, where God is compared to an eagle that stirs up her nest, that flutters over its young, spreading out its wings over the people of Israel, but this comparison seems only to beg the question. If this is indeed the allusion that Jesus wished to make, then why did he draw on the example of a mother hen? Perhaps what is really being offered here is imagery suggesting the advent of a new creation. Jesus, who was with God in the beginning and through whom all things were made (John 1:2–3), would have known intimately the manner in which the spirit of God hovered over the face of the deep on the first day of creation (Gen. 1:2).

The Hebrew word in Genesis 1:2 is much more to the point: God "brooded" over the waters, as a hen might brood over her young. The eagle, a symbol of imperial Rome no less than the image of Herod the fox, really has no favorable place in Jesus' experience as he journeys toward Jerusalem. The foxes have their dens and the eagles their nests, but in the new creation that will soon be effected by the death of this prophet, their houses will be left empty, abandoned.

Jesus is brooding over the face of the deep, as it were, lamenting the excesses of this city's past and anxious about the birth pangs (cf. Rom. 8:22) that he must soon endure there. In the new kingdom of God, the blessed will not be those who come in the name of power and of strength, but rather those who come in the name of the humble and faithful Lord of creation. It is to this end that Jesus must proceed, even amid such inconsequential obstacles to God's will as Herod and Rome.

DANIEL G. DEFFENBAUGH

Pastoral Perspective

capitals) is all too often the place where dreams of a new and more just world die.

If Jesus expects scorn and violence in Jerusalem, he does not return that hateful rage with rage of his own. The opening words of his speech (calling Herod a demeaning name, recalling and predicting murderous actions) could easily lead to a revolutionary diatribe: Kill the prophet-killers! Burn spiteful Jerusalem to the ground! Instead, his oration veers into a motherly lament: "How often I have desired to gather your children together as a hen gathers her brood under her wings, and you were not willing!" (v. 34). At these words, Jesus' original hearers could not have helped but pick up echoes of frequent Old Testament references to the God of Israel as the one "under whose wings you have come for refuge" (Ruth 2:12; see also Pss. 17:8, 36:7, 57:1, 61:4).

With these surprising words, the mighty appear in a new light: Herod, these plotting Pharisees, the power players in Jerusalem, all the first who would be first, then and now—they want to see themselves as masters of the universe, invulnerable and imperial behind their relentless, foxy maneuvering. Jesus calls their death-dealing by name, yet he also sees them as barnyard chicks lost in a storm, too afraid and too stubborn to find shelter under the shadow of mother hen's wings. What these overlords want to be heard as a fearsome canine growl emerges as an almost comic cheeping. The judgment that will yet fall on them, if they do not change their ways, will be the judgment of their own self-destruction: "See, your house is left to you" (v. 35).

The political machinations go on and on, but there is a true and a living God. The foxes are not in control as much as they think they are.

RODNEY CLAPP

Luke understands its significance. Jesus' lament over the city of Jerusalem is less a final judgment on the city and more a call to repentance. The touching metaphor by which Jesus asserts that it is God's will to protect Jerusalem through him is evidence that Jesus is predicting not the city's destruction but its salvation. Both Isaiah (60:4) and Zechariah (10:6–10) use the image of the scattered children of Jerusalem being gathered together to speak of God's unwavering love for Israel. Also, the image of Israel finding shelter under God's "wings" occurs frequently in the Old Testament (see Deut. 32:11; Ruth 2:12; Pss. 57:1; 61:4; 91:4).

Still, Israel cannot remain passive as it awaits God's salvation. Jesus' words challenge Jerusalem to recognize the divine origin of his mission and message. Jesus laments the people's failure to do so in any acceptable numbers. The last verse implies that the day will come when Israel will acknowledge the One who "comes in the name of the Lord" (v. 35). Perhaps Luke here is reflecting the Pauline notion that the Jews are still loved by God because God has not revoked the divine choice of Israel. Like the Gentiles, Israel will enjoy God's mercy at some time in the future (Rom. 11).

The phrase "how often" (v. 34; Matt. 23:37) may allude to multiple visits to Jerusalem by Jesus as found in the Fourth Gospel. The Synoptics have Jesus visit Jerusalem only once. Often John's Gospel is understood as more theological than historical in its presentation of Jesus' ministry. However, it may be that John's description of several trips by Jesus to Jerusalem is more "historical," while the Synoptics' one trip to the city may be more theologically motivated.

LESLIE J. HOPPE

the exile. That prophecy saw the Spirit of God causing good news to be declared, lives changed, and societies transformed. That declaration formed the beginning of a chain reaction of personal and social transformation: "The Spirit of the Lord is upon me, because he has anointed me to bring good news to the poor. He has sent me to proclaim release to the captives and recovery of sight to the blind, to let the oppressed go free, to proclaim the year of the Lord's favor" (Luke 4:18–19 NRSV).

At the beginning of the book of Acts, Jesus tells the disciples that they will be his "witnesses in Jerusalem and in all Judea and Samaria and to the end of the earth" (Acts 1:8 RSV). The beginning of that happening is Pentecost. By the power of the Holy Spirit, the followers of Jesus will walk in his way, sharing in God's work of creating a new humanity in Christ, a new human community born not of blood, but of God.

As the good news of Jesus is declared and the Holy Spirit of God that was on Jesus is poured forth, a new human community emerges from the great variety and diversity of humanity. That very variety is woven into a new tapestry so that the ancient longings of the prophets for a new humanity are realized: "In the last days it shall be, God declares, that I will pour out my Spirit upon all flesh, and your sons and your daughters shall prophesy, and your young men shall see visions, and your old men shall dream dreams; yea, and on my menservants and my maidservants in those days. . . ." (Acts 2:17–18 RSV).

The old slaves realized that the infinite reach and eternal embrace of God's reign was at the core of the gospel message of Jesus. "There's plenty good room, plenty good room, plenty good room in my Father's kingdom."

MICHAEL B. CURRY

Isaiah 55:1-9

¹Ho, everyone who thirsts,
   come to the waters;
and you that have no money,
   come, buy and eat!
Come, buy wine and milk
   without money and without price.
²Why do you spend your money for that which is not bread,
   and your labor for that which does not satisfy?
Listen carefully to me, and eat what is good,
   and delight yourselves in rich food.
³Incline your ear, and come to me;
   listen, so that you may live.
I will make with you an everlasting covenant,
   my steadfast, sure love for David.
⁴See, I made him a witness to the peoples,
   a leader and commander for the peoples.

Theological Perspective

In the modern world, even on Sunday, even in Lent, people crave satisfaction. Perched alertly and anxiously on their pews, the devout seek a word from the Lord. We seek God's face. Afterwards we will rush out to Sunday brunches or loll around poolside regrouping, re-creating, and re-composing ourselves after the helter-skelter hustle of the weekday. All week we have worked and struggled, compromised and sought approval, earning our sustenance and paychecks from a world of competition. All week we have done what was necessary to buy what we need and to produce what is demanded of us. We try to please those over us so we may obtain what we need, what we believe will give us satisfaction. Yet on Sunday we find ourselves spent, drained, and still thirsting for more.

In his essay "The Religion of the Market," David Loy maintains that the traditional religions of the world need not fear that new sects, cults, or sciences will displace them. The new danger, he insists, is the religion of the market.[1] This new religion is a juggernaut, a never-ending mass media, a Madison Avenue–driven machine that insists that we demand and are provided more and more, with no thought to the notion "Enough!"

1. David Loy, "The Religion of the Market," *American Academy of Religion* 65 (1997): 275–90.

Pastoral Perspective

How thirsty are you? Isaiah declares, "Everyone who thirsts, come to the waters." In my home climate of central Florida during the summer, when the humidity is so intense that you step outside and immediately begin to perspire, you know when you are thirsty. You are thirsty all the time! You know your body is dehydrated because you literally see all the liquid leaving it, droplets of perspiration soaking your shirt, dripping off your arms, and running down your forehead. Even if you do not feel thirsty, you know you are thirsty. You drink water before you go outside to exercise. "Everyone who thirsts"—that is me and everybody else—"come to the waters."

In the southwestern United States, where the humidity is low, you may be thirsty and not even know it. Your perspiration evaporates so quickly that you do not realize you are becoming dehydrated. So whether you feel thirsty or not, you drink a little water as often as you can. In Grand Canyon National Park there are signs strategically placed along the trails that remind you to stop and drink water. "Stop! Drink water. You are thirsty, whether you realize it or not."

How could it be that we do not recognize our own thirst?

There are times when we are intensely aware of our needs and desires, including the things we thirst for, and other times when we do not feel the need or

⁵See, you shall call nations that you do not know,
 and nations that do not know you shall run to you,
 because of the L<small>ORD</small> your God, the Holy One of Israel,
 for he has glorified you.

⁶Seek the L<small>ORD</small> while he may be found,
 call upon him while he is near;
⁷let the wicked forsake their way,
 and the unrighteous their thoughts;
 let them return to the L<small>ORD</small>, that he may have mercy on them,
 and to our God, for he will abundantly pardon.
⁸For my thoughts are not your thoughts,
 nor are your ways my ways, says the L<small>ORD</small>.
⁹For as the heavens are higher than the earth,
 so are my ways higher than your ways
 and my thoughts than your thoughts.

Exegetical Perspective

Theologically Isaiah 55 is a central passage in a series of passages proclaiming hope and salvation to the exiles. Exegetically it represents a crucial passage in the current debate regarding the composition of the canonical book of Isaiah. It stands at the nexus of those chapters commonly defined as Second and Third Isaiah and has been variously assigned to the end of a perceived Second Isaiah and the beginning of Third Isaiah. A transitional passage in terms of structure and images, the crucial exegetical issues for preaching lie within the language and formation of the pericope itself.

Writing in a sixth-century exilic context, the writer begins the passage with a cry, "Ho!" catching the attention of all those who thirst, inviting them to come to the waters, and all those who are hungry but without money, to come and buy and eat. Also paradoxically, in verse 1 the parallelism invites them to come and buy wine and milk but without money and without price. Addressed to a people who have been conquered and exiled and who are struggling, the words must first seem frivolous and facile, describing a meal beyond their expectation and hope. At this point the images are concrete items of bread and wine and milk. Scholars have noted in this verse echoes of the street merchant and the language and style of Wisdom, particularly Proverbs

Homiletical Perspective

The preacher who comes to this text hears the story of the prophet's appraisal of the neglect and injustice endured by a community of exiles in Babylon. The image presented here summons the preacher to do some thinking about the doctrine of God. A personal God is depicted at the outset of this passage, one in step with humanity's greatest needs, the solitary source for human renewal and the restoration of life. However, the developing narrative reveals another side of God. In unequivocal expression Second Isaiah insists that mystery, not intellectual comprehension, reflects the divine life. The prophet holds two realities in paradoxical tension: "Come, thirsty one," and "My ways are not your ways, and my thoughts not your thoughts." Language of an elaborate banquet is heard in the opening words of invitation, words spoken over against cultural excesses that never satisfy. Likewise, a radically different vision is perhaps recognized when the preacher stands in the shoes of the handful of exiles being addressed, who themselves were situated on the margins of Israel's exilic community.

The prophet's string of imperatives—"come," "buy," "listen," and "see"—suggests that high significance was given to shaping the content of this oracle. In like manner, contemporary preachers do well to remember their listeners, shaping sermons

Isaiah 55:1-9

Theological Perspective

Perhaps Isaiah received this word from God after visiting a market. Even without mass media, the ancient market square was busy with commerce, with people rushing to buy, struggling to sell, and some, with no assets at all, standing at the margins, perhaps begging for a handout so that they too might taste their daily bread.

Like Isaiah we are all finite creatures beset with daily needs. Never are we free from want. Even in the Lord's Prayer we ask, "Give us this day our daily bread." God could have created us without these needs, without these drives, but God did not. God wants us to depend on him.

Yet the earth is the Lord's and the fullness thereof, and God is near to us with everything we need. Isaiah reminds us, however, that what we really need is God. Why, therefore, do we rush about seeking something that can never fully satisfy? God calls us into ever deeper fellowship. God has the best wine and milk, the best bread and richest fare available. Yet we rush past God, seeking to buy what God has already provided us freely. Only in fellowship with God are we truly fulfilled—yet this is not the theology of the present age.

Ours is an age of reason, science, and markets. These influences are important in their place, but God's wisdom is not found in materialism. God's ways are not our ways, nor are the Holy Spirit's thoughts our thoughts. This is why we must seek the Holy Spirit while she is near. God is always near and willing to fellowship with us. We, however, are like ships that could be firmly anchored, but who wish to set forth on our own adventures. At some point we find ourselves so far from God we cannot feel or hear her.

God says, "Give ear and come to me; hear me, that your soul may live." We are truly alive only in covenant with the God in whom we live and move and have our being (Acts 17:28). God calls us into covenant to be fulfilled and completely satisfied by God. We are called to be the people of God. Our happiness is assured only when we abide in God. Money is insufficient. God's sustenance and blessing are freely given. As the people of God our mission is not one of toil and struggle, but one of joy.

Paradise lost is thereby regained. We are to attract others to God simply by permitting ourselves to be divinely blessed. We are to be endowed with an everlasting splendor—the glory and approval of God—freely given to us. This is our witness to a hurting world. Thus we need not rush about seeking our satisfaction, drinking from fountains that are

Pastoral Perspective

desire for anything in particular. Isaiah's words are like the sign in a dry climate—"Stop! Drink water. You are thirsty, whether you realize it or not." We need to hear and respond to Isaiah, but not on the basis of what we may feel about ourselves at any particular moment. Isaiah is telling us something true about ourselves at every moment of our lives.

Isaiah's offer is unlike anything we know or practice. In his vision, everyone who is thirsty gets water. Everyone who is hungry is invited to eat: buy milk and wine without money! It is like a grocery store where everything is free. In this supermarket, all the people who stand by the side of the road with little cardboard signs that say, "Will work for food," are pushing carts full of groceries through the checkout lines, paying only with a smile and a wave.

In contrast to what is available for free, Isaiah says we are paying for things we do not need in the first place—spending money on what is not bread and laboring for what does not satisfy us. Isaiah says we need a new diet of good and rich food.

Have you ever gone to visit someone at home and as soon as you sit down in the living room your host offers you something to drink? Your answer may be based not on whether you are thirsty but on how long you want to stay. Even if you decline, your host may persist.

"Are you sure? How about a cup of coffee or a soda?"

"No, thank-you, I am just fine."

"Not even a glass of water?"

In this passage, Isaiah leans across the coffee table and says, "Hey. Stop it. Whether or not you are thirsty, whether or not you are hungry, you need what God has to give."

"Incline your ear, and come to me; listen, so that you may live" (v. 3). Isaiah reminds us that a relationship with God based on God's steadfast love for us is our greatest need and the richest nourishment for our lives, but Isaiah's words are not the only offers we hear. We live in the midst of constant promotion. Everywhere we turn we are bombarded with offers and enticements to fill every imaginable want and desire. Even if we do not need anything, it is easy to be convinced we really want something: a new car, a new computer, a glamorous career, a bigger house, a youthful appearance. However the offers are false. They promise to satisfy but turn out to be wasted calories without any nutrition. Any way of life that turns us away from God is a way of life that leads to our starvation and death.

Exegetical Perspective

9.[1] In verse 2 the prophet addresses a people who have wasted their resources and their striving on things that are of no benefit to them. They are seeking in the wrong place, working for the wrong goal. Now they are called to listen and "eat what is good" and take "delight . . . in rich food."

The series of imperatives is continued into the first part of verse 3 with a call for the listener to "incline your ear," to "come" and to "listen" so that "you may live." This call is linked immediately with the promise of a *berit 'olam*, an eternal covenant that is connected to YHWH's steadfast love for David. The idea of this eternal covenant also appears in other prophets of the exilic period (Isa. 61:8, Jer. 32:40; 50:5; and Ezek. 16:60). This, the only mention of David in chapters 40–66, links the hope that the prophet of the exile seeks to kindle with the most powerful and magnificent period to which the tradition testifies. In verse 4 YHWH reminds the listener of what was done for David, making him a witness and commander, but in verse 5 the promise of the restoration of this glory is transferred to the listeners themselves in a second-person address: "you shall call nations . . . and nations . . . shall run to you." The promise of 2 Samuel 7 has been renewed and linked to the continuation and glorification of the nation as a whole. The expansion of the scope of the promise is striking, particularly to a people struggling between hope and despair.

To forestall any presumption that the coming glory is because of the merit of Israel itself, verse 5b follows immediately with the source of Israel's coming glory. It is YHWH who is glorifying Israel; YHWH, the Holy One of Israel, is the source of all good things to come. This reminder leads naturally to the third-person call of verses 6–7, beginning with the imperatives "seek" and "call." It is Israel's part in the covenant to stay close to the source of its glory and power and to return if it has strayed. To stray from YHWH is to become disconnected from the source. Verse 6 opens with a reminder that YHWH is not easily found or summoned if the seeker has performed wickedly or has unrighteous thoughts (v. 7a). However, YHWH can be merciful and pardon the wicked and unrighteous if they return to the holy, divine way (v. 7b).

The difficulty of accepting a promise of future glory for Israel—especially in the surroundings of the exile—or of understanding a God who can

Homiletical Perspective

that not only describe scriptural happenings but also make use of imperatives that address hearers within their social locations. It is one thing to explore homiletically the general tenor of what captivity in Babylon meant in view of the Israelites' mass departure from Jerusalem and the loss of their homeland, yet another to imagine that in Babylonian exile a number of exiles prospered materially as other segments of the population suffered. To read and preach a faithful word from this passage requires paying close attention to its literary features and evident social imbalances. By the same token, one's use of the imagination is crucial for discerning how this inviting word might speak as proclamation (*kerygma*), second-order prophecy (*prophēteia*), or remembrance (*anamnēsis*). Let us consider how a preacher might relate these approaches to three possible themes: providence, grace, and holiness.

A providential word. Second Isaiah is both a prophetic visionary and a sober realist. The prophet has carefully taken into his field of vision a particular community whom he addresses. The meaning of the doctrine of providence has not been without intense debate in Christian understanding. However, providence refers to an understanding of a God-governed creation. This is a lightning-rod text for checking a community of faith's dogmatism and ironclad assumptions. God is both liberating and attuned with suffering while remarkably transcendent. George Lindbeck argues that our doctrinal views and normative convictions may yield more complexity than one might initially imagine. Doctrines function to regulate truth claims, but the logic of their communally authoritative use prevents them from specifying positively what is to be affirmed.[1] Still, a Lenten sermon may explore how the prophet's invitation discourages complacency, challenges power, and evokes remembrance.

A gracious word. O. C. Edwards rightly claims, "There is no activity more characteristic of the church than preaching."[2] However, preaching never stands above the context of Christian worship. Some scholars argue that preaching in the context of the worshiping congregation is inherently sacramental. Imagery in Isaiah 55 is intensely poetic and ritually illuminating. Whether one celebrates "the Lord's

---

1. Claus Westermann, *Isaiah 40–66* (Philadelphia: Westminster Press, 1969), 282.

1. George Lindbeck, *The Nature of Doctrine, 25th Anniversary Edition* (Louisville, KY: Westminster John Knox Press, 2009).
2. O. C. Edwards Jr., *A History of Preaching* (Nashville: Abingdon Press, 2004), 3.

Isaiah 55:1-9

Theological Perspective

bound to run dry. We need not buy and eat bread that is bound to mold and decay.

Our constant striving to satisfy ourselves is doomed to failure. Indeed these are the fruitless efforts, the wicked ways that Isaiah calls us to abandon. Too often, like spoiled children, we become obsessed with our toys and forget their Giver. We must be in the world and participate in its problems. We must work and pay taxes, yet this is not all there is to our lives. In particular, when we reject God's call and strive to serve mammon, we settle for scraps when we could be feasting.

Yet this is not our first or only option. David in this passage is characterized as a commander of a nation. While we need not view ourselves as a martial force, we are still in some respects blessed soldiers in the army of God—soldiers who need not abandon our posts to receive our blessings. This passage predates 1 Peter 2:9. There we are called to be "a royal priesthood, a holy nation, God's own people." So too in Isaiah, we are constantly called to come back to God. No matter what we have done, we can and will be forgiven.

Here we find a divine paradox: although our thoughts are not God's thoughts and our ways are not her ways, although her righteousness is as high above our sinfulness as heaven is above the earth, God is still near! God loves us and is eager and ready to bless us. During this Lenten season, as we relinquish indulgences in order to please God, let us first focus on being with God, spending time with God, drinking the milk and wine he gives us—eating the bread of life. Let us praise him above all the earth so everyone around us will be drawn to the joy and glory of God. In so doing we will be supremely satisfied.

DARRYL M. TRIMIEW

Pastoral Perspective

Lent challenges us to consider the reality of our own sinfulness and our need for repentance. We may not be immediately aware of how we have wandered away from God—how life has lost its meaning in pursuit of a promotion or raise, how we have gotten buried under the demands of economic and social status. Isaiah's words help us to hear the truth so that we can recommit ourselves to God's offer of steadfast love and covenant relationship as the true way for our lives.

In the midst of the false promises for the good life, the full life, the successful life, the happy life, the meaningful life, or the exciting life that are so prevalent in today's world, Isaiah implores us, "Seek the LORD while he may be found, call upon him while he is near; let the wicked forsake their way, and the unrighteous their thoughts; let them return to the LORD, that he may have mercy on them, and to our God, for he will abundantly pardon" (vv. 6–7).

At the end of the movie *Millions*, there is an image of Isaiah's promise of abundant love and mercy. Throughout the movie, in which a little boy finds millions of dollars of stolen money, his family has been trying to use it to get something good for themselves, to enjoy their newfound riches. However their frantic efforts have been tearing them apart. Only the boy Damian has been searching for how he might use the money to help someone else, so that he might find peace and healing following his mother's death. Near the end, when the family realizes the futility of what they have been trying to do, they give the money to build water wells in an impoverished African nation. That endeavor unleashes a great celebration of joy and abundance in which everyone who thirsts, including the family, comes to the waters. It is a reflection of Isaiah's vision, in which the ways of God bring forth life for all.

DANIEL M. DEBEVOISE

punish and forgive absolutely, is addressed in verses 8–9, where the address shifts back to first person and the messenger formula "says YHWH" at the end of verse 8 interrupts the speech to confirm explicitly that it is YHWH speaking. The contrast between human words and deeds and divine words and deeds is absolute and cannot be understood; it can only be accepted. The distance dividing heaven and earth is compared to the distance between God's plans and intentions and human ability to understand those plans and intentions.

While verses 10–13 are not included in the lectionary reading for this date they provide an appropriate conclusion for the call and promise of verses 1–9. The divine speech of verse 10 returns to the concrete, natural images of verses 1–2 and reinforces the power of YHWH to deliver the restoration that is promised. If God's word can send the rain and snow to water the earth and bring forth food to eat, then it can deliver Israel from exile and make them a people to be honored by the nations. Simply put, God's word will accomplish what it promises. Verse 11 foretells the celebration to come upon fulfillment of the promise, a celebration so great that even nature shall join in. The "everlasting sign" of verse 13b echoes the eternal covenant of verse 3b and reinforces the dependability of the promise.

The exegetical issues regarding the formation of the canonical book of Isaiah are not crucial for preaching these verses. Rather, the central message to be proclaimed is the extraordinary nature and dependability of God's promises. Even in the strangeness of a faraway land and in the face of the power of our foes, God promises a restoration and renewal beyond our previous condition. While we may not be able to see the possibility or understand the way, God's word will accomplish its purpose.

RICHARD A. PUCKETT

Supper," "the Eucharist," or "Holy Communion," the words of this passage find some correspondence to modern-day words of invitation at the communion table. In this Lenten text we find words for the broken in spirit deeply reminiscent of King David's invitation to Mephibosheth (2 Sam. 9), anticipating Jesus' call to guests to a great banquet (Luke 14:15–24). More profoundly, Isaiah's "Come . . . I will make an everlasting covenant with you" appears to be a foreshadowing of Jesus' summoning his disciples to his Last Supper just prior to his crucifixion. Proclamation may focus on God's grace-giving word to us, that in God's storage house nothing is lacking. A preacher hoping to sound a prophetic note will inquire about the real physical and spiritual needs of people. To be prophetic might mean that the preacher takes off from the scriptural verse itself: Are you thirsty? Do you hunger? Are your finances dried up? As for remembrance, the preacher need only reflect on how the passage recalls how God made and God kept God's gracious promise.

A holy word. Beyond themes of providence and grace, the prophet in this text trumpets a word that calls his audience to repentance (vv. 6–7). The imperatives are to return to God, to listen, and to seek the Lord while the Lord may be found. Keep in mind the prophet is addressing a mid-sixth-century community who saw themselves as an exilic minority and who were unable to convince others of the way God intended to shepherd the return of the exiles to the land.[3] This text is marked as one offered by the Holy One of Israel, for a people made *hagios* (holy), set apart to do a sacred work. Preaching that matters today bears the marks of such holiness. Second Isaiah is simply an instrument in the divine economy, sent as a herald to bring a message from a covenant-making Sovereign who abundantly pardons sin and who raises up the prophet to offer words of justice, righteousness, and hope. Sermons calling for holiness and repentance during Lent may help us to see our lives in relation to our own exilic situations and to hear again that we are to be "salt and light," striving no longer after things that yield only temporal gratification.

KENYATTA R. GILBERT

3. Robert R. Wilson, "The Community of Second Isaiah," in *Reading and Preaching the Book of Isaiah*, ed. Christopher R. Seitz (Philadelphia: Fortress Press, 1988), 61–62.

Psalm 63:1-8

¹O God, you are my God, I seek you,
   my soul thirsts for you;
 my flesh faints for you,
   as in a dry and weary land where there is no water.
²So I have looked upon you in the sanctuary,
   beholding your power and glory.
³Because your steadfast love is better than life,
   my lips will praise you.
⁴So I will bless you as long as I live;
   I will lift up my hands and call on your name.

⁵My soul is satisfied as with a rich feast,
   and my mouth praises you with joyful lips
⁶when I think of you on my bed,
   and meditate on you in the watches of the night;
⁷for you have been my help,
   and in the shadow of your wings I sing for joy.
⁸My soul clings to you;
   your right hand upholds me.

Theological Perspective

One of the truly great pieces of devotional writing in all of human history, this psalm offers a rich and textured assessment of the divine-human relationship, as well as an assurance of divine help in the time of trouble. The opening appellation—"O God" (v. 1), sparse and laconic—conveys all that is needed to affirm the ultimacy of God. The subsequent affirmation in the same verse—"you are my God"—is a veritable credo, a statement of faith that needful human beings may find access to and security in God, the source of ultimate value.

Against this backdrop of the assertion of divine ultimacy, joined with faith in God to whom the faithful might have access, human vulnerability can be broached without fear throughout the psalm, culminating with assurance of the vindication against enemies in the last verses (9–11). When the ultimacy *of* God and human intimacy *with* God are joined, a powerful bulwark against human vulnerability is thus attained. As beings aware of our contingency, we will always seek that which is ultimate. Thus the psalmist "seeks" God, the ultimate source of existence. Moreover, needful creatures are always mindful of that without which existence is rendered precarious. Our psalmist, no stranger to the inhospitable and arid expanses of land in the Judean plains, gives us poignant imagery to denote

Pastoral Perspective

America loves big. Whatever our income, we love big sales, salaries, vacations, accomplishments, and portfolios. We live in, or hope for, homes that feature double-height entryways, chef's kitchens, oversize garages, master suites, and home theaters where, on our big screens, we cheer on the biggest losers (of weight, that is) or watch the audaciously proportioned Super Bowl. The megamillions jackpot captures the imagination and pocketbook of many, while three-day weekends help others "live large." Our appetites are robust. We love big.

Yet in the midst of this celebration of size, our appetite for God can seem paltry. While we may energetically desire a new car, professional success, or home remodeling, do we yearn for God with similar zest? While we may steadily save for retirement or vacation, do we seek God with the same regularity, intensity, and focus? Do we hunger for God so deeply that our stomachs growl? Do we love God with the kind of spontaneous enthusiasm that we might bring to one of our other loves: jazz, history, NASCAR, photography, or cooking with vine-ripe tomatoes and pungent basil fresh from the garden? Our gusto for God can be remarkably small, particularly when contrasted with the joy and delight in God that we discover in the Psalms.

Exegetical Perspective

Psalm 63 begins with an individual's triple action of crying out to God, invoking the covenant, and undertaking a determined hunt for God: "O God, you are *my God*, earnestly *I* seek *you*" (v. 1, emphasis added). An early riser or perhaps one who has spent a fitful, sleepless night (v. 6), the psalmist seeks God's presence at dawn after the midnight watches. Breaking light refreshes hope and presents a possible relief from difficulties.

The psalm expresses longing (vv. 1–2), praise (vv. 3–5), and confidence (vv. 6–8), judgment on pursuing enemies (vv. 9–10), and a prayer mentioning the king (v. 11, probably voiced by a choir during worship).[1]

The opening eight verses show the king's faith; the closing three express his confidence in his future: he will both live and rejoice. The psalm, applicable to Lent, combines elements of lament and affirmations of faith. The early church used this beloved song to open the singing of the Psalms on the Lord's Day.[2]

The superscription attributes the psalm to David and states he wrote it when he was in the Judean wilderness. Several possibilities arise. The psalm could

Homiletical Perspective

When a Scripture passage is selected, edited, and gathered with other Scripture passages for a given liturgical occasion—in this case the Third Sunday in Lent—the passage is, either by design or by default, transformed by its recontextualization. Its scriptural background still has relevance for the preacher, but the Scripture passage is now being deployed as a liturgical text, with a liturgical purpose. Presuming that the preacher feels some obligation to consider the liturgical demands of the lectionary, one adds the necessity of discerning the liturgical function in the text's new context. What did the editors of the lectionary want to convey with these gathered texts? How do the readings work together? How is the assembly's hearing of a passage shaped by the previous readings? After all, to some degree, context determines content. There are several contexts at work: the biblical context, the Lenten context, the context created by the selection of the several readings, the local parish's context, the liturgical context created by all the other liturgical elements (hymns and prayers, for example), and so on.

In the case of Psalm 63:1–8, how is the psalm affected by editing out the last several verses? How is the reader's hearing of the psalm shaped by preceding readings? How does the psalm as presented in the lectionary prepare the hearer for the

1. J. W. Rogerson and J. W. McKay, *Psalms 51–100*, Cambridge Bible Commentary on the New English Bible (Cambridge: Cambridge University Press, 1977), 65.
2. James Luther Mays, *Psalms*, Interpretation series (Louisville, KY: John Knox Press, 1994), 217.

Psalm 63:1-8

Theological Perspective

human vulnerability and need. Yet even here the needs that humans have for the ultimate transcend mere physical necessities, even the prized water in the desert. Human thirst is for the ultimate—a thirst deeper than that which wells can assuage.

As needful beings, humans must be assured that the God of ultimacy is within reach and is accessible. The psalm eloquently attests to the deep longings of the human heart for God. Yet inherent in this confession of vulnerability is also a testament of hope, a hope that would have been impossible were it not for the earlier attestation of the ultimacy of God, coupled with faith that such a God was accessible. Augustine gives us an insight into this aspect of hope, which is implicit even in the recognition of vulnerability: "But if we acknowledge ourselves as thirsty, we shall acknowledge ourselves as drinking also. For he that thirsteth in this world, in the world to come shall be satisfied, according to the Lord's saying, 'Blessed are they that hunger and thirst after righteousness for the same shall be satisfied.'"[1]

At verse 2, a significant shift occurs when the psalmist couches the deep yearning and thirsting for God within the context of worship in the sanctuary, a feature that has led one commentator to observe that the psalmist's heart has become "a temple of praise."[2] Yet this worship experience is not a self-indulgent kind of mysticism, nor does it intend to shine the light of focus on us humans solely, even in our needy state. Worship is a time in which the focus ought to be on God and on God alone, the God of ultimacy. Moreover, worship, as Evelyn Underhill has observed, "is never a solitary undertaking. Both on its visible and invisible sides, it has a thoroughly social and organic character. The worshipper, however lonely in appearance, comes before God as a member of a great family; part of the Communion of Saints, living and dead."[3] It is in such a context that we bring the affirmation of our thirst for God, and an equal affirmation that this thirst cannot be assuaged on our own terms.

Another significant theological move occurs while the psalmist is within the sanctuary. The thought comes that God is powerful precisely "*because* [God's] steadfast love is better than life" (v. 3, emphasis added). The psalmist realizes that God's power is proportional to and derivative of God's

Pastoral Perspective

In Psalm 63, the psalmist is not simply interested in or respectful of God; rather, the psalmist craves God as a coffee drinker craves the first morning cup. In fact, dire thirst symbolizes the need in verse 1; hunger represents the need in verse 5. The longing for God is so intense that it is experienced physically.

With this profound longing, Psalm 63 exudes utter, rapt joy. Like a young child exhilarated at riding her first bicycle down a steep hill, the psalmist delights in God's presence: "because your steadfast love is better than life, my lips will praise you (v. 3). . . . I will bless you as long as I live; I will lift up my hands and call on your name. My soul is satisfied as with a rich feast (v. 4–5a). . . . you have been my help, . . . I sing for joy (v. 7). . . . My soul clings to you" (v. 8a). Throughout this text, desire for God is clear. If verses 9–11 are included, this gusto for God is even more breathtaking, when it is revealed not as naively flip but as sustained, profound joy that endures threat and danger. Despite the real enemies, opposition, and pain described in verses 9–11, the psalmist is "lost in wonder, love, and praise."[1]

This psalm offers a vision of the faithful life as hungering and thirsting for God, ultimately feasting on God's presence. Centuries later, Jesus similarly advocates big passion for God: "'You shall love the Lord your God with all your heart, and with all your soul, and with all your mind.' This is the greatest and first commandment" (Matt. 22:37–38). The example of faith demonstrated in Psalm 63 invites us to measure ourselves not by how well we care for others, our gifts, our responsibilities, but by what goes on in our deepest being. In a world filled with competition for our affections, allegiance, energy, and love, Psalm 63 challenges the faithful to cultivate gusto for God. The faithful develop our hearts, honing our desires until we find, with Augustine (354–430), that "our hearts are restless until they find their rest in thee."

Unfortunately, as seen in soaring addiction rates, disordered desire is the norm. Sometimes we want wrong things. More often, we want good things in bad ways. We want some things too much and we desire other things too little. Psalm 63 centers the soul, directing desire; thus verses 1–3 provide an excellent opening for a worship service, class, practice, or meeting. Playing up themes of hungering and thirsting, the psalm readily adapts into an opening prayer for a gathering that includes

1. Augustine, *Commentary on the Psalms, Nicene and Post-Nicene Fathers of the Christian Church*, ed. Philip Schaff, vol. 8 (Grand Rapids: Eerdmans, 1974), 258.
2. T. K. Cheyne, *The Book of Psalms* (London: Kegan Paul, 1905), 236.
3. Evelyn Underhill, *Worship* (London: Nisbet & Co., 1951), 81.

1. Charles Wesley, "Love Divine, All Loves Excelling," 1747, in *Lutheran Book of Worship* (Minneapolis: Augsburg Publishing House, 1978), #315.

have been written when a youthful David ran for his life from Saul (1 Sam. 23:14; 24:2) or decades later when as king he fled Jerusalem during his son Absalom's insurrection (2 Sam. 15:23; 16:14) or at another unspecified time. While the desert terrain makes tracking hard, it yields no water.

The psalmist needs immediate help and protection. The psalm juxtaposes his physical need for water with his spiritual thirst for God. Surprisingly, the latter dominates! Although his body wastes from dehydration, his spiritual longing for God takes precedence. Hunted and afraid for his life, the psalmist remembers God's protection and loving-kindness. The psalmist recalls seeing God's power and glory in the sanctuary (v. 2). His soul longs for God.

The psalm presents the ideas that longing is healthy, that thirsting for God's presence invites and brings God's presence, and that God's presence satisfies longings. In addition, God's presence— because of God's nature—always brings more blessings than a supplicant seeks. Because he knows God's character, the psalmist—now energized and prophetic—anticipates a blessing. His longing to look upon God represents a longing for security. With beautiful imagery, the psalmist describes security as being shadowed by the Lord's wings (v. 7).

The psalmist recalls God's *hesed* love, God's loving-kindness (v. 3). *Hesed* denotes the gracious intervention of one of superior power and rank in the life of one of lesser rank. The Psalms associate *hesed* with preserving life (119:149) and as an everlasting quality of God (100:5; 106:1). The psalmist knows that without God's immediate intervention of loving-kindness/*hesed*, he will die. Consequently, he comes again—by force of need and habit—into God's presence. By virtue of living in the world, the psalmist finds himself in yet another life-and-death fix. The psalmist enters God's presence abruptly, his need preempting formalities. Not at all annoyed by the psalmist's predicament, God responds immediately with graciousness.

The psalmist exalts God's love as consistent, unchanging (v. 3). God's true love actively seeks to bless the covenant individual and covenant community. God's love, experienced as God's blessings, leads the psalmist to glorify God energetically with praise. Praise consists of good words that enumerate God's characteristics; this psalm celebrates several: God's power and glory, love, help, and protection (vv. 2–3, 7–8).

The psalmist becomes progressively more excited as he praises God. Speaking God's praises and lifting

subsequent readings, especially the Gospel passage from Luke? In Psalm 63:1–8 we have an exuberant confession of faith, an announcement of complete devotion to God who saves and sustains, a proclamation that God's "steadfast love is better [even] than life" (v. 3a). Edited out of our lectionary passage is the psalm's closing section, verses 9–11, which calls down various sorts of doom on the psalmist's enemies. The tone of these final verses is perhaps overly harsh, even vitriolic and vengeful, for a Sunday morning worship service, especially in comparison with the earlier section. With the predominant Lenten motifs of personal remorse and repentance playing, it may seem uncharitable and out of harmony to vocalize the desire that one's enemies become "prey for jackals." Nevertheless, these latter verses, if they are included, stand as a warning, consistent with other passages selected for this Sunday, which clearly state that there will indeed be a reckoning for those not in line with God's word and way. The major difference is in temperament. The assembly has already heard Isaiah proclaim, "Seek the LORD while he may be found, call upon him while he is near." The notion of seeking has been raised as has the "otherness" of God. Yet God is not perceived as remote: "call upon him while he is near." The assembly will shortly hear Paul warn the Corinthians that they had better learn from the example of the Israelites, that "God was not pleased with most of them [the Israelites], and they were struck down in the wilderness" (1 Cor. 10:5). Jesus likewise warns his audience that, like those who had sinned before and were punished, "unless you repent, you will all perish just as they did" (Luke 13:3). There is still time, but do not tarry.

For those who perceive the good news as eternally comforting in difficult times, these passages could well pose a dilemma. Where is the good news? Where is the grace? Where is the forgiveness? Where are the warm, consoling words on a cold winter night? God is not limited by our puny notions of what makes for divine grace, like bad television scripts that perennially offer, "There, there; everything will be okay." It may work on television, but not in lived life. Instead of hot chocolate for the soul, we sometimes get a cold pool of water. Leaving out verses 9–11 only serves to moderate the temperature of the pool a bit. The grace here is that there is still time; the final judgment has not yet taken place.

The verses of the psalm chosen for the lectionary present a singular, over-the-top devotion to God, unmarred and undeterred by mundane distractions

Psalm 63:1-8

Theological Perspective

love, and not the other way around. Aside from being a totally radical idea in the ancient Near East, this idea still requires some readjustment of human values in contemporary culture. The psalmist affirms both divine ultimacy and the possibility of human companionship with such ultimacy. Only one with such a faith could dare to entertain this extraordinary theological idea: God truly loves those to whom God makes God's self accessible, even to the point of defying human conceptions of power.

Finally, the psalmist resolves to "bless [the Lord] as long as I live" (v. 4). The credo that God is the ultimate value is enlarged upon in rather pragmatic terms in verses 5–8. Quite coincidently, the images of the truly large and full life come forth while the psalmist is still exulting in the glory of God while in the sanctuary. An imagery of fullness—almost to the point of surfeit—is used here to convey just how much the soul feeds on the richness of God, much as a hungry person feeds on a richly laden banquet table: "My soul is satisfied as with a rich feast" (v. 5). It is important to remember that the images used in this meditation on God point to identifiable places within the created order. Homely images of lying in bed and padding about the house in the middle of the night are summoned as examples of places where God would be praised. Every activity, however mundane, is an occasion when the grateful soul can bless God. This is not a picture of an ascetic turning away from the material world, but rather one who delights in offering every moment of existence to God upon the altar of praise.

Therein lies much of the genius of the meditation and even this approach to God in worship. The evocation and worship of God is done precisely within the context where human beings are apt to be found—in this case, as they contemplate the tasks of the day and as they prepare for nightly rest and repose.

SAMUEL K. ROBERTS

Pastoral Perspective

a meal, particularly if everyone can smell the food, has yet to eat, and can relate to hungering and thirsting. After an evening gathering, verses 5–8 provide powerful conclusion, even gently suggesting that those facing insomnia count not sheep but blessings.

If there is anything we need more of in our XXL society, it is more joy and pleasure in God. Loving God more than life (v. 3) still feels foreign to most of us; our desire for God has rarely been so full-bodied that it feels like hunger or thirst. Instead, overwhelmed or embarrassed by the grandeur of the religious passions exhibited by some, we may be tempted to downplay the importance of cultivating zeal for God. Alternatively, gusto for God that is as natural and spontaneous as our enjoyment of life's other loves may seem unrealistic. We may not know how to begin the Lenten discipline of honing and healing our wounded desires or, quite honestly, of deciding whether we want them healed at all.

Fortunately, size is not central with God. For those who worry they are not good enough or who feel isolated or on the outskirts of "real" Christian community, Psalm 63 invites us to start with whatever longing we do have. Whether we genuinely desire to know and enjoy God more, whether we want to desire such a thing, or whether we simply know discontent, restlessness, boredom, or a breaking point, God takes the small and changes the world with it. God did it in choosing a small nation of Hebrew people to be God's own. God did it by sending a vulnerable baby to forever change the world. God did it in healing a wounded creation through the ignominy of a common, crude cross.

Like the proverbial mustard seed, God works with what is—even if it is nothing more than the smallest of desires—and changes the world with it. Even so, the Holy One works with whatever desire for God we do have, and helps us cultivate and grow it, until it too turns into a feast of praise and joy. After all, the whole time we are seeking and thirsting for God, we are held in God's hand (v. 8).

LINDSAY P. ARMSTRONG

his hands in surrender and adoration serve only as preliminaries. He vows to praise God as long as he lives (v. 4). He must sing (v. 5)! Significantly, Judaism and Christianity are singing religions, and singing punctuates corporate, public worship.

Singing God's praise provides a feast for the psalmist's soul. While the choicest foods and coolest water satisfy a hungry person, praise satisfies the longings of this hungry worshiper (v. 5).

The psalmist carries his worship past daybreak. During the day he meditates. He remembers God's past mighty deeds in his life and in the life of the covenant community. Energized, encouraged, and confident because of positive meditation, he proclaims, "You have been my help" (v. 7).

The psalm, however, also carries a sense of desperation. The psalmist clings to God for dear life as to a steady post or a sheltering rock. In God's sanctuary the psalmist, while not free from life's turmoil, nonetheless remains safe while encountering it. The psalmist realizes his body cannot stay in the sanctuary, but his soul can cling to God, and God's right hand will uphold him (v. 8).

The biblical text sees long life as an evidence of God's favor. However Psalm 63 amplifies this teaching: God's loving-kindness, security, and faithfulness are better than life—whether life is long or short (v. 3).

In verses 9–11 the psalmist sketches his current problem: people pursue his life with the intent to kill. However, the psalmist prophesies that they—and not he!—will die by the sword and remain shamefully unburied, food for jackals. Identified here as the king, the psalmist continues under God's protection and continues rejoicing in God. His circumstances have not changed; yes, assassins still pursue. Yet in his refreshed soul, he knows that he will live.

The king and the community who swear by God's name stand on one side, victorious, rejoicing in God. Meanwhile, the opposing community, poetically identified as "the mouths of liars" (v. 11), will be silenced—both by loud praise and by death.

Psalm 63 reveals the psalmist's personality too. Holding himself accountable, on his own initiative he makes a deal. Aware that the Lord's help requires a response—at the very least gratitude—he chooses a lifetime of speaking and singing God's praises. He vows for himself a night-and-day celebration of praise. His mouth will praise God, his hands will be raised, and he will sing loudly! His praise will be public, ongoing, and varied—energizing to himself and enjoyable to God.

ROBIN GALLAHER BRANCH

such as war and corruption, thirst and hunger, whether for body or soul. God is all. The verses form the perfect vision on a distant horizon toward which we continually strive. Leaving off the remaining verses might seem like a nice homiletic gesture, but it really ends up providing an unrealistic image, even a discouraging image, one that in our heart of heart we know is beyond our reach. There is no possible way to accede to that vision by means of our own resources. We may even be driven to despair. While the preacher probably ought not to add the closing verses to the reading of the day, one certainly has some homiletic license to refer to them in the homily itself as providing a realistic trajectory of the life of faith: intense resolve, followed by relapse into revenge, hopefully then followed by a renewed repentance. The complete psalm offers the more realistic ebb and flow of the appropriation of God's grace. Were one capable of completely living into the sort of devotion offered by verses 1–8, there would seem to be no need for verses 9–11. Wrongdoers would be left utterly to the hand of God; indeed they would be out of one's perceptual field. Wishing for the enemy's violent demise seems antithetical to verses 1–8. The final verses, nevertheless, do remind us that those who are not in harmony with God's way will perish, not as a matter of quid pro quo, but as recognition of how things work. If you put your hand in the fire, you are going to get burned. There are choices to be made. That is the message here, anyway.

So we are left with a passage intended to inspire us to surrender our wills, so that we become subsumed by and in God. Let us hope that the verses directly deployed and those implied will move those in the assembly to reckon realistically with their own conflicted stance before God and strive to claim the vision in verses 1–8 as their own while there is still time.

RICHARD C. STERN

1 Corinthians 10:1-13

[1]I do not want you to be unaware, brothers and sisters, that our ancestors were all under the cloud, and all passed through the sea, [2]and all were baptized into Moses in the cloud and in the sea, [3]and all ate the same spiritual food, [4]and all drank the same spiritual drink. For they drank from the spiritual rock that followed them, and the rock was Christ. [5]Nevertheless, God was not pleased with most of them, and they were struck down in the wilderness.

[6]Now these things occurred as examples for us, so that we might not desire evil as they did. [7]Do not become idolaters as some of them did; as it is written, "The people sat down to eat and drink, and they rose up to play." [8]We must not indulge in sexual immorality as some of them did, and twenty-three thousand fell in a single day. [9]We must not put Christ to the test, as some of them did, and were destroyed by serpents. [10]And do not complain as some of them did, and were destroyed by the destroyer. [11]These things happened to them to serve as an example, and they were written down to instruct us, on whom the ends of the ages have come. [12]So if you think you are standing, watch out that you do not fall. [13]No testing has overtaken you that is not common to everyone. God is faithful, and he will not let you be tested beyond your strength, but with the testing he will also provide the way out so that you may be able to endure it.

Theological Perspective

Already in the New Testament, but supremely in the early centuries of the church's life, Christians had begun to read the Scriptures analogically or allegorically. Events and figures in the Old Testament became the types of events and figures of their antitypes found in the New. Our Edenic paterfamilias thus becomes the first Adam, while Christ is the second. Just as Paul calls the church "the Israel of God" in Galatians 6:16, so here he likens the church to the Hebrews who wandered in the desert for forty years (vv. 1–4).

How remarkable! The crossing of the Red Sea was Israel's baptism. The daily manna on which Israel fed (Exod. 16:4) was the body of Christ. The water that gushed from the side of the rock (Exod. 17:6) was the blood of Christ. The rock that Moses struck was none other than Christ himself! That is not all. Christ the new Moses was not only leading Israel under the guise of the old Moses; he was also following them like the hound of heaven, making sure that they arrived in the promised land of salvation. Other ancient commentators also link the day-cloud and the night-fire (Exod. 13:21) to the Holy Spirit's guiding presence. Thus for Paul, we Christians are none other than the original Israel in contemporary form as the ecclesial people of God!

It is wise not to discern easy modern-day parallels between our own situation and Paul's warnings

Pastoral Perspective

John Bach once quipped, "Idolatry is really not good for anyone. Not even the idols."[1] Paul would undoubtedly agree, engineering an extended warning in chapter 10 that culminates with verse 14—a verse, though not included in the Revised Common Lectionary reading, that the pastor might include as it reads more as a climax to this passage than an introduction to the next—"Therefore, my dear friends, flee from the worship of idols."

The warning begins with an adoption. The Gentiles of the Corinthian community are assumed into the family of Israel (v. 1). One wonders, are the Corinthians delighted by this inclusion? If we employ the language of family systems theory, the Corinthians have been adopted not only into the family of God, but also into a family with a ruinous history of idolatry, where the sins of the ancestors are not visited upon the heirs by God's vengeance but in the more traditional, time-honored way—by appropriation. Paul, though, in the manner exercised by every individual who seeks to break a cycle of abuse or violence or idolatry, lifts up the ugliest of the family secrets as a way to embolden the Corinthians to break from the patterns of their spiritual ancestors.

1. Harvey Aranton, "Sports of the Time; For Jordan at Garden, One Last Flashback," *New York Times*, March 10, 2003.

Third Sunday in Lent

Exegetical Perspective

There is a real danger that we will be so fascinated by Paul's interpretation of Israel's wilderness experience that we completely miss his application to the Corinthian issue of fidelity to Christ alone. The apostle's concern for the Christian community and its witness to Christ in relation to the issue of idolatry is clearly seen in today's text. In chapter 8 Paul begins to address the Corinthian position that attendance and participation in the local idol cults are not incompatible with being in Christ. The Corinthians base their argument upon a "superior" knowledge: since idols are really nonexistent, and since there is only one God, such participation is part of normal civic involvement, and their behavior is inconsequential.

Paul's initial response is based upon his concern for the entire Christian community. Some Christians in Corinth do not have the same level of understanding. For them, such activity cannot be done in good faith and with a clear conscience. They believe it to be wrong and so are left in confusion by their fellow Christians' behavior. In chapter 9, Paul argues against idol worship, based upon his own willingness as an apostle to forgo any inherent rights he has as an apostle. His reasoning is based upon his understanding of the nature of Christian life: "For though I am free with respect to all, I have made

Homiletical Perspective

Certain biblical texts read aloud in the Sunday morning gathering create more fear than consolation. These texts are not to be dismissed or ignored. It would be too easy for the preacher to choose another text altogether, or to turn to one of the other lectionary readings (although the Gospel proposed by the Revised Common Lectionary for this Sunday might not be your first choice either!).

One of the questions that challenge every preacher concerns the connection between the text and the lives of the gathered congregation. This is particularly true of the epistles. What is the horizon of the church in this letter? Can the people gathered together on the Third Sunday in Lent hear themselves in the text? One point of connection is found within the liturgical season. Once again we are reminded that the readings for Lent as developed in the current lectionary (which has in its turn tried to recover an ancient liturgical practice) are focused on the baptismal vocation of the children of God. Can a baptismal spirituality help us approach this difficult text?

There are two visible foci in this text. On the one hand, all have passed through the sea but fallen; and on the other hand, God is faithful. Let us look more closely at these two focal points.

1 Corinthians 10:1-13

Theological Perspective

against the idolatry of eating and drinking and dancing, against the immorality that led to the slaughter of twenty-three thousand, against the testing of God that was punished by serpents, or against the grumbling that led to destruction. We will thus be tempted to cite the gross decadence of our twenty-first-century culture as the equivalent evil against which Paul was inveighing in the first century. Thus will we fall prey to the self-righteousness that Paul declares in Romans 2 to be the deadliest of all evils. Such is the subtlety of evil—it corrupts by way of false goodness. Paul is referring not to evils so obvious that we can assure ourselves that we have not committed them, but rather to temptations so great that only the faithfulness of God can enable us to overcome or endure them.

Idolatry is commonly understood to mean the worship or service of some earthly good as if it were divine, to mistake the creature for the Creator, and thus to worship a god who is not *God*. The idolatry that Paul links to hedonic self-abandonment might best be likened to our American mania for the perpetual extension of human existence. Stanley Hauerwas says that, if most Americans were asked, in an unguarded moment, to name the purpose of life, we would answer, "The purpose of life is not to die."

The loss of belief in a resurrected life beyond death, declared the British essayist George Orwell, has done more to sap modern life of ethical excellence than virtually anything else. Orwell was no sort of Christian, but he discerned the deadly effect of mortalism—the notion that we come from nowhere, that we are destined for nowhere, and thus that when we die we rot, as Bertrand Russell famously said. Christians hold to the opposite view. We believe that we have come from and that we will return to the God of Jesus Christ. Our central conviction, therefore, is that the purpose of life is indeed to die—faithfully, graciously, perhaps even in martyrdom—so as to indicate that God's kingdom is indeed our reason for living. The cross is an instrument of death, and Christ bids us to take it up and follow him all the way to the end that is meant to be our real beginning.

When Paul speaks of putting "Christ to the test" (v. 9), it is perhaps appropriate to think of our assumption that, if we are faithful Christians, our lives will turn out well—that we will enjoy prosperity and success, that we will not know suffering and pain, that we will be spared the betrayals and persecutions that afflict others. We grumble against God, therefore, when our pious

Pastoral Perspective

In case the Corinthians object, claiming Christ has freed them from such concerns or has provided them with some special knowledge that enables them to resist the pull of their family's history (consider the debate in chapter 8 about food offered to idols), Paul has reinterpreted that history, arguing that Christ has always been present to the Israelites, even in the exodus—by means of a baptism through Moses, a communion through heavenly bread, and a rock that followed them in their journey and provided for their thirst.

Paul's rhetoric is clear: *all* of our ancestors were shielded by God, *all* passed safely through the sea, *all* received the leadership of Moses, *all* ate spiritual food and drank spiritual drink, but *most* of them failed to please God. Should the church, either at Corinth or in America, think that it is too sophisticated, high-minded, or modern to fall into superstition and idolatry, then it should hear these warnings ringing out from Paul's letter, suggesting that our spiritual practices do not provide the protection from sin that we think they might. Idolatry is still a sin that tests us. In fact, if we return to the language of family systems, idolatry is a profound addiction that adversely inhibits our whole family, creating special hardships for the individuals who would challenge it within our system, the church.

The question also arises, if the Israelites, who were the recipients of so much intercessory activity on God's part, failed over and over in faithfulness (from golden calves to complaints about God's menu), how can the church succeed now—particularly now that whole industries are committed to the making and marketing of idols?

What hope does the church have against magazine ads that celebrate sexuality as an end of its own, or television commercials that suggest busyness (which usually entails the breaking of a Sabbath commandment) entitles you to something special? "You work hard," they scream out, "You deserve it!" Or "You deserve a break today . . . at McDonald's" (Have the golden arches become the new golden calf?). Worse yet is the reinterpretation of the American dream as a race to wealth or an indulgence in material items, an opinion so universally held that it hardly needs to be touched upon here. Can the church stand against such idolatry without lapsing into it?

Our hope for differentiation lies in two places: first, in God, our creator and the creator of Sabbath (we do deserve a break, it seems). With God, nothing is impossible—from the old man who dreams of a

myself a slave to all, so that I might win more of them" (9:19). A significant part of the Lenten call to reflection should engage us at the level of community life. How does our life and practice facilitate or hinder the broader development of the church's mission?

Addressing this issue is crucial for Paul. He demonstrates his concern by showing the Corinthians how the experience of Israel in the wilderness has direct implications for their own experience. Not only is there continuity between the generation that left Egypt and their own, but there is also a corporate lesson to be learned. In the first four verses of chapter 10, the word "all" is repeated five times. As a people, they *all* shared the same experiences of having the supernatural blessings of God in the cloud and sea, in the leadership of Moses, and in food and drink miraculously supplied. This lesson from Scripture is not merely a story unrelated to the Corinthians' history. This story is about "our" ancestors, not about some distant, unrelated generation. The story of Israel is now the Corinthian story as well. Close attention must be paid to the experience of those whose bodies were scattered in the wilderness. They too assumed that idolatry was a trifling matter with God. They discovered that it was not a matter of indifference to God, even though they too had a type of baptism and Lord's Supper.

Type, analogy, and foreshadowing become teaching points of exhortation for Paul. As Moses was Israel's deliverer, so Christ is the Corinthians'. God miraculously supplied food and drink for them. Yet because of the continuity that exists between that wilderness generation and the Corinthians, they are about to repeat the sin of not trusting in God exclusively, and thereby experiencing the judgment of God. Because of their disobedience, the wilderness generation failed to enter the land. Their sin is stated in the strongest of terms: "Nevertheless, God was not pleased with most of them, and they were struck down in the wilderness" (v. 5). Just as God did not tolerate Israel's idolatry, God will not tolerate that of the Corinthians either (v. 6). Now history is dangerously close to repeating itself. We have the opportunity during Lent to seek parallels between our journey and the experience of Israel in the wilderness. What must we do to keep from repeating the untrusting response of that long-ago generation? In what ways do we display the same reliance upon our own strength?

Because of the continuity that exists in God's saving acts of mercy, Paul once again uses the

Passing through the sea. Without making a comparison between the baptism "into Moses" and the baptism into Christ, without falling into the temptation of making claims that can too easily be heard as anti-Jewish, we need to hear Paul's accusations against the ancestors in light of the verse near the end of this passage (v. 12): "So if you think you are standing, watch out that you do not fall." An important qualifier must be added: the judgments Paul makes in verses 1–10 are made against his own people, his own nation, his own upbringing. Paul, as an insider, can make these accusations. We, as outsiders, cannot do the same without serious disclaimers.

The "baptism" that the people claimed in Moses—passing though the sea and under the cloud, drinking from the spiritual rock—all of these blessings were considered by the people as their right, their privilege. Since God had brought them out into the desert, God had better protect and provide for them. They quickly looked after themselves rather than the journey. They looked at what they wanted and needed, rather than asking where God was leading them and how they might follow. In their view, the "baptism" through the sea was solely for their survival, rather than for the proclamation of God's purpose in the world.

As on the Second Sunday in Lent, this Sunday's reading pushes the listener to consider a life that goes beyond the realm of personal and individual need. However the reading goes further. It also pushes the community beyond its self-centered focus. Just as individuals can become enclosed in their own wants and desires, a community can also become enamored by its own blessedness and vitality. Such a community can become closed off from the world by its desire to preserve its own identity, blessing, and life.

Even baptism can become considered a "right"! Pastors may struggle with the issue of a baptismal spirituality in their congregations. Many congregants understand baptism as a family affair, a cute ceremony with a baby in white clothing surrounded by people who are seen once in church and never again, with camcorders and digital cameras busily recording. Has baptism into Christ become our "right," something that we can claim over and against the world?

Paul warns us to think about where we are standing. Are we standing on our own imagined rights and privileges? Does simply being American Christians provide us with complete coverage against falling? Obviously not! Have we become too cozy in

1 Corinthians 10:1-13

Theological Perspective

devotion does not produce happy results. A lady who shared this conception of the Christian life once asked, after I had given a lecture in Cornwall, whether I had noticed that people who do not believe in Jesus come to a sticky end. I could not help replying, "I thought that Jesus himself came to a sticky end." Many of us will indeed die badly—either of disease or accident or disappointment, perhaps even in a terrorist strike. However this is not what matters. What counts is God's own faithfulness to us, enabling us to live faithfully for God amid all the chances and changes of our existence.

One of the shortest sentences in our Lenten reading may be the most essential: "so if you think you are standing, watch out that you do not fall" (v. 12). It is not by chance that the word "humility" is rooted in the Latin *humus*, just plain ordinary dirt. To stand falsely is to be guilty of *superbia*, the pride that holds us literally over others as we look down on them from above, from a stance far removed from the ground. John Calvin regarded humility as the greatest of the virtues, declaring that the only true growth in grace is growth in humility. The greater our humility, the greater our knowledge that we need more of it. The highest pagan enjoyment, declared G. K. Chesterton, is self-enjoyment, extending the ego to infinity. Christians hold to the opposite view, that "the fullest possible enjoyment is to be found by reducing our ego to zero."[1] Thinking oneself sufficient to stand alone is the greatest temptation; the faithfulness of God in sparing us such egotism, replacing it with Lenten humility, is our only hope to live, and thus to die, rightly.

RALPH C. WOOD

Pastoral Perspective

family no longer oriented around cocktail hour to the young woman who breaks the cycle in her family of generations of abuse.

Our second hope is in the church. Here the language of virtue ethics is a helpful guide. In short, virtue ethics is the notion that a community of faith that practices certain disciplines creates members oriented toward certain virtues. For instance, the regular practice of prayer produces gratitude in us— or patience, or humility, or kindness, depending on the foci of those prayers. Similarly, though Paul alerts us that spiritual food and drink are not guarantors of safety, the practice of Communion is a discipline that can bolster us against idolatries. For instance, discovering sufficiency in a meager portion of bread and a limited sip of wine teaches us that our material idols malnourish us. Discovering that all are seated at God's table, from the absurdly wealthy to the pitifully impoverished, teaches us that status idols misrepresent the purpose of life. Discovering unexpectedly that Christ truly does host this table teaches us that our idols of "reality" bankrupt our imaginations.

Additionally, virtue ethics enlist the whole community as an agent to fortify us in pressing times. Therefore, when Paul writes, "No testing has overtaken you that is not common to everyone. God is faithful, and he will not let you be tested beyond your strength" (v. 13), it is critical to recognize that Paul writes to the whole community. As we say in the South, his *you*s are *y'all*s. This grammatical realization lessens the sting often associated with this text—specifically, that of faithful people who fail under the weight of burdens—by redirecting the testing as a burden for the community rather than something that must be borne alone.

This redirection is a verdant ground for pastoral reflection, as it introduces the question of communal support in difficulty: especially, how do our practices create virtues that enable us to endure? The text, of course, also complements the question by providing us a sense of history, an ability to look back upon the practices of our ancestors and notice where they have failed, so that we may learn from them for our future together in God's family.

CASEY THOMPSON

---

1. G. K. Chesterton, *Heretics* (New York: John Lane, 1905), 87.

wilderness generation's experience as a paradigm for the Corinthians: "We must not indulge in sexual immorality as some of them did, and twenty-three thousand fell in a single day" (v. 8). If the wilderness generation failed by rejecting a hidden Christ who sustained them in their journey, how much more will the Corinthians fail if they reject (test) a revealed Christ? These episodes from the wilderness experience serve as instructive lessons for every generation that is tempted to trust in its own strength. Lent also reminds us that God is gracious and merciful to us as we move through the season. This is so because "the ends of the ages" have already come (v. 11) in the life, death, and resurrection of Jesus. It is imperative then that each one of us diligently watch (v. 12) in discernment to see if our loyalties belong to God and God alone. Participating in pagan idolatry rituals and in the Lord's Table are mutually exclusive events. It is dangerous business to cozy up to any idolatry, to any practice that rejects ultimate trust in God alone. God cannot be trifled with on a casual basis in a nonchalant manner.

The entire passage raises the troublesome issue of how the Christian relates to culture. Is it possible to interact with our culture in the same way that we did prior to embracing Christ? Lent says no. The cross looming over this season says that radical, fundamental changes must be made. In fact, there exists the call to challenge cultural assumptions that deal with death as a given. We have options. We can make choices that ultimately reflect living discipleship that relies on God's grace alone, refusing the invitation of the powers to join them. The next verse, left out of this lectionary passage, summarizes the entire point Paul is making: "Therefore, my dear friends, flee from the worship of idols" (v. 14). Life-and-death issues are at stake. Thank God for Lent!

MARK E. HOPPER

our congregations, forgetting about the proclamation of God's purpose of justice and peace for all in the world? Does our sense of privilege trick us into engaging practices of injustice and war? Our baptismal vocation pushes us to think about where we stand and where the boundaries of our community are truly located. Our baptismal vocation pushes us through the doors of the church out into the street.

God is faithful. We may have forgotten our baptisms. We may have neglected growing deeper into a baptismal spirituality, but God is faithful. God continually reminds us that our baptismal journey— through the sea and through the desert (even when it is forty years)—is a continual process. We are baptized once—maybe at birth, maybe later in life— but once we are, life becomes a continual dying and rising with Jesus. Life becomes a call to live this gospel truth.

God is faithful. There is a beautiful Taizé song titled "God can only give faithful love" (in French: *Dieu ne peut que donner son amour*).[1] The text of the antiphon comes from Isaac the Syrian (seventh century CE) and the verses of the song are based on Psalm 103. In his commentary on this text, the Orthodox theologian Olivier Clément notes that for Isaac, God's love is there for all. God wants to be an infinite joy in all people but the fire of God's love is often rejected. Those who reject it "clench themselves up inside" and when God's love is rejected it is "felt as something scorching."[2]

For Paul, God's faithfulness endures and is known in this continual gift of love. If we, however, look only at our right—at our blessing as a type of privilege—then we too risk being "scorched." We close the door upon ourselves. Yet God will always provide a way out, even in the midst of tribulation and testing. A door will always be opened. God will always provide a passage, the same passage Godself endured and opened for us through his cross and resurrection.

DIRK G. LANGE

---

1. *Taizé: Songs for Prayer* (Chicago: GIA Publications, 1998).
2. Olivier Clément, *Taizé: A Meaning to Life* (Chicago: GIA Publications, 1997), 78.

Luke 13:1-9

¹At that very time there were some present who told him about the Galileans whose blood Pilate had mingled with their sacrifices. ²He asked them, "Do you think that because these Galileans suffered in this way they were worse sinners than all other Galileans? ³No, I tell you; but unless you repent, you will all perish as they did. ⁴Or those eighteen who were killed when the tower of Siloam fell on them—do you think that they were worse offenders than all the others living in Jerusalem? ⁵No, I tell you; but unless you repent, you will all perish just as they did."

⁶Then he told this parable: "A man had a fig tree planted in his vineyard; and he came looking for fruit on it and found none. ⁷So he said to the gardener, 'See here! For three years I have come looking for fruit on this fig tree, and still I find none. Cut it down! Why should it be wasting the soil?' ⁸He replied, 'Sir, let it alone for one more year, until I dig around it and put manure on it. ⁹If it bears fruit next year, well and good; but if not, you can cut it down.'"

Theological Perspective

This passage concludes a series of ominous warnings about the urgency of the times, a reality that will have its disruptive effects on family life, economics, religious traditions, and human destiny. In a manner reminiscent of John the Baptist, Jesus is preaching about the complete transformation of the world that is at hand and the need for those who have ears to hear to repent, lest they be left to endure the full force of God's judgment. In order for Jesus to impress this point upon his audience, he needs to address an apparent misconception held by his listeners. With respect to questions of sin and suffering, a common assumption among the people of Israel was that those who experienced pain and affliction were being punished by God, either for their own sins or for those of their ancestors.

This is the force of argument among Job's companions who cannot conceive of their friend's innocent anguish. Jesus himself is confronted by disciples with similar questions as they struggle to understand his ministry of healing and forgiveness: "Rabbi, who sinned, this man or his parents, that he was born blind?" (John 9:2). This question offers a prelude to Jesus' teaching in the final weeks of his life. The Galileans who suffered at the hands of Pilate, as well as the eighteen who were tragically killed when the tower of Siloam fell on them, were

Pastoral Perspective

Self-righteous anger. If emotions were cuisine, this would be the pièce de résistance, the dish we love to linger over and return to, time and time again. Anger by itself does not taste so good. It is bitter and leaves an aftertaste. On the other hand self-righteousness—there is the seasoning that makes plain-old-hamburger anger irresistible. Self-righteous anger goes down smoothly. It makes us feel superior. It elevates us above lesser mortals, not to mention our enemies. So long as we have it on our plates, the confusing grayness of the wearisome world goes away. It is bracingly, refreshingly clear that we are the good guys and those others are the bad guys. If all this were not enough, self-righteous anger also reheats wonderfully; it tastes almost as fine the second or fifth or sixtieth time out of the oven.

However this is Lent, and in the Christian tradition Lent has long been a season that messes with our menus. Such is certainly the case with today's Gospel reading. Jesus is hanging out with his fellow Galileans, his home folk, his people. In these neighborly circumstances, they serve up some self-righteous anger. They tell him "about the Galileans whose blood Pilate had mingled with their sacrifices" (Luke 13:1).

Make no mistake: this would be something to be angry about. It was bad enough to be occupied by

Exegetical Perspective

The recounting of the untimely deaths of several Galileans and Judeans followed by the parable of the Fruitless Fig Tree begins a section of Luke's narrative of Jesus' journey to Jerusalem (9:51–18:14) that focuses on repentance. The unit ends with last Sunday's Gospel reading, which contained the report of Herod's intention to kill Jesus and Jesus' lament over Jerusalem (13:31–35). The pericopes for last week and this week both begin with a report detailing the hostility of a civil authority. Both focus on the threat of imminent death. The number three and the city of Jerusalem figure in both accounts. The centerpiece of the larger unit that begins with verses 1–9 and ends with verses 31–35 contains the parables of the Mustard Seed and Yeast (vv. 18–21) that assert that the reign of God will certainly begin and grow, giving a sound basis for the call to repentance.

The slaughter of the Galileans (v. 1) is not mentioned in any source outside the Gospel of Luke. Though the victims were Galileans, we assume the deaths occurred in Jerusalem, since they were killed as they were offering sacrifice. The only legitimate place for sacrificial worship was the temple in Jerusalem. Evidently the Galileans were on a pilgrimage to the temple. Jesus too would suffer a similar fate at the end of his pilgrimage to the Holy City. As was

Homiletical Perspective

On one level this is a pastoral moment, calling forth a response from Jesus addressed to the deepest thoughts and aches of the human heart. I remember as a child, when a light-hearted occasion of misfortune befell someone, hearing the old folk say in jest, "You ain't been living right." I never heard it said seriously when someone was really hurting. However I have heard the principle behind the saying articulated when things fall apart for someone, when the burden of the heat of the day becomes unbearable, when things seem to go from bad to worse, when someone cries out from a bed of affliction or shrieks in despair from within a vale of tears. "Why?" "Why me?" In the painful struggle of trying to make sense of something senseless, the age-old logic of "You ain't been living right" sneaks into our consciousness.

Common sense suggests that if there is a demonstrable effect, there is an explainable cause. The desire to comfort by explanation is part of who we are as human beings. It comes with the territory. In varying ways the friends of Job reflect that. "As I have seen, those who plow iniquity and sow trouble reap the same," said one to Job when Job's world fell apart (Job 4:8). "If you will seek God and make supplication to the Almighty, if you are pure and upright, surely then he will rouse himself for you," said another (Job 8:5–6). *It could be worse,* another

Theological Perspective

no more egregious in their errors than those who now stand before him. Jesus directs attention away from the perplexing question of theodicy and focuses instead on a doctrine that Paul develops in his Letter to the Romans: "all have sinned and fall short of the glory of God" (Rom. 3:23). Due to the sin of one man in the garden, *all* are now subject to divine judgment, which Jesus has come to announce in no uncertain terms.

Divine judgment, however—understood as the experience of God's wrath apart from God's mercy—is not inevitable. Rather, it is contingent upon repentance, *metanoia*, a complete turning away from former beliefs and actions in faithful acceptance of the proclamation of God's kingdom in the person and work of Jesus Christ. This is the hope offered in Jesus' parable of the Fig Tree. The imagery is reminiscent of the Scriptures in which the people of God are compared to a garden planted and tended by the Lord (Isa. 5:1–7; Joel 2:22). Though some have made attempts to read this allegory literally—understanding the "three years" as representative of Jesus' ministry, the tree itself as the Jewish nation—it is perhaps best to focus simply on the notion that the fig tree is reflective of the apathy and indecision that is widespread among those who hear Jesus' message.

The story is indicative of the socioeconomic circumstances of first-century Palestine with its prevalence of absentee ownership. The master comes to the vinedresser looking for results from his fig tree, which in its barrenness is just "wasting the soil." The tree, however, has an advocate in the gardener, who is willing to provide the special attention it needs in order for it eventually to be productive. The gardener pleads with the owner to grant the tree one more year of life. "Far from offering cheap grace, or forgiveness with no reckoning, the gardener advocates that every chance . . . be given before a final decision is made."[1] The owner agrees and grants the reprieve. This aspect of the story lends symbolic credence to Jesus' emphasis on the urgency of the times, but not to be overlooked is the primary theological insight that God's judgment is tempered by divine mercy. This is especially poignant as we look ahead toward Jerusalem, where we will be confronted with the ultimate paradox of the cross on Golgotha. Jesus' intent in telling this story is to bring home the reality of the unfathomable nature of God,

Pastoral Perspective

Pilate and his Roman minions when they did not commit atrocities, but here was an occasion—have you heard?—when he sent soldiers into the sacred precincts of the temple and had men—our countrymen!—cut down like lambs to the slaughter. No, not simply *like* lambs to the slaughter, but *alongside* sacrificial, slaughtered lambs, so that the blood of holy sacrifices and patriots ran together as one. What could possibly be more violent, more reprehensible, more deserving of condemnation? What could more clearly set us apart from true wickedness?

During World War I, dread stories about the Germans slithered back to the home fronts of those who opposed them. The Hun soldiers were so inhuman that they tossed enemy infants into the air and bayoneted them, it was said. Before the United States militarily ousted Iraq from Kuwait in 1993, Congress heard stories that Iraqi soldiers invaded hospitals and—out of pure malice—removed newborn babies from incubators, leaving them to die on cold tile floors. Both of these stories turned out to be falsehoods, atrocity stories ginned up to fuel martial fury and vengeance. Those who questioned them at the time, who wanted sources checked, were accused of national disloyalty. It is said that anyone who wants to keep enjoying sausage or cheese should never see either one made. The same is true with self-righteous anger. It is a dish best not scrutinized too closely and best partaken of in the company of sure confederates.

We have no way of knowing whether or not the atrocity story the Galileans told Jesus ever happened. What is clear is that it was an appeal to Jesus' nationalistic sympathies.[1] He is expected to hear the story and galvanize in heated moral superiority with his countrymen, very much against the outsider Romans, those inhuman forces of evil. However Jesus will not go along. He does not focus on Pilate or the Romans and their cruelty. Instead, he turns attention back on his inquirers, his countrymen. These Galileans that you say so suffered at Pilate's hand, do you think "they were worse sinners than all other Galileans?" What about those from among us who were innocently building a tower at Siloam, and died when it crashed? Were they any worse than others who were not crushed? Jesus responds to these rhetorical questions unequivocally: "No, I tell

---

1. Sharon H. Ringe, *Luke* (Louisville, KY: Westminster John Knox Press, 1995), 185.

1. On atrocity storytellers and Luke 13:1–5, see Kenneth E. Bailey, *Through Peasant Eyes*, 75–79, in *Poet and Peasant; Through Peasant Eyes*, combined ed. (Grand Rapids: Eerdmans, 1983).

the case with his fellow Galileans, Jesus too will come to his fate because of a decision made by Pilate.

In general, Jewish sources from the first century CE portray Pilate's tenure as characterized by brutality and injustice, but these sources have ideological reasons for such a portrayal. For example, Josephus wishes to show that actions of Pilate were among the provocations that led to the First Jewish Revolt (66–73 CE). While the Gospels do present Pilate as condemning Jesus, they have him appear to be reluctant to do so. He is pushed to an unjust verdict by the insistence of the Jewish religious authorities and the crowd they incite against Jesus. The evangelists had apologetic reasons for this portrait. They sought to minimize the responsibility of Roman authorities for Jesus' death. Still, the Romans did not tolerate any opposition to their rule in Palestine, and Galilee was home to several rebel leaders. Josephus mentions more than a dozen rebels against Roman authority. Perhaps the most notorious was Judas the Galilean, who led a revolt against Roman taxation practices in Judea about the time Jesus was born. Josephus also credits Judas with being the founder of the Zealot party, which urged people to withhold the payment of taxes to Rome. Perhaps the Galileans who came to Jerusalem to offer their sacrifices said or did something to lead Pilate to suspect that they were intent on fomenting rebellious activity in Judea, just as Judas had some years earlier.

Similarly, the collapse of the tower at Siloam (v. 4) is not mentioned elsewhere. The city wall of Jerusalem in Jesus' day did take a turn just above the Pool of Siloam, and it is probable that there was a tower at such a critical point in the wall. In the Fourth Gospel, the Pool of Siloam also figures in a story that raises the question of the connection between sin and a tragic occurrence (see John 9:1–7).

In commenting on the death of the Galileans in the temple and the eighteen people at Siloam, Jesus raises the connection between sin and suffering (vv. 2, 4). That suffering is a punishment for sin is a biblical commonplace (see Deut. 28:15; Job 4:7–8; Prov. 10:24–25; Ezek. 18:26–28). Deuteronomic theology, which had gained wide currency by Jesus' day, asserted that obedience to the Torah brought blessings, but disobedience brought a curse. Here Jesus clearly rejects that view. A person's righteousness or lack of it has nothing to do with any evil that may befall that person. The lesson that Jesus draws from the two unfortunate events is the necessity of

said with these words: "Know then that God exacts of you less than your guilt deserves" (Job 11:6).

So when Jesus spoke to those who came to him telling of a terrible human tragedy, he dealt directly, emphatically, and bluntly with this almost natural human tendency. "Do you think that these Galileans were worse sinners than all the other Galileans, because they suffered thus? I tell you, No'" (Luke 13:2–3 RSV). Frankly, if God was in the business of meting out judgment and curses in relation to our sins, there probably would not be anyone left on the planet. In this text, Jesus says no to simplistic answers to deep and complex questions, no to attempts to solve deep troubles with quick fixes, and no to shallow theological thinking. Clearly Jesus is here responding to a pastoral human ache.

However there is also a missional moment and message here. For after Jesus says no, he goes on to speak of the responsibilities of those who hear his words. "Do you think that these Galileans were worse sinners than all the other Galileans, because they suffered thus? I tell you, No; but unless you repent you will all likewise perish" (v. 2–3 RSV). After applying this understanding to another tragic situation, Jesus tells a parable about a gardener determined to tend a fruitless fig tree because he is open to a future possibility that he does not control or manage.

Facing the reality of mystery and the limits of what we can know is not an excuse to stand still and look sad, as Luke describes some of the disciples, paralyzed at the time of the death of Jesus. Jesus is on a mission. Those who would be disciples of Jesus, who would follow in his way in the power of his Spirit, are on that mission. Much is unknown. Many questions will remain unanswered. In the end, the future is God's, but we share in the mission of unfolding the future. That is clearly where our responsibility lies. "The Spirit of the Lord is upon me, because he has anointed me to preach good news to the poor. He has sent me to proclaim release to the captives and recovering of sight to the blind, to set at liberty those who are oppressed, to proclaim the acceptable year of the Lord" (Luke 4:18–19 RSV).

I once heard the late Dr. Benjamin Elijah Mays, president of Morehouse College, say that "faith is taking your best step, and leaving the rest to God" (my paraphrase). The missional side of this Gospel reading may be that those who would follow in the footsteps of Jesus are charged with witnessing to the world in the name and spirit of Jesus. The results of this witness are not ours to know. The working out of

Luke 13:1-9

Theological Perspective

almost as if to round out Paul's insight quoted above: "they are now justified by his grace as a gift, through the redemption that is in Christ Jesus" (Rom. 3:24).

Yet the gift is not without its price, as Jesus indicates in his emphasis on repentance. The danger here lies in supposing that the sparing of the tree is a once-for-all choice that staves off God's wrath, transforming it into mercy. Returning to our allegory, this assumes that the tree can merely decide as a matter of will to produce its own figs. It is important to note, however, that in the parable it is the gardener who allows for the possibility of fruitfulness, first by pleading his case to the owner of the field, and then by his constant care, digging around the roots, and applying manure. In their predictable scataphobia, commentators have paid little attention to this final act of tilling and keeping (Gen. 2:15) on the part of the advocate, while it offers the greatest potential for producing its own theological fruit.

Augustine was clear on the symbolic importance of manure: "[It] is a sign of humility."[2] Here we find the essence of repentance: the faithful affirmation that "while we still were sinners Christ died for us" (Rom. 5:8). The manure around our roots is the very blood of the one who pleads for our justification before God, the one through whom we may offer up the fruits of the kingdom to our Creator. Lent is the season of *metanoia*, but our sanctifying acts of penance are nothing unless we are able to claim as our own the very humility of Christ, who "did not regard equality with God as something to be exploited, but emptied himself, taking the form of a slave, . . . [who] humbled himself and became obedient to the point of death—even death on a cross" (Phil. 2:6–8).

DANIEL G. DEFFENBAUGH

Pastoral Perspective

you; but unless you repent, you will all perish just as they did" (vv. 2–5).

Jesus does *not* tell his countrymen that the occupying Romans are the epitome of goodness, or that their oppression is anything other than oppression. However he will not have himself or his inquirers defined by their enemies. He will not partake of self-righteous anger with his fellow Galileans. As happens so often in the Gospel of Luke, he confronts those "who trusted in themselves that they were righteous and regarded others with contempt" (18:9). When it comes to judging sin, it is best to look for the log in your own eye before searching for the speck in your neighbor's (6:37–42)—or maybe even your enemy's.

We live in a day—not so unlike that of the atrocity-rumoring Galileans—when everyone wants to blame everyone else for the ills of the world. Christians blame Muslims and Muslims blame Christians. Fundamentalists blame Hollywood, the ACLU, and homosexuals. Liberals blame fundamentalists, militarists, and pharmaceutical companies. Amid the din, Jesus says, "Hold on. Think about a homely old fig tree. One that has not borne much fruit for a long time. The farm owner says, 'Cut that damned tree down.' His head gardener says, 'First, let me aerate the soil around it and throw some manure on the poor thing. After that give the tree one more year, and if does not produce, chop it to the ground'" (see Luke 13:6–9).

So, just when we begin to stir up flattering, heroic images of ourselves in full battle dress, ready to wipe evil off the face of the earth, Jesus knocks off us our moral high horses. He brings us down to earth and back to ourselves, with talk of fertilizer and a scruffy tree. He says, "Ask yourself if you are like that fig tree. Are you bearing fruit or just taking up space?"

It is enough to ruin your appetite for self-righteous anger. It is Lent, though, and Lent does mess with the menu.

RODNEY CLAPP

---

2. Augustine, *Sermon 254.3*, in Arthur A. Just Jr., ed., *Luke, Ancient Christian Commentary on Scripture, New Testament, vol. 3* (Downers Grove, IL: InterVarsity Press, 2003), 223.

Exegetical Perspective

repentance. The untimely deaths of the Galileans and the people crushed by the tower at Siloam ought to remind people that it is a serious mistake to put off repentance. Jesus is calling people to respond positively to his message before it is too late. This urgency reflected in Jesus' words derives from the apocalyptic tenor of much of Jesus' message. Jesus is convinced that the end is coming soon, and a dramatic reversal of fortunes will occur when the reign of God breaks in. To prepare for that fast-approaching end of the age is to repent, remembering that the time available for repentance is very short.

Jesus underscores his message that a day of reckoning is coming with the parable of the Fruitless Fig Tree (vv. 6–9). The parable is reminiscent of two Old Testament texts. Micah 7:1 compares his search for justice in Israel to that of a frustrated harvester who finds no figs or grapes in the vineyard that he oversees. Isaiah's song of the vineyard (5:1–7) also depicts the failure of a well-tended vineyard to produce fruit. The twist that Jesus gives to these familiar images is his emphasis on divine forbearance. Three years should have been enough time for the fig tree to be productive. The logical course of action is to uproot the unproductive tree so that it does not take up valuable ground that could be used to nourish a fruit-bearing tree. Jesus has the person responsible for the vineyard doing something that simply does not make sense under the circumstances, but the extravagant nature of God's mercy is an important motif in Luke's Gospel (e.g., 15:1–32). Still, people need to respond to God's mercy (13:8–9). The fig tree may be given another year to demonstrate its ability to produce fruit, but if it fails to do so, it will be cut down.

LESLIE J. HOPPE

Homiletical Perspective

God's kingdom is not ours to figure out. Our task is to labor, without having all the answers, to acknowledge the deep mystery of it all. The task of the disciple is to witness and then wait, to take our best step and leave the rest to God. We labor now for a future we are not meant to control. Did not Jesus teach us to pray, not "*My* kingdom come," not "*Our* kingdom come," but "*Thy* kingdom come, *thy* will be done"?

No statement of faith says all that could be said; no prayer fully expresses our faith; no pastoral visit brings wholeness; no program accomplishes the church's mission; no set of goals and objectives includes everything that needs to be done. We plant the seeds that will one day grow. We water seeds already planted, knowing that they hold future promise. We lay foundations that need future development. We provide yeast that produces effects beyond our capabilities.

We cannot do everything, and there is a sense of liberation in realizing that. Being freed from managing the results of our actions enables us to do something, and do it well. We may never see the end results, but that is the difference between the master builder and the worker. We are workers, not master builders; ministers, not messiahs. We are prophets of a future not our own.

MICHAEL B. CURRY

Joshua 5:9-12

⁹The LORD said to Joshua, "Today I have rolled away from you the disgrace of Egypt." And so that place is called Gilgal to this day.

¹⁰While the Israelites were camped in Gilgal they kept the passover in the evening on the fourteenth day of the month in the plains of Jericho. ¹¹On the day after the passover, on that very day, they ate the produce of the land, unleavened cakes and parched grain. ¹²The manna ceased on the day they ate the produce of the land, and the Israelites no longer had manna; they ate the crops of the land of Canaan that year.

Theological Perspective

God is always saving people, leading them into new places and new possibilities. Our passage in Joshua details how the forty years of wilderness wandering for the Israelites are coming to an end. Moses has led the people this far, but in this new place they have a new leader named Joshua. They have been wandering for forty years, having escaped the oppression of the Egyptians. They have yet to enter into the land of promise.

The reproach of the Egyptians in this text is their refusal to believe in or obey the God of the Hebrews. God's promise to the Israelites was that they would enter and possess a land of milk and honey. Their entering the land shows that God's promise to them is real and effective.[1] Despite the fact that the Israelites have not always been good, God has always been good to them. In the wilderness they were fed manna, a direct provision from God. They wandered for years in utter dependence upon God. Now the land of promise lies before them, a land of opportunities.

Yet Joshua is aware of the dangers of new opportunities. He understands the danger that God's

---

1. Martin H. Woudstra writes with regard to this passage, "The Lord declares: 'Today, I have rolled away the shame of Egypt from you.' Israel's bondage, which at the Exodus had been broken in principle, was finally and definitively removed now that the people were safely on Canaan's side, no longer subject to the words of shame of which Num. 14:13–16; Deut. 9:28 speak hypothetically" (*The Book of Joshua* [Grand Rapids: Eerdmans, 1981], 102).

Pastoral Perspective

Walk by the display window of any local bookstore and you may see countless titles that have to do with food or cooking: *Thanksgiving 101, A Life of Meals, The Year of Eating Dangerously*. Food is not simply a necessity for us. It is an art form, a lifestyle, an adventure.

Food provides fuel for our bodies, but it also connects us with other sources of power and meaning in our lives. Maybe that is why food is often associated with a significant occasion: a birth, a death, a wedding, a graduation, or a holiday. These times are marked by a specific dish that is served, a specific flavor, taste, or aroma that lingers across the years and is remembered in celebratory reenactments and holiday gatherings.

We often recalibrate our lives by remembering and sharing certain meals and food. Extended families make long treks to gather at Thanksgiving around a table, where we pause and ask those present to name one thing they are grateful for in the past year. In the midst of our daily harried existence, the chance to sit down together at the family dinner table is a chance to connect with each other, even if the best we can do is simply check and compare schedules and to-do lists. When we lose mealtime, we lose touch with each other, and in a sense we lose life.

Exegetical Perspective

Commentators generally agree that the canonical book of Joshua is the result of a final, exilic, shaping of much older materials by Deuteronomistic editors. The primary purpose of this editing is to show the fulfillment of the patriarchal promises in a narrative sequence that begins with the exodus and continues with the taking of the land; it is secondarily to renew that promise for a people disheartened and separated from their tradition by the physical and theological displacement of the exile. Joshua 5:9–12 is a part of chapters 1–5, which describe the preparations of the people for invasion of the land. These chapters include the crossing of the river, sending spies into Jericho and into the house of Rahab the harlot, and cultic preparation for the beginning of the holy war to come. The passage for today includes the recognition of Gilgal as a worship center and the ceremony of Passover, the cultic reminder that YHWH has brought the people to this place.

Verse 9, which begins today's lectionary passage, fits better with the preceding account of the circumcision of Israel immediately after crossing the Jordan. Verses 2–8, the account of the circumcision of the people, constitute the first part of the cultic preparation for taking the land; the second part is the keeping of the Passover in verses 10–12. Verse 9 is the hinge piece of the narrative, giving the etiology

Homiletical Perspective

Novelty has become today's obsession, and that which is novel is oftentimes equated with progress. The OT passage for this Fourth Sunday in Lent presents a contrasting picture. Its words suggest that newness does not come without cost. The probing preacher will investigate this text and seize upon its vitalizing words for hearers who secretly lament the dizzying pace of life, and who have grown uncertain about God's active presence and power in a rapidly changing world.

Joshua 5 depicts God's intimate involvement in ancient Israel's destiny and how this community, through cultic rituals of remembrance, is brought closer to their unsettled yet unambiguous future as they bear in mind their past. Preaching possibilities abound, especially as the preacher-interpreter is attentive to the history and theology both in and around this Scripture. In the face of our culture's disillusionment about and acquiescence to cultural change, we might call attention to three viable homiletical themes: (1) promise and fulfillment, (2) collective misery and divine encounter, and (3) faithfulness and cultic remembrance.

Promise and fulfillment. Israel's survival and beginning strides toward nationhood are centered on this very theme. It is important that the preacher approach the biblical text listening not only for the

Joshua 5:9-12

Theological Perspective

people may commit themselves to the fertility gods of Canaan. The shame and disgrace of the slavery they experienced in Egypt are behind them, but new idolatries lie before them.

Often we find ourselves at this same crossroads. Despite past disgraces, God forgives and presents us with new opportunities for service and faithfulness. The future lies before us, yet we are still far from where we should be. As we reflect in Lent about our relationship to God, it is good to consider Joshua and the first Passover in Canaan.

For these younger Israelites, the exodus is important, but it is history. Their parents celebrated Passover, but most of them died in the wilderness. So these young Israelites know God, but not from the Passover night. They know YHWH as the God of the wilderness—the YHWH of doves and of manna. These people are excited; they are poised to enter the promised land. Jericho is nearby. The land looks good, but it is not empty; it contains great riches, temptations, and resistance. As the people pause upon the plain, Joshua knows that they must reestablish covenant. Before they come into contact with the people of the land—with people who do not know or obey their God—they must clarify their beliefs.

So God has Joshua circumcise these young men. Circumcision reminds the people that they are set apart. It is a symbol of the covenant. It is also symbolic of their commitment to be different from the Egyptians behind them and the Canaanites ahead of them. Joshua makes the men take this step before they enter the promised land. In this land, the old and the new will each have their rightful places. Passover and circumcision remind the people where they came from. Manna also reminds them how God provided for them in the wilderness, but manna is a part of the past in a new land flowing with milk and honey. Manna requires neither settlement nor work; it merely needs to be gathered. The promised land, however, is to be developed. So Joshua and the people feast upon the new food of the new land! Their spirits are high, as well they should be, for the land of promise is finally theirs.

In this Lenten season, we too must be circumcised. We must examine ourselves and do a spiritual and moral inventory. Our old commitments and sins, our spiritual foreskins, must be cut away and cast off. We must confess and repent in order to grow and prosper. In every generation this is our task. The faith of our foreparents cannot be passed by osmosis to us. As Americans, most of us are financially more secure than the rest of the world.

Pastoral Perspective

This passage from Joshua marks a significant turning point in the journey of the Israelites. It denotes a passage of time and life. All the males, all the warriors, who had come out of Egypt had died. None of the people born on the journey had been circumcised. Now standing at the edge of the promised land, this new generation is circumcised, accepting the physical sign of their covenant relationship with God.

This time and place mark a new beginning for them. The Lord declares to Joshua, "Today I have rolled away from you the disgrace of Egypt" (Josh. 5:9). It is language that can propel our hearts forward across centuries to another time and place, where God will again roll something away, a stone from the entrance of a tomb. Neither the disgrace of Egypt nor the darkness of sin and death can finally stand as obstacles to the power of God's love to redeem and give life. God is able to bring forth life out of death and disgrace. In his Second Letter to the Corinthians, Paul declares, "So if anyone is in Christ, there is a new creation: everything old has passed away; see, everything has become new!" (5:17).

This time and place are marked by ritual and remembrance. The Israelites keep the Passover. "On the day after the passover, that very day" they eat (v. 11), and the food opens their eyes to wonder about their journey and their dependence on God, who is the giver of land, food, and life. "On that very day" they eat the produce of the land, unleavened cakes and parched grain. They sample a new cuisine, which tastes like the beginning of a whole new life to them.

On that day the menu changes: no more manna. I wonder if they secretly breathe a sigh of relief. Thank goodness. Wow, I was sick and tired of that stuff. Or maybe they miss it and start to remember it fondly. After all, manna was the gift of life. In either case, the manna ceases and they eat the crops of the land of Canaan. It is a new time, a new stage in life, calling for a different flavor, a new local cuisine. However the message of the food remains familiar. The food is more than fuel for their bodies. The bread points them to the bread giver, who is also the promise giver, who is also the life giver: the Lord.

As part of our celebration of World Communion, members of my congregation bake bread using recipes from all over the world. They bring the bread forward in response to the invitation to the Lord's Table: "Then people will come from east and west, from north and south, and will eat in the kingdom of God" (Luke 13:29). There is an abundance of breads, of all different shapes, sizes, and colors. As I stand at

of the name Gilgal as the end of the account of the circumcision of the people and the introductory setting—linked by the mention of Gilgal in verse 10—of the first Passover in the land. The site—clearly one with cultic significance—was mentioned previously in 4:19–20 as the place where Joshua set up the twelve stones brought out of the Jordan in Israel's crossing. The location of the site is unknown, although Gilgal is the site of various narrative actions in the stories of Saul and David (1 Sam. 10:1–8; 11:14–15; 13:8–14; 15:10–33).

It is here at Gilgal that Israel celebrates its first Passover. The ritual description of the text combines Passover with the feast of unleavened bread (v. 11). Whether this combination is an early occurrence or later in the development of the narrative is unclear, but the combination of deliverance from oppression in Egypt and YHWH's providing from the fruit of the promised land is a natural combination, celebrating YHWH's power to deliver and provide in uncertain and unpredictable circumstances. At this point in the narrative, Passover is a celebration of the congregation and a recognition of the history of the community. For the sixth-century Deuteronomistic editors of the text, the celebration is also a reminder that in another kind of oppression in a foreign land—that of the exile—YHWH has the power to deliver, and even a mighty ruler, whether Pharaoh or Nebuchadnezzar, cannot stand against the divine will for God's people. In the face of destruction and exile it is also a reminder that YHWH can provide the sustenance of life. At this narrative moment of transition in Israel's history, as the produce of the land becomes available for supporting the life of the people, the manna from the desert stops. A new source emerges as an old one ceases—YHWH continues to provide.

The keeping of the Passover here in Joshua 5 is mirrored by the restoration of the celebration by Josiah in 2 Kings 23:21–25. For the Deuteronomistic writer, this bracketing of the narrative of Israel in the land by celebrations of Passover, first by Joshua and then by Josiah, serves to point back again to the total reliance of the people on YHWH's power, and it calls them to return to true worship of the one God. The acknowledgment of the text in 2 Kings 23:22 that "no such passover had been kept since the days of the judges" focuses the importance of the present passage in Joshua as the hinge point in the entry into the land—it is only with YHWH's blessing and support that a people can have a new beginning. The new beginning of entry into the land is reinforced by

secrets related to its literal content, but for its intentional communication as well. Ironically, God's assuring word here that Egypt's reproach has been positively deflated encloses a long-standing promise not made good on that finally catches up with time. Historically, the passage gathers up promises made to relieved recipients Abraham and Sarah. God promised the patriarch a natural born heir, a sizable land endowment, and countless descendants. Out of the same lineage of promise, God's prophetic instrument Moses became the human catalyst of salvation in the sphere of oppression and death. In the present case, fulfillment is realized in the radical destruction of Egypt's present order and the ensuing out-migration of Hebrews.

Against this historical backdrop, we hear this Joshua 5 text saying that the past is never uninformative for the present and future. The story of Joshua commences with this evocative promise: "As I was with Moses, so I will be with you. . . . Be strong and courageous" (1:5b–6). Joshua accomplishes—or better stated, he fulfills—what his predecessor Moses was not allowed to finish. Slavery has ended and wilderness journeying has given way to new beginnings. A new generation of Israelites is consecrated through circumcision, and Joshua leads a new Israel in the process of inheriting the land. The preacher asking historical questions of the text will inevitably be drawn to concerns about the relationship between covenantal obedience and promise bearing. Promises are kept by God, even promises of judgment.

Collective misery and divine encounter. Verse 12 announces that Israel's daily dietary provision of manna has ceased. The image of this "bread from heaven" ending may serve to help hearers understand the significance of trusting God completely each day for sustenance, and what this level of trust demands in spiritual preparation. Manna was edible only on the day when it arrived. New beginnings in the promised land are buttressed by a community's long and arduous journey and experience with manna. Accordingly, Lent calls communities of faith into instructive places that demand some form of sacrifice.

The community's apprehension of prophetic hope is palpable here in Gilgal on the plains of Jericho. Israel is now able to reflect meaningfully on its tragic yet heroic past and to engage in the peculiar possibilities of freedom and inheritance. Passover becomes an opportunity to encounter God anew. A ceremonial ground is consecrated, and the cultus observes its ritual in a visibly public way. On the one

Joshua 5:9-12

Theological Perspective

Yet wealth is both blessing and temptation. It is wonderful to live in a land flowing with milk and honey, but it is also easy to rely more on the land than on the Giver of the land. Our riches can lure us to celebrate ourselves rather than the Holy One who provides for us, calling us to seek our treasures first in heaven rather than on earth. Our truest calling is to watch and pray and work for the reign of God. There we can enjoy milk and honey; there we can even drink living water. First, we must covenant afresh with the God who leads us into new and challenging futures. Before we can begin our new endeavors, ministries, and missions, we must circumcise our hearts, cutting away the old foreskins of past sins and past failures. We must also be careful to dethrone our modern idols. Our reliance upon such idols leaves us open to sudden and terrible reversals. The land still has milk and honey, yet we know that we cannot live on milk and honey—or bread—alone, but only by every word that proceeds out of the mouth of God.

Like Joshua's Israelites, we too must confess that we are not the people we should be. God is still leading people out of disgraceful wandering situations into genuine divine blessings. This way of being in the land requires prayer, meditation, confession of sins, and repentance. Once we have prepared ourselves to follow God into the wonderful provisions of our promised land, we can enjoy both the land and the feast in due time in joy.

DARRYL M. TRIMIEW

Pastoral Perspective

the table the aroma and appearance of the different breads heightens my senses. I begin to anticipate the wonder of different tastes. The variety and plenty of that bread, given and shared by so many, becomes at that moment an embodiment and means of grace for me. Food, bread, given in the name of the one who said, "I am the bread of life," fills me with something much more than fuel for my body. It connects me with the Lord, with the giver of life.

Lent is a time when we reflect on Jesus' journey to Jerusalem and the cross. The people Jesus meets, the places he visits, and the meals he shares along the way are daily reminders that Jesus brings into life the gift and power of God's forgiveness and grace. In the presence of those who complain about the sinners he dines with, Jesus tells a story of an ecstatic father who sees his wayward lost son returning home and declares, "Let's eat the fatted calf for dinner!" From dinner at the door to the promised land to the party for the prodigal son's homecoming, God seems to delight in tying a wonderful meal to the wonder of God's grace and goodness in our lives.

"Stay close to the ground" is sometimes given as healthy diet advice. The idea is that food closer to the ground is less likely to be processed food. The further you get from the "produce of the land," the less nutritional value food has. The spiritual advice from this passage of Joshua may be "Stay close to the food." Savor, remember, and be renewed by the ways God provides for and sustains you, both physically and spiritually. Keeping our connection with the bread and the land, we keep our connection with God who gives us all we need to live.

DANIEL M. DEBEVOISE

the immediate appearance in verse 13 of a man who identifies himself as "commander of the army of the Lord" (v. 14). He proclaims the holiness of the place (v. 15), echoing the encounter of Moses at the burning bush (Exod. 3:5), and the conquest of the land begins in chapter 6 with the taking of Jericho.

The reconstruction of the historical development of Israelite worship with its festival celebrations and corresponding family rituals is beyond the scope of this discussion. However, at some point in Israel's history, probably in the displacement and disorientation of the exile, this communal celebration of Passover was transformed into the more private ritual that celebrated the memory and meaning of the exodus in the more intimate context of the family. When the corporate centers of worship are no longer available, the memory of YHWH's mighty acts continues in the homes of the people.

In summary, the internal structure and narrative placement of this account of the first keeping of the Passover in the land of Canaan emphasizes the place of celebration and ritual in the life of God's people. Faithful celebration belongs at the beginning of every significant undertaking of that people, in this case, entry into the land. Ritual celebration also belongs in the heart of every crisis of the people, as the Deuteronomistic shaping of the text reminds a people in exile. It embodies the mighty acts of God in the history of the people, reminding them of the power of that God to deliver, even in the face of what seem to be overwhelming odds.

RICHARD A. PUCKETT

hand, a sermon reflecting on this symbolism might raise suspicion about the kind of obedience that requires every person's participation in a ritual act. On the other hand, the importance of memorializing past events of God's active involvement on our behalf yields homiletical possibilities. A sermon, metaphorically speaking, might declare God's active role in parting our Red Seas and Jordan Rivers, ending our protracted wildernesses, and delivering us from the identity-bleaching Egypts that hold us captive.

God speaks to Joshua about a past that will no longer put at risk God's preparation for Israel's new experience. Twenty-first-century listeners will hear a sobering word. Though delayed, newness that satisfies comes not to be suddenly out-of-date but to enrich the soul. Preachers who stand in the shoes of these ancient people can perhaps get a glimpse of a community stronger in character for the delay, standing on sacred ground primed for divine encounter. Israel's encounter not only radiates from the revelation of their reproach being lifted, but is indicative of the actualization of Joshua's faith and that of the people as well. Howard Thurman explains: "If our encounters with God are to be satisfying, they must be with one who is seen as holding within his context all that there is, including existence itself."[1]

Cultic remembrance and faithfulness. Inheriting the land was no small challenge of faith for Israel. Joshua and his band were in search of a promised land. As the children of Israel, African Americans and other racial ethnic groups have endured their own Egypts in America. During Lent, African American preachers might relate this passage to their own experiences with racial discrimination and other forms of oppression. Still other communities, especially immigrants, will want to explore the paradoxical realities that surround new freedom in inhabited spaces. Israel had to come to terms with limits in order to trust God to help them possess the land. Gilgal became a sanctuary for them to remember God at every stage of their sojourn.

Inched closer to realizing a dream first articulated to Abraham, Joshua becomes a lens to evoke our awareness of revelation and remembrance of God, which is the basis of Passover itself. Passover represents a new dawn in which makeshift meals of manna end and now the produce of Canaan begins to sustain the faithful.

KENYATTA R. GILBERT

1. Howard Thurman, *The Creative Encounter* (New York: Harper & Bros., 1954), 29.

Psalm 32

[1]Happy are those whose transgression is forgiven,
  whose sin is covered.
[2]Happy are those to whom the LORD imputes no iniquity,
  and in whose spirit there is no deceit.

[3]While I kept silence, my body wasted away
  through my groaning all day long.
[4]For day and night your hand was heavy upon me;
  my strength was dried up as by the heat of summer.   *Selah*

[5]Then I acknowledged my sin to you,
  and I did not hide my iniquity;
I said, "I will confess my transgressions to the LORD,"
  and you forgave the guilt of my sin.   *Selah*

[6]Therefore let all who are faithful
  offer prayer to you;

Theological Perspective

One of the so-called Penitential Psalms, Psalm 32 offers compelling insights into the fruits of penitence, as well as an invitation to live a grace-filled life in response to divine forgiveness. This psalm has had a special place in the lives of notable spiritual giants within the Christian faith. It is said that it was a favorite psalm of Augustine, who supposedly had it written on the wall opposite his bed, his eyes riveted on its words during his last sickness. In Luther's judgment this psalm was among the best. Izaak Walton's life ambition was to live as a man "in whose spirit there is no guile"[1] (v. 2 KJV). While the reasons for the psalm's appeal to these spiritual luminaries might be varied, surely inherent in its appeal is that it is a veritable treatise on the theological experience of forgiveness.

The first two verses of the psalm evoke the essence of human happiness or state of blessedness. "Happy are those whose transgression is forgiven, whose sin is covered. Happy are those to whom the LORD imputes no iniquity, and in whose spirit there is no deceit" (vv. 1–2). There is a theological tension here with respect to the source of such happiness. Does blessedness come from having one's sins

1. Izaak Walton, *The Lives of John Donne, Sir Henry Walton, Richard Hooker, George Herbert and Robert Sandersen* (London: Oxford University Press, 1936), 415.

Pastoral Perspective

Happiness is high on most people's list of priorities. Hunger for happiness drives much of our lives. The ambitions we pursue, the relationships in which we engage, the professions we enter, the hobbies we love, the clothes we wear, the food we eat, and even the way we observe Lent reflect individual beliefs about what brings fulfillment and happiness. Noting the universality of this desire, the Dalai Lama observes:

> Indeed, the more I see of the world, the clearer it becomes that no matter what our situation . . . rich or poor, educated or not, of one race, gender, religion or another, we all desire to be happy. . . . It is in our nature. . . . Our every intended action, in a sense our whole life—how we choose to live it within the context of the limitations imposed by our circumstances—can be seen as our answer to the great question which confronts us all: "How am I to be happy?"[1]

In Psalm 32, happiness comes from being forgiven. It comes not from being important, accomplished, organized, optimistic, or busy. Instead, being happy is a matter of being righteous, and according to Psalm 32, righteousness is not a matter of being sinless. It is about the ego-bruising work of Lent:

1. Dalai Lama, *Ethics for the New Millennium* (New York: Riverhead Books, 1999), 4.

at a time of distress, the rush of mighty waters
shall not reach them.
⁷You are a hiding place for me;
you preserve me from trouble;
you surround me with glad cries of deliverance.   *Selah*

⁸I will instruct you and teach you the way you should go;
I will counsel you with my eye upon you.
⁹Do not be like a horse or a mule, without understanding,
whose temper must be curbed with bit and bridle,
else it will not stay near you.

¹⁰Many are the torments of the wicked,
but steadfast love surrounds those who trust in the LORD.
¹¹Be glad in the LORD and rejoice, O righteous,
and shout for joy, all you upright in heart.

Exegetical Perspective

Psalm 32 exudes vitality. Practical and applicable, it smacks of realism. While reflecting one person's experience, the broadly worded poetry spans generations and genders. Although considered a wisdom psalm, Psalm 32 (a beloved component of corporate worship) contains elements of thanksgiving, joy, and penitence. It opens with Wisdom literature's catch-all word "blessed."

Wisdom literature (Job, Proverbs, Ecclesiastes, Song of Songs, and some psalms) teaches via exaggeration and opposites. Psalm 32's wisdom elements include these words and concepts:

vv. 1–2	blessed/deceit
v. 8	teach/direct
vv. 10–11	wicked/upright

Notice the psalm's straightforward structure:

vv. 1–2	blessedness of the forgiven sinner
vv. 3–4	burden of unconfessed sin
v. 5	confession and pardon explained
vv. 6–7	exuberant affirmation of confession's benefits
vv. 8–9	God's promise of instruction and watch care to the forgiven person
v. 10	comparison between the wicked and the upright
v. 11	corporate command to rejoice

Homiletical Perspective

A persistent question provoked by the so-called parable of the Prodigal Son, the Gospel for this Sunday, is whether the younger son repented before returning home and receiving the father's forgiving embrace. The text does not say that he repented, although many insist that he *must* have repented. How else to receive the father's forgiveness? The discussion can quickly devolve into an insistence on what *we* must do to receive that forgiveness, as opposed to wonderment and awe at what *God* does in forgiving us. Repentance becomes the sinner's gambit, a calculated risk taken by the one asking for forgiveness in order to leverage the forgiver into a position of needing to proffer the desired declaration of forgiveness. In ways more profound than even in the parable itself, Psalm 32 opens up the doorway to understanding in a far deeper way that, while repentance may well be a precondition for receiving forgiveness, it is nevertheless a process in which God is the primary agent. If, in the framework of the parable, the younger son actually did repent, the words of Psalm 32 could well serve as his revelation and his proclamation—perhaps, we might imagine, to his older brother.

In the parable we hear a presumably fictional, albeit masterful, story, a spiritual metaphor, intended to provoke the hearer's response. In the psalm we

Psalm 32

Theological Perspective

forgiven, or is blessedness reserved for those "in whose spirit there is no deceit"? The latter formulation would certainly inspire Pelagians, while those who are indebted to the inherited traditions of orthodoxy would surely gravitate toward the first. At any rate, the remainder of the psalm seems to favor an orthodox reading. Sin is a reality in the human heart. Something is wrong in the human condition and in the conditions that ground human existence. There is no point in a pretension of innocence or hoping that one's natural desires will not eventuate in sinful acts or in a sinful posture away from God. The psalm goes on, however, to outline a marvelous sequence of steps that eventuates in the blessed life and a forgiven state of existence.

First, there can be no divine forgiveness without a sincere and contrite acknowledgment of sin. Interestingly enough, this psalm suggests that acknowledgment of sin must be done well before confession of sin to God. Does the psalmist wish to suggest that a self that has been deluded into believing that it was blameless must now counter such a foolish error by coming to terms with the sin *with oneself*? The notion of a self in critical dialogue with itself is not an exclusively modern notion. Biblical consciousness seems to know a self that can counter itself, even as it attempts to negotiate a moral center of gravity. Without acknowledgment of the sin to oneself, there can scarcely be any confession of sin to God.

Moreover, the psalmist seems to be saying that to ignore human culpability in sin will only exacerbate matters, even to the point of physical impairment. Failure to acknowledge sin in fact informs further deterioration. "While I kept silence, my body wasted away," the psalmist recalls (v. 3). However, by rejecting a theory of naive innocence with respect to human sin, the psalmist opens up the very real possibility that humans will be wracked with guilt, for guilt emerges only when one is cognizant of wrongdoing. Thus the expiation of guilt is critical in this overall moral cleansing such that the psalmist will be able to declare how the Lord "forgave the guilt of my sin" (v. 5). Having affirmed the *bonum* of being released from guilt and other attendant ills emanating from the sinful life, the psalmist can then go on to offer other insights into the richness of the blessed life of being forgiven.

First, in response to God's forgiving act, the faithful assume a posture of prayer. One might ask at this point if the intent is to propose prayers of petition or prayers of thanksgiving. There is a bit of

Pastoral Perspective

acknowledging sin, accepting forgiveness, vigilantly attending to God's teachings, trusting God more than self, and then being happy in the One who steers us toward paths of utter fulfillment.

Undoubtedly, this work is difficult. The confession stage alone is a lonely and tempting place. Culturally, it is popular to assign blame to others and not to assume responsibility ourselves. Sin is accepted readily and dismissed as unproblematic. Alternatively, telling the truth and nothing but the truth about our lives can leave others feeling like lone sinners surrounded by saints. Eventually they withdraw from community and even from God. Still others stay frozen in a state of perpetual horror at their sin, magnifying its importance. Rehearsing their crime repeatedly, as if they alone are guilty of such a thing, they berate themselves repeatedly and ask for forgiveness without repenting because, like rubberneckers staring at a car accident, they are unable to pull their gaze from their sin toward God and the open road of sanctified possibilities lying ahead.

Some sin may be small but haunting, never released but instead hauled everywhere. Much like Augustine's ongoing grief at stealing pears from a neighbor's tree when he was sixteen years old[2] or a friend's ongoing remorse at having intentionally embarrassed an awkward grade-school classmate, some build a past trespass into a paradigmatic representation of the host of failure and sin characteristic of their lives. However, focusing on fault and magnifying its importance is not confession but megalomania, as if we know better than God does that we are undeserving of forgiveness. Such a posture narcissistically keeps the focus on our actions, when what God has done and continues to do is far more important. It involves refusing forgiveness and features failure to follow God's lead into fresh ways of living.

Thus, though Psalm 32 is considered the second of the traditional Penitential Psalms, even this psalm does not stop with confession but pushes past the temptation to dwell on one's crimes, into the essential next steps taken by the righteous. Notably, after verse 6 there is no more mention of fierce faults or forgiven foibles. Instead, the happy acknowledge sin (vv. 5–6), accept forgiveness (v. 7), attend God's instruction (vv. 8–9), trust God more than self (v. 10), and act glad in God (v. 11). Psalm 32 digs beyond the psychologically therapeutic benefits of

2. Augustine, *Confessions*, trans. R. S. Pine-Coffin (New York: Penguin Books, 1961), 49.

Exegetical Perspective

Psalm 32 contains triplicate explanations of forgiveness and sin (vv. 1–2, 5), the triplets balancing each other. The three aspects of forgiveness are being forgiven, the putting away or covering of sin, and God lifting the charge. An evidence of being forgiven is a lack of deceit (v. 2). The three aspects of sin are rebellion against God, wandering away, and depravity. Possible results of these kinds of sin are a loss of vitality and illness (v. 4). As a psalm studied and read during Lent, Psalm 32 teaches the practice of penitence and shows its results.[1] Connecting forgiveness to justification by faith, Paul cites Psalm 32:1–2a in Romans 4:7–8 and writes of the blessedness of the person "to whom God credits righteousness apart from works" (Rom. 4:6 NIV).

Chronologically, the psalm starts backward with the end result of blessedness. Then it tells why the psalmist is blessed: he is both forgiven and restored. The psalm also contains thanksgiving. The reasons for thanksgiving are the psalmist's decision to confess his wrongdoing, his assurance of forgiveness, and the security of God's unfailing love (vv. 1–2, 5, 10). The psalm closes with corporate praise.

The psalmist vividly describes his recent discomfort: "Day and night your hand was heavy upon me" (v. 4). God's heavy-handedness, so to speak, is not arbitrary or churlish but purposeful and merciful. If necessary, it is prolonged until it achieves the desired results. The biblical text consistently presents this fact: God's heavy-handedness lifts in response to human confession and repentance.

One translation describes the pressure the psalmist feels this way: "All the juices of my life dried up."[2] Profoundly uncomfortable, the psalmist wants to change. He acknowledges that he and his actions are the problems. God agrees. However, the purpose of punishment in the biblical text is always restoration—restoring fellowship with God and others. God's grace instigates a desire for confession, and then confession starts the process of God's cleanup.

Confession requires an upright heart. Not undertaken lightly, this serious religious and legal endeavor acknowledges guilt before a judge, but the judge's character is well known. This judge, by his own self-description, is gracious, compassionate, merciful, and slow to anger (Exod. 34:6). Yet knowledge of God's graciousness and willingness to forgive allows no license to continue returning to

1. James Luther Mays, *Psalms*, Interpretation series (Louisville, KY: John Knox Press, 1994), 145–46.
2. Eugene H. Peterson, *The Message* (Colorado Springs, CO: NavPress, 2002), 948.

Homiletical Perspective

hear the narrator's own compelling story told in the first person, with encouraging, grace-filled instruction provided in the light of that experience. Despite homiletic admonitions to avoid the first person in preaching, it can work and does so here. We gratefully do not get lost in the gritty details of the psalmist's situation.

Although it is one of seven Penitential Psalms, this psalm is not actually a confession of sin.[1] Rather, it is a view of confession and repentance from the far side of forgiveness, looking back on, instead of forward to, the reception of forgiveness. It is a reflection on being granted forgiveness and all that that accords, rather than an expression of the need for and the hope for forgiveness. Following two beatitudes, the psalm is a first-person report of what can happen when one tries to hide or deny one's sin, especially from God. The psalm speaks of the festering, corrosive nature of such denial: "my body wasted away through my groaning all day long" (v. 3). It is also, however, a report of what comes when one finally summons the wherewithal to confess and discovers the freeing nature of such an action, throwing off the shackles of a self-imposed imprisonment of shame, betrayal, and mistrust and discovering a freedom that was resident there all along. We are treated to an instruction, based on the psalmist's personal experience, on how to avoid the dire situation in which the psalmist found himself: confess your sins.

The question persists, why do we try to hide and/or deny our sins and our sinfulness, given the repeated calls for repentance in Scripture? We persist in our spiritual blindness, failing to see that the forgiveness has been there all along, that our stubborn insistence on preferring the illusion of self-dependence prevents us from availing ourselves of what is truly freeing—sincere confession, repentance, obedience. The answer that the psalmist provides seems reducible to stubbornness—we are like the horse or mule that needs a heavy hand to keep from willfully straying off course.

It is something of a truism in preaching that one can offer redemption only to the degree that the preaching has exposed and explored the need for redemption. Superficial need results in superficial redemption. The psalmist writes, "Many are the torments of the wicked" (v. 10). I do not know many people who would claim with pride that they are wicked. It could be that I work in too narrow a niche of the population to experience that. As a seminary

1. Artur Weiser, *The Psalms* (Philadelphia: Westminster Press, 1962), 281.

Psalm 32

Theological Perspective

ambivalence here, but one that is theologically suggestive. It could be argued that since the prayer is subsequent to the forgiving act of God, the prayer is one of thanksgiving. Along with this line of thinking would come the rather striking admonition to engage in prayers of thanksgiving even *during* times of distress. This is indeed a brave theological undertaking and tends to upend conventional thinking that distress is a time for almost exclusively petitionary prayers.

At verse 8, there is another aspect in the process toward blessedness. The Lord speaks: "I will instruct you and teach you the way you should go; I will counsel you with my eye upon you." Inherent in a state of blessedness and forgiven existence are the dynamics that attend to character formation and the acquisition of habits consistent with a life that is conformed to the will of God. Grace-filled living presumes a necessary aspect of ethical sensitivity and consciousness of following a path of rectitude that has a divine imprint. Faithful humans will inevitably choose to follow this path charted by God, unlike other creatures for whom the matter of choice cannot be an issue; thus the evocation of the horse or mule, which is "without understanding" and "whose temper must be curbed with bit and bridle" (v. 9). The clear admonition is not to be stubborn as such animals. After all, it is human recalcitrance and moral blindness that have occasioned the sin and guilt which are so problematic.

Finally, the element of trust (v. 10) in the Lord tempers any illusion that the reason for joy is of one's own making. The forgiveness has been offered as a result of God's own pleasure and will. In contradistinction to the malefactor of verse 1, who refused in silence to admit or confess sins, the forgiven one in verse 11 is effusive with praise to God, rejoicing for the gift of forgiveness. The forgiven sing praises of joy as no others can.

SAMUEL K. ROBERTS

Pastoral Perspective

confession to personal change that places God alone at the center of our lives without rival.

The starting point, however, is giving up foolish avoidance of the topic of sin and breaching the silence between self and God. After all, when we keep silent, the consequences are dire. The psalmist had his strength dry up and wither away like torched grass browning in the heat of the summer sun. His mouth kept silent, so his body spoke. It wasted away. Alternatively, we may exhibit extra pounds, knots in our back, higher blood pressure, shorter tempers, or insomnia, but the result is the same: silence about sin makes us sick.

When the only confession we engage in involves prayers that lack specificity, self-examination, and sorrow, there is no bruising of the ego, but neither is there transformation or inner healing. When we let fear or pride infest our lives, we make ourselves at home with distorted views of the nature of humanity and Christian community. At our deepest core, to be human is not to be a sinner but to be loved. To be righteous is not to be sinless but to be forgiven and freed. To be in Christian community is not to downplay brokenness but to accept it and be transformed by the One who healed brokenness on the cross and whose name is and always has been Love.

Liturgically, Psalm 32 invites singing hymns such as "O for a Thousand Tongues to Sing," "What a Friend We Have in Jesus," and "You Are My Hiding Place." During confession, verse 7 provides backbone for a prayer featuring "hiding places" and the innumerable ways we avoid God; alternatively, verse 9 inspires confession centered on ways we are stubborn as mules.

Christian faith is about entering into a way of life that answers the deep human desire for happiness. The entire study of Christian morality is best understood as "training in happiness,"[3] an ongoing initiation into the desires, attitudes, habits, and practices that make for a happy and good life. We may be accustomed to understanding confession— let alone morality or the penitential season of Lent— as life-sapping law, obligation, or rule. However, the witness and instruction of Psalm 32 announces that happiness comes when we are made right with God and engaged in practices such as confession that provide basic building blocks upon which this fundamental friendship flourishes.

LINDSAY P. ARMSTRONG

3. Paul Wadell, *Happiness and the Christian Moral Life* (Lanham, MD: Rowman & Littlefield, 2008), 47.

Exegetical Perspective

sin. The awesomeness of coming before God now deters the psalmist from sin. Remembering the unpleasantness of God's heavy hand likewise warns this psalmist against knowingly sinning again.

Confession makes this a Penitential Psalm. Psalm 32 shares these factors with other Penitential Psalms: (1) sense of sin, (2) knowledge that sin is against God, (3) desire to be changed, and (4) petition to God to deal with the sin and change the psalmist. Psalm 32 gives no leeway for self-righteousness or smugness. The psalmist is not righteous because he confesses. He is righteous because of God's character and magnanimity.

The "confessee" becomes an evangelist for confession, a proponent for corporate prayer. His contagious exuberance is like the joy of recovery after a long illness. He broadcasts confession's benefits in the most public place in town: the sanctuary.

The psalm offers this standard: let joy be an expression of confession! Monitor yourself. If confession becomes dull and joyless, watch out for an attitude of entitlement. Throughout the biblical text, however, God's forgiveness is never cheap grace.

God responds to the psalmist's confession with a prophetic command: Do not be like a dumb animal, a horse or a mule that has to be controlled by bit and bridle (v. 9). The psalmist can choose forcible guidance by God or the more delightful prospect of making God his hiding place and engaging in song together with God (v. 7).

The psalmist invites others to learn from his own arrogance, stubbornness, and long illness. Do not make my mistakes, he advises. Avoid my needless suffering. Choose confession. The psalmist calls on all to intensify their prayer activity (v. 6). They must pray to God in their time of difficulty. Confession and forgiveness have restored the fellowship broken by sin, iniquity, and transgression. The psalmist delights in his new, restored feeling of security in God.

Not prone to repentance, the wicked choose not to confess. The upright, however, confess their sins, thereby acknowledging their membership in faith's household. Receiving the command to rejoice in the Lord (v. 11), the righteous continue worshiping. Joy is the very essence of worship. More than anything else, joy is the language that beckons God. Indeed, Israel's praises enthrone God (Ps. 22:3). Joy strengthens both the individual and the community (Neh. 8:10). Joy focuses individual and community energies on God (Phil. 4:4). Joy transcends circumstances. Joy transforms circumstances. To rejoice is a choice, and joy is the gift.

ROBIN GALLAHER BRANCH

Homiletical Perspective

teacher, I suspect that seminarians recognize that to proclaim loudly and proudly that they are wicked and joyful in their wickedness could be a distinct C.L.M. (career-limiting move). Yet that open acknowledgment and confession—to confess openly our wickedness, our sin and sinfulness, our weakness in the face of sin—are indeed the doorway to forgiveness that has been opened for us. On the other hand, "steadfast love surrounds those who trust in the LORD" (v. 10). In a culture that thrives on being "one up," this psalm is bad news, is countercultural, is threatening to the core. It is disheartening to hear preachers bludgeoning their hearers with their bombastic exhortation to confess their sins, or else . . . or else what? Or else they will be condemned to the eternal fires.

However that is what those hearers are in already when they hide and deny their sinfulness. They are living in their own private hell, constantly in the fear of being found out, lying to others and, even worse, to themselves in order to cover up. Endless distractions are employed to divert their attention from the obvious. Yet the psalmist testifies that the way out of the prison is not denial but confession. Confession is the open doorway to freedom and reconciliation. It is a gift, not an obligation. Imagine having the opportunity to rid one's self of those crushing burdens that weigh heavily on every aspect of one's being. The psalmist knows now that this opportunity exists and wants others to know it as well. In a culture driven by competition, instant gratification, the quest for perfection, and looking out for number one, this psalm offers a world-changing direction.

The preacher will need to make this opportune gift as vivid and compelling as the problems, difficulties, and misdirections that occasioned its need in the first place. Otherwise we, the hearers, will remain stuck in the mire. In these dark, grim, penitential days of Lent, this psalm reorients us to the joy and release that Easter makes possible.

RICHARD C. STERN

2 Corinthians 5:16-21

¹⁶From now on, therefore, we regard no one from a human point of view; even though we once knew Christ from a human point of view, we know him no longer in that way. ¹⁷So if anyone is in Christ, there is a new creation: everything old has passed away; see, everything has become new! ¹⁸All this is from God, who reconciled us to himself through Christ, and has given us the ministry of reconciliation; ¹⁹that is, in Christ God was reconciling the world to himself, not counting their trespasses against them, and entrusting the message of reconciliation to us. ²⁰So we are ambassadors for Christ, since God is making his appeal through us; we entreat you on behalf of Christ, be reconciled to God. ²¹For our sake he made him to be sin who knew no sin, so that in him we might become the righteousness of God.

Theological Perspective

Whether apocryphal or not, there is a splendid story that illustrates the centrality of this Lenten text. It is reported that Karl Barth was once asked what he would say to Adolf Hitler if he ever had the chance to meet the monster who was destroying Europe and who would ruin the whole world if he were not stopped. Barth's interlocutor assumed that he would offer a scorching prophetic judgment against the miscreant's awful politics of destruction. Barth replied, instead, that he would do nothing other than quote Romans 5:8: "While we still were sinners, Christ died for us." Only the unparalleled mercy and forgiveness of God, the unstinted gladness and grace of the gospel, could have prompted the Führer's genuine repentance. To have accused him, though justly, of his manifold abominations would have prompted Hitler's self-righteous defense, his angry justification of his allegedly "necessary" deeds.

If I were brought to a similar pass, I would hope to have the presence of mind to utter these words: "God was in Christ reconciling the world to himself, not counting their trespasses against them, and entrusting to us the message of reconciliation. . . . We beseech you on behalf of Christ, be reconciled to God" (2 Cor. 5:19–20 RSV). The key to this grandest of affirmations may well lie at the beginning of our appointed text. There Paul declares that he will no

Pastoral Perspective

Peter never gets credit for his intelligence. The Gospel writers go out of their way to make him into an idiot. Perhaps this is what happens when you associate with Jesus. You are never the smart one. As far as I am concerned, Peter delivered the definitive line about Paul's letters when he wrote, "There are some things in them hard to understand" (2 Pet. 3:16).

Today we have an example from the Second Letter to the Corinthians on the Fourth Sunday in Lent: "So if anyone is in Christ, there is a new creation; everything old has passed away; see, everything has become new!" (5:17).

Not only is this statement hard to understand; it is hard to swallow once you do—once you can handle Paul's cosmology, once you comprehend how he thinks the world collapsed in Christ's coming and a whole new one sprang up in its place.

"If anyone is in Christ, there is a new creation." It is a beautiful statement—and impossible to preach. The trouble hangs on the "anyone." If anyone is in Christ, there is a new creation—a whole new creation. Everything old has passed away; everything has become new—if anyone is in Christ.

Rhetorically, the promise seems clear: if one person trusts, if one person is in Christ, if one person is an ambassador for Christ, if one person is reconciled to God. Everything hangs on the "if."

Exegetical Perspective

One of the wonderful invitations of Lent is to think of Christ both in his human nature and also in his divine nature. Of course the incarnation of God's reconciling love in Christ cannot be easily teased apart as if it were some kind of layered material. This fabric is woven seamlessly. Yet the text before us bids us consider how this human/divine love makes any kind of difference for us. What can possibly capture us in Lent as completely as it did Paul?

"For the love of Christ urges us on, because we are convinced that one has died for all; therefore all have died. And he died for all, so that those who live might live no longer for themselves, but for him who died and was raised for them" (5:14–15). This is the message of Lent that captures us. Its radical implications beg for a truthful living today.

Those in Christ no longer regard or evaluate people on the basis of their resume, their accomplishments, their position, or their influence (v. 16). If the love of Christ controls us, then we are free to be open and accepting of others on the basis of seeing them through the eyes of Christ, the One who gave himself for everyone. Old standards of judgment such as race, social status, wealth, prestige, and title are obsolete, null and void (cf. Gal. 3:28).

As an example, Paul mentions that he himself had previously evaluated Jesus in terms of his worldly

Homiletical Perspective

Over the past couple of weeks in Lent (esp. Lent 2 and 3), we have seen the focus of Paul's letters concentrating on life as it is lived in community, on the baptismal identity of the people of God. The community that is the church is being invited into a baptismal discipline. Here, then, is our Lenten discipline: not giving up chocolate or skipping lunch, but living into a broad and generous communal vision. All of the spiritual exercises we invent may be good in themselves, but none of them assures us of spiritual perfection or even finding ourselves "right" with God. The Lenten discipline that the epistles for Lent propose directs us away from ourselves, from our own preoccupations, to the God who is present in community.

The reading from 2 Corinthians 5 takes this proposal even further. If there is one word that seems to capture this reading, it is "broadening." Our vision is expanded. The text concerns how we look at our neighbor, and even the world, as a new creation.

The movement we engage is called the "ministry of reconciliation." We become ambassadors of this broadening generosity of the gospel to the world. Paul pushes the community of believers to understand their baptismal vocation as this ministry, a diaconal work of reconciliation. The question posed to the early church and to our churches as

2 Corinthians 5:16-21

Theological Perspective

longer look upon any other person from a human standpoint, just as he has learned to behold Christ himself as the incarnate God, not simply as a Nazarene rabbi. For once we have discerned Jesus to be the Savior of the world, we cannot limit our estimate of other human beings—the born or unborn, exploiters or murderers, terrorists or militarists, frauds or failures—as dwelling beyond his reach. We cannot see any person as anything other than a creature for whom Christ has died and risen, and thus as one meant also to become "a new creation."

Hans Urs von Balthasar, in his splendid little treatise titled *Dare We Hope That All Men Be Saved?* argues that if we deny this hope, then we have no right to confidence in our own salvation.[1] To give up hope for any other person, no matter how wretched their condition may be, is also to give up hope for ourselves. How can we presuppose our own final deliverance from human wretchedness into divine worthiness, while assuming that others cannot be similarly saved? Balthasar also points out that at no time or place in its entire history has the church declared anyone to be definitively damned—not even Judas. By contrast, it has declared many souls to be definitively saved, though not of course presuming on the final judgment of God. Hebrews 11 is the relevant text, with its superb "roll call of the saints," including even Rahab the harlot.

Saints are those who live in the new dispensation, the new epoch, the new creation, since the old eon has ended. In the strict sense, therefore, Christians do not look for the end times, despite the immense popularity of the *Left Behind* novels. We are already living in the final age, the one inaugurated by Christ's life and teaching, his death and resurrection. The kingdom of God is already in our midst, eagerly yearning for its completion. It is thus not quite right to speak of postearthly existence as "life after death." As N. T. Wright observes in his sprightly book called *Simply Christian,* Christians are those who are already living "after death," since Christ has raised us from the grave. We ought more properly to speak of the world to come as "life after life after death."

It is important to notice that God has not reconciled himself to the world, but rather that he has reconciled the world to himself. God does not change. God is the One with whom "there is no shadow of turning" (Jas. 1:17 KJV). Precisely because God is beyond alteration, he can radically transfigure

1. Hans Urs von Balthasar, *Dare We Hope That All Men Will Be Saved?* trans. David Kipp and Lothar Krauth (San Francisco: Ignatius, 1988).

Pastoral Perspective

If the promise hangs on the "if," it turns on the "then"—and it is a big "then." Truthfully, it is the "then'" that is hard to swallow: then, there is a new creation. This promise is extraordinary. New creation is not the sort of weak political catchphrase you throw around. New creation is not "Family Values" or "Green Energy." When Paul employs the phrase elsewhere (which he does only once), he writes: "A new creation is everything" (Gal. 6:15b).

John of Patmos writes about it too, with the same ring of everything:

> Then I saw a new heaven and a new earth; for the first heaven and the first earth had passed away, and the sea was no more. And I saw the holy city, the new Jerusalem, coming down out of heaven from God, prepared as a bride adorned for her husband. And I heard a loud voice from the throne saying,
>
> > "See, the home of God is among mortals.
> > He will dwell with them as their God;
> > they will be his peoples,
> > and God himself will be with them;
> > he will wipe every tear from their eyes.
> > Death will be no more;
> > mourning and crying and pain will be no more,
> > for the first things have passed away."
>
> And the one who was seated on the throne said, "See, I am making all things new." (Rev. 21:1–5a)

All this happens, Paul suggests, if anyone is in Christ.

Pastorally, though, we see the anyones. We have a sanctuary full of anyones—of anyones who trust, of anyones who ache for a new creation, of anyones who live in Christ. We rarely see the new creation, though.

Paul is not just hard to understand; he is hard to swallow as well.

Perhaps Paul's cosmology was confused. Christians have occasionally experienced confusion as a symptom of the Holy Spirit. Perhaps Paul was so wrapped up in the grace of God that he changed, that he was transformed, made new. Perhaps this passage is the preacher preaching to himself. It is because Paul is in Christ that there is a new creation. Everything old to him is now new—mourning and crying and pain are no more. A life of persecuting Christians has given way to a life of pursuing Christ, the persecution doubling back on him hardly a concern. When grace unlevels Christians like this, they find themselves singing in a jail cell like Paul. Everything is now oriented from a God-drenched

status. However when he came to know Christ as Lord, it transformed the foundation of how he viewed himself and others. This new perspective even changed the way he understood who Jesus was. Paul came to know Jesus as the risen Lord, the One who gave himself for all.

The implications of this are stated in verse 17: "So if anyone is in Christ, there is a new creation: everything old has passed away; see, everything has become new!" This transformation that alters our standards of judgment is nothing other than a new creation, a new order of existence. Paul's favorite way to express this new reality is simply to say that we are "in Christ." This is a new creation that relegates to the past the old things like class and prejudices, stereotypes and misconceptions. Such old realities are not part of this new existence in Christ. The perfect tense is used to express the continuing and ongoing nature of this transformation: "the old things became and continue to be new." The old is finished. The new creation has overthrown our human judgments filled with prejudice and bias. The gospel challenges the assumption that human nature cannot change by stating that God can indeed achieve such a transformation in Christ. This is the incredible glory of what Lent suggests is in fact possible. No longer are we held sway by the powers that would destroy us. In Christ we are fully free to experience this grace that created a new humanity, one responsive to the vision of God to bring creation home.

Verses 18–20 form the heart of this text: "All this is from God, who reconciled us to himself through Christ, and has given us the ministry of reconciliation; that is, in Christ God was reconciling the world to himself, not counting their trespasses against them, and entrusting the message of reconciliation to us. So we are ambassadors for Christ, since God is making his appeal through us; we entreat you on behalf of Christ, be reconciled to God." The basic meaning of the word "reconcile" is to make otherwise or to alter. Interestingly, the word is used in the New Testament only by Paul. He uses it to describe the relation between God and humans. The verb "to reconcile" is used only of God's acts. We ourselves are the ones who become reconciled to God. God is the initiator and author of reconciliation, the remover of that which estranges us from God.

Thus our very existence becomes altered in light of the death and resurrection of Jesus. Such graciousness works a decisive change. We are no

well is whether this sign of hope—this ferment of God's peace in the ministry of reconciliation—is central to the life of the community in the place where it is located.

Looking at others. This theme has been present over the past few Sundays. Here Paul reminds us that we look at one another not from our own narrow perspective (Do I like him? Do I agree with her? Oh, he gets on my nerves. She bugs me.). Rather, we are called to look at one another through the waters of baptism. In the community of the church, we look at our pilgrim companions as new creations—not looking at the old—for all have been made new through baptism. Paul adds: "All this is from God" (5:18). We are challenged to discover in the other the call and gift of God.

This new perspective is possible because God has already worked, so to speak, to reconcile us with Godself and with one another. If we translate this reconciliation to life in community, it means that we as individuals are not required through our own work or ingenious methods to "form" or "build" a community. No, the community, the new creation in Christ, already exists. The challenge posed to each and every community is discovering the presence of God already active, already acting in the lives of each member.

Ministry of reconciliation. This discovery is the source of the ministry of reconciliation. Of course, reconciliation goes hand in hand with forgiveness. We are reconciled because we know ourselves to be forgiven. Already the intention of that sometimes impossible gesture of forgiveness—or the desire to live forgiveness in one's heart without being able to speak it in words—opens up a way for the world to hear the good news of reconciliation.

Archbishop Desmond Tutu wrote, "Without forgiveness there can be no future for a relationship between individuals or within and between nations."[1] The call to reconciliation and forgiveness is not a small matter or one that we can easily dismiss. Those who, like Archbishop Tutu, Mother Teresa of Calcutta, or Brother Roger of Taizé, have engaged this path know that the future depends on this ministry. The future for individuals, for nations, for humanity, and for the earth will depend not on staking claims, not on protecting "our" rights, not in guarding boundaries, not in waging war, but in this difficult discipline of reconciling forgiveness.

---

1. "Truth and Reconciliation," BBC *Focus on Africa*, January–March 2000, 53.

2 Corinthians 5:16-21

Theological Perspective

his sin-wrecked world. He does so, among other ways, by means of Christ's atoning death. Paul declares that God subjected the sinless Christ to the whole burden of human sinfulness in order that such crushing weight be lifted from us. The distinction between Sin in the singular and sins in the plural is enormous. The word "sins" describes the many evils, whether great or small, that we commit because we inhabit the ancestral state of "Sin" spelled in the upper case. Sin is our disease, our utter alienation from God. Luther likened it to leprosy, noting that this dread illness cannot be cured "pustule by pustule." Christ's saving sacrifice on the cross is thus the remedy for the contagion of evil. Rather than having us strive vainly to overcome this or that failing (i.e., individual sins), we are meant to become God's own righteousness—his reformed and transformed people called the body of Christ.

This body consists of "ambassadors for Christ." As emissaries and envoys of the gospel, we are not saddled with a dour duty but given the greatest of all honors. My own ministerial exemplar in things Christian, the late Warren Carr, confessed to being troubled by a phrase used by many preachers—namely, that they have "surrendered" to the ministry. The implied assumption, he noted, is that their lives were going swimmingly well until they had to give it all up for something heavy and burdensome. Carr confessed that it was exactly the other way around for him. As a young hellion on the road to misery and destruction, he found himself astonished at the idea that he too might become a proclaimer of this best of all tidings. Figuratively speaking, he took out running after God, chasing him down and grabbing him by the shoulder, asking whether he too might partake of so glad a calling. So too, we are meant not to be dragged reluctantly into God's kingdom, but rather to embrace its ambassadorial call as the unsurpassable privilege.

RALPH C. WOOD

Pastoral Perspective

point of view, even though they once saw everything from a human one. They start describing whole new worlds, worlds that are conceived in imagination, but birthed by lives of faithful discipleship.

In many Christian communities today, the imagination has become impoverished, atrophied, sick, kaput. New creation, however, is conceived in imagination—and imagination begins in prayer, in the images that God plants within us. Prayer, of course, begins in holy silence. When pastors stop talking and start listening, when congregations begin to interpret the subtle movements in their hearts and spirits, then churches will start to hear the call of the new creation. They will stop seeing the world from a human point of view; they will start seeing it with the eyes of Christ.

What marvelous visions await. In prayer, the church can see a world where death and pain and mourning are no more; a world free from addictions; a world where mothers and daughters, fathers and sons, find love where there was mistrust; a world where marriages are joys instead of burdens; a world where everyone has a decent place to live; a world where children can be taught in safety by teachers who do not cry themselves to sleep; a world where people do not suffer in pain because medication is too costly; a world where women are not coerced into lives they cannot bear; a world where children do not settle wars that men create; a world where imagination is as powerful as market indicators and machine guns; a world where everything becomes new by an act of faith, the act of trusting that the futures God whispers to the church can be brought into being.

These visions of a new creation are born when the church listens to God, but this is impractical. Christians cannot have "productive" prayer. If they choose to be silent for twenty minutes a day, they will have 10 percent more clutter in their house. They will not read every op-ed piece in the newspaper. Their dogs will wonder what is wrong with them. However the task of the Christian is not to be effective or to get things done. It is to be faithful. Because mountains are not moved by logistical wizardry, but by faith, and if there is going to be a new creation, some of the mountains will have to go.

CASEY THOMPSON

Exegetical Perspective

longer estranged, at odds, and hostile to God. When we accept it, God's love makes us God's children, God's friends. The basis of such a renewal is that Jesus took upon himself all that estranges us from God. In doing so, he makes it possible for us to experience a new relationship with God based upon trust and love. So transformative is this new relationship that we are now asked to become the visible expressions of this new reality to our world. This ministry of reconciliation awakens us to God's love so that our lives proclaim it. While we are the recipients of this divine love, we also become the agents of God who passionately exhort others to know it for themselves.

Such work can only be called "ministry." It is a ministry of offering to the world that which Christ has given to us—reconciliation. As those who bear witness to this new possibility in Christ, we are its authorized agents, its ambassadors who speak on behalf of their sovereign. This season of the church year, with all its somber occasions to reflect upon the deeper meaning of the cross, still reverberates with powerful and joyful news. The work of Christ was done "for our sake" (v. 21). It was with a view for our well-being that Christ gave himself for us. The good news is not ours to hoard; it is ours to share, to give away, and to live. God's sacrificial love in Christ is an eternal invitation to respond to such grace with faith and also faithfulness. Lent asks each of us to become its ambassador with the invitation: "Be reconciled to God!"

MARK E. HOPPER

Homiletical Perspective

Brother Roger of Taizé embodied this vision of reconciliation in the community he founded at Taizé. Early on he wrote in *The Rule of Taizé*, "Never resign yourself to the scandal of the separation of Christians, all who so readily confess love for their neighbor, and yet remain divided. Be consumed with burning zeal for the unity of the Body of Christ."[2] Brother Roger called the division among Christians a scandal, something that continually divides the body of Christ. The division of Christians nails Jesus back onto the cross.

Of course the ministry of reconciliation has an ecumenical thrust, but it also begins at home, in oneself, in the local church community. Brother Roger did not write that a "scandal" exists because we confess love for God but remain divided. The scandal, he wrote, is that we confess love for our *neighbor* and yet remain divided. It is too easy to say we love God and go about our daily business as if nothing had changed. We cannot say we love our neighbors and not help them in their distress.

Paul opens up for us in this reading a way toward this love of neighbor. The movement of love, the ministry of reconciliation, does not come out of our own strength, nor does it depend on our own effort. God has cleared the way, so to speak, by reconciling all to Godself and inviting us into this large, generous, broad vision of humanity and creation.

We become the "righteousness of God" through the encounter with Christ in the other, in the neighbor, in the person sitting next to me or in front of me or behind me in the pew, in the person standing in the street, in the beggar, in the refugee, in all those calling for help. As ambassadors, we are called out into the street (ambassadors do not stay in their own countries!). The community of believers in every local community is called to live out its baptismal vocation, to become a ferment of hope in the place God has given it, letting God's future break into the world.

DIRK G. LANGE

2. Brother Roger, *The Rule of Taizé* (Taizé: Les Presses de Taizé, 1961), 14–16.

Luke 15:1-3, 11b–32

¹Now all the tax collectors and sinners were coming near to listen to him. ²And the Pharisees and the scribes were grumbling and saying, "This fellow welcomes sinners and eats with them."

³So he told them this parable: . . . ¹¹ᵇ"There was a man who had two sons. ¹²The younger of them said to his father, 'Father, give me the share of the property that will belong to me.' So he divided his property between them. ¹³A few days later the younger son gathered all he had and traveled to a distant country, and there he squandered his property in dissolute living. ¹⁴When he had spent everything, a severe famine took place throughout that country, and he began to be in need. ¹⁵So he went and hired himself out to one of the citizens of that country, who sent him to his fields to feed the pigs. ¹⁶He would gladly have filled himself with the pods that the pigs were eating; and no one gave him anything. ¹⁷But when he came to himself he said, 'How many of my father's hired hands have bread enough and to spare, but here I am dying of hunger! ¹⁸I will get up and go to my father, and I will say to him, "Father, I have sinned against heaven and before you; ¹⁹I am no longer worthy to be called your son; treat me like one of your hired hands."' ²⁰So he set off and went to his father. But while he was still far off, his father saw him and was filled with compassion; he ran and put his arms around him and kissed him. ²¹Then the

Theological Perspective

If the previous section of Luke's Gospel (12:54–13:9) emphasized the urgent need to repent in response to Jesus' message, this series of parables (15:1–32)—of which the story of the prodigal son is the conclusion—offers an insight into how the sinner's *metanoia* is received by God. The context must not be overlooked. The Pharisees and scribes persist in their grumbling as sinners and tax collectors continue to respond positively to Jesus' preaching (vv. 1–2). Speaking more broadly, these "lost and found" allegories are best read in light of Jesus' announcement of "the acceptable year of the Lord," the proclamation he made in Nazareth at the start of his ministry (4:18–19 RSV).

The prospect of releasing captives was indeed good news for those who saw their own story played out in the life of the prodigal son. Here was a young man whose very existence epitomized the depths of sin that most of us know so well, whether we choose to admit it or not. The younger son personifies what appears to be a universal human perception, that worse than death is the feeling of being lost, especially when this condition has been brought on by one's own lust, greed, or arrogance.

In a short time the prodigal son manages to turn his back on his family, forsake the familiarity of his homeland, and lose sight of his religious heritage (as

Pastoral Perspective

In J. R. R. Tolkien's fictional Middle-earth, the diminutive, hairy-footed people known as hobbits have an interesting custom. On a hobbit's birthday, he or she does not receive gifts from family and friends. Instead, the birthday-celebrating hobbit presents gifts—and perhaps throws a party—for all of his or her family and friends. At first blush, this may appear an unappealing practice. "What? *My* birthday and *I* go to the trouble and expense of gifts and a party for everyone else? This is supposed to be *my* day to celebrate and be celebrated!" However stop and consider what this means in terms of the total number of birthday gifts and parties a hobbit participates in every year. Instead of celebrating a birthday—"my birthday"—only once a year, the hobbit celebrates birthdays many times a year, in fact on each and every day a loved one has a birthday.

Their birthday custom suggests the hobbits might understand very keenly the famous story we usually call the parable of the Prodigal Son. As Jesus tells it, a prosperous landowner has two sons. The younger cannot wait until Daddy dies before he gets his inheritance. Despite the insult, the father gives the younger son his share of the family property. The youngest runs off to some first-century Las Vegas, squanders it all, and ends up eating beans and mush alongside the hogs he is reduced to feeding. Then he

son said to him, 'Father, I have sinned against heaven and before you; I am no longer worthy to be called your son.' ²²But the father said to his slaves, 'Quickly, bring out a robe—the best one—and put it on him; put a ring on his finger and sandals on his feet. ²³And get the fatted calf and kill it, and let us eat and celebrate; ²⁴for this son of mine was dead and is alive again; he was lost and is found!' And they began to celebrate.

²⁵"Now his elder son was in the field; and when he came and approached the house, he heard music and dancing. ²⁶He called one of the slaves and asked what was going on. ²⁷He replied, 'Your brother has come, and your father has killed the fatted calf, because he has got him back safe and sound.' ²⁸Then he became angry and refused to go in. His father came out and began to plead with him. ²⁹But he answered his father, 'Listen! For all these years I have been working like a slave for you, and I have never disobeyed your command; yet you have never given me even a young goat so that I might celebrate with my friends. ³⁰But when this son of yours came back, who has devoured your property with prostitutes, you killed the fatted calf for him!' ³¹Then the father said to him, 'Son, you are always with me, and all that is mine is yours. ³²But we had to celebrate and rejoice, because this brother of yours was dead and has come to life; he was lost and has been found.'"

Exegetical Perspective

The very familiar parable of the Prodigal Son is the last in a series of three parables that portray God as seeking out that which is lost. The two others are the parables of the Lost Sheep (15:4–7) and the Lost Coin (15:8–10). The beginning of chapter 15 states that Jesus told these three stories in response to a complaint raised by the Pharisees and scribes concerning Jesus' penchant of associating with people known to be sinners. The parables attempt to show that Jesus had no other choice than to seek the lost.

There are three principal characters in the story of the prodigal son: a father and his two sons. The actions of each are significant. The parable begins by relating the shameful actions of the younger son toward his father. Not only does the younger son reject the value of family solidarity, but he demands his inheritance before his father's death, which is a gross insult to the father. Surprisingly, the father does not exercise his patriarchal authority by demanding that his younger son give up his plans. The older son is silent. Apparently, he does not object to his brother's shameful demands and his father's acquiescence.

The inheritance that the younger son demanded would have been a portion of the family's land holdings. After presumably selling the land, he left home and used the money from the sale to support a

Homiletical Perspective

It is sometimes interesting to look at the entire text of a poem that became a hymn, since there can be surprises in the original version. Such was my experience when I read the full text of Frederick Faber's hymn "There's a wideness in God's mercy." I have been singing that hymn as long as I can remember. "There's a wideness in God's mercy, like the wideness of the sea. There's a kindness in his justice, which is more than liberty."

The hymn speaks of "welcome for the sinner" and "graces for the good." It speaks of "plentiful redemption" and "the sweetness of the Lord." Those stanzas are in most hymnals, but often left out are the stanzas that say:

But we make His love too narrow
By false limits of our own;
And we magnify His strictness
With a zeal He will not own.

Was there ever kinder shepherd
Half so gentle, half so sweet,
As the Savior who would have us
Come and gather at His feet?

Such a vision of the vastness and depth of the love, grace, compassion, and justice of God lies behind Jesus' parable of the Prodigal Son. This

Luke 15:1-3, 11b–32

Theological Perspective

suggested by his intimate knowledge of the swine pen). Devoid of these most basic relationships, he becomes in effect a nonperson. However his is not an experience utterly without hope, for he is still by grace able to utter the single word with which his entire misadventure began: "Father."

Grace lies at the heart of this parable—scandalous grace, grace that defies all earthly rules and conventions. Identifying too closely with the younger son, we risk neglecting the central point of the story: the extraordinary love of the father, who runs to greet his child "while he was still far off." We get the sense here that the spurned parent was in fact keeping vigil, praying for the day his boy would return. Like a shepherd searching for a lost sheep or a woman rummaging for her misplaced coin, the father remained hopeful that the seeds he had once sown in love might yet be harvested in the return of his child.

The economy of such love and grace surprises, even offends, us in its extravagance. While the ways of the world suggest that yes, the son might be welcomed home, but reasonably so—on a ration of bread and water in answer to his deplorable sin—the economy of God is such that rejoicing for the return of a child is simply not enough. Joy must be made all the more complete by abundance: the best robe, the finest ring, the fatted calf. This is the amazing thing about grace, that while we remain bound in both body and soul to Adam's sin, the Spirit of God enables us to utter the word of salvation—"Father"—and God runs out to meet us in the person of his Son. As we once perceived that being lost was a fate worse than death, we can now proclaim in faith that greater than life itself is living with the knowledge that we have been found. The response of God to all of this is unbridled rejoicing.

There is still the figure of the elder son to consider, the ostensibly faithful child who remained at home and "slaved" for his father while his younger brother squandered his inheritance on libidinous excess. Though the context suggests that Jesus' reference to the elder brother was for the benefit of some Pharisees and scribes who disapproved of his associations with so many undesirables, we would do well not to overemphasize the distinction between Gentiles and Jews implied in this parable, which has been typical of theological commentary on this text throughout the centuries. It is perhaps better for us to attend to the way we can so easily resonate with the older son's point of view. Indeed, not to do so would suggest a kind of antinomianism, a belief that

Pastoral Perspective

decides that he might return home—even if his father will not take him back as a son and treats him like a hired hand, it will be better than this.

So home he goes. He is braced for humiliation. However as he comes over the hill in sight of his hometown, his father runs to greet him with open arms. The prodigal cannot even launch into the groveling speech about how he deserves nothing more than hired-hand status—the one he has rehearsed over many weeks and many miles—before the old man is wrapping him in the household's finest robe and putting a ring on his finger. It is the royal treatment, literally.[1] Before he can blink the tears out of his eyes, a fatted calf has been killed and most of the town has been invited into a spectacular party. It is a shindig of, well, biblical proportions.

For us Plain Earth folks, the story would be perfectly satisfying if it ended right there. It would seem that Jesus wants to tell us that the kingdom of God is like a birthday party. You or I or he or she comes back to God, and God celebrates a return for each of us. Not too shabby. However Jesus does not stop the story here. At this juncture he brings the elder son back into the picture—and big brother is miffed. He has not insulted his father. He has not shot his inheritance on prostitutes and good times. He has just slaved away, day after day, year after year, and his father has never even tossed a goat-party for him and a few of his buddies. He is mad. He will not set foot in that big, raucous, rich bash—you can hear the music and the festive noise from out here in the north forty!—now going on around his ingrate brother.

In Plain Earth terms, we can relate to the elder brother. He has been responsible, he has behaved well, he has prudently kept his inheritance secure. Little brother, meanwhile, has sinned profligately and enjoyed it, and for his "punishment," he is getting the party of the year. Does big brother not have a right to at least a little resentment?

In the story as Jesus tells it, the father does not berate and get all censorious with the elder brother. Nor does he defend the younger brother. Instead, he shifts attention away from both of the brothers. The father turns attention to his own love and bounty. There is plenty to go around, he says in so many words. No one will run short—"all that is mine is yours" (15:31). This is not your younger brother's party so much as it is *my* party, the party I throw for many. I am on the lookout for all my loved ones,

---

1. See Kenneth E. Bailey, *Poet and Peasant*, in *Poet and Peasant; Through Peasant Eyes*, combined ed. (Grand Rapids: Eerdmans, 1983), 182–85.

disgraceful lifestyle. Jesus' audience would have been shocked as much by the presumed sale of the land as they would have been by the son's squandering of the proceeds from the sale. It was not just a question of a land-based economy, which led Jewish families to hold on to the ancestral lands. It was also a question of religious belief, since Jews considered their ancestral land holdings to be God's gift to their families.

The crisis on which the story turns is a famine that struck the foreign land where the younger son was living. Because he squandered his wealth, he had no resources available to help him survive the famine. To survive, the younger son humiliated himself by working for Gentiles as a swineherd. Worse than that, he could not assuage his hunger with the food he gave to unclean animals. The son believed that the only way he could survive was to return to his father's house as a hired hand. He knew that he could not reclaim his status as a son.

The setting shifted back to Palestine, and the actions of the aggrieved father were most unexpected. Usually a father who had been so shamed by the actions of his son would have disowned that son. Instead we hear that the father was waiting for his son's return. As soon as he caught sight of his son, he ran out to meet him—something a Palestinian Jewish patriarch would never have done. The father's response to his son's return—the kissing, the gift of a robe and ring, the banquet—was most out of character for someone who had been publicly shamed by his son. The feast that the father arranged for the younger son was necessary to repair the damage caused by the son to his neighbors. They would have regarded his behavior as undermining traditional values and setting a terrible example. The banquet served to ease the younger son back into the good graces of the neighbors.

While the banquet was going on, the elder son reappeared in the story. He was consumed by jealously and resentment. Just as the father reached out to his younger son who was lost, so too did he reach out to the elder son, who was in danger of becoming just as lost as his brother. The father abandoned his guests, which was a breach of etiquette, in order to persuade his older son to rejoice at his brother's return. At this point, the parable ends. We do not know if the elder son came to accept his father's response to his younger brother's return. It is as if Jesus is asking the Pharisees and the scribes if they are going to join him in reaching out to their wayward brothers and

parable points to God's deepest desire, greatest yearning, and passionate dream for all of God's children and the whole of God's creation.

We were made by God to be in loving relationship, harmony, and communion with God, each other, and all creation. Whatever else the story of Adam and Eve is about, this is a bottom-line message. As long as Adam and Eve are in loving relationship with God, each other, and creation, they are in paradise; however, when the primal relationship with God is broken, fragmented, and distorted, their relationship with each other and the rest of the creation is likewise broken, fragmented, and distorted. When all of that happens, they find themselves cast out of paradise.

It is God's dream to renew, reconcile, repair, and restore the creation; that is the magnetic power in the parable of the Prodigal Son pulling the prodigal back home. You know the story. A man has two sons. He divides the inheritance and gives each his share. I like the way the King James Version renders the younger son's behavior, saying that he squandered everything in "riotous living."

In the story things go from bad to worse, and the prodigal finds himself broke, jobless, hungry, and a long way from home. Jesus gives some indication of how far this brother was from home in a telling detail. He says that in order to work he hires himself out to some pig farmer. Moses was clear that swine are not kosher. No good Palestinian Jew would be caught dead near pigs. That is how far this guy is from home.

Then Jesus uses a marvelous turn of a phrase. Wallowing among pigs, the prodigal "came to himself." He realizes the profound discontinuity between who he has become and who he truly is. He does not have it figured out, but he knows something is not the way it is supposed to be.

He is living a nightmare when he is meant to live his father's dream. Something inside of him says, "You were not meant for this." His is the experience reflected in that old gospel song: "There is something within me that holdeth the reign, there is something within me I cannot explain. All that I know is there is something within." So he decides to go home.

The prodigal rehearses what he will say to his father. "Father, I have sinned against heaven and before you; I am no longer worthy to be called your son; treat me like one of your hired hands. . . ." He practices that refrain as he travels, but something strange and unexpected happens. The father shakes

Luke 15:1-3, 11b–32

Theological Perspective

God's grace abounds to such an extent that sin in itself is inconsequential.

Reflecting on the older son's reaction, it is instructive for those of us who have long been part of the church—who have "been with the father always"—to recognize various aspects of our own sinfulness. Pride, jealousy, anger, and self-righteousness are all the more appalling when we know that, as beneficiaries of God's grace through our baptism, we should be engaged in the rejoicing that accompanies the return of a prodigal. Yet sin mars our redemption and hinders our works of sanctification. We assume the worst in others. Like the elder son embellishing his brother's story with "prostitutes," our jealousy often compels us to exaggerate the shortcomings of those in our midst. We think first of how certain turns of events might affect us, instead of how they might benefit the well-being of the body of Christ. We cling to our tried and true ways of doing things, wishing that someone would simply acknowledge our faithfulness, if not with a "fatted calf," then at least with a "young goat." Too often we claim as our own the standards of the world, in which justice is lauded over mercy instead of the other way around.

The parable of the Prodigal Son offers an alternative perspective. It is a view from the kingdom that is often not acknowledged, much less seen clearly. Here, in contrast to "the way things should be," mercy abrogates justice, abundance trumps anger, and wayward children are welcomed home by loving parents. This is the overwhelming scandal of grace, which is cause for great rejoicing.

DANIEL G. DEFFENBAUGH

Pastoral Perspective

near or far. I am working for them and ready to celebrate with them before they even think of responding to me or giving anything back.

Behind Jesus' parable lies profound and overwhelming truth about God and God's kingdom. We humans, we all were lost, mired in sins of sensuality and greed and self-referential resentment, hip-deep in the pig slop of envy. Before we knew it, God reached out in the people Israel and then in the life and death and resurrection of Jesus. God raised us up and called us home. It is just not about you or me, or my sin or your sin, or my deserts or your deserts. It is about God and God's life-giving love and mercy.[2] Every time God's active, stretching, searching, healing love finds someone and calls that person back home, it does not mean there is less for the rest of us. It means there is more. More wine. More feasting. More music. More dancing. It means another, and now a bigger, party.

Maybe those hobbits are on to something.

RODNEY CLAPP

---

2. See Joseph A. Fitzmyer, *The Gospel of Luke X–XXIV*, Anchor Bible (Garden City, NY: Doubleday, 1983), 1084.

sisters, if they are going to rejoice with him over God's most gracious mercy, or if they, like the elder brother, will refuse to enter the banquet room, preferring to be on the outside, thinking of nothing but their resentment over the reconciliation between God and sinners that Jesus came to effect.

The reconciliation between the father and the younger son did not occur because of what the son did, but because of what the father did. Both the younger son and the father acted contrary to the expectations of first-century Jewish culture regarding the behavior of parents and their children. The younger son's flaunting of convention served his selfish purposes. The father's behavior—his dealing with the shame of having been treated so disrespectfully by his son—made it possible for reconciliation to occur. The father and younger son were reconciled as were the neighbors and the younger son. The only person who stood outside the circle of reconciliation was the elder son. The elder son's behavior was another humiliation for the father. Sons owed their fathers loyalty and obedience. The father chose to absorb the shame heaped on him by the elder brother, just as he did for the younger brother. He willingly adopted the stance of pleading with his elder son—a major humiliation for a father from the patriarchal culture of early Judaism.

Chapter 15 begins with a complaint made by the Pharisees and scribes regarding Jesus' willingness to welcome and eat with sinners. It ends with a father's welcome to his erring younger son and a plea to the elder son to join his neighbors and his younger brother for a banquet, marking the restoration of proper relations among the members of the family and the wider community. The parable ends with an implicit question: will the Pharisees and scribes join Jesus in welcoming and eating with sinners?

LESLIE J. HOPPE

off the normal restraint of a Palestinian male and breaks with the social customs defining the roles of fathers and sons. As the prodigal approaches, while he is still far off, the father runs to him, embraces him, and is "filled with compassion." So moved, this father does what few men in his culture would have done. He runs after his son and welcomes him home.

Only then does the prodigal begin his speech. He knows the Palestinian male culture and its rules. So he starts. "Father, I have sinned against heaven and before you; I am no longer worthy to be called your son." So far, so good. This is language the father will understand. The son is making an appeal within the social structure of the time, but before he can finish with the words, "Now make me one of your hired servants," the father interrupts him. Whatever the prodigal has done, he is still his father's son; he can never become his hired servant. "My son was dead, and is alive again; he was lost, and is found!"

As the story unfolds, it is clear that the parable is more about the determined, compassionate, infinite providence of God than it is about the ways of God's prodigal children. In the end, this parable points to the great embrace and deep expansive love, compassion, and justice of God, deeper, wider, and higher than our imaginings.

In *God Has a Dream*, Archbishop Desmond Tutu writes:

> I have a dream, God says. Please help Me to realize it. It is a dream of a world whose ugliness and squalor and poverty, its war and hostility, its greed and harsh competitiveness, its alienation and disharmony are changed into their glorious counterparts, when there will be more laughter, joy, and peace, where there will be justice and goodness and compassion and love and caring and sharing. I have a dream that swords will be beaten into plowshares and spears into pruning hooks, that My children will know that they are members of one family, the human family, God's family, My family.[1]

MICHAEL B. CURRY

1. Desmond Tutu, *God Has a Dream: A Vision of Hope for Our Time* (New York: Doubleday, 2004), 19–20.

Isaiah 43:16-21

¹⁶Thus says the LORD,
    who makes a way in the sea,
    a path in the mighty waters,
¹⁷who brings out chariot and horse,
    army and warrior;
    they lie down, they cannot rise,
    they are extinguished, quenched like a wick:
¹⁸Do not remember the former things,
    or consider the things of old.
¹⁹I am about to do a new thing;
    now it springs forth, do you not perceive it?
    I will make a way in the wilderness
    and rivers in the desert.
²⁰The wild animals will honor me,
    the jackals and the ostriches;
    for I give water in the wilderness,
    rivers in the desert,
    to give drink to my chosen people,
²¹   the people whom I formed for myself
    so that they might declare my praise.

Theological Perspective

In the larger section of Isaiah to which this passage belongs, the overriding concern—both of the prophet and of God's people—is their exile. They had lost everything: their land, their homes, their livelihood, their families; and, to some extent, they felt they had lost God as well. This crisis had raised the most serious of theological questions: Where was God in the midst of this great disaster? Why had God allowed this to happen? What kind of a future did the chosen people of God have now? In other words, God's fidelity, God's goodness, God's omnipotence—indeed, God's very identity—were at stake for the Hebrew people, as they questioned whether God had gone back on God's promises to be with them always.

Into this desperate situation the words of God recorded in Second Isaiah were spoken to God's people, words that are well characterized by the opening verse of Isaiah 40: "Comfort, O comfort my people, says your God." From this verse, we know that Isaiah's message to God's people will be a word of encouragement, a word of consolation, and, most importantly, a word of hope; and from the thirty-nine chapters that precede it, we know that it comes to a people in dire need of a good word from the Lord. No wonder the great Hebrew scholar Abraham Heschel calls the proclamation of Second Isaiah

Pastoral Perspective

Bodies of water serve as both barriers and conveyances of life. In an era of bridges and airplanes, when we can easily drive or fly over bodies of water, it is easy to forget the power the images had for earlier ages. The importance of water barriers is enshrined in the names of towns that end in "ford" or "ferry," and water as a means of conveyance echoes in town names that begin or end in "port." In the ancient world such images were central to the core stories of the Hebrew people.

In this passage the prophet/poet speaking for God employs the images of the sea (as barrier) and rivers (as conveyors of life). Ours is also a time when the glut of information available through a variety of sources numbs us to the power of concrete physical phenomena, especially those drawn from the natural world, to speak of spiritual truths. This text comes from a time when the prophetic and poetic sensibilities are mingled, and some of the most powerful words of God in judgment and comfort are spoken in the concrete imagery of creation. After all, who better could draw from those sources for spiritual insight than the one who spoke them into being in the first place?

The text begins with a reference to God's very identity as one "who makes a way in the sea, a path in the mighty waters" (v. 16), reminding the listener

Exegetical Perspective

The promise of restoration in the Bible finds one of its most vivid expressions in today's reading from the prophet commonly referred to as Second Isaiah (Isa. 40–55). This passage describes the salvific power of the God who saved a covenant people from slavery in Egypt. According to Second Isaiah, this God continues to work during a later age, liberating the exilic community from Babylon during the sixth century BCE. With characteristic rhetorical brilliance, the prophet declares that God is once again giving "water in the wilderness, rivers in the desert, to give drink to my chosen people" (v. 20). Those who have suffered displacement by the fall of Judah and Jerusalem will be restored to their rightful home. This "new exodus" provides the people with an immediate, concrete example of God's abiding love.

The Babylonian exile occasioned a number of responses, as various prophets came to terms with the ruptured promise that Jerusalem would never succumb to foreign invaders. In accounting for historical reality, major figures like Jeremiah and Ezekiel preached oracles of judgment against the people, claiming that the exile was fair punishment for the sins of Judah. Anyone offering a hopeful message was deemed a false prophet (e.g., Jer. 28:16, where the optimistic Hananiah is accused of speaking "rebellion against the LORD"). Yet when

Homiletical Perspective

A sermon on this text will attend to the interplay between what is new and what is old. The obvious focus of the text is found in verse 19, when YHWH says: "I am about to do a new thing."

YHWH's strong claim here recalls the dueling duet from Irving Berlin's *Annie Get Your Gun*. Frank Butler and Annie Oakley sing to teach other: "Anything you can do, I can do better. I can do anything better than you."

God trumps that: "Anything I can do, I can do better." Exodus was good. Return is better still.

God is doing a brand-new thing.

The prophet makes three major claims in moves that may suggest a structure for our sermons.

Moving on to the future. At the center of the text are the promise that God is about to do a new thing and the admonition that Israel is to be on the lookout for God's surprising action. In the context, what YHWH is promising is to bring the people home from exile so that the longings of their hearts will be answered at last.

What Judah experienced as a nation, believers may experience individually. Here the preacher may want to attend to the ways in which members of the congregation themselves feel exiled from the homes they long to see—physically, spiritually, emotionally. The

Isaiah 43:16-21

Theological Perspective

ageless, saying, "No words have ever gone further in offering comfort when the sick world cries."[1]

Indeed, this situation in which the Hebrew people found themselves is a timeless one, not because all of us today understand the experience of exile—though some of us do—but rather because we all have experienced the grim shadow of past tragedies, the way in which those ghosts of past loss, shame, and grief swirl around us and cloud our vision, preventing us from seeing anything but darkness and despair. Sudden deaths, broken relationships, bad decisions, cruelties of others, and cruelties of our own—all these things linger about us and hinder our ability both to see the future and to move into it. What's more, they also raise for us the most serious of theological questions, as they cause us to doubt the promises we have received in Jesus Christ: divine forgiveness, new life, and the love of God.

In this paralyzing situation, Isaiah's words are like a beam of light that scatters the darkness and drives away demons. Just as he did for the Hebrew people so long ago, Isaiah reminds us that our God is the God who has delivered us in the past—the God who parted the sea to lead the Israelites out of their bondage in Egypt—and who will deliver us again. Our God is the God who makes a way where there is no way, who creates streams of living water in the desolate deserts of our landscapes, bringing new life into parched, dry places. Our God is faithful to God's promises, our God does remember the covenant God has made with God's people, and our God will not, will never abandon us, no matter how bad things get.

The great Old Testament scholar Walter Brueggemann calls these words of prophecy "poetry of homecoming," rich, evocative language that uses the power of memory—looking back through the immediate situation of exile to recall the mighty deeds of God in the history of God's people—to stir up a belief in the power of God at work in the future. What God has done for you before, God will do again; hold on, trust in the Lord, and keep faith. What God has in store for you is as miraculous and satisfying as water in the wilderness.

These chapters in Isaiah, and particularly these verses in this pericope, continue to resonate with God's people almost three thousand years after they were written, precisely because we too so often find ourselves in need of a good word from the Lord; because we too so often find ourselves in crisis moments before God, wondering how God will

1. Abraham Heschel, *The Prophets* (New York: Harper & Row, 1962), 145.

Pastoral Perspective

of the intervention of God to allow the Israelite slaves to cross the barrier of the Sea of Reeds. This very same God then closes the water around the forces of Pharaoh: "they lie down, they cannot rise, they are extinguished, quenched like a wick" (v. 17). The story of the escape from slavery through the sea, told in Exodus 14, became an essential part of the identity of both the Israelites and of their God. The God of Israel is the God who makes a pathway through the barriers to freedom, whether they are constructed by Pharaoh or are natural formations like the Sea of Reeds.

What are those barriers, creations of human ingenuity or features of the natural landscape, that stand in the way of our congregation's following God's lead toward freedom? How do we as a congregation listen to the call of God away from whatever would enslave us, whether that is prosperity or poverty, success or failure, growth or decline? What could it mean for us that we follow the God who specializes in making a pathway through whatever barriers would stand in the way of the freedom of the people of God?

Then the prophet/poet makes an unusual turn. God instructs the listeners, "Do not remember the former things, or consider the things of old" (v. 18), which is very unusual, because every time the Israelites forget their history, terrible things happen. They began to worship other gods and neglected widows and orphans. Usually, the prophets encourage their listeners to remember the one who brought them out of Egypt. In fact, did not God just remind us of that fact? Why in the world would God, who keeps reminding the children of Israel of that miraculous escape through the sea, now say that such recollection is not important?

The answer comes in the very next verse. God is "about to do a new thing" (v. 19), and because of that, the imagery shifts from water as a barrier to water as a conveyor of life. The prophet/poet is asking the listener to experience the reversal that God is initiating for the sake of all creation, but the implication is that those who should be listening and responding are not. "Do you not perceive it?" the listeners are asked.

Do we perceive it? Are we prepared for the reversal that God is about to perform? Or will we, like the children of Israel, proclaim that we had it better when we were slaves? Most pastors have heard the phrase, "We've never done it that way before." These words, sometimes called the seven last words of the church, are evidence that we do not perceive

Cyrus of Persia defeated Babylon in 539 BCE, the political situation shifted. The Persian ruler issued a decree that allowed the deported community to return and rebuild. Second Isaiah writes during this later period of open possibility, and he reads the events of his day through a theological lens. He maintains that Jerusalem "has served her term" and paid "double for all her sins" (Isa. 40:2). A new reality has emerged, and God is poised to supersede all previous deeds.

This poetic unit in Isaiah 43:16–21 can be classified as a salvation oracle, introduced by the familiar "Thus says the LORD" formula (v. 16). With regard to phrasing, today's reading is marked by several active participles in Hebrew, which describe the ceaseless, miraculous work of God. If a finite verb expresses a completed action ("I *walked* to the store yesterday"), a participial form conveys ongoing action, something that is still in process ("I *am teaching* my daughter to read"). In Isaiah 43:16–21, such a feature is significant. This passage highlights the work of the Creator who intercedes within history, the God "*who makes* [not made] a way in the sea, a path in the mighty waters" (v. 16), "who brings out chariot and horse" (v. 17), and who is "about to do a new thing" (v. 19). This repeated use of participles shows the present deliverance from Babylon that is now possible and the future glory that awaits the exilic community. For Second Isaiah, earlier deeds are being gloriously replicated in the present.

The most perplexing feature of this unit is the command to the people in verse 18: "Do not remember the former things, or consider the things of old." Is the prophet actually suggesting to the people that they should forget the earlier acts of YHWH? This would seem odd, since Second Isaiah takes great pride in past instances of divine intervention (e.g., 43:9). The prophet's historical context helps us solve this exegetical dilemma. Since the monarchy had collapsed and a number of Judah's citizens had been carted away, many believers would have understood displacement to be a permanent state. Divine rescue might have occurred in the distant past, but a "new exodus" seemed unlikely. To such logic, Second Isaiah responds that the Lord is offering a fresh beginning. This God acts with urgency: "I am about to do a *new* thing; *now* it springs forth" (v. 19, emphasis added). The prophet does *not* want his listeners to forget the earlier acts of deliverance, since he uses them to inspire listeners. In verses 19–21, he alludes to the wilderness wanderings described in the book of Numbers, but his point is not historical recollection.

last line of Isaac Watts's hymn "My Shepherd Will Supply My Need" catches a universal longing: "No more a stranger or a guest, but like a child at home."

Remembering the past. Yet, strikingly, the only way the prophet can describe what is new is by remembering what is old. "Do not remember the old days," he says and then describes YHWH's past acts in ways that are, simply, unforgettable: "Thus says the LORD, who makes a way in the sea, a path in the mighty waters" (v. 16). Isaiah calls for his people not to long for the old exodus, but they can only begin their renunciation by recollection.

For our people too, the way to hope may lie through memory. Preach about the past that is past keeping, but preach about it kindly. Do not just order people to move on; help them on the way.

Every pastor knows that the only way through grief is to go *through* grief, and the only way to move ahead is to name what must be left behind.

Reversing the past. When Isaiah comes to portray the future hope for God's people, he draws on the memories and images from the past, and then simply reverses them. In the first exodus, God made a path through the sea and brought the dry land out of the depth of the waters. In the new exodus, God will make a path through dry land and make water spring forth in the desert: "I will make a way in the wilderness and rivers in the desert" (v. 19).

Anything God can do, God can do better, and backwards and upside down as well.

The preacher helps move the people toward a hope that cannot entirely be described save for the claim that it will be different from last year's hope and that of the year before. In the past, the exodus was God's new thing; in the future, the return from exile will be God's new thing. Isaiah predicts different performances by the same actors, different dramas by the same author.

Our passage preserves the delicate balance between providence and grace. Of course the past was in God's hands, and its benefits are not to be denied. The future will not look like the past, or it will look like the past radically reshaped. Looking back at what has been, we move ahead to what will be—confident in the mercy of God, trusting God's faithfulness, assuming surprise.

Doxology. The oracle ends in the promise of doxology. YHWH's promise to the people is that they will live and prosper to praise YHWH. The

Isaiah 43:16-21

Theological Perspective

reveal Godself and come to us. Thus, what is at stake in this text is the same thing that is at stake for us in our relationship with God today, and that is our very faith. Can we still believe in a good God when awful things have happened to us? Can we still trust that God will be faithful to us, even when God seems absent? Finally, can we hope that God is still at work in our lives, creating a future for us where no future seems possible?

Isaiah, of course, speaks a word from the Lord that answers all these questions in the affirmative, and in so doing, he restores the people's faith in their God and encourages them to believe and hope beyond what they can see, beyond what they can envision for themselves. Because, in fact, these verses are a testimony to the identity of YHWH, the one true God, the Lord of heaven and earth. Here in this passage in particular, Isaiah shows us that God is a God of the future—and not just any future, but a future full of hope and promise. God is the one who brings hope out of desperation, day out of night, and joy out of mourning. God makes a way where there is no way, and God leads us into a bright future that we are able neither to see nor to create for ourselves.

In this season of Lent especially, as we walk the road to Jerusalem and the cross with Jesus Christ, entering further and further into the coming darkness with each week, we too do well to remember this promise of Isaiah and the fidelity of God. In the face of the terrible events of Jesus' betrayal and crucifixion, God not only will raise Jesus from the dead, but will raise us into new life as well—a life with more promise and joy than we ever could have imagined.

KRISTIN JOHNSTON LARGEN

Pastoral Perspective

the new thing that God is doing now. Are we so comfortable in our present self-understanding that we are unable to perceive what God is doing in our midst? Is there a difference between remembering the God who leads us to freedom and clinging to past practices that continue to enslave us?

God is once again going to provide a pathway, this time through the wilderness. (Think of the wildernesses in the lives of your own congregation.) God's new thing will spring forth like rivers that water the desert. Water will once again be a source of life, rather than a barrier. There will be water to drink, to irrigate fields, and to water livestock. The prophet/poet speaks of a God who will cut a path through the water when it gets in the way of the divine call to freedom, and will use water as a pathway through the wilderness of the world toward the new thing that is God's yearning for a beloved (if disobedient) people.

The rivers of water are not intended for humans alone, but for the jackals and the ostriches as well (v. 20a). These are not common creatures, so we might be led to believe that these streams of waters are intended for even the most dangerous and outlandish of God's creatures. We are even told that these wild creatures will honor God for the water that is provided to preserve their lives. Humans could take a lesson from such beasts, the prophet/poet is trying to emphasize.

The chosen of God are offered this way and this source of life for the same reason as the wild beasts. The goal of freedom and new life is to offer praise to the God who provided them in the first place. Has God provided our congregation with a pathway through the wilderness of our world? How will we respond?

MICHAEL E. WILLIAMS

Exegetical Perspective

He suggests that all necessities will be provided in the present and future ("I give water in the wilderness," v. 20), because of the ongoing faithfulness of God. For those who had grown comfortable with life in Babylon, this passage points them toward a necessary return. For those who despaired of ever going home, the message is a hopeful one. By alluding to the earlier exodus and wanderings in verses 19–21, Second Isaiah urges the people to be courageous in envisioning a similar event, a safe passage.

This famous unit is often read by Christians during the season of Lent. This is appropriate, since the poetry in Isaiah 40–55 addresses both anguish and anticipation, human culpability and redemption. Like the Gospel writers and Paul, this prophet refers thoughtfully and reverently to authoritative traditions like the exodus, but he is not afraid to speak a new word for a later age or to press long-established beliefs. Second Isaiah invites readers to affirm the God who is at any point capable of intervening on behalf of individuals and entire groups. This God who long ago made a dry crossing in the midst of a raging sea can also work to turn the arid desert into a well-watered pathway.

All of this movement back to Zion has one central objective. The passage concludes with a striking statement about the ultimate purpose of God's activity: the exiles are to be restored, "so that they might declare my praise" (v. 21). This restoration will encompass the entire creation. Even the obscure and shy animals will join the universal chorus: "The wild animals will honor me, the jackals and the ostriches" (v. 20). Those who have doubted the enduring faithfulness of God can no longer look to earlier events as antiquated or irrelevant examples of divine love. Liberation and a new beginning are guaranteed for the chosen people, so that they can be faithful witnesses to the living God who acts within history and is constantly in motion.

SAMUEL L. ADAMS

Homiletical Perspective

whole passage is divinely self-referential and unashamedly theocentric. Because we are God's people, God promises to redeem us; what God promises to redeem us for is to be God's people.

In the last verses of our passage, Exodus is rounded out by Genesis. The one who keeps bringing people home is the one who made them in the first place. YHWH is the beginning of their journey and the end: true home.

We can also preach this text along with the Gospel and Epistle texts for the day. In the story of the anointing at Bethany in John's Gospel, Mary understands the new thing that God is doing among God's people. Judas continues to see the world in its older form. Jesus reminds the disciples that the poor were here yesterday (alas!) and the poor will be here tomorrow (alas!). There will always be the opportunity to serve the poor, but right now, right here, God is doing a new thing. That new thing is the incarnation, proclamation, and death of Jesus. Mary does right to leave aside the old ways for now and serve the gracious new.

The link to Philippians 3:4b–14 is even stronger. In Philippians, Paul is not saying that the practices of his past were in themselves worthless. He does not deny that God was present in the events and rites and associations that sustained him through the years before he confronted Jesus. However in the light of the new thing God is doing in Jesus Christ, that observant past is relegated to the past. God has done a new thing, and for Paul "whatever gains I had, these I have come to regard as loss . . . because of the surpassing value of knowing Christ Jesus my Lord" (Phil. 3:7–8).

As Lent moves toward Holy Week and Easter, the preacher helps the congregation to remember what God has done and to anticipate the ever-new thing that God is about to do. Always the same God, but not always in the same way.

DAVID L. BARTLETT

Psalm 126

¹When the Lᴏʀᴅ restored the fortunes of Zion,
  we were like those who dream.
²Then our mouth was filled with laughter,
  and our tongue with shouts of joy;
then it was said among the nations,
  "The Lᴏʀᴅ has done great things for them."
³The Lᴏʀᴅ has done great things for us,
  and we rejoiced.

⁴Restore our fortunes, O Lᴏʀᴅ,
  like the watercourses in the Negeb.
⁵May those who sow in tears
  reap with shouts of joy.
⁶Those who go out weeping,
  bearing the seed for sowing,
shall come home with shouts of joy,
  carrying their sheaves.

Theological Perspective

People regularly romanticize the biblical idea of "captivity," as though the captives have chosen to immigrate to another country. We tend to think that, although the immigrants do not have all the privileges of the resident citizen, they are better off in their immigrant situation than in their homeland. That view, however, does not capture the full view of what it means to be in captivity. The difficulty is that most people cannot wrap their minds around the incarceration of an entire people in a foreign land. Captivity in the Bible was not the choice to immigrate to another country. Captivity in the Bible was the exile and imprisonment of a people forcibly separated from their homeland. These captives in exile lived estranged from the most fundamental symbols that gave their lives meaning.

In this age of the prison-industrial complex— where some get rich from the captivity of others— people of course know that millions convicted of crimes are incarcerated throughout the United States of America. Unfortunately, the prison system is a bubble floating beyond the conscious thoughts of most citizens. Even when most people give conscious energy to the reality of the incarcerated, their thoughts are generally associated with a perspective of justice that says the convicts have gotten what they deserve. Those convicted of a crime and

Pastoral Perspective

Psalm 126 is a psalm of two moods. It begins (vv. 1–3) in happiness, with the people of Israel looking back at the good old days, when it seemed that their dreams had finally come true. After years of loss and exile, God made a way for them to come back home—*home!* God restored them to a land they loved and had lost, to livelihoods and neighborhoods. Restoring their city walls and structures was like restoring their very sense of community. People pulled together then. They remembered, and laughter and shouts of joy filled their mouths, filled the air, and floated like helium balloons carrying the message far and wide: "God has done great things for us!" Surrounding nations, though they worshiped other gods, were drawn into Israel's rejoicing and said in response: "The Lᴏʀᴅ has done great things for them" (v. 2).

Many of us know this kind of looking back. Have you ever watched an old home movie and felt overwhelmed by a dreamlike nostalgia? It is a holiday gathering and all of your relatives are there, well and happy on that day. You are a child again and your parents are young and laughing. Siblings and cousins shout with joy, running around in good-natured fun. A grandparent carries a platter of food. An uncle clowns in the background as usual. In those moments of looking back, you remember the

Exegetical Perspective

Returning with joy. Psalm 126 belongs to the collection commonly known as the Songs of Ascent or Pilgrimage Songs (Pss. 120–34). They are so called because the first line of each psalm identifies it as a *shir hamma ʿlot* (song of the ascent or going up). As such, it may have been part of the liturgical procession into the temple during the high feast days. Today's psalm clearly comes from a period after the return from Babylonian exile, as it likens the experience of rescue to waking from a dream. This image prepares us for the explosion of joy and thanksgiving that erupts from this short psalm. After the long dark days of exile, when it seemed that God had abandoned the covenant people, suddenly, as if awaking from a dream, the Judeans find themselves once more in Zion. Laughter and music replace weeping, hope and promise replace despair.

Composed of two strophes (vv. 1–3, 4–6) the psalm is well balanced in structure and complementary in content. There is disagreement regarding the verb tense of verses 1–3. Because of the nature of Hebrew verbs, it is possible to translate these verses either as perfect or completed action or as imperfect or yet to be completed action. If we choose the former, then the exiles have returned and are remembering their experience of liberation. If the latter, then the song reflects a time when the

Homiletical Perspective

As he ascended toward Jerusalem and the temple, the psalmist recalled a time of restoration and dreams fulfilled: "Then our mouth was filled with laughter, and our tongue with shouts of joy." Then the nations marveled at the great deeds God had done for them and they rejoiced (vv. 2–3). Notice, however, that "then" is not "now," that the writer and his community find themselves at a significant distance from those former joyful times. The compassionate preacher will lead her congregation into prayerful reflection on the gap between those experiences. Anamnesis—remembering God's mighty acts—is the lifeblood of Jewish and Christian spirituality, a source that can strengthen and inspire the faithful, especially in difficult times. Grateful Christian communities work at remembering what God has done, both in the biblical past and in their more particular histories.

Such remembering can, however, degenerate into nostalgia. The psalmist hearkens to memories of a better day in the past, something of a golden age perhaps. Sometimes evoking memory becomes a lament more than an enlivening sense of hope. Communities and their leaders remember great days, but insist that the present is a difficult and dry time. As preachers become acquainted with their congregations, they learn stories of their golden ages and

Psalm 126

Theological Perspective

sentenced to prison are not thought to be captives of the system in the same way prisoners of war are thought to be captives. Whereas we expect prisoners of war to seek to escape their captivity, heaven forbid that prisoners of the penitentiary should ever escape their time for doing penance. Yet how often do people conceive the prison-industrial complex as a system of reform?

Most of us have been socialized to see the captivity of the Israelites as God sending the people into exile to teach the people a lesson, in order to promote a more faithful attitude. Do we believe, however, that the people actually learned the lesson? Is captivity mediated justice and a system of reform? These become important questions as we consider the conditions under which many people live life in the United States. What would it mean, for instance, to think of the vast numbers of incarcerated individuals as a population in forced captivity? We are convinced that Israelite captivity was always the result of God's exiling the people because of their unfaithfulness to God. Furthermore, we tend to believe that God sent the Israelites into captivity because they were either unable to learn or unable to maintain the lessons on God's law. In that regard, we characterize the Israelites as repeat offenders. Do we really believe that Israelite captives returned to their homes learned their lessons at a deeper level than ex-offenders do in our own time?

If we shift the context from incarceration within a single physical facility to the institutionalized captivity of an entire people structured by an oppressive society, what populations might we consider living in captivity within the United States yesterday and today? Native Americans were forced into captivity through the reservation system. African Americans were forced into captivity through the American system of slavery. Japanese Americans were forced into captivity through the concentration camp system. Gays and lesbians live in captivity due to most states denying them the status to be legally married. Most Mexican Americans live in the captivity of always being seen as illegal aliens. There are multiple groups being oppressed who might declare a sense of being held, or having been held, captive for generations within the United States.

When captives are set free, it sometimes takes a while for them to realize that the circumstances of their existence have finally changed. It is not that anyone becomes content with captivity; rather, captivity can become the sole focus of one's existence. For those who are forced to focus on their captivity,

Pastoral Perspective

truth of how happy and precious those days were. Other truths are harder to recall—the unseen illness that would later claim one relative or the tensions that ran in low-voltage currents through certain relationships. Communities and cultures can also carry a sense of "collective nostalgia." Churches are not exempt either, as members wistfully remember easier, better days when God was doing great things for them.

Sometimes nostalgic remembrance of the past occurs when the present is unhappy, precarious, or unbearable. On the printed page of Psalm 126 in many Bibles, there is an empty space between verses 1–3 and verses 4–6. Within that space, we step out of a happy past and stand with the psalmist in the present. The silence of that space gives us room to wonder what has happened to the people of Israel. What has taken away their laughter and shouts of joy? What has made their present so unhappy, precarious, even unbearable? We do not know what calamity has occurred, but its effects have been significant for the whole community.

The mood of verses 4–6 now shifts from remembered happiness to expressed sorrow in the present crisis. However, this psalm does not become solely a lament. Though there is a double reference to their sorrow—"sow in tears," "go out weeping"— the psalmist picks up a phrase from verse 2 and uses it twice more to mix present lament with hope for the future. Verse 5's "tears" are transformed into hoped-for "shouts of joy," and the "weeping" that goes out in verse 6 returns likewise as "shouts of joy" before the verse, and the prayer, comes to an end. With growing confidence in God's ability and will to restore, the people move from hope in verse 5 ("*May* those who sow in tears reap with shouts of joy") to an affirmation of faith ("Those who go out weeping . . . *shall* come home with shouts of joy").

The hope and affirmation of faith expressed in these final three verses are crucial, for we believe God has the ability and the will to restore us! It is important, however, to take seriously the very real anguish expressed in verses 4–6. Often we rush ourselves (or others) out of grief and sorrow. We are uncomfortable with tears, impatient with the hard work and slow process healing requires, whether the healing is physical, emotional, spiritual, or all three. The images evoked here are vivid, and it is worthwhile to dwell with them long enough to understand the depth of the sorrow expressed.

The psalmist speaks of the Negeb, a region to the south of Jerusalem, where creek beds dry up from lack

hope of return was still the dream of those in captivity. The NRSV and the New Jerusalem Bible translate the verses as completed action; the New Jewish Publication Society Tanakh translates them as action yet to be completed. The objection that the past tense makes the second strophe unintelligible can be overcome by understanding the second strophe to be a prayer for blessing on the continued restoration of Judean society.

The restitution of things. Twice (vv. 1, 4) the phrase "restore fortunes" appears. In both cases, it introduces the strophe that follows. The phrase carries the sense of "restore to a previous condition." This is clearest in its use in Job 42:10: "And the LORD restored the fortunes of Job when he had prayed for his friends; and the LORD gave Job twice as much as he had before." Job's family, property, prosperity, and respect were restored to a greater degree than previously. This phrase is most often used with reference to God restoring the people to the land (e.g., Jer. 29:14, 30:3; Amos 9:14; Zeph. 2:7, 3:20). Here the repetition of the phrase invokes memory and the prophetic promises of restoration after the bitter experience of exile.

Structurally the psalm is controlled by the repetition of "shouts of joy" (vv. 2, 5, 6). The word (*rinnah*) is used primarily in Isaiah and the Psalms in the context of shouting for joy or singing. There are some uses where it is paired with prayer and translated as "cry." Among its uses, and perhaps reflecting its etymology, the word refers to crying out or raising a voice (e.g., Prov. 1:20; 8:30). Such usage nuances our understanding of this term so that our picture of this joyful singing captures the loud shout characteristic of crying out.

To help us appreciate the contrasts employed in this psalm, we turn to a parallelism similar to 126:6 found in Psalm 30:5: "Weeping may linger for the night, but joy comes with the morning." When we note that weeping is a loud, vocalized expression of grief, we can appreciate that its opposite is a loud, vocalized expression of joy. In the many places where *rinnah* is used, the physical act of weeping, and all that it connotes, gives way to joyful singing. The focus is on the dramatic change from one state of being to another. The mood is exuberant, and the orientation is toward the future. As the final two verses of our psalm anticipate the salvific future of Israel, expressed through the twice-repeated movement from weeping to shouts of joy, it is as if the psalm itself is straining to become a song of joy.

hear dreams, likely romanticized, of a blessed past. They preach in a half-empty church and hear stories of the days when it was full. They serve in communities with rising unemployment rates and hear about times when the local economy prospered. Persons in that community were laughing once and remember what laughing was like, but they are not laughing anymore. Preachers must know if the people in their congregations hearken to any particular golden age, and how they remember that period. While the evoking of such stories can generate energy, it can also mask lament.

This psalm, however, brings the lamentation to the surface as it prays, "Restore our fortunes, O LORD, like the watercourses in the Negeb" (v. 4). This is a hopeful prayer, but hear it carefully. If fortunes need restoring, that means they have fallen. The imagery of dry streambeds stands as a promise. Once they held water, and the reader can presume that they will do so again. On the surface the writer makes prayer for rain, one that calls for God to take action, end the dryness and restore laughter. It is a reasonable request to make of a covenant God, one who has promised steadfast love.

After the image of dry watercourses, however, comes a surprising twist. We might expect an image of clouds gathering for a spring rain, followed by swollen streambeds; rather, we read this image of persons sowing in tears and then reaping with shouts of joy. The tears become the shower that God uses to restore fertility to the desert and send a harvest (vv. 5–6). Weeping is not denied, but God redeems it and transforms it into a means of blessing. The psalm reminds us that we may be surprised by fertility and abundant harvests in places where we thought restoration and healing impossible.

We say that we believe that God can redeem all manner of pain and disappointment, even tears. Such an affirmation may, however, be easier to make when the tears belong to someone else or when the tears result from relatively minor disappointments. Tears shed over losing a championship basketball game or missing a job promotion are not the same as the tears shed over the death of a son or daughter. They are not the same as the bitter tears shed by an abused spouse or the tears shed by refugees who long for a home that they cannot regain. Whatever the cause of one's tears, confident affirmation that God will eventually redeem them must not be preached as a denial of human pain and grief. In Christian proclamation, one speaks of moving *through* pain toward redemption, not *around* it. Such

Psalm 126

Theological Perspective

this focus, if it becomes a myopic view, can sometimes be such an intense gaze that liberation and freedom take on the surreal quality of a dream. If one associates the ending of captivity with the surreal, the ending of one's captivity will forever remain a vain hope of the mind that is never to be imagined as a real possibility. Consequently, if the perceived vain hope is ever realized, it is easy not to recognize that the circumstances of life have, in fact, changed. When captivity is constructed as a vain hope, this might stimulate persons to become repeat offenders, because they live with a deep-seated disbelief that being liberated from their incarceration is not much more than a dream. But should the realized freedom ever sink in, the joyous response of a heart whose burden has been lifted is immeasurable.

Every system, whether good or bad, resists change. People have a tendency to cling to the familiar, even when the familiar is problematic. Consequently, freedom comes with a price. Because of human resistance to change, the price tends to be quite high. Sometimes the price is the loss of security that results from putting oneself in harm's way in order to promote a new reality. At other times the price is the loss of predictability in life, for predictability brings its own sense of security. Furthermore, once freedom is achieved, there is a tall order of responsibility for its maintenance. Truly to release the prisoner and set the captive free, there must be a living into the dream to make it a lived experience for all. It is no wonder that Dr. Martin Luther King Jr.'s "I Have a Dream" speech still provokes the citizens of the United States to live the hope of a more unified future.

LEE H. BUTLER JR.

Pastoral Perspective

of rain. A period of hardship and grief can feel like a drought in the soul. Life recedes; we can become hardened, with cracks appearing in our emotional and physical well-being. The image of sowers weeping as they plant, repeated in verses 5 and 6, vividly reminds us that in grief we struggle to go on living, carrying out tasks and responsibilities. At the end of our own strength, we look to God, as Israel does here. They ask God to relieve the dry, parched places within them, just as God sends rain to the Negeb. They know how suddenly those dry watercourses fill, the waters spilling over the banks into surrounding fields. New life springs up. From ancient Caananite traditions, sowing was associated with tears and harvest with fertility and joy. Israel takes on these same associations in describing themselves as sorrowful in their collective seedtime; their arms are empty, waiting for God to act. They anticipate armfuls of sheaves—an abundance of joy. Verses 4–6, read carefully, remind us that even a dry season or a season of weeping can be fruitful for soil *and* soul if lament and hope in God find a balance within. The attention and care given to such seasons of sorrow and grief may become the ground of new life.

On this fifth Sunday of Lenten repentance and reflection on mortality, Psalm 126 offers encouragement. Remembering God's care for us in the past and enduring this present season thoughtfully and prayerfully can ready us to receive the future God has prepared. Read in this way, Psalm 126 may also encourage us not to rush from a triumphal Palm Sunday ahead into triumphant Easter Sunday, ignoring the pathos of the Holy Week in between. As we move in hope toward Easter, a word that begins each section of this psalm catches our eye: "restore." From our Easter perspective, we know that if we pray only for God to restore life as we have known it in easier or better times, our prayer has fallen short of the hope—and the future—God intends. God has in mind not simply restoration, but resurrection.

KIMBERLY L. CLAYTON

Exegetical Perspective

A harvest of plenty. The second strophe introduces a new image. Somewhat unexpectedly, an agricultural metaphor is used to make an appeal on behalf of Israel's future. Contrasting images are used to illustrate the changing fortunes of Israel in the resettlement of the land. Ezra, Nehemiah, Haggai, and Zechariah make it clear that the initial phases of resettlement were fraught with difficulties, especially for those working the land.

The images used in this psalm correspond to the planting and harvesting seasons, when one depends on the reversal of drought. The psalmist pleads "Restore . . . like the watercourses in the Negeb" (v. 4). The reference is to the wadis of southern Palestine that remain dry practically the entire year. When the winter rains come, just before planting season, the dry wadis become mighty torrents of water signaling hope to those who work the land. After a time of exile, a time when hope dried up, God restored the people to the land and now, once again, they look to God to provide for them in this new situation.

The final image (v. 6) has a wonderful parallelism lost in the NRSV. Literally it is "He walks along and weeping carries the seed bag, he will come in with shouts of joy carrying his sheaves." The actions are separated by time between sowing and harvest, but they are tightly connected linguistically. The psalmist goes out to sow, then comes home with the harvest. At both seed time and harvest, something is carried; first it is the seed, the promise, for sowing, and then the sheaves, the realization of promise, the harvest. What begins with lamentation born of uncertainty, when one must hope that the elements will be favorable, gives way to loud, exclamatory shouts of joy celebrating the successful growing season. At the time of harvest, God's faithfulness is remembered and weeping is a distant memory.

STEVEN BISHOP

Homiletical Perspective

is the insistent message of Lent—one encounters the cross on the way to the resurrection. Do we allow ourselves to see human suffering and disappointment in this nondocetic way? If not, we are avoiding the cross. Preachers should insist that God calls those who hear this psalm to pray it deeply, even with their bodies and their own tears, and to accompany those who mourn until they gather the promised harvest.

Nostalgia about a fondly remembered past, or anamnesis of past triumphs, can mask lament. Laughter and joyfully told stories can be used to suppress the tears that our hearts long to shed. Sensitive preachers will understand that sometimes people laugh to avoid crying. With that in mind, preachers should note the surprising shift in tone found in the transition from verse 3 to verse 4. They should allow it to disarm their hearers and even to release tears that need to be shed. Thus can our lament be confronted, unmasked, and added to this ancient prayer.

In designing a sermon on this psalm, the pastor might begin with memories of the congregation's nostalgically remembered past and then say, "However, it's not that way now, is it?" He would then describe the current aridity while pointing to God's promise for a better future. Just as the psalmist places the image of the sheaves in the mouth of his congregation, so today's preacher will suggest images of what such a redeemed future might look like, beyond the disappointment.

One might also use this text as a way of supporting others in their lamentation. The preacher might acknowledge that the present is a prosperous time for many, that many people are laughing now (see Luke 6:25b). She might say something like "Many of us here feel pretty good about the way life is going right now, but many others are not in that place. Some of those who mourn may be sitting among us today. Others may live far away. This psalm calls us to stand with them in the midst of their tears. Such is the baptismal vocation to which God calls us during this Lent."

MARK W. STAMM

Philippians 3:4b–14

`4b`If anyone else has reason to be confident in the flesh, I have more: `5`circumcised on the eighth day, a member of the people of Israel, of the tribe of Benjamin, a Hebrew born of Hebrews; as to the law, a Pharisee; `6`as to zeal, a persecutor of the church; as to righteousness under the law, blameless.

`7`Yet whatever gains I had, these I have come to regard as loss because of Christ. `8`More than that, I regard everything as loss because of the surpassing value of knowing Christ Jesus my Lord. For his sake I have suffered the loss of all things, and I regard them as rubbish, in order that I may gain Christ `9`and be found in him, not having a righteousness of my own that comes from the law, but one that comes through faith in Christ, the righteousness from God based on faith. `10`I want to know Christ and the power of his resurrection and the sharing of his sufferings by becoming like him in his death, `11`if somehow I may attain the resurrection from the dead.

`12`Not that I have already obtained this or have already reached the goal; but I press on to make it my own, because Christ Jesus has made me his own. `13`Beloved, I do not consider that I have made it my own; but this one thing I do: forgetting what lies behind and straining forward to what lies ahead, `14`I press on toward the goal for the prize of the heavenly call of God in Christ Jesus.

Theological Perspective

Protestant theologians traditionally find in this passage a strong statement of Paul's teaching of the righteousness of faith, and even justification by grace through faith. Martin Luther emphasizes the same sharp contrast between the righteousness of law and the righteousness of faith that he sees at the heart of Paul's Letter to the Galatians. John Calvin calls 3:9ff. "a remarkable passage, if anyone desires to have a good description of the righteousness of faith, and to understand its true nature."[1]

This seems accurate if we also take care to note that our passage does these things in the immediate context of criticizing other understandings of righteousness and the gospel that, in Paul's judgment, threaten the church at Philippi. The question is, how may we obtain true righteousness, a right relation with God, or salvation? Paul's answer is through Christ, "faith in Christ," or even the faithfulness (or faithful obedience) *of* Christ. He contrasts his answer with another: by external marks such as circumcision of the flesh and by works and practices that satisfy the law.

The text. The lectionary passage will be clarified if we also consider 3:2–4a. The letter takes a turn in 3:2

1. John Calvin, *The Epistles of Paul the Apostle to the Galatians, Ephesians, Philippians and Colossians,* trans. T. H. L. Parker, vol. 11 of *Calvin's Commentaries* (Grand Rapids: Eerdmans, 1972), 274.

Pastoral Perspective

If Lent is, among other things, a time to reconsider—a time to set aside distractions in order to focus on our relationship with God and with Christ's church, a time to let the Holy Spirit work on us in order to remold us into the image of God as individuals and as the body of Christ—then this passage from the letter to the church in Philippi brings the season to its peak. This passage encourages us to make a life assessment, creating a ledger as to "losses" and "gains." While there are social, cultural, economic, political, familial values to be cultivated and refined, during Lent we discover other values that outrank those we work so hard to attain. During Lent we look again at what shapes our identity and gives us security and against which we are held accountable. Such Lenten reconsiderations have brought us to this text on the Fifth Sunday in Lent and to the reality that we count as "loss" all that we have striven to achieve, because of *the surpassing worth of knowing Jesus Christ.*

So this text calls us to consider how it is we *know* Jesus Christ. It is clear that *knowing* Christ is more than simply gaining information with the presumption that knowledge yields privilege. This *knowing* calls us to identify so closely with Jesus Christ that we find our security for our past/present/future in Jesus Christ, rather than in our own achievement. This *knowing* calls us to identify so closely with Christ that

Exegetical Perspective

Paul gives us here a rare snippet of autobiography. He does so in order to stress the overwhelming joy of belonging to Christ, in contrast to the great privileges that he possessed as a Jew. In human terms, Paul had every reason to be confident: he was "a member of the people of Israel" (lit. "born a Jew"—i.e., not a convert), had been circumcised on the eighth day, *and* belonged to the favored tribe of Benjamin. The phrase "Hebrew of Hebrews" may mean that Paul was born of pure Hebrew stock, or possibly that he was one of the few Jews who still knew the Hebrew language.

By birth, therefore, Paul had every possible privilege: he had good reason to have confidence "in the flesh." This term covers not only human inheritance but human achievements; here too Paul once possessed every ground for confidence, for he had belonged to the small sect of the Pharisees, who devoted themselves to faithful obedience of the law and were fanatical in their devotion to it. Paul himself had been totally blameless in keeping the law, and his zeal for it had been demonstrated in his persecution of *Christians*.

To us, these may seem strange grounds for boasts regarding birth or achievements, but Paul writes as a Jew, and these were the things he had *treasured, having assumed that they counted* in the sight of God.

Homiletical Perspective

These familiar verses from Philippians activate the "easy-hard" rule for preachers: the easier a passage is for a congregation to hear, the harder a preacher will work to give it a fresh hearing. The lectionary makes the passage even easier to hear by separating it from its launch pad. Beginning in the middle of a sentence, with Paul's admission that he has plenty of reasons to be confident about his religious credentials, the hearer is left innocent of his motive. Just two verses earlier, he has warned his readers to beware of the dogs, the evil workers, "those who mutilate the flesh!"—his unnamed rivals in establishing the Christian gospel, who call Gentiles to become circumcised in their turn toward Christ, the Jewish Messiah and Redeemer of Israel.

A preacher's first decision, then, is whether to include the polemical context for Paul's recital—and dismissal—of his own Jewish credentials. The preacher who does so may discover a sermon at the edge of this passage that is not apparent in the middle: namely, one that calls the present congregation to consider the ways in which they may have become the very people Paul railed against. In Philippians as elsewhere, Paul works hard to persuade tiny renegade churches that they have nothing to fear from taking on the religious establishment of their time. Two thousand years

Philippians 3:4b–14

Theological Perspective

when Paul warns of those who present a message different from his own. Philippians 3:2–6 presents the issue as a disagreement over circumcision and the law or the place of external markers in establishing who belongs to the true people of God. The "dogs" and "evil workers"—Paul's intemperate language signals his personal involvement in the matter—are therefore likely to have been Jewish missionaries and/or Jewish Christians who regarded circumcision of the flesh and right practices according to the law as requirements and signs of membership in the covenant community, true righteousness, and salvation. However Paul insists "it is *we* [emphasis mine]"—those "who worship in the Spirit of God and boast in Christ Jesus and have no confidence in the flesh"—"who are the circumcision" and thus the true community of God's people (v. 3). Or, as Calvin puts it, "we are the true seed of Abraham and heirs of the testament which was confirmed by the sign of circumcision."[2]

Paul illustrates the point autobiographically. He claims that he has more reason than anyone else to place his confidence in circumcision of the flesh and the requirements of the law, since he was circumcised in accord with strict Jewish tradition, a member of "the tribe of Benjamin," a Pharisee rigorously schooled in the law, a zealous persecutor of the church, and "blameless" as to the law. Luther summarizes: "It is as though he were saying: 'Here I may brag openly . . . For if there were any grounds for boasting in the righteousness of the Law, I would have more grounds for boasting than anyone else.'"[3]

Now that Paul is in Christ, these are practices and commitments that lie behind him, and "whatever gains" he has from them, he now regards as loss. Indeed, compared to "the surpassing value of knowing Christ Jesus my Lord," Paul labels all these things "rubbish." They are to be discarded "in order that I may gain Christ and be found in him, not having a righteousness of my own that comes from the law, but one that comes through faith in Christ [or "through the faith or faithfulness of Christ"—a translation that Calvin chooses and that emphasizes Christ's faithful obedience rather than our own efforts], the righteousness from God based on faith" (vv. 8–9).

As one whom "Christ has made . . . his own" (v. 12), Paul now presses toward the goal of resurrection—toward, as Calvin puts it, the

Pastoral Perspective

we seek out where God continues to be at work to bring life into places of death and join in that resurrection. Doubtless there will be suffering in such situations. Yet in *knowing* Christ's resurrection and suffering we are privileged to participate in what God is doing here and now—in individual lives, in the community, in this world—to bring life out of death, to bring light into places of darkness. The privilege of identifying so closely with Jesus Christ calls us to set aside anything we formerly valued because of *the surpassing worth of knowing Jesus Christ.*

What changes when we set aside these other values? Have we experimented with anything during Lent that has caused our perspectives to change? Have we "deprived" ourselves of something and now realize that this is not as important as we thought, not of lasting value? Do we have a different understanding of what we "need"? This is not about setting aside what we already know does not matter and is useless. We are called to set aside what we have counted as our "gain," what we have valued highly, what we have claimed as our achievements, what has given us our status in the community and in the church. We set aside these "gains" because we now realize they give us no advantage. Trusting solely in God's grace, we give up past certainty for future hope, give up measuring our own progress because we recognize there is no righteousness on our own. This is what changes because of *the surpassing worth of knowing Jesus Christ.*

What will never change until we set aside what we have formerly valued? Until we set aside what we formerly considered as our gain, we will still be held captive by how much financial security we think we need; which neighborhood/house/car/school is required; how healthy we assume we should be; the expectations of family, friends, church, nation. As long as we are held captive, we will not know our true identity, security, peace, or *the surpassing worth of knowing Jesus Christ.*

How do we *know* Jesus Christ? How do we find our identity in Jesus Christ? We find our identity the way Jesus found his, by *obedience to the point of death, even death on a cross.* Even if the obedience God demands of us is not as costly as Christ's obedience, how do we find our security? We find our security the way Jesus found his: by trusting in the faithfulness of God, by finding our story to be part of God's larger story of faithfulness. We learn to trust by stepping out into places where we have never been, participating in resurrection. If we stay in places we know well, there is no need to trust

---

2. Ibid., 269.
3. Martin Luther, *Lectures on Galatians, chapters 1–4,* vol. 26 of *Luther's Works* (St. Louis: Concordia Publishing House, 1962), Gal. 1:14.

Exegetical Perspective

He lists his privileges because he fears that those who still treasure them could mislead the members of his churches (3:2–3). He had enjoyed all that these people have—and more!

Nevertheless, he has *abandoned* all these privileges for the sake of Christ. Paul uses the image of a profit-and-loss account. On one side of the ledger are the things that he once treasured but has now written off as worthless. On the other stands what he has gained: Christ (v. 7). He repeats this statement in different language in verse 8a, then again in verse 8b, explaining that he now regards what he once prized as no better than "rubbish" (the Greek word is more forceful, suggesting excrement). He has exchanged it all in order to win Christ (v. 7), to "know" him (v. 8a), and to "gain" him (v. 8b). The repetition serves to emphasize Paul's point and builds up to the climax of verse 9: how can the "rubbish" of birth and achievement compare with what he now has by virtue of being "found in Christ" (v. 9)? Instead of the righteousness that comes from the law (cf. v. 6), he possesses that which comes through "being in Christ." Paul describes this as righteousness "that comes through faith in Christ, the righteousness from God based on faith." Is he again using repetition to stress his point, or do these two phrases say something different?

The answer depends on the way we understand the first phrase, which means literally "the righteousness that comes through the faith of Christ." The Greek word translated "faith" can also mean "faithfulness," and the genitive "of Christ" can refer to both the faith/faithfulness *of* Christ and our faith *in* him. There is much to be said for taking the phrase in the former sense here (as in the NRSV v. 9), since this points us back to Christ's own actions, reminding us of how *he* behaved. A remarkable feature of this passage is the way it echoes what is said about Christ in Philippians 2:5–11. There, we were told how Christ abandoned his privileges and did not consider it appropriate to exploit what he had; because of his self-emptying and death, he has been proclaimed as Lord. Here, Paul tells us about the privileges *he* has abandoned, saying that he did not consider (the verb is the same) them to have any value in comparison with what he has been given in Christ. For Paul, "knowing Christ Jesus" his Lord (v. 8) means becoming like him; to have faith in him (to trust him) means sharing *his* faith in God, and being prepared to trust *God*, even to the point of death.

Paul now explains that knowing Christ means knowing "the power of his resurrection" (v. 10). Experiencing this resurrection, however, depends on

Homiletical Perspective

later, plenty of preachers serve the religious establishments of our time.

If Paul stood before a twenty-first-century North American congregation, whose right to "be found in" Christ Jesus might he defend? If circumcision was the boundary marker that Paul challenged in his own religious community, what boundary marker might he confront in a Gentile Christian community today? Who are the religious renegades this congregation looks down upon, defending its suspicion of them on the basis of its own religious credentials? Preachers who head in this direction will be very careful to point out that today's sermon is not about Jews versus Christians but about those who defend long-established religious teachings and those who go up against them.

Preachers who decide to stay within the bounds of the lection will still have plenty to talk about. Paul's good but difficult news is that those who have found their lives in Christ Jesus have no further use for religious credentials. Whether such marks of distinction are inherited or earned, they simply have no go-power in the economy of God. Preachers who wish to preach the same theme may begin by contemplating their own resumes. Are you the third generation of your family to go into the ministry? Where did you earn your Master of Divinity degree? Were your grades pretty good? Have any of your sermons been published?

None of these things is bad, Paul says. He is not sorry he was born into the tribe of Benjamin, any more than he feels as if he has to apologize for being blameless under the law. It is just that none of those things ever got him one inch nearer where he wanted to go. If anything, they distracted him. Keeping his resume up to date kept him from paying attention to the ways God was working beyond the boundaries of his computer screen. Meeting his quotas kept him from questioning what the numbers really meant. In the end, Paul was on his way to Damascus to demonstrate his zeal for God when God snatched him up, set him down, and gave him a three-day time out to rethink his entire approach.

Churches have resumes too. Some are proud of their long histories and the distinguished preachers who have filled their pulpits, while others focus on gains in giving and membership in recent years. Some can tell you how many members of their youth group have gone on to become ministers themselves, including a couple who became bishops or pastors of tall-steeple churches. None of these things is bad, Paul says. It is just that none of those things will get a

Philippians 3:4b–14

Theological Perspective

completion of salvation after death. He strives but (and this is critical) *not* as one who believes that his relationship to God is primarily a matter of his own striving and performance. "I do not consider that I have made it [the goal of resurrection] my own; but [rather] this one thing I do; forgetting what lies behind [fleshly circumcision and righteousness under the law] and straining forward to what lies ahead, I press on toward the goal" (vv. 13–14).

Contemporary meanings. There is more than a hint of exclusivity and supersession in the negative way Paul describes his own relationship to Israel's traditions—for example, regarding them as rubbish—and this is also reflected in some later theological commentary. Given the history of Christian anti-Judaism and anti-Semitism, it seems wise to balance his language here with his less polemical, more complicated, detailed, and universal statements about Israel in Romans 9–11.

That said, there are a number of other ways to make Paul's basic point. We are familiar with accounts of the meaning and purpose of life that emphasize one's own strenuous efforts, accomplishments, and (alleged) virtues. American fascinations with self-help and success spring to mind. Then again, there is no shortage of preachers who, in effect, emphasize the same thing—for example, moral performance, right worship, and right belief as prerequisites for salvation, the idea that God will dispense God's grace if and only if we deserve it.

Paul stands against this. The most important thing in life (and in death)—our relation to God—is *not* a matter of what *we* do. It is, as the longer theological tradition says, a matter of *grace*. Within the frame of Paul's gospel, then, reliance on God's grace in Christ displaces our frenetic secular and religious efforts to guarantee our own worth and/or divine favor. To say this clearly may be enough for one Sunday, although one may also note that Paul's theology of grace makes for confidence, assurance, and rejoicing (4:4). Musical help making this last point is available from Charles Wesley's hymn "Rejoice, the Lord is King."

DOUGLAS F. OTTATI

Pastoral Perspective

anyone but ourselves. If we venture into what God is doing to bring life into places of death, we realize we are not alone and are able to declare *the surpassing worth of knowing Jesus Christ.*

So, how do we use this passage on the last Sunday in Lent? While there are other compelling texts listed for today, this text is a helpful conversation partner with those texts. Or one may choose to preach from this text, inviting those in the congregation to work through their own life ledger of gains and losses. The preacher might allow this text to complete a season of Lenten confession, a "turning away" from that which keeps us from *the surpassing worth of knowing Jesus Christ.*

The preacher might leave some spaces for silence in a sermon or after a sermon, that the congregation might seriously evaluate their life. This might be a Sunday in which the confession of sin follows the sermon. This might be a Sunday to renew baptismal vows and, following the renunciations, to invite the congregation to turn around physically, to turn away from what was formerly considered a "gain," and to face the opposite direction as they pledge themselves to Jesus Christ the light of the world. The baptismal prayer recounts the story of God's faithfulness from creation, through the flood, bringing God's people across the Red Sea, and on to Jesus' own baptism—a powerful recounting of the privilege that is ours to be part of God's continuing faithfulness. It is also appropriate to allow this passage to encourage us to discover where God is bringing resurrection today and not to shy away from the suffering of participating in such resurrection. In this way we come to *the surpassing worth of knowing Jesus Christ.*

LAURA S. MENDENHALL

Exegetical Perspective

"sharing his sufferings." Paul's understanding of the significance of Christ's death is far removed from the crude substitutionary theories of some later writers. This is no simple exchange; rather, Christ shares our human death and breaks its power over us through his resurrection, so enabling us to share his risen life (cf. Rom. 5:12–21; 1 Cor. 15:12–57). If we are to share that life, however, it is necessary for us to make his death our own (Rom. 6:3–4), and this may well mean sharing his suffering (Rom. 8:17). So Paul must become "like Christ" in death (v. 10)—literally, "be conformed to his death." Christ's humility and death (Phil. 2:6–8) are both the *basis* of Christian life and its *pattern*.

Although Paul already experiences the joy of living in Christ, "resurrection from the dead" (v. 11) still lies in the future: it is something Paul wants to know (cf. Phil. 1:21). The words "if somehow" are not intended to suggest doubt about the outcome, but rather serve to remind us that the goal has not yet been reached. Christians must never be complacent. Paul uses the imagery of the games, which would have been familiar to his readers. Like a good athlete, his aim is to gain the prize, which is "the heavenly call of God" (v. 14). It is not clear whether the call is to heaven or simply comes from heaven. Since Paul will go on to speak of our citizenship in heaven (v. 20), it is probably the former, but however we understand it, the final phrase, "in Christ Jesus," reminds us once again that though Christians must "press on" to "make" the goal their own, they can do so only because Christ has "made" us his own (v. 12). The repeated verb (lit. "to take hold of") reminds us once more that our final victory depends on what Christ has done for us, and is achieved in him.

MORNA D. HOOKER

Homiletical Perspective

congregation one inch nearer where it wants to go. This, of course, raises the question of where a given congregation thinks it wants to go. For Paul, there is only one place worth going: into Christ Jesus, into knowing him and the power of his resurrection, into "sharing his sufferings by becoming like him in his death" (v. 10). If that became a church's mission statement, what aspects of that congregation's ministry would stay and what would go?

First, the congregation would have to decide what all of that language means, at least in their present context. What does it mean to "gain Christ and be found in him"? What does it mean to "know Christ"? Does anyone really want to become "like him in his death"? Phrases such as these roll so beautifully off the tongue that it seems a shame to ask what reality they signify, and yet making that connection is incumbent upon those who wish to speak the words with any kind of authority.

One of the most interesting phrases in the whole lection comes in verse 9. Paul's right relationship with God and neighbor does not come from the law, he says, but through "faith in Christ." This makes faith sound like something that Paul does, but the phrase can also mean "through the faith of Christ." In this view, Paul's only hope of acting right at all is because of Christ's faith in him. This makes faith sound like something that Christ does. A whole sermon lies in this textual variation, dealing with two different understandings of faith.

Finally, the preacher may choose to focus on Paul's famous metaphor of running toward the goal of union with Christ. Verse 14, the most interesting verse in this section, raises the question of whether heaven is a prize for the winner or a call to responsibility for the first one over the line. Either way, the preacher will remember that some in the congregation can no longer run at all, and will therefore stay in the realm of metaphor so that all may join the race.

BARBARA BROWN TAYLOR

John 12:1-8

¹Six days before the Passover Jesus came to Bethany, the home of Lazarus, whom he had raised from the dead. ²There they gave a dinner for him. Martha served, and Lazarus was one of those at the table with him. ³Mary took a pound of costly perfume made of pure nard, anointed Jesus' feet, and wiped them with her hair. The house was filled with the fragrance of the perfume. ⁴But Judas Iscariot, one of his disciples (the one who was about to betray him), said, ⁵"Why was this perfume not sold for three hundred denarii and the money given to the poor?" ⁶(He said this not because he cared about the poor, but because he was a thief; he kept the common purse and used to steal what was put into it.) ⁷Jesus said, "Leave her alone. She bought it so that she might keep it for the day of my burial. ⁸You always have the poor with you, but you do not always have me."

Theological Perspective

This is an appropriate lection for the Fifth Sunday in Lent. Holy Week approaches and the passion and death of Jesus lie immediately ahead, for both the characters in John's Gospel and for the readers. John has alluded in 11:2 to this story about Jesus' visit to Lazarus's home and the reactions of Mary and Judas to him, but he places the story here, at the beginning of chapter 12, as an introduction to Jesus' entry into Jerusalem and the beginning of his passion and death. The story is not only about Mary's preparation of Jesus for his death, but also about Judas Iscariot's objection to what he considers a waste of money that could have been better used if it had been given to the poor.

As John's story turns to the final days of Jesus' life, those who accompany Jesus on his journey to the cross include not only Mary, a faithful disciple who devotes herself and all that she has to Jesus, but also Judas, the unfaithful disciple who steals from the common purse and will betray Jesus. Both are included in John's story of Jesus' death, both the one who is faithful and the one who is not, and their inclusion tells us a great deal about the meaning of the cross and the inclusive nature of God's grace.

Mary serves as a model for Christian discipleship. At the beginning of John's Gospel, John the Baptist witnesses to Jesus as the Christ when he announces,

Pastoral Perspective

Nothing will begin a conversation like an extravagant gift. The preacher who has spent time in church meetings will have plenty of such tales to tell. If the church treasurer announces a large donation, the atmosphere in the room will change.

Suspicions may form about the donor's reasons. The gift may come with strings attached, as someone uses extravagance as a way to peddle influence. Even more controversial is the abundant gift with no restrictions. Not only will the gift spark debate over its use, but it may reveal the otherwise hidden priorities of those who make the decisions.

On the surface, our story in John 12 sounds similar to other anointing stories in the Gospels. One of them raises moral issues about the woman who anoints (Luke 7:36–49), while another reminds us that we can always show kindness to the poor (Mark 14:3–8). The narrative before us is different. As Mary anoints Jesus with costly perfume, it is Judas who is exposed. The Gospel of John cuts him no slack, revealing Judas to be a hypocrite and thief even before he betrays his Lord.

This text prompts the preacher to reflect on the attitudes surrounding an extravagant gift. A gift may provoke suspicion about motives. Others will complain that generosity skewers all of the prevailing complacency. A few may perceive that any criticism

Exegetical Perspective

Lazarus's resuscitation, the imperial context, the divided response to Jesus, Israel's liturgical calendar, and table fellowship provide the setting for Jesus' annointing.

1. Lazarus's resuscitation generates both promises and problems. First, it reinforces the characterization of Jesus as "the resurrection and the life." It points to Jesus' resurrection and the general resurrection, but also to the fullness of life possible through believing in Jesus (11:24–25). Jesus offers this possibility to Lazarus and his family, and they dramatize their fullness of life at a dinner for Jesus (12:2). Second, Lazarus's resuscitation triggers deadly opposition. *Giving life* causes Jesus' *death*!

2. Jesus' death has theological functions for John. It glorifies Jesus as God's agent. However the theological purposes are not divorced from realities of the Roman Empire. Seldom did Judeans experience empire directly. Ordinarily the empire was hidden behind client kings, governors, and some local elite citizens, who both resisted and collaborated with the empire. Caiaphas's discussion with the council reflects resistance to Rome in his desire to maintain some autonomy of the "people" (11:47–50). However resistance also involves collaboration. Only by collaborating can the council maintain its position.

Homiletical Perspective

There are few passages so packed with beauty and truth as this anointing scene at Bethany. Matthew and Mark place it in the house of Simon the leper, and the woman who anoints Jesus is unnamed. John places it in the home of three beloved friends (John 11:5), with Mary as the anointer. The narrative flow and arresting phrases provide the best guide to the sermon's plot.

"Six days before the Passover Jesus come to Bethany." Here is a prelude to the passion, a beautiful domestic scene with a family where the one who had no place to lay his head experienced as much home as anywhere in his ministry.

"There they made him a supper" (RSV). There was Martha, who had made the supreme confession of faith the chapter before (11:27). There was Lazarus, over whom Jesus had wept, whom Jesus raised from the dead, and who was now trying to figure out how to live the rest of his resurrection life. There was Mary, the "ideal disciple" of Luke 10:38–42, who sat at Jesus' feet and learned of him. The supper echoes earlier meals, signs of the inbreaking kingdom, and peers forward to Jesus' Last Supper with his disciples.

Mary's anointing of Jesus. She took the costly perfume and anointed his feet and wiped them with

John 12:1-8

Theological Perspective

"Here is the Lamb of God who takes away the sin of the world. . . . And I myself have seen and have testified that this is the Son of God" (1:29, 34). Unlike John, Mary utters not a word, but her extravagant act, the use of costly fragrance to anoint Jesus' feet, is no less a faithful witness to the even more costly and extravagant act that is about to occur. Jesus has already been anointed for his costly mission (his sending in 3:16) in his baptism by John, and now Mary anoints Jesus for his costly death with her pound of costly perfume. Like John, Mary is a witness and a disciple—not by what she says but by what she does.

The story, however, includes not only faithful Mary but also unfaithful Judas, who is no less a witness and no less a disciple than Mary. Judas is outraged the nard was not sold and the three hundred denarii (perhaps nearly a year's worth of wages) given to the poor. In an aside the author explains to the reader that Judas's true motive was not his concern for the poor but the money he had hoped to steal. Jesus rebukes Judas, although not as strongly as he rebukes Peter in Mark 8:33. In John's story, Judas is the one who betrays Jesus (12:4, 13:21–30, and 18:2–3), and yet Judas is by no means the only apostle who betrays Jesus. Peter also betrays him by three times denying that he is Jesus' disciple (18:15–27). Yet it is to Peter and not Judas, who is apparently concerned about the poor and hungry, that Jesus says, "Feed my sheep" (21:15, 16, and 17).

Karl Barth concludes his five-hundred-page discussion of the doctrine of election with forty-eight small-print pages on the figure of Judas.[1] Is there a redemptive significance even for Judas in the death of Jesus? That is not, he admits, an easy question to answer. Yet Judas, the betrayer, the one who rejects Jesus, although he may not know it, "is still an elect and called apostle of Jesus Christ." In his betrayal and handing over of Jesus to those who would kill him, Judas, no less than any of the other disciples, serves God's great purpose of saving the lost. "Can it be," therefore, "that the 'loving unto the end' of Jesus does not reach him [Judas], the very one who in his person and act simply makes manifest the fact and extent that without His death Jesus had not yet loved His own unto the end?"[2] In other words, if Jesus came to save the lost, surely there is no one in the gospel story who is more lost than the one who betrays Jesus, even if that is what

1. Karl Barth, *Church Dogmatics.*, II/2 (Edinburgh: T. & T. Clark, 1957), 458–506.
2. Ibid., 475–76.

Pastoral Perspective

of generosity is a wonderful way to dodge its power. Some of us should also come clean about money and its enticing power over us.

I will never forget the furor sparked at a stewardship conference at which an ecumenical group of pastors gathered to discuss generosity. One presenter spoke about offering a gift directly to God, and the clergy began to yawn. Then he pulled a $100 bill from his wallet, set it on fire in an ashtray, and prayed, "Lord, I offer this gift to you, and you alone."

The reaction was electric. Clergy began to fidget in their chairs, watching that greenback go up in smoke as if it were perfume. One whispered it was illegal to burn currency. Another was heard to murmur, "If he is giving money away, perhaps he has a few more." There was nervous laughter around the room.

"Do you not understand?" asked the speaker. "I am offering it to God, and that means it is going to cease to be useful for the rest of us." It was an anxious moment.

Certainly we have developed utilitarian approaches to giving. Church members may prefer to earmark their contributions. Major donors may give for the impact of the gift, the name recognition of the accompanying plaque, and the sizable tax deduction. Congregations can designate their benevolences, but a true gift cannot be controlled.

A woman named Mary wasted perfume on Jesus. We can speculate on her reasons, particularly when we hear the description of how she wiped his feet with her hair. Because of the literary context, we can surmise she felt gratitude for his restoration of her brother Lazarus. A student of the Gospel of John would know that the raising of Lazarus would initiate the plot against Jesus (John 11:45–53). If, as Jesus suggests, she purchased it for the day of his burial, the gift was not only six days premature, but unnecessary after his resurrection.

Curiously, Jesus does not take issue with the temporary nature of the gift. He declares it is appropriate in that moment, particularly in light of his impending death. He is gracious enough to receive it with gratitude.

Lots of extravagant gifts are put into the air, where they soon evaporate. A church choir labors to prepare an intricate anthem, and three minutes later it is gone. The teacher prepares the lesson, stands to deliver, and then class is adjourned. Mourners provide large arrangements of flowers to honor those whom they grieve. Saints donate large sums of money for their congregations to spend. Why do they do this? Love has its reasons.

3. Resistance and collaboration are also involved in the divided response to Jesus. Some interpreters portray the Gospel of John as "anti-Jewish" in depicting responses to Jesus. True, in Christian history John's Gospel has been used to vilify Jewish people, but in this text the response of "many of the Judeans" is not negative. Rather, they did a strange thing—they "believed in him" (11:45; 12:11).

Believing in Jesus is strange, because it means heeding his voice like sheep following a shepherd, loving one another like a master washing his disciples' feet, or abiding in him like a vine and its branches. Indeed Martha, Mary, Lazarus, and Jesus dramatize a relationship like a vine and its branches. Believing in Jesus also defies Rome, whose coins proclaimed the emperor "savior of the people" or attributed the abundance of food to him as if he manifested the god of the harvest (Ceres—from which "cereal" comes). Jesus, the bread of life, stands in stark contrast. Believing in Jesus also bypasses Israel's institutions. So Caiaphas takes belief in Jesus as threatening the temple and the nation.

Caiaphas divulges the other half of the divided response: "It is better for you [the council] to have one man die" (11:50). Caiaphas implies that if the council is to maintain power, one man should die. Ironically they also plan to execute Lazarus (12:10). Their strategy doubles. It is better that two should die. Many interpreters think that blaming Jews for Jesus' death is historically indefensible and reflects John's anti-Jewish bias. However, in John the Jewish people as a whole are not involved in Jesus' death. The collaborators are specific Jews, not the nation.

Collaboration with imperial powers to maintain privilege is likely a strategy that most of us adopt to some degree. If, while wearing a coat made in Guatemala or writing on a computer made in Malaysia, I keep silent about the economic injustice in our global village, I participate in systems that take advantage of people who are disadvantaged.

4. Passover is also part of the setting. This is the third Passover in John. On the first, Jesus drives dealers and money changers out of the temple and makes a claim on it as "my Father's house" (2:16). The second is mentioned when Jesus feeds the 5,000 (6:4), which brings into memory the feeding of the Israelites in the wilderness.

The third Passover pops up repeatedly in the last half of John. Perhaps the slaying of Passover lambs in the afternoon of the day of preparation coincides with the crucifixion of Jesus on the same day (19:14), but this does not exhaust the symbolism,

her hair. It was an extravagant act of devotion. Evelyn Underhill writes that worship "is summed up in sacrifice,"[1] the movement of generosity in response to God's sacrificial act of redemption in Christ and our participation in it. There was a sumptuousness about her sacrifice that is true of all saints—a surprising excessiveness in their compassion and generosity.[2] So Mary, counting no cost, anointed him.

In Matthew and Mark, the woman anoints his *head*, a prophetic act anointing him king and Messiah in the empire of Caesar. Think of the prophet Nathan's dangerous act of anointing young David king while Saul was still on the throne.

In John, Mary anoints Jesus' *feet*, another kind of prophetic act, signaling Jesus' imminent death, anointing him beforehand for burial. She could comprehend and accept what Peter and the other disciples could not: the death of their master and Messiah.

Here was also the action of the ideal disciple: the washing of feet. Jesus received from her what he would soon offer to his disciples, she "wiping" his feet with her hair as he will "wipe" (same Greek verb) their feet with his towel. Here is a holy emblem of the disciple's life: washing and being washed.

"And the fragrance filled the room." Did Mary have the Song of Solomon on her lips? (Song 1:12) We do not normally associate acts of witness with the sense of smell, but why not? The smell of freshly baked bread given to another, of a Sunday school classroom full of young children after recess, of a room prepared for a guest. Anne Smith, who began Charlotte Food Rescue, was hauling a station wagon full of donuts to a food shelter. She stopped off to make a pitch to executives of what is now Bank of America. As she rode the elevator to the top floor, someone said, "You smell like donuts!" She laughed and told why, and by the time the elevator door opened, she had recruited another. The fragrance of love's actions is carried on the wind to places we never see.

Judas's objection: "Why was this ointment not sold for three hundred denarii and the money given to the poor?" Judas was counting? Matthew and Mark place the objection on the disciples' lips. John, depicting Judas as moving from the light to the darkness, portrays Judas as the accused. The objection has its

---

1. Evelyn Underhill, *Worship* (London: Nisbet & Co., 1937), 47–48.
2. Edith Wyschogrod, *Saints and Postmodernism* (Chicago: University of Chicago Press, 1990), 146–47.

John 12:1-8

Theological Perspective

Judas is called by God to do. If the Good Shepherd can and does go to any length to save a lost sheep, is Judas beyond the saving grasp of the Good Shepherd? Are there those Jesus is not able to love and save? Is there a limit to the reach of Jesus' saving arm? Barth admits the New Testament does not give us a clear answer. However, Judas is not simply the man who rejects Jesus. Judas shows us who the elect are in the New Testament. "The rejected as such has no independent existence in the presence of God. He is not determined by God merely to be rejected. He is determined to hear and say that he is a rejected man elected."[3]

Judas plays just as important a role in John's story of Jesus' death as does Mary. The choice for the reader is not whether to identify with one or the other. The Christian disciple is neither Mary nor Judas but a paradoxical combination of both. Jesus justifies and sanctifies his disciples, and Mary shows us what sanctification truly is. In the figure of Mary, Christian discipleship is an act of adoration of and gratitude to the one who alone is holy. In her silence, Mary draws our attention not to herself but to the one she anoints. In the figure of Judas, Christian discipleship is God's making righteous or "justification" of those who have rejected and betrayed Jesus. In John's all-encompassing Gospel, Mary is not simply the righteous elect and Judas the unrighteous betrayer. The grace of Jesus Christ includes them both, both the faithful and the unfaithful. Both are included within the bright, transforming light the cross casts in a dark world.

GEORGE W. STROUP

Pastoral Perspective

To reflect on the miracle of generosity will lead us to reflect on Jesus. Throughout the Fourth Gospel, Jesus provides a blessed abundance. At Cana, 180 gallons of new wine are created, even more than a wedding crowd can consume. Five thousand hungry people are fed by the Sea of Galilee, with twelve baskets of leftovers remaining. After fishing all night without results, Simon Peter is instructed by the risen Christ to cast his net on the other side of the boat. Immediately, 153 large fish begin jumping into the net.

As John states, Jesus is the one through whom everything was made. There is abundance wherever he is present. As Mary generously anoints him, he tells her critics to "leave her alone." Generosity breeds generosity. Judas can criticize Mary for what she has done, but the story parenthetically exposes his hypocrisy. Either we love generously, or we do not. Either we are already engaged in providing for the poor, or we are secretly hoarding what might otherwise be shared.

Much of modern religion focuses only on what is useful, practical, and cost effective. Concern for austerity arises when resources seem slim. Yet when it comes to the life of faith, we may discover our hearts are diminished if the budget is our first concern. Should we live spendthrift lives? No. Can we justify the wasting of God's gifts? Not really. However long before a gift can be wasted, it must first be received.

Jesus is the gift of God. According to John's Gospel, Jesus is sent into a world that did not request him, yet he acts entirely for its benefit. He consistently acts on his own terms, always revealing the grace and truth of God. Lazarus was raised from the dead on Jesus' timetable, and not in response to his sisters' wishes. Similarly, Jesus will lay down his life for his people (John 10:17–18), not because he is asked to do so, but because he chooses to give himself.

WILLIAM G. CARTER

---

3. Ibid., 506.

and the Passover setting keeps provoking astonishment as to what it means.

5. The immediate setting for Jesus' anointing is table fellowship. Prior to the dinner, Martha and Mary play prominent roles. They have speaking parts in dialogue with Jesus. Lazarus never speaks.

Mary's anointing of Jesus' feet looks back. This time she has no speaking role, because her action dramatizes what words cannot express—what it means for Lazarus to be restored and reintegrated into the family. This time Judas has the speaking role. Because he cannot hear what words cannot express, he protests—sell the perfume and give money to the poor. If one cannot perceive what Mary's action dramatizes, Judas's logic makes more sense. However the narrator predisposes readers not to side with that logic. Judas was about to betray Jesus and stole money destined for the poor, but before we point at people like Judas, we might need again to remember coats made in Guatemala and computers made in Malaysia.

Jesus' interpretation of Mary's action looks forward. He associates Mary's anointing with his burial. She anticipates Jesus' death as the council does in 11:53, but she is no collaborator. Mary's anointing also anticipates Jesus' entry into Jerusalem. It evokes the anointing of Israel's kings. Yet the enthusiasm of the crowd is motivated by their excitement about the sign Jesus had done with Lazarus (12:18). Mary's anointing arouses complicated motivations and interests among different groups of people in understanding kingship and prepares for a different kind of kingship (18:36; 19:21; cf. 6:15).

Jesus then compares his impending absence with the plight of the poor: "You always have the poor with you, but you do not always have me" (12:8). Incredibly, this has been interpreted to imply that nothing should be done for the poor. Jesus' saying comes from Deuteronomy 15:11, which enjoins Israel to "open your hand to the poor," because "there will never cease to be some in need." This actually means that something should be done because of reversals even when people struggle hard against poverty.

There is yet another dimension to Jesus' saying. He describes the period before his departure as an extraordinary time that supersedes normal activities such as caring for the poor. Mary's anointing expresses what cannot be put into words and makes the five days before Jesus' execution extraordinary.

JAE WON LEE

point. What church serious about discipleship does not struggle with the tension between money spent in beautiful acts of worship and money spent on behalf of the poor?

Jesus' response: "Let her alone!" Here is Jesus' sharp, clear defense of this woman—and his defense of all whose voices and gifts are stifled by the church. He defends her as he did in Luke 10:42. Then he adds, "Let her keep it for the day of my burial." She understood what was coming. She would be there to the end.

"The poor you always have with you" (RSV). The church has used these words both to justify and to condemn complacence toward the needs of the poor. Jesus clearly was not counseling neglect of the poor. His words were a quotation from Deuteronomy 15:11, whose message is unmistakable: "For the poor will never cease out of the land; therefore I command you, You shall open wide your hand . . . to the needy and to the poor, in the land" (RSV). Ethicist and theologian Stanley Hauerwas comments: "The poor that we always have with us is Jesus. It is to the poor that all extravagance is to be given."[3] The true church always has the poor in its midst, always treasures the life of the poor.

"But you do not always have me." So we return to where we began: with a prelude to the passion. Mary's act came and comes in the midst of a world of treachery and betrayal, in the world and among Jesus' followers.

We live our lives in the shadow of the cross, but we also live in the presence of the risen Christ. So here is an invitation to daily companionship with Jesus, at the Table, in extravagant acts of compassion and generosity, in moments of worship. All this in a world which lives by a mind-set of scarcity, rather than a mind-set of abundance, and so tempts us to close in and give little. All this in a world whose violence and cruelty crucify people every day.

H. STEPHEN SHOEMAKER

3. Stanley Hauerwas, *Matthew* (Grand Rapids: Brazos Press, 2006), 215.

SIXTH SUNDAY IN LENT
(LITURGY OF THE PALMS)

Psalm 118:1-2, 19-29

[1]O give thanks to the LORD, for he is good;
   his steadfast love endures forever!

[2]Let Israel say,
   "His steadfast love endures forever."
. . . .
[19]Open to me the gates of righteousness,
   that I may enter through them
   and give thanks to the LORD.

[20]This is the gate of the LORD;
   the righteous shall enter through it.

[21]I thank you that you have answered me
   and have become my salvation.
[22]The stone that the builders rejected
   has become the chief cornerstone.
[23]This is the LORD's doing;
   it is marvelous in our eyes.

Theological Perspective

"Life is a house." Accompanying that understanding is often a description of what are determined to be the important elements for constructing a magnificent life. This metaphor is actually instilled in people fairly early in life. There are frequent references made to describe basic nutrition and early childhood education as "the building blocks of life." Whether or not we actually think of the body as a building, we regularly use language to describe the body and human life as a building under construction. Reflecting on "the stone that the builders rejected" (v. 22) as a statement about community, the builders can be understood as those who maintain the norms of society, no matter how oppressive those norms might be. With this view, the rejected stones are the undesirable, the outcasts, the "abnormal" persons of society. After all, the stone was rejected because it did not conform to a traditional or conventional building block or cornerstone for the building that was envisioned.

This text praises God for the marvelous thing that God has done by taking what was rejected and making it the source of structural integrity. What was this cornerstone? Perhaps the people believed they had been rejected by other peoples of the world, but the salvation of God made them the cornerstone of what it meant to be faithful. Yet joined with this

Pastoral Perspective

Psalm 118 is a festival psalm for both Jewish and Christian communities. It is read during Passover, as the Jewish people recall God's deliverance of them from slavery in Egypt into freedom. For Christians, Psalm 118:1–2, 19–29 is assigned for Palm Sunday in each year of the lectionary. The joyful thanksgiving of this psalm was the liturgy of the faithful as they processed to the temple. Verse 26, "Blessed is the one who comes in the name of the LORD," became the liturgy in all four Gospels for a noisy crowd in Jerusalem welcoming Jesus, who had come to save them. It is still used today for our Liturgy of the Palms as we reenact that first Palm Sunday. We join throngs of worshipers through the centuries as we, too, "bind the festal procession with branches" (v. 27), singing and waving palm fronds.

Psalm 118 begins and ends with a core affirmation of faith: "O give thanks to the LORD, for he is good; his steadfast love endures forever!" This affirmation brackets all that comes in between. In distress, under threat, outnumbered, pushed to the limit—in every circumstance, we are buttressed on all sides by God, who is good and whose steadfast love endures forever. This thanksgiving for God's steadfast love erupts in a cry of confident gratitude at the center of the psalm, "I shall not die, but I shall live, and recount the deeds of the LORD" (v. 17).

²⁴This is the day that the LORD has made;
　　let us rejoice and be glad in it.
²⁵Save us, we beseech you, O LORD!
　　O LORD, we beseech you, give us success!

²⁶Blessed is the one who comes in the name of the LORD.
　　We bless you from the house of the LORD.
²⁷The LORD is God,
　　and he has given us light.
Bind the festal procession with branches,
　　up to the horns of the altar.

²⁸You are my God, and I will give thanks to you;
　　you are my God, I will extol you.

²⁹O give thanks to the LORD, for he is good,
　　for his steadfast love endures forever.

Exegetical Perspective

The Egyptian Hallel Psalms. Psalm 118 concludes a collection known as the Hallel Psalms (Pss. 113–18). This collection recounts and celebrates God's saving action in the exodus from Egypt and is still read during the Jewish Passover celebration. Psalm 118 recalls the Song of the Sea in Exodus 15. Like Exodus 15 it celebrates God's successful rescue of Israel from a powerful nation. Some see in the psalm a recounting of Israel's return from exile or the success of the Maccabean revolt. Early Christians found the psalm apt for understanding the mission of Jesus. All the Gospels and several Epistles quote portions of this psalm.

A composite hymn. This psalm, an exuberant call to praise God, is sometimes described as an anthology of thanksgiving, because it contains numerous allusions to and quotes from other psalms and hymns. Verse 1 is found in 1 Chronicles 16:34, while a variation of verses 8–9 can be found in Psalm 146:3. Other images and metaphors scattered throughout the psalm can be found in other texts. This psalm has also been described as a victory song, because it recites the threats that enemies pose (vv. 10–18). The psalmist gives thanks on behalf of the king or his surrogate in a liturgical procession that celebrates God's protection.

Homiletical Perspective

Preaching occurs within specific liturgical contexts, and the Psalms in particular are often used in dialogue with other lessons, usually texts from the Old Testament. The Revised Common Lectionary follows this pattern, although we should also allow the Psalms to speak to us on their own terms. The lectionary's juxtaposition of texts cannot, however, be overlooked on Passion/Palm Sunday, in which Psalm 118 immediately follows the first Gospel reading (Luke 19:28–40), the text that recounts the entrance of Jesus into Jerusalem. We will want to ask ourselves, to what, and upon what, was Jesus entering, and to what extent do we participate in that journey? How does this psalm help us pray our way into those dynamics and on into the experience of Holy Week?

This psalm itself reflects public liturgical practice. It begins with thanksgiving for God's steadfast love and deliverance (vv. 1–2ff), and then it brings the worshipers in festal procession to the gates of the temple. There they cry, "Open to me the gates of righteousness, that I may enter through them and give thanks to the LORD" (v. 19). This petition is followed by an offering of thanks to God who has become their salvation (v. 21). The full psalm hearkens back to the exodus (vv. 3–18), in which the ancient worshipers participated through this liturgy

Psalm 118:1-2, 19-29

Theological Perspective

statement of the Lord's doing is also a plea for the salvation of God. They had a definition of "righteousness" that they believed themselves to epitomize. So even though there was a sense of having structural integrity—a righteous faith—they wondered why they were being attacked, and whether their walls—their beliefs—were strong enough to withstand an attack. If this were not the case, why was there a fervent request to be successfully delivered from their troubles in the presence of a God who had done marvelously? There seems to be a difference between what God has done and what the people experience as still lacking in their lives. It suggests that no matter how good things are, trouble is always lurking just outside the gates.

In order to stave off the assaults of life, we regularly prepare ourselves to experience the outcomes we desire in life. We regularly engage in activities, and adopt attitudes, that we perceive will result in the things we want for ourselves. We say things like, "Positive thinking yields positive results," "If you can believe it, you can receive it," and "Name it and claim it!" All these attitudes, which can be associated with preparatory activities, can be linked to our understanding of rituals and sacrificial practices. Consequently, the people who lined the festal procession with the palm branches that symbolized victory as they proceeded to the altar were engaging in activities to promote their desired outcome of deliverance and triumph. One of the deep challenges this text presents for us relates to the communal nature of ritual and sacrifice. All too often, we hold rituals to be individual practices, and sacrifices to be for individual purposes. Once we conceive rituals to be communal events, and sacrifices to be communal activities intended for the benefit of many, our power for living is enhanced.

Naturally, when we begin to think and speak of an integrated life, we attend to our spirituality with the language of construction. We often speak of marriage as "building a life together." The wonderful thing about connecting marriage to "the stone that the builders rejected" is that perhaps marriage, as we know it, should be "constructed" in an unconventional way that could actually make it a healthier dwelling with deep spiritual integrity. Reflecting on the building and the cornerstone in this way, a new foundation for encouraging a spirituality of marriage may emerge. Spirituality is an integrative process that restores people to a life of relationships. By extension, emphasizing the

Pastoral Perspective

Psalm 118 was Martin Luther's favorite psalm. He wrote verse 17 on the wall of his study in Coburg castle, where he stayed during an anxious time. During the tumultuous Reformation, Luther's experiences taught him not to place confidence in human beings, in princes or nations. With the psalmist he knew that our only sure refuge, our confidence, is in God alone.

This model prayer is characterized by thanksgiving wholly focused upon the power and goodness of God. Even at verse 19, when the psalmist says, "Open to me the gates of righteousness," the petition is based not on confidence in the psalmist's own righteousness, but on confidence in God's righteousness. The petitioner asks to enter the temple not out of personal worthiness, but in order to thank God, who has come to save and set free. In fact, the psalmist says that God has "become my salvation" (v. 21).

Many years ago in a theology class at Columbia Theological Seminary, Professor Shirley Guthrie was teaching the doctrine of salvation. One student became adamant that not all would be saved; that some were unrighteous and deserved God's eternal condemnation. This student was confident that unrighteous people would receive the punishment they had coming to them. As he continued in this vein, the rest of the class hoped he would not start naming names! After a pause, Dr. Guthrie said in his kind, yet confident manner: "Look, God is *for* us . . . not against us!" That affirmation is the framework within which we live and move and have our being. Our entrance into the temple, into eternal life, is not based on our own righteousness! Our confidence is in God, who has become our salvation.

Why is it so hard for us to live in thanksgiving for God's goodness and love? We mean to live, make decisions, and relate to others in the joyful freedom and salvation God brings. Yet we still act (or react) out of fear instead of faith. Threatened or afraid, we feel that we are on our own to "make it" in this world. We depend on our own power or resources rather than God. Individuals, groups, whole nations turn to economic strength, intellectual prowess, physical or military might to overcome opposing powers. Fearful, insecure, we measure ourselves against others; their judgment becomes our tool of self-assessment, or we judge others as unworthy.

Psalm 118 again turns our attention to God, who apparently sees things differently from the way we often see them. God chooses to use for good what we often reject. A powerful metaphor (vv. 22–23) makes

Exegetical Perspective

The first and last verses of the psalm are identical, producing an *inclusio* or envelope structure. These verses announce the thanksgiving (*todah*) theme of the psalm. A rehearsal of God's saving acts on Israel's behalf shows up between the verses. The psalm opens with a general call to give thanks to God, followed by what appears to be an antiphonal song. The movement of this song is from a broad audience to a narrow audience and finally to a broader audience. Israel is called to give thanks, then the sons of Aaron (priests), and then a wider community made up of those who "fear God." This same pattern also appears in Psalm 115:9–13. One gives thanks to God because God's "steadfast love" (*hesed*) endures forever.

The kindness of God celebrated. *Hesed* (steadfast love) is a rich word in Hebrew and especially favored by the psalmists. One half of all the appearances of this word in the Old Testament are in the Psalter. Older translations render it "lovingkindness." When attributed to God, it speaks of God's capacity to love and to keep covenant. Although God's "kindness" extends to thousands of generations, the psalmist is able to identify in his/her own experience the particular occasion of God's immeasurable kindness.

The tone of the psalm is one of entreaty and invitation. In verse 2 the particle *na'* appears for the first of a number of times. Translating it is difficult, because it communicates tone more than a distinct lexical meaning. At times it is translated "pray," as in "I pray you do this," which carries an urgent tone. In verse 25, it appears in an address to God and is translated "we beseech you." In verses 2, 3, and 4, it is used in an address from the psalmist to humans and reflects the insistent, invitatory nature of the psalm. Typically the particle is not part of a command but a request. The opening verses make the psalm appropriate for use in the Liturgy of the Palms because of its joyful invitation to participate in giving thanks to God.

A liturgy of thanksgiving. Verses 19–29 open with what many scholars identify as a liturgical rubric. The worshiper or leader of the procession calls out to the priest to open the gates of the temple so that they may come in and give thanks to God. Other examples of gate liturgies can be found in Psalms 15 and 24. In both these psalms, there is an extensive description of the one who may enter to worship, but in our psalm it is simplified in verse 20 to the "righteous" (*tsedaqim*). Once the gates are opened, the psalmist declares his/her reason for giving thanks

Homiletical Perspective

of procession.[1] As Christians pray it, it draws them into that original narrative of deliverance and also points them toward the narrative that will unfold during Holy Week. Again, standing on the edge of Holy Week, we should ask about the shape of the journey we are entering. What kind of salvation we are receiving?

The odd saying "The stone that the builders rejected has become the chief cornerstone" (v. 22) should give pause to those who hear it today. It speaks of God's choosing an unlikely instrument, of God's confounding conventional wisdom. It speaks of God's election and call, but of whom? How shall we understand such a calling? What will a God who speaks such things do in our time? Christians have heard these words from Jesus, as he spoke them against the Jewish religious leaders within the parable of the Wicked Tenants (Matt. 21:42; Mark 12:10, Luke 20:17). Peter and John also quote it against the religious leaders (Acts 4:11). First Peter 2:7 presents it as judgment upon those who do not believe. In the liturgical context of Passion/Palm Sunday, the church must hear this text over against Holy Week and the passion narrative. A way of salvation that exalts the weak and powerless will always seems strange, and the way of the cross downright absurd. Preachers must resist attempts to domesticate that strangeness. God indeed works through materials that many prudent architects of society would reject. Can the preacher point to such occurrences, even locally?

Because various New Testament passages (see above) use this text polemically against Jewish religious leaders, contemporary interpreters must make particular effort not to use it in an anti-Semitic way. We are not far removed historically from such tragic use of Scripture within the rites of Holy Week. We need to hear this text about the rejected stone as judgment spoken first to our assemblies and individual lives. How does it call us to reverse our expectations about what faith will do for us, about where God is leading this procession?

The psalmist speaks of the procession entering the temple gates and moving directly to the altar. Liturgical scholars know that processions originally were going somewhere, other than in circles. Sometimes they moved from one stational liturgy to another, sometimes into the streets to pray for the city's protection from earthquake or invaders,[2]

---

1. See discussion by J. Clinton McCann in *The New Interpreter's Bible* (Nashville: Abingdon Press, 1996), 4:1153–54.
2. Robert F. Taft, *The Byzantine Rite, A Short History* (Collegeville, MN: Liturgical Press, 1992), 30.

Psalm 118:1-2, 19-29

Theological Perspective

cornerstone of living together as truly being the work and doing of the Lord further highlights the spirituality of family, community, and all of life.

Given the "on again—off again" debates about marriage and American society, seeing marriage as a spiritual reality instead of a political agenda is critical. Although marriage now tends to be presented as a covenantal relationship blessed by God through a clergyperson, the earliest constructions of marriage were not much more than legal, economic arrangements. Even if one appeals to the New Testament era for describing marriage, there is significant evidence to suggest that marriage, as presented in the Epistles, was the socially acceptable institution for sexual expression. In fact, the popular Pauline admonishment declares, "It is better to marry than to be aflame with passion" (1 Cor. 7:9)—that is, if one cannot control one's sexual desires for the sake of the spirit, then get married.

While there is a frequent feeling that marriage is being assaulted as a rejected stone, there is room to reform our understanding of marriage to move it from a legal, economic institution to a spiritual institution. If the rejected stone becomes the cornerstone for a spirituality of marriage, then there is the hope of building healthier, happier marriages. This might begin by reimagining the ritual of the wedding ceremony. The wedding is understood to be the ritual that precedes the salvation brought by the "holy state of matrimony." Couples regularly approach the altar, down a path lined with petals, with a sense of expectancy about the future. They even see the quality of the ceremony as predictive of the quality of marriage. But rather than the couple taking seriously the communal nature of the event, they regularly isolate the guests as observers and not supporters of the vows they take and make. To transition from a legal basis for marriage to a spiritual basis for marriage, it is vitally important to declare a broad-based definition of spirituality.

LEE H. BUTLER JR.

Pastoral Perspective

it clear that the world's judgments are often wrong, at odds with the judgments and purposes of God: "The stone that the builders rejected has become the chief cornerstone. This is the LORD's doing; it is marvelous in our eyes." The cornerstone of a building is chosen with care, for the weight of the building presses on it from different sides. What looks weak and unworthy to us may be just what God has in mind! Think of Moses and a band of slaves up against Pharaoh and all his mighty army! Today Christians read this metaphor as a reference to Jesus Christ. These verses are often cited in the New Testament (Matt. 21:42; Mark 12:10–11; Luke 20:17; Acts 4:11; and 1 Pet. 2:4–8) to make that connection explicit.

On this Palm Sunday, we join the crowd in Jerusalem, naming Jesus as the one who has come to save us. However because we have lived beyond that first Palm Sunday, we know how the week ahead plays out. We know that the "builders" who reject Jesus as king and cornerstone are not only the chief priests and other authorities, but the crowds also . . . even his own disciples. Though we try to live in faith rather than fear, we are still in the company of those who fall away, fall asleep, betray, deny and doubt him. We still reject what God chooses. Nevertheless, our actions do not determine what God is building! Jesus Christ has become the chief cornerstone, the risen Lord! This is God's doing, not ours. It is marvelous in our eyes. "O give thanks to the LORD, for he is good; his steadfast love endures forever!"

We end where we began: in joyful thanksgiving to God who comes to save us and set us free. Because God has chosen to save us through the life, death, and resurrection of Jesus, we know that, like him, we do not escape or bypass sadness, danger, threat, and death. Knowing that God is for us and not against us, we may live with confidence in God. Our fears are no match for the salvation God brings. Our loudest laments are lost in the litany of thanksgiving: "O give thanks to God!" *"God's steadfast love endures forever!"*

KIMBERLY L. CLAYTON

Exegetical Perspective

to God. God has answered the psalmist and saved him/her out of a desperate situation. This salvation appeared as a reversal of fortunes to all who witnessed it. The stone that the builders rejected ironically became the most important. This architectural imagery links with the previous verses regarding the gates of the temple. The cornerstone is the most important element in the construction of a building and serves as the measuring point for the entire structure. Israel was rejected by the imperial powers (Egypt, Babylon, the Ptolemies) who oppressed it, but now God has vindicated Israel.

In verses 19–29, the tense changes several times; this may be due to its liturgical use. Early Jewish scholars saw in these verses an antiphonal structure of several voices. Verse 19 is the request of the pilgrims or those coming to give God thanks. Someone answers back, perhaps from the temple steps, inviting the righteous to enter through the gates of the temple. Verses 21–22 give the pilgrim's reflection on his/her experience of deliverance and God's elevation of the psalmist, who at one time appeared to be rejected. In verses 23–27 the tense changes from first-person singular to first-person plural; perhaps this signals an extended recitation by the pilgrims who come to the temple.

The first half of verse 26, found in all the Gospels to describe the people's response to Jesus' entry into Jerusalem, looks backward to God's help of Israel and forward to God's doing a new thing. This use of the verse witnesses to the continuity between the Old and New Testaments by demonstrating how readers of the Old Testament find in it a promise of God's continued concern for the faithful. The verb translated "comes" is found also in verses 19–20 and there translated "enter." Verse 26 could be better translated "Blessed is the one who enters in the name of the LORD," which would continue the thought of one entering the temple precincts to worship God.

The psalm ends with a clear description of a liturgical moment in which the procession makes its way to the altar with its sacrifice. The moment is concluded with a confession of loyalty to God.

STEVEN BISHOP

Homiletical Perspective

sometimes into the fields to pray that crops be protected.[3] We retain them for various ceremonial reasons, and sometimes simply because they go well with the hymnody that was written for times when the procession was, in fact, going somewhere other than the church aisles. Thus the wise preacher will ask, where does God wish to lead today's procession? Preachers can point out that the Palm Sunday procession accompanied by this psalm is procession into the nave and also procession into the world where God's mission unfolds. A sermon preached before an ecumenical procession through one's community could make this point with particular clarity, as could a sermon delivered at a common mission site located on the route.

The psalm concludes its remembrance of God's *hesed* with the liturgical affirmation, "This is the day that the LORD has made; let us rejoice . . ." (v. 24). Such a reminder unfolds within all of the church's anamnesis. God's saving work continues. In the midst of this celebration song, the call "Save us, LORD!" may seem like an odd twist, yet it is the ongoing dynamic of life in God. We live at the intersection of remembrance and petition, with visions rooted in God's promise calling us forward. In one sense the assembly always comes to Holy Week needing to be saved again, and so we pray, "Save us!" What shape will such a petition take in your congregation? In what ways do you desperately need God's mercy? How will the call for salvation be about your community?

Some who hear this psalm will be much more attuned to the reality of suffering than others. Many struggle, perhaps unconsciously, against societal pressures that insist on continuous optimism. The preacher must remind her congregation that the story of salvation never denies the reality of suffering, that it bids the faithful pray for help in the midst of trouble.

MARK W. STAMM

3. Martin Dudley, "Rogation Days," in *The New Dictionary of Liturgy and Worship*, ed. Paul Bradshaw (Louisville, KY: Westminster John Knox Press, 2002), 410.

Luke 19:28-40

²⁸After he had said this, he went on ahead, going up to Jerusalem.
²⁹When he had come near Bethphage and Bethany, at the place called the Mount of Olives, he sent two of the disciples, ³⁰saying, "Go into the village ahead of you, and as you enter it you will find tied there a colt that has never been ridden. Untie it and bring it here. ³¹If anyone asks you, 'Why are you untying it?' just say this, 'The Lord needs it.'" ³²So those who were sent departed and found it as he had told them. ³³As they were untying the colt, its owners asked them, "Why are you untying the colt?" ³⁴They said, "The Lord needs it." ³⁵Then they brought it to Jesus; and after throwing their cloaks on the colt, they set Jesus on it. ³⁶As he rode along, people kept spreading their cloaks on the road. ³⁷As he was now approaching the path down from the Mount of Olives, the whole multitude of the disciples began to praise God joyfully with a loud voice for all the deeds of power that they had seen, ³⁸saying,

"Blessed is the king
  who comes in the name of the Lord!
Peace in heaven,
  and glory in the highest heaven!"

³⁹Some of the Pharisees in the crowd said to him, "Teacher, order your disciples to stop." ⁴⁰He answered, "I tell you, if these were silent, the stones would shout out."

Theological Perspective

Luke's Jesus is unintelligible apart from the history of Israel, especially its prophetic literature. At this point in Luke's story Jesus has concluded his journey to Jerusalem (9:51–19:27) and now prepares to enter the city. As at numerous other places in Luke's story, Jesus' words to his disciples are immediately fulfilled in the events that follow. Jesus tells two of his disciples to enter a nearby village, look for a colt that has never been ridden, and bring it to him. If asked what they are doing, the disciples are to say only, "The Lord needs it" (vv. 29–32). The disciples do as they are commanded, and events unfold exactly as Jesus said they would. Like other prophets in Israel's history, Jesus seems to have the power to predict future events.

After the disciples return with the colt, they place blankets on it, and Jesus rides into Jerusalem, fulfilling the prophecy of Zechariah 9:9 ("Lo, your king comes to you; triumphant and victorious is he, humble and riding on a donkey, on a colt, the foal of a donkey") while "the multitude of the disciples" sing the words of Psalm 118:26, "Blessed is the one who comes in the name of the LORD." When Pharisees ask Jesus to silence the crowd, Jesus quotes Habakkuk 2:11 ("I tell you, if these were silent, the stones would shout out"). For Luke, therefore, Jesus is a prophet in a twofold sense: first, he fulfills what

Pastoral Perspective

Since the earliest days of the church, Christians have been shaped by a simple ritual. A worship leader proclaims the blessing, "The peace of the Lord Jesus Christ be with you." Everybody else is invited to respond, "And also with you." This is the echo that we still create every Sunday. Somebody says it to us, and we say it right back. According to Luke's text, this practice dates back at least as far as the first Palm Sunday.

Luke's Palm Sunday account echoes his Christmas story. When Jesus was born, the Gospel writer tells us that angels appeared to sing, "Peace on earth" (Luke 2:14). Now, as Jesus rides his colt toward Jerusalem, the people look to the sky and sing, "Peace in heaven." Heaven sings of peace on earth. Earth echoes back, "Peace in heaven." As the church gathers this day, we are caught in the crossfire of blessings.

For Luke, this is more than a slick literary detail. It is the announcement of what God makes possible in the death and resurrection of Jesus. We hear the story of Jesus approaching Jerusalem from the Mount of Olives, from the spot where tradition held that the Messiah would appear. A gathering of his followers surround him, praising God with exuberant voices. They sing Psalm 118 as their song of deliverance, affirming that God will rescue God's chosen people.

Exegetical Perspective

Luke 19:28–40 contains two distinct responses to Jesus' entrance into Jerusalem. Jesus' disciples acclaim him king and celebrate his entrance into the city that in their tradition was the point of contact between heaven and earth. However "some of the Pharisees" (to avoid negative stereotyping, note that the text speaks of "some" and does not characterize all Pharisees) ask Jesus to restrain the disciples. Jesus' response affirms his disciples: God, who is able to raise up from stones children to Abraham (3:8), could make stones on the Mount of Olives cry out. However this entrance is also the prelude to Jesus' crucifixion.

In the structure of Luke, Jerusalem has been in mind a long time. In the transfiguration, Moses and Elijah talk with Jesus about his *exodus*, which he will accomplish in Jerusalem (9:31). The NRSV translates this as "departure," but given the role of Moses, it is difficult to avoid parallels with Israel's exodus from Egypt—broadly speaking, liberation and identity. If asked, "Who are you?" Israelites might say, "God brought us out of the land of bondage." Is this what Jesus accomplishes—liberation and identity for the children of God?

Two other episodes help to set the context: the story of Zacchaeus and the parable of the Pounds. Zacchaeus is a rich tax collector. First, his wealth is a problem: "It is easier for a camel to go through the

Homiletical Perspective

The perennial challenge for the preacher on Palm Sunday: The kingly procession into Jerusalem will lead to death on a Roman cross. So the preacher must peer forward beyond the joyous praise to the death of Jesus. Many of the congregation may not partake of the coming week's solemn passage until they come fresh-scrubbed and dressed fine on Easter eager to sing, "Christ the Lord is risen today." Verses 39–40 hint at what is to come, but the sermon may well include the prophetic lament and the cleansing of the temple, verses 41–46.

The two processions. Jesus scholars Borg and Crossan give us a riveting image with which to begin: there were the two processions that Passover week.[1] From the west came Pilate draped in the gaudy glory of imperial power: horses, chariots, and gleaming armor. He moved in with the Roman army at the beginning of Passover week to make sure nothing got out of hand. Insurrection was in the air with the memory of God's deliverance of the Hebrew people from slavery in Egypt.

From the east came another procession, a commoner's procession: Jesus in ordinary robe riding on a

---

1. Marcus Borg and John Dominic Crossan, *The Last Week* (New York: HarperSanFrancisco, 2006), 1–5.

Luke 19:28-40

Theological Perspective

the prophets before him have said, and second, Jesus' acts and the events in his life fulfill what he has said.

Christian theologians have long recognized that the Synoptic Gospels use the Old Testament offices of priest and king to describe the significance of Jesus' death and resurrection. This text, like countless others in the Synoptic Gospels, uses the offices of priest and king to interpret the significance of Jesus' death and resurrection. In the Letter to the Hebrews, Jesus is described as "the source of eternal salvation for all who obey him, having been designated by God a high priest according to the order of Melchizedek" (Heb. 5:9–10). In 1 Timothy, Jesus is referred to as "the blessed and only sovereign, the King of kings and Lord of lords" (1 Tim. 6:15).

John Calvin expanded the twofold office of priest and king as a description of Jesus as the Christ and added a third anointed office from the history of Israel—that of prophet. If the offices of priest and king are used to interpret the events of Jesus' death and resurrection, the prophetic office becomes an interpretation of the Gospels' description of Jesus' ministry from Galilee to Jerusalem. Unfortunately, Calvin restricted Jesus' prophetic office to his teaching. "This, however, remains certain: the perfect doctrine he has brought has made an end to all prophecies."[1] To Calvin, Jesus is a prophet in his teaching of "perfect doctrine." Calvin gives little or no attention to Jesus' prophetic actions of healing and of driving out demons, not to mention money changers.

Hans Frei argues that something remarkable occurs in the Gospels' descriptions of Jesus. Luke's description of Jesus' entry into Jerusalem is only one of many scenes in which Luke uses prophetic material from Israel's history in order to interpret Jesus' identity. However, a subtle but important reversal takes place in the course of Luke's story. Jesus is initially interpreted in light of Israel's prophets, but as the story progresses, Jesus, in his particularity (which Frei describes as Jesus' "singularity" and "unsubstitutability"), redefines the office of prophet. Israel's prophets proclaim God's Word to Israel. They preface what they have to say to Israel with the words "Thus says the LORD" and "Hear the word of the LORD." In the Gospels, however, Jesus not only proclaims God's Word; he *is* God's Word. As Frei puts it, "He, the unsubstitutable Jesus, now makes the stylized titles his own. He claims them for himself in his very identity as Jesus

---

1. John Calvin, *Institutes of the Christian Religion*, ed. John T. McNeill, trans. Ford Lewis Battles (Philadelphia: Westminster Press, 1960), 2.15.2.

Pastoral Perspective

Like many peace songs, the psalm provokes anxiety. Some Pharisees want the crowd to hush. We do not know their reasons. Perhaps they think the moment is too political and the empire will retaliate. Or they may disagree with the inference that Jesus is the Messiah. We cannot say for sure. However the Pharisees cannot restrain the crowd. On a day like this, that would be like requesting church choirs to forget about singing Faure's "The Palms."

As Jesus comes around a bend in the road, something changes. He sees the whole city spread out before him. It makes him weep, and we hear him say, "Jerusalem! If only today you knew the things that make for peace, but you do not know them. They are hidden from your eyes."

His words interrupt the echo. Peace on earth, peace in heaven—yet in between, Jesus says there is no peace. His words offer a chilling premonition of what will happen later in Holy Week.

For all its joyful hosannas, Palm Sunday is a day of contrasts. We hear it in the hymns, pivoting as they do between happy triumph and inevitable crucifixion. We see it in Jesus, as the ruler of the universe chooses to ride a borrowed colt. The contrast is clear in the destination, as the city that welcomes him will later scream for his blood. For now, at least, the greatest hopes for peace are hidden from those who wish for it.

We have our own contradictions, of course. Someone tells us the best way to create peace is by initiating a war. The strong are strengthened by holding off the weak. Parents confront fear by buying a handgun for the dresser drawer. Schools encourage competition over cooperation. Governments and businesses seek to win at all costs, even if it bankrupts them. Jesus rides his lowly farm animal through all of it.

Here is what the preacher can ask: What are the things that make for peace? What are the things "hidden from our eyes"?

By asking, we recognize that we do not know the answer. In Luke's Gospel, Jesus indicts again from the cross, saying, "Forgive them, Father, for they *do not know* what they are doing" (Luke 23:34). There is a kind of ignorance, not of the intellect, but of the heart. It is possible to think through a problem without committing to a solution. We can reason our way through a conflict as if it is a game of chess, and totally miss the victims. If we think ourselves superior, we will even miss ourselves.

Years ago, I was studying the New Testament while my father worked for a military contractor.

eye of a needle than for someone who is rich to enter the kingdom of God. . . . Then who can be saved?" (18:25–26). Second, as a chief tax collector, he is a collaborator with Rome. These are matters of oppression and identity. As liberationists have shown, oppressors (and their collaborators) also need to be liberated. Furthermore, as a collaborator, Zacchaeus has compromised his identity. People call him "sinner" (19:7). He has lost identity among the people of God.

The parable of the Pounds is usually interpreted as correcting the expectation of Jesus' disciples "that the kingdom of God was to appear immediately" (19:11). From this perspective, God's kingdom is typically pushed to the eschaton. For Luke, however, there may be a sense in which the kingdom does come with Jesus' entry into Jerusalem. In my view, the parable does not describe God's judgment. Rather, it reflects Israel's situation under Rome, and alludes to Herod Antipas, Rome's client king in Galilee (in Jerusalem at the time of Jesus' crucifixion [Luke 23:7]), who went to Rome to get royal power, and enlisted other collaborators, like the slaves in the parable, and who came back to enforce the flow of revenue upward to the elite of the empire. The parable is not about God's kingdom, but the reality against which Jesus proclaims God's kingdom.

Jesus' entrance follows the plot of Zechariah 9:9: Zion's king comes to Jerusalem triumphant and victorious, humble and riding on a donkey. The disciples' acclamation comes from Psalm 118:26: "Blessed is the one who comes in the name of the LORD," to which Luke adds an explicit reference to Jesus as king. However Luke also adds a comment about peace and glory. The praise of the multitude of angels in 2:14 is about peace on *earth*, and in fact Jesus bestows peace on *earth* (7:50; 8:48; 10:6). Further, the plot of Zechariah 9, which is so strongly played out in Jesus' entry, anticipates God's acts to establish peace for *Jerusalem*.

However Luke 19:38 locates peace in *heaven*. Has peace become otherworldly? It certainly has become complicated, because of the inability of some of Jesus' compatriots to perceive the ways that make for peace, and this portends violence and destruction (19:42–44).

How is it possible to understand the notion of peace? One clue lies in the reason that Jesus' disciples acclaim him king. They praise God for all the deeds of power that they have seen (19:37). The content of Luke up until this point offers a broad selection of deeds of power—healings, exorcisms, resuscitations

young donkey. The careful preparations suggest that Jesus has planned a highly ritualized symbolic prophetic act. Luke has in mind the prophecy of Zechariah 9:9–10, the coming of a new kind of king, a king of peace who will dismantle the weaponry of war.

As Jesus enters, a "whole multitude of the disciples," throng around, spread their cloaks on the road, and lift loud their praise: "Blessed is *the king* who comes in the name of the Lord." "King" has been added to the Hallel Psalm they sing (Ps. 118:26).

Then a couplet of praise is added: "Peace in heaven, and glory in the highest heaven." This is more than a song of heavenly rest and hope in the world to come. It is about the "kingdom of the heavens," as Matthew called it, which has drawn near in Jesus to challenge and change the kingdoms of this world. This "multitude" echoes the song of the "multitude of the heavenly host" in Luke's birth narrative: "Glory to God in the highest heaven, and on earth peace" (2:13–14).

What kind of king? So we have a clash of kingdoms: Caesar or Christ. Caesar's kingdom is based on domination and ruthless power, the kind of kingship Jesus refused when tempted in the wilderness. The kingdom of God Jesus preached is based on justice, mercy, and the love of God (Luke 11:42 and Matt. 23:23). So we have our choice: *Pax Christi* or *Pax Romana*. Our challenge is to show how the gospel of the kingdom has political implications but transcends our everyday political loyalties.

The wild joy of the disciples and the rebuke of the Pharisees. The throng of disciples cannot contain themselves. We think of David stripped to his loincloth dancing before the ark of the Lord as it was brought into Jerusalem.

A group of Pharisees say to Jesus, "Order your disciples to stop."

Are they embarrassed by the wild, ecstatic praise? Are they trying to warn Jesus of the danger of such a demonstration? Earlier in Luke, some Pharisees warn Jesus about Herod's murderous intent: "Get away from here, for Herod wants to kill you" (13:31). Were they afraid that the Roman authorities would smell insurrection and come with terrible vengeance against the nation? Probably.

Jesus' answer: The stones will cry out! Luke's Gospel alone records these thrilling, faith-filled words: "I tell you, if these were silent, the stones would shout out." Here is faith in the sure triumph of God. There are several layers of meaning available in this phrase.

Luke 19:28-40

Theological Perspective

of Nazareth. . . . *Jesus identifies the titles rather than they him.*[2] In other words, Jesus is initially interpreted as fulfilling the words of Israel's prophets; but by the time his identity is fully manifested in his death and resurrection, readers should understand Israel's prophets in the light of Jesus. He identifies them, not they him.

In some forms of contemporary theology, Jesus serves as an example, perhaps even *the* example, of what we already believe about freedom and peace. When this happens, it is our prior notions of freedom and peace that tell us who Jesus is, and Jesus becomes captive to our ideologies. In the Gospels, however, Jesus stands in judgment of all our ideologies. His kingdom is not simply a verification of what we think God's kingdom should be, as Peter discovered in Mark 8:31–33. It is Jesus, as he is given to us in the Gospels, who shows us what freedom truly is (Gal. 5:1) and what, or who, peace really is (Eph. 2:17–22).

The great multitude along the road into Jerusalem declares Jesus to be the one who comes in the name of the Lord and who represents heaven's peace and glory ("Peace in heaven, and glory in the highest heaven!" [v. 38]). In the verses that follow, Luke returns to these words of praise from the multitude. The multitude's praise and joy suddenly turn to great sorrow when Jesus weeps over Jerusalem, because even though the multitude sings of peace and glory in heaven, it fails to recognize the price of true peace, "the things that make for peace!" (v. 42). The multitude sings of peace in heaven without recognizing that Jesus is not an example of some larger notion of peace. He is their peace. Indeed he is the peace of the world—not any peace, but the peace that only he can give—and that peace cannot be found apart from the journey that leads inexorably to Golgotha, both for him and for those that would be his disciples.

GEORGE W. STROUP

Pastoral Perspective

That prompted many interesting conversations during my school vacations. I spoke eagerly about my dreams for world peace, and he listened patiently. Sometimes he noted that it was people like him who put money in the offering plate so that people like me could become preachers.

After one of my rants, he said, "I do not disagree with anything you have said, but we will never have peace on earth until we can quiet the wars within our own hearts." Then he looked at me as if to say, "They should teach you such things at the seminary."

Jesus rides no high horse, just a lowly colt. He chooses to enter a deadly situation without force or protection. He gives himself freely and without reservation. This is a prophetic act, a sign of God's vulnerable love, which risks everything and promises to gain all. This is the means by which God creates peace.

Halfway down the Mount of Olives, there is a small chapel in the shape of a teardrop. It is called Dominus Flevit (Latin for "the Lord weeps"). It is the traditional location where Jesus wept over the city. Pilgrims gather there to share the Eucharist as they move toward Jerusalem. As they view a city still divided, with people of different faiths squabbling over the same real estate, they pass the bread to the words, "This is my body, broken for you." Then they share the cup of wine, saying, "This is the new covenant in my blood, shed for the forgiveness of sins." It is a moment to recall the great cost of reconciliation, as God sent Jesus into the world to bring all back to God's powerful love.

Sometimes we are clueless when it comes to peace. However for those who continue to share the body and blood of Christ, it is common to say, "The peace of the Lord Jesus Christ be with you all."

How does each of us respond? With the words, "And also with you."

WILLIAM G. CARTER

---

2. Hans Frei, *The Identity of Jesus Christ: The Hermeneutical Bases of Dogmatic Theology* (Philadelphia: Fortress Press, 1975), 136 (emphasis added).

of the son of the widow of Nain and of Jairus's daughter, feeding the five thousand. In the context, however, the closest deed of power has to do with Zacchaeus. As 18:25 establishes, saving a rich person is virtually impossible. Moreover, Zacchaeus is a collaborator with Rome. Unlike another rich man, who went away sad (18:23), Zacchaeus's encounter with Jesus converts him, turns him around. He stops serving mammon (16:13), gives to the poor, and makes fourfold restitution for defrauding. Whereas in 18:27 for a rich man to enter God's kingdom is impossible for human beings, for God it is possible. Zacchaeus stops being a collaborator, and Jesus demonstrates his regained identity by calling him a son of Abraham. In the case of Zacchaeus, God has wrought a deed of power through Jesus, and in 19:37 Jesus' disciples praise God for all such deeds of power. Is this the kind of divine, heavenly power that makes for peace?

Would turning around the way empires and their collaborators serve mammon rather than God be a reason to praise God and hail Jesus as a king who makes for peace? The acclamation of peace in heaven and glory in the highest should not be read only in terms of eschatology, especially for people who pray for God's kingdom to come, as in Luke 11:2. Rather, inasmuch as Jerusalem is the point of contact between heaven and earth, affirming peace in heaven should anticipate pouring out peace on earth.

Then Jesus laments that the destiny of Jerusalem is hindered by ways that do not make for peace (19:42). In fact, much of the rest of the story in Luke is about how clients and collaborators of the empire use the violence of crucifixion to try to maintain their distorted version of peace.

JAE WON LEE

First, here is a truth too good to have its mouth shut. It may be temporarily silenced, but not for long.

Second, if disciples fall away by cowardice or complacence, God will raise up more! As John the Baptist said in his message by the Jordan: "God is able from these stones to raise up children to Abraham" (Luke 3:8). Poet Richard Wilbur's Christmas hymn, "A stable lamp is lighted," evokes the wonder of this truth by reminding us that "every stone must cry / every stone must cry."[2]

Third, here is an echo of the prophetic warning of Habakuk 2:9–11. Injustice will not long prevail. The very stones of the house built on corruption "will cry out from the wall." This meaning points to what will happen next in Luke. So we turn to verses 41–46.

The lament over Jerusalem and the cleansing of the temple. Since the lectionary will skip to the passion reading, the preacher may well close by including Jesus' prophetic lament and the symbolic prophetic action at the temple. This is where Jesus has been aiming since Luke 9:51. His own offering of himself, even to death on the cross, must not be disassociated from his prophetic challenge to the ruling elite of his nation who were betraying Torah and God's people. God's saving work on the cross and Jesus' saving work that led to the cross need not be pitted against one another.

So here we have the vivid scene of Jesus weeping over Jerusalem, who would not recognize "the things that make for peace." We have his warning of destruction to come: not one stone left upon another.

Then we have Jesus driving the money changers from the temple and saying, "It is written, 'My house shall be a house of prayer'; but you have made it a den of robbers." Jesus' quotation from Jeremiah makes clear his challenge to the nation's leadership: a call for righteousness and justice. A pondering of Jeremiah 7:3–11 is essential.

Spellbound (vv. 47–48). Every day, as Jesus taught in the temple, religious leaders kept trying to find a way to kill him, but the people who heard him were "spellbound." The crowds that sang and waved palms and laid their garments are still with him, still part of the kingdom movement Jesus brought. Even us.

H. STEPHEN SHOEMAKER

---

2. Richard Wilbur, "A Christmas Hymn," in *New and Collected Poems* (New York: Harcourt Brace Jovanovich, 1988), 225.

SIXTH SUNDAY IN LENT
(LITURGY OF THE PASSION)
Isaiah 50:4-9a

> ⁴The Lord God has given me
>   the tongue of a teacher,
> that I may know how to sustain
>   the weary with a word.
> Morning by morning he wakens—
>   wakens my ear
>   to listen as those who are taught.
> ⁵The Lord God has opened my ear,
>   and I was not rebellious,
>   I did not turn backward.
> ⁶I gave my back to those who struck me,
>   and my cheeks to those who pulled out the beard;
> I did not hide my face
>   from insult and spitting.

Theological Perspective

This text is one of the Suffering Servant songs, which Christians often read as prefiguring Jesus Christ—particularly Jesus' own suffering on the cross and his obedience to the will of his Father. (Remember Jesus' prayer in the Garden of Gethsemane: "My Father, if it is possible, let this cup pass from me; yet not what I want but what you want.") It is no surprise, then, that this text should show up in the lectionary during the Liturgy of the Passion, the time when Christians meditate on Christ's suffering for us and his willingness to be crucified for our sin. In much of traditional Christian interpretation, Jesus Christ is the Suffering Servant sent by God to bear the burden—indeed to die—for human sinfulness and disobedience to God.

This understanding of Jesus Christ is often accompanied by a further interpretation that shares this theme of obedient suffering. As Christians are called to be disciples of Christ and follow in his footsteps, the Suffering Servant figure also has been held up for Christians as a model for bearing one's own suffering—in whatever form that might take—with patience and endurance, believing in God's power of vindication and deliverance for us as well. We see this, for example, in Paul's Letter to the Romans.

While certainly there are facets of both this particular theory of atonement and this model of Christian discipleship that continue to resonate

Pastoral Perspective

Teachers draw upon both knowledge based on information and knowledge based on experience. The "tongue of a teacher" (v. 4a) here clearly leans in the direction of knowledge based on experience. The prophet takes on the voice of the Servant and leaves behind the illusion of judicious objectivity that teaching based on information allows, and that seems so prevalent in seminary education. He takes the immediacy of experience out of the realm of personal excitement or satisfaction (or voyeurism, in the case of so-called reality television). Rather, he prepares to plunge the reader into a terrifying realm of human life that defies information and takes experience into the deep and fearful reality of the human heart.

This teacher's stated purpose is to "sustain the weary with a word," which can be done in a genuinely helpful fashion only by one who has known a kind of bone weariness. The Servant's experience allows for the claim that such weariness is a gift from God that empowers the one who has come through the experience to reach out to those who are still caught in the mire of weariness. To have "been there and done that" does not permit the teacher to dismiss the suffering of another, but calls the Servant to speak a word that can be sustaining to the weary soul.

The unusual turn here is not that the Servant's call to teach stems from experience, nor that the

⁷The Lord GOD helps me;
   therefore I have not been disgraced;
   therefore I have set my face like flint,
   and I know that I shall not be put to shame;
⁸ he who vindicates me is near.
  Who will contend with me?
  Let us stand up together.
  Who are my adversaries?
  Let them confront me.
⁹It is the Lord GOD who helps me;
   who will declare me guilty?

Exegetical Perspective

In a hostile world, the path of a faithful disciple can be perilous and lonely. Such a situation confronts the figure in today's reading from the anonymous prophet called Second Isaiah (Isa. 40–55). By heeding God's daily word to him in the face of withering criticism, this individual must endure the harshest of treatment. Under such trying circumstances, it might be tempting to believe and internalize the aspersions of others. Yet this Servant remains steadfast through the knowledge of one basic fact: "It is the Lord GOD who helps me" (Isa. 50:9).

With regard to the form and context for this passage, this is the third of four Servant Songs found in Second Isaiah. Isaiah 50:4–9a offers an autobiographical portrait of a figure who instructs others in the ways of the Lord, at considerable risk to his well-being. One of the primary models for these descriptions is Jeremiah; today's reading draws on some of the ideas found in this earlier book. In both texts, a prophet suffers shame, only to be "vindicated" by God (compare the language of Isa. 50:8 with Jer. 20:12). This type of scene also appears in certain psalms of lament, where an individual suffers intense persecution on behalf of YHWH (see, e.g., Ps. 22). A major question then becomes the precise identity of the Servant figure in this passage. Possible candidates include Moses or the prophet

Homiletical Perspective

It is safe to say that on Passion Sunday not one of our sermons will focus on the assigned passage from Isaiah. What we can hope for as preachers is to find the ways in which the prophetic passage can enter into conversation with the story of Jesus' arrest, trial, and crucifixion.

It is easy to discern why this Servant song was assigned for this Sunday. For Christian readers, Second Isaiah's description of the fate of the Servant foreshadows the story of Jesus' suffering. Put in other words, looking back on Isaiah in the light of Jesus' passion, we can see themes that resonate with the great texts of Holy Week.

The lectionary stops with verse 9a, although it is quite clear that verse 9b is part of the same oracle. On a Sunday when we remember Jesus as compassionate victim, it is hard to hear the prophet's judgmental pronouncement on those who will judge the Servant: "All of them will wear out like a garment; the moth will eat them up."

Yet any reading of the passion narrative for this day will remind us that it is not only Jesus, the innocent one, who is judged on this Sunday. The judges are themselves judged, condemned, and sentenced, though of course they do not know it. The judgment on Judas is most evident in its fulfillment in Acts 1:18–20. However Pilate and

Isaiah 50:4-9a

Theological Perspective

powerfully with us in the twenty-first century, there are also aspects of them that should trouble us. Particularly complex are the question of suffering in general, both for Jesus and for us, and the relationship between suffering and redemption.

For example, regarding Jesus' own suffering, many feminist theologians and others would challenge the picture of a God who demands the suffering and death of God's own Son as a blood price for the stain of sin. Would a loving, merciful God really demand such a horrible sacrifice? Is another death really the cure for death? What does such a theory say about the life of Jesus? Is it only the death that matters? Is Jesus' life irrelevant to human redemption?

What of human suffering, then? If God ordains Jesus' suffering, is human suffering also ordained by God? If we dare answer yes to this question, it would seem that there is no response in the face of human suffering except, "Grin and bear it. It is God's will, and your suffering will strengthen your faith." Such an answer is no answer at all to a woman who is being abused by her husband, an orphan who has lost both his parents to HIV/AIDS, or a soldier suffering post-traumatic stress syndrome. Whether the answer is true or not, the victim may well cry out, "Yes, but where is God right now?" Such a cry cannot be ignored, as it challenges the core Christian claims that God is loving, and that God is actively at work for good in the realm of human history.

In the context of these difficult issues then, it is worth reflecting upon this particular text anew, to see if it offers any insight, any answer to these pressing theological questions. When we do so, we do find an answer that comes in the form of a word of comfort and a word of hope: comfort that God is not absent in one's suffering, and hope that God will not allow the suffering to go on forever.

First, there is a clear word of *comfort* here, as the prophet recalls his relationship with the Lord, who has been faithful even in the face of oppression. As the prophet describes God's presence with him, we see that the Lord has been for the prophet a giver of life; specifically, the giver of a life-giving word that sustains the weary when they are bowed down with desperation and exhaustion. If the prophet has said any words of encouragement, any words of comfort and support, he freely acknowledges that it is the Lord who is the source of those words, and the Lord who has enabled him to speak them.

Further, the prophet clearly is consoled by the fact that the Lord is the Lord of truth and righteousness;

Pastoral Perspective

experience from which the teaching draws is suffering, Many of the finest teachers have employed their own past difficulties and diseases to help alleviate the suffering of those who were suffering those pains presently. The Servant's case is very different, though. The reversal in this passage is that the Servant is going to use his experience of suffering to benefit those whose had *caused* the Servant's suffering in the first place.

When have the people in our lives employed their suffering so that we might benefit? Who are the teachers or mentors who have helped us through difficult times because they have traveled that way before us? When have members of our congregation or community done the same? Who has suffered at the hands of an individual or group, then used their own suffering to help those who inflicted that pain?

Is it any wonder that the early Christians, who read this and other passages through the lens of the teachings of Jesus and the stories told by and about this most unusual of Messiahs, saw him reflected in the person of Isaiah's Servant? The Servant uses his own suffering as a means to assist others, even those who inflicted the suffering, and Jesus dies by crucifixion after speaking words of forgiveness for those who nailed his hands and feet to the wood of the cross. Even more than the reversals Jesus' disciples had heard and seen in his life and ministry, his humiliating execution, set alongside his compassion toward his executors, linked him firmly with the figure of the Servant. This was the kind of servanthood that Jesus both taught and demonstrated in his life and death.

There is an important distinction between servanthood and servitude. Servanthood is an offering of service to others as a result of a choice made by the one providing the service. Servitude is service of others that is enforced by either custom or coercion. Even service provided because of economic necessity is a form of servitude, not servanthood. Slavery is clearly a form of servitude, but so is the wage slavery of those who are paid so little that they are never able to earn their way out of an abyss of debt. The agricultural methodology of tenant farming and sharecropping that followed the emancipation of the slaves in the American South was no less servitude than the system of slavery that it replaced. So, too, the "company store" system, central to coal mining throughout Appalachia, which forced miners deeper into debt for the very necessities of life.

It is the volitional quality of servanthood that distinguishes it from servitude. The Servant freely

referring to himself. Christian readers have associated the description in Isaiah 50:4–9a with Jesus and his final journey to the cross. This is helpful, since the Servant's courage and experience of humiliation parallel the passion narrative and the Christ hymn in Philippians 2:5–11. For the Servant in these verses and for Jesus, the arduous task of heeding God's voice does not compromise their faithfulness, but reveals it.

This vivid scene in Second Isaiah divides into three logical sections: introduction of the teacher and his divine calling as a prophet (vv. 4–5a); description of suffering in the fulfillment of responsibilities (vv. 5b–6); legal scene in which the servant is vindicated by the Lord against his enemies (vv. 7–9).

Introduction of the "teacher" (vv. 4–5a). The first unit establishes the divine mandate of this prophet, his mission, and its reliability. The opening verse establishes the call: "The Lord GOD has given me the tongue of a teacher." The goal of his efforts is to "sustain the weary with a word." The idea of providing sustenance to those with failing strength is important throughout Second Isaiah, especially in the opening chapter, where "those who wait for the LORD shall renew their strength . . . they shall run and not be weary" (40:31). Historical context is relevant here: this biblical author wrote at the end of the Babylonian exile in the sixth century BCE, when the possibility of restoration would have seemed remote to those exhausted from living abroad. The ability to "sustain the weary with a word" is critical in such a setting. In terms of authenticity, the divine voice comes to this disciple with regularity ("morning by morning"); his testimony is reliable and timely.

Description of suffering (vv. 5b–6). Yet certain detractors have a negative assessment of this individual's calling. This hostile situation tests the determination of the Servant in question, and he does not "turn backward" from his mission. Not only does he accept the burden of his work, but he submits to the unwarranted abuse of others. Jeremiah is roughed up in a similar manner for delivering oracles of judgment (Jer. 37:15). The Servant in Second Isaiah goes even further than Jeremiah, however, because he more willingly accepts his plight: "I gave my back to those who struck me, and my cheeks to those who pulled out the beard; I did not hide my face from insult and spitting." Jesus certainly accepts similar humiliation during his final trials (e.g., Mark 14:65).

Herod too have worn out like a garment. Famous and powerful in their own time, they are now remembered only because they are part of the story of the one who suffered at their hands, their reputations moth-eaten entirely.

Karl Barth suggested that preaching required explication, meditation, and application. Though we may not apply the Isaiah text directly to our Passion Sunday sermons, we would do well to meditate on the themes of Isaiah 50 as they relate to the events of the week of Jesus' death.

The Lord God has given me the tongue of a teacher, that I may know how to sustain the weary with a word (v. 4). Throughout Luke's Gospel, Jesus is portrayed as one whose teaching comes from God and who teaches as he himself is taught. In the passion narrative, as elsewhere in the Gospel, the word he speaks is a sustaining and redeeming word.

At the Last Supper Jesus not only gives the words of institution, as in the other Synoptic Gospels; he also teaches the apostles what the shape of their ministry is to be: they are to learn from his example and be servants of all (Luke 22:24–28). Peter, who will fall far from grace, is commanded—promised—that he will turn back to sustain his weary brothers with a word (Luke 22:31–32). The apostles are encouraged to live courageously, even as they follow Jesus on a dangerous mission (Luke 22:35–38).

The Lord GOD has opened my ear, and I was not rebellious, I did not turn backward (v. 5). The story of the anguish in Gethsemane, perhaps even more powerfully if we include Luke 22:43–44, is the story of Jesus' waiting on the word of the "Father" and his courageous, painful unwillingness to turn backward. As servant, he now serves all the way to the cross.

I gave my back to those who struck me, and my cheeks to those who pulled out the beard. I did not hide my face from insult and spitting (v. 6). In Luke 22:63–65, those who have arrested Jesus mock him and beat him and taunt him saying: "Prophesy! Who is it that struck you?" Of course throughout Luke's Gospel he has prophesied time and again of the fate that awaits him for his faithfulness (see Luke 9:22, 44–45; 18:31–34).

The Lord God helps me; therefore I have not been disgraced. Therefore I have set my face like flint, and I know that I shall not be put to shame (v. 7). Notice the reticence and the power of Jesus before the

Isaiah 50:4-9a

Theological Perspective

and so, even when he is spit on, scorned, and beaten, the prophet is not ashamed, he does not run, he does not give in. He knows that no matter what is happening to him now, justice will win out and the Lord will have the last word. This leads then to the word of *hope* we find in this text. Even though the situation looks very bleak for the prophet right now, he does not despair. Instead, his voice rings out with assurance and defiance: let his enemies do their worst—he will not be shaken, because he knows that the Lord is with him, standing by him as his helper and his defender.

Clearly, in the prophet's view, the Lord is not the instigator of suffering; instead, his suffering comes at the hands of those who do not fear the Lord, who do not love the Lord, and who do not follow the will of the Lord. In short, human evil is the cause of the Servant's suffering—not God. What is more, the Lord is not a passive observer of his suffering, but instead is active in the life of God's Servant, working to redeem him from the threat of death and destruction, and justify his words and deeds of faithfulness. This is the promise revealed to us in this passage of Isaiah: the world can be a dangerous and evil place, and suffering will come, but we can rest assured it is not at the hand of God. Instead, God is at work in our lives for good, for peace, for justice, and for love. Even though we cannot always see the fruit of God's labor, our hope in the Lord will not be disappointed in the end.

KRISTIN JOHNSTON LARGEN

Pastoral Perspective

chooses to act for the benefit of others. This is why it is inappropriate for those who stand in positions of power in a society to preach servanthood to those who do not. The distribution of power is situational; each of us is the more powerful person in certain realms and the less powerful in others. It is the freedom to choose that makes us truly powerful. Perhaps this is the reason that Jesus insists that no one forces him to take the path to the cross. He chooses to take that journey, just as he chooses those who will accompany him on the way.

The irony that the Servant teaches and embodies is the radical reversal of common sense: the only true freedom is to choose to serve others, even those who intend or who do us actual harm. This may involve speaking a word to the weary, even those whose constant needs or demands have made us weary. Is there a pastor of a congregation who would not identify with this situation? In this we follow the example of both the Servant and Jesus Christ, who served those who wearied him with their constant needs and demands and lack of understanding, and who continues to offer us a "word to the weary" in our needs, demands, and lack of understanding. Then he dies asking forgiveness for those who are executing him. Are we willing to go that far?

What audacity to think that this sort of servanthood is where true freedom is found. Yet, this is exactly what Isaiah contends. So the central question may be, "How free are we willing to choose to be?"

MICHAEL E. WILLIAMS

Exegetical Perspective

Legal scene (vv. 7–9a). Such resolve is possible because God assists the Servant in Second Isaiah. Divine aid is vividly illustrated through a legal standoff at the end of today's reading. Regarding the transition to the courtroom scene, the translation in the NRSV ("The Lord God helps me") does not reflect the shift from verse 6 to verse 7 that is apparent in the Hebrew. There is an important conjunction at the beginning of verse 7: "*But* the Lord God will help me" (Jewish Publication Society translation; emphasis added). Although the Servant accepts social rejection and physical abuse, his acquiescence does not indicate guilt. He counters the harsh treatment with a firm dismissal of his opponents' efforts. The reader now understands the reasons for the Servant's steely countenance ("I have set my face like flint"). Firmness is possible because the God "who vindicates" steadfast disciples "is near." The juridical setting highlights the speaker's abiding confidence: "Who will contend with me? Let us stand up together [i.e., participate in a trial]. Who are my adversaries? Let them confront me [i.e., bring charges]." Whatever charges his opponents might bring, the case has already been decided by YHWH, the one true judge.

Reading the third Servant Song as part of the passion liturgy adds important insights to the Christian understanding of Jesus' difficult journey. This passage from Second Isaiah focuses on two central themes: risky servanthood and the sure response of the Lord. Like Jesus, the Servant in these verses understands that acceptance of a prophetic commission will involve tremendous peril. By listening for the word of God "morning by morning," this individual heeds a message that leads him into dire straits. Even with the certainty of vindication, the task is treacherous, lonely, and sad. A "flinty" resolve is possible for this prophet and for Jesus, but this does not alleviate the challenge of advocating for God amid throngs of angry detractors. A Servant who can endure unimaginable sufferings does so through confidence in God. By setting up this dynamic between dangerous obedience and ultimate redemption, Second Isaiah provides a clear depiction of a faithful prophet. This witness can be a message to believers everywhere that true discipleship inevitably involves deep and profound loss.

SAMUEL L. ADAMS

Homiletical Perspective

assembly of the elders: "If I tell you, you will not believe; and if I question you, you will not answer" (Luke 22:67b–68).

Notice his dignity before Pilate. "'Are you the king of the Jews?' He answered, 'You say so'" (Luke 23:3).

Notice that Herod, seeking to judge, is judged by Jesus' silence instead. "[Herod] questioned him at some length, but Jesus gave him no answer" (Luke 23:9). No, he never said a mumbling word.

Jesus is insulted, arraigned, accused, queried, but never put to shame.

He who vindicates me is near (v. 8a). In the Gospels of both Mark and Matthew, the God who vindicates Jesus sometimes seems very far away during this passion scene. "My God, my God," Jesus cries, "why have you forsaken me?" Not so in Luke. Speaking for the vindicating God, Jesus vindicates the believing thief (Luke 23:43). Trusting in the vindicating God, Jesus speaks his last words from the cross: "Father, into your hands I commend my spirit" (Luke 23:46).

It is the Lord God who helps me; who will declare me guilty? (v. 9). The council of the elders of the people declares him guilty: "What further testimony do we need? We have heard it ourselves from his own lips" (Luke 22:71).

Pilate (bowing to political pressure) declares him guilty: "So Pilate gave his verdict that their demand should be granted. He released the man they asked for . . . and he handed Jesus over as they wished" (Luke 23:24–25).

All of them will wear out like a garment, the moth will eat them up (v. 9b). The adversaries do not get the last word in this passion narrative. That word is reserved for the centurion who stands at the foot of the cross. Like the one hanging on the cross, he speaks with the tongue of one who has been taught; his ears have been wakened; his eyes are opened; he speaks the vindicator's word: "Certainly this man was innocent" (Luke 23:47).

DAVID L. BARTLETT

Psalm 31:9-16

⁹Be gracious to me, O LORD, for I am in distress;
   my eye wastes away from grief,
   my soul and body also.
¹⁰For my life is spent with sorrow,
   and my years with sighing;
   my strength fails because of my misery,
   and my bones waste away.

¹¹I am the scorn of all my adversaries,
   a horror to my neighbors,
   an object of dread to my acquaintances;
   those who see me in the street flee from me.

Theological Perspective

A grieving soul. Like the musical traditions of the blues and country, the Psalms are the songs of life. They express the highest joys and the deepest sorrows of life, often within the same, single psalm. The Psalms express the painful truths of the human condition, while simultaneously declaring the most profound hopes of the human spirit. They declare the human spirit's longing for the blessing of the divine presence to shield us against grief and terror.

This psalm cries out from the depths of a grieving soul. Although few people are unaware of stages or cyclical understandings of grief, too many are unaware of the devastating experience of grief. Grief theories tend to focus on symptoms and overlook the distorting effects of grief upon the soul. There tends to be a lack of understanding regarding the way grief has the power to redefine life as a bottomless pit. One of the significant dangers of the grieving soul is the splitting of the self that grief provokes.

Christ prayed "that we may be one." As people reflect on what he meant by his prayer for oneness, a wide range of interpreted meaning has been applied. Most often, the interpretation has emphasized a hope that there would be no division resulting from voicing attitudes of dissension. There is, however, another level of oneness we need always to attend to. We must also attend to the oneness of the individual

Pastoral Perspective

The Sunday before Easter offers two possibilities for the worshiping community: palms or the passion. To celebrate the Liturgy of the Palms is to join the celebratory crowd in Jerusalem welcoming Jesus as king, though his kingship was little understood on that day. For Palm Sunday, a psalm of joyful thanksgiving is assigned in the lection. The Liturgy of the Passion offers a contrasting worship experience. Not moving from one celebration (the triumphal entry into Jerusalem) to another (the resurrection of the Lord), the Liturgy of the Passion ushers us into Holy Week in solemnity. For worshipers who cannot attend services for Maundy Thursday or Good Friday, this may be the only opportunity to read some of Scripture's most poignant passages and to sing some of the church's most exquisite hymns.

Psalm 31:9–16 is assigned each year for the Liturgy of the Passion. This psalm (specifically v. 5) has been connected to the suffering and death of Jesus from the earliest years of the church, as Luke 23:46 records Jesus' last words from the cross: "Father, into your hands I commend my spirit." After Stephen spoke similarly as he was stoned to death, "Lord Jesus, receive my spirit" (Acts 7:59), Psalm 31:5 became the dying words of people of faith through the centuries from Polycarp to Luther. Though written centuries before Jesus' crucifixion, Psalm

¹²I have passed out of mind like one who is dead;
  I have become like a broken vessel.
¹³For I hear the whispering of many—
    terror all around!—
  as they scheme together against me,
    as they plot to take my life.

¹⁴But I trust in you, O Lᴏʀᴅ;
  I say, "You are my God."
¹⁵My times are in your hand;
    deliver me from the hand of my enemies and persecutors.
¹⁶Let your face shine upon your servant;
    save me in your steadfast love.

Exegetical Perspective

A psalm of deliverance. This psalm expresses the forlorn experience of one who has trusted in God yet is surrounded by enemies. Although the threats seem insurmountable, the psalmist still has hope that God will rescue. This psalm is quoted in the Gospel of Luke (23:46). In the Hebrew mind, "Into your hands I commit my spirit" is not a statement of one's soul going to God but an expression of one's life being given up to God, a declaration of trust.

In the Hebrew text, this psalm can be divided into twelve strophes. In English that division is not so clear. The NRSV separates the psalm into nine strophes. The particular verses we are investigating bridge two and a half strophes in the English text. If one does a verse count, then this lectionary division is the numerical center of the psalm. The passages that precede and follow our text are joyful expressions of trust, but our pericope is a description of desperate circumstances. As in many other psalms, the problem concerns personal attacks on the faith of the psalmist. An important clue to reading this section comes in verses 1 and 17. These two sections of confident trust in God's saving provision begin with appeals for rescue from shame. In the Israelite culture of shame and honor, one could experience shame for putting trust in a God who is unable to protect or who appears disinterested.

Homiletical Perspective

The Liturgy of the Passion contradicts the cultural tendency to avoid suffering and suppress lament. Indeed, the Liturgy of the Palms, which begins the classic Passion-Palm Sunday rite, marches us directly toward the way of suffering and does not permit our taking another path toward the joys of Easter. Thus we come to the Liturgy of the Passion and these eight verses from Psalm 31. The full psalm is a prayer for deliverance, that the psalmist not "be put to shame" (v. 1) by the enemies that pursue him. It moves to an expression of lament and ends in thanksgiving for deliverance granted.[1] In today's liturgy, we read the lament (vv. 9–16).

The psalmist acknowledges profound grief. His "eye wastes away from grief, [his] soul and body also" (v. 9). He testifies that his "life is spent with sorrow . . . [his] bones waste away" (v. 10). He is grieved, depressed, and probably physically ill. Here is expression of profound sorrow, of a type that we can rarely admit in our culture. In the wider context of the Passion-Palm Liturgy, a preacher might ask the congregation to imagine themselves praying this lament along with Jesus. As they pray it with him, they also pray it with others who suffer. The

---

1. *The HarperCollins Study Bible, Revised Edition* (San Francisco: HarperSanFrancisco, 2006), 757.

Psalm 31:9-16

Theological Perspective

being, consciously seeking to maintain the harmonious integrity of the body and soul.

One such grieving process that tends to be overshadowed or ignored by our theologies of marriage is the loss and splitting of the soul that often results from divorce. The soul and body, as well as one's entire constructed reality, are shredded by divorce. Not only does a person begin to separate aspects of one's self from all the relationships that were mutually supportive of the marriage; the depth of emotional pain provokes its own internal separations. Furthermore, there is an ostracism of the divorced person by the larger community whereby the divorced person becomes "a reproach" and "an object of dread." The broken relationship truly causes a person to feel like "a broken vessel."

Horror, dread, people fleeing, hearing whispering are all experiences of fear within one's self and others. Fear is a basic human emotion that constricts human behavior. While anger causes us to attack that which is threatening, fear causes us to withdraw from a threat. Fear can range from simple uneasiness to total insecurity. It can make you stop in your tracks, shake in your shoes, and empty your bladder. Fear is stronger than someone on steroids and will make the bravest of people cry. But far more profound than the fear that pervades our existence is the debilitating terror that takes the joy out of life. To live with terror is to live with a constant fear so intense that there is no place where one feels safe.

There are people who tactically make use of terror to control the activities of people. There are people who control their homes through a reign of terror. There are people who control their neighborhoods through a reign of terror. There are people who control countries through a reign of terror. Because terror is a more chronic condition, it causes people to do more than shed a few tears. There is a wailing that goes along with terror, because there is always tragic loss that accompanies terror.

Living with a constant state of terror raises the question, what is provoking the feeling of terror? Terrorism is nothing new to America. When one thinks of terror and terrorism in America, most minds are immediately drawn to the events of recent history, most notably, 9/11. A special edition of the *Chicago Tribune* after the Twin Towers attack read "When Evil Struck America." Terrorism is most often being identified as bombing. Our consciousness has been shaped in such a way that we now think that bombers have always been suicidal Arabs. However, America has a long history of domestic terrorism.

Pastoral Perspective

31:9–16 powerfully evokes images of the suffering Jesus endured in his last days. From the psalmist's time to our own, these verses also have given voice to the nearly unutterable sorrow and pain many have experienced in life. To read and explore Psalm 31 on this Sunday, then, offers the opportunity for reflection on the passion of Christ and may resonate deeply with those who have experienced anguished suffering and grief in their own lives.

The suffering the psalmist describes encompasses the whole person, soul and body. A person who has been doubled over in grief or has endured the exhausting rigors of physical suffering knows the descriptions in verses 9–10 to be true: the eye wastes away from grief; years of sighs, too deep for words, breathe out the heaviness within; there is no energy to get up or go out ("my strength fails because of my misery"); and the sorrow aches in our very bones. These words vividly call up images of Jesus in anguish in the Garden of Gethsemane, on the way to the crucifixion, on the cross. They are our words too for how it feels when suffering and sorrow overwhelm. "Be gracious to me, O LORD," is not too much to ask—God, be gentle, be kind, and *be present*.

The suffering imposed on the psalmist is experienced not only internally, but also externally. In verses 11–13, people on all sides inflict more pain and sorrow, wittingly or not. The psalmist feels scorned by adversaries; but neighbors and friends are not much better. Horror and avoidance seem to be common reactions, even from friends who encounter this one who is in such pain. People are whispering, talking about this suffering person as though he or she is not even there. Their whispers sound like schemes or plots that threaten even further a life already too precarious. We know who these external forces are in Jesus' last days: Judas betrays; the disciples fall away; Peter denies; religious leaders plot; Pilate and Herod wield deadly power; soldiers beat and mock.

Others who have endured long periods of suffering and grief describe the experience of friends falling away or avoiding contact, and of people speaking about them as though they were not in the room. Most of our mistakes in the presence of someone in anguish are made because we feel helpless or uncomfortable, but to the person in pain such actions can seem cruel. Verse 12 is perhaps the most poignant line of all in this section of Psalm 31: "I have passed out of mind like one who is dead; I have become like a broken vessel." Jesus felt abandoned, alone. He, who had held a cup full of

Exegetical Perspective

Addressing God. Verses 9–10 and 14–16 address God directly. The first address requests God's mercy and describes the situation that necessitates this mercy. The parallelism of these first two verses has an internal logic. Because of the psalmist's grief in the experience of distress, the eye, throat, and belly waste away. (The word translated "soul" [*nephesh*] literally means throat or neck.) The movement down the body signifies the debilitating experience of physically wasting away from suffering. We are familiar with this kind of physical response to emotional distress. It is not unusual to hear people describe others as "wasting away" physically when under great emotional duress.

Verses 9–10 use the word "for" (*ki*), which introduces a motive clause that explains the reason for the request. The psalmist cries out to God because his/her life is spent (finished, completed) with sorrow, and the psalmist's years are ended with sighing as strength fails and bones waste away. The psalmist's physical life is slipping away before our eyes.

The parallelism of these verses is evident in that both contain the motive particle *ki* and in both the motive clause is expanded by a description of the physical disabilities suffered by the psalmist. As we become aware of the reason to call for God's gracious intervention, we are confronted by the physical deterioration of eye, throat, belly, strength, and bone.

A moment of inward reflection. Most commentators agree that verses 11–13 are a soliloquy. No longer directly addressing God, the psalmist has turned to inward reflection and rehearses the causes of his/her debilitation. There are enemies nearby who see the psalmist's physical suffering as a sign of God's disfavor or disinterest. Their reaction to the psalmist is not passive; rather, they actively seek to do the psalmist harm, perhaps due to their belief that the psalmist has fallen outside God's concern.

The parallelism of verse 11 reflects the social location of the people who react with astonishment at the psalmist's plight. The adversaries are mentioned first, and one wonders if that is because they are nearest in proximity or nearest in the awareness of the psalmist. The next three groups mentioned all seem to move farther away from the psalmist in proximity and intimacy. The "scorn" that the adversaries have for the psalmist is intensified with the neighbors in an oblique way. The text literally reads "and to my neighbors greatly (*meʾod*)". If we understand that the missing verb is to be borrowed from the preceding line then the neighbors have a more intense reaction

Homiletical Perspective

preacher might ask what one can do when confronted with such lamentation or when experiencing it oneself. In a sense there is little that one can do except hear it in solidarity with the one who suffers, or else speak it oneself. Following that, one can only wait for God to act. Such waiting is an important dynamic of Holy Week spirituality.

Readers may be quick to note the physical suffering attested by the writer, but there are other, perhaps deeper, modes of suffering witnessed in this psalm. The psalmist complains that he has been scorned, plotted against, abandoned, even forgotten (vv. 11–12). Such pain is profoundly psychological, yet it is every bit as real as physical pain. Much of the church's popular piety related to the suffering and death of Jesus has focused on the physical pain that he endured, which was indeed profound. Nevertheless, Jesus endured suffering apart from nails, whips, and thorns—including the suffering of betrayal, abandonment, false accusation, and unjust imprisonment. This psalm, like other texts that we hear within the Passion Liturgy, encourages the faithful to take a deep look at the many ways people suffer. Who are the sufferers that the church is overlooking? Faithful preachers will insist that there is no easy response to suffering, no quick reference to God's redemptive will, no shallow expression of sympathy. We can never understand everything that others suffer. We can, however, stand in solidarity with them.

We might also join them in making demands on God. The preacher might call her congregation to notice the psalm writer's feistiness. After expressing his lament, he makes a turn, saying, "But I trust in you, O LORD; I say, 'You are my God'" (v. 14). This is no vaguely optimistic word of faith, but rather an insistent covenant demand. It is a bold challenge, spoken in anguish, more than a quiet plea. It suggests that, in the context of covenant faith, our lament can be insistent. We insist that God deliver us, that God act on our behalf. What would it sound like to join the afflicted in making such demands? What would we say or do?

The psalmist asks for God's salvation: "Save me in your steadfast love" (v. 16). Given the context of this psalm and the wider context of the Passion Liturgy, preachers will want to inquire as to the shape of such salvation. Often the church has been less than fully biblical in its use of the words "save" and "salvation," associating them primarily with going to heaven after death; but the psalmist is speaking about something more immediate. How should one envision a salvation based on the dynamics of this

Psalm 31:9-16

Theological Perspective

Different peoples have been terrorized in this land for generations, not by Arabs but by other "citizens" believing themselves to be defending America. From massacres to lynching to firebombing, defenders of the faith, militia, military, robed beings, and mobs have led terrorist attacks for generations.

Just as rage is anger at the extreme, terror is fear at the extreme. Terror is a paralyzing emotion whereby one's life is being totally controlled by the terrorizing activities of another. To live with terror is to live under the constant threat of bodily harm, which provokes a hypervigilance. Consider the number of groups who live under constant threat. Salem witch hunts terrorized women. December 16, 1773, the Boston Tea Party was an act of terrorism. November 29, 1864, Colonel John Chivington led 700 men to massacre 700 Cheyenne in Colorado—500 of whom were women and children. In the 1960s, Birmingham, Alabama, was known as "Bombingham" because a series of dynamite bombs struck the homes of African American civil-rights advocates. September 15, 1964, the Sixteenth Street Baptist Church was bombed, injuring twenty and killing four young girls. That same day, a pair of white Eagle Scouts fired their new pistol at two black boys riding a bicycle, killing one who was thirteen years old. April 19, 1995, in Oklahoma City, Oklahoma, a bomb exploded in a federal building, killing 167, of whom 19 were children. Again, to live at the extremes of fear means that even one's relationship with God is defined by the terror one feels. Living under constant threat can also provoke health challenges through self-destructive behaviors.

Although a person may declare complete trust in God, if the basis of that trust has been informed by terror, trust is based upon a hope that God will protect. So, what happens to trust when bad things happen to those who trusted in the Lord? The theodical question is one that cannot be avoided. Moreover, it is imperative that the theodical question be asked with deep integrity, avoiding the tendency of identifying easy scapegoats.

LEE H. BUTLER JR.

Pastoral Perspective

wine and given it to his disciples, became a vessel broken. Broken vessels are thrown out, deemed useless.

If the psalm or the passion of Christ or our own experiences ended there, we would be among those most to be pitied. Yet this psalm, at verse 14, begins to turn us toward God and on this Passion Sunday, therefore, toward the Easter that is to come. By means of the small word "but," the great "nevertheless" of faith, the psalmist gives testimony against all evidence to the contrary: "But I trust in you, O Lord; I say, 'You are my God.'" It is a determined statement of faith—perhaps even a defiant statement of faith, in the face of suffering and sorrow and death. Then this (v. 15): "My times are in your hand."

As we have seen, the psalmist's own hands fail in strength. The hands of others appear as fists that wound or terrorize, but there is God. Gentle, kind, present, and stronger than all else, God holds our days, each rugged day, until there are no more days. Then we find that we are still held. So it is not too much to ask that God's face shine upon us; that God save us in steadfast love. It is not too much to ask, even, that God make a broken vessel into one that is raised up—whole, beautiful, a full-to-overflowing treasure.

While Psalm 31:5 is the moving words of those who die in faith, verse 15 is the moving words of those who live in faith year after year. To say to God, "My times are in your hand," is to trust God with our suffering and anguish, as well as trusting God when all is well. Every time we gather to worship, there are people who bear witness to such faith in their very bodies and lives. They have trusted God to hold them in every circumstance. Each time we take the bread broken and the cup poured out, we hold in our hands the one who has shown us that what is broken will be raised up—whole, beautiful, a treasure.

KIMBERLY L. CLAYTON

of contempt (NRSV, horror) to the psalmist's situation. To the acquaintances (lit. "ones knowing me") the psalmist is an object of dread, and the ones who merely see the psalmist from a distance run away (perhaps in disgust?).

Poignant images appear in verse 12. Though still alive, the psalmist has become like the dead, who are forgotten. Not just forgotten but also useless, the psalmist is like a broken pottery vessel. Why this hopelessness? Another *ki* clause announces the reason for this despair: enemies intend to take his/her life. The expression "terror all around" can be read as something whispered against the psalmist. It can also be read as the psalmist's own interjection into the meditation, a sudden and violent intrusion of a thought often felt but seldom spoken. If we understand this as an interjection, we are given a unique window into the agitated state of mind of the psalmist.

A final declaration of trust. The psalmist is drawn up out of the thoughts of despair and into an affirmation of faith that has been suspended since verse 9. No longer lost in his/her own thoughts, the psalmist resumes addressing God directly and even makes a confession of faith; "You are my God." Verses 9–10 have been noted for their frequent use of body imagery. In verse 15, "hand" is beautifully rendered to provide the image of both safety and deliverance. It is God's hand, and not that of the enemies, that will prevail.

The final verse uses two imperatives to make demands upon God: "Make your face shine on me and rescue me" (my trans.). The psalmist's nearness to God is expressed through the use of imperatives rather than jussives (a wish or desired state, as NRSV translates). When the psalmist speaks against the enemies, it is in the jussive voice, "let my enemies be shamed" (my trans.), but when he/she is speaking to God, the imperative is used ("Incline your ear to me," v. 2). One gets the sense that the psalmist is more comfortable making demands upon God for rescue than demanding the demise of the enemies.

STEVEN BISHOP

psalm? How would we embody it in our communities? Perhaps it would be the reverse of the negative images found in this psalm. It might involve supporting and remembering the weak, including them in community, and not running from their troubles. Preachers can help their congregations notice these dynamics, and they can ask the hard questions that follow upon such noticing.

We live in a society that chronically minimizes grief and looks away from suffering. Lament is not encouraged. It is bad for business, and not a good church-growth strategy. We need to keep things upbeat and positive, say the marketing analysts. Perhaps we should just stop having funerals. We barely know what to do when we hear lamentation, and most of us do not know how to pray it. Can we allow this psalm to call us back to a way of praying that we have largely forgotten?

The lectionary's marking of this pericope, which calls for us to read only verses 9–16, may itself work against such a recovery. Were we to read the wider psalm, we might be surprised by the anger that accompanies the writer's grief, its expression in a prayer for revenge (v. 18, "Let the lying lips be stilled that speak insolently against the righteous"). The pericope, as presented, keeps those words out of the congregation's mouth. Can we speak such difficult words? Can we tolerate hearing them? Could giving permission to speak them be part of the healing work offered by this liturgy?

How might one shape a sermon on this psalm text? We might use it as a lens for praying our way into the passion narrative and the witness to Christ's suffering that we find there. Jesus stands with us, praying in solidarity with all of suffering humanity, while also demanding that his *Abba* grant us a share in the resurrection. Without diminishing the reality of human suffering, the preacher might also posit Christ's identification with a suffering cosmos and his insistent prayer for its redemption.

MARK W. STAMM

Philippians 2:5‑11

⁵Let the same mind be in you that was in Christ Jesus,
⁶who, though he was in the form of God,
   did not regard equality with God
   as something to be exploited,
⁷but emptied himself,
   taking the form of a slave,
   being born in human likeness.
 And being found in human form,
⁸ he humbled himself
   and became obedient to the point of death—
   even death on a cross.

⁹Therefore God also highly exalted him
   and gave him the name
   that is above every name,
¹⁰ so that at the name of Jesus
   every knee should bend,
   in heaven and on earth and under the earth,
¹¹and every tongue should confess
   that Jesus Christ is Lord,
   to the glory of God the Father.

Theological Perspective

The lectionary passage is largely a single lyric, and may well be a hymn that Paul has incorporated into his letter. Regarded independently, its primary purpose is to recount the story of Christ's incarnation, crucifixion, and exaltation, as well as the appropriateness of worshiping Christ and confessing that he is Lord. This is one reason why, in the history of theology, our passage has sometimes been used to claim Christ's divinity and preexistence as well as his two natures. Here, however, Paul puts the lyric to a *practical* use, exhorting the Philippians to live in a manner that conforms to the example and pattern of Christ. This, in fact, is what John Calvin emphasizes in his comments.[1]

The text. This becomes even more apparent when we survey the immediate context. Following an opening salutation, Paul says it is his prayer that the Philippians will grow in love, knowledge, and insight. He mentions that his own imprisonment has served to spread the gospel to "the imperial guard" (!), his satisfaction that "Christ is proclaimed in every way" (if also from a variety of motives), and his conviction that he will remain in the flesh and continue his ministry (1:3–26).

1. *Calvin's New Testament Commentaries*, vol. 11, *The Epistles of Paul the Apostle to the Galatians, Ephesians, Philippians and Colossians*, trans. T. H. L. Parker (Grand Rapids: Eerdmans, 1972), 246–53.

Pastoral Perspective

Will you actually consider preaching on the Philippians text on Palm Sunday? Will you focus on this text when the lectionary provides the powerful and inescapable story of Christ's passion? It will be difficult to resist the Gospel reading, linked as it is to the Old Testament lesson, and leading into the rest of Holy Week. Nevertheless, whether or not you preach from the Epistle reading, the Philippians text will surely be an important conversation partner for the other texts. For with this Philippian hymn the events of Holy Week are put into a larger context and a deeper understanding. With this Philippian hymn the events of Holy Week are given a truer humility and awe and praise. These verses sing of Christ's humiliation that leads to his exaltation, of his death that leads to his life, and so they are listed each year for Palm/Passion Sunday.

Jesus' final days, death, and resurrection are acts of humble service that reveal *his* true vocation. Likewise, they are *our* true vocation. As Paul confronts issues in the church in Philippi, he calls Christians to their vocation, that is, to have the *mind of Christ*. This is the *mind of Christ*—a commitment to serving others, with an unwillingness to seek personal gain. These verses are not a morality lesson leading us to think that if we humble ourselves, then we will become exalted. Such was not the expectation of Jesus. Jesus

Exegetical Perspective

These verses, often described as a hymn because of their rhythmic structure, sum up the good news of Christ's incarnation, life, death, and exaltation. It is possible that they were composed by someone else (and were perhaps already known to Paul's readers), but if so, he has made them his own, using them to express ideas found elsewhere in his letters.

The opening line is ambiguous, as the NRSV note indicates. In Greek there is no verb with the words "in Christ Jesus," but in English we need to supply one. Is Paul simply urging the Philippians to imitate Christ, as the NRSV's "was" might indicate? The answer is surely no, for the Christian life is never mere imitation, but rather is lived "in Christ." This suggests that Paul's meaning may be that Christians should "have the mind" that *is already theirs* (NRSV mg.) *because they are* "in Christ Jesus." This mind is, of course, the mind that belongs to Christ himself and was demonstrated in the way he lived and died (vv. 6–8). His actions are both the basis of their redemption and the pattern for their behavior.

Unfortunately it is not only the introductory line that is ambiguous! Every line of the passage has been endlessly debated, and there are innumerable explanations of its imagery. Here we concentrate on one possible interpretation.

Homiletical Perspective

Whether or not Paul composed or quoted the famous "Christ hymn" in today's Epistle text, its assignment to Palm (or Passion) Sunday makes it a prime text for preaching. For the full details of Jesus' arrest, arraignment, torture, and death, see the Gospel. For the mind of Christ—the attitude that determined his actions every day of his life, including the last—see the Epistle. In this V-shaped piece of poetry, Paul maps the coming to earth of Jesus Christ, his hard hit at the rock bottom of his death, and God's raising him again so that all creation sees who he is (and has been all along).

While the first half of the passage is full of verbs (Jesus emptied himself, took the form of a slave, humbled himself, became obedient), these were not spontaneous actions on Jesus' part. They all arose from the Christ-mind—the way he saw himself in relationship to God and to the world—which involved such total evacuation of his ego that there was all kinds of room for the *egō eimi* (the great "I AM") to act. Upon his death, this is the "I" who exalted him, naming him both Christ and Lord. In the second half of the passage, Jesus does nothing. The verbs all belong to God.

This is Paul's birth narrative, his passion narrative, and his ascension narrative all rolled into one. Preachers wishing to "make sense" of Jesus'

Philippians 2:5-11

Theological Perspective

In 1:27, Paul exhorts the Philippians to live in a manner that is "worthy of the gospel of Christ" so that, whether or not he is able to visit them, he will know that they "are standing firm in one spirit." Indeed, a good portion of the entire letter is taken up in various exhortations (1:27–2:18; 3:1–4:1; 4:4–9). In 2:1–4, Paul exhorts the Philippians to "be of the same mind, having the same love," and then summarizes the turn from self-preoccupation to attentiveness to others that is a hallmark of his teaching about life in Christ. "Do nothing from selfish ambition or conceit, but in humility regard others as better than yourselves. Let each of you look not to your own interests, but to the interests of others" (vv. 3–4). Our passage (vv. 5–11) falls here, and in the verses following it, Paul continues to admonish, for example, "Do all things without murmuring and arguing" (v. 14).

What we find out in 2:5–11 is that Paul's teaching about life in Christ has its theological basis or foundation in "the same mind . . . that was in Christ Jesus" (v. 5). Calvin says this means "the same attitude," although he also links the expression with the imitation of Christ as "the rule of life."[2] We might say that here Paul is pointing to the same disposition and stance in life that was in Christ.

My first professor at divinity school, Joseph Sittler, referred to "the shape of the engendering deed," and this seems critically important to Paul's meaning.[3] God's act or deed in Christ is not barren. It produces and engenders something in us. Moreover, to understand just what this deed does engender, we need to appreciate that it is neither featureless nor bland. The engendering deed has a specific pattern, shape, or texture of humility, of refusing to exploit equality with God, of self-emptying, of taking the form of a slave, and of obedience "to the point of death—even death on a cross" (vv. 7–8). Now it is this particular cross-shaped deed, a deed the world regards as foolish, that proves to be God's true wisdom (1 Cor. 1:20–25). We know this to be so because the one who humbled himself and died on a cross is also the one whom God has exalted and given "the name above every name" (2:9). To let the same mind be in you that was in Christ Jesus, then, is to let this particular deed, its pattern and its wisdom, bring forth in us the same attitude, disposition, or stance.

An alternative ethic. One way to get some of this across in contemporary terms is to say that Paul is

Pastoral Perspective

was simply living out his vocation. Therefore, for a community of faith that had become preoccupied with its own discord, and for individuals who were more concerned with their own self-righteousness, this hymn sang of Christ's true vocation as a reminder of who we are and how we are to live together. Remember who you are!

Are there crises that threaten your own community of faith? If so, what difference could it make if your congregation was to hear Paul's word directly to them? How could your people practice having the *mind of Christ*? What part of your own mind-set would you have to let go of in order to have *Christ's mind*? What would change if you focused on your need to let go of your own mind-set, instead of wishing for others to let go of theirs? How could your congregation find the courage, strength, resolve to be obedient as Jesus was? How did Jesus find the courage, strength, resolve to be *of one mind with God the Father*? How do we as Christians learn to put our minds into a state of trust in God's faithfulness? Perhaps Jesus knew and remembered God's faithfulness better than we do. Yet we do know God's faithfulness and have Jesus' example and one another to prod our memory. The act of worshiping God together is itself part of building memory, in order that we might trust God's faithfulness, remember who we are, and live as ones called to be Christian.

On Palm/Passion Sunday, as we approach Holy Week, it is good to remember who we are and to focus on having the *mind of Christ*, whom we worship and adore, the one who gives us our vocation—calling us together as Christ's church and sending us out in Christ's name to serve others. In any crisis, it is important for the faithful to remember who we are and who we are called to be, lest pettiness seduce us into a preoccupation with ourselves and we lose our identity, our calling, our mission. Christ's true vocation was not to build up himself but to build up others. Our true vocation is not to build up ourselves but to build up others. These verses on the humiliation and exaltation of Christ fit well at any time in the church's life. They are certainly part of the contrast and irony of Palm/Passion Sunday.

While these verses from the letter to the church in Philippi give significant insight at any time of year, to hear them on Palm/Passion Sunday is particularly meaningful. Nevertheless, some of you may forsake preaching altogether in order to read through or dramatize the entire passion narrative. Whether or

---

2. Ibid., 246.
3. Joseph Sittler, *The Structure of Christian Ethics* (Louisville, KY: Westminster John Knox Press, 1998), 24 ff.

Exegetical Perspective

There are two main sections: the theme of verses 6–8 is Christ's self-giving, that of verses 9–11 his exaltation by God. Paul begins with what we would call Christ's incarnation. In the opening line, the NRSV misleads us by using a finite verb ("was"), where the Greek has a participle ("being"), and by adding the conditional "though." The Greek reads simply "Being in the form of God," and the word "form" (*morphē*) means "visible manifestation," suggesting that what Christ did he did *because* he was—and remains—"in the form of God." Christ emptied himself, not *in spite of* being in the form of God, but *because* this is what God is like.

There has been much debate regarding the origin of the imagery, but the background of Paul's ideas is normally found in Judaism, and the language here seems to point to the figure of Adam. Is Paul perhaps drawing a deliberate contrast between Adam, who was created according to God's image and likeness (Gen. 1:26), and Christ, who was "in the form of God"? Adam had grasped at equality with God (Gen. 3:5), but Christ "did not regard equality with God as something to be exploited." Other translations (e.g., NIV) interpret the final phrase as meaning "something to be grasped," as though Adam and Christ were originally equal, and Christ resisted the temptation to reach up. In reaching down, however (v. 7), he *became* man—an idea stated twice—which suggests that *before* his self-humiliation Christ was *greater* than Adam, and that "equality with God" was his by right.

So Christ took the form of a slave. Commentators sometimes link this word to the Servant spoken of in certain chapters of Isaiah (42, 49, 51, 53), but the term refers there to YHWH's servant, and is a title of honor. The Greek word used here (*doulos*) means a slave, and contrasts starkly with the divine status Christ abandoned. He took the "form" (*morphē*) of a slave, the "likeness" (*homoiōmata*) of men, and the fashion (*schēma*) of a man. These three words are not intended to suggest that Jesus was not truly human; rather they point us to the paradox of the incarnation. Adam was created in the likeness of God, and now Christ is born in the likeness of Adam.

In contrast to Adam, however, Christ was not concerned with status but humbled himself. Whereas Adam disobeyed God's command (Gen. 2:17; 3:14, 19), Christ was obedient (cf. Rom. 5:12–19), even to the point of death. Although he did not deserve it, he shared Adam's fate; worse still, he died by crucifixion, the particularly painful and shameful death reserved for rebels and slaves. The final words of verse 8 must have shocked their first hearers

Homiletical Perspective

death this Palm Sunday will find no better script for doing so than these seven verses from Philippians. Jesus' death is no more spontaneous than anything else that happens in his life. He certainly saw it coming. As awful as the manner of his death turned out to be, it was an unsurprising end for one who spent no energy protecting himself. Having emptied himself all of his life, he emptied himself to the end.

Since obedience figures centrally in this passage, preachers will take care with its interpretation. Was it God's will that Jesus die, or was it Jesus' will to be subject to (to obey) the same kind of death that other people died? Rome had crucified thousands of other Jews before it got to Jesus, after all. In many ways, the NIV translation is preferable here: Jesus "became obedient to death." Having taken the form of a slave, he asked for no special pass at the end. He submitted to death the same way he had submitted to everything else that made him fully human.

This is why he can serve as exemplar for the rest of us. "Let the same mind be in you," Paul writes, apparently believing that this is within our reach. On Palm Sunday we do not witness the singular death of a singular child of God. Instead, we witness the kind of self-emptying that we too are capable of. The verbs of our lives can flow from this same Christ-mind, this same way of seeing ourselves in relationship to God and to the world. Sooner or later we too will be called to be obedient to death. In the meantime we are as free as Jesus to decide how we will spend our energy: on self-protection or self-donation, on saving ourselves (and our religious institutions) or giving ourselves away?

Since the individual character of Jesus stands at the center of today's grim and bloody drama, many Palm Sunday sermons focus on the individual dimension as well. Yet today is a good day to ask what it might look like for an entire congregation to embody the mind of Jesus, emptying its corporate self (and coffers) in order to take the form of a slave. How might a whole church become obedient to the point of death? What crosses are right in front of this congregation, just waiting to be picked up?

Preachers who take this tack will note that human volition ends at verse 9. However Christians decide to respond to this Christ hymn, either individually or communally, they die at verse 8. After that, God takes over. Jesus does not exalt himself, any more than Jesus raises himself from the dead. Seeing his "I" on empty, the great "I AM" takes over.

In the NRSV, there is a space between verses 8 and 9 on the page. Preachers may have to work hard

Philippians 2:5-11

Theological Perspective

recommending an alternative ethic. An ethic is a philosophy of life, a kind of wisdom, or a picture of a basic way of going about things. What's more, different ethics and philosophies of life sometimes come to expression in popular sayings. For example, I can remember having heard the following, not too inspiring, advice when I was coming up in New Jersey: "Look out for number one." The basic idea was that one should look out for oneself rather than others, and it was authorized by a view of things that came through in yet another saying: "Do unto others as they would do unto you, but do it first." The world, many believe, is a place filled with people and institutions bent on maximizing their own interests at others' expense and so, when it comes to life on planet Earth, it's every person for himself or herself.

"Let each of you look not to your own interests, but to the interests of others" (v. 4). Paul's exhortation to the Philippians runs clean counter to the conventional Jersey wisdom. However, while it also gains some support from the way things are, for example, the importance of relationships, communities, and mutual responsibilities, it does not require us to be naive. It does not require us to pretend that the world is routinely a happy place chock full of persons and institutions that chronically do what is right and good. That is because, in the final analysis, the exhortation has an alternative basis in the engendering deed.

The alternative nature of Paul's wisdom comes through once again in the claim that at Jesus' name all knees shall bend, even as all tongues shall confess his lordship (vv. 10–11) or, in the words of Isaac Watts's hymn, that "Jesus shall reign where'er the sun . . ." For, as Watts's hymn also suggests, this will be no ordinary empire. Centered not on earthly powers or conventional wisdom, but on the one who "emptied himself, taking the form of a slave" (v. 7), it can only be a great reversal.

DOUGLAS F. OTTATI

Pastoral Perspective

not the verses are a part of a sermon, Philippians 2:5–11 can play a significant role in the service of worship itself. Since these verses are known as a hymn, could you sing the text? Is there someone in the congregation who could put this "hymn" to music for either the congregation or the choir to sing? What might be the impact of hearing God's Word sung on this day? Would singing this early church hymn draw the congregation to the level of praise that Paul intended for the church?

Or could you use the verses as an affirmation of faith to be read together after the sermon or after the reading of the passion narrative? If there are Bibles in the pews, members of the worshiping community might open them to this text and read together to affirm their faith. The entire text could also be printed in the bulletin to be read together. Would you want to consider reading verses 5–8 sitting down and verses 9–11 standing, as a way of accentuating the movement from humiliation to exaltation? Or the verses might be set into a liturgical reading in order to point to theological understandings. If Philippians 2:5–11 is used in one of these ways, there is a natural flow to prayer for the community of faith and for all whom the church is called to serve. In such a prayer, pettiness might be overcome by praise of God. It also would be appropriate following the use of Philippians 2:5–11 to take the offering and to let these verses encourage us to give beyond ourselves and to those whom Christ calls us to serve. In whatever ways the Philippians text is used on Palm/Passion Sunday, this ancient hymn invites us to remember who Jesus is and who Christ calls us to be: obedient servants, confessing together that *Jesus is Lord, to the glory of God the Father.*

LAURA S. MENDENHALL

Exegetical Perspective

beyond measure: was this what "being in the form of God" meant—dying the most gruesome of deaths?!

Why did this happen? Elsewhere, Paul explains that Christ died "for us" (1 Thess. 5:10) or that it was because of "his love for us" (Rom. 5:8). Here, the purpose of Christ's incarnation and death are not spelled out, but if we look at the surrounding verses we realize that the Philippians' life "in Christ" results from Christ's self-emptying and death and his subsequent vindication by God (vv. 9–11). Although the hymn itself does not tell us how these events affect us, the rest of the epistle spells this out, and the final hope, expressed in 3:20–21, is full of echoes of this passage.

Unusually for Paul, verse 9 speaks of exaltation rather than resurrection. God responds to Christ's self-humiliation by "highly" exalting him. What Christ had previously not claimed he is now given, and he is universally acknowledged as "Lord," the name that belongs to God alone. Paul uses a series of superlatives: "highly exalted," "the name that is above every name," "every knee," "every tongue." To be given a name is to be given status and power. What was said of YHWH in Isaiah 45:23 ("To me every knee shall bow, every tongue shall swear") is now said of Jesus. It is "at the name of Jesus" that every knee is to bend, but the name given to him in verse 9 is not "Jesus," since that is the name given him at birth. By using "Jesus" here, Paul reminds us that it is indeed the one who humbled himself and died on the cross who is now acknowledged as "Lord."

Adam was given dominion over the earth, but when Jesus is named, knees above and below the earth will bow. Adam failed to honor God, but Christ's exaltation, far from being a usurpation of what belongs to God, resounds to God's glory. Those who honor Jesus honor God, since Jesus is "in the form of God," revealing to us the very nature of God.

MORNA D. HOOKER

Homiletical Perspective

to keep that space in place, since it is next to impossible for most goal-oriented human beings to separate their actions from their anticipated rewards. For many of us, "therefore" is the most interesting word on the page. If we imitate Christ, therefore we too will be exalted, right? If we humble ourselves, therefore we too will share in the glory of God?

On Palm Sunday, it is appropriate to point out that the space on the page is the equivalent of the grave in which Jesus lay, dead as dead could be—perfectly obedient to death—with no pulse, no thought, no will. In his commentary on this letter, Fred Craddock says, "The grave of Christ was a cave, not a tunnel. Christ acted on our behalf without view of gain. That is precisely what God has exalted and vindicated: self-denying service for others to the point of death with no claim of return, no eye upon a reward."[1]

Here, then, are several theme sentences that Palm Sunday preachers may develop into sermons based on their own congregational contexts:

—Embracing the Christ-mind precedes all Christlike actions.

—Jesus fulfilled his own divine will (to be fully human) by dying on a cross.

—Those who wish to be full of God start by emptying themselves of ego.

—Churches that embody the mind of Christ can expect to die on crosses.

—Emptying yourself and keeping your eye on the prize are mutually exclusive.

—"The grave of Christ was a cave, not a tunnel."[2]

What all of these themes have in common is this: on Palm Sunday, we do not focus on what we believe about Jesus. We focus on what he did, and what we are able to do because he did.

BARBARA BROWN TAYLOR

---

1. Fred Craddock, *Philippians*, Interpretation series (Atlanta: John Knox Press, 1985), 42.
2. Ibid.

Luke 22:14-23:56

[14]When the hour came, he took his place at the table, and the apostles with him. [15]He said to them, "I have eagerly desired to eat this Passover with you before I suffer; [16]for I tell you, I will not eat it until it is fulfilled in the kingdom of God." [17]Then he took a cup, and after giving thanks he said, "Take this and divide it among yourselves; [18]for I tell you that from now on I will not drink of the fruit of the vine until the kingdom of God comes." [19]Then he took a loaf of bread, and when he had given thanks, he broke it and gave it to them, saying, "This is my body, which is given for you. Do this in remembrance of me." [20]And he did the same with the cup after supper, saying, "This cup that is poured out for you is the new covenant in my blood. [21]But see, the one who betrays me is with me, and his hand is on the table. [22]For the Son of Man is going as it has been determined, but woe to that one by whom he is betrayed!" [23]Then they began to ask one another which one of them it could be who would do this.

[24]A dispute also arose among them as to which one of them was to be regarded as the greatest. [25]But he said to them, "The kings of the Gentiles lord it over them; and those in authority over them are called benefactors. [26]But not so with you; rather the greatest among you must become like the youngest, and the leader like one who serves. [27]For who is greater, the one who is at the table or the one who serves? Is it not the one at the table? But I am among you as one who serves.

[28]"You are those who have stood by me in my trials; [29]and I confer on you, just as my Father has conferred on me, a kingdom, [30]so that you may eat and drink at my table in my kingdom, and you will sit on thrones judging the twelve tribes of Israel.

[31]"Simon, Simon, listen! Satan has demanded to sift all of you like wheat, [32]but I have prayed for you that your own faith may not fail; and you, when once you have turned back, strengthen your brothers." [33]And he said to him, "Lord, I am ready to go with you to prison and to death!" [34]Jesus said, "I tell you, Peter, the cock will not crow this day, until you have denied three times that you know me."

[35]He said to them, "When I sent you out without a purse, bag, or sandals, did you lack anything?" They said, "No, not a thing." [36]He said to them, "But now, the one who has a purse must take it, and likewise a bag. And the one who has no sword must sell his cloak and buy one. [37]For I tell you, this scripture must be fulfilled in me, 'And he was counted among the lawless'; and indeed what is written about me is being fulfilled." [38]They said, "Lord, look, here are two swords." He replied, "It is enough."

[39]He came out and went, as was his custom, to the Mount of Olives; and the disciples followed him. [40]When he reached the place, he said to them, "Pray that you may not come into the time of trial." [41]Then he withdrew from them about a stone's throw, knelt down, and prayed, [42]"Father, if you are willing, remove this cup from me; yet, not my will but yours be done." [[43]Then an angel from heaven appeared to him and gave him strength. [44]In his anguish he prayed more earnestly, and his sweat became like great drops of blood falling down on the ground.] [45]When he got up from prayer, he came to the disciples and found them sleeping because of grief, [46]and he said to them, "Why are you sleeping? Get up and pray that you may not come into the time of trial."

[47]While he was still speaking, suddenly a crowd came, and the one called Judas, one of the twelve, was leading them. He approached Jesus to kiss him; [48]but Jesus said to him, "Judas, is it with a kiss that you are betraying the Son of Man?" [49]When those who were around him saw what was coming, they asked, "Lord, should we strike with the sword?" [50]Then one of them struck the slave of the high priest and

cut off his right ear. ⁵¹But Jesus said, "No more of this!" And he touched his ear and healed him. ⁵²Then Jesus said to the chief priests, the officers of the temple police, and the elders who had come for him, "Have you come out with swords and clubs as if I were a bandit? ⁵³When I was with you day after day in the temple, you did not lay hands on me. But this is your hour, and the power of darkness!"

⁵⁴Then they seized him and led him away, bringing him into the high priest's house. But Peter was following at a distance. ⁵⁵When they had kindled a fire in the middle of the courtyard and sat down together, Peter sat among them. ⁵⁶Then a servant-girl, seeing him in the firelight, stared at him and said, "This man also was with him." ⁵⁷But he denied it, saying, "Woman, I do not know him." ⁵⁸A little later someone else, on seeing him, said, "You also are one of them." But Peter said, "Man, I am not!" ⁵⁹Then about an hour later still another kept insisting, "Surely this man also was with him; for he is a Galilean." ⁶⁰But Peter said, "Man, I do not know what you are talking about!" At that moment, while he was still speaking, the cock crowed. ⁶¹The Lord turned and looked at Peter. Then Peter remembered the word of the Lord, how he had said to him, "Before the cock crows today, you will deny me three times." ⁶²And he went out and wept bitterly.

⁶³Now the men who were holding Jesus began to mock him and beat him; ⁶⁴they also blindfolded him and kept asking him, "Prophesy! Who is it that struck you?" ⁶⁵They kept heaping many other insults on him.

⁶⁶When day came, the assembly of the elders of the people, both chief priests and scribes, gathered together, and they brought him to their council. ⁶⁷They said, "If you are the Messiah, tell us." He replied, "If I tell you, you will not believe; ⁶⁸and if I question you, you will not answer. ⁶⁹But from now on the Son of Man will be seated at the right hand of the power of God." ⁷⁰All of them asked, "Are you, then, the Son of God?" He said to them, "You say that I am." ⁷¹Then they said, "What further testimony do we need? We have heard it ourselves from his own lips!"

²³:¹Then the assembly rose as a body and brought Jesus before Pilate. ²They began to accuse him, saying, "We found this man perverting our nation, forbidding us to pay taxes to the emperor, and saying that he himself is the Messiah, a king." ³Then Pilate asked him, "Are you the king of the Jews?" He answered, "You say so." ⁴Then Pilate said to the chief priests and the crowds, "I find no basis for an accusation against this man." ⁵But they were insistent and said, "He stirs up the people by teaching throughout all Judea, from Galilee where he began even to this place."

⁶When Pilate heard this, he asked whether the man was a Galilean. ⁷And when he learned that he was under Herod's jurisdiction, he sent him off to Herod, who was himself in Jerusalem at that time. ⁸When Herod saw Jesus, he was very glad, for he had been wanting to see him for a long time, because he had heard about him and was hoping to see him perform some sign. ⁹He questioned him at some length, but Jesus gave him no answer. ¹⁰The chief priests and the scribes stood by, vehemently accusing him. ¹¹Even Herod with his soldiers treated him with contempt and mocked him; then he put an elegant robe on him, and sent him back to Pilate. ¹²That same day Herod and Pilate became friends with each other; before this they had been enemies.

¹³Pilate then called together the chief priests, the leaders, and the people, ¹⁴and said to them, "You brought me this man as one who was perverting the people; and here I have examined him in your presence and have not found this man guilty of any of your charges against him. ¹⁵Neither has Herod, for he sent him back to us. Indeed, he has done nothing to deserve death. ¹⁶I will therefore have him flogged and release him."

¹⁸Then they all shouted out together, "Away with this fellow! Release Barabbas for us!" ¹⁹(This was a man who had been put in prison for an insurrection that had taken place in the city, and for murder.) ²⁰Pilate, wanting to release Jesus, addressed them again; ²¹but they kept shouting, "Crucify, crucify him!" ²²A third time he said to them, "Why, what evil has he done? I have found in him no ground for the sentence of death; I will therefore have him flogged and then release him." ²³But they kept urgently demanding with loud shouts that he should be crucified; and their voices prevailed. ²⁴So Pilate gave his verdict that their demand should be granted. ²⁵He released the man they asked for, the one who had been put in prison for insurrection and murder, and he handed Jesus over as they wished.

²⁶As they led him away, they seized a man, Simon of Cyrene, who was coming from the country, and they laid the cross on him, and made him carry it behind Jesus. ²⁷A great number of the people followed him, and among them were women who were beating their breasts and wailing for him. ²⁸But Jesus turned to them and said, "Daughters of Jerusalem, do not weep for me, but weep for yourselves and for your children. ²⁹For the days are surely coming when they will say, 'Blessed are the barren, and the wombs that never bore, and the breasts that never nursed.' ³⁰Then they will begin to say to the mountains, 'Fall on us'; and to the hills, 'Cover us.' ³¹For if they do this when the wood is green, what will happen when it is dry?"

³²Two others also, who were criminals, were led away to be put to death with him. ³³When they came to the place that is called The Skull, they crucified Jesus there with the criminals, one on his right and one on his left. [³⁴Then Jesus said, "Father, forgive them; for they do not know what they are doing."] And they cast lots to divide his clothing. ³⁵And the people stood by, watching; but the leaders scoffed at him, saying, "He saved others; let him save himself if he is the Messiah of God, his chosen one!" ³⁶The soldiers also mocked him, coming up and offering

Theological Perspective

Luke's description of Jesus' death is not as popular among contemporary theologians as Mark's or John's account. Of course this may tell us more about the state of contemporary theology than about the significance of Luke's interpretation.

Theologians often reflect the spirit of their age, and in western Europe and North America, after two world wars, numerous smaller wars, the horror of the Holocaust, and numerous smaller holocausts, the question of the absence of God has attracted many theologians to Jesus' cry of dereliction (from Ps. 22:1) in Mark 15:34 ("My God, my God, why have you forsaken me?") as a clearer statement of modern sensibility than Luke's description of Jesus' final words (from Ps. 31:5) in 23:46 ("Then Jesus, crying with a loud voice, said, 'Father, into your hands I commend my spirit'"). In Mark, Jesus appears to die in dereliction—in despair and abandonment. In Luke, Jesus dies in the same way that he began his ministry, by being tempted in the wilderness (4:1–13) but

Pastoral Perspective

Some years ago, during an ecumenical service at which Luke's entire passion story was recited, it was met with the nod of recognition, as the worshipers recalled the Last Supper, the prayerful agony of Gethsemane, the arrest and trial of Jesus, and the crucifixion. But near the end of the account, when the Roman centurion spoke his one line, everyone took notice. Looking to the figure on the cross, he said, "Certainly this man was innocent" (23:47). Many of those present had to take a second look at the text. They remembered all the Jesus films where a centurion exclaims the words from Mark: "Truly this man was God's Son!" (Mark 15:39).

Apparently Luke's primary concern is not Christology but justice. Unlike Mark, he is not disclosing a messianic secret at the last possible moment of Jesus' life. Rather, Luke declares the truth that Rome and Jerusalem would otherwise ignore: Jesus is innocent.

The centurion's word is a deep theme throughout this lengthy text. If one is to preach this day, it might

him sour wine, [37]and saying, "If you are the King of the Jews, save yourself!" [38]There was also an inscription over him, "This is the King of the Jews."

[39]One of the criminals who were hanged there kept deriding him and saying, "Are you not the Messiah? Save yourself and us!" [40]But the other rebuked him, saying, "Do you not fear God, since you are under the same sentence of condemnation? [41]And we indeed have been condemned justly, for we are getting what we deserve for our deeds, but this man has done nothing wrong." [42]Then he said, "Jesus, remember me when you come into your kingdom." [43]He replied, "Truly I tell you, today you will be with me in Paradise."

[44]It was now about noon, and darkness came over the whole land until three in the afternoon, [45]while the sun's light failed; and the curtain of the temple was torn in two. [46]Then Jesus, crying with a loud voice, said, "Father, into your hands I commend my spirit." Having said this, he breathed his last. [47]When the centurion saw what had taken place, he praised God and said, "Certainly this man was innocent." [48]And when all the crowds who had gathered there for this spectacle saw what had taken place, they returned home, beating their breasts. [49]But all his acquaintances, including the women who had followed him from Galilee, stood at a distance, watching these things.

[50]Now there was a good and righteous man named Joseph, who, though a member of the council, [51]had not agreed to their plan and action. He came from the Jewish town of Arimathea, and he was waiting expectantly for the kingdom of God. [52]This man went to Pilate and asked for the body of Jesus. [53]Then he took it down, wrapped it in a linen cloth, and laid it in a rock-hewn tomb where no one had ever been laid. [54]It was the day of Preparation, and the sabbath was beginning. [55]The women who had come with him from Galilee followed, and they saw the tomb and how his body was laid. [56]Then they returned, and prepared spices and ointments.

On the sabbath they rested according to the commandment.

Exegetical Perspective

Surrounding the Last Supper scene, Luke's Jesus teaches the qualitative difference between life under imperial systems and life in God's kingdom, both in the temple precincts (public/outside) and in the upper room (private/inside). Jesus' teaching in the temple confronts elite imperial collaborators (19:45–21:38), and at the Last Supper, Jesus distinguishes his way from living under Gentile kings (22:25–27).

Jesus dies under Pilate's inscription: "This is the king of the Jews" (23:38). For Pilate, this is sarcasm. It mocks Jesus' proclamation of God's kingdom. The crucifixion demonstrates "the reality" of kingdom—Roman supremacy, manifested by Pilate's sentencing Jesus to death. Christians remember this stark political reality every time they say the Apostles' Creed: "Crucified under Pontius Pilate."

Luke's Jesus is a Davidic king (1:32). David's anointing in 1 Samuel distinguishes outward appearances from divine purposes. Similarly, in outward appearances, Jesus parodies a king. However

Homiletical Perspective

Take note of the themes we can explore in Luke's Passion story.

The scandal of the cross. The cross is still a stumbling block, both in its horror and in the fact that a crucified man was made the center of our faith. This form of execution was reserved for the worst offenders: revolutionaries against the state, violent criminals, and low-class thieves. Roman citizens could be crucified only for high treason. No more hideous fate could be imagined.

No wonder Paul called the cross "a stumbling block to Jews and foolishness to Gentiles" (1 Cor. 1:23). Justin Martyr, defender of the faith in the century after Paul, said, "They say that our *madness* consists in the fact that we put a *crucified man* in the second place after the unchangeable and eternal God."

The Roman statesman Pliny wrote about the "perverse and extravagant superstition" of Christians—that a man honored as God would be nailed to a cross as a common enemy of the state.

Luke 22:14-23:56

Theological Perspective

remaining faithful. From the beginning to the end of Luke's Gospel, Jesus is God's faithful Son (3:22), who is also a prophet like Moses. Luke's Jesus not only proclaims God's word, but also enacts it; and the perfect coherence between what he says and what he does makes him a model for those who would be saved (e.g., Zacchaeus in 19:1–10) and for missionaries in the early church (e.g., Stephen in Acts 6:8–7:60).

Because Luke's Jesus dies not in passionate despair but in calm obedience to the one he calls *Pater*, it is not surprising that Mark's Gospel would appeal to a church that finds itself in a new and unfamiliar land, no longer in the center of the public square, but banished to the margins of social power and influence, feeling abandoned and alone. Questions about covenant, the faithfulness of God, and the apparent absence of God cry out for a Christ who knows something of abandonment and despair. Does that mean, however, that Luke's Jesus has nothing to say to a church on the verge of collapse in western Europe and North America? In his description of Jesus' death, it may be that Luke has much to say to a church today struggling to find and understand what discipleship and mission mean in an affluent society that no longer listens to it.

Luke's Jesus is a man in motion, a man on the road, both in Galilee (4:14–9:50) and in his extended journey to Jerusalem (9:51–19:27). Those who would be his disciples have to leave everything behind and travel with him. This Jesus travels light and calls his disciples to do so as well (12:32–34). Jesus travels his path proclaiming the reign of God and the coming of God's kingdom both in what he says and in the wonders he performs. Indeed, in Luke's description of Jesus, there is an extraordinary, unparalleled coherence between what Jesus says about God and what he does in the name of God. That is as true at the beginning of his story about Jesus (in Jesus' temptation by the devil in the wilderness) as at the end (in his death on Golgotha). As Jesus is dying, those around him—the leaders (23:35), the soldiers (23:36), and one of the two thieves crucified next to him (23:39)—mock him. In the midst of it all, Jesus remains faithful to the one he calls "Father."

Peter Hodgson has used the term "homology" to describe the relation between Jesus' words and God's Word. The relation between the two is not one of analogy, but one of homology (literally "the same word"), "a relation of correspondence rather than proportionality."[1] Hodgson understands Matthew

Pastoral Perspective

be sufficient to reflect on Christ's innocence. Listen to Pontius Pilate. No less than three times he declares there is no basis for an accusation against Jesus, much less for a sentence of death (23:4, 14–15, 22) Even at the crucifixion scene, one hardened criminal says to the other, "We are getting what we deserve for our deeds, but this man has done nothing wrong" (23:41).

Jesus has done nothing wrong. He has not led people down the wrong path. He has not rejected the Scriptures. He has not trained terrorists to resist the empire. He has not spoken against God. There is nothing violent about Jesus.

Yet there is something about him that people resist and wish to eliminate. We cannot single out empire or Sanhedrin for blame. There has been something about Jesus that people have resisted from the very beginning.

In Nazareth, he preached to his hometown crowd that God loves the outsider, and his neighbors tried to hurl him over a cliff (4:29). As he taught on the Sabbath in Capernaum, someone with a filthy spirit yelled out, "Jesus, leave us alone!" (4:34). Luke says every time Jesus healed anybody, he had to muzzle the evil forces because they were trying to compromise his mission (4:40–41). From the very beginning of his ministry, Jesus faced opposition to his words and deeds, not because he did something wrong, but because he came in the power of God's Spirit. This was the same Spirit who filled Jesus so that he would "proclaim release to the captives" (4:18). How ironic that he was unjustly condemned!

While we cannot say that the Roman centurion saw the cross through Luke's eyes, we do have his testimony. He declared Jesus to be innocent. That is remarkable, given the conflict and condemnation in the narrative that builds to that moment.

I remember a seminary classmate who worked as a New Jersey prison chaplain. Returning from death row on Sunday evenings, he said, "All the prisoners there insist they are innocent. They say they were falsely accused and unfairly condemned." Pretty soon, he figured that such declarations go with the territory. In the course of a conversation with an inmate, however, Jim discerned that, indeed, the man probably had been unjustly accused. He started to investigate the facts. The details began to fit. Jim took a leave of absence from his seminary studies to research the case, became the man's advocate, and sometime later the prisoner was released.

Of course, Jesus had no such advocate. The centurion said what he did, but did not stop the

---

1. Peter C. Hodgson, *Jesus—Word and Presence: An Essay in Christology* (Philadelphia: Fortress Press, 1971), 101.

from Luke 4:43 on, he proclaims the kingdom of God. This proclamation is subversive, because Rome proclaimed Caesar's rule as the kingdom of the gods. Luke 21 also contrasts appearances and God's kingdom. It appears that elite people contributing to the temple are generous (21:1–4). A poor widow unmasks the myth that the rich are generous. They appear generous out of wealth gained at others' expense (see 20:47). It also appears that the temple's stones ensure enduring order, but its majesty notwithstanding, its end is coming (21:5–6). "Appearances" are that warriors usher in God's kingdom, but God's kingdom lies beyond such devastation (21:7–24).

Rome controls through local collaborators. Luke 22:2 identifies the chief priests and scribes as collaborators who stand against the people, but collaboration also reaches into Jesus' disciples. Judas becomes a collaborator (22:3–6).

References to Passover in Luke 22:1, 7 imply the simultaneity of the conspiracy against Jesus and the Last Supper. Ironically both are preparations for Passover. The supper inside anticipates Jesus' suffering outside, and the presence of Judas reiterates the simultaneity of the collaboration with the announcement of the new covenant and with what Johann Baptist Metz calls "the dangerous memory" of Jesus' crucifixion and resurrection (22:19–20).[1] The disciples' inquiry about who the betrayer might be implicitly exhorts readers to examine themselves to see whether they are collaborators like Judas, even at the Lord's table (22:21–23).

The simultaneity of the Last Supper with the outside conspiracy makes Jesus' saying about Gentile kings a commentary on the conspiracy. A comparison between Gentile king and Jesus' kingdom shows that Jesus' disciples are an unmistakable alternative to empire. It reveals why remembering Jesus is so dangerous. After referring to the new covenant, Jesus declares, "The kings of the Gentiles lord it over them; and those in authority over them are called benefactors. But not so with you" (22:25–26). Acts 4:24–28 offers an interpretation on the event; Pilate and Herod Antipas, it declares, both find Jesus not guilty and still administer justice unjustly. Jesus' band is different from hierarchical political processes and patron/client relationships. Those who dominate others and nevertheless are called benefactors unveil again the myth that the elite are generous. Peter's denial, the enigmatic saying about swords, and Jesus' prayer of anguish all indicate the danger of Jesus' confrontation with imperial powers (22:21–38, 42–46, 54–62).

Some early graffiti discovered on a Roman palace wall near the Circus Maximus, dated 200 BCE, show a man hanging on a cross, except that instead of a man's head there is the head of a jackass, and scribbled underneath in large letters are the words "Alexamenos Worships God."[1]

Preaching the cross ponders how God is redeeming the world in the darkest and most shameful of places.

The costly call of the cross. What is the cross Jesus calls us to take up as we follow? For Dietrich Bonhoeffer, it was to take up the suffering of others. On November 9, 1938, the hidden Nazi violence against the Jews went public. That night, called Krystallnacht, the Night of Broken Glass, there was a rampage of violence against Jewish synagogues, homes, and businesses. That night Bonhoeffer opened his Bible and read Psalm 74. In the margin he wrote: "How long, O God, shall I be a bystander?" The cross will not let us be bystanders.

The two trials.[2] There was the trial of Peter. The judges were the servant-girl and other onlookers. Peter denied Jesus. Seeking to save his life, he lost it, lost it until the risen Jesus revived it again. "Woman, I do not know him," he said (22:57). These words were more than a simple lie; they were also the truth, a confession. He really did not know the man whom he had followed for three years. Is this our confession too?

The second trial was Jesus' trial before Pilate and Herod. Willing to lose his life, he saved it; he stood in majestic silence before his accusers. There was Pilate, who would not take responsibility for the decision but gave it off to others. Murderous coward. Herod, treating Jesus like a plaything, wanting to see his "tricks." The group Pilate brought together into his courtyard—not the Jewish people at large, but the ruling elite and their cronies.

The one handed over. Judas is described as the one who "handed Jesus over" (22:21). The Greek word *paradidōmi* is used, often translated "betray," though the specific word for betray is *prodidōmi*. This broader word "handed over" offers us a moment of spiritual reflection.[3]

Most of our lives we are told that we will make a difference in this life by what we *do*, by our action.

---

1. See Martin Hengel, *Crucifixion* (Philadelphia: Fortress Press, 1977).
2. See Paul Minear, *The Good News according to Matthew* (St. Louis: Chalice Press, 2000), 92ff.
3. See Henri Nouwen, *The Road To Daybreak* (New York: Doubleday, 1988), 156ff.; and W. H. Vanstone, *The Stature of Waiting* (New York: Seabury Press, 1983).

---

1. J. B. Metz, *Faith in History and Society: Toward a Practical Fundamental Theology* (New York: Seabury Press, 1980), 109–11.

Luke 22:14-23:56

Theological Perspective

10:32 ("Everyone therefore who acknowledges me before others, I also will acknowledge before my Father in heaven") to provide evidence "not only for the correspondence between the word of Jesus and the word of God but also for the identity of Jesus' person and his word; he *is* what he says, and his word is event, personal event." Furthermore, "The word with which Jesus' person is identical and which designates his correspondence to God is *faithful* word."[2]

Hodgson might also have explored the sense in which not only Jesus' words but also his acts are homologous with God. For the New Testament, there is not just an analogy, but a correspondence between Jesus' sacrificial love on the cross and the love of God. Hence not only is Jesus what he says, but Jesus is also what he does, and he corresponds to God's word both in what he says and what he does and in the perfect coherence between the two. That is particularly apparent in Luke's description of Jesus' death. In Luke's account, Jesus both lives and dies faithfully—that is, proclaiming and enacting complete trust in the one he calls "Father."

If Jesus' disciples are called to follow his "way," then they too are called to faithful obedience to what Jesus says and does. Only Jesus is without sin, and only in Jesus is there a perfect coherence between what he says and what he does. Jesus' disciples are, without exception, sinners, and one way to understand sin is as an incoherence between what one says and what one does. Those who follow Jesus live by God's grace alone; until God finally transforms all things, there will always be an incoherence between what Christian people say and what they do. As they pursue their own journey to Jerusalem, however, Christians are called in their living and in their dying to struggle for a greater coherence between what they confess with their lips and how they live their lives, a more faithful coherence that is expressed in "Father, into your hands I commend my spirit."

GEORGE W. STROUP

Pastoral Perspective

execution. An innocent man was killed. This is what Luke wants us to see when we look at the cross. Jesus comes to village and city in perfect goodness, and people cannot handle it. In the memorable phrase of Dietrich Bonhoeffer, God "lets himself be pushed out of the world onto the cross."[1]

Throughout the Third Gospel, Luke has reminded us that Jesus speaks like a prophet. He will also die like one. Earlier, when a few friendly Pharisees warned him away from the Holy City, Jesus retorted, "It is impossible for a prophet to be killed outside of Jerusalem" (13:33). He came with the gathering love of a mother hen, yet was met with deadly resistance.

Rather than read the passion narrative as an anti-Semitic vindictive screed, we must read it as an exegesis of the human condition. We resist the love, mercy, and truth of Jesus Christ. We silence the honest voice. We condemn the innocent agitator. We pursue our own agendas for the sake of expediency.

Today we gather before the cross and hear someone say, "This man was innocent." Jesus has done nothing wrong. His way is the true way. If we would follow him, we must honestly appraise the situations before us. We have the choice to push ourselves away from every form of cruelty. Authentic faith takes root when we decide, "For the sake of Jesus, I am no longer going to participate in something that is vindictive, punitive, or evil."

That stand takes great courage. It will certainly provoke its own controversy and opposition, but the way of Jesus is the holy way, the nonviolent way, the discipleship way. It is the narrow way to the reign of God.

Jesus is innocent. He is condemned and killed precisely because he is the one person who was ever totally innocent. He dies between two criminals, at the hand of an oppressive empire, rejected by his neighbors, and abandoned by his friends. Can we live with that?

It may not matter. God will also declare Jesus innocent when the dawn breaks on Easter. Raised from the dead, Jesus will be vindicated. That fact may leave us very unsettled.

WILLIAM G. CARTER

---

2. Ibid., 144–45.

1. Dietrich Bonhoeffer, *Letters and Papers from Prison*, ed. E. Bethge, trans. R. Fuller, F. Clark, et al. (New York: Macmillan, 1971), 360.

Jesus' new covenant does not abandon Israel's history. As Mary, Zechariah, and Peter show (Luke 1:55, 73; Acts 3:22–25), the new covenant is a renewal of the promises to Abraham, Moses, and David.

The high-priestly party, the temple police, and elders are local imperial collaborators. Jesus repudiates a skirmish with swords. Still, he confronts local manifestations of the empire with God's kingdom. Moreover, he interprets his arrest as the "power of darkness" (22:53). Jesus exposes the fascist strategy of empires to hide their repression of difference and portrays such repression as the power of evil.

By refusing to play the role of a defendant on trial, Jesus resists imperial "justice." Jesus' refusal to defend himself (22:66–71; 23:3, 9) challenges both the ground and the appearance of the imperial justice system. Collaboration of local leaders with Rome's client king and governor could hardly be more explicit than in Luke 23:12–13 (see Acts 4:25–27).

On the way to the crucifixion, some women wail for Jesus. Some interpreters suggest that Jesus rebuffs the women (23:27–31), but another take is that he joins their lament but redirects it, by distinguishing again between appearances and reality. Appearances are that his alternative to the conventional is tragic; reality is that the status quo itself is destined for tragedy.

Another prominent part of the crucifixion is the interchange with two other condemned men who forge quite different relationships with Jesus. One mocks, the other pleads to participate in Jesus' kingdom. Jesus assures the second that they will accompany each other in God's reality beyond the conventional social order—he calls it "paradise" (23:39–43). This word, which appears only three times in the New Testament, literally means "garden" and likely refers to a place of blessedness.

Jesus' dying words quote Psalm 31:5, which he likely knew as a bedtime prayer: "Into your hands I commend my spirit." However the prayer has a second line that anyone who knows the psalm would hear implicitly: "You have redeemed me, O Lord, faithful God." Moreover, the psalm expresses hope in God over against worthless things (not "idols," as in Ps. 31:6, NRSV) and confesses confidence in God's faithfulness and mercy. Jesus' words likely imply all of this.

Rome used crucifixion to terrify people who cherished alternatives to dominant imperial values, especially defiant slaves and unruly foreigners. God's kingdom and Caesar's clash when Jesus journeys to Jerusalem. Jesus' trust in the mercy and fidelity of God undergirds this confrontation. So at the moment of his death, he commends his life to this God.

JAE WON LEE

However what we learn this week is that God can make something of our *passion*, that is, what is done to us. Passion comes from the word *paschō*, which means "to be done to," the opposite of *poieō*, which means "to do." God is redeeming the world through both action and passion, because our lives are made up of both what is done to us and what we do.

Jesus is this "one handed over." Judas handed Jesus over, and Jewish leaders handed him over to Pilate, and Pilate is described as handing Jesus over to the will of the crowd (23:25). Paul uses this language as he passes on the Last Supper tradition as it was handed to him: "On the night when he was *handed over . . .*" (1 Cor. 11:23).

Such was the risk of incarnation itself, God handing Jesus over into our hands, Jesus now vulnerable to all the ways life acts upon us: love, rejection, disease, unforeseeable events, beauty, and cruelty.

Such is also the risk of our lives. Can we trust that God can use our passion as much as our action, as God used Jesus' passion for the redemption of the world?

The two prayers. From the cross come two prayers: a prayer for forgiveness ("Father, forgive them; for they do not know what they are doing" [23:34]) and a prayer of relinquishment ("Father, into your hands I commend my spirit" [23:46]). These are the two most important prayers we can offer when crosses come.

Whom was Jesus forgiving? The disciples who deserted him, the Roman soldiers who killed him, the Roman and Jewish ruling elite who condemned him to death, yes. Was he forgiving us all forever, for all our sins? This is the gospel.

Did they "know what they were doing"? Only in part. None of us knows the full extent of our sinning or the full harm we do. God's forgiveness covers all.

In his prayer of relinquishment, Jesus offers to his Abba what he has been offering all along: his life into the hands of God, the faithfulness at the heart of things. This prayer quotes Psalm 31, an evening prayer, and these words may have been the bedtime prayer for Hebrew children and their parents. It is the prayer of "letting go." We say, "O God, take my sticky fingers off the controls, and place my life in better hands than mine."

Can you imagine two better prayers with which to live and die, especially when life has done its worst to us?

H. STEPHEN SHOEMAKER

Isaiah 42:1-9

¹Here is my servant, whom I uphold,
   my chosen, in whom my soul delights;
   I have put my spirit upon him;
   he will bring forth justice to the nations.
²He will not cry or lift up his voice,
   or make it heard in the street;
³a bruised reed he will not break,
   and a dimly burning wick he will not quench;
   he will faithfully bring forth justice.
⁴He will not grow faint or be crushed
   until he has established justice in the earth;
   and the coastlands wait for his teaching.

⁵Thus says God, the LORD,
   who created the heavens and stretched them out,
   who spread out the earth and what comes from it,

Theological Perspective

The fact that Isaiah 42:1–9 is read on the Monday of
Holy Week is an indication that the church has long
connected Isaiah's words with the last days of Jesus'
earthly ministry. The passage is the first of the
Servant Songs of the prophet of Israel's exile and
helped to inform the church's earliest reflection on
the identity and work of the one it called Messiah.
Isaiah's elusive words made it easy for Christians to
make a one-to-one correspondence between Isaiah's
Servant and Jesus. The church, in its liturgy and
music, its prayers and preaching, has continued that
connection down through the ages.

With the rise of critical Bible study, it became
important to take with seriousness the historical
contexts that gave rise to the Scriptures. Toward the
end of the nineteenth century, it was common to
separate chapters 40–55 of Isaiah from the rest of the
book. It was obvious that those chapters were written
during the Babylonian exile of Israel, which began in
597 BCE with an initial deportation of Israelite
leaders and did not end until 539/538 BCE with
Cyrus's defeat of the Babylonians and his annexation
of their empire. An unknown prophet spoke/wrote his
words late in that period, soon after Cyrus's victory.

As historical scholars reflected on the words, the
question that arose was, who was the Servant that
Isaiah had in mind? The church made Jesus the

Pastoral Perspective

Even if interpreters could put a definitive historical
name to the figure at the center of this text, the
ambiguous identity of the Servant of the Lord would
be one of the springs winding the energy of Holy
Week towards its disastrous, then triumphant,
conclusion. As the journey of the week begins, most
worshipers will recognize Jesus in the servant, the
man of sorrows, God's beloved. However if they are
encouraged to listen carefully, a layer or two beneath
the predetermined outcome, they may find
themselves suddenly in the deep water of ambiguity
about who this chosen one of God really is—
ambiguity that, by the end, may nourish both
devotion and discipleship.

To come to worship during the first days of Holy
Week is, perhaps, to be willing to take the weeklong
journey to the cross and the empty tomb one step at
a time—willing to experience those days when, at
least in linear narrative terms, the outcome of
struggle is not yet clear. The first steps, in all three
lectionary years, are steeped in Second Isaiah—to set
up our eventual arrival at the destination of the
week the way the exiles would have arrived in
Jerusalem after their captivity in Babylon. Indeed, to
remove Isaiah 42 from the context of exile robs the
text of prophetic heft and reduces the journey of
Holy Week to a shallow liturgical hop from Palm

who gives breath to the people upon it
  and spirit to those who walk in it:
⁶I am the Lord, I have called you in righteousness,
  I have taken you by the hand and kept you;
I have given you as a covenant to the people,
  a light to the nations,
⁷ to open the eyes that are blind,
  to bring out the prisoners from the dungeon,
  from the prison those who sit in darkness.
⁸I am the Lord, that is my name;
  my glory I give to no other,
  nor my praise to idols.
⁹See, the former things have come to pass,
  and new things I now declare;
before they spring forth,
  I tell you of them.

Exegetical Perspective

The Hebrew Bible lectionary for Holy Week turns to a collection of poems from Second Isaiah, the anonymous prophet of the Babylonian exile whose voice we hear in Isaiah 40–55. These poems (usually identified as 42:1–9; 49:1–7; 50:4–11; and 52:13–53:12) all deal with the Servant of the Lord, an unidentified figure whose mission involves not only the deliverance of Israel, but also the transformation of the world. Outside of the Songs, Second Isaiah uses this title for "Israel, my servant, Jacob, whom I have chosen" (41:8–9; see also 42:19; 43:10; 44:1–2; 44:21; 45:4); therefore, traditional Jewish interpretation and the mainstream of Christian scholarship as well understand the Servant of the Songs to be Israel personified. However, that identification has its problems. In Second Isaiah, Israel is described as stiff-necked and rebellious (48:4), but the Servant in the Songs is responsive and obedient (42:3–4; 50:5). Servant Israel cannot see God at work or hear God's good news of deliverance (42:19); however, the Servant of the Lord says: "Morning by morning he wakens—wakens my ear to listen as those who are taught" (50:4). The most remarkable distinction, however, is that while Israel's exile is a deserved (if extreme) punishment for Israel's sin (40:1–2), the Servant suffers innocently, on behalf of others (53:4–5).

Homiletical Perspective

It is Monday of Holy Week, and already the palms of yesterday's procession have begun to dry out, scattered as they are on sanctuary floors and dining room tables. The cries of "Hosanna, blessed is the One who comes in the name of the Lord," are a part of us still, but the cries fade as quickly as those branches go dry. We awaken to read this word from the prophet Isaiah, from Second Isaiah really, this first of the four Servant poems describing the one who will enact God's plan for this hurting world, bringing justice to the nations—no easy task, Isaiah admits, even for this Servant of God.

If we were to write the script, we would have a few ideas about how God's justice might be accomplished. There would be truth to speak to those in power. There would be a quick and dramatic redistribution of wealth. Those who have profited by their war making, those who have gained material wealth by disregarding an ethic of earth stewardship, those who have oppressed the powerless in nations far away and in homes quite close to ours would all quickly come to know the ways of God. In that knowledge, they would quickly change. Or they would know themselves far distant from the Holy One. That is the way to accomplish justice. That is the way to bring healing to the nations of the earth.

Isaiah 42:1-9

Theological Perspective

answer, but since Jesus had lived 600 years later, speculation about the one (or the many) Isaiah referred to was rampant. However, when we are thinking theologically about Second Isaiah, that question is not the most fruitful one to pursue. The more important question that theology needs to ask is, just what was God up to in the exile of Israel? To that question Second Isaiah gives an unforgettable series of responses.

For Second Isaiah, the first answer is that God has chosen Israel to be God's servant. In one of Second Isaiah's assaults on heathen idolatry, 41:7–10, Israel-servant is contrasted with the created golden object of worship, one "smoothed with a hammer" and "fastened with nails so that it cannot be moved." On the contrary, Israel is "my servant, Jacob, whom I have chosen, the offspring of Abraham, my friend," taken "from the ends of the earth," the one to whom it is said by God, "I have chosen you and not cast you off." The servant Israel has been chosen from afar, has moved a long distance to perform the work of God, is still God's chosen one, despite the horrors of exile and defeat. Second Isaiah speaks to those who have lived in Babylon for more than two generations and urges them to believe that God has never forgotten them but still has a crucial service for them to perform for God and for the whole world.

Second Isaiah begins to spell out the nature of that service in 42:1–9, thus providing the second answer to the question of God's intentions. Perhaps in response to the promise made to Israel in Moses's farewell sermon in Deuteronomy 32:36—that God would "vindicate God's people and have compassion on God's servants, when God sees that their power is gone"—Second Isaiah announces the work of Israel as servant to "bring forth justice to the nations" (42:1). Israel's power is gone in exile; surely such powerless ones have no ability to "bring forth justice" for anyone, let alone the nations! On the face of it, it is an absurd call, but it is only the latest in a long line of God's absurd choices to perform the divine work.

God has always been in the business of choosing the least and the last to act as God's agents in the world: Adam and Eve, Abram, Isaac, Jacob, Joseph, Moses, David, Isaiah, Jeremiah are only the most prominent examples of God's astounding and mysterious choices of servants. Is it not the way of God to choose such as these—powerless, problematic, pariahs among the nations? Exilic Israel now joins their company.

How the servant Israel is to perform the work of justice is also surprising and elusive. Since he has no

Pastoral Perspective

Sunday to Easter. Walter Brueggemann is adamant that "to use the poetry of homecoming without the prior literature of exile is an offer of cheap grace."[1] As Jesus stands at the threshold of both the city and the last week of his life, he is something of an exile himself: on the edge (at Bethany in today's Gospel), mindful of the ambiguous portents of this arrival at the spiritual heart of his culture.

"Here is my servant," the text begins. "*Behold*"— the word anticipates commitment as well as revelation, from Abraham's obedience ("Here I am," Gen. 22:1) to Isaiah's call ("Send me," Isa. 6:8), from Jesus' baptism ("This is my Son, the Beloved," Matt. 3:17)[2] to the consummation of time ("I am making all things new," Rev. 21:5). The word (often invisible in English translations) is an imperative, insisting that we look, see, notice, understand. However, to whom is God pointing, as the voice of the prophet evokes the servant? The focal point of the text shifts from third person (v. 1, "*he* will bring forth justice . . .") to second person ("I have called *you* in righteousness . . .") at verse 6, and images of the Servant shift like a hologram, from a plausible historical figure (Cyrus the Persian—see chap. 45) to Jesus to the faithful community. How should our eyes focus among them?

The ambiguity may be compounded by the assortment of characteristics of servanthood evoked by the prophet. If the focus rests on a historical character at the culmination of the exile, the qualities of subtlety (v. 2, "he will not . . . make [his voice] heard in the street") and spiritual authority (v. 4, "the coastlands wait for his teaching") are hard to impute to an imperial figure. If the focus is on Jesus, then the promise that "he will not . . . be crushed until he has established justice in the earth" (v. 4) is at least ironic, at best unfulfilled. If the focus falls on a whole people chosen to be "a light to the nations," then the intimacy and singularity of the personal images ("my chosen, in whom my soul delights") seem off-target.

However, the journey of Holy Week is, in itself, a journey through ambiguity, toward the liminal place where identities merge and the very nature of servanthood is transformed.

If we ourselves embark upon that journey in all spiritual candor, then we too embark as exiles. When the prophet announces, on God's behalf, that the

---

1. Walter Brueggemann, *Holy Imagination: Prophetic Voices in Exile* (Philadelphia: Fortress Press, 1986), 90.
2. This text from Isaiah 42 also appears in Year A, in the company of Matthew's baptism narrative, on the Sunday of the Lord's Baptism.

Exegetical Perspective

If the Servant in the Songs is not Israel, who could this person be? Prophetic elements in the Songs (particularly 49:1–2, 5; 50:4) have prompted the proposal that the Servant is a prophet—perhaps the prophet who has written these Songs. However the Servant also at times sounds like a king, called and empowered to carry divine justice to the ends of the earth (as is the case in the reading for today; see 42:1, 4, 6). The great Jewish philosopher Martin Buber suggested that the Songs do not describe one particular person, but rather set forth the *way* of the Servant, a way going beyond the old roles of prophet and king to a new understanding of Israel's past and future, particularly as revealed through suffering. The Servant's way is "the work born out of affliction," culminating in "the liberation of the subject peoples, laid upon the servant, the divine order of the expiated world of the nations, which the purified servant as its 'light' has to bring in, the covenant of the people of the human beings with God, the human center of which is the servant."[1]

Christian readers have long seen the Servant of the Lord as a foreshadowing of Jesus Christ (see Acts 8:32–35; 1 Cor. 15:3; 1 Pet. 2:22–25), an understanding that may well go back to Jesus himself. However this does not mean that we must, in traditional fashion, see Second Isaiah as predicting Jesus' coming, as though the prophet's words had no meaning for his own time or people. Second Isaiah set forth the way of the Servant: the path of redemptive suffering, deliberately chosen, which will render the tangled history of God's people meaningful. Jesus deliberately set out to follow that way, stepping into the shoes of the Servant of the Lord. In today's Gospel lesson, Mary's extravagant gift, literally poured out at Jesus' feet (John 12:1–3), points to the way of the Servant. Jesus says that her gift is "for the day of my burial" (John 12:7). The way of God's anointed is the way of selfless, sacrificial love (Heb. 9:12), which leads Jesus inexorably to the cross.

With this understanding, we can turn our attention to today's lection. The role assigned to the Servant in this first Song is strangely conflicted. On the one hand, the Servant is an honored, kingly figure, enjoying the full support of the Divine, and called by God "my chosen, in whom my soul delights" (42:1). Repeatedly, the poem emphasizes the Servant's role in bringing forth and establishing justice (42:1, 3–4), which in the Hebrew Bible is a

1. Martin Buber, *The Prophetic Faith*, trans. Carlyle Witton-Davies (New York: Macmillan, 1949), 229.

Homiletical Perspective

However Isaiah tells of no such thing. No, this Servant will act in ways that are not nearly so satisfying. This Servant will not cry out in the streets, will not lift a voice that any can even hear.

The first to hear Isaiah's words thought that the Servant spoken of might well be Israel itself. Or perhaps it was the prophet, standing in for a reluctant nation. Early Christians made different assumptions when they read these words anew, hearing in Isaiah's song a description of the servant Lord, Jesus.

In Holy Week, even as we are aware that the original context for the prophet's words had everything to do with the covenant people Israel, we find it impossible not to hear in these verses of sadness and of hope a description of the ministry of Jesus, the one who would not cry out with a warrior's call, the one who would not grow impatient with a people who failed to understand, the one who would refuse to harm those he knew to be weak.

Indeed, the God of creation will protect this Servant, Isaiah declares, and the Servant will be a witness, a light, to the nations. Light, to a people who have grown accustomed to the gloom. Light enough even to open the eyes of those whose vision has failed them, light to free those imprisoned in the darkness, light to change the human way of relating to this wonderful and troubled world.

Then, most surprisingly of all, God makes one final claim. It is this: All of these first things have already happened. The new things are not just an idle hope. They are a promise.

It is outrageous, of course. While God's Spirit has surely been present in the Servant Israel and the Servant Jesus, the promised time of change has not yet come. Not even now, after so many centuries have passed.

Why in the world would change have come? These Servants have not held power enough to force change. They have not sought to silence those in control of political systems. They have, rather, done the opposite, insisting on a way unknown by those with power. Yet we know that systems will never respond to the quiet and righteous voice. We know that power yields only to even greater power.

We who stand on this Holy Monday know what is coming in our Gospel story as well, know that we are soon to hear the retelling of betrayal, judgment, torture, and death. That is the way that awaits those who speak softly of God's righteousness. That is the thing that the powers of this earth understand.

Isaiah 42:1-9

Theological Perspective

power, "he will not cry or lift up his voice" (42:2). Nor will he break a "bent reed" or "quench a sputtering wick." Without fail, "he will bring forth justice," not fainting or being crushed until "he has established justice in the earth," until the farthest islands long for "his teaching " (his Torah) (vv. 3–4). With the triple use of "justice" (*mishpat*), Second Isaiah focuses the essence of the servant's task. "Justice" is God's righteous, saving way of life, the correct way for humanity to live in peace and harmony. "Justice" is God's Torah, God's central teaching for humanity, and the servant, Israel, is to announce and deliver that teaching to nations and islands, the entire world. The servant is to do that work without violence, without shouting, with relentless conviction and unchangeable urgency.

God's choice of Israel in exile for this work says little about Israel and everything about God. As Deuteronomy 7:6–8 affirms so clearly, God's choice of Israel in Egypt was based solely on God's unmerited love for them. So here in Second Isaiah, God is in the business of announcing God's plan for the world God created, and Israel has been chosen to be the agent of that announcement. God points to Israel: "Behold, my servant!" as if to say to the world, "In these people you all will see what I have in mind for you." God "holds" Israel up, supports the servant in the relentless task set before them, because God knows that Israel on its own could not do the work assigned.

One can only imagine what Israel in exile thought of this foolish claim that they were to be the agents of God's universal message to the world. Little wonder early Christians made the identity between this servant and the one they believed had come to announce justice to the world. God has ever been in this business of announcing justice and always will be.

JOHN C. HOLBERT

Pastoral Perspective

new order is springing forth, we recognize our own yearning for the passing away of old things that have held us captive. We have known empire and its brutish deployments of power. We have known estrangement, the stretching of ties to the breaking point. We have known disillusionment, when the integrity we counted on was nowhere to be found. We have known death, in the triumph of mortality over desiccated hopes. We have cobbled together a provisional life among the old things. We have known exile.

The journey of Holy Week is fueled by hunger for the justice we have not seen, longing for the confidence we cannot muster, yearning for the Spirit we have not felt. We are beckoned into it by one who comes as a Servant—one beloved of God, in whom the Spirit we crave is palpable, to whom the transformation we need is charged. At first we cannot quite make out who this Servant is—for the contours of the figure before us keep shifting: between power and weakness, between the husks of former things and intimations of new things. Nonetheless we follow.

As the journey deepens, the images of this Servant will darken—from "he will not lift up his voice" to "one deeply despised, abhorred by the nations" (49:7, Tuesday) to "I did not hide my face from insult and spitting" (50:6, Wednesday) and, finally, to the likeness of "a lamb that is led to the slaughter" (53:7, Friday). Then, just at the edge of despair, the dawn of the first day of a new week will unveil the vindication of the Servant. Like stunned exiles stumbling over the threshold of home, we will fall on our knees, but this journey will not end in devotion. Soon the Spirit will come to rest upon *us*, and with it a servanthood commission of our own: to bring forth justice, to free the captive, to breathe peace, to let the light so shine. The contours of our devotion will merge into discipleship. Even now, as the week begins, the Servant, whoever he may finally be revealed to be, is leading us—*behold!*—to the place where revelation and commitment meet.

RICHARD E. SPALDING

Exegetical Perspective

royal obligation (see Pss. 72:1; 99:4; Isa. 9:7; Jer. 22:15; 23:5; 33:15; Ezek. 45:9). Further, the Servant's role is international in scope: "he will bring forth justice to the nations" (42:1), and "the coastlands wait for his teaching" (42:4). The Servant is given by the Lord, not only as "a covenant to the people" (presumably, Israel), but as "a light to the nations" (42:6). The image is not merely royal, but *imperial*; like the Persian emperor Cyrus, whose armies had laid waste the ancient world and conquered Babylon as well (45:1–19), the Servant is described as ruler of the world.

Yet, on the other hand, the Servant's task is accomplished quietly, without kingly pomp: "He will not cry or lift up his voice, or make it heard in the street" (42:2). Further, unlike royal power deriving from the threat of force, and strikingly unlike the ferocious warrior Cyrus, the Servant acts so gently and humbly that "a bruised reed he will not break, and a dimly burning wick he will not quench" (42:3). In a world where might makes right, the way of gentleness and humility seems doomed to failure. To be sure, the Servant's way is not easy; he struggles with weariness, and the powers of this world threaten to crush him (42:4). Yet the God who called this world into being (42:5) guarantees the success of the Servant's mission, "to open the eyes that are blind, to bring out the prisoners from the dungeon, from the prison those who sit in darkness" (42:7).

Sadly, "God is love" (1 John 4:8) has become a cliché, trite and superficial. Yet, in truth, this is the deepest affirmation in all of Scripture. The greatest power in the universe is the power of self-giving, sacrificial love. Despite the scorn of cynics, love works. Indeed, *only* love works. True peace and authentic transformation cannot be imposed by force. They must be discovered, as the astonishing, unlooked-for gifts of God's grace, made real in our midst by God's Servant.

STEVEN S. TUELL

Homiletical Perspective

The passion narrative itself will finally prove Isaiah wrong, finally show what happens, in human terms at least, to anyone who aspires to this Servant's role, to anyone who seeks to be a light to the nations, to restore the sight of a society that has lost its way, to challenge all of the ways we have imprisoned ourselves. There is no future in it, for Isaiah, or for us.

Still, looking directly toward Jesus' betrayal and arrest, trial and torture, looking directly toward the Servant's painful death, are we also able to recall the faithful souls whom we have known during the course of lives spent within Christian communities, who have exhibited the kind of servanthood Isaiah foresees, and whose lives have touched our lives in powerful ways? Have we not all encountered some who proclaim peace, calling out in the midst of this violent world, like the women in black who sit on the front steps of the Methodist church in my town, week after week, singing into the wind? Have we not encountered the good and simple folks whose gentle kindness is its own sort of holy witness? Have we not seen the rare leader who has decided to stand up and make a public witness for the just ways of God, even at the cost of broad popular approval?

They are out there still, in the churches, at the fringes. Seldom do they wield much power, these prophets of every generation. Most often they go largely unseen. However they are there, servants of God, as they have been from the days of exile in Babylon.

Is their witness enough? Or is this finally a story of disappointment, a story of the limitations of the ways of loving-kindness, in a world that mostly celebrates the truly powerful? That will be the struggle for all Christians to encounter yet again, in the week that now begins. Can we really ever believe that love overcomes hate, that peace prevails even in a season of conflict, and that finally a light shines still, through the gloom of night?

WILLIAM GOETTLER

Psalm 36:5-11

⁵Your steadfast love, O LORD, extends to the heavens,
  your faithfulness to the clouds.
⁶Your righteousness is like the mighty mountains,
  your judgments are like the great deep;
  you save humans and animals alike, O LORD.

⁷How precious is your steadfast love, O God!
  All people may take refuge in the shadow of your wings.
⁸They feast on the abundance of your house,
  and you give them drink from the river of your delights.
⁹For with you is the fountain of life;
  in your light we see light.

¹⁰O continue your steadfast love to those who know you,
  and your salvation to the upright of heart!
¹¹Do not let the foot of the arrogant tread on me,
  or the hand of the wicked drive me away.

Theological Perspective

Holy Week liturgically weaves multiple layers of meaning about life as people of faith and about the church. Following Palm Sunday, the Monday, Tuesday, and Wednesday of Holy Week bring new scrutiny to the immediately preceding days of Lent, as well as rich reflections on the meaning of salvation, even as the core Christian story progresses from Jerusalem to Calvary. The scriptural readings during Holy Week have been carefully selected and are closely related one to the other by emphasis on similar or contrasting themes. In a consistent manner, the psalms placed in the readings for this part of the liturgical year reflect a particular intensity, highlighting theological reflections about the meanings of Holy Week and Jesus' passion-death-resurrection. Each reflection intends, liturgically, to form us more fully in our shared Christian identity.

For this Monday of Holy Week, Psalm 36:5–11 serves as one of the building blocks for the other readings of the day. This selection effusively praises God's steadfast love and kindness. The expansiveness of God's loving-kindness reaches to the heavens. The words "abundance" and "delights" in verse 8 indicate the very richness of the feast prepared by God: "They feast on the abundance of your house, and you give them drink from the river of your delights."

Pastoral Perspective

The first three days of Holy Week anticipate the passion and resurrection of Jesus on the days that Christians have come to know as Maundy Thursday, Good Friday, and—later—Easter. The psalms for these days stand in shocking contrast to the tone of Palm Sunday's "Hosannas," though this week is in its totality a far more cosmic victory. However, first must come the trial and crucifixion. Thus it is appropriate that these psalms of lament assigned by the lectionary for Monday, Tuesday, and Wednesday contain both lament and praise. This might seem a somewhat paradoxical combination, were it not for the mystery and paradox of Christianity itself. There are several temptations to avoid in working with these psalms, not the least of which is somehow to see them only in relation to what Jesus underwent. Another temptation is to spiritualize them, and see them only as bespeaking times of nonphysical, *spiritual* crisis.

Turning specifically to Psalm 36, the tone of verses 1–4 and verse 12 is radically at odds with the verses highlighted by the lectionary. The pastor working with this psalm has an opportunity to underscore the way that trust in God's steadfast love is present even when the wicked connive and plot to "get away with murder," assuming as they do that God is not aware of their sin (vv. 1–4). The psalmist

Exegetical Perspective

The psalm as a whole is formed by a series of words or ideas that are repeated at various moments. The location of these repeating elements seems to suggest a concentric structure (A [vv. 1–4]—B [vv. 5–6]—B [vv. 7–9]—A [vv. 10–12]). Although verses 10–12 repeat certain elements present in verses 1–4—"wicked," "evil," "heart," "pride," the act of planning evil while lying in bed (v. 4), in contrast to having been brought down and being unable to get up (v. 12)—there is also presence of words such as *hesed* ("eternal love," "loyalty") and *tsedeq* ("justice," "salvation") in verses 5–9. The sequence is the following: verses 1–4 describe how a wicked person acts. Verses 5–9 tell of who YHWH is and what YHWH does: verses 5–6 speak of YHWH within a cosmic and universal context, and verses 7–9 speak of YHWH within a local context, the temple. The final part, verses 10–12, brings together several of the elements presented previously in order to assemble the psalmist's plea.

There is a marked difference between what compels the wicked person to reject God, to become proud and do evil—sin or iniquity is an oracle that penetrates the innermost part of one's being—and what compels the person who "knows God" and is upright—the divine love (*hesed*) fills the life of the "just" and saturates the entire universe. This contrast

Homiletical Perspective

Psalm 36 provides an excellent opportunity for a preacher to delve into the heart and mind of Jesus as he lived his way faithfully through the events we remember in Holy Week. Many Christians do not have a strong personal relationship with Jesus. One reason for this weak relationship is a failure to connect the feelings and emotions that filled Jesus with the feelings and emotions that fill us. As we connect with the sources of Jesus' spiritual strength, we become strong as well. In this psalm, we hear a word that empowered and reassured Jesus as he walked toward the cross.

If we accept the church's proclamation that Jesus is fully human, we must inevitably come to the conclusion that he was on an emotional roller-coaster in the days leading up to his trial and execution. Some of the emotional ups and downs were externally driven, flowing from large, adoring crowds, on the one hand, and the taunts and harshness of his critics, on the other.

Each of us faces a similar, constantly changing world. We have people who love us, others who are indifferent to us, and some who do not like us at all. Sometimes our lives go well, and we gain approval. Sometimes they do not and we are subject to criticism. Unless we are unhealthy and impervious to the comments and sentiments of people around us, these

Psalm 36:5-11

Theological Perspective

These statements point to God's covenant promises and recall the Garden of Eden's joys. More importantly, these statements point to a journey that takes us beyond the events the Suffering Servant will endure in Jerusalem. God's ultimate promise is salvation for those who are faithful. This covenantal promise is particularly clear with verse 9: "For with you is the fountain of life; in your light we see light."

Yet this Monday continues a mission that will lead the church to reflect on the mysteries of Jesus' passion-death-resurrection. Collectively, the church is reminded of this journey when the psalmist calls out to God for protection against those who would commit evil acts. These evildoers' actions are directly opposite those of God, who acts with mercy and love and kindness. The psalmist characterizes the actions of the plotters: "Do not let the foot of the arrogant tread on me, or the hand of the wicked drive me away" (v. 11). "Foot" and "hand" point to violent, deliberate, and material assaults. These are not accidental or theoretical actions being taken against the psalmist. Instead, the writer anguishes over the personal attacks that have taken a dehumanizing turn. The psalmist is not implying that disagreements should never happen between human beings, but is making a central focus of what happens when human problems turn from tragedy to evil as one group places itself above God. The enemies are described as prideful (the "arrogant"), intent on committing deliberately evil acts (the "wicked"). Arrogance and intentionality imply that the evildoers choose to commit such acts from the basis of false pride, that is, a twisted morality. Rather than acting with honor, these plotters are resorting to violence. Against these actions, the writer seeks refuge.

Yet the central focus of the selection is not the evildoers' activities, mentioned in the last verse, but the love of God: "Your steadfast love, O LORD, extends to the heavens, your faithfulness to the clouds" (v. 5). This psalm selection is ultimately a reminder that God's love is steadfast, a sure refuge even in the face of treachery. The images of feasting, light, and life indicate more than simple protection from bad things; these are visions that look toward the completion of the covenant promises.

God's righteousness and judgment are the keys to understanding this excerpt, as is pointed out clearly at the beginning of this psalm selection: "Your righteousness is like the mighty mountains, your judgments are like the great deep; you save humans and animals alike" (v. 6). God's righteousness is more than simply doing the "right" thing, more than a type of humanly designed code of ethics. In fact, humans

Pastoral Perspective

assures us that, in contrast to the wicked who assume that they can be self-governing, the real governor is the Creator God who comprehends the whole creation (vv. 5–11). God's reality overshadows the trite arrogance of the wicked. God's wings provide a refuge from such wickedness for all.

Several images in the psalm suggest that it was associated with the presence of YHWH above the wings of the cherubim on the sacred ark at the covenant festival. There is an evangelizing reminder to the assembled to remember just who it is that they are worshiping. Read as part of the worship that occurred at the temple in Jerusalem, and also against the background of the destruction of Jerusalem in 587 BCE, there is an appeal on the part of the besieged (or indeed conquered and exiled) to the God of abundance and love. The prayers of the psalm allow us to infer certain things about the needs being expressed. Rather than focus on our own scarcity and weakness, the psalm calls us to focus on the reality of the steadfast love of God that extends to heavens, clouds, mountains, the great deep, animals, and—yes—us. There is true abundance with YHWH.

Although the precise community and situation of composition are lost to us, it is clear that however individually situated the psalm seems to be, the situation is one that is widely shared, an element of corporate worship. In fact, one can see the psalm as addressing the question of why the righteous suffer while the arrogant seem to prosper.

As the psalmist becomes more personal, we see that something profound is going on. He is claiming, or proclaiming, that in fact the people are participating in ("feeding on") the blessings of YHWH. They are experiencing the joy of their salvation in YHWH, which is simultaneously a present deliverance and a transcendent joy. In fact, without God (the wicked live under this illusion) there is no life. Human life without God is exposed as meaningless and off center—disoriented, in the full connotation of that word.

The appeal is for the hearer to focus on the immediate—which is also the ultimate (even eschatological)—reality of God's being in charge. The natural imagery of the psalm—salvation not limited to humans—makes us look to creation, the whole cosmos, the totality of reality. A concern for God's environment, God's creation, is evident in the psalm, and we are a part of God's whole, in contrast to those who think themselves self-made men and women. The wicked are unmindful and deluded.

Exegetical Perspective

is further underlined when verses 2 and 9 are compared. In the Hebrew, both start with the conjunction *kî* ("because"), explaining the source of the behavior of both characters: (1) the wicked person has a personal ego that grants an individualistic view of the world: "in their own eyes"; (2) the "just" person has God as a source, which is called "fountain of life" and "light." The enemies of the psalmist do not "know" ("they have ceased to act wisely and do good," v. 3), and therefore "are set on a way that is not good" (v. 4); the "righteous" person does "know" (v. 10) the Lord and remains whole.

This Holy Week reading spans verses 5–11 and provides the psalm's message with another nuance and a new context. In this context, the liturgical element acquires greater relevance, and the message's weight falls on the declaration of who YHWH is in relation to every living being, especially with human beings—and in particular with those who find themselves very "close" to God, who look to the temple for protection, who "know God" and are "upright."

What is most striking is YHWH's *hesed*, a word that communicates the idea of a "steadfast love" (it appears three times: vv. 5, 7, and 10). It could also be translated as "loyalty." In the psalm's context, *hesed*, as well as *'emunah* ("fidelity"), *tsedeqah* ("justice"), and *yasha^c* ("to save"), is referring to God in a broader context that transcends the people of the covenant. All those manifestations of YHWH embrace every human being and animal in their broadest habitat, the globe that the psalm defines employing three spatial references: the clouds, the highest mountains or the earth's columns, and the great depths. In his worship, the psalmist goes beyond the small dwelling of the temple in order to make the whole of the planet into the "great sanctuary" of God, in which not only the "holy" and the "righteous" have a place, but also every living being that finds refuge and protection in YHWH. In this sense, *hesed* can be translated as "solidarity," a word that in a context of oppression and violence, perceivable in many of our Third-World countries, encompasses the accompanying terms in verses 5–9: justice, loyalty, and salvation. In other words, all of this reading is found within the context of the exodus, the liberating experience wherein the enslaved and oppressed people directly felt all these divine acts that describe YHWH as the God of the exodus. This falls into place nicely with Isaiah 42:1–9 and Hebrews 9:11–15, which accompany this psalm as readings for this day. All living animals are part of this exodus. They too

Homiletical Perspective

external realities affect us. As a result, we may well feel loved, ignored, and despised in the same day.

However in many ways, the external issues are just that: external. Most of us develop inner filtering mechanisms to deal with them in a healthy manner, as did Jesus. We learn to modulate our responses to the world and not overrespond to external stimuli.

However, at times, controlling our inner spiritual life is far more difficult than managing external realities around us. We can cope with the external voices. The inner voices are what trouble and threaten our spiritual journeys.

Jesus teaches us that if we possess a deep, inner spiritual calm, we can deal with the anxiety life produces. Jesus felt anxiety. However, at the core of his being was a calm that kept him from being overwhelmed or misdirected by anxiety.

Filled with a joyous praise of and confidence in God, the spirituality expressed in Psalm 36 was at the spiritual center of Jesus' life. In the face of a troubled, troubling world, where did Jesus and the psalmist find such joy and confidence?

At the beginning of each section of the psalm, the author praises God as "steadfast." In other psalms, God is praised as "our rock." Woven into the fabric of the Psalms is a description of God as certain and constant. Three times in this short passage, the psalmist refers to God's "steadfast love." When everything else disappears, God is still there.

Likewise, belief in a steadfast God is at the heart of Jesus' spirituality. What we observe in Holy Week is a person whose faith was so strong, so certain, that it withstood "the slings and arrows of outrageous fortune." While Jesus was surely shaken by the hostility of his foes and the fear-driven abandonment by his disciples, he remained confident in his God. God was his rock. Jesus' inner calm was on display when he stood before the Sanhedrin, when he dialogued with Pilate, when he said, "Father, forgive them; for they do not know what they are doing" (Luke 23:34).

The belief in a steadfast God brings a joy not always present on the surface of our lives. Nonetheless, it is present in a believer's heart of hearts. Such a belief creates the certainty, as Paul proclaims, that nothing "will be able to separate us from the love of God" (Rom. 8:39).

The same joy in the face of suffering is on display in the lyrics of African American spirituals. For example, the spiritual "I'm Troubled in Mind" ends, "When ladened with troubles and burdened with grief, To Jesus in secret I'll go for relief. In dark days

Psalm 36:5-11

Theological Perspective

often confuse God's judgment with our own, forgetting that God's ways are above ours, and not easily understood. God saves, but not on our own merit. This is the mystery of faith. Over a lifetime, a person may face unbelievable tragedy. Yet God's righteousness saves the sinner, forgives trespasses, and then rewards beyond measure. However where is God's righteousness when "bad things happen to good people"? Through the readings brought to the church this Holy Week, we face our own continued theological dilemma of theodicy.

The law of reciprocal love shapes God's immeasurably generous righteousness. Despite limited and human views, God's righteousness is all-encompassing, embracing humans and animals, recalling from a Christian view how God holds even the sparrows dearly (Luke 12:6–7). In this psalm, we do not get answers that solve the dilemma but one that calls us to participate in the covenantal love of God's righteousness. Throughout the Judeo-Christian theological tradition, God's love brings the faithful to a feast that satisfies fully. The facts of God's righteousness, God's mercy and loving-kindness, and our faith are at times seemingly incompatible. The sometimes difficult theological reflections involved in considering the meanings of the seemingly incompatible ideas of faith may become part of this Holy Week. For instance, we are reminded of our God who is so far above us yet loves us completely. We are reminded of the realities of our mystical and spiritual dimensions, even as we are fully human and therefore finite. The distances between humans and God, along with our spirituality and humanness, comprise internal reconciliatory tasks when we face the dark night of our souls as faith communities this Holy Week. These contrasts comprise some of the lived mysteries of being faithful.

The theology woven into this psalm excerpt is reflected in the words of an eighteenth-century hymn related to and drawing from this psalm: "Rejoice in glorious hope!" "Jesus the Savior reigns, the God of truth and love."[1] The psalmist celebrates God's loving-kindness, even in suffering. The church explores these sacred realities of praise during Holy Week.

STEPHANIE Y. MITCHEM

Pastoral Perspective

They do not realize how dependent they are on the creation. The righteous are aware of how they are sustained by God.

This psalm speaks to those affluent who characteristically believe that they are self-governing. This characterization includes many citizens of affluent countries and contains a warning to those who want to embrace the control of their own lives and also maintain personal righteousness. It warns us not to usurp the place of the one who delights in the deeps of the oceans and sustains the cosmos. The praise of the Great High God, who is the source of all creation, whose righteousness and justice are unfathomable, stands in marked contrast to the wicked who threaten the psalmist. This psalm of praise calls *us* to live with righteousness and justice.

The equation of wickedness and disordered living can find many illustrations among us. Being a law or covenant unto oneself certainly tends to leave behind the rest of the earth community, both human and animal. The psalmist is appealing to us to remember that we are part of the web of God's life, part of the greater reality that is God's future.

The psalm can also be seen as a theological foundation, an argument for upright living, mindful of one's own abundant gifts from a God whose abundance is beyond imagining. It encourages a willingness to share the material and spiritual salvation that God in gracious majesty has given those who seek righteousness. It calls on us to live out that abundance in our dealings with other people and the whole creation. There is another reminder, in verse 12, that the deluded autonomy of the wicked will ultimately fail, because their self-dependence is false. Thus are the hearers warned of the arrogance of not trusting YHWH.

The psalm could shape the liturgy in several ways. Possible themes include ecology, the abundance and steadfast love of God, and the falseness of those who sense that they can control the world, the future. What is crystal clear is that YHWH is a magnanimous and gracious Creator.

L. SHANNON JUNG

---

1. Charles Wesley, "Rejoice, the Lord Is King."

are part of God's salvific plan and receive divine protection and abundance, just as in the creation (Ps. 8:6–8; cf. Hos. 4:1–3), the flood (Gen. 9:9–11), and the messianic kingdom (Isa. 11:1–6).

Verses 7–9 move from the universal context to the local context: the sanctuary. The psalmist does not find a better image for describing God's *hesed*, the divine protection, than that of the maternal figure of the hen that gathers and protects her chicks, even though the expression is referring specifically to the enormous cherubim whose wings extend from wall to wall inside the temple. This image echoes Jesus' lament over sinful Jerusalem (Luke 13:34). From protection we go to provision (v. 8). In YHWH's house, human beings find provisions and never-ending water (see Pss. 23:2; 104:10–14; Ezek. 47:12). The section (vv. 5–9) reaches its climax with verse 9, affirming that YHWH is the never-ending "fountain of life."

The last part (vv. 10–12) reiterates the theme of YHWH's *hesed*, but now in the context of the psalmist's pleading. *Tsedeqah* (justice and salvation) is now added. Yet here the context of divine action is no longer the universal dimension of the planet (animals, human beings; the men and women who could enter the sanctuary); instead, it is those who "know God," those who are "upright of heart." Here, the psalmist (despite speaking in plural [v. 10]) is actually referring to the precarious situation he is experiencing—although all suffering people are also included in his "I"—amid the threat of banishment and oppression by the "evildoers." In verse 11, the expressions "do not let the foot of the arrogant tread on me" and "the hand of the wicked drive me away" are referring to the exile and subsequent oppression by the conquering nation. In order to avoid such demise, the psalmist pleads to YHWH that the *hesed* and the *tsedeqah* may extend YHWH's liberating power. For that to happen, the enemies ("the evildoers") have to be radically annihilated: "they are thrust down, unable to rise" (v. 12)—a contrast to the images in Psalm 15.

EDESIO SANCHEZ

of bondage to Jesus I prayed To help me to bear it, and He gave me His aid."

Preaching on this passage in Holy Week is an opportunity to invite a congregation to look inward. What is our level of confidence in God? Do we see God as steadfast or fickle, constantly present or coming and going in our lives?

A preacher can describe some of the contemporary realities that cause us to question the steadfastness of God—from a terrorist incident to a recent senseless death in the community to a church member learning he or she has cancer. We then link the chaos surrounding Jesus in Holy Week to the chaos that oftentimes surrounds us.

After creating such a description of the external contexts of the original and current Holy Weeks, the preacher can move a congregation inward. In our souls, do we possess the calm certainty in God's love that we see at work in the psalmist and Jesus? Do we have an internal rock of faith upon which we can weather the storms and enjoy the brilliant sunrises of life?

Faith's certainty does not eliminate all doubt. On the cross, Jesus cried out, "Father, why have you forsaken me?" Psalm 36 ends with the psalmist worrying, "Do not let the foot of the arrogant tread on me, or the hand of the wicked drive me away" (v. 11).

Jesus' sense of being forsaken and the psalmist's concern that God was allowing evil to triumph both were rooted in a joyous certainty that God's "steadfast love . . . extends to the heavens . . . faithfulness to the clouds" (v. 5). In a sense they both believed in the face of disbelief, hoped in the face of despair, attempted to keep love alive in the face of hatred and hostility.

As we face the external challenges of life in the twenty-first century and the internal disharmony these challenges can create, we do well to return to Psalm 36 and Jesus' walk to the cross, where we observe a faith that is up to the challenges of life on earth.

JOHN W. WIMBERLY

Hebrews 9:11-15

[11]But when Christ came as a high priest of the good things that have come, then through the greater and perfect tent (not made with hands, that is, not of this creation), [12]he entered once for all into the Holy Place, not with the blood of goats and calves, but with his own blood, thus obtaining eternal redemption. [13]For if the blood of goats and bulls, with the sprinkling of the ashes of a heifer, sanctifies those who have been defiled so that their flesh is purified, [14]how much more will the blood of Christ, who through the eternal Spirit offered himself without blemish to God, purify our conscience from dead works to worship the living God!

[15]For this reason he is the mediator of a new covenant, so that those who are called may receive the promised eternal inheritance, because a death has occurred that redeems them from the transgressions under the first covenant.

Theological Perspective

The Letter to the Hebrews is a commentary on Christ's priestly role. If, as John Calvin suggests, Jesus Christ is prophet, priest, and king, then it is fitting during Holy Week to ponder the priestly office of our Lord. Here we have a description of the high priest entering the Holy of Holies, making a sacrifice on behalf of sinful humanity. In this case, it is not an animal sacrifice, as described in the priestly portions of the Torah, but the priest sacrifices himself; Christ's own blood is shed for us, once and for all.

The old covenant and the new are compared and contrasted in this letter, tempting readers to see Christianity as better than Judaism, the new covenant as improving upon the old, gospel as superseding law. The sacrificial system of the "old" covenant, whereby human priests sacrifice animals offered to God by the faithful for purification, is compared to the "new," wherein Jesus, the high priest, becomes the sacrificial lamb.

We would do well to remind ourselves of the faithfulness behind the Hebrew rituals. The priestly typology can be taken too far. Yet we find in these words some beautiful, passionate, and comforting theology. Jesus the priest is redeemer, mediator, savior. His salvation is once and for all. Christ's gracious death does for us what we cannot do for ourselves.

Pastoral Perspective

The metaphor of Jesus as high priest who came "to make expiation for the sins of the people" (2:17 RSV) is central to the writer of Hebrews. It carries the essential message that, because Jesus Christ intervened on our behalf, we can "with confidence draw near to the throne of grace, [to] receive mercy and find grace to help in time of need" (4:16 RSV). Every generation must define the timely need that grace and mercy will help alleviate. The preacher and interpreter of this passage must ask, in a post-9/11 world, what is our timely need?

The high priest was the mediating factor in the human/God relationship, the proverbial "middle man"—delivering the goods and mitigating the problems. The high-priest metaphor places Jesus squarely between the believer situated in the believing community and God. All the good that God has to offer will come through him (Jesus is high priest of "the good things"). All the "bad" that would prevent us from drawing near to God in relationship is purified through the sacrifice of his blood. The writer of Hebrews draws out this metaphor by telling the story of Israel's worship, giving detailed descriptions of the setting of worship and the actions of the priests and the people.

If the writer of Hebrews were interested in the metaphor of the high priest only, it would have made

Exegetical Perspective

Particularly during this week, as the Gospel of John accompanies us toward Jesus' crucifixion, the christological and soteriological reflections in Hebrews can provide opportunities for insight into some central themes of the Christian gospel. Long before the christological formulations of Nicaea and Chalcedon, the themes of Christ's nature and function are given unique and enduring articulations in Hebrews, whose creative footprints can be seen in subsequent christological paths taken by the church. In today's text, the focus is on Christ as the perfect "mediator of a new covenant" (9:15).

In the Gospels, Jesus' only encounter with the high priest occurs in the passion narrative. In Matthew, Mark, and John—and by implication in Luke—the high priest cross-examines Jesus before his crucifixion. In contrast with this negative function of the high priest in the Gospels, the high-priest Christology of Hebrews may seem somewhat ironic. Yet by providing fruitful tension with the negative role of the high priest in Holy Week, Hebrews portrays Jesus himself as *the* high priest in an entirely positive light.

Having referred to Jesus the high priest in 2:17 and 3:1, the author develops this christological claim in 4:14–5:10, arguing that God has called, appointed, and designated Jesus (5:4–5, 10) as a high priest in the order of Melchizedek (5:6, 10). The chief

Homiletical Perspective

The text is full of imagery from the ancient Jewish ritual of sacrifice, such as a high priest, the tabernacle, the blood of sacrificed animals. Through these images, the author of Hebrews explains the meaning of Jesus' death as a sacrifice for the forgiveness of sin. The language and imagery of Jewish ritual are foreign to us who live in the modern world. Nonetheless, they help us understand how seriously the ancient Jewish people took the problem of sin and how concerned they were about the renewal of the broken relationship between God and humanity caused by human sins. Like the ancient Jewish people, the early Jewish Christians in Hebrews considered the renewal of their identity inseparable from the atonement for their sins.

Many of us, living in the so-called "sinless" society of the industrialized world, may feel uncomfortable with this emphasis on sin. Indeed, the doctrine of sin may be the least attractive doctrine to contemporary preachers. It is often heard, not as the good news, but as the bad news of God's condemnation and punishment. The congregation's immediate reaction to this topic is likely to be defensive: "What sin? Do not call me a sinner. I am every bit a good, responsible citizen!" Some might blame the preacher for raising this subject, and after worship complain, "Why are you

Hebrews 9:11-15

Theological Perspective

Two small phrases in these verses raise two huge theological issues. Jesus' priestly sacrifice is "once for all"(v. 12), a phrase that appears again and again in the Letter to the Hebrews. Yet Christ's death saves only those "who are called," the elect (v. 15). Here we have two petals of the famous TULIP, the U and the L from the five points of Calvinism: unconditional election and limited atonement. If Jesus' sacrifice is really "once and for all," then how can it be limited in any way? If God calls only those who will believe, as the scholastic doctrine of election teaches, then is not Christ's saving grace reserved only for the chosen few? According to Hebrews, Christ's sacrifice is perfect, without blemish, once and for all. Saving grace is for the faithful, the called.

Christ's church continues to grapple with the universality and the particularity of the gospel. The Vatican has continued to reaffirm its claim to be the one true church. Many Reformed churches still insist on the doctrine of double predestination, teaching that God has chosen, from before all time, who will be saved and who will be damned. In a world of interfaith encounters, such views seem more than a little hostile. At the same time, the universality of God's love is an affirmation for many people of faith. That little phrase "once for all" might help us reconcile the particular and the universal as we seek to live our faith in relationship with other faiths and with divisions within Christ's body.

Christian hymnody has at times invoked the blood imagery of Hebrews when singing about salvation. "There is a fountain filled with blood, drawn from Immanuel's veins; and sinners, plunged beneath that flood, lose all their guilty stains." That may be a bit too vivid for some of us, but many of our favorite Holy Week hymns also sing of Christ's physical suffering in a vivid way. These images have become increasingly uncomfortable, even distasteful, for many.

The suffering of Christ has been a point of connection for many believers throughout the ages and throughout our world. The wounds of Christ have kindled passionate love in the hearts of mystics. The physical suffering of Christ has given hope to believers in the midst of pain and loss. The suffering love of Christ is an entry point for many theologies of liberation, where the poor and the oppressed can find comfort and hope. Still, some question this emphasis on the physical suffering of Christ, especially the vivid imagery of blood and wounds. Many feminist and womanist theologians shrink at the violence of Christ's death, violence that adds to oppression, including violence against women and children in our world.

Pastoral Perspective

sense to ground the metaphor in temple worship, with which the writer's contemporaries would have been more familiar. However, by situating the worship of Israel in the tabernacle (the tent, 9:2, 11), the writer means to evoke a context that speaks more directly to the situation and experience of his hearers. Living in an "in-between time," between the promise of Christ's coming again and its fulfillment, the original hearers of Hebrews are wandering, tempted to follow false promises and false gods, losing hope in the face of adversity. There is perhaps no more apt metaphor for the post-9/11 age as well. Many are seeking meaning in an age of uncertainty. Poll after poll reports a majority of Americans believe in a spiritual power beyond themselves and seek spiritual fulfillment. Yet many do not find their way to the church or to Jesus Christ.

Another key to understanding the meaning of the high-priest metaphor for the life of the believer is found in the way the author compares the actions of the high priests of the first covenant, which took place in an "earthly sanctuary" (9:1), and the actions of Jesus, the purveyor of the new covenant, whose actions take place in a "more perfect tent (not made with hands, that is, not of this creation)" (9:11 RSV). While the high priest of the earthly tabernacle had to offer sacrifice continually, and each year enter the Holy of Holies, Jesus entered "once for all into the Holy Place . . . thus obtaining eternal redemption" (9:12). The work of atonement in the first covenant, with its continual demand for expiation, the relentless demand that sins be "paid for" by a blood sacrifice, was a full-time occupation of the faithful.

The writer of Hebrews saw this preoccupation with atoning for the individual's sins (and the sins of the community) as problematic, a burden that interferes with "[running] the race . . . set before us" (12:1). That Jesus would make the atoning action "once for all" meant freedom—freedom from the burden of constantly trying to "make right" with God through the sacrifice of a dead animal. The living sacrifice of Jesus' blood frees the faithful to "serve the living God" (9:14 RSV). Although the focus of the original hearers of Hebrews may have been on the sins of the community, rather than their own particular sins, nevertheless they faced the same danger that we all do, a preoccupation with self that is evident in much of our materialistic culture. While the need for self-justification and redemption may be fulfilled by offering a sacrifice of money and labor to the god of consumer goods and self-gratification, the preoccupation remains the same: what things will make it all right for me and mine?

qualification of Jesus as the mediator par excellence is that he can "sympathize with our weaknesses" and "*in every respect* has been tested as we are, yet without sin" (4:15, emphasis added). This hortatory understanding of Jesus' humanity reinforces the earlier statement that "he had to become like his brothers and sisters *in every respect*, so that he might be a merciful and faithful high priest in the service of God, to make a sacrifice of atonement for the sins of the people" and that "he himself was tested by what he suffered" (2:17, 18, emphasis added). In this way, Hebrews offers the lowest Christology in the NT with respect to the nature of Christ.

At the same time, this low Christology is preceded and accompanied continually by a high Christology rivaling the Logos Christology of John's prologue. Hebrews begins with a Christology not of priesthood but of lofty sonship: Jesus Christ is the Son whom God "appointed heir of all things, through whom he also created the worlds," who "is the reflection of God's glory and the exact imprint of God's very being," and who "sat down at the right hand of the Majesty on high" (1:2–3). Hebrews elaborates this high Christology in a variety of ways, but at its center, both textually and theologically, is the high-priest function of Christ.

These dual aspects of Christology converge and come to expression through the atonement language of 9:11–15. Whereas chapters 7–8 argue that Christ is a better high priest than all the Levitical priests and the mediator of a better covenant, the main point of 9:11–15 is that Christ, as the better high priest of a better covenant, offers a better sacrifice, indeed, the perfect sacrifice of his own blood for all time (7:25, 27; 9:12; 10:10, 12, 14).

The point is not a simplistic supersessionism of the new covenant over against the old one. An understanding of the comparative rhetoric of chapters 8–10 should be accompanied by caution regarding anti-Semitic tendencies. A careful reading would recognize that the a fortiori arguments rely on the Hebrew Scriptures. For example, the "great cloud of witnesses" (12:1) enumerated in the roll call of heroes in chapter 11 is meant to encourage the addressees to "run with perseverance the race that is set before [them]" (12:1). The comparative arguments in Hebrews may wrongly lead some readers, as Marcion did, to view the OT, Judaism, and Israel negatively, as having been simply replaced by the NT, Christianity, and the church. However, the writer of Hebrews thrives on the liturgical language of the tabernacle (e.g., 9:11–12; cf. 9:1–7)

reminding me of all the guilt that I had such a hard time getting rid of in therapy?"

In spite of these potential risks, the text challenges us to reflect on the reality of sin and to talk about it theologically. Some preachers understand sin as a series of personal behaviors that should be avoided, and they preach along the lines of "Do not smoke, do not drink, do not gamble . . ." and force their listeners to repent for their sins, threatening that, if they do not, they will go to hell. Some preachers understand sin in existential terms and preach about human predicaments caused by the individual's fear and anxiety. Yet, in our age of globalization, sin cannot be understood in purely personal terms. Sin is both individual and deeply systemic. Willingly or not, we often participate in distorting and corrupting our relationship with God, with ourselves, with others, and with nature, both collectively and individually. Who knows if my 401(k) retirement plan is supporting transnational corporations that exploit the labor of women and children in developing countries? Our daily use of automobiles and air conditioners contributes to global warming, which can result in the extinction of certain species of animals and plants and threaten the homes of some islanders and coastal people. Our conscious or unconscious prejudices and biases of race, gender, and sexual orientation have sustained a system of social discrimination that can throw our neighbors, family members, friends, and colleagues into the depths of despair and hopelessness. Violent acts occur thousands of times daily, even here in the United States, let alone in Iraq, Afghanistan, and the Middle East.

These sins are inextricably linked to legitimizing greed and lust, and to subtle but devastating public attitudes toward other races, language groups, genders, age groups, and political affiliations. The more we understand the multirelational dimension of our sins, the more helpless we feel.

To us who feel at an impasse when trying to solve the problems of sin, the text reminds us that we can be saved from the forces within us only by something that transcends them, that is, God's radical love revealed by the crucified One. According to the text, the tragic dimension of sin is not the ultimate reality, for God is involved in our sinful world through Jesus Christ, and has solved the problem of sin once and for all. How? Not by force, but by the power of love, by shedding his own blood on the cross as a sacrifice for the forgiveness of our sins.

How, then, can this powerless, suffering Jesus solve the problem of sin? Through his suffering and death

Hebrews 9:11-15

Theological Perspective

"Behold, the Lamb of God, who takes away the sin of the world," announces the Baptist in John's Gospel (1:29 RSV). These words become a mighty chorus, sung as the last movement of the eucharistic meal: "Lamb of God, . . . have mercy on us . . . grant us peace."

John Calvin, writing on these verses in Hebrews, said, "This passage has led many people astray, because they have forgotten that it has to do with sacraments, which have a spiritual meaning. . . . the argument of this verse [v. 13] is from the sign to the reality signified by it."[1] As we think about the priestly office of Christ, we think also about the sacramental nature of priesthood. These verses tell us that Jesus is the high priest and also the sacrificial lamb, the offering without blemish. Calvin reminds us that these verses are open to interpretation. For Reformed churches at least, the typology is not to be taken too literally; the bread and the cup point us to Christ's body and blood. Christ's priestly role is his saving death on the cross. These verses would underscore that connection. Jesus Christ is the model for human priesthood, including the priesthood of all believers.

It is easy to see how human priests, especially in their sacramental role, have come to be seen as mediators, as more holy, more Christlike, than the laity. In the Middle Ages, this association led to a sacramental system that put the faithful at the mercy of their priests. The priest was seen as sacrificing the body and blood of Christ again and again as the bread was broken and the wine poured out. At least this is how Luther and the other reformers saw it in the sixteenth century. Christ's death saves us from "dead works," as Hebrews reminds us. Grace is a free gift, not to be earned or bought. The royal priesthood—Protestants and Catholics, Calvinists and Lutherans—needs to be reminded of that on a regular basis.

REBECCA BUTTON PRICHARD

Pastoral Perspective

Such a preoccupation is "dead works" according to writer of Hebrews. Constantly offering dead animals to fill the need for my atonement is akin to gathering inanimate objects to fill the need for my self-esteem. Preoccupation with dead things does not serve the living God. To rid us of this need to supply dead objects to redeem ourselves, Jesus, the high priest, offers his living blood once for all. Now the occupation of the believer can be one of service, not sacrifice.

There is still a strain of religious expression in America that is preoccupied with getting things right between "me and Jesus." This assumes that "getting things right" between the individual and God is the end and goal of religion and belief. For the writer of Hebrews, it is the beginning of the life of faith; the writer declares that things are right between you and Jesus because Jesus made them right, once for all. Faith is acting on that premise and boldly moving forward in service to a living God. The issue for the writer of Hebrews is the conscience (9:14). When the conscience is free and clear, the person can freely serve others, working for what is pleasing in God's sight (13:21). When the conscience is bound and defiled, the focus is on working toward making things right between the individual and God, and the person will be able only to serve himself or herself. Such action is "dead works" to the writer of Hebrews. It is like running a race with an 800-pound gorilla on your back. To run the race, the runner must set aside all burdens (12:1). To begin an earthly race, the starter shouts, "On your mark, get set, go!" The follower of Christ begins the spiritual race with the shout, "Once for all!"

PETER AND DEBRA SAMUELSON

---

1. John Calvin, *Commentary to Hebrews*, 9:13.

and the soteriological language of atonement (e.g., 9:12–15; cf. 9:6–7, 22) in order to express the meaning of Christ.

While there are only two explicit references to crucifixion in Hebrews (6:6; 12:2), the prominent thread that runs through every chapter, beginning with 1:3, is the cultic vocabulary of tabernacle sacrifice: altar, atonement, blood, Holy of Holies, liturgy, offering, (high) priest, purification, sacrifice, sanctuary, service, worship, tabernacle (or tent). In comparing Christ's priestly service in "the greater and perfect tent (not made with hands)" (9:11, 24; cf. 8:2, 5) with the "earthly sanctuary" (9:1; cf. 13:11), and declaring that Christ's blood effects a clean conscience (9:14; 10:2, 22; 13:18), while animal blood could not (9:9, 12–13), Hebrews uses Mosaic idioms and imagery of Israel's sacrificial cult to offer the church a fresh interpretation of Jesus' crucifixion, that shameful execution Paul calls a "stumbling block to Jews and foolishness to Gentiles" (1 Cor. 1:23).

This cultic language-world is vividly displayed in 9:1–10, where the central motif of blood is introduced as the requirement for access to the Holy of Holies (9:7). Not only does Hebrews contain the highest frequency of the word "blood" in the NT (nearly a quarter of the occurrences); Hebrews 9 contains the highest concentration of "blood" within the book (twelve times). In this regard, today's text is one of the most appropriate, though unpalatable, places for the church's meditation during Holy Week. The efficacious, purifying blood of Christ is the central message of 9:11–15; because of it, the "promised eternal inheritance" (9:15) is within reach of believers.

One thing is clear in Hebrews: Christology is done at the cross. Christology that places an accent on the scandal of crucifixion is *the* way to authenticate a Christian community as one faithful to its calling.[1] The epistle's cross-centered Christology is precisely what keeps it consonant with other attempts in the NT to articulate faith. As difficult as it may be to appreciate or appropriate the blood-sacrificial language of Hebrews, the salvific message of Christ's self-sacrifice is an enduring claim that can help Christians endure in an often hostile world (10:32–34).

KANG-YUP NA

on the cross, Jesus became the mediator of a new covenant between God and humanity. The blood of Jesus, which is the symbol of God's radical love, conformed to the image of God revealed in the crucified One, has sealed a new covenant between God and us. By this new covenant, a new community is born, which is itself the holy place where God dwells. Hence, when we take the problem of sin and its consequences really seriously, we need to talk about Jesus—not the Jesus who is dressed up in fine linen and a golden crown, seated on the royal throne, but the Jesus who suffers on the cross, humiliated, naked, and bleeding, crowned with thorns, to be the mediator between God and humanity.

Actually, talk of the crucified Jesus is not the good news that many who come to church to find a safe haven for their secure lives want to hear. No, talk of suffering is taboo for many contemporary churches that are tempted by strategies that align church growth with the gospel of prosperity. Nonetheless, when we look deeper at human nature and take seriously the contemporary dimensions of human sin, we preachers are obliged to talk about the Jesus who has offered himself as sacrifice for our sins. Only in the crucified Jesus can we see God's solution for the problem of sin, which is God's radical love for humanity. The text further affirms that we, who are forgiven by God's love, are also called to be a new community that forgives others.

Therefore, preaching on sin is ultimately the proclamation of the good news of God's radical love on the cross and an invitation to the ministry of forgiveness. Evidence of this ministry of forgiveness can be found not only in a local church context but also in the larger context of the world. Individual believers, churches, and institutions that are aware of the sinful reality of our world participate in the ministry of forgiveness as peacemakers, caregivers, and witnesses to God's grace and justice, on battlefields, in courtrooms, among refugees, in shelters—every place where humans come into conflict across the globe.

EUNJOO M. KIM

1. See Paul Meyer's "Faith and History Revisited," in *The Word in This World*, ed. John T. Carroll (Louisville, KY: Westminster John Knox Press, 2004), 19–26.

John 12:1-11

¹Six days before the Passover Jesus came to Bethany, the home of Lazarus, whom he had raised from the dead. ²There they gave a dinner for him. Martha served, and Lazarus was one of those at the table with him. ³Mary took a pound of costly perfume made of pure nard, anointed Jesus' feet, and wiped them with her hair. The house was filled with the fragrance of the perfume. ⁴But Judas Iscariot, one of his disciples (the one who was about to betray him), said, ⁵"Why was this perfume not sold for three hundred denarii and the money given to the poor?" ⁶(He said this not because he cared about the poor, but because he was a thief; he kept the common purse and used to steal what was put into it.) ⁷Jesus said, "Leave her alone. She bought it so that she might keep it for the day of my burial. ⁸You always have the poor with you, but you do not always have me."

⁹When the great crowd of the Jews learned that he was there, they came not only because of Jesus but also to see Lazarus, whom he had raised from the dead. ¹⁰So the chief priests planned to put Lazarus to death as well, ¹¹since it was on account of him that many of the Jews were deserting and were believing in Jesus.

Theological Perspective

Following perhaps the most dramatic sign in the Fourth Gospel, the raising of Lazarus, John 12 opens with a countdown to Passover, and marks the beginning of the Passion Week in this Gospel. John 12:1–11 is rich with significant theological themes to explore: (1) the startling image of discipleship; (2) the theological import of "the poor will always be with you" claim made by Jesus; and (3) the theological affirmation that Jesus the giver of life is bound to his death. Let us look at each theme in turn.

Mary as faithful disciple. Before heading to Jerusalem, Jesus pauses to feast at the home of his friends Mary, Martha, and Lazarus, "whom he had raised from the dead" (v. 1). The key scene involves Mary's unconventional act toward Jesus, the anointing of his feet. A version of this story appears in each of the Synoptic Gospels, but the differences between those versions and John's are theologically telling. First, John's version is the only place where the woman is named. Second, in Matthew (26:6–13) and Mark (14:3–9), the woman anoints Jesus' head with the oil, while in Luke (7:36–50) the "sinful woman" anoints Jesus' feet first with tears and then with ointment. Here in John, Mary—whose close relationship to Jesus is made apparent in the chapter 11 story of the dying and rising of Lazarus—does

Pastoral Perspective

Today's lection anticipates what will occur during Holy Week. The setting is in Bethany, in the home of Lazarus, whom Jesus raised from the dead. Not only does the raising of Lazarus foreshadow Jesus' death and resurrection; it is also the event that sets in motion the plot to kill Jesus.

Even in church communities, today miracles of life can attract the attention of those who deal in death. Inner-city ministries become the target of drug dealers who fear they will lose influence in a neighborhood experiencing too much hope. Young church leaders who are successfully reviving a dying congregation are eventually run out by the one bully whom no one is brave enough to challenge. Yet the events that are foreshadowed in this lection are events that conquer death, events that cry, "O death, where is thy sting?" (1 Cor. 15:55 RSV).

There is so much talk of death around the table in Bethany that the preacher might take it as an opportunity to address how people cope with death. Mary pushes the acceptable boundaries of death talk. She opens a jar of costly perfume and anoints Jesus' feet, symbolically anointing him for burial. She enacts a ritual for burial before the person has actually died.

What might it look like today if communities held funeral liturgies for those who are dying? Would it convey a community's confidence in God's

Exegetical Perspective

Preparing to preach John 12:1–11 during Holy Week involves reading the text multiple times. Let me sketch three approaches: reading the anointing of Jesus in conversation with the other Gospel accounts (for which a synopsis of the Gospels is a handy reference), in its context within John, and in the context of Holy Week.

A cursory reading of the four Gospel accounts (see Matt 26:6–13; Mark 14:3–9; Luke 7:36–50) reveals that Matthew and Mark are almost identical, while Luke is remarkably different and John characteristically independent. In John, the first three verses establish the setting: six days before the Passover, in Bethany, with Lazarus, at a dinner where Martha was serving. Matthew and Mark agree that the anointing occurs at Bethany just before Passover, but they place it in the house of Simon the leper, an otherwise unknown character. In Luke, the anointing occurs earlier, in Galilee, in the house of Simon the Pharisee. In Luke, the woman is identified as "a sinner," whereas in Matthew and Mark she is unnamed, and in John she is Mary, the sister of Martha. These two sisters appear elsewhere in the Gospels only in Luke 10:38–42, where again Martha is serving. In Luke, Lazarus is not their brother, but the beggar at the rich man's gate in the parable in Luke 16:19–31. The similarities and differences are

Homiletical Perspective

The Gospel for Monday in Holy Week is like an executive summary of what is going to unfold in the days that follow.

Jesus comes for dinner at the home of Mary and Martha, together with their brother Lazarus, whom Jesus had raised from the dead. Important turning points in the ministry of Jesus tend to take place at dinner tables.

Mary anoints *the feet* of Jesus with precious ointment of great cost. Something very costly is about to unfold and the anointing of feet is a clue. Kings and priests were anointed on the head, and guests were lavished with perfume on the upper body. In preparing a body for burial, the anointing began with the extremities, the hands and feet. The precious ointment heightens our attention to the great cost that Jesus will soon bear in his body. The anointing of Jesus' feet anticipates his burial and the visit of the women to the tomb on resurrection morning to complete the care of his body.

Judas, the treasurer of Jesus' mission, objects to the extravagance of Mary's care for Jesus. Like many who betray, Judas appears to be concerned for others, but in truth he is concerned only for himself. Loyalty to another, even to Jesus, is often limited by our own self-interests and selfish motives. Few things

John 12:1-11

Theological Perspective

not anoint Jesus' feet with oil out of sadness or a need to repent. Rather, the power of Mary's action comes in that it is "an act of faith by a named disciple."[1] Mary's role in this passage has often been underemphasized, but with the rise of feminist theological and biblical scholarship, we see her role in a richer light. Feminist scholars dare to call her a disciple. Mary's faithful act for Jesus functions both as symbolic gesture of thanksgiving for Jesus, who has given new life to her brother, as well as symbolic preparation of Jesus' body for his own burial, as is suggested by Jesus' words in 12:7: "She bought [the perfume] so that she might keep it for the day of my burial."

This image of Mary as faithful disciple does not stand unchallenged within the text, however. Judas Iscariot, the one who will betray Jesus, is also present at this meal, and he objects to Mary's extravagant act, saying, "Why was this perfume not sold . . . and the money given to the poor?" (v. 5). A legitimate question, perhaps, but the narrator quickly clues in the reader that Judas's qualification as faithful disciple or honest questioner is in serious doubt. The narrator explains in verse 6, "He said this not because he cared about the poor, but because he was a thief." Jesus responds to Judas's question, siding unequivocally with Mary. Rebuking Judas, Jesus says, "Leave her alone. . . . You always have the poor with you, but you do not always have me" (vv. 7–8). While Judas carries the official status of disciple, clearly he fails to live up to the role. This unfaithful disciple's challenge to Mary's loyal act serves only to highlight the contrast between the two. A female follower is the one whom Jesus praises as exemplary disciple, offering us an unconventional model of discipleship today.

The poor with us. Before moving to the remainder of the passage, let us pause and consider more fully Judas's question to Jesus. While we can appreciate that Judas's question stems from unreliable motives, asking, why perfume instead of giving to the poor? remains a theologically significant question. Indeed, according to liberation theologians, Christians have all too often embraced Jesus' claim that "the poor will always be with you" as tacit support of the status quo. Is this what Jesus is suggesting? Very likely not. For Jesus' rebuke of Judas is, first of all, in support of Mary's preparation of Jesus for burial. Time before his death is short, and Mary's gesture helps prepare for and signify what lies ahead. Judas, it becomes

1. Dorothy Lee, *Flesh and Glory: Symbol, Gender, and Theology in the Gospel of John* (New York: Crossroad, 2002), 198.

Pastoral Perspective

saving grace? It might encourage the one who is dying. In fact, the Eucharist is such a liturgy: a moment in which the community expresses its confidence in the power of Christ to defeat death, a moment in which each communicant prepares for his or her own death by participating in the death and resurrection of Christ.

Mary's lavish act of devotion is surprising to those around her. Judas condemns Mary for wasting precious resources. We can imagine Martha once again scandalized by her sister, who does not seem to remember how to act like a pious woman. When do such lavish and startling displays of emotion or devotion occur in the church? How permissible are they?

Betty finally divorced her abusive husband and gained full custody of the daughter they had adopted. After years of loneliness, she met her perfect match. He was a deputy sheriff, but of the gentle sort who always made her feel safe. Their courtship was romantic. He adopted Betty's daughter after the marriage. He found a place for Jesus in his heart, only months before they found a tumor in his brain. The pastor baptized the once-hulking deputy, immersing him fully in water, aware of how much his body had already been diminished. After a brief remission, the tumor returned and took Steve from Betty for good. The uptight congregation had bravely surrounded the family with care during Steve's illness, but they were startled by Betty's display at the funeral. Weeping loudly and fainting, she swooned desperately in the pastor's arms as she departed from the casket. They did not know such lavish acts of love were in her.

Doreen was a stately woman with a gift for watercolor painting. She lived with cancer for a long time, long enough to prepare for death. The church needed Easter banners, and she had the perfect idea: large dogwood blossoms in gold and white on a silk baby-blue background. It was not what the pastor had in mind. He would have preferred more obviously Christian symbols of the resurrection. When Doreen's illness progressed faster than expected, several older women in the church took over the sewing. The pastor was surprised by the sacramental feeling in the sewing room—the soft caress in the folds of silk, the beauty of the gold embroidery. Doreen died before Easter that year. When the trumpets sounded on Easter morning and the banners were raised, everyone, including the pastor, gave thanks to God for Doreen and her lavish gift of devotion.

Do we make room for the Marys in our congregations, the Bettys and the Doreens who recognize how closely life and death are connected?

Exegetical Perspective

dizzying, but they confirm that John is drawing on historical tradition.

The reports of the anointing itself are equally tantalizing. In John, Mary takes a pound of costly ointment, pure nard, anoints Jesus' feet, and wipes it away with her hair. The Synoptic Gospels say the ointment is in an alabaster flask. Breaking the slender neck of the flask means that none of the ointment can be held back for a later occasion.

Mark agrees with John in identifying the ointment as "pure nard." Nard was a perfume made from the roots of a plant that grew in India. The value of the fragrance is conveyed by three descriptions, each progressively more specific: "pure" (Gk. *pistikēs*),[1] "precious" (Gk. *polytimou*) (v. 3), and later worth "three hundred denarii" (v. 5). The ointment fills the house with a sweet fragrance. In John, Mary anoints Jesus' feet; in Matthew and Mark, the unnamed woman anoints Jesus' head. In Luke, the woman stands at Jesus' feet; when her tears fall on his feet, she lets down her hair, wipes her tears from his feet, and then anoints them with ointment. In contrast, in John, Mary anoints Jesus' feet and then wipes the ointment off with her hair. Raymond Brown suggests that two historical events lie behind the four accounts.[2] Luke reports a meal in Galilee at the home of Simon, when an unnamed woman creates a scandal by weeping, letting down her hair, and then wiping her tears from Jesus' feet. The other three Gospels report the anointing of Jesus, probably his head, by a woman in Bethany during the week before the Passover. As the two events were recounted, details from one became part of the tradition of the other.

In John, Judas Iscariot protests that the ointment could have been sold for three hundred denarii and given to the poor. The same protest is voiced in Matthew and Mark. In Luke, the protest is raised by the host, Simon the Pharisee, and concerns the woman's character. In the other three Gospels, including John, Jesus defends the woman, connects the anointing with his burial, and observes that they will have many opportunities to aid the poor.

This comparative survey shows that John is distinctive in connecting the anointing with Mary, Martha, and Lazarus; identifying the protestor as Judas; and adding verses 9–11 regarding the crowd, the chief priests, and Lazarus. One other detail

---

1. Frederick W. Danker, ed., *A Greek-English Lexicon of the New Testament and Other Early Christian Literature*, 3rd ed. (Chicago: University of Chicago Press, 2000), 818.
2. Raymond E. Brown, *The Gospel according to John*, Anchor Bible 29 (Garden City, NY: Doubleday, 1966), 450–51.

Homiletical Perspective

are more painful, more costly in human terms, than the betrayal of loyalty.

"Leave her alone" (v. 7). Jesus knows what is coming, and so does Mary. Why else would she go to such extremes? The poor will need our care and concern long after Jesus is no longer with us. We can get back to that in due time. Right now, all of our attention must be on Jesus.

Jesus draws crowds. This simple family dinner in Bethany is drawing a crowd. Some want to see Jesus. More want to see Lazarus to make sure the rumors they have heard about his being raised from death to life are really true. Even in times of great promise, skepticism runs deep. Some find believing easy; others find believing very difficult. Most of us live somewhere in the middle: we want to see Jesus, but we also want to see Lazarus (i.e., what Jesus can do).

The folks in power are threatened. The chief priests have limited vision. In the confines of their world, dead people stay that way. Jesus' raising of Lazarus from the dead was not helpful. It raised too many questions. People were flocking to Jesus. More people were claiming him as their Messiah with each passing day. Lazarus must be put to death, again. The chief priests were worried. What if they caused Jesus to be killed, buried, and his body secured in a rock-solid tomb? This was no time to take chances. It was not just Lazarus that they wanted dead.

This Gospel, coming as it does on Monday in Holy Week, gives us clues about what is coming in the days ahead, heightens our awareness, and calls us to pay close attention to the details as each day of Holy Week unfolds.

Every time I read the story of Mary anointing the feet of Jesus with costly, perfumed ointment, and Judas's reaction to her doing so, I cannot help but recall the church's ministry to the seafarers on the docks of London in the middle of the nineteenth century. It was a desperate time in many ways. The industrial revolution and the mass production of manufactured goods were placing an enormous burden on the English shipping industry. The English colonists around the world were anxious to receive boatloads of comfort and familiarity from home.

Being a dockworker was a dangerous vocation. Loading and unloading the ships was tricky business, and a careless moment of inattention or the simple misstep of a coworker could cause severe injury and often death. The seafarers who worked on the ships would be gone for months at a time, and one never knew when one might be taking their final sailing. The areas around the docks were filled with widows

John 12:1-11

Theological Perspective

clear, cannot accept what it means to live according to the economy of God, where followers like Mary "give as God gives." Rather, Judas is "surrounded by those from whom he takes, victims of his self-centered greed."[2] Jesus' words to Judas—"You always have the poor with you"—illumine the economy to which Judas himself adheres, the this-worldly economy of scarcity, thievery, and death, rather than the economy of God, which offers the promise of life abundant. Jesus does not here approve of poverty. Rather, Jesus points to a different way of being in the world—an extravagant, self-giving love that emerges out of death. We will soon see that this way of being threatens more than simply Judas Iscariot.

Jesus the giver of life. Many would argue that the raising of Lazarus stands at the center of John's Gospel. This event, which does not appear in any of the Synoptics, clearly identifies Jesus as the life-giver to all who believe in him (cf. 1:12; 3:16; 5:24). What are the theological implications of this sign? In verses 9–11, we see that the sign serves to turn us toward the imminence of Jesus' death. In these verses we hear of the growing sentiment among the chief priests to kill both Lazarus and Jesus. Thus, the raising of Lazarus is a "revelation of the identity and mission of Jesus" in and through a concrete action of Jesus.[3] The irony at play here is that the religious authorities commit to killing Jesus because he gives life to others. Yet the paradox remains: his death, the gospel tells us again and again, is what will bring new life to all.

DEANNA THOMPSON

Pastoral Perspective

Judas publicly criticizes Mary and chooses to use her act of devotion as opportunity to call attention to inconsistencies in Jesus' behavior. If Jesus cares for the poor, why does he allow such a colossal waste of resources? However the listener, like the narrator, knows who Judas is and what he will do later in the week.

In response to Judas, Jesus makes that troubling comment about always having the poor with us. The preacher would be wise to attend to it in a pastoral manner. Consider not just the exegetical and theological issues at play here. Consider also how people sitting in the pews who are poor might hear this comment.

It could go either way. A person with few resources might hear Jesus' comment as just another dismissive remark meant to render the poor invisible, or as a welcome respite from being the object of discussion, either derisive or charitable.

Consider a reaction from the latter perspective. There is ample evidence in the Gospels to underscore that Jesus is not saying poverty is part of the natural order of things. Jesus' followers are to care for people in need, especially those who are impoverished, like widows and orphans, and those who are injured or disabled. In fact, his followers are to do more than care for the poor; they are to provide for them.

Perhaps Jesus is saying that it is OK, while caring for the poor, to stop and observe the sacred and to celebrate God's presence. Anyone who has worked or eaten in a soup kitchen will recall moments when folks somehow break through their poverty or their privilege to recognize God in their midst. Perhaps it is the crazy woman whose abrasive singing usually grates on the nerves, but who suddenly issues a beautiful melody. Or the joke that travels around the tables and through the kitchen until everyone, everyone, is laughing. Sometimes a sacred moment centers on a liturgy, a prayer before the meal, a shared Eucharist.

Even in the midst of poverty, even surrounded by death and dying, God is with us.

VERITY A. JONES

2. Anthony J. Kelly and Francis J. Moloney, *Experiencing God in the Gospel of John* (New York: Paulist Press, 2003), 252.
3. Sandra M. Schneiders, *Written That You May Believe: Encountering Jesus in the Fourth Gospel* (New York: Crossroad Publishing, 1999), 160.

Exegetical Perspective

should not be overlooked: John adds that the house was filled with the fragrance of the ointment.

A second reading of the text locates it in its context in John. John links the anointing closely with the raising of Lazarus. John 11 identifies Lazarus as the brother of Mary and Martha, and begins with a reference to Mary's anointing of Jesus (11:2). In turn, John 12 begins with a reference to Bethany as the place where Jesus raised Lazarus. The reader is set up to assume that the dinner was a celebration following the resurrection of Lazarus, which also provides a justification for the lavish anointing of Jesus. The sweet fragrance of the adoration replaces the pungent smell of death (11:39).

Mary, Martha, and Lazarus are representative members of the household of God,[3] who profess faith in Jesus and enjoy table fellowship with Jesus, and whose devotion fills the house with a sweet fragrance. Lazarus is a representative witness and an exemplar of the promise of eternal life. Because of Lazarus, many believe in Jesus (12:11).

John also links the anointing of Jesus with the Last Supper in the next chapter. There, Jesus assumes Mary's role, washing the disciples' feet and wiping them with a towel. Judas again plays a central role as the devil-chosen betrayer (13:2, 27). Whereas Judas steals from the common purse (12:6), Jesus freely offers him the choice morsel (13:26); when Judas leaves, the other disciples assume he is going to give something to "the poor," because he kept the common purse (13:29).

Through these subtle connections, the anointing in John reflects the community's preparation for Jesus' death and departure. It invites readers to gather with brothers and sisters in the household of faith, celebrate the gift of eternal life, offer the Lord their most precious treasures, and prepare for the inevitability of death, while remembering those in need, new believers who come to the household of faith because of the eternal life in us, and those who still plot death. Especially during Holy Week, therefore, the household of faith has much to do when it gathers at table!

R. ALAN CULPEPPER

Homiletical Perspective

and orphans. Poverty and disease was rampant. In many ways it was "progress" at its worst.

In the midst of all this, however, there were beautiful churches adorned with great art and breathtaking stained glass. No expense was spared to provide fine organs and support great choirs. The liturgical vestments were often quite lavish, much grander than in the churches in the wealthy areas. It was all a very costly ointment.

There were soup kitchens too, and church-run schools for the orphans. There were societies for the support of the widows. There were social justice ministries around every corner. The church reached out to "the poor that we will always have with us."

In the dismal surroundings of the London docks, if the people were going to have any beauty in their lives, it was going to have to be at the church. If the people were going to see any great art, it was going to have to be in church. If the people were going to hear any beautiful music, it was going to have to be the organ and choir. If the people were going to be treated to great oratory, it would have to be the great preaching of the church. If the people were going to be anointed with God's beauty, then the church was going to have to provide copious amounts of costly perfumed ointment in the midst of their desperate, needy, seemingly hopeless neighborhood.

Imagine what could have been done if the churches on the London docks had spent all of their resources on something other than costly perfumed ointment. Then imagine what the dockworkers and the seafarers and their families would have missed. Imagine how dreadful our religion might have turned out to be if we did not have Mary of Bethany, and so many like her through the centuries, reminding us by their sacrificial gifts of the extravagance of God.

J. NEIL ALEXANDER

3. Mary L. Coloe, *Dwelling in the Household of God: Johannine Ecclesiology and Spirituality* (Collegeville, MN: Liturgical Press, 2007).

Isaiah 49:1-7

¹Listen to me, O coastlands,
  pay attention, you peoples from far away!
The Lᴏʀᴅ called me before I was born,
  while I was in my mother's womb he named me.
²He made my mouth like a sharp sword,
  in the shadow of his hand he hid me;
he made me a polished arrow,
  in his quiver he hid me away.
³And he said to me, "You are my servant,
  Israel, in whom I will be glorified."
⁴But I said, "I have labored in vain,
  I have spent my strength for nothing and vanity;
yet surely my cause is with the Lᴏʀᴅ,
  and my reward with my God."

⁵And now the Lᴏʀᴅ says,
  who formed me in the womb to be his servant,
  to bring Jacob back to him,

Theological Perspective

Isaiah 49:1–7 comprises the second of the Servant Songs of Second Isaiah and is read during Tuesday of Holy Week, reflecting the church's long tradition of connecting it to the last days of Jesus' life. The passage continues and complements the first Song, 42:1–9. We hear again of the choice of the Servant by God, the fact that the Servant is Israel, and the conviction that the task of the Servant is to bring God's salvation to "the ends of the earth." However, these themes are presented in a fresh way, offering further explorations of the work of God and the Servant in history and theology.

Whereas in the first Song it is God who presents the Servant to the world (42:1), now it is the Servant who speaks in an autobiographical portrait of call and ministry. Here we find parallels with earlier prophetic callings. As in 42:1–9, here the Servant speaks to the farthest reaches of the world, the "coastlands" (or "isles," 42:4; 49:1 KJV). Israel had little connection with the sea, though they lived on the eastern shores of the Mediterranean, so when they spoke of "coastlands," the word was a metaphor for "peoples from far away," as the parallel in 49:1.

Like the prophets of Israel, the Servant was called by God "before I was born," named "in my mother's womb" (v. 1; see Jer.1:5 for a similar idea). Also like them, the Servant was equipped by God with the

Pastoral Perspective

If the first step of Holy Week (in the prophetic text for Monday) is to *behold* the Servant of the Lord, our next charge is to *listen*, as the Servant's own voice is now heard. The journey moves from contemplation —a particular way of seeing the Servant—to engagement: a particular kind of attention to the Servant's own story.

As in the accompanying Gospel text (John 12:20–36), we overhear the Servant working out a redemptive identity. The call begins in the intimacy of the womb, where a name was bestowed (though we never learn it) and gifts for prophetic, redemptive leadership were honed (though only to be hidden). We next learn of the transformation of the Servant's deep discouragement and of the restoration of confidence that comes when human labors are aligned with God's cause. No sooner does the Servant reclaim both identity and mission than this mission is widened to a global scale. It is work that evidently has not yet come to fruition, for the antipathy of the nations persists, and the vindication of the Servant's project remains in the future.

The Servant addresses us as though we are exiles or strangers from the hinterland: "Listen to me, . . . you peoples from far away." Perhaps the distance across which the voice carries accounts for the way the Servant's identity continues to elude focus. The profile

and that Israel might be gathered to him,
for I am honored in the sight of the LORD,
    and my God has become my strength—
⁶he says,
"It is too light a thing that you should be my servant
    to raise up the tribes of Jacob
    and to restore the survivors of Israel;
I will give you as a light to the nations,
    that my salvation may reach to the end of the earth."

⁷Thus says the LORD,
    the Redeemer of Israel and his Holy One,
to one deeply despised, abhorred by the nations,
    the slave of rulers,
"Kings shall see and stand up,
    princes, and they shall prostrate themselves,
because of the LORD, who is faithful,
    the Holy One of Israel, who has chosen you."

Exegetical Perspective

When the boys were small, a neighbor gave my family a picture book, accompanied by a recording, of the story of the Ugly Duckling. The guys loved the present—so much so that over the succeeding weeks, through many, many lively readings, I had the opportunity as never before to immerse myself in this old, familiar tale! You probably know the story: an odd, outsize egg in a mother duck's nest hatches out an odd, outsize duckling, gray and ungainly. Because of his ugliness, the duckling is rejected by everyone in the farmyard. Only when he has grown does he discover the truth about himself: he is not a duck, but a beautiful, graceful swan! Indeed, he had *always* been a swan, with all that beauty and grace locked inside; but he did not know it, and no one else could see it.

Similarly, in the second Servant Song, the Servant of the Lord is born with a great destiny:

Listen to me, O coastlands,
    pay attention, you peoples from far away!
The LORD called me before I was born,
    while I was in my mother's womb he named me.
                                              (49:1)

The language is strongly reminiscent of God's words to the prophet Jeremiah: "Before I formed you in the womb I knew you, and before you were born I

Homiletical Perspective

A story for three voices. First, this is the story of the exiled Jews, living in Babylon. In their voices, across the centuries of time, it sounds like this:

There is still no peace. The day might be coming, we know, when the land will be restored, and the hopes of our people met. However that day is not yet upon us. So, while we wait, while we even dare to hope, we must declare where our hope lies.

And a great hope it is, first given to Abraham and Sarah, and then to Isaac and Rebekah, to Jacob and Rachel. The God of Israel will somehow be known, in the very midst of this people of the covenant. Though we are now a weak and broken nation, with no reason to make claims about God's holy presence, we trust that God is far more powerful than any of the rulers of this earth. We are determined to hold onto this faith, because in the past, we have known a God who loved us. That same God longs for us, God's chosen people, to be redeemed. That redemption has not come easily, but our faith is certain. The one true God will make that clear, in God's own time.

It is not enough that God will simply lead us home again, to the land of promise. No, we are to be a nation whose identity is evident to all, and whose mission is certain. It is not enough that we will be a people free of the oppressors who now confine us. We are to be a light to the nations of the earth. The God who has formed us has a mighty

Isaiah 49:1-7

Theological Perspective

power of the spoken word, metaphorically described as a "mouth like a sharp sword" and "a polished arrow" (v. 2; see Jer. 23:29 for another metaphor of speaking and Jer. 1:9 for God's gift of the word to the prophet; see also three NT passages that describe the word as a sword: Eph. 6:17; Heb. 4:12; Rev. 1:16). These aggressive metaphors are in sharp contrast to the quiet voice of the first Song, a voice that would not break a damaged reed or quench a guttering wick. It might be said that in verse 4 the Servant announces that past attempts at aggressive speaking in response to the call of God have not been finally successful.

If that reading is correct, verse 4 must be a statement of the earlier work of the prophets of Israel, those first servants, whose speeches comprised the oracles of Amos, Hosea, Micah, First Isaiah, and Jeremiah. Though they all spoke truth—their words of warning to preexilic Israel of the anger of God came all too true as exiles well knew—their angry words have led the exilic Servant to despair and hopelessness. "I have worked for nothing; I have spent my strength for emptiness and wind" (v. 4, my trans.). The final two nouns have deep resonance in Israel; the latter is that word that characterizes Ecclesiastes' later convictions that life is at last little more than "wind" ("vanity" in the famous KJV reading), and the former word ("emptiness"—*bohu* in Hebrew) is paired with a rhyming word—*tohu*—in Genesis 1:2 to create a portrait of chaos from which God brings order and light.

Though the chosen Servant of the exile feels profound despair, a tiny ray of light appears in verse 4b: "Still ["without a doubt"], my right [*mishpat*] is with the LORD; my reward is with my God." The key word is the RSV's "right" (NRSV "cause"). This word appears three times in 42:1–4, where it means God's way for the harmony and peace of the world. Though the Servant has felt the failure of prophetic forebears, God still holds the unchangeable content of the Servant's message and the certain final success of the announcement of it. So when God calls the exilic Servant again to the task first given long ago, the Servant listens to the divine voice with the certainty that the task will be successful.

So God speaks to the Servant—the same God who formed the Servant in the womb with the express purpose to "bring Jacob back to God, to gather Israel once again to God" in order to bring honor to God and to show forth God's strength. In the context of the Babylonian exile, this appears to mean that the Servant's role is to gather the exiles

Pastoral Perspective

of the Servant in this thumbnail biography seems to change before our eyes like a Picasso portrait: particular features are familiar, but the composite effect is one of overlapping images sometimes in tension with each other. The Servant speaks with confidence as an actor on the world stage—but confesses to having been a prisoner of self-doubt. The Servant is one whose special relationship to God began even before birth—yet one whom the nations "deeply despise" and "abhor" (v. 7). The Servant remains, apparently, "the slave of rulers," notwithstanding a resemblance to a sharp sword and a polished arrow. As in the first Servant Song, the text accentuates the ambiguity between individual and collective identities of this figure who stands variously for Israel ("you are my servant, Israel"—v. 3), for Israel's redeemer in the theatre of nations ("my servant . . . to restore the survivors of Israel"—v. 6a), and even for the "light to the nations," whose triumph will "reach to the end of the earth" (v. 6b).[1]

In fact, the Song of this Servant is a virtual hymn to paradox. In it, futility is infused with strength—much as the journey of Holy Week discloses the potency of Jesus' overt weakness, his triumph won even in the midst of apparent humiliation. It seems to be in the nature of the Servant both to embody paradox and to resolve paradox: to wield both servanthood and sword, to be despised and honored, to be for one people and for all people.

However, why should God seem to speak the language of paradox so much more fluently than the language of clarity and resolution? Why should God choose to sharpen the prophetic edge of servanthood, only to conceal it in weakness? From the Songs of the Servant to the parables of Jesus, the ways of God seem perennially cryptic, intended to thwart our expectations or knock us off balance. Sometimes we share the anguished longing of the prophet for unequivocal revelation: "O that you would tear open the heavens and come down . . . to make your name known to your adversaries, so that the nations might tremble at your presence!" (Isa. 64:1–2).

In fact, the eloquence of God's dialect of paradox is evident as the journey of Holy Week establishes, step by step, a deep kinship between the Servant and the served. The paradoxes that are etched into the Servant's profile—the tension between weakness and strength, between discouragement and courage, between local focus and global responsibility—are woven just as vividly into our own experience.

1. Much the same dynamic is at work in Isa. 41:1–10.

consecrated you; I appointed you a prophet to the nations" (Jer. 1:5). Later, the apostle Paul would express the confidence that he too had been called before he was born, appointed from the first to proclaim Jesus among the Gentiles: "God, who had set me apart before I was born and called me through his grace, was pleased to reveal his Son to me, so that I might proclaim him among the Gentiles" (Gal. 1:14–15). The Servant's prophetic role, announced on a world stage, is shown as well in the power of his words: [The LORD] "made my mouth like a sharp sword" (Isa. 49:2; cf. Rev. 1:16; 2:16; 19:15, 21, where this image is used for the word of the risen Christ).

However, the Servant's destiny is hidden from the world. Having made the Servant's mouth "like a sharp sword," the Lord hid him away "in the shadow of [God's] hand" (49:2). Though the Lord had fashioned him "like a polished arrow," a beautiful, potent expression of God's intent, the Servant found himself unused, apparently forgotten, hidden away like an arrow in God's quiver (49:2). The hiddenness of the Servant's destiny is a consistent theme of the Songs. So, in 42:1–9, the Servant's activity was so subtle that it would not break an already-bruised and bent reed; so still and quiet that it would not blow out a dim, flickering, all-but-extinguished lamp. This hidden work, however, is most powerfully expressed in the fourth Servant Song, where the nations look on the Servant in bewilderment: "he had no form or majesty that we should look at him, nothing in his appearance that we should desire him" (53:2).

Indeed, not only was the Servant's destiny hidden from the world; it seemed to be hidden even from the Servant himself. Despairing, the Servant cried, "I have labored in vain, I have spent my strength for nothing and vanity" (49:4). In this Holy Week, those words of despair and frustration call to mind the cry of Jesus from the cross, in the words of Psalm 22: "My God, my God, why have you forsaken me?" (Matt. 27:46//Mark 15:34). The way of the Servant is *hard*—as it must be. How, otherwise, could the Servant truly understand the suffering of others, who feel themselves abandoned, forgotten, God-forsaken? Yet, God declares, the Servant will become the means, not only of Israel's redemption, but of the world's transformation:

"It is too light a thing that you should be my servant
   to raise up the tribes of Jacob
   and to restore the survivors of Israel;

plan for us. We will show God's glory, and even those in power will prostrate themselves, so that God may be known, to every tribe and every land.

This is also, for Christian readers, the claim of the servant Jesus. Still, there is no peace in the land. The day of God's redemption is coming, when not just the land but the people of good faith will be restored, and every good hope met.

Surely Jesus is the one who, named while yet in Mary's womb, was brought forth to challenge the powerful, to insist that not they but God was to be glorified. While a Jew, a member of the promised people of Israel, Jesus would recognize it too small a thing to save only one people of God. No, this holy Child of God would be the true light to every nation, the Word of God in every language, to be spoken of in every tongue.

What does it mean for Jesus to speak these words? Though despised by many, though denied and rejected even by those who loved him best, though bound in chains and treated as if he were a criminal, God would be faithful in this holy, human life. From the story of humiliation and powerlessness, in spite of the lessons of human betrayal and fear, the light of Jesus would shine on, first to those who bore witness, then to the gathering crowds who, listening, became believers. Then that light to the nations would break forth, even to the ends of the earth. Yes, this is Jesus' story.

There is one more voice, however, that might claim this text as well, and that voice gives us reason to reflect on this verse once more. What if we as the body of Christ, the church, were to claim the second Servant Song of Isaiah? For this is also the story of the church, in our day.

So try these words again, and consider the role of the church, the holy catholic church of every tradition in every land, as the Suffering Servant. We have been chosen, says the Lord, to be the faithful remnant who know that God alone is our strength. We have been called upon, not just to remember the salvation story of history, not just the Holy Week narrative of a fully human, fully divine Savior in our own lives, but for far more than that.

We are to be a light to the nations. We are to live with such compassion and determination, knowing that God alone is our strength and our salvation, that the ways of the Holy One of Israel will reach to the ends of the earth.

Such a faith affirmation will do more than get our attention. It insists that there are profound

Isaiah 49:1-7

Theological Perspective

back to the land of promise, to reconstitute the scattered nation of Israel. This reading would explain how the Servant can both speak to Israel and be Israel at the same time. In the same way, we can speak in our time of the need for the church to call the church back to its mission for God.

However, the wonder of the call to the Servant now appears, telling the ancients and us that our vision remains too small. "It is too light a thing that you should be my servant to raise up the tribes of Jacob and to restore the survivors of Israel" (v. 6a). One can imagine that to the exiles in Babylon it would have seemed not at all a "light thing" to start the nation again by trekking westward to a place none of them had ever seen. They would have felt like new Abrams, their ancient ancestor who went the same risky way, leaving all he knew, to found Israel, with the promise that he would be a "great nation."

Perhaps Isaiah had this same Abram in mind when he moved the vision beyond nationalistic aspirations to say: "I will give you as a light to the nations, that my salvation may reach to the end of the earth" (v. 6b). God had said to Abram, "I will make of you a great nation. . . . in you all the nations of the earth shall be blessed" (Gen. 12:2–3). You, Israel, "deeply despised, abhorred by the nations, slave of rulers" (v. 7), have now received the task of bringing the light of God's justice, salvation, and hope to those very same nations, those same rulers. God calls the Servant, Israel, far beyond its concern for its own people, to be nothing less than light to the world. Much later, the servant of God, Jesus, will call his followers to be light to the world and, in the words of John, is himself seen as that light.

JOHN C. HOLBERT

Pastoral Perspective

Indeed, if we listen to this text intently, as the Song instructs, we may hear described not only the Servant, but ourselves. The familiar rabbinic parable that we should have two pockets, each containing a scrap of paper—on one written, "I am dust and ashes," and on the other, "For me this world was created"[2]—applies with equal force to God's own chosen Servant and to all of God's people.

The victory that the Servant will finally secure is won by engaging the realities of our existence, one paradox at a time. Thus is the journey of Holy Week an incremental one. On the way of discipleship, toward Easter and then beyond it, we are both the healed and the healers, both the despairing and the elated. As it deepens—as we move from contemplation of this Servant to engagement in this testimony—we may find ourselves drawn into the drama of our own redemption, not as spectators, but as participants in the journey from the gates to the Garden to the cross to the victory, landmarks in the landscape of paradox in which we live. To inhabit the community for which the Servant lives and, ultimately, lays down life, is to know both the anguish and the resolution to which another servant, Paul, testifies: "Wretched man that I am! Who will rescue me from this body of death? Thanks be to God through Jesus Christ our Lord!" (Rom. 7:24–25).

To pay attention as the Servant works out a redemptive identity is, perhaps, to overhear our own experience as exiles, strangers in a landscape of paradox. We may not yet fully grasp the name of the one whom God has chosen to free us. Vindication may still lie on the far side of humiliation and scorn. The victory, when it is revealed, may be like a sword that was hidden in the shadow of death—like an arrow concealed in the quiver of suffering and tribulation.

RICHARD E. SPALDING

---

2. Most attestations of this parable attribute it to Rabbi Simcha Bunim of P'shiskha, based on Gen. 18:27 and Talmud Bavli, *Sanhedrin* 37B.

Exegetical Perspective

I will give you as a light to the nations,
    that my salvation may reach to the end of the
    earth."

                                (49:6)

The audience that first heard these words knew all too well what it was to feel abandoned and forgotten. Through fifty years of exile, they had struggled to preserve their identity in the midst of an alien culture. They were tired, unable to summon the energy to hope for deliverance (see 40:28–31; 43:22–24; 47:12–15; 49:4). No wonder this exilic prophecy begins with a call to encouragement: "Comfort, comfort my people" (40:1), but the message of Second Isaiah is not Pollyanna optimism: all is *not* well. The pain of the people cuts deep. Their despair is real, and *realistic*: experience has taught them not to hope for too much. Yet, God declares, not only will Israel be restored, but in their restoration, the world will be made new. The way of the Servant leads through sorrow into joy, through darkness into light, through death into life.

In today's Epistle, Paul invites his Corinthian audience to look around: "Not many of you were wise by human standards, not many were powerful, not many were of noble birth" (1 Cor. 1:26). Yet, Paul says, "God chose what is low and despised in the world, things that are not, to reduce to nothing things that are, so that no one might boast in the presence of God" (1 Cor. 1:28–29). The message of the cross is that God has come to be present in the midst of suffering, hopelessness, and despair, to reveal the true glory of God's love, life, and goodness in the lives of plain, ordinary, desperate people. We are like a grain of wheat, which contains hidden within it all the potential for the stalk of grain it can become (John 12:24). We cannot know, and the world cannot see, what God dreams for us. However every day, by God's grace, ugly ducklings are transformed into beautiful, graceful swans!

                                  STEVEN S. TUELL

Homiletical Perspective

responsibilities that must be borne by the church and by all who follow in the way of the light of God. Those responsibilities include not just compassionate living, but showing forth such an example that all of the people of the earth will find, in the church's life, reason to delight in the witness of believers and a compelling model for faithful discipleship.

In every reading, our hearts break. Break for the people Israel, lost and nearly hopeless, abandoned in the Babylonian wilderness, yet called upon to be faithful still. Break for Jesus, in this Holy Week, faced with the anguish and the wonder of the days ahead. Could there not have been another way? Would those who would be witnesses to the resurrection even begin to understand that power and the wonder of God's activity?

Finally, if we are honest, our hearts break too for the church—the faithful, failing, faulty church, the body of Christ that seems unable to get out of its own way—the very human institution that too often neglects the gospel calling that is its very reason for being.

The powers of this earth shall see your witness, O church, and stand up. The presidents and prime ministers shall bow before you, because God, who is faithful, the Holy One of every generation, has chosen you. Israel. Christ Jesus. The body of Christ, the church.

                            WILLIAM GOETTLER

Psalm 71:1-14

[1]In you, O Lord, I take refuge;
  let me never be put to shame.
[2]In your righteousness deliver me and rescue me;
  incline your ear to me and save me.
[3]Be to me a rock of refuge,
  a strong fortress, to save me,
  for you are my rock and my fortress.

[4]Rescue me, O my God, from the hand of the wicked,
  from the grasp of the unjust and cruel.
[5]For you, O Lord, are my hope,
  my trust, O Lord, from my youth.
[6]Upon you I have leaned from my birth;
  it was you who took me from my mother's womb.
  My praise is continually of you.

[7]I have been like a portent to many,
  but you are my strong refuge.

Theological Perspective

In some translations, Psalm 71 has a superscription "A prayer for old age." It is the only psalm where old age is mentioned. Because of the Psalms, David can be considered a significant liturgical figure for Jewish and Christian people throughout history. While scholars do not agree about David's direct authorship of this psalm, it is still recognized as part of the Davidic Psalter that was redacted in the postexilic period.[1] This psalm brings aging itself into prayer, has several interesting contrasts, and presents some theological principles, each of which sharpens the focus of reflection for Christians during Holy Week.

The psalm begins with four petitions: "Let me never be put to shame" (v. 1); "Incline your ear to me and save me" (v. 2); "Save me, for you are my rock" (v. 3); "Rescue me . . . from the wicked" (v. 4). These petitions give indication of unspecified dangers—of humiliations and oppressions—as well as God's saving power as refuge and fortress. Four statements of praise follow the petitions: "You are my hope" (v. 5); "My praise is continually of you" (v. 6); "You are my strong refuge" (v. 7); and the strongest of the four, "My mouth is filled with your praise, and with your glory all day long" (v. 8). With these statements

Pastoral Perspective

This psalm contains elements of a classic lament, a genre usually associated with worship. It will be fruitful to point toward some of its distinctive elements. One is clearly the reference to the psalmist's old age and the recollection of a life spent leaning on YHWH. Because the lament genre tends to be in a corporate setting, the topic is not so much personal as public. Will YHWH abandon us in our old age? the psalm seems to ask.

Another distinctive element here is that the worshipers have learned from adversity. He (or she or they) have been tested; they have gone through difficult times. There is some question of what the purpose of that adversity was.

During the course of the psalm, it moves from petition/lament/complaint to praise three times. In concert with the emphasis on adversity or potential adversity, this movement suggests a corresponding movement from fear and urgency to reassurance and trust/praise. Are those characteristics of older age or of the location of the worshipers?

Patrick Miller suggests that a search "for a readily identifiable situation as the context for understanding the laments may . . . be illusory or unnecessary."[1] In fact, it may be impossible. It may

---

1. William L. Holladay, *The Psalms through Three Thousand Years* (Minneapolis: Fortress Press, 1993), 71–72.

1. Patrick Miller, *Interpreting the Psalms* (Philadelphia: Fortress Press, 1986), 8.

⁸My mouth is filled with your praise,
   and with your glory all day long.
⁹Do not cast me off in the time of old age;
   do not forsake me when my strength is spent.
¹⁰For my enemies speak concerning me,
   and those who watch for my life consult together.
¹¹They say, "Pursue and seize that person
   whom God has forsaken,
   for there is no one to deliver."

¹²O God, do not be far from me;
   O my God, make haste to help me!
¹³Let my accusers be put to shame and consumed;
   let those who seek to hurt me
   be covered with scorn and disgrace.
¹⁴But I will hope continually,
   and will praise you yet more and more.

Exegetical Perspective

In this psalm the request for protection and the promptness of worship are interwoven. Although the psalmist starts his prayer asking for salvation, help, and refuge (vv. 1–4), he reminisces about his childhood and youth to proclaim that YHWH has always been his source of refuge and therefore will continue being the object of his praise. Indeed, at the core of the psalm (vv. 9–18), set within the fear of divine abandonment during the time of old age, the psalmist asserts his hope in God, his willingness to praise, the proclamation of divine justice, and the magnificent acts of God, in which salvation is given at all times to God's child.

In all, the psalm finds its framework and center in the theme of shame (vv. 1, 13, and 24), that is, moving *in crescendo* from the psalmist's request never to be ashamed, to the plea that his enemies be put to shame, to even knowing that finally those enemies live in shame and are disgraced. Other topics that help to mark the psalm are wicked and violent enemies, who appear in verses 4, 10, 13, and 24; and divine justice and salvation, which appear in verses 2–3, 15, 19, and 23–24. These themes are found scattered in the three sections that make up the psalm: (a) verses 1–8, (b) verses 9–19a, (c) verses 19b–24. On the other hand, it has long been suggested that Psalm 71 is a kind of anthology

Homiletical Perspective

In a world where crime, terrorism, and faraway violence come into our living spaces via the media, many people come to worship feeling physically and spiritually endangered. Who can forget the tone and tenor of worship the Sunday after 9/11? The list of anxieties we bring to worship is long and diverse—global and personal, real and unreal.

The presence of injustice, inequities, and unfairness in the world and our lives creates within us (1) fear, (2) denial of our own complicity in problems, (3) a sense of isolation in the face of injustice, (4) a desire for vengeance, and (5) anxiety that God has forgotten the faithful in general and, specifically, us. Moving through any one of these realities creates the flow for a sermon.

Holy Week provides a perfect context for discussing the anxieties, explicit and implicit, found in our lives and in the words of the psalmist. After all, in Holy Week we walk with Jesus as he confronts his own fears about his fate. As he walks toward the cross, we observe him feeling increasingly isolated from his followers and even God.

In the hands of a gifted preacher, the concerns of Jesus and the psalmist can become a mirror for our own concerns. The contrasting ways Jesus and the psalmist respond to threats and difficulties can lead us toward the inner security we see at work in the Christ.

Psalm 71:1-14

Theological Perspective

of praise, the faithfulness of the writer becomes one strong basis for hope that God will answer the petitions. Yet the most important reasons for hope revolve elegantly around the very nature of God.

A sharp contrast in this psalm provides powerful imagery for Holy Week. The limit of our humanity, emphasized by the reality of aging, is contrasted with the power of God. Yet we are not expected to be gods to earn God's care; instead, we are held dearly in our human frailty. God is timeless and we are time bound; our state as finite beings is sharply contrasted with God's infinite presence. In this imagery, it is clear that, with God's love, we never need fear aging or facing our own limits. Our hope in this generous God is not irrational, and as we hope, we also praise.

In these statements of praise, verse 7 brings another interesting point forward for clarification. Those surrounding the psalmist are confused: "I have been like a portent to many" (v. 7). The type of portent or sign that others see in the tragedies that beset the psalmist (presumably a good person to whom bad things are happening) is never stated. However, one thing is made crystal clear by this verse: other people will not help resolve the tragedies that cut across the life of the psalmist. The writer's dependence on God is absolute, as stated in verse 3: "You are my rock."

Verse 8 is the strongest statement of praise, but it is also the turning point in the psalm. Verses 9–13 are powerful laments that draw from the previous contrasting sets of four petitions and four statements of praise. Two main themes of lament emerge. First, enemies plot as the writer is less capable due to age: "For my enemies speak concerning me, and those who watch for my life consult together" (v. 10). The psalmist calls for God's restriction of the enemies in verse 13: "Let my accusers be put to shame and consumed; let those who seek to hurt me be covered with scorn and disgrace."

Second, a cry for help is presented in different ways, captured in verse 12: "God, do not be far from me; O my God, make haste to help me!" The need for God's presence is the first plea. To be cut off from God has been described as the truest form of damnation. The plea for God's help in crisis is also needed. The juxtaposition of these two pleas sets up an important theological connection. God is not a magic helper; rather, the believer is in relationship with God. Despite all else, remaining in God's presence is the most important outcome of life and becomes the frame for the petitioner's cries. The praise of God is not falsely presented as a method to

Pastoral Perspective

be truer to the psalm to think of the context as one in which worshipers step into the language of the psalm to give voice to their own lament and hope.

In a church where there are many older disciples, the focus on this movement between adversity and trust can be instructive not only for seniors but also for the young, who experience some of the same fears and need for trust. We may in fact learn something from seniors who believe and trust and hope even when the circumstances point more realistically toward some degree of despair. "I will hope continually, and will praise you yet more and more" (v. 14).

Furthermore, one of the traits of advancing age is a process of loss. Indeed, those psychologists who have studied the process of death and dying suggest that there is a continuum of loss that at one point (unspecified) becomes a process of dying. Reading between the lines here, one can imagine an older psalmist who, in the process of aging, is praising God and also begging God to continue to care for him steadfastly.

There appears to be no wavering in the voice of the psalm but an ongoing appeal to God "the rock and fortress" to deliver and rescue, as God has done in the past. It is as though the congregation is praying for the strengthening of their belief and recalling the many times that YHWH has in fact delivered them. Maybe the psalm envisions the facing of one's own death or invites the worshiper to contemplate facing his or her own death. We could also imagine that a community is undergoing a threat to its continued well-being.

There are elements of the practice of giving testimony or witnessing to the goodness of God at the same time that the author is facing diminishment or death. In his book *Testimony: Talking Ourselves into Being Christian*,[2] Tom Long suggests that language—and especially the language of testimony—shapes the experience, practice, and communal life of Christians. In today's world, which is full of chatter, we yearn for the truthful, meaningful, and compassionate speech that is ultimately grounded in truth about God. Testimony as a form of speech deepens participation in the life of God and, in fact, becomes a form of prayer. This psalm could easily stand as an example of such speech.

The language of the psalm also hints at vulnerability. The image is almost that of someone being hunted down by jackals, enemies lying in wait

---

2. Thomas G. Long, *Testimony: Talking Ourselves into Being Christian* (San Francisco: Jossey-Bass, 2004).

formed from other psalms, mainly Psalms 31 and 22: verses 1–3 from 31:1–3a; verses 5–6 from 22:10–11; verse 12a from 22:1, 11, 19; verse 12b from 38:12 and 40:13; verse 13 from 35:4, 26; verse 17 from 22:10–11; verse 18 from 22:30–31; verse 19 from 36:6; verse 24 from 35:28.

The theological center of the psalm can be found in verse 14. Here the spirit of the entire psalm is summarized: the individual who puts his entire trust and hope in God is permanently willing to worship YHWH. Since today's lesson ends at verse 14, this verse becomes not the central part of the poem but its final point, its climax. The entire experience of the praying psalmist—whether it is inspired by danger, by the need for protection, by trust and hope, or whether it is stemming from childhood, or youth or old age—has its point of reference in this declaration with which the prayer closes.

The person praying this psalm has reached old age and, perhaps due to illness or the frailty that comes with old age, the psalmist finds himself in constant danger. Therefore, he resorts to imperatives: "deliver me," "rescue me," "incline your ear to me," "save me" (vv. 2, 4). He is need of divine help—now! There is no time to waste! This urgency is further intensified when Psalms 70 and 71 are read together. The lack of a Hebrew title in Psalm 71 and the presence of related words and ideas in the two psalms are taken as arguments that confirm their unity. Psalm 70 is full of imperatives that state the situation of imminent danger of the person who is imploring YHWH's aid. Amid this urgency, the psalmist affirms his total trust in his God.

YHWH is called "rock," "fortress," "refuge," "strong fortress." Speaking metaphorically of YHWH's care, these objects of safe haven are considered by the elderly poet as "home" from the moment of his birth until his old age. To his trust and hope in God, the psalmist adds praise and proclamation. What a beautiful picture, in which God is seen as a safe refuge from the moment of birth until the days of old age! A life that is moving from a cry for help, to trust, to praise, to the proclamation of God's marvelous deeds—this, says the psalmist, is the result of a lifelong education in which YHWH has been the divine teacher (v. 17). All of this happens, not in the tranquil life of someone who has every single thing taken care of, but in the life of someone who has lived and lives exposed to frailty, vulnerability, persecution, and violence.

The psalmist's trust and hope are asserted and increased not only with the passing of time, with the

In Psalm 71, the psalmist describes people attacking him. He views his enemies as direct threats to his physical and spiritual well-being. We relate to the psalmist's deep, almost frantic yearning for God's help in combating the forces of evil.

In our preaching, by naming these fears, we can help calm our listeners. We can detail perceived and real threats to the well-being of members of the congregation, ranging from political, economic, and social realities to health problems to interpersonal events in our families. The very act of naming what we are afraid of is healing and empowering.

Next, we move to confession. In the Christian tradition, all truth begins with confession. We are foolish to think unrighteousness is limited to those who attack us. As we name the sinfulness of those who would oppress us, we must also be mindful of and acknowledge our own sinfulness. Confession interjects much-needed humility into our lives as we seek to cope with those who would do us wrong. As we confess, we discover that we are part of the problem.

Surely many of the good people of Jerusalem, Jews and non-Jews, felt oppressed by the Roman government and cried out to God for help. How many of them understood that their silence in the face of Pilate's actions toward Jesus was silence in the face of injustice? Before we invoke God's help in our problems, we need to confess the problems we create for others. The Holy Week story provides a wonderful context for confessing our complicity in contemporary systems of injustice, the same types of systems that enabled Jesus' death.

Having named our fears and confessed our sins, we move to the profound sense of alienation created by fear. We feel this sense of estrangement at work in the psalmist: "Do not cast me off in the time of old age; do not forsake me when my strength is spent" (v. 9). While the psalmist denies that the onslaught of misfortune is having any impact on his faith, in fact, it is obviously having a negative impact. Why else would the psalmist beg God not to forsake him? The psalmist's problems are causing him to wonder whether or not God still cares.

From this sense of estrangement comes a desire within us for God to prove that God is God. Specifically, we want God to prove that God loves *us*. The easiest proof is vengeance. We pray, "God destroy those who would destroy and dishonor me," or, to cite the psalmist, "Let my accusers be put to shame and consumed" (v. 13).

Psalm 71:1-14

Theological Perspective

obtain help against enemies. Praise of God is an expression of the relationship.

It is in this section of lament that old age is placed: "Do not cast me off in the time of old age; do not forsake me when my strength is spent" (v. 9). Old age and failing strength are part of the human condition. That the author faces mortality in a time of trouble and danger stands as a reminder that each human is a finite being. God as Creator is a primary Judeo-Christian theological principle. Faith is built, not on human-determined power, but on the reality of the state of being created by God. Therefore, each person is limited in the ability to *will* situations to preferred conditions. Aging is, again, a reminder of the limits of human power. In this time of weakness from within, other threats come from without, as enemies plot against the psalmist.

As a contrast to the lament of dangers and old age in the second part of the psalm, dedication to God began in the author's younger years. This contrast demonstrates the author's lifelong, faithful commitment to God. This sense defines one of the key aspects of faith, which is trust: "You, O Lord, are . . . my trust . . . from my youth" (v. 5). Trust in God, however, is not an immunization against troubles. At a time that the psalmist lacks personal resources, enemies' plots complicate the problems of aging. The aspect of faithful living that is trust is underscored in this section.

Today's psalm selection ends with a proclamation that moves faith into hope and praise, no matter what the circumstances are: "But I will hope continually, and will praise you yet more and more" (v. 14). The lessons of Holy Week include the one pointed out in this psalm selection: about the full dynamics involved in faithful living, encompassing committed trust, irrational hope, and continual praise.

STEPHANIE Y. MITCHEM

Pastoral Perspective

until the time to strike is most propitious. The anguish of Jesus' being hunted down is a point of connection to Holy Week. To be sure, the faith expressed in the psalm is a strong one, but the fear and danger are also strong. The temptation to spiritualize the violence that seems quite possible to the psalmist is a result of our middle-class sense of immunity to violence. Who knows for sure what will happen?

Do we experience times like this? Did the language of terrorism and war in the wake of 9/11, or the image of the levees breaking as Katrina raged through the Gulf Coast, or the Asian tsunami touch us? Do we remember that?

Who are our enemies these days?

Perhaps they are more subtle. Perhaps they are not those who "pursue and seize that person whom God has forsaken" (v. 11). Rather, the enemies of the affluent may be the voices that call us "not to get involved," "to take it easy," or the voices that advocate the "go along, get along" lifestyle, that urge us to maintain the highest level of comfort possible.

Contrast that, if you will, to the prophetic witness in Scripture. The witness is to be an alternate community, which is both a critique of the present state of things and a hope that things may move in a kingdomward direction. Perhaps the prayer is more a "Let me keep faith, even though I am tempted to abandon you, who have been my rock and fortress" (vv. 2–3). The community itself may be in danger of abandoning YHWH or of losing a strong, vibrant faith. What does it mean for a community to keep faith in our contemporary context? What are the barriers to such faithfulness?

Liturgically this psalm suggests that we remember the faithfulness of God, who does not abandon her children. We are called to be the community that remains steadfast, that does not abandon our vision of the good. We are called not to give up hope, but to remain true to our vision.

L. SHANNON JUNG

arrival of the golden years, but also with life's hard blows (vv. 20–21). What is said regarding the dangers and sufferings that the elderly person faces conjures up the metaphor of the blacksmith's hammer striking metal when shaping it (see Prov. 27:17). He encounters—hence the image of the "hand" (*yad* and *kaf* in Hebrew)—evil, injustice, and cruelty up close (v. 4). He is pursued—like prey by a hunter—and defamed by his enemies, perhaps encouraged by the vulnerability that comes with old age (vv. 9–10). The injuries are nothing but a false interpretation of suffering as an abandonment from God. Therefore, the enemies prepare to attack, thinking that the elderly psalmist has no one who can protect and free him (v. 11).

The end of this elderly psalmist is not, as it would appear, defeat and abandonment. Far from that! Remembering his journey alongside God, in the good times and in the bad, the psalmist declares triumphantly, surrounded by sonorous stringed instruments within a liturgical context, that he has been rescued, and that everyone who had sought the psalmist's demise is now experiencing confusion and shame (vv. 22–24).

The Holy Week texts from the lectionary that accompany this psalm (Isa. 49:1–7; John 12:20–36; 1 Cor. 1:18–31) state that pain and sacrifice are part of an educational process and preparation for a redeeming mission: in the vision of the prophet Isaiah, that is the mission of every one of YHWH's servants; in the Gospel of John, that is the mission of Jesus, the true servant of God; in 1 Corinthians, that is the mission of every Christian, who, amid vulnerability and lack of knowledge, has been chosen by God to proclaim that which may seem offensive to some and foolishness to others.

EDESIO SANCHEZ

In Holy Week, Jesus reveals the profoundly divine alternative, another way, to the very natural, very human desire for vengeance. The other way comes from Jesus on the cross: "Father, forgive them; for they do not know what they are doing" (Luke 23:34). As we watch Jesus overcome his own fears, deal with his own sense of isolation, and reject a desire for vengeance, Jesus teaches us God's way.

Having named and acknowledged the reality of unrighteous behavior we find threatening, as well as our sense of isolation and the desire for vengeance it can produce, we preach the good news. We ask people to believe what the psalmist affirms: God, "you are my rock and my fortress" (v. 3).

Just as this sermon can name the evils that beset contemporary Christians, it can contain illustrations of people who understandably but wrongly interpreted their trials and tribulations as a sign God had forsaken them. There is nothing more powerful than a story of God's love confirmed.

Perhaps we use a biblical illustration about one of the numerous characters in Scripture who thought God had abandoned them. Or we use a story from recent history, such as the story of the Jewish people moving from Holocaust to the establishment of the nation of Israel. Or the illustration is personal, such as a woman who feared God had abandoned her to breast cancer, only to refind God as "a rock of refuge, a strong fortress" as she struggled to beat the disease.

Whatever the illustration, we cannot end our sermons by simply saying, "Keep hope alive." As preachers, we can do better than that. We can show concrete, historical moments where the hope of the faithful was vindicated.

We all observe the powers of injustice appearing to triumph in our world, communities, and personal lives. Holy Week and the psalmist lead us deep into the mystery of how God protects the righteous by empowering them, how God overcomes the forces of darkness by shining light in the world. Psalm 71 gives preachers an opportunity to link the hopes and fears of a Jewish psalmist thousands of years ago to those of contemporary Christians.

JOHN W. WIMBERLY

1 Corinthians 1:18-31

¹⁸For the message about the cross is foolishness to those who are perishing, but to us who are being saved it is the power of God. ¹⁹For it is written,
"I will destroy the wisdom of the wise,
    and the discernment of the discerning I will thwart."
²⁰Where is the one who is wise? Where is the scribe? Where is the debater of this age? Has not God made foolish the wisdom of the world? ²¹For since, in the wisdom of God, the world did not know God through wisdom, God decided, through the foolishness of our proclamation, to save those who believe. ²²For Jews demand signs and Greeks desire wisdom, ²³but we proclaim Christ crucified, a stumbling block to Jews and foolishness to Gentiles, ²⁴but to those who are the called, both Jews and Greeks, Christ the power of God and the

Theological Perspective

The gospel is countercultural and counterintuitive. The gospel is utter nonsense, scandalous even. The central mystery of the Christian faith seems more than a bit foolish at times. Just what is this mystery, this proclamation, this gospel? God chooses what is weak and powerless to communicate love to the world: Christ crucified for us. Salvation and redemption are offered to the whole world through the death of one human/divine person. This is the scandal of particularity. This is the scandal of the cross. Yet it makes a kind of strange sense to those of us who read the Bible, who believe the stories that over and over again show how God uses the weak, the unlikely, the least, the meek to bring hope to the world.

Paul's words evoke a number of knotty theological questions, especially concerning how we are saved and who is saved. There is the question of particularity: Can the one save the many? Or as some feminists have put it, "Can a male savior save women?" For Paul and his heirs, this one is the only one who can. "God became what we are so that we could become what God is," said Athanasius. The God/Man came to satisfy the justice of God, to do what we could not do ourselves, according to Anselm. Christ's sacrifice is sufficient; grace triumphs, Luther reminded us. It is the Lord of glory who died on the cross, Moltmann's "Crucified God." Or as Bonhoeffer put it, "God lets

Pastoral Perspective

In Holy Week the Christian community is invited to contemplate experience according to a different kind of logic: the "logic (word, logos) of the cross" (1 Cor. 1:18). In Holy Week we step from the halls of power, wealth, and wisdom and walk the way of the cross in order to experience what Paul calls "the wisdom of God."

For Paul, this way of understanding the world is a "calling" (1 Cor. 1: 24, 26). We are not schooled to understand the world this way. It is not part of our everyday upbringing. Worldly wisdom operates under a clear, cold logic. Might makes right. Success is sweet vindication. Power moves mountains. Winning is not everything; it's the only thing. Nothing succeeds like success. For the world, to fail, to be overcome in weakness, to be despised and brought low means God was not on your side. God is wisdom, power, and might—not foolishness, weakness, and failure.

Paul says we are called to see the world according to a different kind of logic. In our weakness is God's strength. In our confusion is God's wisdom. On the cross is God's Messiah.

"Cross logic" does not make any more sense to Americans than it did to Greeks and Jews in Paul's day. Take the case of Julie. Her husband was recovering from an accident that had prevented him

wisdom of God. [25]For God's foolishness is wiser than human wisdom, and God's weakness is stronger than human strength.

[26]Consider your own call, brothers and sisters: not many of you were wise by human standards, not many were powerful, not many were of noble birth. [27]But God chose what is foolish in the world to shame the wise; God chose what is weak in the world to shame the strong; [28]God chose what is low and despised in the world, things that are not, to reduce to nothing things that are, [29]so that no one might boast in the presence of God. [30]He is the source of your life in Christ Jesus, who became for us wisdom from God, and righteousness and sanctification and redemption, [31]in order that, as it is written, "Let the one who boasts, boast in the Lord."

Exegetical Perspective

First Corinthians 1:18–31 clarifies the meaning of Christ through an examination of the crucifixion. While Monday's text, Hebrews 9:11–15, deals with *how* the crucifixion of Christ achieves atonement for sins, today's text explores the *that* of the crucifixion, especially regarding its scandal and folly (v. 23). The passage is the beginning of a larger unit that ends in 3:18–23 with a recapitulation of the motifs of worldly wisdom and boasting. As is typical in his letters, Paul's reflections on the cross (esp. 1:26–31) are intended to solve practical problems facing the Corinthian church: "that all of you be in agreement and that there be no divisions among you, but that you be united in the same mind and the same purpose" (v. 10). What is at stake is nothing less than the heart of the gospel, that is, Christ crucified (1:23; 2:2), and the unity of the community it creates (1:10–17; 3:21–23; chaps. 12–14, esp. 12:4–26).

Declaring that Christ sent him to proclaim the gospel "not with wisdom of words" (*en sophia logou,* 1:17 KJV), Paul introduces the "word of the cross" (*ho logos ho tou staurou,* KJV "preaching of the cross," NRSV "message about the cross") as "foolishness to those who are perishing" but "power of God" to those who are being saved (v. 18). It is noteworthy that the word of the cross *as foolishness* is contrasted with the word of the cross not *as*

Homiletical Perspective

To the Corinthian church that is in the midst of a crisis, the apostle Paul contrasts God's wisdom and power, as manifested on the cross, with that of the world. Paul reminds his readers that God has called them, powerless and weak by human standards, through this divine wisdom and power. No one, therefore, can boast of anything before God, except through Christ. According to Paul, the wisdom of the world, which belongs to the wise and the powerful in the world, will not find God, for God's power has been manifested in a most unlikely way, the crucifixion.

The wisdom and power of God revealed in the cross of Jesus Christ may sound foolish to those who boast of being wise, and may seem even scandalous for many believers who adhere to the general social and political dividing lines within the sphere of the church. The foolishness of the gospel is anything but easy to preach, for we live in a competitive society, where the spirit of might, winning, and success dominates our minds and actions. Many of us fall under the spell of the mantra that only dominating forces like imperialism, militarism, and patriarchal hierarchy are powerful enough to save humanity. Moreover, the Christian church, a powerful social institution in the United States and in other countries of Christendom, has difficulty maintaining

1 Corinthians 1:18-31

Theological Perspective

himself be pushed out of the world onto the cross. He is weak and powerless in the world, and this is precisely the way, the only way, in which he is with us and helps us . . . only the suffering God can help."[1]

Not only the particularity of the cross, but the particularity of God's people causes scandal. If some of us believe and receive wisdom and salvation, what of those who continue to view the gospel as foolishness? Who is in and who is out? Who are the elect, the chosen, those who are being saved, and who are the ones who are perishing? If salvation is God's doing, then why bother preaching the gospel at all? If salvation is based on faith, then is belief a wise choice or a gift given only to the few? At different times in history, different groups of believers have wanted to see themselves as among the elect, and to see their detractors as damned.

Propagandists at the time of the Reformation loved to use cartoonlike pictures to convey their ideas. A favorite image shows the blind leading the blind. In one woodcut, the blind leaders are the scholastic theologians and the worldly philosophers—Thomas Aquinas and Plato and Aristotle—guiding the hapless monks and bishops into the abyss. Hopefully we have moved away from such caricatures; nonetheless, this is the kind of picture Paul paints. Some of us get it, and others do not. The good news of the gospel—the surprising, scandalous news of the gospel—makes sense to those of us who believe, even if it seems crazy to those who do not. The bestseller list is full of anti-God, antireligion, anti-Christian books. People of faith are ridiculed as anti-intellectual, unscientific, naive. Can we find comfort in Paul's words? Or is this just another case of rhetorical reframing?

Paul's words make us think about the scandal of the cross, and they make us think about the countercultural nature of the gospel. In Paul's time, it was dangerous to be a Christian, but for much of its history, the Christian church has been at the center of power. Some speak of our age as "post-Constantinian." By this they mean that Christianity is no longer the dominant force, even in so-called Western culture. The power shifts that occur in our postmodern age have placed us at listening posts where we can give these words of Paul a fresh hearing.

Paul's words speak of wisdom and salvation, but they also speak of power and weakness. It is contrary

1. Gustaf Aulén, *Christus Victor* (New York: Macmillan, 1931) offers a summary of various theories of atonement. The quote from Dietrich Bonhoeffer is from a letter dated July 16, 1944 (*Letters and Papers from Prison* [New York: Macmillan, 1953]. 360).

Pastoral Perspective

from working for the past three months. Her daughter, who had a congenital disease that rendered her helpless to care for herself, was becoming more difficult to handle. "Why is this happening to me?" she asked. "Is God testing me? I have been a good Christian my life long. Have I done something wrong? Is this my punishment?" The logic behind her words is that God is wisdom, power, and might. God would make things right for Julie if God wanted to do so. God does not want to do so. Why?

When we walk with Jesus to the cross on Holy Week, we walk with a loser. In the struggle to speak the truth, Jesus was silenced. In the battle to lead the people in the ways of God, Jesus was a casualty. On the stage of power in front of the people, Jesus was mocked. The logic of the cross tells us that, in Christ, God was silenced, God was a casualty, God was mocked. We know this because in Holy Week we live it. We walk the way of the cross.

Paul says we are called to understand God in this way, not just in Holy Week but in every week. It is God's demand on us—our calling. When we accept the logic of the cross and believe that the power of God is expressed in the absurdity of a crucified Messiah, we have a word for Julie. We can invite her to understand that God is in the midst of her life in a powerful way and not far off, not testing her or punishing her or withholding the blessings of God, but bringing God's blessings close through power and wisdom in the midst of suffering. We can say that just as Jesus walked the way of the cross, so Jesus walks with her in the midst of her suffering, questioning, and pain.

We live in an age when the logic of the cross is ridiculed. The prosperity gospel claims God's power will make you rich. Some Christian leaders claim when God's power is wed to the power of the government, God's will is done. Some countries and cultures claim that God is on their side and that their ability to crush the evil opponent proves their claim. In such a context, the claim that God comes in weakness, foolishness, and failure is a tough sell.

Paul says that there is power in this logic, power in the word of the cross—none other than the power of God. That power is experienced when the believer understands the world from the point of view of God's wisdom, the logic of the cross.

For Paul, it begins with the crucified Messiah. The illogic of that event is so overwhelming that it must be a wisdom beyond us, the wisdom of God. Christ looks the fool with the sign "King of the Jews" hanging over his head as he hangs from the cross.

Tuesday of Holy Week

wisdom, but as the "power of God." That is, the preaching of the gospel effects salvation because it is God's power, not because human beings can *become wise* enough to recognize it as wisdom instead of folly. Salvation is not achievable by human means, but by the inbreaking of God's salvific power from beyond human capacity or effort (v. 21).

Also worth noting is 2:5, which contrasts the "power of God" (*dynamis theou*) to "human wisdom" (*sophia anthrōpōn*) as a kind of summary of Paul's argument in 1:19–21. He quotes Isaiah 29:14 to say that God "will destroy the wisdom of the wise," which verse 20 calls the "wisdom of the world" (*hē sophia tou kosmou*) representing "this age" (cf. 3:19). No matter how sophisticated (cf. 13:2), human wisdom stumbles over the foolish proclamation, not because of its unsophistication, but because of the very core of its content, that is, Christ crucified (vv. 21, 23).

Regarding worldly wisdom, verse 21 suggests that its ignorance of God is due to its reliance on human resources rather than on God's power, which is the scandalous word of the cross (1 Cor. 1:18, 24; 2:5; 4:20; cf. Rom. 1:16, 18–32). Gospel preaching of Christ crucified is inevitably foolish to an age and a world founded on their own wisdom (vv. 20–23). The solution does not lie in better marketing of the folly of the cross through clever preaching (v. 17; 2:4). Foolish preaching does not indicate human failure to master good rhetoric; rather, it is the means of revelation that God deliberately chose in order to save believers (vv. 21, 27–28). The "wisdom of God" (vv. 24, 30; 2:7) *is* the foolishness of preaching the crucified Christ (vv. 18, 21, 23; cf. "folly ["foolishness" NRSV] of God" in v. 25).

Thus, the wisdom of God can never be converted into human wisdom to compete among other human wisdoms; nor can there be a method that human beings can use to access God's wisdom (v. 21). Yet that disqualification authenticates it as truly divine, that is, not of human design or subject to human control or possession. If the word of the cross were to satisfy human criteria for approval— whether the Jewish demand for signs (or miracles) or the Greek demand for wisdom or logic—then that revelation would reveal its inauthenticity (vv. 22–24). The word of the cross will, by its divine intent and content (vv. 21, 23), remain insufficient or offensive to a world that can see God's wisdom only as a stumbling block or foolishness.

While verses 18–25 explore the word of the cross in a general way, verses 26–31 deal with the Corinthian community. If the gospel is scandalous

the credibility of this seemingly foolish biblical stumbling block, for such a church does not really have much room for the God who is revealed in the cross, the least expected place on earth. How can a prestigious church proclaim the crucified Christ?

However, looking deeper into the human situation, we cannot but realize the folly of the wisdom and power of the world when we raise the following questions: Who, through a show of force, can eliminate the self-destroying habits of family members and colleagues who have fallen prey to alcohol and hard drugs? Who, through a show of force, can convince young people suffering from chronic or suicidal depression, of life's meaning? Who, through a show of force, can restore the relationship with our "prodigal" children? Who, through a show of force, can bring hope to the desperately helpless in prisons, refugee enclaves, homeless shelters, and nursing homes? What society, through power alone, can break racial, gender, and class prejudices and forge solidarity with the powerless and the marginalized? What nation, through power alone, can ensure world peace? There is no sword that can cut away human problems without hurting people. At best, it can only eradicate one problem by substituting another. We witness our military, whose security demands more and more instruments of destruction and whose budget soars to astronomical heights, without any promise of a better future. Certainly the power of the world cannot win over the human spirit; the wisdom of the world cannot achieve ultimate peace on earth.

Paul convinces us that, in contrast to the wisdom of the world, Christ crucified is real wisdom and that, in contrast to the power of the world, love revealed on the cross is the only real power. In many cases, love is considered powerless because it has of itself no immediate tangible realities. However, God chooses what seems foolish and weak by human standards to make foolish the wisdom of the world and fulfill God's saving work through this. What a paradox! Powerlessness is power—and power is powerlessness. Human powerlessness is the domain of God's power.

The proclamation of this paradox is good news for many believers who themselves identify with the lowly and despised. Mary the mother of Jesus, who is the least of the least in her colonized patriarchal society, perceives a reversal of the world order through divine wisdom and power, and in the Magnificat she praises with joy God's grace granted to her. Her praise has been echoed by other female

1 Corinthians 1:18-31

Theological Perspective

to common sense to think of God's power as weak, to speak of proclamation itself as foolish. Yet this is a recurring theme in Scripture and a theme taken up again and again by theologians. Calvin developed the notion of accommodation to speak of divine condescension. God "babbles" like a nursemaid so that our childish minds might receive a divine word. In Christ, God comes to us as a helpless child, one who grows up to be despised and rejected. The Spirit helps us in our weakness and speaks through fallible human beings. For Calvin, the one who deigns to preach God's Word is the most foolish one of all, but this is the way of the accommodating One. God could have spoken eloquent oracles, could have shouted from the heavens; instead the likes of us are called to preach. As Calvin puts it, "When a puny man risen from the dust speaks in God's name, at this point we best evidence our piety and obedience toward God if we show ourselves teachable toward his minister, although he excels us in nothing."[2]

So Paul is also calling us to examine our theology of preaching and to see our task as preachers as a kind of foolishness, the preacher as clown or jester. This is not to say that the gospel is some kind of divine joke, but to acknowledge the ironic humor in the whole enterprise. We are to enter the pulpit in humility. All Christians are to take the gospel seriously and at the same time to resist the urge to take ourselves too seriously. Those who preach and all who practice the gospel are to be fools for Christ.

REBECCA BUTTON PRICHARD

Pastoral Perspective

Christ is weak, unable to save even himself from a painful death. Christ is despised and brought low. The "called" participate in Christ's life through their own experiences of their lack of wisdom, their lack of power, their failure, and their weakness. According to Paul, it is why they are called; they know something of Christ's experience already from their own lowly positions and lack of wisdom. Only those who have some experience of humility can get the logic of the cross. Paul seems to say, "It takes one to know one."

Understanding experience through the logic of the cross takes practice. Holy Week offers a chance to practice thinking about life according to the wisdom of God. How is it that the Son of almighty God was crucified? How come the powerful were so wrong? Why was it necessary that the Son of Man suffer and die and on the third day rise? What is the power of the cross? These answers come only when we enter into the suffering of Christ and stand with him as he is tried by Pilate and mocked by the soldiers. Shout with the crowd to crucify him. Cry with Mary and the others at his crucifixion and death. These experiences will echo our own humiliation and loss. Through this holy practice, we will know the logic of the cross and find for ourselves the power, the wisdom, and the strength of God.

PETER AND DEBRA SAMUELSON

---

2. John Calvin, *Institutes of the Christian Religion*, ed. John T. McNeill, trans. Ford Lewis Battles (Philadelphia: Westminster Press, 1960), 4.3.1.

Exegetical Perspective

and foolish, then so is the community that the gospel creates under that unifying word of the cross. Thus, the Corinthians should find themselves united in rejecting and relinquishing worldly standards of wisdom, power, or nobility (vv. 26–29) while being judged by the world as foolish, weak, or "low and despised" (vv. 27–28), the purpose of which is to deny the church any foundation for boasting or looking attractive to the world (v. 29). Conversely, if the church finds itself acceptable to the world by offering something to boast about, it proves itself to be false, by virtue of meeting criteria demanded by Jews and Greeks instead of rejecting them (vv. 18, 22–23; cf. Gal. 5:11). The same standard applies to boasting and competition regarding gifts *within* the church that threaten the unity of the church (chaps. 12–14, esp. 12:4–26; cf. 1:12).

Perhaps Ted Turner understood Paul's proclamation of Christ crucified quite well when he told an audience at the American Humanist Association in 1990 that "Christianity is a religion for losers." Not only might Paul concur, but he might add that that judgment by those who are wise, powerful, and of noble birth (v. 26) should lead believers to unite in hearing the word of the cross together again, rather than compete with one another about who is wiser, stronger, or of nobler birth.

However remote the specific problems in Corinth seem today, Paul's bold words can be just as compelling, relevant, and troubling as they appear to have been. Our post-Enlightenment world can be just as skeptical of Christ crucified— for example, see the works of Richard Dawkins, Daniel Dennett, or Sam Harris. Interestingly, such atheists are called the "brights" (cf. 1:20). Likewise, postmodern critics who challenge the very notion or validity of any objective foundation can often deconstruct the crucifixion as a metaphorical cipher for various human desires or societal dynamics, for example, Freud, Marx, or Nietzsche. It would appear that the word of the cross still scandalizes the wisdom of the world, as long as those who are called proclaim Christ crucified, the power of God and the wisdom of God (vv. 23–24).

KANG-YUP NA

Homiletical Perspective

disciples throughout the world: Mary Magdalene, St. Nina of Georgia, Hildegard of Bingen, Sor Juana Inés de la Cruz of Mexico, Sojourner Truth of the United States, Wha Soon Cho of Korea. Paul's paradoxical affirmation about the way God acts in the world has also been witnessed in numerous human activities such as the antislavery and suffrage movements, colonial and postcolonial struggles, the civil-rights and antiapartheid movements, and democratic and human-rights movements against dictatorships in recent history and today. Behind these revolutionary movements, preachers can recognize the divine support of human powerlessness, the subversive power of God's wisdom.

Preaching the wisdom and power of God is the good news, even for those who are boastful by human standards, for it leads them to humility by awakening them to the realization that the source of true power is God and that they may trust God, rather than their own cleverness or personal ambitions. Preaching the foolishness of the gospel is also a reminder for ministers and church leaders, who are tempted to assume that their ministry must be accompanied by triumphant fanfare and enthusiastic approbation. They must remember not to boast in the *presence* of God but instead to "boast in the Lord" (v. 31).

Therefore, preaching the wisdom and power of God in the Christ crucified has power to reorient our thoughts about God and about ourselves by renewing our identity as Christians. Such preaching serves not only to give moral instruction for humility against boasting, but also to call the community again and again to become what it is. Toward this goal, preachers are called to search for God with humility, to see God's radical presence in the last place the world would want to look, and to witness to the subversive power of God, which the wisdom of the world considers to be weakness and folly. In this context, all who listen humbly and attentively to the paradoxical affirmations about the ways God acts in the world will be invited to become agents of God's subversive power and wisdom.

EUNJOO M. KIM

John 12:20-36

²⁰Now among those who went up to worship at the festival were some Greeks. ²¹They came to Philip, who was from Bethsaida in Galilee, and said to him, "Sir, we wish to see Jesus." ²²Philip went and told Andrew; then Andrew and Philip went and told Jesus. ²³Jesus answered them, "The hour has come for the Son of Man to be glorified. ²⁴Very truly, I tell you, unless a grain of wheat falls into the earth and dies, it remains just a single grain; but if it dies, it bears much fruit. ²⁵Those who love their life lose it, and those who hate their life in this world will keep it for eternal life. ²⁶Whoever serves me must follow me, and where I am, there will my servant be also. Whoever serves me, the Father will honor.

²⁷"Now my soul is troubled. And what should I say—'Father, save me from this hour'? No, it is for this reason that I have come to this hour. ²⁸Father, glorify your name." Then a voice came from heaven, "I have glorified it, and I will glorify

Theological Perspective

"The hour has come for the Son of Man to be glorified" (v. 23). Jesus' words to his disciples signal the major theological theme of this passage, that Jesus' glorification is nothing other than his impending death on the cross. What follows is an example of John's paradoxical thinking. Jesus' glorification in death links him to God his Father as well as to his followers, those whom the passage will call "children of light" at its conclusion.

Throughout the passage, we hear references to the hour of Jesus' glorification (v. 23), the glorification of God's name (v. 28), and Jesus being "lifted up from earth" (v. 32). To explain to the crowds what this talk of glorification and being lifted up actually means, Jesus uses the following allegory: "Unless a grain of wheat falls into the earth and dies, it remains just a single grain; but if it dies, it bears much fruit" (v. 24). Here we have yet another instance of paradoxical imagery. How might the preacher help the congregation understand theologically what John speaks of as the glorification of Jesus?

John's Gospel presents in this passage what sixteenth-century reformer Martin Luther later terms "the theology of the cross." According to Luther, the theologian of glory confuses Christ's glory with earthly glory, power, triumph. Indeed, the author of John's Gospel notes a few verses later that

Pastoral Perspective

Tim Douglas is a veteran of World War II. He served in the infantry as a young man. He fought in the Battle of the Bulge in 1944, the bloodiest battle U.S. forces endured in that war. He came home after the war to settle into a teaching career and to raise his children. He is a gentle, thoughtful man, by all accounts. He never talks about the war, but his eyes are haunted.

Friday morning Bible study is not the same without Tim. On the rare occasion when he misses the 7:00 a.m. gathering, someone else has to play his role. However they never do it quite as well; they are too easy on the others. Tim is the skeptic of the crowd, though not a particularly liberal one. His "Yes, but . . ." is usually directed at the young pastor who has just introduced some new idea about that day's lection. She is inclined to wonder aloud about the nature of truth, the divinity of Jesus, the power of forgiveness, the meaning of the cross. Tim's keen mind will hold her ideas up against his more traditional view of faith. "Yes, but . . . what about the 'eye for an eye' commandment? Yes, but . . . if truth is subjective, how can we know or believe anything? Yes, but . . . what is 'the judgment of the world'?"

Tim has a particularly hard time when the pastor uses the phrase "universal salvation" over the course of several weeks. He listens intently to her theological

it again." ²⁹The crowd standing there heard it and said that it was thunder. Others said, "An angel has spoken to him." ³⁰Jesus answered, "This voice has come for your sake, not for mine. ³¹Now is the judgment of this world; now the ruler of this world will be driven out. ³²And I, when I am lifted up from the earth, will draw all people to myself." ³³He said this to indicate the kind of death he was to die. ³⁴The crowd answered him, "We have heard from the law that the Messiah remains forever. How can you say that the Son of Man must be lifted up? Who is this Son of Man?" ³⁵Jesus said to them, "The light is with you for a little longer. Walk while you have the light, so that the darkness may not overtake you. If you walk in the darkness, you do not know where you are going. ³⁶While you have the light, believe in the light, so that you may become children of light."

After Jesus had said this, he departed and hid from them.

Exegetical Perspective

This passage contains what might be called the Johannine Gethsemane, where Jesus confronts his imminent death. It follows closely the Pharisees' comment that the world had gone after him (12:19), the cue for the Greeks who wanted to see Jesus. Philip and Andrew appear together in John (1:40, 44–46; 6:5–9; 12:22). In this scene and in John 6:5–9 Philip seems to be the less perceptive of the pair. Earlier, the authorities speculated that Jesus would go to teach Greeks (7:35; cf. 8:21–22). He was indeed "the Savior of the world" (4:42), but he could not bypass his death in order to go to the Greeks. The coming of the Greeks, therefore, indicated to Jesus that the time of his death, his "hour" (2:4; 7:30; 8:20; 13:1), had come. John speaks paradoxically of Jesus' death as glorification (see 7:39; 12:16; 13:31–32; 17:1, 4–5), and Jesus uses "the Son of Man" as a self-reference when speaking of his return to the Father (3:13–14; 6:62; 8:28; 12:34; 13:31).

Jesus' saying about the grain of wheat does not occur in the Synoptics but has the ring of an authentic parable. When the Greeks requested to see him, Jesus pondered the meaning of their coming in relation to his mission. This led him to express the basic principle of his life: "Unless a grain of wheat falls into the earth and dies, it remains just a single grain; but if it dies, it bears much fruit" (12:24). He came

Homiletical Perspective

Someone should have warned me. It was like a punch in the stomach. I arrived as a cocky young seminarian to preach in place of the pastor who was sick. I was ready. I had something important to say to these people. As I made my way confidently into the pulpit, my eyes fell upon a brass plaque, made shiny from decades of hopeful polishing by a faithful member. Cut into the brass were the words: *We want to see Jesus.* The next fifteen minutes were the hardest time I have ever done in the pulpit.

The story is told of Anthony the Great, the fourth-century leader of Egyptian monasticism. As the story goes, a well-worn monk and a young novice would journey each year into the desert to seek the wisdom of Anthony. Upon finding him, the monk would seek instruction from the great Anthony on the life of prayer, devotion to Jesus, and his understanding of the Scriptures. While the monk was asking all the questions the novice would simply stand quietly and take it all in.

The next year the well-worn monk and the young novice again went into the desert to find Anthony and seek his counsel. Again, the monk was full of questions, while the novice simply stood by without saying a word. This pattern was repeated year after year. Finally, Anthony said to the young novice, "Why do you come here? You come here year after

John 12:20-36

Theological Perspective

the Pharisees "loved human glory more than the glory that comes from God" (v. 43). For John, as a theologian of the cross, Jesus' glorification is precisely the "lifting up" of the Son of Man by means of his willingness to go to the cross. This perspective prompts Luther to insist, "The cross alone is our theology." In the cross, Jesus is glorified, salvation is wrought, God's love for the world is revealed.

In articulating a theology of the cross, Luther demonstrates how theologies of glory try to fool us into thinking that God's glory is akin to the glory of this world. Luther observes, however, "the desire for glory is not satisfied by the acquisition of glory."[1] Therefore, the theology of the cross must come to understand the glorification of Jesus as something altogether different. As the Johannine narrative repeatedly insists, Jesus' glorification comes out of his death—thus the allegory on how the grain of wheat must cease being a grain if it is to bear fruit (v. 24). Only if one hates life "in this world" will that life be kept for eternal life (v. 25). In this paradox, Luther repeatedly explains, lies "the good of the cross."

However, how can glorification wrought through violent death on a cross possibly be good? In John's Gospel, Jesus' death is always interpreted in light of Jesus' life and life-giving work. On the cross, God's glory is both revealed and redefined. For, as we hear in the middle of this passage, Jesus' glorification through the cross is simultaneously the glorification of God the Father (v. 28). In all the Gospel accounts, we see that in going to the cross Jesus must surrender his will to the will of God. Utter surrender to God's will—for anyone, Jesus included—is a deeply destabilizing experience.[2] Verse 27 begins with the "now" of Jesus' troubled soul, knowing what is ahead for himself and his followers. However, missing from the Johannine narrative is Jesus' plea to God that this cup might be removed from him (Matt. 26:39; Mark 14:36; Luke 22:42). It is clear in John's telling of the story that Jesus' glorification, as Jesus himself well knows, is about the self-revelation of God the Father. What is revealed in Jesus' impending death is God's refusal to act with any power other than self-giving love.[3] God's glory is manifest in and through Jesus' startlingly loving gift of himself.

This extravagant act of love also means that "now is the judgment of this world; now the ruler of this

Pastoral Perspective

opining. The idea that perhaps there is no after-death place of eternal punishment, or that such a place might be empty, is difficult for him to reconcile with his worldview. That God refuses to give up on anyone—like a woman looking for her lost coin, or a shepherd abandoning ninety-nine sheep to find the one who strayed, or the father who never gives up hope that his son will return from the far country—sounds nice, but surely it cannot mean that God welcomes everyone, waits for everyone. How can you believe in heaven if you do not believe hell?

Today's lection raises the question of universal salvation. Upon witnessing Jesus enter Jerusalem to crowds shouting, "Hosanna! Blessed is the one who comes in the name of the Lord—the King of Israel!" (v. 13), the Pharisees mutter to each other, "Look, the world has gone after him!" (v. 19). As confirmation of this observation, the next verse points to the presence of Greeks in the crowd, people who represent the world beyond Israel and people beyond Jews. The Greeks inquire about Jesus to Philip, who goes to Andrew, who goes to Jesus for the answer. Jesus responds with an explanation of how he must die an earthly death in order to bring more life to the world: "And I, when I am lifted up from the earth, will draw all people to myself" (v. 32).

How does the notion of universal salvation play in the pews? Not easily in communities deeply rooted in the common cultural acceptance of the existence of heaven and hell. Even nominally religious folks in a congregation will balk when the one thing they thought they understood—good people are rewarded and bad people are punished, if not in this life, then in the next—is challenged. Both the skeptics and the pious are likely to say, "Yes, but . . . without the carrots and sticks, why do we bother with church?"

These are deeply theological issues at stake, but they are likewise deeply pastoral. What does a congregation look like that is so ensconced in reward-and-punishment thinking that even the act of forgiveness becomes a test of faith? Second chances might be offered, but rigid guidelines for bestowing mercy must first be met. That place at the right hand of Jesus might actually be earned, if everything is done just right.

On the other hand, what does a congregation look like that has completely lost the capacity to hold people accountable for unethical behavior and has carried forgiveness to an unhealthy extreme? A truly destructive individual or group could wreak havoc while the merciful just watch, hoping—and praying—that they will change some day.

---

1. Martin Luther, "Heidelberg Disputation," in *Martin Luther's Basic Theological Writings*, ed. Timothy Lull (Minneapolis: Fortress Press, 1989), 45.
2. Anthony J. Kelly and Francis J. Moloney, *Experiencing God in the Gospel of John* (New York: Paulist Press, 2003), 258.
3. Ibid., 268.

then to the existential choice that would make the difference between life and death . . . "What should I say?" He thought of the way of self-preservation: should he say, "Father, save me from this hour"? However that way would mean renouncing his mission. He chose instead the way of self-sacrifice, which was also the way to realize his redemptive vocation: "Father, glorify your name" (12:23–28). To live for the glory of God, that is, to live so as to make known the very character of God, was the purpose of his life (1:18), and he taught his disciples that this was also to be the purpose of their lives (20:21), because to be his disciple is to share his mission.

The principle that "those who love their life will lose it, and those who hate their life in this world will keep it for eternal life" (12:25) is echoed in the other Gospels (Matt. 10:39; Mark 8:35; Luke 17:33). Every person continually makes decisions that force a choice between self-directedness and service to others in the name of Jesus. Do we further our interests, feather our nests, or do we give ourselves in the service of others? What animates our lives? Jesus challenged those who would serve him to follow his example.

In John, there is no account of forty days of temptation, and when Jesus enters the garden across the Kidron, there is no anguish over his coming death. He is one with the Father (10:30), and he is supremely in control (18:11). Following the coming of the Greeks, however, Jesus is troubled (11:33, 38; 13:21). The Johannine Jesus would never pray, "Not my will but yours," because he and the Father are one, and the Son does only what the Father gives him to do (5:19). He entertains the thought of asking the Father to deliver him but rejects it immediately. He was sent to make the Father known (1:18) and to be "the Lamb of God who takes away the sin of the world" (1:29, 36).

The voice from heaven answers enigmatically, "I have glorified it, and I will glorify it again" (12:28). This is the only heavenly voice in John; there is no voice from heaven at Jesus' baptism and no account of the transfiguration. The Johannine Jesus does not need such assurance, however. The voice from heaven was for the benefit of others (11:42), but even this sign was open to interpretation. Some said it thundered; others said they heard the voice of an angel. Human experience is always open to interpretation, and proof never removes the need for faith. Nevertheless, faithfulness opens deeper levels of understanding.

John's "realized eschatology" affirms that our hope for the future is already being realized in Jesus'

year, yet you never ask any questions, you never desire my counsel, and you never seek my wisdom. Why do you come? Can you not speak?" The young novice spoke for the first time in the presence of the great saint. "It is enough just to see you. It is enough, for me, just to see you."

When the Greeks asked to see Jesus, what were they seeking?

Professor Richard C. Hoefler was a taskmaster around those aspects of homiletics he believed to be the most important. He was an endless source of exegetical advice, pastoral insight, and rhetorical instruction. He cared as deeply for his students as for his subject matter. He was never too busy to welcome one more discouraged young preacher into his office, and we always left him sincerely believing that we really could preach in ways that would make a difference in people's lives. While all of our seminary professors had their own gifts and taught us much, Hoefler had a particular gift for connecting with students and inspiring us to be our very best.

Years later, shortly after his death, I attended a reunion with a number of my seminary classmates. As we spent time together reminiscing about our time in seminary, our memories of Hoefler were central to the conversations. It all fell into place for me when one of my classmates commented, "I went to him when I needed to see the answer." That is exactly right, I thought to myself. More than anything he taught us or did for us, Hoefler was able to be transparent, so that everyone who encountered him could see the answer.

In the Gospel for Tuesday in Holy Week, Jesus is transparent about who he is and what is coming. The questions and answers of the dialogue do not provide much new information. What is here we have seen elsewhere, and we know well. This encounter is less about having the answers from Jesus than about seeing Jesus as he makes his way gently toward the cross. All of the dialogue—important exchanges for sure—invites us to see the answer, to see Jesus.

A particularly invitational moment in this Gospel comes when Jesus says, "And I, when I am lifted up from the earth, will draw all people to myself" (v. 32). Is there a certain magnetism that pulls at us when we *see* Jesus? How serious was Jesus when he said "all people"?

Edwin Markham was an American poet in the first half of the twentieth century. His serious poetry is greatly undervalued and has much to commend it.

John 12:20-36

Theological Perspective

world will be driven out" (v. 31). Thus, the glorification of God by way of the cross is inescapably also a judgment on the world's inability to accept the bodily presence of God and the love God offers concretely, in and through the material world. The crowd shows that understanding does not come easily; after hearing about Jesus' glorification and how all people will be drawn to him, Jesus' mission is no clearer to them than before. First the crowd interprets God's voice speaking to Jesus as thunder (v. 29), and after he explains that he must die, the people ask, "How can you say that the Son of Man must be lifted up? Who is this Son of Man?" (v. 34).

The passage concludes with another allegory from Jesus, where he offers his followers a new identity. By embracing Jesus' glorification on the cross, through an acceptance of the cruciform shape of all existence—including their own—they can "become children of light" (v. 36b). Children of the light are, in Luther's language, theologians of the cross. They are followers who know and accept that God's glory is accessible only through the crucified one. In order to serve and follow Jesus, one must live by different rules, where glorification is found in death, and following the glorified one leads directly into a cruciform existence. For Jesus is clear: "Where I am, there will my servant be also" (v. 26b). A theologian of the cross, therefore, not only acknowledges the cruciform nature of Jesus' glorification, but understands that living in close proximity to the cross is an inescapable dimension of following Jesus.

This paradoxical claim refuses tidily to resolve itself, as we see clearly through the final words of the passage: "He departed and hid from them" (v. 36c). This new identity as children of the light also offers comfort in knowing the presence of the light, the glory, the exaltation, even when there is apparent evidence to the contrary.

DEANNA THOMPSON

Pastoral Perspective

Or perhaps a congregation living with the conviction that ultimately God will not let go of anyone, will construe its life to be one of hope and confidence in a final glorious resolution, when God will wipe away every tear from their eyes, and mourning and crying and pain will be no more. Such confidence might propel them to a labor of love, sharing this vision, improving the lives of those around them, and caring for the world that God has created for this time and place. It would not lull them into complacency, but spur them to action, even to loving accountability.

Not all pastoral concerns raised by teaching universal salvation will be congregational. Some, perhaps most, will be much more personal. The threat of eternal punishment is not always directed toward the other. Sometimes it is ourselves we cannot quite forgive, the ones we believe God has abandoned.

Tim Douglas struggles with the notion of universal salvation, not so much because he needs a place to send murderous tyrants. He resists, not because he cannot bring himself to forgive his enemies, but because he cannot completely forgive himself for his own part in the war. He struggles with it because his own damnation somehow helps him make sense of it. He has never spoken about the war, but it haunts his eyes. He says he truly wants to believe that God never gives up on any of us, that none of us is eternally punished, but he cannot quite get there. He is living in his own hell in this time and this place.

Jesus says, "The light is with you for a little longer. Walk while you have the light, so that the darkness may not overtake you" (v. 35).

VERITY A. JONES

Exegetical Perspective

incarnation and death (3:19–21; 5:24–25). The judgment *is now* and the ruler of this world, Satan, *will be* driven out (12:31). Jesus' death will not be humiliation (cf. Mark 10:33–34; Phil. 2:8). Instead, in John, his death is his exaltation, his coronation as king. Jesus therefore refers to his death in three "lifting up" sayings (3:14; 8:28; 12:32). When he is "lifted up," he will "draw all people" to himself (12:32). The coming of the Greeks signaled the time for this global extension of his mission. The *titulus* placed over Jesus on the cross was written in three languages so that all could read it (19:20), and at the symbolically charged catch of fish the same verb "to draw" occurs (12:32; 21:11). Jesus' ministry among such people as Nathanael, Nicodemus, the Samaritan woman, and the man born blind was just a prelude to the universality of the mission of the church.

The crowd responds to Jesus' self-reference, "the Son of Man," recognizing that it is a messianic claim but misunderstanding its application to Jesus and his death. The people did not expect a Messiah who would be put to death, but Jesus used the crowd's lack of understanding to invoke another metaphor. He was the light that had come into the world (1:4–5, 9; 3:19; 8:12; 9:5). "Walking in the light" became a metaphor for living in accordance with Jesus' teachings (1 John 1:7; 2:9–11). Responding to the light in turn confirms the status of the believers as "children of light," a metaphor which the Gospel of John shares with the authors of the Qumran scrolls (1QS 3.13–4.26) and others who saw the world in dualistic categories. The principle remains, therefore, that how we live reveals who we are.

R. ALAN CULPEPPER

Homiletical Perspective

He is best remembered though for a single little verse called "Outwitted":

> He drew a circle that shut me out—
>   Heretic, a rebel, a thing to flout.
> But Love and I had the wit to win:
>   We drew a circle that took him in![1]

I imagine Love (Jesus) drawing the circle that takes everyone in. A well-worn prayer says it this way:

> Lord Jesus Christ, you stretched out your arms of love on the hard wood of the cross that everyone might come within the reach of your saving embrace: So clothe us in your Spirit that we, reaching forth our hands in love, may bring those who do not know you to the knowledge and love of you; for the honor of your Name. *Amen.*[2]

In his novel *The Shoes of the Fisherman,* Morris West writes about an imaginary pope who keeps a secret diary. In that diary can be found these words:

> Yesterday I met a whole man. It is a rare experience, but always an illuminating one. It costs so much to be a full human being that there are very few who have the enlightenment, or the courage, to pay the price. One has to abandon altogether the search for security, and reach out to the risk of living with full arms. One has to embrace the world like a lover, and yet demand no easy return of love. One has to accept pain as a condition of existence. One has to court doubt and darkness as the cost of knowing. One needs a will stubborn in conflict, but apt to the total consequence of living and dying.[3]

As we walk the way of the cross during this Holy Week, are we prepared to walk with Jesus, abandoning the search for security, and reaching out to the risk of living with full arms?

J. NEIL ALEXANDER

1. Online at http://www.theotherpages.org/poems/mark01.html
2. *The Book of Common Prayer* (New York: Seabury Press, 1979), 101.
3. Morris West, *The Shoes of the Fisherman* (New York: William Morrow, 1968), 254.

Isaiah 50:4-9a

⁴The Lord God has given me
  the tongue of a teacher,
that I may know how to sustain
  the weary with a word.
Morning by morning he wakens—
  wakens my ear
  to listen as those who are taught.
⁵The Lord God has opened my ear,
  and I was not rebellious,
  I did not turn backward.
⁶I gave my back to those who struck me,
  and my cheeks to those who pulled out the beard;

Theological Perspective

This third of Second Isaiah's Servant Songs brings something altogether startling: the Servant proclaims that the ministry of the proclamation of God's *mishpat* to the whole world will be performed through suffering. The quiet voice of the Servant in 42:1–4 and the swordlike voice of the Servant in 49:1–9 are now joined by a Servant who decides to suffer when confronted by those who would reject the mission. This idea had immense importance for emerging Christianity and stands at the very center of Christian theological reflection on the ministry of Jesus of Nazareth.

Suffering does not appear in the third Song at first. "The Lord God has given me the tongue of those who are taught" (v. 4a RSV). The phrase, "those who are taught," could be read "disciples," since in Isaiah 54:13 the prophet promises the exiles that "all your children shall be taught by the LORD," shall become God's disciples. The Servant here reiterates in other words that God has made him a disciple.

As before, the Servant-disciple is taught to "sustain the weary with a word," focusing on the act of speaking. The two previous Songs have described the Servant's work as speaking what God has provided, and we might expect the same to occur here. However, suddenly the emphasis shifts. "Morning by morning God wakens my *ear* to listen

Pastoral Perspective

If the Servant Songs from Second Isaiah assigned to Monday and Tuesday of Holy Week have already left the mark of ambiguity and paradox on the journey toward Easter, the way now takes a more dire turn. Tuesday's text described the Servant as "one deeply despised, abhorred by the nations, the slave of rulers" (49:7). Now, as the still-cryptic figure continues the personal narrative of servanthood, the testimony adds a new layer of danger: physical violence, torture, humiliation.

It also adds a crucial new dimension to the Servant's experience: the spiritual discipline of obedience: "I was not rebellious. . . . I gave my back to those who struck me. . . . I did not hide my face" (50:5–6). At a deeper level it intimates two familiar kinds of courage that the Servant has discovered at the heart of the mission. In the inner life of the Servant, the seed of obedience has grown into *resilience*: "I know that I shall not be put to shame" (v. 7). No mortification of flesh or spirit can finally impugn the integrity of one so rooted in the will and presence of God. In the outer life of the Servant—with the stakes escalating toward climactic confrontation—obedience manifests itself as *resistance*.

Obedience becomes resilience as the Servant acquires "the tongue of a teacher" and the opened ear that "listen(s) as those who are taught" (v. 4).

I did not hide my face
　　from insult and spitting.

7The Lord God helps me;
　　therefore I have not been disgraced;
　　therefore I have set my face like flint,
　　　and I know that I shall not be put to shame;
8 　he who vindicates me is near.
　　Who will contend with me?
　　　Let us stand up together.
　　Who are my adversaries?
　　　Let them confront me.
9It is the Lord God who helps me;
　　who will declare me guilty?

Exegetical Perspective

A curious translation problem confronts us in the first verse of today's reading from the Hebrew Bible. The problem is not with the text itself, which seems well-preserved, nor with the word in question, which is fairly common. Instead, translators seem unable to say exactly what the text says! The major English translations vary broadly on the gift the Lord has given to the Servant: is it the "tongue of a teacher" (NRSV), a "skilled tongue" (JPSV), an "instructed tongue" (NIV), or perhaps the "tongue of the learned" (KJV)? Yet, when the same word, *limmudim*, appears later in the verse, it causes little controversy:

> Morning by morning he wakens—
> 　wakens my ear
> to listen as *those who are taught*.
> 　　(Isa. 50:4; emphasis added)

Surely the same word in the same context should be translated the same way both times. The Servant says, "The Lord God has given me the tongue of *those who are taught*."

Perhaps the problem is that Bible translators are usually Bible professors. We believe that teachers talk and students listen, that teachers should speak from authority. Is that really so? My own experience as a teacher has taught me that my teaching is most effective when I am most engaged in the material myself:

Homiletical Perspective

The calls come, late in the night, to every pastor's house. "We're at the hospital," a mother whispers. "Something terrible has just happened," a brother cries. "Can you come right away?" a stranger's voice implores. We go, of course, leave the warmth of home and go, aware yet again that we will arrive with empty hands and sorrowful hearts, and with no answers whatsoever for another family in the midst of trial, in the midst of suffering, in the midst of fear.

We will join the family in their vigil, find hot coffee or ice-cold water, offer an embrace and a calm presence, we hope. There are a few words we have found useful in the past. We recite prayers that we hope will bring solace. We read from a couple of psalms, or recall them by memory. This night at least, we will not dare to offer reasons. Reasons that from one hour to the next a family's story will be forever changed, reasons that some terror has visited nearby? We will have none.

However we do know what we will not say. We will not say that this time of suffering is deserved. We will not suggest that the shooting, the car accident, the act of random violence, will serve some greater purpose, yet to be revealed. Not only would such a claim abuse the pastoral relationship into which we have been invited. We do not believe it to be true. We do not believe that suffering comes to

Isaiah 50:4-9a

Theological Perspective

as a disciple ["one who is taught"]." The Servant is now listener rather than speaker. This changed metaphor is significant. Instead of the word of the Servant speaking for God, the Servant now ceases talking and starts listening, as God "has opened my ear," and perhaps at the same time closed the Servant's mouth. Precisely when the act of speaking is replaced by the act of listening, the astounding introduction of suffering occurs.

"I was not rebellious, I did not turn backward" (v. 5bc). Then, in silence (?), the Servant "gave my back to those who struck me, and my cheeks to those who pulled out the beard; I did not hide my face from insult and spitting" (v. 6). This physical assault on the Servant comes like a blob of the darkest shades onto the portrait Isaiah has been painting. Where does this idea come from? The answer has been much debated.

In the nineteenth century, with the discovery of numerous ancient documents from the Babylonians, a description of a yearly festival was thought to serve as backdrop for Isaiah's reflections. In the festival it was read that the king of Babylon was symbolically murdered, with a slap on the cheek, by the high priest of the cult of the dying and rising god, Tammuz. The king, or perhaps more likely a stand-in, would then fall down, pretending death, to ensure the good growth of the crops. It was assumed that the prophet witnessed this ritual in his Babylonian exile and interpreted it anew for the work of his Servant. In his final Servant Song, Isaiah 52:13–53:12, the Suffering Servant undergoes his blows because of "the transgression of my people" (53:8). As the king "dies" to sustain the grain, so the servant "dies" to sustain the people.

It is now not clear that such a festival with this intent ever occurred in Babylon, though the texts we have do describe a yearly feast wherein the king is struck on the cheek by the priest.[1] However, we are more likely to discover something of the origins of the Servant's suffering in the ancient Hebrew text. Since the figure of Moses, the lawgiver, might already have served as a model on which Isaiah's Servant is based (see Deut. 32:36 and the book of Exodus, where Moses is called "servant" thirty-six times), the unique work of God's greatest Servant could stand behind Isaiah's concept of suffering.

The figure of Moses in the story of the exodus, the central narrative of Israel, rises to an unequaled

Pastoral Perspective

The Servant enacts the fortitude that will be necessary in the coming ordeal by holding fast (as teacher/speaker) to the guidance of God, and by being patient (as listener/learner). Thus the Servant fulfills the exhortations of the two previous Servant Songs: to *behold* and to *listen.*

Two particular qualities of this resilience are immediately apparent. The first is made explicit in the Servant's narrative: resilience is a gift from God. What may appear to us as heroism is actually not about the Servant at all: it is about God. The Servant finds, as we too have often found, that the inner strength that rises in the face of tribulation can only be attributed to divine providence, a theophany of divine love. The attempts of the unnamed adversaries to *dis*-grace the Servant will be finally and conclusively trumped by the grace of God.

The second quality is intimated in the Servant's language: the *beauty* of resilience. The prophet chooses poetry as the vessel for pouring out the promise: "Morning by morning [God] wakens—wakens my ear to listen." The elegant repetition of the words "morning" and "waken" recalls for us the ceaseless daily reenactment of grace in all its simple majesty—the same grace that inspired another exilic prophet to notice that "[God's] mercies . . . are new every morning" (Lam. 3:22–23).

For the Servant, the providential, beautiful gift of resilience makes it possible "to sustain the weary with a word" (v. 4). "In the end," writes Walter Brueggemann, "all we have is the word of the gospel . . . but the word will do . . . because the poem shakes the empire . . . heals, transforms and rescues. . . . Such new possibility is offered in daring speech. Each time that happens, 'finally comes the poet.'"[1] The Servant dares to speak with the tongue of the teacher, knowing the power of word to fortify, to quicken hope, to stir faith—knowing that word, "above all earthly powers," that has the power to defeat the Adversary, as in Martin Luther's towering servant-song: "Lo! his doom is sure, one little word shall fell him."[2] Indeed, the very power of a word to sustain is precisely on display in this text, passed down the generations and into our hands, thanks to the resilience of those who have discovered the courage that it inspires.

So the victory is to be won first at the level of the Servant's inner life. It will be won for us, at the level

1. See *Ancient Near Eastern Texts*, ed. James B. Pritchard (Princeton, NJ: Princeton University Press, 1969), 331–34.

1. Walter Brueggemann, *Finally Comes the Poet* (Minneapolis: Fortress Press, 1989), 142.
2. Martin Luther, "A Mighty Fortress Is Our God" (1529), in *Service Book and Hymnal* (Minneapolis: Augsburg Publishing House, 1958), 150.

Exegetical Perspective

learners teach best! So, too, students learn more when they are actively involved in the process, through discussion, dialogue, projects, and presentations—when, in short, the teacher *surrenders* authority. The Servant says that the Lord's gift was given "that I may know how to sustain the weary with a word" (v. 4). Surely, a word of comfort comes most effectively not from one who stands above me, but from one who kneels beside me—who shares my sorrow, feels my pain, and offers solace as a fellow sufferer.

In this Song, the Servant does not claim authority. The Servant is responsive, obedient—never arrogant:

> The Lord God has opened my ear,
> and I was not rebellious,
> I did not turn backward.
>
> (v. 5)

Far from standing above and apart, the Servant identifies with the outcast and humiliated, to the point of sharing their humiliation and suffering:

> I gave my back to those who struck me,
> and my cheeks to those who pulled out the beard;
> I did not hide my face
> from insult and spitting.
>
> (v. 6)

The suffering of the Servant is a common theme in the Servant Songs (42:4; 49:4), and becomes the major theme of the fourth and final Song:

> He was despised and rejected by others;
> a man of suffering and acquainted with infirmity;
> and as one from whom others hide their faces
> he was despised, and we held him of no account.
>
> (53:3)

The Servant's suffering is never accidental or incidental. Rather, the Servant suffers deliberately, purposively: in solidarity with others. So the vindication of the Servant becomes their vindication as well; when the Servant is strengthened, his fellow sufferers too find strength.

The strength and validation of the Servant comes, not from himself, or from the world, but from the Lord (50:7–9)—and there the lectionary reading ends, leaving the unfortunate implication that trust in God removes all our difficulties. The Servant relies upon the Lord, but that does not make his path clear or easy. Instead, the Servant

> walks in darkness
> and has no light,
> yet trusts in the name of the Lord
> and relies upon his God.
>
> (v. 10)

Homiletical Perspective

sustain us, that suffering is some bizarre and unwelcome gift from a whimsical God.

Unless it is Holy Week. Unless we are reading the texts of Christ's passion. Unless we are standing at the foot of the cross, and trying to create a theological explanation for the terror of unjust crucifixion. Faced with the harrowing story of a suffering Savior, Christian theology has sought to do what Christian practice would never attempt. We have developed a theory of justified suffering, an atonement theology that gives thanks to God for the necessary pain, humiliation, and finally death endured by Jesus.

We turn to these very words in the third Servant Song of Isaiah, and hear in the midst of the brave anguish of the prophet a whisper of Christ's own voice, insisting that vindication is near for the one who endures. At such a moment, it is necessary to remember that atonement theology understands such a sacrifice to be a singular event in human history. The one who endures such pain for every human sin, such theology declares, frees all who follow in his name from the requirement to bear such a debt. The payment has been made on our behalf. That is the real gift of this Holy Week.

The real danger in this text, the real danger in atonement theology for those who have sought to follow Jesus in every way, is that—as has happened far too often in the history of the church—Christ's struggle turns the ongoing reality of human suffering into meritorious activity. The most painful aspects of the human experience, from slavery to genocide to misogyny and racist violence, have been included by some as necessary suffering, just as Jesus suffered. The seemingly smaller struggles known in nearly every human life, from physical pain to tragedies of the heart, will similarly be named, as a necessary part of submission to the powers in our lives. Even torture will lead in the end to redemption, some will preach this week. If it was so for Christ, it will surely be so for us as well. Since Christ suffered, and my suffering is insignificant compared to his, the present trials are but a foretaste of the glory that awaits us.

So it is that too many clergy, faced with the privilege and responsibility of standing in pulpits this week, have upheld, and even sponsored, real harm in the lives of many. Imagining ourselves to proclaim a gospel truth, we have instead preached submission to the evil powers of this world, mistaking them for God's purpose in human history.

We need not read this text in such a way. The key to finding the good news in this Scripture, and the

Isaiah 50:4-9a

Theological Perspective

stature in the tale of his confrontation with God on the sacred mountain after the creation of the golden calf (Exod. 32–34). In sharp contrast to Aaron's boldly hilarious lies and thorough denigration of the people (Exod. 32:21–24), Moses goes back up the sacred mountain to plead with God on their behalf. In the course of that conversation, Moses in effect offers himself in the place of the sinful people; "Alas, this people has sinned a great sin; . . . if you will only forgive their sin—but if not, blot me out of the book that you have written" (Exod. 32:31–32). Moses is not only servant of God; he becomes here servant of the sinful people, willing to die for them.

Could it be that Isaiah, recognizing clearly the weakness and sin of the exiled Israelites, analogous to their sinful forebears at the mountain so long ago, saw that they are in need of a servant, one like Moses, who finally will be willing to offer himself for them all? Unlike the powerful Moses, Isaiah's Servant will make salvation real not through strength, but through the gift of suffering for others. This new Moses is thus both like and unlike the model of the lawgiver.

This Servant will never be rebellious or turn back, but will willingly suffer shame and spitting and humiliation in order to do the work of God. The Servant is able to undergo such assault because of the certainty that God "helps" him (Isa. 50:7). What the world sees as "shame," God will vindicate as part of God's work. Though the world may find the Servant "guilty" (v. 9a), God will declare the Servant innocent and the very model of God's disciple.

The third Servant Song provides a picture of the Servant that includes a willingness to serve by listening (vv. 4–5), a readiness to suffer at the hands of the wicked (v. 6), and a conviction that God's work will be done because God is always there to vindicate God's Servant. The Christian church heard in these words a crucial part of the picture of their Christ.

JOHN C. HOLBERT

Pastoral Perspective

of our inner conviction; as Paul says, "I am convinced that neither death, nor life . . . nor powers, nor height, nor depth, nor anything else in all creation, will be able to separate us from the love of God in Christ Jesus" (Rom. 8:38–39). The Servant's way through the tribulation that now lies just ahead cannot be only a matter of inward disposition. This text warns that the adversaries, the *dis*-gracers, are about to do their worst in a very corporeal way. Spiritual and physical violence must be *resisted* by their opposites: peace and nonviolence. "I have set my face like flint," says the Servant; "Let them confront me" (vv. 7–8). The shamers will end up shaming themselves, for the resilient Servant is now prepared to resist, armed with the conviction that no power or principality can scar the integrity of obedience to the liberating will of God. We, who have shared the servant's experiences of exile, ambiguity, paradox, and even tribulation, can share the Servant's confidence that "[the one] who vindicates me is near" (v. 8) if we too can cultivate the spiritual disciplines of resilience and resistance.

The vantage point of the text on this Servant who accompanies the journey of Holy Week has now shifted from divine introduction ("Here is my servant . . . in whom my soul delights" 42:1) to the Servant's own voice ("Listen to me," 49:1, and "I have set my face like flint," 50:7). There remains another shift: the final Servant Song is cast in *our* voices ("Who has believed what we have heard?" 53:1) in the text for Good Friday.

So we will become more enmeshed with the Servant as the journey of Holy Week deepens. As bread for that journey, we have been offered the Servant's insight that courage is both providential and beautiful—and the assurance that God will instill resilience and inspire resistance in us. Now, with Jesus, we prepare to endure the full force of the power of sin and death with the Songs of our Suffering Servant in our ears and the teaching of God's beloved one on our tongues.

RICHARD E. SPALDING

Exegetical Perspective

When the way is unclear, trust is hard to give. The temptation in dark places is to make our own light, kindle our own torches, become our own guides. However the Servant warns all "kindlers of fire, lighters of firebrands" who "walk in the flame of your fire":

> This is what you shall have from my hand:
> you shall lie down in torment.
>
> (v. 11)

If we play with fire, we will get burned.

In a recent book, pastoral theologian Andrew Purves considers the all-too-common situation of ministers in midcareer, facing a sense of despair, exhaustion, and loss of purpose.[1] The root problem in our ministry, Purves suggests, is that we think of it as *our* ministry, not as Christ's. What would happen, he wonders, if Jesus showed up? Only when "our" ministry is crucified, as it must be, can Christ's ministry flourish in and through us.

The early church read the Servant Songs through the lens of the Lord Jesus. Certainly, in this week, no Christian reader can consider today's Hebrew Bible lection without remembering Jesus' identification with the least. We wince as we read, recalling how Jesus bared *his* back to the smiters and offered *his* cheek "to those who pulled out the beard" (v. 6). In today's Gospel, after Judas leaves the table to go out and betray his Lord, Jesus says, "Now the Son of Man has been glorified, and God has been glorified in him" (John 13:31). Jesus' glory is shown in his betrayal, suffering, and death.

In a few days, the church will rejoice in the celebration of Easter—and rightly so! Let us not hurry though to the empty tomb too quickly. Through this Holy Week, let us stay with the cross awhile, and ask what it might mean for us to follow the way of the Servant, to surrender authority and privilege, and to stand with the suffering and oppressed. The writer of Hebrews calls Jesus "the pioneer and perfecter of our faith, who for the sake of the joy that was set before him endured the cross, disregarding its shame" (Heb. 12:2). What might it mean to follow such a pioneer—in the words of the old gospel hymn, to "go with him, with him, all the way"? What might it mean to say, with Paul, "I have been crucified with Christ" (Gal. 2:19)?

STEVEN S. TUELL

Homiletical Perspective

Gospel passion that in the Christian narrative generally follows it, is to make clear the distinction between the shameful treatment that too many human lives will at some point endure, and the notion that those lives are somehow deserving of such shame.

The Servant in Isaiah 50 has been ridiculed and abused, but there is no redeeming goodness in such treatment. It is undeserved. Throughout this indecent behavior, the Servant trusts in God. In that trust, the Servant is vindicated. When the Lord God sides with the one who is oppressed, there is no earthly power that can prevail.

What of the suffering that has been endured? It brings shame upon itself and upon the ones who have acted with violence, with disdain, with hatred. The oppressed one, be that Isaiah or Israel or Jesus himself, is able to be resolute and faithful because of the absolute certainty that God is not the cause of the hurt. God does not abandon the one who is hurting.

The models of suffering that we have witnessed show this to be true, in every generation. So, we are back to the hospital bed, the accident site, the place of grief late in the night. We are back with the family who grieves, who fears, who wonders where God could possibly be in such a time. "Right here," we are able to affirm. "God is right here, at our side, weeping as we weep, hurting as we hurt." We are certain of God's presence, even in the hardest of times, because of the constant witness in the biblical record that God has ever been at the side of those who are hurting. Never are God's own abandoned. Somehow, because of God's grace alone, we will be able to stand in faith, even on the very hardest of days.

WILLIAM GOETTLER

1. Andrew Purves, *The Crucifixion of Ministry* (Downers Grove, IL: IVP Books, 2007).

Psalm 70

[1]Be pleased, O God, to deliver me.
O LORD, make haste to help me!
[2]Let those be put to shame and confusion
who seek my life.
Let those be turned back and brought to dishonor
who desire to hurt me.
[3]Let those who say, "Aha, Aha!"
turn back because of their shame.

[4]Let all who seek you
rejoice and be glad in you.
Let those who love your salvation
say evermore, "God is great!"
[5]But I am poor and needy;
hasten to me, O God!
You are my help and my deliverer;
O LORD, do not delay!

Theological Perspective

Psalm 70 may be an excerpt from Psalm 40. It could also be the case that Psalm 70 was the original, placed into Psalm 40. Despite the arguments of scholars, what is undisputed is that three successive psalms—69, 70, and 71—are sometimes referred to by scholars as a "theology of the poor."[1] This psalm is spoken from the perspective of the poor and the outcast. Poverty is as real today as it was thousands of years past. This psalm takes us away from sanitized, modern statistics to the pain of people who experience it. "The poor" may lack shelter, clothing, or food, but they become the most vulnerable people in any society—those who are the most easily abused, most often ignored and made invisible. Being poor, this psalm reminds us, involves grief and loss. The reading fits particularly well within the frame of Holy Week, standing starkly with the other readings of the day, pointing to abuse and betrayal. Depending on God's favor is not escapism but faith.

The psalm begins and ends with a cry for God's help, to be swiftly delivered. In verse 1, the call for help is stated: "Be pleased, O God, to deliver me." "Be pleased" indicates that any help is dependent upon God's will. This is the supplication of the ruled to

Pastoral Perspective

The movement in Psalm 70 between the speakers' assurance of faith and their call for God's deliverance seems slightly inconsistent to us, and yet precisely this tension might be highlighted by the preacher. Often in our faith lives we experience this tension between simple belief and periods of doubt. Here the tone is one of the desperation of suffering and even anguish.

It may be difficult for many contemporary believers to feel the sort of urgency that the psalm expresses. "Come *now*, Lord! Deliver me now; do not hesitate an instant! I cannot wait a second longer."

This psalm is associated in the lectionary with Holy Week and also with Advent. On this Wednesday, the taunting use of the "Aha, aha!" in verse 3 is strongly reminiscent of the taunting that Jesus endured at his crucifixion: "He saved others; he cannot save himself" (Matt. 27:42). Let him save himself if he is indeed the Son of God. In this psalm we are hearing the mocking of Psalm 22:6–8 ("scorned . . . despised. . . . all who see me mock at me. . . . let him rescue the one in whom he delights").

There is extreme vulnerability here on the part of the poor and needy who cannot help themselves. (Similar language is found in Pss. 31, 40, 41, and 69.) Those who voice this refrain are caught in a social and economic vise. Compare this with the self-satisfied

---

1. Frank-Lothar Hossfeld and Erich Zenger, *A Commentary on Psalms 51–100,* trans. Linda Maloney (Minneapolis: Fortress Press, 2005), 188.

Exegetical Perspective

This psalm, along with the psalms that precede it and follow it, is a plea for help in which the praying psalmist asks for YHWH's urgent intervention. The entire psalm is basically a series of pleas that begin and end with invocations to YHWH by way of imperatives. The structure of this psalm, which reveals content very similar to that of Psalm 40:14–18, is clearly defined by the series of words that as a whole form a concentric sequence:

A, verse 1   "deliver," "make haste," "help," "God," "YHWH"

B, verses 2–3   "those . . . who seek," "those . . . who desire," "say"

B, verse 4   "all who seek," "those who love," "say"

A, verse 5   "deliverer," "hasten," "help," "God," "YHWH"

The psalm opens (v. 1) and closes (v. 5) in a setting of extreme urgency. The psalmist, who acknowledges himself as "poor" and "needy" (v. 5)—in the biblical theology of oppression both Hebrew words constitute its semantic circle—shows the urgency of his situation and the need for liberation through the synonymous parallelism that is presented in verses 1 and 5. In verse 5, we find intensification of the urgent plea by adding to all the elements present in verse 1 two new ones: "I am poor and needy" and "do not delay." When the

Homiletical Perspective

How many times do members of a congregation visit their pastor's study and ask, "Why is this happening to me?" "Has God abandoned me?" "Have I done something wrong that is causing God to punish me?" The questions may be provoked by relationship problems, a health crisis, or a boss telling a member she has been downsized right out of a job. Whatever the cause, believers today, like the author of Psalm 70, draw a direct line between their problems and their God. They believe God can solve their problems and, to the extent that God does not, God becomes the cause or coenabler of their problems.

The intensity and time-sensitive nature of the psalmist's fear becomes clear in the closing verse, "You are my help and my deliverer; O LORD, do not delay!" While the psalmist does not explicitly state that the problems are God-created, the psalmist wholeheartedly and clearly believes God can put an end to suffering.

In contrast to the psalmist's anxiety, we watch Jesus walk through life with calm determination, confronting the problems that stand in his way. With the exception of understandably anxious moments in the garden of Gethsemane and on the cross, we hear little of the anxiety in Jesus that we pick up in the voice of the psalmist and the voices of members of our congregation.

Psalm 70

Theological Perspective

the ruler; it is important to remember that such ruling relationships were intimate relationships under the cultures of biblical times. The significance of the relationship between ruler (God) and ruled (psalmist) is underscored by the type of help requested.

The cry for help is for "deliverance." Deliverance, however, was not an abstract or intangible concept. The language of deliverance recalls a central facet of the relationship between ruler and ruled: the mercy of the ruler. The ruler's mercy was tangible: local petitioners would line the road or otherwise engineer an encounter during a ruler's visit. The ruler was expected to forgive debts, grant pardons, or alleviate people's suffering in some other way. Being in covenant with God carried the same sense of relationship. God, with loving-kindness, would grant care for the covenanted people, for example, with manna or conversations with angels or unexpected pregnancies. For a people in intimate relationship with God, mercy, whether deserved or not, was expected, and the psalmist draws on this rich tradition. The extravagant love of God will be poured out; thus, the writer of the psalm could state confidently in verse 5: "You are my help and my *deliverer*."

While the first and final verses of the psalm call for God's mercy, the center of the psalm explains the reasons for such pleas through the powerful wording of lamentation. A lament is a powerful way to speak of the heart's anguish, not listing specific grievances but encapsulating grief. In contemporary industrial societies, the practice of grieving often gets short shrift: people are expected to "get over" experiences in efficient and quiet manners. However, grieving—lamentation—is a necessary component of human existence, since there are some events and experiences that are not easily tucked away. To place lament into the public life of prayer becomes a theological statement about the sacredness of human experience. Holy Week becomes a time when lament is reexperienced in the life of the church. For instance, some African American spirituals exemplify laments, and their powerful, emotional cries are the reason for their incorporation into some Holy Week services. The words from one spiritual provide an example: "Sometimes I feel like a motherless child, a long way from home." Like the psalmist, this spiritual does not list specific problems, but feelings. The sense of being a motherless child reflects loneliness and abandonment.

In verses 2 and 3, the psalmist gives voice to the lament by seeking God's deliverance against those

Pastoral Perspective

and self-governed people who are identified as "wicked" in Psalm 36.

It is also instructive that Jesus uses such a lament as his last word from the cross: "My God, my God, why have you forsaken me?" (Mark 15:34; Ps. 22:1). The pervasive intermixture of praise and lament in the Psalms, and also the lament in Jesus's word, deserves attention. Praise and lament are often expressed together as they are here. Indeed, the lament is itself a sign of the trust of the believer.

How are we readers and hearers of this word to identify with it? The psalmist and his community seem already to have been brought to shame. They have been ridiculed. What can we use to capture the emotions of this experience both individually and corporately?

Old Testament scholar Walter Brueggemann's claim about lament in *The Prophetic Imagination* is provocative. He finds prophetic criticism or lament not to be about "carping and denouncing. It is asserting that false claims to authority and power cannot keep their promises . . . in the face of God."[1] Thus, a lament has three aspects: denouncing false authorities (who ridicule and persecute us), praising God, and calling on God for help.

Real lament is a claim that things are not right. It is a bringing to public expression that suffering and death and other negations (divorce, drugs, alcoholism, abuse) are taking place. In some ways, the lament is a way of uncovering the negatives that a "royal consciousness" or official government does not want to acknowledge.

As Americans we live in a "winner take all" society where the point is to succeed. Sometimes that renders us deaf to the cries of the poor and needy—not intentionally, just via the way we are socialized. It may be useful to recall that those who mocked Jesus, according to Matthew, were the soldiers, "those who passed by," "the chief priest and scribes," and "the bandits who were crucified with him."

There is a strong sense in the psalm that the person is being threatened, as well as simply ridiculed ("those who seek my life. . . . who desire to hurt me"). It may not be too much of a stretch to imagine the person undergoing bullying, race-baiting, or physical violence (lynching, gay bashing?). That certainly seems to be a possibility for the author. Such violence is not unknown in our schools, in our homophobic communities, or in

1. Walter Brueggemann, *The Prophetic Imagination* (Minneapolis: Fortress Press, 2001), 11.

second expression is added to the verb "hasten," the urgency of his need for divine liberation becomes much more pressing. The presence of both the generic title "God" and the sacrosanct name "YHWH" in both sections A tells us that the psalmist has no doubt to whom he is directing his plea and that the enemies must not think that they are facing just any deity.

The central parts, the two B components (vv. 2–3 and 4), are interwoven in a game of opposites:

those . . . who seek my life" (to finish me)	"all who seek you" (seek God for refuge)
"those . . . who desire to hurt me"	"those who love your salvation"
"those who say, 'Aha, Aha!'"	"those who . . . say evermore, 'God is great!'"

The oppositions also manifest themselves when verbs referring to YHWH are compared with those referring to the enemies. While YHWH is said to "run," to "not delay" God's arrival in order to aid the poor and needy (v. 5), the enemies are said to have "turned back," and "turn back" (vv. 2 and 3). Besides, by using several Hebrew words that have been translated here as "shame" and "confusion," the psalmist wants to subvert the situation that has forced him to live in poverty and oppression. In fact, the Hebrew word *kalam*, applied here to refer to the enemies, has as one of its accepted meanings "being mistreated."

While the wicked join in shame and punishment, those who seek YHWH amid a joyful and festive liturgy cheer YHWH, "God is great!" and proclaim YHWH as savior and liberator.

In the context of the Psalter, Psalm 70 seems to be a prayer that can be recited by itself, as a short and hasty plea, much like the introductory portion of the extensive prayer that makes up Psalm 71, as a conclusion to Psalm 40 (vv. 14–18). The fact that this psalm can be considered as a separate prayer, or as part of two other prayers, suggests the possibility of having been a short prayer for help for the individual who, in a situation of emergency and urgency, looks to the temple and finds a prayer that is already written and makes it his/her own.[1] How many times could this prayer have gotten someone out of a difficult situation in which prayer was not even a passing thought! At least a handful of these people, who at some point found themselves in dire need, perhaps in a calmer situation turned the psalm

As preachers, how do we compare Jesus' walk through life with the anxiety we hear in the voice of the psalmist? Is one right and the other wrong? Is there perhaps a place for both in our spiritual journeys? Or is Jesus so much stronger than we are that we cannot even identify with his calm approach to life's trials and tribulations?

Throughout the Psalms and in this passage, we hear a yearning for protection by God from enemies. The yearning is rooted in the psalmist's belief that those around him/her are filled with malice and evil intent. The yearning quickly becomes a desire for God to destroy the enemies. In Psalm 70, the psalmist asks of God, "Let those be put to shame and confusion who seek my life. Let those be turned back and brought to dishonor who desire to hurt me." In Jesus, it should be noted that we find no similar desire for enemies to be destroyed. On the contrary, enemies are to be loved.

Creating a connection between the psalmist's yearning to have God protect by destroying/ humiliating enemies and the similar yearnings in our twenty-first-century congregants is key to preaching on this passage. To what extent do listeners to a sermon in the twenty-first century feel a similar threat to their well-being? Does this threat create our own desire to crush our enemies? From what sources come these threats? Are they real or imagined? Who are "the wicked . . . the unjust and cruel" (Ps. 71:4) of today who create the anxiety we hear in the voice of the psalmist? Is it a group of terrorists, a pedophile, a boss who is trying to get us fired?

The petitions of the psalmist raise an interesting, even troubling question: Are we praying for ends (the psalmist prays for the destruction of his enemies) or for means to an end? In other words, are we praying for God to do the work for us or for God to give us what we need to solve or, at a minimum, cope with our own problems? If we are doing the latter, we are praying for wisdom, the spirit of discernment, courage, patience, and other spiritual qualities, rather than a miraculous, divine intervention. If we are doing the former with, say, an illness, we are praying that God will reach inside our body and cure what ails us.

In thinking about illustrations for a sermon on Psalm 70, preachers can lift up situations—in society, in the life of the congregation, or of individuals—where people spend more time brooding over their problems than attempting to solve them with God's help. These illustrations illuminate the all-too-human desire for an externally rather than internally driven solution.

1. James Limburg, *Psalms* (Louisville, KY: Westminster John Knox Press, 2000), 233.

Psalm 70

Theological Perspective

who would do harm. The harm being brought to the psalmist includes violent, mortal threats from those "who seek my life" and "desire to hurt me" (v. 2). The psalmist wants a resolution to the threat against life and limb by seeking deliverance from the perpetrators. The psalmist asks God to confuse and shame them, letting their dishonor be known, so that they will turn back from their destructive course. The threat of assault is compounded by the mockery of "those who say, 'Aha, Aha!'" (v. 3). Those who mock the psalmist would reverse their actions because of shame. In a shame-based culture like that of the psalmist, to cover a person in shame is to exclude him or her from the life of the community. To be excluded from the community is to be excluded from its resources, a horrible fate for the people of that time. The "deliverance" of the psalmist, then, calls for envisioning the life of the community without the violent evildoers, thereby seeking a more wholesome community. The psalmist is calling, not just for personal deliverance, but for that which will make the entire community safer.

The idea of combining personal with communal deliverance is made clearer in verse 4 as the psalmist addresses God: "Let all who seek you rejoice and be glad in you." Those who seek the psalmist's downfall are contrasted with those who seek God. The psalmist identifies with those who seek God, and the evildoers' actions are opposed to that group. The life of the community of believers should be focused on seeking God together, rather than individual agendas or personal glory. God is a personal and communal deliverer.

The final verse of the psalm tersely reiterates several themes. The position of the psalmist as the petitioner who seeks the mercy of the ruler is recaptured: "I am poor and needy." That God is the powerful one in the relationship—the ruler or the deliverer—is also restated with the psalmist's request, "Hasten to me, . . . do not delay!" These themes underline the significance of absolute trust in God to deliver, because the heart of the covenantal relationship is extravagant love.

STEPHANIE Y. MITCHEM

Pastoral Perspective

places where the noose is a symbolic reminder that racism is not dead. There are also communities with few resources, whose voices are not heard and who fear that they will simply fade (even further) into oblivion. Examples include rural communities, neighborhoods of economic refugees from Latin cultures, and cultures of poverty.

There may be a way of identifying with those who cry out as the psalmist does. That is to live with the poor and needy in some way for some amount of time. Roberto Goizueta suggests that it is the needy, the "crucified victim," who can teach us about resurrection, about deliverance, about our own desperate need for healing.[2]

Lament and praise complete one another. The church may have lost its taste or appreciation for lament, which is a serious loss. This loss carries with it a loss of the community's interaction with God. Lament allows the worshiper to complain about injustice, to call on God for deliverance and—here—rescue from danger. Perhaps the community of the well-off has not felt an occasion that calls for lament, or perhaps this represents a capitulation to what the theologian Douglas John Hall calls the "official religion of optimism."[3] If so, that is loss indeed, since part of the optimism points to a determined avoidance of negations of all kinds—substance abuse, betrayal, divorce, suicide, injustice, and death. Might this mean that Christians have neglected one of their central beliefs—resurrection from the dead? and the power of how that belief speaks to and sets death in a penultimate frame?

During Holy Week it may be especially significant to rediscover the place of lament. After all, Jesus uttered one of the most devastating laments of all times, about feeling forsaken by God. This very interaction suggests a dialogue in which God who is our "help and deliverer" does hasten. There is dialogue between crucifixion and resurrection.

L. SHANNON JUNG

2. Roberto Goizueta, "From Calvary to Galilee," *America*, April 7, 2006.
3. See among other sources, Douglas John Hall, "The Changing North American Context of the Church's Ministry," *Currents in Theology and Mission* 22, no. 6 (December 1995): 409.

into a more extended and "well thought" prayer; and so we have Psalm 40 and the prayer that makes up both Psalm 70 and 71. When we view Psalm 70 as part of Psalm 40, we are surprised by its presence as the closing of a prayer in which the praying psalmist has the tranquility to assert a past liberation (Ps. 40:1–3) and lifestyle that the psalmist lives, along with those who are part of his community (Ps. 40:4–10): a willingness to worship, live in accordance to God's will, and proclaim YHWH's unyielding justice, faithfulness, and love. When Psalm 70 is prayed in conjunction with Psalm 71, the setting of urgency in Psalm 70 is affixed to the desire for deliverance from the hands of the wicked, albeit with lesser urgency. The pleading person can at least take the time to declare that YHWH is "rock" and "fortress" and has been from childhood up to the present moment of old age.

In the context of the lectionary's texts for this day, the theme that binds them to the psalm is the enemies' mockery, that "Aha, Aha" (v. 3) that in Hebrew sounds like ridicule and disdain: *heakh-heakh*. Jesus' enemies join in ridiculing him in order to "seek his life" (cf. Ps. 70:2). Isaiah 50:4–9 talks of ridicule and mistreatment of the Suffering Servant, but, just as in the psalm, the Servant declares that in YHWH he/she has a shield that protects him/her from enemies and deriders. John 13:21–32 talks of Judas's betrayal as a main theme, a passage that, when read alongside our psalm, turns Judas into an object of shame and scorn. Finally, Hebrews 12:1–3 revisits the theme of the Suffering Servant, applied specifically to Jesus, who suffered ridicule and violence, but at the end was rewarded by God, and so became paradigm and hope for those who, as in the times of the Epistle to the Hebrews, suffered ridicule and violence for their faith.

EDESIO SANCHEZ

For example, a member of a congregation came to his pastor seeking help for a drinking problem. As they talked, it became clear to the pastor that the member wanted someone/anyone to solve his problem for him. Specifically, the member said it would be great if God would intervene and stop his drinking.

The pastor refused to step into the trap. She directed the member to the only person who could solve the problem: the abusive drinker. She said that she would stand by him. More importantly, God would be a sure and certain help in his time of trouble. However, said the pastor, "God cannot do this for you alone. You have to help God do it."

In Holy Week, we do not hear Jesus complaining about his lot. We do not hear him wishing that God would destroy those who were making his life difficult. Instead, we see Jesus digging deeper for the spiritual resources necessary to walk his walk to the cross. In many regards, it is a striking contrast to the attitude of the psalmist.

As a result, Psalm 70 offers preachers a wonderful opportunity to critique the anxiety-driven, I-am-a-victim mentality that plagues our society from top to bottom. We can contrast our behavior with that of Jesus, who saw himself not as a victim but, rather, as a faithful servant.

Jesus knew there are costs to discipleship. He was fully prepared to pay them. Jesus did ask God to consider removing "this cup." As he did so, however, he refused to impose his desires on God. Instead, tellingly, Jesus ended his request with, "Yet not what I want, but what you want" (Matt. 26:39).

In Psalm 70, the psalmist reveals the event-driven anxiety we all feel at times in our lives. In his walk to the cross, Jesus reveals the way we place our anxieties within the hands of a God who has assured us that we are and always will be protected.

JOHN W. WIMBERLY

Hebrews 12:1-3

¹Therefore, since we are surrounded by so great a cloud of witnesses, let us also lay aside every weight and the sin that clings so closely, and let us run with perseverance the race that is set before us, ²looking to Jesus the pioneer and perfecter of our faith, who for the sake of the joy that was set before him endured the cross, disregarding its shame, and has taken his seat at the right hand of the throne of God.

³Consider him who endured such hostility against himself from sinners, so that you may not grow weary or lose heart.

Theological Perspective

These are encouraging words, following and summarizing those inspiring accounts of the heroes of the Hebrew Bible. We need them and they need us, says the author of Hebrews. The faith of those early readers would be challenged; their very lives were in danger. However, Jesus the high priest, the epitome of faithfulness, stands in a long line of faithfulness, embodying grace under pressure.

Trials and tribulations are part of Christian life. We know the stories of the faithful who have gone before us, the witnesses, *martyroi*, whose endurance engendered faith in others. The word "therefore" at the beginning of chapter 12 takes in the litany of faithfulness in chapter 11 and the remarkable statement that "they would not, apart from us, be made perfect" (11:40). Readers of this letter, then and now, are invited to be part of that cloud of witnesses and to take heart.

These words are often read on All Saints' Day, because they teach us about the communion of saints throughout the ages, even in the ages before Christ. These words remind us that saintliness, sanctified faithfulness, goes way back, that the Christian church did not invent perseverance or holiness or witness. These words also make sense in the midst of Holy Week, as believers walk the Via Dolorosa, the way of the cross that leads to Calvary.

Pastoral Perspective

The writer of Hebrews, a master of metaphor, picks up on a primary way we conceive of life: as a journey or a race. While this is a timeless metaphor, the notion of what the race is all about has changed. The twentieth century began with the dominant idea of progress, that life was progressing logically and inevitably toward a better and better world, a better and better society. With that goal-oriented purposefulness, the race could be run with some confidence, that things can and will get better. Perhaps it was the Holocaust, or Hiroshima. Maybe it was the Vietnam war. Somewhere along the line we were disabused of our belief in progress. The race has since lost its purpose and ending and now has become the rat race: running around in circles, hither and yon, no truth to guide us, no goal to beckon us forward. As we begin the twenty-first century, there is a new notion of what the race might be all about: a fear that the race might soon be over. Terrorist attacks, a quagmire in Iraq, global warming threatening our planet, the oil that fuels our race now becoming scarcer—all these contribute to a sense of an end to the late, great planet Earth.

The writer of Hebrews, however, is not thinking so much of the end of the race. The writer is thinking less of progress, more of process. While most runners are joyful at the end of the race, the

Exegetical Perspective

In these last days of Lent, as the darkest hours of the Christian liturgical year draw near, it is perhaps fitting that the church read the familiar passage in Hebrews 12:1–3. Especially appropriate is the abundance of athletic imagery (cf. 12:11–13; 5:14), giving the impression that the author and addressees of Hebrews have been running a long and difficult marathon and that now, in the last leg of the race, they must dig deep into their reserve of faith to make it to the finish line. In this, one of the most encouraging of biblical texts for believers under persecution (10:32–34), Hebrews leaves a lasting legacy for those in need of faith and hope.

The encomium of faith in chapter 11 warms up with the celebrated articulation of faith as "the substance of things hoped for, the evidence of things not seen" (11:1 KJV). Even though a precise definition is elusive, we can discern the two aspects of faith that interest the author of Hebrews: the first involves the reality (*hypostasis*) of things hoped for, that is, with respect to *time;* the second concerns evidence (*elenchos*) of things not seen, that is, with respect to *perception*. The rest of Hebrews 11 uses examples of biblical heroes to reveal how these two aspects of faith have marked the marathon—or, perhaps better yet, the relay race—of faith that begins with Abel in verse 4.

Homiletical Perspective

The larger context of the text reveals that Hebrews was originally addressed to an oppressed group of early Jewish Christians who lived in the midst of the cosmopolitan Hellenistic culture of the Roman Empire. They were persecuted because of their religious identity. Apostasy or the abandonment of the gospel of Jesus Christ was an everyday threat to their faith community. The previous chapter reminds the audience, who are weary from the demands of the Christian way of life, of stories about "a cloud of witnesses" who had completed their race of faith. In the text, the listeners are encouraged to persevere in their faith in spite of persecution, and to follow in the footsteps of Jesus Christ, who suffered and died on the cross.

The text challenges us to rethink our Christian faith. Christian faith is not a disposable, commodified religion that shoppers pick up on an impulse to satisfy their need for security, only to be discarded when they later feel it is useless. According to the text, such an attitude is sinful (12:1). Actually, Hebrews considers it the greatest sin, one which promises God's fearful judgment (10:26–31). Instead, Christian faith requires of believers a deliberate decision about which is more important to them: worldly satisfaction, or answering the call to live a different life, the life of faith that is "the

Hebrews 12:1-3

Theological Perspective

This walk feels more like a funeral procession than a footrace; we can use these words of encouragement now more than ever. We know the end of the story, but our feet are tired; sin and suffering weigh us down. It is good to know that others have made it and are cheering us on.

The *martyroi* were the witnesses, those who were willing to keep the faith and speak it, even under duress. In those early centuries, bearing witness could lead to very real martyrdom—persecution and death. Just as Hebrews tells the stories of those heroes of the faith, the early church told the stories of the martyrs. The martyrs were considered "athletes," those who had run their race with endurance, who had received their crown of gold. The story of Vibia Perpetua must have been an encouragement to believers who faced such trials. In her account, she tells how the faith of others encouraged her. In her prison cell, the night before her martyrdom, she has a vision. The young mother sees her friend, Pomponius, a deacon, who takes her by the hand and says, "Do not be afraid, I am here, struggling with you."[1]

Modern-day saints have found comfort in the presence and memory of that cloud of witnesses. Most of us have not faced the persecution Perpetua faced, but we know that Christians have endured incredible trials, and still do. In 1984, the Rev. Ben Weir, a Presbyterian minister, was taken captive in Beirut, Lebanon, where he taught. He was held by Shiite extremists for over a year. Ben and his wife, Carol, tell the story of this ordeal in *Hostage Bound, Hostage Free.* Ben describes his surroundings and his spiritual struggles. He looked for the sustaining presence of God in the simple objects around him. "I began counting the horizontal slats of the shutters . . . there were 120. What could those horizontal pieces of wood stand for, so many of them? That's it! Many of them, a crowd! A cloud of witnesses past and present, who through crises and times of trial have observed and perceived the faithfulness of God."[2] Ben remembered these verses from Hebrews and took heart. His story encourages others. We are, all of us, surrounded, always, everywhere.

In the history of the church, there are saints and there are Saints. In Protestant and Reformed traditions, all of us are saints, precious to God,

Pastoral Perspective

Christian finds joy in running the race set before him or her, because the running of the race and the prize at its end are the same, eternal life with God. At the beginning, middle, and end of the race, we already have the prize—surrounded by a cloud of witnesses, we have eternal life with God.

We suggested in the pastoral perspective on Hebrews 9:11–15 (pp. 196–200), that the spiritual race begins not with the traditional, "on your mark, get set, go!" but, rather, with the call "once for all." For the writer of Hebrews asserts that we are not running for the prize; the prize has already been won by the pioneer and perfecter of our faith, once for all. We are running for the joy of running, running while surrounded by so great a cloud of witnesses, running without the weight of sin and every burden, running in presence of the one "seated at the right hand of God."

Through religious influence both within and beyond Christianity, this lesson of Hebrews—that the journey is more important than the destination—has also permeated our culture. However, the culture offers a radically different notion of what the journey is about. As the race nears its end, it is now about getting all you can, taking while the taking is good, fulfilling one's needs and desires. The journey is not about joy but enjoyment, entertainment, and personal gratification. The paradox is that personal gratification is not the best race strategy. It is not a good idea to take on too much before the race.

On an episode of the television comedy *The Office,* the boss has an idea to hold a "Race for the Cure for Rabies" (even though there already is a cure for rabies). The boss, in order to gain an advantage over the other runners, decides to "load carbs" by eating a huge plate of fettuccine right before the race. In the middle of the race, he gets cramps and is nearly unable to finish. The writer of Hebrews could have told him, set aside every burden and sin, and then run the race. This example points out at least four prevailing attitudes that govern modern life, the "running of the race": (1) the race is mostly pointless (there is already a cure for rabies); (2) though pointless, the goal of the race is still to win; (3) one must use every advantage to win; and (4) advantage is gained by consumption.

It is certainly true that our consumption-driven society is burdening us. The list of ills is nearly endless: childhood obesity, global warming, diminishing resources, economic imbalance, joblessness, crime. If the point of the race is to accumulate all you can

---

1. Herbert Musurillo, trans., "The Martyrdom of Saints Perpetua and Felicitas," in *The Acts of the Christian Martyrs* (Oxford: Clarendon Press, 1972), 109–19.
2. Ben and Carol Weir, with Dennis Benson, *Hostage Bound, Hostage Free* (Philadelphia: Westminster Press, 1987), 28–29.

Exegetical Perspective

The temporal aspect of biblical history is illustrated by forerunners who ran their leg of the relay faithfully by following God's promises forward in time, casting their gaze of hope on what was ahead of them. The paradigmatic case is Abraham's hope for procreation despite his old age and Sarah's barrenness (11:11). The perceptional aspect is illustrated by heroes who faithfully obeyed God even though they could not know or see what God did. For example, Noah's building the ark was not something hoped for, but was an act of faithful trust in God's warning of "events as yet unseen" (11:7).

The exemplary faithfulness of Israel's many heroes notwithstanding (11:32–38), the relay race is not yet finished, so that things hoped for still lie ahead of them (11:13, 39). As chapter 11 concludes the litany of faithful obedience, perseverance, and divine favor, several things should be noted for the transition into the final exhortations in chapters 12–13.

First is the respect and purpose with which the Jewish heroes of faith are remembered. The "great cloud of witnesses" enumerated in the roll call of faithful forerunners is meant to encourage the addressees to "run with perseverance the race that is set before [them]" (12:1). The former relay runners have now taken their seat in the stadium of faith as witnesses or spectators, who are there to inspire as well as to cheer the addressees of Hebrews who must now carry the baton forward. This continuity of faith between the old and the new covenants is no trivial point; it ensures that the discontinuities (7:1–10:18) will not degenerate into anti-Semitism.

Second is the ubiquitous theme of suffering and persevering under hostile conditions, a constant fate for the faithful of both the old and the new covenants (see esp. 11:35–38). Faith—which is nearly insepar-able from endurance (e.g., 10:36–39; 12:1–3)—and suffering provide the ties that bind the addressees, baton in hand, with their forerunners. However, supreme among the models of faithful perseverance is Jesus, the "initiator and perfecter" of faithful endurance (v. 2, *archēgos kai teleiōtēs*, my trans.; cf. "Alpha and Omega" in Revelation 1:8; 21:6; 22:13).

Jesus is the beginner and finisher of *faithfulness* in a variety of ways. He can "sympathize with our weaknesses" and "*in every respect* has been tested as we are, yet without sin" (Heb. 2:17, 18; 4:15, emphasis added). Because of his solidarity with humanity and because of his familiarity with humiliation and hostility (12:2–3), Jesus is reliable as a sympathizer, that is, cosufferer, with the addressees, who suffered after they became believers (10:32–34).

Homiletical Perspective

assurance of things hoped for, the conviction of things not seen" (11:1). The text compares this life of faith to running a lifelong race that demands of runners perseverance until they reach their final destination.

Perseverance is one of the most difficult disciplines for many of us, because no one likes to endure pain and hardship. Perseverance may not be counted as a virtue for people living in today's high-tech culture. We value easy answers, immediate results, and tangible benefits, rather than patient discernment, tolerance, and the slow unfolding of understanding. In our pluralistic religious culture, which allows us a range of religious options, perseverance in the course of one's religious life may seem unnecessary. We may be tempted to abandon our religious identity when it causes us to face difficulties, obstacles, or discouragement. Indeed, preaching on perseverance as the essence of Christian faith may even seem inappropriate for contemporary Christians!

However, the text explains perseverance neither as a moral principle nor as an aspect of one's personality or character. Rather, perseverance is theological; it is God's way to love the world. No testimony to God's perseverance is more compelling than that of Jesus, who endured the cross. Just as Jesus and a great cloud of faithful witnesses had run the race with perseverance—even at the cost of their lives—so the text calls us to join that race of faith.

Like the early Christians in Hebrews, many con-temporary Christians are tired of living the Christian way, and they do not want to hear a sermon on perseverance. In parts of the world where religious freedom is forbidden, members of underground churches are persecuted, physically as well as sociopolitically. Many of these believers face the fear of death for themselves and the destruction of their churches on a daily basis. Those who live in a world of suffering from war and violence, hunger and disease, oppression and corruption may seem on the verge of abandoning their Christian faith, especially when God's sovereignty over evil is not yet apparent to them. Even Christian churches in developed, demo-cratic countries may feel exhausted from living a life of faith. While they do not suffer physical persecution, they do experience spiritual hardships when their Christian identity is challenged by materialism and a hedonistic culture of overconsumption. This requires them to choose either God, the crucified One, or mammon as god. Moreover, in a pluralistic culture, many feel burdened with their Christian identity, with

Hebrews 12:1-3

Theological Perspective

eligible to bear witness, made holy by God's grace in Christ. In Roman and Orthodox traditions, those who are honored as extraordinary examples of faithfulness and holiness are beatified, canonized. They are fallible human beings who have transcended their limitations, who are special in their suffering, in their kindness, in their giftedness. They are said to have an extra share of Christ's abundant grace. To many, they have become intercessors, patrons, objects of devotion.

In Celtic prayers, the presence of these saintly souls was invoked for protection, for safety and comfort. Patrick and other Celtic teachers invoked the saints and martyrs in their breastplate prayers, in company with the angels and the forces of nature. In the Gaelic prayers of the Scottish isles, saints are invoked morning, noon and night:

> God and Mary and Michael kindly . . . be shielding me all Three and as One . . .
> I beseech Peter, I beseech Paul, I beseech Mary, I beseech the Son,
> I beseech the trustful Apostles twelve to preserve me from hurt and harm.[3]

The faithful who have gone before us have passed the faith on to us. We would not believe, if it were not for them, and future saints will believe because we keep the faith, because we bear witness, because we follow Jesus Christ.

Jesus is the pioneer and perfecter of our faith. It may be that the older word "author" (v. 2 KJV) makes more sense in an age when pioneers have too often been on the wrong side of the angels. Jesus Christ, the one who wrote the book on suffering love, goes before us and shows us the way. We are invited to lay aside our sins, to grow more faithful, to persevere, to follow. This is a picture of sanctification, of the life-long process of growth in grace. It can be a long, slow, imperceptible course, discouraging at times. Perfection is a goal, a prize, seemingly unreachable, even by biblical saints and heroes. Yet we are urged, encouraged, lured forward by that company of saints and by our faith in Jesus Christ.

REBECCA BUTTON PRICHARD

Pastoral Perspective

before the end, as consumerism would have us believe, the race cannot even be finished, much less won. The wisdom of Hebrews is to be unburdened—free from every weight and sin that clings so closely—in order to run the race with perseverance.

Perseverance. Now there is a countercultural word in a consumption-driven society. The original hearers of the letter of Hebrews faced persecution and even death for their beliefs, and the danger of growing "weary and fainthearted" (v. 3 RSV) in the face of such pressure was real. In their context, it meant "keep on truckin'"—do not let persecution stop you. In our context, when products are built with planned obsolescence, when 50 percent of all marriages end in divorce, when personal fulfillment is the whole point, perseverance is not in fashion. Yet, especially in the face of the meaninglessness and vanity of the modern, consumption-driven life, "keeping the faith" is the way to run the race.

The text gives two crucial assets for the Christian race runner. The first is the "great cloud of witnesses" who, by faith, have persevered. "Surrounding" the runner, they could be seen as spectators in the bleachers, cheering the runner on; or perhaps they are more like a pack of teammates, who run alongside and in front to ease the way. Up ahead is Jesus, in first place, giving us the will to run and showing the way the race goes. We cannot be distracted by the carnival barkers, selling their wares, promising life, health, and beauty. We cannot be discouraged by global warming, terrorist threats, and economic uncertainty. We must persevere. For Jesus has run the race and finished. We look to Jesus, to know not just how to finish, but how to run.

PETER AND DEBRA SAMUELSON

---

3. Alexander Carmichael, *Carmina Gadelica: Hymns and Incantations* (Edinburgh: Floris Books, 1992), 59.

Exegetical Perspective

Jesus initiated the addressees into their suffering faith; he is the source of their faith *and* their suffering. At the same time, Jesus is the one they must look to for inspiration and encouragement (12:2). As one who has been exalted after enduring the cross and "*has taken* his seat at the right hand of the throne of God" (12:2; emphasis added) Jesus is the initiator of faith perfected, i.e., the first to finish the race that was set before him.

The larger point of Hebrews 12:1–3 is the exhortation of the addressees. The purpose for recounting the forerunners of faith (chap. 11) and introducing Jesus as *the* model of faithful endurance is "so that you may not grow weary or lose heart" (v. 3). In more positive terms, the author of Hebrews cheers his audience on to "lift your drooping hands and strengthen your weak knees, and make straight paths for your feet, so that what is lame may not be put out of joint, but rather be healed" (12:12).

During the long season of Lent, the message of faithful endurance is a welcome one, even if it is a difficult call to persevere through the toughest challenges to faith. Such was what the addressees of Hebrews apparently experienced. However, how might Christians and churches that are not being persecuted appreciate and appropriate the rich exhortations of Hebrews? It may help to keep in mind that the Christology of Hebrews 12:1–3, as well as the entire book, does not have primarily abstract theological intentions. The christological claims in 12:1–3 are surrounded by exhortation for the addressees at the beginning and the end, much the same way that the addressees are told that they are surrounded by so great a cloud of witnesses. While the text prepares us for the hostility that Jesus faced on Good Friday, it also provides faith and hope that look ahead to joy that lies ahead.

KANG-YUP NA

Homiletical Perspective

uncertainty about the value of their Christian faith. Above all, in the swirling current of seemingly post-Christian culture, many pastors and church leaders, disheartened by a decrease in membership and finances, do not have the energy to swim against the tide, to hold fast to their commitment to their Christian ministry.

Just like the early Jewish Christians in Hebrews, our identity is challenged; our Christian way of life is doubted. Who can help us lift our tired hands, strengthen our weak knees, and make straight the path under our feet (12:12–13a)? The preacher! Just like the church in Hebrews, our churches need preaching about perseverance, especially when we do not seem to have tangible evidence of God's presence or any vivid sense of hearing God's call as a clear trumpet cry. That is the preacher's task! To those who need to hear the message conveyed in the text, the preacher can say, "You are not the only runner. Do not forget a great cloud of witnesses who have run the course, endured suffering and pain, and finally completed their race of faith. So let us likewise run the race that is set before us with perseverance, looking to Jesus, the pioneer and perfecter of our faith, rather than growing weary or losing heart."

The list of those who have lived the life of faith with perseverance is still incomplete, because God continues to call new runners to join the race. Martin Luther King Jr., Oscar Romero, Fannie Lou Hamer—these are just a few we can name from our recent history who joined the race with perseverance. The preacher can find more whose names can be added to the list, if she looks carefully around at families, friends, colleagues, churches, society, and the larger world. Indeed, all of us are called to join the race of faith. Our identity as Christians is not a burden or an obstacle for our lives, but is rather a gift, given by God to live in a different way, as part of the community of the followers of Jesus Christ. It requires of us perseverance until "Thy kingdom come, thy will be done on earth as it is in heaven."

EUNJOO M. KIM

John 13:21-32

21After saying this Jesus was troubled in spirit, and declared, "Very truly, I tell you, one of you will betray me." 22The disciples looked at one another, uncertain of whom he was speaking. 23One of his disciples—the one whom Jesus loved—was reclining next to him; 24Simon Peter therefore motioned to him to ask Jesus of whom he was speaking. 25So while reclining next to Jesus, he asked him, "Lord, who is it?" 26Jesus answered, "It is the one to whom I give this piece of bread when I have dipped it in the dish." So when he had dipped the piece of bread, he gave it to Judas son of Simon Iscariot. 27After he received the piece of bread, Satan entered into him. Jesus said to him, "Do quickly what you are going to do." 28Now no one at the table knew why he said this to him. 29Some thought that, because Judas had the common purse, Jesus was telling him, "Buy what we need for the festival"; or, that he should give something to the poor. 30So, after receiving the piece of bread, he immediately went out. And it was night.

31When he had gone out, Jesus said, "Now the Son of Man has been glorified, and God has been glorified in him. 32If God has been glorified in him, God will also glorify him in himself and will glorify him at once."

Theological Perspective

"In one sense Judas is the most important figure in the New Testament apart from Jesus. For he, and he alone of the Apostles, was actively at work in this decisive situation, in the accomplishment of what was God's will and what became the content of the gospel."[1] Twentieth-century theologian Karl Barth's interpretation of Judas as carrying out the will of God represents a prominent stream of thought within the history of Christian interpretation of Judas. In John's Gospel generally, and in this passage in particular, John's rendering of Judas lends significant credence to viewing him as the key actor in the divine drama of salvation. A close reading of the text, however, suggests that viewing Judas simply as enactor of God's will is too simplistic.

One consistent theme throughout the Gospel is Jesus' foreknowledge of Judas's role in Jesus' arrest and death. The passage begins with Jesus' words, "Very truly, I tell you, one of you will betray me" (v. 21). Here Jesus verbalizes what we have been told verses before: "For [Jesus] knew who was to betray him" (13:11a). In John 6, Jesus speaks to his disciples, "Did I not choose you, the twelve? Yet one of you is a devil" (6:70). The text goes on to explain that Jesus spoke of Judas, the

Pastoral Perspective

Motives are complicated and often unknown, even to their owners. The story of how Jesus identified Judas as the betrayer is replete with complicated and unknown motives, including the motives of God. This lection not only conveys an important plot development leading to Jesus' passion, but in so doing, it also provides an opportunity to excavate the difficult terrain of congregational life today. Sometimes the stories within our communities have roots and reasons as murky as those the Scriptures ascribe to Judas.

The motives of Judas have never been clear. In fact, Judas has provided Christianity with one of the greatest conundrums of all time. Was he an unlucky pawn in God's plan, his desire to protect the community from a messianic pretender used by God against him? Or was he a calculating villain, perhaps in league with a less honorable supernatural figure, who brought down Jesus Christ?

Such questions about motive will be on the minds of congregants during Holy Week. The Gospel writer John may have been determined to show that God is in charge of the movement toward the cross, but the congregation will hear echoes from other Gospels and even echoes from extrabiblical material such as contemporary movies and musicals as they consider Judas. Taking their questions and concerns

1. Karl Barth, *Church Dogmatics*, II/2, trans. G. T. Thomson (Edinburgh: T. & T. Clark, 1957), 502.

Exegetical Perspective

Repeatedly John indicates that Jesus knew of his coming betrayal and death. He knew what was in the hearts of others (2:24–25), he knew that Judas would betray him (6:70–71), and he knew that his "hour" had come (12:23; 13:1). This scene, set on the evening before Jesus' arrest, follows the footwashing and precedes the Farewell Discourse. As is well known, there is no account of the words of institution of the bread and the cup in John. In addition, the Last Supper in John occurs on the day before the Passover meal (see 18:28).

The reports of Jesus' emotional state are significant. Whereas we are familiar with the Synoptic accounts of Jesus' agony in the Garden of Gethsemane, in John, Jesus is troubled in the story of the raising of Lazarus (11:33, 38), following the coming of the Greeks (12:27), and following the footwashing (13:21). From the time that Judas leaves to betray him, Jesus is supremely in control, and there is no report of his being troubled in spirit, even when he goes out to the garden. Raymond E. Brown pointed out the parallel reference in Psalm 42:5–6: My soul is cast down within me.[1]

1. Raymond E. Brown, *The Gospel according to John*, Anchor Bible 29A (Garden City, NY: Doubleday, 1970), 577.

Homiletical Perspective

If you go to your computer and search for "betrayal," you will find nearly fourteen million sites where you can bone up on betrayal, and the number is growing exponentially. There is everything you might imagine: stories of betrayal, poems and songs about betrayal, articles on how to survive betrayal, and studies on the psychological and emotional costs of betrayal. There are even Web sites that purport to help you be a more effective betrayer and get by with it. You may be surprised at how deep you have to dig before finding any reference to the betrayal of Jesus by Judas. As a preacher, I wrongly assumed that the index of Web sites would go directly to entries that concerned Judas Iscariot. Instead, one discovers tens of thousands of pages of human pathos arising from tragic experiences of betrayal.

The Internet is not the only source of stories about betrayal. Preachers know that in the congregations that sit before us almost everyone has stories of betrayal to tell. They have stories about being betrayed by their spouses, their parents, or their children. They have stories about being betrayed by their employer, their pension fund, or their financial advisor. They have stories to tell about being betrayed by lifelong friends, their "anyway friends" who promised to love them anyway, no matter what. The stories are unending. The pain is

John 13:21-32

Theological Perspective

one who would betray him (6:71). For the writer of John's Gospel, it is vital that readers understand Jesus knows Judas's role from the very beginning.

Further still in John, Jesus' foreknowledge of all that is to come contrasts starkly with the disciples' ignorance at Judas's role. After Jesus proclaims that one of them will betray him, the disciple "whom Jesus loved" asks, "Lord, who is it?" (13:25) When Jesus tells Judas to go quickly and do what needs to be done, the disciples again do not know the meaning behind Jesus' words (v. 28). It is only Jesus who knows the role Judas must play. A few chapters later we hear Jesus speak of Judas's fate: "I guarded them, and not one of them was lost except the one destined to be lost, so that the scripture might be fulfilled" (17:12). Thus, with our passage at its center, the argument can be made that the "will and deed [of Judas] approach what God willed and did in this matter."[2]

Upon further reflection, however, Judas's role may not be quite as tidy as it first appears. Tension exists within the Gospel of John, and within our passage specifically. First, we must attend to the beginning of the passage: "Jesus was troubled in spirit, and declared, 'Very truly, I tell you, one of you will betray me'" (13:21). The portrayal of Jesus as one who calmly accepts Judas's betrayal is offset by this observation. Jesus is not troubled often in John, only at the death of Lazarus (11:33) and at knowing that the hour of glorification had come (12:27). Therefore, Jesus' being troubled by what Judas will do is theologically significant. Perhaps most notably, it points to the love and devotion Jesus has for Judas. We hear in chapter 6 that Jesus chose these Twelve, including Judas. In addition, chapter 13 begins with Jesus washing his disciples' feet, an act typically reserved for a slave. While Peter at first refuses Jesus' gesture of washing (13:8), there is no indication either that Judas objected or that Jesus passed over Judas. Further, Jesus signals Judas's betrayal with yet another intimate act of breaking bread together. Judas, as one of the called, is included in Jesus' acts of love toward his disciples. Despite earlier narrative cues that Judas will betray Jesus, none of the other disciples can imagine who the betrayer might be. Indeed, Judas is at every level one of them. Even when Judas breaks his fellowship with Jesus and the others by going out at night (13:30), the disciples' ignorance and Jesus' love for him remain. These images stand in tension with

2. Ibid., 501, as quoted in Anthony Cane, *The Place of Judas Iscariot in Christology* (Hampshire, UK: Ashgate Publishing, 2005), 68.

Pastoral Perspective

seriously might help uncover some equally difficult motives among members of a congregation.

Looking back on our own actions, or those of the church, we can often see what is really going on underneath in ways we could not see in the moment. Hiding deep reservoirs of anger with superficial criticism. Covering up guilt with heavy-handed charity. Veiling jealousy with gestures of compassion and care. This text might provide the hearers with an opportunity to explore the ways in which they as individuals, and as the church, seek to cover up missteps and sin, rather than open them up to the healing balm offered through Jesus' death and resurrection.

If Judas is simply evil, or in cahoots with something more evil than himself, then we might be quick to write him off as unworthy of consideration. Surely we could spot such an evildoer among us. Even after "Satan entered into him," the betrayer was not recognized by his community, and he was no outsider. Judas was one of the Twelve, loved and trusted by the others, up until the moment of betrayal. The message for the church today is that treachery, even in the innermost circle, is possible. The power and influence that comes with high-ranking leadership in the church is not a guarantee of faithfulness or of loyalty to Christ. Even the most beloved of the church's leaders should not be beyond scrutiny.

What motivates such treachery is harder to pinpoint. Perhaps Judas was bamboozled by the promise of power. Many thought that Jesus was the Messiah who had come to rule Israel. Perhaps Judas understood the Jesus movement as something more political than spiritual, something more historical than eternal, more earthbound than heaven bound. When Jesus began taking things in a different direction, perhaps Judas balked. Perhaps Judas himself felt betrayed by Jesus.

Or perhaps Judas was weak and afraid of what might be done to the Jews if Jesus continued. His motivation may have been the protection of Jews from the wrath of the Romans. Or maybe he was courageous and understood his role in the larger plan, understood that the confrontation with the authorities must come, and come soon, so that Jesus might be glorified.

Equally complicated motives reside in the hearts of church members today. Who can be trusted? Can even a pastor be trusted, if treachery is always a possibility? How do church members hold their leaders accountable without losing faith in the institution, or feeling betrayed themselves by those

Wednesday of Holy Week

Exegetical Perspective

In each of the Gospels, Jesus announces that one of the disciples will betray him (Matt. 26:21; Mark 14:18; Luke 22:21). Jesus uses the unutterably solemn formula "Amen, amen, I say to you" (v. 21) twenty-six times in the Gospel of John, in most cases to introduce a core saying or maxim drawn from tradition. The various accounts of the response of the disciples are revealing: in John they look at one another, "uncertain of whom he was speaking" (v. 22) whereas in Matthew and Mark they ask, "Surely not I?"

The Beloved Disciple is introduced for the first time in the Gospel at this point. Jesus and the disciples were reclining on their left elbows around a mat or low table on which the food was set. The disciple whom Jesus loved was reclining on Jesus' breast (the same phrase used in John 1:18 for Jesus' relation to the Father), hence in front of him or on his right side. The Beloved Disciple is never named in the Gospel of John. Although church tradition from the second century has identified him as John the son of Zebedee, many now hold that he was an eyewitness but probably not John the son of Zebedee.[2] While the Beloved Disciple was closest to Jesus, Peter was down or around the table. Their proximity to Jesus in this scene fits the pattern apparent in the rest of the Gospel in which the Beloved Disciple is at the cross (19:26–27), arrives at the empty tomb first (20:4), is the first to believe (20:8), and the first to recognize the risen Lord (21:7). When Peter motioned to the Beloved Disciple to find out the identity of the betrayer, Jesus answered that it was the one to whom he would give the morsel of bread. The giving of a choice morsel was an act that honored a favored guest (as in Ruth 2:14). Judas may have been just to the left of Jesus. It was "love's last appeal to one on the verge of perdition."[3] The Gospel leaves open the question of whether the Beloved Disciple understood the significance of this act. The giving of the morsel to the betrayer also fulfilled the words of Psalm 41:9, "Even my bosom friend in whom I trusted, who ate of my bread, has lifted the heel against me" (cf. John 13:18).

When Judas Iscariot received the morsel, we are told that Satan entered him (13:27). The reference in John 13:2, that Satan put it into his (Judas's) heart that Judas should betray him, is a Semitic idiom meaning that Satan decided or determined that

2. See James H. Charlesworth, *The Beloved Disciple* (Philadelphia: Trinity Press Int., 1995), 127–224; R. Alan Culpepper, *John the Son of Zebedee: The Life of a Legend* (Columbia: University of South Carolina Press, 1994), 72–85.
3. William E. Hull, "John," in *The Broadman Bible Commentary* (Nashville: Broadman Press, 1970), 330.

Homiletical Perspective

often too deep for words, and even after years of healing, the scars are still visible.

There are also those who sit before us who have done the betraying. Perhaps they betrayed another out of desperation, in a moment of panic, or because it was the only way to preserve their wounded façade. Most human beings have a streak of self-preservation, and when it is put to the test, we will sometimes abandon our promises, loves, and loyalties, to look after ourselves. The guilt runs deep. Just as being betrayed leaves scars, so does being the betrayer. Both betrayed and betrayer identify with these final moments in the upper room. Everyone has been where Jesus is. Many have been where Judas is.

Perhaps the most painful aspect of betrayal is that one nearly always bears it alone. It is difficult for those around us to see it coming. Even when they do, they are often too paralyzed by it to respond on our behalf. It is not surprising then that the disciples had difficulty figuring out what was going on. They were eating the Passover with Jesus. They knew the stories and traditions of the ritual meal. They had tasted the bitter herbs before. They knew what to expect. This was not the first time they had lounged at table with Jesus, dipping morsels of bread into the sauces and chutneys of holy-day cuisine. In the context of the Passover ritual, Jesus' words did not at first seem so out of place. They could not hear the implication of his words. It was impossible for the disciples to imagine that there could ever be among them a betrayal of any kind, especially a betrayal of Jesus.

The disciples were clueless at first about what was happening. That surely made the acts of Judas that much more painful for Jesus. Even after Jesus dipped the bread and gave it to Judas and told him to proceed with the plan, the disciples still were not sure what was happening. Perhaps he was just going on an errand. Perhaps more provisions were needed for the Passover meal. Even with his disciples gathered around him for a community meal, Jesus bore the burden of betrayal alone.

Judas had some burdens to bear as well. He left the upper room alone. He did not even have the comfort of the rest of the disciples being angry with him. He did not have great crowds cheering for him. He had only a few customers whose only interest in him was in what he had to sell. What good is thirty pieces of silver when you are all alone and have no one to spend it on?

Saint Judas. That is not a phrase that falls comfortably off the tongue. Judas is not like the other disciples; we do not name churches after Judas.

John 13:21-32

Theological Perspective

the later claim in John that Judas is the one lost (17:12). From Jesus' troubled spirit to his continued attempt at fellowship with Judas throughout this passage, we have a gripping image of Jesus' refusal to break relationship with Judas, even when Judas turns his back on Jesus.

Adding to the conceptual untidiness of the story, our passage also includes the phrase "Satan entered into him" (13:27). This statement stands in some tension with the chapter 6 claim of Jesus that "one of you is a devil" (6:70b). To say that Satan entered Judas after he received a piece of bread from Jesus is to suggest that Satan was not always in him, that he was not always "a devil." This sequence of events, scholars suggest, indicates that Judas was "a believer like the others."[3] However, with the entrance of Satan, the narrative continues, he takes leave of his communion with Jesus and goes out into the night. Through his actions he becomes, according to the logic of John's imagery, a child of darkness, having left behind Jesus, the light of the world.

Returning to where we began, it is important to note that John's portrayal of Judas is the harshest of the four Gospel accounts. He is identified as a devil early on, named a thief (12:6) and the betrayer whom Satan enters in chapter 13. Judas betrays Jesus "so that scripture might be fulfilled." Yet John's portrayal of Jesus' relationship to Judas is, especially in this passage, intimate, emotional, and loving. Judas clearly occupies the status of one of the chosen, and is treated with love by Jesus; despite this, he turns his back on Jesus, and sets out to hand him over to the authorities. Was it divine providence that led Judas to betray Jesus? Was it Satan? Or was it Judas's own bad choice? The passage encourages us to linger with the questions before offering a definitive response.

DEANNA THOMPSON

Pastoral Perspective

leaders? What of the courage it takes to hold a fellow Christian accountable? What if the one bringing the charge is correct, and yet is "crucified" by others for making "bad news" public? What if the one bringing the charge is misguided and causes harm? Even if we grant good motives to all members of the church, will not some still make mistakes that lead to disastrous ends?

What of God's motives? If the glory of Jesus Christ is the work of God, did God have a plan that included Judas's doing just what he did? Then are we not faced with the question of whether God actively uses people, even hurts people, to accomplish a greater good? If it was not God at work in Judas, then was it Satan? If it was Satan, then did God not have control of the situation? Or could God have known what Judas would do without making him do it, thereby turning an ugly act of betrayal into a beautiful act of resurrection and hope?

These theological and biblical questions have profound pastoral implications. How does a preacher proclaim God's omnipotence, God's grand plan unfolding before us, to the mother in the second pew whose child recently died in a car accident? How can a preacher talk fully and faithfully about God's forgiveness and not include Judas, even the one responsible for Jesus' death? If not Judas, then how can a preacher speak with integrity about forgiveness and reconciliation or even resurrection in the congregation?

It is an incredible story, told by John with great restraint and care. We can see the whispering Simon Peter wanting inside information, and the reclining disciple obliging him. Jesus delivers the answer for all to hear, but not knowing the question asked by the beloved disciple, most of the others miss it. The church has not solved the problem of Judas for 2,000 years, but the quest to understand his motives continues. Perhaps the challenge is learning to ask the right questions.

VERITY A. JONES

---

3. William Klassen, *Judas: Betrayer or Friend of Jesus?* (Minneapolis: Fortress Press, 1996), 149.

Exegetical Perspective

Judas would be the one to betray him. Recognizing that Judas was intent on his plan, Jesus told him to do quickly what he was going to do. Jesus' urging may be connected with his knowledge that his "hour" was at hand.

The theme of the contrast between Jesus' knowledge of all that was happening and the disciples' lack of understanding continues. None of them knew what Jesus meant or what Judas was doing. Some thought Jesus was telling him to buy something they would need for the Passover or to give something to the poor because Judas was the treasurer for the group (see 12:6). Ironically, Judas would give much more to "the poor" than even he realized.

John's note that when Judas went out "it was night" is wonderfully suggestive and dramatic. John uses light and darkness imagery all the way through the Gospel, from the prologue (1:4–5) to the festival of Booths (8:12), the healing of the blind man (9:4), the discovery of the empty tomb while it was still dark (20:1), and the appearance of the risen Lord at first light (21:4). The darkness outside matched the darkness within Judas, but the reference may be a further allusion to Psalm 42: "at night [God's] song is with me" (42:8).

The scene invites searching reflection on our propensity to seek our own ends and our capacity for betrayal of even those we love. Surpassing the abyss of self-love is the depth of Jesus' love, love even for those who betray themselves and others. The poignant scene of Jesus with his uncomprehending disciples on the night before his death reveals all the foundational ironies of the gospel: betrayal revealing divine love, glorification through brutal death, and light shown in the deepest darkness. It beckons us to love while simultaneously announcing grace for those too blind, too deluded, and too self-centered to respond to it. This is the love that marks Jesus' disciples (13:35).

R. ALAN CULPEPPER

Homiletical Perspective

How many people do you know who name their children Judas? Has the time come when we might be more sympathetic to Judas, perhaps seeing him as someone who got caught in competing interests and could not escape? After all, Judas just had a role to play in the drama of our redemption. Someone had to be the bad guy, right? Wrong. Jesus was in plenty of trouble already. There were plenty of accusers standing at the ready, waiting for the opportune moment to put Jesus on trial for all of the crimes he had committed. Jesus did not need Judas to betray him. The die had been cast quite apart from any action of Judas. Jesus needed Judas to pay attention.

When Jesus dipped the morsel of bread and gave it to Judas, perhaps it was more than just a signal to the other disciples. In the story-rich context of Passover, perhaps Jesus was remembering how Boaz treated Ruth: acceptance and respect even in the face of competing realities (Ruth 2:14). Judas and Jesus both recognized their time together was over. With the other disciples they had shared quite a tour of duty as they preached and healed their way through Galilee. Judas had seen and done a great deal as a companion of Jesus, but the end was upon him. Satan had entered into him. It was time for Judas to leave and do what he had to do. When Jesus said to Judas, "Do quickly what you are going to do," those could well have been Jesus' last words of love for Judas. Jesus knew that betraying him was not easy for Judas, that Satan's control had Judas off balance, and the sooner it was over the sooner Judas would be able to see that the saving embrace of the cross included everybody, even him.

J. NEIL ALEXANDER

Exodus 12:1-4 (5-10), 11-14

¹The LORD said to Moses and Aaron in the land of Egypt: ²This month shall mark for you the beginning of months; it shall be the first month of the year for you. ³Tell the whole congregation of Israel that on the tenth of this month they are to take a lamb for each family, a lamb for each household. ⁴If a household is too small for a whole lamb, it shall join its closest neighbor in obtaining one; the lamb shall be divided in proportion to the number of people who eat of it. ⁵Your lamb shall be without blemish, a year-old male; you may take it from the sheep or from the goats. ⁶You shall keep it until the fourteenth day of this month; then the whole assembled congregation of Israel shall slaughter it at twilight. ⁷They shall take some of the blood and put it on the two doorposts and the lintel of the houses in which they eat it. ⁸They shall eat the lamb that same night; they shall eat it roasted over the fire with unleavened bread and

Theological Perspective

The Lord's passing over his people on the way to kill the firstborn of the Egyptians is a most surprising foundation for a festival. It is not, as with other formative events of Israel's history, that the Lord is saving them from the depredations of some foreign power, but rather from the Lord's own threat! (The "destroyer" of 12:23 is only a functionary.) The danger of the Lord to his own people is relatively well attested in the Pentateuch (Lev. 10:1–3; Num. 16:35–50). Especially relevant is God's attack on Moses (Exod. 4:20–26), which is also averted by the application of blood. One of the central messages of the Pentateuch, and especially of the book of Exodus, seems to be that proximity to God is inherently dangerous, because of the intensity of God's holiness (Exod. 19:18–25; 20:18–19).

The application of blood to the doors of the Israelites' houses is a marker to the Lord to spare those within. Everyone else is subject to the divine wrath; even the firstborn of the animals suffer for Pharaoh's hard-heartedness. Analogous situations take place in the present day when innocents suffer for the sins of their leaders. One could even read the text ecologically: the whole created order groans when humans fail in their duty to be shepherds over the earth (Gen. 1:28). Indeed, the Lord's punishment of Egypt is of modest scale by comparison with the

Pastoral Perspective

Maundy Thursday fires the imagination. Like the stain that remains after the dyeing of Easter eggs, the iconic Last Supper is steeped in red—the color of wine, roses, anger, and passion. Christ's Last Supper is a candle-lit valentine of a night, a dangerous tango set against the drumbeat of Jerusalem's crowded streets, rumbling with the urgency of the Passover festival. For Jesus' beloved, it was an evening of fevered emotion and star-crossed longing. In the room where they reclined together, the room they would always remember, Jesus raised the Passover cup, and talked of new blood being poured out. Then Jesus knelt before them with a pail of water. "You must love one another," Jesus commanded ("maundy," from Latin *mandatum*, commandment), as he tenderly dried the dirty water from their feet. In this one startling turn, an unexpected door scraped open, revealing an exodus reinterpreted by Jesus that made sense only in a brokenhearted future.

The motif of reinterpretation might surface as a tension for some ecumenical-minded congregations today, as such a seminal Jewish text—the Passover story of Exodus 12—is appropriated for Christian Holy Week. It may be comforting to note that the priestly writers of Exodus themselves likely reinterpreted the Passover from an ancient spring festival that celebrated the moving of flocks to new

bitter herbs. ⁹Do not eat any of it raw or boiled in water, but roasted over the fire, with its head, legs, and inner organs. ¹⁰You shall let none of it remain until the morning; anything that remains until the morning you shall burn. ¹¹This is how you shall eat it: your loins girded, your sandals on your feet, and your staff in your hand; and you shall eat it hurriedly. It is the passover of the Lord. ¹²For I will pass through the land of Egypt that night, and I will strike down every firstborn in the land of Egypt, both human beings and animals; on all the gods of Egypt I will execute judgments: I am the Lord. ¹³The blood shall be a sign for you on the houses where you live: when I see the blood, I will pass over you, and no plague shall destroy you when I strike the land of Egypt.

¹⁴This day shall be a day of remembrance for you. You shall celebrate it as a festival to the Lord; throughout your generations you shall observe it as a perpetual ordinance.

Exegetical Perspective

Exodus 12:1–14 provides the liturgical instructions concerning the Passover. The final plague, the death of the firstborn of Egypt, has already been announced (Exod. 11:1–6). The distinction has already been drawn between the destruction coming on Egypt and the peace and safety provided to the Israelites (11:7). This twofold format of "announcement of judgment" and "assurance of distinction" has occurred frequently in the preceding plague series (flies, 8:23; disease among the livestock, 9:4; hail, 9:26; darkness, 10:23). In fact, the narrative flow between the announcement of the final plague in 11:1–10 and its fulfillment in 12:29–36 closely parallels the previous plague stories. The instructions in 12:1–14 are, therefore, unnecessary from a narrative point of view. God's ability to make a distinction between Egypt and Israel has, up to this point, never been dependent upon the activities of Israel. These instructions interrupt the narrative flow, slow down the pace of the plague cycle, and, most importantly, refocus and reinterpret the events associated with the exodus from Egypt. What would have otherwise been simply the plague of the death of the firstborn becomes, through these instructions, the Passover of the Lord.

The passage itself is organized into four sections: a reorganization of time (vv. 1–2), instructions about the lamb used in the ritual (vv. 3–11), instructions

Homiletical Perspective

Exodus 12 is a manual for the preparation of the Passover meal. The text merits a careful review to cast the Holy Thursday observance as a commemoration of Jesus' last meal with the disciples. This text delivers several themes for preaching and community life that deserve emphasis, just as Exodus as a whole deserves a thorough gleaning for a tradition that informs and shapes contemporary faith and practice.

Verses 1–10 shape the proper preparation for the feast. It is to be a feast prepared for a household, or shared with a neighbor. The rules for preparation are strict and clear, reflecting a familiar form of sacrifice based on dietary laws for meal preparation. The preacher may find it helpful to refer to a Bible dictionary for the meal customs of first-century Jewish tradition in order fully to understand and interpret the importance of the preparation of the lamb for the Passover meal. This tradition marks the protection of Israel and sets the tone for the final meal of Jesus with his disciples. For the Christian community, Passover becomes the context for the Last Supper, which gives rise to the ritual of Communion (or Eucharist).

In Jewish tradition, the preparation of food and the sharing of a meal not only constitute religious and cultural practice; they also sustain family and community in discipline and adherence to the law.

Exodus 12:1-4 (5-10), 11-14

Theological Perspective

flood (Gen. 7:21–23) or the apocalyptic destruction promised in certain prophetic passages (Isa. 13:5; Luke 21:33–36, etc.).

The association of the paschal lamb with Jesus (e.g., John 1:29, 36; 1 Cor. 5:7) was of central importance to New Testament authors and has been important to Christian interpretation ever since. According to Revelation 7:14 and 12:11, the blood of the Lamb cleanses from sin (cf. also 1 Pet. 1:18–19) and conquers the devil. Following that tradition, John Chrysostom offered a typological interpretation of Exodus 12:13: The blood of the lamb "in its types has washed away sins. And if it had such great power in its types, if death shuddered so much at the figure, how would it not even more so be in terror of the reality itself?"[1] He was speaking about the first Passover—the lamb's blood must have been all the more powerful when actual blood was used; but the observation also has implications for the second coming. If the blood of a lamb protects the people of God from death, how much more will the Lamb of God conquer death on behalf of God's people (e.g., Rev. 21:3–4, 20:13–14)?

Although Christ's death is the once-for-all atoning sacrifice for sin, one might ask, what are the markers of the church today that should protect us from wrath, analogous to the blood on the lintels? Paul calls for his hearers to imitate Christ by offering their bodies "as a living sacrifice," that is, by being transformed and following the will of God (Rom. 12:1–2). Being freed from judgment by Christ's sacrifice, the church has been made free to distinguish itself in this way.

The people are commanded to eat the Passover meal hurriedly, with sandals on their feet and staffs in their hands. In a word, they are commanded to be ready, at any moment, to move with God. Cyril of Alexandria said that it is the duty of Christians "not to have, as it were, their loins ungirt and loose but to be ready cheerfully to undertake whatever labors become the saints."[2] Believers today might ask themselves, Are we prepared to move with God when we receive the command? Are we free to follow God? Or are we weighed down by our possessions and by responsibilities of dubious importance? The festival effectively celebrates things that humans generally find stressful: transience, flight, the absence of possessions. It is a most surprising foundation for

1. John Chrysostom, *Commentary on Saint John the Apostle and Evangelist: Homilies 1–48*, trans. Sister Thomas Aquinas Goggin (New York: Fathers of the Church, 1957), 470.
2. Cyril of Alexandria, *Homilies in the Gospel of Luke*, 92.

Pastoral Perspective

pastures.[1] This original nomadic flavor, with its undertow of movement and the image of a good shepherd moving sheep into a new vista, offers us a revitalizing energy. The patina of thousands of years of ritual and the retelling of the old, old story can lull believers into regarding Holy Week with passive awe, as an iconic work of art, instead of the electric, world-turning force that it is.

Without a doubt, today's lection of Exodus 12 plunges us into wakefulness. Embedded in a plethora of details about how to celebrate the festival, we find some of the most fierce and primal language of our scriptural canon. What are we to make of the angel of the Lord, murdering scores of innocent children and animals in cold blood, all to win a kingly duel with Pharaoh? The picture of Hebrew families smearing lamb blood thickly across their lintels as a cue for God's destroyer to "pass over" their loved ones is hard to embrace. Were the Israelites excited by God's show of might, or were they horrified by the means to the end? The salvific triumph of this story seems to be drowned out by the inescapable sound of weeping Egyptian parents.

A Jewish friend, a cantor in the Reform tradition, remarked recently that this painful conundrum is an age-old Jewish quandary:

> One sensitive midrash (the Jewish interpretive storytelling tradition) turns another similar problem—the drowning of Pharaoh's army—into a teaching moment. In the midrash, as the waters crush the Egyptian soldiers at the parting of the Red Sea, the angels in heaven begin rejoicing in the destruction of Israel's tormentors. God chastises them, saying, "Are you to sing while my children are destroyed?" Even the evildoers of Egypt were human, and God will not tolerate the celebration of human suffering, no matter how deserving the sufferers. For this reason, at our Passover seders, we remove one drop of wine from our glass as we name the ten plagues, reducing our joy in acknowledgment that our freedom was won at the cost of great suffering of others.

It was a costly liberation that freed the Israelites from the chains of Egyptian oppression, and on this Maundy Thursday we are reminded of the terrible price Jesus paid for our own deliverance as well. Even so, the violent imagery of atonement theology is hard for many congregations to enter. It is there-fore all too tempting to tone down the blood, to

1. Judith E. Sanderson, "Exodus," in *The New Oxford Annotated Bible*, 3rd ed. (New York: Oxford University Press, 2001), 98.

about the significance of the ritual as a whole (vv. 12–13), and a concluding notice about the memorial nature of the ritual (v. 14).

"This month will be for you" (vv. 1–2). The refocusing significance of the following passage is hinted at in this introduction. These events, even before they occur narratively, already reorganize time in such a way that the month of Nisan becomes the "first" and—by implication of the Hebrew word *rosh*—the "most important" of the months of the year. These incipient liturgical-historical-narrative events reorganize time.

Instructions concerning the lamb (vv. 3–11). The ritual actions themselves focus almost exclusively on the physical object of the lamb. The Passover lamb is present in every sentence of the instructions and provides the center around which all other activities occur. It—its body, blood, or flesh—consistently appears as a direct object of verbs ("take" in vv. 3, 5, 7; "slaughter" in v. 6; "put" in v. 7; "eat" in vv. 8, 9, 11; "leave over" in v. 10), or as an object of prepositions (usually "from" in vv. 4, 9, 10). The lamb is a consistent, passive object that is used throughout the instructions and the ritual that they outline.

Twice, however, the lamb appears as the subject of a sentence in the instructions. At the beginning of verse 5, the lamb appears as the subject: "Your lamb shall be without blemish, a year-old male." The syntax of the sentence in Hebrew, however, highlights the primacy of the lamb: "A whole, year-old lamb *will be for you [yihyeh lakem]*." Likewise at the beginning of verse 6, the lamb does not stand as an object here (contra NRSV: "You shall keep it"), but rather is the subject: "*And it will be for you* for keeping [*wehayah lakem*]." These sentences show that the lamb, including its blood and flesh, are not only passive objects that are manipulated in the course of the ritual. The real significance of the lamb is in its relationship with the Israelites. The lamb is "for you."

The lamb itself, moreover, provides the central instantiation or symbol of the entire exodus complex. The lamb defines the existence and status of the congregation of Israel in its households (vv. 3–4). Its blood defines the boundaries of those households literally by marking the liminal area between those "inside" and "outside" the house (vv. 5–7). It is roasted and eaten in order to provide strength for the coming trek (vv. 8–10). Its manner of roasting, with head, legs, and organs, defines it as a real meal and not as a sacrifice or offering for

Writing a sermon for Holy Thursday that investigates the preparation of the Passover meal is a preacher's opportunity to remind a faith community of the deep meanings of food for the sacred purpose of sustaining tradition. This is a time to remember the deeply spiritual, cultural, and religious origins of the Last Supper.

The Exodus text invites communicants to understand the power and providence of YHWH in defining the ritual of Passover. The ritual is to be maintained for all of history: "you shall observe it as a perpetual ordinance" (v. 14). Holy Thursday invites the Christian faithful to join with the people of Israel in maintaining the tradition of remembering God's deliverance of the faithful.

Exodus 12 reinforces themes of tradition, history, and memory. Along with the laws of Moses, these themes sustain the religion of the Jewish people. They also provide the preacher with substantive concepts for helping the text stay alive in communities of faith. As we struggle forward in congregations, we must be reminded of the past and its impact on our contemporary challenges and struggles. It is the preacher's task to declare evidence of the foundation of the past, connecting it to the sustenance of community through the continuation of religious ritual. Ritual helps family, community, and religion stay alive. Holy Thursday is the cornerstone of our connection to an ancient faith that thrives as a result of vital and revitalized ritual.

Careful study of verses 1–4 encourages a preacher or teacher to assist those in religious community to look at the importance of tradition both in their observance of religious events and in the context of their own church family. Questions for reflection might include these: what is our origin in this particular place? What holds us together as a practicing faith community? What does our denomination, name, or location teach us about our purpose as a community of believers?

Religious tradition asks those who willingly participate in communities of faith both to follow certain traditions and to sustain those traditions with the addition of creative and sustainable activities that open the community to their deep meaning.

In verse 4 the Exodus text instructs those who would maintain the ritual of the Passover to prepare a lamb for a household—and if the household is too small, to join together with a neighbor. In this way, the text encourages us to invite others to join us in our traditional celebrations, including them in the

Exodus 12:1-4 (5-10), 11-14

Theological Perspective

a festival. For all that, Passover finds clear analogies in the message of Jesus. The parable of the Bridesmaids (Matt. 25:1–13) warns Christians to keep their lamps filled, lest they be unprepared for the coming of the Bridegroom. Like us today, the disciples were often not ready to follow Christ. Even at the moment of his greatest need, they could not stay awake and watchful on his behalf (Mark 14:37–41 and pars.). For a metaphor that speaks to our own world, we might think of having our shoes tied and being ready to run with God. The New Testament authors frequently imagined the walk of faith as a footrace; Hebrews 12:1 exhorts us to "lay aside every weight" so as to "run . . . the race that is set before us" (cf. 1 Cor. 9:24; 2 Tim. 4:7). Moving with God is all the more difficult during Holy Week. Usually we are in one place or another, emotionally—either Good Friday or Easter Sunday—and it is jarring to travel so rapidly from one to the other. The text tries to prepare us for the journey. We may take comfort that at least we, unlike the disciples, have been told the Easter story many times and know what to expect.

Telling the story is also an important facet of the Exodus passage. It ends with the commandment to celebrate the festival of the Passover "throughout your generations" (v. 14). The commandment implies not so subtly that we are prone to forget the mighty acts of God on our behalf. The text does not assume that the rituals it prescribes are immediately comprehensible; in fact, it anticipates that children will ask, "What do you mean by all this?" (v. 26). This question and its answers are still reenacted in the liturgy of the traditional Jewish Passover seder. It is not only children who may struggle with this story; its terror and strangeness pose a challenge to many readers. Some may even recoil at this surprising festival. However, like children who do not choose their family and background, we do not choose our God; rather, we are chosen (Gen. 18:19; Deut. 10:15, etc.). Like the Israelites, we are delivered from slavery and death to serve the Lord (Exod. 3:12).

CHRISTOPHER B. HAYS

Pastoral Perspective

reduce the Easter story to the existential level, presenting Jesus as a wise teacher who became so politically subversive that he was silenced quickly amid a raucous crowd that jammed the city for the holiday. That story, we can buy into.

Our Exodus lectionary passage forces us to a deeper read, as we acknowledge the particularly Jewish history and context of Jesus. Passover was the way Jesus understood his earthly fate, laced through with echoes of Abraham and Isaac, as Jesus willingly allowed himself to be bound to a cross-shaped altar with God's own hand upon the killing knife. For Jesus, unlike Isaac, no substitute ram appeared in the thicket. The Son was not spared. God, in the role of Abraham, was not spared either. A parent's worst nightmare fell without reprieve, just as it had upon the Egyptians in that long Passover night.

The Passover framework reminds us that what is at stake at Easter is not just a beautiful liturgy or a time of joy, but the very crux of life and death itself. Liberation is the point. Christ wants to roll away the stone upon our chests. What is suffocating and killing us? What imprisons us? What do we need to be freed from? Is it the death grip of a culture that perpetuates at every turn a soul-destroying acquisitiveness? Is it the habits of mind that chain us to distractions and hungers that keep our souls bowed to the ground?

What would it mean for each of us to comprehend that we are trapped without a hope in Egypt, toiling in bitter service with no escape? My cantor friend says that the Hebrew word for Egypt is *Mitzrayim*, based on a root akin to the word *tzar*, which means "a narrow place." In our narrow places, what would it be like to witness again the signs and wonders of YHWH, working dazzling power while Pharaoh's magicians flounder? What would it mean for us to finally understand that God's longing for us is so great that God will do anything, going out beyond the limits of human imagination, out to the place of Abraham's homemade altar, to wrest us away from the suffocation of our slavery?

SUZANNE WOOLSTON-BOSSERT

YHWH (cf. Lev. 1:8–9). The meal, as with the lamb, is for Israel. The manner of its being eaten is, likewise, an appropriate symbol for the exodus as a whole: the eater is ready to leave and must eat the meal quickly (*behippazon*; cf. Deut. 20:3). The lamb itself is the subject of the final sentence in the instructions: "It"—that is, the lamb itself—"is the passover of YHWH" (v. 11b; note also v. 21). The whole ritual and the whole event are irretrievably bound up in the lamb.

"The blood will be for you" (vv. 12–13). These verses link the ritual with the wider narrative complex in which they appear. They tie the ritual backwards to the announcement of the plague in 11:5 and the assurance of protection in 11:7, as well as foreshadowing the actual narrative fulfillment in 12:29–30. The blood of the lamb performs a dual role. It is primarily, as with the lamb as a whole, a symbol of the status of Israel; the blood is a sign "for you." It is also, however, a sign for YHWH and the divine distinction that YHWH has between Israel and Egypt. As such, the blood is a symbol not only of the deliverance but of the relationship between YHWH and Israel, the sign that they share in common.

"This day will be for you" (v. 14). The text ends, as it began, with a reordering of time. The day of the Passover and of Israel's deliverance is not simply a past event. It becomes a memorial and a festival. As opposed to most sequences of memorials, this is not simply a past event that people subsequently remember, constructing a ritual to memorialize it. The instructions concerning the Passover of YHWH *precede* the events and memorialize them, in a sense, before they narratively occur! As such, the narrative of the exodus itself becomes one with the ritual, one with the memorial, and those who participate in it become one with those who take and eat in the story itself.[1]

ROY L. HELLER

discussion, practice, and cooperative enactment of religious ritual for the purposes of enlivening faith and education.

A faithful reflection on the text would also include the role of memory in the life of the faith community. Verse 14 reads, "This day shall be a day of remembrance for you." As prescribed by the sacred text, ritual is foundational to sustaining our memory. When we keep the rituals, we preserve the conditions under which faith is both reenacted and continued "as a perpetual ordinance."

At the end of his life, Jesus met with his best friends, commemorating the event of the Passover as an observance in perpetuity for what would turn out to be the emerging community of Christians. In a world that is busy keeping up with movement, technical communication, long-distance family, and changing global realities, the invitation to keep rituals that sustain faith and community becomes a requirement for churches that wish to survive.

Keeping the Passover alive in the memory of a congregation establishes a link for faithful preachers to examine all the kinds of evil that can enslave human beings, including forced immigration, war, famine, inadequate health care, and environmental demise. God calls people of faith to remember God's providence with the renewal of the Passover memory each year, following a prescribed ritual.

For Christians, Holy Thursday is the beginning of new life in faith. In this text from Exodus, the preacher has an opportunity to remind the people of a narrative that maintains religious history and identity for all times and all places. The preacher can encourage the people to remember the narrative of the text, adding to it the faith, struggle, and history of the local community as all move forward together.

Ritual, tradition, history, and memory cannot be frozen in the ancient past. The text speaks the history and tradition of the Jewish people. Holy Thursday invites us into the procession of history and memory by engaging our energies to follow this "perpetual ordinance" in our own time and place.

CLAUDIA HIGHBAUGH

---

1. On this point, see the remarkable exposition by Terence Fretheim in *Exodus* (Louisville, KY: John Knox Press, 1991), 133–39.

Psalm 116:1-2, 12-19

¹I love the LORD, because he has heard
  my voice and my supplications.
²Because he inclined his ear to me,
  therefore I will call on him as long as I live.
. . . .
¹²What shall I return to the LORD
  for all his bounty to me?
¹³I will lift up the cup of salvation
  and call on the name of the LORD,
¹⁴I will pay my vows to the LORD
  in the presence of all his people.

Theological Perspective

Psalm 116 expresses profound religious emotion, the joyful gratitude of one whom God has graciously delivered from the anguish of suffering and imminent death. Now liberated from peril, the psalmist bursts forth in a paean of gratitude and thanksgiving; proclaims God's graciousness, righteousness, and mercy; and promises to make a full public witness of the saving grace that he or she has personally experienced: "I will lift up the cup of salvation and call on the name of the LORD, I will pay my vows to the LORD in the presence of all his people" (vv. 13–14). Divine grace begets human gratitude, commitment, and a boundless sense of freedom and joy in the gift of new life. In this elemental sense, Psalm 116 is the very paradigm of the biblical vision of salvation and a life redeemed through the surprising, unconditioned grace of God, lived freely, lovingly, and joyfully in committed faith and worship.

However, if it is the task of theology to *think critically* about the claims and experiences of faith, an important problem appears throughout the psalm: "I love the LORD, because he has heard my voice and my supplications. Because he inclined his ear to me, therefore I will call on him as long as I live" (vv. 1–2). The sentiment is pure, simple, and heartfelt, like any spontaneous expression of gratitude for an act of

Pastoral Perspective

The members of your congregation who fill the pews on Holy Thursday will long to meet the mystery of God in a way that differs from what is typically offered on Sunday mornings. The decision to attend your service that evening is a choice to enter the dark, which worshipers on that night do literally, as they leave their houses on a winter evening, and spiritually, as they enter the narrative of Jesus' arrest, passion, and death. The readings and rituals of the Triduum—the Three Holy Days that precede Easter Sunday—offer hungry believers an opportunity to participate in a particular union and solidarity with Jesus through their witness to the sacred events retold in the readings and enacted in the foot washing (for some churches), the celebration of the Holy Eucharist, and other liturgical acts such as the stripping of the altar.

It is important to note that the trajectory of the Holy Thursday liturgy overturns both the common pattern of prayer and our expectations about the way God works in the world. Here the familiar sequence of events, in which the forces of chaos and suffering succumb to the limitless power of a faithful God, is thoroughly upended. This night begins with a memory of the Passover—a celebration of the devotion of mighty YHWH—and moves through an account of the Last Supper to the arrest of Jesus, the

15Precious in the sight of the Lord
   is the death of his faithful ones.
16O Lord, I am your servant;
   I am your servant, the child of your serving girl.
   You have loosed my bonds.
17I will offer to you a thanksgiving sacrifice
   and call on the name of the Lord.
18I will pay my vows to the Lord
   in the presence of all his people,
19in the courts of the house of the Lord,
   in your midst, O Jerusalem.
   Praise the Lord!

Exegetical Perspective

Psalm 116 may best be described as a hymn of
thanksgiving (vv. 1–2, 12–19) that brackets a lament
(vv. 3–11). Although the psalm is presented as the
reflections of an individual, it was also certainly
recited in postexilic synagogues and perhaps in the
preexilic temple as well. The affirmation, "I will pay
my vows to the Lord [YHWH] in the presence of all
his people" (vv. 14, 18), as well as the pledge to offer
a sacrifice of thanksgiving in the Jerusalem temple
(vv. 17, 19) suggest the use of the psalm in a cultic
context. The fact that YHWH is referred to in the
third person "he" rather than the second person
"you" also suggests that the psalm was addressed to a
worshiping community rather than being the prayer
of an individual addressed to YHWH himself. Some
scholars have argued that the original psalm was
divided into eight stanzas, each ending with the
phrase "therefore on the name of the Lord [YHWH]
I will call," which due to copyists' errors is now
preserved only in vv. 13b and 17b. Such a
reconstruction suggests that from a very early time
the psalm was used as an antiphonal recitation in the
liturgy of the temple and/or synagogue.[1]

1. Charles A. Briggs and Emilie G. Briggs, *The Book of Psalms*, International
Critical Commentary 19 (New York: Charles Scribner's Sons, 1906), 2:397–99;
Sigmund Mowinckel, *The Psalms in Israel's Worship*, trans. D. R. Ap-Thomas
(New York: Abingdon Press, 1962), 2:31–32.

Homiletical Perspective

This is an appropriate text for the night when we
"lift up the cup of salvation." Given that most
North American congregations worship on Sunday
mornings, this night is different from all other
nights. We worship after nightfall, remembering how
our feet have been scrubbed in Christ's grace, how
our abandonment of Christ has been predicted, and
how our continuing reception of Christ's body and
blood has been instituted. The context shapes our
homiletic.

The lectionary cutting of the text can also shape
the proclamation of it. This psalm thanks God for a
physical healing, but the descriptions of illness and
healing (vv. 3–11) are excised from this text. What
we have is the thank-you note (vv. 12–19).

One homiletical direction would be to preach a
teaching sermon on the Lord's Supper as Eucharist
(thanksgiving), illuminating the heart of the
Communion liturgy by drawing upon the language
of the psalm. Beneath all varied perspectives on the
Christian sacrament, the work of the people is the
same. We gather at the Table to bless God for all
God's works in history, to recall the work of Jesus
Christ, and to call upon the Holy Spirit to fill this
occasion with the presence of the crucified and risen
Lord. Then we receive Christ by breaking the bread
and lifting up the cup of salvation.

Psalm 116:1-2, 12-19

Theological Perspective

unexpected and unconditioned mercy and favor. However, these lines can also be read to suggest the possibility of converting this experience into something like a bargain between ourselves and God. Devotion to God becomes predicated on God's taking favorable actions toward us. In the extreme case, we promise, however subtly or indirectly, to love and serve God in *exchange* for God's continued favor.

While this possibility is not logically or inevitably entailed in the psalmist's song of gratitude, it is a temptation. It offers a way of perverting the sheer grace and gratitude celebrated in the psalm into a manipulative, anxious contract that represents faithlessness, fear, and distrust—pandering to our fears and our unfaith. When we worship and serve God *only* in response to divine benefits delivered (and also covertly threaten to withdraw our support if God fails us), we make God subject to our own agenda and manipulation—an idol. This perversion of faith is not an abstract possibility; it is a pervasive feature of most popular Christian piety and a perennial temptation for all who believe.

This theological issue is part of a broader problem inherent in all forms of devotion and commitment. If we examine the motives and affirmations implicit in any committed relationship, we find, for example, that commitment to one's spouse may be supported by a variety of appealing practical and economic advantages. A marriage based solely on a calculus of self-interest, however, is not truly committed, and is subject to recall if the "terms" of the contract are not fulfilled. A relationship is *committed* to the extent that it has the power to override negativity and failure. Commitment affirms a relationship *intrinsically* as an end or good in itself, and not solely as a means to something else. It is this *intrinsic* affirmation that constitutes a commitment and distinguishes it from a *contract*, whose fundamental purpose is not the relationship itself but some extrinsic good that it seeks to secure.

Ministers and priests are said to be *committed* to their vocation insofar as their loyalty overrides the costs and sacrifices that their vocation entails; they are not "in it" for the money or the prestige—at least not entirely or fundamentally. Of course in the real world, pure commitment—totally unalloyed with self-interest in any form, or even asserted in defiance of self-interest—is rare and arguably a human impossibility. Any loyalty or devotion claiming to be authentically committed will involve a measure of intrinsic affirmation; one cannot be in it entirely for the purpose of gaining an ulterior good.

Pastoral Perspective

world's most famous story of devastation and betrayal. It is into this liturgical framework that Psalm 116 has been set.

Psalm 116:1–2, 12–19 presents an image of the kind of God we want to have and the kind of Christians we long to be. It draws a picture of a Creator who "hears [our] voice and [our] supplications," and a worshiper who responds to the attention and action of God with ecstatic gratitude and a vow of lifelong public devotion. Here is a song of mutual love, loyalty, and care. The psalmist exults in deliverance from great adversity—probably an illness—and celebrates in particular God's availability in a time of desolation. The psalmist rejoices because of the knowledge that he or she matters to God.

The selection of verses 1 and 2, which describe God's empathic listening, and the omission of verses 3–11, which describe God's actual intervention, underscores God's compassion rather than God's might. It draws our own attention to God's ear and not God's arm. Verse 15, "Precious in the sight of the LORD is the death of his faithful ones," echoes this perspective: God mourns but does not prevent the death of a beloved one. Some of your hearers will automatically associate this verse with Jesus. Others, especially those in great crisis, may identify with it themselves.

All who enter your sanctuary that night bring with them their own experience. Some will respond to the psalmist's joy by recalling their own deliverance from tragedy or their gratitude in having been able to endure it. Others may be reeling from the shock of a terminal diagnosis or profound anxiety about financial security. Preachers who serve in congregations that include refugees from countries beset by war or famine, or in areas that have recently suffered natural disasters, will bear in mind parishioners' horrific memories of the loss of loved ones and the experience of being violently uprooted from home.

Like the author of Psalm 116, many of your listeners interpret the events of their lives through the lens of their belief in the willingness and power of God to act on their behalf. The clash between that hope and the realities of their lives may lead to confusion and no small distress, even among the most theologically sophisticated. Although no one has adequately explained why God allows suffering, everyone knows that God does. Verses 1–2, especially in combination with verse 15, can offer comfort. Additionally, few in your congregation will recognize

Exegetical Perspective

As is the case with most of the psalms, it is impossible to definitively identify the author of Psalm 116 or establish when it was composed. Reference to a sacrifice at the sanctuary in Jerusalem (vv. 17–19) suggests a post-Davidic, First Temple period date at the earliest. Some scholars have suggested a date as late as the late Hellenistic period for the composition of this psalm.[2]

Although the authorship and date of composition of Psalm 116 are matters of much speculation and debate, there is general scholarly consensus that (1) the psalm reached its final form around 200 BCE, and (2) when the Psalter reached its final form, the psalm was regularly used in the liturgy of the synagogue.[3]

If one had to identify a few key words or phrases, the most obvious would be the first verse, "I love the LORD, because he has heard my voice and my supplications," and the final word of verse 19 (*halelu-yah*), which translates into English as "Praise the LORD!" This final word, sometimes transliterated in English as "Hallelujah," is expressed in the second-person masculine plural imperative, providing another hint that this psalm was used in worship, as it ends with the command for the congregation to "Praise YHWH!"

From the lectionary reading, it is unclear why the psalmist loves YHWH or why he exhorts his fellow worshipers to praise YHWH. The reason for the psalmist's attitude is clearly stated in the lament (vv. 3–11), which the lectionary reading eliminates. Although the lament decries the psalmist's suffering, it also emphasizes YHWH's faithfulness to the "simple" (v. 6) and ultimately proclaims that "you have delivered my soul from death, my eyes from tears, my feet from stumbling" (v. 8). It is YHWH's faithfulness and protection in the midst of various crises that evokes the psalmist's love for God and prompts him to urge fellow worshipers to praise YHWH. The psalmist does not believe that faith will spare one from life's difficulties, but rather, that it enables one to endure pain and suffering and still maintain hope. In order to appreciate the full impact of the psalm, it is necessary to take into account the lament that the lectionary reading omits. Otherwise, one is left with the impression that this psalm consists of the words of a pious believer whose love of God is unrelated to the suffering and deliverance the psalmist has seen and experienced.

2. Briggs and Briggs, 1:lxxxviii–xcii.
3. Artur Weiser, *The Psalms*, trans. Herbert Hartwell, Old Testament Library, ed. G. Ernest Wright et al. (Philadelphia: Westminster Press, 1962), lxxxix–xcii.

Homiletical Perspective

Even though this is the regular practice of the church, we cannot take it for granted. Children and new adult converts may startle us awake by asking the foundational questions that we answered years ago. Like the person who dared to ask his pastor, "When the bread and wine are distributed in worship, everybody becomes quiet, and it looks like many are praying. So what should I say to God when I pray during the Lord's Supper?"

She pondered the question briefly and replied, "You could do worse than to pray, 'Thank you, God, for all that you have done for us, and for all that you continue to do for the world.'"

This section of Psalm 116 focuses on thanksgiving as the human response to God's saving activity. Most of the verses speak in first-person singular: "Here is what I will do, in response to the bounty of the Lord." The responses have become ritualized as acts of liturgy: lifting up the cup, offering our thanks, paying our vows. The worshiping community gathers all who respond to God's gracious work by doing these things together. Whatever else we can say about it, corporate worship is an expression of human gratitude. The Lord's Supper is rightfully a thanksgiving, offered in return for all God has done for us.

Another direction for a sermon might be to focus on the first four English words of the psalm: "I love the Lord." Loving God is the first of all commandments (Deut. 6:5). It is a binding word that defines the covenant community and precedes every other obligation. We are called to love God with every human faculty: heart, soul, might, and mind. That decree is given six times in Deuteronomy and Joshua and is reaffirmed by Jesus in the Gospels. The people of faith are called to love the God who first loved them.

Curiously, this text may be the only affirmation in all of Scripture when someone actually declares, "I love the Lord." There are, of course, declarations that are more frequent. "Give thanks to the Lord" is a regular phrase of other psalms. "Obey the laws and statutes" is a consistent requirement of the faithful. To speak the words "I love the Lord" is to make obvious what is often taken for granted. As any lover will attest, there is something about saying the words "I love you" that makes them come alive. The spoken words engage the heart; the hidden passion of the soul is voiced in the words.

Most of us can name those who surprised us by speaking of love. In one seminary, for instance, there was a dour theology professor. His intellect was

Psalm 116:1-2, 12-19

Theological Perspective

Theologically, this suggests that in order to be genuine, the love and worship of God must be based in part on a genuine affirmation of the intrinsic goodness, worthiness, and authority of God, and not predicated entirely on what God has done or can do for us in particular situations. It means, in Augustine's terms, "loving God for God's own sake." Such intrinsic affirmation of God is essential to true faith and worship. If it is entirely lacking, faith and worship become self-centered rather than God-centered, and ultimately idolatrous.

This does not mean, however, that faith can or must be indifferent to what we may perceive to be God's acts of mercy and goodness to us. The Bible is clear that faith is fundamentally a response to God's redeeming and forgiving love. There is surely nothing theologically inappropriate in the psalmist's rejoicing over what he or she perceives to be an act of divine deliverance; indeed, not to do so would signal a pitiful, inhuman ingratitude and hardness of heart. The existential problem for faith is to celebrate the unconditioned grace and love of God without converting spontaneous gratitude into a covert, self-centered claim on God—a bargain in which we proffer our allegiance in exchange for divine favor, or assume that we can perpetuate God's favor in future crises by remaining vigorous in our present faith, worship, and obedience. The difference is perhaps subtle, but profoundly important.

In the context of Holy Thursday, Jesus lifts his cup of thanksgiving and worship with his disciples—to "pay [his] vows to the LORD" (v. 14)—on the eve of his betrayal and crucifixion. He trusts and celebrates a God who is not at his or anyone's disposal, but who is nonetheless profoundly and powerfully "for us" in a deep and encompassing sense—unconquerably gracious, righteous, and merciful (v. 5). True, his faith will be severely tested the following day, but at this moment, in the upper room, his impending suffering and death appear to present no ultimate disconfirmation of his faith in a God for whom—as the psalmist says—even the death of his faithful ones is ever precious in his sight (v. 15).

RODNEY J. HUNTER

Pastoral Perspective

this psalm as part of the Egyptian *hallel*, psalms sung, among other times, at the conclusion of the Passover meal. It can be uplifting and encouraging to know that Jesus probably sang these same words with his disciples just before he was handed over to his enemies.

The balance of Psalm 116 describes the author's powerful response to God's compassion. His experience provokes in him a question—"What shall I return to the LORD for all his bounty to me?" (v. 12)—and inflames a deep desire to meet God's mercy with his own public acts of praise (vv. 13, 14, 17, 18, 19) and service (v. 16). This balance of worship and action mirrors the substance of the three readings appointed for this night: Exodus 12, which calls Israel to both ritual and action; 1 Corinthians 11, which recalls Jesus' instructions regarding the bread and wine; and John 13, in which Jesus issues the command to his disciples to love one another.

The very name of this holy night—Maundy Thursday, from the Latin *mandatum*—canonizes obedient action as the proper response to the care of God, and it is every preacher's responsibility to strengthen that consciousness. Authentic gratitude will inspire acts of praise and service (Jas. 2:14–17). If the sermon were taking place on the Third Sunday of Easter in Year A, for which Psalm 116 is also appointed, one could leave it at that. The horrifying events that will be remembered at the end of this night, however, will reframe every promise this psalmist and every Christian has ever made. More specifically to this Psalm 116, Jesus' agonized petition to God that the cup might be taken from him (Matt. 26:39) provides a sobering echo of verse 13. Now "the courts of the house of the LORD" (v. 19) have been reimagined into a garden filled with terror and sorrow, and the challenge of faith will be to stay with Jesus in that garden and follow him into the deeper darkness to come.

MARIA DECARVALHO

Exegetical Perspective

Questions of authorship, date of composition, and final form of the Psalter are all interesting and important issues from an academic point of view, and touching on these questions might help educate one's congregation. But from a practical preaching point of view, they are not the most significant aspects of the passage.

Despite the many questions that surround this psalm, it appears most likely to have been an individual's reflections on the highs and lows of his or her life experiences. The reason for loving God as presented in Psalm 116 may at first strike one as selfish or egocentric. The psalmist loves God because God heard his supplications (vv. 1–2) and delivered him from death (v. 8). The statement in verse 10, "I kept my faith, even when I said, 'I am greatly afflicted,'" could further be interpreted as an indication that because of his great faith, the psalmist feels he deserves the love and salvation YHWH has given. More likely, the psalmist is foreshadowing the words and attitude expressed in 1 John 4:19: "We love because [God] first loved us." In other words, he did not believe that he had earned God's love as a result of his steadfast faith, but rather that his steadfast faith sprang from his experience of God's faithfulness and presence in the midst of adversity.

Whatever the history of the transmission of the psalm, one thing is certain: this psalm survived and ultimately became part of the canon because individuals and the religious community as a whole identified with the challenges, doubts, suffering, faith, and hope that the psalmist so eloquently articulated. In the twenty-first century, this psalm continues to speak powerfully to those who look to God to find meaning in, and relief from, the challenges presented by life and death.

DAVID W. MCCREERY

Homiletical Perspective

intimidating, and many found him unapproachable. He placed great demands on students and graded them harshly if they did not rise to meet them. Students grumbled behind his back. One day he startled them in class as he spoke of God's love for humankind. His eyes filled with tears and his voice choked as he told of God's passion for the world. One student after another had to recalculate their perceptions of their professor. Rather than dislike them, he expected the future servants of the church to give their best efforts on behalf of the gospel. As he never tired of teaching, God's love for the world calls for the full engagement of heart, soul, mind, and strength of all who, in turn, profess their love for God.

"Love" is a powerful word at all times, but especially in the narrative setting of Holy Thursday. Jesus and the Twelve had gathered for a Passover meal, and sang this psalm as part of the Hallel Psalms that are always sung in that setting. They joined the faithful of every time in affirming God's continuing love for the redeemed community, as they shared the matzoh at the seder table and raised the cups of wine. God has loved God's people, no matter what—through slavery and liberation, through wilderness wanderings and homecoming, through rise and fall of the homeland, through exile and Roman occupation.

On this Holy Thursday, as the shadows conspire and suspicions give way to fear, love is at risk of becoming a casualty. Some will approach Jesus with torches and clubs. Others will speak curses and condemnations. One of the people closest to Jesus will react by swinging a sword in violence. All indications are that this could be a moment when love will be crucified by hate; yet it is Jesus who will be crucified, not love. God still loves the world, no matter what.

Through centuries of Christian observance, Holy Thursday has frequently been an evening of darkness and impending doom. Yes, we are moving toward the cross. However, on this night, around this Table, Psalm 116 invites us to live in gratitude and love. We could do worse.

WILLIAM G. CARTER

1 Corinthians 11:23-26

²³For I received from the Lord what I also handed on to you, that the Lord Jesus on the night when he was betrayed took a loaf of bread, ²⁴and when he had given thanks, he broke it and said, "This is my body that is for you. Do this in remembrance of me." ²⁵In the same way he took the cup also, after supper, saying, "This cup is the new covenant in my blood. Do this, as often as you drink it, in remembrance of me." ²⁶For as often as you eat this bread and drink the cup, you proclaim the Lord's death until he comes.

Theological Perspective

How tragically ironic: at the Lord's Table, where the body of Christ is to be most tangibly united in the communion of its members with one another and with their Lord, the body is divided. Divisions at the Table amongst the Corinthian Christians, documented in the preceding verses, are harbingers of much greater divisions that lie ahead for the larger Christian communion, persisting to our own day. The scandal of division at the Lord's Table continues to be manifest wherever people gather there in Jesus' name. The body of Christ was and is a broken body—"By schisms torn asunder, by heresies distressed," in the stark honesty of hymn writer Samuel Stone, portraying the not-so-glorious body of Christ.[1] How far from the apostolic ideal of the "one body" manifest in "splendor, without a spot or wrinkle or anything of the kind" (Eph. 4:4; 5:27)!

Yet it is fitting that the church, as the body of Christ, bear some of the marks of his suffering. The church is broken, even as Jesus' physical body was broken. The church's brokenness is scandalous, even as his was. It is an offense to many, just as Christ's was. None of this, of course, makes it right or good; Jesus' flesh was violated in being broken, and so is

1. Samuel Stone, "The Church's One Foundation," in *Lutheran Book of Worship* (Minneapolis: Augsburg Publishing House, 1978), #369.

Pastoral Perspective

Maybe it is the breathless pace we keep. Maybe it is the absurd rate of change swirling around us. Maybe it is our culture's addiction to novelty, or the overload of data and information that swamps us. For all of these reasons and more, our age is prone to forgetting. On Holy Thursday, we are invited to remember: to remember who we are, and to whom we belong.

We are hardly the first people to be forgetful. While we live in a unique generation, we postmoderns are not alone in our predicament. Though we are separated by nearly two millennia from Paul's original audience, the early Christian community in Corinth, we have much in common with them. Just as we live in a time of explosive globalization wrought by industrialization, air travel, and the Internet, so they also lived in an age of unprecedented international commerce made possible by the Persian road system and the relative peace of the Roman Empire. Just as we inhabit regions immersed in multinational trade and exposed to a world market of ideas, so the Corinthians lived in a seaport churning with multiple peoples, foreign cultures, and exotic goods. Just as we find ourselves experiencing a global village of religious traditions new to us, so they were introduced to manifold novel spiritualities, to mix with whatever traditions they had inherited from their ancestral peoples.

Exegetical Perspective

First Corinthians 11:23–26 is our earliest written reference to the sacramental meal Christians have come to call Communion, the Eucharist, and the Mass. Paul called it "the Lord's Supper" (*kyriakon deipnon,* 11:20). In the Gospels of Matthew, Mark, and Luke (written twenty to thirty years after 1 Corinthians), the story of the meal will be told with more detail than we have in Paul's version. It is set during Passover, just before Jesus' crucifixion; Jesus eats it with his disciples; they are in an upper room, to which Jesus sent disciples to prepare the meal; Jesus foretells Judas's betrayal and the disciples' flight; in Luke's version, Jesus advises the disciples to obtain swords for what is about to transpire. Paul, however, has none of these details. Consequently, he appears not to be concerned with providing the Corinthians with information.[1]

Verse 23 indicates that Paul is in fact reminding the Corinthians of something about which he has already informed them, no doubt having included at least some of the details reported in the Synoptic versions. Referring here to the tradition he has received and passed on (see the similar phrase in 15:3), Paul reduces the tradition to its bare essentials.

1. For a recent treatment of early references to the sacrament of Communion, see Paul F. Bradshaw, *Eucharistic Origins* (New York and Oxford: Oxford University Press, 2004).

Homiletical Perspective

As the saying goes in real estate, so it is with our homiletical approach to this passage in Holy Week, "What matters most is location, location, location." In the case of this text, three kinds of interrelated location merit attention: the location of the passage in Paul's letter to the Corinthians, the location of Maundy Thursday in the Christian year, and the social location of the congregation.

To grasp the larger literary context, it is helpful to recall the tone of Paul's letter to the church at Corinth. Noticeably absent here is the harshness with which he addresses the troublemakers in Galatia, whom he thinks should castrate themselves (Gal. 5:12); but also absent is the abundant pastoral love evident in his correspondence with the church at Philippi (Phil. 1:3). At times in his correspondence with the Corinthians, Paul reacts pastorally to their own concerns on a variety of topics (1 Cor. 7:1), but here, as in the early material on schisms (1 Cor. 1:10–17), he writes in reaction to reports he has received. In other words, while Paul loves this congregation, he is worked up over their behavior. On this occasion it would be good for us to consider our own levels of love and exasperation with the flock we shepherd.

The more immediate literary context is the abuse of the poor by those of means, which has become evident at mealtime in Corinth. It is helpful to recall

1 Corinthians 11:23-26

Theological Perspective

the church. The church's prolonged suffering of brokenness is to be neither celebrated nor tolerated; every effort toward its wholeness is to be pursued with utmost urgency and unfettered hope. Still, it should be no surprise that this brokenness continues.

The scandal of the Corinthians' divisions at the Table does not lead Paul to set aside the Table. Indeed, the divisions the Table occasions heighten the urgency for all to gather precisely there. We live today in a world where baptism and proclamation are shared freely between major Christian communions that nevertheless remain divided at the Table. The Table tells the truth: the church remains sorely divided despite its hopes and claims otherwise. Christians heartily confess their belief and participation in one holy catholic and apostolic church, yet live otherwise. Font and proclamation lift up the hope of that unity, while the Table tells the truth of persisting fragmentation.

Many recent eucharistic liturgies have changed one of the words in the preamble to Christ's institution. Whereas our text relates the words of "the Lord Jesus, on the night when he was *betrayed*," these recent liturgies speak rather of "the Lord Jesus, on the night of his *arrest*." The Greek *paradidōmi* signifies being given up. "Arrest" is administered by external authorities and may be abundantly deserved, but *paradidōmi* is a treacherous act of putative colleagues. "Betrayal" discloses a breach in Christ's company itself. As Jesus shares the cup in Luke's account of the Last Supper, he reveals that the one who will give him up (*paradidōmi*) is seated right there at the table. The raw truth of his betrayal from within his circle is disclosed first at the table, where betrayer and loyalist have equal place. Christ's greatest wound of all is administered by friends, not by religious opponents or Roman executioners. Precisely in the face of *that*, he invites his chosen band, their treachery notwithstanding, "Come to the feast prepared for you." In the same spirit, Paul still invites to the Lord's Table the Corinthians who have betrayed the body of Christ in their exclusionary Table practices.

This invitation comes with a warning to heal the divisions that scandalize the body. Indeed, Paul's invitation to the Table includes a strong admonition to repent of all that betrays the body's unity as the faithful celebrate Holy Communion with one another and their Lord. Unlike Paul, Calvin and other early Reformers begin their eucharistic liturgy with dire warnings against unworthy participation.

Pastoral Perspective

Swept up in such a time, it is easy to forget that we belong to a particular and sovereign God; to forget that our private spiritual experience is not the point of faith; to forget that we do not create our own personalized amalgam of religious practices; to forget that we are not self-made or sustained by our own willpower. So it is not surprising that the early Corinthian Christians had indeed forgotten all of that and perhaps more, as the verses prior to this passage make clear. The result was that many aspects of the church's life, even the Lord's Supper, had become corrupted. At the Lord's Table, each person ate and drank what he or she had brought, as if the point of Communion were personal satisfaction. The people had lost their memory of real communion with each other and with their living Lord.

Our identity-shaping rituals, including the Lord 's Supper, are just one memory away from slipping into empty routine. This is especially true for us, and generations like ours, whose circumstances make us so prone to forgetting. Like the Corinthian Christians, we live in an age of exponential change, when our identity is vulnerable to amnesia. In such an age, we run a keener risk of forgetting who we are and forgetting the deep meaning of even our most sacred acts. Not imagining that this meal might convey something powerful and transformational— something that shapes our corporate identity, something that even transcends space and time—we cling to the *personal* comfort of our rituals as the sum total of their significance.

Paul is writing to a forgetful people, and inviting us to remember: to remember who we are, and to whom we belong. The remembering Paul has in mind is of a particular kind: not merely historical memory, as found in Greco-Roman history or biography, nor the kind of memory associated with nations and heroes, but formative, communal, life-giving memory. Paul's model is the Jewish Passover, the meal that rehearses the Jewish identity shaped by the saving hand of God, who with a mighty hand and outstretched arm brought the people out of slavery. Every time the Passover meal is celebrated, it invites Jewish people of every generation, place, and time to remember—not *as if* they were at the exodus, but that *they were* part of the exodus. The Passover triggers and forms the memory that they were once bound and now are freed, and that they belong to the God who saves them.

So it is for us, in the meal that Jesus offered on the night of Passover, on the night before he was to die. We are invited to remember—especially on Holy

Exegetical Perspective

If Paul is not providing information, though, why does he write of the Supper as he does?

Verses 17–22 points us toward an answer to this question: Paul is concerned about the manner in which the Corinthians "come together" for the Supper. First, Paul notes, the Corinthians are already divided when they come together "as a church" (v. 18). At the Supper, the divisions manifest themselves in sharp disparities among the participants: "each of you goes ahead with your own supper, and one goes hungry and another becomes drunk" (v. 21).

Recent studies have shown that social and economic differences in the Corinthian church contributed significantly to this and other conflicts at Corinth. The Corinthians were modeling their Supper on Roman gatherings (with religious overtones) at which participants in the meal were "wined and dined" according to their social status. The higher the status one enjoyed, the better the food and wine that one was served. Paul finds such behavior "unworthy" (v. 27), since it shows contempt for the church and humiliation for the poor (v. 22). Thus Paul advises the Corinthians to "examine" themselves, to "discern" the body,[2] and to "judge" themselves—so that they need not be judged by God (vv. 28–32).

His final advice seems very mundane, even simplistic: "when you come together to eat [the Lord's Supper], wait for one another" (v. 33). Surprisingly, and somewhat disturbingly, Paul does not advise the Corinthians to supply one another's needs, to ensure that everyone has enough to eat when they come together. He says, rather, that the hungry should eat at home before coming to the assembly (v. 34). Apparently, however, Paul had more to say about this issue than he includes in the letter, for he ends the section on the Lord's Supper by saying that he will take up the "other things" when he comes (v. 34). Paul's collection for the poor among the saints in Jerusalem and his admonitions to "bear one another's burdens" (Gal. 6:2) suggest that he was concerned with the real and practical needs of the poor and addressed them when he saw the issue as pressing.

What are we to say about our passage itself? How does it function in Paul's response to the Corinthians' questions concerning the Lord's

Homiletical Perspective

the early church's seamless blending of ordinary meals with the eucharistic meal of remembrance.[1] As a result, we read this passage not in light of Martin Luther's doctrinal complaints against the church at Rome, but of the apostle Paul's concern for the poor at Corinth. Some preachers might choose to read the larger context or at least explain it, since these "words of institution" are read so frequently apart from the framework in which Paul has set them.

The second sense of location is Holy Week, our present place in the rhythms of the Christian year. Not all worshipers will be cognizant of the meaning of "Maundy," from the Latin for "mandate." On this night the church remembers Christ's mandate to "love one another" as he has loved us (John 13:34). This meal, capable of so many meanings (thanksgiving, remembrance, feast, anticipation, as well as all the nuanced theological debates between denominations), must never be divorced from its first meaning here—the love of Christ for us, which we are enjoined to have toward each other. This is Paul's chief concern, that somehow the meal of love has been replaced by one of social class and distinction. As Gordon Fee rightly notes, we eat this meal in remembrance of the Christ whose life was self-giving, not self-preserving.[2]

The third sense of location is social, which must take into account the situation in Corinth as well as ours today. Gerd Theissen reminds us that Paul identifies two groups of Christians at Corinth, the *haves* and *have-nots*, both in relation to food. Whereas the church as one body is to eat "the Lord's Supper" (11:20), the *haves* are described as eating "their own supper" (11:21).[3] The point does not seem to be that their bread and wine were of higher quality but that they ate a fuller meal in the context of the Lord's Supper. The poor scrounged about while the wealthy ate quite well.

Today, as in Paul's day, distinctions exist in social location, not just between various churches but within the same congregation. We do well to recall how Jesus' self-giving life included feeding the poor as well as dining with the rich, some of them religious (Pharisees, for example), while others were social misfits (tax collectors, for instance). How does the church eat this meal of love when some of its own members struggle to put food on the table? At

---

2. Whether "the body" in v. 29 refers to the church or the bread, the effect is the same. Indeed, for Paul, the body metaphor is so strong in 1 Corinthians that "the body of Christ" has multiple meanings that are tightly interwoven. See chaps. 14 and 15.

1. Dennis E. Smith, *From Symposium to Eucharist: The Banquet in the Early Christian World* (Minneapolis: Fortress Press, 2003), 173–217.
2. Gordon D. Fee, *The First Epistle to the Corinthians*, The New International Commentary on the New Testament (Grand Rapids: Eerdmans, 1987), 556–58.
3. Gerd Theissen, *The Social Setting of Pauline Christianity: Essays on Corinth*, ed. and trans. John H. Schütz (Philadelphia: Fortress Press, 1982), 147–50.

1 Corinthians 11:23-26

Theological Perspective

For Paul, the warnings follow the invitation and institution. Either way, the scandal of betrayal is exposed. Perhaps not coincidentally, the liturgical world that substitutes "arrest" for "betrayal" eliminates from the liturgy the warning against further betrayal that Paul appends to the invitation. This same liturgical world has produced our lectionary, which ends our reading before the warning. Perhaps it is understandable that the Reformers' overemphasis on warning has led their heirs to jettison principled hesitation before the Table. However does it serve the church well to offer such broad and unconditional welcome that betrayal of the church's very identity as the one body of Christ has lost its scandal?

This passage affords a glimpse into Paul's relation to the story of Jesus and Paul's role as one who conveys it to others. It is broadly agreed that Paul's writings antecede the canonical Gospels. This passage is consistent with Paul's claim elsewhere to depend not on the witness of others, but only upon Jesus himself as his source of knowledge (Gal. 2:15–21). "I received from the Lord what I also handed on to you," he contends (1 Cor. 11:23). Paul passes along what Jesus gave him personally. Where and how that happened he does not say. The main point is that Paul considers himself to be delivering firsthand knowledge of Jesus' message and mission, and not mere hearsay. In recounting Jesus' postresurrection appearances, he says, "Last of all, as to one untimely born, he appeared also to me" (1 Cor. 15:8).

Note Paul's use of the past tense—I *handed* this to you. Apparently this telling of the institution of the Lord's Supper is a reiteration of core Christian teaching he already gave the Corinthians during his residence with them, and is thus foundational to his account of the gospel. The Table that seals the communion of the one body with its one Lord is more than an auxiliary aid to gospel living; it belongs to the essence of the church.

The story of the church's divisions at the Table is all too well known. Whether over the precise substance of the bread and wine, or over standards for welcoming people to the Table, deeply entrenched divisions at Christ's Table persist and, despite their scandal, defy easy resolution. Perhaps the best we can agree upon is to join Samuel Stone yet again, "Our cry goes up, 'How long?'"

SHELDON W. SORGE

Pastoral Perspective

Thursday—not *as if* we were present at the Last Supper with our Lord and his disciples, but that *we were* at Table with them. Every time we are at Table, and especially this night, the act of Communion triggers and forms the memory that we were once bound and now are freed, and that we belong to the God who saves us.

As we say "on the night that he was betrayed" Jesus took the Passover bread and gave it to us, we are invited to remember that Jesus offered his life for us not when we were particularly worthy, charming, faithful, or successful, but when we betrayed him.

As we say the words that Jesus said, "This is my body that is broken for you," we are invited to remember—especially on Holy Thursday—that it was not merely some idea or philosophy, or feeling of well-being, or novel spiritual experience, or even wonderful teaching that we received from Jesus, but his very life laid down for us, a new Passover sacrifice to free us from our own slavery to sin and death.

As we say Jesus' words, "This cup is the new covenant in my blood," we are invited to remember that it was not just a thoughtful gesture or passing promise that Jesus left us, but a divine, eternal vow, unbreakable by human failure. The first covenant God made with Moses and the people was sealed by the offering of the blood of animal sacrifices (Exod. 24:8); it was broken by God's people as we failed to be obedient. The new covenant is sealed by the blood of God's own Son: a covenant, therefore, that the worst of our sin and shame can never corrupt.

Who are we, and to whom do we belong? The answers to these questions lie in the memory that we have received, that has been handed on to us, and that we proclaim every time we eat this bread and drink this cup. We are freed from slavery to sin and death. We belong to the Lord, who died for us, so that we might live.

CHRISTINE CHAKOIAN

Supper? There are two clues: Paul's allusion to the Supper in 5:7b–8 and his frequent insertion of an example in the middle of an argument to make his point more clearly.

In 1 Corinthians 5, Paul is dealing with another problem in the church at Corinth—the rather bizarre case of a man living with his stepmother. Paul regards this as so beyond the pale that even the pagans abhor it and sees this act as destructive to the very fabric of the church. Not content with his observation that even the pagans abstain from such sin, Paul refers to the death of Jesus as a paschal sacrifice, the preparation for which is removing all leaven. Paul turns this ritual observance, however, into an ethical argument. Any community that celebrates the death of Christ as its paschal lamb must purge itself of "the yeast of malice and evil," substituting for it "the unleavened bread of sincerity and truth" (1 Cor. 5:8). This is just what Paul does in 11:23–25. The celebration of the Eucharist is not just an act of private devotion, which applies only to the individual. It concerns the entire community, which is nothing less than the body of Christ.

Thus, by inserting the reference to the traditions of Jesus' sacrificial death into his instructions concerning the Corinthians' practice of the Lord's Supper, Paul uses Jesus as a model for how one acts in community. On the very night that Jesus was betrayed, he gave thanks (*eucharistein*) over the bread and referred to it as his body, which is "for you" (v. 24). Likewise, he referred to the cup as "the new covenant in my blood" (v. 25).

By placing these words in the midst of his argument about divisions within the Corinthian community, Paul is providing an example and reminding the Corinthians of what the Lord's Supper is about. The juxtaposition of the Corinthians' conduct and Jesus' conduct could not be more jolting. Waiting for one another when you come together to eat (1 Cor. 11:33) is by no means mundane or simplistic advice. It is following the example of the Lord Jesus, "who on the night when he was betrayed . . ."

OLIVER LARRY YARBROUGH

least a few people gathered on this day will have hurriedly devoured fast food in order to arrive on time, while others may have a reservation at a fine restaurant after the service. What does it mean that all will sit together at this Table during worship?

The Foods Resource Bank offers a helpful image for preachers to consider, inviting us to imagine all the people of earth in a single line from richest to poorest. We must see them as individual persons, not abstractions. On one end is the poorest person in the world, and at the other end the richest. We are all in the line somewhere. Regardless of our place in the line, we have a tendency to look only in one direction—toward those wealthier than us. Perhaps the truest act of worship on this Maundy Thursday is to look in the other direction while eating this sacred meal, recognizing the poor among us and around the world.

In addition to these three issues of location, Paul describes this meal in terms of tradition, highlighting what he "received from the Lord" as well as what he "handed on" (v. 23). Both aspects merit the preacher's attention. While most worshipers will recognize the sacredness of this tradition received from the Lord, some will provide proof that familiarity breeds contempt, or at the very least a yawn. Who in the sanctuary has not heard these words before?

Fresh images of a table big enough for all God's children, the *haves* and *have-nots*, could help preachers on this occasion. We might consider Leonardo da Vinci's masterpiece *The Last Supper*, which so beautifully portrays Christ and his disciples gathered at table. As has been noted throughout the years, they are all on one side of the table, a rather awkward feature; but what has also been noted is how da Vinci's portrayal allows *all* who view this work to join them at the same table.

MIKE GRAVES

John 13:1-17, 31b–35

¹Now before the festival of the Passover, Jesus knew that his hour had come to depart from this world and go to the Father. Having loved his own who were in the world, he loved them to the end. ²The devil had already put it into the heart of Judas son of Simon Iscariot to betray him. And during supper ³Jesus, knowing that the Father had given all things into his hands, and that he had come from God and was going to God, ⁴got up from the table, took off his outer robe, and tied a towel around himself. ⁵Then he poured water into a basin and began to wash the disciples' feet and to wipe them with the towel that was tied around him. ⁶He came to Simon Peter, who said to him, "Lord, are you going to wash my feet?" ⁷Jesus answered, "You do not know now what I am doing, but later you will understand." ⁸Peter said to him, "You will never wash my feet." Jesus answered, "Unless I wash you, you have no share with me." ⁹Simon Peter said to him, "Lord, not my feet only but also my hands and my head!" ¹⁰Jesus said to him, "One who has bathed does not need to wash, except for the feet, but is entirely clean. And you are clean, though not all of you." ¹¹For he knew who was to betray him; for this reason he said, "Not all of you are clean."

Theological Perspective

This entire Gospel can be summed up in the hospitable act of friendship where an extraordinary master takes the place of servant to his own servants (vv. 2b–5). The towel-clad Jesus has extraordinary knowledge, authority, divine origin, and destiny. Yet in this "hour" of anticipated execution and glorification, the disciples will witness what was already declared to some of them by the baptizer John: "Here is the Lamb of God who takes away the sin of the world!" (1:29b, 36b). Will they understand these things?

Do we understand? Where do we locate ourselves in the story of the dirty foot washing? Are we servants of Jesus and God? Or does the demonized figure of Judas live in us as well? The poet Eva Gore-Booth wrote of humankind, "What all men share must all men execrate."[1] Are we as citizens of "this world" the ones who corporately have handed over to imprisonment, torture, and execution the enemies of the state and the religious fanatics who threaten our fanaticism for secular regimes with global reach?

Like Simon Peter, *what if* the act of our teacher and Lord washing our feet, cleansing us from head to toe, is too intimate, too close to erotic love? There

---

1. Eva Gore-Booth, *Shepherd of Eternity and Other Poems* (London: Longmans, Green & Co., 1925), 97, as quoted by Mark Edwards, *John*, Blackwell Bible Commentaries (Malden, MA: Blackwell, 2004), 130.

Pastoral Perspective

Pastorally speaking, the Gospel readings during these last days of Holy Week invite the disciples of Jesus in every age to gather for a meal, have their feet washed, love one another, bid farewell to a dear friend, suffer through his death, and grieve their own loss. Is there anyone among us who has not shared a meal, said good-bye, or suffered a loss? For the preacher who is also a pastor, there may be no better time to gather the people of God around these everyday human experiences, celebrating the common union that is ours in Christ.

The reading for Holy Thursday begins with a meal. Jesus is at the table with his disciples, all of them reclining, propped up on their elbows, dipping pita bread into bowls of savory hummus and smacking their lips, licking their fingers. The sounds of conversation fill the room, punctuated from time to time by loud laughter or the clink of one clay cup against another. Oil lamps flicker, their light reflected in the shining eyes of the disciples, and while all of this is going on Jesus gets up from the table, strips off his outer robe, wraps a towel around his waist, pours water into a basin, and begins to wash the disciples' feet.

It would not be unusual if he were one of the household servants; the disciples have probably had their feet washed before. However this is their teacher, their Lord! As he moves from one to

¹²After he had washed their feet, had put on his robe, and had returned to the table, he said to them, "Do you know what I have done to you? ¹³You call me Teacher and Lord—and you are right, for that is what I am. ¹⁴So if I, your Lord and Teacher, have washed your feet, you also ought to wash one another's feet. ¹⁵For I have set you an example, that you also should do as I have done to you. ¹⁶Very truly, I tell you, servants are not greater than their master, nor are messengers greater than the one who sent them. ¹⁷If you know these things, you are blessed if you do them." . . .

³¹When he had gone out, Jesus said, "Now the Son of Man has been glorified, and God has been glorified in him. ³²If God has been glorified in him, God will also glorify him in himself and will glorify him at once. ³³Little children, I am with you only a little longer. You will look for me; and as I said to the Jews so now I say to you, 'Where I am going, you cannot come.' ³⁴I give you a new commandment, that you love one another. Just as I have loved you, you also should love one another. ³⁵By this everyone will know that you are my disciples, if you have love for one another."

Exegetical Perspective

Johannine commentators commonly recognize chapter 13 as the opening of "Act II" in this Gospel's drama. The action in John 1–12 has revolved around miraculous "signs" of Jesus' identity as God's Son (2:11; 3:2; 4:54; 6:2), eliciting division among his antagonists (5:9b–18; 7:40–52; 9:13–34; 10:19–21; 11:45–53) and extended discourses by Jesus, whose truth sails over his listeners' heads but registers among the Gospel's faithful readers (3:3–21; 5:19–47; 6:35–59; 10:22–39). From chapter 13 onward, the narrative concentrates on the preparation of Jesus' followers for his resolute march to Golgotha, where on the cross his glory will be revealed fully, albeit ironically (17:1–5). The lectionary wisely assigns John 13 for meditation on Holy Thursday. Not only does this passage recount the Fourth Evangelist's version of Jesus' Last Supper with the Twelve; in many ways it crystallizes the dominant theme of John's passion narrative.

Unlike the Synoptic Gospels (Matt. 26:17–19; Mark 14:12–16; Luke 22:7–15), John identifies Jesus' last meal as *prior to* the Passover (13:1a), not as its celebration. John's focus lies elsewhere, namely, on Jesus' washing of his disciples' feet—not described in the Synoptics—and an interpretation of that event's significance. Unfortunately, by excising verses 18–31a, 36–38, the lectionary truncates that explanation. The

Homiletical Perspective

For many congregations, Maundy Thursday is one of the most sacred days of the church year. It is sacred because of the two acts associated with it: Holy Communion and foot washing. It is sacred because it inaugurates the Triduum—the three holy days of Christ's passion, which begin at sundown on Thursday and conclude at sundown on Easter Day. It is sacred because on this evening the family of faith gathers together at table to remember the one whom we, like the disciples in John's Gospel, have dearly loved—and are about to lose to death.

Whatever else happens on Maundy Thursday, preachers need to speak to the heart as well as to the head, to the emotions as well as to reason. This is not a day for academic discourses on atonement theory or for overly rational explanations regarding the meaning of the Lord's Supper. Rather, it is an evening on which to speak to our parishioners out of the same love and compassion we hear echoed in Jesus' voice, as he speaks to "his own" whom he has "loved to the end." It is a day on which to encourage and comfort those we love, even as Jesus encouraged and comforted those who were feeling bereft, because they were about to lose their beloved friend.

While preachers may well scramble for appropriate sermonic images on other days of the year, on Maundy Thursday we are wise to make use

John 13:1-17, 31b–35

Theological Perspective

are boundary issues when it comes to feet. (In historical perspective, "the washing of a master's feet could not be required of a Jewish slave," although on occasion loving disciples might serve their teacher in this way.)[2] Even when the foot washer pronounces us "entirely clean" before "his hour" has run its course, realizing "the end" (eschatology) *before* the execution and resurrection, we turn around and deny we even knew this intimate servant and messenger of God (18:15–18, 25–27). We did not know the one who knew our feet!

When the dirty foot washing in the mixed company of the unclean and clean is over, what do we do with this act of service? Is it merely a moral example of good pastoral, pedagogical, familial, and social behavior? Can such a radical love be proscribed as a formula for action in a world where service debases rather than liberates—where love between those who differ in power often opens the less powerful lover to coercion and abuse?

Sandra Schneiders finds a prophetic and symbolic act in the foot washing and its interpretation by Jesus (13:12–17) that is summed up in "a new command-ment" (13:34–35; 15:12–14). This act of service in the context of Jesus' "hour" was read by the author of John and other NT writers in light of the Suffering Servant Songs in Isaiah (42:1–4; 49:1–6; 50:4–11; 52:13–53:12). However, what is service?

For Schneiders, the ideal is "self-gift . . . an expression of love" that may be taken to the extreme of laying "down one's life for one's friends" (15:13).[3] In ordinary daily life, though, we experience at least three models of service. (1) There is *service as obligation* in a pattern of domination or patriarchy. The server is bound in a relationship of social power to serve a privileged other: children / parents; slaves / masters; woman / man; subject / ruler; the poor / the wealthy. Even when these relations are well intended, the acts of service continually reinforce the imbalance of privilege. Imagine Jesus' facing Pilate in John 19:10–11. (2) In Schneiders's *existential model*, the server acts freely on behalf of the served because of a perceived need that the server has "the power to meet": mother / child, teacher / student, professional / client or patient, clergy / laity, rich / poor, strong / weak. Here again the relations are structured by a fundamental inequality. Children meet our "need to

2. Raymond E. Brown, *Gospel according to John, XIII–XXI*, Anchor Bible 29A (Garden City, NY: Doubleday, 1970), 564.
3. Sandra M. Schneiders, *Written That You May Believe: Encountering Jesus in the Fourth Gospel* (New York: Crossroad, 1999), 170–72. Later Schneiders quotes are from the same source.

Pastoral Perspective

another, they fall silent, until all you can hear is the splash of water being poured into the basin over dusty, callused feet. Peter objects, but Jesus persists. In the end Jesus puts his robe back on to join them at the table. "Do you know what I have done to you?" he asks (v. 12). Apparently not. No one says a word. "I have set you an example," Jesus says. "If I, your Lord and Teacher, have washed your feet, you also ought to wash one another's feet" (v. 14).

On one level this action is symbolic, re-presenting the pendulum swing of the prologue (1:1–18), in which Jesus removes the outer robe of his glory, wraps around himself a towel of human flesh, suffers and dies for the sake of the world, reclothes himself with glory, and resumes his rightful place in the bosom of the Creator. This may be what Peter and the other disciples will understand "later" (13:7). On another level, though, this action is personal and pastoral. The disciples need to have their feet washed. No one else has volunteered to do it. Perhaps, as in the Synoptics, they have been arguing about which one of them is the greatest, and for any one of them to volunteer would be to lose the argument. So Jesus gets up to do it—shocking them all by his disregard for social and cultural convention. As Peter implies by his objection, foot washing is slave labor. However when Jesus has finished he says: "If I, your Lord and Teacher, have washed your feet, you also ought to wash one another's feet" (v. 14).

It is a good reminder for a church that still argues over who is the greatest. We are not here to lord over one another; we are here to wash one another's feet! Sometimes on Holy Thursday we try to do this literally, in the context of worship, and it almost always comes off badly. It is awkward, embarrassing, and in some cases (since the invention of panty hose), practically impossible. Maybe the real problem is that we do not do it often enough to be good at it—not actual foot washing, necessarily, but those countless small acts of humble service Christians can offer to one another on a daily basis.

I still remember talking to a well-respected pastor at a ministers' conference when he looked down and noticed that my shoe was untied. Before I could do anything about it, he had dropped to one knee to tie it for me. I was embarrassed—like Peter—but when he stood up again, he resumed the conversation as if nothing had happened. Maybe that was why he was so well respected. Maybe that is why Jesus says to his disciples: "Do not be afraid to stoop down and offer the most humble service imaginable to one another. It is no more than I have done for you."

point is not merely that Jesus "loved his own who were in the world . . . to the end" (v. 1b), but that he did so in the face of Judas's betrayal (vv. 18–31a) and Peter's eventual denial and abandonment of his Lord (vv. 36–38). That tension between the Son's fidelity to the Father and his followers' infidelity to their Lord is sustained throughout chapter 13 and should not be disregarded.

Among a slave's most menial responsibilities in antiquity was washing the master's feet (see 1 Sam. 25:41; John 1:27). Simon Peter's incredulous protest (13:6, 8a) acknowledges the humiliating impropriety of what Jesus is doing for his disciples. For John, such outlandish flouting of social expectation is significant both christologically and ecclesiologically. The latter is more obvious: Jesus, Lord and teacher, is modeling the radically subservient love that his followers should express toward one another (vv. 12–15). That point is driven home in verses 34–35: Jesus' disciples are so recognized when they love one another precisely as, and to the ultimate degree that, he has demonstrated his love for them (15:12–13).

The basis for the church's conduct does not lie, however, in its natural aptitude. The church can be the church only if it is washed by its Lord and participating in his love (13:8b, 34; 15:9–10). Such self-sacrificial love (*agapē*) looks both backward and forward. It recalls the same love God has expressed in the sending of his only Son for the world's redemption (3:16–17), for the Son speaks only as the Father has taught him (8:28–29; 14:10) and does only the will of the One who has sent him (5:30; 6:38–40). The cross on which Jesus will give his life for the world (see 1:29) is anticipated at 13:4, when Jesus lays aside [*tithēsin*] his garments and takes [*labōn*] a towel: "For this reason the Father loves me, because I lay down [*tithēmi*] my life, that I may take [*labō*] it again" (10:17). The christological and ecclesiological dimensions converge at 13:16: "Truly, truly I say to you: a slave is not greater than his lord, nor an envoy [*apostolos*] greater than the one who has sent him"—even as the Father is greater than the Son (14:28b) and apart from Jesus his disciples can do nothing (15:5).

All this remains true despite the disciples' inability to comprehend it. The answer to Jesus' question, "Do you know what I have done for you?" (13:12) has already been revealed in Peter's fumbling request that his Lord not merely wash his feet but give him a bath (v. 9). In this Gospel, the disciples do not and cannot understand the import of Jesus' actions until after Easter (2:22; 7:39; 12:16; 14:26). Even then, their faith

of the visible liturgical images that are close at hand: a pitcher full of water standing next to a washing basin draped with a towel; a table set for dinner guests with lovely cloths and candles of various sizes, plates and goblets, a loaf of bread, and a carafe of wine. Visuals and actions may well speak as loudly as words on this sacred night, so the wise pastor will attend to them as carefully as to the sermon.

This rich text from John affords many fine options for preaching, even for those who have preached from it many times before. So attending to the particularity of congregational context can be helpful for shaping the preacher's choices.

For instance, if one is preaching in a congregation that tends to favor pietism over activism, or that tends to view itself as a beneficent giver to the poor (rather than a hands-on washer of feet), then a traditional focus on the foot washing act itself, and on Jesus' challenge to the disciples to follow that example (vv. 15–16) may well be in order. Why not bring the community and the world into the sanctuary on this holy evening, asking where it is that people are broken and bruised (from war, poverty, AIDS, abuse, and discrimination) and in need of a healing bath (like the warm whirlpool baths that are frequently given to people with broken limbs during physical therapy)? We can then encourage today's disciples to honor Jesus' life and death by taking up his towel and bathing the world's wounds in his name.

One Christian community in Atlanta, Georgia— the Open Door Community—takes this foot washing command so seriously that they offer a foot care clinic on Thursday evenings, where the homeless of that city can come to have their feet bathed and their foot problems treated by medical volunteers.

If, on the other hand, one is preaching in a congregation that tends to value "doing" over "being," with members already deeply involved in ministries of advocacy and action—perhaps even to the point of denigrating contemplative practices of faith in favor of more activist ones—then she might do well to focus on Peter's refusal to have his own feet washed, and Jesus' challenge to him: "Unless I wash you, you have no share with me" (v. 8b). Just as baptism inaugurates us into Jesus' ministry of tending and washing the wounds of a broken world, we too are in need of the ongoing washing of Jesus and the bathing of our own weary feet if we are to have the strength, compassion, and Spirit to continue that ministry in the world. Indeed, if we do not allow Jesus to bathe us, we may well find that we

John 13:1-17, 31b–35

Theological Perspective

be needed," students feed our egos, clients or patients build up our careers, and laity fill our need to be perceived as "good shepherds." As long as we can keep others in relationships of neediness to us, our self-esteem is validated, while they long for escape or rebellion. (3) The model of *friendship* subverts the obligation of (1) and the privilege of meeting the needs of others less privileged of (2). For "friendship is the one human relationship based on equality." Seeking the good of the friend becomes mutually beneficial. Although friendship may begin between two or more who do not share the same power and prestige, over time the community of friends can subvert the economy of inequality and neediness. The politics of friendship at its best can build bridges over chasms of ideological, religious, racial, and social conflicts. Unfortunately, such friendships are rare and difficult to maintain, as the other models of service structure so many of our daily relationships with others.

Schneiders rereads John's theology of "the hour," the unity of cross and resurrection in light of Jesus' service to the disciples and command to love as friends love. The distinctive motifs of atonement in this Gospel are not the cross as "sacrifice or retribution" but the cross as Jesus' gift of himself to his friends. In this self-gift, symbolized the night before the execution by the foot washing and new commandment, God's love for the world becomes flesh and blood.

Some Christians, looking back over our history of persecution of "the Jews" (13:33), colonization of other religions, and the tendency of our forms of service and family to perpetuate inequality, call our attention to the many and horrific abuses of the cross. Schneiders's close reading of the foot washing that precedes the passion narrative places us on a better path to understand the cross and atonement as the ultimate degree of friendship and beloved community. To live in the light of this cross and this Friend is to seek relations of mutual respect that refuse to use and abuse those less powerful and privileged than ourselves, so that all might become the friends of God.

ROBERT A. CATHEY

Pastoral Perspective

I see this kind of thing in my own church from time to time. One of our members has cerebral palsy, is confined to a wheelchair, and is not able to feed himself. He also has a thousand-watt smile and a wonderful sense of humor, which is good, because when we have potluck luncheons once a month, someone has to volunteer to feed him, and often those people have better intentions than results. I watch out of the corner of my eye as they ease a spoonful of food into his mouth and then dab at his face with a napkin, tentatively. They have never done this before, but they are trying, and he is grinning, and for those who have eyes to see it, some foot washing is going on.

"If I have washed your feet, you also ought to wash one another's feet," Jesus says. Then he goes one better. "If I have laid down my life for you, you also ought to lay down your lives for each other." That is not exactly the way he puts it, of course. He says, "I give you a new commandment, that you love one another," but in the next phrase he says, "Just as I have loved you, you also should love one another" (13:34). Then in chapter 15 he says, "No one has greater love than this, to lay down one's life for one's friends" (v. 13). The connections seem clear: love is laying down our lives for one another; foot washing is one of those small, everyday acts of humble service; and both of these reveal us to be the disciples of Jesus.

JIM GREEN SOMERVILLE

Exegetical Perspective

still falters (20:19–29; 21:20–23). Unlike gnostic writings, in John the disciples' divine election and sustenance do not depend on how much they understand. Their faith is perfected, not in knowledge, but in how much they love their fellow lambs (21:15–19; cf. 1 Cor. 13:12–13).

Some interpreters see in the Fourth Gospel a constriction of love to love "for one's friends" (15:13)—within the church's confines—in contrast with the Synoptic Jesus, who teaches love for one's enemies as well (Matt. 5:44; Luke 6:27, 35). Up to a point that reading is justified, since in John "the world" is a hostile environment that cannot receive the Father's revelation through Jesus (1:10; 15:18–20; 16:33; 17:14, 25). On the other hand, the world, however benighted, is the realm that Jesus has come to save (3:16–17; 4:42; 6:33, 51; 12:47). John does not so much contradict the Synoptics as focus on the love that disciples, in alignment with their Lord, are commanded to offer one another.

The eschatological context in which the Fourth Evangelist locates the foot washing resists all attempts to sentimentalize that episode. The "hour" of the Son's glorification of the Father on the cross has finally tolled (13:31–32; cf. 7:30; 8:20; 12:23–27; 17:1). The devil has commandeered one of Jesus' disciples to betray him (13:2, 11; see also 6:70–71). When Judas leaves the table, "it was night" (13:30), whose darkness is now exposed by "the light of the world" (8:12; 9:5; 12:46; see also 1:5; 3:18–21; 11:9–10). Because Jesus is preparing to return to God, his disciples will soon be unable to see him (13:33; 16:16–28). As the cosmos turns on its hinges, the incarnate Word, who was with God in the beginning (1:1–2, 14), stoops to love to the bittersweet end those whom the Father has entrusted to him (17:24). It is a shattering moment of blessing. "If you know these things, blessed are you if you do them" (13:17).

C. CLIFTON BLACK

Homiletical Perspective

are cut off from the very source of power to serve and heal others in Jesus' name.

Or suppose we know pastorally that some in the congregation are having a hard time forgiving themselves for something they have done, a difficult time accepting the radical grace of Jesus. (In what congregation is this *not* the case?) Then perhaps we turn our attention more toward the people who are gathered at the table with Jesus that night: Judas, whom he knows will betray him; Peter, who will deny him; James and John, who will be unable to keep watch and pray with him; and the others who will forsake him in his hour of darkest need. We will watch in wonder as Jesus' response to this inner circle that has disappointed him over and over and over again is not to chastise or scold or punish, but to take a towel and a basin of water and gently to wash the ugliness of each one in turn. We will remember that the Communion table is a place where we can come—time and time again—to have our own ugliness lovingly touched and washed clean by Jesus.

Finally, in an age when congregations and denominations are significantly divided over doctrinal, social, and other issues, and sometimes have difficulty even gathering at the same table for a meal with one another, the preacher might want to draw attention once again to that *mandatum novum* (new commandment) that Jesus gives his disciples shortly before his death. The fact that Jesus spends his last meal with his friends, pleading that they love one another in spite of their own differences and disagreements, is compelling, to say the least. To ponder what foot washing might look like—not only in relation to the world, but also in relation to those in the church who have hurt us and those we love—might take us very close to the heart of the gospel tonight.

LEONORA TUBBS TISDALE

Isaiah 52:13-53:12

¹³See, my servant shall prosper;
  he shall be exalted and lifted up,
  and shall be very high.
¹⁴Just as there were many who were astonished at him
    —so marred was his appearance, beyond human semblance,
    and his form beyond that of mortals—
¹⁵so he shall startle many nations;
  kings shall shut their mouths because of him;
 for that which had not been told them they shall see,
  and that which they had not heard they shall contemplate.
^{53:1}Who has believed what we have heard?
  And to whom has the arm of the LORD been revealed?
²For he grew up before him like a young plant,
  and like a root out of dry ground;
 he had no form or majesty that we should look at him,
  nothing in his appearance that we should desire him.
³He was despised and rejected by others;
  a man of suffering and acquainted with infirmity;
 and as one from whom others hide their faces
  he was despised, and we held him of no account.

⁴Surely he has borne our infirmities
  and carried our diseases;
 yet we accounted him stricken,
  struck down by God, and afflicted.
⁵But he was wounded for our transgressions,
  crushed for our iniquities;
 upon him was the punishment that made us whole,
  and by his bruises we are healed.

Theological Perspective

So great is the significance of this passage for Christian theology that it has led many interpreters to dub Isaiah a "fifth evangelist." Indeed, it is probably difficult for anyone acquainted with the New Testament not to hear this fourth Servant Song as a description of the suffering and exaltation of Jesus Christ. The difficulty of determining any original historical referent for the Servant in this text has only added to its intrigue.

As Joseph Blenkinsopp points out, a number of the theological ideas of the passage are already nascent in older or contemporaneous biblical texts, such as the suffering of prophetic figures, God's servants as intercessors for the people, and the power of the righteous to influence the fate of the unrighteous.[1] The revelatory nature of the Servant's

1. Joseph Blenkinsopp, *Isaiah 40–55*, Anchor Bible 19A (New York: Doubleday, 2002), 119.

Pastoral Perspective

Despite its universally famous conclusion, Holy Week is a flickering collage of colliding images and mistaken identities. With a suspense plot that keeps us guessing until the very end, a film version of Good Friday might be more M. Night Shyamalan (Academy Award–winning director of *The Sixth Sense*) than Mel Gibson (*The Passion of the Christ*). Despite the way Easter Sunday has grown into a colorful arrangement of lilies and trumpets, pastel eggs and new white Sunday school gloves, underneath it is fed by a dark compost of blood and bone and mystery. Like a Russian nesting doll, the bright painted face of the resurrected Christ is but a final exterior. This is what makes Isaiah's enigmatic fourth Servant Song astonishingly appropriate for Good Friday.

Pastors and scholars have long struggled with this pericope's impenetrable message. Just who is the

⁶All we like sheep have gone astray;
   we have all turned to our own way,
  and the Lᴏʀᴅ has laid on him
   the iniquity of us all.

⁷He was oppressed, and he was afflicted,
   yet he did not open his mouth;
  like a lamb that is led to the slaughter,
   and like a sheep that before its shearers is silent,
   so he did not open his mouth.
⁸By a perversion of justice he was taken away.
   Who could have imagined his future?
  For he was cut off from the land of the living,
   stricken for the transgression of my people.
⁹They made his grave with the wicked
   and his tomb with the rich,
  although he had done no violence,
   and there was no deceit in his mouth.

¹⁰Yet it was the will of the Lᴏʀᴅ to crush him
     with pain.
  When you make his life an offering for sin,
   he shall see his offspring, and shall prolong
     his days;
  through him the will of the Lᴏʀᴅ shall prosper.
¹¹ Out of his anguish he shall see light;
  he shall find satisfaction through his knowledge.
   The righteous one, my servant, shall make many righteous,
   and he shall bear their iniquities.
¹²Therefore I will allot him a portion with the great,
   and he shall divide the spoil with the strong;
  because he poured out himself to death,
   and was numbered with the transgressors;
  yet he bore the sin of many,
   and made intercession for the transgressors.

Exegetical Perspective

The exile (586–538 BCE) was an unspeakably difficult time for Israel. Separated from their land, the exiles found themselves surrounded daily by those who wished them harm. Separated from their temple, they were under the constant peril of religious despair. Moreover, as the exile stretched into multiple decades, the usual and simple view that YHWH was punishing Israel for its sins threatened to give way to the view that YHWH had given up and forgotten Israel. These types of concerns lie at the heart of the oracles of Second Isaiah (chaps. 40–55).

Often the Servant represents faithful Israel, those who trust in YHWH and are hopeful for the future (41:8–9; 42:1; 44:1–2; 45:4). These individuals are, perhaps, to be identified with the community of Second Isaiah, those who treasured these oracles. Occasionally, however, the Servant is identified with

Homiletical Perspective

The focus of today's text is the last Servant Song of the Hebrew Scripture, a passage that evokes emotion, personal connection, and memory. Preached and studied as a text for Good Friday, it conveys the power of the one who suffers in a palpable way.

In the very first verse, the reader is invited to know that what is at once despised is also "lifted up and exalted" by God. The poem moves on to describe in detail the disfigured form of the Servant. The text suggests ugliness in human form, what we might refer to in contemporary language as deformation. Perhaps a good point of reflection on the text is to think about what is difficult to look at in our society. What do we consider disfigured or ugly? What things make us turn away from the sight of them?

Good Friday is a day to consider the people on the earth who suffer. Examples of what it means to

Isaiah 52:13-53:12

Theological Perspective

work—the way it makes the world see and hear (52:15)—also reverses the people's earlier failure to see or hear in Isaiah 6:9 and other verses.

The real theological innovation of the passage is that the suffering of God's innocent Servant can be a *substitute* for that of the truly guilty. That surprising and counterintuitive theme pervades Isaiah 53, but the author expresses it particularly graphically with the image of the *asham* sacrifice in 53:10. That sacrifice is specifically to make atonement with God for sin (Lev. 5:6, etc.); typically it is a sheep, and nowhere else in the Old Testament is the term used in any way comparable to Isaiah 53. Thus, this passage is the key proof text for the image of Jesus as the Lamb of God who by his sacrifice takes away the sin of the world (John 1:29, 36; 1 Pet. 1:18–19; Rev. 5:6; 7:14). The doctrine of Christ's death as a substitutionary, atoning sacrifice was developed most famously by Anselm of Canterbury in *Cur Deus Homo* (*Why God Became Man*). Some theologians have expressed discomfort with substitutionary atonement, as if it made God a "cosmic child abuser," and the idea that "it was the will of the LORD to crush [his Servant] with pain" (53:10) is indeed a potentially troubling one. However, from a Trinitarian perspective, Christ's suffering death is better understood as a gracious choice of God to take on the punishment for human sin. In his *Commentary on John*, Origen of Alexandria[2] combined the references to Christ as sacrificial Lamb with Hebrews 8:1 and John 10:18 to portray Christ as both the sacrifice *and* the high priest who offered it.

The idea of suffering as redemptive can be problematic in other ways, however. First Peter 2:18–25 held up the Suffering Servant as a model for slaves' submission to their masters. In the wake of the Holocaust, both Jewish and Christian theologians have called into question the idea that suffering can be redemptive. Indeed, there are times when suffering is simply evil, and must be resisted rather than embraced. The suggestion that *other people's suffering* is redemptive is particularly dangerous; it risks making the observer complicit in the evil. True imitation of Christ means choosing holiness *for oneself* despite any cost in suffering. Christ's death for our sins does not mean saying thanks and sitting on the sidelines: "If any want to become my followers," Jesus said, "let them . . . take up their cross and follow me" (Mark 8:34).

Pastoral Perspective

Servant prophesied by Isaiah? Jewish interpretation insists that it can be read only as a metaphor for the nation of Israel, despite textual challenges. Christians, for their part, have claimed with utter certainty that Isaiah's Servant is none other than Jesus Christ himself, obviously come to rescue the faithful as an atoning sacrifice ("With his stripes we are healed," Isa. 53:5 RSV).

For Christians, one layer of value in reading Isaiah on Good Friday is the language itself. How easily Christ's heroic efforts are muted by repetition, the sharp edges dulled by time's erosion. It is right and good to slow down and remember the visceral suffering of the (Galilean) Servant, resisting the urge to hop on down the bunny trail to Sunday morning's alleluias. Once our eyes have adjusted to the dim light of that afternoon so long ago, properly recalling and thus honoring the particular suffering, our reading of Isaiah beckons us to submerge to a different depth as well, into the larger landscape of God acting in history. Isaiah brings us to that sweeping canvas by his ancient context. It is an ageless query: What is God doing through something so unrecognizable?

Despite thousands of years of reflection, we still spend an inordinate amount of time reconciling our ideas of our Creator with the movements of God in the world. We think we know how God should act. We pray and wait, impatient for answers. We attempt to tame our unknowing by enclosing God in partisan constructs. In the great polarity between traditionalists and progressives in American Christianity today, for instance, there seems to be more than one Jesus. What is God doing? We think we know.

If snap certitude poisons faith into suffocating religiosity, then as now, Isaiah's prophetic vision is surely an antidote. Because if we are really paying attention, we might just admit that we do not have all the answers. We might just admit that the suffering of Jesus in fact shocks us, just as Isaiah's description of a battered and pitiful Servant leader shocked the Israelites in Babylon. *Behold, your Savior:* marred beyond human semblance, unlovely, undesired, hated, made to suffer such great anguish. As biblical translator Eugene Peterson puts it, "Who would have thought GOD's saving power would look like this?"[1]

Surprise awakens adrenaline and sharpens the senses. Blinking, we sit forward in our seats, suddenly wondering what is to come next. Who is

---

2. Origen, *Commentary on the Gospel according to John Books 1–10*, trans. Ronald E. Heine, vol. 80 in *The Fathers of the Church: A New Translation* (Washington, DC: The Catholic University of America Press, 1989), 242–44.

1. Eugene H. Peterson, Isaiah 53:1, in *The Message: The Bible in Contemporary Language* (Colorado Springs, CO: NavPress Publishing Group, 2002).

Israel as a whole, including those who are either wavering in their trust or who have abandoned hope because of the bleak and cruel circumstances of their captivity (42:19; 43:10; 49:3–6; 50:10).

What is the relationship between these different Servants, and how do they relate to one another? What is the relationship between the faithful community of Second Isaiah and those fearful—or perhaps already apostate—Israelites who do not believe? Are they lost? What is the relationship between Israel as a whole and the wider world—a world where YHWH was also free to choose servants to fulfill the divine will? How does suffering—both suffering for sin as well as innocent suffering—figure in the equation? The poem itself is divided into five movements.

Divine speech: The revelatory Servant (52:13–15). The poem begins with a speech by YHWH, noting the significance of the Servant. The Servant, because of his mangled appearance, will startle many people, including people in positions of power. The Servant, by his experience of suffering, will bring about a revelation (a revolution?) in the way in which people "see" and "contemplate" the world. The identity of the Servant is not made clear here. Is it Israel as a whole and its own sufferings that will be revelatory? Is it the faithful community? Is it, rather, some other individual? In this introduction, the Servant is ambiguous, and intentionally so. For this poem will not let its reader simply define one interpretive option over against another. Relationship and participation will be the watchwords of this poem. No matter who the Servant is, everyone is ultimately involved.

Communal speech: The rejected Servant (53:1–3). While it may be true that in the future many people, including kings, will understand something they had not heard, the community acknowledges that it has already learned something about the Servant and his revelatory quality. In this section, the Servant begins to look more like an individual. This one had no notable qualities, was rejected by people, and was a "man of suffering." This one, most importantly, had no relationship with "us." "We" did not look at him, "we" did not desire him, and "we" did not even "think about him" (*hashabnuhu*; NRSV: "held him of no account"). While it is clear that the Servant is rejected in general, it is important that "we" are the ones who rejected him.

Communal speech: The relational Servant (53:4–6). This central section of the poem provides the hermeneutical key for the whole. Although the

be despised by human beings can be found in the newspaper, in our history texts, and in the routines of daily life. Today the preacher is asked to bring home the horrors of the suffering that some human beings cause others. This not only allows the community of faith to stay connected to suffering; it also allows them to remember that events of horror continue to happen. This is a hard text for people who do not suffer, or who do not own up to the suffering in the world.

In preparation for preaching this text, it will be helpful to form a working definition of the term "servant," both as it refers to the people of Israel and to followers of the Christian faith tradition. In the text at hand, the Servant is the one who bears responsibility for the many, guiding the faithful to God's redemption. The preacher might consider those in the community or larger society whose vocations involve maintaining order and safety. People in public service jobs such as nurses, librarians, and social workers come to mind, as do teachers, firefighters, and those serving in the National Guard. By reflecting on the ways such people respond to those in need, the preacher may be able to help connect the faithful to the supreme sacrifice of Good Friday, even without death.

Out of context, the term "suffering servant" may have no sense of redemption for those who hear it. In this text, however, the Suffering Servant guides the faithful to God's redemption. This story of the Servant is a story of victory for people who work hard to know what it means to be redeemed of God, even when that involves suffering. This calls up many contemporary images. While considering the Suffering Servant of God, the one who redeems us, the preacher might also consider those whose work cuts them off from people in the faith community. Young soldiers fight in wars that many people do not understand. They experience suffering in the line of duty. There is no end to those who are despised and rejected.

In Isaiah, the people of Israel bear the grief and sorrow of the nations. In the Gospels, Jesus' suffering and death become the sacrifice made by God's own for God's people. On Good Friday, Christians see in Jesus the Suffering Servant, taken "like a lamb . . . to the slaughter" (53:7) as the one chosen by God to bear the transgressions of many. The Servant is oppressed and afflicted, yet the Servant does not open his mouth. The Servant has done no violence, but is stricken for the transgressions of the people. This is a harsh punishment. Is it really required of those who work for God's promise? The Isaiah text

Isaiah 52:13-53:12

Theological Perspective

It is possible that Jesus himself invoked this text to explain his mission; in Mark 10:45 he says he came "to give his life as a ransom for many." However in Luke 22:35–37 he uses Isaiah 53:9 to portray himself as a political radical (cf. Matt. 10:34).

When the authors of the New Testament looked to the Scriptures for explanations of the death of the Messiah, Isaiah 52:13–53:12 was one of the most important passages they used. Paul was the first we know of who did this, invoking 53:9–11 to explain atonement in Romans 4:22–25 by identifying Jesus as the one "who was handed over to death for our trespasses and was raised for our justification" (cf. 2 Cor. 5:21; 1 Cor. 15:3–4). Paul also took Isaiah's reference to the incredible news about the Servant (52:14–53:1) to emphasize the importance of spreading the gospel (Rom. 10:14–17; cf. Rom. 15:18–21, which cites the Septuagint translation of Isa. 52:15).

The evangelists also read the passage in new and interesting ways. John found in Isaiah 53:1 an explanation for the disciples' failure to believe despite all the signs that Jesus had performed in their presence (John 12:36–38). The failure of the Servant's contemporaries to understand who he was until after his suffering death is a major theme of the passage, and might press readers to consider the ways in which they too overlook the gifts of those whom society deems deformed or unattractive. As Augustine wrote, "A root is not beautiful, but contains within itself the potentiality for beauty"—that is, it grows into a tree, which Augustine meant to symbolize the church.[3]

Matthew understood Jesus' healings as the fulfillment of Isaiah 53:4's reference to "bearing our infirmities and carrying our diseases" (Matt. 8:14–17). Thus the present-day believers might see this as a warrant for their own ministries of health and healing.

One of the most famous New Testament references to the passage is Acts 8:26–38, in which an Ethiopian eunuch reads Isaiah 53:7–8 and is converted, asking Philip to baptize him. It may not be immediately clear why these verses spoke to the eunuch, but I suggest that he saw himself in the Servant's lack of offspring (Gk. *genea*, "generation," 8:33 NRSV). Extrapolating this point much more broadly, the Song's images of suffering, as applied to Jesus, emphasize Christ's solidarity with those who suffer in many ways.

CHRISTOPHER B. HAYS

Pastoral Perspective

this Servant who restores exiles to God? While remaining mindful of the exegetical tensions of the text, as well as the competing interpretive traditions about the identity of the Servant, perhaps another nesting doll should be pried open to get to the core.

Christian and Jewish believers alike can read Isaiah, celebrating together that the Creator of the world is a God who restores and rescues in awesome ways that we cannot predict and seldom expect. Our task is constantly to ready ourselves for the recognition of Christ's presence where it is manifest, to comprehend the inbreaking—and once we recognize the shape, to imitate it—practicing it with our calendars, not just our aspirations. Following in the wise, nonviolent footsteps of Christ is God's prescription for this ailing planet: bearing one another's grief, carrying common sorrows, working on behalf of those who are languishing in Babylon, cut off and utterly without hope. The pattern of the innocent one standing up courageously against arrayed powers of the status quo is a proven fulcrum for shifting paradigms. Some of the most transformative people in history are those who suffered without losing their vision of truth: Gandhi, King, the monks of Burma. Are we able to recognize God's work when it is right in front of us?

Barbara Brown Taylor captures it this way:

> In the end, it does not matter whether we can name the person Isaiah paints for us, because the portrait already has a name. "God's servant" it says, and that is enough. Whether the words are capitalized or not, they speak to all of us who are God's servants in this world. Whether we like it or not, every one of us is a full-fledged deputy of God's kingdom. Some of us are better at it than others and some of us do more harm than good, but none of us is excused.[2]

It is the ultimate revelation of Eastertide—we are not just saved, we are called. Like the Jewish understanding of Isaiah, we *as a community* are to be the Servant as well. It is the wholly unexpected plot twist, and it is so easy to miss. Who would have thought God's saving power would look like this? God has created something entirely new, something that still startles the nations, causing kings and presidents and CEOs and even ministers to shut their mouths in astonishment. Behold God's handiwork. Behold the cross lifted high, pointing to the largeness of the power of love, a love that shatters every expectation.

SUZANNE WOOLSTON-BOSSERT

3. St. Augustine, *The Works of Saint Augustine: A Translation for the Twenty-First Century*, part 3: Sermons, vol. 2: Sermons 20–50, trans. Edmund Hill, ed. John E. Rotelle (Brooklyn, NY: New York City Press, 1990), 244.

2. Barbara Brown Taylor, "Laboring in Vain," in *Gospel Medicine* (Boston: Cowley Publications, 1995), 159.

community rejected the significance of the Servant, that rejection did not destroy the relationship, but rather defined the relationship in a more forceful and immediate way. The community had interpreted the suffering of the Servant in terms of sin and punishment: the suffering of the Servant was evidence that he was being punished by God. Yet the community comes to realize that a paradigm shift is in order. The theology of retribution and punishment is not the best way to understand the torture and death of the Servant. Instead, the theology of sacrifice—even here with the death of a human being—provides the best lens to understand the Servant's own suffering, the community's suffering, and Israel's suffering. Each instance of suffering and frailty in the Servant is balanced by a positive result in the community, in "us." The poem does not explain or define the way in which this works. It is neither mechanistic nor logical. It is, instead, relational. The Servant relates to the community by taking its iniquities—quite apart from any acknowledgment or request or even awareness on the part of the community.

Communal speech: The redeeming Servant (53:7–11a). The injustice of the suffering and death of the Servant is highlighted in this section. The Servant, however, does not appear at the beginning and end of this section as a completely passive object of derision. Although the Servant "was oppressed," "was afflicted," and was "led," he actively "did not open his mouth" (v. 7). The Servant through his self-imposed silence is the main actor at the beginning of this section. At verse 10, two important changes occur. First, the poem makes explicit the divine initiative in producing the sufferings of the Servant. Second, the poem changes its focus from past events to future hope. The Servant, dead and buried, is not gone. The Servant has offspring (the community?), will cause the "will of YHWH" to prosper, will see the results of his actions, and will be satisfied through knowing those results.

Divine speech: The righteous Servant (53:11b–12). The poem ends as it began, with a divine speech. The Servant, who in his death is identified with the powerful, the transgressors, and the "many," brings all into the reach of his saving embrace. Through identification and relationship, the Servant—whether an individual, a community, or a nation—brings salvation to all by means of willing self-sacrifice.

ROY L. HELLER

raises grave questions about the place of suffering in human life.

Clearly we lament the death of Jesus Christ as those left behind. Is it equally clear that we persist in making separations between people, so that there are still those who are outcast and despised? Why do we ask the innocent to go on suffering affliction? How can the preacher make the connection between the Isaiah text and our continued willingness to sacrifice a few for the comfort of the many? In our own time, it seems sadly true that the nations have not ceased to ask for such sacrifices. When will we put an end to suffering?

Working to make this text live in the sermon and in the congregation will involve asking such hard questions, while at the same time reminding God's people that the Servant in the Isaiah text comes to understand God's purpose. Though he is crushed with pain (53:10), he also sees the light (53:11), discerning the meaning of the suffering.

God's work—the theological work of "bearing away" the sins of many—is done by a people and by Jesus, both of whom bear a legacy of being outcast and despised. Yet the text also promises that the Servant shall prosper (52:13). What, then, is the relationship between the Servant's suffering and his prospering? If the text connects the suffering of the Servant with his prospering, what does this suggest about our own suffering?

The cycle of suffering remains part of human experience, and the role of the Servant is still with us. Even as preachers make connections between the text and those who live lives of service, it is fair to ask how many more Good Fridays we will enact before we accept God's redeeming grace. How, as Christians, might we act on the hope of new life? What connections can we make to those who suffer, without insisting that their suffering continue? What concrete possibilities for healing and renewal might we act upon, so that the redemption of Good Friday is made real? For even on this day we hold the vision of a kingdom where people serve one another— woman to man, person to person—offering one another the gift of peace in a place where pain and suffering are no more.

CLAUDIA HIGHBAUGH

Psalm 22

¹My God, my God, why have you forsaken me?
　Why are you so far from helping me, from the words of my groaning?
²O my God, I cry by day, but you do not answer;
　and by night, but find no rest.

³Yet you are holy,
　enthroned on the praises of Israel.
⁴In you our ancestors trusted;
　they trusted, and you delivered them.
⁵To you they cried, and were saved;
　in you they trusted, and were not put to shame.

⁶But I am a worm, and not human;
　scorned by others, and despised by the people.
⁷All who see me mock at me;
　they make mouths at me, they shake their heads;
⁸"Commit your cause to the Lᴏʀᴅ; let him deliver—
　let him rescue the one in whom he delights!"

⁹Yet it was you who took me from the womb;
　you kept me safe on my mother's breast.
¹⁰On you I was cast from my birth,
　and since my mother bore me you have been my God.
¹¹Do not be far from me,
　for trouble is near
　and there is no one to help.

¹²Many bulls encircle me,
　strong bulls of Bashan surround me;
¹³they open wide their mouths at me,
　like a ravening and roaring lion.

¹⁴I am poured out like water,
　and all my bones are out of joint;
　my heart is like wax;
　it is melted within my breast;
¹⁵my mouth is dried up like a potsherd,
　and my tongue sticks to my jaws;
　you lay me in the dust of death.

¹⁶For dogs are all around me;
　a company of evildoers encircles me.

Theological Perspective

One can scarcely imagine more heartrending images of suffering and destitution than those of the first twenty-one verses of Psalm 22, written from the depths of excruciating pain, the anguish of rejection by valued friends and neighbors, and the fear of abandonment even by God: "My God, my God, why have you forsaken me? . . . Do not be far from me,

Pastoral Perspective

In most Christians' minds the words, "My God, my God, why have you forsaken me?" are identified inextricably with the cross (Mark 15:34 and Matt. 27:46). Although Psalm 22 was in no way composed with Jesus of Nazareth in mind, it would be a mistake to use this day to make that point. During Holy Week, even such generally useful and important instruction

My hands and feet have shriveled;
¹⁷I can count all my bones.
   They stare and gloat over me;
¹⁸they divide my clothes among themselves,
   and for my clothing they cast lots.

¹⁹But you, O Lord, do not be far away!
   O my help, come quickly to my aid!
²⁰Deliver my soul from the sword,
   my life from the power of the dog!
²¹   Save me from the mouth of the lion!

   From the horns of the wild oxen you have rescued me.
²²I will tell of your name to my brothers and sisters;
   in the midst of the congregation I will praise you:
²³You who fear the Lord, praise him!
   All you offspring of Jacob, glorify him;
   stand in awe of him, all you offspring of Israel!
²⁴For he did not despise or abhor
   the affliction of the afflicted;
   he did not hide his face from me,
   but heard when I cried to him.

²⁵From you comes my praise in the great congregation;
   my vows I will pay before those who fear him.
²⁶The poor shall eat and be satisfied;
   those who seek him shall praise the Lord.
   May your hearts live forever!

²⁷All the ends of the earth shall remember
   and turn to the Lord;
   and all the families of the nations
   shall worship before him.
²⁸For dominion belongs to the Lord,
   and he rules over the nations.

²⁹To him, indeed, shall all who sleep in the earth bow down;
   before him shall bow all who go down to the dust,
   and I shall live for him.
³⁰Posterity will serve him;
   future generations will be told about the Lord,
³¹and proclaim his deliverance to a people yet unborn,
   saying that he has done it.

Exegetical Perspective

From a literary point of view, Psalm 22 can be neatly divided into two parts: verses 1–21 consist of a lament and supplication, and verses 22–31 embody a hymn of praise and thanksgiving. The psalmist begins with a bitter cry of despair, questioning why God has abandoned him, followed by a plea for God to intervene on his behalf (vv. 19–21). The hymn of praise and

Homiletical Perspective

As every preacher knows, the first line of Psalm 22 echoes all the way to Golgotha: "My God, my God, why have you forsaken me?" By quoting these words, the dying Christ speaks words that he would have spoken before—not because he "felt" them (he may have), but because they voiced one of the most profound prayers of Israel. The God of covenant is

Psalm 22

Theological Perspective

for trouble is near, and there is no one to help" (vv. 1, 11). Juxtaposed to this cry of torment and plea for help, however, is the rest of the psalm, verses 22–31, which—like Psalm 116 in Holy Thursday's reading—celebrate divine deliverance and the greatness and mercy of God and call the world to sing God's praises. Needless to say, the theological quandary of this psalm lies as much in this extraordinary juxtaposition as in its two starkly contrasting moods.

It is important to note that the psalmist is not asserting the nonexistence of God. There is no question here that God exits, is enthroned, and has delivered the psalmist's ancestors in their time of trouble (vv. 3–5). The psalmist even asserts that God has lovingly cared for himself or herself since birth (vv. 9–10). Nor is there the slightest hint that the suffering is deserved. Instead, the agony of this psalm is more that of a lover's sense of abandonment: how could "my God," who created me and who has repeatedly loved me and rescued me and my people from distress in the past, fail to do so here and now, with me?

There are, of course, possible theological answers. God's ways are not our ways. God has larger purposes hidden from mortal eyes. Faith is being tested or character formed. God will make it all up in the end, eschatologically, or in heaven, or somehow, somewhere. Or perhaps, less traditionally, God really does love and care for us but lacks the power to deliver us from harm. Or, more heretically, maybe God is not entirely good; maybe there is a "shadow side" to God that, like evil itself, must be acknowledged, coped with, and integrated, if possible, into a greater, perhaps mystical wisdom.

However, these and other possible "answers" to the problem, even if true, offer little comfort or help to us in our hour of affliction. Perhaps at a later time (if there is a later time), when a more dispassionate opportunity for reflection presents itself, some of these "answers" may be meaningful and helpful. Not here and now, though, not on the cross. Here there is no answer, only a question; no deliverance, only the experience of abandonment and bewilderment.

Psalm 22 indulges in no clever attempts to defend and explain God's ways to a suffering world. Simply and suddenly, from verse 21b forward, the psalmist simply declares that God has in fact "answered" and "rescued" him or her. The psalm then proceeds to celebrate the greatness and goodness of God and of divine deliverance, as the psalmist vows to worship and praise, with all the earth, the "dominion" of the Lord who "rules over the nations," even (remarkably) "all

Pastoral Perspective

will sound like pedantry. Preaching on Good Friday offers the same extraordinary opportunity that comes with preaching every funeral: occasions that insist on the reality of death find our attention particularly sharp. Even more than when they attend weddings or Sunday morning services, the people gathered before you will listen very closely to what you have to say. They will want to know: what can you tell me about suffering, about death, and about how I can maintain faith and hope when it seems that all is lost?

At first look, Psalm 22 reads like two entirely separate psalms that have adhered to each other by accident, as if two pages of the Psalter had become stuck together at one corner. A close reading shows that the abject desolation expressed in the first twenty-one verses and the ecstatic praise that fills the remaining ten actually enjoy a transcendent unity. In them the psalmist establishes that suffering and deliverance are immutably entwined in the helix of salvation, as are desperate complaint and jubilant thanksgiving. Each is as real and essential a part of life with God and speech to God as is the other. In its expansiveness, this psalm offers both the unwavering truth and the genuine hope for which your listeners long.

The preacher's first task here is to help the congregation avoid two very unhelpful ways of listening to those enormously powerful opening words. One is to confuse familiarity with under-standing, and slip into a sort of pious coma, missing the richness and complexity of the other thirty verses. The other is to identify so strongly with the expres-sions of suffering and desolation the one believes Psalm 22 is actually about one's own personal experience. We are not being invited to interpret this song in light of our own lives. Grace will come to us if we keep our eyes on Jesus and allow ourselves to be both seared and anointed by the truth the evangelists borrow the psalmist's words to tell.

Psalm 22 sets before us a human being whose confidence in God's power to save appears to have been unshaken up to this point. At the very outset, the words "My God" establish that the relationship between the subject and the one he worships has been profound. Verses 3–5 locate him in an ancient and continuing lineage of faith, and verses 9–10 illustrate the intimacy of his relationship with God in the immediate present. We meet him as he is being systematically stripped of (in reverse order) his clothing (v. 18), his flesh (v. 17), his safety and vigor (v. 16), his health (v. 15), and his strength (v. 14). The savage creatures that animate verses 12, 13, and 16 create an environment of desolate terror: all humanity

thanksgiving begins in verse 22, indicating that the psalmist's plea for deliverance has been granted.

The consistent use of the first-person singular "I" throughout the psalm clearly identifies this as an individual, rather than a communal psalm. Although the psalm itself does not provide the identity of the author, the trials described in the lament have led some to suggest Davidic authorship. This is certainly a possibility, but the metaphorical language employed in the lament could easily apply to the suffering of some anonymous individual. The superscription to the psalm indicates that this is a psalm "of David" or "to David" (*ledawid*). Although *ledawid* can be interpreted as being a psalm authored by David, some scholars have suggested that it may rather indicate a collection of psalms that were referred to as the Davidic Psalter —analogous to the Lutheran hymnal—with no claim of Davidic authorship intended.[1]

The meaning of the enigmatic phrase in the superscription, "According to the Deer of the Dawn," has been a matter of much debate. It seems likely that this was the title of a well-known tune or musical arrangement that was to be employed when this psalm was used in worship services.[2] The date of composition and authorship of Psalm 22 continues to be a matter of dispute. Those who defend Davidic authorship argue for a mid-10th-century BCE date, while some scholars suggest a date as late as the Persian or Hellenistic period (ca. fourth century BCE).[3]

Whatever the origins of the psalm, there is consensus that in the postexilic period it played an important role in the liturgy of synagogue worship. The worshiping community identified with the psalmist's feelings of abandonment, tempered by trust in God's faithfulness and the hope of eventual deliverance. Thus what was initially an individual's psalm came to be understood as an expression of the former plight and future hope of the community.

Verse 1 is familiar to most Christians, not because they recognize it as the first verse of Psalm 22, but because they think of Jesus' words from the cross, which according to Matthew 27:46 were uttered at the ninth hour, or around three o'clock in the afternoon. Like the psalmist, Matthew suggests that in the midst of his suffering, Jesus questions why God has abandoned him. Although it is not possible to know precisely why Jesus quoted this psalm, two things are

held to account in the thick of deep trouble and perceived abandonment. Only the bravest of preachers will swim in these waters, knowing that they are in over their heads.

If we preach on this psalm, let us tell the truth about God's silence in the face of our trouble. Gory details from the cross may or may not be necessary, but honesty is required. The preacher must be willing to give field reports of how God has been nowhere to be found. There is no shortage of such stories—but there is a shortage of truthful storytellers. Will we give up every pretension of religious expertise to enter the pathos of this text? Or will we rush to Easter with plastic smiles upon our faces, as if to declare life is easy, pain trivial, and trouble only temporary?

Like most of the biblical laments, Psalm 22 starts sour and ends well. Honest questions precede the theological affirmations. Given the setting of Good Friday, the preacher must not rush to the happy ending. This is a day when the crucifixion of Jesus invites the faithful to consider the threats upon our own lives. We take seriously all mortal pain. While we are Christian people who know that death and destruction will not have the last say upon us, we also recognize that God's power is hidden on the cross. In time the psalmist will shout joyful affirmations at the conclusion of this prayer, but not until the truth is voiced.

Meanwhile, in the thick of it all, God stays quiet. The psalmist cries by day, but hears no answer. The faithful lament by night, but find no rest. Can we simply say this, and leave it there?

Perhaps this would be the occasion for a sermon on the spiritual discipline of restraint. We cannot say everything because it is not ours to say. In no way does this mean that we do not believe in God, but we do honor a God who does not speak too frequently. We abide in silence, trusting what we cannot yet see, affirming what is not yet obvious. This is one way to revere God on God's own terms. We do not say what we cannot say.

When Frederick Buechner learned that his brother was dying, with two weeks to live, he offered to rush to the bedside. His brother replied there was not much to see. So, out of the deepest respect for one another, the two brothers kept their distance. They talked each day on the phone, speaking words of appreciation and love, knowing that neither one could fix the situation. There was little else to do.

1. Artur Weiser, *The Psalms*, trans. Herbert Hartwell, Old Testament Library, ed. G. Ernest Wright et al. (Philadelphia: Westminster Press, 1962), 94–95.

2. Solomon B. Freehof, *The Book of Psalms: A Commentary* (Cincinnati: Union of American Hebrew Congregations, 1938), 55.

3. Charles A. Briggs and Emilie G. Briggs, *The Book of Psalms*, International Critical Commentary 19 (New York: Charles Scribner's Sons, 1906), 1:lxxxix–xcii.

1. Frederick Buechner, *The Eyes of the Heart: A Memoir of the Lost and Found* (New York: HarperSanFrancisco, 1999), 161–63.

Psalm 22

Theological Perspective

who go down to the dust" (vv. 28–29). What begins in a human cry of godforsaken suffering ends in a triumphal vision of divine sovereignty and deliverance for all humankind, including generations unborn.

What are we to make of the psalmist's "answer"? Perhaps verses 21b–31 represent an ancient scribe's pious attempt to assuage the despairing message of verses 1–21a, to dilute and suppress its radical, unanswerable cry—as the keepers of religious traditions and institutions have so often done in response to the hideous, unanswerable existential question of God and human suffering. For such questions know no theological or institutional bounds, subverting every attempt to rationalize and tame them.

There may be another sense in which the two halves of this psalm do belong together. Perhaps the issue, for us as for the psalmist, is not how to explain intellectually the experience of the absence of God, but how to keep on loving God (or for that matter, each other) in the face of an inexplicable failure of God (or our neighbor) to reciprocate our love and trust. For the psalmist, the question is clearly not one of the metaphysical existence, moral goodness, or sovereign power of God, all of which are taken for granted. The problem centers instead on the existential failure of God's love and power to become real here, now, for me. This may be the greater mystery. The most urgent existential question may be to decide whether love itself is a fraud and a deception, not to be trusted, a fool's illusion—or whether, as the Bible claims, love is despite its apparent failure at the core of who God is and consequently at the center of what life is all about (Deut. 6:5; Mark 12:28–31; 1 Cor. 13:13; 1 John 4:7–8). It must be said that this question, which is as pertinent and pressing with respect to love between humans as between humans and God, is indeed at all times and in every circumstance an open question existentially.

In this sense—if we take the psalm in its entirety—the psalmist simply refuses to give up on God's sovereign love and asserts the trustworthiness of that love, even in the face of its apparent failure and defeat. The love affair between the psalmist and God persists, even in the face of its most extreme, disconfirming experience of failure. Surely the endurance and ultimate triumph of the power of love is a matter that only faith can decide in the midst of existential lovelessness and abandonment. It is the only question that really matters—the one crucial question—in every relationship, divine and human, on every Good Friday, God's and our own.

RODNEY J. HUNTER

Pastoral Perspective

is absent. When, in a radio broadcast, an interviewer asked Sherwin Nuland, M.D., author of *How We Die*, "What's the worst way to die?" Nuland answered simply and without hesitation: "Alone." The speaker of this psalm and Jesus, who is made to invoke it, are each about to die in this worst possible way: out of view of the protection of God he had imagined himself able to recruit (vv. 1, 2), abandoned by others (vv. 6–8), and without the least power to protect himself (vv. 14–18). For many of your congregation, Jesus' anguish and death establish his credentials as a human being more firmly than does his birth. Here is irrefutable proof that he is one of us.

Those first twenty-one verses narrate the distillation of a person of faith to his essence: he has lost all that he ever was or has ever had, including the very water and dust that form his body. It is not just that he will cease to exist; all evidence that he ever existed may disappear as well. To all appearances, his frantic petitions find only silence. In what can he—can we—possibly hope?

Those gathered on Good Friday can find genuine comfort in the psalmist's assurance that God "does not despise or abhor the affliction of the afflicted" (v. 24). We will not, however, witness the kind of deliverance celebrated in that same verse until we reconvene for the first service of Easter. Alleluias will find no place in the passion story we are about to hear. Even as we believe that universe-altering redemption will come, we must acknowledge that it is not visible yet. There is no escape from suffering and death, either on this liturgical day or in this world. Yet, the psalmist assures us, there is more than our eyes can see.

Each of the three final verses of Psalm 22 describes a celebration that is still invisible. Verses 30–31 turn our attention to praise offered by people who have not yet entered this life: the echoes of "posterity," "future generations," and "people yet unborn" conjure a chain of worshipers who will exist someday, but do not yet exist. The links also stretch backward: "all who sleep in the earth" and "all who go down to the dust" shall bow down before God as well (v. 29). The chorus will include those who do not exist any more. These images challenge conventional certitude that praise cannot be offered by the dying and the dead (Pss. 30:9; 88:10; 115:17). They suggest that God's reach extends farther than we know, and perhaps that our life does too. When suffering and death distill us, what remains is our essential capacity to praise. When everything is lost, something is left: an unbreakable communion with God.

MARIA DECARVALHO

Exegetical Perspective

certain: (1) he identified with the sense of abandonment experienced by the psalmist, and (2) he must have been very familiar with this psalm. Because of his familiarity, he no doubt knew not only how it began but also how it ended—with the ultimate vindication of the sufferer and affirmation that God had not in fact abandoned him, despite the apparent evidence to the contrary. Viewed in this context, what appears to be a cry of utter despair is in fact an affirmation of God's presence and care, despite human perceptions of what appears to be a hopeless situation.

The New Revised Standard Version renders Matthew 27:35, "And when they had crucified him, they divided his clothes among themselves by casting lots," but notes that other ancient texts add, "in order that what had been spoken through the prophet might be fulfilled, 'They divided my clothes among themselves, and for my clothing they cast lots'" (cf. John 19:24). The complaint raised in Psalm 22:18, "They divide my clothes among themselves, and for my clothing they cast lots," most likely reflects the plundering the psalmist experienced at the hands of his enemies, but this lament is reinterpreted by the Gospel writer as a prophetic reference to the casting of lots for Jesus' garment at the foot of the cross. Clearly, the early Christian church viewed Psalm 22 as foreshadowing both the tragedy and triumph of the passion and resurrection.

Familiarity with texts like this that form the foundation of New Testament texts provides the modern interpreter with a much richer understanding of the message of the early church than is possible by reading the New Testament in isolation.

Another extremely important aspect of this psalm as it relates to the Christian gospel is the lack of animosity toward one's enemies and persecutors that is found in many of the psalms. Despite the trauma caused by his tormentors (vv. 16–18), the psalmist calls not for revenge, but only for deliverance and reassurance of God's presence (vv. 19–21).

The psalm concludes with the restitution of not only the beleaguered psalmist but also the meek, those who seek YHWH, and others who are despised and afflicted (vv. 24, 26). Most surprisingly, "all the families of the nations" (v. 27), "all who sleep in the earth" (v. 29), and "a people yet unborn" (v. 31) will come to recognize YHWH's power and praise him. The enduring influence of this psalm on the Christian understanding of Christology is hard to overestimate.

DAVID W. MCCREERY

Homiletical Perspective

When the end came, the two brothers could only pray to be carried from darkness into light, through pain into peace, through death into life.[1] Anything more would cheapen the truth of the occasion.

Today we look toward a dying man on the cross. Before the preacher fills the air with atonement theories or offers a eulogy of the deceased's good deeds, it is important simply to fix the church's gaze on what is actually going on: Jesus dies in pain, abandoned by friends, mocked by enemies, ignored by others, and God does not rush to fix any of it.

There are other biblical texts that reflect on this particular death, and they can be chosen to proclaim and teach its meaning. As the biblical tradition hears this psalm on Jesus' lips, it affirms both the forsakenness of this moment and his complete trust in the God who saves. Nothing more needs to be said.

If restraint would be too unsettling for the preacher, the form of the psalm suggests a second approach. There is an undulating quality to Psalm 22, as the groans (vv. 1–2, 6–8, 12–18) are matched by affirmations of God's saving love (vv. 3–5, 9–11, 19–31). As the groans lengthen, the affirmations grow even longer. As the listing of personal troubles increase, the declarations of God's saving care are spelled out in greater depth. This is not a bad way to preach—or to pray.

This literary structure suggests a possible structure for the sermon. We could imagine a sermon in similarly aligned sections, as a rhythm is established between the honest expressions of pain and trust. God's apparent absence is answered by the memory of how faithful ancestors trusted and were not abandoned (vv. 1–5). Public scorning and mocking are answered by the promise and memory of God's intimate care (vv. 6–11). The threat of physical disintegration is equalized by God's praiseworthy rescue (vv. 12–31).

Our human experience has a comparable rhythm of divine absence and presence. There is neither too much gloom nor too much sunshine. Mature faith will strive to hold these experiences in dynamic tension, neither rushing too quickly to affirm where God is working nor acquiescing to atheism.

One recalls the old story of the rabbis who gathered to prove that God does not exist. Fed up by long and painful experiences of divine neglect, they were convinced that humanity is completely alone in the universe. Just then, one of them interrupted to say, "We will have to finish this conversation later. It is time for our prayers."

WILLIAM G. CARTER

Hebrews 10:16-25

16 "This is the covenant that I will make with them
  after those days, says the Lord:
I will put my laws in their hearts,
  and I will write them on their minds,"
17he also adds,
  "I will remember their sins and their lawless deeds no more."
18Where there is forgiveness of these, there is no longer any offering for sin.
  19Therefore, my friends, since we have confidence to enter the sanctuary by the blood of Jesus, 20by the new and living way that he opened for us through the curtain (that is, through his flesh), 21and since we have a great priest over the house of God, 22let us approach with a true heart in full assurance of faith, with our hearts sprinkled clean from an evil conscience and our bodies washed with pure water. 23Let us hold fast to the confession of our hope without wavering, for he who has promised is faithful. 24And let us consider how to provoke one another to love and good deeds, 25not neglecting to meet together, as is the habit of some, but encouraging one another, and all the more as you see the Day approaching.

Theological Perspective

The Swiss Reformation bequeathed to the church treasures of remarkable liturgical development. Geneva is more typically acknowledged for its heritage of theological literacy for the whole people of God, and its comprehensive vision of Christian citizenship, rooted in commitment to the lordship and mission of Jesus Christ. Less well recognized is its gift of liturgy, which richly embodies its deepest theological commitments.

Consider its liturgy of confession and pardon. Rather than perpetuate the private confession practiced in the church for centuries, the Reformers brought confession of sin into the open, casting it as corporate confession of the sin in which all God's people are complicit, followed by an assurance of God's pardon to all who confess their sin. Announcement of God's forgiveness of sin in Christ was followed by a most unexpected liturgical rubric —the recitation of the law. Calvin even wanted the law *sung*, of all things. Because of what God has done for us in Christ's ministry of forgiveness and cleansing, we are joyously free to love God and neighbor rightly, which is the essence of God's law. Reception of Christ's atoning work is joined by glad and grateful obedience on the part of those who have been made right with God.

Pastoral Perspective

On Good Friday we are moved to consider the crucifixion of Jesus and the meaning of his suffering and death. Scripture and tradition have provided us with many avenues. We might come near the cross heavy laden with grief, our heads bent low with the shame of our sins and the sins of the world. We might come near to Golgotha to contemplate Jesus' ultimate act of suffering with us, the evidence of God's utter compassion and sympathy for our human frailty. Or we might contemplate the death of Christ as the evidence of evil's staggering, but ultimately penultimate power, a power conquered only by God through the resurrection of our Lord. We join Christians across the centuries in pondering the unfathomable depth of meaning in the cross.

Our reading from Hebrews offers us still another window, through which few of us have beheld Good Friday. Here we see Christ not only as sacrificial lamb (cf. Heb. 9), but also as great high priest before God, whose offering has cleansed us from our sin— not merely for the moment, but once and for all. God has not relaxed divine standards; nor has God become any less perfect, holy, and unutterably divine. Rather, Christ, the archetype of righteousness and purity, has replaced the curtain of the temple with his own flesh, and he has sprinkled the penitent

Exegetical Perspective

Hebrews is a remarkable interweaving of exegesis and exhortation, having long passages of scriptural interpretation immediately followed by moral or spiritual admonitions. One sees this in chapters 1–2, where the author strings together a series of quotations drawn from Jewish Scriptures to show that the Son of God is greater than the angels (1:5–14) and concludes from this that his readers should "pay greater attention to what [they] have heard, so that [they] do not drift away from it" (2:1). Two verses later, he intensifies his warning with a question: "[H]ow shall we escape if we neglect so great a salvation?" that is, one proclaimed by the Son himself and not one mediated by angels (2:3a)?

Hebrews 10:16–25 is part of a similar interweaving of exegesis and exhortation. Verse 16 belongs to the exegetical section that begins at 8:1 and runs through 10:18; the exhortation, which turns on the "therefore" in verse 19, continues through verse 25, reaching a conclusion only at the end of chapter 10. Thus our passage is part of an extended argument and must be carefully set in context. At least three separate themes from the exegetical section appear in 10:16–25: a new covenant, Jesus as high priest, and entrance to the sanctuary. These themes lead to three admonitions:

Homiletical Perspective

If the history of preaching has been caricatured as "three points and a poem," it is for good reason; the pattern survives in many a church today but also to a degree even in Scripture, albeit without the poem. In this part of the sermon that we call the book of Hebrews, the preacher makes three points of application as the climax of an extended section of doctrine. This is no abstract doctrinal rambling on the death of Jesus, however, but a very different Good Friday sermon if we follow the preacher's lead. The "once for all" sacrifice of Christ (Heb. 9:24–26) has communal ramifications, three of them in the form of "Let us . . ." statements (Heb. 10:22–24). Any or all of these could be the focus of our preaching.

The first of these exhortations involves communal worship, the phrases "enter the sanctuary" (v. 19) and "let us approach" (v. 22) relating to the idea of ritual entrance to worship. The image is not far from the tradition of processionals in our own day, when choirs and ministers enter the sanctuary with varying degrees of pomp and circumstance. Of course, the focus is not the manner in which we enter the place of worship but the fact that we do indeed enter.

For the preacher of Hebrews, this entrance takes place through the waters of baptism, "our bodies

Hebrews 10:16-25

Theological Perspective

The Reformers were sometimes accused of antinomianism, on account of their emphasis on the completeness of salvation in Christ apart from all human works. Their liturgy makes clear that those who receive the free gifts of God's grace in Christ are expected to bear the good fruit of living rightly with God and neighbor. Yet this expectation is offered in terms of invitation to the already forgiven, rather than obligation upon those seeking forgiveness.

Among other things, Hebrews is an extended exposition of the unsurpassed gift of Christ's priestly work, setting God's people free to live according to God's intention—not in appeasement of an offended Deity, but in grateful response to the gift of reconciliation already effected for us through the sacrifice of our great high priest, Jesus Christ. This Hebrews theme—God has given us in Christ the full riches of salvation, therefore we are free to live in a way that fulfills God's good intention for us—crescendoes to its climax in today's passage. It is most fitting to turn to it on the solemn day of Jesus' ultimate sacrifice of his own life for the sake of the world.

The resonance of this text with the crucifixion texts from the Synoptic Gospels is unmistakable; in both Hebrews and the Synoptics, the atoning sacrifice of Christ's life is punctuated by the splitting of the veil that separates humanity from God. The word "atone" is exactly right here, meaning to render "at one" that which had been divided—human relations to God, neighbor, and self. "Atonement" is in fact "at-one-ment," the emergence of a divinely enacted wholeness that overcomes all dividedness. The barrier separating God from humankind is torn down—from top to bottom, heaven's action on earth's behalf, according to Matthew and Mark. Our text says that this torn curtain is more than the temple barrier separating God's people from the seat of God's presence; it is nothing less than Jesus' own flesh. The God-man, standing in the gap between humanity and divinity, is broken on the cross, and through his broken body humanity streams across the gap, reconciled to God forever.

This passage's resonance goes beyond the Synoptics; its declaration that through Christ's broken body we enter the divine presence picks up the Johannine teaching that there is no access to God except through the high priesthood of Jesus (John 14:6). References in our text to the blood of Christ, sprinkling of our hearts, and washing with water also resonate—especially on Good Friday—with the Johannine story of water and blood spilling from Jesus' pierced side.

Pastoral Perspective

with the baptismal waters of his own death and rising. Christ has accomplished what no human mediator could achieve: forgiveness so complete that no further sacrifice is needed, reconciliation so unbreakable that we need never fear drawing near to our Most High God.

This invites an approach to the throne of grace different from the one of dishonor, brokenness, and sorrow that we are accustomed to on Good Friday. The posture this reading invites is one of confidence, assurance, and steadfastness. Yet it is no less humble, for it is based not on our own worthiness, but on the sanctification earned by Jesus Christ on our behalf.

What might it mean to us, then, to approach worship on Good Friday this way, with "confidence to enter the sanctuary by the blood of Jesus, by the new and living way he opened for us" (vv. 19–20)? It might mean in part that we allow gratitude and even joy to wash over us—not because Jesus suffered on the cross, but because he has opened a new way forward for us. Like those who participate in 12-step programs, we too know that "we were powerless" over our captivity—not just to sin and death in general, but to their particular manifestations in broken relationships, self-indulgent habits, easy lies, and casual betrayals. We know that the only way we could have become free from our captivity was to turn to one who had power greater than our own—the only one who could open a path to us that we could not walk before. For this, we may find our hearts profoundly glad.

What might it mean to approach the cross "with a true heart in full assurance of faith . . . since we have a great priest" (vv. 22, 21)? It might mean that we rest in the safety and comfort that the work of our salvation is already accomplished. We who strive so hard in our daily lives to achieve success, to complete our endless work, to prove our worth—here at the cross we discover that the most important work of our lives has already been accomplished. "It is finished," Jesus says from the cross in the Gospel of John (19:30); indeed, there is nothing we can add to or subtract from the finished product of our re-creation, completed by Jesus on our behalf.

This passage from Hebrews does not suggest that Good Friday ends with our *approach* to worship at the cross of Jesus Christ, our great high priest. Good Friday also invites us to renew our commitment to life in Christ as we *leave* the altar of his sacrifice for us. In the world beyond the sanctity of worship, it may be harder for us to maintain our faithfulness. The writer of the Letter to the Hebrews is terribly aware of our dashed hopes, our personal failures,

Exegetical Perspective

"let us approach with a true heart" (v. 22); "let us hold fast to [our] confession" (v. 23); and "let us consider how to provoke one another to love and good deeds" (v. 24).

The theme of "a new (or better) covenant" first appears in Hebrews 7:22 and in chapter 8. The author begins our passage with a loose paraphrasing of the section of Jeremiah 31 he quoted in chapter 8, now focusing on verses 33 and 34b. In typical fashion, he cites his proof text in a way that bolsters his argument (compare it to the text of both Jeremiah and Hebrews 8). Claiming in verse 15 that the Holy Spirit is speaking to his own generation through the words of Jeremiah, the writer of Hebrews makes a causal link between Jeremiah 31:33 and 31:34: *because* God writes the law into the hearts and minds of believers in the new covenant, God "will remember their sins and their lawless deeds no more" (v. 17). He pushes this argument one step further: *because* the sins and lawless deeds are remembered no longer, there is likewise no longer any need for sacrifice (literally, "offering for sin," 10:18). In effect he completely nullifies the sacrificial system of the temple in Jerusalem, which, with the exception of a brief interruption after the destruction of Jerusalem in 587 BCE, had dominated Israel's religious consciousness since the time of Solomon.

How can the author of Hebrews make such a radical claim? The answer lies in his treatment of Jesus as priest/high priest/great priest. In our passage, the notion of Jesus as priest appears in 10:21, which refers to Jesus as "a great priest over the house of God." However Jesus as priest/high priest/great priest has been a theme in Hebrews since 2:17. It is taken up again in 3:1; 4:14–5:10; and 7:1–10:14. The exegesis offered in the latter two passages is extremely complicated, as the author draws on many different texts from the Jewish Scriptures dealing with varied priesthoods, most notably represented by Aaron, Melchizedek, the various orders of priests who attended to the daily sacrifices in Jerusalem, and the high priest who officiates on Yom Kippur, the Day of Atonement. Even when readers are not "dull in understanding," the arguments developed here are "hard to explain" (5:11)!

The arguments can be simplified and summarized: because of his resurrection, Jesus, like Melchizedek, is a "priest forever"(see Ps. 110:4 and Heb. 5:6; 7:1–3, 17, 21). Like Aaron, Jesus does not seek the priesthood, but responds obediently when it

Homiletical Perspective

washed with pure water" (v. 22). While modes of baptism vary among traditions, it is generally agreed that all Christians enter the church through the baptismal waters. While means of remembering baptism vary as well, for the preacher in Hebrews, this is how we enter worship, connected to one another in the communal waters of baptism.

The second application concerns believers persevering in the faith (v. 23). Not surprisingly, persecutions among the Hebrews often led to discouragement, even abandonment of the faith by some. The preacher's plea, however, is not self-help psychology but solid theology. This is not a commercial, with multimillion-dollar athletes in expensive running shoes telling us, "Just do it." The preacher's plea is grounded in the faithfulness of God, who has promised to sustain us on our journey.

So much of the church's preaching today forgets the role encouragement can play in sermons. One wonders if many guilt-trip messages are not in some ways the projection of the minister's own frustrations with running "the race that is set before us" (Heb. 12:1). We would do well on this Good Friday to rise above guilt and to offer encouragement for those who are trying hard to live the Christian life, ourselves included.

The final "Let us . . . " statement concerns both a positive appeal (provoking "one another to love and good deeds") and a negative one ("not neglecting to meet together") (vv. 24–25). As for the positive appeal, the essence of Christianity is spelled out in how we treat others. In his *Christianity and the Social Crisis*, Walter Rauschenbusch noted how often Christians allegorize or simply ignore the teachings of Jesus in relating to the poor and outcast. One hundred years later, this is still a relevant word for the church, as evidenced by the updated anniversary publication of Rauschenbusch's classic volume.[1]

In relation to the negative appeal ("not neglecting to meet together, as is the habit of some"), the emphasis on meeting together is a strange text for Good Friday. Obviously, not all of our members attend such services, while on Easter Sunday many will attend who never come through the door of the church any other time of the year. This occasion in the life of the church today is hardly the time to harp on attendance. Besides, the preacher's focus here is much larger than being present on so many Sundays a year.

1. Walter Rauschenbusch, *Christianity and the Social Crisis in the 21st Century*, ed. Paul Raushenbush (New York: HarperOne, 2007).

Hebrews 10:16-25

Theological Perspective

For all the power and majesty of this resounding exclamation of Christ's finished priestly work, the story of atonement does not end with "It is finished" from the cross. Rather, the cross's obliteration of all that divides sinful humanity is only the beginning of the salvation story effected through Jesus Christ. Because of what he has done through his sacrifice on the cross, Hebrews teaches, we are free to move forward in "a new and living way" of freedom, enabled joyously to live according to the life-giving law of God.

This is expressed in our passage in three "let us" invitations. Because of Christ's once-for-all priestly work of atonement, "let us" approach the throne of grace boldly (v. 22), "let us" hold fast to our faith without wavering (v. 23), and "let us" scheme how to incite one another to good deeds for the sake of the world (v. 24). These three invitations are followed by a strong caution not to neglect the assembly of the saints (v. 25).

Even though Christ's work of atonement sets us free to live rightly with God, self, and neighbor, our passage warns us not to neglect the means of grace that help us persist in this blessed way. The *assembly* is the place where means of grace abound to God's people for sustaining their life of appropriate, grateful outworking of their salvation. The means are not specified in this passage, perhaps because they go without saying: the assembly is where the word is read and proclaimed, prayers for the life of the community and for the world are offered, and sacraments are celebrated to seal to us the promises of the gospel. The assembly is not itself a means of grace, let alone a gate to salvation; yet its importance as the setting in which the means of grace are offered to the faithful is inestimable. Indeed, according to Calvin, the meeting of the church to hear the word of God sincerely proclaimed and to participate in the sacraments according to Christ's institution signifies that Christ's true church is present. Wherever the church is, there is salvation, because there word and sacrament always point to Jesus Christ, the one whose broken body is our true and living gateway to God, and whose poured-out gifts of water and blood cleanse us and secure our atonement forever.

SHELDON W. SORGE

Pastoral Perspective

our constant temptations. Rather than chide us for our shortcomings, or insist on our withdrawal from the ever-present sins of the world, he encourages us, saying, "Let us hold fast to the confession of our hope without wavering" (v. 23). Again, this is not because of our own worthiness or strength, but because of the trustworthiness of Christ. "He who has promised is faithful" (v. 23); therefore we have no reason to waver, no matter how the winds of doubt and distress may pound at us.

Most importantly, when we leave the altar of Christ's sacrifice, we leave not alone, but surrounded by the company of witnesses. The Christian faith is not designed as a self-help enterprise; rather, we lean on one another as we ourselves become witnesses of hope to those around us. "Let us consider how to provoke one another to love and good deeds, not neglecting to meet together, as is the habit of some, but encouraging one another, and all the more as you see the Day approaching" (vv. 24–25). On Good Friday, at the cross of Jesus Christ, we discover that we are not alone. Christ has gathered around himself a great cloud of witnesses, not only to give God glory, but also to inspire one another in faithfulness. The cross is never solely a personal matter of individual salvation, but a communal witness of encouragement and hope.

Gathering in worship on Good Friday around this text may evoke a very different feeling than we usually expect: not sorrowful, but joyful; not grieving, but grateful; not introspective, but outward looking, as we look to the accomplishment of Christ, our great high priest.

CHRISTINE CHAKOIAN

Exegetical Perspective

is thrust upon him (Lev. 8:1–9 and Heb. 5:4). It is in comparing and contrasting Jesus to the priests of the temple and to the high priest, however, that the author of Hebrews makes his most telling comments. In contrast to the priests of the temple, Jesus does not make daily sacrifices, but offered a sacrifice once and for all (7:23–25; 10:11–12). Unlike the high priest, Jesus does not have to offer a sacrifice for the people and himself (5:3), but only for the people (7:26–28). Furthermore, while the high priests enter the Holy of Holies with the blood of sheep and goats, Jesus entered with his own blood (9:11–14). For the author of Hebrews, this last point is perhaps the most important, for while he can say on some occasions that Jesus *was offered* (9:28 and 10:10), he more regularly argues that Jesus *offered himself*. He is both priest and sacrifice simultaneously (see 7:27; 9:12–14, 25–26; 10:12–14).

When, in 10:19, the author refers to believers' confidence "to enter the sanctuary," he conflates several readings he treated earlier in other contexts. The first problem in interpreting the phrase is that in temple practice, no one but the high priest could enter the sanctuary (Heb. 9:6–10; Lev. 16:29–34). When Jesus enters the sanctuary to offer his sacrifice, it is not the temple in Jerusalem he enters but the "real" temple in the heavens (9:24). Thus, as "the pioneer and perfecter of our faith" who "has taken his seat at the right hand . . . of God" (12:2), Jesus makes it possible for the faithful to enter the sanctuary, to approach the throne, and to come into the presence of God.[1] As elevated and complex as this exegesis may sound, it has a remarkably practical outcome, expressed in the exhortation: to maintain hope, provoke one another to love and good deeds, to meet together, and to encourage one another as the Day approaches (10:23–25). Is there any better message for Good Friday?

OLIVER LARRY YARBROUGH

Homiletical Perspective

Biblical scholar Craig Koester notes that the phrase "not neglecting" could just as easily be translated "not abandoning." The expression is used elsewhere in Scripture to denote "leaving something vulnerable to destructive forces."[2] The preacher's appeal for church attendance rests upon the communal identity of those gathered.

In a day of rampant individualism, this too is prophetic for our time. Sociologist Robert Putnam refers to this individualism as "the scandal of bowling alone." He noted that between 1980 and 1993 the total number of bowlers in America increased by 10 percent, while league bowling decreased by 40 percent.[3] For Putnam, this trend speaks volumes about valuing the individual over the group, a pattern the church has witnessed as well.

While we might not choose to adopt the preacher's three-point structure to shape our sermon for this Good Friday, there is another facet in this passage worth imitating to varying degrees, namely, the preacher's poetic penchant. While not readily apparent in English, verses 19–25 comprise one long sentence in Greek. We might think of it as a climactic piece of prose near the end of the sermon, akin to the preaching of Martin Luther King Jr. at the Lincoln Memorial or that of other dynamic black preachers.

The preacher also employs symmetry effectively. The section begins with an exhortation for listeners to draw near to God ("since we have confidence to enter the sanctuary" in v. 19) and ends with the promise of God's drawing near to us ("as you see the Day approaching" in v. 25). Although we might not want to scour through a thesaurus in search of terms with which to alliterate our points, the use of well-crafted prose can be quite effective.

In addition, we should not overlook the preacher's own use of a biblical text, a practice still common in Jewish and Christian proclamation. Drawing on Jeremiah 31, the preacher announces that the new covenant now fulfilled in Jesus will be put "in their hearts" and "on their minds" (v. 16). This, of course, is where all good preaching is aimed. Exposition and narration are not mutually exclusive. Neither aspect is to be ignored.

MIKE GRAVES

---

2. Craig R. Koester, *Hebrews*, Anchor Bible 36 (New York: Doubleday, 2001), 445–46.

3. Cited in Robert N. Bellah et al., *Habits of the Heart*, updated ed. (Berkeley: University of California Press, 1996), xvi.

1. Entering the sanctuary also recalls "entering [God's] Sabbath rest," treated in Heb. 3:7–4:16. For the reference in Jewish Scripture, see Ps. 95:7–11.

John 18:1-19:42

^{18:1}After Jesus had spoken these words, he went out with his disciples across the Kidron valley to a place where there was a garden, which he and his disciples entered. ²Now Judas, who betrayed him, also knew the place, because Jesus often met there with his disciples. ³So Judas brought a detachment of soldiers together with police from the chief priests and the Pharisees, and they came there with lanterns and torches and weapons. ⁴Then Jesus, knowing all that was to happen to him, came forward and asked them, "Whom are you looking for?" ⁵They answered, "Jesus of Nazareth." Jesus replied, "I am he." Judas, who betrayed him, was standing with them. ⁶When Jesus said to them, "I am he," they stepped back and fell to the ground. ⁷Again he asked them, "Whom are you looking for?" And they said, "Jesus of Nazareth." ⁸Jesus answered, "I told you that I am he. So if you are looking for me, let these men go." ⁹This was to fulfill the word that he had spoken, "I did not lose a single one of those whom you gave me." ¹⁰Then Simon Peter, who had a sword, drew it, struck the high priest's slave, and cut off his right ear. The slave's name was Malchus. ¹¹Jesus said to Peter, "Put your sword back into its sheath. Am I not to drink the cup that the Father has given me?"

¹²So the soldiers, their officer, and the Jewish police arrested Jesus and bound him. ¹³First they took him to Annas, who was the father-in-law of Caiaphas, the high priest that year. ¹⁴Caiaphas was the one who had advised the Jews that it was better to have one person die for the people.

¹⁵Simon Peter and another disciple followed Jesus. Since that disciple was known to the high priest, he went with Jesus into the courtyard of the high priest, ¹⁶but Peter was standing outside at the gate. So the other disciple, who was known to the high priest, went out, spoke to the woman who guarded the gate, and brought Peter in. ¹⁷The woman said to Peter, "You are not also one of this man's disciples, are you?" He said, "I am not." ¹⁸Now the slaves and the police had made a charcoal fire because it was cold, and they were standing around it and warming themselves. Peter also was standing with them and warming himself.

¹⁹Then the high priest questioned Jesus about his disciples and about his teaching. ²⁰Jesus answered, "I have spoken openly to the world; I have always taught in synagogues and in the temple, where all the Jews come together. I have said nothing in secret. ²¹Why do you ask me? Ask those who heard what I said to them; they know what I said." ²²When he had said this, one of the police standing nearby struck Jesus on the face, saying, "Is that how you answer the high priest?" ²³Jesus answered, "If I have spoken wrongly, testify to the wrong. But if I have spoken rightly, why do you strike me?" ²⁴Then Annas sent him bound to Caiaphas the high priest.

²⁵Now Simon Peter was standing and warming himself. They asked him, "You are not also one of his disciples, are you?" He denied it and said, "I am not." ²⁶One of the slaves of the high priest, a relative of the man whose ear Peter had cut off, asked, "Did I not see you in the garden with him?" ²⁷Again Peter denied it, and at that moment the cock crowed.

²⁸Then they took Jesus from Caiaphas to Pilate's headquarters. It was early in the morning. They themselves did not enter the headquarters, so as to avoid ritual defilement and to be able to eat the Passover. ²⁹So Pilate went out to them and said, "What accusation do you bring against this man?" ³⁰They answered, "If this man were not a criminal, we would not have handed him over to you." ³¹Pilate said to them, "Take him yourselves and judge him according to your law." The Jews replied, "We are not permitted to put anyone to death."

[32]{(This was to fulfill what Jesus had said when he indicated the kind of death he was to die.)

[33]Then Pilate entered the headquarters again, summoned Jesus, and asked him, "Are you the King of the Jews?" [34]Jesus answered, "Do you ask this on your own, or did others tell you about me?" [35]Pilate replied, "I am not a Jew, am I? Your own nation and the chief priests have handed you over to me. What have you done?" [36]Jesus answered, "My kingdom is not from this world. If my kingdom were from this world, my followers would be fighting to keep me from being handed over to the Jews. But as it is, my kingdom is not from here." [37]Pilate asked him, "So you are a king?" Jesus answered, "You say that I am a king. For this I was born, and for this I came into the world, to testify to the truth. Everyone who belongs to the truth listens to my voice." [38]Pilate asked him, "What is truth?"

After he had said this, he went out to the Jews again and told them, "I find no case against him. [39]But you have a custom that I release someone for you at the Passover. Do you want me to release for you the King of the Jews?" [40]They shouted in reply, "Not this man, but Barabbas!" Now Barabbas was a bandit.

[19:1]Then Pilate took Jesus and had him flogged. [2]And the soldiers wove a crown of thorns and put it on his head, and they dressed him in a purple robe. [3]They kept coming up to him, saying, "Hail, King of the Jews!" and striking him on the face. [4]Pilate went out again and said to them, "Look, I am bringing him out to you to let you know that I find no case against him." [5]So Jesus came out, wearing the crown of thorns and the purple robe. Pilate said to them, "Here is the man!" [6]When the chief priests and the police saw him, they shouted, "Crucify him! Crucify him!" Pilate said to them, "Take him yourselves and crucify him; I find no case against him." [7]The Jews answered him, "We have a law, and according to that law he ought to die because he has claimed to be the Son of God."

[8]Now when Pilate heard this, he was more afraid than ever. [9]He entered his headquarters again and asked Jesus, "Where are you from?" But Jesus gave him no answer. [10]Pilate therefore said to him, "Do you refuse to speak to me? Do you not know that I have power to release you, and power to crucify you?" [11]Jesus answered him, "You would have no power over me unless it had been given you from above; therefore the one who handed me over to you is guilty of a greater sin." [12]From then on Pilate tried to release him, but the Jews cried out, "If you release this man, you are no friend of the emperor. Everyone who claims to be a king sets himself against the emperor."

[13]When Pilate heard these words, he brought Jesus outside and sat on the judge's bench at a place called The Stone Pavement, or in Hebrew Gabbatha. [14]Now it was the day of Preparation for the Passover; and it was about noon. He said to the Jews, "Here is your King!" [15]They cried out, "Away with him! Away with him! Crucify him!" Pilate asked them, "Shall I crucify your King?" The chief priests answered, "We have no king but the emperor." [16]Then he handed him over to them to be crucified.

So they took Jesus; [17]and carrying the cross by himself, he went out to what is called The Place of the Skull, which in Hebrew is called Golgotha. [18]There they crucified him, and with him two others, one on either side, with Jesus between them. [19]Pilate also had an inscription written and put on the cross. It read, "Jesus of Nazareth, the King of the Jews." [20]Many of the Jews read this inscription, because the place where Jesus was crucified was near the city; and it was written in Hebrew, in Latin, and in Greek. [21]Then the chief priests of the Jews said to Pilate, "Do not write, 'The King of the Jews,' but, 'This man said, I am King of the Jews.'" [22]Pilate answered, "What I have written I have written." [23]When the soldiers had crucified Jesus, they took his clothes and divided them into four parts, one for each soldier. They also took his tunic; now the tunic was seamless, woven in one piece from the top. [24]So they said to one another, "Let us not tear it, but cast lots for it to see who will get it." This was to fulfill what the scripture says,

"They divided my clothes among themselves,
 and for my clothing they cast lots."

[25]   And that is what the soldiers did.

Meanwhile, standing near the cross of Jesus were his mother, and his mother's sister, Mary the wife of Clopas, and Mary Magdalene. [26]When Jesus saw his mother and the disciple whom he loved standing beside her, he said to his mother, "Woman, here is your son." [27]Then he said to the disciple, "Here is your mother." And from that hour the disciple took her into his own home.

[28]After this, when Jesus knew that all was now finished, he said (in order to fulfill the scripture), "I am thirsty." [29]A jar full of sour wine was standing there. So they put a sponge full of the wine on a branch of hyssop and held it to his mouth. [30]When Jesus had received the wine, he said, "It is finished." Then he bowed his head and gave up his spirit.

[31]Since it was the day of Preparation, the Jews did not want the bodies left on the cross during the sabbath, especially because that sabbath was a day of

Theological Perspective

As Frank Kermode has observed, the well-crafted prose of the Gospel of John reads like a modern novel.[1] Yet amid the realism of the story, today's readers find disturbing differences between our assumptions about the historical figure of Jesus and the divine Revealer, even the "perfected 'Gnostic'" portrayed by the evangelist (to use Rudolf Bultmann's phrase). To read John, we must keep two things in mind: the hymnic, poetic prologue (1:1–18) influences all that follows, and Jesus' passion and death are referred to more often throughout John's Gospel than in any other NT text.

In John, the figure of Jesus is a Jew who is different from other Jews and Gentiles. That difference is signified in several ways, one of which is Jesus' extraordinary knowledge (*eidos*). In foot washing, priestly prayer, the beginning of the passion, and on the cross, Jesus' knowledge includes his union with God and his passion, "all that was to happen to him." So when Judas, the soldiers, and the police find Jesus in the Garden on the Mount of Olives to arrest him, Jesus comes forward and identifies himself as the great "I am." The arrest is turned into a theophany that knocks the armed authorities to the ground.

1. Frank Kermode, "John," in Robert Alter and Frank Kermode, eds., *The Literary Guide to the Bible* (Cambridge, MA: Harvard University Press, 1987), 454–55.

Pastoral Perspective

Many of us have sat at the bedside of a dying friend or relative. Many in our pews are men and women "of sorrows, acquainted with grief." The Gospel reading for Good Friday brings the entire congregation together in a deathwatch as we stand at the foot of the cross, suffer with our friend Jesus, and see him draw his last breath. It is an opportunity to share the experience and to draw strength from one another.

Early in my ministry I visited the home of a parishioner whose husband had just died. "I was in the kitchen," she said. "I heard a noise from the living room, and when I went in, there he was slumped over in his chair." Then she told me again, "I was in the kitchen . . ." In the years since then I have found it to be a common phenomenon: people tend to replay the details of a death, to make sure they get the story straight, I think, but also to make sure there was nothing they should have done that they failed to do. Every year on Good Friday we replay the details of Jesus' death for some of the same reasons: to make sure we get the story straight, certainly, but also to find ourselves in the story and consider our own culpability.

None of us would have done what Judas did, would we? Betrayed Jesus? Unless we believed that he was the political Messiah we had been waiting for,

great solemnity. So they asked Pilate to have the legs of the crucified men broken and the bodies removed. [32]Then the soldiers came and broke the legs of the first and of the other who had been crucified with him. [33]But when they came to Jesus and saw that he was already dead, they did not break his legs. [34]Instead, one of the soldiers pierced his side with a spear, and at once blood and water came out. [35](He who saw this has testified so that you also may believe. His testimony is true, and he knows that he tells the truth.) [36]These things occurred so that the scripture might be fulfilled, "None of his bones shall be broken." [37]And again another passage of scripture says, "They will look on the one whom they have pierced."

[38]After these things, Joseph of Arimathea, who was a disciple of Jesus, though a secret one because of his fear of the Jews, asked Pilate to let him take away the body of Jesus. Pilate gave him permission; so he came and removed his body. [39]Nicodemus, who had at first come to Jesus by night, also came, bringing a mixture of myrrh and aloes, weighing about a hundred pounds. [40]They took the body of Jesus and wrapped it with the spices in linen cloths, according to the burial custom of the Jews. [41]Now there was a garden in the place where he was crucified, and in the garden there was a new tomb in which no one had ever been laid. [42]And so, because it was the Jewish day of Preparation, and the tomb was nearby, they laid Jesus there.

Exegetical Perspective

No portion of John's narrative adheres more closely to the Synoptics than this lengthy section, depicting Jesus' arrest, interrogation, crucifixion, death, and burial. Close study reveals enough variants of detail, however, to confirm that the Fourth Evangelist has impressed upon this account his distinctive concerns, which have left an indelible imprint upon the Christian imagination.

John's account makes many historical claims: some unlikely, others not, still others impossible to verify. Among the latter is "the Passover amnesty" from which Barabbas benefits (18:39–40), a custom uncorroborated in noncanonical sources. Given his portrayal in the histories of Philo (*Embassy to Gaius* 302) and Josephus (*Jewish Antiquities* 18.3.1–2), Pilate's fawning sensitivity to Jewish sensibilities seems out of character. Once again "the Jews" reappear as John's stereotypical villains, as though Jesus, his family, and friends were not equally Jewish (e.g., John 18:36; cf. 7:13; 9:22; 10:31; 13:33). Other features, however, ring true or at least plausible: Jesus' informal interrogation by Jewish leaders (instead of a full-blown trial before the Sanhedrin, as in the Synoptics); their collusion with Pilate in Jesus' crucifixion; and the disappearance (after John 18:3) of the Pharisees, who to this point have been Jesus' principal antagonists (e.g., 7:32; 8:13; 9:13–17; 11:55–57). On

Homiletical Perspective

On this particular Good Friday, the preacher faces several challenges. The first is the sheer scope of the lectionary text from John's Gospel—not only including eighty-two verses, but also taking the reader all the way from Jesus' betrayal and arrest in one garden to his burial in another. Finding a focus for proclamation amid the wealth of possibilities provided can itself be a daunting task.

A second challenge is the fact that in many churches and communities, the tradition on this day is to have a worship service focused on the "seven last words" of Jesus on the cross or perhaps a Tenebrae service (during which candles are extinguished as the passion narrative is read, and the church is left in total darkness). Since such services often bring together a variety of Gospel texts related to the passion (drawn from the Synoptic Gospels and from John), the distinctiveness of each Gospel writer's focus can be diminished. So reclaiming John's unique voice in the midst of the others can also be a worthy goal.

A final challenge is occasioned by the tension between the tone and tenor of the day itself (where sadness, grief, suffering, and death are focal) and John's interpretation of the cross as Jesus' finest hour, the hour of his glorification by God. How do we preach on Jesus' death in John without rushing too quickly to glory (or resurrection)—especially

John 18:1-19:42

Theological Perspective

Throughout the passion narrative, Jesus remains sovereign, the one who knows and remains in charge, while merely human authorities believe they are determining his destiny by trial and execution. The reader was already told about this by Jesus in chapters 10 and 12. This Jesus eludes all our human designs to control how and in whom God will be active in the world to love and give resurrection life. The Word became flesh in a Palestinian Jew, not a Gentile Euro-American Christian.

Amid the turmoil of the late 1960s and struggles for liberation in the early 1970s, Paul Lehmann began to reflect on the confrontation of imperial power with political truth in Pilate's encounter with the so-called King of the Jews. This confrontation ultimately leads to the moment of Jesus' silence before Pilate in the sixth scene of the narrative (19:8–11). Lehmann wrote, "When power crucifies truth, it signals to all the world that it has come to its effective end. When truth confronts the power to crucify with the power of silence, it passes beyond the rhetoric of liberation and signals to all the world the appointed rightness in a revolutionary lifestyle that only silence can express."[2] Lehmann brought into this scene the words of Lucia, a witness to the violent confrontation of "law and order" with student protest at Kent State University:

> I wasn't particularly interested in throwing rocks or anything like that. . . . But I was very much against what [Nixon] did in Cambodia, and I was hoping the rally would produce something, you know, really true. . . . I saw the men firing, and I saw the kids fall, and they looked out over the crowd and there were people carrying, you know, people with blood all over them, downhill and I just couldn't believe it. . . . There's no way to describe the pain that I saw in people's faces or in their voices.

In our times, after the failure of invasions and occupations to secure nation-states and civilians against the threat and reality of terror, we must ask anew what a messianic, revolutionary politics looks like; how best to confront the state with its need for a truth that narrates the violence done in our name, in the name of national security and a "new world order."

Interpreters of this Gospel such as Marit Trelstad are deeply troubled by the abuses of the cross, past and present. Theological-ethical abuses of the cross

Pastoral Perspective

and that all he needed to start the revolution was a good, strong push. Have we ever pushed someone in a similar way because of our own impatience? Is there anything of Judas in us?

None of us would have done what Peter did, would we? Promised to follow Jesus to the grave and then denied him because a silly servant girl asked a question? Who knows what we would really do under the circumstances? Who knows how strong the survival instinct would prove to be? Give Peter credit for wanting to be a better man than he was, for taking a swing at the high priest's servant, for showing up in that chilly courtyard at all.

None of us would have done what Caiaphas did, would we? Made the claim that "it is better for one person to die for the people"? Have we never been guilty of political expediency? Have we never weighed a difficult situation and then chosen the lesser of two evils? Is it any less an evil, just because it is the lesser of the two?

None of us would have done what Pilate did, would we? Shuttled back and forth between Jesus and his accusers, hoping that the easy answer would present itself? How many times have we listened long past the moment when we knew what to do, just because the right thing was neither the easy thing nor the popular thing? How many times have we taken a survey instead of a stand? You can almost feel sorry for Pilate in this story. He wants so much to spare Jesus. However, what can you do when the people have spoken?

None of us would have done what the chief priests did, would we? Shouted out, "Crucify him! Crucify him!" and followed it by saying, "We have no king but Caesar" (19:15 RSV; NRSV "the emperor")? Then again, have you never been part of an angry mob? Have you never called for a president's impeachment? Have you never wished that someone who was making your life difficult would just go away? Have you never done anything to make that departure more likely?

None of us would have done what the soldiers did, would we? Flogged Jesus, dressed him in purple, and put a crown of thorns on his head? None of us would have nailed him to a cross, or gambled for his clothes, or pierced his side, would we? Then again, good soldiers do what they are told to do every day. They are commended for it, decorated. Sometimes innocent people die. We call it "collateral damage."

None of us would have done what Mary did, would we? Stood there at the foot of the cross and watched a son's life drain away? Or risked our lives

---

2. Paul Lehmann, *The Transfiguration of Politics* (New York: Harper & Row, 1975), 66.

balance, John offers a stylized account of Jesus' trial and death, whose spine remains historically straight.

In John 18–19 we may detect three intersecting, theological currents, all of which concern *authority:* its bases, its corruption, and its jurisdictions relative to one another. Who wields power in this story? Whose authority overreaches? Whose is final?

1. Superficially regarded, imperial Rome is in charge. Only its agents, like Pilate, were empowered to crucify political pretenders and other enemies of the state. Thus it is ironic that, in John's narrative, Pilate emerges as the weakest of characters: the archetypal politician attempting to broker compromise between Jesus and his accusers, while fobbing off the disposition of a burdensome case. For John's readers, Pilate's interaction with Jesus is altogether imperceptive: "Are you the King of the Jews?" (18:33, which in Greek can be read as a declaration); "Here is your King" (19:14; also 18:39; 19:15b, 19–22); "Here is the man" (19:5; cf. 1:51; 5:27); "Where are you from?" (19:9; cf. 6:38; 7:27; 8:14; 13:3); "What is truth?" (18:38a; cf. 1:14, 17; 14:6). Not fewer than three times (18:29, 33; 18:38b, 19:1; 19:4, 9) Pilate shuttles outside and inside the praetorium (the governor's residence), caught betwixt an uncooperative defendant and his stubborn accusers. Repeatedly Pilate protests to the chief priests that Jesus is innocent (18:38b; 19:4, 6b) and that, even if he is not, his crime lies in their jurisdiction, not Rome's (18:31a, 35, 39; 19:6b, 12). Finally, when challenged that releasing Jesus would signal infidelity to Caesar, Pilate caves in, allowing the execution to proceed (19:12–13). Although he blusters before Jesus (19:10), no close reader is fooled. Rome's prefect proves most stupid and feckless of all.

2. Though subject to Pilate, this power play's puppeteers are Jerusalem's chief priests (18:3, 35; 19:6, 15, 21). Little is reported about Annas's questioning of Jesus "about his disciples and about his teaching" (18:19). Jesus' interrogation by Caiaphas, "high priest that year" (18:13, 24; cf. Matt. 26:57–66), is not described at all. The chief priests seem selective in justifying their actions by the Torah (John 18:31b; cf. Acts 7:54–60; John 19:7; cf. Lev. 24:16). Beyond their manipulative determination that Pilate execute Jesus (John 18:30), the most ironic aspect of the chief priests' conduct is their scrupulous attention to legal requirements for the Passover's preparation (18:28bc; 19:14) while blatantly flouting its raison d'être: In the moment they affirm "no king but Caesar" (19:15b RSV; NRSV "the emperor"), they embrace a latter-day Pharaoh whose overthrow the Passover is intended to celebrate (Exod. 12:1–28; Deut. 16:1–8).

given the tendency in many North American congregations to prefer this focus to one on suffering and self-giving? How do we sit with the sadness and awful offense of this not-so-good Friday, while also seeing within it Jesus' own ultimate fulfillment of his earthly mission?

Since the wise pastor will be guided, in part, by the worship traditions of the local congregation in discerning a sermon focus, that is as good a place as any to begin thinking about possibilities. For instance, if preaching in a congregation or community where the annual Good Friday service focuses on the "seven last words" of Jesus, the preacher will be pleased to discover that three of those last words appear in John's Gospel: "Woman, here is your son." "[Son], here is your mother" (19:26); "I am thirsty" (19:28); and "It is finished" (19:30). The challenge, however, will be to interpret these texts within a Johannine framework.

For instance, John's is the only Gospel that has three Marys standing near the cross (instead of at a distance), and Jesus entrusting his mother and the Beloved Disciple into one another's care (19:25–26). For John, this act signifies more than that of a dutiful son caring for his mother at his death, or even of a Good Shepherd caring for his own until the end. In this simple act, Jesus also sows the seeds of the new community to come, in which family is redefined in ways that are not restricted to blood kin and in which members of that family are called to be responsible caretakers of one another. Paradoxically, as a beloved son dies, a new community is born. Thus all of those who stand at the cross on Good Friday, weeping over all the unjust, untimely, inhumane, and undeserved deaths they have known, may also find comfort and hope in the new community that Jesus provides for them, even in their moment of greatest grief.

The other two last words from the cross also have new interpretive possibilities when viewed within a Johannine context. According to John, Jesus says, "I am thirsty," in order to fulfill the Scriptures (further evidence that Jesus is fulfilling his God-given mission), and only in John is the sponge full of sour wine that is mockingly offered him placed on hyssop (a probable reference to the Passover story in Exod. 12:22, in which Moses instructs the elders of Israel to slaughter a Passover lamb, dip hyssop in its blood, and spread the blood on the lintel and doorposts of their homes, so that the angel of death will pass over them). In like manner, "It is finished" (19:30) is more than acknowledgment that Jesus' life is coming

John 18:1-19:42

Theological Perspective

may stem from the reduction of its meaning to only one understanding of what atonement is and how it works itself out in human affairs. In the case of John, we find more than one understanding of the cross within the same Gospel. We have already referred to John's correlation of Jesus' condemnation with the slaughter of the paschal lambs (19:14), and John's suggestion of atonement as sacrifice by "fragrance" (or "aroma") in 12:3, as well as by Jesus' final words in 19:30. Ironically, it is high priest Caiaphas in 11:49–52 who prophesies a punitive, substitutionary view of Jesus' death. John's distinctive motifs of atonement include (a) Jesus' gift of himself for his friends, (b) his voluntary and sovereign power over his own death and resurrection, (c) the cross as the revelation of Jesus' identity. Here the words of the Presbyterian Church (U.S.A.)'s Confession of 1967 offer a summary: "These are expressions of a truth which remains beyond the reach of all theory in the depths of God's love for man."

This Gospel refers to "the Jews" seventy-one times, most often in the negative. In the passion narrative, the demonized character of Judas, the chief priests Annas and Caiaphas, the Pharisees, and the temple police arrest Jesus, accuse him before Pilate, and cry out for his crucifixion. We must responsibly preach and teach the passion stories in Holy Week with a full acknowledgment of their history of effects, the centuries of Christian anti-Judaism and replacement theology (supersessionism) that set the stage for and rationalized the Nazi slaughter of one-third of European Jewry. We begin by recognizing that a story that deeply divides us as Jews and Christians, the death and resurrection of a beloved son, also unites us in a deep mythic structure that runs through both testaments.[3] In the Aqedah of Genesis 22, the testing of Abraham, who is commanded by YHWH to sacrifice Isaac, the child of promise, and in the other stories of beloved sons like Ishmael and Joseph, who were given up for dead and then restored to life, we find by analogy the pattern played out in all four Gospels. This may present appropriate times and places for Jews and Christians to come together in the study of Scripture that will be mutually edifying.

ROBERT A. CATHEY

Pastoral Perspective

like the disciple Jesus loved, by standing there with her? Then again, maybe we would. Some of us have watched as loved ones drew their last breath, painful as it was. Some of us have stayed by the bedside in that last hour, risking sleep and sanity. It is not hard to imagine the one who is dying saying to a son or a sister, "Take good care of Mama."

I have been at a hundred bedsides like that. I have sat in hospital waiting rooms sipping bitter, black coffee from Styrofoam cups. I have been part of the deathwatch. Most of the time I have watched and waited with parishioners. On a few occasions I have waited and watched with my own family as someone I loved neared the end. It is not easy, but it is entirely familiar. We sit by the bedside. We speak in whispers. We pat each other and hug. We wipe away tears. We tell stories. Eventually we say our good-byes.

Maybe this is where we need to enter the Good Friday drama, and maybe this is where we need to take our stand: not betraying Jesus, not denying him, not judging him, not condemning him, not rejecting him, not mocking him, not cursing him, not flogging him, not killing him—but standing there at the foot of the cross with others who love him, and putting our arms around each other for comfort and strength, so that when they ask us later what happened we can say, "I was standing at the foot of the cross . . ."

JIM GREEN SOMERVILLE

---

3. See Jon Levenson, *The Death and Resurrection of the Beloved Son* (New Haven, CT: Yale University Press, 1993).

Good Friday

3. By far this narrative's most authoritative figure is the one on trial. "Knowing all that was to happen to him" (John 18:4; 19:28) and his followers (18:15–18, 25–27; also 13:36–38), Jesus steps forward to be arrested (18:1–2, 4) and floors the posse (18:6) with the allusively divine assertion "I am he" (18:5–6, 8a; 8:12, 24, 28, 58; 10:30; 14:10–11). Forthrightly he drinks "the cup the Father has given" him (18:11; 12:27; cf. Mark 14:36), eventually bearing his own cross to Golgotha (John 19:17; cf. Mark 15:21). Jesus does not so much answer his questioners as *he* interrogates *them* (John 18:21, 23, 34); with true judgment he judges his magistrates (18:20, 36–37; 19:11; see 5:30; 8:15–16, 26). Guarding the disciples entrusted to him (18:8–9; 10:28–29; 17:12), Jesus reconstitutes his family at the foot of the cross (19:25b–27) and bestows on it his spirit (19:30). Despite the ridicule and incomprehension of his captors, in this hour Jesus truly is Israel's king (18:36–37, 39; 19:2, 5, 11, 14, 15, 19). Pilate's announcement in three languages (19:19–20) fulfills Jesus' earlier promise that, when lifted up from the earth, he will draw all to himself (12:31–33). During his arrest and crucifixion, Jesus' words and deeds are consistent with his promises (18:9, 32/3:14; 6:39; 8:28; 12:33; 17:12), fulfilling scripture (19:23–25a/Ps. 22:18. John 19:28–29/Pss. 22:16; 69:21. John 19:31–37/Exod. 12:46; Deut. 21:22–23; Ps. 34:20; Zech. 12:10).

Despite the text's insistence on its veracity (19:35), there is no certain interpretation of John 19:34. At minimum, the evangelist correlates his earlier metaphor of life-giving water (4:10–14; 7:38) with Jesus' death (blood; cf. 1 John 5:6). By his death on the cross, Jesus perfectly consummates (*tetelestai*, John 19:30) all things on earth for which his Father in heaven has sent him (5:36; 10:14–15, 17–18; 17:1–5).

Earlier in this Gospel, Jesus has counseled, "Do not judge by appearances, but judge with right judgment" (7:24). This lection for Good Friday is an exercise in discernment. For centuries Christians have bludgeoned their sister and brother Jews with John 18–19. This text, however, stands in judgment of everyone: the threatened pious, craven politicos, faithless disciples. "I can do nothing on my own authority; as I hear, I judge; and my judgment is just, because I seek not my own will but the will of him who sent me" (5:30 RSV). At Skull-Place, would-be accusers do not stand in judgment of the crucified. It is the light shining in darkness that exposes us all for who we are (3:19–21).

C. CLIFTON BLACK

to an end; it is affirmation that Jesus has finished the work God gave him to do, that he has loved his own until the end, and that even in his very act of dying, God is being glorified.

What a fine opportunity these verses—and the whole trajectory of the crucifixion as portrayed by John—provide for linkages with the Eucharist. On this day "Christ our Passover is sacrificed for us." Yet the sacrifice is a voluntary self-offering on Jesus' part, and by this Lamb's blood we are welcomed into life abundant and eternal.

Finally, if he or she is preaching during a Tenebrae service, the preacher's focus may well turn toward the trajectory of the story as a whole, and the way in which God is at work in the midst of Jesus' own deepest hour of suffering to bring hope to the world. Though Jesus is betrayed, falsely accused, mocked, and condemned to death, yet God is sovereign. In the lifting up of Jesus on the cross—with a sign over his head mockingly proclaiming him "King of the Jews" in three different languages—we behold the true ruler of the universe, whose reign is marked by an outpouring of sacrificial love for us all.

Whatever the preacher's focus for proclamation, the cross should be central. On this day, Jesus was crucified. On this day, according to John, the Good Shepherd willingly offered his own life for his sheep. On this day, God won the ultimate victory over death and evil, even as death and evil appeared to have the upper hand.

LEONORA TUBBS TISDALE

Lamentations 3:1-9, 19-24

¹I am one who has seen affliction
  under the rod of God's wrath;
²he has driven and brought me
  into darkness without any light;
³against me alone he turns his hand,
  again and again, all day long.

⁴He has made my flesh and my skin waste away,
  and broken my bones;
⁵he has besieged and enveloped me
  with bitterness and tribulation;
⁶he has made me sit in darkness
  like the dead of long ago.

⁷He has walled me about so that I cannot escape;
  he has put heavy chains on me;

Theological Perspective

Lamentations marked a significant way station in the theological journey of ancient Israel. It was written not only over the physical rubble of Jerusalem, but also over the *theological* rubble of what the nation had understood the promises of God to mean. Probably from ancient times, and certainly by the seventh century BCE, Jerusalem (Zion) had been supposed to be inviolable. YHWH was supposed to have defended it and established it forever (Ps. 48; cf. Ps. 2). Its destruction by the Babylonians crushed all the old certainties. Not only was the remnant of the people humiliated and embittered; it had lost the certainty that it could turn to God for redemption, as one sees the psalmists do so often.

Lamentations is thus a book of waiting for salvation (3:25–26), in the face of a crisis beyond human power to resolve. In much the same way, Holy Saturday is a day of waiting for resurrection, but this waiting is not meaningless or empty. Alan Lewis pointed out that "if it be true that the tomb is empty now, then the gospel's most luminous affirmation and its murkiest enigma relate to what has gone before—to the fact of the tomb's occupancy yesterday and to its occupant's identity. Who must the crucified have been, and why was he buried, if he is now the Risen One?"[1] Holy

1. Alan E. Lewis, *Between Cross and Resurrection: A Theology of Holy Saturday* (Grand Rapids: Eerdmans, 2001), 69; cf. 3.

Pastoral Perspective

Between the cross of Good Friday and the empty tomb of Easter Sunday, something happened. The Greeks have two words for time: *chronos,* the chronological movement of time, measured by clocks and calendars, and *kairos,* the space in between—the white space between words, the pauses between the ticks of the clock. Holy Saturday, although part of the chronological sweep of Holy Week, is a *kairos*-style "in-between" time. Where was Jesus the day we now call Holy Saturday? What was God doing? Why was there a pause before resurrection?

Gospel accounts, scalded into silence by the calamity on Golgotha, hardly register any detail at all. This absence in Scripture makes it tempting to dismiss Holy Saturday as a kind of intermission, a break before the final, glorious act that is Easter. Restless, we wait. In the back row a watch beeps. We shift in our seats. Then, in the midst of our motionless Saturday waiting, the lectionary detonates in our midst . . . *wailing, chaos, sweat, dirt, hammering pulse, and the roaring fear that God is gone.* Lamentations 3:1–9, Jeremiah's great requiem for a city in ruins, takes the stage to give voice to Holy Saturday with devastating power.

The muscular poetry of Lamentations was of course written as a dirge not for Christ but for Jerusalem, destroyed at the hands of invading

⁸though I call and cry for help,
   he shuts out my prayer;
⁹he has blocked my ways with hewn stones,
   he has made my paths crooked.

. . . .

¹⁹The thought of my affliction and my homelessness
   is wormwood and gall!
²⁰My soul continually thinks of it
   and is bowed down within me.
²¹But this I call to mind,
   and therefore I have hope:

²²The steadfast love of the LORD never ceases,
   his mercies never come to an end;
²³they are new every morning;
   great is your faithfulness.
²⁴"The LORD is my portion," says my soul,
   "therefore I will hope in him."

Exegetical Perspective

The book of Lamentations was written as a response to the destruction of Jerusalem in 586 BCE. It is, however, not only a sequence of reports about the immediate annihilation of the city itself; it also traces two additional aspects of that horrible event. First, it reflects upon the long-term consequences of the destruction. In line after line, the author expresses the loss of everything positive that the city had symbolized: earthly beauty, social security, and all those essentials that represented the best of the city—the king, the priesthood, the prophets, happy festivals, and solemn liturgies. All of these elements were not only destroyed, but in the aftermath of the destruction, the void resulting from the loss of these elements was understood as even more devastating than the destruction itself. Nothing, it seems, could make up or replace the loss of the city and what it symbolized.

The second perspective that the book explores concerns the spiritual aspects of the destruction of the city. Delbert Hillers notes, "One such dimension was guilt. Lamentations is also a confession, and testimony to a search for absolution. Those who survived knew or felt themselves, as individuals or as part of an imperfect human community, somehow responsible for the ruin of their city, their land, and their temple."[1]

1. Delbert Hillers, *Lamentations* (New York: Doubleday, 1992), 4.

Homiletical Perspective

Holy Saturday is a day of waiting and watching, a day of putting things into perspective. It is a time to think about the journey of the week past, with the insistent hope that change will come. Holy Saturday is also a day for grieving and lament.

A good beginning for the preacher is to consider a definition of the word "lament." In a theological context, a lament is a process for dealing with and understanding sorrow, loss, or death. Lament is common and explicable, but not commonly explained. It is a biblical tradition, one that allows people as individuals and in communities to grieve.

In today's text from Lamentations, the writer lays out a compelling visual description of his circumstances. God has brought him "into darkness without any light" (v. 1). This gives the reader or listener a sense of being shut off from life, closed off from light, left without any sense of direction. The writer's description of being singled out for the back of God's hand—"again and again, all day long" (v. 3), so that his flesh and his skin "waste away" and his bones are broken—conjures physical abuse and violence. He has been "made to sit in darkness like the dead of long ago" (v. 6) so that there is no escape (v. 7).

As much as the preacher may wish to escape such images, Holy Saturday calls for exploration of this dreadful territory. Reading the text aloud puts the

Lamentations 3:1-9, 19-24

Theological Perspective

Saturday is the day that God spent in the grave. Lamentations 3:6 expresses the despair of those who feel that they are as hopeless and neglected as the dead. Holy Saturday answers that God has in fact not abandoned the dead, but is with them. Christ's resurrection is the firstfruits of God's promise to the dead. How much more will God be with those who only *feel* like the dead!

The Bible does not have a great deal to say about Holy Saturday; Mark 16:10 suggests that Jesus' followers spent it "mourning and weeping." However 1 Peter 3:18–19 asserts that even when Christ was in the tomb, he was "alive in the spirit," and that "he went and made a proclamation to the spirits in prison." Lamentations 3 itself describes the sorrow of the Jerusalemites in terms of imprisonment (v. 7), and also in terms of many other images that describe the sufferings of people in the present day: sickness (v. 4), isolation (v. 14), homelessness (v. 19), even death and mourning (v. 6). In order to practice *imitatio Christi*, then, believers might make this a day of mission to those who are suffering. For those of us who rarely take time to be silent, Holy Saturday can be an opportunity to quiet ourselves enough to hear those who are still crying out all around us today.

Holy Saturday can also be a symbol of the church's now-protracted period of waiting for the return of its Savior to restore justice to the world. It is easy to lose faith under such conditions, the more so when events call God's righteousness into question. Lamentations 3:8 reflects that at such times even prayer can feel useless: "though I call and cry for help, he shuts out my prayer." In *The Institutes of the Christian Religion*, John Calvin viewed the fear that God does not want to receive our prayers as the most harrowing crisis of faith, but he also wrote that God pardons those who have difficulty praying,

> since he often tests his own with sharp trials, as if he deliberately willed to snuff out their faith. Hardest of all is this trial, where believers are compelled to cry out, "How long wilt thou be angry with the prayer of thy servant," (Ps 80:4) as if prayers themselves annoyed God. So when Jeremiah says, "God has shut out my prayer" (Lam 3:8), there is no doubt that he was stricken with violent perturbation. Innumerable examples of this kind occur in scripture, from which it is clear the faith of the saints was so often mixed with doubts that in believing and hoping they yet betrayed some want of faith.[2]

2. John Calvin, *Institutes of the Christian Religion*, ed. John McNeill, trans. Ford Lewis Battles (Philadelphia: Westminster Press, 1960), 3.20.16.

Pastoral Perspective

Babylonians. The incorporation of this Hebrew text into our Holy Week liturgy affords us a far deeper emotional experience of Holy Saturday than anything found in the New Testament. Indeed, the use of Lamentations brings the heartache of the day into sharp relief, offering us a stirring portrait of profound sorrow. Through the use of fragmented sentences and unbalanced meter, the writer employs a sense of language seemingly "broken off in grief."[1] The effect moves us away from an intellectual affirmation of Easter and closer to an experience of the heart. Likewise, the acrostic frame of Lamentations invites emotional exploration by creating a kind of "material, physical container" for the ideas of the narrative, a device that helps "control and contain" the suffering that engulfed the Israelites.[2] In the same way, the use of Lamentations at Easter helps create a space for Christian believers to process their own witness of Jesus' suffering.

The practical import of this device came to mind recently while I was walking my dog in my neighborhood. We happened upon the demolition of a house nearby, the razing of a small wooden residence. Within twenty-four hours, the construction company put up a fence around the site, a demarcation that provided boundaries for the work of raising a new structure. For Christians, Holy Saturday can function as a kind of work site, where we are invited to acknowledge the yawning absence of what once was (so acutely resembling an empty grave), as we await the pouring out of a new foundation.

Viewed properly, the work site of Lamentations in our lectionary can help us explore the complex theological import of this extraordinary final week of Christ's earthly existence. Theologian Sally A. Brown talks about the lament form as having three primary functions: (a) the *critical-prophetic*, which asks complex questions about the nature and origin of violence; (b) the *theological-interrogatory*, which wants to know where God is during times of suffering; and (c) the *pastoral*, wherein we are invited to "rely on God and the community to carry forth hope on our behalf when we ourselves have no hope in us."[3] This model is helpful because it rightly alludes to the complexity of suffering. The implications of Jesus' death can be so discomfiting—especially the torture he endured—that we tend to

1. F. W. Dobbs-Allsopp, "Lamentations," in *The New Oxford Annotated Bible*, 3rd ed. (New York: Oxford University Press, 2001), 1167.
2. Ibid., 1168.
3. Sally A. Brown, "When Lament Shapes the Sermon," in *Lament: Reclaiming Practices in Pulpit, Pew, and Public Square*, ed. Sally A. Brown and Patrick D. Miller (Louisville, KY: Westminster John Knox Press, 2007), 33.

Holy Saturday

This movement from guilt, to acknowledgment, to confession, to assurance, to hope is not a simple process in the book, as it is rarely a simple process in life.

The central poem of the book, chapter 3, is unlike the other four. Instead of focusing on the destruction of the city as an event, this chapter spotlights the suffering of an individual man. The fact that the speaker is explicitly a "man" balances the feminine imagery used to describe Jerusalem elsewhere in the book. Moreover, while the sufferer is portrayed as an individual, the imagery describing his affliction draws on the architectural and civic tropes used to describe the city. Furthermore, the imagery also draws on the traditions of God as the Good Shepherd, but then twists the images in a nightmarish way.

Finally, the whole of the poem of chapter 3 is a highly organized acrostic. In most acrostic poems of the Hebrew Bible, each line or stanza begins with a subsequent letter of the alphabet. This format is represented in the poems found in chapters 1, 2, and 4. In chapter 3, however, not only do the stanzas themselves begin with consecutive letters of the alphabet, but each of the three lines of the stanzas begins with the same letter. The lection for this day includes the stanzas beginning with *alef, bet, gimel* (in vv. 1–9), *zayin*, and *khet* (in vv. 19–24). The intense organizational scheme of this poem provides a way of understanding the "method in the madness," where order can be seen within the chaos and where a movement from beginning to end is a real possibility.

Alef: The horrific shepherd (vv. 1–3). The first stanza draws heavily from the divine shepherd imagery found, for example, in Psalm 23. In that psalm, the shepherd's rod comforts the sheep. The shepherd gently leads the sheep into secure pastures. Even when the sheep wander into darkness, the shepherd stays with them and brings them comfort. Here, however, the shepherd's rod has produced affliction. The shepherd has driven (*nhg;* cf. Ps. 78:52) the sheep into darkness, where there is no light. The shepherd finally has turned and continues to turn his hand against the sheep continually. It is a nightmarish vision of the divine shepherd.

Bet: The body of the sufferer (vv. 4–6). The mention of "hand" in the last line of the first stanza gives way to the fuller notion of the body in the second: this stanza focuses upon the body of the sufferer. God has caused the sufferer's skin and flesh to waste away

hearer in mind of other deep, dark places from which there is no escape. What is it really like to be lost in a cave, locked in a prison dungeon, cut off in a tomb where there is no light, no exit, no way out? Even if the preacher has never been in such a place, the language of Lamentations aids vivid imagination. What is it like to walk a crooked path, the way blocked with hewn stones (v. 9)?

In some congregations, Holy Saturday involves a tradition of prayer vigil. This can be a time when lament and grief join to engage waiting. Communal lament in particular offers worshipers an opportunity to face the deep unknown together, crying out and making a way at the same time. Those familiar with the Wailing Wall in Jerusalem know that it is a place of devotion for Christians as well as Jews. In the public space of a large, urban, interreligious city, people come to the wall every day to pray publicly, crying out to God to remember them, and witnessing to their faith. Some of them pray their prayers out loud, while others write them on small pieces of paper that they tuck discreetly into the crevices of the wall. What might it mean, on Holy Saturday, for the church to become a kind of local Wailing Wall, where people come to cry out to God?

The images of this text support the power of speaking one's pain. A preacher is compelled on this holy day to invite the faithful to full confrontation with their own pain, loss, and isolation. In the places where we live, there are many who speak their tales of horror with authority. Most of us know people in our congregations who have survived darkness and bowed down to hope. Some have survived abuse. Others have endured prison. Few have escaped the loss of friendship, the experience of tragedy, or the sadness of death.

Even those who have been spared the worst kind of darkness still keep memories of slavery, the Holocaust, and September 11, 2001. Holy Saturday is a day for them and for us to face our losses and alienation. It is a day for us to witness to the reality of suffering, even as we call out for God's presence. With the help of the verses assigned for the day, those gathered may be able to open themselves to death and the unknown. They may even discover that what looks like darkness with no apparent way out turns into a confrontation with divine possibility.

When people understand affliction as part of an experience of transition and redemption, meaning can be gleaned from the hardest of times. The preacher who is willing to stay with the reality described by the

Lamentations 3:1-9, 19-24

Theological Perspective

Calvin's comments foreshadow a wrenching revelation of our own times, the news that Mother Teresa struggled with doubt throughout her decades of saintly service. In a 1978 letter to a spiritual confidant, she confessed, "As for me, the silence and the emptiness is so great, that I look and do not see—Listen and do not hear—the tongue moves [in prayer] but does not speak."[3] Although this was treated in the popular media as surprising news, surely many Christians would recognize such struggles and doubts as a part of the walk of faith. In the worst of times it is hard to have conviction that God is with us or that through us God is bringing about the right things. Lamentations is one of the texts in the Bible that demands readers live for a while with such doubts, rather than always pushing them out of our minds.

Nevertheless, just as Holy Saturday is not the end of the Christian story, so Lamentations also looks beyond despair, if only briefly. It does not launch into a new and glorious hymn about the glory of God, but it clings *tenaciously, desperately,* to the old promises, using the formulaic language of God's steadfast love and mercy (vv. 21–24). Those qualities were part of one of Israel's oldest confessions, that YHWH was a God "merciful and gracious, slow to anger, and abounding in steadfast love and faithfulness" (Exod. 34:6, etc.). Lamentations 3 is thus a model of courageous perseverance through a dark night of the soul.

CHRISTOPHER B. HAYS

Pastoral Perspective

skip the difficult parts, merely celebrating that "something" happened that is apparently good news indeed.

Two years ago a member of my congregation lost multiple family members in a tragic accident. I have accompanied her on the journey of mourning, and we talked recently about the effect of reading Lamentations. She told me about a moment in the raw beginning, when her grief was so unbearable that she had the feeling of hitting rock bottom. Everything was stripped away, all the superficial ideas of life, all the things that people say to try to make sense out of the senseless. She said that in that barren place beyond all words, she suddenly had the realization that she was alone with God. She was driving a car, and she felt the bedrock presence of God's Spirit.

"My heart is broken," she cried aloud, "my soul is bereft of peace, I have forgotten what happiness is" (Lam. 3:17). God answered with utter silence, the kind that sounds like truth. My friend felt consoled by the silence, because it seemed to go beyond trying to explain the unexplainable. She felt that God simply understood, enduring her grief with her.

Maybe God understands better than we imagine. This begs a startling midrash musing: what if Holy Saturday was not originally planned? Perhaps the extra day after Good Friday was needed because God was plunged into mourning just like the rest of us—God's Abrahamic role in the death of the Son was too much even for Abba. Perhaps all of heaven was rocked back into traumatized immobility when the nails were pounded into those innocent palms. Dead silence. The ripeness of the in-between, the crucible in which things are torn down and things are raised up.

My grieving friend said, "At a certain point, there is nothing left to say. You just decide to keep walking forward with God." After the worst strikes and scorches the earth, after unexpected horror tears happiness in two like the veil at the temple that black Friday, somehow we pass through the holy *kairos* time of Saturday, knowing that it is not the end of the story. We just keep going forward. "The LORD is my portion, . . . therefore, I will hope in God" (Lam. 3:24).

SUZANNE WOOLSTON-BOSSERT

---

3. Cited by David Van Biema, "Mother Teresa's Crisis of Faith," *Time,* Aug. 23, 2007.

Exegetical Perspective

(*blh*; cf. 1 Chr. 17:9, where the verb applies to Israel as a whole). Furthermore, God has, as with a city, laid siege to the individual, surrounding the sufferer with poison and trouble. Like a captive in prison, the sufferer now sits in the darkness into which God led him (v. 2), with no hope of escape. The sufferer is like the dead, who eternally remain in darkness.

Gimel: The bondage of the sufferer (vv. 7–9). The imagery of the prison in the last line of the previous stanza gives way to the fuller notion of the bondage of the sufferer in the next. Again, using architectural imagery, the poet describes the ways in which God has cut off all possibility of escape. The walls that were intended to provide security (cf. Ps. 48) have denied anyone from leaving the annihilation. As with prisoners, God shackles the sufferer with heavy chains. The temple, once the site of intercession, is now destroyed. This means that God cannot—or perhaps, will not—listen to the people's prayer. Its stones (*gazit*; 1 Kgs. 7:9–12), once so beautiful, now block any chance for escape, trapping the sufferer.

Zayin: Reflection (vv. 19–21). The poem thus far has focused on the suffering of the individual. What purpose does it serve? Why does the poet describe and reflect upon his own suffering? The turn is found initially in this stanza. The expression of pain here allows the poet to turn to hope, quite simply because the poem has focused on how God has brought about the events it describes. While God may be angry and bring destruction, the character of God is not based upon anger, but upon grace and faithfulness, to which the poet turns in the next stanza.

Khet: Faithfulness and hope (vv. 22–24). In the end, there is hope for the sufferer because God's character is one of faithfulness, mercy, and trustworthiness. The rehearsal of the pain and grief of the previous stanzas—real as they are—provides a way of recognizing that the future is still open. This final stanza is not, however, the last word (there are, after all, fourteen more stanzas!). The reflection on the past destruction and the present realization of mercy continues throughout the end of the poem. It is in verses 22–24, however, that the major turn is made.

ROY L. HELLER

Homiletical Perspective

writer—inviting the faithful to wait in the darkness, ask their questions, and voice their laments—points a way to live through isolation and fear.

Today's verses from Lamentations suggest the kind of struggle that is required to move beyond the directionless dark, with its crooked paths and blocked ways. Lament forms a vital part of this struggle. Giving active voice to the experience of loss offers people a way of coping with the worst that can happen to them, enabling them to move through the depths of pain, death, and loss to lives marked by honest witness.

It is easy to anticipate the resurrection, with its renewal of life and restoration of light. It is hard to stay with the experience of being lost in the dark, with all the feelings such an experience engenders. Yet this is the sacred ground of Holy Saturday, where the women waited, prayed, and hoped in remembrance of a life lost to darkness.

How shall we wait and watch this day? What prayers can we make for ourselves and for those who have lost much or are lost to us? How do we enter the sacred spaces of unknowing? The preacher who enters this place of waiting with real depth of soul may enable those who listen to do the same thing. When we interrogate horror, abuse, and fear by speaking our pain, we may find that our bowed-down souls are relieved and lifted up.

As honest as the writer of Lamentations is about the reality of being driven into darkness, he is just as honest about the steadfastness of God's love. God's mercies "never come to an end; they are new every morning" (vv. 22–23). On Holy Saturday, the faithful wait together for that morning, unafraid to give voice to our fear.

CLAUDIA HIGHBAUGH

Psalm 31:1-4, 15-16

¹In you, O Lord, I seek refuge;
  do not let me ever be put to shame;
  in your righteousness deliver me.
²Incline your ear to me;
  rescue me speedily.
 Be a rock of refuge for me,
  a strong fortress to save me.
³You are indeed my rock and my fortress;
  for your name's sake lead me and guide me,
⁴take me out of the net that is hidden for me,
  for you are my refuge.

. . . .

¹⁵My times are in your hand;
  deliver me from the hand of my enemies and persecutors.
¹⁶Let your face shine upon your servant;
  save me in your steadfast love.

Theological Perspective

When in the christological sequence we move from Good Friday to Holy Saturday, we find ourselves beyond the anguish of betrayal and suffering, beyond even a cry of dereliction, beyond life itself, lost forever in the infinite darkness. For now the powers have done their worst. The earthly struggle is lost. The game is over. "It is finished." Human dependency on God is now shown to be radical and total. God alone remains our hope: "My times are in your hand" (v. 15). Exposed to the ultimate vulnerability of human existence in the midst of all that would threaten to undo us, the psalmist cries out to God as our one sure refuge, our strong fortress against the encircling foe, our sole remaining hope against the darkness.

Historically, there is no question that trust in God as ultimate refuge and hope has been and continues to be profoundly meaningful, important, and even lifesaving for millions of faithful persons who cling tenaciously to God as their rock of refuge, as the psalmist does, in the midst of extreme danger, sorrow, and suffering.

What does it mean, though, to claim *God* as "a rock of refuge" (v. 2)? In what sense if any does God *really* provide safety from the storm, a secure hiding place from the principalities and powers that would threaten to undo us? Is faith in God as refuge

Pastoral Perspective

By ten o'clock on Holy Saturday morning, most church sanctuaries are already fragrant with Easter lilies and other spring flowers packed in crates, ready to be rewrapped in gold foil and arrayed around the altar and the pulpit. Members of the altar chapter are lifting the black veil from the cross, covering the table with fresh linens and a white frontal, and buffing every inch of brass they can find. The sacristy smells like silver polish. If there is to be an Easter Vigil service, the materials for the new fire are being collected and arranged at the entrance to the nave. If the choir has started to rehearse, everyone present will hear the alleluias that signal the church's shift to celebration. Absent members of your congregation may well be shopping for party clothes or groceries for the family feasts that follow Easter morning. In all of this, the church behaves as if Holy Saturday were the day before Easter Sunday.

In fact, it is much more significantly the day after Good Friday, which is a very different thing. In terms of worship, this day typically goes unacknowledged—a fact made remarkable because Holy Saturday is unique in the liturgical year. The church identifies it as the sole day on which we are explicitly forbidden from administering the Holy Eucharist. It looks like a day without the possibility of comfort. No wonder we rush to distract ourselves.

Holy Saturday

Exegetical Perspective

In terms of its literary form and context, Psalm 31 is similar to the other Holy Week lectionary readings from the Psalms (Pss. 116 and 22). The phraseology and sentiments of Psalm 31 are also very similar to passages in other psalms and the books of Jeremiah, Lamentations, and Jonah.[1] Whereas many psalms can be neatly assigned to the categories of lament, thanksgiving, praise, supplication, and so forth, this psalm alternates between supplication (vv. 1–2), thanksgiving (vv. 3–8), supplication (v. 9), lament (vv. 10–13), supplication (vv. 14–18), and praise (vv. 19–24). One of the elements that distinguishes this psalm from Psalm 22 is the vindictive attitude the poet expresses toward his tormentors, expressing his hatred of them (v. 6) and calling upon God to punish them (vv. 17–18).

The later superscription in this psalm attributes authorship to David or the Davidic collection of psalms, but there is no evidence within the psalm itself that can be used to determine the identity of the author or the date of the original composition. Some scholars have suggested that this is a late psalm dating to the late Persian or Hellenistic period, around the time the Psalter attained its final form.[2]

1. Solomon B. Freehof, *The Book of Psalms: A Commentary* (Cincinnati: Union of American Hebrew Congregations, 1938), 7.
2. Charles A. Briggs and Emilie G. Briggs, *The Book of Psalms*, International Critical Commentary 19 (New York: Charles Scribner's Sons, 1906) 1:lxxxviii–xcii.

Homiletical Perspective

If a preacher is in the unlikely position of preaching on Holy Saturday, Psalm 31 could be a fruitful text. This psalm sinks into God's protective arms and prays for deliverance. The psalmist both affirms and hopes, moving between the great declarations of God's welcoming presence and anticipation of final deliverance. As with the liturgical date of Holy Saturday itself, this text is the pivot between death and life, despair and hope, humiliation and rescue.

Preachers will have to decide whether they will stay with the lectionary's unfortunate editing of the text or if they will deal with the excised verses. This is a general homiletical truth, but it is particularly important for handling this portion of Psalm 31. For instance, verse 5 ("Into your hand I commit my spirit") is quoted by Jesus in Luke's account of the cross (Luke 23:46) and will be immediately recognized if it is heard by those who know the story.

Not only this; the descriptions of the psalmist's adversity (see esp. vv. 10–13) sound strikingly familiar to those who have heard the passion narratives of the Gospels. For any preacher with the faintest imagination, the whole of Psalm 31 almost sounds like an internal narrative of the Crucified One. Jesus becomes the scorn of his adversaries, a broken vessel, and a horror to his neighbors. He can hear the whispering of those who plot to take his

Psalm 31:1-4, 15-16

Theological Perspective

warranted experientially? If not, is it warranted in some other way—on authority perhaps (Scripture, tradition, reason)? And if so, is such a warrant sufficient to withstand the extreme existential hour of trial? If such faith lacks warrant, is it not then merely a piece of pious, poetic sentimentality, perhaps a nostalgic throwback to memories of intrauterine security?

These questions have been asked and answered in many ways, both existentially and theoretically. Another equally important question, however, is to ask in a more pastoral way how we might distinguish between a mature, theologically profound trusting in God as refuge and defense, and one that is less mature and sophisticated or nuanced theologically. Such a distinction might, for instance, hold that an appropriate expression of faith would not indulge in literalistic or magical beliefs in divine protection or rescue from worldly harm, or seek special guarantees of security to believers against threats that are common to all human beings and perhaps fundamental to our humanity. It would refuse to privilege believers in matters pertaining to basic human conditions and would resist asserting their moral or religious superiority over others. "For he makes his sun rise on the evil and on the good, and sends rain on the righteous and on the unrighteous" (Matt. 5:45).

Nonetheless such faith might affirm that we are ultimately secure in God in some mysterious way beyond space and time, and that even within history we are never beyond the reach of God's indestructible love and embrace. Hence we are never lost to God, whatever evils may come our way. Or a more mature, sophisticated understanding might approach the issue eschatologically by referring specifically to Easter as the first light of a final dawn in which the hidden Rock of refuge becomes manifest as ultimate and unshakable.

However, if we take the cross of Jesus and the dark silence of Holy Saturday as also somehow a revelation of God's total redemptive involvement in evil and suffering, the theological problem becomes even more difficult than conceiving a historically transcendent or eschatological answer to the mystery of suffering and death. For, in committing his spirit to God in his dying moment (Luke 23:46), Jesus lived out the faith of Psalm 31; he clung to God as his refuge and hope; his times were in God's hands. However, where, in that dark hour, was the great Rescuer and Protector of the faithful? What sort of Rock of refuge was this God, who did absolutely nothing to spare Jesus pain or save and protect him from suffering and death?

Pastoral Perspective

Holy Saturday also presents a considerable problem for preachers because, as representatives of a religion whose emblem is a gloriously empty tomb, today we are presented with a tomb that is very much full. This is the only occasion on which the readings insist that we bring our full attention to Jesus' lifelessness, and it first appears that there is no relief in them. Psalm 31, of which we read verses 1–4 and 15–16 on this day, offers us in these verses no news of deliverance. It does, however, offer us the companionship of the psalmist, a model believer. The instruction of this pray-er is critical because we have nowhere else to look. Of the four evangelists, only one offers any information at all about the circumstances or behavior of the disciples after the crucifixion: "On the sabbath they rested according to the commandment" (Luke 23:56).

When the congregation read Psalm 22 during the Good Friday service yesterday, all eyes were on Jesus. Today Jesus is nowhere to be seen. Yesterday's song—witnessed as it was from the foot of the cross—concluded with an ecstatic vision of an eternal kinship of vibrant praise. Today the "I" in verse 1 of Psalm 31 is arresting in its vulnerability and isolation. No community, no matter how faithful and devoted, finally shields us either from the savage truth of death or from the unsettling death of what might have felt very much like truth.

Psalm 31 is the prayer of a believer in great distress who has made a choice where to place her trust (v. 1). The psalmist calls upon God, seeking refuge (vv. 1, 2, 4), guidance (v. 3), and deliverance (vv. 1, 4, 15, 16) from those who are plotting secretly (v. 4) to inflict harm (v. 15). God is called upon as "Lord," with human characteristics—ear (v. 2), hands (v. 15), face (v. 16), as having servants (v. 16); and as a rock (vv. 2, 3) and a fortress (vv. 2, 3), which offer protection simply in their existence. The speaker seeks both the warm responsiveness of a God who is personal and the immutable trustworthiness of a rocky stronghold. These images find their marriage in the final appeal to God's "steadfast love" (v. 16).

There are two things worth noting in this example of prayer at a time of great anguish. First, there is no demand for fierce retribution in the verses appointed for public reading today. We hear no call for God to "whet his sword (Ps. 7:12) or "lift up [his] hand" (Ps. 10:12). There are significant implications to the choice of this psalm on the day after Jesus' death. Even in the verses omitted from public reading, the strong focus of the prayer is on

Exegetical Perspective

Most scholars agree that this prayer was recited in public worship services as part of the liturgy in the postexilic synagogues.[3]

The key verses ("In you YHWH I sought refuge; let me never be put to shame; in your righteousness deliver me" [v. 1, my trans.] and "Let your face shine upon your servant; save me by your grace" [v. 16]) summarize the import of the reading. The poet relies upon God to protect, vindicate, and deliver him. It is interesting to note that the lectionary passage includes only six of the twenty-four verses of the psalm. It is also important to note that the lectionary reading includes only those verses in the psalm that are supplication (vv. 1–2, 15–16) and thanksgiving (vv. 3–4). Not included in the lectionary reading are the lament (vv. 10–13) and hymn of praise (vv. 19–24), which constitute integral elements of the psalm. In the context of Holy Week services, the editors of the lectionary may have felt it necessary to emphasize the positive rather than the negative. This is understandable, but runs counter to the spirit of this psalm in particular and most of the psalms in general. Although the Psalms celebrate the faithfulness and power of God, they do not shy away from dealing head-on with human suffering and feelings of helplessness and hopelessness.

Most surprising is the lectionary's elimination of verse 5, "Into your hand I commit my spirit," recorded in Luke 23:46 as Jesus' last words before dying on the cross. In the context of this psalm, preceding as it does the poet's lament, this is a powerful statement of trust in God despite the suffering and existential angst of the psalmist. In the context of the Christian message, it signifies Christ's submission and trust in God at the hour of his greatest agony. Of all the verses in Psalm 31, the message of verse 5 seems to express an appropriate message of hope on the day following the crucifixion and preceding the resurrection.

Psalm 31 clearly speaks of the physical and emotional torment actually experienced by a pre-Christian individual. Although certain passages can be interpreted as referring to illness (vv. 9–10), most passages identify personal enemies as being the source of persecution from which the poet seeks deliverance (vv. 6–8, 11–18). In his lament, the psalmist also notes that he has become "a horror to my neighbors, an object of dread to my acquaintances," and that "those who see me in the

Homiletical Perspective

life, but ultimately he commits his life and future to YHWH.

For those who work through the whole psalm, therefore, one direction for the sermon might be to receive the psalm as Dietrich Bonhoeffer once suggested: as the prayer of Jesus Christ. In his little book *Psalms: The Prayer Book of the Bible*, Bonhoeffer wrote, "It is the incarnate Son of God, who has borne every human weakness in his own flesh, who here pours out the heart of all humanity before God, and who stands in our place and prays for us."[1] Similarly, as we take Christ's prayer as our own, we participate in his passion and take part in his faithful trust.

A topical sermon on shame might also arise from reflections on this text. The psalmist prays for relief from public humiliation. This is the psalm of someone in public trouble. The probability of embarrassment is high. Scandal is a present threat. In the cultures that use the possibility of shame as an ethical restraint, it can be a powerful motivation—to avoid all shame! It may also spill a nearly unwashable moral stain on those who do not measure up to the society's expectations of behavior.

The apostle Paul was not beyond wagging his finger at those he deemed shameful. In this, he was a child of his culture and a predecessor of our own age. Yet in the light of the cross of Jesus, he was also capable of turning the visceral power of shame on its head. "God chose what is foolish in the world to shame the wise," he thundered to the know-it-all Corinthians, "and what is weak to shame the strong" (1 Cor. 1:27). When Paul recalled how his Hebrew Bible stated, "Cursed is everyone who hangs on a tree," the apostle interpreted the cross by saying, "Christ redeemed us from the curse of the law by becoming the curse for us" (Gal. 3:13).

Perhaps the psalmist's prayer to avoid shame is most realized by the anonymous writer of Hebrews. This early theologian says it is Jesus who endured the cross and disregarded its shame, all for the sake of the joy that was set before him (Heb. 12:2). This lies close to the heart of the good news tucked between Good Friday and Easter. Then the same writer spells out the implications by saying of those who are sanctified by Christ, "Jesus is not ashamed to call them brothers and sisters" (Heb. 2:11).

A third sermon possibility focuses on the theme of time. "My times are in your hand," says the

3. Artur Weiser, *The Psalms*, trans. Herbert Hartwell, Old Testament Library, ed. G. Ernest Wright et al. (Philadelphia: Westminster Press, 1962), 27.

1. Dietrich Bonhoeffer, *Psalms: The Prayer Book of the Bible* (Minneapolis: Augsburg Fortress Press, 1974), 20–21.

Psalm 31:1-4, 15-16

Theological Perspective

Easter may witness to God as the ultimate, invincible Rock of refuge, but that knowledge only comes tomorrow, on Easter. Today, on Holy Saturday, it is death. We can perhaps dare to hope for Easter, but what we *know*, today, is the darkness when faith cries out for a Rock of refuge and no such rock is anywhere in sight. Faith can be hard to come by on Holy Saturday, yet Holy Saturday is fundamental to the biblical story of salvation. It is for good reason that the story of the Christ has this day of total darkness at its center, that Jesus does not go immediately from death to resurrection light, that this Saturday is holy. The Bible owns the unfathomable mystery of death in the very heart of divine redemption, a dark stillness that perhaps penetrates even to the heart and being of God.

If so, perhaps our crying out for a Rock in the storm is in itself already a sign, not only of our own desperate wishful thinking or childish hopes and illusions in the face of fear, but also a sign of our own *imago Dei*, our profound spiritual likeness to God, and our kinship with a God who, reaching out for loving relationship, wholly enters our experience with us. If Good Friday and Holy Saturday are not easy for us, perhaps they are not easy for God, either. Perhaps—just perhaps—God too, in an eternal moment in the eternity of the divine life, is shrouded in darkness with us and for us. Perhaps, at the deepest level of what is meant by *incarnation*, God's cry and our own reach out for each other and touch in the mystery of death. Perhaps, in their convergence, in love, comes the first inkling of the Easter dawn.

RODNEY J. HUNTER

Pastoral Perspective

the psalmist's distress (v. 6) and trust in God's deliverance, not on her anger with her enemies.

Second, it is almost impossible to pray, "for your name's sake lead me and guide me," without wandering to the green pastures and still waters of Psalm 23. Of course there the image of God as shepherd is entirely animate, intelligent, and mobile. Here the psalmist addresses God as "my rock and my fortress" while asking to be guided and led. This suggests a question: Can an inert object like a fortress, built to contain, somehow show us the way to a better place?

Virtually all of us overlook praying these words together, in favor of making preparations for tomorrow morning. In doing so, we miss the opportunity to join our psalmist in seeking the rock-hewn place that moves us toward our salvation. It cannot be by chance that on Holy Saturday we ask God not to be for us an eagle, a warrior, or a king, but to take a form that closely suggests the place where the Crucified One has been laid. The choice of this image reminds us that it is within cold stone walls that salvation happens. With the psalmist we ask God to take us there. If we hope to follow Jesus to Easter morning, this psalm can be an important help in finding the way.

MARIA DECARVALHO

street flee from me" (v. 11). This verse is reminiscent of Job's plight of having his suffering compounded by friends who attributed his ill fortune to punishment from God for his sins.

Psalm 31 takes a dramatic rhetorical turn in verses 19–24. Clearly an indeterminate amount of time has passed since the poet uttered his first supplication and lament, but now his prayer has been answered, as indicated in verse 22, "I had said in my alarm, 'I am driven far from your sight.' But you heard my supplications when I cried out to you for help." The closing verse—"Be strong, and let your heart take courage, all you who wait for YHWH"—sounds like an exhortation of the congregation, which it probably was, supporting the view that the postexilic community adopted this "individual" psalm for use in communal worship. This closing verse may have been used as a benediction at the conclusion of a worship service, and echoes the conclusion of Psalm 27:14, "Wait for YHWH; be strong, and let your heart take courage; wait for YHWH!"

Despite some debate about the authenticity of the sayings attributed to Jesus in the Gospels, there is little doubt that he was steeped in the Hebrew Scriptures and that when he quoted Psalm 31:5, he was thinking not only of this particular verse but of the entire psalm. Since it was part of the synagogue liturgy at the time, Jesus' quotation of verse 5 would have reminded even illiterate disciples of the words of encouragement in verse 24, "Be strong, and let your heart take courage, all you who wait for the Lord (YHWH)."

There are many contemporary lessons we can derive from this psalm, especially when we encounter suffering and the threat of death for ourselves or our loved ones. Both the psalmist and Jesus encourage us not to adopt a fatalistic stance, but to call upon God in our distress, to be strong and take courage, and, in the hour of our weakness, to commit our life/spirit into the loving hands of a faithful God.

DAVID W. MCCREERY

psalmist (31:15). Our temporal experiences are held in God's eternal mercy. This is an appropriate affirmation for a liturgical day when nothing happens. By every human observation, Jesus has entered the great Sabbath of death. On this day, he will not produce anything or engage in any work. He can only lean on the eternal arms and "sleep with the ancestors."

It is difficult for most folks simply to let life rest. A pastoral counselor once observed that the primary reason so many people have a hard time sitting still is their fear of death. Death is the final rest. There are no wages to earn, no routines to maintain, no busyness to fill every available calendar date. Everything stops, and finally we must trust that God will hold it all.

We do not worship any ordinary god. The God of Israel is capable of keeping still, even resting from all work (Gen. 2:2). The faithful are called to mimic the Lord in this regard: six days of labor are followed by a seventh day that is hallowed, blessed, and free from work. When the Sabbath of Holy Saturday comes, God is not in any hurry to raise Jesus from the tomb. The day of rest must be kept before the New Creation begins again.

In the words of one scholar, God is not like any of the minor-league Babylonian gods. There will be no overfunctioning on heaven's throne. The one true God is "so well-established, so surely in charge, so greatly respected by creation, so gladly obeyed by all creatures, that God's governance is not anxiety-ridden or frantic. The world is confidently, serenely ordered as God's good creation."[2]

All of human time—and especially this day—is held securely in the grip of its Maker. This is obvious on Holy Saturday, a day when absolutely nothing happens in a graveyard near Jerusalem.

WILLIAM G. CARTER

---

2. Walter Brueggemann, "The Commandments and Liberated, Liberating Bonding," in *Interpretation and Obedience* (Philadelphia: Fortress Press, 1991), 151.

1 Peter 4:1-8

¹Since therefore Christ suffered in the flesh, arm yourselves also with the same intention (for whoever has suffered in the flesh has finished with sin), ²so as to live for the rest of your earthly life no longer by human desires but by the will of God. ³You have already spent enough time in doing what the Gentiles like to do, living in licentiousness, passions, drunkenness, revels, carousing, and lawless idolatry. ⁴They are surprised that you no longer join them in the same excesses of dissipation, and so they blaspheme. ⁵But they will have to give an accounting to him who stands ready to judge the living and the dead. ⁶For this is the reason the gospel was proclaimed even to the dead, so that, though they had been judged in the flesh as everyone is judged, they might live in the spirit as God does.

⁷The end of all things is near; therefore be serious and discipline yourselves for the sake of your prayers. ⁸Above all, maintain constant love for one another, for love covers a multitude of sins.

Theological Perspective

Holy Saturday is omitted from many Protestant liturgical resources, such as the Presbyterian *Book of Common Worship*. The lectionary moves from Good Friday straight to the Easter Vigil. The silence of death leaves us with little to say, and in part that is as it should be. This is a day for simple, silent grief over the rejection of Life by the powers of this world. Jesus spends this Sabbath resting from his labors, ensconced in swaths of grave clothes. As he breathed his last on Friday, he declared his labors complete. Now he rests.

Was he *really* resting on this Sabbath day? In the days of his ministry he preached, healed, and cast out evil on the Sabbath. If his spirit remained alive when his body was dead, why would he not continue spiritually with his Sabbath pattern of witnessing to the gospel? The apostolic tradition is rich with speculation about what Jesus did in the spiritual realm while his body lay entombed on Holy Saturday. One biblical passage that fuels such speculation is in today's text, 1 Peter 4:5–6. This text is often paired with the passage just a few verses earlier (3:18–20) which teaches that, when he was put to death in the body, Jesus ministered to the spirits "in prison"—those who disregarded Noah's call to repentance and perished in the flood. In today's text there is less detail; it simply says that the

Pastoral Perspective

"He descended into hell," we recite in the Apostles' Creed, repeating the short phrase between Good Friday's "he was crucified, died, and buried" and Easter Sunday's "on the third day he rose again from the dead." "He descended into hell," we recite, but we do not often ponder what it means.

On a Holy Saturday some years ago, the *New York Times* religion writer Peter Steinfels explored the depths of this small phrase's poignant meaning. For first-century Judaism, he said, to be dead was to be confined to Sheol (or Hades)—which was not an addition to or consequence of death, not a place of punishment or torment, but simply a place for those who were dead to await judgment. So it is that 1 Peter can speak of those who "will have to give an accounting to him who stands ready to judge the living and the dead" (v. 5).

Death—and hell, where death resides—is, according to Scripture, quintessentially the experience of nothingness and emptiness. It is the absence of life, the absence of light, the absence even of God. That Jesus himself would experience this descent into "godforsakenness," as Steinfels puts it, gives us a glimpse into his "solidarity with suffering, sinful humanity that [is] central to the Easter mystery. The divine Son has undergone godlessness, total estrangement from his Father," and in doing so has brought

Exegetical Perspective

In the concluding greetings of 1 Peter, the author states that he has written to "encourage" the readers and to "testify" to "the true grace of God" (5:12). Just as Greek and Roman philosophers wrote letters of encouragement to their followers, so Christian leaders wrote to specific house churches (as Paul did to the Thessalonians) or to groups of churches scattered throughout the Greco-Roman world (as the author of James wrote to "the twelve tribes in the Dispersion"). The purpose of these letters was to encourage their readers to remain steadfast, by providing examples they should emulate (or avoid), by describing the conduct appropriate (and inappropriate) for the life they now lived, and by reminding them of the rewards (and punishments) that awaited them. Frequently, letters of exhortation focused on the suffering that adherents were undergoing because of their allegiance, referring to it as a sign of true faithfulness. First Peter has all of these attributes.

The letter is addressed to the "chosen," "destined," and "sanctified" exiles (1:2) in Asia Minor (modern Turkey), an area where the Christian movement grew rapidly in the first and second centuries. The dominant theme is struck in the opening benediction (1:3–10): believers have been given "a new birth into a living hope through the resurrection of Jesus Christ from the dead, and into

Homiletical Perspective

Near the end of our text the author declares, "The end of all things is near" (v. 7). Two thousand years later we realize that eschatological perspective was not quite true. What is true is that much has changed since these verses were penned, and the distance between this passage and our listeners has resulted in a huge gulf that is still growing. As preachers, we might as well acknowledge the distance up front. For starters, there is the historical context of persecution the recipients were encountering (1 Pet. 1:6–7; 4:12). How foreign for most of our congregants! We live in places where politicians often claim the Christian name and seek support from Christians and may be sworn in with a Bible. That is not the case everywhere. In other parts of the world, persecution continues. If our preaching addresses only those who are present in the church this day, we may miss an opportunity to speak on behalf of our brothers and sisters throughout the world. During a time when the church remembers the suffering and death of Jesus, such solidarity might be a timely word. As always, we will have to decide what the sermonic focus is for this occasion.

In addition, the author's theology creates a certain distance between us and the text at several points. This distance, however, need not be viewed negatively. Eugene Lowry and others have noted the

1 Peter 4:1-8

Theological Perspective

gospel was preached to the dead when Christ suffered in the flesh. It does not specifically say that Christ did the preaching, only that the message was preached somehow. These passages, taken together with a handful of others (notably Eph. 4:9–10), show that Jesus' ministry among the dead was deemed significant enough to merit inclusion by most branches of Christianity in the baptismal creed: He "was crucified, dead, and buried; he descended into hell. On the third day he rose again from the dead."

This ancient formulation of baptismal faith—which has come to be known as the Apostles' Creed—is as terse a statement of Christian belief as the early church thought possible. Verbiage is cut to bare essentials. The entire life and ministry of Jesus is collapsed into seven or eight clipped phrases. Nearly his entire career is omitted, but the descent into hell makes this list of absolute essentials. To omit this day liturgically is to pass over something in the church's account of Jesus that has a long pedigree of critical significance.

The few texts that are sometimes taken to refer to Jesus' spiritual ministry on Holy Saturday are enigmatic. Many interpreters reject entirely the notion that these texts are meant to describe what was happening to Jesus on this day. For instance, Calvin suggests that Christ's "descent into hell" is his on-the-cross experience of divine judgment and rejection: "My God, my God, why have you forsaken me?"[1] Whatever was happening to Jesus on Holy Saturday, the apostolic writers make it clear that his disciples are called to follow him through this Saturday journey into the bowels of death. One of the earliest Christian creeds, found in 2 Timothy 2:11, puts it succinctly: "If we have died with him, we will also live with him." The resurrection life of Sunday is impossible to attain without spending some time in Saturday's grave.

First Peter 4 spells out some of what it means to put the carnal self to death in order to be raised with Christ into newness of life. It involves both disposition (the mind) and practice (the flesh). The disposition of mind to which disciples are called is to think like Christ Jesus, to have the "same intention" (v. 1) as the one who gave up all personal rights for the sake of others (see Phil. 2:1–11). The ultimate expression of that disposition was his willingness to die rather than be compromised in his witness. Our text invites us to arm ourselves with the same

Pastoral Perspective

our utter estrangement into "the very inner life of the Godhead." It is no small thing to know that Jesus himself has undergone "the depths of cruelty, absurdity and despair that are all too familiar parts of our inner and outer landscapes," that he himself has felt even the absence of God.[1] Just as Jesus' self-emptying crucifixion is not only a deed of solidarity with everyone who has suffered terrifying violence, so his descent into hell is not only an act of sympathy with those who have experienced death in its ultimate or penultimate forms. Christ's suffering and death are *redemptive.* His descent to hell serves not to leave us there, but to bring us back with him—into life, into light, into the saving presence of God—even at the expense of his own life, even at the cost of his own intimate knowledge of the presence of God.

The posthumous publication of the letters of Mother Teresa of Calcutta reveal the same holy amalgam of astonishing self-emptying and experience of the absence of God, with the same redemptive result of that self-denial. In David Van Biema's *Time* magazine article,[2] he notes that on December 11, 1979, in Mother Teresa's speech accepting the Nobel Peace Prize, this "global beacon of self-abnegating care delivered the kind of message the world had come to expect from her."

"It is not enough for us to say, 'I love God, but I do not love my neighbor,'" she said, since through Christ's death on the cross, he had made "himself the hungry one—the naked one—the homeless one." She encouraged Christians to find and alleviate this hunger, just as Jesus did. As was her custom, Mother Teresa pointed to the great joy that comes from seeing Christ's real presence everywhere: "Christ in our hearts, Christ in the poor we meet, Christ in the smile we give and in the smile that we receive."

Yet beneath her serene presence, her confident faith and radiant joy, lay a care-worn spirit. In her posthumously published letters to her spiritual confidant, Mother Teresa confessed her profound experience of the absence of God: "Jesus has a very special love for you. [However] as for me, the silence and the emptiness is so great, that I look and do not see—Listen and do not hear—the tongue moves [in prayer] but does not speak." In nearly direct contradiction to the message of her Nobel speech, Van Biema tells us, Mother Teresa's sense of God's absence arose precisely when she started her work with the poor, the sick, and the dying in Calcutta.

---

1. John Calvin, *Institutes of the Christian Religion,* ed. John McNeill, trans. Ford Lewis Battles (Philadelphia: Westminster Press, 1960), 2.16.8–12.

1. Peter Steinfels, "Beliefs: The Descent of Jesus into Hell," *New York Times,* April 6, 1996.
2. David Van Biema, "Mother Teresa's Crisis of Faith," *Time,* Aug. 23, 2007.

an inheritance that is imperishable, undefiled, and unfading, kept in heaven for [them]" (vv. 3–4). Nonetheless, they "have had to suffer various trials, so that the genuineness of [their] faith . . . may be found to result in praise and glory and honor when Jesus Christ is revealed" (vv. 6–7).

The exhortations begin almost immediately: "Prepare your minds for action; discipline yourselves; set all your hope on the grace that Jesus Christ will bring you when he is revealed" (1:13). Such lists of short, general admonitions appear throughout 1 Peter (see 2:1, 16–17; 3:8–9, 14–16; 4:7–11a, 15; 5:1–9). In 2:18–3:7, the author employs another kind of exhortation: admonitions to members of an extended household. This household code, like the ones in Ephesians 5:21–6:9 and Colossians 3:18–4:1, is modeled on the many examples in Greco-Roman moral literature. Christian household codes are distinct, however, because they are grounded in theological arguments. Here in 1 Peter, for example, we read that slaves are to "accept the authority of [their] masters," because "Christ also suffered for you, leaving you an example (*hypogrammon*), so that you should follow in his steps" (2:18, 21). The quotation from Isaiah 53 reveals what Christ's example entails: not returning abuse, not threatening, and entrusting oneself to God, who judges justly (2:22–23).

In 3:13–22 the author of 1 Peter returns to the notion of unjust suffering—now, however, addressing all believers. Here again the suffering of Christ is given as an example, but to different effect. On the one hand, the believer who suffers for doing what is right puts the abuser to shame (v. 16). On the other hand, in his suffering Christ "was put to death in the flesh, but made alive in the spirit" (v. 18). It is to this that 1 Peter refers in the opening of our passage.

"Since therefore" directly links 1 Peter 4:1–8 to the argument of 3:13–22, as does the admonition "arm yourselves also *with the same intention*" (v. 1b). The parenthetical statement at the end of verse 1, together with verse 2, clarifies what that intention is: the transformation of life. Thus, just as Christ died in the flesh and was made alive in the spirit (3:18b), so those who hold him as an example and "follow in his steps" (2:21) will no longer live "by human desires" but "by the will of God" (4:2).

The author clarifies this contrast by referencing the time his readers spent "doing what the Gentiles like to do." The vice list that follows enumerates precisely what this means: "living in licentiousness, passions, drunkenness, revels, carousing, and lawless

power of sermons that begin by rhetorically playing with the tension we experience between us and texts. This passage offers much in that regard, and any one of these felt discrepancies might make a good focus. For instance, there is the author's use of battle imagery ("arm yourselves," v. 1), something many Christians find offensive in this overly militaristic world. This might be an appropriate message in light of the violence perpetrated against the Christ and the wars that never seem to cease in our own day. Or we might consider the notion of flesh being evil (vv. 1–2), a gnostic teaching that haunts the church to this day. There is also the troubling description of "Gentiles" (understood here as those who are nonbelievers), who are described as living with no regard for morality (vv. 3–4), when in fact many of the most upstanding persons we know are not Christians. Exploring any of these discrepancies could make for interesting sermon fodder.

Despite the distance between us and the text, there is also much that remains readily available for us preachers to ponder. The overarching emphasis in the passage is on a Christian lifestyle based on the life of Christ, or living "with the same intention" (v. 1). It was a similar passage in 1 Peter 2:21 that led Charles Sheldon to pen his famous novel *In His Steps*, which more recently popularized the expression "What would Jesus do?" We should be quick to note, however, that seeking a martyr's death is not what Jesus would have us do. As the author will later stress, it is a matter of choosing between opposing kinds of behavior, vices and virtues.

The vice and virtue list itself begins with a cataloging of how the recipients lived formerly ("licentiousness," "passions," "drunkenness," and the like [v. 3]). Note, however, that this is not an opportunity for the preacher to rail about a society without moral compass; this is a reminder of how the believers used to live. As Fred Craddock observes, "Christians who tend to be judgmental of others rather than leaving them to God should note here the absence of any triumphant screams over the fence at outsiders."[1] Surely our gathering together on Holy Saturday has a more noble purpose than to shake a bony finger at how "the world" is living these days.

In contrast, those who do seek to live in the pattern of the Christ are enjoined to emulate four positive behaviors, two of which appear in our text (prayer and love in vv. 7–8) and two of which appear

1. Fred B. Craddock, "First and Second Peter and Jude," in *Westminster Bible Companion*, ed. Patrick D. Miller and David L. Bartlett (Louisville, KY: Westminster John Knox Press, 1995), 67.

1 Peter 4:1-8

Theological Perspective

disposition that led Jesus to his death, for only then can we experience true victory over sin.

This disposition frees us to set aside the practices of insistent self-gratification that rule those who live by the laws of sin and death. There is nothing remarkable about the list in verse 3 of practices that are forsaken by those who have died with Jesus; similar lists are scattered throughout the apostolic literature (e.g., Gal. 5:19–21; Jude 7–16; Rev. 21). What stands out is the author's point that those who turn away from such practices will undergo public contempt and false accusation on account of their new way of life—much as happened with their Lord, culminating in his Saturday repose in the bands of death.

The writer does not close the discussion by merely identifying the practices that Christ's followers are to reject. This text is not just about the death of Holy Saturday, but also about the nature of the life that rises from that grave. Those who turn away from the self-seeking of the old nature are invited into a new way of living, marked first and foremost by love for the other, rather than of self. Yet those who seek to put to death the old self discover that its dispositions and practices revive all too easily. Indeed, the community of Christ is marked less by postresurrection purity than by a "multitude of sins." The only way Christ's followers can stay the course of resurrection life amid the throes of this daily death is to love one another persistently through it all. "Love covers a multitude of sins" (v. 8), the text proclaims, quoting Proverbs 10:12. The fact is, the daily lives of Christ's followers more often evince Saturday's grave than Sunday's resurrection. Were it not for a loving community that surrounded sinners with the hope and confidence that besetting sin is not their final word, who would stand? Thanks be to God—there *is* such a community, a community that bears confident witness to the resurrection by loving one another unfailingly through everyone's fits and starts of putting off the ways of death and embracing the way of Life.

SHELDON W. SORGE

Pastoral Perspective

Perhaps it is too much to say that this mystical relationship between self-abnegation and the absence of God is necessarily redemptive. It seems to be no accident that Jesus and the followers who walk after him, undaunted, into the depths of others' suffering—even at the expense of their own joy in God's presence—have done so to retrieve those who would otherwise have no hope. They go in search of the poorest of the poor, the despised on society's margins, the forgotten at the edges of the world— even the dead, who have no advocate but Christ.

In full awareness of this connection, the author of 1 Peter tells us, "This is the reason the gospel was proclaimed even to the dead, so that, though they had been judged in the flesh as everyone is judged, they might live in the spirit as God does" (v. 6). The good news proclaimed to the dead is the same good news proclaimed to the living: everyone indeed is judged according to his or her action, but God's love has covered a multitude of sins. The good news proclaimed to the dead and the living is that God desires us to live—not to indulge ourselves in the distractions of empty passions, or to lose our very selves to our addictions, or to escape into numbing excesses. God desires us to live—really live—in the spirit as God does. As for the dead, they are no longer abandoned to their lonely exile there. As for the living, we are no longer abandoned to our lonely exile here. Whether we are living or dead, Christ has rescued us all. Thanks be to God.

CHRISTINE CHAKOIAN

idolatry" (v. 3). What the author understands by "the will of God" is not addressed until 4:7–11. Our text takes up only the first two verses, mentioning the need to be serious and disciplined and to love one another (vv. 7–8). The next verses are worth noting, however, since they develop the meaning of love for one another. Believers should be hospitable, serve one another with the gifts each has received, speak as if one were speaking the words of God, and always act "so that God may be glorified in all things through Jesus Christ" (4:9–11).

The reference to the "Gentiles" in 4:3 raises an important issue in our passage, namely, the distinction made between "us" and "them." The contrast is sharp, made so not only because of the vice list in verse 3, but also because of the reference to the final judgment in verse 5, when the Gentiles (to whom the readers apparently once belonged, 4:3) will have to give account for their "excesses of dissipation" (v. 4). Equally important for the author, however, they are the cause of the suffering experienced by believers. "Surprised" that believers no longer join them in dissipation, the Gentiles blaspheme, apparently by disparaging the believers' new way of life and the God who called them to it (see 4:14 and 16). The Christian apologists of the second century (such as Justin Martyr) will develop this theme, appealing to the Roman emperors and Senate not to condemn Christians because of the name, but only when they commit specific crimes.

First Peter reflects a world in which Christians are a minority. They feel themselves under threat because of their beliefs and way of life. If 1 Peter derives from the last decade of the first century, some of the suffering referenced in the letter may derive from official acts against perceived threats to the Roman order. Whenever it was written, however, most of the suffering derives from conflicts with neighbors who now regard Christians as outside the norm and therefore appropriate objects of slander and ridicule.

The challenge for most of us preaching from this text is relating it to a historical situation that is decidedly different. Perhaps we should be guided by the admonition in 4:19 and "entrust [ourselves] to a faithful Creator, while continuing to do good."

OLIVER LARRY YARBROUGH

in the verses following (hospitality and exercising spiritual gifts in vv. 9–11). Some preachers will choose to extend the reading through verse 11 on this holy occasion, especially given the doxological nature of verse 11. For those who choose otherwise, there is still plenty of sermon material. A life of prayer and love is an image worth pondering on the night before Easter. The life of prayer is solitary and quiet; "love for one another" means being involved in the messiness of life. While some Christians would like to choose between the two, as Elton Trueblood reminded the church, the most important word in the Bible is "and."

If the truth be told, many of us would rather not preach on Holy Saturday. In some traditions this is a day of silence, recalling the silence of God after the death of Jesus. Besides, who are we to add words to such pain? Some preachers think the liturgy should carry the freight on such holy occasions, that sermons may not be necessary. As Alan Lewis has written, however, Holy Saturday may be a fitting metaphor for the whole Christian life. Lewis observes how we live with one foot in the suffering of Good Friday and the other in the resurrection of Easter Sunday. The fact that he died from cancer while working on his thesis speaks volumes about the reality of his words. Preachers may find much to ponder in Lewis's work.[2]

Lastly, given the prominent baptismal imagery in 1 Peter, Luke Timothy Johnson notes how some scholars believe the epistle may have originated as "a paschal liturgy or even a baptismal ritual."[3] If baptisms were planned for Easter Sunday, then the sermon for this Holy Saturday might acknowledge the significance of the new life into which believers are initiated.

What we hope for in the end is what the author describes in verse 11: "Whoever speaks must do so as one speaking the very words of God." With that charge, let us prepare and so let us preach.

MIKE GRAVES

2. Alan E. Lewis, *Between Cross and Resurrection: A Theology of Holy Saturday* (Grand Rapids: Eerdmans, 2001).
3. Luke Timothy Johnson, *The Writings of the New Testament: An Interpretation*, rev. ed. (Minneapolis: Fortress Press, 1999), 479.

John 19:38-42

38After these things, Joseph of Arimathea, who was a disciple of Jesus, though a secret one because of his fear of the Jews, asked Pilate to let him take away the body of Jesus. Pilate gave him permission; so he came and removed his body. 39Nicodemus, who had at first come to Jesus by night, also came, bringing a mixture of myrrh and aloes, weighing about a hundred pounds. 40They took the body of Jesus and wrapped it with the spices in linen cloths, according to the burial custom of the Jews. 41Now there was a garden in the place where he was crucified, and in the garden there was a new tomb in which no one had ever been laid. 42And so, because it was the Jewish day of Preparation, and the tomb was nearby, they laid Jesus there.

Theological Perspective

Given the variety of speculations and the uncertainty of NT scholarship, Raymond Brown has suggested two possibilities regarding the theological symbolism and the relation of John's independent source(s) to the Synoptic accounts of Jesus' burial in Matthew, Mark, and Luke.

1. In Jesus' last public speech to the Jerusalem crowd before he departs and hides, he speaks proleptically of his death and resurrection: "'And I, when I am lifted up from the earth, will draw all people to myself.' He said this to indicate the kind of death he was to die" (John 12:32–33). Within John's Gospel, "all people" includes both the disciples whose feet Jesus washes, and who are associated with him over against "the Jews," and others: "many, even of the [Jewish] authorities, believed in him. But because of the Pharisees they did not confess it, for fear they would be put out of the synagogue" (12:42). Two of these secret disciples show up after Jesus' death to care for his body: Joseph of Arimathea and Nicodemus (whom the reader met in 3:1–21 and 7:48–53). Given the conflict between devout Jews and early Jewish Christians that occurred in the late first and early second century—the situation in which the Gospel emerged—do the figures of Joseph and Nicodemus serve to call Jewish Christians who still prayed in the synagogues to courageous witness?

Pastoral Perspective

For all the words John writes about the trial, crucifixion, and death of Jesus on Friday (well over a thousand by my count), there is not a word about what happened on Saturday. Not one. The last we hear from John is that Joseph of Arimathea and Nicodemus have secretly slathered Jesus' body in myrrh and aloes, wrapped it in linen cloths, and stuffed it into a nearby tomb. Then, because it was the Day of Preparation, and because it was getting dark, they hurried home for the beginning of Passover. What a Passover it must have been! For those who had known and loved Jesus it would have been the most somber of all celebratory meals. As they shared the Passover lamb, how could they help but think of "the Lamb of God who takes away the sin of the world" (1:29)? The tears would have flowed freely, glistening on their cheeks in the lamplight. Anyone in our congregations who has tried to celebrate Thanksgiving or Christmas after the death of a loved one, or who has come to the birthday of a loved one who has died recently, knows how hard it is, and how empty that empty chair can be.

Here is the shocking truth: Jesus was dead. At least from sundown on Friday night until sundown on Saturday night, he remained dead. If you believe, as John does, that "in the beginning was the Word, and the Word was with God, and the Word was

Exegetical Perspective

The Burial of Jesus

	John 19	Matthew 27	Mark 15	Luke 23
1. *Time:* Day of Preparation				
	vv. 42, 14	vv. 57, 62	v. 42	vv. 54, 56b
2. *Place:* tomb				
	vv. 41–42	v. 60	v. 46	v. 53
3. *Agent(s):* Joseph and Nicodemus				
	vv. 38–39	vv. 57, 59–60	vv. 43, 46	vv. 50–51
4. *Authority:* Pilate's consent				
	v. 38	v. 58	vv. 44–45	v. 52
5. *Implements:* various				
	vv. 39–40	v. 59	v. 46	v. 53
6. *Observers*				
	None	vv. 56, 61	v. 47	vv. 49, 55
7. *Other Details:* burial customs				
	vv. 38, 40	vv. 60, 62–66	16:4, vv. 44; cf. v. 5	vv. 46, 56

As in the Synoptic Gospels, John's description of the burial creates smooth transition between the death of Jesus and the empty tomb. In narrative detail the Fourth Gospel is among the simplest. Less is said about Joseph of Arimathea than in the Synoptics. Though a woman will be first to report the tomb's emptiness (20:1–3), the women do not witness the body's interment in John. That item's omission might suggest that the Fourth Evangelist

Homiletical Perspective

In her book *Thing Seen and Unseen: A Year Lived in Faith*, Nora Gallagher writes these poignant words after a dear friend of hers dies: "Our comfort as creatures is in the body, the warmth of flesh. This is what we count on, what arms and heartens us. And this is the very thing that is impermanent, that is taken away. I say to God, This is unnecessarily cruel."[1]

On Holy Saturday we come face to face with the anguish and cruelty of those times in our own lives when death robs us of the warmth and flesh of one we have known and loved, and when—like the disciples of Jesus—we need hastily to make preparations for what will happen to that cherished body.

In John's Gospel, it is not the women who arrive with spices to prepare Jesus' body for burial on Sunday morning (as in the Synoptic Gospels). Rather, it is two "secret disciples"—Joseph of Arimathea and Nicodemus—who petition Pilate for Jesus' body on Good Friday afternoon, who take it down from the cross, who wash it and anoint it with 100 pounds of spices (more than enough for a royal burial), and who hastily lay that body in a nearby garden tomb before the Passover Day (also the Jewish Sabbath) begins at sundown.

1. Nora Gallagher, *Things Seen and Unseen: A Year Lived in Faith* (New York: Vintage Books, 1998), 174.

John 19:38-42

Theological Perspective

2. Does the burial for which Joseph and Nicodemus prepare Jesus' body (involving the massive amount of myrrh and aloes, and the garden tomb) signify the entombment of the great king? That would be a proper conclusion for "a Passion Narrative wherein Jesus is crowned and hailed as king during his trial and enthroned and publicly proclaimed as king on the cross."[1]

In the context of Holy Saturday, poised between Good Friday and Easter Sunday, what do we make of the identity of the one buried? Do Joseph and Nicodemus bury the body of the human Jesus who has already, in sovereign majesty, given up his spirit on the cross (19:30)? Or do they bury the body of the very Word of God? Does it make sense to confess that the Word of God who became flesh, who became embodied in Jesus of Nazareth (1:14), also tasted death? This christological question has led theologians down two different paths.

In ancient Catholic teaching and John Calvin's theology, the Word of God cannot die, for the Word is coexistent with God and upholds all creation providentially. If the Word of God died on the cross, then there was no Logos to uphold creation between Good Friday and Easter Sunday and no eternal Trinity. Calvin affirmed this ancient doctrine with a sense of awe: "The Son of God descended from heaven in such a way that, without leaving heaven, he willed to be borne in the virgin's womb, to go about the earth, and to hang upon the cross; yet he continuously filled the world even as he had done from the beginning!"[2] This path preserved the majesty of the Word of God from being confined or shut up in the life and death of Jesus.

A different path led from the earthy, bodily language of Scripture and the poetic language of Christian hymns and prayers to Luther's bold theology of the cross: "God is dead." In the passion and death of Jesus, not only did the human nature of the Son of God suffer, but God also suffered the human condition of dying and death, the penalty for our sinfulness. Luther also drew on ancient Catholic teaching: there was an "exchange of properties" between the two natures of the person of Christ, the humanity and the divinity. Luther took this exchange to be both rhetorical (in the language of hymns and prayers) and a realistic feature of God's incarnation in Christ. With Paul the apostle he proclaimed: "I decided to know nothing among

1. Raymond E. Brown, *The Gospel according to John, XIII–XXI*, Anchor Bible 29A (Garden City, NY: Doubleday, 1970), 960.
2. John Calvin, *Institutes of the Christian Religion*, ed. John McNeill, trans. Ford Lewis Battles (Philadelphia: Westminster Press, 1960), 2.13.4.

Pastoral Perspective

God" (1:1), then you must also believe that on the Saturday after Good Friday, in a very real sense, God was dead. Not "God the Father Almighty, maker of heaven and earth," as the Apostles' Creed puts it, but the one who was so much like the Father that he could say to his disciples, "Whoever has seen me has seen the Father" (14:9), and to his opponents, "The Father and I are one" (10:30). The one whom the Nicene Creed insists was "true God from true God" was dead, and no doubt something of God had died with him. We call it Holy Saturday, and much of its holiness certainly is derived from that trembling mystery.

This day provides the congregation an opportunity to come together in its shared grief in a way that is rare in the church. Occasionally someone who is well known and well loved by the entire congregation will die, or the sudden and tragic death of a teenager will pull the community together, but here is an opportunity for all of us to grieve the death of our friend, our Lord, our dearly beloved Jesus.

It may be wise to follow John's lead in this matter—to keep silence, to utter not a word. We might offer to our congregations the opportunity to come to church throughout the day on Holy Saturday and spend some time sitting in the cool, dark, empty sanctuary, reflecting on what it would mean to live in a world without God in it. I remember the community Good Friday service I attended early in my ministry, where the intense young Methodist minister stripped the altar, turned off all the lights, and shouted in the darkness, "Go home and weep; your Lord is dead!" I remember how it felt to stumble out of church on that night with that bleak statement still ringing in my ears, that shocking concept still throbbing in my brain. How would it feel to our congregations to spend Holy Saturday in silent contemplation of the idea that God has died?

Or, instead of silence, we might offer to hold a memorial service in which every participant is encouraged to say a few words. Imagine the poignancy of one person after another rising from the pew to say, "What I loved most about Jesus was . . ." or "What I will never forget about him is . . ." Imagine the way it might bring the death of Jesus home to hold his funeral, to give him a decent burial, as those women wanted to when they came to the tomb on the first day of the week, wondering who would roll away the stone. Without letting the occasion become maudlin or tacky, what would it be like to gather as we do for any other funeral? Why

Exegetical Perspective

and his community were less concerned than others in fending off accusations that the tomb was found empty for reasons simpler than Jesus' resurrection: that the women went to the wrong grave, for instance, or that the body was stolen (esp. Matt. 27:62–66).

Nevertheless, John develops other details. Most obvious is reference to Joseph's "fear of the Jews" (19:38), a recurring theme in this Gospel (7:13; 9:22; 20:19). As Luke clearly knows (23:50), Joseph himself is Jewish, as are the Galileans in John 7:1–13 and Jesus' own disciples in 20:19–23. The term "the Jews" is John's shorthand for authoritative Pharisees and Sadducees who oppose Jesus because he has acted and spoken as though "equal with God" (5:15–18). Those Jews in John who believe in Jesus fear the consequences of openly expressing their faith (7:10–13; 9:18–23; 16:1–4a). While John does not describe him as an influential person, Joseph of Arimathea is among those fearful disciples of Jesus who have kept their allegiance a secret (12:42–43). Here (19:39) Joseph is joined by Nicodemus, whom we meet only in John: a Pharisaic Jewish authority who earlier had paid a night visit to Jesus and had professed him "a teacher . . . come from God," as suggested by the signs Jesus had done (3:1–2).

The position of Joseph and Nicodemus in this Gospel is obscure. On the one hand, they have been drawn together and to Jesus by his death (see 12:31–33), giving the teacher's body an appropriate burial (19:40b, 42). On the other hand, Nicodemus had been left "in the dark" by Jesus (3:3–10; 19:39: "by night"), while only now does Joseph appear, covertly conducting his negotiation with Pilate (19:38). The penumbra occupied by the figures—notable in a Gospel that associates faith with "coming to the light" and unbelief with "love of the dark" (3:17–21)—is captured in their embalming technique, which is equally ambiguous. Although a Roman pound (*litra*) weighed less than that used by modern Americans (11.5 versus 16 ounces), 1,600 ounces of blended myrrh and aloes is excessive preservative for the remains of a single person. It could be that they are offering Jesus a burial fit for the king that he is (1:49; 12:13, 15; 18:33, 37, 39; 19:3, 14–15, 19). On the other hand, by his own testimony, Jesus' kingship is not of this world (18:36). A hundred pounds of burial mixture could suggest lack of comprehension or belief that Jesus and his disciples will be raised from death (2:19, 22; 5:21; 6:39–40, 44, 54; 21:14).

Homiletical Perspective

As I read this account, I am reminded of the way in which my friend Lucy was lovingly anointed for burial after her death some years ago. After a long battle with cancer she died at home—as was her desire. As soon as the word of her passing reached them, her friends began gathering around her bed, patting her cold hands, closing her eyelids, washing her body, and anointing it with oils, before its departure to the funeral home. As the ambulance crew carried Lucy's body away, her friends stood around her empty bed singing "I'll Fly Away."

Caring for the body in this personal way at the time of death is a rare thing in our twenty-first-century culture, where usually the funeral home performs these tasks. In John's Gospel, though, we gain a glimpse into a different era, when anointing the body and providing for a burial place were tangible, personal ways in which to express love for a departed friend. Yet the surprising thing here is that it is *not* the women, nor any of the Twelve, who undertake this task. It is instead two fearful, cowardly, and formerly "secret" disciples (both of them also well-respected religious and community leaders), who somehow—through Jesus' horrific death—gain the courage to come forward, to petition Pilate for Jesus' body, and to declare openly their affection for Jesus in this tangible way.

Fred Craddock suggests that there are two ways to view this act on the part of Joseph and Nicodemus:

> Cynics read the paragraph and observe that many sponsors arrive on the scene after the battle is over. Disciples, not caretakers, are the need of the hour. More generous readers find occasion here to celebrate. In his death, they say, Jesus continues to draw to himself persons who had formerly been hesitant and unbelieving. Had Jesus not said as much when speaking of the cross: in death I will draw all people to myself?[2]

Perhaps, then, Holy Saturday is a day for cowards: a day for those who have been timid and scared to confess the fledgling faith within them, for fear of being ridiculed or falsely judged—and a day for the coward within all of us that has been silent when we should have spoken and immobile when we should have acted. As Craddock indicates, Jesus foretold earlier in this Gospel that even in his death he would draw all people unto himself (12:32). Here, in this act of devotion on the part of Joseph and

2. Fred B. Craddock, *John*, Knox Preaching Guides, ed. John H. Hayes (Atlanta; John Knox Press, 1982), 140.

John 19:38-42

Theological Perspective

you except Jesus Christ, and him crucified" (1 Cor. 2:2). Lutheran scholars of the sixteenth and seventeenth centuries who followed Luther found Calvin's Christology too close to what Luther called a "theology of glory" that failed to proclaim the scandal of the theology of the cross.

In a profound way, John's Gospel warrants both Calvin's conviction of the majesty of the Word of God and Luther's conviction that the incarnation of the Word of God must be understood under the cross of Christ. In proclaiming the gospel in these times, preachers and educators face the challenge of addressing both the "deniers of God" in late modern scientism and the "defenders of God" who are radical traditionalists. Could a Christian theology grounded in John's witness to the mighty Logos become flesh that washes the disciples' feet before being arrested, tried, convicted, and crucified propose a third way between modern atheisms and theisms?

In his doctrine of God, Eberhard Jüngel argues that the gospel of Jesus Christ brings life and death into union under the sign of the cross. This union transforms the very meaning of divinity.[3] In the dispute between traditional theisms and modern forms of atheism, our assumptions about the meaning of the word "God" as a concept and a name must stand under the sign of death and life, darkness and light, the cross of Christ and the mighty Word of God: "I am the good shepherd. The good shepherd lays down his life for the sheep" (John 10:11). In the figure of the Word made flesh who creates all things, washes our feet, lays down his life, and takes up new resurrection life, there is a *Theos*, a God yet unknown to many among the skeptics and defenders of God in the world. Our proclamation and teaching must testify to this *Theos* with the courage of Joseph of Arimathea and Nicodemus, who buried the body of the crucified Jesus.

ROBERT A. CATHEY

Pastoral Perspective

not play the best music we can offer and sing the most hope-filled hymns? If there should be a homily to go along with the eulogies, then let the preacher remind the congregation of how Jesus warned his disciples that he would fall into the hands of sinful men, suffer, and die, but on the third day be raised. If he was right about the first part of that equation, could he not also be right about the second part? How would it feel to walk out of church on Holy Saturday considering that possibility, putting on your hat and buttoning up your raincoat against the weather? Might it not be the perfect minor-key prelude to the major-key hymns of resurrection that will follow on Easter Sunday?

We might choose not to offer any formal services at all, but rather to encourage our parishioners to acknowledge the death of Jesus in the way that seems most appropriate to each of them. I asked my wife, whose father died a few years ago, what she and her family did on the day after he died. She paused long enough to remember and then said, "We went to the funeral home. We picked out the clothes he would wear. We made plans for the funeral service. We welcomed friends and neighbors." Then she paused again before saying, "We wept. Mostly, we just wept."

Holy Saturday is a day for tears.

Is there any eulogy more eloquent than that?

JIM GREEN SOMERVILLE

---

3. Eberhard Jüngel, *God as the Mystery of the World*, trans. Darrell Gruder (Grand Rapids: Eerdmans, 1983), 184–225, 299–396.

Exegetical Perspective

While agreeing with Luke (23:53) that Jesus' remains were put in a tomb where no other body had ever been buried, John alone notes that the grave was new, or fresh (*kainon*, 19:41). Though left undeveloped, this detail chimes with some others in this Gospel. The commandment Jesus gives his disciples on the eve of his death is equally new (*kainēn*: 13:34). The hour of the Son's glorification by the Father has been described as the falling of a grain of wheat into the earth, a death that bears much fruit (12:23–24). Fruit is found in gardens; John alone locates Jesus' fresh grave in a garden (19:41; cf. 20:15). In any case Jesus' grave will not be like that of Lazarus, who was called out of one tomb only to enter another (11:43; 12:9–10).

C. CLIFTON BLACK

Homiletical Perspective

Nicodemus, we see that indeed it is never too late to come to Jesus. His arms of grace and welcome are open to all—even in his death.

Yet given that Holy Saturday is also a day on which some churches reenact that ancient practice of the great Easter Vigil—with its recounting of the redemptive acts of God throughout history, and its culmination in the baptism of those who are openly and publicly professing their faith in Christ—it is also highly possible to see in this act of Joseph and Nicodemus their own inauguration into a new life that will never again be the same. Like those catechumens who will go through the waters of baptism on Easter Eve and become united with Jesus in his death (the baptismal font becoming for them both a tomb of burial and a womb of rebirth), Joseph and Nicodemus have now been united with Jesus in his death, as they have witnessed firsthand his own sacrificial outpouring of love for them on a cross.[3] Chances are good that it has changed them forever. They can no longer hold to a secret and uncertain faith; they must profess it openly. They can no longer hold that faith is simply a manner of private inner conviction; they must somehow engage in the same kinds of public acts Jesus engaged in. They can no longer keep their distance and avoid getting their hands dirty; they must jump with both feet into the waters of cleansing and redemption—following their hearts and Jesus' own Spirit wherever it may lead them.

It is an in-between and all-too-quiet time, this Holy Saturday. A time of waiting and watching and mourning and praying. A time of sitting with the dead, holding their cold bodies, and anointing them for burial. A time when all is still and death seems to have the last word, but even now the seeds of new life are being planted. Soon we will see them blossom in all their Easter extravagance.

LEONORA TUBBS TISDALE

3. When Nicodemus first came to Jesus by night, Jesus told him that unless he was born of water and the Spirit, he would not be able to enter the kingdom of God (John 3:5)

Exodus 14:10-31; 15:20-21

¹⁰As Pharaoh drew near, the Israelites looked back, and there were the Egyptians advancing on them. In great fear the Israelites cried out to the Lord. ¹¹They said to Moses, "Was it because there were no graves in Egypt that you have taken us away to die in the wilderness? What have you done to us, bringing us out of Egypt? ¹²Is this not the very thing we told you in Egypt, 'Let us alone and let us serve the Egyptians'? For it would have been better for us to serve the Egyptians than to die in the wilderness." ¹³But Moses said to the people, "Do not be afraid, stand firm, and see the deliverance that the Lord will accomplish for you today; for the Egyptians whom you see today you shall never see again. ¹⁴The Lord will fight for you, and you have only to keep still."

¹⁵Then the Lord said to Moses, "Why do you cry out to me? Tell the Israelites to go forward. ¹⁶But you lift up your staff, and stretch out your hand over the sea and divide it, that the Israelites may go into the sea on dry ground. ¹⁷Then I will harden the hearts of the Egyptians so that they will go in after them; and so I will gain glory for myself over Pharaoh and all his army, his chariots, and his chariot drivers. ¹⁸And the Egyptians shall know that I am the Lord, when I have gained glory for myself over Pharaoh, his chariots, and his chariot drivers."

¹⁹The angel of God who was going before the Israelite army moved and went behind them; and the pillar of cloud moved from in front of them and took its place behind them. ²⁰It came between the army of Egypt and the army of Israel. And so the cloud was there with the darkness, and it lit up the night; one did not come near the other all night.

²¹Then Moses stretched out his hand over the sea. The Lord drove the sea back by a strong east wind all night, and turned the sea into dry land; and the waters

Theological Perspective

Take note of the last two verses of this reading. Miriam the prophet exalts the Lord, for God destroyed those who enslaved the Israelites. There is no stronger image of liberation: women glorify God for God's liberative action for the weak and vulnerable. Exuberant and joyful sound, voice, and dancing celebrate God's triumph over evil. Evil, represented in the exploitative Egyptians, and particularly in Pharaoh's easily hardened heart (Exod. 14:8), are overtaken by the waters of the Red Sea in a cosmic battle of titans.

How can we praise God for the destruction of others? This text has frequently been used as an argument against the liberation of those who are oppressed. Under the assumption that the oppressed will be as cruel as the oppressors, many Christians have kept silent when significant political and economic transitions affect our daily lives. One assumption has been that our sinful condition, which overwhelms all of humanity, prevents any change, because ultimately those changes are made by people and therefore flawed. In other words, there will always be an oppressor and an oppressed. In the debates surrounding the abolishment of apartheid in South Africa, many Christians condemned the

Pastoral Perspective

There is an old Hasidic interpretation of this story. The Hebrew children are dancing under Miriam's leadership on the far bank of the Red Sea while the Egyptian army and chariots are being "drownded," as the spiritual names their dreadful end. However, in the rabbis' story, the scene is in heaven. All the angels stand near the throne of YHWH and peer down on the action below. When they see the chosen people moving out of the sea that is closing in on the Egyptian military, when they see the people rejoicing (who had been murmuring against God and Moses in fear just hours before), the angels begin their own dance of rejoicing, playing harps, and singing. "Wait," says one of them, "the Creator of the universe is sitting there weeping!" They go to God. "Why are you weeping when Israel has been delivered by your power?" "I am weeping," says the Creator of the universe, "for the dead Egyptians washed on the shore are somebody's sons, somebody's husbands, somebody's fathers."[1]

That story captures, especially at Easter, the problem with this text in the Western or northern

1. Albert C. Winn, "A Way Out of No Way: Exodus 14:5–31," *Journal for Preachers* 14, no. 1 (Advent 1990): 14–18.

were divided. ^{22}The Israelites went into the sea on dry ground, the waters forming a wall for them on their right and on their left. ^{23}The Egyptians pursued, and went into the sea after them, all of Pharaoh's horses, chariots, and chariot drivers. ^{24}At the morning watch the Lord in the pillar of fire and cloud looked down upon the Egyptian army, and threw the Egyptian army into panic. ^{25}He clogged their chariot wheels so that they turned with difficulty. The Egyptians said, "Let us flee from the Israelites, for the Lord is fighting for them against Egypt."

^{26}Then the Lord said to Moses, "Stretch out your hand over the sea, so that the water may come back upon the Egyptians, upon their chariots and chariot drivers." ^{27}So Moses stretched out his hand over the sea, and at dawn the sea returned to its normal depth. As the Egyptians fled before it, the Lord tossed the Egyptians into the sea. ^{28}The waters returned and covered the chariots and the chariot drivers, the entire army of Pharaoh that had followed them into the sea; not one of them remained. ^{29}But the Israelites walked on dry ground through the sea, the waters forming a wall for them on their right and on their left.

^{30}Thus the Lord saved Israel that day from the Egyptians; and Israel saw the Egyptians dead on the seashore. ^{31}Israel saw the great work that the Lord did against the Egyptians. So the people feared the Lord and believed in the Lord and in his servant Moses. . . .

$^{15:20}$Then the prophet Miriam, Aaron's sister, took a tambourine in her hand; and all the women went out after her with tambourines and with dancing. ^{21}And Miriam sang to them:

"Sing to the Lord, for he has triumphed gloriously;
horse and rider he has thrown into the sea."

Exegetical Perspective

The connection of the crossing of the Red Sea with the Easter Vigil is an appropriate one. Just as the death and resurrection of Christ Jesus is the central saving act in the NT, so the crossing of the Red Sea is the main salvific event in the OT. God's actions at that crossing are mentioned throughout the OT, particularly in Israel's hymns of praise (Pss. 78:13, 106:7–11, 114:1–8, 136:13–15).

The narrative in Exodus 14:10–31 is composite, comprising both Priestly (P) and non-Priestly (J) materials. The two stories differ in their details. In the P account, God divides the waters and allows the Israelites to pass through, but afterwards brings the waters crashing back down on the pursuing Egyptians. In the non-Priestly passages, the pillar of cloud protects the Israelites, while an east wind turns the sea into dry ground. In the morning, YHWH throws the Egyptian army into a panic and brings the waters back down upon them. The Israelites remain passive in the non-Priestly version and do not pass through the sea. These two stories have been knit together in such a way as to prevent any clear recon- struction of the events. Instead of a photograph, we are presented with an impressionistic painting of

Homiletical Perspective

Of the several Old Testament readings available for the Easter Vigil, this is the one lesson that is mandated in most liturgies for the service. Hearing this text in the darkness of a church at the Easter Vigil is an occasion for a congregation to engage a crucial portion of Scripture in an environment that provokes fear, wonder, and mystery.

Fear of the advancing army of Pharaoh is the reason for the Israelites' bitter complaint to Moses in 14:11: "Was it because there were no graves in Egypt that you have taken us away to die in the wilderness?" Moses will later become well acquainted with Israelite complaint about lack of water (15:24), lack of food (16:3), and lack of tasty food (Num. 11:5–6). However, here the Israelites stand in fear that they are about to be killed by the army of their Egyptian masters. "In great fear the Israelites cried out to the Lord" (Exod. 14:10b). Terror is not too strong a word for the potential brutality and ruthlessness that could be meted out by the forces of Pharaoh, under whom the people and their ancestors that labored as slaves for generations. These unarmed fugitives now feel a most intense "buyer's remorse." Why did we ever listen to this

Exodus 14:10-31; 15:20-21

Theological Perspective

apartheid system but did not engage and participate in processes to end it. While apartheid was sinful, they believed that no other system could redeem the situation. Ultimately many Christians spoke no words of condemnation and took no prophetic action, for fear of a new oppressive system.

Fear is a force to be reckoned with in this text. On the one hand, the Israelites fear for their lives, raising questions that in the end point to their fear of liberation: "for it would have been better for us to serve the Egyptians than to die in the wilderness" (v. 12b). The text suggests that the fear of the Israelites also comes from the shattering of the shackles of their slavery. The challenges of a new journey are further complicated by the desire of the oppressor not only to gain back what has been lost but also to destroy it. Fear overtakes the Israelites to the point of despair.

On the other hand, verses 5–9 suggest that Pharaoh fears losing what he controls. The question, "What have we done, letting Israel leave our service?" (v. 5b) reveals the sudden recognition that his power over the Israelites has been canceled by God's liberation of God's people. The only choice he has, regretfully, is to destroy the Israelites, "who were going out boldly" (v. 8b). The Israelites' departure becomes a spit in the face of Pharaoh. The text is clear: "the LORD hardened the heart of Pharaoh king of Egypt and he pursued the Israelites" (v. 8a). We are left with the question, did God give Pharaoh any other choice? Moreover, we are left with a problem. How should we act when we lose power, privilege, and comfort for the sake of the liberation of others? Are we given a choice?

While the Egyptians' fear gets them moving to destroy, the Israelites' fear paralyzes them. Moses's faith calls the Israelites not to fear, and to see the deliverance of God. Yet God's words to Moses seem to claim a stronger vision. God asks, "Why do you cry out to me? Tell the Israelites to go forward" (v. 15). Just as God has walked with the Israelites in the desert, God's deliverance is coming. Despite their fear of death, the Israelites are called to move on, to move on faith for liberation and new life. God is fearless in acting on behalf of the Israelites, and expects the Israelites to do the same.

Perhaps we get an insight if we see this battle as a cosmic confrontation between Pharaoh and God, keeping in mind that in the Egyptian religious worldview Pharaoh is also a human-divine being. This battle is between one who dominates and exploits and one who protects and liberates. God's hardening Pharaoh's heart is a suggestive indication

Pastoral Perspective

church. However we expose the gospel and grace in this wonderful story—associated with the Easter festival from antiquity—we need to avoid any note of triumph, any hint that we (the church as the "new" chosen people) are the good guys and the Egyptians (read Arabs, Islamic terrorists) are the bad guys. It is sufficient to recognize that the ancient Egyptians were oppressive overlords and Pharaoh was a genocidal, paranoid ruler who—as all the exegesis on this text unveils—was in a contest with YHWH for glory: "The Egyptians shall know that I am the LORD, when I have gained glory for myself over Pharaoh, his chariots, and his chariot drivers" (14:18).

Neither may we come across as neutral in the face of the violent upheavals all around us, the constancy of arrogance and death, and the use of religion (not only by Islamic terrorists, but by American generals) to justify the battles in which we engage. There is no justice in suicide bombers in Israel or the use of domestic airplanes as weapons, just as there is no justice in the unprovoked invasion of another sovereign nation by the most powerful nation on earth. (If this analysis seems too political, remember that this text is outrageously public/political, affirming the hand of YHWH in the affairs of nations for providential, salvific purposes.)

Having acknowledged the difficulties in interpretation at this particular moment in world history—and because it is Easter—we may approach this text in order to affirm God's triumph in the redemption of Israel, and God's defeat of death in the cross and resurrection of Jesus Christ.

It is, after all, God's triumph over Pharaoh when the Israelites are saved. Miriam recognizes it as such in her song as the women join in with tambourines and dancing and hear her proclaim: "Sing to the LORD, for he has triumphed gloriously; horse and rider he has thrown into the sea" (15:21).

The slaves did not "take up arms against a sea of trouble" (from Hamlet's "to be or not to be" soliloquy). God heard their groaning under Egyptian injustice and sent Moses to ask for their deliverance. With the continued hardening of the ruler's heart, it finally took violence—the death of all the firstborn in Egypt, and the washing away of Egypt's military might—to accomplish God's purpose in the redemption of Israel. However that redemption is sheer gift and grace. "Faith does not assert claims; faith receives [an] undeserved gift." "If we are full of ourselves complaining about what we deserve and do not deserve" (and are full of ourselves claiming to be a special nation, better than all other nations,

what happened.[1] What shines through clearly in both versions—as well as in the composite text—is God's mighty work in saving the Israelites.

The appointed reading opens with the Egyptian army pursuing the Israelites, a situation that has been established in 14:1–10. Pharaoh has decided that the Egyptians cannot afford to lose their labor force (14:5 [J]) because God has hardened the king's heart (14:4 [P]). The location where the Egyptians catch up with the Israelites is unclear. The text calls the body of water the Sea of Reeds (Heb. *yam suf*), which refers either to the Red Sea or to one of the Bitter Lakes, a chain of small lakes stretching north from the Gulf of Suez. The presence of place names such as Pi-hahiroth, Migdol, and Baal-zephon (14:2) do not give clues to the location of the sea, as the sites for these cities have never been determined with any confidence.

As the reading opens in 14:10, the Israelites look up and see the approach of the Egyptian army. Beginning a pattern that becomes the norm for the wilderness period, the Israelites cry out to YHWH and to Moses (cf. Exod. 16:2; 17:2; Num. 11:1; 14:1–2; 20:2). They accuse Moses of bringing them into the desert to die. They claim that this is why they told Moses to leave them alone while they were still in Egypt. Although there is no account of this exact complaint in preceding chapters, it may be a reference to passages such as 5:20–21 and 6:9. Moses responds to the people by telling them to stand firm (14:13). They need merely to keep still, for YHWH will fight for them (14:14). In a play on words, he tells them they should not fear (Heb. *yara'*) because they will see (Heb. *ra'ah*) their deliverance.

With 14:15, the text switches from non-Priestly to Priestly material. Because of the way the two stories have been combined, the command in 14:15 seems to contradict the one given in the previous verses. Now the Israelites are no longer told to stand firm and keep quiet; instead, they are to move out. Moses is instructed to raise his staff over the sea and divide it so the Israelites may go through on dry land. In the dividing of the waters and the appearance of dry land, the text seems to echo the creation account in Genesis 1. With the parting of the Red Sea and the salvation of the Israelites, God is creating a new people who will be God's own.

Although God acts to save the people, this is not the primary goal. Instead, the events at the Red Sea

man Moses? Better to live as slaves in Egypt than to die in the wilderness.

However, slavery and death are not the only alternatives. God has another plan. In a foundational text of Israel's very existence—the exodus—Christians find their most profound foretaste of the message and movement of the Easter Vigil "on this most holy night, when our Savior Jesus Christ passed from death to life."[1] As the crossing of the Red Sea marked Israel's passage from slavery in Egypt to service of the true and living God, so does Christ's resurrection open the way for the Christian's journey from death to life. Radical grace is at work in this saving event. "The LORD will fight for you, and you have only to keep still" (14:14). Many people, whose belief and practice are that salvation is earned, do not find it easy to hear this message. God can make a way when there is no way.

Light and darkness also combine in eerie fashion here. The pillar of cloud, which is an emblem of the living presence of God, moves from in front of the Israelites to behind them so that it comes between the Israelites and the Egyptians. This cloud seems to be an agent of protection, keeping the two peoples invisible to each other all night. Yet it is also said that the cloud "lit up the night" (14:20b). This "luminous darkness" has been spoken of at least as far back as the fourth-century bishop Gregory of Nyssa and served as the title for Howard Thurman's 1965 book, *Luminous Darkness: A Personal Interpretation of the Anatomy of Segregation and the Ground of Hope.* Here too the "segregation" of the Israelites and the Egyptians caused by the cloud, which both darkened and lit up the night, served as prelude to the ground of hope that the Israelites were about to receive.

There is nothing to be gained by seeking natural explanations by which a certain wind blowing a certain way at a certain time of year might expose a portion of more or less dry ground in an already shallow Sea of Reeds. The account states clearly that God caused a strong east wind to blow all night and that it divided the waters such that the waters were a wall for the Israelites to their left and right, just as Cecil B. DeMille portrayed it in his 1956 movie *The Ten Commandments.* "The LORD will fight for you, and you have only to keep still." Let us accept and receive the miracle and the mystery.

The final portion of Exodus 14 is troubling. The soldiers of Pharaoh drown when the wall of water

1. Terence E. Fretheim, *Exodus*, Interpretation series (Louisville, KY: John Knox Press, 1991), 152.

1. *Book of Common Worship* (Louisville, KY: Westminster/John Knox Press, 1993), 297.

Exodus 14:10-31; 15:20-21

Theological Perspective

of God's power over another divine figure. God works behind the scenes on Pharaoh—God's fearless actions for the liberation of the Israelites are to be seen not only in the earthly miracles, but in the subtle ways in which God works on the evildoer. Ironically, the subtle ways in this text push Pharaoh to more violence against the Israelites and limit his choices, but this is exactly the purpose of God. In the cosmic battle, God has restricted Pharaoh's choices to violence and death.

Perhaps we are called to imagine the complexity of a God who is on the side of the persecuted and who knows how obsession with power and profit prevents justice and liberation. Moreover, this text provides a window for us to evaluate where we stand in relation to dramatic transitions in the political and economic lives of our communities. As opposed to Pharaoh, we have choices, and we can choose to be with the God who protects and liberates in any transition.

The legal and constitutional character of South Africa was abolished. A new South Africa was born. While South Africa continues to face cultural, economic, political, and social challenges, the prophetic actions in its history of abolishing apartheid remind us of the boldness of those who struggled for liberation. There is no doubt that liberation gave way to complex situations of tension and reconciliation. Liberation from apartheid—racism—fueled the possibilities of redeeming a people who lived under an oppressive system. Without liberation, reconciliation would have been impossible. Reconciliation continues to be the agenda of God for those who experience fear in the midst of change.

CARLOS F. CARDOZA-ORLANDI

Pastoral Perspective

innocent and good) then "there is no room in our hearts to receive the gift." [2]

Whatever else this text proclaims, it is certain that, in the words of Miriam, the events are to be interpreted as gift, as grace to be received and rejoiced in. The rescue from slavery and death, however, does not derive from Israel's deserving or any claim she puts forward to be God's partner in the defense of liberty and freedom. "For freedom Christ has set us free," therefore, we do not resort to the un-freedom that makes arrogant claims for ourselves, our deserving, our power, or our partnership with God's purpose in saving the world.

Humility is the watchword of this text—in all its jubilation—just as surely as humility is the keynote of the Easter Vigil, when we reflect upon the great gift of Jesus' resurrection. That new life is unasked for and unaided by human design or pretension; it is God's sheer grace, not only for Christians, but for the whole cosmos.

The Easter Vigil invites us "to read and mark in Holy Scripture the record of the wondrous victory whereby death is conquered and life and immortality are brought to light. But first let us pray for the needs of the whole world, and in especial for peace among the nations." So begins a 1952 Scottish prayer book service of lessons and carols for Easter Evening that captures the universal theme of God's mightiest act in raising Jesus from death. So too does the prayer that follows this Exodus lection in the *Book of Common Worship*: "[may this be] a sign for us of the deliverance of all nations through the grace of baptism. Grant that all the peoples of the earth may be numbered among the offspring of Abraham and rejoice in the inheritance of Israel,"[3] until there are no more tears on the face of YHWH over the death of humankind.

O. BENJAMIN SPARKS

2. Richard John Neuhaus, in *God with Us: Rediscovering the Meaning of Christmas*, ed. Greg Pennoyer and Gregory Wolfe (Brewster, MA: Paraclete Press, 2007), 21.
3. *Book of Common Worship* (Louisville, KY: Westminster John Knox Press, 1993), 30.

are the culmination of God's purposes begun when Moses first approached Pharaoh. In Exodus 5:2, Pharaoh says he does not know YHWH, and therefore he will not listen to Moses's demands. Now, in 14:17–18, the Egyptians will find out that YHWH is God (Exod. 6:7, 7:5). In this act, God will be glorified over the Egyptians.

In 14:19–20, the pillar of cloud moves between the Israelites and the Egyptians, preventing the Egyptians from overtaking their former slaves. Moses stretches out his hand, and God sends a strong wind to drive back the waters during the night. The Israelites pass through the sea on dry land. The Egyptians pursue them, but as morning breaks, God looks down from the pillar and throws the Egyptian army into confusion. It is unclear precisely what happens to their chariot wheels (14:25). Various interpreters have suggested they became bogged down in the mud, locked up, or broke off their axles. Regardless of the details, the Egyptians are forced to turn and flee. Moses stretches out his hand again and the waters return, drowning the Egyptians (14:26–28).

These final verses contain a number of touch points with earlier verses. In 14:14, it is said that YHWH will fight for the Israelites, a fact confessed by the Egyptians in 14:25. The Israelites are told they will never again see the Egyptians who are chasing them (14:13). The Israelites do see them one last time, dead on the shore of the sea (14:30). Whereas the reading opens with the people of Israel in fear of the Egyptians (14:10), in 14:31 they stand in reverent fear of YHWH.

The appointed reading ends with two verses from Exodus 15:20–21. These verses attribute to Miriam the Song of the Sea in Exodus 15:1b–18. The Song of the Sea is generally considered the earliest passage that describes the events at the Sea of Reeds. Miriam, who appears only in these two verses in the book of Exodus, is called the sister of Aaron, but not of Moses; this is peculiar, given that Aaron is absent in the story while Moses is the main character. As a prophet, Miriam leads the women of Israel in singing the praise of what God has done for Israel. The verse she sings is a slightly altered form of 15:1b.

KEVIN A. WILSON

falls and covers them. Images of the devastating December 26, 2004, tsunami in Indonesia may come to mind for many. People, vehicles, tree branches swirled together in danger and death. Exodus presents a strong doctrine of divine sovereignty, election, and purpose. God hardens Pharaoh's heart and then visits death upon the Egyptians for Pharaoh's intransigence here at the Red Sea, as on the night of Passover. This deadly side of the story seems to be celebrated as the passage ends and leads into the canticle called the Song of Miriam, which associates God's victory more with "horse and rider thrown into the sea" than with the Israelites' deliverance from slavery.

Jewish midrashic reflection has pondered the problem and questions the joy of the angels at the Hebrews' deliverance by picturing God weeping because "so many of my Egyptian children have perished." The sovereignty of God in the events of the exodus can at last be embraced by those who remember that the purpose of the exodus was not freedom per se, but rather that the Israelites might worship and serve God rather than Pharaoh.[2] Many Christians have found exodus a powerful metaphor for their journey of life—once enslaved by an abusive spouse or an addiction, but now set free. African-born slaves in America made the themes of Exodus the heart of their songs of faith. The liberty of the children of God is glorious, but there is always the danger that freedom becomes license and ultimately a new enslavement. "Whose service is perfect freedom?" is the question to keep on asking. God says, "Mine is."

J. MICHAEL KRECH

2. Exod. 7:16; 8:1, 20; 9:1, 13; 10:3. I am grateful to Rabbi Paul Tuchman of Congregation Or Chadash, Upper Montgomery and Lower Frederick Counties, Maryland, for this insight.

Psalm 114

¹When Israel went out from Egypt,
the house of Jacob from a people of strange language,
²Judah became God's sanctuary,
Israel his dominion.

³The sea looked and fled;
Jordan turned back.
⁴The mountains skipped like rams,
the hills like lambs.

⁵Why is it, O sea, that you flee?
O Jordan, that you turn back?
⁶O mountains, that you skip like rams?
O hills, like lambs?

⁷Tremble, O earth, at the presence of the LORD,
at the presence of the God of Jacob,
⁸who turns the rock into a pool of water,
the flint into a spring of water.

Theological Perspective

Those who hold vigils can have different kinds of experiences. Long ago, I served as a national park ranger. My work was law enforcement, and on a number of occasions I was placed in rather extreme "watchful" situations. Whether trying to outguess a human perpetrator of some inappropriate behavior or working to protect some of our four-legged creatures and people from one another, I recall many stressful vigils.

Looking at it somewhat differently, I have served as a pastor, teacher, university chaplain, and administrator since my ordination over thirty years ago. During this time I have been party to many other kinds of watchful waitings—for the teenager who has run away, for the compromised birth of a newborn, for those whose grip on life is weakening by the hour, for the bright promising student whose life is lost while on a work-study trip, for the gut-wrenching search for and eventual recovery of a body belonging to a person who was in the wrong place at the wrong time and took a bullet.

There is a kind of energetic awakened state during a vigil, often coupled with a sense that this is not a "normal" time. I suspect that it was like this for the ancient Israelites as they fled Egypt: they knew what was behind them, and they knew that if they were to have a future of promise, they needed to

Pastoral Perspective

Psalm 114 creates an evolving landscape for Easter Vigil. The visceral, violent reality of the cross and the bleak finality of the sealed tomb deliver us to a spiritually rich and transcendent moment. During the night on Holy Saturday, we begin celebrating Christ's resurrection, leaping from the physical obviousness of Good Friday to the "empty tomb equals faith" of Easter Sunday. For fear of stranding our congregants in a graveyard at night, Psalm 114 helps us discern subtle changes in the landscape as God makes a way.

As pastors, we are called to help our people discern the subtle changes between where they are and have been and where they hope to be. Through poetry, the psalmist transports us to particular places and times where Israel ached for God's presence. The natural landscapes bear the tension the Israelites experienced during their journey: in Egypt, at the Great Sea, in the wilderness, near the rock at Horeb, at the foot of Mount Sinai, and by the Jordan River.

Earlier on Holy Saturday, the people of God ached for Jesus' presence as he lay in the grave, wondering, "Where is God? God has died and we are stranded in the darkness near Jesus' tomb." Some disciples fled and hid, believing Jesus had disappointed them. His grave is an ominous, volatile, threatening place—a place of no options, a dead

Exegetical Perspective

Psalm 114 is the second of the Egyptian Hallel ("Praise") Psalms (Pss. 113–18) used at several annual feasts of Judaism: Passover, Pentecost, Sukkot (the feast of Tabernacles), and Hanukkah. They are called the *Egyptian* Hallel Psalms because they were sung while the Passover lambs were being slain in the temple. Perhaps because of this connection, Psalm 114 in particular came to be associated especially with Passover, both in the temple and at celebrations in the home. Psalms 113 and 114 are sung at the beginning of the Passover meal, and Psalms 115–18 are sung at the end of the meal (see Matt. 26:30 and Mark 14:26).

The psalm is a hymn celebrating YHWH's great acts of salvation. The psalmist, however, puts a slightly different spin on these events than we usually see. The hymn, which is really a theophany poem—that is, a poem describing God's manifestation or appearance—is divided into four sections: verses 1–2 describe the exodus and settlement in the land; verses 3–4 describe the events in cosmic terms; verses 5–6 ask questions about the actions of the sea, the Jordan, the mountains, and the hills described in verses 3–4; and verses 7–8 present the answers to those questions. Verse 4 contains a possible reference to Mount Sinai, while verse 8 alludes to the famous story of God's providing water from the rock in the wilderness

Homiletical Perspective

At the Great Vigil, the stories of the Bible and the worship of the church collapse as God's single, continuous saving activity. The church ritually joins in the exodus, "when Israel went out from Egypt, the house of Jacob from a people of strange language" (v. 1). Following the paschal candle, the pillar of fire representing the risen Christ, the church journeys from bondage and death through baptismal waters to the promised land of Christ's resurrection.

As a poetic expression of the good news that lies at the heart of the entire Bible, Psalm 114 invites the preacher to proclaim the unity of the vigil. The God of the cosmos reveals God's very self in space and time, to bring order out of chaos, speech out of silence, hope out of despair, freedom from slavery, and life from death. Just as Israel understood the return from exile as a new exodus, so Christians find in Jesus' death and resurrection another—and in fact, the ultimate—instance of God bringing God's people from death to new life.

The Easter Vigil sermon proclaims God's ongoing work, which commenced in the exodus, culminated in the death and resurrection of Christ, and continues in the life of the church, particularly as Christians are joined to Christ's death and resurrection in baptism and share Christ's life in the Lord's Supper. To proclaim this unity, the preacher

Psalm 114

Theological Perspective

leave their familiar but enslaved setting. They had very few clues as to what lay ahead, and got into quite a discussion about whether the God they said they trusted really could be counted on. Evidently enough of them felt compelled to hope that, in leaving and moving on, they would somehow come through their wilderness. So they walked into the unknown, which is what holding a vigil is all about.

Have you ever been expectantly watchful, awaiting something that is both new and deeply familiar? For many of us, the vigil period at Easter presents us with this kind of experience. We may not feel the gut-tightening energy that characterizes other kinds of vigil, perhaps because we already know how the story comes out. Our challenge is to wait as if this vigil really were new, even though the process may feel as comfortable as an old glove. The deep insight that can come to us in a vigil such as this is that God can still provide us with wonderful surprises that can change our lives for the better.

At the Easter Vigil, we are waiting for a remarkable transformation to occur, although we know that in some ways it has taken place time and again over the centuries. It is easy to lose sight of the vibrancy of this time, for its annual return sometimes causes us to treat it as formulaic. However, it is precisely this cyclical frequency that reflects the efficacy of the vigil. Despite being a regular occasion on the church calendar, it can point us to real rebirth, not only in the past, but also in the present. We prevent the vigil from being reduced to the realm of the humdrum by connecting this ecclesial and theological moment with the deep human need to be part of a bigger cycle of life, death, and rebirth—something we live in the presence of daily.

One of the most gripping memories I have of this kind of connection took place about thirty years ago. I was part of a big conference on faith, science, and the future, held at MIT, one of the world's citadels of scientific probity. Though much from those heady days has faded from my memory, I recall several things that were really life shaping and that illustrate a way to connect the psalmist's deep insight to contemporary experience.

One morning, as I was running in the predawn light, I spotted dozens—and then a couple of hundred—of people who were walking without a sound toward an immense building, My curiosity aroused, I cut my run short and followed this silent parade into the central internal corridor of this building, which ran east-west and was about a quarter-mile long. Almost immediately after entering, we were all

Pastoral Perspective

end. This impassable landscape resembles the precarious financial, physical, emotional, and relational terrains that many in our congregations inhabit. Here are the shoreline of the Great Sea with waves before us and an angry army breathing down our necks; a barren desert stretching in every direction; a heaving mountain overshadowing us; a churning river blocking our view of the good life—abundance, security, home.

This is the pastoral landscape *where we begin* Easter Vigil. This is the moment when all Christians are driven to our knees in solidarity with people who are too familiar with such threatening places. Who among us resides in them? Those who are victimized, falsely accused, overpowered, and culturally shunned call such landscape home. People who are poor, but not quite poor enough for us to help, know its shadowy ravines. People who suffer like Christ know this place. From our humble proximity, we relate to the faith story of our ancestors recalled in the psalm.

Israel is led from a familiar landscape of human oppression through unfamiliar and challenging landscapes, challenging us to translate its experience to ours. People of faith touch that cold water and look over our shoulders at the shamed and vengeful army. We sink slightly in the hot sand and realize the view looks dismal, with nothing to indicate the way. We thirst; we face the mountain of judgment. When we find ourselves in desperate, unsalvageable landscapes, we seldom ache for some unseen power. Instead, we want concrete, substantiated bridges and provisions, literal protection, and an obvious way out.

God's people sing Psalm 114 to remember that God makes a way by transforming the landscape. They sing, "The sea looked and fled" (v. 3), reminiscent of the songs Moses and Miriam sang after they crossed to the safe side of the sea (Exod. 15). They sing, "Jordan turned back" (v. 3), recalling the path made through the Jordan River for Israel; "by this you shall know that among you is the living God," proclaims Joshua (Josh. 3:10, 17). During Easter Vigil, we can guide our congregation to look back to *where we have been:* Egypt, where God was listening; the Sea, where God parted the water; the wilderness, where God provided; and Jordan, where God made good on the promise of home and hope. With this hindsight, how do we lead them forward?

We orient our congregants to the story's landscapes. The common feature of the landscapes on which the story unfolds is God. God's presence is the cosmic wedge that transforms the landscape, that

(Exod. 17:1–7; Num. 20:2–13). Thus the poem recounts many of the mighty acts of God on Israel's behalf. The text of Psalm 114 has many echoes and associations with the Song of the Sea in Exodus 15. Both focus on the foundational act of God in the formation of Israel as a people; and both focus on the connection between God's act of freeing the people and the choice of Israel as God's dwelling place.

Verse 1 opens with "When Israel went out from Egypt, the house of Jacob from a people of strange language." As many have noted, the term translated "strange language" often refers to the enemies of Israel (see, e.g., Deut. 28:49; Isa. 33:19; Jer. 5:15). Verse 2 establishes that the exodus event is linked strongly with God's choice of Judah/Israel as the dwelling place of the Divine (see also Exod. 15:17). The term "sanctuary" may refer both to the whole land of Israel as God's dwelling place and to the temple as God's particular home.

Verses 3–4 personify sea, river, mountain, and hill in order to interweave the exodus with creation themes, playing on a mythological account of creation that Israel shared with other ancient Near Eastern traditions. In this account, God (representative of order) creates the world and all that exists after a great battle with the forces of chaos, often represented by the sea, which is usually portrayed as a god in other ancient Near Eastern traditions (cf. Exod. 15:3–12; Ps. 74:12–17; Ps. 104; Job 38:8–11). Once chaos is overcome, God builds a sanctuary on top of God's chosen mountain to represent the divine dominion. In verse 3, the sea looks and flees, and the Jordan runs backward (my trans.; NRSV: "turn back"). Unlike the usual myth, in this psalm the forces of chaos do not fight; rather, they run in the opposite direction, highlighting the complete power of the God of Israel.

Scholars debate whether verse 4 is a reference to the events at Sinai. Some wish to see this psalm as a celebration of the exodus and Sinai events, while others see it as a more general celebration of all God's mighty acts on behalf of ancient Israel. In addition, the actual language, skipping "like rams" and "like lambs," is ambiguous. It could suggest that the mountains and the hills rejoice or that they quake (jump about) in terror. The questions in verses 5–6, which link the fleeing of the sea and the running away of the Jordan with the mountains' actions, tend to lean toward the latter interpretation of verse 4. In any case, verses 1–4, taken as a whole in light of the cosmogonic myth—that is, the above-referenced mythological accounts of the creation of

might pair Psalm 114's poetic allusions to the basic elements of Israel's story with elements of the Easter Vigil. In this approach, the exodus (vv. 1, 3a, 5a) might be paired with the Service of Light and God's provision in the wilderness (v. 8) with the Service of Readings. Most obviously, passing through the sea and crossing the Jordan to enter the promised land (vv. 3b, 5b) corresponds to the Service of Baptism. God choosing the people and establishing them in the land (vv. 1–2) is an intriguing way of considering the Easter Eucharist. God's grace and faithfulness hold these pairings together. In the salvation history of Israel, the cross and resurrection of Christ, and the life and ministry of the church, God chooses God's own, revealing the place of God's dwelling. The preacher might construct a sermon around any of these pairings, or the thread that connects all four.

The psalm provides the preacher words with which to describe both the movement of the vigil and God's saving activity. Verses 1–2 recall the exodus. Lighting the paschal candle, the church begins its own procession, movement, exodus. As the light of the candle pierces the darkness, it speaks of God bringing order out of chaos at creation, and the dawn of the day of resurrection. Following Christ and empowered by his resurrection, the church goes forth in freedom from oppressive powers opposed to God and their strange language, to become God's sanctuary and enter God's dominion.

Sitting through twelve readings in a darkened church can certainly feel like wandering in the wilderness for forty years. The psalm's description of God turning "the rock into a pool of water, the flint into a spring of water" (v. 8) provides a theme to unite these readings. Biblical imagination suggests that the psalmist is alluding to God sweetening the bitter water of Marah and providing water when Moses struck the rock at Horeb (Exod. 15:25; 17:6). The psalmist's description of the God who made "the flint into a spring of water" echoes Moses's description of God, "who led you through the great and terrible wilderness, . . . [and] made water flow for you from flint rock" (Deut. 8:15). While these narratives are not included in the readings this night, the theme of God providing water (refreshment, nourishment, hope, survival) in the wilderness is prominent nonetheless. Isaiah invites all who thirst to come to the water, to incline their ears and listen that they might live (Isa. 55:1–3). For Abraham, water in the wilderness takes the form of God's word, not to lay a hand on the boy or do anything to him, and a ram caught in a thicket (Gen. 22:12–13).

Psalm 114

Theological Perspective

hushed by those who had been there for some time. Directed by their hand gestures to stand with my back against the wall, I watched as the sun rose directly through the center of the glass doors at the far eastern end of the building, causing a wave of awe to run down the corridor. In the heart of one of the more rigorous centers of science in the world, I stood vigil with the members of that community as they awaited dawn on the morn of the summer solstice. They were clearly moved by the powerful experience of seeing the light of a new day—a *centering* new day, being the solstice—even though it had happened countless times before around the planet.

Thinking about it later, I realized that there was even more in play. In a way, it was as if this congregation of very bright people was showing, in a deeply engaged way, that they were willing to wait—mostly in silence, most even without a refreshing cup of coffee—until the dawning of this special day. Though I suspect that a clear majority of the people there were not making an Easter-morn connection with this moment of expectant waiting, they were there just as those of faith await the dawning of Easter, because they felt as if the wait would bear fruit to refresh, renew, and inspire them in their daily experience. Even if the women and men in that hallway were not attuned knowingly to the majesty of God's transforming presence, they were living into the biblical understanding of today's text—for they were embodying the eager and anxious moment so richly depicted by the phrase, "Tremble, O earth, at the presence of the Lord" (Ps. 114:7).

DAVID G. TRICKETT

Pastoral Perspective

opens wide the moment of certain death or utter defeat. Creation understands. Rhetorically, the psalmist asks, "Why is it, O sea, that you flee? . . . O mountains, that you skip like rams?" (vv. 5, 6). The response of these mighty features of creation reveals their obedience to one who is more powerful; they tremble.

In Psalm 114:7 everyone is given the emphatic imperative: "Tremble, O earth, at the presence of the Lord!" Trembling embodies fear and joy at God's presence, where we—members of creation, great and small—succumb to God's sovereignty. As much as we want the thing obstructing our way forward to tremble and part, the "thing" could be ourselves. Like the rest of us, the Israelites repeatedly become their own obstacle to following God's way forward. While Psalm 114 is considered a hymn of praise, we are not invited to praise. Rather, we are called to tremble, letting God work within us. Praise will come. In this instance, though, tremble! Tremble because the God of history works now in the midst of impossible challenge, because now will not last forever for an Easter God who makes a way, who provides, "who turns the rock into a pool of water, the flint into a spring of water" (v. 8).

Easter Vigil ends while it is still night. However, the dark landscape has evolved. As the church sings Psalm 114, the tremble of hope is felt underfoot. God is at work, like the subterranean shifting that constantly makes and remakes the earth. A path is made through an impassable landscape, during what seemed like a divine absence.

Do we trust God is making a way for our salvation? Or do we try to make our own way by swimming, turning back to our captivity, and settling for this side of the Jordan, while God's hope for us awaits fulfillment on the other side? Our congregations want to know, *where are we being led?* Pastors can show them that God cleaves the darkness and leads them into a place of light. They are destined for a promising landscape where God provides them with the bread of heaven and the cup of blessing. Through Psalm 114 they and we recognize the subtle changes of a graveyard—a place where death is planted—that evolves into a garden as Christ rises to life.

M. ASHLEY GRANT

Exegetical Perspective

the world—portrays the exodus events and the settlement in the land as great creative acts of God.

In verses 5–6, the poet questions the sea, river, mountains, and hills about why they behave so strangely—the sea flees, the river turns back (runs in reverse), the mountains skip like rams and the hills like lambs. Verses 7–8 contain the answer to the questions in the form of an address to the earth: lest we have missed the point, it is God's awesome power that has caused the sea and river to run in the opposite direction and the hills to jump in terror. The imperative call to "tremble" has both joyful and fearful connotations, an appropriate mixture of response to God's powerful works. That is not all though. This God is also a God of provision, as the final image of verse 8, an allusion to the wilderness story of God's provision of water from a rock, reveals (see also Num. 20:11).

Like the Passover celebration in Judaism, the Easter Vigil is a reclaiming and reactualizing (making present) of the history of salvation. Each year, participants affirm that God has brought *them* out of Egypt, that God has saved *them*. In addition, there is an "already-not yet" quality to the psalm and the celebration of Passover. The exodus event is celebrated first in Exodus 14 *before* the people are set free and before they enter the land. In Joshua 5, the Passover is the first celebration after their entry into the land, even before they have truly settled in. Psalm 114 would have been an integral part of the Passover celebration that occurred the night before Jesus' death. That fact, along with the psalm's focus on looking both backward and ahead, its concentration on making a past event present to the people reading and/or praying it, and its focus on the mighty acts of God, makes it particularly appropriate for Easter Vigil, when Christians look backward by celebrating the entire history of salvation and look forward to God's greatest act of raising Christ from the dead.

MARY E. SHIELDS

Homiletical Perspective

For Ezekiel, it is God's word of life spoken to a valley of dry bones (Ezek. 37:1–14). God's companionship provides an oasis of safety for three caught in the wilderness of a fiery furnace (Dan. 3:1–29).

Yet the psalm's most compelling description of water is not of springs but seas. The sea fled; the Jordan was driven back (v. 3). The verse is shorthand for the parting of the Red Sea, which brought God's people out of bondage, and for the crossing of the Jordan, which ushered God's people into the land of promise. Early on, the church found the meaning of baptism in these narratives, and baptismal images abound in the readings appointed for the Easter Vigil. God's chosen people pass safely through the water, while God's enemies drown. Ezekiel speaks of God bringing the people into their own land and sprinkling them with fresh water to make them clean (Ezek. 36:24–25). Jonah's sojourn in the belly of a fish is a powerful image of baptismal death and resurrection, which the New Testament reading from Romans makes plain. Paul declares that all who are baptized die with Christ, so that we might walk with Christ in newness of life (Rom. 6:3–4).

Still wet with baptismal water, the church arrives at the Lord's Table—entrance to the land of promise and first taste of the Easter life. The church comes into God's sanctuary and dominion, where Christ is present as the author of life. "The presence of the LORD, . . . the presence of the God of Jacob" (v. 7) turns the rock of human hearts into springs of living water, as surely as God transforms the church's eating and drinking into a share in the life of Christ.

The tone of the psalm, together with the spirit of the Easter Vigil, suggests that the mood of such a sermon is exuberant praise. The congregation's alleluias hardly seem big enough. Psalm 114 invites the mountains and hills to skip like lambs, and the entire earth to tremble at the presence of the Lord.

CRAIG A. SATTERLEE

Romans 6:3-11

³Do you not know that all of us who have been baptized into Christ Jesus were baptized into his death? ⁴Therefore we have been buried with him by baptism into death, so that, just as Christ was raised from the dead by the glory of the Father, so we too might walk in newness of life.

⁵For if we have been united with him in a death like his, we will certainly be united with him in a resurrection like his. ⁶We know that our old self was crucified with him so that the body of sin might be destroyed, and we might no longer be enslaved to sin. ⁷For whoever has died is freed from sin. ⁸But if we have died with Christ, we believe that we will also live with him. ⁹We know that Christ, being raised from the dead, will never die again; death no longer has dominion over him. ¹⁰The death he died, he died to sin, once for all; but the life he lives, he lives to God. ¹¹So you also must consider yourselves dead to sin and alive to God in Christ Jesus.

Theological Perspective

The events of Holy Week lead to the crucifixion of Jesus, and the text before us directs our attention to a uniquely Pauline interpretation of its meaning—an interpretation that involves Paul's understanding of baptism, the cross, and our unity with Christ. As we shall see, that unity is not only an effect of Christ's atoning work and the baptism that binds us to it, but is as well their precondition.

In his *Institutes* Calvin discusses the three classical interpretations of baptism: that it is an "initiation" (analogous to circumcision) by which we are "received into the society of the church"; that it is a sign, "a token and proof of our cleansing" from sin; and that it symbolizes our dying and rising with Christ and therefore our union with him. Of course, Calvin is anxious to distinguish his view from that of the older Catholic sacramental theology. There is here no *ex opera operato* (from the work, the work) as if the action of sprinkling with water accomplished our cleansing. Rather, he insists, there is "no other purification than through the sprinkling of Christ's blood."[1]

It is the third understanding of baptism that Paul has in mind in this passage—that by it we are united

Pastoral Perspective

I once observed a priest giving instruction—misleading and nonsensical instruction, in my opinion—to a group of parents whose babies were going to be baptized at Easter. The priest wanted to make clear that the baptism of these babies was not about cleansing them from sin. Babies were lovely and innocent, he said, proof that the church's historic teaching about sin was misguided. What the priest wanted to do, I think, was counter the notion that the church was somehow saying that the babies needed baptism because they were "bad."

Admittedly, describing babies as "bad" does not get us very far. Victorian valorization of babyhood notwithstanding, babies are not innocent, sweet, and naturally cherubic. What clearer illustration of our sinful natures is there than the willfulness of a squalling baby or an intransigent tot?

"Sin" remains an unpopular word in many of our churches, an embarrassing word, one many of us would like to edit out of the Christian lectionary. Maybe we grew up in homes where the word was wielded like a weapon, designed to prevent everything fun in our lives. Maybe we heard sin preached, but not the goodness of creation. Or maybe we grew up in a church where the concept of sin was deployed not only to keep us in line, but also to inculcate in us a certain pridefulness—we were

---

1. John Calvin, *Institutes of the Christian Religion*, ed. John T. McNeill, trans. Ford Lewis Battles (Philadelphia: Westminster Press, 1977), 4.15.1–6.

Exegetical Perspective

If God has, through Jesus Christ, already accomplished reconciliation with sinful humanity, does it
really matter anymore whether humans continue in
sin? Might it even be the case that the abundance of
God's grace is more evident amid human sinfulness?
As Paul grapples with these questions at the beginning
of Romans 6, he sets forth a tightly structured argument that describes the seismic shift in the divine-
human relationship that has taken place. For Paul to
argue merely that Christians should not sin would not
suffice. Instead he sets forth a more radical claim:
Christians no longer live under captivity to the power
of sin. God's grace, embodied in the death and
resurrection of Jesus Christ, destroys the power of sin
over those who have been baptized into Christ's death
and resurrection. Humankind is not merely rescued
from the power of sin; sin's power itself is nullified.
Paul can thus claim that those who have died with
Christ no longer continue living in sin.

Paul's argument in 6:3–11 has three movements.
In verses 3–4a, Paul recalls his audience's experience
of baptism, on the basis of which he asserts that they
have been baptized with Christ into death. While the
image of baptism plays a prominent role in Paul's
argument, it is not the central topic, as is often
supposed. Rather, Paul affirms Christian freedom
from the power of sin—freedom rooted in the

Homiletical Perspective

This text from Romans represents the avoided "big
elephant" in the commerce of the church growth
movement. As church leaders get excited about slick
packaging of the gospel and attracting a crowd, the
cost of discipleship is often ignored. After all, it is
hard to "win friends and influence people" when you
preach that death is the requirement for following
Christ. The peculiar and spooky idea of dying with
Christ flies in the face of those who view religion as
a positive mental accessory that makes them feel
good. Most Christians, let alone the unchurched, are
far from appreciating the words of Bonhoeffer,
"When Christ calls a man, he calls him to come and
die."[1] Indeed, how do preachers present the
Christian truth of death before life in a culture of
consumers where death is denied at every turn?

A colleague of mine confessed his apprehension
about preaching to his church Paul's idea of dying
and rising with Christ. He assured me that as soon as
he uttered the words "dying" or "death," he would
lose the ears of his affluent congregation. They were
a finicky crowd, he said, and he had to be careful not
to "turn them off." He then remarked with tongue in
cheek that, if forced to preach this text, he would

---

1. Dietrich Bonhoeffer, *The Cost of Discipleship*, rev. unabridged ed. (New
York: Macmillan, 1959), 79.

Romans 6:3–11   343

Romans 6:3-11

Theological Perspective

with Christ in his suffering and rising. Baptism, however, is not Paul's main interest in this passage, although he seems to invest it with an essential significance not apparent in 1 Corinthians 1:14–17. His concern is with the Christian life: "How can we who died to sin go on living in it?" To do so, he argues, is to undertake a form of existence that ought to be impossible, since it was actually overcome and removed by the cross. How was this accomplished?

We need not dwell on the three major theories of the atonement: (1) that the cross of Christ represents a compelling and therefore saving example for Christian life (the "Abelardian view"); (2) that it discloses and accomplishes a victory of God over the evil that threatens us (the so-called *Christus Victor* view); and (3) that it was a sacrifice and punishment that Christ took upon himself on our behalf (the "substitutionary view").[2] While these doctrines are not presented in the ecumenical creeds of the fourth and fifth centuries, they all find articulation in the New Testament, and the latter two especially in Paul. Accordingly, the church has generally held that all three express some necessary part of what Christ did on the cross.

In today's text, Paul presents the substitutionary view, but with a difference. Here, the emphasis is not so much upon Christ's taking our place as it is our being with him at his place on the cross, in the grave, and at the resurrection. Being "baptized . . . into his death . . . we have been buried with him." If Paul modifies these astonishing claims in verse 5, "If we have been united with him in a death *like* his, we will certainly be united with him in a resurrection *like* his," the theme continues to be our unity with Christ, whether past or future. This union with Christ provides for Paul's readers a new and quite different identity.

"If anyone is in Christ," writes Paul in 2 Corinthians 5:17, "there is a new creation." Given his assurances to the Romans in our text, we must regard the "if" as strictly rhetorical. Our being "in Christ," an oft-repeated phrase in Paul's letters, expresses not only our being drawn to Christ by way of his taking our place on the cross, but in a prior sense our possessing an identity with Christ according to his divine/human nature. We must remember that the incarnational Christologies of Nicaea and Chalcedon were explications not only of

Pastoral Perspective

sinless but those other folks down the street were not. Maybe the very concept just seems outmoded, passé. However, baptism presupposes sin. As Charles Clay, an Anglican priest in Virginia about the time of the American Revolution, said in a baptismal sermon, baptism implies a "humble" recognition that the candidate for baptism is defiled; "otherwise there would be no need of washing."[1]

Paul's words in Romans invite us to reflect on the reality of sin—and on the way baptism mysteriously transforms our relationship to sin. I have heard that in some Mexican churches, infants are carried to the baptismal font in a small casket. That sounds macabre, perhaps, but in fact it strikes me as the perfect, stark reminder of what is actually going on in this sacrament. We enter a watery grave with Jesus, and we arise alive, dead to sin.

Here Paul's use of the image of slavery is apt: baptism means that we are no longer enslaved to sin. Through the regenerating love of God and the regeneration of the waters of baptism, we have been freed to choose something else. Baptism is not a magic inoculation that somehow guarantees we will not sin—far from it. We can still choose the allurement of sin, as Paul's next words make clear: "Therefore do not let sin reign in your mortal body so that you obey its evil desires. Do not offer the parts of your body to sin, as instruments of wickedness, but rather offer yourselves to God, as those who have been brought from death to life; and offer the parts of your body to him as instruments of righteousness" (vv. 12–13 NIV). Those of us who have gone down into the watery grave with Christ still have to be wary of sin—and if precedent means anything, we may have to be even more vigilant to guard against sin. After all, when did the devil get really serious about bringing down Jesus? After his baptism, of course.

So we are free to sin, and we are free to turn from sin. When we find ourselves tricked by the devil, we can choose to turn back from sin, toward God—hence the Hebrew and Greek words for repentance, *teshuva* and *metanoia*, mean a complete turning around, a turning around that we are free to choose only because God has freed us to choose it.

Choice, of course, confers responsibility. We cannot simply look at the structural sin of our society—the poisoning of the planet, the degrading commodification of all of life—and throw up our

---

2. Cf. Gustaf Aulen's *Christus Victor* (London: SPCK, 1953) and Colin Gunton's *The Actuality of Atonement* (Edinburgh: T. & T. Clark, 1989).

1. Lauren F. Winner, *A Cheerful and Comfortable Faith: Household Religious Practice in Anglican Virginia* (New Haven, CT: Yale University Press, forthcoming).

community's complete identification with Christ's death and resurrection. Baptism is the ritual setting where this story of Christ's death and resurrection from the dead is told, enacted, and made real in the life of the community of the faithful. The second movement (vv. 4b–7) builds on this claim by extending the correlation between Jesus and Christians to include their unity in resurrection (vv. 4b–5), culminating in a series of assertions about the demise of sin: the body of sin has been destroyed (v. 6b), we are no longer enslaved to sin (v. 6c), and whoever has died is freed from sin (v. 7). The third movement (vv. 8–11) affirms that those who have died with Christ now live "with him" (v. 8) and "to God" (vv. 10, 11). Because of his resurrection, death no longer has dominion over Christ (v. 9). As Christ's death brings an end to the power of sin (v. 10), it renders Christians, like Christ, also "dead to sin" (v. 11).

Modern readers who consider sin primarily a matter of individual choice may have a hard time making sense of Paul's argument in these verses. Here, as throughout most of Paul's letters, the apostle regards sin as an alien power that, like death, exercises dominion over humankind. Fallen humanity under the domination of sin can no more choose not to sin than not to die. From Paul's perspective, both sin and death are inevitable consequences of the fall from grace. There is no path from the world of Adam, the world of sin and death, to God. However, now God has made a way to humankind through the cross and resurrection of Christ, sweeping away the wall of sin and death. Just how is this power over sin extended to Christ's followers?

Paul's logic in this passage assumes corporate identification with Christ; the experience of one, Jesus Christ, stands for the many. Paul has already argued that sin comes into the world through one man, Adam, and death through sin (5:12–14), but that, even more, the free gift of God's grace "abounds for many" through the one man, Jesus Christ (5:15–17). Paul's continued presumption of the corporate identification with Christ of those who are baptized into him is demonstrated by his persistent use in 6:3–11 of correlative prefixes and prepositions. Those who have been baptized into Christ have been, literally, "co-buried with him" (v. 4), united with him (as flesh grows together when a wound heals) in both death and resurrection (v. 5), and "co-crucified with him" (v. 6). They have "died with Christ," and will also "live with him" (v. 8). Paul's argument thus presumes an essential, organic unity between Christ and his followers, first

ignore all the parts about death and focus on resurrection. Candidly, this is the way many preachers would handle this text, but it is not yet Easter, and there is still a cross to bear.

A faithful preacher cannot avoid lifting up death as the prerequisite to life. The gospel is clear that in order to find life we must lose it. There is no resurrection without crucifixion. This is the message of the cross, but it is lost on many who would follow Christ. Most look at the cross and immediately think of forgiveness, redemption, resurrection, and rightfully so, but there are few who gaze at the cross and come to the profound conclusion that to be a disciple one must die with Christ.

On Sundays most preachers look over a crowd that seeks Jesus for the perks and benefits. They want to be on the hopeful side of things. They desire good morals and values for their family, and they want someone powerful they can pray to when they need help or a miracle. They also want good insurance for when they take their last breath. Surely there is nothing wrong with any of these things, but they ignore the essence of Christian discipleship.

How does a preacher effectively communicate the halting idea of dying and rising with Christ in our comfortable, self-indulgent culture? Perhaps it would be good to begin by describing those common but important experiences in life that require sacrifice. Take marriage, for example. The glowing bride and excited groom stand before the minister at the altar and both of them have grandiose thoughts about how the other will make them happy. They pay little attention to the minister who is saying, "Marriage is not to be entered unto unadvisedly, but reverently, discreetly, and in the fear of God." The bride and groom are oblivious when the minister asks them to repeat the words "for better, for worse, for richer, for poorer, in sickness and in health." However, sooner or later, one of them disappoints the other by not living up to expectations, and real marriage begins. One of them gets sick or disabled, and real love and commitment are required. The illusions of marriage die, and the joy of faithful commitment is born.

Perhaps the same couple decides to have children. They think about little people that look just like them. They think of giggles and bubblegum breath. They think of Christmas and ball games and ballet classes. They think of their need of being needed. Then children come, and the real sacrifice of parenthood is required. They get up in the middle of the night with a crying baby. They lose sleep. Their children develop minds of their own, talk back, and

Romans 6:3-11

Theological Perspective

the Logos theology of John 1, but of Paul's understanding of Jesus, to which John was heir.

For Paul, Jesus Christ was "the image of the invisible God. . . . in him all the fullness of God was pleased to dwell. . . . he is before all things . . . [and] in him all things . . . have been created" (Col. 1:15–19)—and those attributes belong to his divine-*human* nature. For this reason Paul in Romans 5 sees the humanity of Christ as prior and superior to the humanity of Adam: "For if the many died through the one man's trespass, much more . . . [has] the grace of the one man, Jesus Christ, abounded for the many" (5:15). It is in Christ and not in Adam that the nature of every human being is established. When Paul speaks of our unity with Christ on the cross, he thinks not only of the reconciliation there achieved, but also of the way in which human beings have always been defined by Jesus Christ. We are who we really are "in him."

This theme was taken up with great power by Karl Barth in the later volumes of his *Church Dogmatics*, where he views the "real" reality of human life in the light of Christ. "There in the eternity of the divine counsel which is the meaning and basis of all creation . . . the decision was made who and what true man is. There his constitution was fixed and sealed once for all. . . . No man can elude this prototype. We derive wholly from Jesus not merely in our potential and actual relation to God, but even our human nature as such."[3]

If we have "died to sin," if we are "baptized into his death," and "united with him in a death like his," this can mean only that, despite the illusions, the so-called facts, by which we try to live and define ourselves and so "continue in sin," we are inseparably bound to the man on the cross. We are there in and with him, because he is, was, and ever will be, in us. "So [we] also must consider [ourselves] dead to sin and alive to God in Christ Jesus" (6:11).

ALEXANDER J. MCKELWAY

Pastoral Perspective

hands in defeat. Instead, we can choose to participate in that sin or to fight it. Too often, by our passivity, we make the wrong choice.

This, it seems to me, is one of the more concrete ways of expressing the good news of Easter. Easter is not about Jesus' triumphing over death in some abstract way. The blessing and the responsibility of Easter is that right here and now, today and tomorrow, we have been freed to choose. When we close this book, when we walk out of church Sunday afternoon, when we get home at the end of a long day—in all of those places we are no longer inevitably bound to sin. We can choose to turn toward God.

Just what is it we reject when we reject sin? And what is it we choose when we choose God? For Paul, "sin" can mean more than just adultery and murder. It can mean simply doing things the old way, the average way. Perhaps, then, our task in preaching this pericope is to give a few examples of what, actually, Christ's love frees us to choose. What does it mean that we choose for God and against sin when we get home after that long day? Does it mean visiting at a homeless shelter at 10 p.m.? Does it mean listening to your spouse with attention and generosity even when "attentive" and "generous" are the last ways you feel?

What is at stake here is more than the burden of having to make a choice between sin and righteousness. What is at stake, in our living and in our preaching, is actually *luxuriating* in what this new righteousness permits Christians to do. The baptismal waters mean that we can aspire to new lives that look something like the new life Christ had. Thus our task in preaching Paul's challenging words may be to help our congregations see, concretely, what aspiring toward an engagement with Christ's love looks like. After all, this is what is so alluring, so captivating, so appealing about the gospel: the choice Paul offers us, the choice God offers us, is a choice to love beyond our limits.

LAUREN F. WINNER

---

3. Karl Barth, *Church Dogmatics*, III/2 (Edinburgh: T. & T. Clark, 1960), 50.

established and embodied at baptism, then demonstrated in this life by freedom from the power of sin (vv. 6c–7), and extending through resurrection to the conquest of death itself.

Paul works from the foundational christological claim that "Christ was raised from the dead" (vv. 4b, 9) to its implications for the followers of Christ. The resurrection of Christ means that he will "never die again" (v. 9), that he has "died to sin, once for all" (v. 10a), and that the "life he lives, he lives to God" (v. 10b). So, too, those who are "buried with him by baptism into death" (v. 4a) "walk in newness of life" (v. 4d), and are both "dead to sin and alive to God in Christ Jesus" (v. 11). Paul does not here present the death of Jesus as a sacrifice for sin, but as the means and model for those who wish to die to the power of sin, that is, to be loosed from sin's tyrannical hold. Even as Christians await the resurrection, they live in the recognition that they are already united with Christ in his resurrection and already set free from sin's power.

What does it mean to be baptized into his death and to die to sin? Those who live under the terms set forth by the world of sin and death organize their lives, societies, and cultures around unsuccessful attempts to keep both sin and death at bay. For Paul, the solution for death and sin lies not in human choice or power, but in the recognition that in Jesus Christ God has already broken the power of sin and death. This is not merely a religious matter, but a recognition that God's grace "once for all" (v. 10) undoes all the systems of human life constructed in the name of Adam ("the old self," v. 6, cf. 5:12–21) and brings to an end the claim of any other power over our imagination and practice, whether economic systems, empires or nations, or even religions.

STANLEY P. SAUNDERS

rebel. Their children stay out all night and worry Mom and Dad sick. Selfish desires die, and the power of selfless giving is born.

When touching on familiar areas such as these, preachers have an entrée into explaining what Paul means by dying and rising with Christ. Reminding listeners that all the important things in life have a cost provides preachers the opportunity to underscore the sacrifice required to "walk in newness of life" with Christ. Real life in Christ begins when control, pride, and stubbornness are sacrificed. People come alive when they relinquish their sinful preoccupations and embrace their need for God. This is what it means to die.

I recall a hospital call while I was in seminary that reminded me of the spiritual death required of all disciples. The supervisor, who was rather unorthodox, and I were visiting patients. He had a way of getting to the truth of things without being abrasive—which is good if you are making your living as a chaplain. We were visiting a patient who was recovering from a drug overdose. He was a prominent man in the community. He said to my supervisor, "I have lost everything—my job, my reputation, and my livelihood. I have lost it all. This is the end for me!" My supervisor responded, "Oh, that's interesting. I see this as just the beginning." "What do you mean, the beginning?" the patient responded. My supervisor replied, "You said you have lost everything? Everything?" The patient said, "Yes, everything that really mattered to me." My supervisor concluded, "Well, that means God has you all to himself. Just think what God can do with you now."

CHARLES D. REEB

Luke 24:1-12

[1]But on the first day of the week, at early dawn, they came to the tomb, taking the spices that they had prepared. [2]They found the stone rolled away from the tomb, [3]but when they went in, they did not find the body. [4]While they were perplexed about this, suddenly two men in dazzling clothes stood beside them. [5]The women were terrified and bowed their faces to the ground, but the men said to them, "Why do you look for the living among the dead? He is not here, but has risen. [6]Remember how he told you, while he was still in Galilee, [7]that the Son of Man must be handed over to sinners, and be crucified, and on the third day rise again." [8]Then they remembered his words, [9]and returning from the tomb, they told all this to the eleven and to all the rest. [10]Now it was Mary Magdalene, Joanna, Mary the mother of James, and the other women with them who told this to the apostles. [11]But these words seemed to them an idle tale, and they did not believe them. [12]But Peter got up and ran to the tomb; stooping and looking in, he saw the linen cloths by themselves; then he went home, amazed at what had happened.

Theological Perspective

The label under the television picture and name of a professor was the single identifier: THEOLOGIAN. The host turned to this guest: "So you are a theologian? Say something theological!" Were he addressing an advanced seminary class on this text, the professor might have said that it is about "the hermeneutics of testimony." Since he was talking to a public on television, just as a preacher talks to a public in church, he instead chose clear language.

Before we interpret the ancient interpreters in the text this week, we must imagine an audience of today. By Saturday of Holy Week, the people in congregations will not have lacked "secular" or God-*less* talk about Easter. They will again this year have heard all about lilies and bunnies and eggs. Also, unless the preacher or teacher successfully has turned things around and helped hearers refocus, many will have gone through the Lenten season without having heard their deepest yearnings addressed and satisfied. Believers, we discern and remember, demand and deserve that rare "word about God," and even more than that. A theological lecture talks *about* God. A sermon *offers* God. The preacher of the word is gracefully gifted with the assignment to tell stories in such a way that the people stand a chance of experiencing the living presence of God and being offered a changed way of life.

Pastoral Perspective

The four Gospel accounts of the discovery of the empty tomb differ famously from each other (as well as from the earlier kerygma of the resurrection appearances found in 1 Cor. 15:3–7), and we who are committed to the principle—or, better yet, the experience—that those variant stories speak truth, might hesitate to call attention to narrative discrepancies. After all, if the lecherous elders in the story of Susanna can be discredited by the detail of a single tree in their story,[1] what happens to the testimony of witnesses who cannot agree on the number of women, the number of angels, the timing of the tomb's opening, the appearance or absence of Jesus, the message entrusted, and all the other points where the stories do not jibe? The story is, in the colloquially exclamatory sense, "incredible," but does such amazement not require credibility, and does credibility not demand consistency?

The Victorian novelist Samuel Butler believed the impossible discrepancies here to constitute disproof of the church's claim of a risen lord. It appeared dishonesty to continue to propagate a faith based on this contradictory testimony, and a strong moral integrity forced him to reject the clerical career that his family had assumed to be his vocation. Yet, over

1. See the short book of Susanna in the Apocrypha, esp. vv. 52–59.

Exegetical Perspective

Chapter 24 comprises five distinctively Lukan episodes, based upon the evangelist's special material, bearing scant resemblance to parallel passages in the Synoptics. There are two reports about finding Jesus' tomb empty, two narratives of postresurrection appearances by Jesus to his disciples, and the account of his ascension (found only in Luke). The narrative is also structured by chronological indicators to suggest the unfolding of events over the course of a single, extended day: "early dawn," "on the first day of the week" (v. 1); "on that same day" (v. 13); "almost evening," the day "now nearly over" (v. 29); "that same hour" (v. 33); "then" (v. 50). The whole is framed by Sabbath rest (23:56) and temple observance (24:53), which betoken the law-abiding piety of Jesus' followers both before and after they had come to believe in his resurrection.

Luke 24:1–11 recounts what seems, on the surface, the familiar story of the women coming to the tomb (cf. Matt. 28:1–10/Mark 16:1–8). However, redaction is everywhere apparent. The women whom the evangelist names (Mary Magdalene, Joanna, and Mary "the mother of James") are, for the most part (Susanna is not explicitly mentioned here), the very ones singled out in 8:1–3 as having provided for Jesus' Galilean ministry "out of their resources." These women from Galilee, who had witnessed Jesus'

Homiletical Perspective

The Gospels are silent about the events that take place between the burial of the body of Jesus in the late afternoon of Good Friday and the visit of the women to the tomb early Sunday morning. It is in this silence that the ancient celebration of the Easter Vigil fits. We wait with the followers of Jesus, remembering how women among them planned to go to the tomb and give Jesus' body a proper cleansing and anointing, a suitable wrapping, and an appropriate burial as soon as the Sabbath ended.

The silence is broken as we begin to hear from Luke of the women's walk to the place where Jesus was laid. We imagine their shadows flitting in and out of the shadows of the landscape of early morning. When they arrive to see the stone at the opening rolled back, we see with them the yawning emptiness of the mouth of the tomb. It is no use pretending at this point that we are surprised—we already know what they will find when they enter.

The very familiarity of the scene hinders our attention to Luke's unique details in his version. For example, we might not notice that Luke talks of two men dressed in luminous clothing in the tomb, not the one figure that Mark and Matthew mention. Matthew even calls him an angel. Surely in Luke they are the same kind of otherworldly messengers. Even more significant, however, is the response of the

Luke 24:1-12

Theological Perspective

Urgent, next, is this question: *which* word about God grows out of this text and then helps the preacher offer the divine presence and benefits? Will a sermon turn out to represent a futile move from God-talk to talk about proofs of the resurrection? Or will it prompt a philosophical or historical lecture on "Who rolled the stone from the tomb?" In a mixed classroom, some of whose students are skeptics, it might be tempting to get into the proving business. In preaching, however, we know that proving is useless and beside the point.

So what does go on in preaching? The main theological issue here falls into the category of *testimony*. A witness sees or experiences something and then is moved to write or tell about it. A whole sequence of testifiers connect us witnesses. Thus today's preacher is testifying to people who will become testifiers. They bring some preconceptions that should make them eager. Today the preacher tells of women in the story who had witnessed and then gave testimony. Even those first observers did not interpret without preconceptions. We are told that they "remembered" (v. 8) earlier witness from Jesus himself. Then these givers of testimony turned the "eleven and all the rest" (v. 9) into potential testifiers. The witnesses did not convince everyone all at once: "These words seemed to [the hearers] an idle tale, and they did not believe" (v. 11).

Sometimes stories are too weird to be taken seriously, and sometimes the tellers of the stories are weirder yet, in which case we would dismiss them. In our story, however, the testimony eventually was believed. Peter and an unnamed "other" disciple heard and became curious, so they went to "see," and Peter "saw"—linen cloths only. These were close enough to what matters to inspire amazement, and amazement is often a first response to testimony.

Third, thanks to these first-day witnesses, there came later sets of witnesses, namely members of a community that kept the saving story alive long enough for Luke to stitch together a rich narrative. Our reading or hearing their story moves "you," whether you are named Mary or Joanna or not. Finally, thanks to all of them, twenty centuries later, the preacher, who was not there to "see," has now also "seen" and gets to pass on the story to people who also were not there and to whom nothing was "proven." They can be amazed and can tell others.

Amazingly, "many believed." They believed not because someone produced and waved the Shroud of Turin, a cloth that some claimed "scientifically" to have been the burial cloth of Jesus. Had there been a

Pastoral Perspective

almost a century and a half since then, the defections from Christianity have not generally had to do with the argument Butler raised about the resurrection, nor has there been much attention given to scriptural inconsistencies from the pew or pulpit. For the most part, Butler's critique went unnoticed. Scholars and theologians, of course, had an obligation to handle these matters, and there were obviously other issues to challenge or to subvert popular faith, but we may wonder why the obvious forensic difficulty in these testimonies has had relatively little effect on Christians. Do we put it down to simple human credulity, to a combination of a will to believe and an intellectual laziness about what is believed? Is it an unwillingness to offend the past, refusal to do to our parents what Samuel Butler did to his? Is it that discrepancies have not been noticed because preachers and pastors have not pointed them out? The possibilities are many, and many seem plausible and even likely part of the truth.

I suggest, however, that alongside these sorry explanations there may be found something more positive. In my experience of the resurrection—as a victory recounted and believed in the church—the particular form in which that news arrives has not been the *object* of faith but the means of its revelation. Because that is so, there is not just practical acceptance but joy in the *plural* variety of witnesses: the *forms* of the resurrection's discovery are not objects of faith but revelations. It may seem laziness and dereliction not to interrogate these witnesses, at least as much as Daniel in Susanna did the lying elders; but is it not also the case that their testimony for the church and the world functions differently from that heard in a courtroom setting? Is this not a case where each speaks and tells of a truth too big and wondrous to fit in a single telling, where each tells what those who welcome it may greet as true without excluding the next peculiar teller of truth? The failure to interrogate the witnesses in this case is not necessarily a result of fear or stupidity; it is rather that the interrogation seems irrelevant, a kind of misunderstanding. That, too, seems part of the situation.

Here we are again, at the great Easter proclamation: "Christ is risen! He is risen indeed!" What are we to say beyond that, we whose vocation is explicitly to be witnesses to the resurrection? Are we tempted to gloss over the variations in the accounts? If we read Luke's tonight and John's tomorrow (or vice versa), shall we assume no one will notice, or be willing to notice, the marked

Exegetical Perspective

crucifixion (23:49), who had seen the tomb and the deposition of his corpse therein (23:55), are the ones who, when "they found the stone rolled away" and the body missing, tell it "to the eleven and to all the rest" (24:2, 9). Surprisingly, not one of their names is found on the slate of candidates put forward to fill Judas' vacancy (Acts 1:21–26), even though they fit all the enunciated eligibility requirements for taking his place in "this ministry and apostleship"!

Indeed, textual tampering in the early part of this chapter works to vitiate the implications of their discovery and their proclamation. The "two men in dazzling clothes," who suddenly appear beside them to ask why they are searching for the living in a grave-yard, are themselves (in some manuscripts, but not Codex Bezae!) allowed to announce Jesus' resurrection: "He is not here, but has risen" (24:5). The Western noninterpolations referenced in the NRSV footnotes should not be ignored.[1] In verse 9 the non-Western witnesses insert the phrase "from the tomb," as if to underscore that the women's report had its origin there, not in some mere apparition. There is an antidocetic *Tendenz* in those texts that have come down to us, which changes the focus of the narrative.

This seems especially true for assessing verse 11. The editorial voice notes that the apostles received the women's word as "an idle tale." The Greek word here, *lēros*, an NT *hapax legomenon*, is usually reserved to describe the ranting of a person suffering from delirium. Seen against Luke's larger narrative, one ought to relish the irony. In 8:2 Mary Magdalene is described as one who was cured by Jesus, as one from whom seven demons had gone out. Mary Magdalene, who had at one time been truly beside herself, is now among those who convey the good news! This would fit it perfectly with one of Luke–Acts' major themes: the unexpected reversal of fortune (cf. 1:46–55).

Verse 12 mutes that theme and is especially problematic. Again, it is lacking in Codex Bezae. Peter sees the linen cloths "by themselves" in the empty tomb; he does not "see" Jesus. This is clearly contradicted by verse 24, which says that "some others" went to the tomb, not just Peter alone. Verse 34 states emphatically that Jesus *appeared* to Simon. Verse 12 is silent about that. Read alongside John 20:3–7, the verse looks suspiciously appended. It does, however, serve to further the antidocetic aims found in the prior modifications of the text. Some would claim that verse 12 additionally functions to provide a

1. See Bart D. Ehrman, *The Orthodox Corruption of Scripture* (New York: Oxford University Press, 1993), 212–61.

Homiletical Perspective

women. In Mark's Gospel, the women are amazed; in Matthew's it is the guards who are fearful. Luke tells us that the women are afraid and bow their faces low to the ground.

In the face of the totally unexpected mystery that confronts them, this abasement seems wholly appropriate. The stone rolled away from the doorway, the body of their teacher gone, the appearance of two strangely bright men—all these things cannot help but elicit their terrified awe. Yet we who are accustomed to this story, who are used to thinking of Jesus as our good buddy, who have tried to make God as knowable and dependable as breakfast cereal, hardly linger at the dreadful silence of these women with their faces in the dirt. Our efforts to tame the holy inure us to their fear. We miss Luke's first preachable lesson in this account: God's ways are not our ways. They are beyond human comprehension; they subvert what we expect; they demand the impossible. They are holy precisely because they are not of our own making. When we encounter God's ways, our first response should acknowledge that fact with more than a nod.

Luke's second lesson comes only moments later. "Why do you look for the living among the dead?" the angelic figures say to the tops of the women's heads. We are just as guilty of such a fruitless search. We too want to tend the corpses of long dead ideas and ideals. We cling to former visions of ourselves and our churches as if they might come back to life as long as we hold on to them. We grasp our loved ones too tightly, refusing to allow them to change, to become bigger, or smarter, or stronger. We choose to stay with what we know in our hearts to be dead, because it is safe, malleable, and so susceptible to burnishing through private memory. The words of the unworldly messengers are a challenge to stop hanging on to the dead and to move into new life. They are reminders that the Holy One dwells wherever new life bursts forth.

The third preachable lesson from Luke is also found in the mouths of the two angelic beings. "Remember how he told you," they tell the women, "that the Son of Man must be handed over to sinners, and be crucified, and on the third day rise again" (v. 7). This memory connects the empty tomb with the very human Jesus who ate and talked, suffered and died. In Alan Culpepper's words, "Remember what Jesus had done and what he had taught. Remember the meals in Jesus' fellowship, his healings and his parables, the bent woman and the ten lepers. Would you understand the meaning of

Luke 24:1-12

Theological Perspective

cloth for the taking, and had the disciples taken it to Jerusalem and Asia Minor and said, "He is risen, and we can prove it scientifically. Here is his shroud," who would have believed? Hearers did not look at such artifacts or wave cloths and claim proofs. What *do* witnesses do when they testify? They put their lives on the line.

We get a clue from Acts, another book by Luke. He told about Antioch, the first place where people were called Christians. They heard a variety of testimonies. Was it time to check them out, time to call for the burial cloths to make the point? No. We read that the apostles instead sent Barnabas, "a good man, full of the Holy Spirit and of faith. And a great many people were brought to the Lord" (Acts 11:24).

So we have pictured that a Barnabas-like "hermeneutics of testimony" was developing. Today, if the teller is a deceiver, liar, or skunk, he is not "good," and it is hard to picture that "many people" would be brought to the Lord through such a witness. It was becoming clear that the once-frightened people in Antioch, now disciples like the spice-carrying women at the tomb or one of those who had first heard it all as an "idle tale" (v. 11), gave the story a chance.

It helps when the witness as the testifier is known for her truthfulness, her ability to sort out stories, and her readiness to put her life on the line, which is what believers were doing daily in the Roman Empire. Reading the story in a Gideon Bible in a hotel room has its place for helping people "remember," just as the disciples had remembered. As for coming to faith, however, the main human agents then were and today are parents, preachers, sufferers, people of action, banquet-goers whose perception begins with an amazement that leads them to "tell all this," and thus to encourage a new round of witnesses. With words and actions under the Holy Spirit they get to help the testimony ring true today.

MARTIN E. MARTY

Pastoral Perspective

differences? Should we hope they do not, for our sake and for theirs? Or should we anticipate their noticing and take the initiative, providing possible harmonizations or apologetic defenses for the credibility of the texts?

Let us make neither of those approaches our primary one. Instead, let us exhibit our faith and our joy, not defensively or dishonestly, but with bold confidence. Such proclamation, excitedly retelling the story and being unafraid to love the peculiar ways in which each witness tells it, serves the community. The community that saw the risen Lord, not dead but alive (as in 1 Cor. 15), and that came to know him in the reunderstanding of the Scriptures and in the breaking of the bread (as in Luke's Emmaus story), retells the discovery again as it encounters the tomb of his burial. In Matthew, there is the drama of an earthquake and the stone rolling away to reveal the tomb *already* empty. In Mark, there is an empty tomb and an open, potentially unheeded, command to hurry up where Jesus has gone. In John, there is Mary Magdalene and her grief and yearning, along with a host of other details in each book.

Here in Luke's narrative, the one that gives us the angelic challenge to both church and soul—"Why do you look for the living among the dead?"—and the one in which we find that angels like disciples seem to need companions when they are sent on a mission, it is the unique details as well as the barest outline of the story that speak the truth. (The classic analogy comes to mind: true as an arrow is true, for it hits the mark.) The preacher can thus speak with enthusiasm of the diversity of details among the various accounts, not to explain them away but to caress their different insights, focusing on the one at hand but celebrating them all, excitedly sharing the wonder that gave rise to them all, the glory refracted in each.

JOHN K. STENDAHL

Exegetical Perspective

second witness to support the testimony of the women, an apologetic attempt to counter sentiments expressed by Luke's contemporary Josephus (*Antiq.* 4:8.15): "From women let not evidence be accepted, because of the levity and temerity of their sex."[2]

When one reads all of chapter 24, bracketing for a moment the antidocetic, feminine-pejorative accretions, a different pattern emerges. The Easter message entails three component parts: experience, memory, and exegetical insight. The women who had witnessed everything about Jesus' ministry concretely were confronted at the tomb with a reality that defied concretion. The "angels" (24:6–8a) urge them to *remember* Jesus' words, his passion predictions in Galilee (9:21–22, 44; 18:31–33). Memory corroborates experience, but memory is not enough. Jesus' words are veiled; their experiences are opaque. They must be complemented by exegetical insight (cf. 9:45; 18:34b).

The report in verse 10 is but the beginning of the *euangelion* coming to articulation. When the risen though unrecognized Jesus engages Cleopas and the other, unnamed follower on the walk to Emmaus, they too recall quite vividly Jesus' career that culminated in his death. They had been stirred by his prophetic word, but memory and the "astounding" testimony of the women are not enough to revive their sagging hope. Jesus chastises, "Oh, how foolish you are, and how slow of heart to believe all that the prophets have declared!" Then, Luke says, the resurrected Jesus, "beginning with Moses and all the prophets, interpreted to them the things about himself in all the scriptures" (vv. 25–27). Exegesis completes their memory, transforms their experience. Similarly, at the end of the day, when Jesus nearly bowls over the disciples with the raw physicality of his appearance, they are nevertheless "disbelieving" (cf. John 20:27), "still wondering" (Luke 24:41). Again, Jesus commences to "open their minds to understand the scriptures (v. 45).

Experience, memory, exegesis. Followers of Jesus recognize him as the risen Lord when the three are brought together. "Were not our hearts burning . . . while he was opening the scriptures to us" (v. 32)? His final missionary charge to his disciples continues to recall his words and to contextualize their experience, both with scriptural explanation. The women's delirious-sounding message, now grounded in the entirety of the scriptural witness, brings to an end this long day's journey into enlightenment.

GREGORY A. ROBBINS

Homiletical Perspective

the empty tomb? Remember Galilee."[1] The admonition to remember grounds the mystery of resurrection in the everyday world of human living as well as in the demanding communal ethic that Jesus taught.

This means that the boundless gift of the empty tomb cannot be separated from the words and actions of Jesus. Resurrection, after all, is not some buoyant ideal, unconnected to the real world. It is an invitation to live as Jesus lived, a doorway to a life in which meals are shared with enemies, healing is offered to the hopeless, prophetic challenges are issued to the powerful. Only now it is not Jesus who does these things—it is we ourselves who see at last the subversive power of the resurrection in order to live it now. On that first dim Easter morning, when women cowered in the dust and angels picked them back up, pointing them out the door of a tomb into the full light of morning, the power of God was no longer unspoken. The silence was broken, and the women rushed back to tell the others about what they had seen. No matter that the others did not believe at first. Who *could* believe, under the circumstances? No matter that Peter had to test the women's story by running to the tomb, seeing for himself the linen clothes, and wondering all the way back home about what he had seen. The women knew. The women remembered. The women believed. The women responded by breaking their own silence to speak their own truth. Which is, after all, exactly what God asks of us.

NANCY CLAIRE PITTMAN

1. R. Alan Culpepper, "Luke," in *The New Interpreter's Bible* (Nashville: Abingdon Press, 1995), 9:473.

2. See Charles H. Talbert, *Reading Luke* (New York: Crossroad, 1989), 228.

Isaiah 65:17-25

¹⁷For I am about to create new heavens
  and a new earth;
 the former things shall not be remembered
  or come to mind.
¹⁸But be glad and rejoice forever
  in what I am creating;
 for I am about to create Jerusalem as a joy,
  and its people as a delight.
¹⁹I will rejoice in Jerusalem,
  and delight in my people;
 no more shall the sound of weeping be heard in it,
  or the cry of distress.
²⁰No more shall there be in it
  an infant that lives but a few days,
  or an old person who does not live out a lifetime;
 for one who dies at a hundred years will be considered a youth,
  and one who falls short of a hundred will be considered accursed.

Theological Perspective

Isaiah launches the reader into God's new creation. New life in this text is defined in terms of "new heavens and a new earth." God's new creation is cosmic, and a new order is at hand. While many believers circumscribe the resurrection to life after death, the prophet reminds us that resurrection is God's power to create a new reality for all creation. This new creation reconfigures relationships. Here the prophet points to a new cosmic matrix: the new cosmos reveals how the transformation of relationships and the transformation of space and time are mutually dependent. Relationships change because space and time change; space and time change because relationships change. Context and relationships embody God's creative power. This matrix is not a linear, sequential, and cumulative progression of goodness, in which relationships transform context or context transforms relationships. God's creative power transforms both, unleashing the goodness of God's power on God's new cosmos.

God's new cosmos has at least three dimensions: (1) the joy of God in creating new heavens and a new earth; (2) the transformed character of life in God's new cosmos; and (3) the reordering of cosmic relationships in the new creation. Perhaps the preacher can focus on one of these characteristics or allow them to interact with each other, emphasizing

Pastoral Perspective

"They shall not labor in vain or bear children for calamity," God declares through the prophet, in the Jerusalem that will be created as a joy. There people will rejoice when women no longer bear children to be kidnapped into militias, or to take up swords, or to be shattered by invasion, war, conquest, or deportation. Male children will not have their arms chopped off if they do not sign up as boy soldiers, nor will female children be gang raped or sold into slavery. These calamities greet many children in this world on Easter morning.

"Bear children for calamity" flickers on and off like a searchlight today, begging for an interpretation that cries for justice—not only for peace, not only for personal resurrection or the rebirth of spring (which is not a biblical notion). Isaiah captures creation's part in the rejoicing of a restored Jerusalem. New heavens and a new earth herald this action of God, which concludes with the friendship of predators and prey, and defanged serpents. There will be no more torture or destruction (of animals or humans) on the holy mountain of the Lord.

Yet suddenly it is Easter Day, with new frocks, suits, and ties; lamb or pork on the table; parades, dancing, and games in the streets; and folk on front porches drinking mimosas and Bloody Marys. Elsewhere in the world, children are born, not for

21They shall build houses and inhabit them;
    they shall plant vineyards and eat their fruit.
22They shall not build and another inhabit;
    they shall not plant and another eat;
    for like the days of a tree shall the days of my people be,
    and my chosen shall long enjoy the work of their hands.
23They shall not labor in vain,
    or bear children for calamity;
    for they shall be offspring blessed by the LORD—
    and their descendants as well.
24Before they call I will answer,
    while they are yet speaking I will hear.
25The wolf and the lamb shall feed together,
    the lion shall eat straw like the ox;
    but the serpent—its food shall be dust!
    They shall not hurt or destroy
    on all my holy mountain,

                      says the LORD.

Exegetical Perspective

The setting of Isaiah 65:17–25 is difficult to determine. As a part of what scholars have termed Third Isaiah (Isa. 56–66), it can be roughly placed in the early postexilic period following the return of the exiles from Babylon. The general tone of these chapters suggests the first century of Persian rule (538–424 BCE).[1] The exiles who returned to the province of Yehud (Judah) had high expectations of a renewed Jewish existence, expectations that were fed by the prophecies of Second Isaiah (Isa. 40–55). The realities of postexilic life failed to live up to these expectations, however, leading to a rethinking of the Isaianic tradition. Drawing on earlier passages in the book of Isaiah, Isaiah 65:17–25 is full of hope, offering a vision of the new world that God is creating.

The text appointed for this Sunday opens with language that draws heavily on the Priestly creation story in Genesis 1. The same verb for creation is used in both passages (Heb. *bara'*). This word is found frequently in the Isaianic tradition, particularly within Second Isaiah, where it refers not only to the creation of the world but also to YHWH's creation of Israel (Isa. 40:26–28; 41:20; 42:5; 43:1, 7, 15; 45:7–8, 12, 18; 48:7; 54:16). Here

---

1. Joseph Blenkinsopp, *Isaiah 56–66*, Anchor Bible 19B (New York: Doubleday, 2003), 42–43.

Homiletical Perspective

Leading a service of worship in witness to the resurrection is the minister's task both on Easter Day and at funerals. Every funeral service seeks to bring pastoral care and comfort to the grieving, but the circumstances of the person who has died may make that task vary in difficulty. If the funeral is for a person who has lived to "a ripe old age," whose family can look back across a life of accomplishment and blessing, then death may seem to be less the unwelcome intruder. In the case of a young person who dies suddenly or violently, the grieving are more likely to say, "She had her whole life ahead of her." Pastoral care must be attentive to these differences, while the proclamation of the resurrection remains urgent.

Isaiah 65:20 takes some account of the life span issue. It agonizes over "an infant that lives but a few days" and proclaims, "No more." Even the long and well-lived life—at whose ending North American culture may often judge that excessive grief is unseemly, if not unwarranted—this too is protested: "One who falls short of a hundred [years] will be considered accursed."

The Old Testament reading for Easter Day is not likely to be the primary preaching text, but it portrays the new heaven and new earth in images familiar to the present earth: inhabiting one's own house and eating the fruit of one's own vineyard.

Isaiah 65:17-25

Theological Perspective

the cosmic matrix—the transformation of context and relationships—made possible by God's creative power for new life, rather than limiting this power to the individual hope for life after death.

The joy of God in creating new heavens and a new earth. God delights in creating a new space, a new context, a new Jerusalem. The old space, the old Jerusalem, is not to be remembered. The new Jerusalem is full of joy. God's joyful nature overwhelms God's created new space. God is joy. God's new space, the new Jerusalem, is joy. "*Mi Dios es alegre*" (My God is joyful) says the refrain of a popular rhythmic hymn sung in many congregations in the Latin Caribbean. People sing the refrain over and over, assuring the community that the nature and character of God is joy. Congregational space becomes party space, because the reign of God is a party. God delights in the joy of a new space that celebrates God's creative power.

The character of life in God's new cosmos. The new Jerusalem is not an abstract ideal, and Isaiah gives us strong grounding for God's joy. First, God's new creation generates *good* life. With new space come new relationships. Sobs of distress are heard no more, and weeping is unreal in the new Jerusalem. We may imagine a space where the conditions of evil and suffering are eliminated; in this new place, our relationships can engender only goodness and joy.

Time is also transformed. Any student of astrophysics recognizes that a change in space produces a change in time. *Chronos*, our linear time frame, collapses. Time becomes unending, eternal, but not in the sense of something *otherworldly* juxtaposed against the *this-worldly*. God's new creation is a total transformation of the spatial and chronological setup of our daily lives. Life is long, abundant, and joyful. God transforms the context.

The cosmic relationships in the new creation. Who could live long if deprived of shelter and food? Who could live joyfully if exploited? Who could enjoy work, only to come home to poverty and misery? Who could rejoice in a newborn, if the future held only suffering and death? Such questions show the interplay between context, content, space/time configuration, and relationships.

In Guatemala, many Amerindian mothers do not name their children until the age of three years. The marginalization and exploitation of Amerindian communities create an uncertainty of life for the

Pastoral Perspective

dancing and new dresses, but for bloody, heart-wrenching calamity.

What does Easter—beyond personal resurrection and the promise of eternal life—have to do with justice? This text invites us to declare that resurrection has become the key to understanding justice and restoration as God's way in a tortured world. Resurrection is the act of God, the beginning of a new creation. With the resurrection of Jesus from death, God has answered definitively, before we called. God has spoken with finality, while we were standing at the tomb in doubt and fear, or were muttering to each other and to the seemingly ignorant stranger on the road to Emmaus.

We did not expect resurrection. The women were on their way with spices and ointments to minister to the corpse of Jesus. Things were as they had always been: the powerful crushing the innocent; the fearful finding a scapegoat to assuage their anxiety about social upheaval and persecution; the energetic followers running away at the moment of crisis; and the one who loudly claimed to be the most loyal of all the disciples denying that he ever knew the man who was charged with blasphemy and sedition. We did not expect resurrection. Human life was unfolding, as T. S. Eliot wrote, "from birth to copulation to death," with the more than occasional ordinary acts of public and private cruelty interrupting the course of ordinary days.[1]

Yet when the resurrection came, everything was "thrown off balance," as Flannery O'Connor's Misfit said of Jesus. "Jesus is the only One that ever raised the dead . . . and He shouldn't have done it. He thrown everything off balance. If He did what He said then it's nothing for you to do but to throw everything away and follow Him, and if He didn't, then it's nothing for you to do but enjoy the few minutes you got left the best way you can—by killing somebody . . . or doing some other meanness to him."[2]

God threw the cosmos off balance by raising Jesus Christ from death. The world was turned upside down. Things have never been the same since: not the stars in their courses, not the future of this planet, not the relationship of human life to the rest of creation, and not the people of God—who are now defined by relationship to Jesus Christ in Word and water, bread and wine. God not only entered the

---

1. T. S. Eliot, "Fragment of an Agon," in *The Complete Poems and Plays 1909–1950* (New York: Harcourt, Brace & World, 1952), 80.
2. Flannery O'Connor, "A Good Man Is Hard to Find," in *The Complete Stories* (New York: Farrar, Straus, & Giroux, 1971), 132. I first saw this used in a similar fashion by Buddy Ennis in a sermon printed in *Journal for Preachers*.

Exegetical Perspective

God is said to be creating new heavens and a new earth. The new creation will be so spectacular that the Israelites will no longer remember "the former" (Heb. *ri'shonoth*), an obvious allusion to the original creation "in the beginning" (Heb. *re'shith*, Gen.1:1).

In verse 18 the Israelites are called to rejoice over the new creation, for it is not just the world that is being renewed. Both Jerusalem and the Israelites are being recreated as well. The verbs for rejoicing alternate with the verb for creation, creating a chiastic structure in this verse:

But be glad (*sisu*)	A
and rejoice (*gilu*) forever	B
in what I am creating (*bore'*);	C
for I am about to create (*bore'*)	C'
Jerusalem as a joy (*gilah*)	B'
and its people as a delight (*masos*).	A'

Due to the different English words used to translate the noun and verb forms of the words for being glad / delight (*sis*) and rejoicing / joy (*gil*), the chiasmic structure does not come through in the NRSV. In verse 19a, it is God's turn to rejoice over Jerusalem. God's pleasure is expressed using the same words as in the previous verse (Heb. *sis* and *gil*), which unites God and the people in their happiness over the new creation.

In verses 19b–24, the specifics of life in God's new creation are laid out. No more will weeping or the cry of distress be heard in Jerusalem. Although crying would have been found in Jerusalem in any period, no doubt the first readers would have thought back to the weeping and distress found in Jerusalem after its destruction at the hands of the Babylonians in 587 BCE. In verse 20, the people are promised long life. As with much of the creation language employed in this passage, the promise of long life calls to mind the conditions of the primeval history (Gen. 1–11), when lifespans often covered several centuries. God's new creation will reflect the ideal life that was found after the first creation.

With verses 21–22 the passage turns to the idea of security within the home. No longer will people build houses and plant vineyards, only to have them taken away by someone else. The loss of home and the fruits of one's labor are frequently mentioned as calamities in the Old Testament (Lev. 26:16; Deut. 28:30), but given the location of this passage in the postexilic period, it is likely that the original hearers would have thought back to the destruction of Jerusalem in 587 BCE, when their ancestors' houses and vineyards, for which they had worked so hard, had been taken away for generations. Third Isaiah

Homiletical Perspective

The text thereby addresses a theological question on the mind of the Easter Day worshiper, whether that worshiper is present every Sunday or on Easter only. It is the old question that refuses to go away: why is there suffering, injustice, and death in a world fashioned by a good Creator? That question per se may not be best answered in the Easter sermon. Preachers may save theodicy for another time, but the Isaiah text is aware of the problem. In it, suffering, injustice, and death make the human heart long for God's new creation.

Both preacher and hearer may detect some discontinuity between the tangible and this-worldly vision in Isaiah 65 and the less easily grasped truths found in the Easter Gospel and Epistle. The proclamation of and belief in the resurrection of Christ teeter between the familiar and the utterly novel. In Isaiah 65, at least, the concepts are readily understandable: babies no longer die (v. 20); children no longer suffer (v. 23b); work is always rewarded and rewarding (v. 22b–23a); weeping and cries of distress are no more (v. 19b). The passage even proclaims a new thing throughout the animal kingdom, in an echo more associated with Advent: "The wolf and the lamb shall feed together."

Some will be so bold as to ask, if Christ is raised from the dead, then why are these promises in Isaiah not found among the benefits of the resurrection here and now? Alas, the burden and the glory of preaching consist in proclaiming things that are not yet fully realized, but the hope for them holds a powerful grip upon the faithful imagination. By following where the risen Christ leads, some of the faithful have realized portions of Isaiah's vision in some measure, in some places. More children do live longer and freer of disease, and more people have useful, creative work, because of advances achieved in places where the Gospel of Christ has been proclaimed and received. As expressed in the Confession of 1967, "Already God's reign is present as a ferment in the world, stirring hope in men and preparing the world to receive its ultimate judgment and redemption. With an urgency born of this hope the church applies itself to present tasks and strives for a better world."[1]

However in the not-yet-ness of the Easter proclamation, heaven has not yet arrived on earth. We receive the vision of Isaiah 65 by faith and in hope that remains beyond our reach here below. As the Confession of 1967 continues, "It [the church]

---

1. "The Confession of 1967," in *The Book of Confessions* (Louisville, KY: Office of the General Assembly of the Presbyterian Church (U.S.A.), 2002), 262.

Isaiah 65:17-25

Theological Perspective

young. Mothers resist naming their children, creating a shield of love against love itself. Their strategy is to keep a human and emotional distance from the pain of the child's imminent death. On the one hand, this distant relationship between mother and child prevents further pain. There is already enough pain when most Amerindian mothers "bear children for calamity." On the other hand, it resists the temptation to surrender life to a cynical cycle of tragedy. Amazingly and as a testimony of faith, these women expect the blessing of the Lord upon them and their descendants.

Just imagine these Amerindian women reading Isaiah: "No more shall there be in it an infant that lives but a few days. . . . They shall not labor in vain or bear children for calamity" (vv. 20a, 23a). Isaiah nourishes the hope of longevity with the goodness that comes from justice: time and relationships are embodied in the image of a child growing old, not in the frequently justified theology of life after death, when injustice is the cause of death.

This new cosmic creation reconfigures the way we relate to God and God relates to us. God responds to our needs even before we name them, because God knows. From a Christian perspective, the resurrected one is also the one who has lived among us, suffered among us, and died among us. Jesus' resurrection is not only a witness to the promise of life after death. It is also a testament to the promise of resurrection grounded in a life given to others against all manifestations of evil.

This new cosmic order reshapes the natural order. Predator and prey eat together. The two are reconciled. Once more, spatial dynamics are reconfigured to radiate an image of new cosmic relationships. Context and content embody no hurt or destruction. In the new cosmic matrix, relationships embody the joy of God's creative power.

How might our communities participate in God's joy of the new cosmos this Easter season? Will it be necessary to change our configuration of space and time, our architecture, the setup of our seats, our worship time? Will it be necessary to develop new relationships? How might we embody God's creative joy in our midst, as we live into the reality of new heavens and a new earth?

CARLOS F. CARDOZA-ORLANDI

Pastoral Perspective

created order as a human being, God overcame the "meanness" that we did to the Incarnate One.

Just so, the prophet declared that God was doing something new—that in God's new world order there would be no more meanness, no more crying and lamentation, but a new heaven and a new earth, with a new social order that excluded not only war between humans but also war among the creatures. All creation (thrown off balance by human disobedience) is now at peace with itself and thereby reflects the character of Israel's God.

Is this merely pious nonsense for returned exiles or the church? Is this salve that soothes burdened cynicism, helping the poor and those with tender consciences endure the troubles of this world while we await the resurrection? Is such yearning what Marx claimed, and what the "new atheism" declares, to be the opiate of the people? Or is this trustworthy verbal evidence—backed up by hopeful actions all over the world, even in the glutted despair of the overdeveloped world—that human life does not and has never completed itself?[3] The prophet knew that reality, and so declared God's salvation. The church maintains that faith and—here and there, now and then—makes real the claims of resurrection by our obedience. In spite of the arrogance and danger to life of all fundamentalisms everywhere, there arise Martin Luther King Jr., Desmond Tutu, Mother Teresa, and Mahatma Gandhi (and hundreds of thousands of unknown faithful people) who give evidence that the Spirit of God is completing what God intends for all creation.

It is a challenging business to preach on an apocalyptic Old Testament text when the church celebrates resurrection. However, the reward is rich and sure. We proclaim a God who is the same today, yesterday, and forever, until the wolf and the lamb shall feed together.

O. BENJAMIN SPARKS

---

3. Paul D. Hanson, *Isaiah, 40–66*, Interpretation series (Louisville, KY: John Knox Press, 1995), 241–46.

Exegetical Perspective

promises a new creation in which this loss can never be repeated.

Neither shall they bear children only to see them die. Instead, verse 23 promises that the birth of children will be a blessing. The Israelites are to be a seed blessed by YHWH. Although the connections with creation language are not strong in this verse, it is possible—though far from certain—that the reference to the offspring ("seed," Heb. *zeraʿ*) echoes the language of the curse after the fall in Genesis 3:15. Isaiah 65:23 may be alluding to a creation in which the curse of the fall is reversed. In verse 24, God promises that the Israelites' prayers will be heard and answered even before they finish speaking.

The final verse in this passage picks up on the imagery employed in Isaiah 11:6–9. In both of these passages, the authors foresee a future in which the conditions of the first creation have been reestablished. In Genesis 1:30, God gives plants to the animals as their food. Although it is not explicitly stated, the implication is that they do not eat meat. Isaiah 65:25 sees a return to that ideal. No longer will animals eat one another. Instead, even the fiercest of them—the wolf and the lion—will dine on vegetation. The restoration of the heavens and the earth is a blessing not only for humans but for the animal world as well. No one, whether animal or human, will hurt or be hurt on God's holy mountain, that is, Mount Zion in Jerusalem. The location of this ideal existence in Jerusalem picks up on earlier traditions in Isaiah that point to a future in which Jerusalem will be the center of the world (Isa. 2:2–3), an image reflected in the new Jerusalem of Revelation 21:1–2.

KEVIN A. WILSON

Homiletical Perspective

does not identify limited progress with the kingdom of God on earth, nor does it despair in the face of disappointment and defeat. In steadfast hope, the church looks beyond all partial achievement to the final triumph of God."

As part of the scriptural witness to Easter, Isaiah 65 "fleshes out" the believer's response to faith in the resurrection. The preacher may move the focus of the sermon beyond the scientific plausibility of Christ's resurrection and beyond even the need, as some see it, of putting away our critical thinking for this grand hour of Easter worship. Isaiah 65 engages the issue of what difference the Easter message will make to those who have heard it on the day *after* Easter. Will those who are convinced of the resurrection of Christ understand that it has effects beyond the gift of life in a world to come for the individual? Resurrection faith sends its adherents toward work and witness here and now, in the service of Isaiah's vision of the redeemed life of creation.

The Easter sermon that keeps some focus on Isaiah 65 can be just the occasion to connect a congregation's faith and works. Imagine that belief in the resurrection of Christ energizes a church to share the risen life of Christ and support a shelter for victims of domestic violence or begin an after-school tutoring program for children in the nearby public school. So "shall be offspring blessed by the LORD— and their descendants as well" (v. 23). Dare we also hope that the Easter-only worshiper actually comes back to worship the next Sunday as well? Then we may well "be glad and rejoice forever in what I am creating" (v. 18).

J. MICHAEL KRECH

Psalm 118:1-2, 14-24

¹O give thanks to the Lord, for he is good;
   his steadfast love endures forever!

²Let Israel say,
   "His steadfast love endures forever."
. . . .
¹⁴The Lord is my strength and my might;
   he has become my salvation.
¹⁵There are glad songs of victory in the tents of the righteous:
   "The right hand of the Lord does valiantly;
¹⁶ the right hand of the Lord is exalted;
   the right hand of the Lord does valiantly."
¹⁷I shall not die, but I shall live,
   and recount the deeds of the Lord.
¹⁸The Lord has punished me severely,
   but he did not give me over to death.

Theological Perspective

This psalm is filled with a sense of joy that is grounded in gratitude. It is a song of deliverance, with a central theme that is both ancient and much needed today, as we look forward toward the many challenges facing all communities of faith. Most simply put, one of the messages of this text—and this day—is that no matter what challenges, privations, and sufferings we may know, we are nonetheless upheld by the loving mystery we know as God, who will not let us get lost forever. The psalmist wants us to know that God has great things in store—for example, the chance to allow the transformative power of divine grace to live in us. Such a vocation draws us forward to live ever more effectively as vessels through which that grace is shared with the world.

My present point of view is shaped in part by virtue of the reality that I am charged with helping to prepare women and men to be effective transformational leaders. That is a genuine challenge and one I do not take lightly. Such language is not generally used by a number of my colleagues elsewhere to describe the somewhat rarified world of graduate theological education, but I have found there is a critical need for us to shape sustainable communities of faith with a sense of joyful accountability. This task requires us to think in terms of effectiveness and transformation.

Pastoral Perspective

If there is one day when pastors can integrate dynamics into worship, unsettling our members from their pews for theological and pastoral reasons, it is Easter. Mainline churchgoers usually refuse to be moved by Sunday worship. The cultural imperative of Monday through Saturday bids them to work hard and play hard. Conversely, come Sunday, congregants sit in uncomfortable pews and listen to lazy tempo hymns, while offering is as optional as are their voices in the liturgy. Many Christians refuse to be moved—except perhaps on Easter!

On Easter, churches break out the brass, hire soloists, decorate the cross; even the air is drenched with sweet aroma from lilies lavishing the altar. Who participates in this aesthetic expression and sensory interpretation of the text? The pastor, altar guild, choir, and ushers. If the celebration is for everyone, how can pastors more fully include the congregation in the worship of the day, embodying the story we aim to share? While the resurrection story may be the text for the service, Psalm 118 lends liturgical direction for Easter Day worship, helping us to draw all God's people into this life-giving story.

Psalm 118 is one of a cluster of praise psalms (Pss. 113–118) used at Jewish festivals of Passover, Tabernacle, and Weeks. Consider the elaborate liturgies of these festivities: pilgrims traveling great

¹⁹Open to me the gates of righteousness,
   that I may enter through them
   and give thanks to the Lord.

²⁰This is the gate of the Lord;
   the righteous shall enter through it.

²¹I thank you that you have answered me
   and have become my salvation.
²²The stone that the builders rejected
   has become the chief cornerstone.
²³This is the Lord's doing;
   it is marvelous in our eyes.
²⁴This is the day that the Lord has made;
   let us rejoice and be glad in it.

Exegetical Perspective

The final psalm sung as part of the Passover celebration, and the last of the Egyptian Hallel (praise) Psalms, Psalm 118 was also clearly written for use in the temple. In fact, along with Psalms 113–17, it was recounted at the three main annual festivals, including the Passover. It is unfortunate that the lectionary uses only a selection from the psalm, since the whole is equally appropriate for use at Easter. Portions of Psalm 118 also comprise the lection for Passion/Palm Sunday.

The psalm itself has a liturgical framework (vv. 1–4, 29) surrounding a song of thanksgiving (vv. 5–28). The final form is a thanksgiving processional liturgy that begins outside the gates of the temple and moves inside. The psalm itself is quite complex in structure, combining several speakers and ritual actions. Verses 1–4 are set up antiphonally, with the celebrant calling all to give thanks to YHWH in verse 1, followed by three specific groups in verses 2–4: Israel, the priests, and finally, anyone who fears YHWH. The fourfold call is all-encompassing, four being the number of completion. The first verse is most appropriately envisioned as sung by the leader, setting forth both the call and response, with the first line of verses 2–4 being sung by the leader and the refrain, "His steadfast love endures forever," sung by the group called upon to give thanks.

Homiletical Perspective

Psalm 118 is appointed for Easter because the church finds in this psalm both an allegory for Jesus' destiny and a way of expressing the great reversal that is Christ's resurrection. "The stone that the builders rejected has become the chief cornerstone" (vv. 22–23). Today, Psalm 118 also calls the church to a reversal in much Easter preaching.

Many Easter sermons move too quickly from what God is doing in raising Christ Jesus from the dead to what we ought to do because of or in response to what God has done. Many preachers pause at the empty tomb just long enough to say, "Christ is risen," and then send people on their way. "Like the women at the tomb," the preacher declares, "we are to go and tell." Or, we are to live in the power of Christ's resurrection. Or, we are to be the risen Christ's presence in the world. The Easter sermon becomes pep talk or marching orders. The appointed psalm stops such sermons right in their tracks. Confronted with the good news that "Christ is risen indeed," the psalm demonstrates that our first and most important response is to thank and praise God for the gift of new life.

"This is the day that the Lord has made," the psalmist declares. What a day this is! This is the day on which God did not give Jesus—and us—over to death. This is the day on which God opens Christ's

Psalm 118:1-2, 14-24

Theological Perspective

From a theological perspective, effectiveness correlates directly with the ancient notion of bearing fruit. It connotes a sense that God's mysterious power embraces us, turns us around (remember the Christian notion of *metanoia*), and sets us on a deliberate path in life. We are held accountable for living in a renewed, or transformed, way: rather than focus as we once did primarily on what serves us and brings us gain, we are turned outward to serve others—and, in so doing, to serve the God who frees us from ourselves. Whereas we once thought it most important to look in the mirror, we are now led to see that looking out the window is the path for us. We are turned from inward-serving to outward-serving, and one of the most important fruits we can bear is the sharing of our hope with others.

The Psalter text for today assumes an effective deliverance and a transformed life. Why is it so difficult for us to live into that same reality today? Whether we are called as clergy or laity, each of us is given a role in God's redeeming present and future. Each of us is to be an agent of renewal, transformation, and reconciliation. This vocation requires joyful and grateful passion from us, issuing forth in our sense of responsibility for passing on this way of being and doing in the world. There is no reason why those of us in theological education cannot be agents of this renewal too!

Sometimes we can learn from those in the field far better than we can from other sources. Congregations, agencies related to the churches, business organizations, governmental agencies, and the wide world of not-for-profit groups hold within them women and men, older and younger alike, who are filled with passion for living the biblical experience. From them we can learn a great deal about what it means to walk through the shadows of loss and death into new life. With them, we can be vehicles for rekindling that passion where it has become too tame or sterile; but it will require that we have no failure of nerve.

What might this experience look like? There are many possible ways of framing it, but for some years now I have been struck with insights from several strands of what is now referred to as "positive psychology." This is not the same thing as the "positive thinking" that was popular a half-century ago; it is far from it. One core insight provides a wonderfully rich contemporary translation of what this biblical text is pointing to: by looking beyond ourselves, we can come to new understanding of who we are and how we function in the world.

Pastoral Perspective

distances to worship at the temple in Jerusalem; special meals and sacrifices symbolizing elements of the Jewish people's story; communities celebrating; worshipers processing to the temple and reenacting stories. The festivals allowed people whole-body worship experience as they passed on their faith story. Psalm 118 offers us a chance for unbridled joyful worship, which we embody when we enact the text, give thanks, testify, and rejoice as a community.

We enact the text. In discussions of experiential worship and liturgics, most attention is paid to the word—spoken, sung, or prayed. Seldom in mainline settings is attention focused on physical movement. Lutheran pastor Bob Rognlien advises, "When we learn to worship God physically, we discover that our bodies can help our hearts, souls, and minds to love God more completely."[1] Psalm 118 guides us in physical worship. The psalmist requests entry through "the gates of righteousness (v. 19)," into the temple in order to give thanks to the Lord. A response follows, "the righteous shall enter" (v. 20). We then get a sense of processing into the sanctuary, where thanksgiving is offered more fully through praise of God's sovereignty and saving work. Further along, the procession and activity around the altar are specified: "Bind the festal procession with branches, up to the horns of the altar" (v. 27).

How could we integrate such congregational movement in Easter Day worship? In the Easter morning story, everyone stirs: the women journey somberly to the tomb and run anxiously to tell the good news; angels roll the stone from the tomb and speak with startled mourners; Jesus gardens, soon to appear among the followers; John and Peter sprint to the tomb. How much more fully can *we* grasp the revelation of resurrection if we physically interpret the story, reflecting the human search for God in procession through the sanctuary and up to the altar! From the altar, the congregation encounters God afresh. The psalmist proclaims, "The stone that the builders rejected has become the chief cornerstone" (v. 22).

We give thanks. A leader calls the community to give thanks to God (v. 1), and the choir responds, "God's steadfast love endures forever." God's *hesed* gives us reason to be thankful. Israel attests to God's *hesed* (v. 2); the priests attest to it (v. 3); all who fear God are thankful (v. 4). Many voices rise to proclaim God's faithfulness and merciful love. This is the God we seek to encounter.

---

1. Bob Rognlien, *Experiential Worship: Encountering God with Heart, Soul, Mind, and Strength* (Colorado Springs, CO: NavPress, 2005), 63.

Exegetical Perspective

Verses 5–18 contain the actual thanksgiving, which includes a summary of the situation (v. 5), a statement of trust in the Lord (vv. 6–7), and two proverbial sayings (vv. 8–9). The recounting of the psalmist's situation and God's response is followed by the psalmist's request for entry into the temple (v. 19). The invitation of the priest (or temple personnel) is given in verse 20, which is followed by the psalmist's gratitude to YHWH for that invitation in verse 21. Verse 22 can be seen as another proverbial saying, the completion of the psalmist's response, or the beginning of the people's speech. The syntax changes beginning with verse 23, where, instead of a single speaker, the whole community speaks, acknowledging God's gracious acts of salvation and asking for blessing (vv. 23–25), which is given in verse 26. Verse 27 combines a corporate confession (v. 27a) with a ritual instruction that could link this psalm directly with the feast of Sukkot (the feast of Tabernacles), in which interwoven branches are brought in and waved (v. 27b). Verse 28 contains the speaker's last words of praise; verse 29 repeats verse 1 and is best viewed as being sung by the leader once again.

While the identity of the speaker in verses 5–19 is debated, given its final form as a thanksgiving liturgy, the speaker must be a representative of the people. The logical candidate is the king, which makes added sense in light of its use in Judaism as a messianic psalm, as well as its appropriation by the early church to refer to Jesus.

After verses 1–2, the lection continues with verses 14–24, skipping the description of the psalmist's situation (the psalmist was surrounded by enemies) and the psalmist's attribution of salvation to YHWH (v. 13). Verse 14 is more appropriately translated: "The LORD is my strength and my song [NRSV: "might"]; he has become my salvation." Verses 15–16 use the term "the right hand of the LORD" three times, almost as a refrain. This phrase echoes Exodus 15:6, which also pictures YHWH intervening to save Israel. The term "hand" in Hebrew is a euphemism for power, so verses 16–17 attribute the deliverance of the psalmist to God's power. Moreover, these verses suggest that the victory is to be celebrated by the whole community ("there are glad songs in the tents of the righteous," v. 15).

Verse 17 declares that the psalmist has escaped a life-and-death crisis and owes his or her life to God. The response of gratitude and spreading the word ("I will recount the deeds of the LORD") is a common response in the thanksgiving psalms. Christians have often read resurrection into this

Homiletical Perspective

tomb, the day on which God opens to us the gate of righteousness and we enter through it. This great good news is the core of Easter preaching. The psalmist prevails upon us to preach celebration, to inspire the congregation with our praise to acknowledge our salvation as an act of God. In the language of the psalm, Easter is a time for singing "glad songs in the tents of the righteous." On this day, the church breathes in and basks in the good news that "I shall not die but live." We proclaim, "I shall not die, but I shall live, and recount the deeds of the LORD" (v. 17). We might conceive of the Easter sermon as a "glad song." With the psalmist, our first response to Easter dawn is to sing praises to God for answering us and becoming our salvation.

With thanksgiving the church joins Israel in saying, "God's steadfast love endures *forever*." We celebrate the new life that God brought before Christ rose from the dead, as well as the new life that comes after. The expression "the right hand of the LORD," which appears three times in this reading (vv. 15–16), reminds us of God's ongoing work of bringing new life. The phrase is scriptural shorthand for God's power, exercised among both human beings and nations. It connects Christ's resurrection with God's saving acts recorded in the Hebrew Scriptures.

For example, Scripture recalls that by a strong hand God brought Israel out of the house of slavery; God stretched out God's right hand and shattered the enemy. The image of the right hand of the Lord points to both the exodus and the return from exile. These mighty acts inform what we celebrate on Easter. Christ's resurrection does more than overcome physical death. Christ's resurrection is God's victory over all the powers of death at work in our lives and the life of the world. This good news makes our glad song even louder, as the church recalls all God's saving acts and celebrates Christ's resurrection in the context of God's ongoing work of salvation, rather than as an isolated event.

Finally, Psalm 118 encourages the church to sing a glad song by helping to recover a sense of Easter's unexpectedness. Today we travel to the tomb knowing exactly what we will find. We will find the stone rolled away from the tomb, and we will not find the body (Luke 24:2–3); in response we will surely sing, "Jesus Christ is risen today." Psalm 118 invites us to shake up the celebration by reminding us that Easter is the reversal of everything we expect.

"The stone that the builders rejected has become the chief cornerstone" (v. 22). The church has used

Psalm 118:1-2, 14-24

Theological Perspective

This hope-filled insight focuses on what we *can* be and do, not on our inabilities. Athletes and artists discover the truth of it when they find themselves "in the zone" or "in flow." We can also see it at work when we are nurtured to develop the strengths that each of us brings to the world simply by virtue of who we are. By growing those strengths, we are able to express a greater capacity to make a difference, to have courage in trying circumstances. Doing so, we find that this frame of reference naturally leads to deeper passion, joy, and gratitude that spill over to the others with whom we share our experience.

Such a perspective represents a shift in our expectations, which is what Easter is all about. We see in transformed ways both ourselves and the world into which we fit. It is as if our old norms and fingerposts (think of finding your way in the dark on country pathways, and you will remember the importance of fingerposts) have been replaced. We see with fresh eyes, and can make new sense of that ancient text, "the stone that the builders rejected has become the chief cornerstone" (v. 22).

Easter re-presents us with our vocation to share God's grace with the world. Facing outward instead of inward, we are able to live in relationships that have been turned around. Discovering the strengths and talents that God has given us, we are able to share with others what transformed life is all about. Planting seeds of hope and inspiration in them, we are able to invite them to join us in grounded, passionate reconnection with the life-giving grace of God that Christian folk see in the living Jesus. What a claim to own—and pass on—as Easter dawns!

DAVID G. TRICKETT

Pastoral Perspective

We testify. Through many voices, one voice rises in testimony of the lived experience of God's steadfast love in the face of dire circumstances: "All nations surrounded me . . . like bees . . . I was pushed hard, so that I was falling" (vv. 10–13). The psalmist is won over and sings, "The LORD is my strength and my song; he has become my salvation" (v. 14 NIV). This victory is not only personal but communal, as when Moses sang the same words after God delivered him and the Israelites from Egypt (Exod. 15:2). "Glad songs of victory" build among those worshiping, not because of human agency, but because of God, who "does valiantly" and "is exalted" (vv. 15–16). God's victory opens both person and community to a new lease on life, "I am not going to die after all! I will live and choose life in giving thanks to God and in proclaiming God's works."

We rejoice. While many open worship with verse 24 ("This is the day that the LORD has made; let us rejoice and be glad in it!"), joy is in itself a revelation born from relationship with God. Psalm 118 declares God's ongoing work, which gives us reason for joy and gladness. This psalm points to the daily-ness of giving thanks to God and of choosing to live, not as people fearful of abusive human powers, but as people who side with God. Our joy flourishes in relationship with God, whose steadfast love endures.

Russell Mitman, pastor and intentional worship leader, writes, "God *moves* in a mysterious way in the encounter with God's people, and they discover at the conclusion of the worship event they are at a different place spiritually than they were when they were first called into encounter. . . . People are moved."[2] The congregation who first came searching for God now encounters God. How do we lead our people forward from this *moving* encounter? For our worship truly to embody the faithful life described in Psalm 118, we must "recount the deeds of the LORD" (v. 17). In searching and then giving thanks, we process into the sanctuary, and in joy we recess from the holy place, setting out to proclaim our faith: Christ has died, Christ is risen, Christ will come again.

M. ASHLEY GRANT

---

2. F. Russell Mitman, *Worship in the Shape of Scripture* (Cleveland: Pilgrim Press, 2001), 47.

Exegetical Perspective

verse (resurrection was a concept foreign to ancient Israel; the idea of resurrection did not develop until late in the Persian Period, around 200 BCE and thereafter). Verse 18 treats both the situation of distress and God's deliverance as the acts of God.

In verse 19, the psalmist approaches the entrance to the temple and asks for admittance. Verse 20 gives the gatekeeper's response: the righteous are allowed to enter. "The righteous" here refers to anyone whom YHWH has delivered. Verse 21, the last individual word of the psalmist in the lection, is appropriately a statement of thanksgiving.

Probably the most famous verse in our familiar lection is verse 22: "The stone that the builders rejected has become the chief cornerstone" (lit. the head of the corner). In its context, this verse encapsulates what God has done for the psalmist and shows a dramatic reversal. What was insignificant and unwanted has become one of the key foundations for the entire building. It is this verse that led to the psalm's use in messianic interpretation. It is quoted in several places in the NT (Matt. 21:42; Mark 12:10; Luke 20:17; Acts 4:11; Eph. 2:20; 1 Pet. 2:4–7), each time referring to Jesus, who was rejected by civil and religious leaders, but who has become the key to salvation.

The final verses of our lection, verses 23–24, represent the community's response: first comes the acknowledgment that it is God who has rescued the psalmist; it is followed by gratitude and praise. In verse 24, the phrase "this is the day that the LORD has made" connects this act of deliverance with God's creative acts. It is fully appropriate, then, that this is a reading for Easter, the day in which God made all things new through raising Jesus from the dead. Jesus' death and resurrection represent new life and a new beginning for worshipers and, indeed, for all of creation. Verse 22 also reminds us that we cannot experience the resurrection (Jesus as the chief cornerstone) without the crucifixion (the stone that the builders rejected). The ending note of praise and rejoicing is the only appropriate response, both then and now, to God's amazing acts.

MARY E. SHIELDS

Homiletical Perspective

this verse as a metaphor for Jesus for so long that it may have lost its power. What image can we offer to help our hearers recapture Easter surprise? For the women who went to the tomb and those who received their testimony, the resurrection of Jesus was unexpected. That Jesus' death and resurrection both represents and is an expression of the power of "the right hand of the LORD" was surprising—like a stone that the builders cast aside as useless turning out to be the perfect fit for the cornerstone, the most important component of the building. Even though we know what to expect on Easter, experiencing God's bringing life out of death often surprises us as surely as the empty tomb surprised those women. The psalmist reminds us that death transformed into new life could only be the Lord's doing. It is "marvelous to our eyes," the wonderful, unexpected sort of thing that only God could do. What image might we offer to help our hearers *experience* as well as understand Christ's resurrection in this way?

Easter is "the day that the LORD has made." By the powerful and unexpected act of raising Christ Jesus from the dead, God made a day, a special occasion on which we are to "rejoice and be glad" (v. 24). An Easter sermon that is a glad song rather than a pep talk will inspire and empower the church to join in singing both, "God's steadfast love endures forever," and "I shall not die, but I shall live, and recount the deeds of the LORD." Caught up in the song, the church does what it sings. The church goes and tells. The church lives in the power of Christ's resurrection. The church is the risen Christ's presence in the world.

CRAIG A. SATTERLEE

Acts 10:34-43

³⁴Then Peter began to speak to them: "I truly understand that God shows no partiality, ³⁵but in every nation anyone who fears him and does what is right is acceptable to him. ³⁶You know the message he sent to the people of Israel, preaching peace by Jesus Christ—he is Lord of all. ³⁷That message spread throughout Judea, beginning in Galilee after the baptism that John announced: ³⁸how God anointed Jesus of Nazareth with the Holy Spirit and with power; how he went about doing good and healing all who were oppressed by the devil, for God was with him. ³⁹We are witnesses to all that he did both in Judea and in Jerusalem. They put him to death by hanging him on a tree; ⁴⁰but God raised him on the third day and allowed him to appear, ⁴¹not to all the people but to us who were chosen by God as witnesses, and who ate and drank with him after he rose from the dead. ⁴²He commanded us to preach to the people and to testify that he is the one ordained by God as judge of the living and the dead. ⁴³All the prophets testify about him that everyone who believes in him receives forgiveness of sins through his name."

Theological Perspective

While the major text for this Easter must certainly be John's account of the resurrection, Peter's sermon in Acts 10 reminds us of the centrality of the resurrection for Christian faith. It is not, as some suppose, one of the more extravagant of the Bible's miracle stories, which for that reason might best be set aside. Nor, as others suppose, should the story of Jesus' rising from the grave be transmuted into a symbol or metaphor—as if it only points to the renewing power of faith, or of nature itself. Still less, we might add, is the resurrection of Jesus a singularly striking example of universal immortality with which humanity is endowed. As Paul makes clear in 1 Corinthians 15, our only hope for life beyond the grave depends upon Christ's victory over death. We do not possess it on our own. This is the message of Easter.

Generally speaking, technical theological discourse has little place in preaching. "Theology," in that sense, best serves as background that (1) can alert us to various dimensions of the content of the gospel, and (2) can provide a test as to whether what we are saying is consistent with it. If a sermon is not the place for theological argument, it is also not the place for arguments taken from philosophy, natural science, or other aspects of our own experience. This is especially true for preaching on Easter, when what ought to be a forthright *proclamation* of Jesus'

Pastoral Perspective

Here, in his last sermon in Acts, Peter realizes something essential about the God with whom he has always lived in relationship: God does not show partiality or favor. Rather, God offers restoration and salvation to all people, Jews and Gentiles alike. For Peter, the new insight is about the inclusion of Gentiles in God's program. Peter took for granted that Jews were included in God's love.

The question of God's partiality is a tricky one. In congregations, our struggle with partiality often comes up when we read and discuss certain passages in Hebrew Scripture. Indeed, as early as Cain and Abel, the troubling question of partiality arises. Why does one brother's sacrifice please God and the other's sacrifice does not? Then there is the problem of election. Why does God elect one nation and not others?

Of course the extravagant and universal love that Peter comes to understand through his encounter with Cornelius is there in Hebrew Scripture too, in the whispers of universality that offer a counterpoint to the decided particularity of election. Abraham's covenant includes, at its very inception, a promise of blessing to all nations; thus God's radical exclusion ends up in radical inclusion, which we see in Isaiah 2:1–5.

The news of God's impartial love is not just abstract information about God. It places a clear

Exegetical Perspective

Peter's sermon in the household of Cornelius is the most complete, concise articulation of the gospel in the book of Acts. The sermon has two main elements: (1) opening and closing statements that affirm God's impartiality (vv. 34–35) and offer forgiveness to all (v. 43) and (2) a recitation of the gospel story from its inception with the ministry of John, through Jesus' ministry, death, and resurrection, to the calling of the disciples as witnesses (vv. 36–42). These two elements serve a single, integral purpose: the articulation of the universal reach of God's actions through Jesus Christ. For Luke, the gospel apparently does not end with the story of Jesus, but includes all that has happened since, not only among the people of Israel, but among everyone who fears God in every nation (v. 35). The gospel history that Peter recites is thus a living, still-unfolding expression of God's impartiality, the dimensions of which are still dawning fresh on Peter.

Peter's sermon embodies the tension between the universalistic implications of the claim of divine impartiality and the particularity of the Judean setting of the gospel story as Peter has heretofore experienced it. We might expect that Peter would tailor the message to his Gentile audience, but instead he emphasizes the Jewish roots and setting of

Homiletical Perspective

As preachers read through this commentary during this most profound week of the church year, perhaps they are asking the all-too-familiar question, "How can the Easter message be preached yet again with freshness?" This is a common struggle for many preachers. Those who are called to stand behind the holy desk are constantly trying to find new and clever ways to communicate the gospel. This quest for sacred novelty reaches its most challenging point during weeks such as this one. What can be said about Easter that has not already been said?

Perhaps there will be preachers who find themselves wandering away from the assigned Gospel text for Easter to seek another text that might offer a unique perspective. At first glance, the assigned reading in Acts does not seem to deliver much marrow for the preacher. On the surface it appears to be just a snippet of a sermon from Peter where he summarizes the ministry of Jesus. All the key points are mentioned. God anointed Jesus with the Holy Spirit when he was baptized by John the Baptist. He went about doing good and healing the oppressed. He was crucified. God raised Jesus from the dead on the third day. Everyone who believes in him will be forgiven of sin. A concise summary, but what unique perspective does it offer the preacher who is moving ever closer to the big Sunday when everyone will be in church?

Acts 10:34-43

Theological Perspective

resurrection is often obscured by vain attempts to prove that it really happened.

For this Sunday, it is enough to proclaim the resurrection as the central fact of Christian faith, with attention to Acts 10 to present some aspects of its meaning for Christian life.

Concerning the centrality of the resurrection, we should remind ourselves that the Gospel narratives describing it are the basis for every other account of Jesus' life and ministry. Since the Enlightenment, this has often been forgotten by Protestant theology. Under the influence of the so-called age of reason, the Bible was subjected to a historical-critical method of interpretation whereby reports of the miraculous were regularly discounted as myths, so that what was left of the gospel was merely Jesus' ethical teaching. Permutations of this approach may be found in Rudolf Bultmann's reduction of the New Testament to an existential message of hope, and more recently to the well publicized work of the Jesus Seminar, in which the historically reliable portions of the Gospels are further reduced to a social ethic amenable to the needs of modern life. In all of these, the actual resurrection of Jesus plays no part.[1]

Such neglect renders the New Testament largely inexplicable. Given the apostles' earlier insistence upon Jesus' rising from the dead, how can we understand the Gospel writers' portrayal of his miraculous birth, the event of his baptism, the significance of his death, or the special authority assigned to his sometimes unoriginal teaching, if the church's recollection of these things was not seen in the light of Jesus' resurrection? If God had not "raised him on the third day and allowed him to appear . . . to us who were chosen by God as witnesses" (vv. 40–41), none of Jesus' life activities could have been understood as they are in the New Testament. The resurrection, far from being a rather unbelievably happy ending tacked onto the life of Jesus, is, in fact, the indispensable precondition of its telling.[2]

The meaning of the resurrection encompasses the whole of the gospel. It is *the* revelatory event that attests to the truth of Christian faith. Without it, the divine humanity of Jesus could not be asserted, nor could the saving grace of his life and death be believed. Regarding the latter, Peter's address to Cornelius and his friends suggests several

---

1. Cf. Rudolf Bultmann et al., *Kerygma and Myth* (New York: Harper & Row, 1961), esp. chap. 1. For the conclusions of the Jesus Seminar, see John Dominic Crossan, *Jesus: A Revolutionary Biography* (San Francisco: HarperSanFrancisco, 1994).
2. See Karl Barth, *Church Dogmatics*, IV/2 (Edinburgh: T. & T. Clark, 1967), 140–51.

Pastoral Perspective

demand on us, to love impartially as God loves. Peter enacts God's impartial love by eating with Gentiles. At the table, Peter actively works out reconciliation with Gentiles; he actively seeks peace with them.

It is no coincidence that the message Peter focuses on here is the "good news of peace through Jesus Christ" (v. 36 NIV). The theme of peace runs throughout the New Testament. Jesus himself promises peace in his Farewell Discourse in the Gospel of John: "My peace I give to you." Paul told the Ephesians that he was preaching the gospel of peace. The peace that Jesus, Peter, and Paul are talking about is an active, reconciling kind of peace. Through his abject pacifism on the cross, Jesus restored peace between God and God's creatures. It is that peace between God and people that makes possible peace between and among people. This is one thing that Jesus' resurrection means. Suddenly, what seemed absurd before Easter is now a real possibility. This church—the early church with which Peter was concerned, and our church today—can become a community of active peacemaking, a community of radical reconciliation between men and women, rich and poor, Jew and Gentile.

Peter's insight into God's impartiality is not supposed to make us preen. We are not supposed to hear Peter's proclamation of God's cosmopolitanism and feel good about ourselves because we know and love a God who knows and loves all. Rather, Peter's insight—what really might be termed Peter's conversion—should chasten us. The words should strike us as a critique. God wants to be in relationship with all kinds of people. Because God loves all people, we are able—indeed called—to expose ourselves to those people too. Because God is the God of impartiality, we are called to be a people of impartiality. Because God makes peace with us and with all, we are called to make peace with other people.

Yet do we?

I do not. I would like to think I do, but I do not. In fact, much of the time I act like God is partial and, unsurprisingly, my God mostly favors me and my way of doing things.

Rather than actively making peace with other people, we are implicated in our own partiality over and over in the church: in the kinds of families we welcome into the church preschool; in the churches we are willing to engage in ecumenical work; in the distinctions we draw between the people we break bread with at the Communion table and the people we invite home for a dinner party.

the gospel ("the message . . . sent to the people of Israel," v. 36; "Judea" and "Galilee," v. 37; "Judea" and "Jerusalem," v. 39; "the prophets," v. 43). The apparent tension between the Jewish flavor and Gentile audience of the sermon reflects Peter's understanding of his vocation as "witness." The message sent to the people of Israel is that Jesus Christ is "Lord of all" (v. 36), and the message for the Gentile Cornelius is that the one he has been praying for is the Jewish Messiah, put to death on a tree in Jerusalem (v. 39b). Whether the audience is Jewish or Gentile, the gospel Peter preaches carries both potential offense and reason for hope.

Peter's opening statement, "I truly understand that God shows no partiality," suggests a change in his own awareness. Assertions of divine impartiality or universalism were not novel concepts for first-century people, but now Peter's perception of the dimensions of God's impartiality is taking on new clarity and force. In the larger context of Acts 10, Peter's statement is the public pronouncement of his own continuing conversion and, with this, the transformation of the church's understanding of its vocation (cf. 11:1–18). Realization of the gospel clearly entails the transformation of the missionary as well as those who are the objects of mission. This mutual conversion of both Peter the Jew and Cornelius the Gentile is a necessary aspect of the proclamation of peace through Jesus Christ (v. 36, cf. Luke 2:14, 19:42). By naming clearly what Peter has known, if not fully understood, about God, Peter's sermon opens up imaginative space for the continuing conversion of the church and for the mission to the nations.

Peter's growing insight into God's impartiality (vv. 34–35) has its christological corollary in the primary assertion of verse 36: "Jesus is Lord of all." The "message [God] sent to the people of Israel" (v. 36) recalls first of all the divine announcement to the shepherds (Luke 2:8–20) about Jesus' birth, and probably also refers to the good news that Jesus himself proclaimed and embodied throughout his ministry. In Luke 2:10–11, the announcement of good news for "all the people" is associated with "the Lord" who is "Savior" and the Davidic "Messiah." The shepherds who heard that message would have presumed that "all the people" referred to Israel. Peter's conception of "all" (Acts 10:36, 43) expands along with his perception of the dimensions of God's impartiality. The promised messianic peace, announced to the Jewish people and realized in the ministry of Jesus, is now extended to all people, in every nation, who believe in him (v. 43).

A bit of reflection on this text will remind preachers what they already know about how to preach the Easter message effectively. Initially, what is made plain in this text is that Peter is not concerned with the contemporary preacher's malaise of "effective illustrations for sermons." Peter is so compelled to preach the good news to the Gentiles that he gets right to it. He assumes his listeners do not know why the good news is so good. Peter sees his primary responsibility as simply telling the gospel story. No decorations. No fanfare. Just the story of Jesus.

This is an important lesson for preachers as they prepare their sermons for Easter. After all, studies show that most preachers can no longer assume that the majority of their listeners are familiar with the Bible. On Sunday, preachers may find a congregation expecting to hear something about a special man coming out of a tomb, but they may not be expecting to hear a preacher boldly proclaim the truth that because this man was raised from the dead, their sins can be forgiven and their lives forever changed. This is the Easter message that Christ commanded Peter and every other preacher to proclaim.

Easter is an opportunity for preachers to lay bare the good news of Jesus Christ and get out of the way. Too often, preachers, in their well intended desire to create "dynamic" sermons, inadvertently prevent listeners from hearing about the resurrection power of Christ. Like some commercials during the Super Bowl—everyone remembers the humorous content but nobody remembers the product advertised—so too our sermons can become entertaining discourses without any clear, convicting message about the life-giving and life-changing power of Christ. What is the message of Easter if it is not a resoundingly clear and passionate proclamation that there is new life in Christ?

Preachers may be surprised at what occurs within listeners when the good news of Easter is unashamedly preached. During Peter's simple sermon, the Holy Spirit came upon those who were listening, and the circumcised believers were "astounded" that the Holy Spirit had been given to the Gentiles (vv. 44–45). Many preachers may also be astounded at how the Holy Spirit works through an honest exhortation of the gospel. Perhaps some people the preacher thinks least likely to hear and respond to the word of God will actually come alive. Is it too much for preachers to expect this to occur? Through the years, many preachers have commented

Acts 10:34-43

Theological Perspective

dimensions of this grace that we can here only briefly mention under the heading of "freedom."

We must not ignore the context of Peter's sermon, namely, his obedience to the divine command to reach out beyond the boundaries of Judaism to preach the gospel to Gentiles. The divinity of Christ, so powerfully displayed in his resurrection, caused Peter to perceive that "God shows no partiality," that beyond the confines of biblical history the "acceptance" and grace of God extends to "every nation" (vv. 34–35). Today, when the political rhetoric of freedom runs afoul of religious presumptions on all sides, it is important to recognize that if the risen and ascended Christ lives, he lives as God lives—free of any constraints or limits we might set to his work of salvation. The church witnesses to that grace, but neither the church, nor its scriptures, nor its confessions can contain, control, or own it.

As we are freed by the freedom of the risen Christ from the religious exclusivity that threatens our world today, so are we freed from the guilt and despair that accompany both our corporate and our personal lives. While the reader of this commentary needs no help defining our corporate and personal sins, it is worth remembering that the forgiveness achieved on the cross and confirmed in the resurrection is not only a personal matter, but is directed as well to communities. This is plainly the case among the prophets of the Old Testament, where the promise of forgiveness is applied to the nation Israel. If prophetic criticism creates the need, the promise of forgiveness creates the possibility for amendment of life—not only for individuals, but also and even for a nation-state whose prideful miscalculations have caused much suffering and death.

We have much to answer for, but "the one ordained by God [to be] judge of the living and the dead" (v. 42) is the one God raised up on the third day to make manifest and confirm the fact that on the cross he really did take—and take away—the sins of the world. This, and not political rhetoric, promises real freedom. This too is the message of Easter.

ALEXANDER J. MCKELWAY

Pastoral Perspective

One of the most heinous instances of the church's partiality is our long history of doing violence in the name of Christ to Jewish communities. Eastertide— just a few weeks after we have proclaimed the Johannine passion narrative, a text that has been deployed to quite violent ends over the centuries—is perhaps an especially appropriate time to educate our congregations about that long history, and to consider whether today our churches actively reflect God's love for, and God's choice of, Jews.

Too often our churches fail on this score. When we casually talk about "legalism," or when we associate the Old Testament with "law" (bad) and the New Testament with "love" (good), or when we use "Pharisee" as shorthand for the worst kind of rigidity and bigotry, we fail to reflect what Peter took for granted: that Jews are perforce included in God's love and restoration. I was recently given a story cube, a small toy that tells the story of Easter to tots. I noticed that all the bad guys—the ones crucifying Jesus—were wearing yarmulkes. They were, in other words, marked visually as Jews. Jesus and his followers were not. What does that story cube teach small children? That Jesus rose from the dead, to be sure. Also that the people who killed Jesus were Jews, but somehow Jesus and his disciples were not.

Peter was surprised that God's love included even the Gentiles. Perhaps the surprising word in the church today is that God's love includes the Jews. Throughout church history, we have been guilty of reversing Peter's formulation and concluding, in a supersessionist bent, that God's love does not any longer include Jews, but only Christians. Perhaps Peter's words may today be read as an invitation to redress this in our churches, and consider how we can once again become a body devoted to impartiality and reconciliation, and especially a body in which Jews and Christians are reconciled to one another.

LAUREN F. WINNER

Exegetical Perspective

The concise recitation of the gospel narrative in verses 37–42 both recalls the main elements of Luke's account of Jesus' ministry and highlights the role of the disciples as witnesses (vv. 39, 41, 42). All of these events are elements of "the message"—that Jesus is Lord of all—that spread throughout Galilee and Judea, beginning already with John's call to baptism. The claim that God anoints Jesus of Nazareth with the Holy Spirit and with power (v. 38a) refers particularly to Jesus' articulation of his call in Luke 4:16–30, as well as to his baptism (Luke 3:21–22; cf. Luke 4:1, 14). Jesus' power is also evident in his healing ministry and his exorcisms, which liberate the people from sickness and the oppressions of the devil (Acts 10:38), and demonstrate that "God was with him" (v. 38c). God is the primary force in all that has happened, including the events that have brought Peter to the house of Cornelius. In 10:39–40, Peter's focus shifts to the death and resurrection of Jesus, which both secure forgiveness for all (v. 43) and establish Jesus as "judge of the living and the dead" (v. 42), that is, the universal judge of all people, regardless of their ethnicity and status. From beginning to end, this series of divine actions constitutes the gospel message that God has announced to the people of Israel and that Peter now announces to Cornelius.

Peter gives particular attention to his role as witness. The disciples have witnessed everything Jesus did both "in Judea and in Jerusalem," including his death and resurrection on the third day (vv. 39–40). The risen Jesus appears not to everyone, but only to those who are "chosen by God as witnesses" (v. 41a) and who "ate and drank" with the resurrected Jesus (v. 41; see also Luke 24:42–43). Here Peter indicates that his testimony bears witness to both the living and crucified Jesus and the Jesus who has been resurrected from the dead. Peter has witnessed the reality of Christ's life and power on both sides of the crucifixion. Eating and drinking with the resurrected Jesus reaffirms Luke's assertion that hospitality and table fellowship provide the settings where the crucified and resurrected Jesus is still discovered (see Luke 22:14–23; 24:13–35). It is therefore perfectly fitting that Peter's witness in the house of Cornelius will be sealed by the coming of the Spirit and by extended hospitality and table fellowship (Acts 10:48; 11:3).

STANLEY P. SAUNDERS

Homiletical Perspective

on the simplicity of Billy Graham's sermons. There is nothing creative or clever about them. He has never attempted to make the gospel more palatable for his listeners. Like Peter, Graham has simply preached the salvation message of Christ and been wise enough to leave the rest to God.

After reading and reflecting on this text, some preachers may come to the conclusion that what they need for Easter is not some clever idea or gimmick but a renewed passion to preach the gospel of Jesus Christ. There is an old story about a saint named Abbot Joseph who lived during the fourth century CE. He offered wisdom to many young monks who were trying to find their way. One day a frustrated monk sought the abbot for guidance. The young monk explained that he was doing everything he was told to do but still felt a void. He fasted and prayed. He spent time in contemplative silence and meditated on the Scriptures. He did his best to cleanse his heart of bad thoughts. He did all he knew to do, but there was still something missing. Desperate, he asked the abbot, "What more should I do?" The abbot rose up in reply and lifted his hands to heaven. Suddenly, his fingers became like ten lamps of fire. As the young monk looked on with amazement, the abbot said, "Why not be totally changed into fire?"[1]

What has been said about Easter that has not already been said? A lot! Like Cornelius and the rest of Peter's crowd, there will be plenty of people in churches on Easter who will be saying in their hearts, "All of us are here in the presence of God to listen to *all* that that the Lord has commanded you to say" (Acts 10:33). Dare a preacher be turned into fire this Sunday?

CHARLES D. REEB

---

1. Barbara Brown Taylor, *Gospel Medicine* (Boston: Cowley Publications, 1995), 131–32.

John 20:1-18

¹Early on the first day of the week, while it was still dark, Mary Magdalene came to the tomb and saw that the stone had been removed from the tomb. ²So she ran and went to Simon Peter and the other disciple, the one whom Jesus loved, and said to them, "They have taken the Lord out of the tomb, and we do not know where they have laid him." ³Then Peter and the other disciple set out and went toward the tomb. ⁴The two were running together, but the other disciple outran Peter and reached the tomb first. ⁵He bent down to look in and saw the linen wrappings lying there, but he did not go in. ⁶Then Simon Peter came, following him, and went into the tomb. He saw the linen wrappings lying there, ⁷and the cloth that had been on Jesus' head, not lying with the linen wrappings but rolled up in a place by itself. ⁸Then the other disciple, who reached the tomb first, also went in, and he saw and believed; ⁹for as yet they did not understand the scripture, that he must rise from the dead. ¹⁰Then the disciples returned to their homes.

Theological Perspective

The Easter texts were written and told in order first to bring judgment on a hopeless world and then to save a faithless one. Such texts are prophetic, and those who preach them are called to be prophets. Prophets? We should use that title cautiously. Novelist Saul Bellow, who back in the 1960s heard many civic activists referred to as "prophets," wearied of such use of the term. Many of them were sincere and well-intentioned speakers, but as he heard them, most activists of any sort were people who talked not about God but about themselves, their causes, or the evil of their foes. I heard Bellow say in a lecture, "Being a prophet is nice work if you can get it. But to be a prophet, sooner or later you have to talk about God."

Preachers can easily get in the habit of forgetting that "*sooner*." It is tempting for them to talk first about themselves and their opinions or about world affairs or movies. They may then forget about God entirely, or speak in such unsure and muffled tones that no one hears or gets the point or experiences God's power from them. So the corrective reminder has to be emphatic: it *is* more efficient and effective to talk about God *sooner*. Notice that the theological theme that prompts the "God-talk" of this text from John 20 focuses on the crucial theme of what God does to turn an ancient story into a prophetic word that will help make the conversion of humans possible.

Pastoral Perspective

The narrative here seems almost two separate stories, that of the woman Mary and that of the two men, Peter and the other disciple, the one whom Jesus loved.

I call the disciples "men," but the word that comes more quickly to mind is "boys." There seems such a childish competition between them. When they get word of the missing body, they run to the tomb, but their racing is not presented just as a run to arrive: it is reported as a race, with care taken to tell that the "other disciple," the one with whom the author identifies, outran Peter and got there first. He won the race, even though Peter, typically brash, was the one who forged first into the tomb. So yes, the common claim that Peter was the first of the male disciples at the actual site of the resurrection may have some truth, but only by a technicality. The other one, John, was really first, and the faster runner. Besides, he was the one whom Jesus loved. Perhaps I overstate the comic quality of John's account here, but it is hard to ignore at least the suggestion of such childish, such boyish, competition between these two iconic figures.

The story of Mary Magdalene, on the other hand, has nothing of such comedy. Arguably, there *is* something of comedy in the classic sense in the confusion about Jesus and the gardener, but that is

¹¹But Mary stood weeping outside the tomb. As she wept, she bent over to look into the tomb; ¹²and she saw two angels in white, sitting where the body of Jesus had been lying, one at the head and the other at the feet. ¹³They said to her, "Woman, why are you weeping?" She said to them, "They have taken away my Lord, and I do not know where they have laid him." ¹⁴When she had said this, she turned around and saw Jesus standing there, but she did not know that it was Jesus. ¹⁵Jesus said to her, "Woman, why are you weeping? Whom are you looking for?" Supposing him to be the gardener, she said to him, "Sir, if you have carried him away, tell me where you have laid him, and I will take him away." ¹⁶Jesus said to her, "Mary!" She turned and said to him in Hebrew, "Rabbouni!" (which means Teacher). ¹⁷Jesus said to her, "Do not hold on to me, because I have not yet ascended to the Father. But go to my brothers and say to them, 'I am ascending to my Father and your Father, to my God and your God.'" ¹⁸Mary Magdalene went and announced to the disciples, "I have seen the Lord"; and she told them that he had said these things to her.

Exegetical Perspective

John's Easter morning sequence is surely one of the most memorable. In the Synoptics, Mary Magdalene is accompanied by other women to the tomb (see Matt. 28:1; Mark 16:1; Luke 23:55–24:1, 10). Here, she is alone. Mary comes while it is still "dark." This may be John's way of underlining, once again, the dark/light symbolism first announced in 1:5. The time of Mary's arrival may also be seen to mirror both the darkness of her despair and the depth of confusion her discovery engenders.

That Mary found the tomb's stone "removed" invites comparison with the circumstances surrounding Jesus' raising of Lazarus (11:38–41), where the stone needed to be taken away. Mary's alarm, her summons to Peter and the "other" disciple ("the one whom Jesus loved," the Beloved Disciple), suggest that she fears the work of grave robbers.

Those who detect a rivalry between Peter and the Beloved Disciple in what follows overlook the sheer narrative energy this passage manages to convey— *and* the ambiguity with which it concludes. Peter leaves for the tomb first, followed by the "other disciple." Then, for a time, they are running together. What amounts to a footrace ensues, with the other disciple outrunning Peter, arriving at the tomb first. He looks in, balks, but does not enter. Peter does. He observes the particulars of the evidentiary remains,

Homiletical Perspective

This text is privileged in the Revised Common Lectionary; every year it is listed as the Gospel reading for Easter worship. Although it is by no means the earliest account of the resurrection (that honor belongs to the creedal statement quoted by Paul in 1 Cor. 15:3–5), it has held great influence throughout the ages. This is true not only because of its place in the lectionary but also because of the author's fine attention to dramatic and narrative detail, drawing readers into its scenes and offering them the same choices once given to Mary, Peter, and the Beloved Disciple. Countless hymns have been composed and pictures painted about this scene at the tomb. So it remains the Easter classic. Each preacher will have to determine whether she or he can preach it every year or turn to another Gospel's account of Jesus' followers at the empty tomb.

In the first two verses, the narrator reintroduces the three characters whose responses dominate John's version of the story. Mary Magdalene finds the tomb with its stone rolled away. When she runs to tell the others that the body has disappeared, Peter and the Beloved Disciple take off to see for themselves before Mary returns to make her own discoveries. It is in the responses of these three model disciples that we find homiletical riches for our Easter preaching.

John 20:1-18

Theological Perspective

So we talk about conversion. To make a textbook case out of this, we recall that the Hebrew word for "convert" is *shub*, meaning to "turn back," to "return," or that the Greek is *metanoia*, which also implies a 180-degree turning. Both indicate the involvement of the heart and not just the head—though conversion includes a change of mind or intellectual dimension. This conversion can occur when people hear testimony as the word is preached, become aware of the presence of God in the sacraments, or are moved by the generous activity of people who have already turned or been turned. Christians believe that their baptism represents and effects such a turning, a newness in Christ.

In the tradition of the Reformation, which was in some continuity with older Catholic interpretations, while conversion occurred in churchly contexts of preaching and the sacraments, special stress was placed on the personal dimension, in which divine grace worked in the human heart. Sometimes conversion occurred in an instant, as in this text. Here we find the model of Mary Magdalene's conversion, and then that of a disciple and Peter. They turned or were turned from being uncomprehending to knowing emphatic faith. For other people through the ages, conversion resulted from a long process that might involve resistance before there is acceptance. Believers come to know and to testify that conversion, the opening of the eyes and hearts plus the openness to faith and hope and love, is not something one can accomplish through her own purpose or strength. Converts like to speak, instead, of the Holy Spirit being active.

Now we can look more closely at the story that suggests this theological theme. If we remember that conversion refers to turning around, to being turned, we will be informed and moved by two case studies here. The first is that of Mary Magdalene. She had to be converted from the sincere and well-intended business she had generously undertaken, to take charge in a hope-less memorial act for the dead Jesus. Then, we are told, she looked and "saw." Did she really yet see? Notice that there was no reference to God, no God-talk in her statement to Peter and the other disciple. No, she said that an anonymous "*They* have taken the Lord out of the tomb" (v. 2), and "*they*" must have laid him somewhere. So, unturned, unconverted, she quite naturally wept outside the tomb, engulfed in her puzzlement and her grieving. When asked about what was going on, we heard her say again that "they" must have done something, not that God *had* done something and

Pastoral Perspective

very different from the boys-will-be-boys rivalry that brings a smile of recognition at the footrace. What we have in the Magdalene story, rather, is deep and intimate emotion. Unlike the empty-tomb stories of the other evangelists, John's account gives us just one woman, one who comes to the tomb alone. She comes out of her own desire to be where the body of Jesus is. She is bereft that he has been taken away, not just by death but by the disappearance of his body. She grieves, she yearns, she weeps. Her words are poignant, and we can feel the hurt and longing in them: "They have taken away my Lord, and I do not know where they have laid him" (v. 13).

Try as I might, I cannot help but hear a resonance of the Magdalene's voice in *Jesus Christ Superstar*, that of the amazed and devoted lover of the man who has moved her so deeply. Volumes have been written on all that is problematic with that tradition of imagining Mary Magdalene, both as it has diminished her likely importance as an apostle in her own right and as it has played out as a paradigmatic male fantasy about women. This story, like other images of feminine devotion to a messianic male figure, is fraught with danger, with both a history of and a potential for misappropriation. Let the teller of the tale take care! Cognizant of such risk, however, I am moved once more by this woman who loves with such longing for a lost beloved. Lurid legends or prurient speculation about the Magdalene set aside, this *does* seem the depiction of an intimate and deeply embodied affection.

Is it not both curious and wonderful that these two stories—one of the boys and one of the woman, the comic and the passionate—sit here, one within the other? While we might opt to preach primarily from the one or the other, why not let both play upon us, reminding us that the encounter with the resurrection can be experienced differently by different people at different times, its music in different keys and danced in different ways?

The empty tomb found by the disciples is a place pregnant with potential meaning not yet understood. What it means is still unknown, but what it will mean transforms both past and future for the eager disciples who run to it. They see nothing within but empty wrappings, the leavings of one who left, and only later will they understand what presence that absence bodes.

Mary, on the other hand, has not raced with curiosity or hope, but has come to pay grief's necessary homage to one she loved. When she looks

Easter Day

apparently concurring with Mary's initial assessment (grave robbery). The Beloved Disciple weighs the material effects differently.

The disposition of the burial cloths is peculiar. Again, a contrast with Jesus' raising of Lazarus (11:41–44) is surely meant to be drawn. Not only did Lazarus's stone have to be removed; Lazarus emerged from the tomb "bound hand and foot" in grave clothes, his face wrapped with a cloth. Onlookers were charged with the task of disentangling him. For the Beloved Disciple, this tidiness augurs for an interpretation other than a case of mere robbery. It seems not to be a matter of resuscitation.

The Beloved Disciple "believes"—but what? The discovery, as it presents itself, does not yet add up to a fully articulated belief in Jesus' resurrection. The evangelist underscores this by noting that "as yet they did not understand the scripture, that he must rise from the dead" (20:9). Indeed, the men return to their homes. Their investigation of the tomb has *not* served, as many claim, to corroborate or to provide a legally valid (Deut. 19:15) confirmation by two male witnesses of an insufficient, singular, inferior, female report.

Mary remains at the tomb, outside, distraught. When she peers in, grave clothes do not arrest her attention. The tomb is no longer empty! There are "two angels in white, sitting where the body of Jesus had been lying, one at the head and the other at the feet" (v. 12; cf. Mark 16:5; Matt. 28:2–3; Luke 24:4). The angels, whom Mary does not acknowledge as such, are reverencing an empty space. Perhaps this cenotaphic tableau is an *ironic* evocation of the ark of the covenant: God's presence is absent in this place of death. When they ask her why she is crying, she persists in her assumption that a heist has occurred.

Mary backs out of the tomb, turns around, and encounters a human figure. She thinks it is the "gardener" (Gk. *kēpouros*—a *hapax legomenon* in the NT and LXX). Is this meant to evoke the rather different garden encounter between God, Adam, and Eve in Genesis 3:8? Sticking to her guns that the body of Jesus has been relocated, she begs him for information of its whereabouts. We anticipate a Homer-like recognition scene (e.g., Odysseus's nurse catches sight of the hero's telltale scar and welcomes his return). Rather, Jesus calls her by name: "Mary!" Suddenly, it is clear to her: she is face to face with the (literally "my") "Teacher." The reader is expected to remember that when Jesus was teaching in Jerusalem before his death, he said, "I am the good shepherd,"

The Beloved believes. The minute the beloved disciple hears Mary's news, he jumps up to see what has happened, arriving at the tomb before Peter. His actions seem perfectly understandable, since in the Fourth Gospel he always represents the most appropriate way to respond to Jesus and his message. After all, he stayed with Jesus all the way to the bitter end; why would he not want to see what has happened now? Because the Beloved Disciple serves as the faithful witness, the source of the irreplaceable knowledge for belief in this Gospel, he must see for himself the linen cloths and the bodyless tomb. He instantly believes without full comprehension or explanation of what it all means.

We know people like this today; every church needs them to survive. These are the people who have no evidence to believe that the boy who messes up the sound equipment in the sanctuary will be anything but trouble, yet insist that he is headed toward a brilliant career in sound engineering. These are the people who see service possibilities in broken-down playgrounds and faded fellowship halls. These are the people who require no proof that eternal life trumps death and smile inwardly every time they hear the word "resurrection." Although they may often annoy us with their boundless optimism and refusal to face facts as we see them, we secretly cheer for them and draw strength for our own faith journeys from their unwavering trust that God will work good, even out of a crucifixion.

Peter runs. Peter's reaction to Mary's news about an open tomb is less easy to understand in this Gospel. We are not sure why he joins this outlandish footrace to Jesus' tomb; after all, he has just spent the last few days running away from Jesus. Why is he running toward him now? Although the Fourth Evangelist does not speculate, we may make some guesses. Perhaps it is simple jealousy, a desire to prove that he is as good as the faithful Beloved Disciple. Or perhaps guilt motivates Peter to run out the door so that he can say he is sorry—for denying Jesus after boasting about his loyalty, for not being present at the cross, for running away when the chips were down. Or maybe Peter felt a hopeful curiosity. With all the other disciples, he was present at the raising of Lazarus. Could it be possible that the same thing has happened to Jesus?

Many of us live with Peter in this complex of emotions. We harbor petty jealousies in our souls for those who seem so blessed by the love of God, so full of confidence and joy. We are resentful of the success

John 20:1-18

Theological Perspective

was doing it now. Her response was passive and ordinary. Then when she turned around, she saw Jesus; but still, with unconverted eyes and heart, she did not recognize him. She believed in the presence of a gardener, but had not yet believed in or felt the presence of God in the risen Christ. She heard an ordinary word, simply, her name, but it was spoken with a theological intention, to quicken her faith and hope: "Mary!" Then, *"She turned"* her face to him (v. 16) and then really "turned," which is exactly what conversion means and is about. She now had to tell others.

In the process, she had gotten ahead of them, so she turned before those two disciple insiders got there. They began to "see," in a beginning of conversion, but this is still not the end of our story. The process next took several turns. The first of two disciples peeked into the tomb, "but he did not go in" (v. 5) to where the action had been and the evidence lay. (You cannot be converted if you are not open to stirrings and signs.) Then, we hear, when Peter *did* go in, he saw something, and did some deducing. Whatever it was that Peter did moved the first disciple to open himself and now to explore. This disciple "went in, and he saw and believed" (v. 8).

The process still was only half completed. The disciple and Peter did not know what to make of the experience, "for as yet they did not understand the scripture, that [Jesus] must rise from the dead" (v. 9). They simply and sadly went home. They did not yet do what Mary Magdalene could do and did, for she "went and announced to the disciples, 'I have seen the Lord!'" (v. 18). She told them that he had said certain things to her, thus providing a case study in the phenomenology of conversion and its positive consequences.

MARTIN E. MARTY

Pastoral Perspective

in, she sees not only the emptiness but the angels who make the slab no longer a mere place of absence but a vision of the mercy seat and the ark of God's presence (Exod. 25:17–22). Yet, after responding to the angels and telling her grief, Mary turns *away* from the tomb; even with angels, with religious symbolism, with supernatural promise and implications, it cannot hold her interest. It does not compensate for the reality of Jesus, does not dissolve her grief. He is not there, and she turns away. It is when she turns around that she encounters the one whom she seeks, in reality and not just potential. At first she does not recognize him—we may think of all the different reasons we also do not recognize our Christ—but he calls her by name. Then she sees and exclaims her greeting in return, "*Rabbouni*, my teacher."

There is tenderness of affection here and the joy of a real presence, but there is finally that *Noli me tangere* and a new incompleteness: she may not hold on to him, perhaps not even touch him. He is going away, and as she seems to reach for him, he retreats from her. She will be his apostle to the disciples, but he does not stay to be held. That withdrawal is also part of the story.

There is much that may engage our reflection here, much familiar from our parish experience—comedy and devastation, symbol and realities, encounters and absences, the dance of nearness and distance in relationships—all of it laid out, not as the tired story of human life through the generations, but as it shines in the transfiguring light of the resurrection morning. May we preachers see it, and show it, so freshly new.

JOHN K. STENDAHL

Exegetical Perspective

who "calls his own sheep *by name* and leads them out" (10:11, 3). They follow him because they "know his voice" (10:4). Jesus needed to call Mary by name for her to recognize him.

However, recognizing Jesus is not the same as apprehending his resurrected nature. Apparently, Mary attempts some sort of physical confirmation. How so? We are not told exactly; the text is silent (even if many commentators—and novelists—are not). This we do know: she is *rebuffed*. "Do not keep on trying to hold me," Jesus says, in effect. Mary learns from her Teacher that she is being caught up into a larger drama that includes Jesus' death, resurrection, *and* ascension. This is *not* merely a story about a reunion, case solved. It is about ultimate destinies: Jesus' and Mary's—and the disciples' destinies too. Jesus tells her: "I am ascending to *my* Father and *your* Father, to *my* God and *your* God" (20:17). The story has not concluded; it is still unfolding. She must relate *that* to the disciples.

In John's Gospel, the evangelist wants his audience to recognize that Jesus is, utterly, a "God-related being."[1] Jesus has a uniquely intimate relationship with God, whom he calls "Father." The evangelist is also at pains to make clear that God is a "Jesus-related Being," that is, God works redemptively in and through all that Jesus does and undergoes. Hence, Jesus is the Father's "Son," but the Gospel goes further. It says that those who have the eyes of faith to perceive this can themselves become "children of God"—both "God-related" *and* "Jesus-related" persons. "To all who receive him, who believe in his name, he [gives] power to become children of God, . . . born, not of blood or of the will of the flesh or of the will of man, but of God" (1:12–13).

That is why Mary cannot hold on to Jesus. Her story and his, his experience and hers, cannot be anchored in the past. Nor is it singular. Instead, he calls her by name to announce to the disciples—and, by extension to all who would believe—a new creation, an unimaginable future. The good news that she reports to the disciples is only the beginning of an ongoing revelation of what resurrection and its implications might mean.

GREGORY A. ROBBINS

Homiletical Perspective

of others. Or we promise ourselves that we will not fall away from whatever God has given us to do, but the minute we are threatened in some way, we leave. With Peter we are hurrying to confess our shortcomings. Or maybe we remember something remarkable and life-giving from our past, running to see if it might happen again, if new life is possible even for those of us caught in a web of conflicting feelings and actions.

Mary speaks. Then there is the Magdalene who shows up at the tomb after her male companions have returned home, weeping for what is gone. She obviously expects nothing to happen; she has come to mourn the loss of life, of a body to touch, and to bid good-bye. In her grief she can hardly think clearly. She sees two angels and does not recognize their otherworldly origins. She sees Jesus and mistakes him for the gardener. Then he speaks her name, and she suddenly knows exactly who this mysterious stranger is. She responds to the call of her name; "Teacher," she replies. Then Jesus commissions her to go and tell what she has seen, just as he commissioned the woman at the well way back at the beginning of his ministry.

Scholars often remind us that the resurrection narratives are really commission stories, sending believers out into the world to tell everyone that death is not the last word. Otherwise, no one would ever know what happened, and Easter would be just a reunion story with tears and hugs all around. However, Mary obeys the risen Jesus, fighting her impulse to cling to a familiar body, and leaves the garden to tell what she knows to be true. An expected ending is now a beginning—of telling the truth about life to those who want to deal only in death, of offering living water and the bread of life to those who want only to buy and sell commodities that perish. Mary speaks, and in her speaking we find our own voice.

NANCY CLAIRE PITTMAN

---

1. To use David H. Kelsey's felicitous turn of phrase in *Imagining Redemption* (Louisville, KY: Westminster John Knox Press, 2005).

Acts 5:27-32

²⁷When they had brought them, they had them stand before the council. The high priest questioned them, ²⁸saying, "We gave you strict orders not to teach in this name, yet here you have filled Jerusalem with your teaching and you are determined to bring this man's blood on us." ²⁹But Peter and the apostles answered, "We must obey God rather than any human authority. ³⁰The God of our ancestors raised up Jesus, whom you had killed by hanging him on a tree. ³¹God exalted him at his right hand as Leader and Savior that he might give repentance to Israel and forgiveness of sins. ³²And we are witnesses to these things, and so is the Holy Spirit whom God has given to those who obey him."

Theological Perspective

What does it mean to "obey God rather than any human authority" in today's world? Many preachers focus their preaching on this section of the text, reminding Christians of our call to follow the gospel of Jesus Christ. To claim to follow the gospel is usually not the challenge. The challenge is to discern and act upon what we believe is obedience to God rather than any other force.

A superficial reading of the text might lead a reader to hold Jews responsible for the death of Jesus and only further anti-Semitism. However, simply dismissing this text on the basis of its apparently anti-Semitic tone would also be a mistake. In Luke through Acts, the Roman Empire is Jesus' executioner. The *leaders* of Israel, under Rome's colonial rule, were trapped in a conspiracy to kill the prophet from Nazareth. From the beginning of Acts to chapter 6, we find Israel's *leaders*, the Sadducees, wrestling with the political consequences of playing the Roman Empire's conspiracy game. A detailed reading of the text shows that the *people*, in this case mostly Jews, were listening to the apostles, and some were following their footsteps. The text is clear: "but the *people* held them in high esteem. Yet more than ever believers were added to the Lord, great numbers of both men and women" (vv. 13b–14, emphasis added).

Pastoral Perspective

George MacLeod (founder of the Iona Community in Scotland) was fond of saying that the "church is most beautiful to God when she is bloody"; and the church is bloody when it is being persecuted, as Jesus said, for righteousness' sake. Whether MacLeod gleaned that wisdom from an ancient writer (Tertullian?) or whether it was his own inspired utterance, his words foreshadow the gathering storm over the heads of the apostles in this short periscope from the fifth chapter of Acts. The blood of the martyrs would not flow until Stephen had preached, been arrested, and been stoned to death, all of which occurs in the next two chapters. However, hints come in the words of Peter and the apostles when they are taken from their preaching on the temple steps and brought before the council: "We must obey God rather than any human authority." Missing from this lectionary selection is the council's reaction to Peter's and the apostles' speech: "When they heard this, they were enraged and wanted to kill them" (v. 33).

Their desire to kill was grounded in their envy of the dazzling success of the Holy Spirit, working through these apostles to heal the misery of the suffering masses. Their reaction was further fueled by the rest of Peter's testimony before the council, in which he declared that the God of their ancestors had raised up from death Jesus, the one whom they

Exegetical Perspective

The book of Acts is structured according to the command of Jesus in Acts 1:8, "You will be my witnesses in Jerusalem, in all Judea and Samaria, and to the ends of the earth." Whereas in the Gospel of Luke the action moved inevitably toward Jerusalem, the action in Acts begins in Jerusalem and moves out into the wider world. Following the giving of the Holy Spirit at Pentecost (Acts 2), the disciples are witnesses in Jerusalem (3:1–7:60), in Judea and Samaria (8:1–11:18), and throughout the rest of the Roman Empire (11:19–28:31). Today's reading is part of the larger story of the apostles' preaching in Jerusalem.

Acts 5:27–32 is a small section of a larger pericope that is found in Acts 5:12–42. The narrative begins with a summary of the apostles' work in Jerusalem (vv. 12–16). This leads to the decision by the high priest that the apostles should be arrested (vv. 17–18). That night, an angel comes to the apostles, opens their prison doors, and commands them to return to preaching in the temple (vv. 19–21a). When the apostles return to proclaiming the message of Christ, they are arrested again and brought before the Sanhedrin (vv. 21b–26). The passage in Acts 5:27–32 comprises the accusation of the high priest against the apostles and the apostles' response to the charges.

In verse 27, the apostles stand before the Sanhedrin, the central council of the religious authorities

Homiletical Perspective

Early on, Luke states his purpose for his two-volume work on the gospel of Jesus Christ: "I too decided, after investigating everything carefully from the very first, to write an orderly account for you" (Luke 1:3). Those preaching from Luke–Acts have noticed the author's tendency to report events as more orderly and peaceful than life as actually lived tends to be. The marked difference between Luke and Matthew in their respective reports of the childhood of Jesus is an example of Luke's faith that God will "carry out in tranquility the plan of salvation."[1] For Luke, Jesus' childhood is an orderly progression of temple-centered devotion, whereas Matthew's account shows the holy family running for their lives to Egypt to escape the murderous intentions of King Herod.

Luke generally likes to "accentuate the positive."[2] This tone is continued in Acts. Tom Long reports a student who likened the genre of Acts to the work of a pious local church historian: "The Reverend John Smith preached his first sermon at Trinity Presbyterian Church on September 1, 1935. The church was filled to capacity and every heart was stirred."[3]

Luke's interest in portraying the early church as moving from strength to strength requires the

1. From the Good Friday liturgy in the Gelasian Sacramentary.
2. Popular song by Johnny Mercer/Harold Arlen.
3. Tom Long, lecture, January 15, 2006, Nashville, TN.

Acts 5:27-32

Theological Perspective

Moreover, verse 26 captures the tension of this religious and political situation: "Then the captain went with the temple police and brought them [the apostles], but without violence, for they were afraid of being stoned by the people." In this text it is evident that obeying "God rather than any human authority" shows the complexity of living the gospel faithfully in a context of multilevel political forces.

What does it mean to "obey God rather than any human authority" in today's world? In the in-betweenness of multiple political forces, is there a way to discern God's mission and invitation to coparticipate in God's salvation to creation? Perhaps a brief case study may give us insight to answer the questions above.

Is China a mission field or a witness of faithfulness? Not a few Christians and Christian parachurch organizations from all over the world strongly believe that Communist China needs Christian missionaries. The Chinese government, however, does not allow missionaries into its territories. Nevertheless, political and economic opportunities have opened China's doors to financial and technological investment, developing a growing commodity trade with developed countries. Christian businesspeople, involved in partnership transactions, consultations, and investments, have used their professional visas as a way to share the gospel of Jesus Christ with the Chinese people.

Aware of Chinese law, Christian mission organizations and many Christian business leaders have embarked on the evangelization of the new emerging China. They have used multiple strategies: "smuggling" Bibles, handing out tracts, inviting partners to dinner to talk about religion, and many others. Despite the fact that these activities are considered illegal in China, many organizations and Christian businesspeople-missionaries claim that, "We must obey God rather than any human authority." They believe they are being faithful to a higher order, to a higher law.

Unfortunately this higher order seems to be silent about the consequence of these actions for Chinese Christians who are "evangelized." For instance, because the Chinese government has very strict laws and regulations regarding religious activities—and is on edge with any religious movement that might go beyond its control—many Chinese Christians and people who interact with missionaries have experienced harassment, persecution, and even imprisonment. The "successful" evangelistic stories of these well-intentioned Christian businesspeople

Pastoral Perspective

had killed on the cross—for the sake of Israel's salvation and the forgiveness of sins.

So here is a short proclamation of the Easter gospel that is so prevalent in the first chapters of Acts, but told in a larger story (5:12–42) of the healings, the arrest and imprisonment of the apostles, their release by an angel, and their being hauled away from their preaching and back before their accusers. After much deliberation and a face-saving approach suggested by Gamaliel, a respected member of council, the authorities brought the apostles back, had them flogged, and let them go, forbidding them to speak the name of Jesus again. Their threats and abuse were useless. God's word would not be hindered—nor the work of the Holy Spirit.

If the full story is used, there are at least three implications for the church and the believer. What we see first is the recapitulation of the life of Jesus Christ in the early days of the church. We are the body of Christ in the world, and our faithfulness will always evoke the reaction that brought Jesus to doom. However, just as God raised Jesus from death, so God is always raising the church from death: whether it is the death of long-term apostasy or death by persecution for arousing the envy of the world, provoking the world's enmity toward God. This story reminds the church—especially in times of betrayal, persecution, mockery, and abuse—that God is sovereign and that "gates of hell can never 'gainst that church prevail."[1]

Second, there is a challenge here that, even as absorbed as we are in the secular and religious norms of the beginning of the twenty-first century, we are to obey God rather than human initiative. There is no substitute for the faithful proclamation of the word. When the Holy Spirit takes hold, manifesting obedience, healing, and joy through the followers of Christ, we will face opposition. The fact that so few of us, and so few congregations, face terrifying opposition in this choice-driven, liberty-loving culture begs us to ask a question that grows out of George MacLeod's assertion: Are we beautiful to God? Or is the church in the developing world beautiful, with manifold healings and severe persecutions showing us the way to truth and life? Remember, the apostles in this story were not attacking the religious establishment; in fact they were going "about (in the power of the Spirit) doing good" (cf. 10:38). On a universal scale, such a story recalls the Cain and Abel story writ

1. Sabine Baring-Gould, "Onward Christian Soldiers," in *Lutheran Book of Worship* (Minneapolis: Augsburg Publishing House, 1978), #509.

in Jerusalem. This is not the first time the apostles have been arrested. In addition to the arrest in Acts 5:17–18 that begins this pericope, Peter and John are also arrested in Acts 4:1–22. In that passage, the two are brought before the council to answer the charges against them. As in today's reading, it is Peter who delivers a speech proclaiming the gospel. The disciples are arrested frequently in the book of Acts, at the hands of both the Jewish and Roman authorities (12:3–5; 21:33; 28:17).

The high priest announces the charges against the apostles in verse 28. They have been told not to teach in "this name" (4:17–18), yet they persist in doing so. The high priest here seems purposefully to avoid referring to Jesus by name.[1] The apostles are accused of filling Jerusalem with their teaching. Whereas the high priest views this negatively, the reader knows that the apostles are fulfilling the command of Jesus in Acts 1:8.

Beginning in verse 29, Peter and the apostles respond to the charges. Their first defense is that they must obey God rather than human authorities. This statement reflects not only the defense Peter gave in Acts 4:19, but also a statement by Plato to his accusers: "I shall obey the god rather than you."[2] The apostles' claim to be obeying God stems from the command given to them by the angel when they were released from prison in 5:20.

In verses 30–32, the apostles move from defending their actions to proclaiming the gospel. Although their speech is shorter than previous proclamations in the book of Acts, it contains a number of the same elements. The apostles note that the God of their ancestors (lit. "fathers," cf. Acts 3:13) has raised Jesus, who was killed by hanging on a tree. The reference here seems to be to Deuteronomy 21:23. A similar reference is made in Acts 10:39, as well as in Paul's letter to the Galatians (Gal. 3:13). The connection is not made explicit here, but the irony of God blessing the one who was cursed by being hung on a tree would probably have been apparent to the original audience.

The apostles claim in verse 31 that God has exalted Jesus at his right hand, a common image (Rom. 8:34; Eph. 1:20; Col. 3:1; Heb. 1:13; 1 Pet. 3:22) that has already been invoked by Peter during his sermon on the day of Pentecost (Acts 2:33–35). Jesus is here given the titles of "Leader and Savior."

---

1. Hans Conzelmann, *Acts of the Apostles*, Hermeneia (Philadelphia: Fortress Press, 1987), 42.
2. Plato, *Apologia* 29d.

preacher to interpret as accurately as possible the accounts of persecution, such as Acts 5:27–32. Has Luke in any way demonized Jewish opposition to the first Christians in order to cover the "heroes" of the story with greater glory?

That there were tensions both between various factions of first-century Judaism and between some of them and Jesus and the early church cannot and need not be denied. However, many preachers and hearers are now more sensitive to the church's history of anti-Semitism and agonize over accounts such as this one. Acts 5:28 echoes the troubling words of Matthew 27:25, where the crowd responds to Pilate's washing his hands of the situation, "His blood be on us and on our children!" Casting stones at twenty-first-century Jews or caricaturing Jewish belief and practice then or now, as overly legalistic or consistently resistant to new ideas, is neither accurate nor loving. Indeed, as this account proceeds beyond this pericope, the distinguished Pharisee Gamaliel will prove to be wise in counsel (5:34–39).

Here in Acts, Jewish and Roman authorities do have the upper hand, and Christians meet opposition and persecution from them. The crucial homiletical question becomes how to appropriate the courage shown by Peter and the apostles in answering, "We must obey God rather than any human authority" (v. 29).

Some Christians will find this most preachable verse relevant to the real or perceived culture war between "secular humanists" and "people of faith." They will see as heir to Peter's boldness the public high school valedictorian who inserts a prayer into her speech at graduation, despite being warned by the school principal not to do so, thus obeying God rather than human authority. Other Christians will see as closer to the spirit of Peter the protesters whose placards and chants of "No War for Oil" break up a congressional committee hearing on Department of Defense appropriations.

In nations where governments are fairly chosen by the will of the people and orderly processes exist to hear grievances, it may be appropriate that the protesters who interrupt a congressional committee's proceedings be removed from the room. In nations where the constitution and national heritage encourage mutual respect for people of various faiths and those who hold no religious faith at all, the school principal really is correct. Praying your prayer to a captive audience at a public school graduation is not an act of courage but of bad manners.

Acts 5:27-32

Theological Perspective

do not give the whole picture. What is usually missing is that "obeying God rather than any human authority" ends up putting at risk the lives of people who might honestly be seeking God. It is ironic that Christian businesspeople might rejoice in their missionary work while the text clearly describes that "as they [the apostles] left the council, they rejoiced that they were considered worthy to suffer dishonor for the sake of the name" (v. 41). *Suffering in solidarity with others* may be "a criterion of obeying God rather than human authority."

What is faithfulness to God? During the late half of the 1990s, the China Christian Council (CCC) faced a very difficult decision. Christianity in China continued (and still continues) to grow. Household and village Christian communities began to come together to celebrate worship services and engage in mission activity, with very few theologically trained leaders. The theology and ecclesiology of many of these Christian communities—heavily syncretistic and blurring the line between folk religion and Chinese Christianity—were and continue to be questionable. The Chinese government was well aware of all of these emerging Christian communities and their activities and wanted to maintain oversight over their development. The government needed to see a "stamp" of legitimacy from official religious organizations such as the CCC.

The debate was intense and contentious in the CCC. The *leaders* of the organization debated the theological and ecclesial consequences of recognizing these emerging Christian (or even pseudo-Christian) communities under the official umbrella of the respected CCC. The leaders faced the serious religious ramifications of such a political decision on their part. They were caught between the government and the people. After much discussion and debate, the CCC recognized many of these emerging Christian communities, including them in the list of official Christian organizations protected by the CCC. This meant more responsibility for the CCC, but it also meant *protection of people*, of many new Christians who might not have had adequate theological training and whose practice of faith might therefore have been questionable. The integrity of what some would call orthodoxy was secondary to the protection of sisters and brothers in the faith.

Faithfulness requires discernment, wisdom, and risk. Learning how to "obey God rather than any human authority" may demand a hard look at the witness of Christians at the margins, rather than our own assumptions of higher Christian order and law.

CARLOS F. CARDOZA-ORLANDI

Pastoral Perspective

large—after the resurrection, which is the harbinger of God's mercy and salvation for the whole cosmos. Lives of faithfulness in and through the Word will provoke religious and secular powers. Is the church up to the challenge?

Third, embedded in this story is something uniquely Christian. After the apostles have been flogged, forbidden to speak of Jesus, and released, they rejoice. "As they left the council, they rejoiced that they were considered worthy to suffer dishonor for the sake of the name" (5:41).

As this shocking (at least to modern, Western ears) fact is contemplated, care must be taken to remind hearers that this action by the apostles does not justify or promote self-sought victimization, and certainly not martyrdom. There is a sickly assumption in much Christian writing, thinking, and speaking that knows and even yearns for persecution.

Some persons are masters at making themselves (or others) victims for their own self-aggrandizement, for the sake of "winning" whatever cause they are espousing. People provoke others on purpose, and then cry that they have been mishandled or abused, when in fact, if they had quietly gone about their own (and even God's) business, without calling attention to themselves or hating their opponents, they would have escaped unnoticed. On no account does this unique verse justify such behavior. The apostles were not confronting the authorities. They did indeed choose to obey God, and the Holy Spirit "chose" them to manifest the "new world order" that was growing out of the resurrection of Jesus Christ. When they suffered on account of the name, *they rejoiced*, because they were privileged to begin to bear on their bodies the marks of the one who had saved, empowered, and anointed them to preach the gospel. They were not gloating; they were filled with joy. Between those two emotional/mental states, there is a world of difference.

O. BENJAMIN SPARKS

Exegetical Perspective

Although "savior" is a common epithet for Jesus, "leader" (Gk. *archēgos*) occurs only four times in the New Testament. "Leader" is perhaps not the best translation of the term, as the word carries more the idea of a founder or originator. The NRSV of Acts 3:15 comes closer to the meaning with its translation of the term as "author," while Hebrews 2:10 and 12:2 use "pioneer."

The apostles close their defense by claiming that they are witnesses to the events to which they testify. Being a witness is the major function of the apostles throughout the book (Acts 1:22; 2:32, 3:15; 6:13; 7:58; 10:41; 13:31; 22:15; 22:20; 26:16). Witnesses in this sense are not simply passive observers of an event; they must actively make known what they have seen. In claiming their roles as witnesses, the apostles once again allude to the command of Christ in Acts 1:8, but they are not alone. They also proclaim that the Holy Spirit—the primary actor in the book of Acts—is a witness of these things as well. The Holy Spirit is given to those who believe, a reference to the events of Pentecost in Acts 2.

This pericope concludes in the verses that extend beyond today's reading (vv. 33–42). In response to the apostles' testimony, the council seeks to kill them. They are saved by the wise advice given by a Pharisee named Gamaliel, who is identified in Acts 22:3 as the teacher of Saul/Paul. Quoting historical precedents (vv. 34–37), Gamaliel suggests that the council not oppose this new movement centered on Christ. If it is of human origin, he says, it will fail; however, if it is of divine origin, then the council will be in the position of opposing God (vv. 38–39a). The council is convinced by his advice. After flogging the apostles and commanding them not to speak in the name of Jesus anymore, the council releases them (vv. 39b–40). The apostles rejoice at having suffered for Christ, but immediately return to the business of proclaiming Jesus (vv. 41–42).

KEVIN A. WILSON

Homiletical Perspective

Where then does this boldness of the apostles find a voice today? At least in the pulpit, one hopes. The preacher's greatest censor is not the first-century Jewish high priest or Roman governor; it is the chair of the finance committee or the prickliest member of the pastor-parish board. The first people who need to be persuaded of Peter's bold call to "obey God rather than any human authority" are we who are called to proclaim God's truth to God's people in God's house. Acts 5:27–32 pronounces judgment on the timidity and dilettantism of too much of our preaching. The pastor's reasons for these habits in preaching may not be so craven as concern over next year's salary increase or even continued service in the present church. A genuine pastoral heart may be inclined to pull punches in the pulpit, not wanting to further burden people whom we already know to be at near-crisis level in their personal lives.

However, preaching is not saying what people want to hear; it is saying what people want to say. Beneath their roles as lay leaders of an "institution," and even beneath the personal burdens they bear, people keep coming to church every Sunday to hear a truth that no one else will tell them. Ours is a deep truth, which when spoken with love and with conviction has the power to transform burdens and transcend everyday life. Those who listen to our preaching hunger for living expression of the grace of the Lord Jesus Christ, the love of God, and the fellowship of the Holy Spirit.

This pericope for the Second Sunday of Easter may be less about what to preach than how to preach—with boldness, but without wounding anyone in mean-spirited payback; with relevance, but without betraying a vow of pastoral confidentiality; with authenticity, but without calling undue attention to oneself.

When the preacher speaks with the boldness of Peter and the other apostles, it does, at least over time, encourage our hearers to take principled if unpopular stands in the workplace and helps lead us all to be seekers of truth and agents of reconciliation.

J. MICHAEL KRECH

Psalm 150

¹Praise the LORD!
  Praise God in his sanctuary;
    praise him in his mighty firmament!
²Praise him for his mighty deeds;
    praise him according to his surpassing greatness!

³Praise him with trumpet sound;
    praise him with lute and harp!
⁴Praise him with tambourine and dance;
    praise him with strings and pipe!
⁵Praise him with clanging cymbals;
    praise him with loud clashing cymbals!
⁶Let everything that breathes praise the LORD!
    Praise the LORD!

Theological Perspective

This is certainly a prime season for thanksgiving to
God, even though such language no longer makes
sense for an increasing number of people. Many folks
in churches may wonder at such a claim, but I suggest
we think about why so many congregations are getting
smaller and may not last much longer. What does this
say about a faith that proclaims rebirth, new life, and
transformation? Why are we unable to embody what
we say is so important for us? I suggest that it is
because a growing number of perfectly normal people
no longer see a vibrant connection between the
language of faith and their daily experience—of stress,
of trauma, and of the unmet yearnings of their hearts.
Worse, we do not know how to make that translation
for them. What are we to do in the face of this reality,
especially during Easter season?

Clearly, we must name this truth and not shy from
it. Many of us have not done a good job of
connecting ancient insights with the real-life
experiences of our day. Yet we assert that expressions
such as those in today's Psalter text are somehow
important: "Praise [God] for his mighty deeds" (v. 2).
On the one hand, we speak of a majestic and loving
God who is truly mighty; on the other, we watch as
our communities of shared conviction shrivel.

Many of us have lost sight of the difference
between a vital, living tradition and a sterile,

Pastoral Perspective

Many a pastor has fantasized about walking into
Sunday morning worship to find the congregation
praising God. Trumpets blare. Choir voices boil over
into the congregation, who dance in the aisles. Cymbals crash. The church lovingly recognizes God,
having moved beyond all inhibitions, and every
member breathes, "Praise the Lord!" We do not have
to preach because our aim and hope as pastors—
God's praise—has been fulfilled.

Psalm 150 realizes our fantasy. The only problem is
that our congregation does not realize it with us! *If we
take seriously Psalm 150, then we are called to disarm
our congregations of their inhibitions for God's praise.*

Firstly, contemporary culture inhibits churchgoers.
Biblical scholar Walter Brueggemann powerfully
disarms those who are preoccupied by the cultural
expectation of utility when he asserts, "Psalm 150 . . .
is the extreme case of inutility. It asks nothing. Indeed
it almost claims nothing. It nearly says nothing."[1]

"Praise is useless!" Post that on the sermon board
for the Second Sunday in Easter and even the most
beloved pastor's phone would ring off the hook.
Deacons would be up in arms. Music directors and
choir members would weep. Visitors would attend

1. Walter Brueggemann, *The Psalms and the Life of Faith*, ed. Patrick D. Miller
(Minneapolis: Fortress Press, 1995), 125.

Exegetical Perspective

Psalm 150 is the last of a collection of psalms beginning and ending with the words, "Hallelu Yah!" (Praise YHWH). The collection comprises Psalms 146–50. In addition, this psalm forms a bookend with Psalm 1; that is, Psalms 1 and 150 provide the introduction and conclusion to the whole Psalter. Walter Brueggemann calls this psalm a good match for Psalm 1, since "the expectation of the OT is not finally obedience but adoration."[1] This psalm, with its resounding, all-encompassing call to praise, forms an eminently appropriate doxological conclusion.

As several scholars have noted, the psalm contains four parts, the first section announcing *who* is to be praised (v. 1); the second proclaiming *why* God is to be praised (v. 2); the third describing *how* YHWH is to be praised (vv. 3–5); and the final segment setting forth *who* is to do the praising (v. 6). In addition, the psalm contains a tenfold imperative call to praise representing a complete number, which rounds off to twelve (a venerable number in Israelite tradition) when the first and last lines of the psalm are included. The number twelve is reminiscent of the twelve sons of Jacob and the twelve tribes of Israel. In addition, it is a multiple of four, the number of

Homiletical Reflection

Psalm 150 is the Easter alleluia "turned into an entire psalm."[1] It is packed with imperative forms of the verb "praise." More than calling the congregation to sing the alleluia with gusto, an Easter sermon based on this psalm inspires the assembly to participate in Christ's resurrection by offering itself to God in a life of praise. An effective strategy for preaching such a sermon on the Second Sunday of Easter—when people expect to hear about Thomas and may be feeling like his twin—is to connect the psalm to the appointed Gospel reading.

One fruitful way of connecting Psalm 150 and John 20:19–31 is to name the contradiction in the tone of these readings. Psalm 150's rousing and enthusiastic call to praise surely stands in stark contrast to the mood in the house where the disciples met on the evening of the first day of the week (John 20:19). This contradiction is not limited to the lectionary. In many congregations, worship on the Sunday after the crowds have gone similarly pales in comparison to services on Easter Day. More to the point, many people return to their lives after glorious Easter worship, only to find that the powers of death at work in the world continue to reign.

1. Walter Brueggemann, *The Message of the Psalms: A Theological Commentary* (Minneapolis: Augsburg Press, 1984), 167.

1 James Luther Mays, *Psalms*, Interpretation series (Louisville, KY: John Knox Press, 1994), 449.

Psalm 150

Theological Perspective

doctrinally "correct" traditionalism. Meanwhile, many of those who have spurned us—saying that we are not relevant to their lives—can see what we cannot: we have often let our efforts to clarify, define, and control people's understandings and behaviors get in the way of God's gracious, loving resilience. Speaking words of praise and love, we continue to disregard—or actively abuse—fellow human beings both near and far, usually those who are somehow different from us. Our praise sounds shallow and tinny to those who see our racist blindness, our gender callousness, and the other subtle controlling tactics that some of us exhibit. In response, many of those we wish to reach are just walking away. They will offer praise, such as they can, elsewhere.

If we are to reclaim space for the grace and deeply transformative love of God that can change lives and nations, we must find fresh ways to connect with the daily experiences of people. There is a kind of spontaneous joy reflected in today's Psalter reading that can fill us up. It can spring up in some unlikely places, including the bond of mutual trust and then affection that can grow between adversaries who have been on opposing sides of life-and-death struggles for generations.

We must find ways to translate the words of our forebears into language and behavior that can touch both head and heart. Only by doing this can we live into our calling, which is to help ensure that God's embrace is returned by folks who did not know it was there. This embrace is on offer to each of us without price—except, of course, the requirement that we commit our lives to it.

The question for the preacher is how we might talk *today* with meaning about the outpouring of thanks to God that the Psalter shows. For one thing, we can find guidance in certain general principles that actually undergird many of our confessional traditions. These are pretty fundamental, and the specific language used to capture them is not nearly as important as their actual connection with real lives today. These principles do not require a postgraduate degree to understand, nor do they require a religious expert (or ordained leader) to interpret them. Many of them are lively and undomesticated and connect deeply with our hearts.

Take courage, for instance. At the seminary where I teach, we were able to touch the lives of a wide public by focusing on the witness of nine teenagers who desegregated Central High in Little Rock half a century ago. Their willingness to embody God's lure to freedom in the midst of great social uncertainty

Pastoral Perspective

the stone church down the street whose marquee promises, "Jesus is back! Just ask Thomas."

Psalm 150 draws the entire Psalter to conclusion with a simple though dramatic call to praise that is unqualified and unapologetic. There is no divine promise, no mention of covenant, no allusion to judgment, just "useless" praise to God. By summoning "everything that breathes" to praise God, Psalm 150 asks believers to do something apparently pointless—the thing most antithetical to our culturally conditioned understanding of human industry. If secular culture defines us so that we hope through praise to gain something tangible—wealth, health, happiness, or fame—then we will find praise useless and the act of praising superficial. However, if we understand praise as our ultimate expression of loving recognition to God, then we can begin to imagine our part in what God receives as Psalm 150 crescendoes among creation.

Secondly, preoccupation with self hinders response to Psalm 150. I once watched a junior choir singing an anthem, using all sorts of accompanying gestures. The young girls timidly watched each other for precision while they were being watched by the whole congregation. In worship many of us feel as if we are "being watched." Parishioners think their sacred acts must be perfect, which amplifies their feeling of unworthiness. Moreover, society and culture dissuade them from submissive gestures or claims of dependence, even in worship, which creates tension between who they are as people of faith and who they are as secular beings, vying for power and independence.

Christians ought to remember that praise is not primarily about us; it is about God. That will disarm many Christians who are sold on a self-centered religious perspective. Psalm 150 begins and ends with, "*Hallelu Yah!*" (vv. 1, 6), framing ten additional invitations to praise God. While lacking the elaborate litany of God's deeds and character found in other praise psalms (Pss. 144–49), this one simply offers "God's acts of power" and "surpassing greatness" (v. 2) as sufficient reason to give praise. This praise liberates self-conscious worshipers, either by suspending their concerns or at least by prioritizing those concerns relative to God.

Lastly, while a hermeneutic of suspicion can be a healthy trait for a mature religious identity, suspicion can stifle our joyous praise. Paying excessive attention to doubt and distrust draws attention inward and away from God. Christians sometimes doubt their own interpretations of the biblical text used in worship, or

Exegetical Perspective

completion. The associations are therefore richly allusive, an indication that every part of the psalm was carefully and theologically crafted. The call to praise is plural in form; it is not directed to an individual, but to the community.

Verse 1 opens with the imperative call to praise the Lord. The second half of the verse describes where YHWH is to be praised: first in the sanctuary and second in the entire firmament. The word "firmament" describes the dome of the heavens in Hebrew cosmology (see, e.g., Gen. 1:6–8) and thus indicates that the whole world is the realm for praising God (cf. Ps. 19:1). Because most Hebrew poetry is synonymous parallelism, the parallel between "firmament" and "sanctuary" has led some scholars to debate over the referent of the term "sanctuary." The term most often refers to the temple, the actual place of YHWH's dwelling, but in some contexts it represents all of Israel. The ambiguity of the poetry allows for all these connotations to be in the reader's mind. Verse 2 gives the reasons for praise: both God's actions and God's very being (God's "surpassing greatness") demand the worshiper's response of praise.

In verses 3–5, a whole symphony is used to praise God, including horns, strings, wind instruments ("pipe"), and percussion. While there have been many attempts to discern the exact nature of the instruments used, we have little specific information on many of these. We often do not even know how they looked or sounded. What is most important in these verses, however, is that every type of instrument is included, just as every voice is called upon to sing this praise to God in verse 6. The whole creation, as represented by the all-inclusive list of musical instruments, is therefore symbolically called upon to worship God.

Note that in the middle of this symphony, the people are called to praise YHWH with tambourine and dance (see also Ps. 149:3). One of the ways Israel celebrated victories over enemies was through tambourine and dance (see Exod. 15:20–21; Judg. 11:34; and 1 Sam. 18:6–7). The inclusion of dance links the call to praise with the reason given in verse 2: God's mighty deeds. In the OT, it was women who celebrated Israel's victories with tambourine and dance, so the reference to tambourine and dance may also be an explicit inclusion of women in this call to praise, an appropriate reference, given the universal call in verse 6.

Verse 6 is the climax of the hymn, calling every living being (lit. "everything that has breath") to join

Homiletical Perspective

They find that Easter has come and gone, but fear and doubt remain. So vibrant praise might legitimately seem out of place on this second Sunday of the season.

The preacher might then reconcile this contradiction by prescribing praise as the Easter antidote for fear and doubt. Might praise be the catalyst through which the power of Christ's resurrection works in our lives and in the world? Thomas certainly praises Jesus: "My Lord and my God!" (John 20:28). Might praise be a way those who have not seen and yet believe experience and express faith in the risen Christ? Psalm 150 answers a resounding yes. We are to praise God for God's mighty deeds and God's surpassing greatness (v. 2). These are apt descriptors for Jesus' rising from death to new life and passing through locked doors to stand with frightened disciples. We praise God's mighty deeds—particularly God's mighty deed of raising Christ from the dead. The psalmist calls for praise without considering how people might be feeling or what is happening in the world, because praise is not a reflection of us. When praise is grounded in God, rather than in our feelings and circumstances, praise is participation in God's mighty deeds.

This kind of praise certainly begins with singing the alleluia, but it does not stop there. Psalm 150–style praise is offering one's whole life and self to God; this is certainly the sort of praise that Jesus has in mind when he breathes the Holy Spirit into the disciples and commissions them to forgive and retain sins (John 20:22–23). While our Easter praise starts in worship, it continues as God's people go forth into the world. Our praise extends from our worship to every aspect and arena of life.

To make this point, the preacher might join the psalmist in musing about the church's worship as a beautiful melody, a siren song that entices the orchestra of the cosmos to join in. The church's worship summons every section of creation's orchestra—strings, horns, pipes, and percussion—to share in the Easter symphony. The song of resurrection spills out of the house where disciples gather until it fills all of creation. On that day when creation offers itself as an Easter hymn to the risen Christ, doubt and fear will disappear. The barriers that separate people from one another and humanity from God and the rest of creation will be as ineffective as the locked doors that separated Jesus from the disciples.

This is only possible because even our Easter praise is not our doing. God gives the melody of resurrections, as surely as Jesus gave the disciples the

Psalm 150

Theological Perspective

helped us realize that thanks-giving, or praise, is not a verbal activity alone. Instead, it is a deeply value-laden commitment that requires a great deal of courage to live out.

Go check with a member of the "millennial" population group. Have you ever wondered why law firms and business schools in North America are having a devil of a time employing the highly talented graduates they have historically secured? It is because these young people want to serve something far more encompassing than a bottom line. Increasingly, they want to work with organizations committed to social responsibility. God is working in society, even apart from the church!

This work is also taking place inside churches. In the biblical witness, Jesus himself spoke about the importance of *doing*, and not just *speaking*, the truth—and of not being held hostage to yesterday's seeming truths. So it is with the basic experience of giving thanks. Such praise is happening, both inside and beyond the churches. Will church folk see and affirm it? What can we learn from it?

To give thanks to God is a kind of performative utterance that embraces us and leads us to see that, among other things, it is important not to harm others. Moreover, we are also charged to do all that we can to help others. We can do both of these things because we are deeply attracted to the mysterious yet loving reality that people of faith have long called God—the reality that is our beginning and our end, the source and the object of our thanks-giving. People of biblical faith claim that God is gracious, whether we consciously confess it or not; yet we also maintain that knowing this relationship immeasurably enriches our capacity to see a bigger picture and find deeper fulfillment along our life's pathway. To live with this understanding gives us a sense of the sheer joy-in-relationship with God and others of which the psalmist wrote. Come, let us celebrate, be glad in it, and translate it effectively for the wider world that is so hungry for this love.

DAVID G. TRICKETT

Pastoral Perspective

they distrust the antiquated language used in the liturgy. Some doubt God's motive for loving them and distrust the people in the next pew who seem untroubled. Like Thomas, churchgoers can guard their belief, withholding the recognition of "My Lord and my God!" until God satisfies their conditions of presence (John 20:24–29). What is missing in Psalm 150 speaks loudly. The first community singing this psalm most likely knew Israel's history with God. Their relationship with God developed through years of religious convictions and laws embodied in their daily life. They praised a God they had already experienced as Creator, Comforter, Savior, and Sovereign.

Part of disarming our suspicions involves validating our contemporary experience of God. Just as the Israelites grew to know God, so also have our congregations. Being in and part of creation reaffirms their belief in God as Creator. Many in our parishes will attest to God as Sustainer and Comforter. They have encountered the unbearable loss of a child, spouse, or covenanted relationship, and yet they cope by grace they cannot fully comprehend. God is Sovereign. No matter what political mandates, economic systems, or environmental barriers those in the congregation impose or support, time reveals the insufficiencies of those structures, so that the faithful rediscover God's reconciling embrace. Pastorally speaking, what are we doing for every person in our congregation to foster the deeper relationship with God that motivates them to praise?

The daunting challenge for spiritual leaders implicit in verse 6 is to orchestrate and build on the praise that has already begun but will not reach fulfillment until "everything that breathes" praises God. Do we allow ourselves to praise God publicly, or are we too inhibited by our preoccupation with the details of leading worship, our self-conscious unworthiness under our liturgical garb, or our wavering trust in God? To give up such inhibitions would almost be like coming to church naked—like King David dressed in a loincloth (2 Sam. 6:14)—with no watch, no sermon notes, nothing to identify ourselves as clergy. There we stand, dance, and sing God's praise, exposed before God's people, revealing our adoration, dependence, and confidence in God. Few of us would claim that fantasy, which is disarming indeed! Yet our people need our own example and permission, as well as our persistent invitation to disarm them for divine praise.

M. ASHLEY GRANT

Exegetical Perspective

in this praise. This is not only a fitting conclusion to the book of Psalms, but also an apt reading for the Second Sunday of Easter, a day on which Christians continue to celebrate Christ's death and resurrection, the greatest of God's mighty deeds.

MARY E. SHIELDS

Homiletical Perspective

Spirit and authority to forgive sins. Just as Jesus expands the apostolic circle to include "those who have not seen and yet have come to believe" (John 20:29), so Psalm 150:2 expands the sphere of the risen Christ's presence and power from the house of frightened disciples to God's "sanctuary" and "mighty heavens" (NIV). The risen Christ is present and powerful throughout creation. Both the disciples' and the church's praise is insufficient; all creation must join in. The preacher joins the psalmist in inviting all creation to praise God by joyously giving itself to God. The result is nothing less than God's symphony of resurrection.

In liturgical traditions, the proper Preface for the Easter season, which is sung or spoken by the presiding minister as part of the celebration of Holy Communion, is an excellent example of this kind of proclamation. The Preface exalts the glorious resurrection of our Savior Jesus Christ, the true Passover lamb, who in dying destroyed death and in rising brought us to eternal life. The Preface then calls the assembly and all creation to praise: "And so, with Mary Magdalene and Peter and all the witnesses of the resurrection, with earth and sea and all their creatures, and with angels and archangels, cherubim and seraphim, we praise their name and join their unending hymn."[2] The congregation responds with songs and lives of praise.

Christians have included the Easter Preface in worship for centuries; God's people have sung Psalm 150 even longer. Both hymns remind us that, though the call to praise is extended to us, the song of praise does not begin with us. God's people have sung and lived praise since God brought life. We join our lives and song to theirs, which even a small gathering of frightened disciples can do.

CRAIG A. SATTERLEE

---

2. Evangelical Lutheran Church in America, *Evangelical Lutheran Worship, Leaders Desk Edition* (Minneapolis: Augsburg Fortress Press, 2006), 404.

Revelation 1:4-8

[4]John to the seven churches that are in Asia:

Grace to you and peace from him who is and who was and who is to come, and from the seven spirits who are before his throne, [5]and from Jesus Christ, the faithful witness, the firstborn of the dead, and the ruler of the kings of the earth.

To him who loves us and freed us from our sins by his blood, [6]and made us to be a kingdom, priests serving his God and Father, to him be glory and dominion forever and ever. Amen.

[7]Look! He is coming with the clouds;
   every eye will see him,
  even those who pierced him;
   and on his account all the tribes of the earth will wail.
So it is to be. Amen.

[8]"I am the Alpha and the Omega," says the Lord God, who is and who was and who is to come, the Almighty.

Theological Perspective

"Jesus Christ . . . the firstborn of the dead. . . . Look! He is coming with the clouds; every eye will see him . . ." When John of Patmos wrote these words a generation or two after the Easter event, the redeeming and triumphal power of Jesus' death and resurrection were already set as the twin pillars upon which the Christian faith rested. By the light of these events the church interpreted the past, so that all of history, especially that found in the Old Testament, moved toward Easter. In that same light the future revelation of the Son of God as past event present in the life of the church must also be seen as a future event in the outworking of human history.

This is the idea that controls the Revelation of John, with its kaleidoscope of strange visions and symbolic creatures. This John, unlike the writer of the Gospel, does not seem aware of Paul's teaching regarding the divinity of Christ. We still find here an impressive, if less developed, Christology. While the passage begins and ends with an evocation of the eternal God, "who is and who was and who is to come," it turns out that this God is "his Father," and Jesus, himself, because he was resurrected, is "the firstborn of the dead," whose blood "has freed us from our sins." Thus, Jesus is so related to the Father that to him, also, are to be given "glory and dominion forever." Since the eternality ascribed to the Father is

Pastoral Perspective

The third Eucharist I ever attended—this was still months before I would be baptized, before I would receive Communion for the first time—happened at a small theological college in England. The preacher was the woman who would eventually baptize me. The text was something about Mary. I do not recall the sermon, but I do remember people coming up to the preacher afterward and saying how nice it had been to see a woman preach on the passage in question.

What I remember most clearly is a typo in the bulletin:

Christ has died.
Christ is risen.
Christ has come again.

I had not attended seminary yet, of course, so I did not know enough to think something clever, such as, "This gives proleptic proclamation a whole new meaning!" Instead, I thought, "Hmmmm. I know I am relatively new to this Christianity thing, but have I missed something crucial?" Afterward, someone helpfully confirmed that the typo was, in fact, a typo.

Every day brings reminders that the promises of Easter are not yet fully realized. You pick up the newspaper and read about the war your country

Exegetical Perspective

John here develops an epistolary salutation as a liturgical dialogue, incorporating the voices of (1) John himself (v. 4a, and perhaps v. 7), (2) God, the seven spirits, and Jesus Christ (vv. 4b–5a), (3) the congregation (vv. 5b–6), and (4) God's own voice in direct address (v. 8). This greeting invokes the congregation's participation in worship of God and Jesus Christ, worship to which they will be called again and again throughout Revelation. This political and theological confession sets the stage for all that follows.

The greeting (vv. 4–5a). Revelation identifies itself as an "apocalypse" (v. 1), but to this generic frame John has added a prophetic note (v. 3) and now employs formal elements of ancient letter writing. The letter form evokes a sense that the performance of Revelation in the worshiping assembly gives voice to and makes present one who is otherwise absent. The salutation identifies John as the sender and the seven churches of Asia as the addressees. John will name these seven churches in the individual letters collected in 2:1–3:22, but here "the seven churches" may represent all the churches of western Asia Minor (modern-day Turkey). Rome exerted its imperial control in Asia Minor by political, economic, and military means, but especially through the manipulation of religious practice and

Homiletical Perspective

By now the Easter lilies have started to wilt. The "church alumni" have come and gone and will not be back until Christmas. The preacher is exhausted. Those who help lead worship are worn out. Yet another Sunday is coming and the gospel must continue to be preached.

Preachers who are reading this particular section of the commentary do not have the luxury of taking this Sunday off, as many do. For whatever reason, those reading these words will be in the pulpit this Sunday, attempting to match the same level they or someone else offered the congregation on Easter. This may seem like a daunting task to some. After all, there are times when parishioners give the impression that preachers are only as good as their last sermon. Secretly, most preachers feel the same way and are haunted by the fact that Sundays just keep coming. What can preachers say this Sunday that will keep the flame alive?

Ideally, the Second Sunday of Easter is an opportunity for the faithful to bask in the glow of the resurrection. Jesus is risen, and we live in the power of his resurrection. We are Easter people, so every day is Easter day! However, most of the evidence is to the contrary. Sure, on Easter the church was covered with vibrancy. There was life in all that was shared, prayed, sung, and preached.

Revelation 1:4-8

Theological Perspective

seen to belong also to the Son, and since John seems to know the Lukan tradition of Jesus' ascension, he, with the whole church, believed that Jesus' return would replicate his departure: "he is coming with the clouds." Here, as elsewhere in Revelation, it is best not to dwell on the imagery, but expound as best we can the truth to which those images point.

As in the other texts assigned for this Sunday after Easter, our attention is drawn again to the church's witness to the resurrection. The early traditions regarding Jesus' postresurrection appearances are reflected in John 20, and the fact that accounts of the resurrection were a well-known and essential part of early apostolic preaching is found in Acts 5: "The God of our ancestors raised up Jesus, whom you had killed" (v. 30). The text from Revelation witnesses to the resurrection as an established and saving fact in the life of the church at the close of the first century, and the assigned texts from John's Gospel and from Acts provide what came to be seen as *evidence* for the truth of the report. In Acts 5 the evidence has to do with the acceptance of the claim by many in Jerusalem. In John 20 the evidence is found in the experience of those present—Thomas and others who saw the risen Christ. A few verses later we are told that Jesus presented himself publicly to his disciples in "many" ways "which are not written in this book. But these are written so that you may come to believe" (John 20:30–31). In the early days of the church and for almost two thousand years thereafter, the testimony of these witnesses was considered crucial and convincing. That, however, is no longer the case.

In a prescientific age, the parameters of what was possible—and even likely—were quite extensive, and for almost two thousand years the resurrection of Jesus inspired little doubt. With the Enlightenment of the eighteenth century, however, doubts began to rise, as philosophical empiricism and the advent of modern science caused a "paradigm shift" concerning what counts as real and true. David Hume insisted that uniform and repeated experience was necessary for any claim to be true, and since a "miracle" by definition is a *unique* event, it cannot, on this principle, be "true."[1] This attitude was reinforced by Newtonian physics, which saw the natural order as uniform and predictable, with no room at all for mystery or the supernatural.

Thus, for the past two centuries Christian faith has confronted a dominant worldview that denies

Pastoral Perspective

started. You are beckoned to the funeral of a friend's child. The fight you have been having with your sister for seventeen years keeps on going.

I think about this every year at Eastertide. Looking around church, I see these faithful people of God proclaiming *Alleluia!*—proclaiming that *Christ is risen indeed!*—as they trade Good Friday's red for Easter's white, as they sip champagne after the Easter Vigil. I see them genuinely celebrating, even if their lives are falling apart.

In a class I took on Revelation, the professor pointed out that here, at the outset of this letter, it is clear that John knows quite intimately the churches to whom he writes; otherwise he would have identified himself with more detail. Similarly, we preach in congregations where we are privileged to know intimately the struggles of faithful men and women. We preach Easter's resurrection in congregations where many people feel like the disciples on the road to Emmaus before they recognize Jesus. They feel defeated.

There is, to be sure, plenty of genuine Easter spirit in my community. Mark and Sarah are about to leave for South America, to bring home the baby they have been waiting on for years. Susan will be dead in two months, she knows it, and she feels a peace that passes all understanding. My friend Catherine says the most Easterish thing she is doing this month is marching in a rally in Washington; God is in the business of redeeming the world, and this rally is her way of participating in that redemption. So, yes, there is plenty of Easter triumph here. There is deep confidence that God is doing a great work in the world, and that we have graciously been invited to join in.

However, I know that some of us are living in a long Holy Saturday. I know that Rose, sitting two pews from the altar, has just learned that her cancer has come back. I know it is hard for her to trust in the *Alleluias* of Easter. I know that Steven, perched in a pew at the back of the sanctuary, has felt nothing but God's absence for three years. He is telling the truth when he proclaims Christ's resurrection, but it is a truth he has not felt in a long time. I know that Katie, whose parents have just split up, is not sensing God's triumph very clearly this week.

I know that sometimes it is hard for me to lay claim to the reality and promise of the Easter season. Sometimes I look out the window and see resurrection everywhere, but sometimes I just see brokenness. Sometimes that is all I see when I look in the mirror, too. On those days it is hard to remember that Christ

---

1. David Hume, *An Inquiry concerning Human Understanding*, ed. Charles W. Hendel (New York: Prentice Hall, 1955), 123.

imagery in order to represent its rule as both inevitable and divinely ordained. John uses this epistolary introduction to assert, in contrast, the rule of God and Jesus Christ over all other powers, including Rome.

John's simple self-designation in v. 4 (he will reveal more about himself in v. 9) keeps the focus resolutely on those from whom the greetings of grace and peace actually come: God, the seven spirits before the throne, and Jesus Christ (vv. 4b–5a). The identification of God as "the one who is and who was and who is to come" in verse 4 and in verse 8 forms an *inclusio* around this unit and, with the corresponding identification of Jesus Christ in 22:12–13, provides a frame for the whole performance. This designation of God echoes Exodus 3:14, where the God who will liberate Israel from bondage bears the name "I am who I am" or "The one who is."

God's presence and power transcend all human notions of time, yet God is at work in present experience, in the memory of the people, and in hope. John does not name God as the one "who will be," that is, in terms of the abstract future, but rather as "the one coming" (my trans.), who will end the injustice and suffering of the world. This identification of God also provides a direct link to the designation of Jesus as the "one coming with the clouds" (1:7; cf. 22:7, 12, 20). "The seven spirits who are before God's throne" constitute a fluid image, incorporating aspects of divine power, insight, and presence both in heaven and on earth. In 3:1 they are associated with seven stars, in 4:5 with "seven flaming torches," and in 5:6 with "the seven eyes" of the lamb, "sent out into all the earth."

John designates Jesus Christ, the third figure named in the greeting, by means of three titles corresponding to three dimensions of his person (the same elements occur in connection with David in Ps. 89). He is "the faithful witness" (or "martyr") in his ministry and especially in his death. In his resurrection, he is "the firstborn of the dead," vanquishing the power of death and inaugurating a fresh creation. As "the ruler of the kings of the earth" Jesus now exercises God's sovereignty even over those who, like Caesar, seem to manifest absolute power and invincibility and who demand that they be worshiped.

The doxology (vv. 5b–6). John's discourse shifts to the first-person plural, marking the beginning of the liturgical dialogue. The first element is a doxology—"To him be glory and dominion forever and ever. Amen" (v. 6b)—directed to Christ and emphasizing

However, when the last car left the church parking lot after Easter services were over, things went back to life as usual. People have returned to backbreaking jobs in order to pay off debts that drain the life out of them. Car accidents still happen. Divorce papers continue to be filed. Children continue to starve around the world. People continue to kill and be killed. Destruction and death continue to march on.

The original audience of the assigned text in Revelation felt the disparity between being Easter people and living in the realities of a cruel world. The Christians in Asia Minor were being persecuted, and they needed help making sense of their faith in the midst of such trying times. How were they supposed to be faithful when being discouraged made better sense? Revelation was written to encourage these persecuted Christians to live in the power of the resurrection when evil seemed to be the only power at work in their world.

This text marks the very beginning of the peculiar odyssey of encouragement known as the Revelation to John. Appropriately, the writer of Revelation begins by reminding the reader that God is in charge of the world and God will have the last word. The two pronouncements of God "who is and who was and who is to come" in verses 4 and 8 serve as solid bookends to a short but penetrating text on the sovereign power of God. From beginning to end, this text is saturated with words and images of God's complete dominion. Perhaps what is most striking about this text is the motivational vision in verse 7 of the "comeback" of the Lord. It ends with the beautifully arrogant statement, "So it is to be. Amen."

If the preacher is using this text for Sunday, the central task is to help listeners bridge the gap between the celebration of Easter and the coming of the kingdom. Theologically, Christians know that, on Easter, God in Christ defeated evil, but the reality is that evil is still very much alive. How do preachers encourage congregations to be faithful as Easter people when it still feels like Good Friday to many of them? This week congregations (and preachers too!) will be coming down from the high of Easter, and many will enter worship with the question, "Now what?"

The encouraging feel of the text gives preachers an idea about the attitude their sermons might adopt this coming Sunday. Congregations need to be encouraged by the fact that God indeed defeated evil on Easter, and everything that is experienced until kingdom come is simply a "mopping up" effort. Evil is a sore loser and does not take defeat very well. The

Revelation 1:4-8

Theological Perspective

the possibility of God's miraculous activity in the world. Now, however, that scientific worldview has been replaced by another "paradigm shift."[2] In the theories of relativity and quantum mechanics has emerged a new view of reality that constitutes the ineluctable parameters of contemporary science—whether or not theologians and even some scientists recognize that fact. The new science understands the cosmos to include such Newtonian inadmissibles as uncertainty (we can never know both the position and velocity of subatomic particles), paradox (electrons appear as both particles and waves), and relativity (things heretofore thought to be absolute, like space and time, are found to be what they are only in relation to something else).

About these matters two points should be made. First, it would be a mistake to imagine that the new science provides any proof of biblical claims. The mysteries of the cosmos are not the mysteries of God. The Creator and creation are radically different. Nor should the puzzlements of science inspire another kind of "stop-gap" theology, as if the authority of faith is dependent upon the uncertainties of science, or could be confirmed by various parallels between its conceptions and those of science. Second, the new science does, however, remove from theology and preaching a worldview thoroughly antagonistic to its work, and this means that those whose business it is to proclaim the truth of the gospel need not assume its knowledge to be inferior—less reasonable or less real—to that of science.

The reason and reality known to the church is found in the word of God, where it "tells us the story of how there was an empty grave, that the new life beyond death did become visible."[3] That word will establish all the certainty we need, and while science cannot confirm the truth of Easter, neither can it now presuppose it is false.

ALEXANDER J. MCKELWAY

Pastoral Perspective

has triumphed, already, over all of this. There will come a day when I will look out the window and be unable to see any brokenness, because all my attention will be fixed on Christ's glorious return in the clouds. That day is not yet here though.

Here, at the beginning of Revelation, there is a clear sense of expectation precisely because, as John's audience knew well, God's triumph is not finished yet. The challenge of Easter preaching is to preach resurrection and triumph without evading real, present suffering. John's tripartite sense of time may help us. *Christ has done this, and Christ is doing this, and Christ will do this.* He was, and is, and is to come. Christ's "was" is not canceled out by his "will be." This may be read as an acknowledgment that the future does not cancel out the past or the present. Put differently, Eastertide is not the eschaton, and the meaning of Easter is not the elimination of suffering.

In terms of preaching, this means that we cannot permit our proclamation to proclaim *through* difficulty; rather, our proclamation must *address* difficulty. In fact, perhaps we need even to *proclaim* difficulty. Easter needs Good Friday, because we cannot appreciate the fullness of Christ unless we appreciate what he assumed—unless we appreciate the real, authentic pain he experienced. The acknowledgment of Katie's suffering and Steven's suffering and Rose's suffering is thus not a counterpoint to Easter; it is part of the proclamation of Easter.

So this is part of what we are privileged to remind one another, here on the Second Sunday of Easter with John. We do not simply say Christ is risen. We say there is more coming down the pike.

We say:

> God loves us.
> God has already freed us from our sin (and we know there is still brokenness aplenty in this beautiful Easter world).
> God will come back, with the clouds, to finish the work Easter unleashed.

LAUREN F. WINNER

---

2. Cf. Hans Küng and David Tracy, eds., *Paradigm Change in Theology* (New York: Crossword Press, 1989).
3. Karl Barth, *Dogmatics in Outline* (New York: Harper & Row, 1959), 123.

Exegetical Perspective

Christ's ongoing love for the community of faithful, his redemption of them from the world of sin (v. 5b), and finally, the reconstitution of those who speak into a kingdom (or "empire") (v. 6a). They are not a kingdom made up of priests, but a people who manifest God's rule in and for the world (see 5:10; 20:4, 6; 22:5), much as Israel was constituted at Sinai (Exod. 19:1–6) as a priestly nation. They bear witness to God's authority, unmasking illegitimate human authorities. Whether it is the congregations of Asia Minor who utter these words, or John on their behalf, the effect is the same: as the doxology names the love, liberation, and community-forming power of Jesus Christ, it also brings into existence the people of which it speaks (as the Pledge of Allegiance constitutes a people). Christ's rule, shared with his faithful witnesses, is the focus of this doxology. The rest of Revelation develops this message in detail.

The prophetic announcement (v. 7) and divine oracle (v. 8). In response to the community-forming doxology of verses 5–6, yet another voice announces that Christ is coming with the clouds (v. 7). This image draws from Daniel 7:13 (one coming with the clouds) and Zechariah 12:10 (people mourning the one they have pierced). Christ's coming is not for a chosen few, for every eye will see him. His coming brings judgment to those who opposed him and to all "the tribes of the earth," whose wailing denotes despair or, perhaps, repentance. In 18:9 the merchants of the earth wail over the destruction of Babylon, the symbol of human, imperial orders like that of Rome. The coming of Jesus is certain, visible, decisive, and world changing. The community constituted by the preceding doxology watch for his coming, ready to name Christ's advent for all.

The double confirmation, "Yes. Amen," at the end of verse 7 may be the audience's response to the acclamation of Christ's coming, or the words of God, confirming the certainty of what has been announced. In verse 8, however, it is clearly God who speaks, one of two occasions in Revelation where God speaks directly (see 21:5–8). In both passages God is "the Alpha and the Omega," the origin and goal of creation. Jesus himself will adopt the names spoken here for himself in 22:13. God's identity and sovereignty are thus inseparable from the certainty of Jesus' love, redemption, and coming in power.

STANLEY P. SAUNDERS

Homiletical Perspective

job of the church is to crash the pity party of evil by announcing that the Lord God is "Alpha and Omega." The promise of Easter is that Christ is truly alive and is empowering the church to embody the victory of God.

Preachers should think concretely about how listeners can embody Easter. What kind of daily choices can be made at work, home, or play that will reflect God's presence and power? What do relationships look like for Easter people, and how can behavior reveal the conquering love of God? What issues, locally and globally, should the church stand behind or against, and how is such courageous action a foretaste of the kingdom of God? The text begs preachers to answer these and similar questions and, in doing so, to remind congregations that being faithful as Easter people means reflecting the God who is in charge and the kingdom that "is to be."

The bold confidence exuded in the text comes from the writer's knowledge of how the script ends. Therefore, the underlying message of the text is that Christians should live their Easter faith boldly, because all the struggles of this present life are simply a prelude to "feasting at the heavenly banquet." This is not unlike watching a movie with a happy ending. Those who have not seen the movie watch with trepidation and fear of the unknown. Those who have seen the movie watch with a grin, because they know how it all comes together at the end. As trouble befalls our world, Christians can go about their business with a grin, because they know who has the last word. This grin will make the discouraged curious. People always want to know what is behind a grin.

CHARLES D. REEB

John 20:19-31

¹⁹When it was evening on that day, the first day of the week, and the doors of the house where the disciples had met were locked for fear of the Jews, Jesus came and stood among them and said, "Peace be with you." ²⁰After he said this, he showed them his hands and his side. Then the disciples rejoiced when they saw the Lord. ²¹Jesus said to them again, "Peace be with you. As the Father has sent me, so I send you." ²²When he had said this, he breathed on them and said to them, "Receive the Holy Spirit. ²³If you forgive the sins of any, they are forgiven them; if you retain the sins of any, they are retained."

²⁴But Thomas (who was called the Twin), one of the twelve, was not with them when Jesus came. ²⁵So the other disciples told him, "We have seen the Lord." But he said to them, "Unless I see the mark of the nails in his hands, and put my finger in the mark of the nails and my hand in his side, I will not believe."

Theological Perspective

So frequent are the mentions in these readings of "seeing" and "touching" the risen Lord that we could expect the theologian to say that this text is about "empirical verification." That is not a word combination restricted to theological classrooms, as an Internet search yields almost two million usages. Why do those two long and forbidding words become so prominent in vocabularies, one might ask? The answer is clear: in our scientific age, more than ever, we are trained to verify by trusting sense experience, *empeiria* meaning "experience." Sight and touch make very strong impressions and provide evidence to be tested.

There is no reason to attack such senses and tests, especially because in this text Jesus invites such examination: "Put your finger here and see my hands. Reach out your hand and put it in my side. Do not doubt but believe." Touch and see: the command could be a mantra wherever people must experiment. The counsel is clear: do not accept something just because people traditionally have done so. Science is creatively disrespectful of such traditions. Scientists reason that if they are to heal, they must probe, criticize, evaluate, and seek to discover. "Touch and see." Just in case, they could add smell to senses that aid in verifying.

Hearing and seeing are crucial in this passage. Peter and another disciple saw the empty tomb.

Pastoral Perspective

"[Jesus] breathed on them" (v. 22).

Consider engaging that sentence with incarnational imagination: What did that breath smell like? Was it sweet with the scent of springtime? Was there something of heaven in it, beyond ordinary experience? Or was there still the smell of the wine and the food he had shared with them three nights before? Or maybe the disciples smelled what they recognized from all those meals back in Galilee—fish and olives and bread perhaps. Or was it the gall he had been given to drink on the cross, or the heavy odor of the spices with which he had been anointed for burial? Was there something of the grave that clung to him still now—as they could also see the wounds in his hands—even as he stood so wonderfully alive again before them?

Each such possibility makes the story slightly different, but of course none is decisively entailed by either text or dogma, and neither is any of this speculation vital to the gospel. Thinking about it may seem trivial, wasteful, and mistakenly grounded in a naive literalism. Nevertheless, I have suggested this meditative exercise for the preacher, not as proposed sermon content, but as preparatory reflection, because it drives the metaphor of *inspiration* back to the flesh-and-blood experience involved, namely, that the Holy Spirit given to us is the breath, the *pneuma*,

26A week later his disciples were again in the house, and Thomas was with them. Although the doors were shut, Jesus came and stood among them and said, "Peace be with you." 27Then he said to Thomas, "Put your finger here and see my hands. Reach out your hand and put it in my side. Do not doubt but believe." 28Thomas answered him, "My Lord and my God!" 29Jesus said to him, "Have you believed because you have seen me? Blessed are those who have not seen and yet have come to believe."

30Now Jesus did many other signs in the presence of his disciples, which are not written in this book. 31But these are written so that you may come to believe that Jesus is the Messiah, the Son of God, and that through believing you may have life in his name.

Exegetical Perspective

The vignettes presented in chapter 20 of John's Gospel are paradigmatic (but not exhaustively so) of the diverse ways those who have encountered Jesus can become believers. Prior to his crucifixion, Jesus performed "signs," or miracles, which served as vehicles for eliciting belief (2:11). The crucifixion itself is a sign; it is Jesus' glorification (17:1). After Good Friday, there are new sorts of signs—*and* transformed belief: belief in Jesus as the resurrected Son of the Father. For some, the evidence of the empty tomb points the way. For others, a peculiar arrangement of burial wrappings sparks the imagination (the Beloved Disciple). Angelic appearances may not convince. A voice uttering one's name *can*—as it does with Mary Magdalene. Ultimately, the Gospel writer hopes that the power of the stories themselves, *singly and combined*, will foster belief among *readers* (20:31; cf. 21:25) who live at some remove, both physically and temporally.

With Jesus' appearance to the ten, the intended "sign" would be the fulfillment of promises made earlier. Darkness again prevails; it is "evening." The disciples are sequestered, "locked up," for "fear of the Jews." Apparently, the persecution Jesus had predicted (15:18–24; 16:1–4) has come to pass. By "coming" and "standing" among them, Jesus fulfills the very oaths proffered in the Farewell Discourse

Homiletical Perspective

In John Irving's novel *A Prayer for Owen Meany*, the narrator John has a number of conversations with his friend Owen Meany about the meaning of belief. In one scene at the schoolyard, Owen illustrates his faith in God by pointing to a gray granite statue of Mary Magdalene as twilight falls. When it has become so dark that the statue is no longer visible, Owen asks John if he knows that the statue is still there. (To convey the unusual quality of Owen's voice, Irving capitalizes his speech.) John says that of course he knows. Owen keeps pushing:

> "YOU HAVE NO DOUBT SHE'S THERE?" [Owen] nagged at me.
> "Of course I have no doubt!" I said.
> "BUT YOU CAN'T SEE HER—YOU COULD BE WRONG," he said.
> "No, I'm not wrong—she's there, I know she's there!" I yelled at him.
> "YOU ABSOLUTELY KNOW SHE'S THERE— EVEN THOUGH YOU CAN'T SEE HER?" he asked me.
> "Yes," I screamed.
> "WELL, NOW YOU KNOW HOW I FEEL ABOUT GOD," said Owen Meany. "I CAN'T SEE HIM—BUT I ABSOLUTELY KNOW HE IS THERE!"[1]

1. John Irving, *A Prayer for Owen Meany* (New York: Ballantine Books, 1989), 451.

John 20:19-31

Theological Perspective

Mary Magdalene heard her name called. On the day of the resurrection, Jesus said, "Peace be with you" (John 20:19, 21), and there was peace among the disciples who were there. He taught them the words of forgiveness, and told them that these would effect forgiveness. Thomas had not seen, touched, smelled, or touched Jesus as the others had, and he had not heard the words.

The story of Thomas is so dramatic that we tend to tell it in such a narrow way that Thomas acquires the nickname "doubting." He often gets disdained or scolded: Why did he not catch on right away? Was he an agnostic, a skeptic, a professional doubter? Hardly. He simply had been absent, beyond the sight and sound of Jesus' presence.

This story is not about Good Friday or Easter Day or earlier the evening of the second Sunday. It marks our opening to new stages of faith and church life. Up until the story, faith came in the face of Jesus' physical presence. Here, in the word to Thomas, the Jesus of this Gospel sets us up theologically for the experience of God *not* based solely on sight. Decades after these words were written, the last disciple died. Never again on earth would physical eyes or noses or tongues certify Jesus' presence. Yes, Christians are still to "taste and see that the Lord is good," but related to symbols. They could "taste" in the bread and wine of the Lord's Supper, but that was sacramental.

The one direct call for verification in this text came through hearing. "Faith comes by hearing." Thomas, who is not the last doubter among the old-school disciples, gets to be the one to whom it is announced first that, from now on, hearing would do it all. Notice: Jesus *spoke* an invitation to touch and see. We are not told whether Thomas ever did touch. What matters is that, having heard the words of Jesus, he gasped, "My Lord and my God!" He occasions a blessing that still comes to us in Asia, Africa, Australia, and the Americas: "Blessed are those who have *not* seen and yet have come to believe" (v. 29).

A few hundred or thousand believers could come to faith in Jesus's lifetime. Literally, however, billions have come to faith through the centuries after, when Jesus was not seen except figuratively in pictures, or in vaporous visions. "Jesus said . . . Thomas answered." The word did it; touching had become irrelevant, perhaps even rude and offensive.

Recognizing that verification after the time of Thomas depends upon hearing (or seeing on scrolls or in books) what was or is to be said, theologians busy themselves with the meaning of speaking and

Pastoral Perspective

of the crucified and risen Jesus. He gives it not as words on a page, but breathing it out, breath that is partly the shaped exhalation of speech but also air for our lungs, life for our lives. As God breathed into a creature of dust, and humanity first came to life, so here the Christ enlivens these disciples. This is of course a metaphorical use of language, but to begin an abstracted discussion of what it means risks divesting it of its full meaning, "spiritualizing" the Spirit and divorcing resurrection from the incarnation. Let us not discard or discount the reality that this gospel, and our apprehension of it, involves real breath and real flesh. Let us consider, let us seek to feel and believe, that the breath we now draw into our lungs is infused with that of the risen Lord.[1]

If this breath of ours is indeed that of Jesus, moreover, it is not in our lungs only for the purpose of sustaining our flesh with life-giving oxygen. It is there for us to breathe out as well, giving it the shape of words, expressing it in speech and sign to inspire others. That also is part of this incarnational metaphor. Jesus appears in the locked room of fear and speaks his word of peace. He displays the wounds in his flesh, and with his breath he explicitly gives his disciples the Holy Spirit; but thereby he also makes them his apostles, his sent ones—"As the Father has sent me, so I send you." His breath thus appears to be both equipment and investiture for that mission. Immediately Jesus elaborates what they are to do, the tasks for which they now have his breath. He empowers them to speak words of forgiveness and of judgment, words that will not be mere expressions of personal emotion but declarations of divine fact.

The idea of bearing Christ's life-breath may sound attractive, but two problems commonly arise at just this point. The first is with the mission, a notion that Jesus is here creating a corps of magistrates to go out into the world and busily dispense sentences of condemnation to some or grace to others by the authority of heaven. So juridical a construction of this mandate to the apostles not only misses the spirit by which the Spirit is given but risks prideful dishonor to the wounded humanity that Jesus so patently shares. The authority is more simply to speak, as he would, the words of peace—both sharp challenge and abundant forgiveness, comfort to the afflicted and

---

1. Even if we or our hearers cannot feel or believe that, we might remember the example of Thomas, whose inability to believe could have put him outside the circle of the disciples, but who is still among them now a week later. We do not know whether it was hope or friendship or despair in other options that kept him from leaving, but let it be noted that the fellowship of the disciples was elastic enough that he could be there.

Exegetical Perspective

(chaps. 14–17): that after he had gone away he would return (14:18–19, 28); that his "peace" would indeed perdure (14:27; 16:33); that their pain would "turn to joy" and that it would be "complete" (16:20–24); that the Spirit would be bestowed upon them (14:16–17, 25–26; 15:26; 16:13–14); and that they would be empowered to "testify," to "bear witness" on Jesus' behalf.

It is tantalizing to speculate about the relationship between John and the Synoptics when considering this pericope.[1] Jesus' promise in Luke 24:49 and its fulfillment in Acts 2:4 seem to be captured in this one scene. When one links Jesus' valedictory remarks in 16:8 with verses 21–23 here, one may hear canonical echoes of the Great Commission in Matthew 28:19 and Jesus' granting to Peter and the disciples the powers to "bind and loose" (Matt. 16:18–20; 18:18). Regardless of the interrelationship of the traditions (redactional indicators are disappointingly sparse), the author of the Gospel of John compresses Good Friday, Easter, and Pentecost into one theologically rich narrative.

The passage is replete too with OT allusion. Jesus "breathes" on them and says, "Receive the Holy Spirit." The verb for "breathe" here (*emphysaō*) is not common. In LXX it occurs in Genesis 2:7 and Ezekiel 37:9. Jesus, sent by the Father, "animates" the dust-bound, fear-slain, boney-faithed disciples with the life-giving Spirit.

Thomas's initial, "unbelieving" response to the disciples' claims about Jesus' resurrection should *not* be seen as singular. As noted above, the signs Jesus performed during his public ministry were intended to elicit faith/believing (1:50; 10:38; 11:15, 40; 14:11). Others, not just Thomas, expected signs as a precondition for belief (4:48; 6:30). Elsewhere, the disciples responded to the message of Jesus' resurrection with disbelief (Matt. 28:17; Luke 24:11, 24, 38, 41). The Thomas narrative is part and parcel of a post-resurrection tradition that none of the Gospels seeks to suppress. Indeed, if the possibility of connections between John and the Synoptics is pursued, one might very well consider 20:26–28 a re-working, a personalizing (with Thomas as the lead character) of Jesus' appearance to the disciples in Luke 24:36–43, where Jesus himself invites the disciples to press the flesh, and further challenges their incredulity by polishing off a piece of broiled fish. Literarily too, the obvious parallel between Thomas's demand and Mary

Homiletical Perspective

The character Owen Meany is an exemplar of the kind of faith that the Fourth Evangelist celebrates in the second half of John 20. Because Owen believes so fully and completely in God, he stakes his life on his conviction. He does not need to see; he does not need signs and wonders; he believes and orients his whole life around this belief.

To understand this kind of faith as the central message of Thomas's encounter with Jesus, we have to notice that practically everyone in John 20 sees the resurrected Jesus. Surely Mary Magdalene does, but so do the disciples who encounter Jesus behind closed doors later that same day. They converse with him in the afternoon as Mary did in the morning. Like Mary, they receive a commission for service.

So why should we be so hard on Thomas for demanding the same opportunity to see Jesus that everyone else had? If he insists that there is no way he will believe such an unbelievable story, why do we fault him? Yet year after year, as this story shows up on the Sunday after Easter, we preach against poor doubting Thomas for not having enough faith to believe without seeing. There is good reason to single out Thomas for inadequate faith, but the fact that he wanted what almost everyone else got, is not it.

Here is the real problem with Thomas. In rejecting the disciples' good news about what they have seen, he rebuffs the very friends with whom he has shared life for so long. In fact, throughout John's Gospel, and in the Johannine Epistles that grow out of it, love and trust within the faithful community are the significant expression of the work of Christ in their midst. Yet Thomas's words, especially in the Greek, carry a powerful sting; "there's no way I will believe unless I see it for myself" is the original force.[2] Thomas abrogates the work of Christ in their midst through his proud words of doubt. *Their* eyes and *their* fingers are not enough for him; he must see and touch *for himself*. Thus the community that Jesus has tried so hard to build throughout the Gospel is threatened from the beginning by Thomas's skepticism.

This kind of radical suspicion of our companions in faith tears at the fabric of our churches today. We can list occurrences of such distrust in our midst. There is the detractor who will not accept the trustworthiness of the deacons who count the offerings. There is the disparager who wonders if people who do not accept all lines of his creed are really Christian.

---

1. See D. Moody Smith, *John among the Gospels*, 2nd ed. (Columbia: University of South Carolina Press, 2001).

2. Bernard Brandon Scott, "A New Voice in the Amphitheater: Full Fidelity in Translating," in *Fidelity and Translation: Communicating the Bible in New Media*, ed. Paul A. Soukup and Robert Hodgson (Franklin, WI: Sheed & Ward and New York: American Bible Society, 1999), 115.

John 20:19-31

Theological Perspective

hearing. They are aware that many believers are hearing-impaired, but know that the deaf use sign language or technology to start conversations with them. Christians are not to be trained to be gullible, regarded as suckers, blinded in naiveté. They are to hear and study, "testing the spirits." They are to compare testimonies.

In a theology or philosophy classroom, we are involved with rhetoric. The master of rhetoric, which is persuasive speech intended to produce effects, was Aristotle. His work still informs preachers. He noted several elements. First was the credibility of the speaker: you do not likely trust "truths" from someone you *know* to be a hypocrite or liar. The philosopher called that *ethos*, namely, "character." Second, you are alert to the disciples in this story: people afraid, eager, some still bereft. Aristotle calls this *pathos,* as in "sympathy" and "empathy." The preacher deals with a community that is open to "seeing" the Lord, for they have suffered, felt abandoned, been distracted, and he or she must identify with them. Third is the "word," *logos:* one must have something to say. Jesus' *logos* on the day of this story led him to speak the healing word to Thomas, who was probably being considered a second-class citizen disciple.

The theologian who preaches or the preacher "doing" theology (=making God-talk) lives most of life like everyone else, "empirically testing" thermometers, scales, and claims alike. Yet in the act of preaching, "under the Holy Spirit," using perhaps bad grammar, telling bleak anecdotes, fighting to be seen as credible even as he "runs an institution," the key element for the speaker is the word, the spoken word wherever possible, something to be tested and confirmed. When things line up right and match, there can be a response, such as "My Lord and my God!"

After that is spoken, heard, and exchanged, believers can go about their work, their Sabbath rest, their finding opportunity to relate to others and to do the works of love in such a way that they will be exemplifying that the lives of believers, "empirically" or visibly, are and are to be tested as they are asked whether they embody the new life that comes with Christ's resurrection.

MARTIN E. MARTY

Pastoral Perspective

affliction to the comfortable—as we Lutherans say, in flawed shorthand, both law and gospel. We are to speak what is needed, what God needs spoken, for the sake of those who might otherwise perish. The principle of divine authority in this *can* be an opening for arrogance, but it can and should instead be a caution to use our speech with holy responsibility, both with compassionate care and with urgent attention, not to our own feelings and interests but to what God wants spoken.

The second potential problem in this breath-borne commissioning lies in the restriction of agency in the mission that Jesus entrusts to his followers. Is it just to those called apostles and their successors in office, or is the paradigm here for the whole church and for each able believer? The debate is classic: just who has the keys of which Jesus spoke to Peter? Our various traditions have not dealt with that question identically, but perhaps we may agree that it would be an impoverishing shame to make Jesus' actions here paradigmatic only for priests and preachers. Our ministry is emblematic of the purposes for which others are to use their resurrection breath, speaking and doing the gospel of mercy and justice. May Jesus breathe in our words, but also let our hearers speak in kind. Perhaps we will be among those who need their speaking.

JOHN K. STENDAHL

Exegetical Perspective

Magdalene's rebuffed attempt to "keep holding onto" Jesus (20:17) should not be missed.

Thomas is mentioned only in passing in the Synoptic lists of the Twelve and in Acts (Matt.10:3; Mark 3:18; Luke 6:15; Acts 1:13). In John, he gains more prominence as a character with a distinct voice (11:16; 14:5; 20:24–29; 21:2). "Thomas" is not a proper name, but a nickname that means "twin" in Aramaic/Syriac. According to the *Gospel of Thomas*, his given name is Judas. So, when John identifies him as the one "who was called the Twin" (Gk. *Didymus*), he is providing a Greek translation of a nickname intended to distinguish him from Judas Iscariot. Whose twin is he? In the gnostic Gospel, Jesus reveals to Thomas that "whoever drinks from my mouth will become as I am, and I myself will become that person, and the mysteries shall be revealed to him" (*Gos. Thom.*, Log. 108). Elaine Pagels is convinced that, for the *Gospel of Thomas*, encountering the "living Jesus" means recognizing "oneself and Jesus as, so to speak, identical twins."[2] The Gospel of John counters that tradition by offering a "Thomas," a "Twin," who is unbelieving, who comes to faith reluctantly. Perhaps he is *our* "twin"?

Thomas's demand and Jesus' acceding to it make any docetic reading of the crucifixion or the resurrection implausible. Introduced for the first time in the passion narrative are *fulfillment formulae* ("this was to fulfill what the scripture says . . .") and explicit quotations of the OT (19:24, 28, 36–37). Matthew is distinguished by this technique.[3] John reserves it for the end. The quotations (Ps. 22:18; Ps. 69:21; Zech. 12:10) underline the *physical* reality of Jesus' suffering and death. Jesus' anguish and demise were not apparitional; they were foretold in Scripture. The Thomas account, however, cannot be read as another riff on the Homeric recognition of identity based on evidence of a scar (*Odyssey* 19.467–73). The empty tomb, the grave cloths, the presence of angels, Jesus' exchange with Mary, the appearance on the evening of the first day of the week and, now, the revelation to Thomas—taken together—can demand only one response: christological confession, "My Lord and my God!" (cf., LXX, Ps. 34:23). This is the most explicit one in the Gospels (cf., Acts 2:36; Titus 2:13; Heb. 1:8ff.). Read within the context of John's prologue, it is both the climax of the Gospel and its logical conclusion.

GREGORY A. ROBBINS

2. Elaine Pagels, *Beyond Belief* (New York: Random House, 2003), 57.
3. O. Lamar Cope, *A Scribe Trained for the Kingdom*, CBQ Monograph Series 5 (1976).

Homiletical Perspective

There are the cynical personnel committee members who dismiss the stories of young girls who say the youth minister has approached them sexually. "If you cannot prove it to me with evidence that I can verify on my own, I refuse to accept the truth you are presenting here," these skeptics say dismissively to those in our midst who speak a different truth. They echo Thomas when they say these things, refusing to believe something that might force them to reexamine their comfortable preconceptions or do things that might upset others.

It is Thomas's community-shattering doubt that the Gospel of John rejects. For at some point, if our churches are to be faithful to the risen Christ, we must stop distrusting our friends in Christ. At the very least, we must stop questioning motives, doubting dedication, and thinking the worst of our companions when they state a different opinion or offer a contradictory version. We must learn to believe not simply in the goodness of the Lord, but in the goodness of one another—even when they deliver the strangest news, "We have seen the Lord."

Ultimately in the Gospel of John, it is those who believe without seeing who are the true followers of Jesus. This is confirmed in the words that Jesus speaks, over the head of Thomas, to those readers who will not be able to see in the years ahead, "Blessed are those who have not seen and yet have come to believe" (v. 29). The only one who does this within John's resurrection narrative is the Beloved Disciple, who runs to the tomb, sees absolutely nothing, and believes. It is he who verifies the truth of these written words at the end of the Gospel: "This is the disciple who is testifying to these things and has written them, and we know that his testimony is true" (21:24).

In *A Prayer for Owen Meany*, Owen believes in God and God's work in his life, without clear-cut evidence or proof. His lifelong friend John does not have the same solid conviction. What John has is a confidence in his friend that carries him through his own skepticism and into a new life.

NANCY CLAIRE PITTMAN

Acts 9:1-6 (7-20)

[1]Meanwhile Saul, still breathing threats and murder against the disciples of the Lord, went to the high priest [2]and asked him for letters to the synagogues at Damascus, so that if he found any who belonged to the Way, men or women, he might bring them bound to Jerusalem. [3]Now as he was going along and approaching Damascus, suddenly a light from heaven flashed around him. [4]He fell to the ground and heard a voice saying to him, "Saul, Saul, why do you persecute me?" [5]He asked, "Who are you, Lord?" The reply came, "I am Jesus, whom you are persecuting. [6]But get up and enter the city, and you will be told what you are to do." [7]The men who were traveling with him stood speechless because they heard the voice but saw no one. [8]Saul got up from the ground, and though his eyes were open, he could see nothing; so they led him by the hand and brought him into Damascus. [9]For three days he was without sight, and neither ate nor drank.

[10]Now there was a disciple in Damascus named Ananias. The Lord said to him in a vision, "Ananias." He answered, "Here I am, Lord." [11]The Lord said to him, "Get up and go to the street called Straight, and at the house of Judas look for a man

Theological Perspective

The famous Damascus Road story is usually read as a description of the transforming personal encounter that changed the course of Saul's life. As such, the event described is a prototypical conversion experience. This narrative is also Luke's introduction of Saul (afterward to become Paul, see Acts 13:9) as a leading actor in the apostolic mission to the ends of the then-known earth. It is also presented by the narrator, and confirmed in other terms by Paul himself (1 Cor. 15:8), as involving a postascension appearance of the risen Christ.

For Luke, this experience was clearly something different in principle from the preascension bodily and quasi-bodily appearances of Jesus to his disciples described in all four Gospels. Luke does not doubt the words attributed to Ananias, "Brother Saul, it was the Lord Jesus who appeared to you on the road." However, for Luke, this occurs after the "forty days." Jesus has been "lifted up" into a cloud, out of sight (Acts 1:9). According to Luke, this late resurrection encounter—being different from the one on the road to Emmaus, for instance (Luke 24:13–35)—does not give Paul status comparable to that of "the Twelve" (Matthias substituting for Judas), who accompanied Jesus during his earthly ministry and then became "witnesses to his resurrection" (Acts 1:22). Luke's theological purpose with respect to Saul in Acts 9

Pastoral Perspective

In his book *Why Preach? Why Listen?* William Muehl suggests that on any given Sunday when you look out at a congregation, you can imagine that many of those sitting in the pews almost did not come that day. They considered staying home because in their minds their faith does not measure up to the faith of others in the congregation.[1] The passage from Acts 9, often called "the Conversion of Saul," contributes to this "faith inferiority complex."

When people tell about their faith journeys, most share a narrative that begins something like this: "I was raised in the church and never knew a time when I was not a Christian." There is something comforting about having such an early faith identity. There is nothing wrong with such a faith statement unless you compare it with Acts 9; then it lacks drama and may seem woefully inadequate.

If the truth be known, we have some discomfort with the story of the conversion of Saul, so we become defensive and say, "Even though I never had a Damascus Road experience, I still believe God has been at work in my life." This reflects the feeling of what I am calling "faith inferiority."

1. William Muehl, *Why Preach? Why Listen?* (Philadelphia: Fortress Press, 1986), 11.

of Tarsus named Saul. At this moment he is praying, [12]and he has seen in a vision a man named Ananias come in and lay his hands on him so that he might regain his sight." [13]But Ananias answered, "Lord, I have heard from many about this man, how much evil he has done to your saints in Jerusalem; [14]and here he has authority from the chief priests to bind all who invoke your name." [15]But the Lord said to him, "Go, for he is an instrument whom I have chosen to bring my name before Gentiles and kings and before the people of Israel; [16]I myself will show him how much he must suffer for the sake of my name." [17]So Ananias went and entered the house. He laid his hands on Saul and said, "Brother Saul, the Lord Jesus, who appeared to you on your way here, has sent me so that you may regain your sight and be filled with the Holy Spirit." [18]And immediately something like scales fell from his eyes, and his sight was restored. Then he got up and was baptized, [19]and after taking some food, he regained his strength.

For several days he was with the disciples in Damascus, [20]and immediately he began to proclaim Jesus in the synagogues, saying, "He is the Son of God."

Exegetical Perspective

The importance of Saul's (= Paul's) Damascus Road encounter with the risen Jesus is indicated by its repetition in Acts, here in the narrator's voice and twice again in Paul's voice in defense of his mission and message (cf. 22:3–16; 26:4–23). The present reader of this narrative triad need not try to harmonize the discrepancies found among them but rather consider how the narrative's repetition in Acts supplies a more fully nuanced portrait of the Paul of Acts and his importance for the future of the church.

Luke tells the story of Saul's conversion with familiar irony: his opposition to the early church (8:1–3) occasions Philip's successful mission beyond Jerusalem to the north. The rousing success of the church's mission beyond Jerusalem prompts Saul to aim his hostilities northward toward Syrian Damascus, following a path marked out by the stupendous effects of the gospel (8:4–40). The geographical reversal that begins this powerful drama signals Saul's spiritual reversal: on his way to destroy "the disciples of the Lord" (9:1), Saul encounters the living Jesus and becomes one of his disciples instead.

Before taking up the story of Saul's conversion, the careful reader will recall the strategic moment when Saul is introduced in Acts: immediately before Stephen's petition for the forgiveness of those, now including Saul, whose ignorance has resulted in his

Homiletical Perspective

Preaching is translating Scripture from its ancient context and helping us see that the same human themes are at work in our lives. Paul's conversion on the Damascus Road is so dramatic as to be off-putting. It is far easier to "leave it back then" as both ancient and irrelevant. Yet preachers have to find ways to help our hearers see how our lives intersect with the text, and how God intervenes in our lives today.

There is nothing more difficult to preach to twenty-first-century persons than the "unbelievable," and this passage surely pushes the envelope. Did this really happen to Saul? Do things like this happen to people today? Occasionally, we will hear people describe some metanoic experience in their lives that is so unusual, so pronounced, as to be nearly unbelievable. So we are left with a choice. If we believe that God truly intervenes in such blinding, definitive ways, then why has it never happened to me or to thousands of others? Does God pick favorites? Am I coasting along in such normality that God need not "turn me around" so graphically? Why does it happen so rarely?

Not many of us are "breathing threats and murder" against our opponents. However, we have all been on wrong paths that have been injurious to ourselves and others. We have all been headstrong, stubborn, blinded to our own ambition, selfish to meet our own need, caught in addictive behaviors,

Acts 9:1-6 (7-20)

Theological Perspective

looks not backward to the constitution of this authoritative group, but forward to the validation of the Pauline missionary journeys Luke is about to describe.

First Corinthians 15 is another passage altogether, but we must allude to it in order to have an adequate theological understanding of what is and is not said in Acts 9. Paul is concerned in his letter to Corinth with establishing the continuity of his own experience of the risen Christ with the preascension appearances to the disciples and others, as handed down in the tradition, and hence with the continuity of his teaching with theirs. He seeks to do for himself what Luke does not, that is, retrospectively to establish his apostolic status. Paul too is an apostle, if only the least of them—not because his late experience of the resurrection is in any way lacking, but because he formerly persecuted the church (1 Cor. 15:9, alluding to what is described in Acts 9:1–2). It is as if Paul saw the resurrection and the ascension as one continuous event, with no distinction between appearances during the "forty days" and his own experience afterward. Paul's insistence in 1 Corinthians 15 that the resurrection body is not composed of flesh and blood but is a spiritual body (1 Cor. 15:44) is compatible with, if not the same as, Luke's description of the nature of Paul's experience on the Damascus Road.

Although we may infer that Paul's letters, in written form, actually preceded the composition of the Acts of the Apostles, it would seem probable that Luke used oral traditions like that behind Acts 9:1–20, that were even older than the letters. In any case, the Damascus Road narrative shows no evidence of having been influenced by 1 Corinthians 15 and thus goes back to an independently circulating account of the beginning of Saul's missionary career, now spliced with other sources onto other subjects in Luke's narrative of the apostolic age. It is of interest to ask how Luke uses this older story to explain the origins of the mission to come.

How, for example, does the just-converted Saul so quickly grasp the content of the gospel that he is about to preach? It is often assumed that—taken blind into Damascus, then healed, baptized, and filled with the Spirit—Saul must then have undergone a crash course in early Christian teaching. The story does not say so though. It says only that Christ's purpose for Saul—"to bring my name before Gentiles and kings and before the people of Israel," and to "suffer for the sake of my name" (vv. 15–16)—has been revealed to Ananias in a vision.

Pastoral Perspective

It is important to remember that what happened to Saul was noteworthy precisely because it was *not* typical of the way most people became converts. Luke goes out of his way to let us know the significance of this conversion by giving us three accounts of it (Acts 9:1–20; Acts 22:3–21; Acts 26:2–23). Since Luke was a concise writer, this repetition stands out.

"Damascus Road experience" is a phrase used to describe many religious experiences that bear little resemblance to what happened to Saul. In his commentary on Acts, William Willimon encourages us to pay careful attention to this story so that we may gain new insight for our lives. He suggests that the story is so familiar that its meaning may be taken for granted and therefore misunderstood. He cites an interesting quote by Flannery O'Connor, who once said of Paul, "I reckon the Lord knew that the only way to make a Christian out of that one was to knock him off his horse."[2] Never mind that the story in Acts does not say Paul was on a horse.

Despite her addition of a mount for Paul, Flannery O'Connor guides our attention in the right direction. The main character in this and every conversion story is God. It is God who changes lives. The one thing clear about Saul's Damascus Road experience is the power of God that turned him from someone "breathing threats and murder against the disciples of the Lord" (9:1) to someone who "proclaimed Jesus" so that "all who heard him were amazed" (vv. 20–21). Saul's conversion was not something he decided to do on his own. It was God's doing.

African American preachers sometimes ask their congregations, "Can I get a witness?" God needed a witness to carry the good news of Jesus Christ to the Gentiles, the powerful, and the people of Israel. God chose someone who had been a witness *against* the followers of Christ to become a powerful witness *for* Christ. Thus the story is not so much about Saul as it is about the way God works to change lives.

Luke places today's text in a series of conversions, including Samaritans and an Ethiopian. Following Saul's story, Luke moves on to tell the story of the conversion of a Roman centurion. In all of these stories, God touches the lives of unlikely people from diverse backgrounds to spread the gospel to the ends of the earth.

It is easy to identify with Ananias in this story. When the Lord tells him in a vision about what is going on with Paul, Ananias is dubious, to say the

---

2. William H. Willimon, *Acts*, Interpretation series (Louisville, KY: John Knox Press, 1988), 73.

tragic lynching (7:58–60). Saul's initial appearance in the narrative world of Acts prompts a deeply theological reading of his subsequent conversion and commission. That is, even as Saul approaches Damascus "breathing threats and murder" (see 7:51–52), God's steady perspective on human destiny is that Saul is a forgiven man. This inclination toward Saul's story helps explain not only why Jesus should meet with him but that his stunning turn to Jesus somewhere on the Great North Road cashes in a faithful Stephen's promissory note (cf. 22:20).

Saul's persecution of believers in Jerusalem has concluded, and he now travels northbound to extend his hostilities in Damascus against those "who belong to the Way" (v. 2), a messianic movement within Judaism that believes the risen Jesus is God's Messiah (4:26). Damascus was an important Syrian city about 135 miles north of Jerusalem and a leading commercial center of the Roman Empire. Josephus reports that the city was home to a large population of Jews.[1] While the historical circumstances of Saul's opposition to believers in Damascus remain uncertain, the council's interest in policing the city's synagogues suggests "the disciples of the Lord" have settled in Jewish neighborhoods and now threaten the faith of their congregations. Saul's holy mission is to ferret out and "bind" any religious renegade he finds there and return them to Jerusalem for a religious inquisition.

The sudden appearance of "a light from heaven" (9:3; cf. 22:6, 9; 26:13; 2 Cor. 4:4–6), though, interrupts Saul's plans. The light "flashed around him" (9:3; cf. 22:6; 26:13) as the special effect of a theophany when God makes an urgent house call on a prophet in visional form (cf. Exod. 19:16; Ezek. 1:4, 7, 13, 28; Dan. 10:6). Appropriately, Saul's response to what he sees and hears recalls Ezekiel, who had a similar experience with God and "fell to the ground" in preparation to hear "the LORD" speak (cf. Ezek. 1:28).

Biblical stories of God's visitations of Israel or Israel's prophets also include auditions (Exod. 3:4–10; Luke 9:35), which typically disclose God's instruction. Famously, for example, God calls Moses to broker Israel's future in an extraordinary theophany of a burning bush (Exod. 3–4). As with Moses before him, Saul does not initially recognize the voice that addresses him and asks, "Who are you, Lord?" (9:5a). While Saul is not yet a believer and does not recognize the speaker as the "Lord" Jesus, he does understand the importance of the Lord's

1. Josephus, *Jewish Wars*, 2.20.2.

and oblivious of the true cost to others or to ourselves. Here are some examples:

—The hard-driving businesswoman who is so determined to get a promotion that she loses her marriage
—The teenager, angry and hurt, who cannot forgive a parent's error
—The man who is so locked up in his emotions that he cannot express his love for his spouse
—The ever-pleasing wife who is so accommodating as to allow her husband's alcoholism to destroy their children
—The revengeful lover who would do harm rather than seek reconciliation
—The employer whose cultural values prevent him from promoting women equally
—The partisan political leader incapable of compromise
—The sports enthusiast incapable of sporting behavior
—The hard, demanding parent who cannot give a child a break

On this level, we have all been on the wrong path. We have been closed-minded. We have been stubborn. The preacher asks, "What happens when we see the light?" What happens when we open our hearts and minds to discover our error? What happens when, suddenly or gradually, we find ourselves walking the path that leads to life? In Matthew 7:13–14, Jesus reminds us how wide is the road that leads to destruction and how narrow the gate that leads to life. How do we find the "road less traveled"? The task of the preacher is to take what first appears unbelievable and help our hearers realize that this is the *stuff* of everyday life.

The next question becomes, "What was your blinding light?" What changed your mind? What caused you to see reality anew? What finally caused you to see where your addictive behavior would lead? What got through to you so that you saw the chaos your stubborn refusal was creating? Sometimes it is a risk-taking friend who has that soulful confrontation with us, or the partner who finally tells us the truth, or the child who heroically tells it like it is. Sometimes it is just the vacancy of our own souls in the middle of the night that finally convinces us.

The task of the preacher is to ask, "Was God in this?" Where was God in your conversion experience? Is God in the "business" of changing lives? It is often only in the past tense that we can identify the hand of God upon our lives. From that vantage, we can see the Spirit at work. For it is not the honest friend, the

Acts 9:1-6 (7-20)

Theological Perspective

Strangely, there is no record that this message was passed on to the convert, even if we assume that it must have been. We proceed immediately to what can only be described as an act of ordination. Ananias lays hands upon Saul and proclaims, in the name of the Lord Jesus, that he is to regain his sight and receive the Holy Spirit. "Something like scales" then fall from Saul's eyes. Is Saul's ability to see again intended as a metaphor for his ability now to see differently? We may conjecture so. Soon Paul is proclaiming Jesus in the synagogues, saying that Jesus is the "Son of God" and, later, "proving that Jesus was the Messiah" (vv. 20, 22).

What does this passage tell us about Saul's degree of understanding of his mission at this moment? He cannot have been much acquainted with what the original disciples knew so well: the story of Jesus' life and preaching and the details of his passion. Paul's letters, some written years later, show little knowledge of such things. How, then, can he have grasped the gospel message so well, and with such theological sensitivity and creativity as to transform the early church and deeply impact the world of his time? We can only assume that the knowledge of the Way that served Saul as a zealous a persecutor was now turned on its head to serve him as a zealous advocate. However, a mere redirection of zeal from destructive to constructive purposes would ordinarily leave many things poorly or incompletely understood.

Thus Luke's version of the story of Saul's conversion ends without telling us how Paul becomes the theologian he turns out to be. There is a hint in Acts 11:26. We read there that Saul and Barnabas spent a year together with the church in Antioch, teaching "a large company of people." Anyone who has ever offered a team-taught course knows that this is the best way to learn!

LEWIS S. MUDGE

Pastoral Perspective

least. "You must be kidding! This guy is out to get us." Experience teaches us to be cautious about peoples' ability to change. It is hard "to teach old dogs new tricks." However, a consistent theme in the Bible is that when God is the agent of change, all things are possible. This story is a helpful reminder that conversion is not primarily about us, but about God.

There is no one religious experience that fits all. What happened to Saul on the Damascus Road was dramatic and had a significant impact on the church. Our task is to remain open to what God is doing in and around us. Even when we feel uneasy like Ananias, we can remember that he nevertheless did what God asked.

In the congregation I serve, when we train new officers to lead the congregation, we ask each one to tell about his or her faith journey. I am always impressed by the variety of experiences. I marvel at the myriad ways God has been working in their lives. There are usually other people who have assisted them along the way. At this point, William Muehl provides an essential insight: "The roads to Christian faith are as varied as the people who profess it."[3] As we remember and celebrate the Damascus Road experience of Paul, we should be grateful to God for the variety of conversion experiences that enrich the community of faith.

Let us pray that God will open our eyes, as God opened Paul's, to the new reality created by the life, death, and resurrection of Jesus Christ. The image of light is powerful in this story. It blinds Paul initially; then, when his sight is restored, he has a new way of seeing. It is this vision that he shares to bring others into the light of God's love. Our religious experience is not a private affair. Whatever shape or form it takes, it is for spreading the gospel and building up the church.

JOSEPH S. HARVARD

---

3. Muehl, *Why Preach? Why Listen?* 17.

Exegetical Perspective

address and knows he must be absolutely attentive to what is said next: "I am Jesus, whom you are persecuting" (v. 5b). Jesus instructs Saul, "Get up and enter the city, and you will be told what you are to do" (v. 6).

Significantly, Jesus introduces the stated purpose of their meeting by the intensive *alla*, which normally links together sharply contrasting statements: "But [*alla*] get up and enter the city" (v. 6a). In this case, however, the *alla* of Jesus makes emphatic the importance of his surprising return to meet with Saul. As the readers shortly will learn, Jesus has come again to redirect Saul into his future mission as God's chosen instrument.

Jesus concludes his brief speech by what Acts scholars often call "the *dei* of divine necessity": "and you will be told what you are to do [*dei*]" (v. 6b; cf. 22:10; 26:14). Often in Acts, as here, the use of *dei* in a speech stipulates what is necessary for one to do in realizing Scripture's revelation of God's redemptive plans. According to the theological beliefs that shaped Acts, God's salvation is not something that happens by chance or good fortune, but is a work of the Sovereign One that unfolds according to the prophets' revealed script. While it is impossible to deny the transforming effect Jesus' visitation has on Saul, his turn toward Jesus is only one element of a biblical pattern of conversion that concludes in a call to bear witness to the risen one. The real climax of this story is not Saul's conversion from moral morass to virtuous living or from Judaism to Christianity; nothing like this is found in Acts. Saul's turn to Jesus rather rights him for a future scripted by God as "a chosen instrument to bring [Jesus'] name to the Gentiles and . . . the people of Israel . . . [and to] suffer for the sake of my name" (9:15–16). The rest of Acts narrates the dramatic fulfillment of the Lord's stunning prediction.

ROBERT W. WALL

Homiletical Perspective

heroic child, or our soul's vacancy that actually turns us around. It is a light that turns on within us—and it is our willingness to take the risk of seeing anew that makes the turnaround possible. We stood at a crossroads. We had a choice. We could have launched blindly forward, or tarried. We tarried, and that made all the difference.

Many people experience God in those crucible moments: "Were it not for God, I cannot imagine how I could have made this transition." Emilie Griffin writes, "It is clear that conversion begins with a restlessness of the human heart which can find no resting place on earth."[1] Griffin wisely observes that often our disenchantment "comes not from failure but from success. It is success that disappoints us because we had so thoroughly expected it to be the crown of life."[2] We get what we want, and we find it lacking.

In the past tense, most people can relate to taking the wrong path, experiencing a turnaround, and finally discovering the gate that leads to life. What happened to apostle Paul on the road to Damascus happens to all of us. Scripture is not overstated.

Conversions happen all the time and need to happen all the time. The preacher and the people are still stubborn. We remain caught in yet another addictive pattern of behavior. We are still blind and need the light. We are all walking the Damascus Road breathing threats and destruction. The bumper sticker is trite but true: "God isn't done with me yet." Certainly, God was not "done" with Paul once he first saw the light. Converted, he remained stubborn and blind. Converted, we remain stubborn and blind.

Preaching connects when the people ask, "Where is God at work right now within my life? Where do I need to open my eyes and see the light? In what way am I on the wrong path? Where do I stand in need of *metanoia*?"

Preaching also demands that we help people see our cultural blindness and our social bias. Paul's failure represented an uncritical way of thinking that condemned all Christians as a threat to his spiritual status quo. As preachers connect with this conversion text, it causes us to ask how our cultural bias is blinding us, causing us to "breathe threats and destruction" where God is calling us to breathe life and invitation.

STEPHEN D. JONES

---

1. Emilie Griffin, *Turning, Reflections on the Experience of Conversion* (Garden City, NY: Doubleday, 1980), 48.
2. Ibid., 31.

Psalm 30

[1]I will extol you, O Lᴏʀᴅ, for you have drawn me up,
 and did not let my foes rejoice over me.
[2]O Lᴏʀᴅ my God, I cried to you for help,
 and you have healed me.
[3]O Lᴏʀᴅ, you brought up my soul from Sheol,
 restored me to life from among those gone down to the Pit.

[4]Sing praises to the Lᴏʀᴅ, O you his faithful ones,
 and give thanks to his holy name.
[5]For his anger is but for a moment;
 his favor is for a lifetime.
 Weeping may linger for the night,
 but joy comes with the morning.

[6]As for me, I said in my prosperity,
 "I shall never be moved."
[7]By your favor, O Lᴏʀᴅ,
 you had established me as a strong mountain;

Theological Perspective

Psalm 30 gives voice to the theology that grounds biblical faith and worship. The poet praises God for God's deliverance from "a sickness unto death." The congregation is invited to join the song—an invitation, we confess, that includes the church at worship, listening for the word of the Lord, on the Third Sunday of Easter.

Undergirding and informing this and other such prayers of praise and thanksgiving are God's sovereign grace and steadfast love, God's faithfulness to save and to bless, God's correcting judgment and redeeming purpose. Here is the God to whom each life is precious and who initiates the relationship that makes possible this prayer. God says to the individual and to the community, "Call on me in the day of trouble; I will deliver you, and you shall glorify me" (Ps. 50:15). Just so, God is ready, indeed eager, to be sought and to act in grace and favor. To this God, who is already at work to save, the psalmist has cried out (30:2a, 8–10), and God has come to deliver (vv. 2b–3, 11).

To worship such a God is to realize that prayer itself is God's gift—that in electing to be God with and for us, and not without us, God enables us, encourages us, teaches us to pray. This theology refutes the notion of prayer as essentially a technique born of human desire or necessity, whereby we enlist a useful god to meet our needs and satisfy our wants.

Pastoral Perspective

Psalm 30 is steeped in a variety of experiences familiar to pastors and to our people. The "foes" of the opening verse are not prevailing at the moment, and so the speaker pauses to praise God, to recall what has happened, and to commit to continue giving thanks "forever"—regardless of what may yet occur. Such a response on the part of an individual relies on a worshiping community for witness, accountability, and support. The difficulties encountered (and, by implication, anticipated) make this clear. This psalm is simultaneously the testimony of one who has come through big trouble, looking back with gratitude, and an affirmation that enables one to conform one's self to hope and trust, in the midst of potential hopelessness. When we explore them, the variety of familiar experiences invite our people to precisely these faith responses of their own.

Pastors frequently find ourselves working with individuals, families, and communities that find themselves down in the Pit. We are often the only ones who can find a way to ask the key question, how can trust and hope arise in the midst of all this? Further, we help our people find their way to answering the question, once they have asked it. Psalm 30 provides one model for answering; while the word "hope" is not used in the psalm, hope arises in the repeated movement from difficulty to thanks.

you hid your face;
  I was dismayed.

⁸To you, O Lᴏʀᴅ, I cried,
  and to the Lᴏʀᴅ I made supplication:
⁹"What profit is there in my death,
  if I go down to the Pit?
  Will the dust praise you?
  Will it tell of your faithfulness?
¹⁰Hear, O Lᴏʀᴅ, and be gracious to me!
  O Lᴏʀᴅ, be my helper!"

¹¹You have turned my mourning into dancing;
  you have taken off my sackcloth
  and clothed me with joy,
¹²so that my soul may praise you and not be silent.
  O Lᴏʀᴅ my God, I will give thanks to you forever.

Exegetical Perspective

Psalm 30 is filled with movement—from the present
to the future, and then back to the past before
returning to the initial present moment. The
psalmist has experienced a life-changing event and
wants to relate that event to the totality of his or her
existence over time.

The psalm commences with a report about difficulties that have been resolved (vv. 1–3). As is typical
of many psalms, the individual refers to multiple
problems. The psalmist confronted enemies (v. 1); the
psalmist apparently experienced ill health out of
which healing could occur (v. 2). Enemies (of what
kind we are not told) and illness symbolize the social
and bodily challenges that can confront a person.
When they happen at the same time, the very life of
the individual seems threatened. Of these two negative
forces, illness, which remains unnamed, seems to be
the primary problem. The psalmist praises God for
not having let the enemies celebrate the difficulties,
that is, the psalmist does not report having been
attacked by enemies. They remain an audience rather
than active perpetrators. The anonymous enemies
witness the suffering of the psalmist.

In the first three verses, the psalmist also attests to
physical movement—having been "drawn up," (v. 1),
"brought up" (v. 3). After reading the first verse, it is
not clear from whence the psalmist has been lifted.

Homiletical Perspective

Psalm 30 begs to be preached, so much so that it
essentially provides the preacher with all the moves
and examples necessary for a compelling and
convincing homily. "Joy comes with the morning"
(v. 5). That will preach. "You have turned my
mourning into dancing" (v. 11). That will too. In
fact, the whole psalm will. How? With as much
enthusiasm as the preacher can muster. We will
come back to that.

The tradition has taken a psalm of personal
thanksgiving and suggested in the superscription that
it was or should be used by the whole community.
That is an excellent idea, and not only for this
particular psalmist's experience. In most communities, most of the time, finding a way truly to celebrate
the blessings of its individual members is a chore,
when it might be joy. We will come back to that too.

Homileticians often advise that the trajectory of
the biblical text should shape the trajectory of the
sermon. Most of us nod our heads yes and then go
our own way, but this time perhaps not, because the
trajectory of Psalm 30 is like a good novel: things get
bad, things get worse, things resolve. The psalmist was
flying high, full of his or her own importance, and
then crashed. However, it was not crash and burn,
because there was still hope—in God. So the psalmist
called on God, offered a reasonable argument for

Psalm 30

Theological Perspective

By contrast, both the psalm in particular and Scripture as a whole declare that we belong to one whose eagerness to be sought is infinitely greater than our seeking (Isa. 65:1) and who will answer even before we call (Isa. 65:24). Moreover, God's desire to be sought is unqualified. God wants the prayers of us all, whether faith is for us a joyful confidence, a constant struggle, an earnest but elusive hope, a shallow superstition, a distant memory, or something we had but lost, or never had.

The theology expressed in Psalm 30 is given systematic treatment in Karl Barth's development of the doctrine of creation in *Church Dogmatics*, III/1. Barth regards God's desire to be God with and for us as the very presupposition of creation. God calls the universe into being so that in time and space and in relation to the world and those who dwell in it, God can become flesh and dwell among us as Emmanuel.

Its post-Easter setting in the lectionary reflects the history of Psalm 30, reinterpreted in the liturgy and life of the church. Both in its understanding of God and its reference to deliverance from death, the psalm strains forward to the Christ event. Death is the "trouble" the psalmist faces. The poet likens God's deliverance to being "brought up . . . from Sheol" and "restored . . . to life from among those gone down to the Pit" (i.e., the grave, v. 3). This surely is what led Augustine to describe this psalm as "to the end, a Psalm of the joy of the resurrection . . . the renewing of the body . . . not only of the Lord, but also of the whole church."[1] The psalm offers no doctrine of resurrection in the New Testament sense. We do see here, however, the sovereignty of God over the power of death, of which the resurrection is the defining instance. Indeed if the Son's "cry of dereliction" (Mark 15:34) is for us the quintessential calling upon God, resurrection is the Father's making good on God's promise to deliver.

God's desire for humanity must not cause us to dismiss God's judgment as of little account, nor does the psalm do so. The psalm describes judgment neither as God's dramatic lashing out at us nor as God's angry denunciation of us, but as God's reluctantly letting us go our own way and attain our own goal—only to realize that God is not a part of it. The psalmist is not cast off or abandoned but allowed to learn that self-centeredness and self-sovereignty are self-defeating. Often it is the case

1. Augustine, *Expositions on the Book of Psalms*, in Philip Schaff, ed., *A Select Library of the Nicene and Post-Nicene Fathers of the Christian Church*, 1st series, vol. 8 (Grand Rapids: Eerdmans, 1979), 67–68.

Pastoral Perspective

The psalm text moves from trouble to relief and thanks no less than four times. The sheer repetition of the pattern fosters hope that this time too, God will respond. Rehearsing what God has done again and again helps us remember the many ways in which we have experienced healing, and the faithfulness of God on which our trust is based.

Sometimes our pastoral task is helping folks accurately identify the true nature of the foes who hold our hope captive. They are readily apparent in a health crisis or life-sapping chronic condition. Less obviously, the foes of verse 1 may be individual and internal, or social and external, depending on the community of faith and its social location. In more affluent contexts, our tendency may be to see even external forces as a reflection of internal patterns and failings. While there *are* internal foes that bring us down—from addictions to relational habits—the external foes that trigger or intensify those internal situations can be substantial. It can take a loving community to help one push back at those external, culturally supported, foes.

The combination in Psalm 30 of individual struggle celebrated in the context of a community at worship invites exploration of actual community struggles and naming the pitfalls together. The list of external foes might include consumerism, workaholism, unsustainable use of the natural environment, expecting service from others rather than building community, racism. The list is as long as the consequences of sin that fall on others rather than ourselves, and can be identified in those terms.

Verse 5 points toward another familiar experience—difficulty accepting divine forgiveness. Divine "anger is but for a moment"; divine "favor is for a lifetime." If we are still feeling judged, distant, or estranged from God, the issue is within *us*, not from God, according to the psalmist. God forgives; the issue is whether we are willing to accept divine forgiveness and its implications. Attention to this experience invites pastors to rehearse again with the community of faith the common ways in which we resist forgiveness. We are unwilling to commit to changing our behavior, unwilling to change our self-image, unwilling to acknowledge we need help (even to recognize the problem!), unwilling to be dependent for forgiveness on One whom we do not control.

The nature of our dependence on God is named more fully in verse 7: "you hid your face." We are not in control of what God does, no matter how much or how well we pray. This is not to say that we are out of control of ourselves, but to say that our

Only in verse 3 does the poet identify that location as Sheol/the Pit. Those two nouns refer to the same place—the underworld where the dead continue to exist in "the land of gloom and deep darkness" (Job 10:21).

Was the psalmist actually dead or just as good as dead? Certainly the latter. The NRSV makes it sound as if the psalmist had been "restored" to life. JPS offers a more likely translation, "preserved me from going down into the Pit" (v. 3b). One might imagine that the person had approached a physical and psychological reality similar to "the gates of death," the entrance to the underworld, but was rescued just as the gates were about to swing open. This psalmist had experienced death in life—social death through having enemies and physical near death due to illness. Describing this experience of feeling dead while still alive is one of the hallmarks of this psalm. For this psalmist, only God could move the person back to real life.

Verses 4–5 move to the future, a time for song and giving thanks. Based on personal experience, the psalmist now admonishes God's "faithful ones" to sing. These are imperative verbs. The psalmist is not recommending, but commanding the community to sing. Perhaps the most surprising element in these verses is the new rationale. One would have assumed that the psalmist was commanding praise because of having been saved from death. Instead, the psalmist has apparently experienced the "anger" of the Deity, but now attests that it was a fleeting experience.

Only in the next two verses (vv. 6–7) do readers learn the way in which the psalmist perceived God's anger. These verses are, apparently, a flashback—to a time before there were any difficulties, a time when the poet had said, "I shall never be moved." These words stand in considerable contrast with that which is described in this psalm. The person who was thought to be immovable experiences radical change. The poet had gone down and had been lifted up. Now the poet is moving both forward and backward in time.

This psalmist reports that the prior belief in personal immovability was theologically grounded. The psalmist believed that God had made the poet "as a strong mountain" (v. 7), presumably immovable. It was for good reason that the psalmist believed that he or she was settled for life.

Then life changed. One may presume that illness struck the psalmist. When the psalmist sought help from God, the Deity did not respond: "you hid your face" (v. 7). God could not "see" the poet's plight.

deliverance, and was saved. The response? What it might have been in the first place: "O LORD my God, I will give thanks to you forever!" (v. 12).

The psalm is filled with the ebb and flow of the life of faith, as contemporary as it can be. Good things ("I said in my prosperity, 'I shall never be moved,'" v. 6) are followed by bad things ("you hid your face; I was dismayed;" v. 7). To make matters worse, everyone is watching (v. 1). The psalmist has the same choice that we and our audiences do: trust or despair? The psalmist chooses trust, calling on the name of the Lord, presumably with confidence, but also with a good argument for deliverance: if I am not around to sing your praises, who or what will? The dust (v. 9)? The argument works! So now what?

Here is one possible crux for the homily: now what? What will we do with all that God has done for us? Shall we pat ourselves on the back for our wisdom in accepting the grace of God, or shall we jump with joy? Sadly, the church seems more filled with back-patters than with jumpers. A homily on Psalm 30 could invite a more enthusiastic response than is frequently common.

Now what? I will give thanks to you forever—that is what. Whether lying at death's door, facing unemployment, worried about a child's marriage, waiting for the results of a crucial exam—academic, professional, or medical—almost everyone in the house has felt what the psalmist is talking about. Save me, O God, because I sure cannot do it myself. Then to our absolute delight, we are saved. Now what? If a thank-you note is not an adequate response to what God has done, then what is?

Some years ago a young pastor from a free-church tradition found herself, while on vacation, in intensive care after an anaphylactic reaction to medication. A friend happened to know a priest in that town and asked him to visit the pastor. After the usual pastoral pleasantries, the priest said, "I brought oil for anointing, and the Eucharist."

"Oh no, that's all right," the pastor said. "If you could just pray, it would be fine." They looked at each other for a moment, and then the pastor said, "No, no, that's not what I meant at all. I want everything you have!"

"I want everything you have." That is how one responds to deliverance. The psalmist ironically asks, "Will the dust praise you?" (v. 9) and the answer is obvious. However, I am not certain we do much better, confining our praise to a few poorly sung hymns on Sunday morning. That is hardly giving thanks forever.

Psalm 30

Theological Perspective

that, in God's economy, we are punished not so much *for* our sins as *by* our sins.

Even so, God's invitation, "Call on me," is not withdrawn. As with the prodigal son in Jesus' parable, the psalmist turns in the day of trouble to one who is "merciful and gracious, slow to anger and abounding in steadfast love" (Ps. 103:8). Albert Outler, the Methodist historian and theologian, described the working of God's judgment in this way:

> God-with-us: in life's turmoils and drudgery, its vigils and sunburst, unraveling and reweaving the strands of our memories and hopes, judging, thwarting, leaving us to suffer for our own misdeeds and those of others and yet never forsaking us even in our sufferings. God-with-us: not to dominate but to bless and yet also to prevent the final triumph of our resistance to his righteous rule. God-with-us: endlessly patient, endless concerned, endlessly resourceful.[2]

God's judgment is infinitely more searching than we know, yet God's grace keeps pace and ultimately outreaches judgment, turning weeping into joy and mourning into dancing (vv. 5, 11; cf. Isa. 54:7–8).

This invincible grace is what underlies the glad testimony of verses 5 and 11–12. Whether in the life of the individual, the church, or the world, God's way of being God, set forth in the Bible and supremely in the life, death, and resurrection of Jesus Christ, enables us to lift our voices and offer our lives in the joyful worship and grateful service that constitute the chief end of human life in this world (cf. John 21:1–19; Acts 9:1–20) and the next (cf. Rev. 5:11–14).

JOHN B. ROGERS

Pastoral Perspective

relationship with God is a *real* relationship—meaning God is making choices too. Realizing this is threatening as well as exhilarating. It leads the psalmist to attempt to persuade God based on God's investment in the relationship: "What profit is there [to You] in my death?" (v. 9). Such an attempt at persuasion is based on profound trust that the speaker of the psalm matters to God, that God attends to this relationship. As we speak the psalm, we simultaneously cultivate that trust, even as we release illusions about our ability to predict what God will do. Claiming to know in advance how God will respond is simply another way to maintain the illusion of our own control; if we can predict how God will act, we will always be ready, hence, in control. Trust allows us to live fully in relationship.

Psalm 30 invites us to express and to examine a wide variety of strong feelings in the context of a community of faith. The psalm refers to rejoicing, crying for help, thanksgiving, anger, weeping, joy, pride, hiding, dismay, supplication, praise, mourning, and dancing for joy. These move back and forth between celebration and desperation, danger and help. The psalm never stays long in either, reflecting the ambiguity of human life. "Where am I now, *really*?" one might ask. Is this a time of despair or of joy? The psalm invites individuals and communities to acknowledge the depths of our emotional experience and to attend to where we are at this moment, so that we may express it in our prayer. The actual references are to physical expressions of prayer, not just words: weeping, wearing sackcloth, singing, and dancing.

When we notice that we have been avoiding the expression or acknowledgment of these strong emotions in our community's worship, the psalm encourages us. Divine power and faithfulness is the context within which all human emotions may be addressed. Neither the community nor the individual is lost when our expression of feelings begins with praise for how God has repeatedly provided safety, healing, and restoration in the past. We discover that instead of feeling lost, we see hope and trust arise yet again.

CATHERINE L. KELSEY

---

2. Albert C. Outler, *Who Trusts in God* (New York: Oxford University Press, 1968), 105–6.

Exegetical Perspective

Hence the psalmist begins to argue with God, offering three questions, all of which work together to make one basic point: God, if you let me die, I will not be able to praise you. The psalmist presumes that God wants to be praised and therefore appeals to that part of God's psyche. Once having made that point, the psalmist cries out for mercy and help.

The final section of the psalm clearly implies that the psychological tactics of this worshiper have worked. Though the psalmist does not report that the Deity responded verbally to the three questions—they were rhetorical questions after all; the answer to each one was no—the psalm does rehearse the Deity's actions.

The final two verses begin with understandable but odd imagery. The psalmist is mourning, but for whom? Perhaps the psalmist was mourning his or her own near death. God moves the psalmist from a time of mourning to a time of dancing and joy. (One hears echoes of the great poem in Eccl. 3:4, "a time to mourn and a time to dance.") God not only changes the psychological world of the psalmist, God also changes that person's clothes. "Joy" is now the poet's attire. God cares for the entirety of this person.

The first portion of verse 12 is very difficult to translate. It might be rendered, "so that glory may praise you." KJV, "to the end that my glory may sing praise to thee," is close to this, though the first-person pronoun, "my," is not present in the Hebrew text. The noun *kabod* ("glory") sometimes means physical/psychological appearance (so Ps. 45:3). This sense, "my entire being," would fit well here, expressing the notion that the psalmist, dancing and reclothed, will praise God.

Vocabulary of "praise" is important in this psalm. It occurs in the first ("extol") and final ("give thanks") verses. Perhaps more important, the same Hebrew word for praise appears in verses 4, 9, and 12, and it is this word that the psalmist uses to put pressure on God, arguing that there will be no praise from the psalmist if that person dies. It is fitting, therefore, that the psalmist praises God after having been rescued (v. 12).

DAVID L. PETERSEN

Homiletical Perspective

However, what is? We can exhort, chide, and chastise all we want, but the truth is that very few of our listeners understand what a life of thanksgiving looks like. It is not enough to quote 1 Thessalonians 5:18 ("Give thanks in all circumstances") or remind them of their Westminster Shorter Catechism ("The chief end of humanity is to glorify God and to enjoy God forever"). If we cannot help our listeners *see* that the glorifying is both an appropriate and fulfilling response, we might as well sit back down.

It helps, of course, if we happen to believe that ourselves, and it helps even more if we practice what we believe. The example of prayerful, thankful preachers, though, may only confirm the suspicion that only professional holy people need apply. Nor can we roll out the usual suspects—Mother Teresa, Martin Luther King, and so forth. What we need is the example of a life of thanksgiving that looks like the lives of the people we are preaching to. You are going to have to make that up, but do not let that stop you.

I remember a saint whose life was ravaged and finally taken by breast cancer. The eighteen months from diagnosis to premature death were a painful struggle. Yet even in the last days, do you know what her song was? "God is so good, God is so good, God is so good, so good to me."

What about the athletes we see crossing themselves before they step to the plate or the free-throw line, or who kneel and point to heaven after a goal or touchdown? We hard-nosed types tend to scoff at such public displays, but why? Have we ever waded imaginatively into their lives, wondering what calls forth such acts of devotion? I suspect there are stories just waiting to be told. Why don't you tell one?

WILLIAM F. BROSEND

Revelation 5:11-14

¹¹Then I looked, and I heard the voice of many angels surrounding the throne and the living creatures and the elders; they numbered myriads of myriads and thousands of thousands, ¹²singing with full voice,
"Worthy is the Lamb that was slaughtered
to receive power and wealth and wisdom and might
and honor and glory and blessing!"
¹³Then I heard every creature in heaven and on earth and under the earth and in the sea, and all that is in them, singing,
"To the one seated on the throne and to the Lamb
be blessing and honor and glory and might
forever and ever!"
¹⁴And the four living creatures said, "Amen!" And the elders fell down and worshiped.

Theological Perspective

Revelation is the only full representative of the apocalyptic genre in the New Testament. A rich symbolic text with a complex narrative structure, it engages our theological imaginations in ways that are distinct and troubling, uniquely confronting our worlds of common sense in its attempt to reveal hidden realities that include the vulnerability of sin and the power of God's grace.

For all of Revelation's stunningly Byzantine poetic, intertextual, liturgical, structural, and cosmological complexity, it is also disarmingly simple. That is because, as the first three words of Revelation indicate, its focus is the "revelation of Jesus Christ." The book articulates what was revealed about God in the historical event of Christ crucified and risen. The book of Revelation, in other words, tells less about the *future* than most of us think it does. We often assume that the big apocalyptic events lie somewhere ahead of us. Yet it was clear to John, as it was to other New Testament theologians, that the great apocalyptic events lay *behind* him, in the suffering, death, and resurrection of Jesus. Whatever denouement lies ahead in the future pales in comparison to the events of the cross that reveal the very heart of God, as well as God's intent for us. The solid foundation that undergirds the many

Pastoral Perspective

Those looking for words about the bloody judgment day when the "evil" are slashed, tormented, and finally dragged away to their death, will not find today's text a welcome passage—for in this vision from John we encounter every creature in heaven and earth and in all the seas singing together and worshiping God. This crowd does not include just some creatures. It includes all creatures, including those from under the earth, in Hades, and in the sea that is known for its roiling chaos. "Then I looked, and I heard the voice of many angels surrounding the throne and the living creatures and the elders; they numbered myriads of myriads and thousands of thousands, singing with full voice" (vv. 11–12a). John's vision offers a comprehensive picture of inclusivity—which may not be exactly what those who want to separate the chaff from the wheat, the goats from the lambs, and the good from the bad want to hear. There is no description of a bloody judgment day here.

One of the challenges of the text, then, is to read it in light of what has presumably come before it. Many may prefer to focus on God's judgment and division, articulated so vividly in Matthew's Gospel. Yet these verses in Revelation describe the culmination of the gospel story. In the scene before us we see what God's final word will be—and it is not about division.

Exegetical Perspective

Revelation 5:11–14 presents two hymns of praise, one to the Lamb and one to God ("the one seated on the throne") and to the Lamb. Acclamation and worship from the heavenly court respond to these hymns. Following the Lamb's initial appearance in Revelation, these hymns acknowledge the Lamb's great deeds. The Lamb is worthy of praise, having won sovereign authority over the fate of all things and having ransomed an elect people by means of its death and resurrection.

The lectionary excerpts these two hymns from a larger unit, Revelation 5:1–14. In verses 1–10 we encounter the scroll with seven seals that holds the destiny of the cosmos: "Who is worthy to open the book and to unbind its seals?" (v. 2, my trans.). With no one worthy in heaven, on earth, or even under the earth, John weeps greatly. Yet one of the elders in the heavenly court announces: "Behold, the Lion of the tribe of Judah, the Root of David, has conquered, so that he is worthy to open the book and to unbind its seven seals."

The Lion, of course, does not appear. Instead, for the first time we encounter the Lamb, "standing as if it had been slain" (v. 6). Once the Lamb has taken the book, the four living creatures and the twenty-four elders fall down in worship and break out into

Homiletical Perspective

One of the strongest challenges facing preachers during the season of Easter will simply be sustaining the interest of congregations for celebrating the resurrection of Jesus from the dead. After all, many of the most important events in our culture require only a short attention span rather than long-term contemplation. However, on the Third Sunday of Easter, the surprising news of the crucified and risen Jesus should still be very much on our minds.

Rather than seeing this state of affairs as a homiletic liability, the preacher is afforded a span of fifty days for announcing, explicating, and celebrating the great news that constitutes the heart of the gospel: that by the raising up of crucified Jesus, the God of Israel has exalted him to be Lord and Christ. This Sunday's reading continues in a series of five lessons from John's Apocalypse, the book of Revelation. Surprisingly, these lessons do not fit many of the stereotypical views of this strange-sounding book. Rather, they cut right to the heart of the matter: worship is central to our identity and mission as God's people, since it is worship that shapes the human community in response to the God of Jesus Christ.

Today's lesson turns our attention away from our immediate concerns, especially ourselves, in order to look, see, and be taken up in wonder, love, and

Revelation 5:11-14

Theological Perspective

reversals of the apocalypse of Revelation is, in other words, a "theology of the cross."[1]

These final verses of chapter 5 point backward to the introduction of the Lamb in 5:6 and forward to the glorious consummation of the Lamb's coenthronement with God as sovereign Lord of the new heaven and the new earth that God's Word calls forth (21:5), a consummation that is prefigured already in Daniel 7:9–14. One important key to the interpretation of Revelation is found in the *manner* in which the Lamb is introduced. Christ, though announced as the "Lion of . . . Judah" (5:5), actually appears as "a Lamb standing as if it had been slaughtered" (5:6). Only the one slain is worthy to open the scroll's seven seals.

In highly symbolic language, one encounters here the same theology of the cross that Paul articulates in 1 Corinthians 1:23–25, paraphrased in the aphorism "God's weakness is stronger than human strength." Throughout Revelation this insight energizes a consistent and thoroughgoing criticism of two interconnected human projects that John experienced: (1) the socioeconomic world constructed by the ideology of Roman imperial might and (2) the idolatrous public worship that legitimated this regime in the imperial cult. The revelation of God on the cross—of Christ *crucified*—turns upside down the usual ideas of what constitutes power as well as sacrifice.

On the one hand, the ever-present threat of violence that enforced the *Pax Romana* is laid bare, associated as it is with the dragon/beast who is worshiped because of its might (13:4). On the other hand, the apparent victory of such violence in the slaughter of the Son of God is also revealed to be temporary and hollow. Who is the Lord of this world and worthy of worship? Is it the Roman emperor and all that he stands for? Or is it the crucified one? The central claim of Revelation is that the power and honor that Rome take for granted actually belong to the slain one: "Worthy is the Lamb that was slaughtered to receive power and wealth and wisdom and might and honor and glory and blessing!" (5:12). Assigning worship to Christ dethrones the everyday rule of violence. Whatever wrath comes from God in this world turned upside down by the cross is the "wrath of the Lamb" (6:16). It is the

---

1. Martin Luther, based on his study of Paul, coined the term "theology of the cross" (*theologia crucis*) in the Heidelberg Disputation of 1518, in opposition to what he called a "theology of glory." See, e.g., Douglas John Hall, *The Cross in Our Context: Jesus and the Suffering World* (Minneapolis: Fortress Press, 2003) and Gerhard O. Forde, *On Being a Theologian of the Cross: Reflections on Luther's Heidelberg Disputation, 1518* (Grand Rapids: Eerdmans, 1997).

Pastoral Perspective

Instead, it is about the great myriads and myriads and thousands and thousands surrounding the throne of God. Numbers like those do not speak of separation and damnation. Instead, they describe the gathering together of every creature in heaven and on earth—and even under the earth, where some of the faithful might argue the most terrible of terrible creatures reside. Yet even those who come from under the earth and from the great turmoil of the sea have voices with which to praise: "To the one seated on the throne and to the Lamb be blessing and honor and glory and might forever and ever!" (v. 13b).

Clearly, this Third Sunday of Easter is not a day to proclaim judgment. Instead, it offers the faithful an opportunity to join "every creature in heaven and on earth and under the earth and in the sea, and all that is in them" (v. 13a) in praising the loving God who reaches out not just to the upright but to all God's children, including the least, the lost, and the lonely.

This passage reminds us too of the power of the cross. The thousands of thousands who surround the throne sing the worthiness of "the Lamb that was slaughtered." Some preachers may be tempted to use this passage to point to the Trinity. It is safer simply to emphasize its message about how God is able to work through suffering, for there is powerful consolation here for those who know brokenness. Later we will learn that "these are they who have come out of the great ordeal; they have washed their robes and made them white in the blood of the Lamb" (7:14b). This is why they are before the throne of God (7:15a), rising to the promise that "God will wipe away every tear from their eyes" (7:17b).

This passage carries a great message of comfort to the broken. In all of our brokenness, we are never too damaged for God to use us. During Eastertide, when we redefine what it means to "win," we find another passage that reminds us how the cross has changed our understanding of victory. Victory is not reserved for those who do the wounding (or who manage to escape being wounded). Victory is given to the wounded, leading us to learn that it is not through our own physical power or our triumph over others that we win anything. Only in God are we made worthy. Recognizing the worthiness of the Lamb that was slaughtered, we find our own path to worthiness. Insecure, self-doubting human beings cannot hear that message too many times.

John's powerful vision of worship is given to us to be read in the midst of our own worship. In its proclamation should be the clear message that ultimate power does not belong to those who appear

song. The song praises the Lamb who is worthy to take the book, for the Lamb has ransomed people from "every tribe and people and tongue and nation" with its own blood (v. 9).

The twin blessings of Revelation 5:11–14 can stand independently, yet the larger context is critical for their interpretation. These hymns represent the second and third of a three-hymn set. The songs of praise occur in response to the revelation of the Lamb's sovereign authority, won by means of its death. The Lamb has redefined messianic power, not roaring as a lion but creating a freed people by means of its death and resurrection.

The scene occurs in the heavenly throne room, to which John was transported in 4:1. The heavenly court includes God, seated upon the throne and surrounded by four living creatures and twenty-four elders. The scene concludes when the Lamb opens the first seal (6:1), unveiling the eschatological sequence of seals, trumpets, and bowls. The trumpets and bowls ultimately unfold from the seals; thus, the Lamb exercises the authority to reveal the destiny of all things.

Attention to their literary context indicates that these are no generic blessings; rather, they respond to the Lamb in three particular respects. This is the Lamb's first appearance in Revelation, and the hymns set forth his most fundamental attributes. First, the Lamb has won the authority to unseal the scroll of destiny, from which the rest of Revelation unfolds. Second, the Lamb has won this authority by ransoming a people through his own death. Though Revelation features fearsome judgment, the Lamb conquers by passing through death to life and by the word of its testimony (1:16; 19:15, 21). In imitation of the Lamb, its followers also conquer by means of their own faithful testimony, even to the point of death (12:11). Third, the Lamb makes this ransomed people into a dominion of kings and priests who reign upon the earth. All these accomplishments have been celebrated in the first hymn, 5:9–10.

Such songs of praise merit special attention, given the religious and imperial context of Asia Minor. Touring the main streets of Ephesus or Pergamum, even a resident of the Bible Belt, familiar with "a church on every corner," would be taken aback by the overt signs of religion. The cities of Asia Minor won fame for their devotion to the emperor, including groups of singers specially appointed to sing during festivals for the imperial household.[1] In Ephesus,

praise by gazing upon the throne of God in heaven. This heavenly scene is liturgical, or doxological, a vision of cosmic scope that is an expression of Christian orthodoxy, or "right praise," having at its center the crucified and risen Jesus, "the Lamb who was slain." It will be helpful for the preacher to take a brief backward glance at verses 1–10, since John has articulated deep anxiety over his inability to find a person possessing sufficient authority for opening the seven seals on the scroll of history, an action that would reveal and determine creation's final destiny. John's weeping ends only when he is summoned to turn and to see the "Lion of the tribe of Judah" who has conquered and is able to break the seals to interpret the scroll. At 5:6, however, there is a sudden and surprising shift from the conquering Lion to a slain Lamb. Here, in two messianic images, lie rich possibilities for powerful Easter proclamation.

This sudden turn is as unexpected as the resurrection of dead Jesus, the one condemned as a common criminal and executed by the combined efforts of religion, politics, and popular opinion. Amazingly, John summons us to turn with him to contemplate the truth of God's wisdom and ways with the world in light of Jesus, born of a Jewish peasant girl named Mary. He suffered under Pontius Pilate and was crucified, died, and was buried, and yet, by his "weak power," revealed the dominion of God that moves the world. This is truly astounding news that must be proclaimed, an announcement so earth shaking, so life changing, as to be all but incredible. Amazingly, in spite of—or perhaps because of—his suffering and death on a cross, the risen Jesus is truly worthy to be worshiped, and to possess all power, wealth, wisdom, strength, honor, glory, and blessing. In other words, in Jesus Christ we are turned to "see" the truth, goodness, and beauty of God, imitating the one whom we know, love, and adore.

As doxological speech, preaching is the work of the whole church, which, drawn by the Spirit in response to the living Word, the risen Lord, offers itself in prayer and praise and so constitutes itself, and is constituted as, the body of Christ. The saving power of God's revealed speech is experienced and rooted in worship; so, animated by divine grace, the church attends to the gospel in its speech and enactment, offering affirmation and adoration evoked by an astonishing glory, goodness, and love. The proclamation of the Easter gospel is public speech that acclaims God's glory for the redemption and completion of all creation, the "love, wonder,

---

1. Steven J. Friesen, *Imperial Cults and the Apocalypse of John: Reading Revelation in the Ruins* (New York: Oxford University Press, 2001), 105–13.

Revelation 5:11-14

Theological Perspective

identity of the Lamb that reveals the nature of God's wrath, and not vice versa.

An apocalypse unveils that which otherwise remains hidden. That which is hidden to the world is the victory won in the death of Christ. Yet, one might ask, where is that hidden victory to be found? Where is it to be touched, grasped as real? One of Revelation's answers to this question of "practical theodicy" is that the liturgy of the church makes real the victory of Christ for those with the eyes and ears of faith. In worship, the Lamb's eschatological reign is already experienced, in the praise of the God who was, is, and is in the process of coming (1:4, 8; 4:8; cf. 17:8, 11).

All of creation joins in this hymn of praise (5:12–13), bringing together what was kept separate by the orders of creation, time, geography, and by the everyday reality of empire ("divide and conquer"). Angels, living creatures, the elders sing in "full voice" as does "every creature in heaven and on earth and under the earth and in the sea" (cf. Phil. 2:6–11). One of the sacramental signs of the inbreaking kingdom of God of the early church, then, was that its worship brought together those who were otherwise separated by the highly segregated society of the Greco-Roman world: slaves/free, Jews/Greek, men/women, haves/have-nots, those with honor/those with culturally inscribed shame, pure/impure. A diverse, multicultural community came together to sing its praise to the victory of the Lamb and the revelation of God's judgment upon the oppressive socioeconomic values of empire. Though the consummation of God's reign lies in the future, its beginning resides in a multilayered past made accessible by a holy Scripture read in the light of the cross of Christ. In the present, that reign is most powerfully experienced in the worship of the only God, the Alpha and the Omega, and the praise of God's Christ, the "Lamb who was slaughtered," experienced "in the spirit on the Lord's day" (1:10).

ERIK M. HEEN

Pastoral Perspective

most powerful, but instead to those who appear wounded and broken like the Lamb. Despite all of our inclinations to think otherwise, that means every one of us. Like it or not, we are all invited to be part of the glorious choir of those singing praise and honor to God both now and in the moment of final victory.

The preacher has a dual challenge in dealing with this passage. Working to help those who are less likely to see themselves as broken to claim their brokenness, the preacher will also work to help those who cannot get past their brokenness to see their wholeness in God. Either way, we will miss the point of this passage if we do not also include a triumphant note in our interpretation of it. There is great celebration in these verses, punctuated by at least three exclamation points. The song this crowd sings is a new song (v. 9), sung in full voice (v. 12). Yet this triumph is not exclusive. As John describes it, the victory celebrated in these verses is entirely inclusive. A sermon true to his vision will end as the passage ends, with joyful proclamation—for the Lamb that was slaughtered has received "power and wealth and wisdom and might and honor and glory and blessing!"

"And the four living creatures said, 'Amen!' And the elders fell down and worshiped" (v. 14).

DANA FERGUSON

Exegetical Perspective

where the temple to Diana captured international fame, our tourist would pass temples dedicated to Augustus and Domitian. Revelation exalts the unqualified sovereignty of God and the Lamb, standing in direct opposition to the piety directed toward "the one seated on the throne" (5:13) in Rome.

While these hymns sing directly to the imperial and religious realities of their own time and place, in another sense they transcend ordinary time. Those who sing include, first, the Lamb's allies: the four living creatures, the twenty-four elders, and a numberless crowd (5:11). The second chorus, however, includes "every creature" in heaven, on earth, and under the earth (5:13; see Phil. 2:10–11). The hymns transport Revelation's vulnerable audience from a time of cultural pressure to a view that comprehends all things, when "every creature" sings the Lamb's praises.

Revelation's hymns foreground the political and theological implications of worship. As worship names that which is worthy, it also dismisses competing claims upon our loyalty. Wise preachers must address a society that enfolds expectations of loyalty to nation and culture within fidelity to Christ. Nevertheless, Revelation's hymns pose an ethical problem for interpreters. The songs of Revelation 15:3–4 and 16:4–7 celebrate the righteous judgments of God. One wonders if they are designed to mitigate any potential offense readers might take in response to the horrific judgments that surround them. With respect to Revelation 5:11–14, the hymns celebrate the Lamb's faithfulness even as they portend the tribulations to come.

Some Christian traditions define their identity, some their worship, in terms of praise. Yet here praise has theological content. Revelation 5:11–14 demonstrates that praise responds to the saving action of God, demonstrated in specific ways. In particular, this passage names the Lamb as the one who sets his people free, makes them a people, and owns their destiny.

GREG CAREY

Homiletical Perspective

and praise" that witnesses to the living communion enjoyed by the church, through the presence of Christ and the Spirit, for the good of the world.

Such dramatic announcement and communal celebration is indeed the work of evangelism, the "publicity" or astounding news that in the call of Israel and the life, death, resurrection, and exaltation of Jesus Christ, God has defeated the false gods and powers of this world and enthroned him as Lord of heaven and earth. Joined with Christ by the Spirit who illumines the witness of Scripture to make him known, the church's liturgical celebration of the gospel through word and Sacrament is both a witness and blessing to the nations, a compelling invitation and urgent summons to join the great vocation of praise for "the Lamb who was slain."

Prayerful attentiveness to John's vision of the slain Lamb, enthroned and ruling over and in all things, is still able to move us to rethink how we might presume such things could be irrelevant for our preaching. John's witness is the confession of a people "evangelized" over time by what they have heard proclaimed, and which is demonstrated in the gift of repentance, the purification and redirection of all human desire toward God's self-gift in Christ. Such transformation occurs in hearing the one Word God is and speaks; a living "away" from ourselves to what is beyond our control or our possession; contemplating the crucified Lord whose presence with us is mediated by the Spirit. Such listening is a gift bestowed and received within a way of life created, formed, and sustained by the gospel that—according to the wisdom of the world—may sound so odd and strange that many will claim it could hardly be "good news": the announcement that "God has made both Lord and Christ this Jesus who was crucified."

MICHAEL PASQUARELLO III

John 21:1-19

¹After these things Jesus showed himself again to the disciples by the Sea of Tiberias; and he showed himself in this way. ²Gathered there together were Simon Peter, Thomas called the Twin, Nathanael of Cana in Galilee, the sons of Zebedee, and two others of his disciples. ³Simon Peter said to them, "I am going fishing." They said to him, "We will go with you." They went out and got into the boat, but that night they caught nothing.

⁴Just after daybreak, Jesus stood on the beach; but the disciples did not know that it was Jesus. ⁵Jesus said to them, "Children, you have no fish, have you?" They answered him, "No." ⁶He said to them, "Cast the net to the right side of the boat, and you will find some." So they cast it, and now they were not able to haul it in because there were so many fish. ⁷That disciple whom Jesus loved said to Peter, "It is the Lord!" When Simon Peter heard that it was the Lord, he put on some clothes, for he was naked, and jumped into the sea. ⁸But the other disciples came in the boat, dragging the net full of fish, for they were not far from the land, only about a hundred yards off.

⁹When they had gone ashore, they saw a charcoal fire there, with fish on it, and bread. ¹⁰Jesus said to them, "Bring some of the fish that you have just caught." ¹¹So Simon Peter went aboard and hauled the net ashore, full of large

Theological Perspective

Our story opens with the disciples gathered together, presumably before nightfall, on the shore by the Sea of Tiberias. Peter says to the others in verse 3, "I am going fishing," and they respond, "We will go with you." From the outset of the story, Peter is portrayed as the leader of the small band.

The disciples caught nothing "all through the night," notes the close of verse 3, but verse 4 opens with Jesus on the beach "just after daybreak." Night has passed and a new day is beginning. From the beach, Jesus calls to them, but the disciples do not yet recognize him. He knows they have caught nothing, and when the disciples confirm this, he urges them to "cast the net to the right side of the boat." When the disciples' nets begin to tear from the great weight of the fish now caught, the Beloved Disciple is the first to recognize Jesus in the wondrous event that has just occurred: "It is the Lord!" Directly in response to hearing those words Simon Peter "put on some clothes, for he was naked, and jumped into the sea."

A number of things are worth pointing out about this passage and how it might be a theological focal point for preaching. Many ancient authorities or church fathers find in this story of the Beloved Disciple and Peter two distinct but necessary aspects of Christian faith. John Chrysostom writes in his *Homilies on the Gospel of John*:

Pastoral Perspective

For many people today, the experience of sensory and emotional overload is a regular feature of their lives. Increasingly graphic images of sex and violence greet us in the print media, as well as on the Internet and television, and it seems that the decibels are rising in radio advertisements and in the ordinary noise of the street. Times of peace and quiet have become much less frequent for many, and the stress some people feel at work is matched only by the stress they feel as they commute on overcrowded streets and subways. One might wonder if much about our daily lives has contributed to a numbing of the human spirit, so that we require increasingly loud or shocking experiences to get through to us.

This is the general landscape of daily life for many, but the experience of emotional overload for some might finally come when they suddenly receive news of a grim medical diagnosis or when a spouse walks out of the marriage. Perhaps a child suddenly falls prey to an eating disorder, the boss gives notice, or a tragedy takes the life of a loved one. Experiences like these can overwhelm the human spirit, and many people will at such times seek comfort, almost mindlessly, in a variety of familiar activities. Some take refuge in the solitary labor of gardening, and others reach for chocolate or go shopping. Some escape by losing themselves in television or late

fish, a hundred fifty-three of them; and though there were so many, the net was not torn. [12]Jesus said to them, "Come and have breakfast." Now none of the disciples dared to ask him, "Who are you?" because they knew it was the Lord. [13]Jesus came and took the bread and gave it to them, and did the same with the fish. [14]This was now the third time that Jesus appeared to the disciples after he was raised from the dead.

[15]When they had finished breakfast, Jesus said to Simon Peter, "Simon son of John, do you love me more than these?" He said to him, "Yes, Lord; you know that I love you." Jesus said to him, "Feed my lambs." [16]A second time he said to him, "Simon son of John, do you love me?" He said to him, "Yes, Lord; you know that I love you." Jesus said to him, "Tend my sheep." [17]He said to him the third time, "Simon son of John, do you love me?" Peter felt hurt because he said to him the third time, "Do you love me?" And he said to him, "Lord, you know everything; you know that I love you." Jesus said to him, "Feed my sheep. [18]Very truly, I tell you, when you were younger, you used to fasten your own belt and to go wherever you wished. But when you grow old, you will stretch out your hands, and someone else will fasten a belt around you and take you where you do not wish to go." [19](He said this to indicate the kind of death by which he would glorify God.) After this he said to him, "Follow me."

Exegetical Perspective

Whether they are heading for the pulpit or not, readers of this passage can easily become lost in a series of exegetical and historical questions. The opening story, in which Jesus appears to Peter and other disciples as they are fishing and they all gather for breakfast on the beach, has confounded readers for two thousand years. In contrast, the second story in which Jesus and Peter discourse about love is one of the more popular stories in the Bible. It seems straightforward in its intentions.

When readers of the Gospel of John come to chapter 21, many things seem to change. The obvious change in rhetorical style and theological imagery has occasioned endless discussion about the origin of the chapter, as to whether it comes from the same hand or the same time as the rest of the Gospel. Some scholars suggest rather plausibly that the Gospel was not composed by one hand at one moment but by many hands over a period of time. The question this poses for the preacher is whether the passage should be read in the larger context of the Gospel or as a separate piece with its own history and purposes.

The scene is Galilee at the Sea of Tiberias. The Galilean setting raises the question of the tension in early Christian resurrection stories between those set in Jerusalem and those set in Galilee. John gives a rather curious list of disciples who are gathered on the

Homiletical Perspective

When you finish reading the last verses of John 20, it sounds as though you have come to the end of the book. The story wraps up with the resounding words, "These [signs] are written so that you may come to believe that Jesus is the Messiah, the Son of God, and that through believing you may have life in his name" (John 20:31). What a great ending! However, just when it sounds as if it is all over, there is yet one more story. It is like a play when the curtain comes down and an actor steps out on the front of the stage to deliver an epilogue, a postscript to the drama that has unfolded before us. There seems to be some fear that we might not have gotten the meaning of all that we saw and heard, and so, one more unforgettable story is offered.

The fact that someone other than John may have composed the epilogue does not lessen its insight or its liveliness. Whoever added the epilogue has read and thoroughly digested John's work. We will never identify exactly what this anonymous editor intended, but when we read the epilogue closely, it awakens one flashback after another of what took place earlier in the drama. Themes, insights, and scenes from the full story keep replaying themselves as we attend closely to the epilogue.

Hearing that the risen Christ appears at the Sea of Tiberias and feeds the disciples fish and bread stirs

John 21:1-19

Theological Perspective

When they recognized him, the disciples Peter and John again exhibited their different temperaments. The one was fervent, the other more contemplative. The one was ready to go, the other more penetrating. John is the one who first recognized Jesus, but Peter is the first to come to him.[1]

If the Beloved Disciple is the first to understand, recognize, or hear the Lord—something that is utterly necessary for faith—such recognition is not yet manifest in action. If Peter is the first to act—which symbolizes for these classic interpreters the human response of committed faith—such action must always be grounded in authentic recognition. Neither understanding nor action alone constitutes authentic faith, and thus one needs to unite the best of Peter and the best of the Beloved Disciple if one is to be a person of true faith.

One might focus on another theological point by turning this classic interpretation in a slightly different direction. Rather than focusing on the allegorical attributes that each figure represents (i.e., understanding for the Beloved Disciple and action for Peter), one might underscore the point that the church needs a variety of gifts in order to respond fully to Christ. From this perspective, one could draw attention to the multiple gifts, perspectives, and theologies in both the local and the wider church that need to be honored in order for our personal—and corporate—faith to be whole. Insofar as Peter and the Beloved Disciple are frequently posed as rivals for authority in the post-resurrection community, this reading of the two figures suggests that they—and we—need to set aside our claims of priority and work together in patience, forgiveness, and devotion to the Christ.

A third theological focus would be to concentrate on Peter and what he does (v. 7b) in response to the Beloved Disciple's recognition of the Lord. "When Simon Peter heard that it was the Lord, he put on some clothes, for he was naked, and jumped into the sea." While a number of commentaries suggest that Peter was not completely naked but stripped to his loincloth, the inclusion of the detail of his nakedness is a thought-provoking one.

The writer of this Gospel, who we know from the prologue is no stranger to reimagining the beginning of Genesis, may allude here to Adam's hiding from God in the garden in Genesis 3. If so, John, or the redactor of this added material in chapter 21, may

1. John Chrysostom, *Homilies on the Gospel of John* 87.2, in *John 11–21*, ed. Joel C. Elowsky, vol. IVb of *Ancient Christian Commentary on Scripture: New Testament*, ed. Thomas C. Oden (Downers Grove, IL: InterVarsity Press, 2007), 380.

Pastoral Perspective

nights at the office, and others turn to alcohol or drugs.

For the disciples, the general landscape of life over the last week of Jesus' life had been overwhelming. The tension-filled, emotional high of their entry into Jerusalem was followed by extraordinary events in the temple, a Passover meal unlike any other, an intense experience in the Garden of Gethsemane, an unexpected betrayal, an armed arrest, a series of denials, a mock trial, a jeering mob, and a bloody execution. Surely in the hours following Jesus' death, the disciples were crushed and numb. The human spirit can take only so much. Then came the events that brought an emotional overload of another sort altogether—news of the empty tomb and resurrection appearances that had to be seen to be believed. These events would not only overwhelm and change the lives of the disciples forever; these events would change the entire world forever.

In the immediate aftermath of these events, surely the disciples needed some time and emotional space to assimilate what they had experienced. Following Peter's lead, the disciples returned to their familiar trade. "I am going fishing," Peter announced, and the others said they would go with him. It is a detail of the Gospel narrative that seems quaint and even quirky, coming as it does in the midst of such world-altering events. However, this is how human beings often respond to emotional overload, and the disciples' decision to return to their former life and trade sets us up to realize that, in some ways, there is no longer any escape. Wherever they go, the Lord will be with them. The ordinary and the routine will no longer be either ordinary or routine. As the psalmist asks so poignantly, "Where can I go from your spirit? Or where can I flee from your presence?" (Ps. 139:7). For, even as the disciples retreat to their familiar trade, as we might retreat to the office or to the mall or to the garden, what they ultimately discover is that Jesus is there, and he is waiting to serve and nourish them.

Of course, we have to have eyes to see, and it is notable that only one of the disciples recognizes Jesus on the shore. All of them see the Lord, but only one of them, the Beloved Disciple who reclined at Jesus' breast at the Last Supper, recognizes the Lord. The pastoral implications of this are potentially enormous. Could it be that "reclining with Jesus," spending tender time with the Lord in prayer, resting our mind at his heart and breast . . . could it be that such quiet immersions of ourselves in the presence of God are the key to recognizing God in our daily

shore, one of whom turns out to be the Beloved Disciple. From this point, the story parallels closely the account in Luke 5:4–11, raising the questions of the origin of each and the relationship between the two stories. In Luke the miraculous catch leads to discipleship; in John it leads to recognition: Peter jumps into the water and rushes to the shore to greet Jesus.

The account of the meeting on shore is more than a little curious. It is a subdued and awkward encounter, lacking in the expected celebration. Jesus has bread waiting and his own fish cooking on a small fire. He asks for some more fish. We are told that there were 153 fish and that the net did not break. Jesus then invites the others to breakfast. No one says anything. Jesus passes out the fish and bread without comment. The scene ends with the note that this was Jesus' third appearance since being raised from the dead.

Readers have long wondered how to read this puzzling story. Typically the Lukan account provides the initial key. The fish, or at least the ones caught from the Sea of Tiberias, are seen as symbols of people, as they are in Luke. The initial scene is then read as a call to mission. However, there is no hint in the story that the fish are really people or that any of this has anything to do with mission. The only direct hint in the story about the fish is their number. Numerous attempts to explain the symbolism of the number, both in antiquity and modern times, have proven unconvincing. The number is probably given simply to underline the size of the catch. All of this suggests that the point of the opening scene is its miraculous character. As with all the miracles in John, its central purpose is to point to Jesus. In the miracle Jesus is revealed and recognized as the Lord.

If this is so, then the scene on the beach becomes more important. Amid the curious narrative of the awkward encounter between Jesus and the disciples, the meal that Jesus has ready and offers to the disciples serves as the focal point of the encounter. The symbolism and purpose of this meal are not made explicit in the story. There are two somewhat distinct meal trajectories in early Christianity that employ fish and bread. Both Jewish and Christian accounts of eschatological banquets have fish as the main meal. In addition, early Christian iconography tended to picture the Eucharist with images of fish and bread rather than with cup and bread. Whatever the precise symbolism, this is a sacred meal in which Jesus feeds his disciples.

Read this way, the story, for all its awkwardness, becomes quite classical in its theology. In the midst

up the memory of John 6:1–14, when Jesus blessed five loaves and two fish and fed a crowd of five thousand on the shores of the same lake. If we have wrongly concluded that Christ's abundant generosity belongs to the past and not the present, the epilogue gives witness that the risen Christ continues to bless and feed us.

Hearing that the disciples cast their net on the right side of the boat as the risen Christ instructs them, we may be stirred to remember that the disciples never catch a fish in any of the Gospels without the help of Christ. Although this memory involves moving beyond the bounds of John's narrative, at least one scholar has remarked about "a similar picture but couched in different words" in Luke 5: 6–7.[1] The original readers and hearers of John's Gospel and the epilogue probably knew the traditions of the disciples having nothing to show for their labors until Christ guided them. The epilogue says in effect: if you are going to fulfill the mission entrusted to you (John 20:21), you will need the risen Christ guiding and feeding you.

Hearing that none of the disciples at first recognize the risen Christ when he appears on the shore and calls to them, we remember that Mary mistook him for the gardener when she first encountered him at the empty tomb (20:15). If we have concluded, "Well, that was Mary's problem—she was lost in grief," then the epilogue reminds us that the failure to recognize the risen Christ continues to plague the disciples even after he has greeted them behind locked doors (20:19–23), and after he has again appeared to them in the presence of doubting Thomas (20:24–29). If we are tempted to leave John's drama thinking that we would never be so obtuse in identifying Christ, the epilogue warns not to be so sure. There is a good chance we will be as slow to recognize his presence as the disciples in the boat.

Hearing that Jesus invites them to breakfast and feeds them bread and fish recalls the earlier scene of his being at table with them when he washes their feet and delivers his Farewell Discourses. This early morning meal on the shore corrects any misunderstanding that the Last Supper was the final meal Christ ate with his disciples. The risen Christ continues to share in the table fellowship of the church, continues to supply the strength and nurture we need for our lives and work.

1. Raymond E. Brown, *The Gospel according to John, XIII–XXI* (Garden City, NY: Doubleday & Co., 1970), 1071.

John 21:1-19

Theological Perspective

imagine the significance of the resurrection as undoing the shame of Adam. Yes, Peter, in verse 7b, puts on his clothes—he is aware of his sin and shame. In contrast to Adam, Peter does not allow his shame to stop him from moving toward the one he loves. Peter does not hide any longer in shame but leaps toward the risen one in joyful desire. For the reader who catches the allusion to Adam, Jesus' later questions about Peter's love (21:15–17) confirm what is already glimpsed in this scene of immediate responsiveness.

Preaching this portion of the text in the celebration of Easter involves being able (1) to locate stories of how shame shuts us down as persons and closes us off to growth and (2) to locate those liberating moments of grace when, in response to God's call, we have broken free from that shame to leap toward healing and wholeness.

In the latter part of the reading, Jesus addresses Peter, asking him three times, "Simon Peter, do you love me?" This portion of the story is often read either as Jesus' rehabilitation of Peter (following his threefold denial) or as the commissioning of Peter (along the lines of Matt. 16:18–19), and sometimes both. To be sure, the threefold repetition of the question suggests that Jesus is testing the depths of Peter's conviction. While that threefold structure may play off of Peter's denial in John 18:15–27, the content of the question echoes the love command of Jesus' final discourse (14:1–16:33). Moreover, Jesus' response to Peter to "feed my sheep" reaches back even earlier in the Gospel to Jesus' assertion, "I am the good shepherd. I know my own and my own know me" (10:14). In John, as noted earlier with respect to the Beloved Disciple and Peter, knowing and loving are ultimately one. If Peter is being called to leadership in the passage, he is also being told that he must be ready to risk all that he knows and loves.

JOSEPH A. BESSLER

Pastoral Perspective

lives and ordinary routines? Could it be that our more impetuous inclinations—wanting to build three booths on the mount of transfiguration or needing to go fishing just to keep busy—could it be that our need to stay on the move and remain productive, instead of "wasting time with God" in prayer, often keeps us from recognizing the presence of the Lord in our lives?

In the end, perhaps the risen Lord offers the Peter in each of us still another way to recognize and encounter the Divine in the day to day, as the Lord tells the impetuous and active disciple three times to feed his sheep. It is as if our denials of God are somehow redeemed by our loving encounters with God in the hungry and poor. However, surely there is a Beloved Disciple and an overactive Peter in each of us, and this Gospel passage gives us some guidance in surviving, and even overcoming, circumstances that threaten to overwhelm us. Reclining at the breast of Jesus in prayer, periodically resting in the Lord's heart—this sharpens our spiritual vision and helps us to recognize the nurturing presence of the Lord, even in the most routine and familiar circumstances of our over-busy lives. Feeding the Lord's sheep is a tangible way of staying in relationship with the Lord, as well as the surest way to express our love for him, "not only with our lips, but in our lives."

GARY D. JONES

Exegetical Perspective

of our labor, Jesus calls us and feeds us. The food is the Eucharist; the meal is a banquet in God's kingdom. The fish we eat are gathered from our own labor and are given by God.

While the second story contains its own set of puzzles, its basic meaning seems clear enough. The story is a call to Peter to love and feed the followers of Jesus. Its threefold repetition recalls Peter's threefold denial. Nearly every reader has seen the story as a combination of a rehabilitation of Peter and an installment of Peter as leader of the community. The story builds upon classic Johannine notions of love wherein the followers of Jesus love Jesus by loving one another.

In recent years some readers have suggested that the change in the Greek terms for the words for "love" (from "friendship love" to "agape love") and for "sheep" (from a term that refers only to sheep to one that refers to cattle in general) indicates a subtle intensification of the exchange. This certainly could be true. However, the Gospel of John and early Christianity used the two words for love interchangeably. The shift in terminology is probably stylistic and signals nothing theologically. Also puzzling is the peculiar phrasing of Jesus' first question to Peter: "do you love me more than these?" The comparison may function as an intensive, not as an attempt to rank love.

Perhaps even more curious is Jesus' prediction about the future of Peter, wherein someone will tie a belt about him and lead him where he does not want to go. While it is not clear whether it is Jesus or Roman persecutors who are leading Peter, the saying points to a violent death. Jesus first calls Peter to love and care for his followers and then predicts his violent end. Love, it seems, offers no security.

LEWIS R. DONELSON

Homiletical Perspective

Finally, hearing Christ ask Peter three times if Peter loves him, we recall Christ's prediction that Peter would deny him three times (13:38) and the sad scenes in which the prediction is fulfilled (18:15–17, 25–27). If we have carried away from the Gospel the idea that the final thing to remember about Peter is his unfaithfulness, the epilogue reminds us that far more important than Peter's denials is the grace of Christ: the divine willingness to engage and entrust the ministry, even to someone whose life so far has been marked by impetuosity and denial.

In short, the epilogue is a dramatic appeal to us not to reduce Christ and the wonders of his ministry to a story in the past, not to leave the gospel in a time and place long ago and far away. The epilogue returns us to the dynamism of the prologue, to the resilience and vitality of God's word. The epilogue affirms, through its story of the risen Christ on the shore of the Sea of Tiberias, what the prologue affirms as the story of Christ's earthly ministry begins: "The light shines in the darkness, and the darkness did not overcome it" (1:5).

The epilogue awakens memories of the darkness —the darkness of our hunger, the darkness of our failure to recognize Christ, the darkness of our denial—but at the same time it reminds us that none of this darkness has overcome the light. For the risen Christ still calls, still feeds, still empowers even doubters and deniers for the ministry.

The epilogue tells us: the curtain may have come down on John's narrative, but the real-life drama of Christ is continuing. Everything John has shown you continues past the last scene into the present moment and beyond.

THOMAS H. TROEGER

Acts 9:36-43

³⁶Now in Joppa there was a disciple whose name was Tabitha, which in Greek is Dorcas. She was devoted to good works and acts of charity. ³⁷At that time she became ill and died. When they had washed her, they laid her in a room upstairs. ³⁸Since Lydda was near Joppa, the disciples, who heard that Peter was there, sent two men to him with the request, "Please come to us without delay." ³⁹So Peter got up and went with them; and when he arrived, they took him to the room upstairs. All the widows stood beside him, weeping and showing tunics and other clothing that Dorcas had made while she was with them. ⁴⁰Peter put all of them outside, and then he knelt down and prayed. He turned to the body and said, "Tabitha, get up." Then she opened her eyes, and seeing Peter, she sat up. ⁴¹He gave her his hand and helped her up. Then calling the saints and widows, he showed her to be alive. ⁴²This became known throughout Joppa, and many believed in the Lord. ⁴³Meanwhile he stayed in Joppa for some time with a certain Simon, a tanner.

Theological Perspective

Suddenly the topic in Acts shifts from the conversion of Paul to Peter's miraculous raising of Tabitha. It is hard to find profound theological meaning in this passage taken in isolation. Seeing the Tabitha story in a larger context helps. In Acts 3 we read of Peter's earlier healing of a lame man at the Beautiful Gate of the temple, a narrative accompanied by elaborate theological explication. Peter uses this earlier occasion to preach a sermon containing most of the main themes of the early apostolic message. This healing, Peter says, was not performed by the apostles in their own power as human beings, but by the power of the God of Abraham, Isaac, and Jacob and in the name of the crucified Jesus Christ, the "Holy and Righteous One" (3:14). The sermon goes on to show how all of this has been foretold by the prophets, setting up the lengthy Lukan narrative to follow.

The Tabitha story no doubt presupposes all this, but it contains no explanatory sermon, nor even an invocation of the name of Jesus Christ, at the moment of the miracle. It is unusual too that Peter excludes the mourners from the "upper room" where Tabitha lies. This could explain Peter's seeming failure to call openly on Jesus' name, there being no others present to hear it. Perhaps the name was spoken in Peter's silent prayer. On the other hand, much attention is paid to Tabitha's former good works, even to the point

Pastoral Perspective

In the first half of Acts 9 we have the most familiar story in Acts, the conversion of Saul. The scene then shifts to Peter, who is another strong witness to the power God let loose in the world in the resurrection of Jesus Christ and the sending of the Holy Spirit. In the verses just before those assigned for today, a paralyzed man named Aeneas is healed when Peter announces, "Jesus Christ heals you." With this radical proclamation, Aeneas rises, becoming a witness to the power of God who leads many to the Lord.

If you find this event strange or even embarrassing, just wait for Peter to raise Tabitha from the dead! Luke wants to make sure we get the message. The God who created the world and raised Jesus from the dead is still active in the world, bringing healing to the diseased, hope to those in despair, and life where death seems to reign.

Acts is not a narrative that fits easily into our contemporary worldview. Most of us have adjusted our lives to the go-along and get-along ways of the world. As Charles Taylor says in his excellent book, *A Secular Age*, almost everyone would agree that we live in a secular world. This is a world in which belief in God cannot be taken for granted.[1] We live and move and have our being in communities inhabited

1. Charles Taylor, *A Secular Age* (Cambridge, MA: Belknap Press, 2007), 3.

Exegetical Perspective

Acts is a literary tapestry, weaving together different narrative strands of the church's mission to the end of the earth. The reader understands these separate strands are the warp and weft of a whole cloth that gives texture to the entire narrative. If Peter's story is the warp of Acts, then Paul's is its weft. Both are prophets-like-Jesus who execute their commissioned tasks in different places with similar authority and effectiveness. For this reason, the interpreter should recognize the narrative interplay between Saul, who departs to prepare for his future mission (9:30–31), and Peter, whose mission beyond Jerusalem prepares the reader for Saul's future mission to the nations (9:15–16).

The new snapshots of Peter added to his portraiture in Acts commend his personal powers, which are actually *increasing* and are in no way diminished by the Lord's prediction of Saul's important ministry. In fact, Peter soon becomes Israel's principal witness to the Spirit's "Gentile Pentecost" (10:44)—an event that confirms God's plan to allow repentant pagans to share in the blessings promised to Israel according to the Scripture (see 10:44; 11:15–18; 15:8–11).

This passage narrates the second of two healing stories. The first is of the paralytic Aeneas in Lydda (9:33–35; see 3:1–8) and the second is of the

Homiletical Perspective

As preachers, we have to find a way to approach this text so that it becomes accessible to our congregants. We could begin with the miraculous aspect, focusing on the raising from the dead of Tabitha (or Dorcas) by Peter. We might better begin with the healing aspect, focusing not only on the act but also on the role of a healing community.

What we have in this text is a community torn over illness, disease, and loss. Dorcas "became ill and died" (v. 37a). What congregation has not been wracked by illness, disease, and loss? Is there a family that has not been touched by one or more of those realities? What we find in Joppa among these early Christians is found as well in McMinnville, Toronto, Joplin, El Paso, and Springfield. Strong advances have been made in medicine, and yet cancer and other diseases seem to be impacting more people. We unknowingly eat injurious ingredients, breathe questionable air, and live with levels of stress, carelessness, and dysfunction that breed illness and disease.

The congregation in Joppa lost one of its pillars. Dorcas was a beloved saint. Her ministry was apparently to serve among the widows, making them tunics and other articles of clothing, as she supported them with her love and devotion. "She was devoted to good works and acts of charity" (v. 36b). The women in this text do not seem to be professional

Acts 9:36-43

Theological Perspective

of displaying garments she produced, as if somehow to justify the miracle. This is highly unusual. We do not read encomiums to the personal character or economic output of Lazarus before Jesus brings him back from the dead (John 11)!

So the account of the raising of Tabitha omits elements that are present in most other New Testament miracle stories and adds at least one element that is not. It seems that the Tabitha story is an atypical example of the miracle tradition. If we read it just as it stands and in isolation, its theological yield is both meager and confusing. These traits not only frustrate interpreters; they exacerbate the basic challenge of belief. The less a text tells us about the *message* a miracle bears, the more difficult it is for us to come to terms with the miracle as such. Of course, a miracle performed without interpretation still makes an impression. However, what impression is that? We are told here (9:42) that people hear of Tabitha's return to life and *believe*, but what do they believe? The story, as offered by Luke, would probably lead people to believe that Peter is a wonder worker or magician (not an uncommon occupation at that time, as in Acts 13:6–12) and that merit in the patient's past life helps empower the magic (an early form of "works righteousness"?). Perhaps Peter closes the door to mourners in order to protect his trade secrets? However, this is not the New Testament message, any more than it is Luke's intention. To avoid such misunderstanding, the miracle needs to be clothed in explicit theological meaning. Absent such meaning, we can be misled by wishful thinking or simple credulity, or we can be forced to disbelieve the tale in the name of intellectual integrity.

Even with gospel meanings intact, belief in miracles has been difficult enough—not just in the modern world, but down the centuries. One approach, traces of which some interpreters find as early as 1 Corinthians 13:8–11, has been to say that the biblical miracles, as expressions of the power of the resurrection, were among God's ways of launching the new age; that accomplished, miracles were no longer needed. Similarly, it has been suggested that miracles were thought in the early church to be signs of the nearness of the Parousia. With acceptance of the Parousia's delay, miraculous events lost this important meaning and were less often reported. Others have said that miracles are just as possible today as they ever were. The reason we see so very few is that people do not have sufficient faith.

A variant on this position is found in the requirements for sainthood in the Roman Catholic

Pastoral Perspective

by people we know and respect who do not share our faith claims. In such a context it is not easy for us to sustain our faith.

To enter into the world described in Acts, we do not need to leave our minds at the door, but it is necessary for us to accept the assumption that God is still working through God's Spirit in the lives of people and in human society to restore this broken world.

Today's story about a woman being raised from the dead challenges our assumption that we are left to our own devices to fix our predicaments—or, more to the point, that our predicaments are not fixable at all. We live in a world where the familiar nursery rhyme about Humpty Dumpty has tremendous influence. Humpty Dumpty is broken, and the common assumption is that putting him back together again is an impossible task. That is just the way it is—but not according to Acts.

Acts tells us that those who belonged to the Way (9:2) were empowered to "turn the world upside down" (17:6). So in Acts we keep reading stories about conversions, healings, and life after death. This community empowered by the Holy Spirit was not content with the status quo.

During periods of racial oppression in the United States when African Americans suffered the indignities of injustice, they came together to worship God. In the black church, people who lived in a society that questioned their value were free to imagine a world where God was at work to set them free from oppression and valued them as children of God. After long years of suffering, the vision sharpened as the God of Moses and Jesus began to create a new reality. Hearing the stories of that era in church, along with the biblical stories that inspired them, not only challenges our worldview; it begins to transform it and encourage us to live into a new reality.

Tabitha was a disciple, Acts says, employing the first and only use in the New Testament of the feminine form (*mathētria*, v. 36) of the Greek word for disciple (*mathētēs*). (Have you heard the argument that women cannot be leaders in church because it is not "biblical"? Somebody forgot to tell Luke!) Tabitha was a woman who was a widow. In her day, women were not valued by the culture at large, and widows had no one to stand up for them, so they lived on the margins of society. The story says that Tabitha was a do-gooder, "devoted to good works and acts of charity" (v. 36). She was a woman who served others, and then she died. "Too bad, but that is the way it is in this world, right?"

deceased Tabitha/Dorcas in Joppa (9:36–42). Peter restores both in a manner reminiscent of Jesus (see Luke 5:17–26) and the prophets before him (see 1 Kgs. 17:17–24; 2 Kgs. 4:19–37). In this manner, then, Peter's religious authority is reestablished, even enhanced. These healing stories not only reestablish Peter's authority but also place this prophet-like-Jesus strategically in Jonah's Joppa (9:43) for his mission to the Gentile Cornelius (10:1–48) and subsequent meeting in Jerusalem (11:1–18).

The situation in Joppa, however, is considerably more urgent: another "disciple" had become "ill and died" (9:37). Luke not only uses the feminine form for "disciple" (*mathētria*)—the only time it is used in the NT—but supplies Dorcas's Aramaic name, Tabitha, along with her impressive spiritual résumé, "she was devoted to good works and acts of charity" (v. 36b). No doubt this healing miracle only confirms God's favor and reserves for her a place in Luke's narrative!

Perhaps her importance to the congregation in Joppa explains why it sends two witnesses of her demise to Peter, with the extraordinary appeal to "come to us without delay" (v. 38b). Peter's wide-spread reputation as a healer, coupled with biblical accounts of dramatic healings that Luke's narrative echoes, have cultivated an optimism of grace that believes even a dead woman already prepared for burial—"they had washed her and laid her out" (v. 37, my trans.)—can be resuscitated by the apostle. The fact that Luke does *not* mention that her body was "anointed" with burial salts, as expected by Jewish convention, may well indicate the community's confidence in her imminent resuscitation.

There is more at stake, though, in Tabitha's restoration than in Aeneas's prior case, as the details of her résumé make clear to the reader: she is renowned for "good works and charity." The widows of her congregation cry out to Peter, showing him the clothes she had made for them (v. 39b). The middle voice of the participle "showed" (*epideiknymenai*) indicates that the widows are actually wearing clothes made for them by Tabitha, who also distributed them among the most needy of the community in keeping with the community's principle of shared goods (see 2:42–47; 4:32–35). Her loss is felt more severely, then, and her resuscitation is desired more keenly, because of the community's responsibility for its needy widows (cf. 6:1–2).

Against this background, which the reader brings to this story, her healing bears an additional witness to the importance of the community of shared goods. Yet the story's spotlight remains fixed on Peter,

mourners called in to weep over the loss of a stranger. They are crying over the loss of a beloved friend, a saintly and charitable leader. The fact that we are told her Aramaic name (as she was likely known within the faith community) and her Greek name (as she may have been known in the wider community) may suggest that her good works and acts of charity were widely and publicly practiced.

Our congregations are drawn toward healing because brokenness is so much a part of our lives. We have all become ill and lost hope. We have all either stared into death's eyes ourselves or done so alongside beloved family members and friends. The congregation in Joppa was making communal intercession for the healing of one of its members, hoping earnestly for her wholeness by reaching out to her with the spiritual resources at hand.

Christians today are more aware than ever of the power of holistic healing—the intersection of prayer, hopeful attitude, and the resources of medicine. We are more aware than ever that no one should face disease alone. Prayer partners and spiritual advocates can support us, complementing medical treatment. Communities are powerful healing partners in helping us overcome illness and brokenness. This was true for Dorcas, and it remains true for us today.

The emphasis in this text is not upon Peter. It is upon the community that yearned for a hopeful outcome for Dorcas as they implored Peter, "Please come to us without delay" (v. 38). They lovingly cared for Dorcas's body. They brought all the tunics and clothing that she had made for the widows, tangible symbols of her compassion. They shed communal tears. They waited prayerfully outside while Peter was with their friend, ready to be called back to Dorcas's side.

This congregation of resurrection hope had reason to believe in a God who transcends the categories of birth, life, and death. We do not hold the keys that unlock these mysteries. We do not know God's will as it pertains to Dorcas or to our loved ones. The helpful distinction is between praying for a cure, which seems to dictate to God our desired outcome, and praying for healing, which can come in a hundred unexpected ways. God's Spirit will intervene on behalf of our prayers, yet the healing that comes often surprises us and causes us to catch our collective breath.

Communal healing requires that we overcome the intense privacy and individualism that are the cultural icons of our day. There is a tendency within all of us, when facing a crisis or catastrophe, to pull

Acts 9:36-43

Theological Perspective

Church. Two miraculous acts, fully supported by scrupulously examined evidence, are needed. The assumption here is that miracles are still possible for persons of extraordinary saintly virtue, who are accordingly extremely rare. Many modern believers try to keep scriptural miracle stories, ancient or modern, out of their consciousness, arguing to themselves that faith does not require them to take any position, pro or con, concerning their veracity. Still others come to the question by trying to explain miracles, or explain them away, using today's superior knowledge of the physical world.

None of these approaches is satisfactory. The heart of the question remains the relationship between miracle and meaning. We are more able to take a positive view of a miracle if it helps, in the text and in our understanding, to say something theologically important. This, rather than taking miracles as sheer wonders in face of which we grit our teeth and believe, is what counts. As Paul says, "If Christ has not been raised, . . . you are still in your sins" (1 Cor. 15:17). The question then becomes what *kind* of an event is needed to mark the theological point? Consider Paul's own struggle in 1 Corinthians 15 to clarify the *kind* of "body" that rises after physical death. We can think of there being a range of positions along a continuum between event and meaning. Some will say that securing the meaning requires a certain emphasis on the miraculous event that marks it (like downgrading preaching in favor of the Eucharist). Others will lean toward the meaning side, judging that the event merely instantiates the power already inherent in the gospel itself (like emphasizing the preached word and seeing the eucharistic act as mainly symbolic).

The Tabitha miracle account is not a helpful statement of either viewpoint. Its theological value lies in its atypicality. It leads us not to take the usual form of miracle stories for granted but rather to appreciate the importance of the theological elements that usually accompany their expression.

LEWIS S. MUDGE

Pastoral Perspective

Wrong! The disciples sent for Peter. Without telling him why, they requested his presence, "Please come to us right away!" What did he find upon arrival? A dead widow surrounded by mourning widows who—like the women who went to the tomb of Jesus—were preparing her for burial. Peter entered the room and knelt to pray. Then he told Tabitha to get up, and she did!

The Spirit of God who raised Jesus from the dead brings back to life this faithful woman whose acts of compassion are central to the new reality of God's reign. This is a strange turn of events according to our standards, but God has a different value system. It should not surprise us if we have been listening to Mary's song about how God "lifted up the lowly" (Luke 1:52). Later Paul will describe a new distribution of power where God uses what is lowly and despised in the world to bring about a new reality (1 Cor. 1:26–31).

Have you ever met Tabitha? I have known her in every church I have ever served. She has no wealth or power except her deep and abiding commitment to give expression to God's compassion for those in need. She is tenacious about practicing her faith by serving others. She prays a simple prayer: "Lord, help us to help those in need, and make us sensitive to what they really need." Tabitha's work is too important to die, and I am grateful that the story records God's agreement as well, by empowering Peter to keep her alive. Tabitha is still alive in almost every church I know.

JOSEPH S. HARVARD

who "sends them all out of the room" (v. 40). Perhaps the reader has reason to wonder how he will respond to the weeping widows, given the earlier failure of the Twelve to respond adequately to the welfare of Hellenist widows. In his ministry beyond Jerusalem, Peter's response is more direct and empathetic than before: he hears the widows' lamentation, prays, and then resuscitates Tabitha (vv. 40–41).

Peter's command, "Tabitha, get up" (*anastēthi*), and the narrator's refrain, "he presented her to them alive," recall the resurrection of Jesus (see 1:3). This refrain also glosses Peter's similar command of Aeneas (see v. 34b); thus we now suppose that his earlier claim that "Jesus Christ heals you" (see v. 34a) is implied here as well and underwrites Peter's prophetic role of announcing the availability of the Lord's healing power to those marginal ones who believe (cf. Luke 8:49–56). Peter's power to heal is not an exercise of magic but a function of his close communion with the Lord of glory. Once again, the action of "helping her up" (v. 41) and returning her to the "saints and widows" confirms the resuscitation. Again, as a result of this healing, "many people believed in the Lord" (9:42b; see 9:35). The catalytic character of "signs and wonders" is characteristic of Acts; however, it would be exceptional that dramatic healings should produce mass conversions. Luke's narrative summaries of conversions are characteristically gapped and should be filled out with additional details culled from similar missionary episodes. In this way, the reader knows that the inference of every conversion is that people "turn to the Lord" (v. 35) and "believe in the Lord" (v. 42) in response to the proclamation of the gospel.

The impression left by the final verse of this lection is one of pause in preparation for the story's next episode. Two details are important in this regard. First, Peter "stayed in Joppa." The repetition of the city in the following story of Cornelius's conversion (10:6, 17, 32) commends its importance to the story's theological meaning: Peter, "son of Jonah" (Matt. 16:17), departs from Joppa as did the OT Jonah before him, both on missions to Gentiles that resulted in their surprising salvation. Second, Peter stays "with a certain Simon, a tanner" (9:43). Luke's keen interest in what is kosher or not in his telling of Cornelius's story (10:14) is introduced here by reference to Simon's trade, since a tanner carries the odors and blood of animals that would make him unclean.

ROBERT W. WALL

in, to draw in, to hunker down, to go private. Novelist and author Frederick Buechner writes,

> When it comes to putting broken lives back together—when it comes, in religious terms, to the saving of souls—the human best tends to be at odds with the holy best. To do for yourself the best that you have it in you to do—to grit your teeth and clench your fists in order to survive the world at its harshest and worst—is, by that very act, to be unable to let something be done for you and in you that is more wonderful still. The trouble with steeling yourself against the harshness of reality is that the same steel that secures your life against being destroyed secures your life also against being opened up and transformed by the holy power that life itself comes from.[1]

The congregation at Joppa was vulnerable. They stood together, using all the tools and spiritual resources available to them—weeping together, hoping together, and celebrating together. They were unafraid to wade into each other's lives in transforming ways. These can be rare marks in twenty-first-century Christian communities. The role of the preacher is to find ways to identify, energize, and celebrate the marks of a healing community in today's individualistic culture.

Dorcas will not live forever. This is not her day to die, or at least to remain dead, but Dorcas is not immortal in her earthly pilgrimage. Peter will not return time and again to revive her. Even Peter will not live forever. The emphasis of this text is not upon a return from death, but upon a community honing all of its spiritual strength and resources passionately upon life and wholeness.

STEPHEN D. JONES

---

1. Frederick Buechner, *The Sacred Journey* (San Francisco: Harper & Row, 1982), 46.

Psalm 23

¹The Lord is my shepherd, I shall not want.
² He makes me lie down in green pastures;
he leads me beside still waters;
³ he restores my soul.
He leads me in right paths
for his name's sake.

⁴ Even though I walk through the darkest valley,
I fear no evil;
for you are with me;
your rod and your staff—
they comfort me.

Theological Perspective

In the image of God as shepherd, Psalm 23 provides a powerful metaphor for the reality behind God's name: YHWH—"I am who I will be . . . I am the one who is and who will be present with you and for you" (see Exod. 3:14). The name declares God's promise to be effectively present as God in the life and history of Israel for the blessing of all people (cf. Gen. 12:3). What does it mean to be those for whom God is present to bless and keep, to guide and direct, to discipline and redeem? How might one speak of this one whose name is not a definition we can master, but a promise we must trust? The psalmist answers: "The Lord is my shepherd" (v. 1).

James L. Mays writes: "A metaphor used for theological purposes is very serious business. It does not simply describe by comparison; it identifies by equation."[1] The metaphor of the shepherd is pastoral, political, and personal. In it we learn about the nature and character of YHWH as God and king. Indeed, as the one who inspires the metaphor, YHWH controls and gives it content. While ancient Near Eastern rulers were often pictured with a mace and a shepherd's crook as official symbols, the shepherd of Psalm 23 is defined neither by the culture's norms nor by the

1. James L. Mays, *Psalms*, Interpretation series (Louisville, KY: John Knox Press, 1989), 116.

Pastoral Perspective

The Twenty-third Psalm is certainly the best-known biblical text among the older generations in our congregations. It is usually held in memory in the King James Version of the text, even among younger folks, but it is less and less likely to be held fully in memory by those whose Sunday school experience was spotty. Neither the hymnody of our traditions nor contemporary praise songs reproduce the psalm exactly. Since music is now a primary vehicle for what memorization commonly occurs, many in our congregations will be familiar with the images but will not have the actual text in mind. This combination of familiarity and unfamiliarity allows rich engagement with the text.

"I shall not want." The God who is named and then addressed in Psalm 23 is trustworthy—with our lives, with our choices, with our fears and losses. Living out of a fundamental attitude of trust is counterintuitive, even countercultural, in modern Western cultures. To say with the psalmist, "I shall not want," directly challenges all of the advertising that is designed to create a felt need that a particular product can satisfy. It is not easy for us to resist all of the voices that seek to heighten our sense of dissatisfaction with the gifts we have from God: life itself, community/communion with persons and with all creation, the capacity to feed and shelter and

⁵ You prepare a table before me
   in the presence of my enemies;
you annount my head with oil;
   my cup overflows.
⁶ Surely goodness and mercy shall follow me
   all the days of my life,
and I shall dwell in the house of the LORD
   my whole life long.

Exegetical Perspective

"The LORD is my shepherd." As soon as he or she hears these words, the worshiper typically moves on to "I shall not want." Familiarity does not so much breed contempt as it does a quick recitation of this psalm. Such a well-known psalm, however, deserves a more deliberate reading. The metaphors and message it presents are rich and powerful.

"The LORD is my shepherd" offers both a negative and a positive claim. The latter is, of course, that YHWH functions as a shepherd. Equally important is the former claim: that no other person, human or divine, plays that role. There were options. Baal, a Canaanite god, might have been construed as a shepherd. Even more likely, a king could be viewed as a shepherd. That metaphor appears both in the OT and in extrabiblical texts to depict the king as protector of his people (e.g., Ps. 78:70–72; Isa. 44:28; Jer. 23:1–4; Ezek. 37:24). Hammurabi's famous stele (it preserves an ancient Mesopotamian law code) includes the following claim by that famous Babylonian king: "I am Hammurabi, the shepherd." For this psalmist, however, no god other than YHWH, no earthly king, plays the role of shepherd. Strikingly, this view of God as shepherd does not appear frequently in the Psalter (only elsewhere in 28:9; 80:1). In Psalm 28:9 and 80, God is the shepherd of all Israel, not the shepherd of an individual, as is the case in this psalm.

Homiletical Perspective

I often wondered if Psalm 23 is as important for Jewish devotional and liturgical practice as it is for Christians. While serving a parish in Rochester, New York, I had an unusual opportunity (or at least location) to find out—the steam room of the Jewish Community Center, a wonderful place to receive an after-workout education. Not long after I joined the center, my calling was revealed, and soon I was widely referred to as "Reverend." My Jewish friends were as curious about my faith practices as I was about theirs, and it was rare that they did not ask me about something, from papal pronouncements to wacko evangelists.

I was acutely aware of one frequent, visible distinction between me and my generally older interlocutors: I did not have numbers tattooed on my arm. So it took me a while to ask survivors of Nazi work/death camps if the Twenty-third Psalm was important to them, but I am glad I did. It led to the same kind of recitations, albeit in Hebrew or Yiddish, that one might hear in English at a nursing home or funeral service.

Why is that? Why is Psalm 23 so popular, yet inevitably associated with death? It is a psalm of deliverance, and while the best translation of the tense of the Hebrew is a matter of some dispute, the NRSV puts almost everything in the present tense:

Psalm 23

Theological Perspective

community's desires. Rather, YHWH is self-defined as shepherd "for his name's sake" (v. 3b) through the unfolding of salvation history: in the exodus and wilderness sojourn, in the giving of the Law and land, and in establishing the nation, in the exile and restoration. This one, and no other to whom poet or people might be drawn, is the shepherd of Israel. Psalm 23 is fraught with political implications, not only for those who first sang it, but also for the people of God today.

The psalm reflects YHWH's provision for the nation's needs, though not their desires (v. 1; cf. Deut. 2:7). It acknowledges YHWH's guidance and discipline (vv. 2–3). It affirms YHWH's presence and protection when death threatens (v. 4). It describes YHWH's making a place of nurture and safety when enemies lurk (v. 5).

Of particular importance is the image in verse 6 of YHWH's goodness and mercy pursuing the poet throughout his life, not waiting for him to seek or call. John Calvin saw in verse 6 an expression of God's prevenient grace, which anticipates our unwillingness to turn to God and yet, like the "hound of heaven," follows steadily, tirelessly after us and brings us home (cf. Luke 15:5).[2] At stake theologically in this image is the conviction that even faith is a gift—the fruit of God's grace at work in us—not an accomplishment for which we can take credit. We are justified *by* the gift of grace *through* the gift of faith. Both prepositions express God's faithfulness in and for us and are crucial to the way we understand the doctrine of justification.

What might it do to our understanding of God, and to the way we live with life's joys and sorrows, if we took seriously that God always takes the initiative with us—a shepherd leading us toward himself, following us in our wanderings so that we never get beyond the love that will not let us go?

The readings for the Fourth Sunday of Easter witness to the church's conviction that the shepherd of Psalm 23 has become flesh in Jesus Christ, the good shepherd who lays down his life for his sheep (John 10:11–16, 27–30; cf. Luke 15:3–7; Matt. 18:10–14), even sheep not of the particular fold one may currently envision. Because Jesus is "good news of great joy for all the people" (Luke 2:10; cf. Gen. 12:3), because Jesus Christ is Emmanuel, the church claims, confesses, and sings the whole reality set forth in Psalm 23.

The postresurrection placement of the psalm in the lectionary offers intriguing theological possibilities

2. John Calvin, *Institutes of the Christian Religion,* ed. John T. McNeill, trans. Ford Lewis Battles (Philadelphia: Westminster Press, 1960), 2.3.12.

Pastoral Perspective

cherish each being in community. Because the rest of the psalm is powerful, we can easily rush past these opening words, "I shall not want." When we do move on to the line about the "valley of the shadow of death" (KJV) or the "darkest valley" (NRSV), these words may unintentionally elicit this cultural pressure to feel needy, when the shepherd has fully provided for our real needs. "I shall not want" is a statement of fact, based on trust, that is a reality check against our feelings of neediness.

In a similar way, doing anything in the presence of our enemies also runs counter to most contemporary cultural expectations. We are repeatedly told it is unsafe. Clearly, the psalm invites us to articulate our assumptions and feelings about safety and to examine them in the presence of the one who is our true safety. In the political environment in which this essay is written, feelings about safety are frequently manipulated for a variety of purposes. Without the verse about our enemies, the psalm could have avoided reflection on such public and political fears. Psalm 23, however, does not allow an evasion of political space. Our fears are no longer easily manipulated when we recognize that God brings us safely into the presence of our enemies—if we are willing to trust God. It is not an accident that folks reciting the psalm from memory are most likely to forget what comes next when they arrive at the beginning of this verse!

The public nature of Psalm 23 may be further explored through experimenting with who the speaker might be. Readers of Psalm 23 almost always interpret the first-person singular "my" as an individual person. Without changing the language of the text itself, we can fruitfully posit other entities as the "I" who speaks and trusts. Try reading the psalm with the planet Earth as the speaker, the one who claims the Lord as shepherd. Try reading it together as a civic community or as a congregation—not as a multiplicity of voices, "*our* shepherd," but as *one* voice, "I, Christ's Church, Anywhereville, the Lord is my shepherd." The experience of divine care begins to expand with such public readings.

Turning to another kind of approach to Psalm 23, the abundant vivid metaphorical images in the psalm make it a wonderful text for meditative prayer. *Lectio divina* with this psalm seems quite natural to folks, who are inclined to hold on to one phrase or another in the text anyway. Liturgy or preparation for worship might specifically invite such meditative reading and list some of the metaphors: our God is our shepherd, we are sheep, lying down in green pastures, being led by still waters and along straight

Exegetical Perspective

If God is a shepherd, then the worshiper is a sheep or goat. That is the symbolic world presented in verses 1–2, or at least the first part of verse 2. This animal not only lies in a fertile pasture; it also has a safe and quiet place to drink water. God "leads" the animal. This same image and word—God as shepherd "leading" sheep—occurs in Isaiah 40:11. There, God leads particularly vulnerable sheep, those who are nursing their young. God leads those needy sheep on good trails. On the rocky terrain of Syria-Palestine, it was not always easy to find the proper or safe trail. Here, God takes care of the sheep by not letting them stray or stumble.

Verse 4 marks a minor transition in the psalm. (One might well translate, "I will fear no adversity," instead of "I will fear no evil." In the metaphoric world of the shepherd and sheep, sheep would fear harm, not "evil.") The psalmist is still describing terrain, "the darkest valley," but now, instead of talking about God as shepherd, the psalmist speaks directly to God. The sheep now says, "You are with me." This image of a talking sheep begins to fracture the metaphor that, up to this point, has undergirded the psalm. Verse 4 is the final place where the imagery of shepherd/sheep is at play. The shepherd's implements—one to guide the sheep, the other to drive off predators—as well as the very presence of the shepherd, offer comfort.

Verse 5 signals a major change in the poetry. The psalmist, once a sheep, now becomes a human being. The Deity, once a shepherd, now becomes a gracious host. The dangers of the natural world now become enemies.

What does not change is the benevolent action of God, who "spreads" a table. The imagery may, in fact, be that of spreading a woven mat on the ground. Whether textile or wood structure, it is in full view of the psalmist's enemies. (The motif of enemies is prominent in the Psalter; this same phrase appears in Pss. 6:10; 7:6; 31:11; 42:10; 69:18.) These are the adversaries who have elsewhere been quoted as saying "Where is your God?" (Ps. 42:10). That question is now answered, since they can see God taking care of the person whom they had oppressed. Does this mean the psalmist simply feels safe, or is she or he gloating? The psalm does not answer that question.

When at table, the psalmist is utterly comfortable. Anointing with oil, of course, can refer to the ordination of a priest or the coronation of a king. On the latter occasion, Israelites spoke as if God anointed the Davidic king (Ps. 45:7). One may therefore say that, in Psalm 23, the psalmist is treated

Homiletical Perspective

The Lord *is* my shepherd, who *leads* and *restores*; I *fear* no evil; your rod and staff *comfort*; you *prepare* and *anoint*. Only verse 6 is translated with future (or subjunctive) force: *shall follow, shall dwell.* So why, if I say, "Psalm 23," do you ask, "Who died?" That makes about as much sense as treating 1 Corinthians 13 as if Paul wrote it for a wedding liturgy.

The first important homiletical issue in treating Psalm 23 is that the metaphors and images are mostly about the present, not the future. The second issue, noted and emphasized by James Luther Mays, is the uniquely personal nature of the relationship described in the text. "Psalm 23 is completely unique. No other psalm says, 'My shepherd.' In all other psalms where 'shepherd' is used as a metaphor for the deity, the relationship is to the community . . . it is always 'our shepherd.' What is going on in Psalm 23 is the location and recapitulation of God's relation to his people in the living of one individual person."[1]

The psalm is both present and personal. Would that more preaching were so. Instead, we are generic and future, speaking of what "everyone can hope for." If Psalm 23 is any guide, that is a very unbiblical understanding. What are you and God up to these days? That is a much more biblical question, and a much more faithful way to preach about Psalm 23. What exactly might that look like?

Start with the root metaphor of this psalm—actually the root metaphors, because both "Lord" and "shepherd" are metaphors, which is something of a problem. We speak metaphorically in order to inform and enrich our understanding of one thing or idea by comparing it to something well—or at least better—understood. However, Scripture often likes to generate meaning more intensely by compounding the metaphors.

For example, every time Jesus begins a parable, "The kingdom of God is like," and goes on to speak of sowing seed, leavening dough, or searching for pearls, we misunderstand if we forget that kingdom is itself a metaphor, not a place. So to refer to God as Lord is to call up one cluster of metaphorical meaning—ruler, sovereign, benefactor, and the like. To then say this Lord is my shepherd conjures another set of meanings by which the psalmist and the preacher describe just what kind of Lord we understand God to be. The task in the sermon is to recreate this metaphorical process imaginatively for listeners, not by telling them everything there is to

---

1. James L. Mays, in *Preaching and Teaching the Psalms*, ed. Patrick D. Miller and Gene M. Tucker (Louisville, KY: Westminster John Knox Press, 2006), 120.

Psalm 23

Theological Perspective

for preaching and teaching. In the Psalter, it follows Psalm 22—the Good Friday lection for every year. The one who cried out from the cross in God-forsakenness is risen. Psalm 23 might be seen as the Son's own filial confession of gratitude to the Father who brought him through the darkness of death and hell. The church in turn praises God "who brought back from the dead our Lord Jesus, the great shepherd of the sheep" (Heb. 13:20), and confesses the Son as the incarnation of the Father's love and presence in the hymnal version of Psalm 23, "The King of Love My Shepherd Is."

Psalm 23 has long provided a powerful witness in the worship of the Christian funeral. In death's shadow and darkness, Christ accompanies us. Into the hell of God-forsakenness he descended, so that even when we make our beds in hell, we will not be without him. As the messenger at the empty tomb announced, "He is going ahead of you" (Mark 16:7), not only to prepare a dwelling place for us at the end of life, but also to prepare a table in the midst of life, with all its joys and sorrows, its hopes and fears. Christ has promised to remain with us as the good shepherd even to the end of time, so that in life and in death we may be confident that we belong not to the powers of evil, sin, and death, but to him of whom we can say with confidence and trust: "The LORD is my shepherd."

In the dramatic movement of worship in Eastertide, Psalm 23 further identifies the one to whom the poet in last week's Psalm 30 prays. Moreover, it is, as Karl Barth noted, "a summary of the whole Psalter,"[3] and leads forward to the universal praise sounded in Psalm 148, appointed for the Fifth Sunday of Easter.

JOHN B. ROGERS

Pastoral Perspective

paths, being restored by rest, moving through dark valleys, relying on rod and staff for safety, sitting before a full meal, sitting with enemies, being anointed, watching one's cup be filled to overflowing, dwelling safely, living in the house of God. Inviting folks to allow their minds to wander as they explore one of these images and to freely link it with others gives meditative space for the Spirit to move in their hearts and minds in powerful ways.

Some persons in our congregations have difficulty using the honorific name "Lord" as address to God. The richness of the author's reference to God in Psalm 23 might be evoked through naming persons with whom God has been in relationship. For example, "The God of Abraham and Sarah, of Paul and Mary Magdalene, of Martin Luther King Jr. and Dorothy Day is my shepherd; I shall not want." Such a reading evokes their trusting faith in the one who is faithful. It invites us to dwell metaphorically in a flock whose stories and whose preferred name for the One-Who-Shepherds are as varied as our own.

Finally, Psalm 23 is the most familiar of the many psalms that reassure us of God's continuing presence, no matter what is happening to our bodies, our relationships, our community, or our world. It is easy in the midst of trauma to give our confidence over to doctors or leaders as if they hold everything in their hands. They do not. Psalm 23 helps us retain perspective in the midst of trauma, perspective that retains our agency in relation to those who intend to help us. We seek to discern the hand of God in the work of those who help in times of trauma, but we do not expect them to do everything on our behalf. Many of us forget this when we are frightened about our health in particular. Psalm 23 helps restore us to our selves; we are active as ones who trust in God. Through it all, God and God alone is our true safety, our true shepherd.

CATHERINE L. KELSEY

3. Karl Barth, *Church Dogmatics*, IV/I (Edinburgh: T. & T. Clark, 1956), 608.

royally. This verse probably refers to the use of olive oil to beautify one's hair and skin (Ps. 104:15; Eccl. 9:8). Moreover, the psalmist's drinking vessel is utterly full. (Note the prominence of liquid imagery throughout the psalm: water, oil, drink.)

From the leisure of that scene, the psalmist gazes into the future and sees a time when enemies will no longer chase him or her (cf. Ps. 143:3, "For the enemy has pursued me, crushing my life to the ground"). Instead, personified "goodness" and "steadfast love" (NRSV "mercy") will pursue the psalmist (the Hebrew verb has a stronger meaning than "follow"). Where will that chase end? On the one hand, the psalmist suggests it will continue. They will pursue the psalmist "all the days of my life." On the other hand, the psalmist reports that "I shall dwell in the house of the LORD." This motif is attested elsewhere in the Psalter, for example, "to live in the house of the Lord all the days of my life." One could imagine the psalmist running around the temple courtyard forever, but that would be to absolutize the imagery in verse 8—being pursued and dwelling. (A literal translation of the Hebrew in verse 6 would be "I will return to the house of the LORD for many days." That would be consistent with the emphasis on movement in the earlier part of the verse.)

Different though the two primary metaphors are (God as shepherd and God as host), they share one element: God providing nurture, especially to those in distress. To be near God is to be fed. Both Judaism and Christianity have recognized the importance of such divinely provided food. Jews celebrate the meal of Passover, whereas Christians experience the ultimate communal meal of the Eucharist.

DAVID L. PETERSEN

know about ancient Israelite animal husbandry, but by recontextualizing the imagery.

We do this best by demonstrating how the leading secondary metaphors—lead, guide, provide, and so forth—may have meaning in the lives of our hearers. The preacher needs to translate the ancient and beloved pastoral imagery into compelling and contemporary experiences of the goodness of God's love without sliding into sentimentality. That is done by focusing on the central insights of the homiletical exegesis of the psalm, the twin ideas of present and personal. What is God doing in the lives of your listeners?

Because of the intimacy of the psalm itself, our preaching has license to be intimate in a way many sermons do not. However, we do not want thereby to turn the Deity into a cuddly teddy bear. That is not intimacy; that is schmaltz. Intimacy is Paul praying for deliverance from the thorn in the flesh and God responding, "My grace is sufficient for you" (2 Cor. 12:9). Intimacy is Jesus washing the disciples' feet and breaking bread on the night before his death (John 13), pouring his soul out in the garden (Mark 14:34–35), and giving himself on the cross. Intimacy is tough stuff, and the preacher needs to treat it as such.

We keep faith with Psalm 23 if we remain present and personal, but this does not mean ignoring the last, luminous line: "I shall dwell in the house of the LORD my whole life long." What happened to "forever"? Because we are conditioned by the King James and Revised Standard Versions, "my whole life long" does not sound long enough. However, it is not a question of chronology. It is promise affirmed. What God has done for the psalmist is what the psalmist trusts God will continue to do. A sermon that invites the listener to share such trust, a sermon that is personal and present, responds well to the daunting task of preaching a text as familiar as Psalm 23.

WILLIAM F. BROSEND

Revelation 7:9-17

⁹After this I looked, and there was a great multitude that no one could count, from every nation, from all tribes and peoples and languages, standing before the throne and before the Lamb, robed in white, with palm branches in their hands. ¹⁰They cried out in a loud voice, saying,

"Salvation belongs to our God who is seated on the throne, and to the Lamb!"
¹¹And all the angels stood around the throne and around the elders and the four living creatures, and they fell on their faces before the throne and worshiped God, ¹²singing,

"Amen! Blessing and glory and wisdom
and thanksgiving and honor
and power and might
be to our God forever and ever! Amen."

Theological Perspective

In the book of Revelation there are clear tensions between the community that worships the Lamb and the world that has been pulled into the cult of the emperor. For instance, the claim in verse 10—that "salvation belongs to our God who is seated on the throne, and to the Lamb"—defies the official propaganda of the Roman Empire. This propaganda claimed that salvation—understood as rescue from danger and the enjoyment of peace and well-being by the inhabitants of the empire—had its source in Rome. Revelation sees through such pretensions of benevolence to the brutal rule of violence that lies within. The "great multitude" (v. 9) that cries out the hymn of praise to God and the Lamb, then, represents among other things the dominion of God that stands firmly against the imperial project that is Rome.

Revelation expresses the conviction that witness on behalf of the gospel of Christ crucified will bring one into direct conflict with the powers of this world of empire (1:9). In 7:14 this conflict is referred to as "the great ordeal," often translated as "the great tribulation" (e.g., RSV, NIV). It is evident to John that the great tribulation has already begun and coincides with the mission of the church, an insight cherished for much of the church's history. Augustine, for instance, argued that the millennium—the reign of Christ referred to in 20:4—and the tribulation are

Pastoral Perspective

We Christians are wont to imagine that God's job is to keep us and our loved ones safe from all harm. This misguided belief causes more lives of faith to crumble than any other that I have known. Today's vision from Revelation to John clearly lets us know that pain and suffering will be a part of any Christian life. Those standing "before the throne and before the Lamb" have "come out of the great ordeal; they have washed their robes and made them white in the blood of the Lamb" (v. 14). They are in need of shelter (v. 15). They have known hunger and thirst and scorching heat (v. 16). They have tears in their eyes (v. 17). The preacher who attends to these details lets the Christian community know that God never promised we would not suffer. Suffering has always been part of the Christian story, and we are not immune.

However, that is only a part of the story and never The End. This passage moves through its important message about suffering to a vision of how victory is finally won. This vision is counter to the visions of victory offered to us by our culture:

"The one with the most toys wins."
"The one with the most money and the biggest house wins."
"The one with the most power wins."

¹³Then one of the elders addressed me, saying, "Who are these, robed in white, and where have they come from?" ¹⁴I said to him, "Sir, you are the one that knows." Then he said to me, "These are they who have come out of the great ordeal; they have washed their robes and made them white in the blood of the Lamb.
¹⁵For this reason they are before the throne of God,
    and worship him day and night within his temple,
    and the one who is seated on the throne will shelter them.
¹⁶They will hunger no more, and thirst no more;
    the sun will not strike them,
    nor any scorching heat;
¹⁷for the Lamb at the center of the throne will be their shepherd,
    and he will guide them to springs of the water of life,
    and God will wipe away every tear from their eyes."

Exegetical Perspective

The acclamation in Revelation 7:9–17 recalls that of Revelation 5:11–14, read during the Third Sunday of Easter. However, while the whole of Revelation 5 emphasizes the revelation of the Lamb and *why* the Lamb merits worship, Revelation 7 is more interested in *who* voices the praise. The identity of the ones who praise poses a major problem for interpretation.

The lectionary's omission of 7:1–8 significantly limits our appreciation of this pericope. Revelation 7:1–8 introduces the 144,000, twelve thousand from each of Israel's twelve tribes. As with other figures in Revelation, their number does not indicate a literal accounting of the redeemed Israel; rather, their appearance evokes the eschatological hope for Israel's eventual reconstitution.[1] In contrast, the multitude of 7:9 has no number and consists of people from "every nation."

It is likely that John is redefining eschatological Israel. He does so by sliding from one image (the 144,000 Israelites) to another (the countless multitude from every people) without explicit interpretation. Two considerations justify this interpretation. First, John makes a similar move when he introduces the Lion. The Lion never appears but is replaced by the

Homiletical Perspective

During the past generation, "church growth" has been a popular emphasis in North American Christianity, exported by means of a global market. It is significant, then—during a time when we are warned of continuing decline in church membership, attendance, resources, and influence—that John invites us to join him in contemplating a most impressive sight. John's Revelation does not tell us to do, but to see, to become attentive recipients of, a vision given by God. What we see is a huge throng standing before the throne of the Lamb. How is that for "church growth"? The multitude we see is innumerable. The whole creation is represented, with members from all nations, tribes, races, and languages. John summons us to look beyond our own fearful conditions and circumstances to behold the glorious completion of God's saving promises, which began with the call of Abraham and Sarah.

Moreover, the crowd that surrounds the throne of God and the slain Lamb is not only impressively large; it is also diverse, brought together and united as one people whose life is centered in the praise of God. Even more impressive, however, is that this diverse gathering is united around the Lamb, moved to ecstatic speech and shouts of praise by the beauty of such generous, self-giving love. It is here that preachers are given a wonderful opportunity to

1. For a long list of passages that voice this hope, see David Aune, *Revelation 6–16*, Word Biblical Commentary 52B (Nashville: Thomas Nelson, 1998), 436.

Revelation 7:9-17

Theological Perspective

actual in the ongoing experience of the church. Yet this is not how many understand the "tribulation" today. One apocalyptic model that has gained currency in recent years is "pretribulation premillennialism," which lies, for example, behind the popular *Left Behind* series. In this reading of biblical texts, the great tribulation and Christ's reign lie largely before us.

Premillennialists agree on the basic outline of these future events. At the end of the present age, human society will grow worse and worse until the antichrist will gain control, throwing the world into a reign of terror. This is the "great tribulation." At the end of the tribulation, the reign of the antichrist will be destroyed at the battle of Armageddon by the triumphant return of Christ. Having disposed of the antichrist and his forces, and having bound the power of Satan, Christ will establish his millennial kingdom, which will end after a thousand years with an easily subdued revolt by Satan. The resurrection of the dead will follow, as will the judgment and the creation of a new heaven and a new earth.

While most premillennialists agree on this script for the future, they disagree on the exact timing of the church's "rapture." The rapture is the "catching away" of the church to meet Christ in the air (1 Thess. 4:15–17). Pretribulationists believe that the church will be raptured before the rise of the antichrist and before the beginning of the tribulation. That is, the true believer will escape all of the pain and suffering of the tribulation period. By contrast, a close reading of Revelation reveals that those who publicly witness to the power of the gospel to confront evil, wherever it might be found, inevitably encounter tribulation rather than escape it.

The salvation (i.e., "rescue") that followers of Christ experience in Revelation is of a different order than that found in pretribulation premillennialism. It is grounded in faith's ability to resist evil and endure its counterattack. It is a salvation that is possible only in Christ (7:10), made real only by faith in the promises of God. The only weapon the faithful have in this war against evil is the word of God (1:16; 2:12; 19:21). From the perspective of the world, this is a weak weapon indeed. Yet for those with faith, as Paul says, the gospel "is the power of God for salvation" (Rom. 1:16), but not from suffering on account of the gospel.

Revelation refers to some Christians who have lost their lives for the gospel (e.g., 2:13; 6:10; 12:11; 16:6; 17:6; 18:24). Severe threats, however, come to the churches not only from without, but also from

Pastoral Perspective

In Revelation we hear again the Christian message that none of these definitions of victory matches the victory of the Christian life. For John, ultimate Christian victory comes in death. This claim is important to hear during the days of Eastertide, when we proclaim again and again exactly what the death of Christ means for Christians. Dying and rising in Christ is how we become victors. We are conquerors not because we escape persecution—Christ did not escape it—but because like him we are God's children. Joining the great multitude in John's vision, we too recognize our shepherd in "the Lamb at the center of the throne" (v. 17), who will guide us to springs of living water, where "God will wipe away every tear from" our eyes.

Listening to the promise in this text we learn a lot about letting go—of the definitions of victory reinforced by our culture, of our great need to control all the circumstances of our lives, including their ultimate outcome. John's vision reveals how many illusions we have, both about our own power and about what God "owes" us by seeing that no harm comes our way. Every person in this passage has come through a great ordeal. Every robe needs washing. "For this reason they are before the throne of God" (v. 15a). Their suffering has prepared them for worship and for victory—but victory by God's definition and not their own. Reading this passage in public worship, we might well wonder how we too are being prepared for the challenges that will come to us, both individually and in community, as we open ourselves to God's future for us.

As I was preparing for intense medical treatment for cancer, I was told by my doctors to gain as much weight as I could. I scanned the grocery shelves for the highest caloric foods I could find, deciding on King Don's individual chocolate dessert cakes, along with some protein powder and lots of ice cream. As I sat forcing down one King Don after another and washing them all down with milkshakes, the cakes did not seem as yummy as they had been during my kindergarten years. Yet the doctors told me the cakes would get me through to the end. They would help strengthen me for the ordeal ahead.

Whatever ordeals we are facing, some of our preparations will be like that—accepting the food that God offers us, even when it does not taste as good as we had hoped. On other days, the food will be delicious, as we study, pray, and worship together, putting on "spiritual weight" for whatever lies ahead. Ordeals are not *all* God has in store for us, after all. There is also joy, as we share in the beloved lives of

first appearance of the Lamb (5:5–6). This move redefines messianic identity from what we might call Lion power to Lamb power. Second, John's allusion to "those who say they are Jews but are not" (2:9; 3:9) suggests a struggle for Israel's inheritance. Whereas John claims this inheritance for himself and his churches, Jews outside the churches reject this claim. Thus the slide from 144,000 Israelites to a countless number from every tribe may indicate John's claim that those who follow the Lamb constitute the New Israel.[2]

This argument is theologically and ethically sensitive. If Revelation defines Israel in terms of those who follow Jesus, this passage clearly packs anti-Jewish potential. This dangerous possibility is hardly mitigated by the probability that John himself is a Jewish follower of Jesus. Nevertheless, Christians must confess their place in the trajectory of God's covenant with Israel.

The transition from the 144,000 Israelites to the countless multitude also transforms the identity of those who follow the Lamb. The census in 7:5–8 suggests an army. Biblical census taking is associated with preparing an army for war, and the reappearance of the 144,000 in 14:1–5 identifies the group as entirely male. In contrast, the countless multitude is not gender specific. Their white garments, washed in the blood of the Lamb, combine with their passage through the "great persecution" (NRSV "ordeal") to suggest that this multitude consists of faithful witnesses to Jesus. They have risked—or lost—their lives in faithful testimony (see 12:11).[3] As a result of their witness, we learn, they stand ever before God's throne, shepherded, kept, and comforted by the Lamb.

The image of white garments suggests purity from a corrupt world. Followers of Jesus are to keep their garments clean in the here and now. For their faithfulness they receive white garments in the age to come (3:4). This is particularly true of the martyrs (6:11).

This multitude has passed through "the great persecution" (7:14), perhaps simply an eschatological period of general distress or alluding to persecution. Revelation, it seems, interprets that period as a time of persecution for the saints.

We do not know the extent or nature of persecution in Asia Minor during the late first century, nor

2. Richard Bauckham notes that both in 5:5–6 and 7:4–14 this slide accompanies a transition between what John *hears* and what he *sees* (*Theology of the Book of Revelation*, New Testament Theology [New York: Cambridge University Press, 1993], 76).
3. Bauckham indeed identifies them as martyrs (*Theology of the Book of Revelation*, 77).

proclaim the resurrection of the crucified Jesus in a manner that challenges claims that the Easter faith of the church is only an "ideal."

We will do so by inviting listeners to join a heavenly celebration in which salvation is ascribed to God who sits on the throne and to the Lamb. The fruit of this victory is made visible by witness that is congruent with the character of the one who has triumphed. Moreover, the heavenly congregation to which we belong by the gift of our baptism is large, diverse, and one. These identifying marks are not so much tasks that have been assigned for us to accomplish by our plans and efforts—get larger, be more diverse, become united—as they are indicative of the way things are in heaven and are now being realized on earth among those who have turned to see and sing the glory of the slain Lamb of God.

There is indeed much good news in this lesson, and preachers would do well to invite our listeners to turn, see, and join in becoming glad recipients of what God has accomplished in the life, death, and resurrection of Jesus. Moreover, John shows us that those who sing the praises of the Lamb include those who have been called to join him by participating in his suffering. There is indeed a great mystery, inviting serious attention to the reality of cross and resurrection, that illumines what God has done for us and what God is doing with us for the sake of the world. The church celebrates the victory of the Lamb in a rather strange manner, by sharing in the humility by which his victory was won: through the "weak power" and "foolish wisdom" of a crucified Lord (1 Cor. 1:18–31). While we cannot produce this life, it is the gift we receive from the one who freely shares himself when we gather in his presence.

John's vision of the victorious Lamb and the joyful multitude that surrounds him cannot be separated from the reality of suffering that accompanies loving obedience to God. As the church continues to journey through the Great Fifty Days, the most festive season of the Christian year, it remembers that the victory we celebrate was won in, with, and through—not apart from—rejection, suffering, and death. At the same time, there is ample opportunity for extending comfort, since the Lamb is also a Shepherd who provides, protects, cares for, and lovingly leads his flock. Amazingly, the humble Shepherd is the risen Lord who rules heaven and earth through intimate involvement in the affairs of his people for the sake of the whole world. We are compelled to proclaim this hope in the darkest of circumstances, since the one who conquered sin, evil,

Revelation 7:9-17

Theological Perspective

within. There are teachings in circulation that do not concur with the rule of faith as understood by the writer (e.g., 2:15, 20). There is also the danger that comes with a lukewarm reception of the testimony of Jesus in the churches themselves (e.g., 3:2, 15). The possibility of being reassimilated into the web of power and influence of the Roman imperial project is real. According to John, one cannot be loyal to both the values of Rome and the values of Christ. The baptized, then, are exhorted to stand firm in their resistance to the seductive lure of the entitlements that come with imperial domination. The two-edged sword of the word of God does battle on these fronts within the walls of the churches.

John reminds the churches of the great cost of forgiveness and the promise of the new creation that is in Christ. Disciples of the Crucified One, he notes, "have washed their robes and made them white in the blood of the Lamb" (7:14). It is this very same victim of human sinfulness who, in an odd reversal, has become the Shepherd who leads the faithful through their own encounters with evil. As foretold in Isaiah 49:10 and emphasized again in Revelation 21:4, when all is finally made new, this Christ will guide the weary to the healing waters of life, waters experienced already in the church's sacrament of baptism. They will be nourished by food that satisfies the deepest hunger, a meal already experienced in the sacrament of the body and blood of Christ.

God's millennial reign, John tells us, is made real through these gifts given by Christ and received by "every nation, . . . all tribes and peoples and languages" to make one people out of what were many. God's restoration of all things is inaugurated through the assembly that has been gathered around the altar of God and the Lamb, nourished by the sacramental word made visible by grace. Thus transformed, these same saints are sent out into the world they resist to witness that "salvation belongs to our God who is seated on the throne, and to the Lamb."

ERIK M. HEEN

Pastoral Perspective

those around us and celebrate the good things of life. All of these are ways that we feed ourselves and God feeds us as we live in between times.

As Christians work together to define our path in the midst of so many other paths offered by our society and our world, John's words of revelation can serve as water pouring freely over us during the parched times of our lives. We can help our congregations distinguish between reality and illusion—between what God has promised and what God has not—not imagining that our lives will be free from suffering but trusting that in God we will find strength, courage, and solace enough to sustain us until that time when we too become victors in and over death.

Preachers might spend some time thinking of concrete stories from the local or global community that illustrate how people facing great ordeals are sustained in the wilderness by the grace of God and their neighbors. What kind of "cakes" does the Christian community eat in order to keep up its weight? What are some of the differences between this food and the food the world offers? What kinds of hungers does each food feed (or fail to feed)?

In these days of Eastertide, the preacher's job is to proclaim boldly that there will be a day when hunger and thirst will be no more. With John, we can paint the glorious picture of the church triumphant, so filled with joy and thanksgiving greater than any suffering in life that all fall down before God singing, "Thanksgiving and honor and power and might be to our God forever and ever! Amen" (v. 12).

DANA FERGUSON

Exegetical Perspective

can we document any widespread or official persecution in the region during that period. Yet Revelation frequently expresses concern with persecution. After all, Jesus is the "faithful witness" (1:5) whose testimony led to his own death. The letters to the churches acknowledge the concern with persecution (2:9–10, 13). Moreover, Revelation 6 assumes a number of martyrs from the past, even as it anticipates even more martyrs "soon to be killed" (6:11).

Chapters 7 and 5 of Revelation are intricately linked. Chapter 7 attributes to the Lamb power, wealth, wisdom, might, honor, glory, and blessing. Chapter 5 invests God and the Lamb with blessing, honor, glory, and might. Both chapter 7 and chapter 5 contain hymns that frame the Lamb's opening of the scrolls.

Revelation 7:9–17, like the rest of Revelation, calls its audience to identify with the faithful witnesses to Christ. To witness, in Revelation, is to risk one's life by testifying faithfully to the ways of God in a hostile world (1:5; 2:13; 12:11; 17:6). Thus Revelation 7:9–17 celebrates those followers of Jesus whose faithfulness endures a hostile cultural context. It invites its audience to identify with the countless multitude of faithful witnesses.

Contemporary preachers must weigh carefully how to interpret Revelation's call to discipleship. The Apocalypse judges its own cultural context in an absolutely hostile way. On the one hand, it anticipates persecution; on the other, it regards involvement in the larger society as defiling (3:4; see 18:4). Most readers of this volume will not so thoroughly distance themselves from their own social context, nor will they anticipate active persecution. Yet we should heed the challenge posed by the countless multitude in Revelation 7. Who will bear faithful testimony to the ways of the Lamb in a society defined by countless Beast-ly practices?

GREG CAREY

Homiletical Perspective

and death has neither rejected nor abandoned the world that continues to reject and abandon him. The subject of suffering will require careful thought that can benefit from the rich imagery of John's vision. The lesson does not provide a theodicy, nor does it lend itself to easy explanations. More importantly, however, it proclaims hope in the living God whose great love, as revealed in the humble obedience of Jesus, draws us to see God's goodness in the face of overwhelmingly contradictory evidence. A sermon on this day will be hard pressed to capture the immense joy that is the fruit of such extravagant love. John's witness provides the preacher with a splendid opportunity for pointing to the Lamb and Shepherd who calls us to be made witnesses, or martyrs, by participating in the power of his goodness: "I am the good shepherd." As John Howard Yoder writes,

> The point that apocalyptic makes is not only that people who wear crowns and who claim to foster justice by the sword are not as strong as they think—true as that is, we will sing: "O where are Kings and Empires now of old that went and came?" It is that people who bear crosses are working with the grain of the universe. One does not come to that belief by reducing social processes to mechanical and statistical models, nor by winning some of one's battles for the control of one's own corner of the fallen world. One comes to it by sharing the life of those who sing about the Resurrection of the slain Lamb.[1]

MICHAEL PASQUARELLO III

1. John Howard Yoder, "Armaments and Eschatology," *Studies in Christian Ethics* 1, no. 1 (1988): 58; cited in Stanley Hauerwas, *With the Grain of the Universe: The Church's Witness and Natural Theology* (Grand Rapids: Brazos Press, 2001), 6.

John 10:22-30

²²At that time the festival of the Dedication took place in Jerusalem. It was winter, ²³and Jesus was walking in the temple, in the portico of Solomon. ²⁴So the Jews gathered around him and said to him, "How long will you keep us in suspense? If you are the Messiah, tell us plainly." ²⁵Jesus answered, "I have told you, and you do not believe. The works that I do in my Father's name testify to me; ²⁶but you do not believe, because you do not belong to my sheep. ²⁷My sheep hear my voice. I know them, and they follow me. ²⁸I give them eternal life, and they will never perish. No one will snatch them out of my hand. ²⁹What my Father has given me is greater than all else, and no one can snatch it out of the Father's hand. ³⁰The Father and I are one."

Theological Perspective

Our story begins by situating the debate that Jesus is having with his religious opponents. They are walking in the portico of Solomon in the temple, at the time of the feast of Dedication—what we know as the celebration of Hanukkah, the feast that recalls God's reclaiming of Jerusalem through the heroic faith of the Maccabees. Celebrated with lighted lamps, the feast is a joyous one for Israel. Ironically, however, the talk around Jesus in this passage is anything but joyous. For John's faithful reader, the ironic contrast between the feast's call for joy and the opponents' attack upon Jesus is deepened because the Logos, Wisdom, and Light of the world is walking in the portico of Solomon, unrecognized by Jesus' critics. What follows in the text is a centerpiece of Johannine theology.

"The Jews," as the author of the Gospel refers to them, want Jesus to say plainly whether he is laying claim to being the Messiah—a loaded political question at any time, but especially so during a celebration that recalled the victorious Maccabean revolt against the Seleucid Empire in 167 BCE. In response Jesus says, "The works that I do in my Father's name testify to me" (v. 25b); his opponents, he says, do not "believe" the testimony of Jesus' works, "because you do not belong to my sheep" (v. 26). Jesus' answer appears cryptic. First, he says

Pastoral Perspective

"If you are the Messiah, tell us plainly" (v. 24). Whether it is politicians deriding their opponents for "fuzzy, Washington math," or preachers denigrating Christians who have a hard time putting their faith into words, we are all familiar with the appeal of "plain-talking leaders." The trouble, of course, is that talking "plainly" about that which is inherently complex, or even beyond our understanding, is misleading to the hearer and demeaning to the subject of the discussion. The trouble with talking plainly about the things of God is that the things of God are anything but plain. When a person begins speaking with unequivocal certainty about God, this is a sure sign that the person is no longer speaking about God. We can speak with unequivocal certainty about things our minds can grasp, but God is not one of those things. God grasps us; we do not grasp God.

Oftentimes our desire for plain talk in the realm of faith is manifest in Bible studies where participants seem bent on finding out "what the Bible means." The operative mind-set in such Bible studies is not that Holy Scripture invites us to experience and participate in rich stories with multiple meanings, but that Holy Scripture contains a coded message that can be cracked, if only one is persistent and has right faith in God. Those who try thusly to discern "the plain meaning of Scripture"

Exegetical Perspective

This passage, like many in John, is filled with theological images that receive fuller treatment elsewhere in the Gospel. In some ways, we have to read the entire Gospel of John in order to read this passage. The question of the messiahship of Jesus, which is the organizing theme of the passage, is also a dominant theme in the Gospel itself. The role of festivals, the imagery of sheep, the promise of eternal life, the issue of election, and the unity of the Father and the Son—all explicit issues of the passage—are also part of larger discussions in the Gospel. In fact, this entire interchange closely parallels that in John 7. Nevertheless, in the midst of this deep intercon-nectedness to the rest of the Gospel, this passage has a special role. It introduces the unity of Jesus and the Father in a new way and, in doing so, anticipates much of the debate that follows in the Gospel.

The setting is the festival of Dedication. This festival commemorated the rededication of the temple by the Maccabeans in 164 BCE, after its desecration by Antiochus IV, when he erected therein an image of Zeus. This feast, best known by its Hebrew term Hanukkah (which means "dedication"), is of course still celebrated in Jewish communities. Beginning in chapter 5, the Gospel of John builds its narrative around a sequence of festivals that Jesus attends in Jerusalem. As readers have long noted, by

Homiletical Perspective

People who like black-and-white answers and who prefer plain meaning to subtlety and allusion may find reading the Gospel of John frustrating. For others, however, the ambiguity and nuance of John's stories will resonate with their struggles to understand exactly who Jesus is and what he means for their lives. John 10:22–30 is a case in point.

I can imagine a sermon that begins by considering the question that the Jews ask Jesus: "How long will you keep us in suspense? If you are the Messiah, tell us plainly" (v. 24b). The Greek suggests two strikingly different ways to understand the tone of the question. The questioners may be open to Jesus, honestly seeking to understand who he is. They are "'in sus-pense'" about Jesus' true identity. Or it may be that the Greek that is translated in the NRSV "How long will you keep us in suspense?'" ought to be rendered "How long will you annoy us, or vex us?"[1] If this is the case, then the questioners are adversaries, troubled by Jesus' failure to give them an unambiguous basis for attacking his claims.

There are arguments in favor of each translation, but none is conclusive. In the two verses preceding this passage, we learn that "the Jews were divided"

1. For a concise but thorough discussion of these two possibilities, see C. K. Barrett, *The Gospel according to St John: An Introduction with Commentary and Notes on the Greek Text* (London: SPCK, 1967), 316.

Theological Perspective

that his "works" constitute public evidence that he bears the mantle of the Messiah. He then invokes a metaphor about sheep to explain why "the Jews" fail to understand and believe that testimony. That is the cryptic part.

Jesus' answer becomes less murky once one recognizes that the imagery of the shepherd is a powerful messianic image in Israel's collective memory. In contrast to the wicked shepherds of Ezekiel 34, John portrays Jesus as the good Shepherd, the authentic bearer of God's caring authority. When Jesus says to his critics, "You do not belong to my sheep," he implies that they are wicked. They cannot see the truth of his testimony because they follow wicked shepherds, wicked leaders.

Jesus says that the sheep of his fold "hear [his] voice" and "follow [him]" (v. 27). It is the unity of hearing *and* doing that binds the sheep of Jesus' fold to him. In that unity, the disciples' relationship to Jesus is similar to Jesus' relationship to the Father. Jesus rewards their faithfulness with "eternal life" (v. 28). As the Maccabean martyrs are immortal—evidenced by the feast of the Dedication of Jerusalem—so the disciples of Jesus' flock will be immortal because of their dedication to Jesus.

In verses 28–30 Jesus makes a remarkable claim that in turn opens onto the climactic statement, "I and the Father are one." After saying his sheep "will never perish," Jesus says, "No one will snatch them out of my hand." This is an amazing image of salvation: being in the protective hands of Christ, hands that would be so horribly wounded at the cross. Jesus then underscores his own dependence on the Father: "My Father, who has given them to me, is greater than all; no one can snatch them out of my Father's hand" (v. 29 NIV). While it is possible to see in these verses an argument for limited atonement—that Jesus "saves" only the elect given to him, and not all of the world—John's theological points are, first, that Jesus and the Father are unified in their common purpose,[1] and, second, that because they are in Jesus' "hand," which is to say within Jesus' power, the disciples will remain faithful to him and continue his work. Jesus' conclusion, "I and the Father are one," is not a metaphysical claim but a claim to unity of purpose.

In her commentary on the Gospel of John in *The New Interpreter's Bible*, Gail O'Day says, "The Greek word 'one' . . . is neuter not masculine, so that Jesus

1. See Jesus' comment in John 5:17, "My Father is still working, and I also am working."

Pastoral Perspective

might discover that there is nothing plain about a God who speaks from a burning bush and is named "I AM WHO I AM." The plain-speaking Baptist preacher Will Campbell once remarked that if Moses had reported this experience to his family and friends, they would likely have said, "It's time for Thorazine."

In this passage from John's Gospel, Jesus says to his demanding inquirers that he has already told them plainly what they need to know. The trouble is that the way Jesus has told them is through his works. In other words, it seems that Jesus' role and identity cannot be reduced to a title; instead, his role and identity must be experienced. This becomes clear in the analogy of the sheep and shepherd. The sheep know and trust the shepherd, not because they have gone through any sort of rational, intellectual discernment, but because they have experienced the shepherd and his "works." In the same way, a child knows and trusts his or her mother because of experience, not reason, and it is not an accident that Jesus elsewhere says, "whoever does not receive the kingdom of God as a little child will never enter it" (Mark 10:15; Luke 18:17).

Surely there will always be a role for Christian apologetics. After all, the first and great commandment is, "You shall love the Lord your God with all your heart, and with all your soul, and with all your mind" (Matt. 22:37; Mark 12:30 and Luke 10:27 add "with all your strength"). Our minds must be engaged in the discernment of faith and the ways of God, but many of us are still trying to exorcise the ghost of Descartes ("I think, therefore I am") by recognizing that we have relied overly much on the intellect as the primary faculty in the Christian life. Some of the bestselling books of our day, written by self-proclaimed atheists, are devoted largely to exposing what the authors perceive as intellectual fallacies in traditional religious teachings. To many of their arguments, faithful Christians who believe that God is beyond all human ideas and concepts can say, "Amen." However, fighting about who believes the right things about God can keep faithful people entangled with words about God, instead of walking in the ways of God. Without denying the importance of the mind in faith, pastors today should perhaps focus on helping Christians return to an authentic experience of God, recognizing that this experience will be beyond our understanding and powers of description. After all, the early church grew dramatically, not because multitudes were convinced of the truth of creeds and dogmas, but because

placing the ministry of Jesus in the festival context, John not only elevates the status of Jesus, but questions the ongoing power of the traditional festivals. The conflict with religious traditions that is created by the arrival of the Messiah is a central theme not only of John but of all the Gospels. If the Messiah has come, then the center of God's activity, God's righteousness, and God's holiness may have shifted from the temple and its work to the Messiah and his work.

Jesus' response to the demand by the Jews at the festival to declare if he is the Messiah seems at first to be clear and unequivocal. Even if the sentence "I have told you" points to an exchange in the past that cannot be identified with certainty, it is nonetheless an affirmation. However, as is typically the case in John, simple affirmations never turn out to be very simple. Jesus adds, "You do not believe," and thereby undoes the force of both the question and the answer. The correct answer to whether Jesus is the Messiah becomes almost beside the point.

Again, as is typically the case in John, the question of Jesus' identity evokes a variety of images and theological strategies. Jesus first points to his work. This is Jesus' most common response to the issue of his identity. Throughout the Gospel of John, Jesus' unity with the Father consists, first, of a unity of words and deeds. Jesus says what the Father is saying and does what the Father is doing. Thus the primary argument in John for the messiahship of Jesus is the character of Jesus' deeds.

However, in the theological logic of the Gospel of John, neither Jesus' words nor his deeds lead to a full recognition of who he is. While belief may emerge in part from the data of Jesus' deeds, data alone does not result in faith. To make this point, Jesus returns to the imagery that opened the chapter. As he noted in verses 3 and 16, sheep recognize the voice of their own shepherd and gatekeeper. Thus the reason people do not have faith in Jesus as Messiah is because he is not their shepherd and they are not his sheep. The Gospel of John does not see faith as simply a human deed. Faith includes the action of God. John's well-known doctrine of election surfaces here. In John, belief in Jesus depends upon being chosen by God to be one of Jesus' flock.

While election seems to exclude certain people, it affords enormous blessings to others. The affirmation in verse 28 of eternal life and security from enemies anticipates Jesus' prayer in chapter 17. In the theology of the Gospel of John, eternal life and security are not simply promises. To be a sheep

(v. 19) about what Jesus had said and done. So it makes sense to understand that their question arises from both perspectives. Some are genuinely seeking to know who Christ is, and some want him to make a claim that will give them unquestionable cause to reject him.

This nuanced reading of the situation makes for a more complex interaction between Jesus and his religious questioners, one that empowers preachers to deal with the varied ways that listeners throughout history have approached the issue of who Jesus is, from friendly inquiry to hostility. Homiletical attention to the different possible inflections of the question might help the congregation acknowledge their own ambiguities about acknowledging Jesus as the Messiah. In a congregation whose ethos suppresses doubts and questions, such a sermon may not be welcome. In many congregations, though, having the pulpit express the divided way that Jesus is received may give listeners the honesty of soul that is a prerequisite for hearing the nuance and complexity of Jesus' response as recounted by John.

Jesus' initial reply does not instantly clear things up. It is not without its own ambiguities. He says, "I have told you, and you do not believe" (v. 25a). In fact, at this point in the Gospel of John, there is only one person to whom Jesus has acknowledged straight out that he is the Messiah: the Samaritan woman at the well (4:26). The Jews who are now questioning him have received more oblique indications: they know about his healing the blind man and his claim to be the good shepherd, but they have not yet heard what they consider to be a conclusive claim that he is the Messiah. Instead, Jesus points them to his actions: "The works that I do in my Father's name testify to me" (10:25b). However, the people who are questioning him are not able to perceive the meaning of those works because they "do not belong" to Christ's sheep (v. 26). This kind of statement can drive modern rationalist listeners to their own hostility toward John, if not toward Jesus. It seems terribly unfair: Christ is doing works that testify to who he is, but some who are asking him about his identity will never understand or believe, simply because they do not belong to his flock. Faithful, gracious preaching needs to take seriously these concerns, because anti-Semitism and sectarian wars among Christians have often fed on such patterns of theological thought.

Without reinforcing engrained distortions and the animosities they breed, there is a major

John 10:22-30

Theological Perspective

is not saying that he and the Father are one person, nor even of one nature or essence. Rather, he is saying that he and God are *united* in the work that they do. It is impossible to distinguish Jesus' work from God's work, because Jesus shares fully in God's work."[2]

O'Day cautions against a metaphysical reading of the statement "I and the Father are one," because that has been the most prevalent way of interpreting this passage over the course of Christian history. O'Day, of course, does not mean to disparage the notion of the Trinity or of the incarnation, but only to point out that the meaning of John's text cannot be reduced to the doctrinal interpretation.

What complicates our own hearing and preaching of this text is the long history of anti-Judaism that is both *in* the text—in John's endless invective against "the Jews"—and *beyond* it in the history of Christian interpretation and practice. The problem here is not simply the diminishment of "the Jews" as the "killers of Christ" but the long history of Christian supersessionism at work in the doctrines of the incarnation and the Trinity.

Reflecting on our salvation in Christ this Sunday, it might be helpful to dwell on the image of being in the "hand" of Jesus. Just as Easter is proof for Christians that Jesus is ultimately in the hands of God, not in the hands of the emperor or in the hands of death, so in our celebration we claim that we are in Jesus' hands, not in the hands of other powers. What might it mean for us to live out of that confidence and trust, and so become the hands of Christ in the world? Whom are we willing to hold on to, as we are in the hands of Christ? Whom are we to hold?

JOSEPH A. BESSLER

Pastoral Perspective

multitudes experienced the living Lord and a new life that was foolishness to the wise (1 Cor. 1:27). Perhaps in our day we have been too stuck in our heads.

The Jesuit priest Anthony DeMello told a parable he entitled "The Explorer," which illustrates our predicament. In it, a person leaves his home village to explore the faraway and exotic Amazon. When he returns to his village, the villagers are captivated as the explorer tries to describe his many experiences, along with the incredible beauty of the place, with its thundering waterfalls, beautiful foliage, and extraordinary wildlife. How can he put into words, though, the feelings that flooded his heart when he heard the night sounds of the forest or sensed the dangers of the rapids? So he tells them they simply must go to the Amazon themselves. To help them with their journey, the explorer draws a map. Immediately the villagers pounce on the map. They copy the map, so that everyone can have his or her own copy. They frame the map for their town hall and their homes. Regularly they study the map and discuss it often, until the villagers consider themselves experts on the Amazon—for do they not know the location of every waterfall and rapids, every turn and bend?

People will often press their pastors and fellow Christians to "tell us plainly" about the things of God, and the ability to speak eloquently of one's faith and journey is a wonderful gift. The most important task, however, might be to encourage and support others in making their own personal journeys and experiencing the living Lord themselves. For, as DeMello suggests in his parable, there can be a certain futility about drawing maps—however plain and explicit they might be—for armchair explorers.

GARY D. JONES

---

2. Gail R. O'Day, "The Gospel of John," in *Luke, John*, vol. 9, *The New Interpreter's Bible*, ed. Leander Keck et al. (Nashville: Abingdon Press, 1995), 667.

Exegetical Perspective

in Jesus' flock is to have eternal life already and to be eternally safe already. The syntax of verse 28 betrays this collapsing of the future and the present. Jesus gives (present tense) eternal life now. This affirmation leads in verse 29 to the rather puzzling affirmation that "what the Father has given me is greater than all." There are actually five reasonable versions of this sentence in the ancient texts. In fact, the somewhat less puzzling version of the sentence, the "Father, who has given them to me, is greater than all" (NIV), has the most support. One version affirms the value of the sheep; the other affirms the superiority of God.

All of this culminates in the famous claim "The Father and I are one" (v. 30). It is significant that in the Greek the adjective "one" is in the neuter form, not the masculine. Thus, in spite of the theological tendency to read this affirmation as declaring that the Father and the Son are one person, the Greek does not really permit this. This does not mean that traditional Trinitarian notions of one person are incorrect or without support; it simply means that this particular text does not say this. As noted above, the unity affirmed in this passage is a unity of deeds. Jesus does the works of the Father.

The affirmation of oneness between Jesus and the Father is perhaps the core theological claim of the Gospel of John. This oneness determines the character of both the Father and the Son. To see the deeds of the Son and to hear his words is to see and hear God the Father. The story of Jesus reveals the character of God. This oneness also reveals the character of those who belong to Jesus. For instance, as the passage notes, this oneness means that the sheep of Jesus cannot be snatched away.

LEWIS R. DONELSON

Homiletical Perspective

theological principle that nurtures a more sympathetic reading of John. The evangelist is eager to preserve the elemental belief that God is the one who initiates a relationship to us. God seeks us out long before we seek God. Christ makes us his sheep; we do not make him our shepherd. The initiative and sovereignty of God, though transfigured into Christian terms by the gospel, has ancient roots in the Hebrew Scriptures, particularly the great pastoral passages in the Psalms: "The Lord is my shepherd. . . . He makes me lie down in green pastures; he leads me beside still waters" (Ps. 23:1–2), and "Know that the Lord is God. It is he that made us, and we are his; we are his people, and the sheep of his pasture" (Ps. 100:3).

In a real sense John is affirming the divine initiative and sovereignty that are characteristic of the very tradition that Jews love and honor, including the Jews who are questioning Jesus! For John, this ancient pattern finds its most perfect expression in the incarnation and ministry of Christ. Tragically, that Christian commitment and the first-century conflicts that it occasioned have clouded the relations between those who accepted Jesus as the Messiah and those who did not.

To read John and to find ourselves addressed and transformed by the word of God does not require that we continue the conflicts that were part of his community's milieu. Instead, we can ask in our sermon for the grace we need in order not to replicate the animosities of the past. We can profess anew what both Jews and Christians affirm: the initiative and sovereignty of God. We can unambiguously affirm our gratitude for the eternal life Christ gives us, for the enduring assurance that no matter what the future holds, God's hand is holding us and nothing can snatch us away (vv. 28–29).

THOMAS H. TROEGER

Acts 11:1-18

¹Now the apostles and the believers who were in Judea heard that the Gentiles had also accepted the word of God. ²So when Peter went up to Jerusalem, the circumcised believers criticized him, ³saying, "Why did you go to uncircumcised men and eat with them?" ⁴Then Peter began to explain it to them, step by step, saying, ⁵"I was in the city of Joppa praying, and in a trance I saw a vision. There was something like a large sheet coming down from heaven, being lowered by its four corners; and it came close to me. ⁶As I looked at it closely I saw four-footed animals, beasts of prey, reptiles, and birds of the air. ⁷I also heard a voice saying to me, 'Get up, Peter; kill and eat.' ⁸But I replied, 'By no means, Lord; for nothing profane or unclean has ever entered my mouth.' ⁹But a second time the voice answered from heaven, 'What God has made clean, you must not call profane.' ¹⁰This happened three times; then everything was pulled up again to heaven. ¹¹At that very moment three men, sent to me

Theological Perspective

In this passage Peter seeks to justify to the "circumcision party" in Jerusalem his having eaten with (an unspoken implication of his having accepted their hospitality) the Roman centurion Cornelius and his family in Caesarea (Acts 10:24–29). That Cornelius and others received the Spirit and were baptized in the name of Jesus Christ, inaugurating a mission to the Gentile world, seems at first to have been lost on these headquarters conservatives. They first focus on Peter's apparent violation of Jewish dietary laws (see Lev. 1–11). True, Peter describes his vision of the great sheet filled with clean and unclean animals and the command to kill and eat, but for him the point is that God has given Cornelius and his companions the same gift of the Spirit received by the apostles when they first believed (Acts 11:17). This is a pivotal realization, on which the rest of the book of Acts turns.

That such a revelation came first to Peter rather than to Saul, soon to be Paul, helps explain subsequent events. Had the recent convert (Acts 9) originated the Gentile mission he subsequently pursued so effectively, he would likely have been long, if ever, in gaining acceptance from the Jerusalem church. The result might well have been schism rather than assimilation. However, for Peter, of all people, to have concluded that God intended the inclusion of the Gentiles—and for him to have defended this

Pastoral Perspective

Several years ago, I went to Israel on an interfaith journey with members of a Jewish congregation, an African American congregation, and the congregation I serve. We went to experience together the places that were important in our sacred stories, and it was an incredible trip for all of us. This is not "A Pastor's Travelogue on His Trip to the Holy Land." I mention the trip because Joppa was our first stop after landing in Tel Aviv. My traveling companion, Rabbi John Friedman, said he knew that I wanted to see the house of Simon the tanner where Peter had his vision. Jews know many Christian stories, and my friend knew this one was crucial to the development of the early church.

The visit to Simon's house was a great place to start our journey. Our trip was in the summer of 2001, shortly before the events of September 11. In the years since then, I have come to realize how Peter's story has taken on even more significance since 9/11.

The text from Acts begins with Peter reporting to the church leaders in Jerusalem. It sounds as if he was being called on the carpet for breaking the rules. He had been eating with "the uncircumcised." A similar change had been leveled against Jesus for eating with sinners (Luke 15:2). So Peter was in good company, but that did not make his confrontation with the Jerusalem leaders easy.

from Caesarea, arrived at the house where we were. [12]The Spirit told me to go with them and not to make a distinction between them and us. These six brothers also accompanied me, and we entered the man's house. [13]He told us how he had seen the angel standing in his house and saying, 'Send to Joppa and bring Simon, who is called Peter; [14]he will give you a message by which you and your entire household will be saved.' [15]And as I began to speak, the Holy Spirit fell upon them just as it had upon us at the beginning. [16]And I remembered the word of the Lord, how he had said, 'John baptized with water, but you will be baptized with the Holy Spirit.' [17]If then God gave them the same gift that he gave us when we believed in the Lord Jesus Christ, who was I that I could hinder God?" [18]When they heard this, they were silenced. And they praised God, saying, "Then God has given even to the Gentiles the repentance that leads to life."

Exegetical Perspective

Readers of biblical narratives must be on the lookout for repeated words and events. Repetition cues theological importance. In Acts, the story's signal events are repeated three times—scholars call these "Lukan triads." Changes made within each successive narration add layers of meaning to that particular episode that clarify its theological importance. The story of Cornelius's conversion forms one such Lukan triad.

In Luke's second telling of this story in Acts 11, Peter is compelled to provide testimony to a council of church leaders in Jerusalem (vv. 1–3). Evidently, some believers are upset by reports that uncircumcised "Gentiles had also accepted the word of God" (v. 1; cf. 8:14). Ironically, their criticism of Peter echoes his own hesitancy to obey the visionary directive to eat nonkosher foods (10:13–16) and his subsequent anxiety in visiting a nonkosher household (cf. 10:28). Peter's rehearsal of Cornelius's conversion (11:4–14) does not seek to defend his own actions but the actions of God, who has saved a nonkosher Roman Gentile from sin (vv. 15–18).

The irony of the present story is nicely captured by Luke's clever repetition of *diakrinō*, used first in reference to the Spirit's injunction for Peter to hear out Cornelius's emissaries and accompany them "without hesitation" (10:20), and now here of Peter's

Homiletical Perspective

This story was so important to the early church that it is told in chapter 10 and retold in chapter 11 as Peter testified in Jerusalem before a feisty group of critics. No issue was more debated by early Christians or more important to them than whether their newfound faith was intended only for Jews or whether it was to include Gentiles while allowing them to remain Gentiles. The circumcised believers were critical of Peter, asking, "Why did you go to uncircumcised men and eat with them?" (11:3). What most disturbed the circumcised believers was table fellowship with Gentiles—entering their homes, breaking bread at their tables.

We learn from the early church that believers were not reluctant to voice their differences. Peter entered the Jerusalem church and squarely faced his critics. Too often, we try to be nice at church. We try not to be confrontational. We try to sidestep controversy. We closet our differences. We paint smiles on our church faces, even as we realize irreconcilable issues. This text reminds us that controversy needs to be voiced, not avoided, and conflict needs to be transformed, not ignored.

We really have no need in chapter 11 to repeat, almost word for word, a story we have been told in the preceding chapter. We already know about Peter's vision. We know about the large sheet coming down

Acts 11:1-18

Theological Perspective

proposition with so full a recital of his understanding of the gospel—gave this step a chance with the Jerusalem conservatives. Besides, Peter could truthfully say that he did not take the initiative in any of this. The vision *came* to him. He was called by *others* to come, heal, preach, and baptize. God was speaking *through* him. Who was he to resist God (11:17)?

It is significant, nonetheless, that the near-term struggle turned on the issue of clean and unclean meats. One would expect both Peter and his opponents to have focused on the notion of legitimate Israelite descent. After all, in his sermon at the Beautiful Gate (Acts 3), Peter stressed the power of the "the God of Abraham, the God of Isaac, and the God of Jacob, the God of our ancestors" (v. 13). Cornelius and his friends and family had no claim to *this* sacred history. Apparently it was *easier*, if still not simple, for Jews of the time to overlook issues of Israelite genealogy than to overcome their sense of revulsion at persons who ate the flesh of "unclean" animals.

To grasp what is involved here, there can be no better example than the revulsion felt by many (but of course far from all) Christians across the globe today at same-sex relationships and practices. Nothing could seem, from their point of view, more "unclean." Revulsion, either in the ancient world or now, does not respond to theological argument. A change of heart comes when one sees the Spirit at work in the stories of strangers, recognizing in them the same Spirit that is working in one's own life. People need first to see God at God's surprising work. Theological reflection comes afterward, either to bring what has been *seen* into coherence with past thinking, or to make a reasoned break with that thinking. In the ancient world, one would search the Scriptures in order to find a place in them for the new insight. Then one would seek principles for integrating the new vision in practice, a task undertaken at the "Council of Jerusalem" described in Acts 15.

An important lesson to be learned from this episode and its consequences is that, while conversion changes the convert, the convert also brings a new perspective to the message. Bringing people of a new culture into the faith community calls for restatement of the gospel in terms that speak to that new culture, and so it has been throughout church history. It is extremely significant that an authorization of such cultural restatement lies here, within the NT narrative, preparing the way for Paul's letters and establishing the principle canonically. Such restatements continue as Christian faith becomes integrated into the Roman Empire of the west and

Pastoral Perspective

Have you ever been to a church meeting when you could feel the tension in the air? Such meetings often center around who is "in" and who is "out." In the present case, the tension was between those drawing a narrow circle of inclusion around the gospel and others who were busy expanding the circle until all God's children had a place at the table.

Would the Gentiles have a place? That was the question hanging in the balance along with the integrity and expansion of the early church. Fortunately, God had a witness. Peter was the pivotal figure, the rock, whose confession changed the dynamics of Jesus' relationship with his followers and opened the door to discipleship. Remember the promise that the risen Lord made to his disciples, that they would receive the power of the Holy Spirit (Acts 1:8)? The fulfillment of this promise is nowhere more evident than in the boldness of Peter's testimony in Jerusalem. God empowered Peter, an ordinary fisherman, to play a significant role in the mission of the church.

God enables ordinary people to be witnesses to the gospel. This can be frightening, because it voids our excuses that we are not gifted enough, not old enough, not good enough to get the job done. God has always had the audacity to choose ordinary people to do extraordinary things in the service of God's reign. Such a realization should give us hope and strengthen our resolve to join the cloud of witnesses from Abraham, Sarah, and Moses to Esther and Jeremiah, Peter and Paul.

Peter gave testimony to the church leaders about a vision he received while praying on the roof. He saw a sheet being lowered from heaven with a variety of creatures on it. He was told to "kill and eat." Peter refused because the food was "profane" and "unclean." Then he heard the crucial line, "What God has made clean, you must not call profane" (10:15). This cycle repeated three times, and then everything was taken up into heaven.

This vision was followed by the arrival of three men from Caesarea who appeared at the door. Peter was instructed by the Spirit to go with them and not distinguish between "them and us" (11:12). When he arrived at Cornelius's house and preached, the Spirit led the Gentiles present to salvation. Peter concluded that God had given them the same gift God had given to Jewish believers. Then he asked the profound question, "Who was I that I could hinder God?" (v. 17).

Think about the astonishing insight contained in that question. If God so loved the world that Jesus came not to condemn the whole world but to save it,

opponents in Jerusalem who "criticize" (11:2) him for doing so: if the anxiety of traditional Jews is that they will become as Gentiles by sharing table fellowship with them, then the salve of their concern is to enjoin any Gentile to become as Jews by circumcision and purification. The reader of Acts must take their anxiety seriously, since it reflects a firm commitment to maintain the community's hallmark "one heart and soul." Now, however, the internal conflict does not arise over sharing goods (5:1–11; 6:1–7), but whether to share the Holy Spirit with uncircumcised Gentiles.

Peter's response to his opponents is characterized by Luke as an "explanation" (*ektithemai*, v. 4). Such speeches set forth in chronological order a straightforward report of a contested event in order to set the record straight. Peter does so in the first person as the principal witness and so a trusted interpreter of this event.

Peter's speech makes two substantial additions to the initial narration of the episode in Acts 10. The first is his reference to "these six brothers [who] accompanied me [when] we entered the man's house" (v. 12; cf. 10:45–48). Even though it remains unclear from the earlier account whether they had agreed with Peter's actions, he now skillfully transforms the six into multiple witnesses who can confirm his report as trustworthy. The second and more important change comes with Peter's retelling of Cornelius's report of an angelic visitation (11:13–14; cf. 10:30–32). Only now does Peter disclose heaven's confirmation that his house call would become the means "by which you and your entire household will be saved" (11:14).

Such visionary episodes function as a literary trope in Acts for disclosing new directions in God's redemptive plan. The church's prior belief that Gentiles must be purified—by circumcision and Torah observance—to be initiated into the covenant-keeping community is now rewritten by divine revelation to include uncircumcised Gentiles. God's plan is disclosed to Peter neither by kerygma nor by Scripture but by religious experience. His prior claim of divine impartiality (10:34) is learned by a series of timely revelations, climaxed by his observation that "God gave them the same *gift* that he gave us when we believed in the Lord Jesus Christ" (11:17; cf. 11:15b). Even though a nonproselyte Gentile, Cornelius evidently received blessings promised by God to Israel, including "the gift of the Spirit."

The Jewish response to Peter's report and stunning conclusion is silence (v. 18a): the initial

from heaven. We know about the four-footed reptiles, beasts, and birds of prey, all forbidden as food for faithful Jews. We already have heard the voice from heaven saying, "What God has made clean, you must not call profane" (10:15b; 10:28b).

What changes in chapter 11 is the confrontation with "the apostles and the believers" in Jerusalem. Peter has been called before them, has heard their criticism, and now responds to it. His response is not argumentative or tightly reasoned. Rather, his response is to tell a story, a story that we have already heard but that is repeated in detail. Now we know that the Jerusalem leaders have heard everything that happened to Peter. It is the story, not argumentation, which changes their hearts. The text says, "they were silenced" by Peter's story (v. 18). Actually, only their criticisms were silenced. For the next verse states, "And they praised God" as they recognized the authenticity of the repentance of the Gentiles.

Stories, not arguments, change lives. We are told this story again so that we know exactly what changed the minds and hearts of the Jerusalem leaders. Had Peter come to argue theological points with them or debate doctrinal differences, he might not have been able to change their hearts. Generally, arguments tend only to crystallize differences. Debates tend to keep two sides apart. In debates and arguments, there are winners and losers. Peter could have charged angrily into the Jerusalem court and argued, "Is it fair that we keep the gospel to ourselves? Does not God also love Gentiles? Cannot Gentiles approach God directly without first becoming like us?" One can imagine such an argument going on for days.

However, a story changes hearts and lives, because stories are powerful. A story invites people across the separating chasm, making everyone the winner. Jesus knew this as he changed so many hardened hearts with parables. His parables often left people with questions for them to explore, rather than theological issues for them to debate.

Jesus' parables were powerful to his first-century agrarian audiences, for they were about vineyards, seeds, robbers, barns, and lilies of the field. They were stories that held powerful sway with his hearers. While modern hearers of Jesus' parables live in a different world, the same realities of jealousy, greed, and forgiveness are also at play in our lives. The stories we tell also have to be believable. They have to be stories that could as well be told of us.

Peter's story was told in such a way that it could have happened to any of the apostles. He was not

Acts 11:1-18

Theological Perspective

into the Byzantine civilization of the east. They go on in relation to Aristotelian thought in the Middle Ages, and again as the Reformation marks the indigenization of the faith into northern Europe. We have for decades celebrated the further indigenization of faith in multiple ethnic and cultural groups. Now we witness a massive reindigenization of faith taking place across the global South. What happens when we realize that almost all of this has been the work of representatives of only half the human race? Fully integrating the voices of women is once again revolutionizing our understanding of the gospel.

Just how far can this indigenization go before the original faith becomes unrecognizable? Peter and Paul, were they on earth today, might already find it so. Or are there forms of expression—the Scriptures and creeds, for example—that cannot be altered in the indigenization process? Both Scriptures and creeds, as we know them, are products of indigenization as well. Perhaps the gospel itself, as we understand it, can be seen as an indigenization of the mind of God into the narrow confines of human understanding. Indigenization and incarnation become one—"accommodation" to our human limits, Calvin called it.

Yet in every age we see human resistance to each new thing, including the gospel that "everything has become new" (2 Cor. 5:17). Is there anything in the faith that does not change? If Peter's preaching is the criterion, then the changeless elements are speaking the name of Jesus, bearing witness to his resurrection, and acknowledging the transforming power of the Holy Spirit. We may add to this the foundational principle recorded in Acts 11, where notions of clean and unclean as ways of separating people from one another are ruled antithetical to Christian faith forever, invalidating any attempt on our part to reinstate them, in any form, ever again.

LEWIS S. MUDGE

Pastoral Perspective

who are we to try to limit the mission of God to redeem humanity? Every time we exclude someone from full participation in the redemptive efforts of God, Peter's question should trouble us and the church. What if the church had closed the door to the Gentiles, and Christianity had remained a sect within Judaism? Peter was persuaded that God the creator did not intend to exclude anyone from the community of God's care. His conclusion was revolutionary.

Those in the faith community often use the word "discernment." Peter discerned the connection between his vision and the three visitors who asked him to travel to Caesarea with them. Luke makes it clear that the gift of discernment is the work of God's Spirit. If there is hope for the church in these days when there is so much dissension and division in faith communities, then we must pray to have visions that bring us together to receive the gift of discernment. We need to be open to the work of God's healing and reconciling Spirit.

More amazing than Peter's vision and discernment was how the leaders in Jerusalem responded. They listened and were open to the new reality Peter envisioned. They could have said, "You are out of your mind, and this is wrong!" Instead, the Holy Spirit gave them the ability to listen and to change.

As we go about our business in the church, the world is watching. Do we have anything to offer that differs from other groups characterized by dissension and division? Can we listen to each other and seek to discover where God's Spirit is leading? Can we broaden the table so everyone has a place?

JOSEPH S. HARVARD

objection (v. 3) is considered an irrelevancy by the apostle, who has skillfully turned the occasion into a theological platform to sound a programmatic note about Israel's mission to pagan nations. However, the full importance of their judgment that "God has granted even the Gentiles repentance unto life" (v. 18b NIV) is gleaned from two texts found earlier in Acts. The initial pairing in Acts of "repentance" with the reception of both "forgiveness of sins" and "the gift of the Spirit" famously frames Peter's altar call on the day of Pentecost (2:38). If that earlier text glosses this one, the implied verdict is that the requirements and results of Gentile and Jewish repentance are the same, because their experience of the Spirit is the same: God has "*granted* even the Gentiles *repentance* unto life." The full implication of this verdict comes later in Acts when they reconvene following Paul's first mission (Acts 13–14) to consider the question of table fellowship within the mixed congregations his mission has formed beyond Palestine. Peter will tell the story of Cornelius yet again, this time to commend "purity of the heart" as the only condition of Christian fellowship (Acts 15:6–11).

The second alluded text is Acts 5:30–32, where Peter famously addresses the Sanhedrin with the affirmation that "we must obey God rather than any human authority" (5:29). Peter goes on to explain that his obedience is predicated on "the *God* of our ancestors [who] raised up Jesus" (5:30) in order to "*give repentance* to Israel and forgiveness of sins" (5:31) . . . and give the Holy Spirit "to those who obey God" (5:32). That is, God's plan to restore repentant Israel is signaled by its reception of the Holy Spirit. Behind this present verdict, then, lies the critical recognition that Cornelius's repentance and Spirit baptism are not at odds with Israel's God but actually *agree* with God's way of mapping the history of salvation. In fact, Cornelius's conversion is but a promissory note that still must be cashed in the subsequent narrative, when Paul's destiny prophesied by Jesus (9:15–16) is realized.

ROBERT W. WALL

seeking to break the rules. He was not trying to go outside accepted norms. He was not trying to cause a disturbance or a ruckus. God intervened in his life, speaking to him in a vision and a voice, calling Peter to overcome his stereotypes and distinctions and see his mission in more universal terms. Peter's message was, "This is my story, but it could as easily have been your story. This could have happened to you. What would you have done, if God had appeared and spoken to you in this way? Would you, could you, have acted differently?"

It is hard to argue or split theological hairs with a compelling story. Preachers are called to be compelling storytellers, and so are Christians today. It is not only the old, old story but also the story of how God has acted in our lives, speaking to us in that still small voice, forcing us to overcome our stereotypes and to see our mission in more universal terms. Stories change lives, then and now.

As followers of the rabbi from Nazareth whose primary teaching was through parables, we sometimes forget the power of stories today. We rarely tell our children the stories of how we have experienced God. We rarely tell our young people stories of how God changed our minds, redirected our paths, and opened new horizons for us. We do not tell the stories because we do not want to appear manipulative or better-than-thou or self-righteous, or to speak of holy places and times for which words are not always adequate. We do not want to appear weird or fanatical. So we keep our stories to ourselves, telling them only in the most careful contexts and in the most measured ways.

This is not the message of Acts 11. Many Christians shy from evangelism, fearing the "hard sell." If we would only learn to be storytellers and tell compelling stories in our preaching, we could leave the rest up to the Spirit who takes up where stories end.

STEPHEN D. JONES

Psalm 148

¹Praise the LORD!
  Praise the LORD from the heavens;
    praise him in the heights!
²Praise him, all his angels;
    praise him, all his host!

³Praise him, sun and moon;
    praise him, all you shining stars!
⁴Praise him, you highest heavens,
    and you waters above the heavens!

⁵Let them praise the name of the LORD
    for he commanded and they were created.
⁶He established them forever and ever;
    he fixed their bounds, which cannot be passed.

⁷Praise the LORD from the earth,
    you sea monsters and all deeps,

Theological Perspective

"My mouth will speak the praise of the LORD, and all flesh will bless his holy name forever and ever" (Ps. 145:21). Ending with that promise, Psalm 145 serves as an overture to the symphony of praise with which the Psalter concludes (Pss. 146–50). Psalm 148, featuring the universe in chorus, is the symphony's central movement and makes a wonderful Eastertide cantata.

Praise is central to biblical faith. What does it mean to praise God? What happens when we heed the psalmist's exhortation to "praise the Lord"? First, we direct our praise exclusively to God. The Lord God Almighty alone is both subject and object of praise. When we praise God, we fulfill the purpose for which, according to the Westminster Shorter Catechism, we are created; namely, "to glorify God and to enjoy God forever." When we lift our voices in praise to God, the name we utter identifies the One whose reality is the deepest truth about the universe and about every life.

Praise testifies to the initiative of God in creation and redemption. Praise confesses God as the source of all life, as the one whose purpose and presence order and sustain creation in accord with the divine intention, and as the one whose faithful providence issues in acts of blessing and salvation for his people, and through them for all the families of the earth. This one alone, YHWH, is Creator and Sustainer,

Pastoral Perspective

All created things, that is, *all* things, are called out to praise God by Psalm 148. Humans are put into perspective; we are one small part of all that God has created. So we too are challenged to praise through our collective being as humans. Furthermore, those who speak Psalm 148 are blessed by God in the unfolding of history. In history, peoples and individuals are particular, unique. Hence, we are challenged to praise through our particularity as well as through community.

Living into a life of praising God is complicated by normal features of consumer cultures; in advertising rhetoric, words of praise are easy and quickly become empty, even to the one speaking them. In such cultural contexts, engaging in praise requires careful attention and intention. A reflective pastor can identify at least five actions that contribute to attention and intention as people of faith turn to praise God.

1. Praise requires *noticing* both what has occurred in the past and what is going on in the present. Psalm 148 demonstrates the wide breadth of such noticing: in spiritual realms beyond our direct access, in the wide universe of sun and moon and stars, in the almost invisible depths of the oceans, among monstrous things that threaten us, in the uncontrollable weather, in wild places and among

^{8}fire and hail, snow and frost,
　　stormy wind fulfilling his command!

^{9}Mountains and all hills,
　　fruit trees and all cedars!
^{10}Wild animals and all cattle,
　　creeping things and flying birds!

^{11}Kings of the earth and all peoples,
　　princes and all rulers of the earth!
^{12}Young men and women alike,
　　old and young together!

^{13}Let them praise the name of the Lord,
　　for his name alone is exalted;
　　his glory is above earth and heaven.
^{14}He has raised up a horn for his people,
　　praise for all his faithful,
　　for the people of Israel who are close to him.
　Praise the Lord!

Exegetical Perspective

The final five psalms of the Psalter share a striking feature. All of them begin and end with the same refrain, "Praise the Lord!" (*halelû yah*). (Psalms 106, 113, and 135 share this same pattern.) There can be little doubt that those who created the Psalter wanted to conclude this collection of songs by emphasizing praise of God. Further, the Masoretic Text prints these lines as if they did not belong to the poetic structure of the psalms that they surround. The refrains appear as brackets that surround the psalm and, in so doing, create a frame of praise. One might therefore say that the Psalter, which itself is divided into five books, concludes with a little Pentateuch of praise: five psalms that are enclosed by imperative verbs calling the community to praise God.

Despite this common refrain of praise, each of these five psalms bears distinctive features. Psalms 146–49 offer various reasons to justify this call to praise. Psalm 150, in contrast, simply reiterates, in various ways, the call to praise. In Psalms 146–49, the justification for praise is utterly diverse. YHWH should be praised because "he upholds the orphan and the widow" (146:9), "he hurls down hail like crumbs" (147:17), "his glory is above earth and heaven" (148:13), "the Lord takes pleasure in his people" (149:4). It is appropriate to praise God because of what God is, because of God's creative

Homiletical Perspective

A wondrously repetitive psalm of praise, Psalm 148 echoes much of what came before it in the Psalter. It too is echoed later in the tradition, most notably in the apocryphal addition to the Greek version of Daniel known as the Song of the Three Jews, found in the *Book of Common Prayer* as Canticles 1 and 12, "Song of Creation." Other than saying "Amen!" to the call of the psalm to praise the Lord, what are the homiletically significant dimensions of the text? I think there are at least four, each of which could produce an effective homily, depending on how preacher and listeners are likely to hear the psalm.

1. One focus is on the impact praise has on the one offering it, because the act of praise presents a wonderful gift to the one doing the praising. It takes the focus off ourselves. Whether we consider our culture to be uniquely narcissistic, or just typically so, the fact is that we spend a good bit of time wrapped up in our own little worlds. Even when coming to church and listening to the wonderful sermons we preach, our listeners are conditioned to ask, "What is in this for me?" Common as it is, that is not really an especially helpful question to guide one through life. The act of praise—and it is important to be reminded that "praise" is an action, not an idea—inherently thwarts this vicious cycle and says, "Hey, it's not always about you!"

Psalm 148

Theological Perspective

Lord and Savior. Biblical praise is offered only to this one who is self-named: YHWH (Adonai, Lord).

Praise proclaims the universal sovereignty of God. In calling heaven and earth, stars and angels, fauna and flora, people and princes to take up the song of praise to YHWH, there is a clear evangelistic note. Here is evangelism in the true sense: not the manipulative use of threats and fear to secure a conversion, but a joyful invitation to join the chorus of praise to the Creator and Redeemer.

There are two particular issues at stake here in this all-inclusive invitation to praise YHWH as Lord and King. On the one hand, the Psalter's way of dealing with the gods of the nations is a lesson in early apologetics. While "other gods" are denied a place of equality with YHWH or even a lower place in a pantheon, the realities and powers of which they are personifications are acknowledged, in their noble, righteous expressions, to be blessings of YHWH. The Bible's prohibition against idolatry is unwavering, but the hopes and fears, the longings and loves that dwell deep in the human spirit are incorporated into YHWH's sovereignty of steadfast love. Note, for example, in Psalms 82; 86:8, 10; 89:6; 95:3, how other gods are denied divinity but not existence.

On the other hand, in this invitation to universal praise the people of God are reminded that YHWH's sovereignty is not limited to the life of the covenant community. Rather, YHWH's freedom for all humanity requires freedom from any limiting or confining particularities. The good news is that the particulars of God's sovereign grace and steadfast love are all-inclusive.

All of these characteristics of praise are represented in Psalm 148. The psalm envisions all creation and all creatures joining in chorus. Praise sounds from the heavens and beyond (vv. 1–6) and from the ends of the earth (vv. 7–14). No one is left out. In a thrilling testimony to the comprehensiveness of biblical faith and the unlimited nature of God's salvation, the psalmist pictures creation and humanity reconciled to God and to each other. William P. Brown points out how the traditional enemies who show up in the Psalter—foreign rulers, feral animals, "the wicked"—are at peace in the psalm's depiction of salvation as redemption and reconciliation rather than as a victorious conquest.[1] The doctrine of the atonement is too rich and comprehensive to be limited to one expression, but

1. William P. Brown, *Seeing the Psalms: A Theology of Metaphor* (Louisville, KY: Westminster John Knox Press, 2002), 162–66.

Pastoral Perspective

wild creatures large and small, among humans who lead and young persons expected to follow. In all these places and among all these beings, God has been active! Those who are called upon to praise are always noticing, always asking themselves, "What is God already doing here in this place, in this moment?"

Christians name the divine activity as creative, redemptive, and sustaining. Psalm 148 directs our attention primarily to God's creative activity, but calls us to praise all that we can see when we look carefully around us. It is often easier for our people to identify the redemptive and sustaining activities of God in their own individual experiences. The psalm invites testimony to the multiple transformations God works in the course of our journeys—normal development as we grow, as well as healing of old wounds, of harmful patterns of behavior, of injuries, and of illness. Redemption leads on into all these features of sanctification. It is helpful for there to be occasion for public naming of what God has done for us and with us. Not all of these occasions must be in the context of a community's worship, but any occasion where God is praised will become a moment of worshipfulness. Testimony is one public practice of noticing.

2. Praise becomes empty words when noticing does not move into *gratitude* for what we see. We resist gratitude in those moments in which we are unwilling to acknowledge our dependence on God. More commonly, we resist gratitude when we are unwilling to acknowledge our interdependence with the rest of the creation in which God has placed us. Hence, in a culture that celebrates independence, it is not surprising to find ourselves avoiding gratitude. Acknowledging our interdependence reminds us of the fragility of our lives. Psychologically and spiritually, we resist knowing our vulnerabilities. It is easier for us not to notice what God is doing than to trust that God's activity in the interconnected web of life will sustain us. Gratitude brings our noticing into the spiritual realm of trust, deepening our relationship with God by acknowledging our dependence on God and on the rest of creation.

3. Through its attention to the particularity of portions of creation, Psalm 148 implies that our practices of praise should *use our particularity*. Individuals praise through the intentional cultivation of the unique combination of gifts and opportunities we have been given by our Creator. If all the features of creation are called to praise, we and our people are invited to ask ourselves how all

activity, and because of what God has done on behalf of God's people. Psalm 148, though referring briefly to God's people in verse 14, focuses on the world of creation and people beyond Israel's borders.

Psalm 148 commences in an unusual fashion. When hearing the refrain, "Praise the LORD!" one normally expects that the community or individual psalmist is being commanded to offer such praise. Not so in Psalm 148:1–2. The human audience will overhear praise being offered to God in the heavens. Praise will be offered both "in" and "from" the heavens. One might imagine the divine council (cf. Job 1–2; Isa. 6) functioning as a choir. Or one could think about a great cathedral in which the choir is singing from a balcony far above the worshipers. Such praise is awesome, beyond the capacity of typical mortals.

That same theme is struck in verses 3–6. The imagery is still of praise from the heights, but now those heavenly heights are associated with personified celestial objects. The sun, moon, and stars are all commanded to praise God. One biblical tradition clearly lies behind these verses—that of creation as attested in Genesis 1. That text, which depicts a heavenly ocean above the "dome" (Gen. 1:6–7), helps readers understand the mandate for the "waters above the heavens" to praise God. The allusion to creation becomes explicit in verses 5–6. The notion of God setting limits on the astral objects is noteworthy, especially since the sun, moon, and stars were worshiped in other ancient Near Eastern societies. For Israel, those potential sources of veneration stand under YHWH's clear control.

Praise of God could involve praising "the name of the LORD." One might translate this phrase, "Let them praise the name YHWH." The very name of God could be the object of praise. (See Ps. 113:1–3 for marked attention to the divine name. The name of God could be associated with the temple, see, e.g., Deut 12:11; Isa. 18:7.)

Verses 7–10 move down to the earth. A remarkable choir will praise God. Choristers include sea monsters, snow, mountains, fruit trees, insects, birds, and animals. All elements of the earth, including objects that one normally thinks of as inanimate, such as mountains (cf. Hab. 3:10 for mountains seeing and writhing), are to praise YHWH. These verses emphasize, by citing such diverse components of the earth, that everything that humans encounter—the contours of the earth itself, water, weather, and all life, whether animal or plant—is to be in a posture of praise. Here again,

2. The act of praise puts the focus where it belongs, on God. How do we keep the focus where it belongs? In my Anglican tradition it was long noted and bemoaned that worship was cold, distant, and, frankly, boring. The liturgical renewals of the last century seriously addressed these concerns, pushing the altar forward and turning the celebrant around to face the people, eschewing Latin, chant, and organ for simple phrases, catchy melodies, and popular instrumentation. There is nothing wrong with any of that, as long as the familiar does not become a vehicle for the self-indulgent, and the focus remains where it should be, on God.

As a seminary professor I have opportunity to worship, preach, and celebrate in a variety of Episcopal parishes. It is interesting to note how churches have adapted architecturally to liturgical renewal, some sliding the altar just far enough away from the frontispiece for a skinny celebrant to stand, others leaving the high altar intact and creating a new space in the midst of the nave. Such efforts attempt to address the question of focus, as do our musical, ritual, and liturgical innovations. Architectural and liturgical focus can only do so much, however. Our hearts and souls must follow, taking the focus off ourselves and putting it on God.

3. Praise changes things, especially the life of the praiser. Don Saliers says this much better than I ever could.

> The rich and complex practice of singing our lives takes many forms, some of them only coming into being. One thing can be said of them all, however: where people sing of God, an embodied theology— a way of living and thinking about life in relationship to God—is formed and expressed. Through this practice, music lends its power to all the other practices that shape and express who we are.[1]

In our praise, and especially in our praising together within community, we grow, we connect, and we become more fully who we are called to be. Well and good for those of us with voice to sing, but the psalm calls for much, much more—for the praise of all creation.

4. All creation praises God. "Will the dust praise you?" asks the author of Psalm 30 (v. 9), and apparently the answer is, "No!" The author of Psalm 148 seems to see things differently. Sun, moon, stars, waters, sea monsters, the elements, mountains and

---

1. Don Saliers, "Singing Our Lives," in *Practicing Our Faith: A Way of Life for a Searching People*, ed. Dorothy C. Bass (San Francisco: Jossey-Bass, 1997), 193.

Psalm 148

Theological Perspective

salvation as reconciliation has promise as the metaphor that could be most inclusive of other metaphors, and most able to find expression in the life of a community of faith that reflects, however imperfectly, the triune life of God.[2]

Psalm 148 is especially poignant read or sung in an Easter context. Indeed, with the undoing of death in Christ's resurrection, yet another voice is added to the chorus of Psalm 148. Francis's "Canticle of the Sun," the basis of the hymn "All Creatures of Our God and King," invites death, its power broken, to praise God.

> And thou, most kind and gentle death,
> Waiting to hush our latest breath,
>   O praise him! Alleluia!
> Thou leadest home the child of God,
> And Christ our Lord the way hath trod.
>   O praise him, O praise him,
>   Alleluia! Alleluia! Alleluia![3]

This canticle would be an appropriate opening hymn of praise on the Fifth Sunday of Easter.

The psalm's vision of the final consummation of all things complements the eschatological note in the resurrection, which is reiterated in another lection for the day, Revelation 21:1–6. The reconciled universe pictured in the psalm finds fulfillment in the Christian affirmation that, in Jesus Christ, God has set forth that purpose intended, from the foundation of the world, to unite all things in him (cf. Eph.1:3–10). Accordingly, a fitting conclusion to worship might be Charles Wesley's "Love Divine, All Loves Excelling." In that hymn God is praised as "Alpha and Omega"—the "end of faith as its beginning"—and God's new creation, brought now to completion, matches the chorus of Psalm 148, being "lost in wonder, love, and praise."

JOHN B. ROGERS

Pastoral Perspective

the features of our lives might be brought together in our living praise. This includes not only the features we delight in; it also includes features that we consider negative or that we would change if we could, but we cannot. If we deeply trust God's activity in and through creation and redemption, then we might begin to trust that even the negative features of our lives might contribute to our praise. We readily acknowledge this possibility when we look at the lives of the saints and consider their peculiar quirks and how God used them. (Think of your favorite saint here, and you will easily come up with an example!) We too are called upon to praise God explicitly through our uniqueness as individuals and our uniqueness as communities of faith, just as Israel is called out by the psalm text to praise through its unique community experience, both positive and negative.

4. We can go one step further with this last form of praise by *encouraging other persons* to cultivate their unique combination of gifts. We can generate praise, not only in our own lives, but by naming and welcoming and encouraging it in others as they live into their creative possibilities. Sometimes encouragement may be in the form of challenging habits of living that get in the way. Other times encouragement may be in the form of accountability or "checking in." Psalm 148 suggests that the creation works together in and through its diversity to praise God. We take the psalm seriously when we also work together and encourage our diverse lives of praise.

5. Finally, because we are creatures with language, we *speak our praise*. We do this in gathered worship, in prayer, at meals, on awakening, at moments of wonder, in delight. We speak to notice together. We speak to intensify gratitude. We speak to name our living as praise. We speak to invite others to living praise. We speak in order to recognize ourselves in God's holy presence. Speaking our praise gives us life in God's presence. Praise the Lord!

CATHERINE L. KELSEY

2. See Colin E. Gunton, *The Actuality of Atonement* (London: T. & T. Clark, 1988), 173–203.
3. Francis of Assisi, "All Creatures of Our God and King," trans. William H. Draper, in *Service Book and Hymnal* (Minneapolis: Augsburg Publishing House, 1958), #173.

these elements are understood to be subject to Israel's God. The "stormy wind" exists to fulfill God's command (v. 8).

Just as Genesis 1 reaches its climax with the creation of humanity, Psalm 148 concludes by referring to people. They too shall praise the Lord from the earth. This human praise knows no national boundaries; kings and all peoples are to praise God, as are men and women, young and old.

Verses 13–14 provide the final admonition to praise within the poem. Verse 13 begins with the same words as verse 5. If verse 5 refers to the heavenly choir, then the "them" of verse 13 probably refers to the earthly choir, all those entities named in verses 7–12. At this point, the poet is obviously interested in uniting the two choral groups and does so by mentioning both earth and heaven in verse 13.

Only in the last verse does Israel appear! One might presume that they too will be commanded to praise the Lord. Amazingly, that does not happen. Instead, the psalmist attests to God's past behavior. The Deity has "raised up a horn for his people." "Raising a horn" means "to strengthen" or "to exalt" someone. For example, the final line of 1 Samuel 2:10, which NRSV translates as "and exalt the power of his anointed," reads literally "and raise the horn of his anointed." YHWH, whose name and being everything and everyone in the universe is commanded to praise, has raised up "praise for all his faithful" (v. 14). Put simply, though everyone except Israel praises God, God has created praise for Israel, the people "who are close to him." Since no one else will praise that special people, God will have to do it. Praise for God has turned into praise for Israel. The only words that it makes sense for Israel to say at that point are the standard refrain, "Praise the LORD!"

DAVID L. PETERSEN

hills, trees, animals, even creepy-crawly things are called on to "Praise the Lord!" How does that happen? How do inanimate and inarticulate objects and creatures "praise"? They do it very well, as a matter of fact, if we just listen—and let them. When we see a beautiful sight or hear a lovely sound in nature, what happens? We slow down, look and listen more carefully, admire, and, quite often, give thanks for the beauty and wonder we have just experienced. Nature, splendid or sublime, delicate or devastating, calls for our praise of its praiseworthiness.

What happens, though, when our indifference to creation, and our exploitation of it, causes creation itself to groan (Rom. 8:22) and even become silent? When we cannot see the stars give their praise through the haze of pollution, when species are driven to extinction by overdevelopment and their song is silenced, do we not find ourselves condemned by the psalmist's call to praise? I take verses 5–6 seriously. "Let them praise the name of the LORD, for he commanded and they were created. He established them forever and ever; he fixed their bounds, which cannot be passed." Can we truly claim to exercise dominion over God's gift of the earth and all that is in it (Gen. 1:26) when our actions diminish the praises of earth and heaven?

I am not advocating you weigh in on an increasingly complex debate about global climate change, but . . . OK, I am. In a discussion that rightly includes concern for the economies of developing nations, the needs of endangered species as well as thirsty people, Psalm 148 also asks us to think about our responsibility to protect creation's capacity to praise its Creator. "Let them praise the name of the LORD, for his name alone is exalted; his glory is above earth and heaven" (v. 13). Yes, let them.

WILLIAM F. BROSEND

Revelation 21:1-6

¹Then I saw a new heaven and a new earth; for the first heaven and the first earth had passed away, and the sea was no more. ²And I saw the holy city, the new Jerusalem, coming down out of heaven from God, prepared as a bride adorned for her husband.

³And I heard a loud voice from the throne saying,
"See, the home of God is among mortals.
He will dwell with them;
they will be his peoples,
and God himself will be with them;
⁴ he will wipe every tear from their eyes.
Death will be no more;
mourning and crying and pain will be no more,
for the first things have passed away."

⁵And the one who was seated on the throne said, "See, I am making all things new." Also he said, "Write this, for these words are trustworthy and true." ⁶Then he said to me, "It is done! I am the Alpha and the Omega, the beginning and the end. To the thirsty I will give water as a gift from the spring of the water of life."

Theological Perspective

Heaven is eternal, in the cosmology into which many of us have been socialized. On earth things change—people are born and die, historical periods come and go, entire cultures disappear, and species become extinct. Death is intimately connected with life. In heaven, at least in our imagining of it, one is spared such vicissitudes and the sorrows that come with them. This clear antithesis between the eternal realm (heaven) and the imperfect earth, however, is not the cosmology of the book of Revelation.

In Revelation, the heaven and the earth that characterize this age must pass away before all things are made new (21:1). Far from being separate realities, heaven and earth have an open door between them in the present age (3:8; 4:1). Events in heaven can determine the course of human events, and vice versa. Satan's expulsion from heaven comes as a result of the death of Jesus on the cross (12:5, 7); the same fallen angels work their revenge on the saints of God (12:9, 17). In the present age, then, there is a stunning reciprocity that connects the world above with that of the world below. This is perhaps most strongly evidenced in Revelation with regard to the liturgy of the church on earth. In its worship, the church actively participates in the high liturgy in heaven before the divine throne (e.g., 4:6b–11; 7:9–10).

Pastoral Perspective

"I am the Alpha and the Omega, the beginning and the end." Here we have the key to the new Jerusalem. We humans spend a lot of time conjuring up images in our minds of the physical nature of the place—heavenly mountains or beaches, divinely paved roads or rolling soft hills. In the Revelation to John, that image is revised. The new heaven is plainly and simply the place where God is. This is the first and most important detail: heaven is the place where God is and humans are fully united with God.

John goes on to describe a holy city. Why a city? Because cities are places where people live together in dependence upon one another. A city works when everyone in it does something to contribute to its welfare. It is the welcome place where people arrive home at the end of a long and confusing journey. It is where God lives.

John describes this particular city by noting what is *not* in it. After the first heaven and the first earth have passed away, he says, "the sea [is] no more" (v. 1b). A powerful biblical symbol for chaos, the sea also represents what separates humans from one another. So part of the beauty of this dry, new Jerusalem is that there are no stormy seas to separate people from one another. Here God and human beings live in harmonious relationship with one another.

Exegetical Perspective

With the revelation of the bride, foreshadowed in 19:7, we reach Revelation's narrative resolution. Opposition to the Lamb has been crushed. The dragon, along with the beast and the false prophet, have been cast into the lake of fire. The arrival of the bride, the Holy City, marks the fulfillment of the blessed hope.

The personification of great cities as women was a familiar convention in the ancient world. Enticing in appearance, some women generate commerce even as they enslave other peoples. The tradition depicts their judgment in terms of sexual violence. Revelation's characterization of the whore explicitly draws upon this convention (17:1–18:24). She creates commerce, adorns herself in purple and scarlet, and drinks from a golden cup.

Babylon was a golden cup in the LORD's hand, making all the earth drunken; the nations drank of her wine, and so the nations went mad (Jer. 51:7). Babylon's fate resembles those of Tyre and Nineveh (Ezek. 26:1–28:19; Nah. 3:4–7): stripped and made desolate, she is devoured by her supposed allies (Rev. 17:16).

More pointedly, Roman iconography employed the image of the goddess Roma to depict the imperial city's glory and virtue. Like other texts from the period, Revelation clearly calls its ancient

Homiletical Perspective

I am accustomed to reading or hearing this passage from the book of Revelation at funerals and have had many occasions to do so over the years. However, I have often wondered if limiting our use of Revelation to dealing with disaster, at the end of life or the time of death, might actually limit our vision of God dwelling in our midst in the present. The vision disclosed in today's lesson reveals the true end or goal of life, the destiny of creation that has been taken up into the life of Jesus Christ, the risen Lord. John provides us with a stunning picture of the living God dwelling among us through the Spirit's power.

While the story of the Bible begins with a garden, it ends in a city, a Holy City, the new Jerusalem, which is illumined by the glory of the Lord, who is surrounded by the praise and adoration of redeemed humanity. What if preachers were to read John's vision with imaginations shaped by the word and sanctified by the Spirit? What if we were to look not only *at* John's vision, but to look *through* John's vision to contemplate the end, the glorious destiny for which the mystery of grace presses in on us who live somewhere in the middle, between the beginning and the end of the story?

As disciples of a crucified Lord, Christians have been called to walk by faith and not by sight, which is

Revelation 21:1-6

Theological Perspective

What, then, distinguishes the new heaven and new earth from those of the old age? Why is it necessary for God to create anew? In 21:1 we are given a hint. John, observing the new creation, notes, "The sea was no more." Exegetes have long recognized that this is a reference to no ordinary sea, but to the sea of primordial chaos of Genesis, out of which evil (Leviathan; the dragon) continually threatens to undo the goodness of God's creation (e.g., Ps. 74:13–14; Isa. 27:1). Remarkably, here in the last book of the Christian canon, the ancient motifs of the Old Testament story of primal creation return. The ending of all is prefigured in the beginning of all. Like the Pauline notion that through our baptism into Christ (the new Adam) the old Adam is destroyed so that we might enjoy the "newness of life" (Rom. 6:4; cf. 1 Cor. 15:21–22), so too the Apocalypse returns to Genesis to indicate how in Christ all of creation has been radically renewed (cf. Rom. 8:18–23).

Previous to chapter 21, the "sea" in Revelation has been the site of intense struggle between God and Satan. It is, for example, the place of the emergence of the beasts of chapter 13. In addition, the disruptive influence of these waters extends into heaven itself. There it emerges as the sea of glass before the throne of God (4:6; 15:2). It is a sea subdued, but still potentially destructive. In (the first) heaven, then, the saints experience no more than an "inaugurated eschatology." Even in heaven, the kingdom of God and the Lamb—though *already* present—is *not yet* fully realized. Only after God's word spoken anew brings about the creation of the new heaven and the new earth is the threat of evil removed from the very heart of heaven itself (21:5).

Revelation's use of Genesis creation motifs impresses upon us the fact that earth has been and will continue to be the focus of God's ultimate concern. Given the current environmental crisis, it is important to reflect upon how passionately God desires the healing of all creation. The atonement brought about through the death of Jesus—and the power for reconciliation that flows from it—is intended by God to extend through a restored humanity to all creation. Indeed, as the vision of the new creation continues to unfold in Revelation, the distinction between heaven and earth simply falls away. Heaven quite literally descends to earth, radically renewing it (21:2). In the process, all life on earth is restored to God's intent for it. One might legitimately ask, then, what role the saints have in this process (cf. 2 Cor. 5:18–19).

Pastoral Perspective

In the context of Easter season, this passage may be understood as providing strength and hope in desperate times. It is not a rosy description of heaven, leading hearers to say, "Oh, does that not look lovely," as they pass by a particularly attractive window and move on down the street. Instead, John offers us a vision we can sit down in front of, taking in all that he shows us about it. That way, when it is time for us to stand up again, we may be able to move on from whatever devastating place we have been, strengthened with the knowledge that something new lies ahead. With the vision of the new Jerusalem fixed firmly in our minds—the place where the God we love and worship stands right beside us—we can continue walking until we arrive at that city where God makes God's home among us.

At the individual level, John's words can be particularly important for persons who are grieving the death of a loved one. The promises in this text are not just for those in the pews. They are also for those who have come before us and who have gone on ahead of us. They are for everyone who longs for assurance that there is a place where death and mourning, crying and pain, will be no more—not for any of us at all, ever again.

In a world where people often think that the worst that can happen to them is death, this is a vital message. Whether death comes early or late, slowly or suddenly, it is not the worst thing that can happen to those who join the heavenly host. We cannot be reminded of this too often, as we yearn for those whom we have loved and lost. In John's vision, they have come to a place where there is no more pain and suffering. They have laid down the burdens they carried like knapsacks full of rocks. They have been released from the cares that bound them like graveclothes. While that message alone is worth preaching, there is more to say about this passage.

A number of years ago, I lay in a hospital bed with the news that I had cancer. It was a particularly vicious and sneaky kind of cancer for which there were no survival rates. The morning after I received the news, a doctor I had come to know during the course of my long journey to a diagnosis heard of my situation and came to visit me. He did not come to share his medical knowledge with me. During that visit, he was no longer my doctor. He came to offer his support.

"Will I survive this?" I asked him.

"Yes," he replied, "but you will have to fight." Those words had great meaning to me at that moment. Yet I had no idea how much they would

Exegetical Perspective

audience to identify "Babylon" with Rome, the "city on seven hills" (17:9). Rome revels in its glory and generates unfathomable wealth for some, but Revelation insists that the imperial city is gaudy, corrupt, murderous—and doomed.

The contrast between the whore and the bride invites attention. Whereas Babylon is a prostitute, the bride is, well, a bride. Purple and scarlet adorn Babylon, while the new Jerusalem is adorned modestly and in white, "as a bride adorned for her husband."[1] The whore wears gold and jewels and pearls, while the new Jerusalem features even greater glory. The whore rides the beast, while the bride marries the Lamb. Revelation calls its audience to "come out" from the whore (18:4), whereas it envisions the bride with open gates and "the nations" walking about in her streets (21:24–26).

In comparison with the whore, the bride's appearance offers a peculiar kind of hope. The whore promises luxury, but her opulence depends upon violence and exploitation. That luxury calls attention to itself, yet its days are numbered. The bride, on the other hand, offers a permanent luxury without ostentation. Her wealth brings healing and restoration. No more tears, no death, no mourning and crying and pain (21:4). Her gifts are for all to enjoy.

The Revised Common Lectionary includes only 21:1–6, rather than 21:1–8 or 21:1–22:5. The omission of verses 7–8 eliminates notes of triumphalism and exclusion from the passage and focuses our attention on the blessed hope embodied in the bride. The entire description of the Holy City would make for long reading, yet interpreters may wish to consider some details from that larger context. For example, the new Jerusalem needs neither temple nor illumination, since God and the Lamb provide both its holiness and its light. Bright water and a variety of fruits suggest the lushness of this new reality. The detailed, almost architectural, description of the heavenly city recalls Ezekiel's lengthy account of the restored temple and revived Israel (chaps. 40–48). This sort of eschatological poetry invites an audience to take an imaginary stroll in such a spectacular and blessed setting.

The image of the bride poses one irresolvable problem for interpretation. All of Revelation's female characters are defined in terms of their sexuality. Jezebel and Babylon are promiscuous; their judgment takes the form of exposure and rape. The

1. For a bride's modest appearance, see Lynn R. Huber, *Like a Bride Adorned: Reading Metaphor in John's Apocalypse*, Emory Studies in Early Christianity (New York: T. & T. Clark, 2007), 130–33.

Homiletical Perspective

to live in the middle of the story. While we believe God is at the beginning of all things, we believe too that God is at the conclusion of all life, or in John's striking words: God is "the Alpha and the Omega" (v. 6), the beginning and the end. Moreover, it is common for us to assume that the beginning was good ("God saw everything that he had made, and indeed, it was very good," Gen. 1:31), and we agree the conclusion will be good ("Then I saw a new heaven and a new earth," Rev. 21:1). This would seem to say that everything in between the beginning and the end is also good, but we know this is not the case.

Yet because of the Easter gospel, we who preach have no need to deny the innumerable ways our expectations for uninterrupted goodness are regularly interrupted. In recent memory, such events as the World Trade Center bombings, the widespread disaster wreaked by Hurricane Katrina, and the protracted involvement of the United States in Iraq are only three large-scale, unforgettable examples among countless unnoticed, forgotten, and smaller forms of loss, death, and the diminishment of life. Relationships grow cold, sour, and end; hurt and disappointment come from those we love; life seems to be unjust or senseless; decisions or answers are not as readily evident as we would hope; failure and discouragement accompany our noblest intentions. As John reminds us, we know all too well the reality of tears, pain, sadness, darkness, suffering, and death.

A good example of this was evident after the terrible bombings on September 11, 2001. Each night I tuned in to the national news to get an update. The anchor was busy at work interpreting for the whole nation, announcing news—a particular kind of gospel—making large claims that sounded rather like the end-time vision of John. This well-known commentator, and others like him, repeated with such authority and finality, "The terrorist bombings of September 11 have changed our lives forever; our life will never be the same."

In light of John's end-time vision, the preacher of an Easter gospel must question the source of this news, asking just whose story is being read and whose vision has been seen. This is the position in which the church finds itself during the season of Easter, when we proclaim the gospel of Jesus Christ among many other competing gospels, each with its respective interpretations, explanations, and speculations. A variety of competing stories are being told, and if we listen carefully, we can discern their contributions to helping us make sense of God, ourselves, and the world in light of the risen Lord, Jesus Christ.

Revelation 21:1-6

Theological Perspective

Once creation is restored, "death is no more." Here is the early Christian understanding that death is not "natural," because it is not intended by God. It is, rather, a consequence of a good creation disturbed by evil (Gen. 3). As in Paul, death in the Apocalypse is the last enemy to be overcome (1 Cor. 15:26). Of the many differences between the theology of Revelation and the premises of modernity, one of the most striking is evident at this point. Such a belief ("death is not natural") flies in the face of evolutionary biology, in which the forward movement and differentiation of species depends upon death. Death and natural selection are two sides of the same coin.

Theological challenges emerge at this point. Various reductionistic responses have been proposed. Among them are mirror-image projections: (1) The Bible is wrong, death is part of the natural order; and (2) natural science is wrong, death is not natural. A third alternative, however, is to take the understandings of both science and the word of God as appropriately descriptive. That is, in the present age, death is part of the natural order of things, and its power cannot be denied (science). Nevertheless, death is not the "intent" of God; it is not part of God's design for life (revelation).

If both of these premises are true, then one can only marvel at the freedom God has given, not only to human beings, but also to all of creation. This freedom has resulted in a glorious universe that has life at its very heart, yet also carries within itself remarkably deep sorrow and grief. The Apocalypse reveals that the pain that comes with life as we know it is acknowledged by a God who, once mortally wounded by our sin, continues to stand in solidarity with us in the midst of the suffering experienced by all of creation (21:3). Revelation also informs us that it is only when God's word is spoken over this deeply troubled creation—yet once again—that evil is banished, hope is restored, and all things are made new, including our understanding of the immutability of heaven itself.

ERIK M. HEEN

Pastoral Perspective

grow in value over the next eighteen months as I lay in bed struggling for my life. They had seemed simple words at the time. Their profundity grew each day as I mustered all the strength I had simply to get out of bed and attempt to make it through another day. As I did, I heard those words ringing in my head: "You will have to fight." So that is what I did, leading me into a new day that dawned many long months later.

The words that we hear today in Revelation have the power to become such life-altering words for God's people, especially for those who find themselves in the midst of struggle and turmoil. "It is done! I am the Alpha and the Omega, the beginning and the end" (v. 6). These are words that matter at the very heart of life, where we ask who we are, who God is, and what is the value of the Christian pursuit. They tell us that there will be a new day when we live face to face with God. All that has hindered, hurt, and hampered us will be gone. What will be left is a life with God, filled with relationships of joy and strength with God's people.

So do not pass by these words lightly, as if window-shopping God's promises. Stop and sit down a while. Take in all that John is showing you. Think of those whose ability to stand has depended on their trust in this vision. Then stand up yourself in the midst of God's people, and proclaim a message with power to sustain them through all the days to come.

DANA FERGUSON

Exegetical Perspective

woman clothed with the sun is a mother, whose activity consists in flight from the dragon. The new Jerusalem arrives as a bride, whose adornment is for her husband. Some interpreters attempt to redeem this pattern. They argue that the female images are simply a stock device of ancient political discourse, and that they serve not to condemn women but to resist imperial violence. That is true, of course, but contemporary readers must engage the text as it presents itself—including the imagery of sexual violence against women. The bride's description locates women's redemption in purity and in preparation for marriage.

Many reject Revelation on the grounds that it either rejects worldly matters or places its hope in a pie-in-the-sky future. That objection misses the point of the new Jerusalem on two counts. First, the new Jerusalem comes down from heaven to earth. It celebrates the embodied life of culture, food, and beauty. Apocalyptic poetry imagines a "new heaven and a new earth" in terms of transformation and healing, not simply obliteration. Second, the new Jerusalem evokes faithful discipleship in the present, rather than an empty hope that sits and waits. The comparison between the new Jerusalem and Babylon encourages cultural critique rather than abject dissatisfaction.[2] This accounts for Revelation's appeal among some liberationist readers.

Revelation calls believers to reject any association with the imperial system of their day. One cannot overemphasize how much pressure such radical discipleship would have brought upon the believers in places like Smyrna, Pergamum, and Laodicea. How would a believer in the contemporary United States entirely avoid implication in this nation's military systems? One can hardly begin to imagine. Allusions to John's *Christian* opponents in the letters to the churches (Balaam, 2:14; the Nicolaitans, 2:6, 15; and Jezebel, 2:20) suggest that many believers in Asia did not share John's point of view. The glories of the new Jerusalem call John's audience to imagine the blessings that attend their resistance and faithful witness under immense cultural pressure. The bride's appearance challenges preachers to adopt the visionary voice. How *might* things look, should believers follow the Lamb faithfully over against cultural resistance?

GREG CAREY

Homiletical Perspective

Situated within the story of Scripture, we are able to see the world through the eyes of John's vision, the vision of a Holy City, the new Jerusalem that the living God is now bringing into being, a city whose citizens surround the throne of the suffering Lamb who was slain and who takes away the sins of the world. Our life and destiny are illumined within a story we not only read but inhabit, a story authored by the God who is Alpha and Omega, the beginning and end of all that is. Eugene Peterson writes,

> The biblical story began, quite logically, with a beginning. Now it draws to an end, not quite so logically, also with a beginning. The sin-ruined creation of Genesis is restored in the sacrifice-renewed creation of Revelation. The product of these beginning and ending acts of creation is the same: "the heavens and earth" in Genesis, and "a new heaven and new earth" in Revelation.[1]

The center of this story is Jesus Christ—his life, suffering, death and resurrection, and promised return in glory—the focal point on which the destiny of the universe turns. Apart from God's gracious Word and gift of self-giving love through him, we could never know these things on our own, since our minds are so deeply colored by the world's heart-breaking news.

On this Lord's Day the preacher is authorized to announce on behalf of the one seated on the throne: "Behold, I am making all things new!" We need imaginations nourished by the word and sanctified by the Spirit to connect what is visible and invisible—the reconciliation of heaven and earth— seeing the past, present, and future of all things through the light of God's glory in Christ.

MICHAEL PASQUARELLO III

2. Barbara R. Rossing has articulated a world-affirming interpretation of Revelation that is sensitive to ecological concerns. See her *The Rapture Exposed: The Message of Hope in the Book of Revelation* (Boulder, CO: Westview, 2004).

1. Eugene H. Peterson, *Reversed Thunder: The Revelation of John and the Praying Imagination* (San Francisco: Harper & Row, 1988), 169.

John 13:31-35

³¹When he had gone out, Jesus said, "Now the Son of Man has been glorified, and God has been glorified in him. ³²If God has been glorified in him, God will also glorify him in himself and will glorify him at once. ³³Little children, I am with you only a little longer. You will look for me; and as I said to the Jews so now I say to you, 'Where I am going, you cannot come.' ³⁴I give you a new commandment, that you love one another. Just as I have loved you, you also should love one another. ³⁵By this everyone will know that you are my disciples, if you have love for one another."

Theological Perspective

On this Fifth Sunday of Easter, the church asks us to recall a moment prior to the crucifixion in John's Gospel. The passage opens with Jesus' statement, "Now the Son of Man has been glorified, and God has been glorified in him." Christian commentators including Tertullian and Hilary of Poitiers read this passage as evidence of the Trinity. Hilary argues: "The Father glorifies him [the Son], not with a glory from without but in himself. By taking him back into that glory that belongs to himself and that [the Son] had with him before, the Father glorifies [the Son] with himself and in himself."[1] Here one should be cautious of reading Christian doctrines of the fourth century into John's words. John's emphasis on the word "Now" suggests that all that has happened up to this point, and all that Jesus has announced in the discourses of the preceding chapters, is coming to fulfillment. Recalling that Jesus has said, "I lay down my life for the sheep" (10:15), as evidence of being "the good shepherd," John's Jesus views his approaching death as glorification, as a luminous proof of his messianic role—seeing the work of his Father to its completion.

1. Hilary of Poitiers, *On the Trinity* 9.40–42, in *John: 11–21*, ed. Joel C. Elowsky, vol. 4b of *Ancient Christian Commentary on Scripture: New Testament*, ed. Thomas C. Oden (Downers Grove, IL: InterVarsity Press, 2007), 111.

Pastoral Perspective

Judas had gone out, the Gospel lesson says. The hour had come. There was no turning back now. The betrayal had been set in motion and could not be stopped now.

Judas had gone out, and Jesus knows what this means. However, he also knows the disciples are not going to understand the implications of what has just happened and what is about to happen. In fact, although it is too late, the disciples are going to fight and resist, and eventually run away. So this is Jesus' last opportunity to say what he wants to say. Instead of addressing the disciples as students, he addresses them with an intimacy that conveys the poignancy of this special moment in his life. "Little children," he says to these grown men, "listen to me now. I am getting ready to go to a place where you cannot come, so it's important that we have this time together now."

Many of us have experienced something similar—a final, intensive conversation with someone we love who knew that he or she would not be with us much longer. This is a truly sacred time that we are supposed to remember for the rest of our life. In the same way, we are meant to remember these words of Jesus in a way that befits the circumstances in which he spoke them.

Jesus has decided to get right to the point. Laying aside his usual way of speaking in parables and

Exegetical Perspective

It would be difficult to overestimate the importance of this passage in Christian thought. The love command that Jesus here gives to his disciples is typically understood as both the center of Jesus' teaching and the center of the Christian life. Christian ethics is commonly described as a love ethic, in large part because of this passage. Most readers of the Gospel of John also see this passage as pivotal to the structure and theology of the Gospel.

The literary context of the passage is crucial to its meaning. As a transition from Jesus' public ministry to the farewell conversations with disciples, the passage offers fundamental clues to the identity and character of the Jesus community. This community is characterized by John's peculiar notions of glory and love. The immediate context of the passage is that of betrayal, both by Judas and by Peter. The dynamics of betrayal change the character of glory and love.

As Judas disappears into the night, Jesus announces the glorification of both God and the Son of Man. It is not exactly clear in the Greek who is being glorified when and by whom. Nevertheless, it is clear that eventually both God and Jesus are glorified in the events of Jesus' life. The concept of glory is crucial to the theological narrative of John, although it is never explained. At its root, glory

Homiletical Perspective

Glory and fame are the currency of American pop culture. In preparation for a sermon on this lection, I suggest you purchase current issues of magazines that feature the hottest figures in entertainment and sports. Go online to the mass-appeal Web sites. Watch the celebrity television shows with the highest ratings. Listen to the interviews with the heroes and stars of the day.

The pursuit of glory and public fascination with those who attain it are as ancient as human civilization. These passions are not the invention of our electronic world, no matter how much the media may feed them. Two thousand years ago in the cosmopolitan cultures of the Mediterranean basin, people paid attention when someone rose to glory and prominence. According to John, Jesus himself had a moment of high public acclaim. In an earlier passage that is significant to understanding this Sunday's reading, the Pharisees observe: "Look, the world has gone after him!" (12:19b).

Immediately afterward "some Greeks" come asking to see Jesus. Given the placement of their appearance in John's narrative, it is reasonable to suppose that the Greeks are eager to see the one whom the world has "gone after." It is at this point that Jesus introduces the theme that he will later elaborate in today's Gospel. Jesus begins radically to

John 13:31-35

Theological Perspective

"Little children," says Jesus, "I am with you only a little longer" (v. 33). As he begins to prepare the disciples for his death, he speaks tenderly to them, knowing how this will leave them feeling orphaned. While he promises in John 14:18 not to leave the disciples "desolate," and even later (15:15) calls the disciples "orphaned," and not children, his words of encouragement call attention to the despair that is about to engulf them. It will not feel like glorification—for him or for them.

Jesus' declaration of a "new commandment" in verse 34 is clearly the focal point of our reading. The commandment to love one another draws on both the explicit tenderness and the implicit suffering expressed in the preceding verse. Jesus urges the disciples to be patient with one another in the days ahead. Coming on the heels of the story of Jesus' washing the disciples' feet and of Judas's betrayal, Jesus' "command" has the tone of an earnest plea—to care for one another, forgiving one another in the wake of Jesus' death, even as he will forgive his tormentors from the cross. His commandment echoes his words to Peter in John 13:8b, "Unless I wash you, you have no share with me." His new commandment is not so much a legal or military order as it is a profound plea and hope that the disciples will "abide" in Jesus' way of life and love.

Among ancient authorities, Jesus' love command raised an important question. Cyril of Alexandria, Augustine, and others were well aware that Leviticus 19:18 had already commanded Israel to "love your neighbor as yourself." What, they asked, was *new* in Jesus' love command? Some, like Augustine, suggested that the difference in Jesus' command was a difference in *kind* from the Jewish command. Jesus commanded a spiritual love distinguished "from all carnal affection," calling his disciples "to love one another as those who are God's."[2] Others, like Cyril, argued for a difference in *degree*:

> The law of Moses mandated the necessity of loving our brothers as ourselves, yet our Lord Jesus the Christ loved us far more than he loved himself. Otherwise, he would have never descended to our humiliation from his original exaltation in the form of God and on an equality with God the Father, nor would he have undergone for our sakes the exceptional bitterness of his death in the flesh, nor have submitted to beatings from the Jews, to shame, to derision, and all his other sufferings too

Pastoral Perspective

paradoxes, he simply decides to give an order, "I give you a new commandment," he says so simply, "that you love one another." That is it.

As one modern New Testament scholar observed: "[This] new command is simple enough for a toddler to memorize and appreciate, and it is profound enough that the most mature believers are repeatedly embarrassed at how poorly they comprehend it and put it into practice."[1]

"By this everyone will know that you are my disciples, if you have love for one another" (v. 35). How embarrassing it is for many of us who call ourselves Christian to recall that Jesus wanted to make it easy for us by having us focus on this one thing; yet we have found so many other ways to identify true believers and often have a hard time putting this commandment into practice even in our own family lives.

Jesus does not talk about the importance of the Bible or a carefully constructed creed. The New Testament would not even be written until two generations after Jesus' death, and the Nicene Creed would be hammered out by combative theologians over the next 350 years. The Bible and the creed would become terribly important to human beings over the years, while the one thing most important to Jesus would get lost as Christians wrestled with power and orthodoxy.

What Jesus wanted us to know, apparently, was that although people would fight wars over who held correct beliefs, this was not Jesus' primary concern. Jesus' way was the way of little children, not the way of learned theologians and intelligent preachers.

"Little children," he said, "I give you a new commandment, that you love one another." The commandment is not about what you believe; it is about how you live.

In her autobiographical work, *The Spiral Staircase*, Karen Armstrong notes that in most religious traditions, faith is not about belief, but about practice. "Religion," Armstrong writes, is not about having to believe or accept certain difficult propositions; instead, religion is "about doing things that change you."[2]

This came home to her especially when she wrote her first book on Islam. Muslims, she came to understand, are not expected to accept a complex creed. Instead, they are required to perform certain

1. D. A. Carson, *The Gospel according to John* (Leicester, England: APOLLOS, 1991), 484.
2. Karen Armstrong, *The Spiral Staircase: My Climb Out of Darkness* (New York: Alfred A. Knopf, 2004), 270.

2. Augustine, *Tractates on the Gospel of John* 65.1, in *John: 11–21*, 114.

means reputation, and to be glorified means to acquire good reputation. When glory refers to God and even to the status of followers of Jesus, it takes on aspects of heavenly splendor and the wonders of God's kingdom. Thus, when the Gospel of John refers to the glorification of God and Jesus, it is probably referring to the manifestation and recognition by the world of their proper heavenly status.

However, there is a powerful irony in the Gospel of John around the notion of glory, because it is in the cross that Jesus (and God) are glorified. Thus, Judas, disappearing into night while plotting betrayal, and Peter, in anticipation of his denial promising to give his life for Jesus, are not unfortunate and extraneous additions to the story of Jesus' glorification. Death and betrayal belong to the core of Jesus' glory. Given this, it is fitting that this passage, after announcing the coming glory, immediately announces Jesus' departure.

The issue of Jesus' departure has already provoked puzzling and antagonistic discussions with "the Jews" in 7:32–36 and 8:21–24. Both of these discussions overlay Jesus' death on the cross with a narrative of Jesus' return to the Father. The same overlay is occurring here. In fact, it is Jesus' announcement that "where I am going, you cannot come" (13:33) that leads to Peter's doomed promises and to the fuller discussion of Jesus' departure in chapter 14. In 14:1–4, Jesus' departure becomes Jesus' arrival: "And if I go and prepare a place for you, I will come again and will take you to myself, so that where I am, there you may be also" (v. 3). The tenderness of Jesus' naming his disciples "little children" (13:33) connects to the terror created by Jesus' death and the comfort created by Jesus' return. In this way, betrayal and the cross become moments in Jesus' departure and return—all of which leads to glory, not only for God and Jesus but for Jesus' followers as well.

These brief sentences also connect to the central theological themes, issues, and questions of the Gospel as a whole. Much of the christological labor in the Gospel focuses on the nature of divine presence. Even if Jesus manifests "the Father," he does so in a way that reinforces God's mystery and otherness. Jesus himself is notoriously and persistently beyond the grasp and understanding of the humans who pursue him. The constant interplay between presence and absence is evoked here in the ironies of a glory that is displayed in suffering and a departure that is an arrival.

transform the meaning of glory: "The hour has come for the Son of Man to be glorified. Very truly, I tell you, unless a grain of wheat falls into the earth and dies, it remains just a single grain; but if it dies, it bears much fruit" (12:23–24). This is not the kind of glory that the world has in mind. It does not make for the grandeur of marble monuments in the ancient world or glitzy magazine covers and titillating interviews on talk shows in the media world.

However, to be fair, it is not just the world that has difficulty grasping the kind of glory that Christ reveals in the Gospel of John. Even his disciples, and in particular Peter, are initially embarrassed and uncomprehending. When Jesus, in a scene leading up to our lesson, wants to wash Peter's feet, the baffled disciple exclaims: "'You will never wash my feet'" (13:8). Peter cannot hold together his understanding of how to honor Jesus and Jesus' understanding of how God is glorified through humble and sacrificial action.

Because John's Gospel operates simultaneously at two different levels—the unfolding story line of Jesus' ministry, and the life and concerns of John's community—today's reading may reveal how the church was continuing to struggle with Jesus' radically transformed understanding of glory. The church at this point in history is still a relatively peripheral movement amid the global economic and military might of the Roman Empire. (We might not think of the Roman Empire as "global" nowadays, but it must have felt global to those who lived under its rule.) For John's community, the signs of Caesar's worldly glory abound. His head is on the coins they exchange, his standards are carried by occupying troops, his governors and proconsuls live in splendor. How can the church, living in such an environment and feeling the pressure of its material and cultural forces, begin to understand why Jesus would say at the moment of his betrayal to suffering and death: "Now the Son of Man has been glorified, and God has been glorified in him" (John 13:31)?

I go to a current American dictionary to see if since the Roman Empire any of Jesus' transformed understanding of glory has entered into common parlance. The dictionary gives eight definitions. Every single one of them is a variation on the first definition: "Exalted honor, praise, or distinction accorded by common consent; renown: 'For what is glory but the praise of fame'" (Milton)."[1] The

---

1. William Morris, ed., *The American Heritage Dictionary of the English Language* (Boston: Houghton Mifflin Co., 1976), 561.

John 13:31-35

Theological Perspective

numerous to mention. . . . It was indeed something new for love to go as far as that! (9)[3]

Later theologians noted a tension between John's "love one another as I have loved you," Matthew's formulation of the great commandment (Matt. 22:34–40), and Luke's story of the Good Samaritan. The issue, framed in large part by the emerging traditions of Christian orthodoxy and heresy—as well as by various formulations of "election" theology—asked whether Christ died for "his own" (i.e., the elect only) or for all humanity (i.e., the stranger or the neighbor), and therefore whether Christians should be concerned principally with loving one another or with loving "the world."

Verse 35 extends John's concern with testimony that we heard in the Gospel reading from the Fourth Sunday of Easter. "By this everyone will know that you are my disciples, if you have love for one another." *If* the disciples love one another in the midst of the suffering that is to come, Jesus says, *then* they will have proven themselves faithful to him. If the disciples can love another in that situation, then they will have proven that they understand by *doing* what Jesus taught them.

To preach this text, one needs to find one's way into a group's fear—its sense of anxiety, of being threatened—exploring the way fear causes us to pull apart from one another and ignore the common good. The group can be as small as a couple of people or as large as a nation. Exploring those dynamics, we may be able to hear more deeply the tenderness and compassion of Jesus for his friends and for us as well.

JOSEPH A. BESSLER

Pastoral Perspective

ritual actions, such as the hajj pilgrimage and the fast of Ramadan, which are designed to change them. Muslims are to prostrate themselves in prayer facing Mecca several times a day as an act of surrender. Muslims are commanded to give alms to the poorer and more vulnerable among them, as a way of cultivating the kind of generous spirit that makes them want to give graciously, as God does. Armstrong says these repeated actions are intended to lead to personal transformation. "The point is that this was not a belief system, but a process. The religious life . . . made people act in ways that were supposed to change them forever."[3]

The Christian religion, of course, has its own share of ancient practices and rituals that shape our lives in the image of Christ. Although Christians today are often concerned about who is orthodox and who is revisionist in faith, perhaps the more important concern has to do with who most effectively evinces the love of Christ in their lives. After all, Jesus did not say, "They will know you are my disciples if you believe the right things."

There is a story in Isak Dinesen's book *Out of Africa* about a boy named Kitau. He appeared at the author's door one day to ask for a job as a domestic servant. She hired him but was surprised when after three months he asked her for a letter of recommendation to Sheik Ali bin Salim, a Muslim who lived in a nearby town. Dinesen offered to raise Kitau's pay in order to keep him, but money was not his interest. Kitau had decided to become either a Christian or a Muslim, and his purpose in working for Dinesen had been to see, up close, the way a Christian lived. Now that he had worked for Dinesen and seen the ways of Christians, he would go and observe Sheik Ali to see how Muslims behave; then he would decide. The author remembers how she wished Kitau had told her that before he came to live with her.

Judas had gone out. This was Jesus' last opportunity to get his point across to the disciples. No more parables or paradoxes, just a simple commandment: "Little children, love each other. This is how everyone will know that you are my disciples."

GARY D. JONES

---

3. Cyril of Alexandria, *Commentary on the Gospel of John 9*, in *John: 11–21*, 114.

3. Ibid., 281.

Exegetical Perspective

It is, of course, the love command that has provoked the most response and has had the most influence over Christian thought. The setting of this passage has long reminded readers of a covenant ceremony. It reads as if the announcement of Jesus' departure, the giving of a new command, and the note that obedience to this command is the public mark of the new community, comprise John's version of the new covenant that the Synoptics place at the Lord's Supper. The love command is both the organizing force and the sign of the Jesus community.

This covenant context is probably why Jesus calls the commandment "new." It is obviously not new in the sense that a command to love has never been given before. Rather, it is new in the sense that a new community emerges from its giving. In the context of covenant, the command to love one another is probably a command to love others in the community. However, Christians have always read the command as universal, connecting it, for instance, to Jesus' command to love one's enemies (Matt. 5:44). Love, we say, does not limit itself according to the social profile of the person.

The content of love is not detailed. The passage simply points to Jesus as the model: "Just as I have loved you, you also should love one another." Readers naturally think of Jesus' constant solicitude and compassion for those he meets, of his weeping over Lazarus, of his commitment to the security of his flock. However, the command to love transcends such examples. As Jesus notes in 15:13, "No one has greater love than this, to lay down one's life for one's friends." This is what Jesus does; he lays down his life for his friends. Having Jesus as a model undoes all the limits. Whatever love might mean in a given moment, it asks for everything. Love does not calculate the costs.

Finally, readers have long puzzled over the psychological discord of commanding people to love. Can love be commanded? Love feels more like a gift, an event, than an act of obedience. Thus, in the theology of John, love between humans belongs to God's presence. In the language of covenant, Jesus is present through the love of the disciples. In the language of theological presence, to live in Jesus is to love and to love is to live in Jesus (15:1–11).

LEWIS R. DONELSON

Homiletical Perspective

dictionary offers not the slightest inkling of Christ's transformed understanding of glory.

How then can people grasp the transformation of glory through the death and resurrection of Christ? Whether we lived in the Roman Empire two thousand years ago or live in American pop culture today, the answer clearly requires more than words. In common speech the meaning of glory stubbornly persists as honor, praise, renown. We cannot verbally argue people into a transformed understanding of glory. That is why Christ instructs the disciples: "I give you a new commandment, that you love one another. Just as I have loved you, you also should love one another" (John 13:34).

The newness of the commandment is not that love has never before been commanded (Lev. 19:18). The newness is in the source that feeds this love: the humility of the Almighty as revealed through Christ's death, the transformation of the meaning of glory from worldly renown to Godly compassion. We are not simply to use words to tell people about the meaning of the cross and resurrection; we are to love one another as a way of embodying the truth that Christ reveals through his death and resurrection. There is a way of translating this verse that makes even clearer the causal connection between the loving action of Christ and the community's loving one another: "I have loved you in order that [*hina* in Greek] you also love one another." I prefer this translation to the NRSV's "you also should love one another," because the "should" sounds like a moral commandment divorced from the gracious action of Christ that makes possible our love.

When we allow the love of Christ to take deep root in us, so that it flourishes in all that we do and say to one another, it is the first step in helping the world to understand how Christ has transformed glory. We give witness to what no purely verbal argument can ever accomplish: the glory of God breathing through the life of a Christ-centered community.

THOMAS H. TROEGER

Acts 16:9-15

⁹During the night Paul had a vision: there stood a man of Macedonia pleading with him and saying, "Come over to Macedonia and help us." ¹⁰When he had seen the vision, we immediately tried to cross over to Macedonia, being convinced that God had called us to proclaim the good news to them. ¹¹We set sail from Troas and took a straight course to Samothrace, the following day to Neapolis, ¹²and from there to Philippi, which is a leading city of the district of Macedonia and a Roman colony. We remained in this city for some days. ¹³On the sabbath day we went outside the gate by the river, where we supposed there was a place of prayer; and we sat down and spoke to the women who had gathered there. ¹⁴A certain woman named Lydia, a worshiper of God, was listening to us; she was from the city of Thyatira and a dealer in purple cloth. The Lord opened her heart to listen eagerly to what was said by Paul. ¹⁵When she and her household were baptized, she urged us, saying, "If you have judged me to be faithful to the Lord, come and stay at my home." And she prevailed upon us.

Theological Perspective

We know almost nothing about Lydia, but what we know fascinates us. Who was this woman making her way independently in a world run by men? Who was this Gentile who sought the God of Judaism? The text tells us only that she was a "seller of purple goods, who was a worshiper of God." However, in just those two phrases, Scripture with its stunning brevity show us that work and worship both had their place in the life of this remarkable, busy woman.

So she rises from the text and stands before us even today as a kind of narrative icon, contemplative Mary and active Martha in one, her heart set on God even while her work gets done.

She came to the riverside, to a secluded place of prayer. Perhaps she expected to meet other women, Jewish worshipers or Gentile seekers, for prayer together. Perhaps she came regularly. What she did not know was that on this particular day outside the city gates, she would be met by Paul and his companions, missionaries looking for anyone who was seeking God in this hidden place of prayer. There at the riverside, Lydia found the God who was finding her.

It almost did not happen. Recall for a moment all the contingencies of history, that long list of improbable events that led to Lydia's encounter with Paul. Think back to the controversy in the early church over the preaching of the gospel to the

Pastoral Perspective

Visions are surprising things. When we talk of "God's vision" today in church, we typically mean strategic planning, as one step in a congregation's planning process. Perhaps we are comfortable with talking about God's vision in this way because it seems manageable to us. We can discover what the vision is by following logical steps: (1) pray, (2) thank God for working in our congregation, (3) discern God's vision for us by calling a consultant, and so on. In a way, Paul's vision in Acts 16 does move him and his companions to Macedonia, "being convinced that God had called us to proclaim the good news to them" (Acts 16:10). However, our well-conceived *scripting of* God's vision, if it is even that, is a very different affair from *receiving from* God a vision.

In the biblical witness, visions from God are not the exception but the norm. Beginning with Adam and Eve and moving throughout the Scriptures to the Apocalypse at the end, God is demonstratively engaged with human affairs to catch our attention and transform us. Yet transformation is often difficult and painful, especially when we know the way we want to head. Maybe this is why we like logical planning steps to name God's vision; it gives us the false idea that God is predictable and controllable. When God does visit us, however, we are undeniably changed. Clearly, in Paul's life, Jesus'

Exegetical Perspective

Paul's mission to Europe. Fresh from the first general church council in Jerusalem (Acts 15), Paul resumed his missionary activities. Heading west from Jerusalem, he traveled through the Roman provinces of Syria and Cilicia (15:41) and into Asia Minor (present-day Turkey), revisiting Derbe and Lystra (see Acts 14 for Luke's account of his earlier visits there). In Lystra, Paul visited Timothy, a disciple whose mother was Jewish and whose father was Greek (Gentile). From 2 Timothy 1:5 we learn that both Timothy's mother Eunice and his grandmother Lois were Hellenistic Jewish Christians. Since Timothy had earned a good reputation among the Christian communities of Lystra and nearby Iconium, Paul wanted to enlist him as a missionary companion.

It may seem odd that Paul, the missionary to the Gentiles, had Timothy circumcised—something his mother and grandmother seem to have overlooked. It is also interesting that this oversight was apparently not a problem for local Christian communities. Nevertheless, Paul had him circumcised "because of the Jews who were in those places" (16:3). This was probably done for pragmatic rather than religious reasons. In describing Paul's missionary work, Luke offers a predictable pattern. When visiting a town, Paul would seek out the local synagogue to present his message about Jesus the Messiah, and the

Homiletical Perspective

In the season of Easter we ask: What do we do now that Jesus is risen? Something significant, we hope, in response to such a transformative event. The book of Acts follows the outgrowth of ministry in the early church as a fruit of the resurrection. In Acts 16:9–15, the apostolic "crossing over" to Macedonia and Lydia's conversion are examples of inspired decisions that result in creative ministry. Acts offers particular accounts of people coming to genuine faith, allowing us to see the work of redemption that follows from Christian service. After the intense experience of Easter, the apostles push ahead to the work God has for them. At the midpoint of the church's story in Acts, we find ministry taking shape through journeys that progress only through prayerful discernment.

The route change is inspired by Paul's vision of a Macedonian man pleading for help. After arriving in Philippi, they venture outside the gate, supposing to find there a place of prayer. Paul and others meet Lydia, a solid result in this missionary venture after days of proceeding by faith. As we read and talk about this passage in worship, we might accent the adventurous nature of the action and its characters. The first-person plural voice of this passage stands out in contrast to the omniscient voice found in most biblical narrative. The "we" emphasizes the personal engagement of people traveling together

Acts 16:9-15

Theological Perspective

Gentiles (Acts 15) or how Paul had to be nudged and redirected again and again to get him to Philippi (16:1–8). It was not enough for the Spirit to guide Paul and his companions. Twice the text tells us that the Spirit prevented Paul from going the wrong way (16:6–7). We can only imagine what it is like to have the experience of the Holy Spirit stopping us from doing something.

Then, of course, there is Paul's vision of the "man of Macedonia" who pleads for help. Only when Paul discusses the vision with his companions do they conclude that they must go to Philippi, and they leave immediately. Did they ever meet the "man of Macedonia," or was Lydia the one to whom the Spirit was guiding them?

It almost did not happen, this meeting of the businesswoman and the missionaries, and it surely would not have happened were it not for the inexplicable convergence of human faithfulness and divine guidance. Paul and Lydia and the Holy Spirit all work together in this event, this "chance" encounter by the river. Paul would not have been guided to this place at this moment, were he not first of all at God's disposal, open to being guided, sensitively attuned to being steered in one direction and away from all others. Lydia would not have arrived at this place or time, had she not first of all been a worshiper of God, a seeker already on her way.

Paul does his part and Lydia hers, but it is God who guides all things and works in and through all things, not just for good but for what would otherwise be impossible. It is the Spirit who brings Lydia to Paul so that she can hear the gospel.

However that is only half of what is required. True, Lydia must first hear the words of good news, and to do that she must meet Paul. She also must hear the words as truth, as gospel, as the answer to her search. It is the Spirit of the Lord Jesus Christ who prepares Lydia's heart to hear, receive, and understand. "The Lord opened her heart to give heed to what was said by Paul" (v. 14).

Here is the center of the story, the moment of intersection between human obedience and divine initiative. Longing and grace meet there on the bank of the river. The longing heart of a faithful woman is opened by the gracious impulse of a faith-giving God in an action that, like the incarnation itself, is at once fully human and fully divine. Like Lydia we are astonished when, looking back, we can say only that our steps were guided and our hearts opened.

Lydia was baptized and her household, the text tells us almost in passing (v. 15). Then she opens her

Pastoral Perspective

visit to him on the road to Damascus radically changed Paul's direction (Acts 9:3–9).

As in chapter 9, God sets Paul's course in Acts 16 through a vision by vetoing Paul's strategic plan. After being forbidden to travel to Asia (v. 6) and Bithynia (v. 7), Paul hears "a man of Macedonia pleading with him and saying, 'Come over to Macedonia and help us'" (v. 9). The route Paul finds himself on is "to Philippi, which is a leading city of the district of Macedonia and a Roman colony" (v. 12). This Spirit-led route—sailing from Troas and straight to Samothrace, then to Neapolis (v. 11)—brings Paul to Europe for the first time to continue witnessing to the gospel "to the ends of the earth" (Acts 1:8). As recorded in Acts, this will be Paul's first visit to Philippi, where fond relationships will be forged, ones for which he will thank God with joy every time he remembers them (see Phil. 1:3–11).

Now that Paul's attention has been set on Philippi, he puts in motion his ministerial plan for the city. Once Paul and his unknown traveling companions reach Philippi, they remain "in this city for some days" (v. 12), waiting for the "sabbath day" (v. 13), and thus discover who the devout Jews in the city are. Visiting with devout Jews in a new city is the way Paul typically meets people and introduces the gospel. However, instead of meeting a man of Macedonia, Paul sits down and speaks to the women gathered there (v. 13). Yet again, God's mission takes a different course. The first convert recorded in Philippi is not "a man of Macedonia" but "a woman named Lydia . . . a dealer in purple cloth" (v. 14).

In New Testament times, visions from God were not strange occurrences, but a woman cast in a role beyond that of being property was exceptional. In Acts we hear several stories of women responding to God's vision with the same faithfulness as their male counterparts. These women—like Rhoda, Tabitha, Eunice, Priscilla, and Lydia—lead the first-century church with integrity, energy, and command.

Lydia is a "dealer in purple cloth" (v. 14), an extravagant textile affordable only to the wealthy. She is a businesswoman of no small stature and is in charge of her own household. Notice that Lydia is not associated with a man, indicating that she is in full command of her property. She does not depend on a man to confer her status. She is a financially independent woman who is Paul's first convert in Europe. More important than her station, however, is Lydia's vision of what God is doing.

In verse 14, we learn that Lydia worships God and that the Lord has "opened her heart to listen eagerly"

response to him would be mixed. Some agreed with what he had to say but others did not, so that he had to discontinue his teaching in the synagogue and find another venue, perhaps the household of a sympathetic believer (for example, see the establishment of the Corinthian church in Acts 18:1–11). Therefore for Paul—and Timothy—to be creditable to a Jewish audience, both needed to be fully Jewish.

Luke continues the travelogue of Paul and Timothy as they journey toward the west coast of Asia Minor. It would be helpful to consult a map to see where Paul *intended* to go (the Roman province of Bithynia in the northern part of Asia Minor) and where the "Spirit of Jesus" led him—across the beautiful blue Aegean waters to Europe. It was in Troas, on Asia's west coast, that Paul had his famous dream in which a man pleaded with him to "come over to Macedonia [modern-day Greece] and help us" (v. 9). It is impossible to know the identity of the man in Paul's vision. He was probably not Jesus (would Jesus plead to come "help us"?). The man might have been Luke inserting himself into the story. The pronouns of the very next verse switch from third person ("he/they") to first person ("we/us"), and for the remainder of the narrative Paul's travels are told from the perspective of an apparent eyewitness. At any rate, the man in the vision was effective in bringing Paul and Timothy to Greece, where they made their way to the town of Philippi.

Lydia (vv. 11–15). Luke has accurately described Philippi as "a leading city of the district of Macedonia and a Roman colony" (v. 12). Ancient Greece was composed of two Roman provinces: Macedonia in the north and Achaia in the south. Philippi was founded in 356 BCE by Philip of Macedon (father of Alexander the Great), but remained an insignificant village until it was "rediscovered" by Emperor Augustus as an ideal place for retired army officers who had faithfully served him during the battle of Actium (31 BCE). Peter Oakes[1] offers an excellent description of the social composition of the city with a population of about 15,000. Oakes approximates that the elite comprised 3 percent of the population; landowning farmers and pensioned colonists made up 25 percent; skilled workers, merchants, and service providers amounted to 45 percent; and the poor comprised the remaining 27 percent. Slaves (about 20 percent of the total

1. Peter Oakes, *Philippians: From People to Letter* (New York: Cambridge University Press, 2001).

and plotting their next move, and as readers we are granted a sense of immediacy, of being there.

For Paul, the known spiritual disciplines and sources of divine inspiration lead to the unknown. By following the known script they are led to encounters and experiences, and new scripts begin to write themselves. In Philippi, Paul follows the weekly tradition of Sabbath prayer, which is how he meets Lydia. We are reminded of the basic power of relationships in ministry, and how each person adds to the capacity for ministry within the community. With each convert and each travel stop, the church was becoming more diverse in culture and geography. The experience in Philippi begins to form a theory and practice that produces the kind of Hellenistic missiology found in Paul's address in Athens (Acts 17).

Long before any organized church structure took shape, believers gathered and God's Spirit moved them, often taking them far from the established patterns of their own religious life. Macedonia represents a missionary frontier, and crossing over that threshold is a symbolic and real gesture in support of the gospel's expansive character. Paul and his companions at this point appear stalled and in search of divine guidance, and so this crossover constitutes a tremendous leap of faith.

The story of the early church takes these first missionaries outside the circle of the known and the comfortable. The text supplies place names of a sailing itinerary (Troas, Samothrace, Neapolis, v. 11), so we cannot miss that they are on an extended journey far from home. The description of Philippi as "a leading city of the district of Macedonia" (v. 12) suggests the book's cosmopolitan scope, written for an audience at a cultural or geographical distance from the events. Telling the story of the early church, the book of Acts models in its narrative a cultural openness that goes beyond the point of view of a single region or ethnic group. The personal plea of a man from Macedonia to "come over . . . and help us" (v. 9) diverts the apostles and provides the opportunity for them to meet Lydia. Authentic mission is always a response to a need within the community, not simply the missionary's need to proclaim. Congregations and individual Christians looking for ways to engage in innovative ministry can look to this passage for examples of the transformative role of prayer and worship.

On the Sabbath Paul went looking for the place of prayer outside the city gate. On this cultural frontier the only audience they found that day was outside the gate and so, outside the establishment. They did

Acts 16:9-15

Theological Perspective

house as a base for Paul and his companions, insisting that they stay there while continuing their work in Philippi. In fact, she attaches a condition to her request that makes it difficult for Paul to say no. Come and stay, she says, "if you have judged me to be faithful to the Lord." How could Paul argue with that? More than hospitality, however, is at stake. By hosting the missionaries, she becomes one of them, a new convert already in the business of converting others. We can only imagine how many heard the good news while gathered at Lydia's house.

God opened her heart, and immediately she opened her home. Apparently without any hesitation, she is baptized and turns her house into a base for the spread of Christianity in Europe. Almost as if in a single action, her faith leads to baptism, which issues immediately in hospitality and in sharing in all the risks of the mission enterprise. What is remarkable for us is how decisive Lydia appears to be. Unlike so many of us, she sees the truth before her and decides what course to take, and it is done.

Lydia is decisive because she is discerning, able to see through the events on the surface to the deeper workings of God's Spirit. She is discerning because God has opened her heart to a new level of perception. God has given her this ability to perceive because she comes to worship. She comes to worship because she is hungering for something more in life, something beyond the commercial success she has apparently achieved. She is hungering for more because that restless Spirit, who is surely in us all before we ever know it, has stirred up a holy longing in her soul. Every step of the way, the Spirit prompts and calls and blesses her and, through her, blesses us.

RONALD COLE-TURNER

Pastoral Perspective

to what is said by Paul. For Lydia, God uses a foreigner, a stranger to Philippi, as the one who brings the good news. The vision Lydia receives moves her, and indeed her whole household, toward the greatest Christian expression of transformation, namely, baptism (v. 15). This prominent dealer in purple cloth, who has been in full command of her life, is now a humble servant of God. This change is evident in Lydia's gracious hospitality when she urges Paul and his companion to "come and stay at my home" (v. 15) and later, in chapter 16, when after leaving prison Paul goes to Lydia's home again (v. 40).

Visions from God are surprising things, for they utterly transform us and alter our course. In the early 1990s, George Gallup Sr. asked Presbyterians whether they had ever experienced a vision from God. Surprisingly, half of the church members he asked said they had had a vision from God, and even a higher percentage of clergy said the same thing.[1] Perhaps one reason this statistic is surprising is because we simply do not talk about our visions from God—and maybe for good reason. If we were to talk openly about God's involvement in our lives, we could not control the plan, as we do in strategic planning. On the other hand, if we *did* share our visions from God, we might find ourselves with open hearts that readily receive the gospel that forever changes us, even to the point of providing hospitality to foreigners and those just freed from prison.

DAVID G. FORNEY

---

1. George Gallup Sr., public lecture, Princeton Theological Seminary, March 1992.

Exegetical Perspective

population) were included in the households of the first three groups (elites, farmers, and colonists had several slaves for a variety of tasks; families in the service class might have had one or two slaves per household). The church that eventually formed at Philippi probably had a modest membership of perhaps seventy-five to one hundred persons who mirrored the general population. Paul's letter to the Philippian Christians also sheds light on this congregation. The tone of his letter is joyful (in spite of his imprisonment) and full of thanksgiving for the Philippians' generosity toward him, which reflects a measure of their social and economic status.

This social schema is in the background of Luke's narrative. He recounts that on the Sabbath "we went outside the gate by the river" looking for "a place of prayer." It may be that Paul and his companions were searching for the local synagogue, a place Paul would typically visit on his first Sabbath in town. The reader is not told exactly where Paul was when he "sat down and spoke to the women who had gathered there." This sentence contains a couple of fascinating details. First, Paul sat down to speak—the typical posture of a teacher at work. Second, it is a bit of a surprise that this well-known Pharisee and teacher from Jerusalem would carry on a serious discussion with a group of women.

One of the women listening to Paul was Lydia, a "worshiper of God . . . and dealer in purple cloth." Again, Luke has included significant details. As a "God worshiper," Lydia was a Gentile attracted to Judaism, but not yet ready to make the full commitment of conversion. As a "dealer in purple cloth," she was a businessperson accustomed to dealing with the elite class of Philippi, who were allowed to wear the color purple. Moreover, she was head of her own household (no small feat in the exceedingly patriarchal Roman Empire), and finally, she was Paul's first convert in Europe!

After her baptism (a rite symbolizing conversion to this messianic sect of Judaism), she implored Paul and his companions to enjoy her hospitality. As if to put a fine point on her significant status, Luke notes that Lydia asked them to stay at "my house" (*ton oikon mou*, v. 15). Our narrator notes that "she prevailed upon us." Who would dare decline such an invitation?

PAUL W. WALASKAY

Homiletical Perspective

not enter and take charge, addressing great crowds and gaining large numbers of converts. Rather, they went to where they might find an audience willing to hear, if only a small group. The bond with Lydia is immediate and strong, and though Paul came to help, he found help himself in Lydia's generous hospitality. As a God-fearer, she actively pursued worship, even if it placed her at the margins. This dealer of purple cloth had financial resources to share, but most importantly she was receptive and willing to listen. Just as Paul had been open to a change of course to Philippi, Lydia was open when visitors arrived at her place of prayer.

People from distinctly different backgrounds are often brought together in Acts. Those once separated by barriers of language and geography are brought together. Sermons on this passage will encourage those travelers who are part of our mobile society, whose lives are constantly marked by new places and new contacts. At the same time, Acts inspires a more concerted effort within the local church (places of prayer) to consider mission and outreach within our own neighborhoods.

Luke emphasizes the role of women, and Lydia becomes a model of female spirituality and leadership at the outset. Lydia listens eagerly and is baptized, and she continues to take an active role by inviting the visitors to come and stay in her home. The force of her invitation is noted in the concluding verse: "And she prevailed upon us" (v. 15).

The centrality of worship is confirmed by the important role of the place of prayer outside Philippi. It becomes a gathering place where the missionaries can share their message. Those who bring good news have the opportunity to go outside the city in order to find a place of prayer. How do we identify the places where people are waiting to hear the word? In our visions, do we hear the calls to come over, and do we have courage enough to cross over and help? When we do, we may well find our mission field and our best listening partners.

RICHARD M. LANDERS

Psalm 67

¹May God be gracious to us and bless us
  and make his face to shine upon us,   *Selah*
²that your way may be known upon earth,
  your saving power among all nations.
³Let the peoples praise you, O God;
  let all the peoples praise you.

⁴Let the nations be glad and sing for joy,
  for you judge the peoples with equity
  and guide the nations upon earth.   *Selah*
⁵Let the peoples praise you, O God;
  let all the peoples praise you.

⁶The earth has yielded its increase;
  God, our God, has blessed us.
⁷May God continue to bless us;
  let all the ends of the earth revere him.

Theological Perspective

The opening of this psalm echoes the familiar words of the priestly benediction found in Numbers 6:24–26: "The LORD bless you and keep you; the LORD make his face to shine upon you, and be gracious to you; the LORD lift up his countenance upon you, and give you peace." As a reading during the Easter season that precedes Ascension of the Lord Sunday, this text invites us to interrogate the theological meaning of blessing in the context of salvation history.

According to scholars, there are at least two reasons to explore the meaning of this blessing as alluded to and as written in the psalm. First, the original priestly benediction is clearly to be bestowed by Aaron and his sons to convey God's blessing of the people Israel as God's covenanted people. Here it is less clear whether the blessing is solely for Israel because of its unique relationship to God or because of its position in the world among other nations. Second, is the connection between the blessing of the land and its harvest premised upon the cycles of creation, or is it of historical significance?[1]

Scholars answer the two queries about the meaning of the blessing in this psalm in the

1. Eep Talstra and Carl J. Bosma, "Psalm 67: Blessing, Harvest, and History: A Proposal for Exegetical Methodology," *Calvin Theological Journal* 36, no. 2 (2001): 300, 312–13.

Pastoral Perspective

The season of Easter pulses with the joy of God's astonishing blessings in the resurrection of Christ. Psalm 67 gives expression to this joy and locates it in the experience of God's faithful people from generation to generation. The psalm begins and ends with joyful benediction and blessing. "May God be gracious to us and bless us," the people sing, "may God continue to bless us until all the ends of the earth revere him." Thought to be a harvest festival song, this psalm bubbles over with wonder and awe for all the gifts of a gracious and good God. The people exult, as does the whole of the earth. "The earth has yielded its increase; God, our God, has blessed us" (v. 6).

For many contemporary worshipers in the Northern Hemisphere, the earth itself is bursting forth with new life in the springtime of the year, the greening life of running sap, blooming bulbs, and blossoming flowers. God's people are caught up in the delight of it all. Nature witnesses to God's generosity and love. The song of joy of the whole creation is spontaneous and heartfelt. Surely God *has* blessed us wondrously and powerfully and given us new life. It is as if only music can adequately express such deep gratitude and praise. Humans and nature sing together. "All nature sings, and round me

Exegetical Perspective

The lectionary texts for this Sunday insist on the cosmic scope of God's blessing. Paul sails to Philippi and, after sharing the gospel with women gathered at a river, baptizes Lydia, who is, as far as we know, the first European to convert to Christianity (Acts 16:9–15). In Revelation, an angel carries John to a mountaintop where he glimpses the new Jerusalem and "the nations" who stream through its open gates, find healing at the tree of life (Rev. 21:10; 21:22–22:5). In Psalm 67, the psalmist understands God's blessing of the community ("us," vv. 1, 6–7) to be inseparable from that of the world ("*all* the peoples," "*all* the ends of the earth," vv. 3, 7, emphasis added). Like a steady heartbeat, the psalmist's use of the plural and repetition of "all" resists any small-minded notions we might have of God's saving power.

Psalm 67 may be outlined as a concentric structure of five units, two of which are the psalm's refrain (B, B'):

A. Prayer for blessing (vv. 1–2)
    B. Refrain: "Let all the peoples praise you" (v. 3)
        C. Reason for praise: God is judge/guide (v. 4)
    B'. Refrain: "Let all the peoples praise you" (v. 5)
A'. Prayer for blessing (vv. 6–7)

Homiletical Perspective

The most difficult instrument to play in a symphony orchestra is second fiddle. No one will notice how well you play it—but make a mistake, and all will notice and remember it. This psalm, as it is placed in the lectionary, plays second fiddle to the passage from Acts 16:9–15. When used as a response in the liturgy or as a text for a sermon, its message is strengthened by its relationship to the Acts passage. Even though it is second fiddle, it does not give an uncertain sound. The gospel is ours not to keep but to give away. This lection, used in conjunction with the lesson from Acts 6:9–15, makes it clear that God's intention for God's people is for them to see a larger vision. The lesson from Acts makes the call to Macedonia across the Aegean Sea and into Europe a call for the followers of the risen and ascended Christ to move beyond their comfort zones into unfamiliar territory. We have the privilege of seeing that the seeds planted by that small beginning grew through the centuries to become a major harvest.

Psalm 67 is a response to this lesson and affirms this direction for the gospel. This gospel is for all people, all nations, just as the earth has given its increase to God's people. So God's people must tell of God's love and care for all people and take this message to all nations. The preacher of this text has

Psalm 67

Theological Perspective

following way. From an explication of the text that places verse 5 at the center of their reading, Psalm 67 is described as a song of the community in response to a particular blessing experienced in history. Here the text holds in tension a meaning of the earth as the habitation of peoples (e.g., vv. 3a and 5b) and the earth as cultivated land yielding a harvest (e.g., v. 6a). This tension between the two meanings thus leads these scholars to emphasize a theological frame that can be compared to postexilic prophecy— especially as found in Zechariah—of blessing, harvest, and history. Harvest is a sign that points toward the new beginning made after the exile (see Zech. 8:12). In Psalm 67 the blessing thus derives from Israel's unique relationship to God and is of historical significance, but it also signifies God's blessing as God, Israel, the peoples/nations, and the earth interact in the harvest season.[2]

The meaning of blessing in the context of salvation history is that a blessing is always a gift from God. Perhaps the gift of blessing is bestowed following our labors, as in the work of cultivating the land to produce a harvest, but it is not our labors that cause the blessing. The harvest is a sign pointing to God. God gives the blessing as confirmation of God's continuing relationship to us as people of God, who have a larger role to play in God's unfolding salvation history with all peoples and nations of the earth.

It is this larger role in God's unfolding salvation history that must capture our attention during the season of Easter. Like the people Israel, Christians as people of God must remain aware of all the actors in God's salvation history. Peoples of other faiths, nations of the world, and the earth itself are all actors with whom Christians interact through the blessing of the gift of Jesus. God gave Jesus, God's only Son, out of love in order to reconcile the world to God's self. The response of Christians to God's gift thus has everything to do with reconciliation.

How are Christians in the United States to know when they are in the season of harvest and being blessed by God? Our season of harvest will be marked in two concrete ways. First, Christians will be engaged in ministries of reconciliation; the reconciling work of Jesus Christ through his death and resurrection makes this an explicit vocation for Christians. In the twenty-first century, this vocation of reconciling ministries means that we will not merely tolerate peoples and nations of other faiths;

2. Ibid., 303–13.

Pastoral Perspective

rings the music of the spheres," the hymnwriter phrased it.[1]

Yet even in Eastertide, not everyone will be cheerful or joyful. Internal rhythms and personal circumstances are sometimes out of harmony with the mood of the season. There will be those in worship for whom life seems dreary and sad, for whom grief abides and whom fear pursues. Within their aching hearts and shadowed souls, the season's relentless cheerfulness can seem empty, heartless, and even cruel. This can create a painful dissonance within them. They can feel isolated and alone in their sorrow and out of sync in their despair. They perceive their own darkness as a painful and embarrassing indictment of faithlessness. These anxious and self-conscious worshipers are in the season of a Psalm 42 more than of a Psalm 67. In Eastertide, may they hear again the assurance that for them, compassionately, the risen Christ still shows his wounded hands and side. The one who has been raised up is the one who has borne our griefs and carried our sorrows (Isa. 53:4).

In such seasons of life, the prayerbook that is the book of Psalms becomes a special gift, a trusted means of lovingly yet efficaciously drawing worshipers out of themselves and into the shared experience of God's people over time and space. The psalm lifts individual worshipers from their own immediate situation and places their lives in the context of the whole of God's people and God's work. For the cheerless worshiper, there is no imperative to feign joy in such times, but simply the invitation to remember and to trust through the witness of the psalm.

Even if the fullness of the light is too much to embrace just yet, even if its promise seems in vain, there comes the memory that for some, somewhere, joy is real, even now. Somewhere, rejoicing is sincere. For some, even now, thanksgiving is heartfelt, and that is enough. The psalm works in this way to form Christians as people who can hold on to hope in the midst of despair and trust through times of loss and desolation. "Weeping may linger for the night, but joy comes with the morning," the psalmist has proclaimed (30:5). God has been faithful and will be again. God has blessed and will bless again. God does not stay distant or silent forever. For Christians this is the deepest promise of Easter, that nothing will separate us from the love of God in Christ, as

1. Maltie D. Babcock, "This Is My Father's World," in *The Worshipbook* (Philadelphia: Westminster Press, 1970), #602.

The refrain summons worldwide praise of God (vv. 3, 5). Its twofold use of the verb "to praise" or "to give thanks" (*ydh*) urges adoration that springs from gratitude for who God is and/or what God has done (e.g., Pss. 28:6–7; 35:17–18; 57:9–10 [Heb. vv. 10–11]). The second line intensifies "peoples" to "*all the peoples*" (lit. "peoples, *all of them*"), emphasizing that everyone should participate. (Note the psalm focuses on worship by humanity, only one part of the cosmos; elsewhere the psalmist beckons other parts of the cosmos to praise, e.g., Pss. 96:11–13; 98:7–9.) Finally, placement of the vocative ("O God") in the center of the refrain literally surrounds God with the vast and reverent chorus.

The refrain frames verse 4, the heart of the psalm and its only three-line verse. There, the psalmist explicitly names the motivation for all-encompassing praise: *for* (*kî*) God judges with equity and guides the world (v. 4bc). Affirmations of God's sovereignty often include celebration of God's role as judge (e.g., Ps. 82:8; 94:2; 96:10–13; 98:9; cf. Gen. 18:25), while the verb "to lead" or "to conduct" calls to mind a particular expression of divine power, namely, God's guidance of Israel through the wilderness (e.g., Exod. 13:21; Deut. 32:12; Ps. 78:14, 53, 72). The psalmist painstakingly measures out God's sovereignty by "nations . . . peoples . . . nations," referring to "peoples" or "nations" no less than seven times in verses 5–7, a number that signifies completeness. Because God is just and God reigns, the psalmist contends, every corner of the world can rejoice and sing.

The outermost units of the psalm draw a straight line from God's blessing of Israel to worldwide knowledge of and reverence for God (vv. 1–2, 6–7). Prayer for the community (for "us") has implications for all peoples. The psalmist first seeks God's favor *so that* "all nations" might know God's saving power (vv. 1–2). The logic recalls God's promises to Abraham and Sarah ("I will bless you . . . *so that* you will be a blessing. . . . in you all families of the earth shall be blessed," Gen. 12:2–3; cf. Exod. 9:16), and the language evokes the priestly benediction: "The LORD bless you and keep you, the LORD make [the LORD's] face to shine upon you, and *be gracious* to you" (Num. 6:24–25; cf. 6:22–27).

Divine favor is frequently described as God's face shining on the community—God's face by synecdoche represents the full presence of God, which is turned toward the community, while its "shining" attributes to God a sunlike radiance (e.g., Pss. 4:6 [Heb. v. 7]; 31:16 [Heb. v. 17]; 44:3 [Heb. v. 4]). God's light on Israel, the psalmist contends,

ample warrant to declare that the blessings of our God are not just for us. We are blessed in order to bless others. God's goal is the entire world. Preaching this passage, the preacher is empowered by its picture of the completed harvest as an illustration, which is what the psalmist seeks to communicate in this hymn.

The bountiful harvest is an apt picture for those who originally sang this hymn. It may not communicate well to those of us who live surrounded by asphalt and concrete, securing our food at the supermarket. However, people who live close to the earth and whose quality of existence is defined by the harvest understand clearly that this is a call to evangelism. In preaching this, it is important that we bring the symbol of the harvest into the life of the twenty-first century.

In his groundbreaking book *The New Face of Christianity: Believing the Bible and the Global South*, Phillip Jenkins notes that the church is growing rapidly in Africa and South America, whereas it is stagnant in Europe and North America. The reason for this is that the global south is closer to the metaphors of the Bible, in this case, the harvest and praising God for it. This presents a challenge for the preacher of this text. For those who live close to the earth and depend upon its gifts for life, strength, survival—seeing its abundance as a manifestation of the goodness and grandeur of God—there can be only one response; that is to tell all nations of God's goodness, that they too may fear and honor God and receive God's blessings.

Our psalmist makes clear three declarations: (1) that God has mercy on God's people and gives them God's blessings; (2) that God gives them God's presence (shines on them); (3) that this is done so that earth may understand God's ways and all nations may know God's deliverance. Therefore, all people will praise God.

When this psalm was used in corporate worship, verse 5 was the confessional response of the congregation. They affirmed that God's blessings are universal. How can any congregation not see from this psalm and its supporting lessons (Acts 16:9–15) that the gospel is to be shared? This text is a clear call to the preacher to ask the question of the congregation: *how big is your God?* God will not be restricted to people who look like us. Anything less than the entire world is not worthy of the death, burial, and resurrection of our Lord. God refused to be the private possession of one group of people in the New Testament, and God certainly cannot be contained or

Psalm 67

Theological Perspective

we will come to embrace them, striving to love them as we invite them to praise our God: "Let the peoples praise you, O God; let all the peoples praise you" (v. 5). If other peoples and nations join us in praising God as Christians, it shall be God's work ("your saving power among all nations," v. 2a) and not our efforts to convert others through coercion.

Second, the relationships between Christians and peoples and nations of other faiths will be relationships of justice. "Let the nations be glad and sing for joy, for you judge the peoples with equity and guide the nations upon earth" (v. 4). The justice of God is to be the standard for justice among the peoples and nations of the earth. This means that the uneven application of human law cannot be tolerated. If there is to be an international court where perpetrators of crimes against humanity are tried, then all nations must make appearances before that court. The torture and annihilation of any nation's people must be judged by norms of a global common morality; no nation gets to claim moral superiority and thus the right to dispose of others deemed less than human by actually substituting military might for moral authority. We Christians in the United States will know we are in a season of harvest when our rhetoric about being a Christian nation is experienced by peoples and nations of other faiths, within our borders and beyond, as ministries of reconciliation and equitably applied justice.

"May God be gracious to us and bless us and make his face to shine upon us" (v. 1). Jesus Christ is risen! God has been gracious to us. The justice of God through this act of resurrection makes feasible our living together on the earth through ministries of reconciliation. The question is whether or not we are willing to cultivate the earth through such ministries, so as to have a season of harvest.

MARCIA Y. RIGGS

Pastoral Perspective

Paul put it. God's face is shining upon all in Eastertide, in our darkness as well as in our light. God is blessing us all.

Fundamentally, Psalm 67 rejoices that God is present with God's people. God is blessing the people with God's very self. This is the deepest longing of the human heart: to know with assurance the loving, living, abiding presence of God. The blessing that will come to all people is that very knowledge of God and God's loving-kindness, God's saving power that will come upon all peoples and all nations of the earth.

In so doing, Psalm 67 proclaims that God intends to take all this much farther than our own feelings and perspectives readily or comfortably embrace. This is part of the psalm's important work of contextualization as well. Here the scope of God's purpose is revealed to encompass the whole globe. God is blessing all the nations, not just the Hebrew people. God is blessing and judging all the peoples. This revelation turns narrow or selfish associations with God's judgment inside out. No one is exempt, and no one is excluded from its span. God's work of righteousness proceeds without regard to any parochial boundaries. It is not subject to human calculation or even comprehension. God's judgment is God's trustworthy gift to all peoples and all nations. Therefore it calls forth thanksgiving and praise.

In this, the depth of the people's rejoicing is revealed. The psalm has shifted the focus from the worshiper to God. The great stretch of God's saving love embraces the private hurts and needs and joys of each parishioner, even as it reaches to include the whole of humankind and all the nations of the earth. God's righteousness will be made manifest for the whole of the world, God's way made known upon earth. Salvation is for all.

"Let the peoples praise you, O God; let all the peoples praise you" (v. 3). At the heart of it all is trust—trust in God to act and to save God's people and God's world, and in so doing, to bless.

PATRICIA FARRIS

illumines for everyone God's "way" and "saving power" (v. 2). God's "way" may refer to the history of God's activity in the world (e.g., Deut. 32:4; Prov. 8:22) and/or the "way" God expects God's people to conduct themselves (e.g., Gen. 18:19; Jer. 5:4). Both testify to God's "saving power," to God's intent to establish justice and peace for all (e.g., Exod. 15:2; Isa. 51:5). Through God's blessing of Israel, the world comes to know and worship God.

The concluding prayer for blessing (vv. 6–7), which begins and ends with the word "earth" (*'erets*), points to the earth's bounty as evidence of God's favor. (Some interpreters posit that Psalm 67 was once associated with a harvest festival.) The ancients celebrated seasonal rains and good harvests as divine gifts, even as droughts and poor harvests signaled God's judgment (e.g., Lev. 26:4, 20; Deut. 11:17; Ps. 85:12 [Heb. v. 13]; Ezek. 34:27; Hag. 1:10). One imagines the psalmist pointing to piles of barley, wheat, and dried fruits, to jugs of wine and olive oil, exclaiming "God is good!" and praying that God continues to be so. Such abundance from the earth, the psalmist concludes, should stir "all the ends of the earth" (cf. Pss. 2:8; 72:8; Isa. 52:7–10) to "revere" (lit. "fear") God.

In this Easter season, as we proclaim that "God so loved *the world*" (John 3:16a), that God sent Jesus Christ not to condemn the world, but "in order that *the world* might be saved" (John 3:17), Psalm 67 insists we never forget the wideness of God's sovereignty and love. The psalmist reminds us that the scope of God's salvation and blessing is communal *and* cosmic, particular *and* global—for "us" and most certainly for "them." God's blessing of Israel is inextricable from God's blessing of the whole earth.

CHRISTINE ROY YODER

controlled by any one group now. God is for all nations, then and now. The preacher could ask the question again, *how big is your God?* Suburban Christianity has reduced God to a provider of soccer games, cell phones, SUVs, cookouts, and entertainment. Too often, urban Christianity has been reduced to self-help and success theology. Too many sermons are basically motivational speeches decorated with one or two Scriptures. The mission the Bible has for God's people calls this into question.

When this text is used as a congregational response to the lesson for the day (Acts 16:9–15), its power is intensified. The psalmist wants God's "ways" to be known on all the earth. God wants the whole earth to know and live his way. Every God substitute is evidence that we want to know God's way but have missed the mark. The world has lost its way, morally and spiritually, and the people of God have the knowledge that can bring it back. For the church, the events of the book of Acts are not on a side street but on the main road. They are a part of God's plan from the days of Abraham and Moses. This text, taken to heart, demands that the preacher give her congregation a wider view. It lifts our horizons and pulls the church forward, giving the church a world to serve and a life wish. If anything smaller than this text is preached, the church will experience a death wish instead.

The harvest of the church is the gathering in of all nations (Matt. 9:35–38). "God of grace and God of glory, on thy people pour thy power."[1]

WILLIAM L. SELF

1. Harry Emerson Fosdick, "God of Grace and God of Glory," in *Baptist Hymnal* (Nashville: Convention Press, 1991) 395.

Revelation 21:10; 21:22-22:5

21:10And in the spirit he carried me away to a great, high mountain and showed me the holy city Jerusalem coming down out of heaven from God. . . .

22I saw no temple in the city, for its temple is the Lord God the Almighty and the Lamb. 23And the city has no need of sun or moon to shine on it, for the glory of God is its light, and its lamp is the Lamb. 24The nations will walk by its light, and the kings of the earth will bring their glory into it. 25Its gates will never be shut by day—and there will be no night there. 26People will bring into it the glory and the honor of the nations. 27But nothing unclean will enter it, nor anyone who practices abomination or falsehood, but only those who are written in the Lamb's book of life.

22:1Then the angel showed me the river of the water of life, bright as crystal, flowing from the throne of God and of the Lamb 2through the middle of the street of the city. On either side of the river is the tree of life with its twelve kinds of fruit, producing its fruit each month; and the leaves of the tree are for the healing of the nations. 3Nothing accursed will be found there anymore. But the throne of God and of the Lamb will be in it, and his servants will worship him; 4they will see his face, and his name will be on their foreheads. 5And there will be no more night; they need no light of lamp or sun, for the Lord God will be their light, and they will reign forever and ever.

Theological Perspective

The final weeks of Eastertide concentrate our attention upon Jesus' constitution of the church, for they mark the time of transition between his physical presence with the disciples and the "last days" following his ascension, which is the ecclesial era. So, for example, the Gospel for the Sixth Sunday of Easter is taken from John's account of Jesus' promise to the disciples that when he is no longer with them, the Father will send the Holy Spirit in his name (John 14:26). This bestowal of the Spirit is the church-constituting act par excellence, which makes of it a sacramental body: Christ will be present in and through the church by the indwelling of the Spirit.

The lectionary's pairing of John 14 with Revelation 21 and 22, in which the writer is shown a vision of the holy city Jerusalem descending out of heaven, thus suggests an ecclesiological theme at the heart of this Sunday's place in the liturgical cycle. Although we read in this lesson only a portion of these two chapters, the vision that is developed throughout these chapters revolves consistently around the image of the new Jerusalem. So if one reads this text with an ear for its ecclesiological significance—taking the new Jerusalem (as did the early Christians) as a metaphor for the church—then one is immediately struck by the fact that the community of the faithful is not regarded as trapped

Pastoral Perspective

The opening verse of this text carries the reader away, literally, into the heights of a mountain from whose summit one may witness the descent of the holy city. We are watching a divine construction site. From this vantage point, the dramatic changes being brought about through God's action can be seen with clarity. We have been positioned in hard hats to witness the culmination of God's plan for humanity.

The high points of mountains are looked upon as traditional "thin places," offering a closer mingling of the Divine and the mortal. The Bible provides multiple narratives in which persons climb toward the heavens in order to commune with the Almighty. For many of us, travel into the mountains is connected with time for personal re-creation, retreat, and study. We ascend to gain perspective and a different angle of vision. What can only be discerned piecemeal or partially from ground level can be better grasped from on high, where it might be seen whole and complete. Ground-level living contends with obstacles and impediments. To see clearly we must rise higher. In our opening text it is God who provides the means for doing so. Perhaps there is a message here, witnessing to God's provision of perspective. It does not have to include a physical mountain. It may involve a spiritual one, granted through worship, or through prayer and

Exegetical Perspective

This text offers a rare glimpse of how an early Christian hoped for the future. Inspired by passages such as Isaiah 65–66 and Ezekiel 40–48 (the latter especially evident in the verses omitted), the author looks forward to heaven on earth, when the throne of God is no longer in heaven (as in Rev. 4) but on earth (22:1).

The visionary character of John's experience is hinted at by the phrase "in the spirit" (21:10), reminding us that we are dealing with a very different sort of literature here. John's vision, like many other strands of the New Testament, sees the physical temple of God on earth as redundant after it is found in the lives of men and women committed to Jesus. The absence of the temple indicates the lack of need to enclose the divine presence, for it will pervade the whole city (21:22). It is possible that there is no need for a temple because the city is a perfect square and is a sanctuary in itself, but Almighty God and the Lamb are the temple (v. 22). If a temple separates divine presence from the rest of the world, then here the divine is immediately present, without a preserve to guarantee and identify holiness. Christ's presence in the world, found in a variety of different places, takes the place of the temple in sharing the holiness of God. Heaven and earth meet no longer in the temple but "outside the camp," a place of former shame and reproach.

Homiletical Perspective

Great poetry can suffer from explanation and elucidation. So perhaps it would be understandable if a preacher were tempted to read this text, invite the congregation into silent meditation on its eloquent imagery, and take a seat. However, we are, after all, talking about preachers here, and Revelation begs to have its mysteries unpacked.

John's vision of the inbreaking of the new continues in this passage with a view from a high mountain, a supreme vantage point for holy revelations. From here, he sees the "new Jerusalem" coming down from heaven. No detail is spared in the description of this splendid city, made of pure gold and adorned with every jewel imaginable. It is a sparkling, priceless gem of a place.

Of note is the absence of the temple in this Jerusalem. The focal point for faithful generations, the temple was considered the dwelling place of God. However, now God has become the dwelling place—the permanent, central fixture in this new city. Because that is so, the city is a place of life, healing, and hope.

John employs a cornucopia of images to make this point. This new Jerusalem is flooded with perpetual light, so that no sun or moon or lamps are necessary. Its gates are always open. From the throne at its center flows a river, and on its banks stands the

Revelation 21:10; 21:22-22:5

Theological Perspective

in the fallen, corrupt world of human experience. Rather, it is already part of the new heaven and earth that God will bring to completion at the end of time—the new creation that brings the first creation to its perfection.

For those who observe the Great Vigil of Easter Eve, this language of re-creation hearkens back to the final collect of the vigil's Liturgy of the Word, where the congregation prays that God will "look favorably on your whole Church, that wonderful and sacred mystery." Through that blessing, the whole world may "see and know that things which were cast down are being raised up, and things which had grown old are being made new."[1] This is the ecclesiological significance of the image of the new Jerusalem: the church is the embodiment, already coming into being, of a restored creation into which all things and all people will be incorporated. (No wonder, then, that this same text is often read at funerals!)

Moreover, the particular verses appointed for this Sunday are those that especially develop the image of the city as a symbol of the church. Cities, of course, have always held a strong place in the collective imagination of human beings—whether as dens of corruption or as oases of culture and civilization. The new Jerusalem in John's Revelation, however, makes unambiguous appeal to the latter strain of imagery; here the city is no longer a dense, dark collection of human vices, but a renewed community that "has no need of sun or moon to shine on it" (21:23), for it is now the light of God that illumines its streets.

This is an image of the city as the place where human nature can find its perfection. As Eugene Boring writes in his commentary on Revelation, "A city is the realization of human community, the concrete living out of interdependence as the essential nature of human life."[2] The new Jerusalem is thus a place of safety and inclusion (its gates are always open) and a beacon of hope to all people (nations will walk by its light). This, then, is the vision held out for us of the church's own life: it is a place of consummation for the purposes for which God created humanity.

Yet this theologically lofty vision is, in our own time, hard to relate to. The city has become a place of almost insurmountable problems: urban sprawl, environmental degradation, and paralyzing gaps between rich and poor. Indeed, contemporary

1. *The Book of Common Prayer* (New York: Church Hymnal Corporation, 1979), 291.
2. M. Eugene Boring, *Revelation* (Louisville, KY: John Knox Press, 1989), 219.

Pastoral Perspective

contemplation, as it did for the writer of these verses of Scripture.

A common lamentation with the gaining of such a "vision" is that one must inevitably descend to the valleys and fields, where life is lived from fragmented moment to moment. The full glory of what was glimpsed whole dims in memory. All of us have had this experience, when a "mountaintop" revelation is followed by a return into the mundane and muddled everyday slog of living. We are unable to hold to what we received "on high." With the passing of time we might question whether the experience that once enraptured us was even real. Too many intervening struggles eclipse and obscure what we once grasped so clearly.

In this instance, however, the text assures us that the vision provided is not going to diminish or fade into the recesses of memory. This is not some vague fanciful outline for the future, but is instead a multidimensional revelation of what is to become the concrete and corporate reality. As the text continues in chapter 22, we learn that through the action of God, the mountaintop experience and the commonplace will come together and be joined permanently.

The holy city of Jerusalem has settled upon the earth. The eternal is established within the landscape of history. The symbols used throughout the bridging text linking the lectionary verses are vivid in their explicitness. We read of precious stones and precise dimensions. Rivers, which have served throughout the biblical narrative as obstacles to be crossed, are no longer barriers. The tree of life that stood in the Genesis garden is found to be growing on both sides of a single watercourse that flows from the throne of God. No one is to be left out. There is access for everyone without partition. Political realities are dissolved.

From the ground-level perspective of our present world, characterized more by division than unity, the images offered are striking and parabolic. We know our human capacity for duplicity and subterfuge, our penchant for disguising and hiding our true designs. In the city depicted in the text, this no longer occurs. There is no night, no darkness or shadow present for hiding motivations or intentions. The revealing light of God illuminates every corner and every closet. There is no longer a place for pretence or deception. Such ideas have no purchase here, being alien to the very nature of what God brings into being.

The garden that was the beginning home of humanity is again a shared dwelling place where

Sixth Sunday of Easter

The universal hope expressed here (21:24–25) contrasts with the rhetoric of exclusion (21:27). The fact that some names are not written in the book of life suggests that humans can do nothing about their eternal lot, but this is not the case. Rejecting the lure of the beast and Babylon is the criterion for inclusion in the new age (20:13; cf. 13:8; 13:15–17). Sharing the divine reign is a key feature of the eschatological future. This is something already glimpsed by those who share the life of Jesus and are a kingdom of priests (1:6).

The climax of John's vision comes with possession of the divine name, when the servants of the Lamb will share his character by bearing his name on their foreheads (22:4). Possession of the name is promised from the very start of the vision (7:3). Wearing it enables the confession of the faithful and the entry of their names into the book of life.

The whole passage uses contrasts between darkness and light (21:23; 22:5) to evoke the all-pervading presence of God in the new age. There is little need of light in the city because of the radiance of divine glory. This contrasts with the darkness of Babylon (16:10; 18:23). The reference to the lamp of the Lamb (21:23) offers an additional light alongside and, in some sense, subordinate to the glory of God. God will shine upon the servants of the Lamb, and they will reign forever (22:5). In the millennium, God's servants share God's reign (cf. 3:21); they constitute a kingdom of priests who serve God's throne.

The nations are guided by this glorious light (21:24), in contrast with earlier descriptions of their delusion (14:8; 18:3). The kings of the earth now reappear (21:24), hitherto thoroughly under the spell of the beast but now under the King of kings and Lord of lords. They bring their glory into the city. People follow them, bringing "the glory and honor of the nations" (21:26). Compare Isaiah 60:11, where the kings bring their wealth into a city whose gates are always open; "day and night they shall not be shut." The city of John's vision will not include anything that is unclear (v. 27), nor any one whose name is not written in the book of life.

At the very heart of the city John sees a river that contains the water mentioned in 21:6. Its life-giving quality stands in strong contrast with the rivers poisoned in the eschatological catastrophes. This river evokes paradise, the garden of Eden (Gen. 2:10).

As mentioned earlier, the throne of God and the Lamb (7:17) will be in the city. The throne in 4:1 is in heaven, but here God's dwelling is with humanity on earth, where God's servants will perform their

tree of life, whose fruit is never out of season. The inhabitants of this city will see the face of God, upending the traditional understanding that no one can see God's face and survive. They will bear God's name on their foreheads, indicating that they are sealed for eternity by God's protection.

Pervading all of these images is a sense of permanence. This is not surprising, given that the destruction of Jerusalem and its temple, in 587 BCE by the Babylonians and again in 70 CE by the Romans, signaled dispersion, exile, captivity, repression, and tenuous existence for the faithful. The new Jerusalem is indestructible—a shining light for all nations, which stream to her gates and lavish the city with honor.

Images of exile and devastation may be quite foreign to the experience of many congregations in this country, but for the millions of people who are undocumented, uninsured, unsheltered, or unemployed, feeling like exiles in a land of plenty is daily fare. For those in other parts of the globe who are in the crosshairs of U.S. military and economic policies, security, consolation, and survival are familiar longings.

Revelation unfolds as an indictment of the domination and corrupting power of the Babylonian and Roman empires and, by implication, of all empires. In 1960, theologian Reinhold Niebuhr spoke of Americans "frantically avoiding recognition of the imperialism that we in fact exercise."[1] In the decades since, and especially in the post-9/11 era, the notion of American Empire has gained currency among theologians and social analysts.

Historian Michael Ignatieff asks,

> What word but "empire" describes the awesome thing that America is becoming? It is the only nation that polices the world through five global military commands; maintains more than a million men and women at arms on four continents; deploys carrier battle groups on watch in every ocean; guarantees the survival of countries from Israel to South Korea; drives the wheels of global trade and commerce; and fills the hearts and minds of an entire planet with its dreams and desires.

The aspiration to empire is no longer considered an offense. Joseph Nye, dean of Harvard's Kennedy School of Government, wrote in *The Washington Post*, "Not since Rome has one nation loomed so

---

1. This quotation and the one in the next paragraph are quoted in Michael Ignatieff, "The Burden," *New York Times Magazine*, January 5, 2003.

Revelation 21:10; 21:22-22:5

Theological Perspective

urbanists regard the city as something so complex and out of control that it can no longer be meaningfully studied or planned—only passively observed. The Dutch architect Rem Koolhaas has described this situation as "the apotheosis of urbanization," which is "glaringly obvious and mathematically inevitable."[3] The biblical appeal to an idealized image of the city thus may not ring very true to our ears. Rather, the mood of our current culture often turns back toward more transcendentalist yearnings—wishing to find peace and inspiration in the natural, rather than the urban, environment. Yet cities are also an inescapable fixture of contemporary life: in 2008, for the first time, more than half of the world's population, more than three billion people, lived in towns and cities. Moreover, today's metropolises can no longer even be described by so tame a word, but must now be thought of as a "megalopolis." So, does the image of the ideal city go the way of the good shepherd, as totally unrelated to the realities of our contemporary existence?

Here we are driven back to the biblical text, to discover the other dominant metaphor of Revelation 21: Christ is "the Alpha and the Omega, the beginning and the end." Christ is is the Lord not just of a beguiling simplicity—the idyllic beginning of humankind in the garden of Eden—but also of the complexities of our most intractable problems. If urban life has become almost unimaginably complex, that does not mean that God is somehow exiled from its stark realities. No. John's Revelation insists that in Christ "the home of God is among mortals" (21:3). If the hard reality of Jesus' human life was to be born of poor humble parents in a small provincial village, the hard reality of Jesus' life with us now is to be homeless in city streets, to struggle for survival in an urban shantytown, to be isolated and lonely in suburban sprawl. It is to these places that the church must now bear Christ's presence, relating even the most apocalyptic urban environments to the God who is all in all.

JOSEPH H. BRITTON

Pastoral Perspective

God and God's people are together in mutual relationship. The tree offers fruit for every month. It is ever flourishing, ever bearing. There is no barren period when it will not produce, nor weeks of the year when its branches are void of fruit. There is diversity and abundance without division and limitation. Even the leaves of the tree of life are meant for healing, serving as reminders of the shade and solace available from God.

The symbolic particulars of the descended city of Jerusalem are revealing. They capture aspects of the biblical narrative that have become concretized in the hymns and prayers of generations of Christian believers. We have heard these descriptions so often that, for many, their power to awe has been lost. With a revisited awareness we move outside the limits of the words themselves and experience them anew as indicators of a reality beyond our imagining. They point us beyond any glory we can bring to mind. The contextual horizon of these magnificent assertions reminds us of the mortal eyes of the author, who told us in the opening chapter of the book of Revelation that these narrated visionary descriptions have been seen "in the spirit." This recognition opens the interesting question of the idiosyncratic character of all biblical revelation. It suggests that while the fundamental nature of God's eschatological action is unaltered, the particulars in which it is clothed may appear differently, depending on the one to whom the vision is offered.

Such recognition allows us fully to embrace and celebrate the divine character and fulfillment of God's will, without being bound to the exacting specifications of a spiritual vision as interpreted by a single individual or community. We are empowered to view this revelation through eyes shining with new astonishment as we identify aspects of the holy city that reach beyond those detailed by John. We are invited to encounter unique applications of God's construction of the heavenly city for the brokenness of our own lives. There is a street address here for everyone where stands a dwelling place that is furnished with grace specific for each one's needs.

PAUL "SKIP" JOHNSON

3. Rem Koolhaas and Bruce Mau, *S, M, L, XL* (New York: Monacelii Press, 1995), 963.

service (cf. 7:15). They will see God's face, the ultimate privilege. Not even Moses was allowed to do that (Exod. 33:20). According to John the evangelist, no one has seen God at any time, and it is only the Logos incarnate who has made God known (John 1:18; cf. 14:9). In Matthew 5:8 it is the pure in heart who will see God, but in Revelation 22:3–4 it is God's servants who have not worshiped the beast or committed fornication with Babylon who will see God's face.

There is a difference between the throne here and that in Daniel 7:9–10 (cf. *1 Enoch* 14:19), where the seer sees a throne of "fiery flames" with "a stream of fire" issuing from it. No mention is made of any stream of fire in Revelation 4, though the throne produces lightning, thunder, and voices (4:5). The fiery character of the stream in Daniel, hinted at perhaps in Revelation 4:5 and 15:2, is replaced in the new Jerusalem by the stream of living water proceeding from the throne and running down the street of the city (22:2). Life-giving water is also a feature of the new Jerusalem in Ezekiel's vision, where water flows from the entrance of the temple fructifying the land (Ezek. 47:1–12). Leaves and fresh fruit each month are characteristic of the trees irrigated by the water that runs from the temple in Ezekiel 47:12 (cf. Rev. 22:2). The emphasis in today's text on healing for the nations contrasts with the iron rod that will be wielded against the nations elsewhere in Revelation (e.g., 12:5). Still, nothing accursed enters into the city (22:3), which is in line with the sentiments expressed in 22:11, 15 (cf. 21:8, 27).

CHRISTOPHER ROWLAND

large above the others. Indeed, the word 'empire' has come out of the closet."[2] William Kristol is chair of the Project for the New American Century, a powerful, neoconservative think tank committed by its own description to "accept[ing] responsibility for America's unique role in preserving and extending an international order friendly to our security, our prosperity, and our principles." The Project's papers lay out the vision of an "American peace" (Pax Americana) based on "unquestioned U.S. military pre-eminence." Affirmation of such an aspiration even appeared on Vice President Dick Cheney's 2003 family Christmas card: "And if a sparrow cannot fall to the ground without His notice, is it probable that an empire can rise without His aid?"[3]

In this empire, unilateral decision making rules, preemptive war is admissible, "occupiers" are labeled "liberators," torture is redefined, and the world's goods are ours to exploit. The war on terrorism is pitched as a righteous clash between good and evil, and God is on our side. The notion of America as the "new Israel," God's new chosen people—first embraced by the founding Puritans—has been resuscitated in this era. It is a far cry from the new Jerusalem—an image of justice and consolation for the exiles, the captives, and the oppressed.

How to preach in such a time? Methodist Bishop Peter Storey of South Africa offers some help:

> I have often suggested to American Christians that the only way to understand their mission is to ask what it might have meant to witness faithfully to Jesus in the heart of the Roman Empire. . . . America's preachers have a task more difficult, perhaps, than those faced by us under South Africa's apartheid, or by Christians under Communism. We had obvious evils to engage. . . . You have to expose and confront the great disconnect between the kindness, compassion, and caring of most American people and the ruthless way American power is experienced, directly and indirectly, by the poor of the earth. You have to help good people see how they have let their institutions do their sinning for them.

The challenge is ours to accept.

JOYCE HOLLYDAY

2. This quotation and the one about an American peace are quoted in Jim Wallis, "Dangerous Religion—Bush's Theology of Empire," informationclearinghouse.info, December 19, 2003.
3. This quotation and the longer one of Bishop Storey are quoted in Ray McGovern, "Hijacking God for Empire," buzzflash.com, December 29, 2003.

John 14:23-29

²³Jesus answered him, "Those who love me will keep my word, and my Father will love them, and we will come to them and make our home with them. ²⁴Whoever does not love me does not keep my words; and the word that you hear is not mine, but is from the Father who sent me.

²⁵"I have said these things to you while I am still with you. ²⁶But the Advocate, the Holy Spirit, whom the Father will send in my name, will teach you everything, and remind you of all that I have said to you. ²⁷Peace I leave with you; my peace I give to you. I do not give to you as the world gives. Do not let your hearts be troubled, and do not let them be afraid. ²⁸You heard me say to you, 'I am going away, and I am coming to you.' If you loved me, you would rejoice that I am going to the Father, because the Father is greater than I. ²⁹And now I have told you this before it occurs, so that when it does occur, you may believe."

Theological Perspective

Today's text breaks open assumptions about our relationship to God and raises new questions. Jesus refuses to fit neatly within the confines of historic formulas. He testifies here to a powerful unfinished encounter with God that presses beyond language. Yet he promises a complete communion between the human and divine. This reflection will touch on three of the challenges that emerge in reading John 14:23–29.

The first challenge arises out of Jesus' promise of the Holy Spirit, the "Counselor" (NRSV "Advocate"). John's Jesus can see what his disciples cannot, while he looks forward to a time when they will finally "get it." Jesus tells his followers he is about to leave, and breaks the news to them that they are going to be receiving a teacher who will clarify all that remains hidden. They will remember, he tells them, and therefore believe. Yet their transformed remembrance will come not just by their doing, but through a Counselor who will "teach . . . everything."

Does the Spirit impart new knowledge of Jesus or just clarify what is already known? Is God's revelation complete in the crucified and risen Jesus Christ, or is there more to be revealed of Christ today? How does that *more* relate to the Jesus of history?

The second challenge in this passage is an ancient one. Jesus' statement that he is going to the "Father,"

Pastoral Perspective

A pastoral perspective on John's Farewell Discourse will bear in mind the realities of separation and death in the lives of everyone listening to a sermon. While most people who are listening will not remember the first time their parents left them alone, almost everybody will have some memory of being left: with a childcare provider, on the first day of school, at the end of a relationship, upon the death of someone beloved. As Jesus takes leave of his disciples, such experiences will not be far from the consciousness of many in the congregation. Even in the midst of Easter worship, anticipatory or remembered grief will cast its shadow.

A preacher may comment on the resources for addressing grief within the passage itself. The Advocate is coming to remind the disciples of Jesus and his teaching (v. 26). Jesus reminds his followers that they need not be fearful or have anxiety (v. 27), and that rejoicing is appropriate for this departure (v. 28). There are dangers of making reference to these resources without further comment, however. We risk sounding as though we believe that in the face of loss we can find either a replacement or some other compensation to make us feel better. Alternatively, we can sound as though we are mouthing pious platitudes filled with "shoulds," like: "You really should be happy about your loss, because

Exegetical Perspective

It is not easy to preach from a segment of a longer text, yet that is the task set before us by the lectionary text from John. The text is part of a larger rhetorical segment of the Gospel, namely, the Farewell Discourse of Jesus to his disciples (13:1–17:26). John 14 can be divided into four segments:

verses 1–4	opening discourse
verses 5–7	Thomas's question
verses 8–21	Philip's question
verses 22–31	Judas's question

Today's text is taken from the section of the discourse triggered by Judas's question, "Lord, how is it that you will reveal yourself to us but not to the *kosmos* [world]?" This is a clear reminder that the Farewell Discourse is intended for Jesus' disciples only and not for the curious outsider. This is privileged conversation.

John's Gospel was probably written in Ephesus during the 80s or early 90s of the first century, the period of time when the house churches were being evicted from the synagogue. Hostility was high, and mutual suspicion reigned. (See John 9:22; 16:2; 20:19 for historical echoes in John.) The fledgling house churches were keeping clear boundaries that separated them both from the synagogue and from the Roman temples in Ephesus. Conflict can sharpen differences, as well as motivate groups to clarify their

Homiletical Perspective

Maintaining the energy and excitement of Easter preaching is difficult. Once the filled worship spaces of Easter Sunday begin to return to "comfortably full" or "disappointingly empty," the preacher faces what some congregations experience as "business as usual." Into that context comes this bad news/good news text. The bad news is that Jesus is going away (v. 28). The good news is that the Holy Spirit will come to restore the presence of the absent Jesus (v. 26). Having just celebrated the resurrection, listeners might not expect a reading that points toward the death of Jesus.

The glimpses of the Trinity in this Gospel reading give the preacher one possible approach to the sermon: Who is God, the Father (vv. 23, 26, 28)? Who is God, the Son? (vv. 23, 24, 26)? Who is God, the Holy Spirit (v. 26)?

God, the Father. The power of this nomenclature is certainly not in its masculinity. Although the temptation for some is to envision God as male, to do so is to miss how our Lord used the term "Father." The word "Father" is used to depict the relationship within the Godhead, characterized by love (v. 23), by provision (vv. 23, 26), and by welcome (v. 28). Jesus' use of the word "Father" is not about gender; it is about relationship.

John 14:23-29

Theological Perspective

alongside the news of the coming "Holy Spirit," paved the way historically for the doctrine of the Trinity. His announcement of the indwelling of both the "Father" and himself in the community of believers, through the Spirit, seems at first to justify that trajectory. At the same time, the passage contains a challenge to the doctrine.

Ancient interpreters struggled with what it meant for Jesus to say God as his parent was *greater* than he, over against Trinitarian teachings that insisted on coequal persons. Doing battle in the fourth century CE with Christians who would not accept the doctrine of Christ as divine, Basil the Great was very concerned that the "greatness" of the "Father" be understood only as a comparison of two beings with the same "Substance." He was concerned that there be no inference that Jesus the "Son" was of a different essential nature than the "Father."[1] Writing considerably later, John of Damascus went further, arguing that the "Father" was only the "cause of the Son," the origin, without implying a coming earlier in time or exhibiting "superiority in nature." For John of Damascus, "greater" meant merely that the "Son" was begotten by the "Father" and not the reverse.[2]

Such ancient arguments hint of the wider debate behind them regarding the humanity and divinity of the Christ. Varying understandings of God may be brought to—and broken by—this passage from scripture. With the simple word "greater," John's Gospel opens a chink in the walls of a theological edifice for which it is a foundation. For better or worse, the text contains no question, "What do you mean by 'greater'?" for Jesus to answer.

A third challenge is raised by the query from the "other" Judas just prior to our reading (v. 22). Why do only Christ's followers see him for who and what he is? Judas is puzzled, and so are we. The verses selected for this Sunday are framed by this question, one that has haunted the history of Christianity. Judas seems to feel that Jesus is *choosing* not to manifest himself to the world. Jesus' response, "Whoever does not love me does not keep my words," throws the question wide open. Is human love for God a choice? Why do some love God, and others hate—or simply fail to perceive? Would a loving God make it so?

For early Christians facing persecution for their beliefs, the problem was surely more than

Pastoral Perspective

the one who has left you is so much better off." The context of Jesus' sayings here is the whole of the Farewell Discourse, including the earlier promise of the indwelling of the Holy Spirit (vv. 17, 23) and the promise that the disciples will not be left orphaned (v. 18).

While Jesus' departure may involve grief and loss, the discourse is about his continuing presence, which distinguishes this time from other times when sadness is appropriate. The 1979 *Book of Common Prayer* of the Episcopal Church contains a note to the burial rites that talks of Easter joy and goes on to say, "This joy, however, does not make human grief unchristian. The very love we have for each other in Christ brings deep sorrow when we are parted by death. Jesus himself wept at the grave of his friend."[1]

Many in our congregations have great anxiety around what to say and what not to say to people who are grieving, and this lection may present a pastoral opportunity to address that anxiety.

Anxiety, fear, and troubled hearts are much on Jesus' mind (v. 27b). The antidote to such fear is the peace given by Jesus, and not peace as the world gives (v. 27a). Many people yearn for peace in the world's terms: cessation of conflict, whether psychological tension or warfare; a sense of calm or serenity of spirit. The peace that Jesus promises as he takes leave might include such things, but the peace that Jesus gives is nothing less than the consequence of the presence of God. When God is present, peace is made manifest. Communities that include a sign of peace during worship often place it immediately following prayers of confession and absolution. When they do so, they are enacting the truth that where sin is forgiven, the new (eschatological) community of peace is a reality. This gift of peace is bound up with all that makes for righteousness or right relation: love, forgiveness, reconciliation, and thanksgiving.

Freedom from anxiety is directly related to our putting our whole trust in God's grace and love, which becomes possible as we remember that love created us for love. The terminology of family-systems theory developed by Murray Bowen and introduced to faith communities through the work of Edwin Friedman[2] has gained currency in many parts of the church in recent years. Friedman talks of how we may become nonanxious presences through self-differentiation. As we become clear about who

1. Basil the Great, "On the Holy Spirit," quoted in Joel C. Elowsky, ed., *Ancient Christian Commentary on Scripture IVb: John 11–21* (Downers Grove, IL: InterVarsity Press, 2007), 156.
2. Ibid., 145–46.

1. *The Book of Common Prayer* (New York: Seabury Press, 1979), 507.
2. See Edwin H. Friedman, *Generation to Generation* (New York: Guilford Press, 1985); *A Failure of Nerve: Leadership in the Age of the Quick Fix* (New York: Seabury Books, 2007).

identity. Jesus' Farewell Discourse reflects this historical context and contributes to these two tasks. This is why the farewell takes the form it does. The disciples' questions reflect the questions harbored by the members of the Johannine community, and, in the guise of answering them, Jesus addresses the members of John's house churches as well.

The lectionary text is puzzling in that it begins with Jesus' answer (v. 23) to Judas's question (v. 22) while omitting Judas's question, a significant omission, because the question frames the discourse that follows. The question is also needed because of the paradoxical answer it elicits. Jesus does not seem to answer Judas's question at all. What is the relationship between 14:22 and 14:23–24? This kind of discourse is common in John's Gospel. The disciples speak at one level (the view from the *kosmos*), while Jesus speaks at a spiritual level. The interplay between these two levels is distinctive of John's Gospel. Whatever can be said about the discourse, Judas must have posed an important question, because Jesus offers an extended answer (14:23–31).

Quite likely, Judas asked the question to construct the barrier between the house churches and the larger world or cosmos. Why did you choose us over them? Why is this special revelation reserved for us? Jesus' answer subtly undermines the question by indicating its irrelevance. There is something more important than dividing the house between us and them. Pay attention to the basic tasks of a disciple. What are they? The vocabulary of the passage is larded with Johannine language pointing to the task of disciples. Jesus speaks of "keeping" his word (*ton logon*, v. 23) and then of "keeping" his words (*tous logous*, v. 24). What is the difference? Are these two ways of saying the same thing?

It seems that for every responsibility the disciples have, Jesus and the Father provide the resources they need to carry out their tasks. In this case, Jesus and the Father will "make their home" with the disciples. The imagery is from the building trades. To build (*poieō*) a home could be translated to "craft or fashion" a home. Of course the home being discussed is not a building under construction. But John's community is very much a work in progress that needs a home, now that the synagogue can no longer function as a home for them. As the disciples nurture the word/words of Jesus, so Jesus and the Father not only craft a "home" for them but provide the very word/words they are to study and hold firm.

One more item needs to be mentioned about verses 23–24: this is an example of John's

These words of Jesus are in response to a question (v. 22). How reassuring it is to recognize the openness of the Lord to questions! It is okay for the church to be a community of questions, as well as a community of answers. Jesus responds to the inquiry by contrasting the world with those who keep the word sent by the Father (v. 24). Love is the currency of faithfulness. The absence of love suggests the absence of the relationship that brings love. Where love is, Jesus and the Father are at home (v. 23).

God, the Son. Jesus is clear that he and the Father are on the same page; they are singing from the same sheet of music (vv. 23–24). Jesus has lived out what he taught his disciples to pray: "Your will be done, on earth as it is in heaven" (Matt. 6:10). The loving commands of the one who sent Jesus are the very things Jesus has lived and taught. If we want to meet and experience the fullness of God, we will meet and experience Jesus. It is no accident that when Christians make the sign of the cross, they do so in the name of the full Godhead: Father, Son, and Holy Spirit. The love from the cross is the love from God. These verses anticipate the prayer of Jesus in John 17:21–22: "As you, Father, are in me and I am in you, may they also be in us, so that the world may believe that you have sent me. The glory that you have given me I have given them, so that they may be one, as we are one." The invitation to the disciples—to us—is to participate in the community that is at one with God, a community of full love.

Verse 28 jumps out, takes the preacher by the arm, and says, "Do not chase this rabbit!" There is indeed a pull to ignore Jesus' statement that "the Father is greater than I." Does this mean Jesus is less than the Father? Over the centuries, students of the Bible have pursued numerous (and variant) explorations of the text. A sermon that lingers too long on this verse is likely to become an interesting (or not!) theological lecture. Nevertheless, Jesus' declaration gives the preacher a handle for speaking of the humanity of our Lord (fully human, fully divine). He has shared our humanity, and, indeed, these verses that begin to point toward his impending death remind us of that humanity. Verse 28 is a connecting point between our own life journey and the mountains and valleys of Jesus' life (and death): "I am going away, and I am coming to you."

The Christ Jesus of Philippians 2:5–8, who "did not regard equality with God as something to be exploited," invites us to have the same mind as Christ does. It is a mind of full love of God and full

John 14:23-29

Theological Perspective

theoretical! Why could their detractors, or even their families, not understand and share their faith? The dilemma had the edge of a sharp sword.

The question of why some can see and others cannot, why some believe and others hate, has faced people of faith in many times and places since. If few postmodern Christians are concerned with the relative greatness or Being of the three persons of God, this nest of issues has still become a theological obsession for others.

In modernity the struggle over why some believe and others do not has taken an intellectual twist. Skeptics have asserted that all religious claims are empty because they cannot be scrutinized through any kind of public means. The question has been raised in various forms: is religious language meaningful if it makes sense only to its adherents? Is private truth really truth at all? The repeated challenge of secular critics has dominated much of theology.

Honesty compels our generation to acknowledge with the "other" Judas the apparent hiddenness of God, and the painful division occasioned by faith. In some ways Jesus seems to heighten the tension! Yet he then offers another starting place, insisting that his followers start living out love by "keeping my word," assuring us it comes ultimately not from Jesus alone but from one who sent him.

Wrestling with how to *talk* comprehensibly with others about beliefs must not distract us from the business of the *practice* of incarnate faith. Faithfulness in human action will, Jesus assures, lead to a firsthand experience of divine indwelling presence. We need to begin with following the path of Christ. We can invite others to try that practical, intimate path! The route to knowing God is to live the word of Jesus, which in turn will, with the Spirit's aid, lead to a living experience of the love of Jesus and the one who sent him.

In the absence of a physically present Christ, our daily practice makes real the living presence and love of God. Love in action is the route to experiencing Love's grace-filled indwelling. Love in action is the closest we come to *evidence* of God. The problem of "Why some and not others?" is unresolved. However, the first step in engaging it is not theory but practice, not argument but passionate love.

PETER J. B. CARMAN

Pastoral Perspective

we are and where we stand in life, we are better able to stay nonanxious in a variety of situations.

Most families know what it is like to be at a family gathering wondering whether great aunt so-and-so will have too much to drink or uncle whoosit will have one of his "spells." In the same way, most families know how everyone calms down when father gets home from work or when mother steps in and takes charge. The capacity to be nonanxious helps others to calm down as well. This is not unlike what happens in the presence of God or in a time of peace that is not as the world gives. We see this reality at work in the ministry of the risen Jesus. Consider that occasion after the resurrection when the disciples were afraid and gathered behind locked doors. "Jesus came and stood among them and said, 'Peace be with you'" (20:19). Jesus was and is the nonanxious presence of God.

Jesus' own capacity for setting aside anxiety by putting his whole trust in God's grace and love is shown here when he refers to the "ruler of this world" (v. 30). Jesus' conflict with the religious authorities of his day was introduced near the beginning of John's account, in the story of the cleansing of the temple (2:13–22), and anyone who has followed the story thus far must expect that there will be no happy ending. Even Jesus is aware that he is probably going to his death.

John does not show us his agony in the Garden of Gethsemane (Matt. 26:30–56; Mark 14:26–42; Luke 22:39–46). Instead, he shows us a Jesus who is confident that as he is with God, so the ruler of this world will not be able to exert power over him. When he says, "Rise, let us be on our way" (v. 31), Jesus is speaking of the way that will lead to his death, the way of the cross, and is confident that death is not the worst fate in life. The worst fate would be to act without integrity, breaking faith with the source of his life.

GEOFFREY M. ST. J. HOARE

"eschatology." When John says, "My Father and I will come to them and build a home in their midst" (v. 23, my trans.), he is not speaking about the Parousia or about the resurrection of the dead, but about the spiritual indwelling of the Father and the Son in the lives of disciples. It is another example of how John views things through his own particular (perhaps peculiar) lens.

However, this is a Farewell Discourse, and the danger of such a discourse for John's community is that it leaves them feeling empty and perhaps a bit abandoned. Is absence all they have to look forward to? The answer, of course, is a hearty no! Jesus' departure will bring a new presence to the community. In a world where members of marginal groups were subjected to Roman "justice," an advocate was a welcome addition to the community. Yet the primary task of the Paraclete was to teach, not defend. (See Ps. 25:5, 9.) If so, the role of the Advocate is to activate the memory banks of the community so that they can remember Jesus' teachings. The Holy Spirit will "teach you everything" and "remind you of all that I have said to you" (v. 26). So the community will have help in "keeping" Jesus' word and words.

In fact, there is a continuum involving the Father, Jesus, and the Holy Spirit. As Jesus departs, indeed *because* Jesus will depart, the Holy Spirit will come. As Jesus is reunited with the Father, the community will be united to the Spirit. This is an unusual Farewell Discourse. Its yield is "peace" to encourage troubled hearts ("troubled" connotes fear and anxiety, perhaps leading to cowardice). Faith is not for the fainthearted. The verb *aphiēmi* ("my peace I leave with you," v. 27) could be translated "bequeath." Although the ruler of this world lurks in the background, this Farewell Discourse testifies to the resources and riches that the disciples stand to inherit if they stand firm. There will be no surprises, because the Advocate will tell them all things in advance. Against such spiritual resources, the ruler of the world does not stand a chance.

WILLIAM R. HERZOG II

love of neighbor. We might dare say that if that is good enough for Jesus, it ought to be good enough for us!

God, the Holy Spirit. In this reading, the Holy Spirit is described as teacher and reminder (v. 26). What characterizes our favorite teachers? Mostly frequently, those teachers we remember fondly are those who established a caring relationship and those who expected (and saw) the best in us. The Holy Spirit is our Advocate, Helper, Companion, and Comforter. That sounds like one who expects (and sees) the best in us!

The Holy Spirit reminds us who Jesus is (v. 26). Jesus is one who sees a person open to salvation when the world sees only Zacchaeus, a conniving tax collector. Jesus is one who sees a foundation for the church when the world sees only Peter, a man of flimsy faith. Jesus is one who sees someone who can reclaim a pure life, when the world sees only a woman caught in adultery. What does Jesus see when he looks at me?

The Holy Spirit brings Jesus' actions into the present tense. The same one who sent Jesus as the Word made flesh (v. 24; also 1:14) is the one who sends the Holy Spirit as the reminder (refresher) of that presence (v. 26). No wonder the persons of the Trinity all seem cut from the same piece of cloth!

Another approach. This Gospel lesson is filled with "preachable verses." Jesus has announced that he is on the way to his death (John 13:36). What surrounds that pronouncement is a kind of summary of the Lord's teaching: If you love me, you will do what I say (14:23); I give a kind of peace that the world cannot give (or take away) (v. 27); you need not be fearful in the face of new tomorrows (v. 27). Any one of these themes lends itself to a full day in the pulpit.

F. BELTON JOYNER JR.

Acts 1:1-11

¹In the first book, Theophilus, I wrote about all that Jesus did and taught from the beginning ²until the day when he was taken up to heaven, after giving instructions through the Holy Spirit to the apostles whom he had chosen. ³After his suffering he presented himself alive to them by many convincing proofs, appearing to them during forty days and speaking about the kingdom of God. ⁴While staying with them, he ordered them not to leave Jerusalem, but to wait there for the promise of the Father. "This," he said, "is what you have heard from me; ⁵for John baptized with water, but you will be baptized with the Holy Spirit not many days from now."

⁶So when they had come together, they asked him, "Lord, is this the time when you will restore the kingdom to Israel?" ⁷He replied, "It is not for you to know the times or periods that the Father has set by his own authority. ⁸But you will receive power when the Holy Spirit has come upon you; and you will be my witnesses in Jerusalem, in all Judea and Samaria, and to the ends of the earth." ⁹When he had said this, as they were watching, he was lifted up, and a cloud took him out of their sight. ¹⁰While he was going and they were gazing up toward heaven, suddenly two men in white robes stood by them. ¹¹They said, "Men of Galilee, why do you stand looking up toward heaven? This Jesus, who has been taken up from you into heaven, will come in the same way as you saw him go into heaven."

Theological Perspective

When we proclaim the ascension as part of the gospel, what exactly are we proclaiming? What is at stake theologically when we say that Jesus Christ not only rose from the dead but ascended?

Before we can even begin to address these questions, we have to admit that the ascension poses a special challenge for today's preacher, one that some of us would rather avoid. We understand the problem well enough. We do not, as a matter of fact, believe that Jesus ended his earthly ministry with the equivalent of a rocket launch, rising a few hundred miles above the earth. Nor do we think Jesus was the first to be "beamed up," to use the term made so familiar by the television series *Star Trek*.

In part, the problem we face arises from the profound change in worldview that occurred with the coming of modern science. Christians never really did believe the earth is flat, but until Copernicus, nearly everyone believed that planet Earth sat firmly fixed at the center of the universe and that celestial bodies—the sun, moon, and stars—all rotated around us. For Jesus to go "up," then, may have been mysterious but not wholly inconceivable. The great religious art of medieval Europe showed Jesus just above the clouds. We could stand here, point up, and say that Jesus went *there*, thinking that he could look down on us through the

Pastoral Perspective

Many stained-glass windows depict Jesus coming from heaven amid the clouds. The clouds themselves seem almost to dissolve into the background, with Jesus' penetrating eyes looking directly at us. In the church my wife grew up in, this scene is captured in the sanctuary's main window, with Jesus extending a hand to viewers, bidding us to come. The window is magnificent, warm in hue, and welcoming. It sets our eyes on heaven and the second coming of Christ. Yet the two men in white robes who suddenly appear in the first chapter of Acts ask, "Why do you stand looking up toward heaven?" Indeed, why do we sit in our pews Sunday after Sunday, looking to the heavens?

The beginning of the book of Acts is, of course, not the beginning of the story. While Luke blazes a trail through the uncharted territory of the first-century church, he relies on "the first book" of his Gospel to tell how this crew of eleven arrived at this moment of staring into heaven. Instead of just picking up the story with their being "continually in the temple blessing God" (Luke 24:53), Luke provides the reader Theophilus with an update. Like a "Previously on *E.R.* . . . ." plot summary, Acts 1:1–9 recaps Jesus' ascension. Luke ends his Gospel with Jesus' blessing the eleven disciples and then being "carried up into heaven" (Luke 24:51).

Exegetical Perspective

From Jesus to church (vv. 1–5). Luke begins his second volume, the Acts of the Apostles, with a brief transition. He offers his readers a synopsis of the Gospel in which he wrote about "all that Jesus did and taught from the beginning until the day when he was taken up to heaven" (vv. 1–2). Luke also offers a peek at what is to come in this volume. "John baptized with water, but you will be baptized with the Holy Spirit not many days from now" (v. 5). Then he launches his story about the powerful effects of the Holy Spirit on the community of Jesus' followers.

Luke reminds his readers of the centerpiece of Jesus' preaching—the kingdom of God, which might be rendered "reign of God." What might life be like if God truly reigned in our lives, in our communities, and in our churches? The book of Acts offers stories that attempt to answer this question. As the reader works her way through these stories, she is challenged to see her community of faith in light of these first Christians.

In an almost offhanded way, Luke notes that Jesus appeared to his apostles for forty days after his "suffering." Bible readers, both in Luke's time and ours, immediately recall that the number forty occurs in several Old Testament stories. It rained for forty days and nights while Noah and his family

Homiletical Perspective

The book of Acts opens with Jesus taking leave of the apostles. The ascension of Jesus is a moment of loss and transition, as well as a moment of glory. We read Acts 1 with mixed emotions, reliving the grief of the apostles as Jesus is taken from them, while we also look forward with hope to the work God has prepared for us. Transitions are a constant feature of our existence, but those transitions that involve losing and gaining people can be among the most significant. We are often engaged in the back-and-forth between encounter and dismissal, greeting and farewell. The ascension initiates a new era when Jesus is no longer present in the flesh, and when the community looks outward and begins adding to its numbers.

Jesus leaves only after preparing the apostles over a period of forty days, so his departure is not abrupt. That this story appears in Luke 24:44–52 and again in today's text, with further theological detail regarding the future church, suggests a concern not to gloss over the departure. In Luke, the parting words center upon continuity with Hebrew Scripture as fulfilled in Jesus' death and resurrection, and the church's call to proclaim to all nations. Like the psalmist who exalts the Lord who is "king over all the earth" with songs of joy (Ps. 47:1–2), the apostles are joyful after the ascension, as they return to worship in Jerusalem.

Acts 1:1-11

Theological Perspective

clouds, as we might from the window of an airplane. Thanks to Copernicus, however, going "up" is no longer a coherent idea. Today there is no more "up," if by that we mean a fixed spatial location always over our heads.

Against the backdrop of such challenges and in the context of science fiction, it is our task to proclaim the gospel of Jesus Christ, who lived, died, rose again, and ascended to glory. The danger before us is that in the face of the problems of modern cosmology, we will avoid the ascension altogether or, worse, deny its truth by first denying its relevance to the gospel. We need to see that modern cosmology is actually beneficial, because it sets us free from the rather silly medieval idea that Jesus Christ is suspended a few hundred miles overhead, staring down on us like a prince in a castle turret.

The text, of course, does say that the disciples watched as Jesus went up. What were they witnessing, if not the first stage of something that resembled a launch? Note carefully, however, that this text links ascension with resurrection. According to the text, Jesus "presented himself alive after his passion by many proofs, appearing to them during forty days" (v. 3 RSV). Thus the liturgical calendar places ascension forty days after Easter. The significance of Easter (resurrection) and ascension (exaltation) are tied together as two parts of a single whole. Together they constitute one sweeping forty-day movement that brings the obedient Christ not just from the grave to the skies but from hell and godlessness to the place of highest honor at the right hand of God the Father (Phil. 2:6–11). The distance bridged in this movement of resurrection and exaltation is not measured in the number of miles from earth to heaven but in the amount of evil and destruction that separates us from God. It is not the force of gravity that must be overcome, but the forces of sin, death, hell, and annihilation.

The theologian Jürgen Moltmann poses the question: "*Where* was Jesus raised *to*?" He agrees that Jesus does not simply go up into the sky. Nor is it right to say that Jesus is simply moved into the future and is thereby removed from our space because he is removed from our time. "Jesus was raised into the coming glory of the Father," Moltmann writes. "Jesus is risen into the coming kingdom of God."[1]

Precisely at this point, the recent renewal of Trinitarian theology led by Moltmann and so many

Pastoral Perspective

However, here in Acts, instead of the disciples' minds being opened "to understand the scriptures" (Luke 24:45), they receive the promise of the Holy Spirit. Thus, in a short recap, Luke moves us from the first book's focus on the work of the second person of the Trinity to the second volume's focal point, the work of the third person, the Holy Spirit.

Jon Walton, the pastor of First Presbyterian Church, New York City, says that this is both good news and bad news:

> The bad news is Jesus is no longer among us bodily on earth. He has ascended to heaven, as we say in the creed, where he sitteth on the right hand of God, the Father Almighty, from whence he shall come to judge the quick and the dead; which is all well and good in the great by and by, but for now he is gone from our sight. The good news is that God is still with us in Spirit and in truth, even as we look to next Sunday when we celebrate Pentecost, the gift of the Holy Spirit to the early church, the continuation of God's presence, comfort, and power among us.[1]

In the Acts account of the ascension, the disciples hope that the bad news will not come, that Jesus will not leave them to cope hopelessly by themselves. It was, after all, only forty days earlier that they were lost and dismayed with Jesus' torturous departure. Moreover, they are still anticipating the promised kingdom.

"So when they had come together, they asked him, 'Lord, is this the time when you will restore the kingdom to Israel?'" (Acts 1:6). For forty days, they have received the peace of Christ, and now they are ready for the kingdom to come. "Has Jesus not been speaking of the kingdom?" they ask each other while waiting in Jerusalem. For forty days Jesus has been talking about the kingdom, and now he has "ordered them not to leave Jerusalem, but to wait there for the promise of the Father" (v. 4). They reason that he must mean the promised kingdom. So, longing to be with Jesus forever, they ask him, "Is it time?" However, the kingdom they ask about is not the kingdom of which Jesus has been speaking. For forty days, Jesus has taught about the kingdom of *God* (v. 3), whereas the disciples want to know about the kingdom of *Israel* (v. 6).

Sitting in our pews on Sundays, our focus is often like that of the disciples, fixed on our preconceived

---

1. Jürgen Moltmann, *The Trinity and the Kingdom*, trans. Margaret Kohl (San Francisco: Harper & Row, 1981), 88.

1. Jon M. Walton, "Why Are You Standing Looking to Heaven?" sermon preached at First Presbyterian Church, May 20, 2007, accessed at http://www.fpcnyc.org/sermons.html.

Exegetical Perspective

were safely aboard the ark. The Hebrews wandered the Sinai wilderness for forty years. Both Moses and Elijah went into the wilderness for forty days and nights to discover the will of God (Exod. 34:28; 1 Kgs. 19:8–12). The reader might also remember that Luke's first volume contained a story in which Jesus was led into the wilderness, where he was tested by the devil for forty days and nights. Jesus, full of God's Spirit, prevailed over the prince of darkness and returned with the good news of God's reign among us.

Three items are common in these stories: (1) Moses, Elijah, and Jesus went alone into the wilderness to discover the power of God, (2) all three fasted in preparation for their mission, and (3) all three came to represent major aspects of God with us. Moses unveiled God's will as Torah, Elijah proclaimed God's prophetic word, and Jesus preached the good news of God's reign. The opening verses in Acts offer yet a fourth story of forty days with God's representative, but this time with significant differences. First, Jesus does not fast. An alternate reading of verse 4 would translate the word *synalizomenos* as "eat [salt] with" (see NRSV footnote). Second, Jesus spends forty days in Jerusalem, not the wilderness. Finally, Jesus is not alone, but continues to instruct his disciples.

Power play (vv. 6–8). The apostles are well acquainted with Jesus' message about the reign of God, and they take it literally as "kingdom of God." The first question they ask their risen teacher indicates this. "Lord, is this the time when you will restore the kingdom to Israel?" Yes, it is well and good to speak about the reign of God, which can be rather soft and squishy, full of love and turning the other cheek, but what about the hard political (not to mention economic) realities of life? Let us talk about Israel's liberation from the oppressive rule of Rome. Let us talk about power. The apostles might have reminded Jesus of his own words: "You are those who have stood by me in my trials; and I confer on you, just as my Father has conferred on me, a kingdom, . . . and you will sit on thrones judging the twelve tribes of Israel" (Luke 22:28–30). It is time for Jesus to make good his promise.

Twice in history, Israel has been a kingdom, first under David and his dynasty (1000–583 BCE) and later under the Hasmoneans (165–63 BCE). Babylon destroyed the first kingdom, and Rome put an end to the second. Nevertheless, hope still smoldered among ordinary Jews of the first century. With God's help, they believed, Roman rule could be

Homiletical Perspective

The powerful symbolism in the phrase "he was lifted up" (v. 9) conveys the ascension as a moment of glory. We remember that the one who was lifted up (humbled) on the cross is now exalted to a place of oversight at the genesis of the early church. The glorious ascension itself created a pastoral void among the followers of Jesus who were so fixed on his return.

Ascensions and moments of divine encounter can dazzle us so that we forget the surrounding world. We glory in the moment, only to find that God has moved on, and so must we. While taking seriously a congregation's sense of divine presence or absence, preachers can through this text remind the faithful of the need for shared vocation. In community we live together through intense moments of divine revelation, and we stand together when God is hidden from our gaze.

The role of the Holy Spirit is affirmed in Jesus' instruction to remain in Jerusalem. Just as baptism initiates Jesus' earthly ministry, the baptism of the Spirit at Pentecost becomes the triggering event in the life of the church. While opening its doors to Gentiles, the church interprets itself in light of Hebrew Scriptures. Hans Conzelmann writes: "Jerusalem represents the continuity between Israel and the church."[1] The beginning of the church is found in a city with strong ties to a shared religious past.

Before Jesus is taken from them, the disciples ask: "Is this the time when you will restore the kingdom to Israel?" (v. 6). In his response Jesus places this knowledge of "times or periods" (v. 7) under divine authority, and he calls them instead to be witnesses through the power of the Holy Spirit. The widening pattern described in verse 8 ("in Jerusalem, in all Judea and Samaria, and to the ends of the earth") is played out as Acts unfolds.

For those who have struggled with the absence or distance of Jesus in their lives, these stories demand that we consider the tremendous faith required of us. The loss of the apostles resonates with other biblical passages where God seems distant or veiled. By returning to the time Jesus left, we can understand that we need resources found in community and through the Spirit. Still, it is a challenge to serve the living Christ who has ascended. Emily Dickinson writes in one of her poems (#377):

At least—to pray—is left—is left—
Oh Jesus—in the Air

---

1. Hans Conzelmann, *Acts of the Apostles* (Philadelphia: Fortress Press, 1987), 6.

Acts 1:1-11

Theological Perspective

others makes a decisive difference in our entire orientation to this text. Jesus Christ, sent from the very heart of God, is raised in power and exalted in glory. Resurrection and ascension, tied together as they are, are themselves part of a larger narrative of the triune God, a revealed history of interaction among the three identities of the Trinity, traditionally known as the Father, Son, and Holy Spirit.

The triune God is active love, reaching out to the creation and bringing the whole creation into fellowship. The story of this outreach stretches from the sending of Christ to the ascension. From there the story of divine love goes on to include the sending of the Holy Spirit, whose work is the transformation of the creation until all things are gathered up in the endless fellowship of the living God.

In the whole sweep of this narrative, the ascension stands as a critical movement. Just as the incarnation reveals to us the outreach of the love of God, so the ascension reveals to us the transfiguration and the gathering up that is to come at the end. What happens to Jesus Christ—death, resurrection, and being raised in exaltation to glory—will happen to us all. The ascension is a crucial moment of revelation, showing us the larger story of God's loving action. It is a reminder that our lives are caught up in something far more grand than we can imagine.

One more point must be made about the importance of ascension. This doctrine is the presupposition for the profoundly important belief that right now Jesus Christ is interceding for us, praying for our salvation. Jesus our high priest, who knows exactly the temptations and the trials of our human condition, bears up our prayers with his own, assuring that our feeble prayers reach far beyond the limits of our power to project them. For while we await our own ascension, our prayers ascend even now with the exalted Christ to the very heart of God.

RONALD COLE-TURNER

Pastoral Perspective

notions of the kingdom. For the disciples, the political reconstitution of Israel is paramount. When Israel is once again made the preeminent nation that it was under King David, then they will surely be in God's favor. Of course, they will also have autonomy and wealth and will be able to hold their heads high as God's chosen people with other peoples and nations. So, Jesus, is this the time of your return?

What descriptor best expresses your congregation's understanding of the kingdom? Perhaps your congregation is looking for the kingdom of *survival.* "We are a small congregation that desperately needs young families to join our gray-haired church so that we will survive." Or perhaps your congregation is anticipating the kingdom of *activity.* "With more than thirty opportunities a week for people to come and serve, we are busier than ever!" I suspect that most congregations are seeking the kingdom of *consumption,* constantly striving to provide bigger, better, and more entertaining worship services, so that those who come on Sundays will feel good about the pastor's performance. When we ask Jesus when God will restore the kingdom to the good old days—to the way we think church ought to be, or to the way that best satiates us—Jesus points not to the future but to the power of the Holy Spirit in the present.

The opening of the book of Acts is a two-layered transition. The top layer is a transition from the Gospel of Luke to the Acts of the Apostles. Underneath this layer is a far more important transition. In it, we are moved from passively waiting for Jesus to come and fix things in the end times to actively participating in the work of the Holy Spirit now. If we sit staring into heaven looking for Jesus, then we cannot be God's witnesses "to the ends of the earth" (v. 8). Perhaps our stained-glass windows should be plain clouds, so that our attention is turned to those around us who are in need of knowing the good news of the gospel.

DAVID G. FORNEY

overthrown. So the disciples looked to Jesus, who had miraculously survived even Roman crucifixion: "Lord, is this the time when *you* will restore the kingdom to Israel?"

In the Gospel stories, Jesus often probes beneath the surface. While the disciples perhaps even piously wish for the restoration of God's rule in Israel, what they really crave is power—to sit on those promised thrones. Jesus' response is probably not what they want to hear. Only God knows the times and periods that God alone has set. Nevertheless, Jesus says, "Your wish is granted. Yes, you will receive power [*dynamin*]." They will receive *power* from the Holy Spirit to be "my witnesses" (*mou martyres*). To be sure, this is not quite the kind of power the apostles have in mind. However, the realm of their power will rival even that of the Roman Empire, for it extends from Judea to Samaria, even to the "end of the earth"—which may be understood either geographically or temporally.

Lift off (or left behind) (vv. 9–11). As Jesus begins to leave this earth, two men in white robes appear to the disciples on Mount Olivet. The reader may easily infer that Moses and Elijah are here to comfort the apostles, the same two who appeared on a mountain in shining white garments at the transfiguration of Jesus (Luke 9:28–36). There are also "two men in dazzling clothes" who comfort the women at the empty tomb (Luke 24:4). Here, the men bring words of assurance and promise to the apostles: "This Jesus, who has been taken up from you into heaven, will come in the same way as you saw him go into heaven" (Acts 1:11).

First-century readers had heard stories of Moses and Elijah ascending into heaven, so they might have expected those exemplars to accompany Jesus in his return to their realm. The apostles who have witnessed the ultimate power of God now return to Jerusalem to begin their exercise of power as witnesses for Jesus Christ.

PAUL W. WALASKAY

I know not which thy chamber is—
I'm knocking—everywhere—[2]

The absence of the earthly Jesus leads us to search for a God who is nevertheless present in the world.

When Jesus is taken out of their sight, the disciples are left "gazing up toward heaven" (v. 10). This posture of expectation represents their belief in the immediate return of their Lord. Two messengers ask them, "Why do you stand looking up toward heaven?" (v. 11), implying the need to move ahead in the practice of ministry. The two messengers do not comfort or counsel by dwelling on the apostles' loss, but rather urge them ahead to active engagement in a new era.

In order to embrace their role as witnesses, the apostles would need to relinquish some of their expectations. They could not expect to take the world by force or earthly strength. Jesus had said, "The good news of the kingdom of God is proclaimed, and everyone tries to enter it by force" (Luke 16:16). Deeds of power, miracles, and wonders had marked the experience of the community of faith, but these were gifts of God not subject to human command. Next steps would involve openness and waiting for the Spirit to move, often without tangible success or a sense of assurance. A ministry stretching to include Gentiles would require great boldness and faith. The Spirit moves the apostles to visit unusual places and takes them in some rather unexpected directions. As a result of their constant witness, they are accused of "turning the world upside down" (Acts 17:6).

Today we have traditions and institutions, rules and procedures that govern the life of the church. It is instructive while reading Acts to return to the beginning, to a time before these human orders (helpful as they are) took shape. We have an opportunity to examine how the divine movement toward human redemption shaped the structures we now take for granted. Our processes must allow room for the Spirit of God, just as they did at the formation of the church.

RICHARD M. LANDERS

2. Emily Dickinson, *The Poems of Emily Dickinson*, ed. R. W. Franklin (Cambridge, MA: Belknap Press, 1998), 173.

Psalm 47

¹Clap your hands, all you peoples;
 shout to God with loud songs of joy.
²For the Lᴏʀᴅ, the Most High, is awesome,
 a great king over all the earth.
³He subdued peoples under us,
 and nations under our feet.
⁴He chose our heritage for us,
 the pride of Jacob whom he loves.   *Selah*

⁵God has gone up with a shout,
 the Lᴏʀᴅ with the sound of a trumpet.

Theological Perspective

Upon first reading this psalm, we are caught up in its liturgical commands to clap and shout with joy and its cadences of doxology: "Sing praises to God, sing praises; sing praises to our King, sing praises" (vv. 5–7). Indeed, the tenor of the psalm is one of invitation to worship God because of what God has done for God's people. Theologically, we can thus draw a connection between doxology and historical memory. As Israel remembers God's actions on their behalf, they are compelled to praise God. Historical memory is therefore understood as the linchpin of liturgy. Like Israel, we contemporary people of God acknowledge that the community of faith's relationship with God is historically grounded, and our worship derives from such. In other words, the call to worship in our churches is both a recall of God's activity in the past and a call to praise God for God's past, present, and future active presence with us.

At the next level of reading of the psalm, we are drawn to the central image of God provided therein. The image of God as king captures our attention: "a great king over all the earth" (v. 2), "our King" (v. 6), and "king over the nations" (v. 8). In the first instance (v. 2), we are reminded that God is the creator and provider of the natural world. In the next instance (v. 6), we are reminded that God elected a people, Israel. On behalf of Israel, God

Pastoral Perspective

The worship of the people on Ascension Day celebrates Christ being lifted up to the right hand of God, King of kings and Lord of lords. Psalm 47, an enthronement psalm, provides essential grounding and background for an understanding of the kind of king Christ is to be, as well as the nature of his reign and his realm. Several of the psalm's important themes focus the claims of Christ's realm on both the allegiance and the hearts of worshipers.

The first of these themes is the assertion that "kingship" or ultimate authority is the purview of God and God alone. "For God is the king of all the earth; sing praises with a psalm" (v. 7). Although images of monarchy may be somewhat foreign to a contemporary mind-set, there is even so within the faithful a deep yearning for conviction and assurance that God is indeed God and that God's ways will prevail on this earth. People are constantly bombarded by so much that testifies to the contrary: poverty, violence, war, deceit, crime, disease, greed, arrogance, corruption. As a result, temptations toward cynicism, apathy, and depression are real and ever present.

God's people become worn down. In many ways, on many levels, they surrender to the status quo. In effect, they give up on God. Turning inward seems the only prudent course of action, their only sure

^{6}Sing praises to God, sing praises;
  sing praises to our King, sing praises.
^{7}For God is the king of all the earth;
  sing praises with a psalm.

^{8}God is king over the nations;
  God sits on his holy throne.
^{9}The princes of the peoples gather
  as the people of the God of Abraham.
For the shields of the earth belong to God;
  he is highly exalted.

Exegetical Perspective

"Taken up to heaven" (Acts 1:2), "lifted up . . . out of their sight" (Acts 1:9), "seated . . . at [God's] right hand in the heavenly places" (Eph. 1:20), "carried up into heaven" (Luke 24:51). The lectionary texts for this Sunday sweep our gaze again and again to the heavens as we gather to celebrate the wonder and mystery of Jesus' ascension. At the same time, like the two men in white robes who ask the disciples, "Why do you stand looking up toward heaven?" (Acts 1:10–11), the texts encourage the Christian community to get on with the worship and mission of God: to wait for empowerment by the Holy Spirit (Acts 1:5, 8); to "be my witnesses" (Acts 1:8; cf. Luke 24:48); to "proclaim in [Jesus'] name to all nations" (Luke 24:47); to pray and hope (Eph. 1:15–19); and to worship God continually (Luke 24:53).

Struggling to express the inexpressible—to describe the miracle of Christ's exaltation and its implications for believers and the whole world—the early Christian community turned to ancient Israel's celebration of YHWH's enthronement, a tradition reflected in Psalm 47 (cf. Pss. 93, 95–97, 99). The psalm may be outlined in three units: verses 1–4, 5–7, and 8–9. Each unit includes one verse that explains the psalmist's imperatives or observations (cf. the Hebrew word "for" [ki] in 47:2, 7, 9b).

Homiletical Perspective

The ascension of Jesus from the Mount of Olives is easily pushed aside so that the preacher can get to what is commonly believed to be more important matters, such as the coming of the Holy Spirit and the mission of the church. However, without the ascension, the story is incomplete, and these important matters are diminished.

The ascension, which was largely a hidden act in Jesus' day, moves us to dangerous but exciting territory. In preaching this text, the church must be reminded that Jesus was far more than a brilliant peasant teacher or religious iconoclast. Rather, he ascended to the Father and now reigns with him. He is more than just an historical figure. He is Lord of heaven and earth. The ascension ushers us into the post-Easter time and the coming of the Holy Spirit with power to fulfill the mission of the church.

This challenges the preacher to call the church to mission in the world, to lead them to become more than just admirers of Jesus as a historical figure, as we would admire Socrates or Abraham Lincoln. The church is called to see Jesus as God's Son, triumphant over sin and death, and to follow the post-Easter Jesus into all the world, which is God's domain. Here is an opportunity for the preacher to focus on and celebrate the worship of the church, the power of the gospel, and the mission of the church.

Psalm 47

Theological Perspective

subdues peoples and nations (v. 3). "He chose our heritage for us, the pride of Jacob whom he loves" (v. 4). In the final instance (v. 8), we are reminded that God oversees the political world, the world of human affairs.

Theologically, it is the theme of God's sovereignty that thus comes to the fore. Here the awesome creative, relational, and political power of God is disclosed as a reason why God is worthy to be praised. Likewise, doxology and the sovereignty of God should intersect in our worship in the churches; we must praise in theocentric perspective, especially in the wake of the celebration of Easter. For Christians, the resurrection of Jesus Christ is surely the boldest witness to the sovereignty of God as maker of heaven and earth, as protector of God's people, and as overseer of human affairs.

Holding these two initial readings of the psalm together, another important feature of this psalm's theological frame emerges. Along with the themes of doxology and the sovereignty of God, there is a missiological theme that is particularly significant for Christians on Ascension Sunday. This missiological theme is most evident in the second part of the psalm (vv. 6–9). In these verses, especially verse 9, a universal God is being praised. One scholar explicates this universal God with reference to a fourfold Christian missiological interpretation of the psalm: (1) Other nations are included in the people of God in verse 9, and thus we are called to accept others as God accepts them. (2) In eschatological perspective, the enthronement of God can be read in light of the ascension of the risen Christ, and the church is called to live into the resurrection power of the Lord. (3) Living God's future doxologically in the present assures us that God is really governing the whole world for the good of the world. (4) The psalm concludes with an all-embracing vision like the one found in Revelation 5:13.[1] Likewise, the promise of the Spirit to the disciples as Jesus ascends (Luke–Acts account) and the subsequent work of the Spirit in spreading the gospel to Jews and Gentiles supports a missiological theme of inclusivity.

The theological frame of Psalm 47—doxology, sovereignty, missiology—is the basis upon which we ask our final question: What is the most faithful reading of this psalm by twenty-first-century Christians? The tragic events of September 11, 2001, have left churches to wrestle theologically with an

1. Jannie du Preez, "Interpreting Psalm 47: Some Notes on Its Composition, Exegesis, and Significance for the Church's Mission at the Turn of the Century," *Missionalia* 25, no. 3 (1997): 308, 318–20.

Pastoral Perspective

source of security and happiness. Coping strategies include houses and cars that insulate against others; bank accounts and retirement plans that promise security; and small, tight circles of family and a few close friends that constrain real community. These are among the many responses of a people who are, in their hearts, resigned to their own powerlessness and insignificance.

Psalm 47 refutes the mighty chorus of "the more things change, the more they stay the same," what the contemporary American author John Irving has called "the undertoad," the undertow of apathy and negativity relentlessly pulling one's spirit down and under. In contrast to that resignation, Psalm 47 proclaims, "God Rules!" to use the ultimate compliment of youth. Despite every attempt to thwart God's power, God's ways will indeed triumph upon the earth, and God's people will see the Lord in the land of the living. Jesus' prayer, "Your kingdom come, on earth as it is in heaven" (Matt. 6:10), is grounded in this ancient affirmation of faith.

The affirmation that God is king, and that Christ is the Lord of life, forms within the worshiper a deep assurance of security and trust. It gives a perspective on all of life that is seen only through the eyes of faith. This perspective can calm the anxious mind. It can orient the believer's attitudes toward all the challenges of life. It can ground the disciple in the courage necessary to withstand any temptation to misplace one's allegiance in any unholy or penultimate contender.

For this new orientation to be possible, some verses within Psalm 47 need to be critically examined and explicitly addressed, lest worshipers by confused and misled by them. Certain verses reveal the tension that OT scholar Walter Brueggemann has described between the two themes of God's universal sovereignty and God's particular selection of Israel. God, described as "king over all the earth" (v. 2), has "subdued peoples under us, and nations under our feet" (v. 3). If this tension is not addressed directly, people may not be equipped to make distinctions between the covenant with the Hebrew people and contemporary nation-states. Without comment or qualification, verse 3 could be taken to mean that violent repression of one's enemy is God's will and intent.

Examining Psalm 47 in the context of Ascension Day offers a rich and intriguing teaching moment in which all claims of kingship and conquest can be explored in light of the reign of Christ, Prince of Peace. The very nature of Christ's realm is one of

Exegetical Perspective

Verses 1–4. The first unit weaves together celebration of God's sovereignty over the whole world and God's particular care for Israel. The psalmist exhorts "all the peoples" to "Clap!" and "Shout!"—and explains ("for . . . ," v. 2) that the imperatives are motivated by YHWH's distinctiveness. First, YHWH, the name of God first revealed to Moses (Exod. 3:13–15; 6:1–9), is God "Most High" (*'elyon*), a common epithet in Semitic languages for the supreme Deity, and thus a title to which many may assent (e.g., Pss. 83:18; 97:9). Second, God is "to be feared" (NRSV "awesome"). The fitting human response, given the mystery, power, and righteousness of God (e.g., Ps. 97:2, 6, 10–12), is grateful awe, trembling, and reverence. As this psalm and others attest, "fear of the LORD" does not terrify or squelch joy. Rather, by casting out all other fear, "fear of the LORD" inspires worship and delight—shouting, clapping, and singing (e.g., Pss. 34:11; 96:4; 111:1–10). Lastly, God is the "great king" whose authority and kingdom, that of "all the earth," far exceeds that of any human power or government. It is no wonder, then, that the psalmist urges "all you peoples" (v. 1) to rejoice, and *loudly*, before the God of "all of the earth" (v. 2).

Israel's voice in the global chorus should be especially pronounced, the psalmist continues, because YHWH, God "Most High," has long acted on Israel's behalf (vv. 3–4). With repetition of first-person plural suffixes ("under *us* . . . under *our* feet . . . *our* heritage for *us*"), verbs that convey God's fierce protection and intimacy ("subdued . . . chose . . . loves"), and mention of a divinely appointed "heritage" (v. 4), a term that denotes kinship and a future, the psalmist sets Israel apart as a people for whom God has particular concern. The psalmist also refers to the community collectively as Jacob (e.g., Deut. 32:9; Ps. 44:4; Isa. 10:21; 40:27; Jer. 10:25)—a move that calls to mind the stories of the eponymous ancestor of Israel who survives by his wits and God's blessing (Gen. 25–36), and whom God promises never to abandon: "Know that I am with you and will keep you wherever you go, . . . I will not leave you until I have done what I have promised you" (Gen. 28:15; see 28:10–17).

Verses 5–7. Shouts of praise by all peoples (v. 1) merge with a resonating shout "God has gone up!" as the psalmist next invites readers to participate in God's enthronement. The scene is easy to imagine. Amid great pomp and circumstance, God ascends slowly to the throne while the crowd, standing on its toes to see, shouts and cheers. Over the din rises a

Homiletical Perspective

Psalm 47 originally served to accompany a joyous procession to be sung before the act of worship. This is a psalm that celebrates God's triumphant reign in three areas: before battle: "He shall subdue the people under us and the nations under our feet" (v. 3 KJV); in battle: "God has gone up with a shout" (v. 5); and after the battle: "For the shields of the earth belong to God" (v. 9). Because of this, we shout for joy.

In a day when worship can become the battleground for churches, we need to be reminded that this has always been an issue. Remember, the first murder was over how to worship (Cain and Abel). While seeker services and entertainment evangelism are commendable and laudable goals, it is a misnomer to call *services* "worship" if their purpose is to attract people rather than to adore God.

This psalm gives the preacher an opportunity to teach and define worship. People of all ages in our churches will gladly receive more depth, due to the shallowness of our world. Yet often worship does not satisfy our deepest need. A sermon on this psalm could lead people to see that worship is not judged by what we get out of it, but rather what God gets out of it. What does God experience in our worship? The preacher may remind the people of Kierkegaard's analogy that God is the audience and we are on the stage, and that the preacher is just off the stage, giving cues to the congregation about worship. God does the judging, not the congregation.

In preaching this, the preacher should remind the congregation that worship is more than a service to attend, a program to be judged, or a performance to be evaluated. Rather, we bring the reality of our lives into the worship of God. This bubbles up out of Psalm 47. The operative word here is "liturgy," which means *work of the people.* True worship results in liturgy, or service, and energizes the church and the individual to do God's work.

Worship encouraged by this psalm has passion: "Clap your hands, all you peoples; shout to God with loud songs of joy." There is no lifeless, limp expression here! This passion is pure ecstasy, joy and victory, moving us to triumph and to mission. Every pastor knows her people are beaten down by life. They carry the world on their backs. They must be reminded that God is the *awesome* in their lives. Passion for God transforms life and raises oppressively low ceilings. True worship leads the people from selfishness and self-centeredness to an understanding of God as King of all the earth. A walk with God will replace our own anxiety with trust.

Psalm 47

Theological Perspective

interpretation of the sovereignty of God that breaks with previous and current interpretations—those that use God's sovereignty as justification for violence against persons within and without the Christian community who are deemed heretical, or those interpretations that champion imperialism—the subjugation and conquest of non-Christian peoples and nations. The theological frame of Psalm 47 offers us a way to disrupt such interpretative rationale for violence and imperialism.

If we will remember that authentic praise happens when we acknowledge fully the way that the sovereign God oversees the whole world—the earth, God's chosen people, and other peoples—then our worship can form us into people who will interact with those of other faiths, as God does in this psalm. It is neither the denial nor the affirmation of Israel as the people of God, but the eschatological inclusion of all peoples and nations, that makes Psalm 47 a theological under-pinning for twenty-first-century Christians. Those who confess their sins of exclusion and conquest to the sovereign God of Psalm 47 will be compelled to witness to a vision of an inclusive people of God.

How shall we profess a risen Christ in a twenty-first-century world of religious violence? If we take seriously Psalm 47, we will first acknowledge that our sovereign God is the God of Israel who delivered that people, and that the God who elected a particular people is also the sovereign God over all peoples and the earth. If we take seriously Psalm 47, we will exalt this sovereign God, because this God honors both particularity and universality. If we take seriously Psalm 47, we will profess a risen Christ by respecting peoples and nations of other faiths, because we are witnesses to a God who oversees and loves the whole world.

MARCIA Y. RIGGS

Pastoral Perspective

reconciliation and forgiveness. The liberating power of Christ's reign comes in contrast to the repressive power of Caesar, which oppresses and subjugates. Providing critical perspective, understanding, and insight enables worshipers to let the biblical perspective fully inform contemporary situations and choices.

The psalm points to the new reality, indeed a new heaven and a new earth, being ushered in by God. "The princes of the peoples gather" and even "the shields of the earth belong to God" (v. 9), the psalmist reveals. Psalm 47 implies that human ways of violence and war will be no more in God's kingdom. In God's new realm, as the prophet proclaimed, "they shall beat their swords into plowshares, and their spears into pruning hooks; nation shall not lift up sword against nation, neither shall they learn war anymore" (Isa. 2:4). God's people are formed by the regular reminder that peace is more than a dream, precisely because of the kind of king God is and because of the kind of realm God intends, on earth as in heaven.

Ascension Day is indeed a festal day and an occasion for raucous celebration. As Psalm 47 indicates, polite music alone is not enough to express the fullness of this joy. The marvelous, salvific assertion that "God Rules!" calls for shouting with loud songs, the clapping of hands, and the sound of trumpets. The mood of this day's worship should reprise the rowdy joy of Palm Sunday, that day when grown-ups delight to join in revelry with all the children of the congregation. Imagine party hats and noisemakers, tambourines and joyous laughter, and a procession of liturgical dancers waving banners high. This is a day to let joy burst forth, a day to set all doubting and reticence aside. This is a day to say "No!" to all the powers of darkness and to proclaim with assurance that God's ways will triumph. "For the LORD, the Most High, is awesome" (v. 2a). This is the day to get the children and youth to join in and sing "Our God Is an Awesome God"[1] with gusto. It should all sound delirious with joy and resplendent with praise.

PATRICIA FARRIS

---

1. Rich Mullins, "Awesome God," BMG Songs, 1988.

Exegetical Perspective

long, full blast of the shofar (NRSV "trumpet"), an instrument with considerable military (e.g., Josh. 6:1–20; 1 Sam. 13:3; Jer. 6:1, 17) and liturgical significance, including use during royal coronations (1 Kgs. 1:34, 39, 41; 2 Kgs. 9:13). The psalmist spurs on the celebration, repeating the plural imperative "Sing!" five times in verses 6–7, and dancing back and forth between epithets for God that are distinctive to Israel and others that are broadly inclusive ("God . . . YHWH . . . God . . . our King . . . God is the king of all the earth," vv. 5–7). Everyone sings because ("for . . . ," v. 7) God reigns over all.

Verses 8–9. The psalm closes with a snapshot of the world order after God's enthronement. The coronation of God transforms sociopolitical and power structures. God presides "over the nations" (v. 8), and the leaders of those nations gather before God, presumably to pay tribute (v. 9). The psalmist's depiction of them as "the people [ᶜam] of the God of Abraham," although surprising and debated (LXX, for example, reads "with [ᶜim] the God of Abraham"), evokes God's promises to Abraham and Sarah—including that they and their descendants will be a means of blessing for all peoples (Gen. 12:1–3). Earthly rulers thus gather in God's throne room, apparently without conflict, to acknowledge God's sovereign power and to identify themselves with God's promises. "The shields of the earth" (v. 9b) may refer metaphorically to the world leaders (i.e., those who protect the people) or literally to the world's defenses. Either way, the powerful recognize ("for . . . ," v. 9b) that the protection of *all* nations is the purview of the one who is "greatly elevated" (NRSV "highly exalted") over them. So they come from the ends of the earth and gather before God.

Psalm 47 leaves us in the divine throne room this Sunday, dramatically reminded that God (and the ascended Jesus) sits enthroned over the world, and that God's authority and power surpass that of all worldly powers and governments (cf. "far above all rule and authority and power and dominion, and above every name that is named," Eph. 1:21). May we grow hoarse from our singing and shouting. May our hands sting from the clapping. May our ears ring from the clamor of joy.

CHRISTINE ROY YODER

Homiletical Perspective

Ascension Day tells us how to look at life in the world. Israel, though a small nation surrounded by major powers, believed that God lived in their midst. This changed everything for them. We cannot be the church unless we believe the ascended Christ lives in his church. If this is preached, our sense of being overwhelmed by our world will be diminished, and our mission in and to the world will be embraced. On this day, the faithful preaching of this text will lift burdens, stretch horizons, refocus the church on its place in God's plan, and empower the community to a larger task. The sensitive preacher, looking through this text to the ascension, will find new strength for her people and remind them again that they are the living embodiment of the victory of Jesus. Our power is quiet power, based upon a confident belief that Jesus has ascended to the Father and completed his mission. Our expression of this is in our vital and mature understanding of worship and mission. Our community of faith reflects the living presence of the Lord Jesus and his mission in our humble acts of obedience.

This psalm is a message our churches need. We serve not a weak and defeated God with a limited mission. Our reason for being is for more than our personal development. We exist to continue God's work in a fallen world, to roll back the darkness, and we are empowered for this mission. For this reason, we can "shout with a voice of triumph," for "we are more than conquerors through him who loved us" (Rom. 8:37). Or, in the spirit of today's psalm and the book of Revelation, sing praises to God, sing praises. Sing praises to the Lamb upon the throne. Sing praises to God. Sing praises, for God is greatly exalted.

WILLIAM L. SELF

Ephesians 1:15-23

¹⁵I have heard of your faith in the Lord Jesus and your love toward all the saints, and for this reason ¹⁶I do not cease to give thanks for you as I remember you in my prayers. ¹⁷I pray that the God of our Lord Jesus Christ, the Father of glory, may give you a spirit of wisdom and revelation as you come to know him, ¹⁸so that, with the eyes of your heart enlightened, you may know what is the hope to which he has called you, what are the riches of his glorious inheritance among the saints, ¹⁹and what is the immeasurable greatness of his power for us who believe, according to the working of his great power. ²⁰God put this power to work in Christ when he raised him from the dead and seated him at his right hand in the heavenly places, ²¹far above all rule and authority and power and dominion, and above every name that is named, not only in this age but also in the age to come. ²²And he has put all things under his feet and has made him the head over all things for the church, ²³which is his body, the fullness of him who fills all in all.

Theological Perspective

Ascension Day is not, for most Christians, a day of any great importance. Among the great feasts of our Lord such as Christmas and Easter, Ascension Day has no particular traditions associated with it (even liturgical ones), nor is it regarded as a holiday around which families or communities gather. Theologically speaking, however, the day is of utmost importance, for without it all the other events of Jesus' life dangle like unresolved plot lines in a poorly constructed novel. The reason for the ascension's centrality is this: Jesus' ascent into heaven brings "closure" both to his prophetic teaching ministry and to the mystical meaning of his death and resurrection, by incorporating it into the life of God from whence it came. That is to say, were Jesus' kenotic self-emptying (Phil. 2:5–11) in the incarnation not completed at the other end by his return to the Father, then the trajectories of his teaching and resurrected life—however dynamic and dramatic—would stretch indeterminately out into time and space like one of those arbitrary rocket launches into the cosmos, rather than standing as a conclusive witness to the dwelling of God in creation.

Archbishop of Canterbury Rowan Williams tries to explain it in this way: imagine what it is like when you first wake up in the morning. When you put on the light, all you are conscious of is the brightness of the light itself. Only gradually do your eyes adjust

Pastoral Perspective

Today's text asserts the writer's hope and prayer for the community receiving the letter. It is an informed hope that is spoken with poised assurance, kindled by a firm and sure confidence in what is possible within the Christian life. The writer proclaims the power and authority of Christ in dramatic fashion. This power, which is above all others, will be shared with those who believe. It is an inheritance of all the saints. In contrast to understandings of Christian life that focus on dramatic conversion experiences (turning confessing believers into paragons of spiritual wisdom), this text proposes that knowledge and discernment of Christly power come as believers progress in their relationship with Christ.

In other words, being a Christian is a formative process—a journey—not a "once and done" dramatic revelation. The Christian life as expressed in this text is about being shaped and fashioned over time. It is not a magic act in which a wand is waved and all is different. The text tells us, instead, that there is a participatory, communal element to Christian faith that enlightens the eyes of the heart in the midst of the saints. This is not esoteric knowledge to be gained by intellectual study. The vision of the faithful life contained in this text is learned and lived within community and expressed through relationships. It is not a faith lived in

Exegetical Perspective

This passage from Ephesians connects the life in Christ with the position of the ascended Christ (1:20). In it the writer (widely believed to be a follower of Paul rather than Paul himself) describes the prayers for the saints. It starts with a prayer for spiritual enlightenment (vv. 3, 8, 17) that comes as the result of the power set free from the resurrected Christ (vv. 19–20). This passage is full of evocative language in which the consequences of the session of Christ at God's right hand are explored. The long sentences evident in the Greek are one of the characteristics of this epistle. Scholars have noted connections with other Christian texts, such as the opening verses of 1 Peter (1 Pet. 1:3–5; cf. Eph. 1:1–14) and also some of the liturgical texts from the Dead Sea Scrolls, such as the Hymns (in Hebrew *Hodayoth*, 1QH, where the writer speaks of his divinely given insight in ways similar to what we find in Ephesians). The text divides into two units: the nature of conversion (vv. 15–19) and God at work in Christ (vv. 20–23).

First, the writer explores the nature of conversion. This is described in terms of an intellectual enlightenment, where the mind undergoes a transformation. The language used describes renewed vision. It is parallel to the sort of language used in authentic Pauline passages such as Romans 12:2: "Do not be conformed to this world, but be

Homiletical Perspective

On Christmas Eve, in an overnight shelter for homeless women in Washington, DC, an argument erupted. Sheila accused Mary of stealing her coat while she slept. Mary called Sheila a liar, followed by a long string of creative synonyms for "prostitute." Sheila told Mary she was a "no-good-good-for-nothing." Mary shot back, "Oh yeah? I am better than you will ever be. I am an aristocrat of the highest order—with the Rothschilds on my mother's side and the Three Wise Men on my father's." That was the end of the discussion. Sheila could not top that.

The words of this modern Mary echo those of an ancient Mary, the mother of Jesus, who—pregnant with child and with hope—proclaimed that the powerful would be put off their thrones and the lowly lifted up, that the rich would be sent away empty and the hungry filled (Luke 1:52–53). The predicted social upheaval was fulfilled symbolically in that women's shelter, as a claim of royalty, of power, of "somebodyness" issued forth out of homelessness, brokenness, and powerlessness.

Luke is the only Gospel writer to include Mary's hymn of praise, known traditionally as the Magnificat, in his birth narrative. He is also the only one (if we accept Mark's shorter ending as the historically accurate rendering) to end his account with a description of the ascension of Jesus

Ephesians 1:15-23

Theological Perspective

sufficiently to the light that you are able to make out other objects. After a few moments, however, you cease to be conscious of the light itself, and start to see what else is in the room, as it is illumined by the light. The Gospel accounts of Jesus' resurrection, says Williams, show him to have been like that initial morning light: at first Jesus' resurrected self was so blinding that the disciples could be conscious only of him. The ascension, however, is that moment when the light itself recedes into the background, so that Jesus becomes the one through whom we see the rest of the world. "He is the light we see by; we see the world in a new way because we see it *through* him, see it with his eyes."[1] Moreover, this new perspective works in two ways: not only do we see the world as the place where *Jesus* has promised to be, but we also see it as the place where *we* are committed to be.

The importance of a right perception lies at the heart of the Epistle for this day. Paul's prayer for the Ephesians is that God will give to them "a spirit of wisdom and revelation . . . so that, with the eyes of your heart enlightened, you may know what is the hope to which he has called you" (vv. 17–18). Paul is eager that the Ephesian Christians see the world from the unique perspective of faith, which, though it experiences the world as corruptible, is nevertheless filled with hope; and though it encounters the powers of death as invincible, knows nevertheless that they are defeated by the stronger power of God's love. There is here a deliberate juxtaposition of contradictory forces—God's power contravenes what otherwise seems so obvious in our experience. Evil is subject to good, and death submits to life. However, this is the very paradox that is sealed by Christ's ascension: because Jesus' life can now be seen to be bound up with the life of God, heaven and earth are also bound together in a single continuum, so that the realities of heaven (love and life) can be seen through Christ as the final word on the evil and death of this world. Such a hope is clearly reflected in the church's hymnody for its observance of Ascension Day.

To reiterate, the key to the authenticity of this hope in Christ is, as Paul puts it, that God "put all things under his feet and has made him the head over all things for the church" (v. 22). Easter, of course, is usually preached as the source of this hope: because Christ is risen, our hope is secured. Still, as Williams points out, the resurrection accounts actually reflect a certain ambivalence. The

Pastoral Perspective

isolation. It does not involve gaining political power or substantial material goods. It is an illumination of the heart that grows as one proceeds along a spiritual path, revealing to believers nuances of the world that would be otherwise impossible for them to grasp. It is a participatory enlightenment that takes place within community, shaping wise knowledge of true and mature hope. The Christian life is thus about Christian formation and the gaining of heart knowledge through the spiritual realities of hope and of power.

In the 1983 Oscar-winning film *Tender Mercies*, Robert Duvall plays Mac Sledge, a middle-aged country-and-western singer whose successful career and life have collapsed into an alcoholic haze. Out of hope and opportunities, bitter and cynical in attitude, he becomes a handyman working for a young widow who runs a modest roadside motel in rural Texas. As the narrative moves forward, Mac marries the widow and is baptized at the local church, sharing the baptismal pool that Sunday with the young boy who is the widow's son. Riding back home from the service, Mac and the boy are playfully inquisitive with each other, pondering any differences in themselves that they can feel or see, now that they have been baptized. Both agree that they seem pretty much the same. By the film's conclusion, however, the viewer knows without a doubt that these characters are very different from who they were at the film's beginning. As in today's text, there has been a growth of grace and discernment among the saints. Hope and a spirit of wisdom have been born of water and community.

In another scene from the same film, Mac is walking toward his pickup truck on the main street of the local town. A woman carrying groceries on the sidewalk is watching him and calls out as he passes, "Hey mister, were you really Mac Sledge?" Mac glances back as he gets in his vehicle.

"Yes ma'm, I guess I was."

With emphasis on the enlightenment of the eyes of the heart, the writer of Ephesians reminds us that in our maturity as believers we will see and judge differently. This ties us directly to numerous biblical stories where God's choices illustrate an ability to see beyond the material surface. When God instructs Samuel to pick David as the future king of Israel, we are told explicitly that God sees beyond outward appearance, looking upon the "heart" (1 Sam. 16:7). Today's text from Ephesians generates anticipation that such depth of vision is available for all who come to know Christ more completely.

---

1. Rowan Williams, "Ascension Day," in *A Ray of Darkness* (Cambridge, MA: Cowley Press, 1995), 69.

transformed by the renewing of your minds, so that you may discern what is the will of God—what is good and acceptable and perfect." The concentration in Ephesians is on intellectual, rather than ethical, transformation. The ethical is important, as becomes apparent in the rest of the letter, but here inner transformation is given priority, for it is the inner person who is the source of ethical rectitude. Thus, in Matthew 15:16–20, the heart is seen as the source of either good or evil, and here it is the "eye of the heart" (v. 18) that is enlightened so that the whole of life is illumined (cf. Luke 12:2–3).

The writer uses the language of wealth and inheritance to describe salvation. This parallels language in Colossians 1:12–13 (Colossians and Ephesians have many affinities) and 1 Peter 1:4. "Among the saints" is probably a reference to both humans and divine beings. "Holy ones" is a way of referring to angels (e.g., Dan. 7:18), and it is angelic beings that are referred to in Colossians 1:12. However, this is also the way Paul refers to Christians, as is evident in many of his addresses (e.g., 1 Cor. 1:2), and it is the way Ephesians opens (1:1).

God's power is at the root of hope. God's power is "great" and "immeasurable," and it is God's power that is at work among believers (v. 19). "God put this power to work in Christ" when God raised him from the dead and seated him at God's right hand (v. 20). This is a reminder of the importance attached by early Christians to the work of the Spirit, both as a force for illumination (1 Cor. 2:10–16) and as a power at work in the world (Acts 2:17–21), drawing on the rich tradition of energetic activity that typified the life of characters like Samson or Saul in the Hebrew Bible (Judg. 14:19 and 1 Sam. 10:6–13).

The climax of this passage comes in the focus on Christ "in the heavenly places" (v. 20). This is a phrase that is distinctive to Ephesians. Elsewhere it is not used solely of Christ, but includes those linked with him who are privileged to share his lot. This is the basis of their activity: to make known the divine mystery to the powers (3:10) and to recognize that the spiritual life is a struggle against flesh and blood (6:10). The theological understanding here is not limited to a body of people separate from the whole world. Christ is head of the whole creation, and the resurrected Christ is Lord over all (1:22). The whole of creation will be subject to the rule of Christ (picking up on widespread ideas the writer shared with Jews about the messianic age from passages like Isa. 11 and Zech. 8:20–23, where the messianic rule affects all people).

(24:44–53). These two events frame a Gospel that is preoccupied with issues of power, making the case over and over that those on the margins of society are inheritors of the realm of God.

The momentum of the Gospel culminates with Jesus' promise to his followers that they will be "clothed with power from on high" and his disappearance into heaven. This rendering forms a bridge to an even more detailed account of the ascension at the opening of Luke's second volume, the Acts of the Apostles (1:6–11), a book imbued with the power of the Spirit at work in the church and in the world.

The Letter to the Ephesians reverberates with similar themes: the shift from aliens to heirs, the enduring presence of the Spirit, the greatness of God's power. The chosen text from the first chapter pairs nicely with Luke's account of the ascension for preaching. It offers a cosmic vision of Jesus' place in creation and in the church.

The author of Ephesians, likely a disciple of the apostle Paul, acknowledges the pervasiveness of the powers and principalities that serve death. The point is made most trenchantly in the sixth chapter, with the exhortation to "put on the whole armor of God" in the spiritual battle against "the rulers, . . . the authorities, and . . . the cosmic powers of this present darkness." The enlightened and prepared Christian will walk into the world wearing "the belt of truth," "the breastplate of righteousness," "the shoes . . . of peace," "the shield of faith," "the helmet of salvation," and "the sword of the Spirit, which is the word of God" (6:11–17).

Ephesians 1:20–23 is the announcement that this battle has already been won. It celebrates "the immeasurable greatness of God's power" (v. 19). God raised Jesus from the dead, breaking death's grip on the world. Christ sits "far above all rule and authority and power and dominion" (v. 21). Through his resurrection, the powers and principalities that serve death have been vanquished.

United Methodist pastor and theologian Bill Wylie-Kellermann says of the events surrounding Jesus' death, "Authority is truly the question of the hour."[1] The chief priests and Pharisees asked Pilate for troops to guard the tomb, "an appeal to the authority of death." The sealing of the tomb, Wylie-Kellermann believes, is widely misunderstood.

The traditional Sunday school version is a matter of rolling a big stone over the gaping entrance and

---

1. This quotation and all following are from Bill Wylie-Kellermann, *Seasons of Faith and Conscience* (Maryknoll, NY: Orbis Books, 1991), 186.

Ephesians 1:15-23

Theological Perspective

elusive Jesus, who comes and goes at will, appearing and reappearing quite unpredictably, evokes in the disciples a certain "surprise and disorientation." Yet is it not then that their hearts are set on fire with the recognition of God's power that makes them apostles? As Paul reminds us in the text from Ephesians, that power is fully set in motion by God, who both raises Christ from the dead *and* seats him "at his right hand in the heavenly places, far above all rule and authority and power and dominion" (vv. 20–21). It is as if a rising tide that is set in motion by the resurrection reaches its conclusion only in the ascension, when both heaven and earth are filled by Christ's presence, "the fullness of him who fills all in all" (v. 23).

Indeed, this is the reading of the centrality of the ascension that is reflected in the church's liturgy: one of the collects for this day begins by invoking God's blessed Son, who "ascended far above all heavens that he might fill all things," echoing Paul's own text.[2] If all things are now filled by Christ's presence, then the consequence for Christian living is that nothing and no one can be taken as insignificant or of no importance. Our commitment to God means that we are also committed to what God is committed to: the whole of creation, as it has been filled by Christ's presence. That is why, says Williams, "Christians are going to be a nuisance in any imaginable human society."

JOSEPH H. BRITTON

Pastoral Perspective

Lee Atwater was a highly successful consultant and political strategist of the 1980s who is often credited with raising negative campaigning in the United States to the level of a political art. He assisted with George Bush's election to the presidency in 1988 and became chair of the Republican National Committee. Atwater was at the height of his power and influence when he was diagnosed with a brain tumor in 1990. Before he died, he wrote a number of letters to former political foes, asking for their forgiveness for his earlier actions against them, speaking of his regret about the material orientation of his life and the lack of "heart" that led him to attack others for political gain.

Atwater offers a public example of the corruption that is possible with undue focus on worldly, material power. He writes about the antithesis of the power being lifted up in these verses from Ephesians, where "riches" and "greatness" are redefined. Such misuses and misunderstandings of power are manifest every day on the private stage of our own lives. We can discern them in our work and family relationships as well.

The writer of Ephesians speaks of power in a fundamentally different way, understanding it as a spiritual reality that raises the dead and has dominion both within and without time. This is power far beyond the political. Its expression is formed and made manifest in the life, death, and resurrection of Jesus. Such power of life and hope is the inheritance of those who grow in the knowledge of Christ, developing the eyes of their hearts and learning to see as God sees.

PAUL "SKIP" JOHNSON

---

2. *The Book of Common Prayer* (New York: Church Hymnal Corp., 1979), 226.

Exegetical Perspective

The language of Christ's headship of a body, unlike language elsewhere in the Pauline corpus (e.g., 1 Cor. 12 and Rom. 12), seems here not identified solely with the church, but describes the fullness of what is still being completed. The exegetical question is whether (as one would naturally suppose in the light of usage elsewhere) "his body" (v. 23) refers solely to the church, or if the explanatory conclusion extends to "all things" in 1:22. Either way, the universal lordship of Christ is stressed here and, as elsewhere in Ephesians, also the consequences of this lordship for Christians, including the significance of their role on earth as the extension of the cosmic Christ (Eph. 4:11–16). The passage expresses the writer's hope of greater vision, which places the eschatology of Ephesians alongside that of Revelation 20–22 and indeed Romans 8:18–24, as offering a more universal and cosmic scope to the work of Christ.

The enigmatic words "the fullness of him who fills all in all" (v. 23), which picks up on Pauline language already used of eschatological fulfillment in 1 Corinthians 15:28, suggest that Christ is an anticipation of something that is to be completely filled in the future. That kind of pattern is typical of Pauline language both about the resurrection (1 Cor. 15:20) and the Spirit (2 Cor. 1:22). Thus a spiritual actuality, already fulfilled, will extend to a wider group of people. Indeed, the promise could be even wider to include the whole of creation.

CHRISTOPHER ROWLAND

Homiletical Perspective

cementing it tight. The seal is viewed as "something like first-century caulking—puttying up the cracks to keep the stink in." Not so, according to Wylie-Kellermann. This was a legal seal, with cords strung across it to indicate any tampering. It was an echo of the seal put over the lions' den with Daniel inside, marked with the king's own signet; and of the seals on the scroll of history in Revelation, which only the Lamb was worthy to break. The seal, says Wylie-Kellermann, is a legal lock on the tomb door—"not air tight, but politically tight. To remove the stone and break the seal is a civil crime. The resurrection is against the law."

Jesus' resurrection broke the authority of imperial Rome and subdued the power of death. After this victory, carried into heaven by the Spirit, Jesus took his place above all earthly powers as the head of the church. However, if our understanding and our preaching on this passage remain in the cosmic realm—if they stay in the clouds without ever touching the ground—we lose some of the text's power. To borrow a phrase from the passage, we need to use "the eyes of the heart" (v. 18) to see the full picture.

Jesus is indeed the one who is "seated at God's right hand in the heavenly places" for eternity (v. 20), but he is also the one who walked the earth and brought good news to those who suffered, to those who lived on the margins: to the diseased and the outcast and the oppressed who were the victims of the powers of death. He still brings good news to the likes of Sheila and Mary, whose "glorious inheritance" (v. 18) is far richer than the wealth of the Rothschilds or the wisdom of the magi.

Because Christ is enthroned in heaven, we can expect the earthly thrones to be vacated by the abusive, imperial rulers, just as Mary the mother of Jesus predicted two thousand years ago. We can trust that all will unfold "according to the working of God's great power" (v. 19). This is indeed part of "the hope to which God has called" us (v. 18).

JOYCE HOLLYDAY

Luke 24:44-53

⁴⁴Then he said to them, "These are my words that I spoke to you while I was still with you—that everything written about me in the law of Moses, the prophets, and the psalms must be fulfilled." ⁴⁵Then he opened their minds to understand the scriptures, ⁴⁶and he said to them, "Thus it is written, that the Messiah is to suffer and to rise from the dead on the third day, ⁴⁷and that repentance and forgiveness of sins is to be proclaimed in his name to all nations, beginning from Jerusalem. ⁴⁸You are witnesses of these things. ⁴⁹And see, I am sending upon you what my Father promised; so stay here in the city until you have been clothed with power from on high."

⁵⁰Then he led them out as far as Bethany, and, lifting up his hands, he blessed them. ⁵¹While he was blessing them, he withdrew from them and was carried up into heaven. ⁵²And they worshiped him, and returned to Jerusalem with great joy; ⁵³and they were continually in the temple blessing God.

Theological Perspective

When we try to recall Jesus' commission of his disciples, it is the well-known words from Matthew that first come to mind. So it is helpful to take a fresh look at Luke's version. Christ's final words here are very different from Matthew's Great Commission. If we listen to Luke's risen Jesus, we may have to start all over again in how we view repentance and forgiveness, sin and salvation.

Jesus finishes presenting his life's historic purpose with a promise that "repentance and forgiveness of sins is to be proclaimed in his name to all nations, beginning from Jerusalem" (v. 47). Most traditional understandings of sin and repentance are personal and individual, so we need to read Jesus' brief promise carefully in light of Luke's consistent message of repentance and forgiveness. If we do, we may hear a new prophetic word.

Perhaps because Luke's Jesus begins this passage with opening the disciples' minds to the way in which his suffering, death, and resurrection have fulfilled the Scriptures, it is tempting to read verse 47 as a call to inward transformation leading to personal forgiveness for individuals. When it comes to salvation, many jump to the afterlife: God's forgiveness leads all who accept it to a home in heaven!

Bede the Venerable offered one such take on Luke's closing words. A Benedictine monk who lived

Pastoral Perspective

If this lection is being read in public worship, then we assume the emphasis of the day is on the departure of Jesus and its meaning. A pastor may well face an incredulous congregation who are not helped by some of the classical images of art and imagination in which Jesus' feet, complete with stigmata, are shown disappearing into a cloud. Whatever the mode and manner in which Jesus' postresurrection appearances came to an end, the import of the ascension is found in what precedes it: his last teaching for the disciples, the commission to bear witness and wait for "power from on high," and the final blessing.

For the purposes of Luke's story, the ascension brings Easter Day to a close. He will follow a different scheme in Acts 1:1–11, also read on this day, which gives rise to the tradition of placing the observance of Ascension Day forty days after Easter, and the pouring out of the Holy Spirit ten days after that on Pentecost. For some congregations, Luke's use of the ascension as a literary device (suggested by the differing schemes he uses in Luke and Acts) will be pastorally helpful. This may be especially so in light of the other Gospels, which treat crucifixion, resurrection, ascension, and the gift of the Holy Spirit as a single movement or event.

In some settings a pastor may need to take this opportunity to address the nature of scriptural

Exegetical Perspective

Although the Emmaus Road incident has received more attention than the passage before us this week, the commissioning of the disciples and the ascension of the Lord embody Luke's distinctive contribution to understanding the Easter event and season. The passage can be divided into five sections:
Commissioning the witnesses for mission
- 24:44–46   rereading scripture (christologically)
- 24:47–48   the mission and the witnesses
- 24:49   waiting for the mantle of power
Jesus' blessing and ascension
- 24:50–51   ascension at Bethany
- 24:52–53   return to Jerusalem (the origin)

It will be useful to examine each section briefly.

Verses 44–46. Like John, Luke is concerned with Jesus' words, but for Luke, the primary purpose of Jesus' words is to interpret the Law of Moses, the Prophets, and the Psalms, so that what Scripture teaches about the Christ/Messiah might be fulfilled. Jesus is teaching the disciples to reread the Scriptures through the lens of his ministry, so that it will be clear how his ministry "fulfills" this christological pattern, which includes suffering and resurrection. The use of *dei* with *plērōthēnai* ("it is necessary to fulfill") indicates that this pattern exists by divine necessity. It is Jesus' role in God's unfolding salvation history.

Homiletical Perspective

Quick! What is the appropriate liturgical color for celebrating the ascension of the Lord? Many Protestant traditions have given only minor attention to this holy day. Observed forty days after Easter, Ascension Day does not fall on a Sunday but on a Thursday. Some customs commemorate the Lord's ascension on the Sunday following Ascension Day. So a preacher might find this Gospel text being proclaimed on a weekday or a Sunday. The Revised Common Lectionary uses the same lessons in all three years of the cycle.

The account of the ascension in Luke 24:44–53 falls into three time frames: past, present, and future. Although such an outline might seem a bit too neat, it does capture the range of what Luke has recorded. Each preacher will have to decide whether or not to pursue the differences between what Luke has written in Acts and what Luke has written in the Gospel narrative.

Past. There is a lure in twenty-first-century culture to give priority to contemporary values while diminishing the roots from which those values have grown. Jesus offers a countercultural view, pointing the disciples to the past ("everything written about me in the law of Moses, the prophets, and the psalms," v. 44).

Tradition becomes a feeding tube by which God's work in days long ago is delivered to our own time.

Luke 24:44-53

Theological Perspective

in Britain in the seventh and eighth centuries, Bede wrote in one of his *Homilies on the Gospels*, "There was certainly a necessary sequence. First Christ had to shed his blood for the redemption of the world. Then through his resurrection, and ascension, he opened to human beings the gate of the heavenly kingdom. Last, he sent those who would preach to all nations throughout the world the word of life and administer the sacraments of faith. By these sacraments they could be saved and arrive at the joys of the heavenly fatherland."[1]

Bede succinctly summarized a lovely, even commonsense reading of this passage. However, in the larger message of Luke, we discover that the call to repentance and the forgiveness of sins has a sharp this-worldly dimension.

Luke's Gospel contains a prophetic summons to repentance from systemic domination. At its heart is a demand to the powerful to forgive the acute debts of the poor, debts that were in Christ's day keys to enslavement. Jesus pronounces a day in which God will set free those in bondage, turning upside down the power arrangements of a world in which debtors' property could be seized and their bodies sold.

This proclamation runs throughout the Gospel. The expectation of redemption from bondage begins with Mary's prophetic recitation of a jubilee reversal of human power structures in the Magnificat (Luke 1:46–55). In chapter 4, Jesus announces the fulfillment of Isaiah's vision of one sent to preach good news to the poor, release to the captives, recovery of sight to the blind and, in culmination, "the acceptable year of the Lord." The proclamation continues with the "blessings and woes" (6:20–26) of the Sermon on the Plain. This theme emerges repeatedly in the parables of Luke too. Within this "jubilee" context, repentance and forgiveness are both economic and spiritual.

In a recent article by Ivoni Richter Reimer, we find a compelling depiction of a Roman colonial world in which overwhelming debt was a central feature of the lives of the poor. In particular, she describes the crushing weight of numerous taxes on everyone. "For thousands of people . . . the loss of everything, imprisonment on account of their debts, and slavery on account of their debts, presented real threats to the everyday reality of their lives."[2]

Pastoral Perspective

authority, discussing how Jesus "opened [his listeners'] minds to understand the scriptures" (v. 45). In most instances the congregation will be eager to hear more about the instruction, commissioning, and promise of blessing in these brief creedal statements of Jesus according to Luke.

A pastor may need to be aware that, in a setting sometimes described as "post-Christendom," these creedal statements call for interpretation if we are to be authentic in bearing witness. The phrase "post-Christendom" is a shorthand reference to the perceived reality that the alliance of church and empire has come to an end. For those who live in such a reality, the relationship of the church to the world is one of increasing ambivalence, requiring great clarity as Christians articulate their faith for others.

One pastoral task is to help those who listen to us appropriate the story of Jesus for themselves, moving from inherited or derivative faith to owned or lively faith. A meditation on "rising" or "being raised" could be useful. This would allow some reference to the single movement of Jesus being lifted on the cross, raised from the dead, and ascending into heaven in the other Synoptic Gospels, as well as explicit reference to the categories of exaltation or glorification in John's Gospel. (In all three years of the lectionary cycle, the ascension lections fall between Johannine passages prescribed for the Sixth and Seventh Sundays of Easter.)

For those who listen to us, being raised might be compared to being justified, healed, and redeemed, or—especially in this context—being forgiven after repentance (v. 47). In communities that kneel for confession, the response to the proclamation of forgiveness is usually to rise and stand. This hearkens back to "the days of yore," when a loyal subject being made a knight first knelt before the king in an act of obeisance, then received a gift or honor from the king, and was finally commanded to rise into his new status. As the story of Jesus becomes our own, so we are, in many and varied ways, "raised with Christ."

As the story becomes our own, so we become "witnesses of these things" (v. 48), and a pastor may wish to address the challenges of Christian witnessing. The disciples are commissioned to wait in the city until they have been "clothed with power from on high" (v. 49). The implication is that the promised power will be for the purpose of proclaiming to all nations the good news of which they are witnesses (v. 46–47). In Acts, Luke will go on to show that this commission to preach to all

---

1. Bede, *Homilies on the Gospels*, in Arthur A. Just Jr., ed., *Ancient Christian Commentary on Scripture III: Luke* (Downers Grove, IL: InterVarsity Press, 2003), 389.

2. Ivoni Richter Reimer, "The Forgiveness of Debts in Matthew and Luke," in *God's Economy: Biblical Studies from Latin America*, ed. Ross Kinsler and Gloria Kinsler (Maryknoll, NY: Orbis Books, 2005), 164.

Exegetical Perspective

The order of the sentence is important and reads: "everything must be fulfilled . . . concerning me." This is not about finding a general pattern of promise and fulfillment but a concern that the Scriptures "concerning [Jesus]" (NRSV "about") be interpreted and understood. When Jesus "opens [the disciples'] minds," he focuses on the mystery of Jesus' suffering and resurrection. However, what passages of Scripture can Jesus or Luke have in mind? The Servant Songs of Second Isaiah (Isa. 42:1–4; 49:1–6; 50:4–11; 52:13–53:12) or a scattering of psalms come to mind.

Verses 47–48. Up to this point Luke has been concerned with reinterpreting the Scriptures in the light of Jesus. Now his focus shifts to the outcome of Jesus' ministry—the mission that the disciples will conduct in his name. The content of their message is clear: to proclaim "repentance for the forgiveness of sins in Jesus' name." There is a textual variant here. Some manuscripts speak of repentance *and* (*kai*) forgiveness while others speak of repentance *for* (*eis*) the forgiveness of sins. The latter is preferred, since it identifies the purpose of repentance and makes repentance part of a larger process. The scope of the mission is clear: "to all nations." The starting line is equally clear: Jerusalem. Finally, the role of the disciples is clear: they are witnesses (*martyres*). This means that Jesus' resurrection is not the end but the beginning of a new mission.

When the risen Lord tells the disciples, "You are witnesses of these things," he is referring to everything from the suffering and resurrection of the Messiah (v. 46) to the proclaiming of repentance for the forgiveness of sins (v. 47). The proposed reinterpretation of Scripture is in the service of this mission. It might be interesting to examine Luke's Gospel to see how he reinterprets passages from the Law of Moses, the Prophets, and the Psalms. This is the only time "the Psalms" fill in for the third of the tripartite division of Scripture into Law, Prophets, and the Writings, and the Psalms are probably meant to stand on their own, not as shorthand for the Writings. This means that Luke seems to be elevating the Psalms to a status similar to the Law and the Prophets.

Verse 49. Up to this point, the passage appears to be gaining a certain momentum: reinterpret Scripture and launch the mission. Rather than issue a clarion call to action, the disciples/witnesses are told to wait. The verb, *kathisate*, carries the connotation of "standing quiet or calm." Wait, yes, but wait for what? The answer is forthcoming, "until you have been

Homiletical Perspective

Old is good. The Law of Moses tells how God wants God's people to live. The Prophets alert God's people to ways in which God's people miss the mark. The Psalms share the fullness of the feeling of God's people, whether in praise, lament, confusion, doubt, or hope. God has not just arrived at the party! We are not the first to encounter the living God. When we draw on tradition, we ask those who walked the mountain before us to let us know where the rocks are, where the fresh streams are, and where the dangerous animals hide.

Jesus acknowledges that the past contains much that is good. Indeed, Jesus says that it "must be fulfilled" (v. 44). As Luke tells the story, this Jesus is clearly the eternal Word (John 1:14), God's prime presence (Col. 1:17), and the one who is beyond all we know (John 21:25). To deny the past is to deny who God is.

Present. After Jesus acknowledges the truth of the Law of Moses, the Prophets, and the Psalms, he moves into a mode of contemporary application (v. 45). The disciples know that Jesus is on target because they have seen the things of which he speaks (v. 48). Where is God's truth seen as "real" in the twenty-first century? Where is grace being experienced? Where is forgiveness being accepted? Where is healing breaking through brokenness? Where is reconciliation happening? Where is the gift of faith being received?

God provides means of grace, avenues through which God makes God's transforming presence accessible in this day. Those means include public and private prayer, personal and corporate worship, studying and hearing the Scriptures, fasting, frequent sharing in the Lord's Supper, and holy conversation (or holy conferencing). When today's disciples practice these means of grace, God ordinarily brings God's gracious gifts. Luke calls it "open[ing] their minds to understand the scriptures" (v. 45). We might call it "being available to where God is today."

Future. Jesus is clear that the story does not end with this conversation. He tells the eleven disciples to "stay here in the city until you have been clothed with power from on high" (v. 49). Reporting this call from Jesus, Luke sets the stage for the Pentecost events he describes in Acts 2. God makes good on God's promises. If God says power will be given, power will be given! In this sense, the resurrection of Jesus is an appetizer (or foretaste) of a future in which all in God's family are given new life.

Luke 24:44-53

Theological Perspective

If we read this passage as the culmination of a prophetic call to the nations to repent from exploiting of the poor, rather than a promise of personal atonement, then why does the passage speak of the forgiveness of sins? The term for forgiveness in the Greek is literally and technically a term for liberation from captivity, or repayment or cancellation of financial obligation. To find the close parallelism between the sins of the powerful and the debts of the powerless, we need look no further than Luke's version of the Lord's Prayer, which reads: "Forgive us our sins, as we ourselves forgive everyone indebted to us." The two are so tightly connected as to be inseparable.

Regardless of how much we want to sustain a purely spiritual understanding of redemption, we need to acknowledge at least that Jesus in Luke is deeply committed to the literal redemption of those chained by economic structures. Our traditional understanding of repentance and forgiveness needs to be brought back to earth by placing it in the context of release for the captives and hope for the poor.

Once we plant our theology on the ground, we see the words of Jesus to his disciples in a whole new light. They are to be sent out to proclaim to the nations a challenge from the same God who sent Elijah, Elisha, John the Baptist, and the young girl Mary. This is God's challenge to the mighty to repent of their old habits of crushing the poor. It is God's invitation to the disciples to begin to practice the kind of debt forgiveness that is ultimately required of all.

A jubilee reading of the ending of Luke leaves us with a host of questions. What is the risen Christ's pronouncement to our own day? What are the systemic debts we need to forgive, and the systemic sins (and debts) for which we need forgiveness? What is our place in the church's call to offer the gospel of repentance to the nations?

Jesus asks his disciples to wait until they receive collective and personal empowerment from the Spirit of God to go forth from Jerusalem to the nations. Sheer duty is never enough to sustain the hard work of discipleship—it takes more, a spiritual empowerment. When do we wait and when do we act? What are we waiting for?

PETER J. B. CARMAN

Pastoral Perspective

nations gives rise to the first major controversy of the church, namely, the question of whether "all nations" includes the Gentiles. The promise of power gives rise to a second challenge that has been and continues to be a temptation for Christians of many stripes. This temptation is to think that somehow the power that is promised becomes our own, to be used for our own purposes—rather than a gift from God, to be used for the purpose of God.

The proclamation that the power of God is made manifest in weakness, and the commission to preach a suffering Messiah (v. 46), can serve as a built-in corrective to the temptation to abuse power by diverting it to ourselves. A pastor may wish to address the human love affair with power and those whom we perceive as powerful by reminding the faithful that we bear witness with our whole lives. Something as simple as relating our belief in Jesus to some personal or political consequence can lead us to become the focus of a conversation—an apologist for the faith—and therefore vulnerable to the challenges and criticisms of others.

As a final act before his departure, Jesus blesses his disciples, offering yet another window for addressing pastoral concerns. A blessing is a bestowal of material or spiritual good. Conduct an informal survey of what churchgoers consider a blessing, and you may hear answers such as, "I am not exactly sure what constitutes a blessing, but I know that it is better to have a blessing than not."

In today's text, the blessing is best understood as a sacerdotal or prophetic act in which the thing pronounced becomes true through its being pronounced. In other words, when Jesus blesses the disciples, they are made happy by the act of blessing. Both the presence of the blesser and the promise of the blessing sustain them so that they worship with joy (v. 52) and bless God in return (v. 53). They enjoy the attention of God even as they await the fulfillment of the promise. This is a powerful message to those who recognize that not all is right with the world or their lives, but who live in a reasonable and holy hope that God's purposes will be fulfilled.

GEOFFREY M. ST. J. HOARE

clothed with power from on high." Like Elisha, who waited for Elijah's mantle to fall on him, so the witnesses/disciples must wait for this divine mantle to fall on them (1 Kgs. 19:19–21; 2 Kgs. 2:9–14; see also Ps. 93:1–2).

This means that the complete picture is still shrouded in mystery. What is this divine power from on high? Of course, for Luke this phrase refers to the descent of the Holy Spirit manifest at Pentecost. However, for the disciples, that is not clear. They know only the next step they are to take: "stay in the city until the Father's promise (*epangelian*) falls upon you."

Verses 50–51. Once the disciples know what they are to do (wait calmly) and on what authority they are to do it (reinterpret the Law, the Prophets, and the Psalms), they are prepared. Jesus now turns to some unfinished business in the guise of blessing the disciples. The Gospel of Luke opened with the stories about Zechariah, who saw a vision in the temple and was struck dumb. Therefore, he could not utter the priestly blessing for the people gathered for the blessing (1:21–23). Now Jesus utters the blessing that Zechariah could not.

The blessing occurs in Bethany. It is as though the risen Lord took the disciples to the trail head that would lead to the Gentile mission but prevented them from beginning their journey until they were clothed with power from on high. Just as Jesus disappeared from the disciples and was carried into heaven (the ascension), so in the Emmaus story, Jesus disappeared from the sight of the disciples (vv. 30–31), but this time he vanished not to return. It is Luke's distinctive contribution to understanding the resurrection that he distinguishes the postresurrection appearances from the ascension.

Verses 52–53. Only after Jesus has ascended into heaven does Luke say that "they worshiped him," because he has ascended to the Father. Neither resurrection nor ascension is about human longing for life after death. Resurrection is a call to mission. Nothing is said about the disciples' resurrection. Indeed, they are focused on waiting in Jerusalem, so they worship daily in the temple, returning to the familiar after their sense of the familiar and the ordinary has been stretched to the limit and beyond all limits. They stand calmly, but they also engage in expectant waiting, until the mantle passes to them and the power from on high endows them for the mission ahead.

WILLIAM R. HERZOG II

One church bulletin board carried this message: "PUSH = Pray Until Something Happens." In this Gospel lesson, there is a tilt toward tomorrow: something is going to happen. When today's disciples learn to live with that sort of expectancy, they can experience the excitement and anticipation of a child who sees a still-unopened package under the Christmas tree. What is the surprise that God will give? When we get to the tomorrows of our lives, God is already there, and God's grace is sufficient.

The ascension. Does God sometimes seem absent, even while God is blessing us? Jesus left the disciples even as he was blessing them (v. 51). In the earliest depictions of the ascension, the apostles see the hand of God reach down in a cloud to grasp the hand of Jesus.[1] A cloud is often a biblical symbol for the presence of God. When early artists wanted to make sure viewers understood that God was involved in what was happening in the ascension, they painted a cloud. Luke makes the same point by writing that Jesus "was carried up into heaven" (v. 51). Note the difference between the active voice (Jesus did something) and the passive voice (something was done to Jesus).

In the end, there is only one way to respond to the mystery of the ascension: with worship, joy, and praise of God (vv. 52–53). Already looking to the next gift, the disciples do just what Jesus has asked them to do—they return to Jerusalem (v. 52). Do they fully understand what they have just seen? Not likely. However, aware that God has been at work among them, they remember the past, they acknowledge the present, and they claim the future.

A hymn. Charles Wesley penned these words to capture the fullness of the ascension: "See! The heaven its Lord receives, Alleluia! Yet he loves the earth he leaves, Alleluia! Though returning to his throne, Alleluia! Still he calls the world his own, Alleluia!"[2]

F. BELTON JOYNER JR.

1. "Ascension," in David Lyle Jeffrey, ed., *A Dictionary of Biblical Tradition in English Literature* (Grand Rapids: Eerdmans, 1992), 58.
2. Charles Wesley, "Hail the Day That Sees Him Rise," in *The United Methodist Hymnal* (Nashville: United Methodist Publishing House, 1989), #312.

Acts 16:16‑34

¹⁶One day, as we were going to the place of prayer, we met a slave-girl who had a spirit of divination and brought her owners a great deal of money by fortune-telling. ¹⁷While she followed Paul and us, she would cry out, "These men are slaves of the Most High God, who proclaim to you a way of salvation." ¹⁸She kept doing this for many days. But Paul, very much annoyed, turned and said to the spirit, "I order you in the name of Jesus Christ to come out of her." And it came out that very hour.

¹⁹But when her owners saw that their hope of making money was gone, they seized Paul and Silas and dragged them into the marketplace before the authorities. ²⁰When they had brought them before the magistrates, they said, "These men are disturbing our city; they are Jews ²¹and are advocating customs that are not lawful for us as Romans to adopt or observe." ²²The crowd joined in attacking them, and the magistrates had them stripped of their clothing and ordered them to be beaten with rods. ²³After they had given them a severe flogging, they threw them into prison and ordered the jailer to keep them securely. ²⁴Following these instructions, he put them in the innermost cell and fastened their feet in the stocks.

Theological Perspective

This series of stories begins with the perplexing tale of the slave girl. To be honest, most of us are probably troubled by the details of this story. The slave girl follows Paul and his companions and announces that they are "servants [NRSV "slaves"] of the Most High God, who proclaim to you the way of salvation" (v. 17). We are left to wonder whether Paul finds this helpful at first. Her cry certainly would have gathered an audience.

This goes on for many days, and only then Paul was "annoyed" (v. 18). He turns to the girl but talks right past her, addressing the spirit of divination that is in her and commanding it to come out. He never speaks to the girl. He is annoyed at the spirit, but appears to show no outrage at her being a slave. He frees her from her possession, but does nothing to free her from being a possession. Matters are made worse after the authorities realize they have violated his rights as a Roman citizen, and Paul demands an apology for his mistreatment. Are we right to be troubled by these things? Or is more going on here, perhaps not justifying what troubles us, but putting the story on a different level?

Note how the slave girl's owners take the first step in moving the story up to a higher level. They might have brought a complaint under Roman property law for the loss of the value of their slave. Instead,

Pastoral Perspective

God's intention is that we may be one, as the triune God is one. The Gospel reading for this Seventh Sunday of Easter (John 17:20–26) is Jesus' high-priestly prayer, telling of God's intent that all be one. "As you, Father, are in me and I am in you," says Jesus, "may they also be in us" (John 17:21). It is this relationship among the three persons of the Trinity that epitomizes Jesus' desire for us and that raises the pastoral question, what does this intention look like in the life of believers?

In other words, what are some concrete examples of the relationship Jesus describes in John 17:23—"I in them and you in me, that they may become completely one"? In today's text from Acts, we have two interrelated stories that provide us with two different manifestations of God's aim. In the healing of a slave girl and the salvation of a jailer, we witness how God brings about healing, wholeness, and unity in two particular lives, witnessing what it means to move toward becoming completely one.

Paul and his companions travel to Europe for the first time after Paul receives a vision of a Macedonian man pleading with him, saying, "Come over to Macedonia and help us" (Acts 16:9). There are several interesting aspects to Paul's nighttime vision. One feature is that, while it is a man who implores him to come over and help, it is two women who are the first

^{25}About midnight Paul and Silas were praying and singing hymns to God, and the prisoners were listening to them. ^{26}Suddenly there was an earthquake, so violent that the foundations of the prison were shaken; and immediately all the doors were opened and everyone's chains were unfastened. ^{27}When the jailer woke up and saw the prison doors wide open, he drew his sword and was about to kill himself, since he supposed that the prisoners had escaped. ^{28}But Paul shouted in a loud voice, "Do not harm yourself, for we are all here." ^{29}The jailer called for lights, and rushing in, he fell down trembling before Paul and Silas. ^{30}Then he brought them outside and said, "Sirs, what must I do to be saved?" ^{31}They answered, "Believe on the Lord Jesus, and you will be saved, you and your household." ^{32}They spoke the word of the Lord to him and to all who were in his house. ^{33}At the same hour of the night he took them and washed their wounds; then he and his entire family were baptized without delay. ^{34}He brought them up into the house and set food before them; and he and his entire household rejoiced that he had become a believer in God.

Exegetical Perspective

Slaves (vv. 16–18). In this passage, as in Luke's other writing, he gives the reader little sense of passing time. This episode simply begins, "One day" (*egeneto de*, which the KJV renders in an Old Testament–like phrase, "and it came to pass"). Once again, Paul and his friends are on their way to "the place of prayer" when they meet a woman at the other end of the social spectrum from Lydia (vv. 11–15). Far from being a householder, this unnamed young woman (*paidiskēn*) is a "slave girl" who has "owners" (*kyrioi*). As if to draw a deep contrast with Lydia, Luke includes plenty of details about this young woman. We have already noted that she is nameless. She is possessed with a spirit of divination (*pneuma pythōna*), literally "a spirit, a snake," an allusion to the snake that symbolized the Greek god Apollo at Delphi. Like those young women at Delphi, she divines the future (she is a *mantike*, a mantic) for anxious souls who are willing to pay. Apparently she is very good at her craft, for her owners live well off her gift.

She has also identified (and perhaps identified with) fellow slaves, recognizing Paul and his companions as "slaves of the Most High God." Not only that, but these slaves proclaim "a way of salvation." Many of her petitioners have asked about a way out of a difficult situation, a way of rescue, a way of salvation (*hodon sōtērias*). While she has the

Homiletical Perspective

The presence of God's Spirit is the occasion for freedom, including the liberation of our true selves. Paul writes to the church in Corinth: "Now the Lord is the Spirit, and where the Spirit of the Lord is, there is freedom" (2 Cor. 3:17). Jesus inaugurated his ministry as the proclamation of freedom to captives (Luke 4:18–19). The apostles take up this mantle with instructions from Jesus at the ascension, and through the power of the Holy Spirit poured out at Pentecost. While still in Philippi, Paul and Silas are arrested for casting out a spirit of divination as they are en route to the local place of prayer, an aside that turned out to be the main event. In fact, their ministry brings freedom to captives, even in an incidental sidewalk healing on the way to somewhere else.

As we examine the lives of those transformed by the gospel message, we see them in a movement from subservience to service, from work that delimits to work that coexists with their delight in God's way. Christians come to worship with pressures of work weighing on their hearts and minds. Indeed, how we earn a living constitutes a significant portion of our identities. Worship is a time to clarify our values and motives, and to see all we do and all we are in light of the gospel message. When we engage the gospel, we disengage from

Acts 16:16-34

Theological Perspective

they complain to the authorities that Paul and Silas are political subversives, undermining Roman order with Jewish customs. It is almost as if the text is warning us today that if the church challenges unjust economic systems, it will be accused of political offenses. From a relatively straightforward matter of civil property law, the slave owners make Paul and Silas the most dangerous of all criminals, those that threaten the order of the state. The charge is not unlike accusations made of Jesus.

Because the authorities agree that they are subversives, Paul and Silas are beaten and thrown into prison, where they pray and sing until midnight. Then follow the earthquake, the release of the shackles, the opening of the door, and the jailer's decision to kill himself rather than be dragged before the authorities to explain why all the prisoners were gone. Paul stops him just in time, whereupon the jailer asks one of Scripture's most profound questions, "What must I do to be saved?" (v. 30).

Whenever the jailer's question is asked, the obvious counterquestion is, "Saved from what?" Sword in hand, the jailer was probably thinking about how to be saved from the wrath of the authorities. However, his question has come to mean much more, depending on who is asking it.

"What must I do to be saved?" is a personal question in search of a personalized answer. What must I do to be saved from what destroys me? What must I do to be saved from my particular bondage, my oppression addiction, emptiness, or boredom? There are countless ways to lose our way in this world or to be in bondage, just as there are many different threats from which we need to be saved.

While the aftershocks still rattled the walls, the jailer knew he needed saving. The threat to his well-being was clear, tangible, looming. We, on the other hand, sometimes have only a vague sense that we are in trouble, that our lives are falling apart, or that we are losing our way. We learn to hide these thoughts, either with diversions or with shallow hopes that things will get better. The jailer's situation was unique only in its immediacy. We all need to be asking, "What must I do to be saved?"

Whatever the jailer may have meant by his question, Paul's answer is deceptively simple. Here we arrive at the key step in the story where Paul takes the action up to a yet higher level. The slave owners were partly right: the gospel subverts oppressive order. For Paul, even that level does not get at what is really going on. The story in which Paul and the jailer and all these other characters play

Pastoral Perspective

to receive Paul's help. The first is Lydia, the independent businesswoman who has command of her purple dye trade and her household (vv. 13–15). As a worshiper of God, Lydia finds that the Lord opens her heart (v. 14), so that she and her household are baptized (v. 15).

Up to this point in Acts, Paul has been primarily preaching in the synagogues of the Diaspora. In Philippi, we observe the manifestations of Jesus' high-priestly prayer in marketplaces with possessed slaves and in the heart of a prison with the dutiful jailer.

The next person to receive God's grace through Paul is a slave girl who has "a spirit of divination" and brings her owners "a great deal of money by fortune-telling" (v. 16). When she sees Paul and Silas, she cries out, "These men are slaves of the Most High God, who proclaim to you a way of salvation" (v. 17). Day after day, the spirit wails this truth (for Paul is a slave of the Most High God) until Paul, in annoyance, exorcises the spirit. "I order you in the name of Jesus Christ to come out of her," he says (v. 18), and it is done. Paul's motivation is to alleviate himself of this aggravating tagalong; God's yearning, though, is to bring wholeness to the slave so tormented.

While the text does not provide us an account of the slave girl's life after that, we do know she was no longer exploited as property to satisfy the greed of her owners. By the power of Jesus Christ, her torment was turned to health, her slavery to freedom. The slave girl was made whole, neither because of Paul's impulse nor because of her faith, but because of Jesus' prayer that "all may be one."

The plotline of the passage continues directly from this exorcism, since "her owners saw that their hope of making money was gone" (v. 19). Their loss of income results in Paul and Silas's severe flogging and imprisonment. It is in prison, however, that we see a second example of God's intention of unity. Paul and Silas find themselves at the center of captivity: they are in the innermost cell, feet fastened in stocks, at the darkest hour, midnight (vv. 24–25). It is precisely here, in complete darkness, that Jesus' prayer is answered.

Paul and Silas are praying and singing hymns to God, with their fellow prisoners listening to them, when there is a violent earthquake that shakes the foundations of the prison. "Immediately all the doors" are opened, and everyone's chains are "unfastened" (vv. 25–26). Freedom is brought to all those inside. Now, in a chapter from previous jail breaks in Acts, none of the prisoners take flight.

Exegetical Perspective

spirit of the python, which may or may not be accurate in its predictions, she is able to recognize that these "slaves" are directly connected with the God who rules the heavenly realm, *tou theou tou hypsistou*. It may be that she has the realm of Zeus in mind, or she may be using the typical non-Jewish designation for the Jewish divinity. After many days of following Paul with such mantic declarations, she is silenced. The annoyed apostle put an end to her disruptions by casting the spirit out of her.

When income dries up (vv. 19–24). The slave girl's owners, now deprived of their source of income, haul Paul and Silas into the marketplace, where the city court can be convened. Paul and Silas are charged with disturbing the city and, being Jews (a hint of typical first-century anti-Semitism here), advocating customs that are not lawful for Romans. It is impossible from the text to know just what unlawful customs Paul and Silas are advocating. Nevertheless, the magistrates have the missionaries stripped and beaten with rods, the kind of beating intended to teach a lesson prior to kicking troublemakers out of town. One might expect Paul and Silas simply to be beaten, escorted to the city gates, and ordered never to return. Instead they are thrown into prison.

Who is Lord? (vv. 25–34). The story that follows is familiar: as Paul and Silas pray and sing hymns in jail, an earthquake shakes the foundations of the prison, doors spring open, shackles fall to the floor, and one expects prisoners to flee for the exits. This is what the jailer expects. Since the prisoners are his responsibility and he has been unable to prevent their escape, why not end it all right here, right now? However, Paul shouts, "Do not harm yourself, for we are all here." Rather than falling on his sword, the jailer prostrates himself before Paul and Silas and cries out, "Sirs (*kyrioi*), what must I do to be saved?"

Has there been a more potent question flowing through Christian history? His cry of desperation might have been a commonsense plea: "How will I ever survive this mess?" While his concern may be for the moment, Paul and Silas address a much larger issue. They offer rescue that transcends the darkness of the moment. Their response also penetrates the whole history of Christian witness: "Believe on the Lord Jesus (*kyrios Iesous*), and you will be saved, you and your household" (v. 31). The story continues in the jailer's house, where Paul and Silas "spoke the word of the Lord (*kyrios*)."

Homiletical Perspective

confining assumptions about work, including the assumption that we are the sum of our work.

Part of our vocational identity requires Sabbath rest and an encounter with God through prayer and worship. On their way to pray, the ranting that is a distraction becomes the cause for which Paul and Silas will be arrested. They sing and pray in jail, creating Sabbath conditions in captivity. The earthquake shakes the foundations of the prison, freeing captives. The night concludes with the washing of wounds, professions of faith at baptism, and the breaking of bread. The hospitality of a godly household brings everyone safely into a new dawn.

Paul acts out of annoyance because the girl had called out day after day: "These men are slaves of the Most High God, who proclaim to you a way of salvation." Only later do the missionaries learn that their healing by exorcism got in the way of those who were making a great deal of money because of her fortune-telling. Moved by annoyance rather than compassion, their action brings unintended results. Without the spirit of divination she is no longer useful to her owners, so this healing is an act of liberation.

Dragged to the marketplace, Paul and Silas are publicly accused of "disturbing" the city, though by legal standards the charges remain vague. Also, a cultural argument is leveled against them: they are Jews advocating anti-Roman customs. Indeed, Paul was a Jew, but also a Roman citizen who demanded the rights of citizenship. His insulted reaction to the arrest (see Acts 16:35–40) exemplifies a larger effort in Luke–Acts to show the legitimacy of the Christian movement. However, as this turns to a mob scene ("the crowd joined in attacking them," v. 22), they are beaten and jailed in the innermost cell, where they are put away with stocks on their feet. The form and manner of their humiliating incarceration is shown in stark contrast to the form and manner of their subsequent liberation.

We see here the concern for justice in the early church. Though hope for a restored political order lies beneath the surface, the daily work of the church is seen in Paul's demand for justice for himself. In Luke–Acts, repeatedly the falsely accused Christians struggle for vindication and recognition under the law. Martin Hengel writes that Luke is an apologist who argues for "public toleration" of a new religious group.[1] These daily battles, in unfavorable or hostile

1. Martin Hengel, "Unfashionable Reflections on Luke as a Theological Historian," in *Acts and the History of Earliest Christianity*, trans. John Bowden (Philadelphia: Fortress Press, 1980), 60.

Acts 16:16-34

Theological Perspective

their role is, in truth, a theological story, one in which God is acting and Christ is saving. Paul's answer, "Believe in the Lord Jesus Christ," is an invitation to the jailer, and indeed to everyone, to tune in to the level of God's action.

In its simplest form, Paul's answer seems terribly inadequate, as if what the jailer (and all of us) really need is some carefully worded strategic plan or some tested method of self-improvement. Might we not complain that Paul's answer to the question of salvation seems to encourage passivity? We are simply told to trust that Jesus Christ is saving us, not to do anything to save ourselves. Even worse, Paul's answer seems to ignore the personal or individual circumstances from which each one of us needs to be saved. How can one answer fit us all?

The answer is simple—and saving—precisely because it is *not* a program of self-improvement. The secret is that Jesus Christ is saving us. Believing it means tuning in to the highest level of the story line of what is going on. It means becoming decisively aware that our small lives are swept up into a great drama, God's story line. God is indeed reaching out to us in Jesus Christ, taking our lives into the gospel story of transformation and redemption. Trusting in this truth means that we give up efforts to save ourselves by solving our problems.

To be sure, there are still many problems to be solved in this world. We have much yet to do to bring release to captives, justice for the oppressed, and peace for those ravaged by conflict. As important as these actions are, they are only a part of a higher, more important action, the saving action of a sovereign God who enters our humanity to take it up and redeem it to its final destiny.

RONALD COLE-TURNER

Pastoral Perspective

Rather, they stay until the jailer wakes up—an awakening from both physical and spiritual unconsciousness.

Until this point in the jailer's life, he has derived all meaning from his profession; consequently, he plans to fall on his sword because of his failure to guard his prisoners. Yet oneness with God does not come from professional fanaticism but from Jesus Christ. Upon learning that the prisoners are still in their cells, he asks, "Sirs, what must I do to be saved?" to which the prisoners answer, "Believe on the Lord Jesus, and you will be saved, you and your household" (vv. 30–31). The irony is that those who seem to be in prison are actually free in Christ, and the jailer, who supposedly has the keys to freedom, is actually the one shackled by his duty.

What duties shackle us today? Is it our jobs, in which we go through the motions but are not generative? Perhaps it is an insatiable need for entertainment that prompts us to leave the TV, or the computer, or the radio on from the time we wake up till we fall asleep. What holds us captive?

At the start of this passage, there are three different types of captivities; in the end, there is only one. In the beginning, there is, first of all, Paul and Silas's captivity to the Most High God. Second, there is the girl's slavery to a spirit of divination that makes her a prime target for exploitation. Third, there is the jailer's sense of duty, leading him nearly to take his life when he seems to have failed at his assignment. In the end, we find Jesus' prayer answered, with all of these captives finding their freedom in being bound to God. Or, in the prayerful words of Jesus, "I in them and you in me, that they may become completely one" (John 17:23).

DAVID G. FORNEY

Exegetical Perspective

Note the many times the term *kyrios* is used throughout this episode at Philippi. Titles are important in Roman culture; they reflect status and honor. *Kyrios*, "master," is the title that rises above all others. In Philippi it can refer to petty masters—the owners of a pitiful slave girl. Far above these pathetic *kyrioi* is the master of the realm—Lord Caesar, from whom all other lordships derive. It is in this context that Paul and Silas speak boldly about another Lord, Jesus.

At the end of the story, a double washing takes place. The jailer washes the physical wounds of Paul and Silas; "then he and his entire family were baptized without delay" (v. 33). Once again Paul is offered the warm hospitality of a grateful host. They eat together and the "entire household rejoiced that [the jailer] had become a believer in God" (v. 34).

At some point before morning, Paul and Silas return to the prison, which may be attached to the jailer's living quarters. In the morning the city magistrates order the release of Paul and Silas, and for the first time the reader learns of Paul's own high status. He is a Roman citizen (at 22:28, we learn that he is a birthright citizen) who demands an apology for his shameful treatment by the city officials. After the apology is given, Paul and Silas return to Lydia's house before moving on to Thessalonica, the capital of the province.

Acts 16 is a very important chapter in Luke's history of the early church. Our narrator has skillfully expanded Paul's groundbreaking statement in Galatians 3:28 into an elegant story. "There is no longer Jew [Paul and Silas] or Greek [Lydia, the mantic, the jailer], there is no longer slave [the mantic] or free [Lydia, Paul], there is no longer male [Paul, Silas, the jailer] or female [Lydia, the mantic]; for all of you are one in Christ Jesus." Amen!

PAUL W. WALASKAY

Homiletical Perspective

circumstances, were fought with quiet faithfulness. The story of Paul and Silas is an inspiration to advocates for justice on many fronts, and it predates attitudes of triumphalism associated with Christianity as it joins the ranks of the establishment.

The worshipful posture of the prisoners suggests that they are not defeated by arrest and flogging. Prayer and hymns seem out of place for such a dire setting. We wonder why they are still awake singing at midnight. However, their praise (with other prisoners listening in) shakes the foundations of the prison—doors are opened and chains are unfastened. Just as the Gerasene demoniac was loosed from his chains by Jesus (Luke 8:35), and the young woman was freed from exploitation, all the prisoners, including Paul and Silas, are loosed. The work of the Spirit brings freedom to all who are captive.

In Acts, a person's work, the way she or he makes a living, is often highlighted. Vocational choices were important to figures like the apostle Paul, who was also a tentmaker to provide for living expenses. Perhaps the fortune-teller and jailer featured in this passage represent extremes of vocational imbalance. The girl was released from bondage to those who would exploit her gifts. The jailer, who was ready to end his own life because of a job-related failure (brought on by an act of God), is spared dishonor and shame. In this moving scene, the jailer washes their wounds; then Paul and Silas baptize him and are invited as guests into his home. The violence and confinement of the first part of the account are reversed, and instead we find freedom, hospitality, and faith.

Conversion in Acts is distinct and unique to individuals as God's word is freshly delivered to them. What they receive is not a stale repast of something ratified at a church council meeting (Acts 15). Rather, the message is shown in the imaginative lives and sacrifice of those who bring God's proclamation into every corner of the world. The church came into being and flourished through the movement of the Spirit, which took apostles to remote places and sometimes into close confining cells. Wherever the Spirit moves, the work of worship and witness by faithful people brings freedom to all who believe.

RICHARD M. LANDERS

Psalm 97

¹The LORD is king! Let the earth rejoice;
  let the many coastlands be glad!
²Clouds and thick darkness are all around him;
  righteousness and justice are the foundation of his throne.
³Fire goes before him,
  and consumes his adversaries on every side.
⁴His lightnings light up the world;
  the earth sees and trembles.
⁵The mountains melt like wax before the LORD,
  before the Lord of all the earth.

⁶The heavens proclaim his righteousness;
  and all the peoples behold his glory.

Theological Perspective

This psalm continues theological themes of Psalms 67 and 47: blessing and salvation history; doxology, sovereignty, and missiology, respectively. These themes are, however, given meaning in Psalm 97 under the umbrella theme of God's reign, evoked beginning in verse 1a, "The LORD is king!" This umbrella theme, God's reign, is perhaps one of the most traditional ways in which to envision God's relationship to the world. God as the king of the universe controls natural elements ("clouds and thick darkness," "fire," "lightnings," "the mountains"—vv. 2a, 3a, 4a, 5a), using them to mystify Godself as well as to destroy enemies of God. Consequently, it is the way that the theme of God's reign has been interpreted that is the basis of this theological reflection. How are we in the twenty-first century to appropriate this envisioning of God's relationship with the world? If not this traditional interpretation, what metaphor and interpretation can be true to this biblical metaphor, while at the same time recognizing that humans enamored with the power of a conquering God/King soon equate their conquests of other humans with God's will?

James Luther Mays's discussion of the language of the reign of God is an appropriate point of departure for this reflection. Mays begins by reminding us that this language in the Psalms reveals a narrative plot

Pastoral Perspective

Today's psalm speaks to a variety of pastoral needs and situations on this last Sunday in Eastertide. If for some worshipers the week has been difficult, renewal may be found in the forceful, powerful decrees of this psalm. They will find great comfort and encouragement in the opening assertion of verse 1: "The LORD is king! Let the earth rejoice; let the many coastlands [that is, the far-flung places] be glad!" This is a psalm to be sung to the accompaniment of trumpets, cymbals, and tympani, a psalm of brash proclamation. Sometimes, in the midst of sorrow or simply the emptiness of feeling becalmed and listless, a good dose of the energy of God's power and might proves to be healing and rejuvenating. Certainly the vibrancy and assertiveness of this psalm could come as a tonic to drooping spirits with flagging enthusiasm for life and faith.

Other parishioners will relate readily to the powerful nature imagery of Psalm 97, which locates awareness of God's righteousness and justice in the fire, the lightning, the clouds, and the melting mountains (vv. 2–4). Many people find God in sunsets, storms, waves, the beauty of the forest, or even the stark barrenness of the desert. In nature they experience deep feelings of gratitude, mystery, reverence, and joy. Many people are much more inclined to experience and name the presence of

⁷All worshipers of images are put to shame,
   those who make their boast in worthless idols;
   all gods bow down before him.
⁸Zion hears and is glad,
   and the towns of Judah rejoice,
   because of your judgments, O God.
⁹For you, O Lord, are most high over all the earth;
   you are exalted far above all gods.

¹⁰The Lord loves those who hate evil;
   he guards the lives of his faithful;
   he rescues them from the hand of the wicked.
¹¹Light dawns for the righteous,
   and joy for the upright in heart.
¹²Rejoice in the Lord, O you righteous,
   and give thanks to his holy name!

Exegetical Perspective

The lectionary readings for this Sunday testify variously to trust and hope in God's sovereignty, particularly in circumstances in which God's rule may be in doubt. Beaten severely and shackled in the innermost cell of a prison in Philippi, Paul and Silas, for example, pray and sing hymns to God in the midnight darkness (Acts 16:25). The concluding verses of Revelation urge the faithful to persevere in the midst of crisis, trauma, and oppression by Rome because Jesus' return is imminent (Rev. 22:12–21). Here, the psalmist declares "YHWH reigns!" (v. 1) and "Rejoice!" (vv. 1, 12) and observes with equal clarity that God has adversaries, and God's people are in need of God's protection and rescue from the wicked (v. 3, 10). Weaving exuberant confidence with eyes-open urgency, Psalm 97, one of the so-called enthronement psalms (see Pss. 47, 93, 95–99), unfolds in three units: a description of God enthroned over the whole creation (vv. 1–5), the acknowledgment of God's reign by all humans and other gods (vv. 6–9), and implications of God's reign for God's people (vv. 10–12).

Painting with vibrant brushstrokes, the psalmist begins with a description of God's reign as cosmic and awe inspiring (vv. 1–5). The framing verses of the opening unit establish the expansive scope of God's kingdom—"the earth . . . the many coastlands"

Homiletical Perspective

Psalm 97 is a continuation of a theme that runs through the Psalms. It is a theme that gives us courage and delight. As the sun rises with great regularity every morning, so this theme reoccurs with regularity. Psalm 97 contains nothing new in content and structure, and its structure has a familiar appearance. Nevertheless, the thoughts themselves are like living water to which thirsty people turn with eternal gratitude. This psalm continues the theme that the foundation of our faith is secure because "The Lord reigns. Let the people rejoice."

The sovereignty of God is foundational, not only to our faith statement but to our lives. Our churches need to reaffirm this at every possible opportunity—thus the repetition. Our faith does not have depth or power, nor do our lives have stability, until they have this certainty in them. The preacher has no other sure foundation for her ministry than this. Our people are battered by every imaginable faith claim from the false gods of our culture, and the only sure defense is to know without equivocation that "the Lord reigns."

Sometimes the Lord's hand is covered. "Clouds and thick darkness are all around him; righteousness and justice are the foundation of his throne" (v. 2). When that happens, we are thrown back on our faith. God usually approaches us indirectly. Most of

Psalm 97

Theological Perspective

that discloses God's role ("The LORD is king"), kingdom activity ("The LORD reigns"), and an event ("The LORD has become King"). The reign of God is about the story of creation and the history of salvation as the activity of God in bringing order and harmony to the cosmos and to human society. In the Psalms the language of the reign of God presents a litany of the comprehensive power of God: God controls the spheres of the cosmos, history as salvation history, and the disorder of human society (i.e., violence, deceit, and greed). Importantly, the power of God even comprehends time; it too is eternal.

Furthermore, according to Mays, modern hearers of the language of the reign of God often miss the power of the language because we interpret it using the sensibilities of modernity rather than poetry. To appreciate the power of this poetic language of the Psalms, we need to suspend our dependence on notions of the scientific, compartmentalization, a sovereign self, liberal democracy, psychology, and general values; we would instead embrace metaphor, unity, a sovereign God, monarchy, human trust, and good and evil, righteousness and wickedness. In sum, according to Mays, to understand fully the language of the reign of God in the Psalms, we must embrace the dissonance and acknowledge the language of the Psalms as the language of faith.[1]

Mays's discussion is important for us because it reminds the modern reader that his or her interpretation of the psalm is biased by a culturally nurtured worldview premised upon twentieth- and twenty-first-century ideas and experiences. Although his discussion does not make sufficient note of the cultural biases of the worldview of the text, the larger point about how the language of faith is powerful because it is metaphorical should not be lost. Metaphorical language touches us cognitively and emotionally. Thus, the quests of liberation theologians (e.g., Latin American, Hispanic, womanist, feminist) for revised metaphors for the reign of God, such as the kin-dom of God, make sense. When the histories and current experiences of peoples and nations represented by the liberation theologians are filled with the exploitation of feudal lords, conquest of explorers on behalf of a king, and frequently foreign-funded dictators or presidents, it is important to have a metaphor for God's rule of the world that does not align with those historical and current experiences.

Pastoral Perspective

God in nature than in history or in the complexities of human interaction. Psalm 97 provides ways to invite these worshipers into theological reflection and spiritual formation around their own experiences of revelation and insight, found in the beauty, majesty, and awe of God's creation.

However, Psalm 97 presents some challenging and paradoxical images of God as well. Some of these images might prove to be a different kind of balm, less familiar to worshipers and therefore unexpectedly welcome. These images can be especially evocative when read in this brief span of days between the ascension and Pentecost. This little season of days can be thought of as a time of the absence of God's presence. Between the departure of the risen Lord and the coming of the Holy Spirit, these pregnant days are a time of a strangely unfamiliar waiting for God to be revealed in new ways to God's people. This is a liminal time, an unsettling time, a time for difficult and sometimes disturbing truths to be revealed. It is a season that invites truth telling about experiences of the absence and the elusive mystery of God.

This is a season for people who wrestle with a God who is, for them, more mysterious than familiar and comfortable, a God who is more often hidden than revealed. These are people who find it hard to talk about God, hard to pray to God, hard to grasp and sustain a faithful relationship with a God who keeps coming in and out of focus. Scripture and worship rarely address their situation face on. Psalm 97 offers ways to do so.

We find in verse 2 the theophany of God's appearing in clouds and thick darkness, hidden from our eyes. Rowan Williams, before becoming archbishop of Canterbury, wrote a little book titled *A Ray of Darkness*.[1] Drawing on the writings of a fifth-century Syrian monk, Dionysius, Williams describes ways in which God breaks into our limited understandings with a ray of darkness. This darkness reveals the God who cannot be fully known and cannot be contained by the limitations of human conjecture and formulation. God's ray of darkness comes to deepen the mystery within God's people, hinting at God's presence but refusing neatly to categorize or contain the numinous mystery of a God who remains beyond all human telling.

Still other worshipers may be put off by the psalm's stark polarities and contrasts between the pious and the idolatrous, the righteous and the

---

1. James Luther Mays, "The Language of the Reign of God," *Interpretation* 47, no. 2 (April 1993): 117–26.

1. Rowan Williams, *A Ray of Darkness* (Boston: Cowley Publications, 1995).

Seventh Sunday of Easter

Exegetical Perspective

(v. 1), "the mountains . . . all the earth" (v. 5)—and, in between, the psalmist points again to "the earth" and to the "mainland" or "continent" (v. 4, NRSV "the world"). These references, coupled with the psalmist's animation of the earth and mountains before God ("sees and trembles," v. 4; "melt like wax," v. 5), emphasize that God rules over the whole creation. God's presence is astounding. Evoking language typical of a theophany, or appearance of God (e.g., Exod. 19:16–20; 20:18–21; Ps. 18:7–15), the psalmist characterizes God's presence as a storm—"clouds and thick darkness . . . fire . . . lightning"—while repetition of the terms "surrounding" (*sabib*, v. 2 [NRSV "all around"], v. 3 [NRSV "on every side"]), and "before" (*lipne*, vv. 3, 5 [2x]) contribute to the storm's swirling immensity. The result is an image of God as undeniably and powerfully present, yet also elusive—obscured from view by darkness, fire, and cloud.

Although storm imagery may convey wild, indiscriminate force, the psalmist is clear that God wields God's fierce power to a specific end: the establishment of justice. God's throne is founded on "righteousness and justice" (v. 2; cf. Pss. 9:7–8; 89:14), the heavens declare God's righteousness (v. 6a), and, as the second unit of the psalm tells us, God's justice is that to which the whole world responds (vv. 6–9). Shifting our attention from mountains and earth to humans and gods, the psalmist dances between the global ("*all* the peoples" [v. 6b], "*all* worshipers of images" [v. 7a], "*all* gods" [v. 7c], "*all* the earth" [v. 9a], "*all* gods" [v. 9b]) and the particular (Zion and the towns of Judah, v. 8), to argue that *everyone*—from the many to the few—acknowledges God's reign.

For some, the acknowledgment triggers disillusionment and shame as, arguably, they see the gods they worship bow down before YHWH (v. 7). For others, God's rule and justice sparks joy (v. 8). However, for everyone, God alone is sovereign, a conviction the psalmist underlines in verse 9 with repetition of the phrase "over all" and twofold use of the Hebrew root meaning "to ascend" (*ʿlh*)—God is "Most High," a common epithet in ancient Semitic languages for the supreme Deity, and God is "greatly elevated."

God's sovereignty and commitment to justice, the psalmist concludes, have implications for God's people (vv. 10–12). The Hebrew of verse 10a, "those who love YHWH hate evil" (see NRSV footnote; also Prov. 8:13; Amos 5:14–15), requires the faithful to align themselves with God's disposition and

Homiletical Perspective

us are very familiar with cloudy days. The most prominent examples of this are doubting Thomas and Simon Peter during Holy Week. We need to listen for and to the voice of God, most particularly on cloudy days. We must stay the course and believe that on a cloudy day you *can* see forever and experience God's presence and support. This psalm repeats the theme that God is sovereign, and the foundation of our faith is secure.

The value of our faith depends on the strength of our idea of and experience with God. If our churches reflect this strong belief in the sovereignty of God, they will be strong churches. Anything less is utterly insufficient to meet the needs and wants of our people. Strong churches cannot be built on a weak God. A great faith demands a great God. Here is the starting point of this psalm, and thus the starting point of our preaching. Charles Spurgeon, the famed British preacher of the nineteenth century, noted that "the people listened with one ear and read with one eye."[1] In our hectic world, this is doubly true. Therefore, the message of this psalm must be constantly repeated in the life of the church.

God and this psalm claim the entire world. The lesson in Acts 16:16–34 reaffirms that salvation is for everyone, everywhere, anytime. This God who reigns is all-powerful and worthy of worship. If our people serve lesser gods, they will be put to shame and embarrassed (v. 7). We become like the gods we worship.

The preacher may wish to remind her people that in spite of the violence and apparent irrationality of God, God is consistent, just, and righteous. Verse 7 addresses the issue of false gods and those who "make their boast in worthless idols." Shame comes to those who worship these impotent false gods. Every pastor sees the results of worshiping the false gods of our culture. Every generation must face this. The calf worship connected with Aaron reappeared in the days of Jeroboam. Throughout the Old Testament we find allusions to astrology and sun worship.

The Old Testament prophets focused their wrath against these gods. Anything that separates the soul and God is idolatrous and is to be shunned. We find in our generation that people are quick to worship the false gods of our culture, whether they be professional athletics, corporate culture, gross commercialism, or the "celebrity of the month." Christian people are constantly allured into the

1. C. H. Spurgeon, *Lectures to My Students* (Grand Rapids: Zondervan Publishing House, 1962 reprint), 321.

Psalm 97

Theological Perspective

Moreover, Mays's insistence that the language of the Psalms is the language of faith is critical. Again, however, his insight is most helpful when we remember that the language of this psalm is the language of faith that undergirds an eschatological vision. The twenty-first-century Christian reading and interpretation of Psalm 97 during the Easter season must be mindful that the truth (its power to provoke and sustain faith) of the biblical metaphor, the reign of God, is for us about the relationship between the resurrection of Jesus Christ and an already-and-not-yet future.

Through the resurrection of Jesus Christ, the reign of God is this interim time in which the earth is being called upon to rejoice because God does control time, cosmos, the historical and social spheres. However, our response to that call requires certain things of us. We must unmask our idols of consumption and warfare ("worshipers of images are put to shame, those who make their boast in worthless idols," v. 7); turn away from what is expedient and seek to do justice ("the LORD loves those who hate evil," v. 10a, "light dawns for the righteous," v. 11a); and live gratefully ("Rejoice in the LORD, O you righteous, and give thanks to his holy name!" v. 12).

How are we in the twenty-first century to embrace the reign of God as metaphor for God's relationship to the world? Is it possible for humans to shout, "The Lord is king!" and not think that they are surrogate kings with the power of God? My answer is a qualified yes to both questions. Two professions of faith must always determine the yes answer. First, the reign of God can provide us with a check upon the human will to power in that it is about God being in control of all the earth, of all of us. God's control does not have to speak to us of conquest; it can speak to us of God's overwhelming love, for God so loved the world that God gave his only Son, and that Son ascended to heaven and sits at the right hand of God. Second, as we make that profession of Jesus' ascension, we relinquish any claim to be surrogate kings for God on earth. For on Easter Sunday morning, we proclaim, "Christ the King!"

MARCIA Y. RIGGS

Pastoral Perspective

wicked, the faithful and the adversary, the wise and the foolish. To them, the world seems much more complex and nuanced. Their choices do not seem as clear-cut or obvious. For these people, an explanation of the worldview of the psalmist might be helpful, a worldview that often presents distinct choices between life and death, faith and faithlessness, fidelity and apostasy. Into this dichotomized worldview comes the contemporary worshiper negotiating daily a complex world of competing claims, nuanced distinctions, and compromised choices. For these worshipers, the writings of the German theologian Paul Tillich about ambiguity as a fruitful source of religious contemplation might prove helpful. People ponder questions such as these: How does one live a faithful life in a complicated world? What equips one to wrestle with less than optimum options? How does the Christian lead a faithful life?

In the midst of nuance and ambiguity, Psalm 97 nevertheless calls for faithful living. The psalm makes this personal in a manner that is lost in most English translations. It is found in the grammar of the Hebrew of verse 11. The first clause of the verse is written in the singular and the second clause in the plural. "Light dawns for the righteous *tsaddiq* [one] and joy for [all] the upright in heart" (my trans.). This language points to the critical importance of each individual's choice for good, to live as a righteous person in a world of moral ambiguity and compromise. The medieval Jewish scholar and rabbi Maimonides taught that the individual's decision has the capacity to tip the scale of the world toward life. In the worldview of Psalm 97, even while God's lightning lights up the whole sky, the one lighted candle held by one faithful soul has the power to make all the difference in the world—however much the hand that holds it may tremble.

PATRICIA FARRIS

Exegetical Perspective

purposes, and assumes they do so in a context of considerable opposition and struggle. Evil threatens the "lives of [God's] faithful"; the wicked seize them (v. 10bc). The psalmist does not downplay the profound risk of faithfulness, but meets it with reassurance that God "guards" and "rescues" the faithful (v. 10bc). Indeed, light and joy are "sown" for them, a verb that suggests God scatters seeds of delight far and wide for the righteous to reap (v. 11a; also Gen. 26:12; Deut. 22:9; NRSV reads with the Greek). For the psalmist, the promise that God plants joy (*simkhah*) for the faithful (v. 11) prompts the imperative "Rejoice (*simkhu*) in YHWH!" today (v. 12). God's reign and God's rescue of God's people are certain.

As we read or sing Psalm 97 this Sunday of the Easter season, we testify, as generations have before us, that even when circumstances in the world suggest God does *not* reign—warfare and violence, poverty, oppression and exploitation, devastation of the environment, and so on—we believe that God most certainly *does*, and that God's sovereign power is evident once again in the life, death, and resurrection of Jesus Christ. At the psalmist's urging, we rejoice that God by God's wisdom sustains the cosmos, guiding it surely and ultimately in the direction of God's justice and peace, a justice that the heavens proclaim and the whole world acknowledges.

Such audacious joy persists and is possible only because we are convinced that, as Martin Luther King Jr. once eloquently stated: "There is a creative force in this universe working to pull down the gigantic mountains of evil, a power that is able to make a way out of no way and transform dark yesterdays into bright tomorrows. Let us realize that the arc of the moral universe is long, but it bends toward justice."[1] Wickedness may prosper, and evil may have its day, but such moments are not the last word—because God, God's creation, and God's people labor for justice, goodness, and joy.

CHRISTINE ROY YODER

Homiletical Perspective

temples of these gods. The hardest thing for any pastor to do is to keep the attention of her people away from the false gods and focused on the God revealed in the Bible. Idolatry remains a great evil that cannot be ignored. In preaching this text, we must make sure we understand that true worship is the only real antidote for the worship of false gods.

This God also delivers God's own from the power of the wicked. Being reassured that God is sovereign will bring calm and peace to a troubled life. God orders our steps through temptations, joys and sorrow, the places we occupy, and the works we do. "The LORD reigns." He is not only holy but also loving. This needs to be taught, preached, and reinforced in every way. It should be shouted from the rooftops, from the very skies. "The heavens proclaim his righteousness; and all the peoples behold his glory" (v. 6).

The Lord loves, guards, and rescues the faithful (v. 10). This constitutes encouragement for those who trust in God's ultimate triumph over evil. In these final verses we see the reward to be received by the righteous, which includes joy in seeing the God they worship vindicated in the eyes of the world and in their own lives. Whatever happens to us, including all difficulties and hardships, comes because of God's will, but that will is loving and perfect. "The LORD reigns."

It follows that we must love the Lord, and evidence of that love would be the hating of evil. There is not a word here that would affirm the spirit of the church at Laodicea (Rev. 3:15, 16). A passionate love of God and the fierce hating of evil cannot be hidden under a bushel.[2] "The LORD reigns."

WILLIAM L. SELF

---

1. Martin Luther King Jr., "Where Do We Go from Here?" n.p. [cited July 30, 2008]. Online: http://www.stanford.edu/group/King/publications/speeches/Where_do_we_go_from_here.html.

2. *Interpreter's Bible* (Nashville: Abingdon Press, 1955), 4:524–25.

Revelation 22:12-14, 16-17, 20-21

12"See, I am coming soon; my reward is with me, to repay according to everyone's work. 13I am the Alpha and the Omega, the first and the last, the beginning and the end."
14Blessed are those who wash their robes, so that they will have the right to the tree of life and may enter the city by the gates. . . .
16"It is I, Jesus, who sent my angel to you with this testimony for the churches. I am the root and the descendant of David, the bright morning star."
17The Spirit and the bride say, "Come."
And let everyone who hears say, "Come."
And let everyone who is thirsty come.
Let anyone who wishes take the water of life as a gift. . . .
20The one who testifies to these things says, "Surely I am coming soon."
Amen. Come, Lord Jesus!
21The grace of the Lord Jesus be with all the saints. Amen.

Theological Perspective

If the twenty-first chapter of Revelation revolves around a strong ecclesiological theme, then the twenty-second chapter is predominantly christological in nature. Here it is clearly Jesus himself who speaks, affirming once again that he is "the Alpha and the Omega, the first and the last, the beginning and the end" (v. 13). Adding to this assertion of the comprehensive and eternal nature of his existence, Jesus goes on to say, "I am the root and the descendant of David" (v. 16), indicating (as the sixth-century commentator Oecumenius says) that he is both the root and cause of all things in regard to his deity, but also the shoot and offspring in regard to his humanity. As Oecumenius puts it, "And so he is Immanuel, of divinity and of humanity, possessing both [natures] perfectly, according to the traditional language, unconfusedly, unchangeably, immutably, really."[1]

These biblical affirmations of what the early church defined as Christ's two natures in one person set up a tension between longing and fulfillment that is reflected in the liturgical sources for this day as well. On one hand, Christ's work is now fully

1. Oecumenius, *Commentary on the Apocalypse*, quoted in William C. Weinrich, ed., *Ancient Christian Commentary on Scripture: Revelation* (Downers Grove, IL: InterVarsity Press, 2005), 405. Oecumenius wrote the earliest existent Greek commentary on Revelation.

Pastoral Perspective

Coming at the very end of the book of Revelation, as well as being the words that close the Christian Bible, this text has interested the church for centuries. The proclaimed words of promise draw a portion of their power from their familiarity to us. They bring to mind experiences that all of humanity shares. They invoke memories of long-distance separations stained with tears and weighted with heavy hearts, when we wondered if and when our loved ones might be seen again. They acknowledge protracted periods of waiting and yearning for the presence of another, and then comes the phone call, the telegram, the letter, the e-mail message, the announcement that the wait is almost over. Our experience of separation will soon be ending. Arrival of the loved one is imminent.

Yet rather than be caught up in the emotions of anticipation, the text carries explicit instructions for those who are waiting. "Blessed are those who wash their robes, so that they will have the right to the tree of life and may enter the city" (v. 14). It is an odd directive. It points us away from sky gazing and orients us toward the everyday work of the faithful, in ways that can be interpreted both practically and metaphorically. Doing laundry is not glamorous or exciting. It can be mundane and tedious labor. Yet it is necessary.

Exegetical Perspective

No exegete will be able to accept with equanimity this selection of verses from the close of John's Apocalypse. It is true that 22:6–21 is a collection of sayings, loosely related to the theme of the book with invocations (vv. 17, 20), threats (vv. 12, 15), and promises (v. 14). They do offer a glimpse into the peculiar authority that the book possesses.

Christ announces that he is coming soon to reward everyone according to deeds (22:12). The theme of reward for works is important for the Apocalypse (20:12). Just as the climax of John's vision has a return to paradise in the new Jerusalem (21:1–2), so the nature of Christ as Alpha and Omega is a theme of the book (1:8; 4:8; 11:17).

There is another blessing here in plural form on those who wash their robes (22:14). In 7:14 that washing has been done in the blood of the Lamb, probably indicating the witness of those who have stood firm in the face of the threat of the state beast (12:11). This echoes the challenge to the angel at Sardis (3:4), where there are still a few persons "who have not soiled their clothes."

"Washing robes" will give the right to the tree of life (22:2). Jesus identifies himself with "the bright morning star," Lucifer (22:16). The fact that Satan can be an angel of light and Christ can be Lucifer takes us to the heart of one of the main themes of

Homiletical Perspective

People carry all sorts of expectations into the pews on Sunday mornings. Some bear personal wounds or burdensome responsibilities that have them panting for a word of comfort and consolation. Others are plagued with an awareness of their frailties and shortcomings and come seeking assurance. Still others bring a hunger to follow Jesus more passionately into the places where the Word and the world intersect, longing for a message of inspiration and hope. Or they bring the simple desire to experience the familiar joy of connecting with others who are on the same journey. At heart, we all want to hear the good news.

The best worship services give space and voice to all these longings: confession and pardon, petition and praise, conscience and communion. The best sermons offer a point of connection for all who listen, whatever prompts them into the pews. The epilogue of John's lengthy apocalyptic vision, Scripture's closing word, opens wide onto a spectrum of human longings and theological assurances. The passage is rich with declarations and symbols from which themes for preaching can be drawn.

Faithfulness rewarded. The passage begins with Christ's announcement that he is returning soon. While such a declaration usually carries overtones of judgment, John uses the language of reward. Christ

Revelation 22:12-14, 16-17, 20-21

Theological Perspective

complete and revealed: this is the Sunday after the ascension, when God has raised Christ to his throne in heaven, where the wholeness of his humanity is confirmed in the richness of his divinity. The Collect of the Day begins, "O God, the King of glory, you have exalted your only Son Jesus Christ with great triumph in heaven."[2] In that sense of finale the church and all creation rejoices; yet at the same time there is also an undercurrent of longing and expectation that runs just below the surface. For although Christ is enthroned in heaven, the promised gift of the Holy Spirit (John 14) has yet to come. So, just as the book of Revelation ends with the urgent prayer, "Come, Lord Jesus!" the church prays urgently on this day for the gift of Christ's presence through the Spirit: "Do not leave us comfortless, but send us your Holy Spirit to strengthen us, and exalt us to that place where our Savior Christ has gone before."

Revelation ends on a brief benediction: "The grace of the Lord Jesus be with all the saints. Amen." Although the ancient sources vary (some omitting "all," while others omit "the saints"), the thrust of these final few words of the New Testament is that, through Christ, God has established a dialogical interplay of divine grace and human longing that is now fully realized. The final few verses of Revelation offer an insistent refrain of invitation to participate in this divine/human exchange: "The Spirit and the bride say, 'Come.' . . . And let everyone who is thirsty come" (v. 17). Although the inconsistency of the sources makes it unclear whether this grace is given universally or only to those found worthy of it, the invitation is nonetheless clearly into that place of holiness that is the meeting point between the human and the Divine.

The American Jewish theologian Abraham Heschel described the person who lives such a place of holiness as pious. While piety is often a pejorative word in common speech (suggesting a certain superciliousness), for Heschel it refers to a person whose life is lived in a manner that is "compatible with God's presence."[3] Piety for him is about the response humankind makes to God, and the pious man or woman is someone who recognizes the divine presence as a reality that irresistibly breaks into the most ordinary of human circumstances with an overwhelming

Pastoral Perspective

The adrenaline high that is generated by speculations of Christ's return date is exciting. Every generation since Christ's ascension has seen the rise of religious leaders offering numerical calculations of a calendar date for Christ's return. In the United States of 1844, thousands of followers of William Miller gathered together in fervent anticipation on October 22, in response to the prediction that the day of return had arrived. As later noted by Hiram Edson, one of those participants, "Our fondest hopes and expectations were blasted, and such a spirit of weeping came over us as I never experienced before. . . . We wept and wept, till the day dawn." In the early 1970s the author Hal Lindsey published a hugely successful book, *The Late Great Planet Earth*, which cobbled together an assortment of twentieth-century international events that were loosely matched to Scripture, in order to determine a date of Christ's return. The result of his book and related others was an eschatological orientation among many Christians of the late twentieth century that served only as a distraction from the practices and work of the faithful in a broken world. The instructions for those who are waiting are to concentrate on the tasks at hand and to be about the work of cleansing a world made unclean.

A significant aspect of the text is the relational orientation of the speakers. The verses can be experienced as a call-and-response, back-and-forth exchange that sets the reader in the midst of urgency and anticipation. Jesus announces his return and provides instructions. The Spirit and the bride reply. Then all who hear are urged to join in as well. We listen to this text, not as passive receivers, but as active participants asked to be prepared to enter into the community. This is a call to ministry, not a ticketed invitation to sit in a stadium and watch a spectacle. It is a reminder that being a Christian assumes an active disposition and an attitude of grace-filled practice within the community of faith.

Another powerful note of the text comes in the universality of the announcement of return and its accompanying invitation to the waters of life. Everyone who is thirsty is told to come. No qualifications or prerequisites are given, outside of the request for attention to laundry washing. No limitations are posted regarding who is allowed to enjoy the drink of salvation. "Let anyone who wishes take the water of life" (v. 17d). It creates a marvelous cinematic image of countless people of all nationalities, ages, languages, classes, and so forth drawing out water that is freely given as a gift.

---

2. This and the sentence at the end of the paragraph are from *The Book of Common Prayer* (New York: Church Hymnal Corporation, 1979), 226.

3. Piety is, for example, a unifying theme of Heschel's classic work *Man Is Not Alone* (New York: Farrar, Straus & Giroux, 1951); see esp. the concluding chapter, "The Pious Man."

John's vision: that which is good and that which is evil are often hard to distinguish from one another, as the Lamb and the beast are described in similar terms (5:6; cf. 13:4). The discernment of the difference between the two is at the heart of the challenge of the vision.

The omission of verse 15 may soften the unpalatable language of this section of Revelation, but it diminishes the impact of the apocalyptic message that entry into the new Jerusalem is not a done deal. Ambiguity remains. "Dogs" (v. 15) is a term for outsiders, which Paul uses elsewhere as a term of abuse for (apparently) Jewish opponents (Phil. 3:2). Readers of Revelation are faced with a challenge, a crisis, from beginning to end, even after they put the book down. Divine assurance of ultimate salvation is not part of the book of Revelation.

In verse 16 Jesus speaks of the mission of his angel to bear witness to these things, possibly a reference to Christ as Son of Man. The book continues the activity of testimony by the one who has been the faithful witness (1:5), but it is the witness of Jesus that is at the heart of prophecy (19:10). Prophecy, witness, and the life of Christ are bound together in Revelation, reminding its readers that there is a price to pay for such commitments and activities. The Davidic pedigree, asserted in 22:16, is linked, ironically, with Balaam's prophecy (Num 24:17).

The Spirit and the bride now speak in response to Jesus in a kind of divine antiphon (22:17). The voice of the bride, the new Jerusalem, is heard only here. The Spirit and the bride plead with Jesus to come (v. 17). Whether that coming is with clouds (1:7) or as a thief (16:15), it is coming soon (2:16; 22:7, 12). This plea is important enough to be made again: "And let everyone who hears say, 'Come'" (v. 17b).

John's testimony (22:18–19) emphasizes in solemn terms the authority of the words of the prophecy of this book. Revelation is a writing like the law of Moses or the prophecy of Isaiah; the only parallels in the New Testament are the Gospels of Matthew (1:1) and John (20:30). The final book of the canon contains words that, like those of the book of life (13:8), are of utmost significance, echoing the words of Deuteronomy:

So now, Israel, give heed to the statutes and ordinances that I am teaching you to observe, so that you may live to enter and occupy the land that the LORD, the God of your ancestors, is giving you. You must neither add anything to what I command you nor take away anything from it, but keep the com-

is coming "to repay according to everyone's work" (v. 12). He will come to reward his followers for their faithful labor on behalf of the gospel.

Christ's enduring presence. The first proclamation is followed by a second: "I am the Alpha and the Omega, the first and the last, the beginning and the end" (v. 13). The redundancy serves to reinforce the truth of Christ's existence from the beginning of time and his promise to be present for all eternity. He encompasses the whole range of human history, the entire alphabet of life's experience, "the beginning and the end." Nothing—no wound, no sorrow, no joy—lies outside of Christ's enduring and embracing presence.

Salvation at hand. Verse 14 reprises the themes of the tree of life and the gates of the city that are regular features in John's vision: "Blessed are those who wash their robes, so that they will have the right to the tree of life and may enter the city by the gates." This blessing is a word of reassurance. No one comes to the end of life unmarked, free of stains and smudges, but all can symbolically "wash their robes" (translated by some ancient authorities as "do his commandments") and, by doing so, have access to salvation.

The robe is the symbol of worthiness of heaven. The tree of life is the metaphor for salvation and eternal life, an echo of the access denied to Adam and Eve in the garden but restored to those who are righteous and worthy. The tree stands on the bank of the river of the water of life. "Let everyone who is thirsty come. Let anyone who wishes take the water of life as a gift" (v. 17). Those who thirst for justice and hope are invited to quench their heart's longing in the life-giving water. Drink, wash, be baptized and healed.

Those who are thirsty for salvation will receive it as a gift, as the Samaritan woman at the well received the "living water" from Jesus: "Those who drink of the water that I will give them will never be thirsty. The water that I will give will become in them a spring of water gushing up to eternal life" (John 4:14). Those who receive this salvation are ushered through the gates into the city of God. To enter by the gate is to enter as a citizen of the new Jerusalem, the city without fear, without tears, without pain. To enter by the gate is to enter as a forgiven and beloved child of God.

The fulfillment of justice. In verse 16, Jesus identifies himself as the one who sent the angel who brought the vision to John and the testimony to the churches.

Revelation 22:12-14, 16-17, 20-21

Theological Perspective

deluge of both grace and judgment. God seeks out human beings to be in partnership with God's purposes of justice and mercy—yet God also reacts with dismay at the indifference and aggression of human beings toward one another and toward the creation. The pious person desperately wants to be part of God's activity in the world, and so prays fervently (in a manner not unlike that of the concluding verses of Revelation) that the Lord will come.

Yet there is a more radical idea contained in Heschel's notion of piety as well. We usually think of ourselves in subjective terms, with God being the object of our thought and devotion; for Heschel, the subject/object relationship is reversed. God is the subject, and we are the objects of God's passion and concern. This is what piety ultimately means for Heschel: a profound awareness that we are creatures entirely beholden to the God who has created us. The ethical consequences for the religious life are immediately apparent: as objects of the divine subject, we are categorically responsible to God for every aspect of our lives (hence Heschel's definition of piety as a life compatible with God's presence).

Seen in this light, the final invocations in Revelation for the Lord to come would be understood not from our perspective, as a desire for Christ to be known to us, but more as an act of acknowledgment of the dominion exercised by Christ as the beginning and end of all things, and our desire to be included in it. To paraphrase the well-known eucharistic prayer, we pray not only for the risen Lord to be known to us in the breaking of the bread, but also that we will be known to him in a reciprocal act of self-offering. Indeed, such a eucharistic reciprocity is suggested in verse 20, where Christ promises to come soon, and humankind responds, "Yes, come, Lord Jesus!"

JOSEPH H. BRITTON

Pastoral Perspective

It brings to mind a personal memory of a morning spent on the banks of the Ganges River in India as thousands of brightly clad pilgrims descended stone steps in the city of Varanasi to draw out water from a river that is considered holy. The sun was rising, and moving toward the stream were men and women old and young, prosperous and poor, with shadings of every skin color. Children were assisted by older siblings. Mothers carried babies, and the infirm were helped by friends and family. Differences were of no matter. What was of importance was the coming to the sacred waters.

Far too often we emphasize the particularity of Christ's return and grasp it as the personal possession for a favored community of which we claim membership. These closing verses of our Bible suggest, to the contrary, that such exclusivity is a manufactured interpretation that is truly separate from the design and will of the returning Christ. Perhaps this is part of the washing that the text is referring to, a cleansing of our own prejudices and assumptions, which must be addressed before we may enter the heavenly city that has descended to us.

Southern writer Flannery O'Connor addressed these matters repeatedly in her fiction. In her well-known short story "Revelation," she brings this biblical message to the fore through a character whose narrow-mindedness and intolerance for others are revealed through the unexpected (and undesired) experience of a divine vision that comes to her in the waiting area of a doctor's office. The character's pride and self-importance are mortally punctured as she glimpses a celestial bridge to the heavens filled with persons that she judges to be unworthy and grotesque. It is an ironic apocalyptic vision borrowed from John that points to our own need of preparation to be worthy of Christ's greeting.

PAUL "SKIP" JOHNSON

mandments of the LORD your God with which I am charging you. (Deut. 4:1–2, alluded to in Rev. 22:18)

This is a warning for the present. Offenders are threatened with plagues (cf. Deut. 29:19–20), or with loss of entry into the holy city and participation in the tree of life (22:19). Thus any ill treatment of the book, for instance by addition or subtraction, brings a curse. Unlike Deuteronomy, however, what is contained in this book is not law but prophecy (22:19).

The penultimate word comes from the one who bears witness (22:20), who asserts that he comes quickly (22:7,12 cf. 1:7). The response, "Amen. Come, Lord Jesus," echoes the response found in early liturgies such as the *Didache*: "Remember, Lord, thy Church, to deliver it from all evil and to make it perfect in thy love, and gather it together in its holiness from the four winds to thy kingdom which thou hast prepared for it. For thine is the power and the glory for ever. Let grace come and let this world pass away. Hosanna to the God of David. *If any man be holy, let him come! If any man be not, let him repent: Maranatha, Amen*" (*Didache* 10:5–6).

There is also the enigmatic *Maranatha* in 1 Corinthians 16:22: "Let anyone be accursed who has no love for the Lord. Our Lord, come! (*Maranatha!*)" John's apocalyptic prophecy ends with a prayer that the grace of the Lord Jesus be with all (the main text of the NRSV does not represent the inclusiveness of the Greek in its translation "with all the saints"; the alternative, more inclusive reading, which is favored in modern editions of the Greek New Testament, omits "the saints"). As in 1:4, there are many similarities with the greetings of the Pauline letters (e.g., 2 Cor. 13:13).

CHRISTOPHER ROWLAND

"I am the root and the descendant of David," Christ proclaims, confirmation of the messianic mantle he wears. The "bright morning star," a messianic symbol, conjures images of the nativity star that rested over the stable and guided the magi to the scene of the miraculous birth.

This Messiah was an early disappointment—not the crusading warrior on a mighty steed that the Jews hoped would rout the brutal Roman occupiers, but a baby, naked and vulnerable, his only crib a feeding trough. Yet he is the one who announces the reign of justice, who turns the social order on its head and creates a community of compassion among those who have been marginalized, rejected, and despised: "He has scattered the proud in the thoughts of their hearts. He has brought down the powerful from their thrones, and lifted up the lowly; he has filled the hungry with good things, and sent the rich away empty" (Luke 1:51b–53).

The gift of grace. How marvelous that the last word in Scripture is a bestowal of grace: "The grace of the Lord Jesus be with all the saints. Amen" (v. 21). Grace is perhaps the greatest longing in human hearts and the most difficult gift to accept. Too many of us are like the older brother in Jesus' parable of the Prodigal Son—the one who stayed home, worked hard, kept out of trouble, and resented his father's lavish love for the wandering, squandering son. Where is the party for the tireless, faithful one? Where the luxurious robe and the gold ring?

We covet a fatted calf and overlook the fact that we have been given the keys to the kingdom. Grace upon grace. We do not get what we deserve. Thank God. "Come, Lord Jesus!"

JOYCE HOLLYDAY

John 17:20-26

²⁰"I ask not only on behalf of these, but also on behalf of those who will believe in me through their word, ²¹that they may all be one. As you, Father, are in me and I am in you, may they also be in us, so that the world may believe that you have sent me. ²²The glory that you have given me I have given them, so that they may be one, as we are one, ²³I in them and you in me, that they may become completely one, so that the world may know that you have sent me and have loved them even as you have loved me. ²⁴Father, I desire that those also, whom you have given me, may be with me where I am, to see my glory, which you have given me because you loved me before the foundation of the world.

²⁵"Righteous Father, the world does not know you, but I know you; and these know that you have sent me. ²⁶I made your name known to them, and I will make it known, so that the love with which you have loved me may be in them, and I in them."

Theological Perspective

How do we pass on the message of faith to those who did not share the original connection and numinous grace of a direct encounter with Christ? Will we ever be able to be truly one, given the diversity of our religious experiences?

In the last words of the farewell prayer for his original disciples, Jesus foresees that their circle will some day expand to include many others. Hence his prayer is not only for them but for those to follow—all of us! His words anticipate a tough dilemma. Will later generations of Christians, who were not part of the circle who first encountered Jesus, be able to experience the same kind of unity with God and with Christ as those through whom they came to faith (vv. 20–21)? That completeness of sacred experience and communion among believers across the generations is Jesus' expressed desire.

Verses 22–23 indicate that Christ's *glory* is given both to his first disciples and just as fully to their later sisters and brothers, a unity not merely for its own sake, but as a witness to the whole world. "The glory that you have given me I have given them, so that they may be one, as we are one, I in them and you in me, that they may become completely one, so that the world may know that you have sent me and have loved them even as you have loved me."

Pastoral Perspective

Jesus draws his high-priestly prayer to a close by returning to the theme of unity among his followers introduced earlier (v. 11b). We do not know whether division threatened John's community or what the cause of such division might have been. We do know that Jesus is interested in making clear the unity and continuity between the present and the future (post-Easter), between the disciples with him in Galilee and those who will later come to believe through their proclamation (v. 20). These disciples, present and future, are in continuity with one another, even as Jesus is in continuity with the Father. This same unity and continuity will be perceived by the church in relation to the Holy Spirit to be poured out at Pentecost.

Before moving too quickly to the modern use of this prayer to address the reality of divisions among Christians and the scandal of disunity in the face of Jesus' missionary imperative, it may be helpful as a pastoral matter to spend some time holding up a vision of unity that transcends historical boundaries. These are complicated subjects that do not lend themselves to easy description in the homiletic form.

According to John, Jesus' historical reality within creation is in unity and continuity with the Creator, and the proclamation of later disciples is in

Exegetical Perspective

Today's text is the culmination of Jesus' Farewell Discourse in the Gospel of John (13:1–17:26). Just as scholars have suggested that John 14 could stand on its own as a rhetorical segment, so scholars believe that John 17 could stand on its own and might have been a unified discourse. The discourse divides into two sections:

13:1–16:33	words/"the word" addressed to the church
17:1–26	words/"the word" addressed to heaven

In turn, the second segment of the discourse further divides:

17:1–19	words/"the word" addressed to the disciples
17:20–26	words/"the word" addressed to future generations

Today's text forms an appropriate conclusion to Jesus' Farewell Discourse. It ends not only by looking to the past as a summing up, but by looking to the future of the Johannine community as house churches were being expelled from the synagogue.

The discourse describes this moment of conflict as the confrontation between "the world" (*kosmos*) and the "word" (*logos*) given to the community. In the parlance of John's Gospel, "the world" is not a

Homiletical Perspective

In a red-letter edition of the Bible (with the words of Jesus printed in red), this lesson closes out four chapters of almost solid red. Jesus has defined leadership as servanthood (13:1–20); he has told about the upcoming betrayal (13:21–30). Then John unleashes verse after verse of the teaching of Jesus. Chapters 14–16 have the feel of a dying leader calling together all the followers for one last round of instruction: "Make sure you remember these things."

Then, in John 17, the Lord switches to prayer. A good question for a preacher to ask is, would you rather have Jesus talking to you or praying for you? (That is not a trick question; there is no "right" answer.) Although John's Gospel account continues for four more chapters, this prayer contains the penultimate words of the Lord. Once again, Jesus models the truth that the deepest moments of life are those when our hearts and habits are wide enough to include others. John 17 is called a "priestly" prayer because in that chapter Jesus intercedes for others before God, as a priest would.

Three themes emerge in this prayer: (1) belief, (2) oneness, and (3) love. A preacher could explore any or all of these in a sermon near the end of Easter season.

John 17:20-26

Theological Perspective

The purpose of Jesus' prayer is unity not for its own sake, but for the sake of witness to the love of God and the authenticity of Christ as the one "sent." It is a prayer needed as much in the divided and fragmented world of twenty-first-century Christianity as in the churches of the first centuries after Christ.

Such a prayer has been perennially relevant in the feisty history of Christianity. John Chrysostom, bishop of Constantinople in the late fourth century, paraphrased Jesus to say that if disciples would but keep the peace among themselves that they had learned from him, the people around them "would know the teacher by his disciples." He went on to suggest pointedly that the quarrelsomeness of those same disciples would cause others to "deny that they are the disciples of a God of peace and will not allow that I [Jesus], not being peaceable, have been sent from you."[1] The bishop, no stranger to church fights, seems to have spoken with the wry voice of experience.

In the ancient world and in ours, the very prayer for unity with God and with one another has had the power to divide. At the heart of long-standing controversies have been questions such as whether communion with God and other people is a product of human will or divine grace or both. The quarrels have included sometimes bloody debates over whether Christ's nature is the same as the nature of the One who sent him (fully divine) or the same as that of the humans whom he is bringing into communion with God.

Yet, despite differing and sometimes sharply conflicting theological perspectives, a longing for a deeper unity among followers of Christ keeps surfacing. As early as the third century CE, Origen of Alexandria, bringing together Greek philosophy and Christian faith, suggested that church unity prefigures the future unity of all humankind. In other words, the unity of the disciples is a "form" of the eventual restoration of unity for all of humankind.[2]

When Christians are one with one another, their unity surely allows the world to see the "peaceable" teacher, Jesus, as one embattled bishop of Constantinople suggested. We glimpse with Origen the ways in which unity among the followers of Christ may offer a model of a better world for all of humanity, a healed human race, yet to come. Our moments of unity with God and with our neighbors

Pastoral Perspective

continuity with the proclamation of those who walked with Jesus in his ministry before Easter.

Some images may be helpful. This is the same unity that the living enjoy with the dead and the church professes in the classical creeds. Time and place are part and parcel of creation. The Creator transcends the created order and is therefore, in some sense, outside of time. We might say that all moments in history are accessible to God at once or "in the twinkling of an eye" (1 Cor. 15:51–52). We sometimes talk of the "nearer presence of God" as what we will know after death, the firstfruits of which we sometimes taste even now. Few have grasped this notion of God being outside of time (and so our being in continuity with all that has been, is, and is yet to come) more eloquently than T. S. Eliot in his *Four Quartets*.[1] Such thoughts, inherent in Jesus' high-priestly prayer, lend themselves to reflections on death, on our continuity with those who have gone before, and on the communion of saints in whose midst we worship.

The unity for which Jesus prays (v. 21) is founded in reciprocal love (v. 23, 26), the kind of self-giving love seen in the life of Jesus. This mutual and reciprocal love is the kind of love that is as much a decision and choice as it is a feeling. It is the kind of love that can be commanded (13:34; 15:12, 17), love that is sometimes easy and graceful, having the character of a gift, and is at other times more about being faithful to our commitments through decision or choice. The difficulties Christian communities experience staying in visible unity with one another are mirrored in the difficulties that many people have in keeping their own vows of commitment to one another.

A pastor might reflect on the essential reciprocity of the love revealed in Jesus' prayer, with its challenge to be enough of a self to engage in self-giving love. Helpful here may be the image of a dance, in which couples sometimes dance together and sometimes apart. A failure to live in unity is usually a failure of reciprocity. A pastor may wish to examine some of the things that lead to such failure and how often those things revolve around issues of power or control. For couples, this might include differences over anything from housekeeping to managing money. Differences between Christian communities flow from notions of doctrinal purity and consequent practices of church discipline. "It

---

1. John Chrysostom, in Joel C. Elowsky, ed., *Ancient Christian Commentary on Scripture IVb: John 11–21* (Downers Grove, IL: InterVarsity Press, 2007), 257.
2. Origen, in ibid., 256.

1. "A people without history/ Is not redeemed from time, for history is a pattern/ Of timeless moments." From *Little Gidding*, in T. S. Eliot, *Four Quartets* (New York: Harcourt, Brace & World, 1943), 58.

Exegetical Perspective

geographical term as much as it is a theological term to describe all the forces, spiritual and historical, arrayed against the work of the Father through the Son. The world, whether the world of the Roman Empire or the world of a temple-laden urban center like Ephesus or the world of the synagogue, is implacably opposed to the work of the Father. This is why Jesus says, "Righteous Father, the world does not know you, but I know you" (17:25). This is the central conflict the community of house churches must face.

Being under siege by "the world," a community may become more cohesive or more splintered. This is why Jesus is so concerned about the unity of the community. Throughout today's text, Jesus' speech reflects a wordplay in Greek between "in" (*en*) and "one" (*hen*). Unity begins with the mutual indwelling between the Father and the Son, "that they may all be 'one' . . . as you, Father are 'in' me, and I am 'in' you" (v. 21). It is easy to misconstrue Jesus' words here, converting them into a personal mysticism or spiritual formation, but Jesus' words are addressed to the community. If there is any mysticism in John's Gospel, it is a community-oriented mysticism, not mysticism for the individual believer.

John is concerned about the spiritual formation of the community, for the distinctive witness of the Johannine community is rooted in the nature of the community itself. The indwelling of the Father and Jesus models the unity needed by the community "so that they may be 'one' as we are 'one'" (v. 22). The community's cohesion bears witness to its divine origin "so that the world may believe that you have sent me" (v. 21). If the community breaks into fragments, its chaos will undermine its mission to the world.

We often think of mission as individuals going to mission fields for their work, but John speaks about another witness in which the community itself is missional. Therefore, to attend to the well-being of the community is part of its mission to the world, and to nurture its unity is a form of witness to a divided world. Nurturing healthy communal life is an expression of an outgoing mission. The two imply each other.

John's Gospel has been characterized as a Gospel of glory expressing a theology of glory. So when Jesus says, "The glory that you have given me I have given them" (v. 22), it sounds as though this is the case. A closer look reveals that Jesus' glory is seen most vividly and vibrantly on the cross. The theology of glory incorporates the theology of the cross; they cannot be separated in John's Gospel.

Homiletical Perspective

Belief. Jesus prays for those who have believed in him (v. 20), for those who will believe because of the witness of the disciples (v. 20), and for the world, that all might come to belief (v. 21). Here the evangelistic task of the local community of faith begins to breathe. Of primary concern is the nurture and growth of those within the family of faith (v. 26). Next there is an outreach in word and deed to those whom the church community encounters directly (v. 26). Third, there is witness, service, and mission in the world—both the world nearby that does not yet share the heartbeat of Jesus and the world far away that might not yet have a name for the grace in life (v. 25).

Belief here means more than accepting cognitive information. Belief means recognizing that Jesus has been sent by the one he called "Father" (v. 23). John Chrysostom (ca. 347–407) argued that the world could come to such belief by observing the transformed lives of the followers of Jesus. He wrote, "And how will they believe this? 'Because,' Jesus says, 'you are a God of peace.' And, if therefore the (disciples) keep that same peace that they have learned (from me), their hearers will know the teacher by the disciples, however, if they quarrel, people will deny that they are the disciples of a God of peace and will not allow that I, not being peaceable, have been sent from you."[1] The challenge of living faithfully is not only a call to personal goodness; it is a call to let our lives invite others to follow Jesus.

Oneness. The unity within the community of the triune God is the unity to which Jesus points (v. 21). Jesus prays for nothing less than oneness for believers (v. 21). Can we imagine what the Lord felt as he moved inexorably toward his own death and still saw squabbling and power plays among his followers? For that matter, can we imagine what the Lord feels today as he observes denominational bigotry and internecine disarray?

The importance of unity among believers is that such oneness leads the world to believe (v. 23). The counterpoint of that truth is that the world does not believe in Jesus because the world sees partitions among the followers of Jesus. Jesus prays that the eleven disciples and those who come to belief because of the disciples be unified into one body (v. 20). There is to be no second-class citizenship among the people of faith. Ecumenism—the economy of God by which God organizes the whole

---

1. Chrysostom, "Homilies on the Gospel of John," in Joel C. Elowsky, ed., *Ancient Christian Commentary on Scripture, NT vol. IVb, John 11–21* (Downers Grove, IL: InterVarsity Press, 2007), 257.

John 17:20-26

Theological Perspective

allow us hope for the eventual reconciliation and unity of all humankind. The modern ecumenical movement has sought both to live into a vision of united church and into a vision of a reconciled, just, and peaceful humanity. Both efforts are in keeping with the spirit of Jesus' prayer. Even as we work ardently for unity among Christians, and for a more just and peaceable world, we need to be aware of the costliness of the unity Jesus prays for. Two words in this brief passage deserve to be underlined: "glory" and "love."

Jesus speaks in this passage of sharing his *glory* with his disciples. Yet as we look in John's Gospel at the placement of this prayer, the final words before the account of the betrayal of Jesus, we remember that Christ's glory is inseparable from Christ's suffering and cross. The unity that Christ is invoking for his disciples may include the disciples' cross. Unity with Christ throughout history has often meant suffering at the hands of unjust powers, for the sake of love and of integrity. Christ's glory is not always the world's glory. At the cross, it is a shattering reversal of all our conventional expectations of glory.

The last word is *love*. Jesus does not call for doctrinal unity, organizational unity, or political unity. So often, Christ's prayer for his disciples has been used to sanctify those ends, and even to justify the harsh imposition of artificial unity. Yet this prayer is for unity that grows out of the *love* of God, received and shared among his followers, leading to an experienced *unity in love* between Jesus and his followers, and with the one from whom Christ comes. In moments of communion, surely the debates about the nature of God and humanity, the questions of whether divine grace or human will is the means of unity, all of these must fade away, leaving only the burning vision of a cross and the words "For God so loved the world . . ."

If we were to take such love to heart, would our divisions and hostilities melt away? Would we be willing, for love's sake, to embrace a more costly glory? Such are the hopes that course through Jesus' prayer for us.

PETER J. B. CARMAN

Pastoral Perspective

would be easy for everyone to live in reciprocal love and unity if only everyone would follow the rules that I lay down."

The unity that constitutes the glory given to the disciples (v. 22) is the unity of God-given love, which, to borrow from Paul, "binds everything together in perfect harmony" (Col. 3:14). Our awareness of disunity, brokenness in relationship, and the pain that accompanies such may serve to call us back to recognizing our dependence on God for life and to embracing repentance, divine forgiveness, and restoration. Our manifest difficulty at living into our God-given unity may lead to pastoral reflections on such themes as loss and restoration, exile and homecoming, wilderness and promised land, repentance and forgiveness.

As Jesus draws his prayer to a close (v. 24–26), he sets everything in the context of hope of life with God. Many commentators assume that the state of being with Jesus (v. 24) is the state that inheres after death, but in any event it is a state to be fully realized in the future, even though it has been revealed in the present (v. 26). An old psychoanalytic rule of thumb suggests that if a person tends to depression, her or his fundamental issue is meaning. If a person tends to anxiety, her or his fundamental issue is death. Jesus' prayer—found in John immediately before the story of the passion and resurrection and read here in light of yet another departure following Ascension Day—can become an occasion to address anxiety by pointing to a reasonable and holy hope of life in the nearer presence of God. One way to point to the reasonable reality of such a hope is to discuss the nature of God as trustworthy, revealed in history, with such revelation notably recorded in Scripture and made manifest in Jesus. In other words, we can give people permission to find unsatisfactory some of the classical depictions of "afterlife" (including angels, harps, and streets of gold) while still affirming the faith in God that gives rise to such visions.

GEOFFREY M. ST. J. HOARE

This is particularly important since this culmination of the Farewell Discourse looks to the future proclamation of "the word." Indeed, John 17:20–26 could be seen as an abbreviated manual on discipleship and witness. What appears to be a triumphal community wrapped up in glory is, in truth, just the opposite. It is a place where the "word" brings together the theology of glory (Jesus' peculiar glory) and the theology of the cross (where Jesus' peculiar glory shows most clearly).

John's Gospel and its Farewell Discourse raise serious questions for church communities. Do we proclaim as full a gospel as John does? Have we been faithful to the vision of this community and the fullness of its gospel? Do we balance the theology of the cross and the theology of glory as well as John did?

The concern for future generations reminds us that this is not just a Farewell Discourse but a transitional discourse as well, for it witnesses to an imminent change. Just as Moses's farewell led to the emergence of Joshua, and Elijah's exit led to the entrance of Elisha, so the departure of Jesus will lead to the coming of the Spirit. What matters most for John is that the experience of the indwelling remains available to the community, for the unity of the Johannine community is based not on dogma but on a communal experience of indwelling that is analogous to the relationship between Jesus and the Father. This is what the community witnesses to the world. Their mission is to keep this experience of faith alive in the community, so that they can offer it to a broken and fractured world.

In verse 24, Jesus petitions the Father to let the disciples "be with me where I am, to see my glory," perhaps an allusion to John 14:1–7 or an allusion to the cross. Whatever the case, the disciples never go to the "many rooms" (NRSV "many dwelling places"), but Jesus and the Father come to make their home with the disciples (14:23). This is a reminder that the discourse remains unfinished, pointing in a distinctively Johannine way to an eschatology beyond the indwelling on which it has focused. There is "a glory beyond the glory" of which Jesus has spoken, but that glory can be found only beyond the hour of the glory of the Son of Man.

The discourse ends with love (v. 26). The purpose of the Father's indwelling is the imparting of love to the disciples. Now they carry in their community the experience of that love, a power strong enough to remake the world.

WILLIAM R. HERZOG II

world—becomes the single effort to express the unity to which Christians are called. The ultimate unity of the church is not in human maneuvering but in the oneness of God (v. 21). We find our unity in our common acceptance by Christ. As Fred Kaan has written, "Help us accept each other as Christ accepted us; teach us as sister, brother, each person to embrace. Be present, Lord, among us, and bring us to believe we are ourselves accepted and meant to love and live."[2]

Love. Five times within these six verses, Jesus names "love" as the key descriptor of divine relationships (vv. 23, 24, 26). Love is the bond within the Godhead (vv. 23–24). Love is the divine gift to the disciples (v. 23). Love is the magnetic grace through which God seeks to attract the world (vv. 25–26). Love is the ingredient that the Lord prays will be within his followers (v. 26).

These prayers might seem like sentimental mishmash if we did not know how the story ends. The love for which Jesus prays is cross-shaped love. There is indeed glory in this loving unity (v. 22), but the glory cannot be separated from the crucifixion. It is self-giving love that is resurrected into new life. The Song of Solomon 8:6 claims that "love is strong as death." The eternal Christ (v. 24) prays that his disciples might be "with me where I am" (v. 24). This is no small matter, considering that he was on his way to his death.

Pentecost. Finally, the preacher might recall that this lection on unity is followed by the Pentecost accounts. Barriers and boundaries fall and unity breaks out when the Holy Spirit comes (Acts 2:1–4).

F. BELTON JOYNER JR.

2. Fred Kaan, "Help Us Accept Each Other," in *The United Methodist Hymnal* (Nashville: United Methodist Publishing House, 1989), 560.

Contributors

Samuel L. Adams, Assistant Professor of Old Testament, Union Theological Seminary and Presbyterian School of Christian Education, Richmond, Virginia

J. Neil Alexander, Bishop, Episcopal Diocese of Atlanta, Georgia

Katherine E. Amos, Resident Faculty of Spirituality and the Arts, Wake Forest University Divinity School, Winston-Salem, North Carolina

Lindsay P. Armstrong, Associate Pastor for Christian Education, First Presbyterian Church, Atlanta, Georgia

David L. Bartlett, Professor of New Testament, Columbia Theological Seminary, Decatur, Georgia

Joseph A. Bessler, Robert Travis Peake Associate Professor of Theology, Phillips Theological Seminary, Tulsa, Oklahoma

Steven Bishop, Assistant Professor of Old Testament, Episcopal Theological Seminary of the Southwest, Austin, Texas

C. Clifton Black, Otto A. Piper Professor of Biblical Theology, Princeton Theological Seminary, Princeton, New Jersey

Robin Gallaher Branch, Professor of Biblical Studies, Crichton College, Memphis, Tennessee

Joseph H. Britton, Dean, Berkeley Divinity School at Yale, New Haven, Connecticut

William F. Brosend, Associate Professor of Homiletics, School of Theology, University of the South, Sewanee, Tennessee

Lee H. Butler Jr., Professor of Theology and Psychology, Chicago Theological Seminary, Chicago, Illinois

Carlos F. Cardoza-Orlandi, Professor of World Christianity, Columbia Theological Seminary, Decatur, Georgia

Greg Carey, Professor of New Testament, Lancaster Theological Seminary, Lancaster, Pennsylvania

Peter J. B. Carman, Pastor, Lake Avenue Baptist Church, Rochester, New York

Nick Carter, President, Andover Newton Theological School, Newton Centre, Massachusetts

William G. Carter, Pastor, First Presbyterian Church, Clarks Summit, Pennsylvania

Robert A. Cathey, Professor of Theology, McCormick Theological Seminary, Chicago, Illinois

Christine Chakoian, Pastor, First Presbyterian Church, Lake Forest, Illinois

Rodney Clapp, Editorial Director, Brazos Press, Wheaton, Illinois

Kimberly L. Clayton, Director of Lifelong Learning, Columbia Theological Seminary, Decatur, Georgia

Ronald Cole-Turner, H. Parker Sharp Professor of Theology and Ethics, Pittsburgh Theological Seminary, Pittsburgh, Pennsylvania

R. Alan Culpepper, Dean, McAfee School of Theology, Atlanta, Georgia

Thomas W. Currie, Dean, Union Seminary and Presbyterian School of Christian Education at Charlotte, North Carolina

Michael B. Curry, Bishop, Episcopal Diocese of North Carolina, Raleigh, North Carolina

Daniel M. DeBevoise, Co-Pastor, Park Lake Presbyterian Church, Orlando, Florida

Maria DeCarvalho, Founder, Another Way, Providence, Rhode Island

Daniel G. Deffenbaugh, Associate Professor of Religion, Hastings College, Hastings, Nebraska

Lewis R. Donelson, Ruth A. Campbell Professor of New Testament Studies, Austin Presbyterian Theological Seminary, Austin, Texas

Patricia Farris, Senior Minister, First United Methodist Church of Santa Monica, California

†Dana Ferguson, Executive Associate Pastor, Fourth Presbyterian Church, Chicago, Illinois

David G. Forney, Pastor, First Presbyterian Church, Clarksville, Tennessee

547

Kenyatta R. Gilbert, Assistant Professor of Homiletics, Howard University School of Divinity, Washington, D.C.

William Goettler, Pastor, First Presbyterian Church of New Haven, Connecticut

M. Ashley Grant, United Church of Christ Pulpit Supply Pastor, Milford, Connecticut

Mike Graves, Wm. K. McElvaney Visiting Professor of Preaching, Saint Paul School of Theology, Kansas City, Missouri

Lori Brandt Hale, Associate Professor and Director of General Education, Augsburg College, Minneapolis, Minnesota

Joseph S. Harvard, Pastor, First Presbyterian Church, Durham, North Carolina

Christopher B. Hays, D. Wilson Moore Assistant Professor of Ancient Near Eastern Studies, Fuller Theological Seminary, Pasadena, California

Erik M. Heen, Professor of New Testament and Greek, The Lutheran Theological Seminary at Philadelphia, Pennsylvania

Roy L. Heller, Associate Professor of Old Testament, Perkins School of Theology at Southern Methodist University, Dallas, Texas

William R. Herzog II, Dean and Professor of New Testament Interpretation, Andover Newton Theological School, Newton Centre, Massachusetts

Claudia Highbaugh, Dean of Religious and Spiritual Life, Connecticut College, New London, Connecticut

Elizabeth L. Hinson-Hasty, Associate Professor of Theology, Bellarmine University, Louisville, Kentucky

Geoffrey M. St. J. Hoare, Rector, All Saints' Episcopal Church, Atlanta, Georgia

Kenneth G. Hoglund, Professor of Religion, Wake Forest University Divinity School, Winston-Salem, North Carolina

John C. Holbert, Lois Craddock Perkins Professor of Homiletics, Perkins School of Theology at Southern Methodist University, Dallas, Texas

Joyce Hollyday, Co-Pastor, Circle of Mercy, Asheville, North Carolina

Morna D. Hooker, Professor of Theology and Fellow, Robinson College, Cambridge, United Kingdom

Leslie J. Hoppe, Adjunct Old Testament Studies Professor, Catholic Theological Union, Franklin, Wisconsin

Mark E. Hopper, Pastor, First Baptist Church, Bowling Green, Kentucky

Rodney J. Hunter, Professor of Pastoral Theology Emeritus, Candler School of Theology, Emory University, Atlanta, Georgia

Callista S. Isabelle, Associate University Chaplain, Yale University, New Haven, Connecticut

Paul "Skip" Johnson, Adjunct Assistant Professor of Pastoral Theology and Care, Columbia Theological Seminary, Decatur, Georgia

Gary D. Jones, Rector, St. Stephen's Episcopal Church, Richmond, Virginia

Stephen D. Jones, Pastor, Second Baptist Church of St. Louis, Missouri

Verity A. Jones, Publisher and Editor, *Disciples World*, Indianapolis, Indiana

F. Belton Joyner Jr., Retired United Methodist Pastor, Bahama, North Carolina

L. Shannon Jung, Professor of Town and Country Ministries, Saint Paul School of Theology, Kansas City, Missouri

Catherine L. Kelsey, Dean of the Chapel, The Iliff School of Theology, Denver, Colorado

Eunjoo M. Kim, Associate Professor of Homiletics, The Iliff School of Theology, Denver, Colorado

J. Michael Krech, Pastor, First Presbyterian Church, Somerville, Tennessee

Richard M. Landers, Associate Minister, Hyde Park Union Church, Chicago, Illinois

Dirk G. Lange, Assistant Professor of Christian Assembly, The Lutheran Theological Seminary at Philadelphia, Pennsylvania

Kristin Johnston Largen, Assistant Professor of Systematic Theology, The Lutheran Theological Seminary at Gettysburg, Pennsylvania

Jae Won Lee, Assistant Professor of New Testament, McCormick Theological Seminary, Chicago, Illinois

W. Eugene March, A. B. Rhodes Professor of Old Testament, Louisville Presbyterian Theological Seminary, Louisville, Kentucky

Martin E. Marty, Fairfax M. Cone Distinguished Service Professor Emeritus, The University of Chicago, Illinois

Peter W. Marty, Senior Pastor, St. Paul Lutheran Church, Davenport, Iowa

David W. McCreery, Professor, Department of Religious Studies, Willamette University, Salem, Oregon

Alexander J. McKelway, Retired Presbyterian Minister, White Stone, Virginia

Laura S. Mendenhall, Senior Philanthropy Advisor, Texas Presbyterian Foundation, Austin, Texas

Stephanie Y. Mitchem, Associate Professor, Director of African American Studies Program, University of South Carolina, Columbia, South Carolina

Lewis S. Mudge, Robert Lighton Stuart Professor of Theology Emeritus, San Francisco Theological Seminary and the Graduate Theological Union, Berkeley, California

Donald W. Musser, Professor of Religious Studies, Stetson University, DeLand, Florida

Kang-Yup Na, Professor, Department of Religion, Westminster College, New Wilmington, Pennsylvania

Douglas F. Ottati, Craig Family Professor of Reformed Theology and Justice Ministry, Davidson College, Davidson, North Carolina

Michael Pasquarello III, Granger E. and Ann A. Fisher Professor of Preaching, Asbury Theological Seminary, Wilmore, Kentucky

Pheme Perkins, Professor of New Testament, Boston College Department of Theology, Chestnut Hill, Massachusetts

David L. Petersen, Professor of Old Testament, Candler School of Theology, Emory University, Atlanta, Georgia

Nancy Claire Pittman, Assistant Professor of the Practice of Ministry, Phillips Theological Seminary, Tulsa, Oklahoma

Rebecca Button Prichard, Pastor, Tustin Presbyterian Church, Tustin, California

Robert W. Prim, Pastor, Nacoochee Presbyterian Church, Sautee-Nacoochee, Georgia

Richard A. Puckett, Director of Public Relations and Development, United Methodist Children's Home, Decatur, Georgia

Charles D. Reeb, Senior Pastor, Pasadena Community Church (United Methodist Church), St. Petersburg, Florida

Marcia Y. Riggs, J. Erskine Love Professor of Christian Ethics, Columbia Theological Seminary, Decatur, Georgia

Sharon H. Ringe, Professor of New Testament, Wesley Theological Seminary, Washington, D.C.

Gregory A. Robbins, Associate Professor of Religious Studies, University of Denver Department of Religious Studies, Denver, Colorado

Samuel K. Roberts, Anne Borden and E. Hervey Evans Professor of Theology and Ethics, Union Theological Seminary and Presbyterian School of Christian Education, Richmond, Virginia

John B. Rogers, Retired Presbyterian Minister, Montreat, North Carolina

Christopher Rowland, The Dean Ireland Professor of the Exegesis of Holy Scripture, University of Oxford, Queen's College, Oxford, United Kingdom

Debra Samuelson, Pastor for Evangelism and Outreach, Lutheran Church of the Redeemer, Atlanta, Georgia

Peter Samuelson, Pastor, Emmanuel Lutheran Church, Atlanta, Georgia

Edesio Sanchez, Translation Consultant, United Bible Societies, República Argentina

Craig A. Satterlee, Axel Jacob and Gerda Maria (Swanson) Carlson Chair of Homiletics, Lutheran School of Theology at Chicago, Illinois

Stanley P. Saunders, Associate Professor of New Testament, Columbia Theological Seminary, Decatur, Georgia

William L. Self, Senior Pastor, Johns Creek Baptist Church, Alpharetta, Georgia

Mary E. Shields, Associate Professor of Old Testament/Hebrew Scriptures, Trinity Lutheran Seminary, Columbus, Ohio

H. Stephen Shoemaker, Senior Minister, Myers Park Baptist Church, Charlotte, North Carolina

Archie Smith Jr., James and Clarice Foster Professor of Pastoral Psychology and Counseling, Pacific School of Religion, Berkeley, California

Jim Green Somerville, Pastor, First Baptist Church, Richmond, Virginia

Sheldon W. Sorge, Associate Director, Louisville Institute, Louisville, Kentucky

Richard E. Spalding, Chaplain, Williams College, Williamstown, Massachusetts

O. Benjamin Sparks, Retired Presbyterian Minister, Richmond, Virginia

Mark W. Stamm, Associate Professor of Christian Worship, Perkins School of Theology at Southern Methodist University, Dallas, Texas

John K. Stendahl, Pastor, Lutheran Church of the Newtons, Newton, Massachusetts

Richard C. Stern, Professor of Homiletics, Saint Meinrad School of Theology, St. Meinrad, Indiana

George W. Stroup, J. B. Green Professor of Theology, Columbia Theological Seminary, Decatur, Georgia

Barbara Brown Taylor, Butman Professor of Religion, Piedmont College, Demorest, Georgia; Adjunct Professor of Christian Spirituality, Columbia Theological Seminary, Decatur, Georgia

Casey Thompson, Associate Pastor for Congregational Life, Idlewild Presbyterian Church, Memphis, Tennessee

Deanna Thompson, Associate Professor and Chair, Department of Religion, Hamline University, St. Paul, Minnesota

Leonora Tubbs Tisdale, Clement-Muehl Professor of Homiletics, Yale University Divinity School, New Haven, Connecticut

Jeffery L. Tribble Sr., Assistant Professor of Ministry, Columbia Theological Seminary, Decatur, Georgia

David G. Trickett, President and Henry White Warren Professor of Ethics and Leadership, The Iliff School of Theology, Denver, Colorado

Darryl M. Trimiew, Chair, Philosophy and Religious Studies, Medgar Evers College, The City University of New York, Brooklyn, New York

Thomas H. Troeger, Lantz Professor of Christian Communication, Yale University Divinity School, New Haven, Connecticut

Steven S. Tuell, Associate Professor of Old Testament, Pittsburgh Theological Seminary, Pittsburgh, Pennsylvania

Kimberly M. van Driel, Pastor, Immanuel Evangelical Lutheran Church, Naugatuck, Connecticut

Paul W. Walaskay, Professor of Biblical Studies, Union Theological Seminary and Presbyterian School of Christian Education, Richmond, Virginia

Robert W. Wall, Paul T. Walls Professor of Scripture, Seattle Pacific University School of Theology, Seattle, Washington

Michael E. Williams, Lead Pastor, First United Methodist Church, Hendersonville, Tennessee

Kevin A. Wilson, Lecturer in Biblical Studies at Wartburg College, Lawrence, Massachusetts

John W. Wimberly, Pastor, Western Presbyterian Church, Washington, D.C.

Lauren F. Winner, Assistant Professor of Spirituality, Duke University Divinity School, Durham, North Carolina

Ralph C. Wood, Professor of Theology and Literature, Baylor University, Waco, Texas

Suzanne Woolston-Bossert, Associate Pastor, The United Parish Church of Brookline, Massachusetts

Oliver Larry Yarbrough, Tillinghast Professor of Religion, Middlebury College, Middlebury, Vermont

Christine Roy Yoder, Associate Professor of Old Testament, Columbia Theological Seminary, Decatur, Georgia

Scripture Index

Author Index

Numerals indicate numbered Sundays of a season; for example, "Lent 1" represents the First Sunday in Lent, and "Easter 2" the Second Sunday of Easter.

Rodney Clapp — Lent 2 G PP, Lent 3 G PP, Lent 4 G PP

Kimberly L. Clayton — Lent 5 PS PP, Liturgy of Palms PS PP, Liturgy of Passion PS PP

Ronald Cole-Turner — Easter 6 NT TP, Ascension NT TP, Easter 7 NT TP

R. Alan Culpepper — Mon. of Holy Wk. G EP, Tue. of Holy Wk. G EP, Wed. of Holy Wk. G EP

Thomas W. Currie — Ash Wednesday OT TP, Lent 1 OT TP

Michael B. Curry — Lent 2 G HP, Lent 3 G HP, Lent 4 G HP

Daniel M. DeBevoise — Lent 2 OT PP, Lent 3 OT PP, Lent 4 OT PP

Maria DeCarvalho — Holy Thursday PS PP, Good Friday PS PP, Holy Saturday PS PP

Daniel G. Deffenbaugh — Lent 2 G TP, Lent 3 G TP, Lent 4 G TP

Lewis R. Donelson — Easter 3 G EP, Easter 4 G EP, Easter 5 G EP

Patricia Farris — Easter 6 PS PP, Ascension PS PP, Easter 7 PS PP

†Dana Ferguson — Easter 3 NT PP, Easter 4 NT PP, Easter 5 NT PP

David G. Forney — Easter 6 NT PP, Ascension NT PP, Easter 7 NT PP

Kenyatta R. Gilbert — Lent 2 OT HP, Lent 3 OT HP, Lent 4 OT HP

William Goettler — Mon. of Holy Wk. OT HP, Tue. of Holy Wk. OT HP, Wed. of Holy Wk. OT HP

M. Ashley Grant — Easter Vigil PS PP, Easter Day PS PP, Easter 2 PS PP

Mike Graves — Holy Thursday E HP, Good Friday E HP, Holy Saturday E HP

Lori Brandt Hale — Ash Wednesday G TP, Lent 1 G TP

Joseph S. Harvard — Easter 3 NT PP, Easter 4 NT PP, Easter 5 NT PP

Christopher B. Hays — Holy Thursday OT TP, Good Friday OT TP, Holy Saturday OT TP

Erik M. Heen — Easter 3 NT TP, Easter 4 NT TP, Easter 5 NT TP

Roy L. Heller — Holy Thursday OT EP, Good Friday OT EP, Holy Saturday OT EP

William R. Herzog II — Easter 6 G EP, Ascension G EP, Easter 7 G EP

Claudia Highbaugh — Holy Thursday OT HP, Good Friday OT HP, Holy Saturday OT HP

Elizabeth L. Hinson-Hasty — Ash Wednesday PS TP, Lent 1 PS TP

Geoffrey M. St. J. Hoare — Easter 6 G PP, Ascension G PP, Easter 7 G PP

Kenneth G. Hoglund — Ash Wednesday PS EP, Lent 1 PS EP

John C. Holbert — Mon. of Holy Wk. OT TP, Tue. of Holy Wk. OT TP, Wed. of Holy Wk. OT TP

Joyce Hollyday — Easter 6 NT HP, Ascension E HP, Easter 7 NT HP

Morna D. Hooker — Lent 5 E EP, Liturgy of Passion E EP

Leslie J. Hoppe — Lent 2 G EP, Lent 3 G EP, Lent 4 G EP

Richard A. Puckett	Lent 2 OT EP, Lent 3 OT EP, Lent 4 OT EP	H. Stephen Shoemaker	Lent 5 G HP, Liturgy of Palms G HP, Liturgy of Passion G HP
Charles D. Reeb	Easter Vigil E HP, Easter Day NT HP, Easter 2 NT HP	Archie Smith Jr.	Ash Wednesday OT PP, Lent 1 OT PP
Marcia Y. Riggs	Easter 6 PS TP, Ascension PS TP, Easter 7 PS TP	Jim Green Somerville	Holy Thursday G PP, Good Friday G PP, Holy Saturday G PP
Sharon H. Ringe	Ash Wednesday G EP, Lent 1 G EP	Sheldon W. Sorge	Holy Thursday E TP, Good Friday E TP, Holy Saturday E TP
Gregory A. Robbins	Easter Vigil G EP, Easter Day G EP, Easter 2 G EP	Richard E. Spalding	Mon. of Holy Wk. OT PP, Tue. of Holy Wk. OT PP, Wed. of Holy Wk. OT PP
Samuel K. Roberts	Lent 2 PS TP, Lent 3 PS TP, Lent 4 PS TP	O. Benjamin Sparks	Easter Vigil OT PP, Easter Day OT PP, Easter 2 NT PP
John B. Rogers	Easter 3 PS TP, Easter 4 PS TP, Easter 5 PS TP	Mark W. Stamm	Lent 5 PS HP, Liturgy of Palms PS HP, Liturgy of Passion PS HP
Christopher Rowland	Easter 6 NT EP, Ascension E EP, Easter 7 NT EP	John K. Stendahl	Easter Vigil G PP, Easter Day G PP, Easter 2 G PP
Debra Samuelson	Mon. of Holy Wk. E PP, Tue. of Holy Wk. E PP, Wed. of Holy Wk. E PP	Richard C. Stern	Lent 2 PS HP, Lent 3 PS HP, Lent 4 PS HP
Peter Samuelson	Mon. of Holy Wk. E PP, Tue. of Holy Wk. E PP, Wed. of Holy Wk. E PP	George W. Stroup	Lent 5 G TP, Liturgy of Palms G TP, Liturgy of Passion G TP
Edesio Sanchez	Mon. of Holy Wk. PS EP, Tue. of Holy Wk. PS EP, Wed. of Holy Wk. PS EP	Barbara Brown Taylor	Lent 5 E HP, Liturgy of Passion E HP
		Casey Thompson	Lent 2 E PP, Lent 3 E PP, Lent 4 E PP
Craig A. Satterlee	Easter Vigil PS HP, Easter Day PS HP, Easter 2 PS HP	Deanna Thompson	Mon. of Holy Wk. G TP, Tue. of Holy Wk. G TP, Wed. of Holy Wk. G TP
Stanley P. Saunders	Easter Vigil E EP, Easter Day NT EP, Easter 2 NT EP	Leonora Tubbs Tisdale	Holy Thursday G HP, Good Friday G HP, Holy Saturday G HP
William L. Self	Easter 6 PS HP, Ascension PS HP, Easter 7 PS HP	Jeffery L. Tribble Sr.	Ash Wednesday G PP, Lent 1 G PP
Mary E. Shields	Easter Vigil PS EP, Easter Day PS EP, Easter 2 PS EP	David G. Trickett	Easter Vigil PS TP, Easter Day PS TP, Easter 2 PS TP